D1760668

AMERICA

ALL

The University

DETAIL OF ENGRAVING BASED ON
THE CHASM OF THE COLORADO
BY THOMAS MORAN

AMERICA

A NARRATIVE HISTORY

Brief Eighth Edition

GEORGE BROWN TINDALL

DAVID EMORY SHI

W · W · NORTON & COMPANY · NEW YORK · LONDON

W. W. Norton & Company has been independent since its founding in 1923, when William Warder Norton and Mary D. Herter Norton first published lectures delivered at the People's Institute, the adult education division of New York City's Cooper Union. The firm soon expanded its program beyond the Institute, publishing books by celebrated academics from America and abroad. By mid-century, the two major pillars of Norton's publishing program—trade books and college texts—were firmly established. In the 1950s, the Norton family transferred control of the company to its employees, and today—with a staff of four hundred and a comparable number of trade, college, and professional titles published each year—W. W. Norton & Company stands as the largest and oldest publishing house owned wholly by its employees.

Editor: Jon Durbin
Manuscript editor: Abby Winograd
Project editor: Melissa Atkin
Emedia editor: Steve Hoge
Print ancillary editor: Rachel Comerford
Production manager: Christine D'Antonio
Book design by Antonina Krass
Editorial assistant: Jason Spears
Composition by TexTech, Inc.
Manufacturing by Worldcolor, Taunton

Copyright © 2010, 2007, 2004, 1999, 1996, 1992, 1988, 1984 by W. W. Norton & Company, Inc.

All rights reserved
Printed in the United States of America
Since this page cannot legibly accommodate all the copyright notices,
the Credits constitute an extension of the copyright page.

Library of Congress Cataloging-in-Publication Data

Tindall, George Brown.
America : a narrative history / George Brown Tindall,
David Emory Shi.—8th ed.
    p.   cm.
Includes bibliographical references and index.
ISBN 978-0-393-93408-3
1. United States—History.   I.   Shi, David E.   II.   Title.
E178.1 .T55 2009   2009024625
973—dc22

W. W. Norton & Company, Inc., 500 Fifth Avenue, New York, NY 10110
www.wwnorton.com

W. W. Norton & Company Ltd., Castle House, 75/76 Wells Street, London W1T 3QT

1 2 3 4 5 6 7 8 9 0

WITHDRAWN
UNIVERSITY OF
CANCELLED
GLASGOW
LIBRARY

Short Loan Collection

FOR BRUCE AND SUSAN
AND FOR BLAIR

FOR
JASON AND JESSICA

GEORGE B. TINDALL late of the University of North Carolina, Chapel Hill, was an award-winning historian of the South with a number of major books to his credit, including *The Emergence of the New South, 1913–1945* and *The Disruption of the Solid South.*

DAVID E. SHI is a professor of history and the president of Furman University. He is the author of several books on American cultural history, including the award-winning *The Simple Life: Plain Living and High Thinking in American Culture* and *Facing Facts: Realism in American Thought and Culture, 1850–1920.*

CONTENTS

Part Two / B U I L D I N G   A   N A T I O N

Part Five / GROWING PAINS

Part Six / MODERN AMERICA

Part Seven / THE AMERICAN AGE

MAPS

PREFACE

This edition of *America: A Narrative History* marks the twenty-fifth anniversary of the book. I very much regret that George Tindall is not alive to celebrate with me. He died on December 2, 2006, in Chapel Hill, North Carolina. He was eighty-five. George was a meticulous, pathbreaking, award-winning scholar. He was also an eloquent writer, an engaging teacher, and a caring mentor. And, of course, he wrote a wonderful history of America!

George Tindall developed the idea for a distinctive American history textbook nearly four decades ago. He set out to write a compelling narrative history of the American experience, a succinct narrative that would be animated by colorful characters, informed by balanced analysis and social texture, and guided by the unfolding of events. Those classic principles, combined with the book's handy format and low price, have helped make *America: A Narrative History* a book students like to read and teachers like to teach. It was my good fortune to join George in this worthy endeavor beginning with the second edition.

My duty as the new co-author on *America* at that time was to create the first brief edition. Making sure that the very first brief edition remained a coherent narrative was my overriding concern. Up to that time, most instructors complained about the choppy and incoherent nature of all the brief histories of America. Many of us still do today. We want to do the right thing for our students by purchasing a briefer, more affordable text, but too often we feel like we sacrifice quality to gain those other advantages. This is not the case when you choose the Brief Edition of *America*. We overcame that criticism by bringing it in at a length that gave us a workable balance between breadth and depth in the way we covered the topics and periods. The first brief edition was a big success!

The new Brief Eighth Edition of *America: A Narrative History* is better positioned than ever to meet the needs of today's teachers and students.

America's briefer, coherent narrative voice provides a clear path through the complexities of American history. New, carefully crafted pedagogical features have been added to the Eighth Edition to further help guide students through the narrative. New focus questions and chapter summaries work together seamlessly to highlight core content. Other text features include easy-to-read, full-color maps, new chapter chronologies, and new lists of key terms. Even with all these noteworthy improvements, we remain the lowest priced brief edition in full color in the marketplace!

We also continue our tradition with the new Brief Eighth Edition of creating thematic based revisions that are designed to show how politics, economics, culture, and society interact to shape the American experience. New themes in previous editions have included the role of immigration, the western experience, work, and the environment. This Brief Eighth Edition of *America* features the theme of religion and its myriad effects on history and society. Religion, of course, is one of the most powerful forces in human life, and it has played a crucial role in the development of the United States. Americans have always been a peculiarly religious people. Native American cultures centered their societies on spiritual life. And most of the first European colonists saw themselves as "a chosen people," agents of divine providence with a mission to spread the gospel to the so-called New World. In 1831 and 1832 the astute Frenchman Alexis de Tocqueville toured the United States and reported that there "is no country in the world where the Christian religion retains a greater influence over the souls of men than in America."

Yet Christianity in America has always assumed many forms. Religious freedom has been as valued a principle as religious belief. And in recent years the United States has witnessed a surge in non-Christian religions. "We are a religious people," said Supreme Court Justice William O. Douglas in 1952. Yet thirteen years later he added that America had become "a nation of Buddhists, Confucianists, and Taoists." Islam, in fact, is the nation's fastest-growing faith; there are more Muslims in America than Episcopalians. The United States is fast becoming a pluralistic, multireligious nation in which toleration is an ever-important outlook. More than the members of any other industrialized society, the vast majority of Americans (90 percent) believe in God, pray, and attend religious services at churches, synagogues, temples, and mosques. To a remarkable degree, many Americans fashion their personal conduct upon their religious principles and their social relationships upon their religious beliefs. Thus diversity characterizes American religious life. There are many different faiths and also quite different expressions of the same faith. Although the U.S. Constitution creates a "wall of separation" between religion and government, Americans are also more apt to mix faith and politics than citizens of other countries. In other words, religion continues to be one of the most dynamic—and most contested—elements of American life.

Some of the additions to the Eighth Edition relating to religious history are outlined here:

- Chapter 1 includes discussions of Aztec religious beliefs and rituals, sixteenth-century European religious life, and Spanish efforts to convert Native Americans to Catholicism.
- Chapter 2 examines the English Reformation and the distinctive characteristics of Anglicanism (the faith of the Church of England), the Native Americans' reverence for nature, and Judaism in British North America.
- Chapter 3 describes the important role of women in colonial religious life, the popularity of Deism among many key Revolutionary leaders, and the social aspects of the Great Awakening.
- Chapter 4 details the impact of the Jesuit missionaries in New France.
- Chapter 8 analyzes the logic of the First Amendment's emphasis on the separation of church and state.
- Chapter 13 explores the changes in religious life during the early nineteenth century.
- Chapter 15 includes new material on religious life in the Old South.
- Chapter 16 features the religious revival of 1857–1859.
- Chapter 17 shows that the armies fighting the Civil War engaged in frequent religious services and revivals.
- Chapter 18 details the role played by religious life in the Reconstruction of the South after the Civil War.
- Chapter 22 summarizes the role that religious fervor played in the populist movement of the 1890s.
- Chapter 23 discusses the role of religion in justifying American imperialism at the end of the nineteenth century.
- Chapter 24 highlights the role of religion in the motives of "progressive" social reformers.
- Chapter 32 describes the efforts of Congress and President Dwight Eisenhower to reaffirm America's belief in God.
- Chapter 33 stresses the crucial role played by religion in the development of the civil rights movement of the 1950s and 1960s.
- Chapter 36 explains the rise of the Republican conservatives and the role that the major revival of evangelical religion played in the conservative ascendancy in American politics.

As a thank you to our adopters and to highlight our new theme on religion, we are pleased to offer adopters the *Norton American History Digital Archive,* a 7-DVD set, including a new DVD on religion.

Beyond those explorations of religious history, I have introduced other new material throughout the Eighth Edition, including new segments on Native Americans, African Americans, women, and minorities. In addition, I have incorporated fresh insights from important new scholarly works.

Also revised is the outstanding support package that supplements the text. *For the Record: A Documentary History of America,* Fourth Edition, by David E. Shi and Holly A. Mayer (Duquesne University), is the perfect companion reader for *America: A Narrative History.* The new edition has been brought into closer alignment with the main text, and the price has been reduced by nearly 50 percent. *For the Record* now has 225 primary-source readings from diaries, journals, newspaper articles, speeches, government documents, and novels, including a number of readings that highlight the new theme of religion in *America.* If you haven't looked at *For the Record* in a while, now would be a good time.

America's StudySpace (http://wwnorton.com/studyspace) provides a proven assignment-driven plan for each chapter. Highlights include chapter outlines, quizzes in the the new Quiz Plus format, iMaps and new iMap quizzes, map worksheets, flashcards, interactive timelines, new U.S. History Tours powered by Google Earth map technology, research topics, and several hundred multimedia primary-source documents. The *Norton Instructor's Resource Disk* provides enhanced PowerPoint lecture outlines with images from the text, four-color maps, the U.S. History Tours in a slide-show format, additional images from the Library of Congress archives, and audio files of historic speeches.

The *Instructor's Manual and Test Bank,* by Stephen Davis (Kingwood College), Edward Richey (University of North Texas), Michael Krysko (Kansas State University), Brian McKnight (Angelo State University), and David Dewar (Angelo State University), includes a test bank of short-answer and essay questions, as well as detailed chapter outlines, lecture suggestions, and bibliographies. Finally, Norton coursepacks deliver all the instructor materials in a ready-to-use format for your course management system (Blackboard, WebCT, Angel, Moodle, and so on).

It's easy now to see why *America* continues to set the standard, even after twenty-five years, when it comes to providing a low-cost book with high-value content. Your students will read it, and they will save money when you use it.

In preparing the Eighth Edition, I have benefited from the insights and suggestions of many people. Some of those insights have come from student readers of the text, and I encourage such feedback. I'd particularly like to thank Eirlys Barker (Thomas Nelson Community College), who was a reviewer for us and worked on the wonderful new pedagogy in the text. Likewise, I'd like to thank Stephen Davis for his work on the *Instructor's Manual and Test Bank.* I'd like to give special thanks to Brandan Franke (Blinn College, Bryan) for his work on the new PowerPoint lectures. Numerous scholars and survey instructors advised me on the new edition:

Heather Abdelnur (Augusta State University), Alan Autrey (Lamar University), Frank Bagolione (Tallahassee Community College), Mario Bennekin (Georgia Perimeter College), William Bush (University of Nevada, Las Vegas), David Castle (Ohio University, Eastern), Craig Coenen (Mercer County Community College), Alice Colbert (University of Arkansas, Fort Smith), Alice Connally (Purdue University, North Central), Scott Cook (Motlow State Community College), Amy Darty (University of Central Florida), Wade Derden (Pulaski Technical College), Mark Goldman (Tallahassee Community College), James Good (North Harris College), Shane Hamilton (University of Georgia), Yolanda Orizando-Harding (University of Central Florida), George Hatfield (Clayton State University), Marc Horger (Ohio State University), Charles Killinger (Valencia Community College), Margaret (Peggy) Lambert (Lone Star College, Kingwood), Pat Ledbetter (North Central Texas College), Robby Luckett (University of Georgia), Lisa Morales (North Central Texas College, Corinth), Bret Nelson (San Jacinto College, North), Michael Nichols (Tarrant County College, Northwest), George Pabis (Georgia Perimeter College), Thomas Price (State University of New York, Ulster County Community College), Brooks Simpson (Arizona State University), John M. Wegner (Eastern Michigan University), Joe Whitehorne (Lord Fairfax Community College).

Once again, I thank my friends at W. W. Norton, especially Steve Forman, Jon Durbin, Steve Hoge, Karl Bakeman, Nicole Netherton, Melissa Atkin, Christine D'Antonio, Rachel Comerford, Abigail Winograd, Stephanie Romeo, and Jason Spears for their care and attention along the way.

Part One

A NEW WORLD

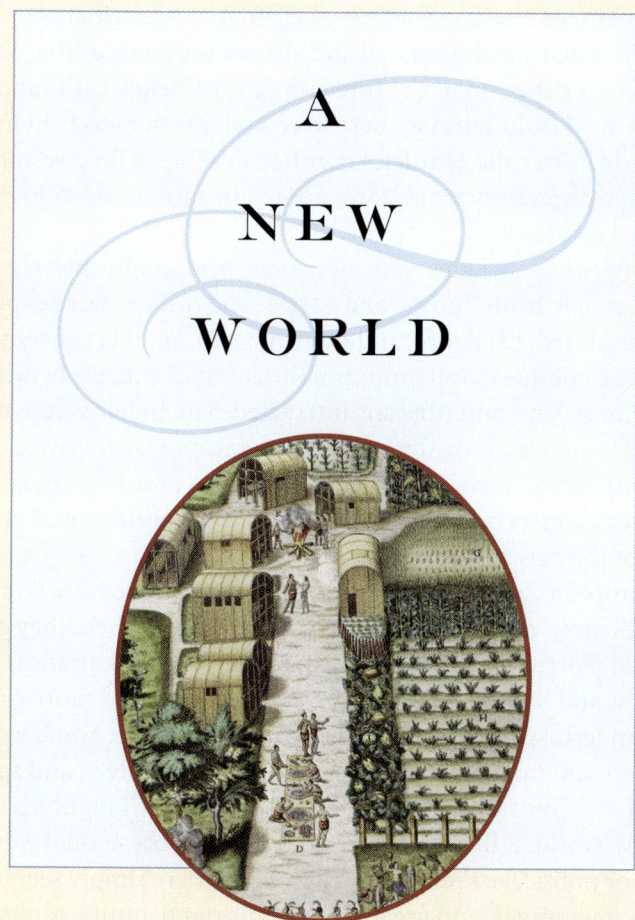

Long before Christopher Columbus accidentally discovered the New World in his effort to find a passage to Asia, the tribal peoples he mislabeled Indians had occupied and shaped the lands of the Western Hemisphere. By the end of the fifteenth century, when Columbus began his voyage west from Europe, there were millions of natives living in the "New World." Over the centuries they had developed diverse and often highly sophisticated societies, some rooted in agriculture, others in trade or imperial conquest.

The indigenous societies were, of course, profoundly affected by the arrival of people from Europe and Africa. The Indians were exploited, infected, enslaved, displaced, and exterminated. Yet this conventional tale of tragic conquest oversimplifies the complex process by which Indians, Europeans, and Africans interacted. The Indians were more than passive victims; they were also trading partners and rivals of the transatlantic newcomers. They became enemies and allies, neighbors and advisers, converts and spouses. As such they participated in the creation of the new society known as America.

The Europeans who risked their lives to settle in the New World were themselves quite varied. Young and old, men and women, they came from Spain, Portugal, France, the British Isles, the Netherlands, Scandinavia, Italy, and the various German states. A variety of motives inspired them to undertake the harrowing transatlantic voyage. Some were adventurers and fortune seekers eager to find gold, silver, and spices. Others were fervent Christians determined to create kingdoms of God in the New World. Still others were convicts, debtors, indentured servants, or political or religious exiles. Many were simply seeking a plot of land, higher wages, and greater economic opportunity. A settler in Pennsylvania noted that "poor people (both men and women) of all kinds can here get three times the wages for their labour than they can in England or Wales."

Yet such enticements did not attract enough workers to keep up with the rapidly expanding colonial economies. So the Europeans began to force Indians to work for them, but there were never enough laborers to meet the unceasing demand. Moreover, the captive Indians often escaped or were so rebellious that their use as slaves was banned. The Massachusetts legislature outlawed forced labor because Indians were of "a malicious, surly and revengeful spirit; rude and insolent in their behavior, and very ungovernable."

Beginning early in the seventeenth century, colonists turned to the African slave trade for their labor needs. In 1619 white traders began transporting captured Africans to the English colonies—in very large numbers. This development would transform American society in ways that no one at the time envisioned. Few Europeans during the colonial era saw the contradiction between the New World's promise of individual freedom and the expanding institution of race-based slavery. Nor did they imagine the problems associated with introducing into the new society a race of people they considered alien and unassimilable.

The intermingling of people, cultures, plants, and animals from the continents of Africa, Europe, and North America gave colonial American society its distinctive vitality and variety. In turn, the diversity of the environment and the climate spawned quite different economies and patterns of living in the various regions of North America. As the original settlements grew into prosperous and populous colonies, the transplanted Europeans fashioned social institutions and political systems to manage growth and control tensions.

At the same time, imperial rivalries among the Spanish, French, English, Portuguese, and Dutch triggered costly wars. The monarchs of Europe struggled to manage often unruly colonies, which, they discovered, played crucial roles in their European wars. Many of the colonists brought with them to the New World a feisty independence, which led them to resent government interference in their affairs. A British official in North Carolina reported that the residents of the Piedmont region were "without any Law or Order. Impudence is so very high, as to be past bearing." As long as the reins of imperial control were loosely applied, mother countries and their colonists maintained an uneasy partnership. But as the British authorities tightened their control during the mid–eighteenth century, they met growing resentment and resistance, which escalated into revolt and culminated in revolution.

1

THE COLLISION
OF CULTURES

FOCUS QUESTIONS   wwnorton.com/studyspace

- What civilizations existed in pre-Columbian America?
- Why were European countries, such as Spain and Portugal, prepared to embark on voyages of discovery by the sixteenth century?
- How did contact between the Western Hemisphere and the "Old World" change through the exchange of plants, animals, and pathogens?
- What were the Europeans' reasons for establishing colonies in America?
- What is the legacy of the Spanish presence in North America?
- What effect did the Protestant Reformation have on the colonization of the New World?

The "New World" discovered by Christopher Columbus was in fact home to civilizations thousands of years old. Until recently, archaeologists had long assumed that the first humans in the Western Hemisphere were Siberians who some 12,000 to 15,000 years ago crossed the Bering Strait on a land bridge to Alaska made accessible by receding waters during the last Ice Age. Over the next 500 years the Asian migrants fanned out in small bands from the Arctic Circle to the tip of South America. Recent archaeological discoveries in Pennsylvania, Virginia, and Chile suggest that humans may have arrived by sea much earlier (perhaps 18,000 to 40,000 years ago), however, from various parts of Asia—and some of them may even have crossed the Atlantic Ocean from southwestern Europe.

PRE-COLUMBIAN INDIAN CIVILIZATIONS

Whatever their place of origin and time of arrival, the first peoples in the Western Hemisphere spread across North and South America, establishing new communities and cultures. In the high altitudes of Mexico and Peru, Mayas, Aztecs, Incas, and others built great empires and a monumental architecture, supported by large-scale agriculture and far-flung commerce.

INDIAN CULTURES OF NORTH AMERICA   The pre-Columbian Indians of the present-day United States created three distinct civilizations: the Adena-Hopewell culture of the Ohio River valley (800 B.C.–A.D. 600), the Mississippian culture of the Southeast (A.D. 600–1500), and the Hohokam-Anasazi culture of the Southwest (400 B.C.–present). None of these developed as fully as the civilizations of the Mayas, Aztecs, and Incas to the south. Like the tribes of Mexico and South America, the North American Indians often warred with one another. They also enslaved other Indians, tortured captives, and scalped victims. Some tribes practiced ritual cannibalism. Yet they also created sustainable cultures that were as diverse, dynamic, and mobile as those of the peoples of Europe. The Native American tribes of North America shared some fundamental myths and beliefs, especially concerning the sacredness of nature, the necessity of communal living, and respect for elders, but they developed in different ways at different times and in different places. In North America alone, there were probably 240 different tribes when the Europeans arrived.

The Adena-Hopewell culture in what is today the American Midwest left behind enormous earthworks and hundreds of elaborate burial mounds, some of them elaborately shaped like great snakes, birds, and other animals. The Adena and, later, the Hopewell Indians were gatherers and hunters. Evidence from the burial mounds suggests that they had a complex social structure featuring a specialized division of labor. Moreover, the Hopewells developed an elaborate trade network that spanned the continent.

The Mississippian culture, centered in the southern Mississippi River valley, flourished between 900 and 1350. It resembled the Mayan and Aztec societies in its intensive agricultural economy, which was based on growing corn, beans, and squashes. The Mississippians built substantial towns around central plazas and temples. Like the Aztecs, they developed a highly stratified social structure and spiritual death cults, which involved ceremonial human torture and sacrifice. Like the Hopewells to the north, the Mississippians developed a specialized labor system, an effective governmental structure, and an expansive trading network. The Mississippian culture peaked in the fourteenth century and succumbed first to climate change and finally to pandemic diseases brought by Europeans.

The arid Southwest spawned irrigation-based cultures, elements of which exist today and heirs to which (the Hopis, Zunis, and others) still live in the adobe cliff dwellings (called *pueblos* by the Spanish) erected by their ancestors. About A.D. 500, Hohokam Indians migrated from present-day Mexico into today's southern Arizona. They developed sophisticated irrigation systems in order to grow corn and other crops, and they constructed temple mounds similar to those in Mexico. For unknown reasons, the Hohokam society disappeared during the fifteenth century.

The most widespread and best known of the Southwest cultures were the Anasazi ("Enemy's Ancestors" in the Navajo language). In ancient times they developed extensive settlements in the "four corners," where the states of Arizona, New Mexico, Colorado, and Utah meet. In contrast to the Mesoamerican and Mississippian cultures, Anasazi society lacked a rigid class structure. The religious leaders and warriors labored much as the rest of the people did. In fact, the Anasazi engaged in warfare only as a means of self-defense (*Hopi* means "Peaceful People"). Environmental factors shaped Anasazi culture and eventually caused its decline. Toward the end of the thirteenth century, a lengthy drought and the pressure of migrating Indians from the north threatened the survival of Anasazi society.

NATIVE AMERICANS IN 1500 When Europeans began to arrive in North America in the sixteenth and seventeenth centuries, as many as 4 million Indians lived on a continent crisscrossed by trails and rivers that formed an extensive trading network. The scores of tribes can be clustered according to three major regional groups: the Eastern Woodlands tribes, the Great Plains tribes, and the Western tribes. Although the tribes differed by geography, language, and customs, they shared many attributes and assumptions. They believed that sacred spirits live within plants and animals, and the daily challenge was to keep the spirits satisfied so as to ensure good weather, bountiful harvests, abundant game animals, and victory in battle. Not the least of their shared assumptions was that the European explorers and settlers were trespassing on their lands.

The Eastern Woodlands peoples tended to live along the rivers coursing through primeval forests. They included three distinct regional groups: the Algonquian, the Iroquoian, and the Muskogean. The dozens of Algonquian-speaking tribes stretched far beyond the Eastern Woodlands; those living in the East included the Lenni–Lenape (the Delaware), the Lumbee, the Mahican, the Mohegan, the Pequot, the Narragansett, the Wampanoag, and the

Powhatan tribes making up the Confederacy. Their settlements reached from the New England seaboard to lands along the Great Lakes and into the upper Midwest and south to New Jersey, Virginia, and the Carolinas. The Algonquian tribes along the coast were skilled at fishing; the inland tribes excelled at hunting. All of them practiced agriculture to some extent, and they frequently used canoes hollowed out of trees ("dugouts") to navigate rivers and lakes. Most Algonquians lived in small round shelters called wigwams. Their villages typically ranged from 500 to 2,000 inhabitants.

West and south of the Algonquians were the Iroquoian tribes (including the Seneca, Onondaga, Mohawk, Oneida, and Cayuga, and the Cherokee and Tuscarora in the South), whose lands spread from upstate New York south through Pennsylvania and into the upland regions of the Carolinas and Georgia. The Iroquois's skill at growing corn led them to create permanent agricultural villages. Around their villages they constructed log walls and within them they built enormous bark-covered longhouses, which housed several related family clans. Unlike the patriarchal Algonquian culture, Iroquoian society was matriarchal. In part, the matriarchy reflected the frequent absence of Iroquois men. As adept hunters and traders, the men traveled extensively for long periods. Women headed the clans, selected the chiefs, controlled the distribution of property, and planted and harvested the crops.

The third major Indian group in the Eastern Woodlands were the Muskogean-speaking chiefdoms of the South. They included the Creek, Chickasaw, and Choctaw tribes. West of the Mississippi River were the Indian peoples living on the Great Plains and in the Great Basin (present-day Utah and Nevada), many of whom had migrated from the East.

The Native Americans of the Great Plains, the Plains Indians, were a diverse lot. The Blackfeet, Cheyenne, and Arapaho were Algonquian-speaking tribes. The Comanche were Shoshonean, the Apache were Athabaskan, and the Teton Sioux and Crow were Siouan. All were nomadic tribes whose culture focused on hunting the vast herds of bison and growing corn.

The Western tribes, living along the Pacific coast, depended upon fishing, sealing, and whaling. Among them were Salish tribes, including the Tillamook; the Chinook; and the Pomo and Chumash, both speakers of a Hokan language.

Over the centuries the Native Americans of North America had adapted to changing climates and changing environments. Their resilience was remarkable. But they were unprepared for the arrival of Europeans, who were intent upon conquering, converting, exploiting, enslaving, and destroying them. The results were devastating and tragic. Epidemics wiped out millions.

Thousands more were killed by European guns and swords. Many Indians were forced to become Christians and to abandon their traditional lands, folkways, and customs. Yet amid the chaos and the carnage, Native Americans proved to be resourceful and resilient. Survivors banded together to reunite families, form new communities, preserve their traditions, and absorb the massive changes transforming their world. What for years was viewed as a simple process of conquest and displacement was in fact much more complex and nuanced. In the process of changing and adapting to new realities in accordance with their own traditions, Native Americans played a crucial role in shaping America and the origins of the United States.

FIRST CONTACTS

The discovery of the Western Hemisphere coincided with the spread of European power and culture around the world. The expansion of Europe derived from, and in turn affected, the peculiar patterns and institutions that distinguished modern times from medieval: the revival of ancient learning and the rise of the inquiring spirit; the explosive growth of trade, towns, and modern corporations; the decline of feudalism and the rise of national states; the religious zeal generated by the Protestant Reformation and the Catholic Counter-Reformation; and, on the darker side, some old sins—greed, conquest, racism, and slavery.

By the fifteenth century these forces had combined to focus European eyes on new lands to conquer or settle and on new peoples to convert, civilize, or exploit. Europeans were especially attracted by the lure of Asia, a near-mythical land of silks, jewels, and millions of "heathens" to be Christianized. Equally valued were the spices—pepper, nutmeg, clove—so essential to the preservation of food, especially in southern Europe, where the warm and humid climate accelerated spoilage.

THE VOYAGES OF COLUMBUS Asia's wealth tantalized Christopher Columbus, a gold-loving, God-fearing adventurer. Born in Genoa, Italy, in 1451, the son of a weaver, Columbus took to the sea at an early age. During the 1480s he hatched a scheme to reach Asia by sailing west. After years of disappointment and disgrace, he finally won the financial support of Ferdinand and Isabella, the enterprising Spanish monarchs whose marriage united the kingdoms of Castile and Aragon to form the nation of Spain.

In 1492, Columbus chartered one small ship, the *Santa María*, and the Spanish city of Palos supplied two smaller caravels, the *Pinta* and the *Niña*.

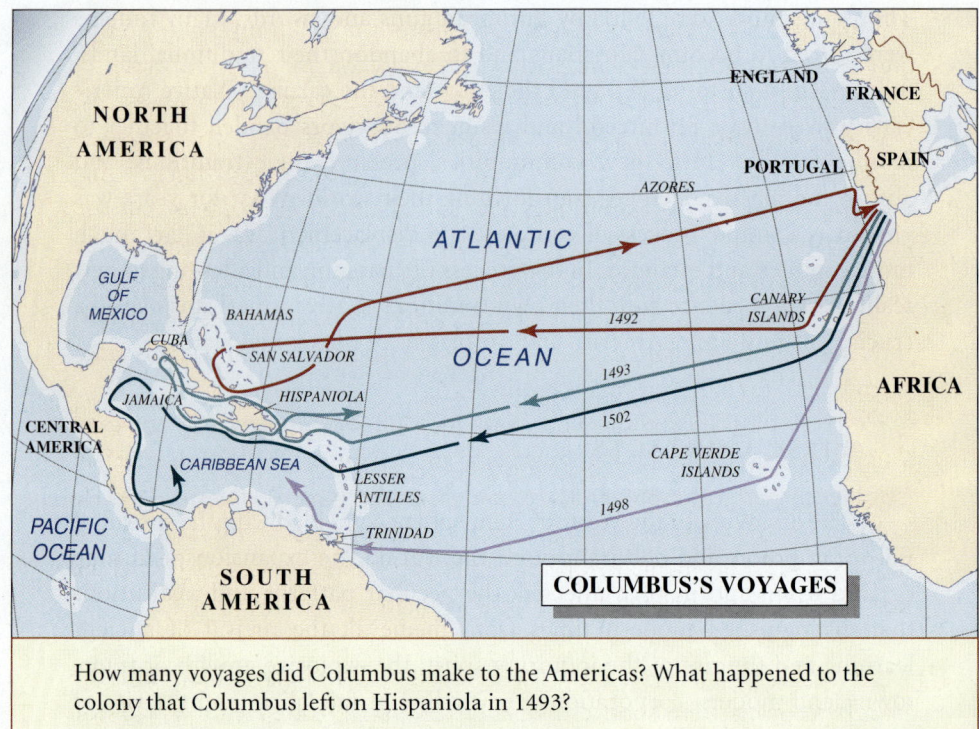

COLUMBUS'S VOYAGES

How many voyages did Columbus make to the Americas? What happened to the colony that Columbus left on Hispaniola in 1493?

From Palos this little squadron, with eighty-seven men, set sail on August 3. Early on October 12, a lookout called out, *"Tierra! Tierra!"* (Land! Land!) He had sighted an island in the Bahamas that Columbus named San Salvador (Blessed Savior). Columbus assumed they were near the Pacific "East Indies," so he called the islanders *Indios*, Indians. Their docile temperament led him to write in his journal that "with fifty men they could all be subjugated and compelled to do anything one wishes." It would be easy, he said, "to convert these people [to Catholicism] and make them work for us."

At the moment, however, Columbus was not interested in enslaving "noble savages"; he was seeking the East Indies and their fabled gold and coveted spices. He therefore continued to search through the Bahamas down to Cuba and then eastward to the island he named Española (or Hispaniola), where he first found significant amounts of gold jewelry. On the night before Christmas in 1492, the *Santa María* ran aground off Hispaniola. Columbus, still believing he had reached Asia, decided to return home. He left about forty men behind and seized a dozen natives to present as gifts to Spain's royal couple. After Columbus reached Palos, he received a hero's welcome.

The news of his remarkable discovery spread rapidly throughout Europe, and Ferdinand and Isabella instructed him to prepare for a second voyage.

Columbus recrossed the Atlantic in 1493 with seventeen ships, livestock, and well over 1,000 men, as well as royal instructions to "treat the Indians very well." Once back in the New World, however, Admiral Columbus discovered the Europeans' camp in chaos. The unsupervised soldiers had run amok, raping women, robbing villages, and as Columbus's son later added, "committing a thousand excesses for which they were mortally hated by the Indians." The natives struck back and killed ten Spaniards. A furious Columbus attacked the Indian villages, after which he loaded 550 Indians onto ships bound for the slave market in Spain.

Columbus made two more voyages to the New World. Ironically, however, the land was named not for its European "discoverer" but for another Italian explorer, Amerigo Vespucci, who traveled to the New World in 1499. He sailed along the coast of South America and reported that it was so large it must be a new continent. European mapmakers thereafter began to label the new world using a variant of Vespucci's first name: America.

THE GREAT BIOLOGICAL EXCHANGE   European contact with the place Europeans were soon calling the New World produced a worldwide biological exchange that had profound consequences. If anything, the plants and animals of the two worlds were more different from each other than were the peoples and their ways of life. Europeans had never seen such creatures as the iguana, the flying squirrel, the catfish, and the rattlesnake, nor had they seen anything quite like several other species native to America: bison (buffalo), cougars, armadillos, opossums, sloths, anacondas, toucans, condors, and hummingbirds. Turkeys, guinea pigs, llamas, and alpacas were all new to Europeans. Nor did the Native Americans know of horses, cattle, pigs, sheep, and goats, which soon arrived from Europe in abundance.

The transfer of plant life transformed the diet of both hemispheres. Before 1492, maize (sweet corn), potatoes (sweet and white), and many kinds of beans (snap, kidney, lima, and others) were unknown in the Old World. Columbus returned to Spain with a handful of corn kernels, and within a few years corn had become a staple crop throughout Europe. The white potato, although commonly called Irish, actually migrated from South America to Europe and reached North America only with the Scotch-Irish immigrants of the 1700s. Other New World food plants include peanuts, squash, peppers, tomatoes, pumpkins, pineapples, papayas, avocados, cacao (the source of chocolate), and chicle (for chewing gum). Europeans in turn brought to the New World rice, wheat, barley, oats, wine grapes, melons, coffee, olives,

A land Sort of the Savages esteeme above all other Torts

Unfamiliar wildlife

A box tortoise drawn by John White, one of the earliest English settlers in America.

bananas, "Kentucky" bluegrass, daisies, dandelions, and clover.

The beauty of the biological exchange between Old and New Worlds was that the food plants were more complementary than competitive. Indian corn spread quickly throughout the world. Plants initially domesticated by Native Americans now make up about a third of the world's food crops.

Europeans also adopted many Native American devices, such as canoes, snowshoes, moccasins, hammocks, kayaks, ponchos, dogsleds, toboggans, and parkas. The rubber ball and the game of lacrosse have Indian origins as well. Still other New World contributions include tobacco and several other drugs, among them curare (a muscle relaxant), coca (for making cocaine), and cinchona bark (for making quinine).

By far the most significant aspect of the biological exchange, however, was the transmission of infectious diseases from Europe and Africa to the New World. European colonists and enslaved Africans brought with them deadly pathogens that Native Americans had never experienced: smallpox, typhus, diphtheria, bubonic plague, malaria, yellow fever, and cholera. In dealing with such diseases over the centuries, people in the Old World had developed antibodies that enabled most of them to survive infection. Disease-toughened adventurers, colonists, and Africans arriving in the New World thus carried viruses and bacteria that consumed Indians, who lacked the immunity that forms from experience with the diseases.

The results were catastrophic. Far more Indians died from contagions than from combat. Major diseases such as typhus and smallpox produced pandemics in the New World on a scale never witnessed in history. In the face of such terrible and mysterious diseases, panic-stricken Indians fled to neighboring villages, unwittingly spreading the diseases in the process. Unable to explain or cure the contagions, Indian chiefs and religious leaders often lost their stature. As a consequence, tribal cohesion and cultural life disintegrated, and efforts to resist European conquest collapsed.

Smallpox was an especially ghastly disease in the New World. In central Mexico alone, some 8 million people, perhaps a third of the entire Indian population, died of smallpox within a decade of the arrival of the Spanish. Disease became the most powerful weapon of the European invaders. A

Spanish explorer noted that "half the natives" died from smallpox and "blamed us." Many Europeans, however, interpreted such epidemics as diseases sent by God to punish Indians who resisted conversion to Christianity.

EXPLORATION AND CONQUEST OF THE NEW WORLD

Excited by Columbus's remarkable discoveries, professional explorers, mostly Italians, probed the shorelines of America during the early sixteenth century. The first to sight the North American continent was John Cabot, a Venetian sponsored by King Henry VII of England. Cabot crossed the North Atlantic in 1497. His landfall at what the king called "the newe founde lande," in present-day Canada, gave England the basis for a later claim to all of North America. During the early sixteenth century, however, the British became so preoccupied with internal divisions and conflicts with France that for several decades they failed to follow up Cabot's discoveries.

During the sixteenth century the New World thus was a Spanish preserve, except for Brazil, which was a Portuguese colony. The Caribbean Sea served as the funnel through which Spanish power entered the New World. After establishing colonies on Hispaniola and at Santo Domingo, which became the capital of the West Indies, the Spaniards proceeded eastward to Puerto Rico (1508) and westward to Cuba (1511–1514). Their motives were explicit. Said one soldier, "We came here to serve God and the king, and also to get rich."

A CLASH OF CULTURES The often-violent encounter between Spaniards and Indians in the New World brought together quite different forms of technological development. Whereas Indians used dugout canoes for transportation, Europeans sailed oceangoing warships and brought steel swords, firearms, explosives, and armor, as well as fighting greyhound dogs, which the Spaniards used to guard their camps. The Europeans' horses, pigs, and cattle served as sources of food and leather. Horses provided greater speed and introduced a decided psychological advantage in battles.

The most dramatic European conquest of a major Indian civilization began in 1519, when the Spaniard Hernán Cortés and 800 men landed on the east coast of Mexico. Cortés then set about a daring conquest of the Aztec Empire. The 200-mile march from the coast through difficult mountain passes to the magnificent Aztec capital of Tenochtitlán (the site of present-day Mexico City) and the subjugation of the Aztecs, who thought

Cortés in Mexico

Page from the Lienzo de Tlaxcala, a historical narrative from the sixteenth century. The scene, in which Cortés is shown seated on a throne, depicts the arrival of the Spaniards in Tlaxcala.

themselves "masters of the world," were two of the most remarkable feats in human history. Tenochtitlán, with some 200,000 inhabitants, was by far the largest city in North America, much larger than Seville, the most populous city in Spain. Graced by wide canals and featuring beautiful stone pyramids and other buildings, the fabled capital seemed impregnable.

Cortés, however, made the most of his assets. His invasion force had landed in a region where the natives were still resisting the spread of Aztec power and were ready to embrace new allies, especially those who possessed powerful weapons. By a combination of threats and deception, Cortés and his thousands of Indian allies entered Tenochtitlán peacefully and made the emperor, Montezuma II, his puppet. This state of affairs lasted until the spring of 1520, when the Aztecs rebelled, took over the city, and stoned Montezuma to death. The Spaniards' Indian allies remained loyal, however, and the remarkable Cortés gradually regrouped his forces; in 1521 he took the city again.

Within twenty years the Spanish conquistadores (soldiers), had established a sprawling empire in the New World. Between 1522 and 1528 various lieutenants of Cortés's conquered the remnants of Indian culture in the

Yucatán Peninsula and Guatemala. Then, in 1531, Francisco Pizarro led a band of soldiers down the Pacific coast from Panama toward Peru, where they brutally subdued the Inca Empire. From Peru, conquistadores extended Spanish authority through Chile and Colombia.

SPANISH AMERICA   The Spanish conquistadores transferred to America a system known as the *encomienda*, whereby favored officers became privileged landowners (*encomenderos*), who were expected to protect and care for Indian villages or groups of villages and support missionary priests. In turn they could require tribute from the villagers in the form of goods and labor. Spanish America therefore developed from the start a society of extremes: wealthy European conquistadores at one end of the spectrum and native peoples held in poverty at the other end.

By the mid-1500s, Indians were nearly extinct in the West Indies, killed more often by European diseases than by Spanish exploitation. To take their place, the colonizers as early as 1503 began to import enslaved Africans. In all of Spain's New World empire, the Indian population dropped from about 50 million at the outset to 4 million in the seventeenth century, slowly rising again, to 7.5 million, by the end of the eighteenth century. Whites, who

Missionaries in the New World

A Spanish mission in New Mexico, established to spread the Catholic faith among the native peoples.

totaled no more than 100,000 in the mid–sixteenth century, numbered over 3 million by the end of the colonial period.

The Indians, however, did not always lack advocates. Some Catholic missionaries offered a sharp contrast to the conquistadores. They ventured into remote areas, often without weapons or protection, to spread the gospel—sometimes risking their lives. Where conquistadores sought to wrest gold, land, and labor from the Indians, the Spanish missionaries wanted their souls, and they had a tremendous impact upon Native American culture. At their worst the missionaries were bigots determined to rid "heathen" people of their native religion and many of their cultural practices. At their best, however, missionaries were impassioned defenders of the Indians.

THE SPANISH HERITAGE   Throughout the sixteenth century much of what is now the United States belonged to Spain, and Spanish culture etched a lasting imprint upon American ways of life. Spain's colonial presence lasted more than three centuries, much longer than either England's or France's, and its possessions were much more far-reaching. The vice royalty of New Spain was centered in Mexico, but its frontiers extended from the Florida Keys to Alaska and included areas not currently thought of as formerly Spanish, such as the Deep South and the lower Midwest. Spanish place-names—San Francisco, Santa Barbara, Los Angeles, San Diego, Tucson, Santa Fe, San Antonio, Pensacola, and St. Augustine—survive to this day, as do Spanish influences in art, architecture, literature, music, law, and cuisine.

Although Spain's influence was strongest from Mexico southward, the "Spanish borderlands" of the southern United States, from Florida to California, preserve many reminders of the Spanish presence. The earliest known exploration of Florida was made in 1513 by Juan Ponce de León, then governor of Puerto Rico. He sought the mythic fountain of youth but instead found alligators, swamps, and abundant wildlife. Meanwhile, other Spanish explorers skirted the coast of the Gulf of Mexico from Florida to Mexico's Yucatán Peninsula, scouted the Atlantic coast from Key West to Newfoundland, established a town at St. Augustine, Florida, and a mission at Santa Fe, New Mexico, and planted a short-lived colony on the Carolina coast.

Spain established provinces in North America not so much as commercial enterprises but as defensive buffers protecting its more lucrative trading empire in Mexico, the Caribbean, and South America. During the seventeenth century the Spaniards were concerned about French traders infiltrating from Louisiana, English settlers crossing into Florida, and Russian seal hunters wandering down the California coast. Yet the Spanish settlements in what is today the United States never flourished. England and France surpassed

Spain in America because Spain failed to embrace what the other imperial powers decided early on: that developing a thriving Indian trade in goods was more important than the conversion of "heathens" and the often fruitless search for gold and silver.

THE SPANISH SOUTHWEST Spain eventually founded other permanent settlements in present-day New Mexico, Texas, and California. Eager to

SPANISH EXPLORATIONS OF THE MAINLAND

- Núñez de Balboa, 1513
- Ponce de León, 1513
- Cortés, 1519
- Narváez, 1527–1528
- Pizarro, 1531–1533
- Cabeza de Vaca, 1528–1536
- de Soto, 1539–1542
- Coronado, 1540–1542

What were the Spanish conquistadores' goals for exploring the Americas? How did Cortés conquer the Aztecs?

pacify rather than fight the Indians of the region, the Spanish used religion as an instrument of colonial control. Missionaries, particularly Franciscans and Jesuits, established isolated Catholic missions where they imposed Christianity upon the Indians. The soldiers who were sent to protect the missions were housed in presidios, or forts, while their families and the merchants accompanying the soldiers lived in adjacent villages.

The land that would later be called New Mexico was the first center of mission activity in the American Southwest. In 1598, Juan de Oñate, the wealthy son of a Spanish family in Mexico, received a land grant for the territory north of Mexico above the Rio Grande. With an expeditionary military force made up of Mexican Indians and mestizos (sons of Spanish fathers and Indian mothers), he took possession of New Mexico, established a capital at San Gabriel, and dispatched expeditions to look for gold and silver. He promised the Pueblo leaders that Spanish dominion would bring them peace, justice, prosperity, and protection.

Some Indians welcomed the missionaries as "powerful witches" capable of easing their burdens. Others tried to use the Spanish invaders as allies against rival tribes. Still others saw no alternative but to submit. The Indians living in Spanish New Mexico were required to pay tribute to their *encomenderos* and perform personal tasks for them, including sexual favors. Disobedient Indians were flogged by soldiers and priests. In 1598 the Pueblos revolted. During three days of fighting, the Spanish killed 500 Pueblo men and 300 women and children. Survivors were enslaved.

During the first three quarters of the seventeenth century, Spanish New Mexico expanded very slowly. The hoped-for deposits of gold and silver were never found, and a limited food supply dulled the interest of potential colonists. In 1608 the Spanish government decided to turn New Mexico into a royal province. Two years later the Spanish moved the province's capital to Santa Fe, the first permanent seat of government in the present-day United States.

Franciscan missionaries claimed that 86,000 Pueblo Indians had been converted to Christianity. In fact, however, resentment among the Indians increased with time. In 1680 a charismatic Indian leader named Popé organized a massive rebellion. Within a few weeks the Spaniards had been driven from New Mexico. Almost 400 of the Europeans were killed in the uprising. The Indians burned churches, tortured and executed priests, and destroyed all relics of Christianity. It took fourteen years and four military assaults for the Spaniards to subdue the region. Thereafter, except for sporadic raids by Apaches and Navajos, the Spanish exercised stable control over New Mexico.

HORSES AND THE GREAT PLAINS   Another major consequence of the Pueblo Revolt was the opportunity it afforded Indian rebels to acquire hundreds of coveted Spanish horses (Spanish authorities had made it illegal for Indians to own horses). The Pueblos in turn established a thriving horse trade with the Navajos, Apaches, and other tribes. By 1690, horses were evident in Texas, and they soon spread across the Great Plains, the vast rolling grasslands extending from the Missouri River valley in the east to the base of the Rocky Mountains in the west.

Horses were a disruptive ecological force in North America. Prior to the arrival of horses, Indians hunted on foot and used dogs as their beasts of burden, hauling supplies on travois, devices made from two long poles connected by leather straps. Dogs, however, are carnivores, and it was difficult to find enough meat to feed them. Horses thus changed everything, providing the pedestrian Plains Indians with a transforming source of mobility and power. Horses are grazing animals, and the grasslands of the Great Plains offered plenty of forage. Horses could also haul up to seven times as much weight as dogs, and their speed and endurance made the Indians much more

Plains Indians

The horse-stealing raid depicted in this hide painting demonstrates the essential role horses played in Plains life.

effective hunters and warriors. In addition, horses enabled Indians to travel farther to hunt, trade, and fight.

Horses transformed the economy as well as the ecology of the Great Plains. Tribes such as the Arapaho, Cheyenne, Comanche, Kiowa, and Sioux reinvented themselves as equestrian societies. They left their traditional woodland villages on the fringes of the plains and became nomadic bison hunters, using virtually every part of the bison they killed: meat for food; hides for clothing, shoes, bedding, and shelter; muscles and tendons for thread and bowstrings; intestines for containers; bones for tools; horns for eating utensils; hair for headdresses; and dung for fuel.

In the short run the horse brought prosperity and mobility to the Plains Indians. Horses became the center and symbol of Indian life on the plains. Yet the Indians began to kill more bison than the herds could replace. In addition, horses competed with the bison for food, depleting the grass and compacting the soil in the river valleys during the winter. And as tribes traveled greater distances and encountered more people, infectious diseases spread more widely. Other problems ensued. Horses became so valuable that they intensified intertribal warfare. And as the herds of bison dwindled, the value of buffalo hides increased and hunters began to practice polygamy, because more wives could process more buffalo. The rising economic value of wives eventually led Plains Indians to raid other tribes in search of captive brides as well as horses. The introduction of horses into the Great Plains, then, was a decidedly mixed blessing. By 1800 a white trader could observe that "this is a delightful country, and were it not for perpetual wars, the natives might be the happiest people on earth."

CHRISTIAN EUROPE

Sixteenth-century European life was centered on religion. It was an age of faith, in which spiritual concerns were all-encompassing and deeply felt. In matters of faith, the Roman Catholic Church and the Bible were the pervasive sources of authority. Cathedral spires dotted every city, and the peal of church bells reminded the faithful of their daily duty to pray. Weekly activities were organized around worship services, prayer rituals, and religious festivals and ceremonies. People believed fervently in heaven and hell, devils and witches, demons and angels. Europeans also took for granted the collaboration of church and state; political leaders required religious uniformity and enforced conformity. Heresy and blasphemy were not tolerated. Christians were deadly serious about their faith. They were often willing to kill and die for their beliefs. During the Reformation, Catholics and Protestants persecuted, imprisoned, tortured, and killed each other—in large numbers.

One of Spain's primary motives in exploring the New World was to convert the "heathens" to Catholicism. Through the various evangelical orders—Augustinians, Dominicans, and especially Franciscans and Jesuits—the Roman Catholic Church, together with the Spanish government launched a massive effort to convert the Indians. During the sixteenth century, thousands of Catholic priests fanned out across New Spain (and, later, New France). The missionaries ventured into the remotest areas to spread the gospel, often suffering terrible torture and martyrdom for their efforts. Many of them decided that the Indians of Mexico could be converted only by force. "Though they seem to be a simple people," a Spanish friar declared in 1562, "they are up to all sorts of mischief, and are obstinately attached to the rituals and ceremonies of their forefathers. The whole land is certainly damned, and without compulsion they [the Mayans] will never speak the [religious] truth." By the end of the century, there were over 300 monasteries or missions in the New World, and Catholicism had become a major instrument of Spanish imperialism.

CHALLENGES TO THE SPANISH EMPIRE   The success of Catholic Spain in exploring, conquering, and exploiting the New World spurred Portugal, France, England, and the Netherlands to develop their own imperial claims in the Western Hemisphere. The French were the first to pose a serious threat to the Spanish monopoly in the New World. In 1524 the French king sent the Italian Giovanni da Verrazano in search of a passage to Asia. Sighting land (probably at Cape Fear, North Carolina), he ranged along the coast as far north as Maine, but it would be another seventeen years before the French would make their first effort at colonization. Jacques Cartier explored the Gulf of St. Lawrence and ventured up the St. Lawrence River as far as present-day Montreal. Near Quebec he established a short-lived colony in 1541.

Thereafter, however, French interest in Canada waned, as the French were preoccupied with the religious civil wars wracking their country. Not until the early seventeenth century, when Samuel de Champlain established settlements in Acadia (Nova Scotia) and at Quebec, along the St. Lawrence River, did French colonization in America begin in earnest. Enterprising French traders negotiated with Indians for their fur pelts, and French Jesuit missionaries cultivated their souls.

Acquiring furs and ministering to "heathens" took the French southward as well. In 1673, Louis Jolliet and Père Jacques Marquette, a Jesuit priest, explored the Mississippi River, but fearing an encounter with the Spaniards,

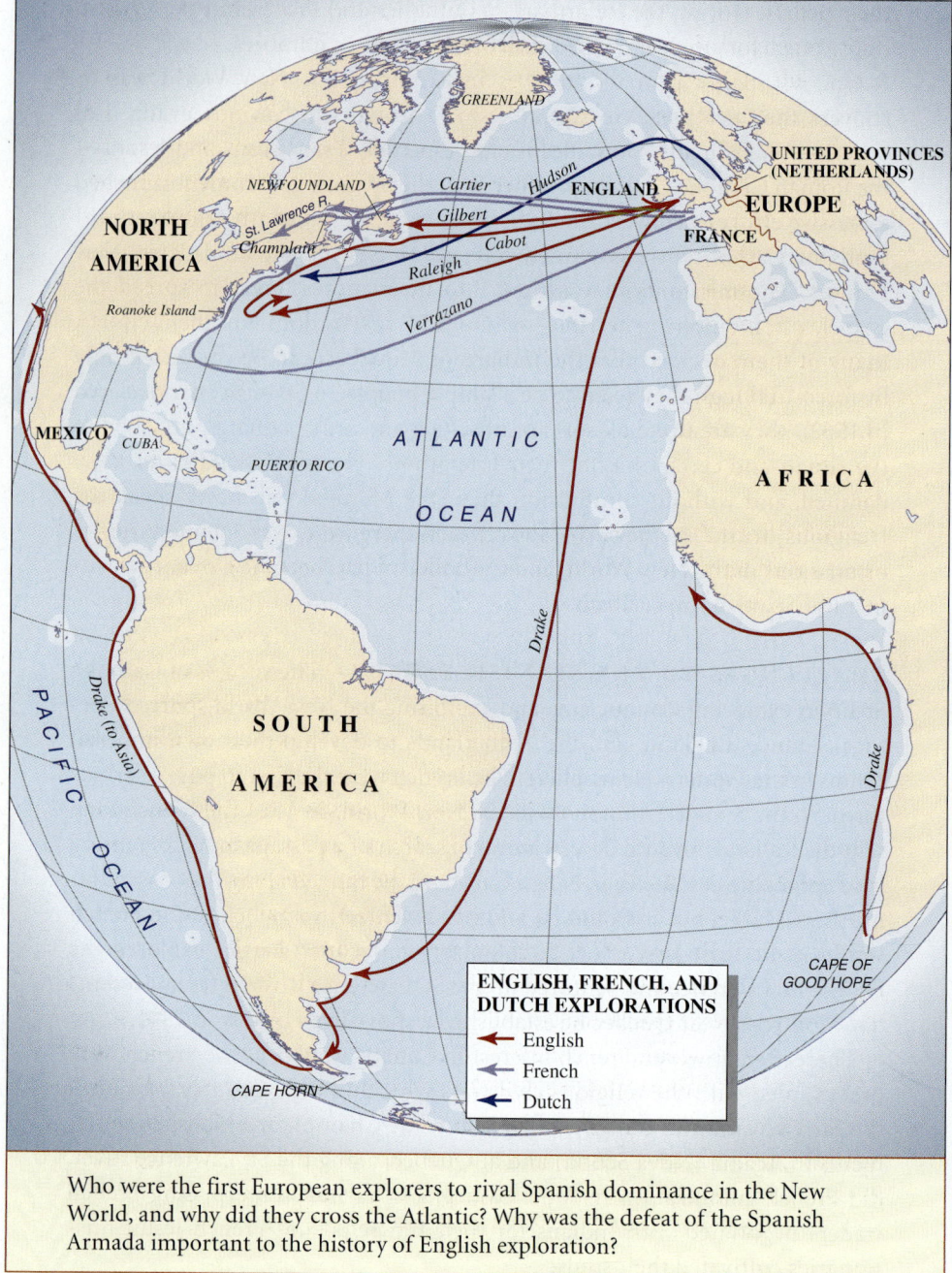

ENGLISH, FRENCH, AND
DUTCH EXPLORATIONS

— English
— French
— Dutch

Who were the first European explorers to rival Spanish dominance in the New World, and why did they cross the Atlantic? Why was the defeat of the Spanish Armada important to the history of English exploration?

they turned back before reaching the Gulf of Mexico. Nine years later René-Robert Cavelier, sieur de La Salle, did the same, but he ventured all the way to the Gulf of Mexico. There, near the river's delta, the French in the early eighteenth century would establish a settlement called New Orleans. The French thereby came to control not only Canada but also the major inland waterway in North America, the Mississippi River. But because the French monarchy emphasized the fur trade and Catholic missionaries rather than permanent settlement, French America remained only sparsely populated.

From the mid-1500s greater threats to Spanish power in the New World arose from the growing strength of the Dutch and the English. The prosperous provinces of the Netherlands, which had passed by inheritance to the Spanish king and had become largely Protestant, rebelled against Spanish Catholic rule in 1567. A prolonged, bloody struggle for independence ensued; Spain did not accept the independence of the Dutch republic until 1648.

Almost from the beginning of the Dutch revolt against Spain, Dutch privateers plundered Spanish ships. The Dutch raiders soon had their counterpart in England's "sea dogges": John Hawkins, Francis Drake, and others. While Queen Elizabeth of England steered a tortuous course to avoid open war with Spain, she encouraged both Dutch and English sea captains to attack Spanish vessels. In 1577, Francis Drake set out on his famous adventure around South America to raid Spanish towns along the Pacific coast. Three years later he returned in triumph.

Sporadic British piracy against the Spanish continued until 1587, when Queen Elizabeth had her Catholic cousin, Mary, Queen of Scots, beheaded for her involvement in a plot to kill the English queen and elevate herself to the throne. In revenge for Mary's execution, Spain's King Philip II vowed to crush Protestant England and began to gather his ill-fated invasion fleet, called the Armada. The ambitious enterprise quickly became a case of incompetence and mismanagement accompanied by bad luck. The heavy Spanish warships could not cope with the smaller, faster English vessels, and a ferocious storm destroyed much of the Spanish fleet. Defeat of the Spanish Armada convinced the English that the Spanish navy was no longer invincible and cleared the way for English colonization of the Americas. England at the end of the sixteenth century entered the springtime of its power, filled with a youthful zest for the new worlds and their wonders.

End of Chapter Review

CHAPTER SUMMARY

- **Pre-Columbian America** At the time of contact, Native American tribes, such as the Aztecs and Mayas of Central America, had developed empires sustained by large-scale agriculture and long-distance trade. North American Indians, however, were less well organized. Those Indians in the Ohio and Mississippi Valleys did establish important trading centers sustained by intensive agriculture.

- **Age of Exploration** By the 1490s, Europe was experiencing a renewed curiosity about the world. New technologies led to the creation of better maps and navigation techniques. Nation-states searching for gold and glory emerged; and Europeans desired silks and spices from Asia.

- **Great Biological Exchange** Contact resulted in a great biological exchange. Crops such as maize, beans, and potatoes became staples in the Old World. Indians incorporated into their culture Eurasian animals such as the horse and pig. The invaders carried pathogens that set off pandemics of smallpox, plague, and other illnesses for which Native Americans had no immunity.

- **Colonizing the Americas** When the Spanish began to colonize the New World, the conversion of Native Americans to Catholicism was important but the search for gold and silver was primary. In that search, the Spanish demanded goods and labor from their new subjects. As the Indian population declined, the Spanish began to "import" enslaved Africans.

- **Spanish Legacy** Spain left a lasting legacy in the borderlands from California to Florida. Catholic missionaries contributed to the destruction of the old ways of life by actively exterminating "heathen" beliefs in the Southwest, a practice that led to open rebellion in 1598 and 1680.

- **Protestant Reformation** The Protestant Reformation shattered the unity of Catholic Europe. By the time of Elizabeth I of England, religious differences had led to state-supported plunder of Spanish treasure ships, then to open hostility with Spain. England's defeat of the Spanish Armada cleared the path for colonization in North America.

CHRONOLOGY

by 12,000 B.C.	Humans have migrated to the Americas, most of them from Siberia
A.D. 1492	Columbus, sailing for Spain, makes first voyage of discovery
1497	John Cabot explores Newfoundland
1503	First Africans are brought to the Americas
1513	Juan Ponce de León explores Florida
1517–1648	The Protestant Reformation spurred religious conflict between Catholics and Protestants
1519	Hernán Cortés begins the Spanish conquest of the Aztec Empire
1531	Francisco Pizarro subdues the Incas of Peru
1541	Jacques Cartier, sailing for France, explores the St. Lawrence River
1588	The Spanish Armada is defeated by the English
1680	Popé leads rebellion in New Mexico

KEY TERMS & NAMES

2

BRITAIN AND
ITS COLONIES

FOCUS QUESTIONS wwnorton.com/studyspace

- What were Britain's reasons for establishing colonies in North America?
- Why did the first English colony, at Jamestown, experience hardships in its first decades?
- How important was religion as a motivation for colonization?
- How did British colonists and Native Americans adapt to each other's presence?
- Why was it possible for England to establish successful colonies by 1700?

English colonization of North America began in 1584, when Sir Walter Raleigh led an expedition that explored the Outer Banks of North Carolina and discovered Roanoke Island. Three years later about 100 settlers arrived, including women and children, under the leadership of Governor John White. After a month in Roanoke, White returned to England to get supplies, leaving behind the other colonists, including his daughter Elinor, her husband, and her baby, Virginia Dare, the first English child born in North America. White, however, was long delayed because of the war with Spain. When he finally returned, in 1590, he found the village of "Ralegh" abandoned and pillaged, possibly by Indians or Spaniards. No trace of the "lost colonists" was ever found, and there were no English settlers in North America when Queen Elizabeth died, in 1603.

SETTLING THE CHESAPEAKE

With the death of Queen Elizabeth, the Tudor family line ended, and the throne fell to Elizabeth's cousin James VI of Scotland, the son of the ill-fated Mary, Queen of Scots. The first of the Stuarts, he ruled England as James I, as Elizabeth had planned. The Stuart dynasty spanned most of the seventeenth century, a turbulent time of religious and political tensions, civil war, and foreign intrigues. During those eventful years in English history, all but one of the thirteen North American colonies were founded. They were quite diverse in geography, motives, and composition, a diversity that has since been a trademark and a strength of American society.

In 1606, having made peace with Spain, thereby freeing up resources and men for colonization, James I chartered what was called the Virginia Company, with two divisions, the First Colony of London and the Second Colony of Plymouth. The Virginia Company was a for-profit enterprise. The stockholders viewed the colony as a source of gold, wine, citrus fruits, olive oil, and forest products needed for England's navy. Many also still hoped to discover a passage to India. Few if any investors foresaw what the first English colony would become: a fertile place to grow tobacco. — key crop

From the outset the pattern of English colonization diverged significantly from that of Spanish activities in the New World. The autocratic Spaniards regulated all aspects of colonial life. The English had a different model, based on their settlements, or "plantations," in Ireland, which they had conquered by military force under Queen Elizabeth. Within their own pale (or limit) of settlement in Ireland, the English had set about transplanting their familiar way of life insofar as possible. Thus the English subjugated the Indians of North America much as they had the Irish in Ireland. In America the English settled along the Atlantic seaboard, where the native populations were relatively sparse. There was no Aztec or Inca Empire to conquer.

VIRGINIA   The London group of the Virginia Company planted the first permanent colony in Virginia, named after Elizabeth I, "the Virgin Queen." On May 6, 1607, three tiny ships loaded with 105 men reached Chesapeake Bay after four storm-tossed months at sea. They chose a river with a northwest bend—in the hope of finding a passage to Asia—and settled about forty miles inland to hide from marauding Spaniards.

The river they called the James and the colony, Jamestown. After building a fort, thatched huts, a storehouse, and a church, the colonists began planting, but most of them were townsmen unfamiliar with farming or "gentlemen" adventurers who scorned manual labor. They had come to find gold, not to live as homesteaders. Ignorant of woodlore, they did not know how to exploit the area's abundant game and fish. Supplies from England were undependable, and only John Smith's firm leadership and trade with the Indians, who taught the colonists to grow maize, enabled them to survive.

The Indians of the region were loosely organized. Powhatan was the charismatic chief of some thirty Algonquian-speaking tribes in eastern Virginia. The tribes making up the so-called Powhatan Confederacy were largely an agricultural people; corn was their primary crop. Powhatan hoped to develop a lucrative trade and military alliance with the English; he realized too late that the newcomers intended to seize his lands and subjugate his people.

"Ould Virginia"

A 1624 map of Virginia by John Smith, showing Chief Powhatan in the upper left.

The colonists, as it happened, had more than a match for Powha.. Captain John Smith, a soldier of fortune with rare powers of leadership and self-promotion. With the colonists on the verge of starvation, Smith imposed strict discipline and forced all to labor, declaring that "he that will not work shall not eat." Smith also bargained with the Indians and mapped the Chesapeake region. Despite his efforts, only 38 of the original 105 colonists survived the first nine months.

John Smith's efforts to save the struggling colony abruptly ended when he suffered a gunpowder burn and sailed back to England in 1609. More colonists were dispatched, including several women. The colony lapsed into anarchy and suffered "the starving time," the winter of 1609–1610, during which most of the colonists, weakened by hunger, fell prey to disease. A relief party found only about sixty settlers still alive in 1610.

For the next seven years the colony limped along until it gradually found a reason for being: tobacco. In 1612, John Rolfe had begun to experiment with the harsh-tasting Virginia tobacco, and by 1616 a smoother-tasting variety of the weed had become a valuable export. As Virginia's tobacco production soared, planters purchased indentured servants (colonists who exchanged their labor for the cost of passage to America), thus increasing the flow of immigrants to the colony. Meanwhile, Rolfe made another contribution to stability, by marrying Pocahontas, the daughter of Powhatan. Their marriage helped ease deteriorating relations between the Indians and the English settlers.

In 1618, officials in London initiated a series of reforms intended to shore up their struggling American colony. They first inaugurated a new "headright" policy. Anyone who bought a share in the company or could transport himself to Virginia could have fifty acres and fifty more for any servants he might send or bring. The following year the company relaxed its tight legal code and promised that the settlers would have the "rights of Englishmen," including a representative assembly. On July 30, 1619, the first General Assembly of Virginia met in the Jamestown church and deliberated for five days, "sweating and stewing, and battling flies and mosquitoes." It was an eventful year in two other respects. During 1619 a ship arrived with ninety "young maidens" to be sold to husbands of their own choice for the cost of transportation (about 125 pounds of tobacco). And a Dutch warship dropped off "20 Negars," the first Africans known to have been brought to English America.

Yet the English foothold in Virginia remained tenuous. Some 14,000 people had migrated to the colony since 1607, but the population in 1624 stood at a precarious 1,132. The king appointed a commission to investigate the running of the struggling colony by the Virginia Company, and on the commission's recommendation a court dissolved the company. In 1624, Virginia became a royal colony.

Relations with the Indians continued in a state of what the governor's council called "perpetual enmity" until the Indians staged a major attack in 1644. The English suffered 350 casualties, but they put down the uprising with such ferocity that nothing quite like it happened again. The combination of warfare and disease decimated the Indians of Virginia. The 24,000 Algonquians who inhabited the colony in 1607 were reduced to 2,000 by 1669.

MARYLAND   In 1634, ten years after Virginia became a royal colony, a neighboring settlement appeared on the northern shores of Chesapeake Bay. Named Maryland in honor of Queen Henrietta Maria, it was the first so-called proprietary colony, granted by the king not to a joint-stock company but to an individual, Lord Baltimore. Sir George Calvert, the first Lord

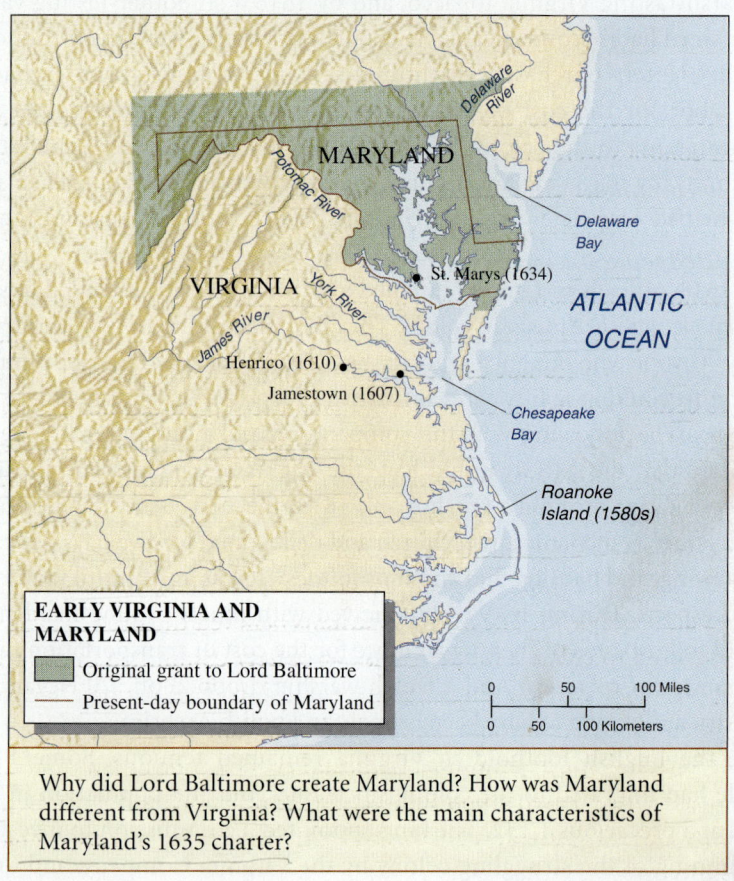

EARLY VIRGINIA AND MARYLAND

▇ Original grant to Lord Baltimore
— Present-day boundary of Maryland

Why did Lord Baltimore create Maryland? How was Maryland different from Virginia? What were the main characteristics of Maryland's 1635 charter?

Baltimore, had announced in 1625 his conversion to Catholicism and sought the colony as a refuge for English Catholics, who were subjected to discrimination at home. The charter for such a colony was finally issued in 1632, after his death.

His son, Cecilius Calvert, the second Lord Baltimore, founded the colony in 1634 at St. Marys, on a small stream near the mouth of the Potomac River. Calvert brought along Catholic gentlemen as landholders, but a majority of the servants were Protestant. The charter gave Calvert power to make laws with the consent of the freemen (all property holders). The first legislative assembly met in 1635 and later divided into two houses, with governor and council sitting separately. The charter also empowered the proprietor to grant huge manorial estates, and Maryland had some sixty before 1676. But the Lords Baltimore soon found that to draw large numbers of settlers, they had to offer small farms, most of which planted tobacco.

SETTLING NEW ENGLAND

Meanwhile, far to the north of the Chesapeake Bay, quite different English colonies were emerging. The New England colonists were generally made up of middle-class families who could pay their own way across the Atlantic. The Northeast, unlike the Chesapeake colonies, had relatively few indentured servants, and there was no planter elite. Most male settlers were small farmers, merchants, seamen, or fishermen. New England also attracted more women than did the southern colonies. Although its soil was not as fertile and its farmers not as wealthy, New England was a much healthier place to settle. Because of its colder climate, the region did not experience the infectious diseases that ravaged the southern colonies. Life expectancy was much longer. By 1700, New England's white population exceeded that of Maryland and Virginia.

Most early New Englanders were devout Puritans, who embraced a much more rigorous Protestant faith and simpler rituals than did the Anglicans of Virginia and Maryland. The zealous Puritans believed themselves to be on a divine mission to create a model Christian society committed to the proper worship of God. In New England these self-described "saints" sought to purify their churches of all Catholic and Anglican rituals, supervise one another in practicing a communal faith, and enact a code of laws and a government structure based upon biblical principles. Such a holy settlement, they hoped, would provide a beacon of righteousness for a wicked England to emulate.

PLYMOUTH   The Pilgrims who established the Plymouth colony were bent not on finding gold or making a fortune but on building a Christian commonwealth. They belonged to the most uncompromising sect of Puritans, the Separatists (Nonconformists), a small group that had severed all ties with the Church of England. The Church of England, according to the Puritans, had retained too many vestiges of Catholicism. Viewing themselves as "the godly," they demanded that the Anglican Church rid itself of "papist" rituals—no use of holy water, no elegant robes (vestments), no bejeweled gold crosses, no worship of saints and relics, no kneeling for Communion, no "viperous" bishops and archbishops, no organ music. The Separatists went further. Concluding that the Church of England could not be fixed, they resolved to create their own godly congregations separate from the established church. Such rebelliousness infuriated Anglican officials. During the late sixteenth century, Separatists were "hunted & persecuted on every side." English authorities imprisoned Separatist leaders, three of whom were hanged, drawn, and quartered. Persecuted by King James I and Anglican officials, the Separatists fled to Holland in 1607.

They grew uneasy with Dutch folkways, however, and decided to move to America. These "Pilgrims" secured a land patent from the Virginia Company, and in 1620, about 100 men, women, and children, led by William Bradford, crammed into the *Mayflower* for the transatlantic voyage. Only half the voyagers were Pilgrim "saints," Christians recognized as having been elected by God for salvation; the rest were non-Pilgrim "strangers": ordinary settlers, hired hands, and indentured servants.

A stormy voyage led them to Cape Cod, off the coast of Massachusetts, far north of Virginia. Exploring parties chose for their settlement a place they called Plymouth. Since they were outside the jurisdiction of any organized government, forty-one of the Pilgrims entered into a formal agreement to abide by laws made by leaders of their own choosing—the Mayflower Compact of November 21, 1620. Used later as a model by other New England settlers, the compact helped establish the distinctive American tradition of consensual government.

Throughout its separate existence, until it was absorbed into Massachusetts in 1691, the Plymouth colony's government grew out of the Mayflower Compact, which was not a formal constitution but an agreement among members of a religious group who believed that God had made a covenant (or agreement) with them to provide a way to salvation. Thus the civil government evolved naturally out of the church government, and the members of each were initially identical.

Nearly half the Pilgrims died, but friendly relations with the neighboring Wampanoag Indians proved their salvation. In the spring of 1621, the colonists met Squanto, who showed them how to grow maize. By autumn the Pilgrims had a bumper crop of corn, a flourishing fur trade, and a supply of lumber for shipment. To celebrate, they held a harvest feast with the Wampanoags, an annual ritual that would later be dubbed Thanksgiving.

MASSACHUSETTS BAY   The Plymouth colony's population never rose above 7,000, and after ten years it was overshadowed by its larger neighbor, the Massachusetts Bay Colony. That colony, too, was intended to be a holy commonwealth made up of religious settlers bound together in the harmonious worship of God and the pursuit of their "callings." The colony got its start in 1629, when a group of Puritans and merchants persuaded King Charles I (son of James I) to grant their newly formed Massachusetts Bay Company an area north of the Plymouth colony for settlement. Leaders of the company at first looked upon it mainly as a business venture, but a majority faction, led by John Winthrop, a respected lawyer animated by intense religious convictions, resolved to use the colony as a refuge for persecuted Puritans and as an instrument for building a "wilderness Zion" in America.

Winthrop was a courageous leader who reflected the strengths and weaknesses of the Puritan movement. In 1629, at forty years of age, he found himself managing a floundering English estate that could not support his seven sons. Even more unsettling was the government's heightened persecution of Puritans and other dissenters. Hence he eagerly supported the idea of establishing a spiritual plantation in the New World, and he agreed to head up the enterprise. Winthrop shrewdly took advantage of a fateful omission in the royal charter for the Massachusetts Bay Company: the usual proviso that the company maintain its home office in England. Winthrop's group took its charter with them, thereby transferring government authority to Massachusetts Bay, where they hoped to ensure local control.

In 1630 the *Arbella*, with John Winthrop and the charter aboard, embarked with ten other ships for Massachusetts. There were 700 Puritans on board. Some 200 of the exiles died in the crossing. In "A Modell of Christian Charity," a speech delivered on board, Winthrop told his fellow Puritans that they were a God-chosen people on a divine mission: "We must consider that we shall be a city upon a hill"—a shining example of what a truly godly community could be. By the end of 1630, seventeen ships bearing 1,000 more colonists

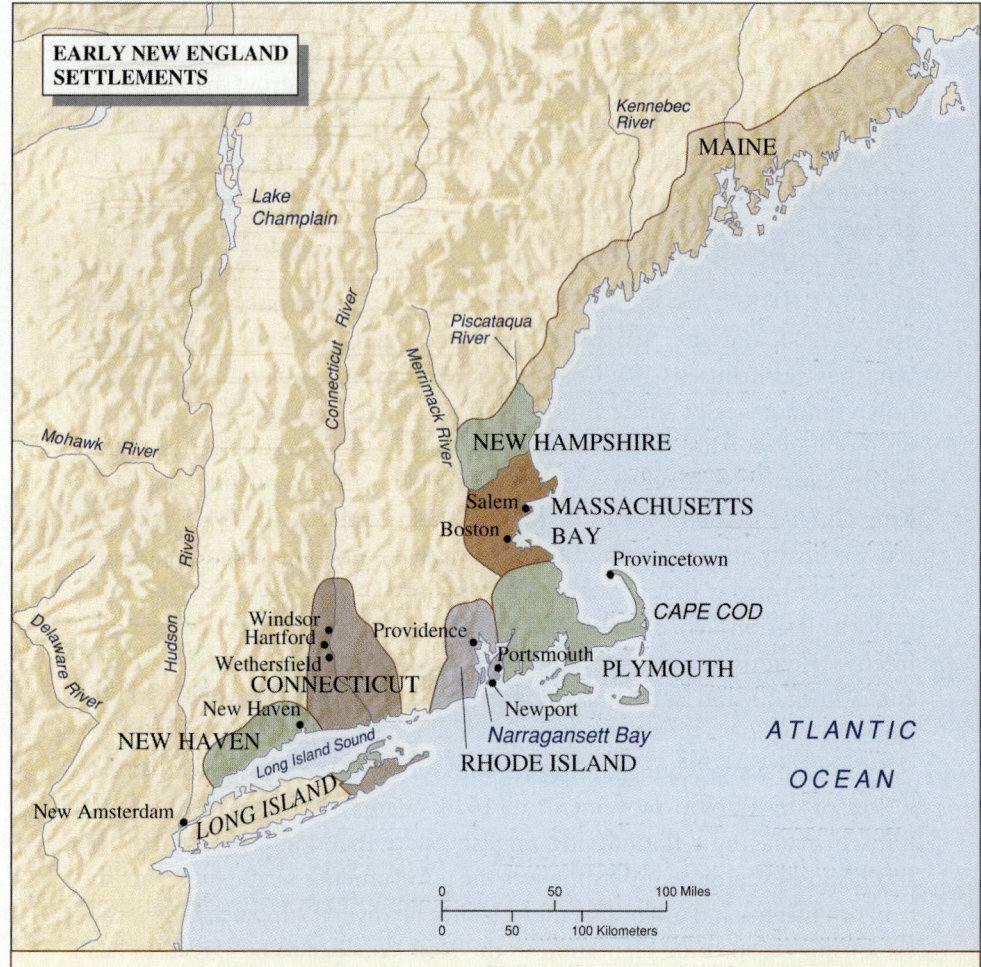

EARLY NEW ENGLAND SETTLEMENTS

Kennebec River

MAINE

Lake Champlain

Connecticut River

Merrimack River

Piscataqua River

Mohawk River

NEW HAMPSHIRE

Salem

Boston

MASSACHUSETTS BAY

Provincetown

CAPE COD

Delaware River

Hudson River

Windsor
Hartford
Wethersfield
CONNECTICUT
New Haven

Providence

Portsmouth

PLYMOUTH

NEW HAVEN

Newport

Long Island Sound

LONG ISLAND

Narragansett Bay
RHODE ISLAND

New Amsterdam

ATLANTIC

OCEAN

0   50   100 Miles

0   50   100 Kilometers

Why did European settlers first populate the Plymouth colony? How were the settlers of the Massachusetts Bay Colony different from those of Plymouth's? What was the origin of the Rhode Island colony?

had arrived in Massachusetts. As settlers—Puritan and non-Puritan—poured into the region, Boston became the chief city and capital.

The transfer of the Massachusetts charter, whereby an English trading company evolved into a provincial government, was a unique venture in colonization. Under this royal charter, power rested with the Massachusetts General Court, which consisted of shareholders, called freemen (those who had the "freedom of the company"), but of those who came, few besides

Winthrop and his assistants had such status. Such a small inner circle suited Winthrop and his friends, but soon other settlers demanded a share of political power. Rather than risk trouble, the inner group invited applications and finally admitted 118 additional freemen in 1631. The inner group also stipulated that only official church members, a limited category, could become freemen.

At first the freemen had no power except to choose "assistants," who in turn elected the governor and deputy governor. In 1634, however, the freemen converted themselves to a representative body with two or three deputies to represent each town. A final stage in the evolution of the government, a two-house legislature, came in 1644, with the deputies and assistants sitting apart and all decisions requiring a majority in each house.

John Winthrop

The first governor of Massachusetts Bay Colony, in whose vision the colony would be as "a city upon a hill."

Thus over a period of fourteen years, the Massachusetts Bay Company, a trading corporation, evolved into the governing body of a holy commonwealth. Membership in a Puritan church replaced the purchase of stock as a means of becoming a freeman, which was to say a voter. The General Court, like England's Parliament, became a representative body of two houses, with the House of Assistants corresponding roughly to the House of Lords and the House of Deputies corresponding to the House of Commons. Although the charter remained unchanged, the government differed considerably from the original expectation.

RHODE ISLAND More by accident than design, Massachusetts became the staging area for the rest of New England as new colonies grew out of religious quarrels. Puritanism created a volatile mixture: on the one hand, the search for God's will could lead to a rigid orthodoxy; on the other hand, it could lead troubled consciences to embrace radical ideas.

Young Roger Williams, who had arrived from England in 1631, was among the first to cause problems, precisely because he was the purest of Puritans, a Separatist troubled by the failure of the Massachusetts Nonconformists to repudiate the "whorish" Church of England. Williams held a brief pastorate in Salem, then moved to Plymouth. Governor Bradford found him gentle and kind in his personal relations and a charismatic speaker but noted that he "began to fall into strange opinions." A quarrel with the authorities over their treatment of Indians led Williams to return to Salem. There he continued to challenge social and religious norms. Williams's belief that a true church must have no relations with the English government, the Anglican establishment, or the unregenerate eventually led him to the conclusion that no true church was possible, unless perhaps one consisting of his wife and himself.

In Williams's view the purity of the church required complete separation of church and state and freedom from all coercion in matters of faith. "Forced worship," he declared, "stinks in God's nostrils." Such radical views prompted the church of Salem to expel him, whereupon Williams charged that the churches were "ulcered and gangrened." In 1635 the General Court banished him to England. Williams and a few followers headed into the wilderness in the dead of winter and were eventually taken in by the Narragansetts. In the spring of 1636, he bought land from the Indians and established the town of Providence at the head of Narragansett Bay, the first permanent settlement in Rhode Island and the first in America to legislate freedom of religion.

Thus the colony of Rhode Island, the smallest in America, grew up as a refuge for dissenters who believed that the government had no right to coerce religious belief. In 1640 the colony's settlers formed a confederation and in 1643 secured their first charter of incorporation as Providence Plantations. Roger Williams lived until 1683, an active, beloved citizen of the commonwealth he founded. During his lifetime at least, Rhode Island lived up to his principles of religious freedom and a government based on the consent of the people.

Roger Williams was just one of several prominent Puritan dissenters. Another, Anne Hutchinson, quarreled with the Puritan leaders for different reasons. She was married to a prominent merchant and had given birth to thirteen children. Strong-willed and articulate, she also worked as a healer and midwife and hosted meetings in her Boston home to discuss sermons. Soon, however, those discussions turned into well-attended forums for Hutchinson's commentaries on religious matters. She claimed to have had direct revelations from the Holy Spirit that convinced her that only two or three Puritan ministers actually preached the appropriate "covenant of grace." The others, she charged, were godless hypocrites, deluded and incompetent. They were promoting a "covenant of works" that led people to believe that good conduct would ensure their salvation.

Hutchinson's beliefs were provocative for several reasons. Puritan theology presumed that people could be saved only by God's grace rather than through their own willful actions. But Puritanism in practice also insisted that ministers were necessary to interpret God's will for the people so as to "prepare" them for the possibility of their being selected for salvation. In challenging the very legitimacy of the ministerial community as well as the hard-earned assurances of salvation enjoyed by current church members, Hutchinson was undermining the stability of an already fragile social system and theological order. What made the situation worse in such a male-dominated society, of course, was that a *woman* had the audacity to make such charges and assertions. Anne Hutchinson had both offended authority and sanctioned a disruptive self-righteousness.

A pregnant Hutchinson was hauled before the General Court in 1637, and for two days she verbally sparred with the presiding magistrates and testifying ministers. Her skillful deflections of the charges and her ability to cite chapter-and-verse biblical defenses of her actions led an exasperated Governor Winthrop to explode, "We do not mean to discourse with those of your sex." He found Hutchinson to be "a woman of haughty and fierce carriage, of a nimble wit and active spirit, and a very voluble tongue."

As the trial continued, an overwrought Hutchinson was eventually lured into convicting herself by claiming direct divine inspiration. Banished in 1638 as "a woman not fit for our society," she walked through the wilderness and settled with her family and a few followers on an island south of Providence, near what is now Portsmouth, Rhode Island. The arduous journey had taken a toll, however. Hutchinson grew sick, and her baby was stillborn, leading her critics in Massachusetts to assert that the "monstrous birth" was God's way of punishing her for her sins. Hutchinson's spirits never recovered. After her husband's death, in 1642, she moved to what is now New York, then under Dutch jurisdiction, and the following year she and five of her children were massacred during an Indian attack.

CONNECTICUT, NEW HAMPSHIRE, AND MAINE Connecticut had a more orthodox beginning than Rhode Island. It was founded by Massachusetts Puritans seeking better land and access to the fur trade farther west. In 1636 three entire church congregations trekked westward by the "Great Road," driving their hogs and cattle before them, and settled the Connecticut River towns of Wethersfield, Windsor, and Hartford.

Led by Thomas Hooker, they organized the self-governing colony of Connecticut in 1637 as a response to the danger of attack from the Pequot Indians, who lived nearby. In 1639 the Connecticut General Court adopted the Fundamental Orders, a series of laws providing for a "Christian Commonwealth" like that of Massachusetts. In the Connecticut colony, however, voting was not limited to church members. The Connecticut constitution specified that the Congregational churches would be the colony's official religion, supported by tax revenues and protected by the government. The governor was commanded to rule according to "the word of God."

Although it would later become part of Connecticut, a separate colony was initially established in New Haven. A group of English Puritans led by their minister, John Davenport, had migrated first to Massachusetts and then, seeking a place to establish themselves in commerce, had settled in New Haven, on Long Island Sound, in 1638. Like all the other offshoots of Massachusetts, the New Haven colony lacked a charter and maintained its independence. In 1662 it was absorbed into Connecticut.

To the north of Massachusetts, most of what are now the states of New Hampshire and Maine was granted in 1622 by the Council for New England to Sir Ferdinando Gorges and Captain John Mason. In 1629, Gorges and Mason divided their territory at the Piscataqua River, Mason taking the southern part, which he named New Hampshire, and Gorges taking the northern part, which became the province of Maine. In the 1630s, Puritan immigrants began filtering in, and in 1638 the Reverend John Wheelwright, one of Anne Hutchinson's followers, founded Exeter, New Hampshire. Maine consisted of a few small, scattered settlements, mostly fishing stations, the chief of them being York.

INDIANS IN NEW ENGLAND

The English settlers who poured into New England found not a "virgin land" of uninhabited wilderness but a developed region populated by over 100,000 Indians. The white colonists viewed the Native Americans as an alien race and an impediment to their economic and spiritual goals. To the Indians the newcomers seemed like magical monsters, and they coped with their changing circumstances in different ways. Many resisted, others sought accommodation, and still others grew dependent upon European culture. The interactions of the two cultures involved misunderstandings, the mutual need for trade and adaptation, and sporadic outbreaks of epidemics and warfare.

Indian religious beliefs differed dramatically from Christianity. Native Americans believed that nature was suffused with spirits. Animals, plants, trees, rivers, and stones harbored spiritual power, and human beings were very much dependent upon such supernatural forces. Indian rituals, ceremonies, and taboos acknowledged their dependence upon the workings of nature. Rain dances, harvest festivals, and pre-battle ceremonies were all intended to honor the spirits at work in nature. The Puritans dismissed such animistic beliefs as superstitions fostered by Satan. The Bible, after all, said that Christians were separate from and superior to the natural world, and this reading gave English settlers a biblical rationalization for taking lands from the Indians. God had, after all, granted his faithful dominion over "every living thing that moveth upon the earth."

In general, the English colonists adopted a strategy for dealing with the Native Americans quite different from that of the French and the Dutch. Merchants from France and the Netherlands were preoccupied with exploiting the fur trade. Thus they established permanent trading outposts, which led them to nurture amicable relations with the Indians, who were far more

Algonquian ceremony

As with most Indians, the Algonquians' dependence on nature for survival shaped their religious beliefs.

The Broiling of Their Fish over the Flame

In this drawing by John White, Algonquian men in North Carolina broil fish, a dietary staple of coastal societies.

numerous than they. In contrast, the English colonists were more interested in pursuing their "God-given" right to fish and farm. They sought to manipulate and exploit the Indians they encountered rather than deal with them on an equal footing. Their goal was subordination rather than reciprocity.

Initially the coastal Indians helped the white settlers develop a subsistence economy. They taught the English settlers how to plant corn and use fish for fertilizer. They also developed a flourishing trade with the newcomers, exchanging furs for manufactured goods and "trinkets." The various Indian tribes of New England fought among themselves, usually over disputed land. Had they been able to forge a solid alliance, they would have been better able to resist the encroachments of white settlers. As it was, they were not only fragmented but also vulnerable to the infectious diseases carried on board the ships transporting European settlers to America. Epidemics of smallpox devastated the Indian population, leaving the coastal areas "a widowed land." Between 1610 and 1675 the Abenakis, a tribe in Maine, declined from 12,000 to 3,000 and the southern New England tribes from 65,000 to 10,000.

THE PEQUOT WAR Indians who survived the epidemics and refused to yield their lands were forced out. In 1636, settlers in Massachusetts accused a Pequot of murdering a colonist. Joined by Connecticut colonists, they exacted their revenge by setting fire to a Pequot village on the Mystic River. As the Indians fled their burning huts, the Puritans shot and killed them— men, women, and children. Sassacus, the Pequot chief, organized the survivors among his followers and attacked the English. During the Pequot War of 1637, the colonists and their Narragansett allies killed hundreds of Pequots. Most of the survivors were sold into slavery in Bermuda. Under the terms of the Treaty of Hartford (1638), the Pequot Nation was declared dissolved.

RENEWED SETTLEMENT

By 1640, English settlers in New England and around Chesapeake Bay had established two great beachheads on the Atlantic coast, with the Dutch colony of New Netherland in between. After 1640, however, the power struggle between king and Parliament, the Church of England and the Puritans, which erupted in religious civil war in 1642, distracted attention from colonization. As a result, migration to America dwindled to a trickle for more than twenty years. During the time of the English Civil War (1642–1646) and Oliver Cromwell's Puritan dictatorship (1653–1658), the struggling colonies were left pretty much alone. Virginia and Maryland remained almost as independent from British authority as New England was.

The Restoration of King Charles II in 1660 triggered few changes in colonial governments. Immigration rapidly expanded the population of Virginia and Maryland. Fears of reprisals against Puritan New England on account of the reestablishment of the Anglican Church as the official church of England proved unfounded, at least for the time being. The charter of Massachusetts was reconfirmed in 1662, and Connecticut and Rhode Island received their first royal charters in 1662 and 1663. All three colonies retained their status as self-governing corporations.

The Restoration also opened a new season of enthusiasm for colonial expansion. Within twelve years the English would conquer New Netherland, settle Carolina, and nearly fill out the shape of the American colonies. In the middle region, formerly claimed by the Dutch, four new colonies sprang into being: New York, New Jersey, Pennsylvania, and Delaware. Without exception, the new colonies were proprietary, awarded by the king to "proprietors," men who had remained loyal during the civil war.

THE CAROLINAS Carolina from the start comprised two widely separated areas of settlement. The northernmost part, long called Albemarle, remained a remote scattering of settlers along the shores of Albemarle Sound. The eight lords proprietors to whom the king had given Carolina neglected Albemarle from the outset and focused on more promising sites to the south. Eager to find settlers who had already been seasoned in the colonies, they looked first to the Caribbean island colony of Barbados. In 1669 three ships left London with about 100 settlers recruited in England; they sailed first to Barbados to pick up more settlers and then north to

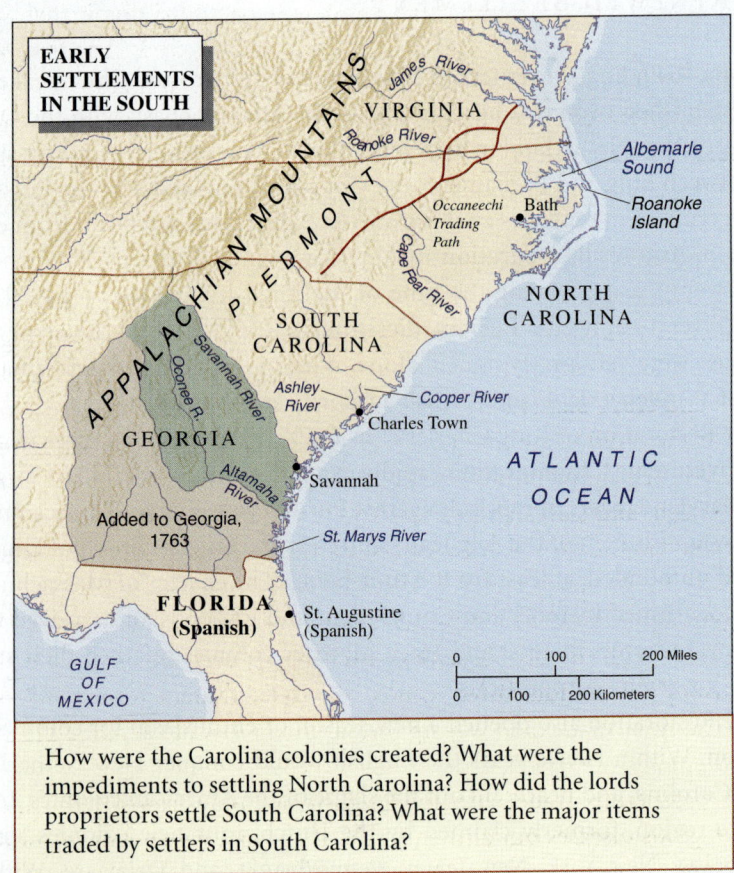

EARLY SETTLEMENTS IN THE SOUTH

How were the Carolina colonies created? What were the impediments to settling North Carolina? How did the lords proprietors settle South Carolina? What were the major items traded by settlers in South Carolina?

Bermuda. The expedition landed several miles up the Ashley River, at a place that they named Charles Town (later known as Charleston).

The government of South Carolina rested upon one of the most curious documents of colonial history, the Fundamental Constitutions of Carolina, drawn up by one of the eight proprietors, Lord Anthony Ashley Cooper, with the help of his secretary, the philosopher John Locke. Its cumbersome form of government and its provisions for an almost feudal social system and an elaborate nobility had little effect in the colony except to encourage a practice of large land grants. From the beginning, however, smaller headrights (land grants) were given to immigrants who could afford the cost of transit. The provision in the Fundamental Constitutions that had the greatest effect was a grant of religious toleration, designed to encourage immigration, which gave South Carolina a distinctive degree of openness (extending even to Jews and "heathens") and ethnic pluralism.

Ambitious English planters from sugar-rich Barbados dominated South Carolina and soon organized a major trade in Indian slaves. The first major export other than furs and slaves was cattle, and a true staple crop was not developed until the introduction of rice in the 1690s. South Carolina became a separate royal colony in 1719. North Carolina remained under the proprietors' rule for ten more years, when they surrendered their governing rights to the Crown.

THE SOUTHERN INDIANS The English proprietors of South Carolina wanted the colony to focus on producing commercial crops for profit (staples). Such production took time to develop, however. Land had to be cleared and crops planted and harvested. These activities required laborers. Some of the South Carolina planters from Barbados brought enslaved Africans and British indentured servants with them. But many more workers were needed, and slaves and servants were expensive. The quickest way to raise capital in the early years of South Carolina's development was through trade with the Indians.

Beginning in the late seventeenth century the Creeks developed a flourishing trade with the British settlers, exchanging deerskins and slaves from rival tribes for manufactured goods. By 1690, traders from Charleston, South Carolina, made their way up the Savannah River to arrange deals with the Indians.

The prosperous trade with the English not only exposed the Indians to contagious diseases but also entwined them in a dependent relationship that would prove disastrous to their way of life. The English traders began

A war dance

The Westo Indians of Georgia, pictured here doing a war dance, were among the first Native Americans to obtain firearms and used this advantage to enslave other Indians throughout Georgia, Florida, and the Carolinas.

providing the Indians with firearms and rum as incentives to persuade them to capture members of rival tribes to be sold as slaves. While colonists themselves captured and enslaved Indians, most tribes captured other Indians and exchanged the captives for British trade goods, guns, and rum. Colonists, in turn, put some of the Indian captives to work on their plantations. But because Indian captives often ran away, the traders preferred to ship them to New York, Boston, and the West Indies and import Africans to work in the Carolinas.

The complex profitability of Indian captives prompted a frenzy of slaving activity among British settlers. Slave traders turned Indian tribes against one another in order to ensure a continuous supply of captives. As many as 50,000 Indians, most of them women and children, were sold as slaves in Charleston between 1670 and 1715. More enslaved Indians were exported during that period than Africans were imported. Thousands more captured Indians circulated through New England ports. The burgeoning trade in enslaved Indians caused bitter struggles between tribes, gave rise to unprecedented colonial warfare, and spawned massive internal migrations across the southern colonies.

During the last quarter of the seventeenth century, the trade in enslaved Indians spread across the entire Southeast. Slave raiding became the region's single most important economic activity and a powerful weapon in Britain's global conflict with France and Spain. During the early eighteenth century, Indians armed with British weapons and led by English soldiers crossed into Spanish territory in south Georgia and north Florida. They destroyed thirteen Catholic missions, killed hundreds of Indians and Spaniards, and enslaved over 300 Indians. By 1710 the Florida tribes were on the verge of extinction. In 1708, when the total population of South Carolina was 9,580, including 2,900 Africans, there were 1,400 enslaved Indians in the colony.

SETTLING THE MIDDLE COLONIES AND GEORGIA

NEW NETHERLAND BECOMES NEW YORK   During the early seventeenth century, having gained its independence from Spain, the tiny nation of the Netherlands (Holland) emerged as a maritime giant. By 1670 the mostly Protestant Dutch had the largest merchant fleet in the world and the highest standard of living. Blessed with extraordinary ports and direct access to the Rhine River and the North Sea, they controlled northern European commerce and became one of the most diverse societies in Europe. The Dutch welcomed exiles from the constant religious strife in Europe: Iberian and German Jews, French Protestants (Huguenots), and English Puritans. The extraordinary success of the Netherlands also proved to be its downfall, however. Like imperial Spain, the Dutch Empire expanded too rapidly. Netherlanders dominated European trade with China, India, Africa, Brazil, and the Caribbean, but they could not efficiently manage their far-flung possessions. It did not take long for European rivals to exploit the weak points in the lucrative Empire. By the mid–seventeenth century, England and the Netherlands were locked in ferocious commercial warfare.

In London, King Charles II resolved to pluck out that old thorn in the side of the English colonies: New Netherland. The Dutch colony was older than New England, having been started when the two Protestant powers, England and the Netherlands, allied in opposition to Catholic Spain. The Dutch East India Company (organized in 1602) had hired an English captain, Henry Hudson, to seek the elusive passage to China. In 1609, Hudson had discovered Delaware Bay and had explored the river named for him to a point probably beyond Albany, where he helped initiate a lasting trade between the Dutch and the Iroquois Nations. In 1610 the Dutch established fur-trading posts on Manhattan Island and upriver at Fort Orange (later Albany). In the 1620s a newly organized Dutch West India Company began to establish permanent settlements. In 1626, Governor Peter Minuit purchased Manhattan from the Indians, and the new village of New Amsterdam became the capital of New Netherland.

The colony's government was under the almost absolute control of a governor sent out by the West India Company. The governors depended upon a small army garrison for defense, and the inhabitants (including a number of English on Long Island) showed almost total indifference in 1664 when Governor Peter Stuyvesant called them to arms against a threatening British fleet. Almost defenseless, the old soldier Stuyvesant blustered and stomped about on his wooden leg, but he finally surrendered to the English without firing a shot.

The plan of conquest had been hatched by Charles II's brother, the Duke of York, later King James II. When he and his advisers counseled that New Netherland could easily be conquered, Charles II simply granted the region to his brother. The English transformed New Amsterdam into New York and Fort Orange into Albany, and they held the country thereafter, except for a brief Dutch reoccupation in 1673–1674. Nonetheless, the Dutch left a permanent imprint on the land and the language. Whereas the Dutch vernacular faded away, place-names like Wall Street (named for the original wall that provided protection against the Indians) and Broadway (Breede Wegh) remained, along with family names like Rensselaer, Roosevelt, and Van Buren.

JUDAISM IN NORTH AMERICA In September 1654, ten years before the English took control of the Dutch colony of New Netherland, a French ship named *Sainte Catherine* arrived in New Amsterdam (New York) Harbor. On board were twenty-three Sephardi, Jews of Spanish-Portuguese descent. Penniless and weary, they had come seeking refuge from Brazil, where they had earlier fled from Spain and Portugal after being exiled by the Spanish Inquisition. When Portugal took Brazil from the Dutch, they again had to flee the Catholic Inquisition. They were the first Jewish settlers to arrive in North America, and they were not readily embraced. Leading merchants as well as members of the Dutch Reformed (Calvinist) Church asked Peter Stuyvesant, the dictatorial Dutch director general of New Netherland, to expel them. Stuyvesant despised Jews, Lutherans, Catholics, and Quakers. He characterized Jews as "deceitful," "very repugnant," and "blasphemous." If the Jews were allowed in, then "we cannot refuse the Lutherans and Papists." Stuyvesant's employers at the Dutch West India Company disagreed, however. Early in 1655 they ordered him to accommodate the homeless Jews, explaining that he should "allow every one to have his own belief, as long as he behaves quietly and legally, gives no offense to his neighbor and does not oppose the government."

The autocratic Stuyvesant grudgingly complied, but the Jews in New Amsterdam thereafter had to fight for civil and economic rights, as well as the right to worship in public. For example, the refugees were not allowed to serve in the city militia. Instead, they had to pay a tax to support it. One of the New Amsterdam Jews, Asser Levy, protested and won the right to participate in the town guard in November 1655. He later persuaded officials to let Jews own weapons. On April 21, 1657, Levy became the first Jew to obtain

Jewish heritage

A seventeenth-century Jewish cemetary in New York City.

citizenship in New Netherland. He developed a prosperous butcher shop and became a prominent merchant and real estate investor. In 1671 he provided a loan for the construction of the first Lutheran church in New York.

Yet anti-Semitic prejudice remained, although it was much less pronounced than in Europe. It would not be until the late seventeenth century, long after the English had taken over New Netherland and renamed it New York, that Jews could worship in public. Such restrictions help explain why the American Jewish community grew so slowly. In 1773, over 100 years after the Jewish refugees arrived in New Amsterdam, only 242 Jews resided in New York, and Jews represented only a tenth of 1 percent of the entire colonial population. On the eve of the American Revolution, there was not yet a single rabbi in British America. Not until the nineteenth century would the American Jewish community experience dramatic growth.

THE IROQUOIS LEAGUE One of the most significant effects of European settlement in North America during the seventeenth century was the intensification of warfare among Indian peoples. The same combination of forces that weakened the Indian populations of New England and the Carolinas affected the tribes around New York City and the lower Hudson

River valley. Dissension among the Indians and susceptibility to infectious disease left them vulnerable to exploitation by whites and other Indians.

In the interior of New York, however, a different situation arose. There the tribes of the Iroquois (an Algonquian term signifying "Snake" or "Terrifying Man") forged an alliance so strong that the outnumbered Dutch and, later, English traders were forced to work with the Indians in exploiting the lucrative beaver trade. The Iroquois League represented a federation of five tribes that spoke related languages: the Mohawk, Oneida, Onondaga, Cayuga, and Seneca (a sixth tribe, the Tuscaroras who lived in the Carolinas, joined in 1712). When the Iroquois began to deplete the local game during the 1640s, they used firearms supplied by their Dutch trading partners to seize the Canadian hunting grounds of the neighboring Hurons and Eries. During the so-called Beaver Wars the Iroquois defeated the western tribes and thereafter hunted the region to extinction.

During the second half of the seventeenth century, the relentless search for furs led Iroquois war parties to range across eastern North America. They gained control over a huge area from the St. Lawrence River to Tennessee and from Maine to Michigan. The Iroquois's wars helped reorient the political relationships in the whole eastern half of the continent. Besieged by the Iroquois League, the western tribes forged defensive alliances with the French.

In the 1690s the French and their Indian allies gained the advantage over the Iroquois. They destroyed crops and villages and infected the Iroquois with smallpox. Facing extermination, the Iroquois made peace with the French in 1701. During the first half of the eighteenth century, the Iroquois maintained a shrewd neutrality in the struggle between the two rival European powers, which enabled them to play the British off against the French while creating a thriving fur trade for themselves.

NEW JERSEY Shortly after the English conquest of New Netherland, the Duke of York granted his lands between the Hudson and Delaware Rivers to Sir George Carteret and Lord John Berkeley and named the territory for Carteret's native island of Jersey. In East Jersey, peopled first by perhaps 200 Dutch, new settlements gradually arose: disaffected Puritans from New Haven founded Newark, and a group of Scots founded Perth Amboy. In the west, facing the Delaware River, a scattering of Swedes, Finns, and Dutch remained, soon to be overwhelmed by swarms of English Quakers. In 1702, East and West Jersey were united as a royal colony.

PENNSYLVANIA AND DELAWARE The Quaker sect, as the Society of Friends was called in ridicule (because they were supposed to "tremble at the word of the Lord"), became the most influential of many radical religious groups that sprang from the turbulence of the English Civil War. Founded in Great Britain by George Fox in about 1647, the Quakers carried further than any other group the doctrine of individual spiritual inspiration and interpretation—the "inner light," they called it. They discarded all formal sacraments and formal ministry, refused deference to persons of rank, used the familiar *thee* and *thou* in addressing everyone, declined to take oaths, claiming they were contrary to Scripture, and embraced simple living and pacifism. Quakers experienced intense persecution—often in their zeal they seemed to invite it—but never inflicted it upon others. Their tolerance extended to complete religious freedom for everyone and to equality of the sexes, including the full participation of women in religious affairs.

Quaker meeting

The presence of women at this meeting is evidence of Quaker views on gender equality.

The settling of English Quakers in New Jersey encouraged others to migrate, especially to the Delaware River side of the colony. And soon across the river arose the Quaker commonwealth, the colony of Pennsylvania. William Penn, the colony's founder, was raised as a proper English gentleman but in 1667 became a Quaker. In 1681, King Charles II gave Penn a huge tract of land in America and named it Pennsylvania (literally, "Penn's Woods"). William Penn vigorously recruited settlers of all faiths to his new colony, and religious dissenters from England and the Continent—Quakers, Mennonites, Amish, Moravians, Baptists—flocked to the region. Indian

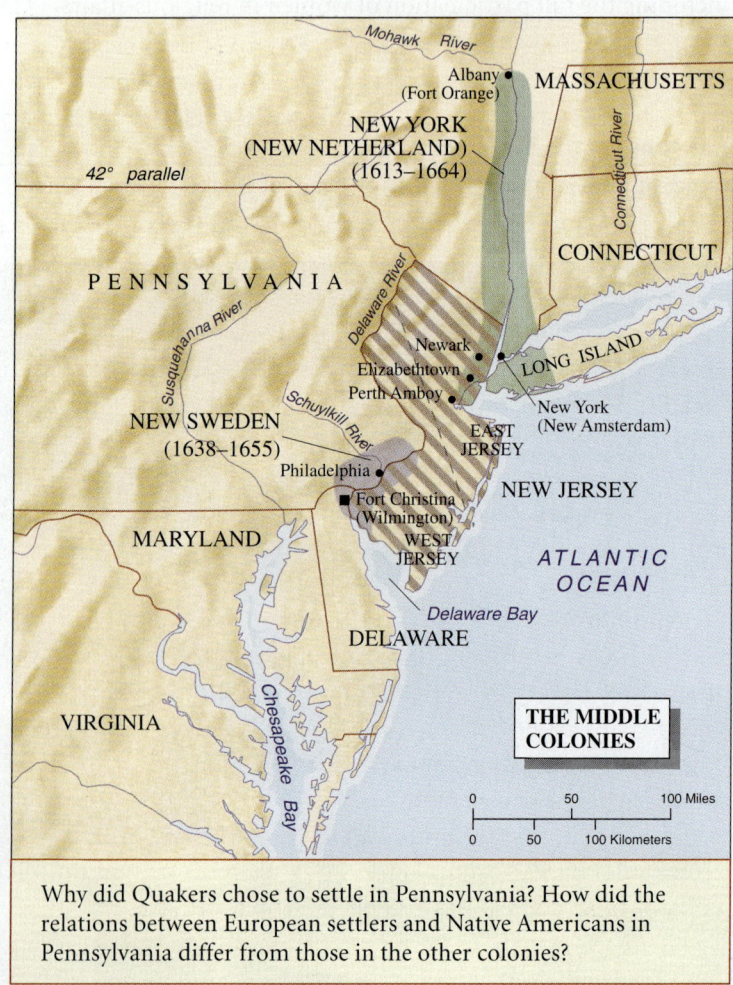

Why did Quakers chose to settle in Pennsylvania? How did the relations between European settlers and Native Americans in Pennsylvania differ from those in the other colonies?

relations were good from the beginning because of the Quakers' friendliness and Penn's careful policy of purchasing land titles from the Indians.

Pennsylvania's government resembled that of other proprietary colonies except that the councillors as well as the assembly were elected by the freemen (taxpayers and property owners) and the governor had no veto—although Penn, as proprietor, did. "Any government is free . . . where the laws rule and the people are a party to the laws," Penn wrote in the 1682 Frames of Government. He hoped to show that a government could run in accordance with Quaker principles, that it could maintain peace and order without oaths or wars, that religion could flourish without official government support and with freedom of belief.

In 1682 the Duke of York also granted Penn the area of Delaware, another part of the former Dutch territory. At first, Delaware became part of Pennsylvania, but after 1704 its settlers were granted the right to choose their own assembly. From then until the American Revolution, Delaware had a separate assembly but shared Pennsylvania's governor.

GEORGIA   Georgia was the last of the British colonies to be established in North America—half a century after Pennsylvania. In 1732, King George II gave the land between the Savannah and Altamaha Rivers to the twenty-one trustees of Georgia. In two respects, Georgia was unique among the colonies: it was intended to be both a philanthropic experiment and a military buffer against Spanish Florida. General James Oglethorpe, who accompanied the first colonists as resident trustee, represented both concerns: he served as a soldier who organized the colony's defenses and as a philanthropist who championed prison reform and sought a colonial refuge for the poor and the religiously persecuted.

In 1733, General Oglethorpe and about 120 colonists founded Savannah near the mouth of the Savannah River. Soon thereafter they were joined by Protestant refugees from central Europe, who made the colony for a time more German than English. The addition of Welsh, Highland Scots, Sephardic Jews, and others gave the early colony a cosmopolitan character much like that of Charleston, South Carolina.

As a buffer against Spanish Florida, the colony succeeded, but as a philanthropic experiment it failed. Efforts to develop silk and wine production foundered. Landholdings were limited to 500 acres, rum was prohibited, and the importation of slaves forbidden, partly to leave room for servants brought on charity, partly to ensure security. But the utopian rules soon collapsed. The regulations against rum and slavery were widely disregarded

Lake Superior

Lake Michigan

Lake Huron

Lake Erie

SAUK

FOX

WINNEBAGO

KICKAPOO

POTAWATOMI

FOX

WYANDOT

ERIE

MIAMI

Ohio River

SHAWNEE

CHEROKEE

APPALACHIAN

Mississippi River

Savannah River

CHICKASAW

GEORGIA

FALL

YAMASEE

CREEK

Altamaha River

CHOCTAW

FLORIDA (Spanish)

APALACHEE

GULF OF MEXICO

Why did European settlement lead to the expansion of hostilities among the Indians? What were the consequences of the trade and commerce between the English settlers and the southern Indian tribes? How were the relationships between the settlers and the members of the Iroquois League different from those between settlers and tribes in other regions?

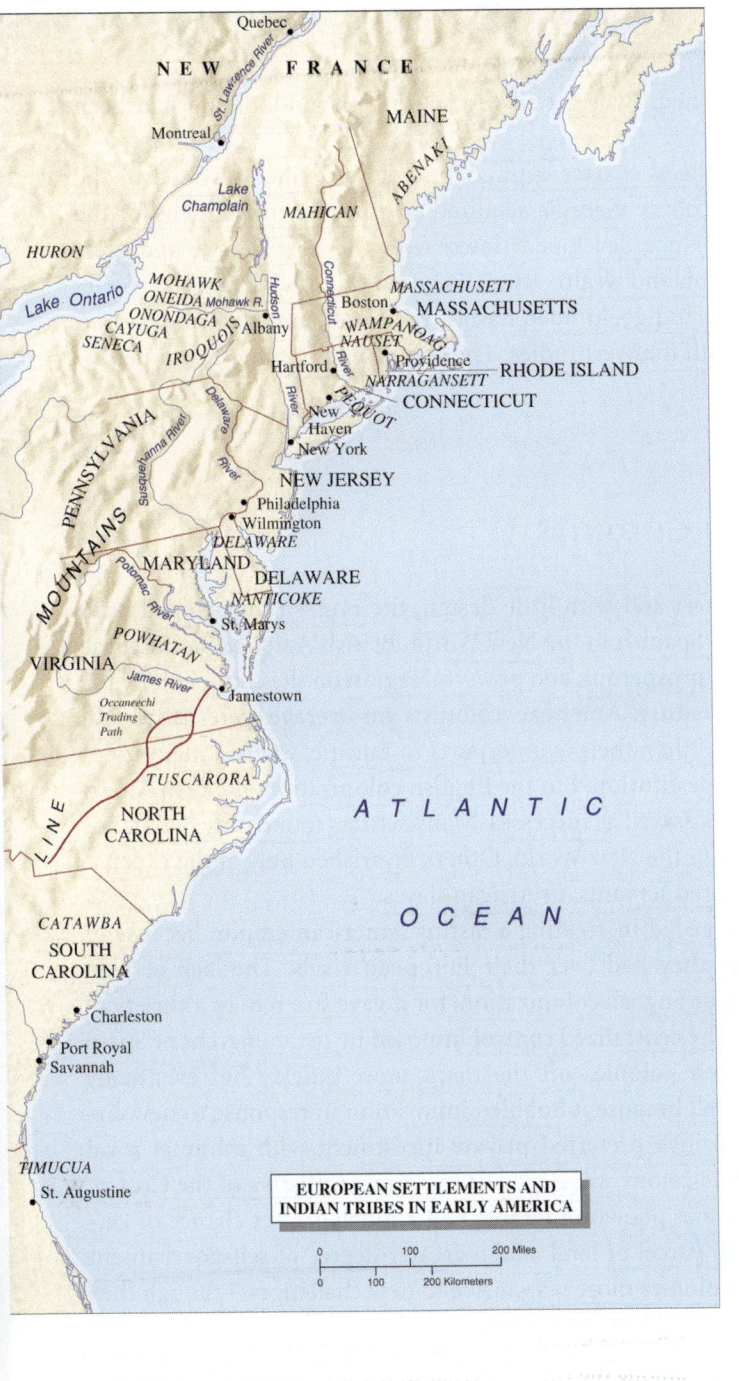

EUROPEAN SETTLEMENTS AND
INDIAN TRIBES IN EARLY AMERICA

0   100   200 Miles

0   100   200 Kilometers

and finally abandoned. By 1759 all restrictions on landholding had been removed.

In 1754 the trustees' charter expired, and the province reverted to the Crown. As a royal colony, Georgia acquired an effective government for the first time. The province developed slowly over the next decade and grew rapidly in population and wealth after 1763. Instead of wine and silk, Georgians exported rice, indigo, lumber, naval stores, beef, and pork and carried on a lively trade with the West Indies. The colony had become a commercial success.

THRIVING COLONIES

After a late start and with little design, the English outstripped both the French and the Spanish in the New World. British America had become the most populous, prosperous, and powerful region on the continent. By the mid–seventeenth century, American colonists on average were better fed, clothed, and housed than their counterparts in Europe, where a majority of the people lived in destitution. But the English colonization of North America included failures as well as successes. Many settlers found only hard labor and an early death in the New World. Others flourished only at the expense of Indians, indentured servants, or African slaves.

The British succeeded in creating a lasting American empire because of crucial advantages they had over their European rivals. The lack of plan marked the genius of English colonization, for it gave free rein to a variety of human impulses. The centralized control imposed by the monarchs of Spain and France got their colonies off the mark more quickly but eventually caused their downfall because it hobbled innovation in response to new circumstances. The British preferred private investment with minimal royal control. Not a single colony was begun at the direct initiative of the Crown. In the English colonies poor immigrants had a much greater chance of getting at least a small parcel of land, and a greater degree of self-government made the English colonies more responsive to new challenges—though they were sometimes hobbled by controversy.

Moreover, the compact model of English settlement contrasted sharply with the pattern of Spain's far-flung conquests and France's far-reaching trade routes to the interior by way of the St. Lawrence and Mississippi Rivers. Geography reinforced England's bent for the concentrated settlement of its colonies. The rivers and bays indenting the Atlantic seaboard served as veins of communication along which colonies first sprang up, but no great river offered a highway to the far interior. For 150 years the western outreach of British settlement stopped at the slopes of the Appalachian Mountains. To the east lay the wide expanse of ocean, which served not only as a highway for the transport of European culture to America but also as a barrier that separated old ideas from new, allowing the new to evolve in the new environment.

End of Chapter Review

CHAPTER SUMMARY

- **British Colonization**   Profit from minerals and exotic products was the overriding motivation for the joint-stock Virginia Company, organized to finance the 1607 Jamestown venture. Proprietary colonies, such as Maryland and the Carolinas, were given to individuals who desired wealth but did not usually become colonists themselves. The colonies were also an outlet for Britain's poor.

- **Jamestown Hardships**   The early years of Jamestown were grim because food was in short supply except when the Powhatans provided corn. However, relations with the Indians deteriorated, culminating in an Indian uprising in 1622. English investors searched for profits from minerals and trade with Indians, not from agriculture. A high mortality rate caused a scarcity of labor.

- **Religion and Colonization**   Religion was the primary motivation for the founding of several colonies. The Plymouth colony was founded by separatists on a mission to build a Christian commonwealth outside the structure of the Anglican Church. The Massachusetts Bay Colony was created by Puritans who wished to purify the established church. Rhode Island was established by Roger Williams, a religious dissenter from Massachusetts. Maryland was a refuge for English Catholics. William Penn, a Quaker, founded Pennsylvania and invited Europe's persecuted religious sects to his colony. The Dutch, with their policy of toleration, allowed members of all faiths to settle in New Netherland.

- **Native American Relations**   Settler-Indian relations were complex. Trade with the Powhatans in Virginia enabled Jamestown to survive its early years, but brutal armed conflicts occurred as settlers invaded Indian lands. Puritans retaliated harshly against Indian resistance in the Pequot War of 1637 and in King Philip's War from 1675–1676. Only Roger Williams and William Penn treated natives as equals. Conflicts in the Carolinas—the Tuscarora and Yamasee Wars—occurred because of Indian slave trade and other abuses by traders. France and Spain used natives to further their imperial ambitions, which allowed the Native Americans to play European powers against each another.

- **British America**   By 1700, England was a trading empire. British America was the most populous and prosperous area of North America. Commercial rivalry between the Dutch and the English led to war, during which the Dutch colony of New Netherland surrendered to the English in 1664. Native allies, such as the Iroquois, traded pelts for English goods. By relying increasingly on slave labor, the southern colonies provided England with tobacco and other plantation crops.

CHRONOLOGY

1584–1587	Raleigh's Roanoke Island venture
1607	Jamestown, Virginia, the first permanent English colony, is established
1620	Plymouth colony is founded; Pilgrims agree to the Mayflower Compact
1630	Massachusetts Bay Colony is founded
1634	Settlement of Maryland begins
1636	Rhode Island is established
1637	Pequot War
1642–1651	English Civil War
1666	Restoration of the English monarchy
1681	Pennsylvania is established
1733	Georgia is founded

KEY TERMS & NAMES

3

COLONIAL WAYS OF LIFE

FOCUS QUESTIONS wwnorton.com/studyspace

- What were the social, ethnic, and economic differences among the southern, middle, and New England colonies?
- What was the attitude of English colonists toward women?
- How important was indentured servitude to the development of the colonies, and why had the system been replaced by slavery in the South by 1700?
- How did the colonies participate in international and imperial trade?
- What were the effects of the Enlightenment in America?
- How did the Great Awakening affect the colonies?

Those who colonized America during the seventeenth and eighteenth centuries were part of a massive social migration occurring throughout Europe and Africa. They moved for different reasons. Most were responding to powerful social and economic forces: rapid population growth, the rise of commercial agriculture, and the early stages of the Industrial Revolution. Others sought political security or religious freedom. Many came as indentured servants, exchanging several years of labor for access to freedom in America. Millions of Africans, of course, were captured and transported to new lands against their will.

THE SHAPE OF EARLY AMERICA

Those who settled in colonial America were mostly young (over half were under twenty-five), and most were male. Almost half were indentured servants or slaves. England also transported some 50,000 convicted felons to the North American colonies. Only a third of the newcomers journeyed with their families. Most immigrants were of the "middling sort," neither very rich nor very poor. Whatever their status or ambition, however, this extraordinary mosaic of ordinary yet adventurous people created America's enduring institutions and values.

SEABOARD ECOLOGY   America's ecosystem was shaped by both Native Americans and European settlers. For thousands of years, Indian hunting practices produced what one scholar has called the "greatest known loss of wild species" in American history. In addition, the Native Americans burned trees and undergrowth to provide cropland, ease travel through hardwood forests, and nourish the grasses, berries, and other forage for the animals they hunted. This "slash-and-burn" agriculture halted the normal forest succession and, especially in the Southeast, created large stands of longleaf pine, still the most common source of timber in the region.

Equally important in shaping the ecosystem of America was the European attitude toward the environment. Whereas the Native Americans tended to be migratory, considering land and animals communal resources to be shared and consumed only as necessary, many European colonizers viewed natural resources as privately owned commodities. Settlers quickly set about evicting Indians; clearing, fencing, improving, and selling land; growing surpluses; and trapping game for furs to be sold or traded.

European ships brought to America domesticated animals—cattle, oxen, sheep, goats, horses, and pigs—that were unknown in the New World. By 1650, English farm animals outnumbered the colonists. Rapidly multiplying livestock reshaped the environment and affected Indian life in unexpected ways. Farmers allowed their cows, horses, and pigs to roam freely through the woods, since the labor shortage made it too expensive to pen the animals in barnyards or fence them in pastures. Over time, the failure to constrain farm animals denied the planted fields dung for use as a valuable fertilizer. The fertility of the soil declined with each passing year.

Many of the farm animals turned wild (feral), ran amok in Indian cornfields, and devastated native flora and fauna. In New England, rooting pigs devoured the shellfish that local Indians depended upon for subsistence. As livestock herds grew, settlers acquired more land from the Indians. Trespassing livestock and expanding colonial settlements caused friction with the Indians, which occasionally ignited in violent confrontations. One historian, in fact, has referred to roaming English livestock as four-legged "agents of empire" invading Indian land. As a frustrated Maryland Indian charged in

Colonial farm

This plan of a newly cleared American farm shows how trees were cut down and the stumps left to rot.

1666, "Your hogs & cattle injure us. You come too near us to live & drive us from place to place. We can fly no farther. Let us know where to live & how to be secured for the future from the hogs & cattle."

POPULATION GROWTH England's first footholds in America were bought at a fearsome price. Many settlers died in the first years. But once the brutal seasoning phase was past and the colonies were on their feet, Virginia and its successors grew at a prodigious rate. After the last major Indian uprising, in 1644, Virginia's population quadrupled, from about 8,000 to 32,000 over the next thirty years, then more than doubled, to 75,000, by 1704. America's plentiful land beckoned immigrants and induced them to replenish the earth with large families. Where labor was scarce, children could lend a hand and, once grown, find new land for themselves if need be. Colonists tended, as a result, to marry and start families at an earlier age than their European counterparts.

BIRTHRATES AND DEATH RATES The initial scarcity of women in the colonies had significant social effects. Whereas in England the average age of women at marriage was twenty-five or twenty-six, in America it dropped to twenty or twenty-one. Men also married younger in the colonies than in the Old World. The birthrate rose accordingly, because women who married earlier had time for about two additional pregnancies during their childbearing years. Given the better economic prospects in the colonies, a greater proportion of American women married, and the birthrate remained much higher than in Europe.

Equally important in explaining rapid population growth in the New World was the much lower death rate, at least in the New England colonies (in the South, death rates remained higher due to malaria, dysentery, and other warm-climate diseases). After the difficult first years of settlement, infants generally had a better chance of reaching maturity, and adults had a better chance of reaching old age, than did their counterparts in Europe. This greater longevity resulted less from a more temperate climate than from the character of the settlements themselves. Since the land was initially bountiful, famine seldom occurred after a settlement's first year. Although the winters were more severe than those in England, firewood was plentiful. Being younger on the whole—the average age in the colonies in 1790 was sixteen!—American adults were less susceptible to disease than were Europeans. More widely scattered, they were also less exposed to infectious diseases. That began to change, of course, as cities grew and trade and travel increased. By the mid–eighteenth century the colonies were beginning to experience levels of contagion much like those in Europe.

WOMEN IN THE COLONIES   Colonists brought to America deeply rooted convictions about the inferiority of women. God and nature, it was widely assumed, had stained women with original sin and made these "weaker vessels" smaller in stature, feebler in mind, and prone to both excited emotions and psychological dependency. Women were expected to be meek and model housewives. Their role in life was clear: to obey and serve their husbands, nurture their children, and maintain their households. Governor John Winthrop insisted that a "true wife accounts her subjection [as] her honor and freedom" and would find true contentment only "in subjection to her husband's authority."

Most women accepted their subordinate status in a male-dominated society. A Virginia woman explained that "one of my first resolutions I made after marriage was never to hold disputes with my husband." Both social custom and legal codes were designed to keep women deferential and powerless. They could not vote, preach, hold office, attend public schools or colleges, bring lawsuits, make contracts, or own property except under extraordinary conditions. In the eighteenth century, "women's work" typically involved activities in the house, garden, and yard. Yet there were exceptions to these prevailing gender roles. Circumstances often required or enabled women to exercise leadership outside the domestic sphere. Elizabeth Lucas Pinckney (1722?–1793), for example, emerged as one of America's most enterprising horticulturalists. Born in the West Indies, raised on the island of Antigua, and educated in England, she moved with her family to Charleston, South Carolina, at age fifteen. The following year her father, a British army officer and colonial administrator, was called back to Antigua as another war erupted between England and Spain. He left young Eliza to care for her ailing mother and younger sister—and to manage three plantations worked by slaves. Intelligent and plucky, Eliza assessed her agricultural options and decided to try growing indigo, a West Indian plant that produced a much-coveted blue dye for fabric. Within six years she had reaped a bonanza. Exporting indigo became fabulously profitable for her and for other planters on the Carolina coast who sought to mimic her success. She later experimented with other crops, such as flax, hemp, and silk.

In 1744 vivacious Eliza Lucas married widower Charles Pinckney, a prominent attorney and civic leader who was twice her age. Because her husband traveled frequently, she continued to manage the household and the plantations. Within five years she had given birth to four children. She was a devoted wife and loving mother. Her two surviving sons, Charles Cotesworth and Thomas, would play major roles as generals in the American Revolution, in the drafting of the Constitution, and in the political leadership of the new United States of America (both Federalists, they remain the only two brothers to have campaigned for the presidency). When Eliza Pinckney died, she was so revered that President George Washington served as a pallbearer at her funeral.

WOMEN AND RELIGION During the colonial era, women played a crucial, if restricted, role in religious life. No denomination allowed women to be ordained as ministers. Only the Quakers let women hold church offices and preach ("exhort") in public. Unlike Puritans, who characterized women as "weak vessels" who had succumbed to the original sin in the garden of Eden, Quakers viewed women as equal to men and allowed them authority in their meetings and communities. But the Quakers were unusual in this regard. Most churches (except those of the Baptists and Quakers) did not allow women to vote on congregational issues, such as the appointment of a minister. Puritans cited biblical passages claiming that God required "virtuous" women to submit to male authority and remain "silent" in congregational matters. Governor John Winthrop demanded that women "not meddle in such things as are proper for men" to manage.

Women who challenged ministerial authority were usually prosecuted and punished. Yet by the eighteenth century, as is true today, women made up the overwhelming majority of church members. Their disproportionate attendance at church services and revivals was a frequent cause of ministerial concern. A feminized church was deemed a church in decline. In 1692 the magisterial Boston minister Cotton Mather observed that there "are far more *Godly Women* in the world than there are *Godly Men*." In explaining this phenomenon, Mather put a new twist on the old notion of women being the weaker sex. He argued that the pain associated with childbirth, which had long been interpreted as the penalty women paid for Eve's sinfulness, was in part what drove women "more frequently, & the more fervently" to commit their lives to Christ.

The religious roles of black women in colonial America were quite different from those of their white counterparts. In most West African tribes, women were not subordinate to men, and women frequently served as priests and cult leaders. Furthermore, some enslaved Africans who were transported to North America had already been exposed to Christianity or Islam in Africa, through Portuguese Catholic missionaries or Arab merchants and slave traders. Most of them, however, tried to sustain their traditional African religion once they arrived in the colonies. Unlike Christianity or Islam, African religions had no sacred scriptures or writings. Their beliefs were passed on through generations by custom, ritual, and oral history. Africans believed in one supreme God (a "Creator") and lesser deities; they

The First, Second, and Last Scene of Mortality

Prudence Punderson's needlework (ca. 1776) shows the domestic path, from cradle to coffin, followed by most colonial women.

also assumed that there was an afterlife. They engaged in ancestor worship, expecting the spirits of their dead relatives to live on in the activities of the family or clan. African religions, like Indian religions, also held that spirits resided in rocks, rivers, trees, and the sky. West Africans also believed in magic. Conjurers, or "diviners," both men and women, used various objects with which to communicate with the spirits. Once in America, African women (and men) were often excluded from church membership for fear that Christianized slaves might seek to gain their freedom. To clarify the situation, Virginia in 1667 passed a law specifying that children of slaves would be slaves even if they had been baptised.

The acute shortage of women in the early years of colonial settlement made them more highly valued than they were in Europe, and the Puritan emphasis on a well-ordered family life led to laws protecting wives from physical abuse and allowing for divorce. In addition, colonial laws gave wives greater control over property that they contributed to a marriage or that was left after a husband's death. But the traditional notion of female subordination and domesticity remained firmly entrenched in America. As a Massachusetts boy maintained in 1662, the superior aspect of life was "masculine and eternal; the feminine inferior and mortal."

SOCIETY AND ECONOMY IN THE SOUTHERN COLONIES

CROPS The southern climate enabled colonists to grow exotic staples (profitable market crops) prized by the mother country. In Virginia, tobacco production soared. After 1690, rice became the most profitable staple crop in South Carolina. The southern woods also provided lumber and naval stores (tar, pitch, and turpentine). From their early leadership in the latter trade, North Carolinians would later derive the nickname of Tar Heels.

The economy of the southern colonies centered on a fundamental fact: land was plentiful, and laborers were scarce. The low cost of land lured most colonists. In 1614 each of the Virginia Company's colonists received three acres, and this policy marked the beginning of a "headright" system that provided every settler in the colony with a plot of land. In 1618 the company increased the land grants, giving 100 acres each to those already in the colonies and 50 acres each to new settlers or anyone paying the passage of immigrants (for example, indentured servants) to Virginia.

If one distinctive feature of the South's commercial agriculture was a ready market in England, another was a trend toward large-scale production.

Virginia plantation

Southern colonial plantations were constructed with easy access to oceangoing vessels, as shown on this 1730 tobacco label.

Those who planted tobacco discovered that it quickly exhausted the soil, thereby giving an advantage to the planter who had extra fields in which to plant beans and corn or to leave fallow. With the increase of the tobacco crop, moreover, a fall in prices meant that economies of scale might come into play—the large planter with the lower cost per unit might still make a profit. Gradually he would extend his holdings along the riverfronts and thereby secure the advantage of direct access to the oceangoing vessels that moved freely up and down the waterways of Chesapeake Bay. So easy was the access, in fact, that the Chesapeake colonies never required a city of any size as a center of commerce.

INDENTURED SERVANTS AND SLAVES The plantation economy depended upon manual labor, and voluntary indentured servitude accounted for probably half the white settlers in all the colonies outside New England. The name derived from the indenture, or contract, by which a person agreed to work for a fixed number of years in return for transportation to the New World.

Although many servants saw the opportunity to go to the New World as a chance to better themselves, not all went voluntarily. The London underworld developed a flourishing trade in "kids," who were "spirited" into servitude. On occasion, orphans were bound off to the New World, and from time to time the mother country sent convicts into colonial servitude. Once an indenture had run its course, usually after four to seven years, a servant claimed the freedom dues set by law—some money, tools, clothing, food—and often took up landowning.

Slavery, long a dying institution in Europe, evolved in the Chesapeake after 1619, when a Dutch vessel dropped off twenty Africans in Jamestown. Some of the first slaves were treated as indentured servants. Those who worked out their term of indenture gained freedom and a fifty-acre parcel of land. They themselves sometimes acquired slaves and white indentured servants. But gradually the practice of perpetual black slavery became the custom and the law of the land.

AFRICAN ROOTS AND BLACK CULTURE   Enslaved Africans came from lands as remote from one another as the Congo is from Senegal, and they spoke Mandingo, Ibo, Kongo, and countless other languages. For all their differences, however, the many peoples of Africa did share similar kinship and political systems. African societies were often matrilineal: property and political status descended through the mother rather than the father. Priests and the nobility lorded over the masses of farmers and craftspeople. Below the masses were the slaves, typically war captives, criminals, or debtors.

Most of the Africans who arrived in British North America during the seventeenth century did not come directly from Africa, however. Instead, they were first brought to the sugar-producing colonies in Brazil and the Caribbean. Once in North America, slaves often worked alongside white indentured servants, and personal relations between the two groups tended to be more open and casual than they would be a century later. A surprising number of the early slaves were able to earn money on the side and buy their freedom. Thus, the enslaved Africans of the seventeenth century had a more fluid and independent existence than would their successors.

During the eighteenth century, with the rapid development of a plantation economy in the Chesapeake Bay region and coastal South Carolina, the demand for slaves grew so quickly that a much higher proportion came directly from the African interior. Captured by ruthless European, Muslim,

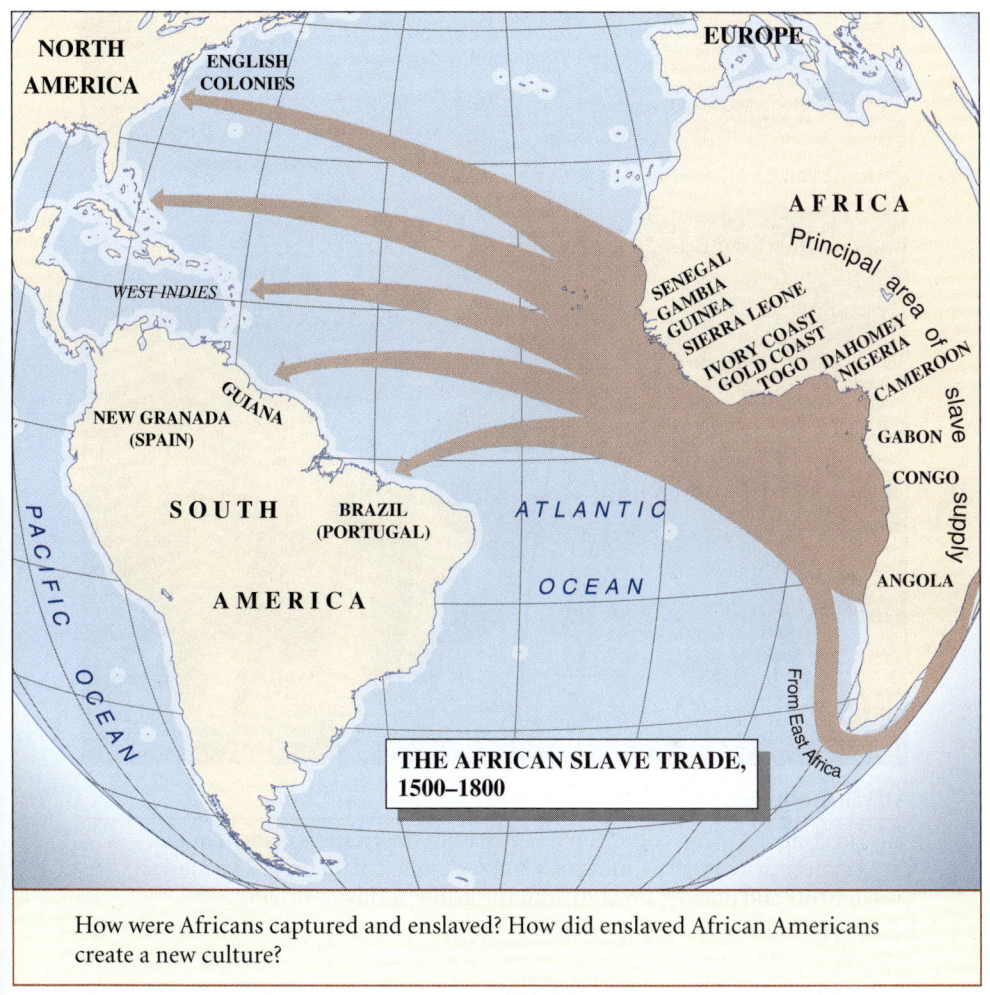

NORTH AMERICA

ENGLISH COLONIES

EUROPE

AFRICA

Principal area of slave supply

SENEGAL
GAMBIA
GUINEA
SIERRA LEONE
IVORY COAST
GOLD COAST
TOGO DAHOMEY
NIGERIA
CAMEROON

WEST INDIES

NEW GRANADA (SPAIN)

GUIANA

SOUTH

AMERICA

BRAZIL (PORTUGAL)

ATLANTIC

OCEAN

PACIFIC

OCEAN

PACIFIC OCEAN

GABON

CONGO

ANGOLA

From East Africa

THE AFRICAN SLAVE TRADE, 1500–1800

How were Africans captured and enslaved? How did enslaved African Americans create a new culture?

or African traders, the people destined for slavery were packed together in slave ships and subjected to a grueling transatlantic voyage that killed one in seven of them. Planters wanted field hands, so most of these newer slaves were young males who had had no exposure to European culture or languages, a factor that discouraged relations between the races.

Some of the enslaved blacks rebelled against their new masters, resisting work orders, sabotaging crops and tools, or running away to the frontier. In a few cases they organized rebellions, which were ruthlessly suppressed. "You would be surprised at their perseverance," noted one white planter. "They often die before they can be conquered." Those still alive when recaptured frequently faced ghastly retribution. After capturing slaves who participated

African heritage

The survival of African culture among enslaved Americans is evident in this late-eighteenth-century painting of a South Carolina plantation. The musical instruments and pottery are of African (probably Yoruban) origin.

in the Stono Uprising in South Carolina in 1739, enraged planters "cutt off their heads and set them up at every Mile Post."

SLAVE CULTURE   In the process of being forced into bondage, diverse blacks from diverse homelands forged a new identity as African Americans while entwining in the fabric of American culture more strands of African heritage than historians and anthropologists can ever disentangle. Most important are African influences in music, folklore, and religious practices. On one level, slaves used songs, stories, and sermons to distract themselves from their toil; on another level these compositions conveyed coded messages of distaste for masters or overseers. Slave religion, a unique blend of African and Christian beliefs, centered on the theme of deliverance: God, slaves believed, would eventually free them and open up the gates to the promised land. The planters, however, sought to strip slave religion of its liberationist hopes.

Africans brought to America powerful kinship ties. Although most colonies outlawed slave marriages, many masters believed that slaves would work harder and more reliably if allowed to form families. Though many couples were broken up when one partner was sold, slave culture was remarkable for its powerful domestic ties. It was also remarkable for developing sex roles distinct from those of white society. Most enslaved women were by necessity field workers as well as wives and mothers responsible for household affairs. They worked in proximity to enslaved men and in the process were treated more equally than were most of their white counterparts.

Americans gradually incorporated slave labor into virtually every activity within the dramatically expanding colonial economy. To be sure, the vast majority of slaves worked as field hands. As the number of slaves grew, however, so, too, did the variety of their labors and the need for different skills. Virginia and Maryland planters favored slaves from the Bight of Biafra, on the Gulf of Guinea, and the Congo, where yam cultivation resembled the cultivation of tobacco. Fulani from West Africa were prized as cattle herdsmen. Sugar growers requested Hausa tribesmen from northern Nigeria because of their expertise in producing sugar from cane. South Carolina rice planters purchased slaves from Africa's "Rice Coast," especially Gambia, where rice cultivation was commonplace.

RELIGION   After 1642, Virginia's royal governor, William Berkeley, decided that his colony was to be officially Anglican. He created laws requiring "all nonconformists . . . to depart the colony." Puritans and Quakers were hounded out. By the end of the seventeenth century, Anglicanism predominated in Virginia and Maryland, and it proved especially popular among the largest landholders and wealthiest colonists. During the early eighteenth century, Anglicanism became the established (official) religion in all the southern colonies. In America, however, the Anglican Church evolved into something quite different from its parent, the Church of England. The scattered colonial population, the absence of bishops, and the uneven quality and commitment of ministers made centralized control of religious life difficult.

Anglicans were very different from Puritans and Quakers, Baptists, and Methodists. They did not require members to give a personal, public account of their conversion. Nor did they expect members to practice self-denial. Anglicans disliked "fire-and-brimstone" sermons. They preferred ministers who stressed the reasonableness of Christianity, the goodness of God, and the responsibility of people to help others in need.

SOCIETY AND ECONOMY IN NEW ENGLAND

TOWNSHIPS   In contrast to the seaboard planters, who transformed the English manor into the southern plantation, the Puritans transformed the English village into the New England town, although there were many varieties. Land policy in New England had a stronger social and religious purpose than elsewhere. The headright system of the Chesapeake never took root in New England. There were cases of large individual grants, but the standard practice was one of township grants to organized groups. A group of settlers, often already gathered into a congregation, would petition the general court for a town and then divide the parcel according to a rough principle of equity—those who invested more or had larger families or greater status might receive more land—retaining some pasture and woodland in common and holding some for later arrivals. In some early cases the towns arranged each settler's land in separate strips after the medieval practice, but with time land was commonly divided into separate farms a distance from the central village, to which landholders would move.

ENTERPRISE   New England farmers and their families led hard lives. The growing season was short, and the harsh climate precluded profitable cash crops. The crops and livestock were those familiar to the English countryside: wheat, barley, oats, some cattle, swine, and sheep. With abundant fishing grounds that stretched northward to Newfoundland, it is little wonder that New Englanders turned to the sea for their livelihood. New England's proximity to waters rich in cod, mackerel, halibut, and other varieties of fish made it America's most important maritime center. Whales, too, abounded in New England waters and supplied oil for lighting and lubrication, as well as ambergris, a secretion used in perfumes.

New England's fisheries, unlike its farms, supplied a product that could be profitably exported to Europe, with lesser grades of fish going to the West Indies as food for slaves. Fisheries encouraged the development of shipbuilding, and experience at seafaring spurred commerce. This in turn led to wider contacts in the Atlantic world and prompted a degree of self-indulgent materialism and cosmopolitanism that clashed with the Puritan credo of plain living and high thinking. In 1714 a worried Puritan deplored the "great extravagance that people are fallen into, far beyond their circum-

Profitable fisheries

Fishing for, curing, and drying codfish in Newfoundland in the early 1700s. For centuries the rich fishing grounds of the North Atlantic provided New Englanders with a prosperous industry.

stances, in their purchases, buildings, families, expenses, apparel, generally in the whole way of living." But such laments failed to stop the material growth of the New England colonies.

SHIPBUILDING   The abundant forests of New England represented a source of enormous wealth. Old-growth trees were especially prized for use as ships' masts and spars. At the same time, English officials encouraged the colonists to develop their own shipbuilding industry. American-built ships quickly became prized by European traders for their quality and price. It was much less expensive to purchase ships built in America than to transport American timber to Britain for ship construction, especially since a large ship might require the timber from as many as 2,000 trees.

Nearly a third of all British ships were made in the colonies. By the mid–seventeenth century bustling shipyards had appeared in many New England towns where rivers flowed into the ocean. By the eighteenth century, Massachusetts was second only to London in the number of ships produced. Shipbuilding was one of colonial America's first big industries, and it in turn nurtured many related businesses: timbering, sawmills, iron foundries, sail lofts, fisheries, and taverns.

Architectual drawings used in shipbuilding

An architectual drawing of a ship from eighteenth-century New England.

TRADE   By the end of the seventeenth century, America had become part of a great North Atlantic commercial network, trading not only with the British Isles and the British West Indies but also—and often illegally—with Spain, France, Portugal, Holland, and their colonies. Since the colonists lacked the means to produce goods themselves, they imported manufactured goods from Europe. Their central economic problem was finding the means to pay for those imports—the eternal problem of the balance of trade.

The mechanism of trade in New England and the middle colonies differed from that in the South in two respects: the northern colonies were at a disadvantage in their lack of cash crops to exchange for English goods, but the success of their shipping and mercantile enterprises worked in their favor. After 1660, in order to protect England's agriculture and fisheries, the British government placed prohibitive duties (taxes) on certain major products exported by the northern colonies—fish, flour, wheat, and meat—while leaving the door open to timber, furs, and whale oil. As a consequence, in the early eighteenth century, New York and New England bought more from England than they sold there, incurring an unfavorable trade balance.

The northern colonies addressed the trade imbalance in two ways: they used their own ships and merchants, thus avoiding the "invisible" charges by middlemen, and they found other markets for the staples excluded from England, thus acquiring goods or coins to pay for imports from the mother country. These circumstances gave rise to the famous "triangular trade"

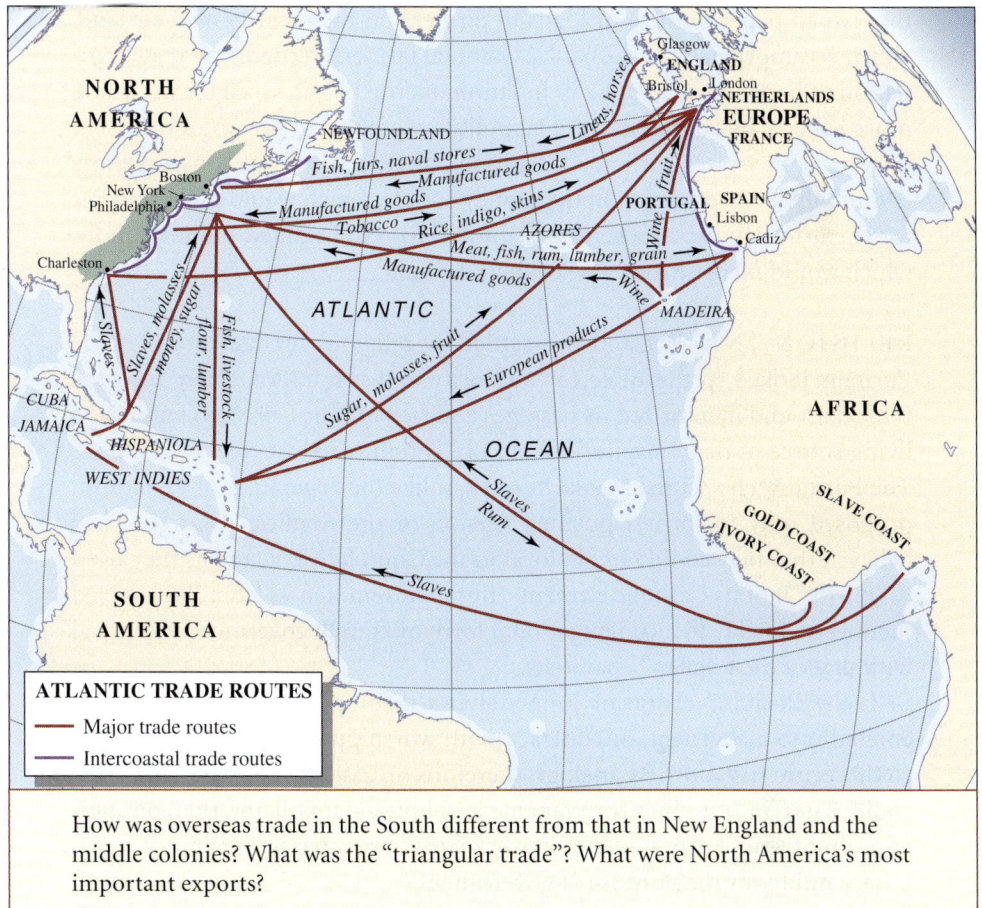

How was overseas trade in the South different from that in New England and the middle colonies? What was the "triangular trade"? What were North America's most important exports?

(more a descriptive convenience than a rigid pattern), in which New Englanders shipped rum to the west coast of Africa, where they bartered for slaves; took the slaves on the "Middle Passage" to the West Indies; and returned home with various commodities, including molasses, from which they manufactured rum. In another version they shipped provisions to the West Indies, carried sugar and molasses to England, and returned with goods manufactured in Europe.

The generally unfavorable balance of trade left the colonies with a chronic shortage of hard currency (coins), which drifted away to pay for imports. Various expedients met the shortage of gold or silver coins: Most of the colonies at one time or another issued bills of credit, on promise of payment in hard currency later (hence the dollar "bill"), and most set up land banks that issued paper money for loans to farmers on the security of their land, which was mortgaged to the banks. Colonial farmers, recognizing that an inflation of paper money led to an inflation of crop prices, asked for more and more paper. Thus began in colonial politics what was to become a recurrent issue in later times: currency inflation. Wherever the issue arose, debtors commonly favored growth in the money supply, which would make it easier for them to pay debts, whereas creditors favored a limited money supply, which would increase the value of their capital.

RELIGION   New England was settled by religious fundamentalists. The Puritans looked to the Bible for authority and inspiration. They read the Bible daily and memorized its passages and stories. The Christian faith was a living source of daily inspiration and obligation for most New Englanders. The Puritans who settled Massachusetts, unlike the Separatists of Plymouth, proposed only to form a purified version of the Anglican Church. They believed that they could remain loyal to the Church of England as they tried to "purify" it of its Catholic elements. But their remoteness from England led them very quickly to a congregational form of church government identical with that of the Pilgrim Separatists.

In the Puritan version of John Calvin's theology, God had voluntarily entered into a covenant, or contract, with worshippers through which they could secure salvation. By analogy, therefore, an assembly of true Christians could enter into a church covenant, a voluntary union for the common worship of God. From this idea it was a fairly short step to the idea of a voluntary union for the purpose of government.

The covenant theory contained certain kernels of democracy in both church and state, but democracy was no part of Puritan political thought, which like so much else in Puritan belief began with original sin. Innate human depravity made governments necessary. The Puritan was dedicated to seeking not the will of the people but the will of God. The ultimate source of authority resided in the Bible, but the Bible had to be explained by "right reason." Hence, most Puritans deferred to an intellectual elite for a true knowledge of God's will. Church and state were but two aspects of the same unity, the purpose of which was to carry out God's will on earth. Although Puritan New England has often been called a theocracy, the church in theory was entirely separate from the state. By law, however, each town had to support a church through taxes levied on every household. And every resident was required to attend midweek and Sunday religious services. The average New Englander heard over 7,000 sermons in a lifetime.

DIVERSITY AND SOCIAL STRAINS   The harmony sought by Puritans settling New England was elusive. Increasing diversity and powerful disruptive forces combined to erode the consensual society envisioned by the founding settlers. Social strains and worldly pursuits increased as time passed, a consequence primarily of population pressure on the land and increasing disparities of wealth. Initially fathers exercised strong patriarchal authority over their sons through their control of the land. They kept their sons in town, not letting them set up their own households or get title to their farmland until they reached middle age. In New England as elsewhere, the tendency was to subdivide the land among all the children. But by the eighteenth century, with land scarcer, younger sons were either getting control of the property early or moving on. Often the younger male children were forced, with family help and blessings, to seek land elsewhere or new kinds of work in the commercial cities along the coast or inland rivers. With the growing pressure on land in the settled regions, poverty and social tension increased in what had once seemed a country of unlimited opportunity.

Sectarian disputes and religious indifference also fractured many communities. The emphasis on a direct accountability to God, which forms the base of all Protestant theology, led believers to challenge authority in the name of private conscience. Massachusetts repressed such heresy in the 1630s, but it resurfaced during the 1650s among Quakers and Baptists, and in 1659–1660 the colony hanged four Quakers who persisted in returning after they had been expelled. These acts caused such revulsion—and an investigation by the Crown—that they were not repeated, although heretics continued to face harassment and persecution.

More damaging to the Puritan utopia was the growing materialism of New England, which strained church discipline. More and more children of the "visible saints" found themselves unable to testify that they had received the gift of God's grace. In 1662 an assembly of ministers at Boston accepted the Half-Way Covenant, whereby baptized children of church members could be admitted to a "halfway" membership. Their own children could be baptized, but such "halfway" members could neither vote nor take Communion. A further blow to Puritan convention and control came with the Massachusetts royal charter of 1691, which required toleration of dissenters and based the right to vote on property rather than church membership.

NEW ENGLAND WITCHCRAFT   The strains accompanying Massachusetts's transition from Puritan utopia to royal colony reached a tragic climax in the witchcraft hysteria at Salem Village (now the town of Danvers) in 1692. Belief in witchcraft pervaded European and New England society in the seventeenth century. Prior to the dramatic episode in Salem, almost 300 New Englanders (mostly lower-class middle-aged spinsters or widows) had been accused of practicing witchcraft, and more than 30 had been hanged.

Still, the Salem episode exceeded all precedents in its scope and intensity. The hysteria began when a few teenage girls became entranced by African tales told by Tituba, a West Indian slave, and began acting strangely—shouting, barking, groveling, and twitching for no apparent reason. The town doctor concluded that they had been bewitched, and the girls pointed to Tituba and two older white women as the culprits. Town dwellers were seized with panic as word spread that the devil was in their midst. At a hearing before the magistrates, the "afflicted" girls rolled on the floor in convulsive fits as the three women were questioned. Tituba then shocked everyone by not only confessing to the charge but also divulging that many others were performing the devil's work.

Tituba's confession spurred the crazed girls to accuse dozens of residents, including several of the most respected members of the community. Within a few months the Salem jail overflowed with townspeople—men, women, and children—all accused of practicing witchcraft. Before the hysteria ran its course ten months later, nineteen people (including some men) had been hanged, one man—stubborn Giles Corey, who refused to plead either guilty or not guilty—was pressed to death by heavy stones, and more than 100 others were jailed.

But as the net of accusation spread wider, extending far beyond the confines of Salem, colonial leaders feared that the witch hunts were out of control. When the afflicted girls charged Samuel Willard, the distinguished pastor of Boston's First Church and president of Harvard College, the stunned magistrates had heard enough. Shortly thereafter the governor intervened when his own wife was accused of serving the devil. He disbanded the special court and ordered the remaining suspects released. Nearly everybody responsible for the Salem executions later recanted, and nothing quite like it happened in the colonies again.

What explains the witchcraft hysteria at Salem? Some historians have argued that it represented nothing more than a contagious exercise in adolescent imagination intended to enliven the dreary routine of everyday life. Yet adults pressed the formal charges against the accused and provided most of the testimony. This fact has led some scholars to speculate that long-festering local feuds and property disputes may have triggered the prosecutions. One of the leaders of the young girls, for instance, was twelve-year-old

Anne Putnam, whose older male kinfolk pressed many of the complaints. The Putnam clan were landowners whose power was declining, and their frenetic pursuit of witches might have served as a psychic weapon to restore their prestige.

More recently, historians have focused on the most salient feature of the accused witches: almost all of them were women. Many of the accused women, it turns out, had in some way defied the traditional roles assigned to females. Some had engaged in business transactions outside the home; others did not attend church; some were curmudgeons; many were worried about Indian attacks. Most of them were middle-aged or older, beyond child-bearing age, and without sons or brothers. They thus stood to inherit property and live independently. The notion of autonomous spinsters flew in the face of prevailing social conventions. Whatever the precise cause, there is little doubt that the witchcraft hysteria reflected the peculiar social dynamics of the Salem community.

SOCIETY AND ECONOMY IN THE MIDDLE COLONIES

AN ECONOMIC MIX   Both geographically and culturally the middle colonies stood between New England and the South, blending their own influences with elements derived from the older regions on either side. In so doing, they more completely reflected the diversity of colonial life and more fully foreshadowed the pluralism of the American nation than did the other regions. Their crops were those of New England but more bountiful, owing to better land and a longer growing season, and they developed surpluses of foodstuffs for export to the plantations of the South and the West Indies: wheat, barley, and livestock. The region's commerce rivaled that of New England, and indeed Philadelphia in time supplanted Boston as the largest city in the colonies.

Land policies in the middle colonies followed the headright system of the South. In New York the early royal governors carried forward, in practice if not in name, the Dutch device of the patroonship, granting influential friends vast estates on Long Island and up the Hudson and Mohawk River valleys. These realms most nearly approached the medieval manor. They were self-contained domains farmed by tenants who paid fees to use the landlords' mills, warehouses, smokehouses, and wharves. But with free land elsewhere, new waves of immigrants avoided these autocratic patroonships in favor of broader opportunities in the promised land of Pennsylvania.

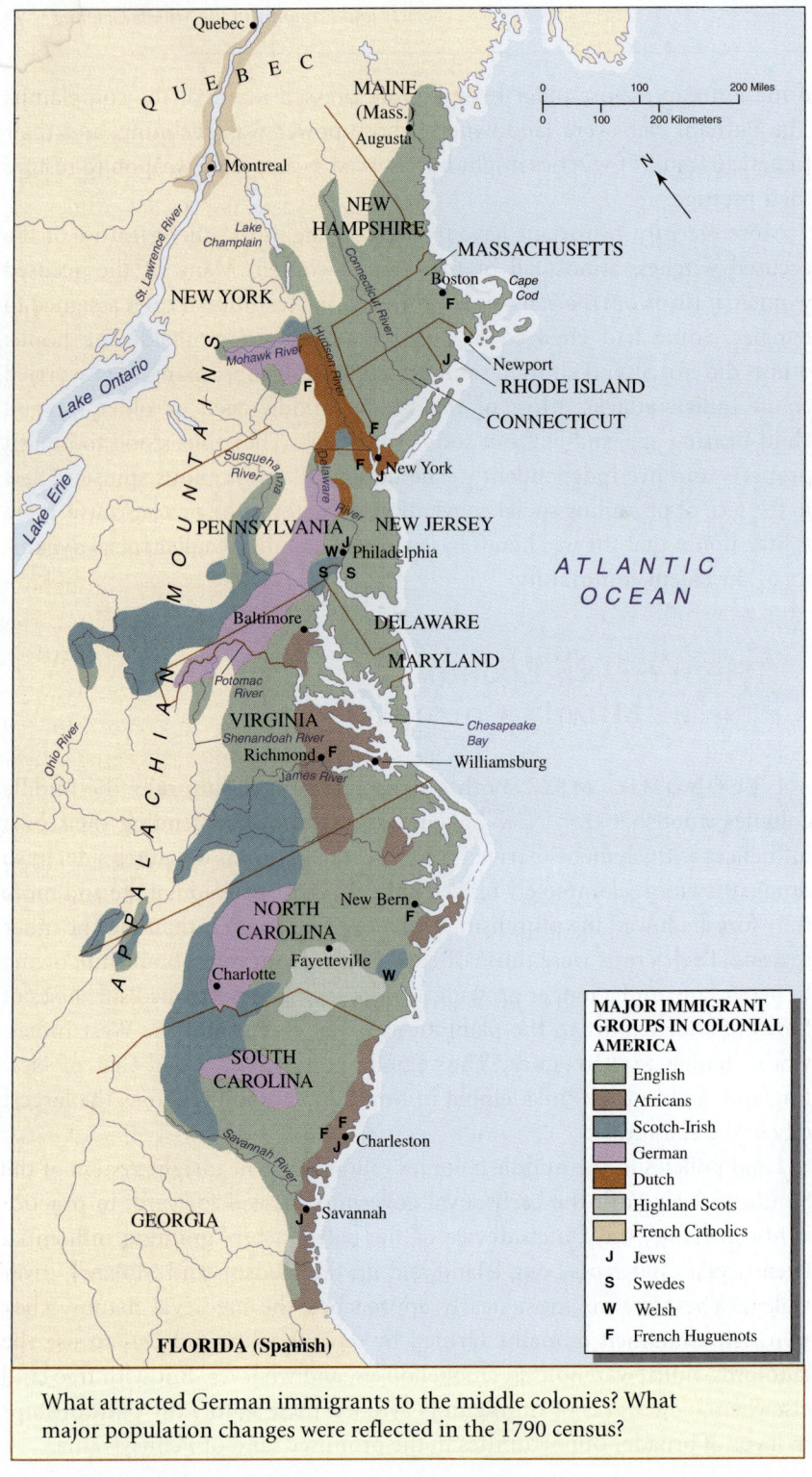

Quebec

QUEBEC

MAINE
(Mass.)

Augusta

Montreal

Lake
Champlain

NEW
HAMPSHIRE

MASSACHUSETTS

Boston
F

Cape
Cod

St. Lawrence River

NEW YORK

Mohawk River

F

Susquehanna
River

Lake Ontario

APPALACHIAN MOUNTAINS

Lake Erie

Ohio River

PENNSYLVANIA

F
F

F
J

New York

Delaware River

W
S

J

S

Philadelphia

NEW JERSEY

DELAWARE

Baltimore

Potomac
River

MARYLAND

Newport

RHODE ISLAND

CONNECTICUT

Connecticut River

Hudson River

J

ATLANTIC
OCEAN

VIRGINIA

Shenandoah River

Richmond

F

James River

Chesapeake
Bay

Williamsburg

NORTH
CAROLINA

Charlotte

Fayetteville

W

New Bern

F

SOUTH
CAROLINA

Savannah River

F
J

F

Charleston

GEORGIA

J

Savannah

**MAJOR IMMIGRANT
GROUPS IN COLONIAL
AMERICA**

English

Africans

Scotch-Irish

German

Dutch

Highland Scots

French Catholics

J Jews

S Swedes

W Welsh

F French Huguenots

FLORIDA (Spanish)

What attracted German immigrants to the middle colonies? What
major population changes were reflected in the 1790 census?

AN ETHNIC MIX   In the makeup of their population, the middle colonies stood apart from both the mostly English Puritan settlements of New England and the biracial plantation colonies to the south. In New York and New Jersey, for instance, Dutch culture and language lingered, along with the Dutch Reformed Church. Up and down the Delaware River, the few Swedes and Finns, the first settlers, were overwhelmed by the influx of English and Welsh Quakers, followed in turn by Germans and Scotch-Irish.

The Germans came mainly from regions devastated by incessant war. The promise of religious freedom in the New World appealed to persecuted sects, especially the Mennonites, whose beliefs resembled those of the Quakers. West of Philadelphia thrifty immigrant farmers and artisans created a belt of settlement in which the "Pennsylvania Dutch" (a corruption of Deutsch, meaning "German") predominated. The Scotch-Irish began to arrive later and moved still farther out into the backcountry throughout the eighteenth century. (Scotch-Irish is an enduring misnomer for Ulster Scots, Presbyterians transplanted from Scotland to confiscated lands in northern Ireland to give that country a more Protestant tone.) The Scotch-Irish fled economic disaster and Anglican persecution. They settled first in Pennsylvania and then fanned out across the fertile valleys stretching southwestward into Virginia and Carolina. With the Germans they became the most numerous of the non-English groups in the colonies, but others also enriched the diversity of the population in New York and the Quaker colonies, including Huguenots (French Protestants), Irish, Welsh, Swiss, and Jews. By 1790 barely half the nation's inhabitants could trace their origins to England.

Colonial Cities

Since commerce was their chief reason for being, colonial cities hugged the coastline or, like Philadelphia, sprang up on rivers that could be navigated by oceangoing vessels. Never having more than 10 percent of the colonial population, they exerted an influence on commerce, politics, and culture out of proportion to their size. Five port cities outdistanced the rest. By the end of the colonial period, Philadelphia had some 30,000 people and was the largest city in the colonies, second only to London in the British Empire; New York, with about 25,000, ranked second; Boston numbered 16,000; Charleston, South Carolina, 12,000; and Newport, Rhode Island, 11,000.

THE SOCIAL AND POLITICAL ORDER Merchants formed the upper crust of urban society, and below them came a middle class of craftspeople, retailers, innkeepers, and artisans. Almost two thirds of the adult male workers were artisans, people who made their living at handicrafts. They included carpenters, shoemakers, tailors, blacksmiths, weavers, and potters. At the bottom of the pecking order were sailors and unskilled workers. Such class stratification in the cities became more pronounced during the eighteenth century and thereafter.

Problems created by urban growth are nothing new. Colonial cities were busy, crowded, and dangerous. They required not only paved roads and streetlights but regulations to protect children and animals from reckless riders. Other regulations restrained citizens from tossing their garbage into the street. Devastating fires led to building codes, restrictions on burning rubbish, and the organization of fire companies. Rising crime and violence required more police protection. Also in cities the poor became more visible than they were in the countryside. Colonists responded according to the English principle of public responsibility for the needy. Most of the aid went to "outdoor" relief in the form of money, food, clothing, and fuel, but almshouses also appeared to house the destitute.

THE URBAN WEB Transit within and between early-American cities was initially difficult. The first roads were Indian trails, which themselves often followed the tracks of bison through the forests. Those trails widened with travel, then were made into roads. Land travel was initially by horse or by foot. The first stagecoach line for the public opened in 1732. From the main ports good roads might reach thirty or forty miles inland, but all were dirt roads subject to washouts and mud holes.

Taverns were an important aspect of colonial travel, since movement at night was risky. By the end of the seventeenth century, there were more taverns in America than any other business, and they became the most important social institution in the colonies—and the most democratic. By 1690 there were fifty-four taverns in Boston alone, half of them operated by women.

Colonial taverns and inns were places to drink, relax, read a newspaper, play cards or billiards, gossip about people or politics, learn news from travelers, or conduct business. Local ordinances regulated the taverns, setting prices and usually prohibiting them from serving liquor to African Americans, Indians, servants, or apprentices.

Taverns served as a collective form of social discourse; long-distance communication, however, was more complicated. Postal service in the seventeenth century was almost nonexistent—people entrusted letters to travelers

Taverns

A tobacconist's business card from 1770 captures the atmosphere of late-eighteenth-century taverns. Here men in a Philadelphia tavern converse while they drink ale and smoke pipes.

or sea captains. Massachusetts set up a provincial postal system in 1677 and Pennsylvania in 1683. Under a parliamentary law of 1710, the postmaster of London named a deputy in charge of the colonies, and a postal system eventually extended the length of the Atlantic seaboard. Benjamin Franklin, who served as deputy postmaster for the colonies from 1753 to 1774, sped up the service with shorter routes and night-traveling post riders, and he increased the volume by lowering rates.

More reliable mail delivery gave rise to newspapers in the eighteenth century. Before 1745 twenty-two newspapers had been started: seven in New England, ten in the middle colonies, and five in the South. An important landmark in the progress of freedom of the press was John Peter Zenger's trial for seditious libel, for publishing criticisms of New York's governor in his newspaper, the *New York Weekly Journal.* Zenger was imprisoned for ten months and brought to trial in 1735. English common law held that one might be punished for criticism that fostered "an ill opinion of the government." The jury's function was only to determine whether the defendant had published the opinion. Zenger's lawyer startled the court with his claim that the editor had published the truth—which the judge ruled an unacceptable defense. The jury, however, agreed with the assertion and held the editor not guilty. The libel law remained standing as before, but editors thereafter were emboldened to criticize officials more freely.

THE ENLIGHTENMENT

By the middle of the eighteenth century, the thirteen colonies were maturing. People increasingly referred to themselves simply as Americans. The population was exploding, fed both by natural increase and by a constant stream of immigrants from diverse lands. Schools and colleges were springing up, and the standard of living was rising as well. More and more colonists had easier access to the latest consumer goods—and the latest ideas percolating in Europe. Through their commercial contacts, newspapers, libraries, and other channels, colonial cities became the centers for the discussion of new ideas. Most significant was a burst of intellectual activity known as the Enlightenment. Like the Renaissance, the Enlightenment prized rational inquiry, scientific discoveries, and individual freedom. Unlike their Renaissance predecessors, however, many enlightened thinkers were willing to discard orthodox religious beliefs in favor of more "rational" ideas and ideals.

DISCOVERING THE LAWS OF NATURE   One manifestation of the Enlightenment was a scientific revolution in which the prevailing notion of an earth-centered universe was overthrown by the sun-centered system that had been described by the sixteenth-century Polish astronomer Nicolaus Copernicus. The scientific revolution climaxed in 1687, when England's Sir Isaac Newton set forth his theory of gravitation. Newton had, in short, challenged biblical notions of the natural order by depicting a mechanistic universe moving in accordance with natural laws that could be grasped by human reason and explained by mathematics.

By analogy to Newton's view of the world as a machine, one could reason that natural laws govern all things—the orbits of the planets and the orbits of human relations: politics, economics, and society. Reason could make people aware, for instance, that the natural law of supply and demand governs economics or that the natural rights to life, liberty, and property determine the limits and functions of government.

Much of this new enlightened thought could be reconciled with established beliefs: the idea of natural law existed in Christian theology, and religious people could reason that the worldview of Copernicus and Newton simply showed the glory of God. Yet Deists carried the idea to its ultimate conclusion, reducing God from a daily presence to a remote Creator, a master clockmaker who planned the universe and set it in motion. Evil in the world, one might reason further, resulted not from original sin so much as from an imperfect understanding of the laws of nature. People, the English philosopher John Locke argued in his *Essay Concerning Human Understanding* (1690), reflect the impact of their environment, the human mind being a blank tablet at birth that gains knowledge through experience. Corrupt society therefore might corrupt the mind. The best way to improve both society and human nature was by the application and improvement of Reason, which was the highest Virtue (Enlightenment thinkers often capitalized both words).

THE ENLIGHTENMENT IN AMERICA   However interpreted, such "enlightened" ideas profoundly affected the climate of thought in the eighteenth century. The premises of Newtonian science and the Enlightenment, moreover, fitted the American experience, which placed a premium on observation, experiment, reason, and the need to think anew. America was therefore especially receptive to the new science.

Benjamin Franklin epitomized the Enlightenment. He rose from the ranks of the common folk and never lost the common touch, a gift that accounted for his success as a publisher. Born in Boston in 1706, Franklin was the son of a maker of candles and soap and a descendant of Puritans. Apprenticed to his older brother, a printer, Franklin left home at the age of seventeen and relocated to Philadelphia. There, before he was twenty-four, he owned a print shop, where he edited and published the *Pennsylvania Gazette*. When he was twenty-six, he published *Poor Richard's Almanack*, a collection of homely teachings on success and happiness. Before he retired from business, at the age of forty-two, Franklin, among other achievements, had founded a library, organized a fire company, helped start the academy that became the University of Pennsylvania, and organized a debating club that grew into the American Philosophical Society. Franklin was devoted to science. Skeptical and curious, pragmatic and irreverent, he was a voracious reader and an inventive genius. His wide-ranging experiments traversed the fields of medicine, meteorology, geology, astronomy, and physics. He developed the Franklin stove, the lightning rod, and a glass harmonica.

Franklin's love of commonsensical reason and his pragmatic skepticism clashed with prevailing religious beliefs. Although raised as a Presbyterian, he became a freethinker who had no patience with religious orthodoxy and sectarian squabbles. Franklin prized reason over revelation. He was not

Benjamin Franklin

Shown here as a young man in a portrait by Robert Feke.

burdened with anxieties regarding the state of his soul. Early on, he abandoned the Calvinist assumption that God had predestined salvation for a select few. He found the doctrine of original sin "unintelligible," was skeptical of the divinity of Jesus, and did not accept at face value the Bible as God's word. Franklin quit attending church as a young man, yet he retained a belief in God. Like the European and English Deists, he grew skeptical of biblical revelation and came to believe in a God that had created a universe animated by natural laws, laws that inquisitive people could discern through reason. The Deistic God was a distant Creator, not a providential force in human life. Franklin decided that Christian morality, not theology, was the basis of a good life—and a meaningful religious outlook.

Benjamin Franklin and other like-minded thinkers, such as Thomas Jefferson, James Madison, and Thomas Paine, derived an outlook of buoyant hope and confident optimism from the discoveries of modern science. Unlike Calvinists, they believed people have the capacity to unlock the mysteries of the universe and thereby shape their own destinies. "The rapid Progress *true* Science now makes," as Franklin wrote, led him to regret being "born too soon." Jefferson concurred. He, too, envisioned a bright future for humankind: "As long as we may think as we will and speak as we think, the condition of man will proceed in improvement." The evangelical religiosity of traveling revivalists disgusted Jefferson. His "fundamental principle" was that reason, not emotion and "blindfolded fear," should inform decision making, and virtue should trump piety: "We are saved by our good works, which are within our power, and not by our faith, which is not in our power." Jefferson warned against those "despots" in religion and politics who resisted change and still wanted to dictate belief.

Such enlightened thinking, founded on freedom of thought and expression, could not have been more different from the religious assumptions shaping Puritan New England in the seventeenth century. The eighteenth-century

Enlightenment set in motion self-assured intellectual forces that challenged the reality of revealed religion and the logic of Christian faith. Those modern forces, however, would inspire stern resistance in the defenders of religious orthodoxy.

EDUCATION IN THE COLONIES   The heights of abstract reasoning were of course remote from the everyday concerns of most colonists. For the colonists at large, education in the traditional ideas and manners of society—even literacy itself—remained primarily the responsibility of family and church. Conditions in New England, however, proved most favorable for the establishment of schools. The Puritan emphasis on reading Scripture, which all Protestants shared to some degree, implied an obligation to ensure literacy. In 1647 the Massachusetts Bay Colony required every town of fifty or more families to set up a grammar school (a "Latin school" that could prepare a student for college). Although the act was widely evaded, it set an example that the rest of New England emulated.

In Pennsylvania the Quakers never heeded William Penn's instructions to establish public schools, but they did respect the usefulness of education and financed a number of private schools, where practical as well as academic subjects were taught. In the southern colonies, efforts to establish schools were hampered by the more scattered population and, in parts of the backcountry, by indifference and neglect. Some of the wealthiest southern planters and merchants sent their children to England or hired tutors, who in some cases would also serve the children of neighbors. In some places wealthy patrons or the people collectively managed to raise some kind of support for academies.

The Great Awakening

During the early eighteenth century, the American colonies were "awash in a sea of faith," as one historian has written. Hundreds of new congregations were founded between 1700 and 1750. Most Americans (85 percent) lived in colonies with an "established" church, meaning that the colonial government officially sanctioned—and collected taxes to support—a single preferred denomination. Anglicanism was the official church in Virginia, Maryland, Delaware, and the Carolinas. Congregationalism was the official faith in New England. In New York, Anglicanism vied with the Dutch Reformed Church for control. Pennsylvania had no official church, but Quakers dominated the legislative assembly. Like Pennsylvania, New Jersey and Rhode Island had no official denomination and hosted numerous sects.

Each of the three major denominations—Anglican, Presbyterian, and Congregational—sought to enforce their religious monopoly in their colonies. Most colonies with an established church organized religious life on the basis of well-regulated local parishes, which defined their borders and defended them against dissenters and heretics. No outside preacher could enter the parish and speak in public without permission. Then, in the 1740s, the parish system was thrown into turmoil by the arrival of outspoken traveling (itinerant) evangelists, who claimed that the official parish ministers were incompetent and unregenerate. Many of the evangelists also insisted that Christians must be "reborn" in their convictions and behavior; traditional creeds or articles of faith were unnecessary for rebirth. By emphasizing the individualistic strand embedded in Protestantism, the so-called Great Awakening ended up invigorating—and fragmenting—American religious life. Unlike the Enlightenment, which affected primarily the intellectual elite, the Great Awakening appealed to the masses, including Native Americans and enslaved African Americans. It was the first popular movement before the Revolution that spanned all thirteen colonies. As Benjamin Franklin observed of the Awakening, "Never did the people show so great a willingness to attend sermons. Religion is become the subject of most conversation."

EDWARDS AND WHITEFIELD   In 1734–1735 a remarkable spiritual revival occurred in the congregation of Jonathan Edwards, a Congregationalist minister in Northampton, in western Massachusetts. One of America's most brilliant philosophers and theologians, Edwards had entered Yale in 1716, at age thirteen, and graduated as valedictorian four years later. In 1727, Edwards took charge of the Congregational church in Northampton and found the congregation's spirituality at a low ebb. Edwards claimed that the young people of Northampton were addicted to sinful pleasures, such as "night walking and frequenting the tavern," and indulged in "lewd practices" that "exceedingly corrupted others." He was convinced that Christians had become preoccupied with making and spending money and that religion had become too intellectual and in the process had lost its animating force. "Our people," he said, "do not so much need to have their heads stored [with education] as to have their hearts touched." He added that he considered it a "reasonable thing to endeavor to fright persons away from hell." His own vivid descriptions of the torments of hell and the delights of heaven helped rekindle spiritual fervor among his congregants. By 1735, Edwards could report that "the town seemed to be full of the presence of God; it never was so full of love, nor of joy."

The true catalyst of the Great Awakening, however, was a young English minister, George Whitefield, whose reputation as a spellbinding evangelist preceded him to the colonies. Congregations were lifeless, he claimed, "because dead men preach to them." Too many ministers were "slothful shepherds and dumb dogs." To restore the fires of religious fervor to American congregations, Whitefield reawakened the notion of individual salvation. In the autumn of 1739, Whitefield arrived in Philadelphia and late in that year preached to huge crowds. After visiting Georgia, he made a triumphal procession northward to New England, drawing great crowds and releasing "Gales of Heavenly Wind" that dispersed sparks throughout the colonies.

Whitefield enthralled audiences with his unparalleled eloquence. The English revivalist stressed the need for individuals to experience a "new birth," a sudden and emotional moment of conversion and salvation. By the end of his sermon, one listener reported, the entire congregation was "in utmost Confusion, some crying out, some laughing, and Bliss still roaring to them to come to Christ, as they answered, *I will, I will, I'm coming, I'm coming.*"

Jonathan Edwards heard Whitefield preach and wept through most of the sermon. Thereafter he spread his own revival gospel throughout New England. The Great Awakening in New England reached its peak in 1741 when Edwards delivered his most famous sermon. Titled "Sinners in the Hands of an Angry God," it represented a devout appeal to repentance. Edwards reminded his congregation of the reality of hell, the omnipotence of God's vision, and the

George Whitefield

The English minister's dramatic eloquence roused American congregants, inspiring many to experience a religious rebirth.

certainty of his judgment. He warned that God "holds you over the pit of hell, much as one holds a spider, or some loathsome insect, over the fire, abhors you, and is dreadfully provoked . . . he looks upon you as worthy of nothing else, but to be cast into the fire."

Women, both white and black, were reported to be more susceptible to fits of spiritual emotion than men. Whitefield and other traveling evangelists targeted women because of their spiritual virtuosity. These ecstatic evangelists believed that conversion required a visceral, emotional experience. Convulsions, shrieks, and spasms were the physical manifestation of the Holy Spirit at work, and women seemed more willing to let the Spirit move them. Some of the revivalists, especially Baptists, initially loosened traditional restrictions on female participation in worship. Scores of women served as lay exhorters, including Bathsheba Kingsley, who stole her husband's horse in 1741 to spread the gospel among her rural neighbors after receiving "immediate revelations from heaven." Sarah Osborn, a Rhode Island Congregationalist widow, was so inspired by the preachings of Whitefield and Gilbert Tennent (another leader of the Great Awakening) that she organized a women's prayer group that same year. By the 1760s her home in Newport had become the locus of a sustained revival. Hundreds of people, white men and women, free and enslaved blacks, converged in her home to pray and embrace Christ. Despite a male friend's advice to "shut up . . . [her] Mouth and doors and creep into obscurity," Osborn persisted. Similarly, Mary Reed of Durham, New Hampshire, so enthralled her minister with her effusions of the Holy Spirit that he allowed her to deliver spellbinding testimonials to the congregation every Wednesday evening for two months. Such ecstatic piety was symptomatic of the Awakening's rekindling of religious enthusiasm. Yet most ministers who encouraged public expressions of female piety refused to link such enhanced participation to the more controversial idea of allowing women to participate in congregational governance. Churches remained male bastions of political authority.

The message and technique of Edwards and Whitefield were infectious, and imitators sprang up everywhere. Once unleashed, however, spiritual enthusiasm was hard to control, and in many ways the Great Awakening backfired on those who had intended it to bolster church discipline and social order. Some revivalists began to court those at the bottom of society— laborers, seamen, servants, and farmers. The Reverend James Davenport, for instance, a fiery New England Congregationalist, set about shouting, raging, and stomping on the devil and beseeching his listeners to renounce the

Sarah Osborn's house

Osborn's house in Newport, Rhode Island, was visited by hundreds of people who came to pray and embrace Christ.

established clergy, whom he branded unconverted, and become the agents of their own salvation. The radical revivalists, said one worried conservative, were breeding "anarchy, levelling, and dissolution."

PIETY AND REASON   Whatever their motive or method, the revivalists succeeded in awakening the piety of many Americans. Between 1740 and 1742 some 25,000 to 50,000 New Englanders, out of a total population of 300,000, joined churches. The Great Awakening also contributed to the fragmentation of spiritual life. It spawned a proliferation of new religious groups and sects that helped undermine the notion of state-supported churches and the authority of conventional ministers. Everywhere the revivals induced splits, especially in the more Calvinistic churches. Traditional clergymen found their position undermined as church members chose sides and either dismissed their old ministers or deserted them.

By the middle of the eighteenth century, New England Puritanism had completely fragmented. The precarious balance in which the founders had held the elements of piety and reason was shattered, and more and more Baptists, Presbyterians, Anglicans, and members of other denominations began establishing footholds in formerly Puritan Congregationalist communities. Yet the revival frenzy scored its most lasting victories along the chaotic frontiers of the middle and southern colonies. In contrast, in the more sedate churches of Boston, rational religion ultimately got the upper hand in a reaction against the excesses of revival emotion. The rationality of Newton and Locke—the idea of natural law—crept more and more into the sermons of Boston ministers, who embarked on the road to Unitarianism and Universalism.

In reaction to taunts that the "born-again" revivalist ministers lacked learning, the Great Awakening gave rise to the denominational colleges that became characteristic of American higher education. The three colleges already in existence had their origins in religious motives: Harvard College, founded in 1636 because the Puritans dreaded "to leave an illiterate ministry to the church when our present ministers shall lie in the dust"; the College of William and Mary, created in 1693 to strengthen the Anglican ministry; and Yale College, set up in 1701 to serve the Puritans of Connecticut, who believed that Harvard was drifting from the strictest orthodoxy. The College of New Jersey, later Princeton University, was founded by Presbyterians in 1746 as the successor to William Tennent's Log College. In close succession came King's College (1754) in New York, later Columbia University, an Anglican institution; the College of Rhode Island (1764), later Brown University, which was Baptist; Queens College (1766), later Rutgers, which was Dutch Reformed; and the Congregationalist Dartmouth College (1769), the outgrowth of a school for Indians. Among the colonial colleges only the University of Pennsylvania, founded as the Academy of Philadelphia in 1751, arose from a secular impulse.

The Great Awakening, like the Enlightenment, set in motion powerful intellectual and spiritual currents that still flow in American life. It implanted permanently in American culture evangelical energies and the appeal of revivalism. The movement weakened the status of the established clergy, encouraged believers to exercise their own judgment, and thereby weakened habits of deference generally. The proliferation of denominations heightened the need for toleration of dissent. In some respects the Great Awakening, characterized by piety and emotion, and the Enlightenment, dominated by reason and rationality, led by different roads to similar ends. Both movements emphasized the power and right of individual choice and popular resistance to established authority, and both aroused millennial hopes that America would become the promised land in which people might approach the perfection of piety or reason, if not both. Such hopes had both social and political, as well as religious, implications. As the eighteenth century advanced, fewer and fewer people were willing to defer to the ruling social and political elite, and many such rebellious if pious folk would be transformed into revolutionaries.

End of Chapter Review

- **Colonial Differences** Agriculture diversified: tobacco was the staple crop in Virginia, and rice and naval stores were the staples in the Carolinas. Family farms and a mixed economy characterized the middle and New England colonies, while plantation agriculture based on slavery became entrenched in the South. By 1790, German, Scotch-Irish, Welsh, and Irish immigrants had settled in the middle colonies, along with members of religious groups such as Quakers, Jews, Huguenots, and Mennonites.

- **Women in the Colonies** English colonists brought their belief systems with them, including convictions about the inferiority of women. The initial shortage of women gave way to a more equal sex ratio as women immigrated—alone and in family groups—thereby enabling a dramatic population growth in the colonies.

- **Indentured Servants** In response to the labor shortage in the early years, Virginia relied on indentured servants; by the end of the seventeenth century, enslaved Africans were the norm in the South. With the supply of slaves seeming inexhaustible, the Carolinas adopted slavery as its primary labor source.

- **Triangular Trade** British America sent raw materials, such as fish and furs, to England in return for manufactured goods. The colonies participated in the triangular trade with Africa and the Caribbean, building ships and exporting manufactured goods, especially rum, while "importing" slaves from Africa.

- **The Enlightenment** The attitudes of the Enlightenment were transported along the trade routes. Isaac Newton's scientific discoveries and John Locke's idea of natural law culminated in the belief that Reason could improve society. Benjamin Franklin, who believed people could shape their own destinies, became the face of the Enlightenment in America.

- **The Great Awakening** Religious diversity in the colonies increased. By the 1730s a revival of faith, the Great Awakening, swept through the colonies. New congregations formed as older sects were challenged by evangelists, who insisted that Christians be "reborn." Individualism, not orthodoxy, was stressed in this first popular movement in America's history.

CHRONOLOGY

1619	First Africans arrive at Jamestown
1636	Harvard College is established
1662	Puritans initiate the Half-Way Covenant
1662	Virginia enacts law declaring that children of slave women are slaves
1691	Royal charter for Massachusetts is established
1692	Salem witchcraft trials
1730s–1740s	Great Awakening
1735	John Peter Zenger is tried for seditious libel
1739	Stono Uprising
1739	George Whitefield preaches his first sermon in America, in Philadelphia
1741	Jonathan Edward preaches "Sinners in the Hands of an Angry God"

KEY TERMS & NAMES

4

THE IMPERIAL
PERSPECTIVE

FOCUS QUESTIONS wwnorton.com/studyspace

- How did the British Empire administer the economy of its colonies?

- How were colonial governments structured, and how independent were they of the mother country?

- How did the presence of the French in North America affect Britain and its colonies?

- What were the causes of the French and Indian War?

- How did victory in the Seven Years' War affect the British colonies in North America?

For the better part of the seventeenth century, England remained too distracted by the struggle between Parliament and the Stuart kings to perfect either a systematic colonial policy or effective agencies of imperial control. The English Civil War of the 1640s ushered in Oliver Cromwell's Puritan Commonwealth and Protectorate, during which the colonies were given a respite from royal control. After the Restoration of King Charles II and the Stuart dynasty in 1660, the British government slowly developed a new plan of colonial administration. By the end of the seventeenth century, however, it still lacked coherence and efficiency, leaving Americans accustomed to rather loose colonial reins.

ENGLISH ADMINISTRATION OF THE COLONIES

Throughout the colonial period the British monarchs exercised legal authority in America, and land titles derived ultimately from royal grants to individuals and groups. All important colonial officials held office at the pleasure of the monarch. The British government regarded English colonists as citizens, but it refused to grant them the privileges of citizenship. It insisted that Americans contribute to the expense of maintaining the colonies, but it refused to allow them a voice in shaping administrative policies. Such inconsistencies bred tension that festered over time. By the mid–eighteenth century, when the British tried to impose on their American colonies the kinds of controls that were reaping profits in India, it was too late. British Americans had developed a far more powerful sense of their rights than had any other colonial people, and they were increasingly determined to assert and defend those rights.

THE MERCANTILE SYSTEM   In developing a national economic policy, Restoration England under King Charles II adopted the mercantile system, or mercantilism, which was based on the assumption that the world's supply of gold and silver remained essentially fixed, with only a nation's share in that wealth subject to change. Thus one nation could gain wealth only at the expense of another—by seizing its gold and silver and dominating its trade. To acquire gold and silver, a government had to control all economic activities, limiting foreign imports and preserving a favorable balance of trade. A mercantilist government therefore had to encourage manufacturing, through subsidies and monopolies if need be, to develop and protect its own shipping and to exploit colonies as sources of raw materials and markets for its finished goods.

During the English Civil War of the 1640s, Dutch shipping companies had taken over the trade with England's colonies. To win it back, Oliver Cromwell persuaded Parliament in 1651 to adopt the Navigation Act, which required that all goods imported by England or the colonies arrive on English ships and that the majority of the crews be English.

With the Restoration, Parliament passed the Navigation Act of 1660, which added a twist to Cromwell's policy: ships' crews had to be three-quarters English, and "enumerated" products not produced by the mother country, such as tobacco, cotton, and sugar, were to be shipped from the colonies only to England or other English colonies. Not only did England (and its colonies) become the sole outlet for these profitable colonial exports, but the Navigation Act of 1663 required that all ships carrying goods from

Europe to America dock in England, be offloaded, and pay a duty before proceeding. A third major act rounded out the trade system. The Navigation Act of 1673 (sometimes called the Plantation Duty Act) required that every captain loading enumerated articles in the colonies pay a duty, or tax, on them.

ENFORCING THE NAVIGATION ACTS The Navigation Acts supplied a convenient rationale for a colonial trading system: to serve the economic needs of the mother country. Their enforcement in far-flung colonies, however, was another matter. In 1675, Charles II created the Lords of Trade, who were to make the colonies abide by the mercantile system and make them more profitable for the Crown. The Lords of Trade named colonial governors, wrote or reviewed the governors' instructions, and handled all reports and correspondence dealing with colonial affairs.

Between 1673 and 1679, English collectors of customs duties arrived in all the colonies, and with them appeared the first seeds of colonial resentment. New England's Puritan leaders in particular harbored a persistent distrust of royal intentions. The Massachusetts Bay Colony not only ignored royal wishes; it also tolerated violations of the Navigation Acts. This led the Lords of Trade to try to revoke the colonial charter in 1678. The issue remained in

Boston from the southeast

This view of eighteenth-century Boston shows the importance of shipping and its regulation in the colonies, especially in Massachusetts Bay.

legal snarls for another six years; in 1684 the Lords of Trade won a court decision annulling the Massachusetts charter.

THE DOMINION OF NEW ENGLAND   In 1684 the Massachusetts Bay government fell under the control of a special royal commission. Then, in 1685, King Charles II died and was succeeded by his brother the Duke of York, as King James II, the first Catholic sovereign since Queen Mary (r. 1553–1558). Plans long maturing in the Lords of Trade for a general reorganization of colonial government coincided with the autocratic notions of James II, who asserted power more forcefully than his brother had. The new king therefore readily approved a proposal to create a Dominion of New England, which included all the colonies south through New Jersey.

The Dominion was to have a government named by royal authority; a governor and council would rule without any colonial assembly. The royal governor, Sir Edmund Andros, appeared in Boston in 1686 to establish his rule, which he soon extended over Connecticut and Rhode Island and, in 1688, over New York and East and West Jersey. Not surprisingly, a rising resentment greeted Governor Andros's measures, especially in Massachusetts. Andros levied taxes without the consent of the General Court, suppressed town governments, enforced the trade laws, and clamped down on smuggling. Most ominous of all, he and his lieutenants took over one of Boston's Puritan churches for Anglican worship. Puritan leaders believed, with good reason, that he proposed to break their power and authority.

But the Dominion of New England was scarcely established before word arrived that the Glorious Revolution of 1688 had erupted in England. King James II, had aroused resentment by instituting arbitrary measures and openly parading his Catholic faith. In 1688 parliamentary leaders, their patience exhausted, invited James's Protestant daughter Mary and her husband, the Dutch leader William III, to assume the throne as joint monarchs. James II fled to France.

THE GLORIOUS REVOLUTION IN AMERICA   When news reached Boston that William and Mary had landed in England, the city staged its own Glorious Revolution. Governor Andros and his councillors were arrested, and Massachusetts reverted to its former government, as did the other colonies that had been absorbed into the Dominion. All were permitted to revert to their former status except Massachusetts Bay and Plymouth, which after some delay were united under a new charter in 1691 as the royal colony of Massachusetts Bay.

The Glorious Revolution in England had significant long-term effects on American history. The Bill of Rights and the Toleration Act, passed in England in 1689, limited monarchical powers and affirmed a degree of freedom of worship for all Christians, thereby influencing attitudes—and the course of events—in the colonies. The overthrow of James II also set a precedent for revolution against the monarch. In defense of that action, the English philosopher John Locke published his *Two Treatises on Government* (1690), which had an enormous impact on political thought in the colonies. Locke's contract theory of government argued that people are endowed with natural rights to life, liberty, and property. When a ruler violates those rights, the people have the right—in extreme cases—to overthrow the monarch and change their government.

AN EMERGING COLONIAL SYSTEM William and Mary revised the Navigation Acts and the administrative system for regulating the American colonies. The Navigation Act of 1696, officially called the Act to Prevent Frauds and Abuses, required colonial governors to enforce the Navigation Acts, allowed customs officials to use "writs of assistance" (general search warrants that did not have to specify the place to be searched), and ordered that accused violators be tried in admiralty courts, because colonial juries habitually refused to convict their peers. Admiralty cases were decided by judges whom the royal governors appointed.

Also in 1696, King William III created a Lords Commissioners of Trade and Plantations to take the place of the Lords of Trade. Intended to ensure that the colonies served England's economy, the new Board of Trade oversaw the enforcement of the Navigation Acts and recommended ways to limit manufacturing in the colonies and encourage their production of raw materials needed by England. From 1696 to 1725, the Board of Trade sought to bring more efficient royal control to the administration of the colonies. After 1725, however, its energies and activities waned. The Board of Trade became chiefly an agency of political patronage, studded with officials whose main interest was their salaries.

THE HABIT OF SELF-GOVERNMENT

Government within the American colonies, like colonial policy, evolved essentially without plan. In broad outline the governor, council, and assembly in each colony corresponded to the king, lords, and commons in England. At the outset all the colonies except Georgia had been founded by trading companies or feudal proprietors holding charters from the Crown, but eight colonies eventually relinquished or forfeited their charters and became royal provinces. In these the Crown named the governor. Connecticut and Rhode Island were the last of the corporate colonies; they elected their own governors to the end of the colonial period. In the corporate and proprietary colonies and in Massachusetts, the charter served as a rough equivalent to a written constitution. Over the years certain anomalies appeared as colonial governments diverged from trends in England. On the one hand, the governors retained powers and prerogatives that the king had lost in the course of the seventeenth century. On the other hand, the assemblies acquired powers, particularly with respect to government appointments, that Parliament had yet to gain for itself.

POWERS OF THE GOVERNORS   The Crown never vetoed acts of Parliament after 1707, but the colonial governors, most of whom were mediocre or incompetent, still held an absolute veto over the assemblies, and the Crown could disallow (in effect, veto) colonial legislation. As chief executive, the royal governor in each colony could appoint and remove officials, command the militia and naval forces, grant pardons, and as his commission often put it, "execute everything which doth and of right ought to belong to the governor," which might cover a multitude of powers. In these respects, his authority resembled the Crown's, for the king still exercised executive authority and had the power to name administrative officials.

POWERS OF THE ASSEMBLIES   Unlike the governor and members of the council, who were appointed by either king or proprietor, the colonial assembly was elected. Whether called the House of Burgesses (Virginia), or Delegates (Maryland), or Representatives (Massachusetts), or simply the assembly, the lower houses were chosen by popular vote in counties, towns, or, in South Carolina, parishes. Religious requirements for voting were abandoned during the seventeenth century. The chief restriction on voting rights was a property qualification, based upon the notion that only men who held a "stake in society" could vote responsibly. Yet the property qualifications generally set low hurdles in the way of potential voters. Property holding was widespread, and a greater proportion of the population could vote in the colonies than anywhere else in the world of the eighteenth century. Women, Indians, and African Americans were excluded—few then questioned this—and continued to be excluded for the most part into the twentieth century.

The Boston State House
Built in 1713.

By the early eighteenth century the colonial assemblies, like Parliament, held two important strands of power. First, they controlled the budget by their right to vote on taxes and expenditures. Second, they held the power to initiate legislation. Throughout the eighteenth century the assemblies expanded their power and influence, sometimes in conflict with the governors and sometimes in harmony with them. Often in the course of routine business, the assemblies passed laws and set precedents the collective significance of which neither they nor the imperial authorities fully recognized. Once established, however, these laws and practices became fixed principles, part of the "constitution" of the colonies. Self-government in the colonies became first a habit, then a "right."

TROUBLED NEIGHBORS

Self-government was not the only institution that began as a habit during the colonial period. The claims of white settlers on Indian lands had their roots in the first English settlements, where relations between the colonists and the Indians were at times cooperative and at times hostile. Indian-white relations transformed the human and ecological landscape of colonial North America, stirred up colonial politics, and disrupted or destroyed the fabric of Indian culture. Relations between European settlers and North American Indians were themselves agitated by the fluctuating balance of power in Europe. The French and the English each sought to use Indians to their advantage in fighting each other for control of New World territory.

DISPLACING THE NATIVE AMERICANS   The English invasion of North America would have been a different story had the Native Americans been able to organize greater resistance. Instead, the Indians in the coastal regions were scattered and often at war with one another. The English adopted a policy of divide and conquer. Whether tempted by trade goods or the promise of alliances or intimidated by a show of force, most Native Americans let matters drift until the English were too entrenched to be pushed back into the sea.

During the first half of the seventeenth century, the most severe tests of the colonists' will to prevail came with the Virginia troubles in 1644 and Connecticut's Pequot War of 1637. In both colonies, Indian leaders engaged in last-chance efforts to save their lands; in both instances they failed. For the Pequots the result was virtual extermination—Puritans killed Pequots with such savagery that they offended their allies, the Narragansetts, who had never seen such total war. In Virginia, according to a census taken in 1669, only eleven of twenty-eight tribes described by John Smith in 1608, and only about 2,000 of some 30,000 Indians, remained in the colony. Indian resistance had been broken for the time.

Then, in the mid-1670s, both New England and Virginia went through another time of troubles: an Indian war in New England and a civil war masquerading as an Indian war in Virginia. The spark that set New England ablaze was the murder of John Sassamon, a "praying Indian" who had attended Harvard, strayed from the faith while serving King Philip (Metacomet) of the Wampanoag tribe, and then returned to the Christian fold. When Plymouth tried and executed three Wampanoags for Sassamon's murder, King Philip's tribesmen attacked.

Thus began King Philip's War, which the land-hungry leaders of Connecticut and Massachusetts quickly enlarged by assaulting the peaceful Narragansetts at their chief refuge in Rhode Island, a massacre the Rhode Island authorities were helpless to prevent. From June to December 1675, Indian attacks ravaged the interior of Massachusetts Bay and Plymouth, and guerrilla war continued through 1676. Finally, depleted supplies and the casualty toll wore down Indian resistance. Philip's wife and son were captured and sold into slavery. In August 1676, Philip himself was tracked down and killed. Sporadic fighting continued until 1678 in New Hampshire and Maine. Indians who survived the slaughter had to submit to colonial authority and accept confinement to ever-dwindling plots of land.

BACON'S REBELLION   The news from New England heightened tensions among colonists in the sparsely settled Virginia interior and contributed to the tangled events thereafter known as Bacon's Rebellion. The roots of the revolt grew out of a festering hatred for the domineering colonial governor, William Berkeley. Appointed by the King in 1641, he served as governor for most of the next thirty-five years. Berkeley was an unapologetic elitist who limited his circle of friends to the wealthiest and most ambitious planters. He granted them most of the frontier land and public offices, and he rarely allowed new elections to the assembly for fear that his cronies might be defeated. The large planters who dominated the assembly levied high taxes to finance Berkeley's regime, which in turn supported their interests at the expense of the small farmers and servants. With little nearby land available, newly freed indentured servants were forced to migrate westward in their quest for farms. Their lust for land led them to displace the Indians. When Governor Berkeley failed to support the aspiring farmers against the Indians, the farmers rebelled.

The discontent turned to violence in 1675 when a petty squabble between a frontier planter and the Doeg Indians on the Potomac River led to the murder of the planter's herdsman. Frontier militiamen retaliated by killing ten or more Doegs and, by mistake, fourteen Susquehannocks. Soon a force of Virginia and Maryland militiamen laid siege to the Susquehannocks and murdered five chieftains. The enraged Indian survivors took their revenge on frontier settlements. Scattered attacks continued down to the James River, where Nathaniel Bacon's overseer was killed.

In 1676, Bacon defied Governor Berkeley's authority by assuming command of

STRANGE NEWS

FROM

VIRGINIA;

Being a full and true

ACCOUNT

OF THE

LIFE and DEATH

OF

Nathanael Bacon Efquire,

Who was the only Caufe and Original of all the late
Troubles in that COUNTRY.

With a full Relation of all the Accidents which have
happened in the late War there between the
Chriftians and Indians.

LONDON,
Printed for *William Harris*, next door to the Turn-
Stile without *Moor-gate.* 1677.

News of the Rebellion

A broadsheet printed in London, provided details about Bacon's Rebellion.

a group of frontier vigilantes. The vain, ambitious, and hot-tempered Bacon had a talent for trouble and an enthusiasm for terrorizing peaceful Indians. After threatening to kill the governor and the assemblymen if they tried to intervene, Bacon began preparing for a total war against all Indians. Berkeley opposed Bacon's genocidal plan not because he liked Indians but because he wanted to protect his lucrative monopoly over the deerskin trade with them. To prevent any government interference, Bacon ordered the governor arrested, thus pitting his own followers (who were largely servants, small farmers, and even slaves) against Virginia's wealthy planters and political leaders. Berkeley's forces resisted—but only feebly—and Bacon's men burned Jamestown in 1676. But Bacon could not savor the victory long; he fell ill and died a month later.

Governor Berkeley quickly subdued the leaderless rebels. In the process he hanged twenty-three men and confiscated several estates. For such severity the king recalled Berkeley to England. A royal commission then made treaties of pacification with the remaining Indians, some of whose descendants still live on tiny reservations guaranteed them in 1677. For the colonists the fighting had opened new lands and confirmed the power of an inner group of established landholders who sat on the Virginia council.

SPANISH AMERICA IN DECLINE   By the start of the eighteenth century, the Spanish were ruling over a huge colonial empire spanning much of North America. Yet their settlements in the borderlands north of Mexico were a colossal failure when compared with Spanish Mexico and the colonies of the other European powers. The Spanish failed to create thriving colonies in the American Southwest for several reasons. Perhaps the most obvious was that the region lacked the gold and silver, as well as the large native populations, that attracted Spain to Mexico and Peru. In addition, the Spanish were distracted by their need to control the perennial unrest in Mexico among the natives and the mestizos (people of mixed Indian and European ancestry). Moreover, those Spaniards who led the colonization effort in the borderlands were so preoccupied with military and religious control that they never produced viable settlements with self-sustaining economies. Only rarely, for example, did the Spanish send many women to their colonies in North America. Even more important, they never understood that the main factor in creating a successful community was a thriving market economy. Instead, they concentrated on building Catholic missions and forts and looking—in vain—for gold. Whereas the French and the English based their Indian policies on trade (that included supplying Indians with firearms), Spain emphasized conversion to Catholicism and stubbornly adhered to an outdated mercantilism that forbade manufacturing within its colonies and strictly limited trade with the natives.

NEW FRANCE   Permanent French settlements in the New World began in 1608, when the French explorer Samuel de Champlain founded a settlement at Quebec. From there he pushed his explorations into the Great Lakes as far as Lake Huron and southward to the lake that still bears his name. There, in 1609, he joined a band of Indian allies in a fateful encounter, firing his gun into the ranks of their Iroquois foes and thereby kindling a hatred that pursued New France to the end. Thenceforth the Iroquois stood as a buffer against any French designs to move toward the English of the middle colonies and as a constant menace on the flank of the French waterways to the interior.

From the Great Lakes, French explorers moved southward down the Mississippi River. The French thus enjoyed access to the great water routes that led to the heartland of the continent. Yet French involvement in North America never approached that of the British. In part this was because the French-held areas were less enticing than the English seaboard settlements. Few Frenchmen were willing to challenge the interior's rugged terrain, fierce winters, and hostile Indians. In addition, the French government impeded colonization by refusing to allow Huguenots to migrate; New France was to

Champlain in New France

Samuel de Champlain firing at a group of Iroquois, killing two chiefs (1609).

remain Roman Catholic. It was also to remain a howling wilderness, home to a mobile population of traders, trappers, missionaries—and, mainly, Indians. In 1750, when the English colonists in America numbered about 1.5 million, the French population was no more than 80,000.

In some ways, however, the French had the edge on the British. Their relatively small numbers forced them to develop cooperative relationships with the Indians. Unlike the English settlers, the French established trading outposts (to trade European goods for furs) rather than farms, mostly along the St. Lawrence River, on lands not claimed by Indians. Thus they did not have to confront initial hostility. The heavily outnumbered and disproportionately male French settlers sought to integrate themselves with Indian culture rather than eliminate it. Many French traders married Indians and raised families, in the process exchanging languages and customs. This more fraternal bond between the French and the Indians proved to be a source of strength in the wars with the English. French governors could mobilize for action without any worry about quarreling assemblies or ethnic and religious diversity. New France was thus able to survive until 1760 despite the lopsided disparity in numbers between the colonies of the two powers.

THE JESUITS IN NEW FRANCE The lucrative fur trade enticed the French to settle in Canada, but it was the activities of Catholic missionaries that gave New France its dynamism. Like Spain, France aggressively sought to convert the Indians to Catholicism, in part because Christian Indians would become more reliable trading partners and military allies. Jesuit missionaries led the way in New France. The Society of Jesus (the Jesuits), had been founded in 1539, when Ignatius of Loyola, a Spanish soldier and nobleman, and six companions, pledged to lead lives of poverty and chastity—and to defend the Roman Catholic Church. A year later the pope officially recognized the Jesuits as a new religious order and urged them to undertake missionary work among the "pagan people." The Jesuits became famous for their religious fervor, intellectual force, and personal courage. They served as the "shock troops" of the Catholic Counter-Reformation, fighting the spread of Protestantism and traversing the globe as earnest missionaries. Some 3,500 Jesuits served in New Spain and New France.

With remarkable tenacity and resilience, French Jesuits in distinctive black robes fanned out from Quebec, walking and canoeing hundreds of miles across the Great Lakes region and down the Mississippi River. Unlike their Spanish counterparts, they were rarely accompanied by soldiers. And unlike the Spanish Franciscans, who required Indian converts to move to missions, many Jesuits lived among the Indians. Jesuits and Indians borrowed from each other's practices and belief systems while never fully abandoning their own ways. Many of the Indian converts, for example, tolerated the Jesuits but never fully embraced them and their teachings.

THE COLONIAL WARS

For most of the seventeenth century, the French and the British Empires in America developed in relative isolation from each other; for most of that century, the homelands remained at peace. After the Restoration in 1660, Charles II and then James II pursued a policy of friendship with Louis XIV. The Glorious Revolution of 1688 abruptly reversed English diplomacy, however. William III, the new British king from the Calvinist Dutch republic, had engaged in a running conflict with the ambitions of Catholic Louis XIV in Europe. His ascent to the throne brought England almost immediately into a Grand Alliance against the French in the War of the League of Augsburg, known in the colonies simply as King William's War (1689–1697). This was the first of four great European and intercolonial wars to be fought over the next seventy-four years.

Thereafter the major European wars of the period were the War of the Spanish Succession (known in the colonies as Queen Anne's War, 1702–1713); the War of the Austrian Succession (known in the colonies as King George's War, 1744–1748); and the Seven Years' War (known in the colonies as the French and Indian War, which lasted nine years in America, from 1754 to 1763). In all except the last, the battles in America were but a sideshow accompanying greater battles in Europe, where British policy aimed to keep a balance of power with the French. The multinational alliances shifted from one fight to the next, but Britain and France were pitted against each other every time.

So for much of the century after the great Indian conflicts of 1676, the colonies were embroiled in global wars and rumors of war. The effect on much of the population was devastating. The New England colonies, especially Massachusetts, suffered more than the rest, for they were closest to the battlefields of French Canada. It is estimated that 900 Boston men (about 2.5 percent of the men eligible for service) died in the fighting. One result of such carnage was that Boston's population stagnated through the eighteenth century while the population of Philadelphia and New York continued to grow, and Boston had to struggle to support a large population of widows and orphans. Eventually the economic impact of the four imperial wars left increasing numbers of poor people in New England, and many of them would participate in the popular unrest leading to the Revolutionary movement. Moreover, these prolonged conflicts led the English government to incur an enormous debt, establish a huge navy and standing army, and excite a militant sense of nationalism. These changes would ultimately lead to a reshaping of the relationship between the mother country and its American colonies.

THE FRENCH AND INDIAN WAR   Of the four major wars involving the European powers and their New World colonies, the climactic conflict between Britain and France in North America was the French and Indian War. It began after enterprising Virginians during the early 1750s had crossed the Allegheny Mountains into the upper Ohio River valley in order to trade with Indians and survey 200,000 acres granted them by King George. The incursion by the Virginians infuriated the French, and they set about building a string of forts in the disputed area.

The Virginia governor sent an emissary to warn off the French. An ambitious young officer in the Virginia militia, Major George Washington, having volunteered for the mission, received a polite but firm French refusal. In the spring of 1754, the Virginia governor sent Washington back to the disputed region with a small force to erect a fort at the strategic fork where the Allegheny and Monongahela Rivers meet in southwestern Pennsylvania to form the Ohio River. The twenty-two-year-old Washington, hungry for combat and yearning for military glory, led his 150 volunteers and Iroquois allies across the Alleghenies, only to learn that French soldiers had beaten them to the strategic site and erected Fort Duquesne, named for the French governor of Canada. Washington decided to make camp about forty miles from the fort and await reinforcements. The next day the Virginians ambushed a French detachment. Ten French soliders were killed, one escaped, and twenty-one were captured. The Indians then scalped several of the wounded soldiers as a stunned Washington looked on. Washington was unaware that the French had been on a peaceful mission to discuss the disputed fort. The mutilated soliders were the first fatalities in what would become the French and Indian War.

Washington and his troops retreated and hastily constructed a crude stockade at Great Meadows, dubbed Fort Necessity, which a large force of vengeful French soliders attacked a month later, on July 3, 1754. After a day-long battle, George Washington surrendered, having seen all his horses and cattle killed and a third of his 300 men killed or wounded. The French permitted the surviving Virginians to withdraw after stripping them of their weapons. Washington's blundering expedition triggered a series of events

The first American political cartoon

Benjamin Franklin's exhortation to the colonies to unite against the French in 1754 would become popular again twenty years later, when the colonies faced a different threat.

that would ignite a world war. As a prominent British politician exclaimed, "The volley fired by a young Virginian in the backwoods of America set the world on fire."

In London, government officials had already taken notice of the growing conflict in the American backwoods. The British decided to force a showdown with the French in America, but things went badly at first. In 1755 a British fleet failed to halt the landing of French reinforcements in Canada. The British buttressed their hold on Nova Scotia by expelling most of its French population. Some 5,000 to 7,000 Acadians who refused to take an oath of allegiance were scattered through the colonies, from Maine to Georgia. Impoverished and homeless, many of them desperately found their way to French Louisiana, where they became the Cajuns (a corruption of the term *Acadians*) whose descendants still preserve elements of the French language along the remote bayous and in many urban centers.

A WORLD WAR For two years, war raged along the American-Canadian frontier without igniting war in Europe. In 1756, however, the colonial war merged with what became the Seven Years' War in Europe. In the final alignment of European powers, France, Austria, Russia, Saxony, Sweden, and Spain fought against Britain, Prussia, and Hanover. The onset of world war brought into office a new British government, with the popular, eloquent William Pitt as head of the ministry. Pitt's ability and assurance ("I know

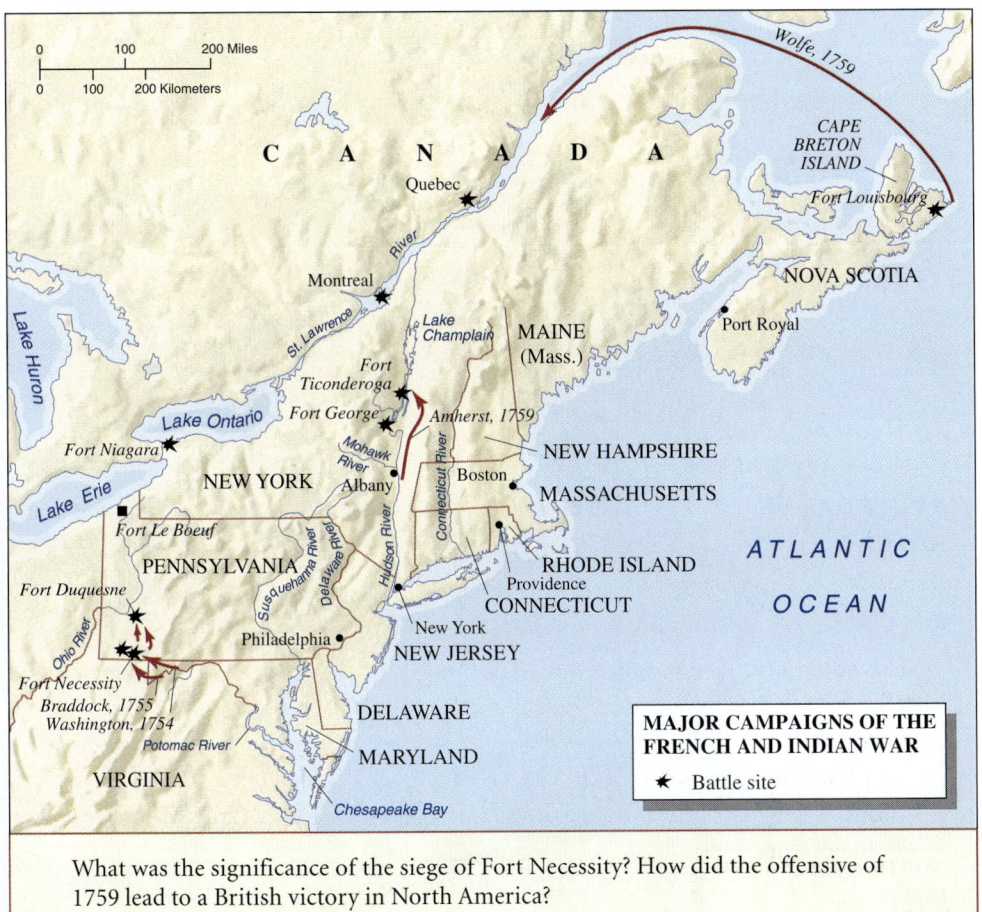

MAJOR CAMPAIGNS OF THE
FRENCH AND INDIAN WAR

★   Battle site

What was the significance of the siege of Fort Necessity? How did the offensive of 1759 lead to a British victory in North America?

that I can save England and no one else can") instilled confidence at home and abroad.

British sea power cut off French reinforcements and supplies to the New World—and the goods with which they bought Indian allies. In 1758 the tide began to turn. Fort Louisbourg in Canada fell to the British. When a new expedition marched against Fort Duquesne, the outnumbered French burned the fort and fled the scene. On the site arose the British Fort Pitt and, later, the city of Pittsburgh.

In 1759 the decisive battle of the French and Indian War occurred at Quebec, in Canada. Commanding the British expedition up the St. Lawrence River was General James Wolfe, a dedicated professional soldier who, at the age of thirty-two, had already spent more than half his life in military service.

NORTH AMERICA, 1713
- England
- France
- Spain

What events led to the first clashes between the French and the British in the late seventeenth century? Why did New England suffer more than other regions of North America during the wars of the eighteenth century? What were the long-term financial, military, and political consequences of the wars between France and Britain?

For two months, Wolfe probed the French defenses of Quebec, seemingly impregnable on its fortified heights and manned by alert forces under General Louis-Joseph de Montcalm. Finally Wolfe's troops found a path up the cliffs behind Quebec. During the night of September 12–13, they scrambled up the sheer walls and emerged on the Plains of Abraham, athwart the main

NORTH AMERICA, 1763

- England
- Spain
- Proclamation line of 1763

RUSSIANS

UNEXPLORED

HUDSON BAY

HUDSON'S BAY COMPANY

NEWFOUNDLAND

ST.-PIERRE ET MIQUELON (France)

NOVA SCOTIA

QUEBEC

NEW ENGLAND

THE THIRTEEN COLONIES

VIRGINIA

OREGON

Disputed by Russia and Spain

LOUISIANA

INDIAN RESERVE

Mississippi River

PACIFIC OCEAN

ATLANTIC OCEAN

CAROLINAS

NEW SPAIN

EAST FLORIDA

WEST FLORIDA

GULF OF MEXICO

CUBA

HISPANIOLA

GUADELOUPE (France)

HAITI (France)

MARTINIQUE (France)

BRITISH HONDURAS

CARIBBEAN SEA

NEW GRANADA

NEW GRANADA

0 500 1000 Miles
0 500 1000 Kilometers

How did the map of North America change between 1713 and 1763? How did Spain win Louisiana? What were the consequences of the British winning all the land east of the Mississippi?

roads to the city. There, in a battle more like conventional European warfare than a frontier skirmish, the British forces allowed the French to advance within close range and then fired two devastating volleys that ended French power in North America for all time. News of the victory was clouded by word of Wolfe's—and Montcalm's—deaths in the battle.

The war in North America dragged on until 1763, but the rest was a process of mopping up. In the South, where little significant action had occurred, belated fighting erupted with the Cherokees, but a force of British regulars and provincials broke their resistance in 1761.

Just six weeks after the capture of Montreal in 1760, King George II died, and his twenty-two-year-old grandson ascended the throne as George III. The new king took a more active role in colonial affairs than his Hanoverian predecessors had. The new king yearned for peace, which entailed forcing his chief minister, William Pitt, out of office. Pitt had wanted to declare war on Spain before the French could bring that other Bourbon monarchy into the conflict. He was forestalled, but Spain belatedly entered the war, in 1761. During the next year the Spanish met the same fate as the French: in 1762, British forces took Manila in the Philippines and Havana in Cuba. By 1763 the French and the Spanish were ready to negotiate a surrender. Britain ruled the world.

THE PEACE OF PARIS The war culminated in the Treaty of Paris of 1763. It ended French power in North America, and Britain took all of France's North American possessions east of the Mississippi River (except New Orleans), several islands in the West Indies, and all of Spanish Florida. The English invited the Spanish settlers to remain and practice their Catholic religion, but few accepted the offer. The Spanish king ordered them to evacuate the colony and provided free transportation to Spanish possessions in the Caribbean Sea. Within a year most of the Spaniards had sold their property at bargain prices to English speculators and begun an exodus to Cuba and Mexico. When the Indian tribes that had been allied with the French learned of the 1763 peace settlement, they were despondent. Their lands were being given over to the British without consultation. The Shawnees, for instance, demanded to know "by what right the French could pretend" to transfer Indian territory to the British. The Indians also worried that a victorious Britain had "grown too powerful & seemed as if they would be too strong for God itself." The Indians had hoped that the departure of the French from the Ohio River valley would mean that the area would revert to their control. Instead, the British cut off the trade and gift-giving practices that had bound the Indians to the French. British forces also moved into the French frontier forts. In a desperate effort to recover their autonomy, tribes struck back in the spring of 1763, capturing most of the British forts around the Great Lakes and in the Ohio River valley. They also raided colonial settlements in Pennsylvania, Maryland, and Virginia, destroying hundreds of homesteads and killing several thousand people. In the midst of the Indian attack on Fort Pitt (formerly Fort Duquesne), English troops distributed smallpox-infested blankets and handkerchiefs from the fort's hospital to the

Indians besieging the garrison. Such efforts at germ warfare were intended, in the words of the English commander, to "extirpate this execrable race" of Indians.

Called Pontiac's Rebellion because of the prominent role played by the Ottawa chief, the far-flung attacks on the frontier forts convinced most colonists that all Indians must be removed. The British government, meanwhile, negotiated an agreement with the Indians that allowed redcoats to reoccupy the frontier forts in exchange for a renewal of trade and gift giving. Still, as Pontiac stressed, the Indians asserted their independence and denied the legitimacy of the British claim to their territory under the terms of the Treaty of Paris. He told a British official that the "French never conquered us, neither did they purchase a foot of our Country, nor have they a right to give it to you." The British may have won a global empire as a result of the Seven Years' War, but their grip on the American colonies grew ever weaker.

In compensation for the loss of Florida, Spain received Louisiana (New Orleans and all French land west of the Mississippi River) from France. Unlike the Spanish in Florida, however, few of the French settlers left Louisiana after 1763. The French government encouraged them to stay and work with their new Spanish governors to create a bulwark against further English expansion. Spain would hold title to Louisiana for nearly four decades but would never succeed in erasing the region's French roots. The French-born settlers always outnumbered the Spanish.

The loss of Louisiana left France with no territory on the continent of North America. After 1763, British power reigned supreme over North America east of the Mississippi River. In gaining Canada, however, the British government put in motion a train of events that would end twenty years later with the loss of the rest of British North America. Britain's success against France threatened the Indian tribes of the interior because they had long depended upon playing the two European powers off against each other. Now, with the British dominant on the continent, American settlers were emboldened to encroach even more upon Indian land. In addition, victory on the battlefields encouraged the British to tighten their imperial control over the Americans and demand more financial contributions from the colonists to defray the cost of British army troops. Meanwhile, humiliated France thirsted for revenge. In London, Benjamin Franklin, agent for the colony of Pennsylvania from 1764 to 1775, found the French minister inordinately curious about America and suspected him of wanting to ignite the coals of controversy. Less than three years after Franklin left London and only fifteen years after the conquest of New France, he would be in Paris arranging an alliance on behalf of Britain's rebellious colonists.

End of Chapter Review

CHAPTER SUMMARY

- **Mercantilism** Lords Commissioners of Trade and Plantations administered the economy of the British Empire. The Navigation Acts decreed that enumerated goods had to go directly to England and discouraged manufacturing in the colonies. Raw materials were shipped to the mother country to be processed into manufactured goods. These mercantilist laws were designed to curb direct trade with other countries, such as the Netherlands, and keep the wealth of the empire in British hands.

- **"Salutary Neglect"** Lax colonial administration by the mother country allowed the colonies a measure of self-government. The dynastic problems of the Stuart kings aided the New England colonists in their efforts to undermine the Dominion of New England. The Glorious Revolution of 1688 resulted in a period of "salutary neglect." The American colonies pursued their interests with minimal intervention from the British government, which was preoccupied with European wars.

- **The French in North America** Even though the French were more interested in trade than settlement, and in converting natives to Christianity, the British feared their further expansion. During the European wars of the period, New France and the British colonies engaged in armed conflict, with allied Indians fighting on both sides.

- **The French and Indian War** Four wars took place in America between 1689 and 1763 as the British and French confronted each other throughout the world. The Seven Years' War (1754–1763), known as the French and Indian War in American colonies, was the first world war and was eventually won by the British. A plan to unify all of Britain's American colonies, including those in Canada, proposed by Benjamin Franklin at the Albany Congress, failed to gain colonial support.

- **The Effects of the Seven Years' War** At the Peace of Paris in 1763, France lost all its North American possessions. Britain gained Canada and Florida, while Spain acquired Louisiana. With the war's end, Native Americans were no longer regarded as essential allies and so had no recourse when settlers squatted on their lands. The Treaty of Paris set the stage for conflict between the mother country and the American colonies as Britain tightened control to pay for the colonies' defense.

CHRONOLOGY

1608	Samuel de Champlain founds Quebec
1651, 1660, 1663, 1673	Navigation Acts
1675–1676	King Philip's War
1676	Bacon's Rebellion
1684	Dominion of New England is established
1688	Glorious Revolution
1754	Washington is defeated at Fort Necessity
1754–1763	French and Indian War
1759	Quebec falls to the British
1763	Peace of Paris
1763	Pontiac's Rebellion

KEY TERMS & NAMES

mercantile system p. 95

"enumerated" goods p. 95

Navigation Acts p. 96

Glorious Revolution p. 97

Lords Commissioners of Trade and Plantations (the Board of Trade) p. 98

New France p. 104

Jesuits p. 105

French and Indian War p. 107

Fort Necessity p. 107

Pontiac's Rebellion p. 113

5

FROM EMPIRE TO INDEPENDENCE

FOCUS QUESTIONS wwnorton.com/studyspace

- How and why did British colonial policy change after 1763?
- How did Whig ideology shape the colonial response to the new British policy?
- Name the events that led to a break with the mother country.
- Who were the main proponents of revolution, and how did they justify their position?
- How did the individual colonies finally unite to embrace the idea of independence, and how was the goal achieved?

Seldom if ever had England thrilled with such pride as it did during the 1760s. The military victories of 1759 had delivered Canada and India to British control. In 1760 young King George III had ascended the throne. And in 1763 the Treaty of Paris declared England the victor in the Seven Years' War and confirmed its ownership of a vast new global empire. The end of the French imperial domain in North America opened the prospect of British development of the sprawling region between the Appalachian Mountains and the Mississippi River, from the Gulf of Mexico north to Hudson Bay in Canada.

The American colonists shared in the euphoria of victory over the French, but the celebration masked festering resentments and new problems spawned by the war. Underneath the pride in the sprawling British Empire, a sense of an American nationalism was maturing. For over a generation the colonists had essentially been allowed to govern themselves and were beginning to think and speak of themselves more as American than as English or British.

George III

At age thirty-three, the young king of a victorious empire.

Now, with vast new western lands to exploit, they could look to the future with confidence.

THE HERITAGE OF WAR

Fighting a major war with such success gave the colonists a new sense of importance. Many in the early stages of the war had lost their awe of the British soldiers, who were vigorously inept at frontier fighting. American colonists were also dismayed by the sharp social distinctions between officers and men in the British army. The provincials, by contrast, presumed that by volunteering, they had formed a contract with a particular American officer from their community.

During the war many colonists became convinced of their moral superiority to their British allies. Although they admired the courage and discipline of British redcoats under fire, New Englanders abhorred the carefree cursing, whoring, and Sabbath breaking they observed among the British troops. Most upsetting were the brutal punishments imposed by British officers on their wayward men. The war thus heightened the New Englanders' sense of their separate identity and of their greater worthiness to be God's chosen people.

In the aftermath of victory, the British Empire stood supreme, but the British government faced massive new problems. How should it manage the defense and governance of the territories acquired from France? How was it to pay the huge debt built up during the war and bear the new financial and administrative burdens of greater colonial administration and more far-flung global defense? What should be done with the lands inhabited by Indians but coveted by colonists? As an Ojibwa chief told a British trader, "Although you have conquered the French, you have not yet conquered us." And—the thorniest problem of all, as it turned out—what role should the colonies play in all this? The problems were of a magnitude and complexity to challenge men of the greatest statesmanship and vision, but those qualities were rare among King George III and his aides. The king himself, while a conscientious and deeply religious man, was obstinate, unimaginative, and overly dependent upon his advisers.

In the British government of the eighteenth century, nearly every politician called himself a Whig, as did the king. *Whig* was the name given to those who had opposed James II, led the Glorious Revolution of 1688, and secured the Protestant Hanoverian succession in 1714. The Whigs were the champions of liberty and parliamentary supremacy over the monarchy, but with the passage of time Whiggism had drifted into complacency, and leadership settled upon an aristocratic elite of the Whig gentry. In the absence of party organization, parliamentary politics hinged upon factions bound together by personal loyalties, family connections, local interests, and the pursuit of royal patronage in the form of government appointments. Throughout the 1760s, George III turned first to one and then to another mediocre prime minister, and the government grew more unstable just as the new problems of colonial administration required forceful solutions. Colonial policy remained marginal to the chief concerns of British politics. The result was inconsistency and vacillation followed by stubborn inflexibility—and revolution.

Western Lands

No sooner was peace arranged in 1763 than the problem of America's western boundaries overlapping with Indian lands provoked a crisis in the British government. The Indians of the Ohio River valley, fearing the arrival of British settlers, joined Ottawa chief Pontiac's attempt to renew frontier warfare. Within a few months, Indians had wiped out every British post in the Ohio River valley except Forts Detroit and Pitt. They then launched a series of devastating assaults on British settlements along the Appalachians and the Great Lakes.

To secure peace on the frontier, the government in London postponed further colonial settlement of the western lands. The immediate need was to stop Pontiac's warriors and pacify the Indians. The king had signed the Royal Proclamation of 1763, which drew an imaginary line along the crest of the Appalachians, beyond which white settlers were forbidden to go. It also established the new British colonies of Quebec and East and West Florida.

But Pontiac did not agree to peace until 1766, and Britain's proclamation line did not remain intact for very long. Hardy pioneers pushed over the Appalachian ridges. By 1770 the town of Pittsburgh had twenty log houses, and four years later Daniel Boone and a party of settlers cut the Wilderness Road through the Cumberland Gap, in southwestern Virginia, to the Kentucky River.

GRENVILLE'S COLONIAL POLICY

As the Royal Proclamation of 1763 was being drafted, a new ministry in London began to grapple with the complex problems of imperial finances. The new chief minister, George Grenville, faced sharply rising costs for the defense of the American colonies on top of an already staggering government debt.

CUSTOMS AND CURRENCY   Because Britons paid more in taxes than the colonists did, Grenville reasoned that the prosperous Americans should share the cost of their own military defense. He also learned that the royal customs service in America was amazingly inefficient. Smuggling and corruption were rampant. So Grenville issued stern orders to colonial officials and dispatched the navy to patrol the North American coast in search of smugglers. Parliament agreed to create a new maritime court in Halifax, Nova Scotia, granting it jurisdiction over all the colonies. Decisions would be made by judges appointed by the Crown rather than by juries of colonists sympathetic to smugglers. The old habits of "salutary neglect" in the enforcement of the Navigation Acts were coming to an end, to the growing annoyance of American shippers.

The Great Financier, or British Economy for the Years 1763, 1764, 1765

This cartoon, critical of Grenville's tax policies, shows America as an Indian (fourth from the left) groaning under the burden of new taxes.

The Molasses Act of 1733 had set a sixpence-per-gallon customs duty on molasses in order to prevent trade with the French sugar islands. New England merchants evaded this tax, smuggling in French molasses to make rum. Recognizing that the molasses duty, if enforced, would ruin the rum distillers, Grenville put through the Sugar Act (1764), which cut the duty on molasses in half. This, he believed, would reduce the temptation to smuggle or to bribe customs officers. In addition, the Sugar Act levied new duties on imports of foreign textiles, wine, coffee, indigo, and sugar. The act, Grenville estimated, would bring in enough revenue to help defray "the necessary expenses of defending, protecting, and securing" the colonies. For the first time, Parliament had adopted taxes on trade explicitly designed to raise revenues in the colonies rather than just regulate trade.

Another key element in Grenville's colonial program was the Currency Act of 1764. The colonies faced a chronic shortage of coins, which kept flowing overseas to pay debts in England. To meet the shortage, they issued their own paper money. British creditors feared receiving payment in such a depreciated paper currency, however. To alleviate their fears, Grenville prohibited the colonies from printing money. This caused the value of existing paper money to plummet, since nobody was obligated to accept it in payment of debts, even in the colonies. The deflationary impact of the Currency Act, combined with new duties on commodities and stricter enforcement, jolted a colonial economy already suffering a postwar slump.

THE STAMP ACT   Grenville's strategy to raise revenue from the colonies entailed one more key provision. Because the Sugar Act would defray only part of the cost of maintaining British troops along the western frontier, he proposed another provocative measure to raise money in America, a stamp tax. Enacted by Parliament on February 13, 1765, the Stamp Act called for revenue stamps that were to be purchased and attached to printed matter and legal documents of all kinds: newspapers, pamphlets, almanacs, bonds, leases, deeds, licenses, insurance policies, ship clearances, college diplomas, even playing cards. The requirement was to go into effect on November 1.

In March 1765, Grenville persuaded Parliament to pass the final measure of his new program, the Quartering Act, which required the colonies to supply British troops with provisions and provide them barracks or submit to their use of inns and vacant buildings owned by colonists. The Quartering Act applied to all colonies but affected mainly New York, headquarters of the British forces.

THE IDEOLOGICAL RESPONSE   The cumulative effect of Grenville's measures outraged colonists. Unwittingly he stirred up a storm of protest and set in motion a profound exploration of colonial rights and imperial relations. By this time the radical ideas of the so-called Real Whig minority in England had slowly begun to take hold in the colonies. The Real Whigs sought to safeguard citizens against government abuse of power.

Whigs attacked the government's efforts to tighten colonial regulations. They charged that Grenville had loosed upon the colonies the very engines of tyranny from which Parliament had rescued England in the seventeenth century. A standing army, Whigs believed, encouraged despots, and now, with the French gone and Chief Pontiac subdued, several thousand British soldiers remained in the colonies. Among the fundamental English rights were trial by jury and the presumption of innocence, but the new vice-admiralty court in Halifax excluded juries and put the burden of proof on the defendant. Most important, the English had the right to be taxed only by their elected representatives. Now, with the Stamp Act, Whigs argued, Parliament sought to usurp the colonial assemblies' power of the purse strings. This could lead only to tyranny and enslavement.

PROTEST IN THE COLONIES In a flood of colonial pamphlets, speeches, and resolutions, critics of the Stamp Act repeated a slogan familiar to all Americans: "no taxation without representation." The Stamp Act became the chief target of colonial protest because it burdened all colonists who did any kind of business. And it affected most of all the articulate elements in the community: merchants, planters, lawyers, printer-editors—all strategically placed to influence public opinion.

Through the spring and summer of 1765, popular resentment of Grenville boiled over at meetings, parades, bonfires, and other demonstrations. Calling themselves Sons of Liberty, colonial militants met underneath "liberty trees"—in Boston a great elm, in Charleston a live oak. One day in mid-August 1765, nearly three months before the Stamp Act was to take effect, an effigy of Boston's royal stamp agent swung from the city's liberty tree. In the evening a mob carried it through the streets, destroyed the stamp office, and used the wood to burn the effigy. Somewhat later another mob sacked the homes of the lieutenant governor and the local customs officer. The stamp agent in Boston, thoroughly shaken, resigned, and stamp agents throughout the colonies felt impelled to follow his example.

The widespread protests encouraged colonial unity, as rebellious Americans discovered that they had more in common with each other than with London. In May 1765 the Virginia House of Burgesses struck the first blow against the Stamp Act with the Virginia Resolves, a series of resolutions inspired by the young Patrick Henry. Virginians, the burgesses declared, were entitled to all English rights, and the English could be taxed only by their own representatives. Virginians, moreover, had always been governed by laws passed with their own consent. Newspapers spread the resolutions throughout the colonies, and other assemblies followed Virginia's example. In June 1765 the Massachusetts House of Representatives invited the colonial assemblies to send delegates to confer in New York about the Stamp Act.

Nine responded, and in October the twenty-seven delegates of the Stamp Act Congress issued a Declaration of the Rights and Grievances of the Colonies, a petition to the king for relief, and a petition to Parliament for repeal of the Stamp Act. The delegates argued that Parliament might have powers to legislate the regulation of colonial trade, but it had no right to levy taxes, which were a gift granted by the people through their elected representatives.

By November 1, its effective date, the Stamp Act was a dead letter. Business activities were conducted without the revenue stamps. Newspapers appeared with the skull and crossbones where the stamp belonged. Colonial rebels were beginning to sense their power. After passage of the Sugar Act, rebels began to boycott British goods rather than pay the new import duties. Now colonists signed nonimportation agreements promising not to buy British goods. By shutting off imports from the home country, they could exercise real leverage.

REPEAL OF THE STAMP ACT   The storm had scarcely broken before Grenville's ministry was out of office, dismissed not because of the colonial turmoil but because of tensions with the king over the distribution of lucrative government appointments. In July 1765 the king installed a new minister, the Marquis of Rockingham, leader of the "Rockingham Whigs," who sympathized with the colonists' views. Rockingham resolved to end the quarrel with America by repealing the Stamp Act, but he needed to move carefully in order to win a majority. Simple repeal was politically impossible without some affirmation of parliamentary authority over the colonies. When Parliament assembled early in 1766, the powerful parliamentary leader William Pitt demanded that the Stamp Act be repealed "absolutely, totally, and immediately," but he urged that Britain's authority over the colonies "be asserted in as strong terms as possible," except on the point of taxation.

In March 1766, Parliament repealed the Stamp Tax but passed the Declaratory Act, which asserted the full power of Parliament to make laws binding the colonies "in all cases whatsoever." It was a cunning evasion that made no concession with regard to taxes but made no mention of them either. To be sure, the Sugar Act remained on the books, but Lord Rockingham reduced the molasses tax from threepence to one pence a gallon, less than the cost of a bribe.

The Repeal, or the Funeral Procession of Miss America-Stamp

This 1766 cartoon shows Grenville carrying the dead Stamp Act in its coffin. In the background, trade with America starts up again.

FANNING THE FLAMES

Meanwhile, King George III continued to play musical chairs with his ministers. After Rockingham lost the king's confidence, William Pitt formed a ministry that included the major factions of Parliament. Soon thereafter, however, Pitt slipped over the fine line between genius and madness, and he resigned in 1768. For a time in 1767, the guiding force in the ministry was Charles Townshend, chancellor of the exchequer (treasury). The witty but erratic Townshend took advantage of Pitt's mental confusion to reopen the question of colonial taxation.

THE TOWNSHEND ACTS   In 1767, Townshend put his plan through the House of Commons, and in September he died, leaving a bitter legacy: the Townshend Acts. With this legislation, Townshend had sought to bring the New York assembly to its senses. That body had defied the

Quartering Act and refused to provide beds or supplies for the king's troops. Parliament, at Townshend's behest, had suspended all acts of New York's colonial assembly until it would yield. New York finally caved in, inadvertently confirming the British suspicion that too much indulgence had encouraged colonial bad manners. Townshend had followed up with the Revenue Act of 1767, which levied duties on colonial imports of glass, lead, paints, paper, and tea. Next, he had set up a Board of Customs Commissioners at Boston, the hotbed of colonial smuggling. Finally, he had reorganized the vice-admiralty courts, providing four in the continental colonies: at Halifax, Boston, Philadelphia, and Charleston.

The Townshend duties increased government revenues, but the intangible costs were greater. The duties taxed goods exported from England, indirectly hurting British manufacturers, and they had to be collected in colonial ports, increasing collection costs. More important, the new taxes accelerated colonial resentment and resistance. The Revenue Act of 1767 posed a more severe threat to colonial assemblies than Grenville's taxes had, for Townshend proposed to use the revenues to pay the salaries of royal governors and other officers and thereby release them from financial dependence upon the colonial assemblies.

DICKINSON'S "LETTERS" The Townshend Acts inspired the colonists (including women who called themselves Daughters of Liberty) to boycott British goods and to develop their own manufactures to reduce their economic dependence upon Britain. Once again the colonial press spewed out protests, most notably the essays of John Dickinson, a Philadelphia lawyer who hoped to resolve the dispute by persuasion. Late in 1767 his twelve "Letters from a Farmer in Pennsylvania" (as he chose to style himself) began to appear in the *Pennsylvania Chronicle,* from which they were copied by other newspapers. He argued that Parliament might regulate American commerce and collect duties incidental to that purpose, but it had no right to levy taxes for revenue.

SAMUEL ADAMS AND THE SONS OF LIBERTY But British officials could neither conciliate moderates like Dickinson nor cope with firebrands like Boston's Samuel Adams, who was now emerging as the supreme genius of revolutionary agitation. Born in 1722, Adams graduated from Harvard and soon thereafter inherited the family brewery, which he proceeded to run into bankruptcy. His distant cousin John Adams described Sam as a "universal good character," a "plain, simple, decent citizen, of middling stature, dress, and manners" who prided himself on his frugality and his distaste for ceremony and display. Politics, not profit, excited his passion, and he spent most of his time debating political issues with sailors, roustabouts, and stevedores at local taverns. Adams insisted that Parliament had no right to legislate for the colonies. Massachusetts, he declared, must return to the spirit of its Puritan founders and defend itself from a new royal conspiracy against its liberties.

Adams became a tireless agitator. He whipped up the Sons of Liberty, writing incendiary newspaper articles and letters and organizing protests at the Boston town meeting and in the provincial assembly. The royal governor called him "the most dangerous man in Massachusetts." Early in 1768, Adams and Boston lawyer James Otis formulated a letter that the Massachusetts assembly dispatched to the other colonies. It restated the illegality of parliamentary taxation, warned that the new duties would be used to pay colonial officials, and invited the other colonies to join in a boycott of British goods.

In mid-May 1769 the Virginia assembly reasserted its exclusive right to tax Virginians, rather than Parliament, and called upon the colonies to unite in protest. Virginia's royal governor promptly dissolved the assembly, but the members met independently and adopted a new set of nonimportation agreements. Once again, as with the Virginia Resolves against the Stamp Act, most of the other colonial assemblies followed suit.

THE BOSTON MASSACRE   In Boston roving gangs enforced the boycott of goods from England, intimidating Loyalist merchants and their customers. This led the governor to appeal for military support, and two British regiments arrived from Canada. The presence of British soldiers in Boston had always been a source of provocation, and now tensions heightened. On March 5, 1770, in the square before the customhouse, a mob began heaving taunts, icicles, and oyster shells at the British sentry, whose call for help brought reinforcements. Then somebody rang the town fire bell, drawing a larger crowd to the scene. Among the mob was Crispus Attucks, a runaway mulatto slave who had worked for some years on ships out of Boston. The riotous crowd began striking at the troops with sticks, and it knocked one soldier down. He rose to his feet and fired into the crowd. Others fired too, and when the smoke cleared, five people lay dead or dying, and eight more were wounded.

The cause of colonial resistance now had its first martyrs, and the first to die was Attucks. News of the Boston Massacre sent shock waves through the colonies. The incident, remembered one Bostonian, "created a resentment which emboldened the timid" and "determined the wavering." But late in April 1770, news arrived that Parliament had repealed all the Townshend

The Bloody Massacre

Paul Revere's partisan engraving of the Boston Massacre.

duties save one. The cabinet, by a vote of 5 to 4, had advised keeping the tea tax as a token of parliamentary authority. Colonial rebels insisted that pressure should be kept on British merchants until Parliament gave in altogether, but the nonimportation movement soon faded. Parliament, after all, had given up most of the taxes, and much of the colonists' tea was smuggled from Holland anyway.

For two years thereafter, colonial discontent remained at a simmer. The Stamp Act was gone, as were all the Townshend duties except that on tea. Yet most of the hated regulations remained in effect: the Sugar Act, the Currency Act, the Quartering Act, the vice-admiralty courts, the Board of Customs Commissioners. The redcoats had left Boston, but they remained nearby, and the British navy still patrolled the coast, looking for smugglers. Each remained a source of irritation and the cause of occasional incidents. As Sam Adams stressed, "Where there is a Spark of patriotick fire, we will enkindle it."

DISCONTENT ON THE FRONTIER

Many colonists showed no interest in the disputes over British regulatory policies raging along the seaboard. Parts of the backcountry had stirred with quarrels that had nothing to do with the Stamp and Townshend Acts. Rival claims to lands east of Lake Champlain pitted New York against New Hampshire. Eventually the residents of the area would simply create their own state, Vermont, in 1777, although it was not recognized as a member of the Union until 1791.

In Pennsylvania a group of frontier ruffians took the law into their own hands. Outraged at the unwillingness of the Quaker-influenced assembly to suppress Chief Pontiac's rebellion, a group called the Paxton Boys took revenge by massacring peaceful Susquehannock Indians in Lancaster County, then threatened the so-called Moravian Indians, a group of Moravian converts near Bethlehem. When the Moravian Indians took refuge in Philadelphia, some 1,500 Paxton Boys marched on the capital, where Benjamin Franklin talked them into returning home by promising more protection along the frontier.

Paxton Boys

A depiction of the Paxton Boys preparing to attack the Susquehannock Indians.

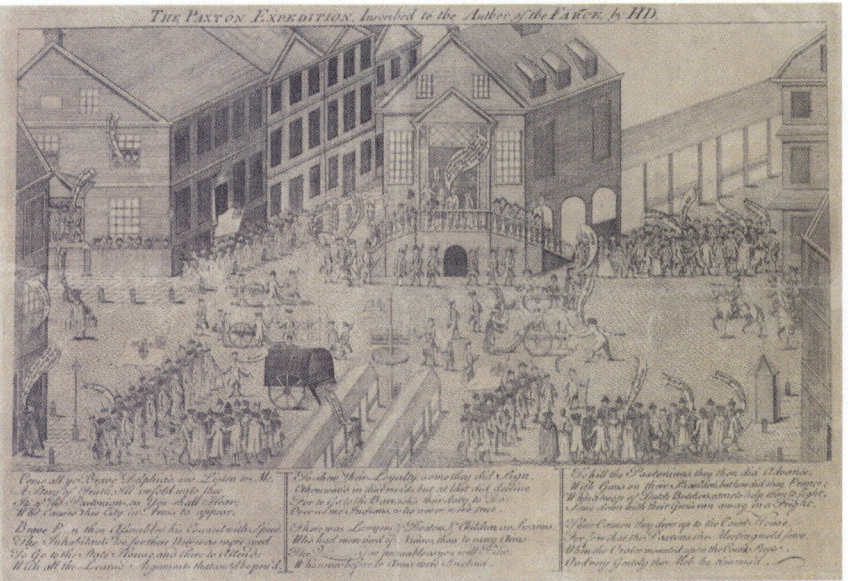

Farther south, settlers in the South Carolina backcountry complained about the lack of protection from horse thieves, cattle rustlers, and Indians. They organized societies called Regulators to administer vigilante justice in the region and refused to pay taxes until they gained effective government. In 1769 the assembly finally set up six circuit courts in the region and revised the taxes, but it still did not respond to the backcountry's demand for representation in the colonial legislature.

In North Carolina the protest was less over the lack of government than over the abuses and extortion by government appointees from the eastern part of the colony. In 1766, farmers organized to resist, but their efforts were more pitiful than potent. In the spring of 1771, the royal governor and 1,200 militiamen defeated some 2,000 ill-organized Regulators in the Battle of Alamance. The pitched battle illustrated the growing tensions between backcountry settlers and the wealthy planters in the eastern part of the colony, tensions that would erupt again during and after the Revolution.

These disputes and revolts within the colonies illustrate the fractious diversity of opinion and outlook evident among Americans on the eve of the Revolution. Colonists were of many minds about many things, including British rule. Frontier conflicts in colonial America also helped convince British authorities that the colonies were inherently unstable and required firmer oversight, including the use of military force to ensure civil stability.

A Worsening Crisis

Two events in June 1772 shattered the period of calm in the quarrels with the mother country. Near Providence, Rhode Island, *Gaspee,* a British schooner patrolling for smugglers, ran aground. Under cover of darkness, colonial rebels boarded the ship, removed the crew, and set fire to the vessel. Three days after the burning, Massachusetts's angry royal governor, Thomas Hutchinson, told the provincial assembly that his salary thenceforth would come out of customs revenues. Massachusetts Superior Court judges would be paid from the same source and would no longer be dependent upon the assembly for their income. The assembly feared that this portended "a despotic administration of government."

To keep the pot simmering, in November 1772 Sam Adams convinced the Boston town meeting to form the Committee of Correspondence, which issued a statement of rights and grievances and invited other towns to do the same. Similar Committees of Correspondence soon sprang up in other colonies. In March 1773 the Virginia assembly proposed the formation of such committees on an intercolonial basis, and a network of committees spread across the colonies, maintaining contact, mobilizing public opinion, and keeping colonial resentments at a simmer.

THE BOSTON TEA PARTY   Frederick, Lord North, who had replaced Townshend as chancellor of the exchequer, soon brought colonial resentment to a boil. In May 1773 he contrived a scheme to bail out the foundering English East India Company. The company had in its British warehouses some 17 million pounds of unsold tea. Under the Tea Act of 1773, the government would refund the British duty of twelve pence per pound on all tea shipped to the colonies and collect only the existing threepence duty payable at the colonial port. By this arrangement, colonists could get tea more cheaply than the English could. North miscalculated, however, in assuming that price alone would govern colonial reaction.

The Committees of Correspondence, backed by colonial merchants, alerted colonists to the British conspiracy to purchase their loyalty and passivity with cheap tea. Before the end of the year, large shipments of tea had gone out to major colonial ports. In Charleston it was stored in warehouses—and later sold to finance the Revolution. In Boston, however, Governor Hutchinson and Sam Adams engaged in a test of will. The ships' captains, alarmed by the rebel opposition, proposed to turn back, but Hutchinson refused permission until the tea was unloaded and the duty paid. Then, on December 16, 1773, a group of colonial Patriots, disguised as Mohawk Indians, boarded the three ships and threw the 342 chests of tea overboard—cheered on by a crowd along the shore. One participant later testified that Sam Adams and John Hancock were there.

Given a more tactful response from London, the Boston Tea Party might easily have undermined the radicals' credibility. Many people, especially merchants, abhorred the wanton destruction of property. British authorities, however, had reached the end of their patience. They were now convinced that the very existence of the empire was at stake. The rebels in Boston were inspiring what could become a widespread effort to evade royal authority and imperial regulations. A firm response was required. "The colonists must either submit or triumph," George III wrote to Lord North, and North hastened to make the king's judgment a self-fulfilling prophecy.

THE COERCIVE ACTS   In April 1774, Parliament enacted four harsh measures designed by Lord North to discipline Boston. The Boston Port Act closed the harbor from June 1, 1774, until the lost tea was paid for. An Act for the Impartial Administration of Justice let the governor transfer to England

The Able Doctor, or America Swallowing the Bitter Draught

This 1774 engraving shows Lord North, the Boston Port Act in his pocket, pouring tea down America's throat and America spitting it back.

the trial of any official accused of committing an offense in the line of duty. A new Quartering Act directed local authorities to provide lodging for British soldiers, in private homes if necessary. Finally, the Massachusetts Government Act made all of the colony's governing council and law-enforcement officers appointive rather than elective, declared that sheriffs would select jurors, and stipulated that no town meeting could be held without the governor's consent, except for the annual election of town officers. In May, General Thomas Gage replaced Hutchinson as governor of Massachusetts and assumed command of the British forces in the colonies.

Designed to isolate Boston and make an example of the colony, the Coercive Acts of 1774 instead cemented colonial unity and emboldened resistance. At last, it seemed to the colonists, their worst fears were being confirmed. If these "Intolerable Acts," as the colonists labeled the Coercive Acts, were not resisted, they would eventually be applied to the other colonies.

Further confirmation of British "tyranny" came with news of the Quebec Act, passed in June 1774. That act provided that the government in Canada would not have a representative assembly and would be led by an appointed royal governor and council. It also gave a privileged position to the Catholic Church. Americans viewed the measure as another indicator of British authoritarianism. In addition, colonists pointed out that they had lost many lives in an effort to liberate the trans-Appalachian West from the control of

French Catholics. Now the British seemed to be protecting papists at the expense of their own Protestant colonists. What was more, the act placed within the boundaries of Quebec the western lands north of the Ohio River, lands that Virginia and Connecticut had long claimed.

Meanwhile, colonists rallied to the cause of besieged Boston, taking up collections and sending provisions. When the Virginia assembly met in May 1774, a young member of the Committee of Correspondence, Thomas Jefferson, proposed to set aside June 1, the effective date of the Boston Port Act, as a day of fasting and prayer in Virginia. The irate British governor thereupon dissolved the Virginia assembly, whose members then retired to a nearby tavern and resolved to create a Continental Congress to represent all the colonies. Similar calls were coming from Providence, New York, Philadelphia, and elsewhere, and in June the Massachusetts assembly suggested a September meeting in Philadelphia. Shortly before George Washington left to represent Virginia at the meeting, he wrote to a friend that "the crisis is arrived when we must assert our rights, or submit to every imposition that can be heaped upon us, till custom and use shall make us as tame and abject slaves, as the blacks we rule over with such arbitrary sway."

George Washington's reference to slavery revealed the ugly contradiction in the inflamed rhetoric about American liberties. Many colonial leaders who demanded their freedom from British tyranny were quite unwilling to give freedom to slaves. In 1774 in Boston, Phillis Wheatley, an enslaved African-born woman of about twenty-one years of age who had become an accomplished poet, highlighted the hypocrisy of slave-owning patriots when she wrote in a newspaper essay that "the Cry for Liberty" did not extend to her and other slaves. The Revolution was for whites only.

THE CONTINENTAL CONGRESS On September 5, 1774, the First Continental Congress assembled in Philadelphia. It endorsed the radical Suffolk Resolves, which declared null and void the recent acts of Parliament intended to coerce the colonies, urged Massachusetts to arm for defense, and called for economic sanctions against British commerce. The Congress also adopted a Declaration of American Rights, which denied Parliament's authority with respect to internal colonial affairs and proclaimed the right of each assembly to determine the need for troops within its own province.

Finally, the Congress adopted the Continental Association of 1774, which recommended that every county, town, and city form committees to enforce a boycott of all British goods. These committees became the organizational and communications network for the Revolutionary movement, connecting every locality to the leadership. The Continental Association also advocated the nonimportation of British goods (implemented in December 1774) and the nonexportation of American goods to Britain (to be implemented in September 1775 if colonial grievances were not addressed).

In London the king fumed. In late 1774 he wrote his prime minister that the "New England colonies are in a state of rebellion," and "blows must decide whether they are to be subject to this country or independent." British critics of the American actions reminded the colonists that Parliament had absolute sovereignty. Power could not be shared. Yet amid all of the furious rhetoric, many colonial militants still balked at the idea of armed conflict with Britain. In a December 1774 letter, Mercy Otis Warren, sister of James Otis and the colonies' first female playwright, observed that "America stands armed with resolution and virtue; but she still recoils at the idea of drawing the sword against the nation from whence she derived her origin. Yet Britain, like an unnatural parent, is ready to plunge her dagger into the bosom of her affectionate offspring."

In early 1775, Parliament declared Massachusetts in rebellion and prohibited the New England colonies from trading with any nation outside the empire. Lord North's Conciliatory Resolution, adopted on February 27, 1775, was as far as the British government would go to avert a crisis. Under its terms, Parliament would levy taxes only to regulate trade and would grant to each colony the duties collected within its boundaries, provided the colonies would contribute voluntarily to a quota for defense of the empire. It was a formula not for peace but for new quarrels.

Shifting Authority

Events were already moving beyond conciliation toward conflict. All through late 1774 and early 1775 the defenders of American rights were seizing the initiative. The unorganized Loyalists (or Tories), if they did not submit to nonimportation agreements, found themselves confronted with tar and feathers. The Continental Congress urged each colony to mobilize its militia. The militias organized special units of "Minutemen" to be ready for quick mobilization. Royal and proprietary officials were losing control as provincial congresses assumed authority and colonial militias organized and gathered arms and gunpowder. Still, British military officials remained smugly confident that the colonists would be inept revolutionaries. Major John Pitcairn wrote home from Boston in March, "I am satisfied that one active campaign, a smart action, and burning two or three of their towns, will set everything to rights."

LEXINGTON AND CONCORD   Major Pitcairn soon had his chance. On April 14, 1775, General Thomas Gage, the British commander, received orders to suppress the "open rebellion." Gage decided to seize Sam Adams and John Hancock in Lexington and destroy the militia's supply depot at Concord, about twenty miles northwest of Boston. But local Patriots got wind of the plan, and on April 18 Boston's Committee of Safety sent silversmith Paul Revere and tanner William Dawes by separate routes on their famous ride to spread the alarm. Revere reached Lexington about midnight and alerted John Hancock and Samuel Adams. Joined by Dawes and Samuel Prescott, who had been visiting in Lexington, Revere rode on toward Concord. A British patrol intercepted the trio, but Prescott slipped through and continued to deliver the warning.

At dawn on April 19, the British advance guard of 238 redcoats found Captain John Parker and about seventy Minutemen lined up on the Lexington village green. Parker apparently intended only a silent protest, but Major Pitcairn rode onto the green, swung his sword, and brusquely yelled, "Disperse, you damned rebels! You dogs, run!" The Americans had already begun backing away when someone fired a pistol shot, whereupon the British soldiers loosed a volley into the Minutemen and then charged them with bayonets, leaving eight dead and ten wounded.

The Battle of Lexington

Amos Doolittle's impression of the Battle of Lexington as combat begins.

The British officers hastily reformed their men and proceeded to Concord. There the Americans had already carried off most of their valuable supplies, but the British destroyed what they could. In the meantime, American Patriots were swarming over the countryside, eager to wreak vengeance on the hated British troops. At Concord's North Bridge the growing American militia inflicted fourteen casualties on a British platoon, and by about noon the exhausted redcoats had begun marching back to Boston.

By then, however, the road back had turned into a gauntlet of death as the rebels from "every Middlesex village and farm" sniped at the redcoats from behind stone walls, trees, barns, and farmhouses all the way to the Charlestown Peninsula. By nightfall the redcoat survivors were under the protection of the fleet and army at Boston, over 250 having been killed or wounded; the Americans had lost fewer than 100. A British general reported to London that the rebels, though untrained, had earned his respect: "Whoever looks upon them as an irregular mob will find himself much mistaken."

THE SPREADING CONFLICT   The Revolutionary War had begun. When the Second Continental Congress convened at Philadelphia on May 10, 1775, British-held Boston was under siege by Massachusetts militia units. On the very day that Congress met, a force of "Green Mountain Boys" under Ethan Allen of Vermont and Massachusetts volunteers under Benedict Arnold of Connecticut captured the strategic Fort Ticonderoga in upstate New York. In a prodigious feat of daring energy, the Americans then transported sixty captured British cannons down rivers and over ridges to support the siege of Boston.

The Continental Congress, with no legal authority and no resources, met amid reports of spreading warfare; it had little choice but to assume the role of the Revolutionary government. The Congress accepted a request that it "adopt" the motley army gathered around Boston and on June 15 named George Washington to be general and commander in chief of a Continental army. Washington accepted on the condition that he receive no pay. The Congress fastened on the charismatic Washington because his service in the French and Indian War had made him one of the most experienced officers in America. That he was from influential Virginia, the most populous province, heightened his qualifications.

On June 17, the very day that George Washington was commissioned, the colonial rebels and British troops engaged in their first major fight, the Battle of Bunker Hill. While the Continental Congress deliberated, American and British forces around Boston had increased. Militiamen from Rhode Island, Connecticut, and New Hampshire joined in the siege. British reinforcements

View of the Attack on Bunker Hill

The Battle of Bunker Hill and the burning of Charlestown Peninsula.

included three major generals: William Howe, Sir Henry Clinton, and John Burgoyne. On the day before the battle, Americans began to fortify the high ground of Charlestown Peninsula, overlooking Boston. Breed's Hill was the battle location, nearer to Boston than Bunker Hill, the site first chosen (and the source of the battle's erroneous name).

With civilians looking on from rooftops and church steeples, the British attacked in the blistering heat, with 2,400 troops moving in tight formation through tall grass. The Americans, pounded by naval guns, watched from behind hastily built earthworks as the waves of brightly uniformed British troops advanced up the hill. Ordered not to fire until they could see "the whites of their eyes," the militiamen waited until the attackers had come within fifteen to twenty paces, then loosed a shattering volley. Through the cloud of oily smoke, the Americans could see fallen bodies "as thick as sheep in a fold." The militiamen cheered as they watched the greatest soldiers in the world retreating in panic.

Within a half hour, however, the British had re-formed and attacked again. Another sheet of flames and lead greeted them, and the vaunted red-coats retreated a second time. Still, the proud British generals were determined not to be humiliated by the ragtag rustics. On the third attempt, when the colonials began to run out of gunpowder and were forced to throw stones, a bayonet charge ousted them. The British took the high ground, but at the cost of 1,054 casualties. American losses were about 400. "A dear bought victory," recorded General Clinton, "another such would have ruined us."

The Battle of Bunker Hill had two profound effects. First, the high number of British casualties made the English generals more cautious in subsequent encounters with the Continental army. Second, the Continental Congress recommended that all able-bodied men enlist in a militia. This tended to divide the male population into Patriot and Loyalist camps. A middle ground was no longer tenable.

While Boston remained under siege, the Continental Congress held to the dimming hope of a compromise. On July 6 and 8, 1775, the delegates issued two major documents: an appeal to the king, thereafter known as the Olive Branch Petition, and a Declaration of the Causes and Necessity of Taking Up Arms. The Olive Branch Petition, written by John Dickinson, professed continued loyalty to George III and begged him to refrain from further hostilities pending a reconciliation. The declaration, also largely Dickinson's work, traced the history of the controversy, denounced the British for the unprovoked assault at Lexington, and rejected independence but affirmed the colonists' purpose to fight for their rights rather than submit to slavery. "Our cause is just," he declared. "Our Union is perfect." Such impassioned rhetoric failed to impress George III. On August 22 he declared the defiant colonists "open and avowed enemies." The next day he issued a proclamation of rebellion.

Before the end of July 1775, the Congress had authorized an ill-fated attack against British troops in the walled Canadian city of Quebec. One force, under General Richard Montgomery, advanced toward Quebec by way of Lake Champlain; another, under General Benedict Arnold, struggled through the Maine woods. The American units arrived outside Quebec in September, exhausted and hungry. Then they were ambushed by a silent killer: smallpox. "The small pox [is] very much among us," wrote one soldier. As the deadly virus raced through the American camp, General Montgomery faced a brutal dilemma. Most of his soldiers had signed up for short tours of duty, many of which were scheduled to expire at the end of the year. He could not afford to wait until spring for the epidemic to subside. Seeing little choice but to fight, Montgomery ordered a desperate attack on the British forces at Quebec during a blizzard, on December 31, 1775. The assault was a disaster. Montgomery was killed early in the battle. Over 400 Americans were taken prisoner. The rest of the Patriot force retreated to its camp outside the walled city and appealed to the Continental Congress for reinforcements.

By May 1776 there were only 1,900 American soldiers left outside Quebec, and 900 of them were infected with smallpox. Sensing the weakness of the American force, the British attacked and sent the ragtag Patriots on a frantic retreat up the St. Lawrence River to the American-held city of Montreal and eventually back to New York and New England. The sick were left behind, but the smallpox virus traveled with the fleeing soldiers.

Quebec was the first military setback for the Revolutionaries. It would not be the last. And smallpox would continue to bedevil the American war effort. The veterans of the failed Canadian campaign brought home both smallpox and demoralizing stories about the disease, spreading the epidemic to civilians and making the recruitment of new soldiers more difficult. Men who might risk British gunfire balked at the more terrifying thought of contracting smallpox in a military camp.

As the fighting spread north into Canada and south into Virginia and the Carolinas, the Continental Congress appointed commissioners to negotiate peace treaties with Indian tribes, organized a Post Office Department, and formed a navy and marine corps.

When George Washington arrived outside Boston to take charge of the American forces after the Battle of Bunker Hill, the military situation was stalemated, and so it remained through the winter, until early March 1776. At that time, American forces occupied Dorchester Heights, to the south of Boston, bringing the city under threat of bombardment with cannons and mortars. General William Howe, who had long since replaced Gage as British commander, reasoned that discretion was the better part of valor and retreated with his forces by water to Halifax in Canada. The last British troops, along with fearful American Loyalists, embarked from Boston on March 17, 1776. By that time, British power had collapsed nearly everywhere, and the British faced not the suppression of a rebellion but the reconquest of a continent.

COMMON SENSE   In early 1776, Thomas Paine's stirring pamphlet *Common Sense* was published anonymously in Philadelphia, transforming the revolutionary controversy. Born of Quaker parents, Paine had distinguished himself in England chiefly as a drifter, a failure in marriage and business. At age thirty-seven he had sailed for America with a letter of introduction from Benjamin Franklin and the purpose of setting up a school for young ladies. When the school did not work out, he moved into the political controversy as a freelance writer, and with *Common Sense,* he proved himself the consummate Revolutionary rhetorician. Until his pamphlet appeared, the squabble had been mainly with Parliament, but Paine directly attacked allegiance to the monarchy, the last frayed connection to Britain. The "common sense" of the matter, to Paine, was that King George III and his advisers bore the responsibility for the malevolence toward the colonies. Americans should consult their own interests, abandon George III, and declare their independence: "The blood of the slain, the weeping voice of nature cries, 'TIS TIME TO PART."

INDEPENDENCE

Within three months more than 100,000 copies of Thomas Paine's pamphlet were in circulation across the colonies. "*Common Sense* is working a powerful change in the minds of men," George Washington noted. One by one the provincial governments authorized their delegates in the Continental Congress to take the final step. On June 7, 1776, Richard Henry Lee of Virginia moved "that these United Colonies are, and of right ought to be, free and independent states." South Carolina and Pennsylvania, however, initially opposed severing ties with England. After feverish lobbying by radical Patriots, the dissenters changed their minds and the resolution passed on July 2, a date that "will be the most memorable epoch in the history of America," John Adams wrote to his wife, Abigail. The memorable date, however, became July 4, 1776, when Congress adopted the Declaration of

The Coming Revolution

The Continental Congress votes for independence on July 2, 1776.

Independence, an eloquent statement of political philosophy that still retains its dynamic force.

JEFFERSON'S DECLARATION   Although Thomas Jefferson is often called the author of the Declaration of Independence, he is more accurately termed its draftsman. In June 1776 the Continental Congress appointed a committee of five men—Jefferson, Benjamin Franklin, John Adams, Robert Livingston of New York, and Roger Sherman of Connecticut—to write a public explanation of the reasons for colonial discontent and to provide a rationale for independence. The group asked Adams and Jefferson to produce a first draft, whereupon Adams deferred to Jefferson because of the thirty-three-year-old Virginian's reputation as a superb writer.

During two days in mid-June 1776, in his rented lodgings in Philadelphia, Jefferson wrote the first statement of American grievances and principles.

The Declaration of Independence

Members of the Continental Congress made eighty-six changes to Jefferson's draft.

He drew primarily upon two sources: his own draft preamble to the Virginia Constitution, written a few weeks earlier, and George Mason's draft of Virginia's Declaration of Rights, which had appeared in Philadelphia newspapers in mid-June.

Jefferson shared his draft with the committee members, and they made several minor revisions to the opening paragraphs and to his listing of the charges against King George III. They submitted the document to the entire Congress on June 28, whereupon it was tabled until July 1. Over the next three days the legislators made eighty-six changes in Jefferson's declaration, including shortening its overall length by a fourth. Jefferson regretted many of the changes, but the legislative editing improved the declaration, making it more concise, accurate, and coherent—and, as a result, more powerful.

The Declaration of Independence is grounded in John Locke's contract theory of government—the theory, in Jefferson's words, that governments derive "their just Powers from the consent of the people," who are entitled to "alter or abolish" those that deny their "unalienable rights" to "life, Liberty, and the pursuit of Happiness." The appeal was no longer simply to "the rights of Englishmen" but to the broader "laws of Nature and Nature's God." The document set forth "a history of repeated injuries and usurpations, all having in direct object the establishment of an absolute Tyranny over these States." The "Representatives of the United States of America," therefore, declared the thirteen "United Colonies" to be "Free and Independent States."

"WE ALWAYS HAD GOVERNED OURSELVES"   So it had come to this, thirteen years after Britain had won domination of North America. Historians have advanced numerous explanations of what caused the Revolutionary controversy: "unfair" regulation of trade, the restrictions on settling western lands, the tax controversy, the debts to British merchants, the growth of a national consciousness, the lack of representation in Parliament, the ideologies of Whiggery and the Enlightenment, and the abrupt shift from a mercantile to an "imperial" policy after 1763.

Each factor contributed something to the collective colonial grievances that rose to a climax in a gigantic failure of British statesmanship. A conflict between British sovereignty and American rights had come to a point of confrontation that adroit statesmanship might have avoided, sidestepped, or outflanked. Irresolution and vacillation in the British ministry finally gave way to the stubborn determination to force an issue long permitted to drift. The colonists saw these developments as the conspiracy of a corrupted oligarchy—and finally, they decided, of a despotic king—to impose an "absolute Tyranny."

Perhaps the last word on how the Revolution came about should belong to an obscure participant, Levi Preston, a Minuteman from Danvers, Massachusetts. Asked sixty-seven years after Lexington and Concord about British oppressions, the ninety-one-year-old veteran responded: "What were they? Oppressions? I didn't feel them." When asked about the hated Stamp Act, he claimed that he "never saw one of those stamps" and was "certain I never paid a penny for one of them." Nor had he ever heard of John Locke or his theories. "We read only the Bible, the Catechism, Watts's Psalms and Hymns, and the Almanack." When his exasperated interviewer asked why, then, he had support the Revolution, Preston replied, "Young man, what we meant in going for those redcoats was this: we always had governed ourselves, and we always meant to. They didn't mean we should."

CHAPTER SUMMARY

- **British Colonial Policy** After the French and Indian War, the British government was saddled with an enormous national debt. In order to reduce that imperial burden, the British government concluded that the colonies ought to help pay for their own defense. Thus the ministers of King George III began to implement the Navigation Acts and impose new taxes.

- **Colonial Justification to Resistance** Whig ideology was based on the writings of John Locke and others who justified the Glorious Revolution of 1688. American colonists adopted that ideology to justify their resistance to increasing royal control over the colonies. They viewed their opposition to King George an outgrowth of Parliament's long constitutional struggle to preserve life, liberty, and property against royal tyranny.

- **Road to the American Revolution** Colonial reaction to the Stamp Act of 1765 was the first intimation of real trouble for imperial authorities: colonists argued that citizens should be taxed only by their elected representatives. Conflict intensified when the British government imposed additional taxes in the form of the Townshend duties. Spontaneous resistance led to the Boston Massacre, and organized protesters staged the Boston Tea Party. The British response, the Coercive Acts, sparked further violence. Compromise became less likely, if not impossible.

- **Taxation without Representation** Colonists based their resistance to the Crown on the idea that taxation without direct colonial representation in Parliament violated with rights as Englishmen. They viewed George III as a tyrant who had ignored the contractual nature of government. Patrick Henry protested the Stamp Act in Virginia on those grounds; Samuel Adams and the Sons of Liberty used the same arguments to incite mobs. It was Thomas Paine, in *Common Sense*, who first argued clearly that independence was not only necessary in response to royal actions but also economically viable.

- **Declaration of Independence** The main tie connecting the thirteen very different colonies that would become the United States was their link to England. They were united through what was increasingly regarded as the unreasonable and unconstitutional demands that the mother country had made on them since 1763. George III's refusal to compromise after violence erupted at Concord alienated many among the colonial elite who might have argued for restraint. Paine's *Common Sense* further persuaded many colonists to abandon their vindictive king. In June 1776, Richard Henry Lee introduced a motion for independence at the Continental Congress. Its passage, on July 2, 1776, created a new country, the United States of America. Lee's motion has been overshadowed throughout history by the document issued two days later, the Declaration of Independence.

CHRONOLOGY

1760	King George III accedes to the throne
1763	French and Indian War ends
1764	Parliament passes the Revenue (Sugar) Act
1765	Parliament passes the Stamp Act; colonists hold Stamp Act Congress
1766	Parliament repeals the Stamp Act, passes the Declaratory Act
1767	Parliament levies the Townshend duties
1770	Boston Massacre
1772	*Gaspee* incident
1773	Colonists stage the Boston Tea Party
1774	Parliament passes the Coercive Acts; Colonists hold First Continental Congress
1775	Battles of Lexington and Concord
1775	Colonists hold Second Continental Congress
1776	Thomas Paine's *Common Sense* is published; Declaration of Independence is signed

KEY TERMS & NAMES

Part Two

BUILDING

A

NATION

While it was one thing for Patriot leaders to declare America's independence from British authority, it was quite another to win it on the battlefield. Barely a third of the colonists actively supported the Revolution, the political stability of the new nation was uncertain, and George Washington found himself in command of a poorly supplied, untested army.

But the Revolutionary movement would persevere and prevail. The skill and fortitude of Washington and his lieutenants enabled the Americans to exploit their geographic advantages. Even more important was the intervention of the French on behalf of the Revolutionary cause. The Franco-American alliance, in 1778, proved decisive. In 1783, after eight years of sporadic fighting and heavy human and financial losses, the British gave up the fight and their American colonies.

Amid the Revolutionary turmoil the Patriots faced the daunting task of forming new governments for themselves. Their deeply ingrained resentment of British imperial rule led them to grant considerable powers to the individual states. As Thomas Jefferson declared, "Virginia, Sir, is my country." Such powerful local ties help explain why the colonists focused their attention on creating new state constitutions rather than a national government. The Articles of Confederation, ratified in 1781, provided only the semblance of national authority. All power to make and execute laws remained with the states.

After the Revolutionary War ended, the flimsy federal government authorized by the Articles of Confederation proved inadequate to the needs of the new—and expanding—nation. The obvious weaknesses of the new national government led to the Constitutional

Convention of 1787. The process of drafting and ratifying the new constitution prompted a debate on the relative significance of national power, local control, and individual freedom that has provided the central theme of American political thought ever since.

The American Revolution involved much more than the apportionment of political power, however. It also unleashed new societal forces and posed volatile social questions that would help reshape the very fabric of American culture. What would be the role of women, African Americans, and Native Americans in the new republic? How would the contrasting economies of the various regions of the new United States be developed? Who would control the vast territories to the west of the original thirteen states? How would the new republic relate to the other nations of the world?

These controversial questions helped crystallize the first national political parties in the United States. During the 1790s, Federalists, led by Alexander Hamilton, and Republicans, led by Thomas Jefferson and James Madison, engaged in a heated debate about the political and economic future of the new nation. With Jefferson's election as president in 1800, the Republicans gained the upper hand in national politics for the next quarter century. In the process they presided over a maturing society that aggressively expanded westward at the expense of the Native Americans, ambivalently embraced industrial development, fitfully engaged in a second war with Great Britain, and ominously witnessed a growing sectional controversy over slavery.

6

THE AMERICAN REVOLUTION

FOCUS QUESTIONS

   wwnorton.com/studyspace

- What were the military strategies and problems for both the Americans and the British?
- What were the war's major turning points?
- Who were the Loyalists; and what became of them?
- Why was it possible to gain European allies; and how important were European allies to the war's successful conclusion?
- To what extent was the American Revolution a social revolution in matters of gender equality, race relations, and religious freedom?

F ew foreign observers thought that the upstart American Revolutionaries could win a war against the world's greatest empire and most powerful military force. The Americans lost most of the battles in the Revolutionary War but eventually forced the British to sue for peace and grant the colonists their independence. The surprising result testified to the tenacity of the Patriots, to the importance of the French alliance after 1778, and to the peculiar difficulties facing the British as they tried to conduct a demanding military campaign thousands of miles from home.

The American Revolution unleashed powerful political, economic, and social forces. While securing American independence, the Revolution generated a new sense of nationalism and created a unique system of self-governance; it also began a process of societal definition and change that has yet to run its course. The turmoil of revolution disrupted traditional class and social relationships and helped transform the lives of people who had long been relegated to the social periphery—African Americans, women, and Indians. In important ways, then, the Revolution was much more than simply a war for independence. It was an engine for political experimentation and social transformation.

1776: WASHINGTON'S NARROW ESCAPE

On July 2, 1776, the day that the new Congress voted for independence, British redcoats landed on Staten Island, across New York Harbor from Manhattan. By mid-August, British Major General William Howe had some 32,000 men at his disposal, including 9,000 Hessians (German soldiers hired by the British), the largest force mustered by the British in the eighteenth century. General Washington transferred most of his men from New York to Boston, but he could muster only about 19,000 poorly trained soldiers and militiamen. Such a force could not defend New York, but Congress wanted it held. This meant that Washington had to expose his men to entrapments from which they escaped more by luck and British caution than by any strategic genius on the part of the American commander. The inexperienced Washington was still learning the art of generalship, and the New York campaign taught him some costly lessons.

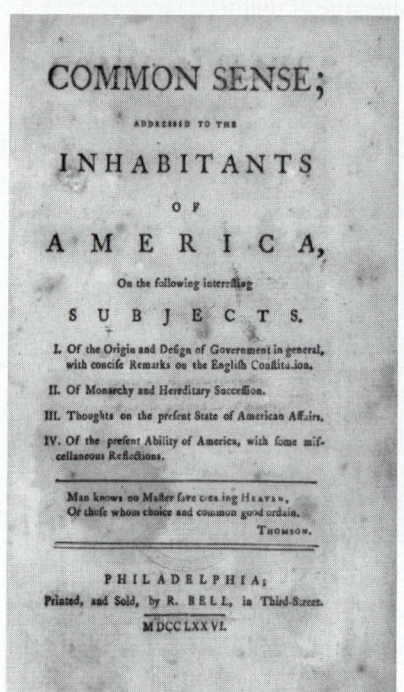

Common Sense

Thomas Paine's inspiring pamphlet was originally published anonymously because of its treasonous content.

FIGHTING IN NEW YORK AND NEW JERSEY By occupying New York, the British sought to sever New England from the rest of the rebellious colonies. In late August 1776 the British forced Washington to evacuate Long Island. Only a timely rainstorm kept the British fleet from destroying

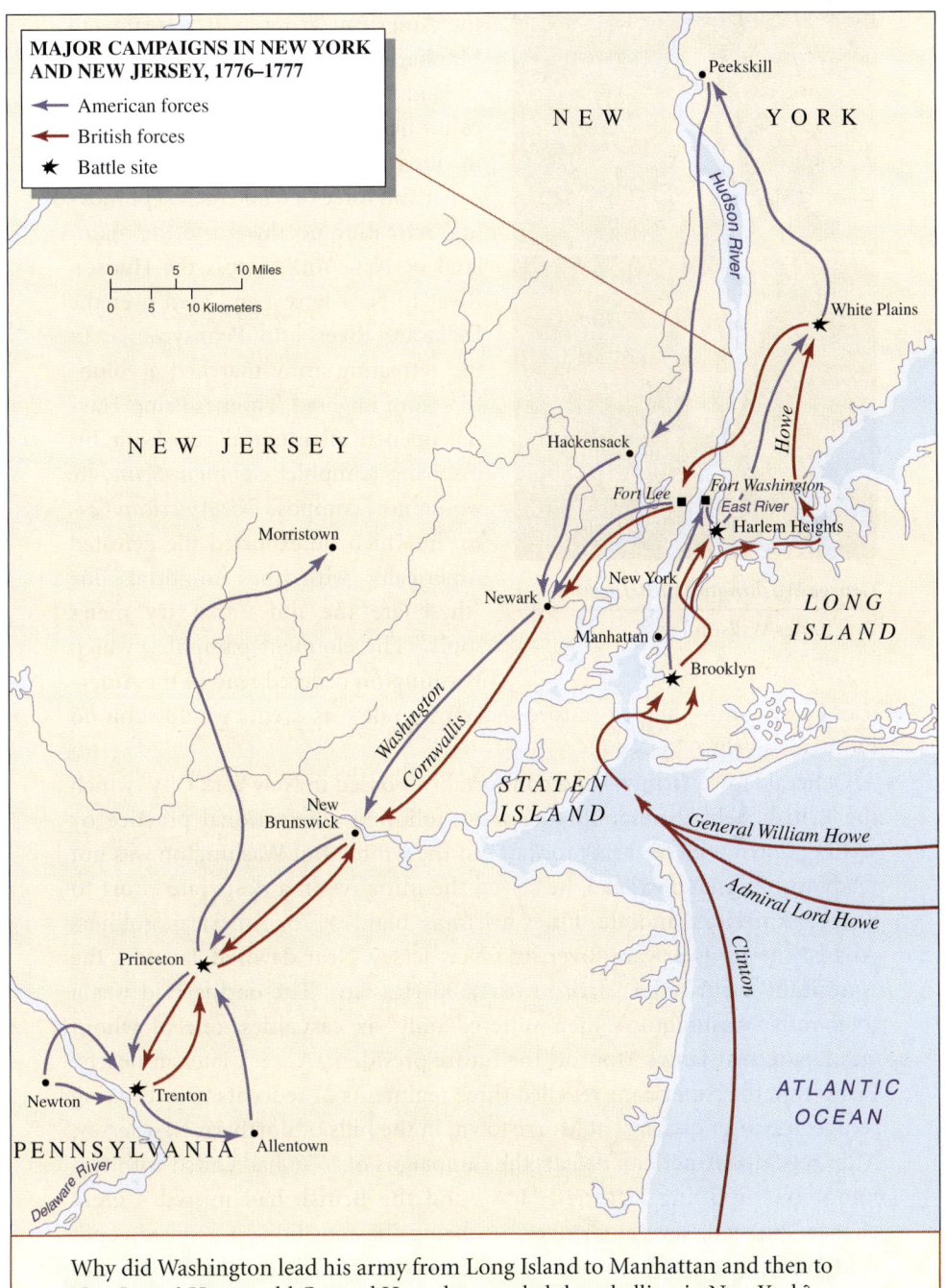

MAJOR CAMPAIGNS IN NEW YORK
AND NEW JERSEY, 1776–1777

→ American forces

→ British forces

★ Battle site

NEW YORK

Peekskill

Hudson River

0   5   10 Miles

0   5   10 Kilometers

White Plains

NEW JERSEY

Hackensack

Howe

Fort Lee

Fort Washington

East River

Harlem Heights

Morristown

Newark

New York

Manhattan

LONG
ISLAND

Washington

Brooklyn

Cornwallis

STATEN
ISLAND

General William Howe

New
Brunswick

Admiral Lord Howe

Clinton

Princeton

ATLANTIC
OCEAN

Newton

Trenton

Allentown

PENNSYLVANIA

Delaware River

Why did Washington lead his army from Long Island to Manhattan and then to
New Jersey? How could General Howe have ended the rebellion in New York?
What is the significance of the Battle of Trenton?

George Washington at Princeton

By Charles Willson Peale.

the American army as it retreated to Manhattan.

Had the British moved quickly, they could have trapped Washington's army in lower Manhattan. But the main American force of 6,000 men kept moving, retreating northward to the mainland of New York, across the Hudson River to New Jersey, and then over the Delaware River into Pennsylvania. In the retreating army marched a volunteer from England, Thomas Paine. Having opened an eventful year with his inspiring pamphlet *Common Sense,* he would now compose *The American Crisis,* in which he exhorted the defeated Americans with the immortal line "these are the times that try men's souls." The eloquent pamphlet, which Washington ordered read in the American army camps, helped restore shaken morale—as events would soon do more decisively.

General Howe, firmly—and comfortably—based in New York City (which the British held throughout the war), followed conventional practice by settling down with his army to wait out the winter. But Washington was not ready to hibernate; instead, he seized the initiative in a desperate effort to restore American morale. On Christmas night 1776, American soldiers crossed the icy Delaware River into New Jersey. Near dawn at Trenton, the Americans surprised a garrison of 1,500 Hessians. The daring raid was a total rout. Washington's men suffered only six casualties, one of whom was Lieutenant James Monroe, the future president. A week later, at nearby Princeton, the Americans repelled three regiments of redcoats before taking refuge in winter quarters at Morristown, in the hills of northern New Jersey. After repeated American defeats the campaigns of 1776 had ended with two minor but uplifting victories. Howe and the British had missed a great chance—indeed, several chances—to bring the rebellion to a speedy end. And Washington had learned that the only way to defeat the British was to avoid major battles and wear them down in a long war of attrition and exhaustion.

AMERICAN SOCIETY AT WAR

CHOOSING SIDES   After the British army occupied New York, many civilians assumed that the rebellion was collapsing, and thousands hastened to sign an oath of allegiance to the Crown. But the events at Trenton and Princeton reversed the outlook, and New Jersey quickly reverted to rebel control. Nonetheless, many colonists remained Tory in outlook. During or after the war roughly 100,000 of them, more than 3 percent of the total population, left the thirteen colonies for Canada or Britain. American opinion concerning the Revolution divided in three ways: Patriots, or Whigs (as the Revolutionaries called themselves), Tories, and an indifferent middle group swayed by the better organized and more energetic radicals.

Tories were concentrated mainly in the seaport cities, but they came from all walks of life. Almost all governors, judges, and other royal officials were loyal to Britain; most Anglican ministers also preferred the mother country. Where planter aristocrats tended to be Whigs, as in North Carolina, many backcountry farmers leaned toward the Tories. When Patriots took control of an area, Loyalists faced a difficult choice: flee with the British and leave behind their property, or stay behind and face the wrath of the Patriots. In this sense the War of Independence was very much a civil war that divided families and communities and unleashed bloodcurdling atrocities in the backcountry of New York and Pennsylvania and in Georgia, where Tory militiamen and their Indian allies went marauding against frontier Whigs. Whigs responded to the Loyalists in kind.

MILITIA AND ARMY   Since the end of the French and Indian War, the colonies had required all adult males between the ages of fifteen and sixty to enroll in their local militia company, attend monthly drills, and turn out on short notice for emergencies. When fighting erupted between the British and the Revolutionaries, members of community militias had to choose sides.

American militiamen served two purposes during the Revolution. They were a home guard, defending their community, and they augmented the Continental army. Dressed in hunting shirts and armed with muskets, they preferred to ambush their opponents or engage them in hand-to-hand combat rather than fight in traditional formations. They also tended to kill unnecessarily and to torture prisoners. To repel an attack, the militia somehow materialized; the danger past, it evaporated, for there were chores to do at home.

The Continental army was on the whole better trained and more motivated than the militias. Although many soldiers were attracted by bounties

American militia

This sketch of militiamen by a French soldier at Yorktown, Virginia, shows one of those ubiquitous American frontiersmen turned soldier (second from right), and it is also one of the earliest depictions of an African American soldier.

of land or cash and some later deserted, most of those who persevered were animated by genuine patriotic fervor and a thirst for adventure that enabled them to survive the horrors of combat and the tedium of camp life. Unlike the full-time professional soldiers in the British army, George Washington's Continental army, which fluctuated in size from 2,000 to 20,000, was populated mostly by citizen soldiers, poor native-born Americans or immigrants who had been indentured servants or convicts.

FINANCIAL STRAINS AND SMALLPOX The new Continental Congress struggled to provide the army with adequate supplies. None of the states contributed more than a part of its designated share, and Congress reluctantly let army agents take supplies directly from farmers in return for certificates promising future payment. To pay for the war, Congress and the states printed paper money. With goods scarce, prices rose sharply.

During the harsh winter at Morristown, New Jersey (1776–1777), Washington's army nearly disintegrated as terms of enlistment expired and deserters fled the brutally cold weather, inadequate food supply, and widespread disease. Smallpox continued to wreak havoc among the American armies. By 1777, Washington had come to view the virus with greater dread than "the Sword of the Enemy." On any given day, a fourth of the American troops were unfit for duty, usually because of smallpox. The threat of smallpox to the war effort was so great that in early 1777 Washington ordered a mass inoculation, which he managed to keep secret from British intelligence. Inoculating an entire army was an enormous, risky undertaking. Washington's daring gamble paid off. The successful inoculation of the American army marks one of his greatest strategic accomplishments of the war.

Only about 1,000 soldiers stuck out the winter in New Jersey. With the spring thaw, however, recruits began arriving to claim the bounty of $20 and 100 acres of land offered by Congress to those who would enlist for three years or for the duration of the conflict, if less. With some 9,000 regular troops, George Washington in 1777 began challenging British forces in northern New Jersey.

BEHIND THE LINES   Civilians saw their lives profoundly changed by the Revolutionary War. British forces occupied the major cities (Boston, New York, Philadelphia, Charleston, Savannah); towns and villages were destroyed; crops and livestock confiscated; families disrupted; and husbands and fathers killed, maimed, or reported missing. The poor suffered most amid the war's disruptions and skyrocketing prices. A bushel of wheat that had sold for less than $1 in 1777 brought $80 two years later. Many consumers appealed to the authorities to institute price controls so that they could afford basic necessities. Others took more direct action. In Boston, women paraded through the streets; and merchants were accused of hoarding. The specter of mechanics and laborers exercising political power horrified most Revolutionary leaders. The American people, John Adams insisted, must accept social inequality and defer to the leadership of their betters. The "one thing" absolutely required of a new republic was "a decency, and respect, and veneration introduced for persons of authority."

1777: SETBACKS FOR THE BRITISH

Indecision, overconfidence, and poor communications plagued British military planning in the campaigns of 1777. The profoundly confident General John Burgoyne proposed to bisect the colonies. His men would advance southward from Canada to the Hudson River while another force moved eastward from Fort Oswego, on Lake Ontario, down the Mohawk River valley in New York. At the same time another British army would move against the Patriot capital, Philadelphia, expecting the Pennsylvania Tories to rally to the Crown and secure the colony.

What were the consequences of Burgoyne's strategy of dividing the colonies with two British forces? How did life in Washington's camp at Valley Forge transform the American army? Why was Saratoga a turning point in the American Revolution?

Washington withdrew most of his men from New Jersey to meet the new threat. At Brandywine Creek, southwest of Philadelphia, the British out-maneuvered and routed Washington's forces on September 11, and fifteen days later British troops occupied Philadelphia. Washington's army retired to winter quarters at Valley Forge, Pennsylvania, while General Howe and the British remained in the relative comfort of Philadelphia, twenty miles away (eighteenth-century armies rarely fought during the winter months). Howe's plan had succeeded, up to a point. He had taken Philadelphia—or as Benjamin Franklin put it, Philadelphia had taken him. But the Tories there proved fewer than Howe had expected, and his decision to move on Philadelphia from the south, by way of Chesapeake Bay, put his forces even farther from Burgoyne's army in the north. Meanwhile, Burgoyne's northern British expedition was stumbling into disaster in New York.

SARATOGA   In 1777, General Burgoyne moved south from Canada toward Lake Champlain with about 7,000 men, his mistress, and a baggage train that included some thirty carts carrying his personal trappings and a large supply of champagne. A powerful force on paper, the expedition was in fact much too cumbersome to be effective in the dense forests and rugged terrain of upstate New York. Burgoyne sent part of his army down the St. Lawrence River with Lieutenant Colonel Barry St. Leger, and at Fort Oswego they were joined by a force of Iroquois allies. The combined group then headed east toward Albany. When they met the more mobile Americans, the British suffered two serious reversals.

At Oriskany, New York, on August 6, 1777, a band of Patriot militiamen thwarted an ambush by Tories and Indians and gained time for Benedict Arnold to bring 1,000 soldiers to the relief of Fort Stanwix, which had been under siege by St. Leger. Convinced that they faced an even greater force than they actually did, the Indians deserted, and the Mohawk River valley was secured for the Patriot forces. To the east, at Bennington, Vermont, on August 16, New England militiamen repulsed a British foraging party. American reinforcements continued to gather, and after two sharp clashes, Burgoyne pulled back to Saratoga, where American forces under General Horatio Gates surrounded him. On October 17, 1777, Burgoyne, resplendent in his scarlet, gold, and white uniform, surrendered to the plain-blue-coated Gates. The victory at Saratoga proved critically important to the American cause.

General John Burgoyne
Commander of Britain's northern forces. Burgoyne and most of his troops surrendered to the Americans at Saratoga on October 17, 1777.

ALLIANCE WITH FRANCE   In early December 1777, news of the surprising American triumph at Saratoga reached Paris, where it was celebrated almost as if it were a French victory. Its impact on the French made Saratoga a decisive turning point of the war. In 1776 the French had taken their first step toward aiding the colonists by sending fourteen ships with military supplies crucial to the Americans; most of the Continental army's gunpowder in the first years of the war came from France. Besides weapons and ammunition, the French had also secretly sent clothing, shoes, and other supplies to help the Americans. After Saratoga the French saw their chance to strike a sharper blow at their hated enemy, Britain, and entered into serious negotiations with the Americans.

On February 6, 1778, France and America signed two treaties. The first officially recognized the United States and offered trade concessions, including important privileges to American shipping. The second agreed, first, that if France entered the war, both countries would fight until American independence was won; second, that neither would conclude a "truce or peace" without the consent of the other; and third, that each guaranteed the other's possessions in America "from the present time and forever against all other powers." France further bound itself to seek neither Canada nor other British possessions on the mainland of North America.

By June 1778, British vessels had fired on French ships, and the two nations were at war. The French decision to join the infant United States in its war for independence became the most important factor in America's winning the Revolutionary War. In 1779, Spain entered the war as an ally of France. The following year, Britain declared war on the Dutch, who persisted in carrying on a profitable trade with the French and the Americans. The rebel farmers at Concord had indeed fired a shot "heard round the world." The American fight for independence had expanded into a world war, and the fighting now spread to the Mediterranean, Africa, India, the West Indies, and the high seas.

1778: BOTH SIDES REGROUP

THE REVOLUTIONARY ARMY AT VALLEY FORGE   For George Washington's army, bivouacked at Valley Forge, near Philadelphia, the winter of 1777–1778 had been a season of intense suffering. The American force, encamped in crowded, lice-infested huts, endured cold, hunger, and disease. Some troops lacked shoes and blankets. Their makeshift log-and-mud huts offered little protection from the howling winds and bitter cold. Most of the army's horses died of exposure or starvation. By February, 7,000 troops were

Valley Forge
During the winter of 1777–1778, Washington's army battled starvation, disease, and freezing temperatures.

too ill for duty. More than 2,500 soldiers died at Valley Forge; another 1,000 deserted. Fifty officers resigned on one December day. Several hundred more left before winter's end. By March, however, the once-gaunt troops at Valley Forge saw their strength restored. Their improved health enabled Washington to begin a rigorous training program designed to bring unity and order to his motley force. By the end of March, the ragtag soldiers were beginning to resemble a professional army. Moreover, as winter drew to an end, the army's morale gained strength from congressional promises of extra pay and bonuses after the war and from the news of the French alliance.

PEACE OVERTURES AND THE EVACUATION OF PHILADELPHIA

After Saratoga, Lord North, the British prime minister, knew that winning the war was unlikely, but the king refused to let him either resign or make peace. On March 16, 1778, the House of Commons adopted a program that in effect granted all the demands made by the American Patriots prior to independence. Parliament repealed the Townshend tea duty, the Massachusetts Government Act, and the Prohibitory Act, which had closed the colonies to commerce. It then dispatched a peace commission to negotiate an end to the war, but its members did not reach Philadelphia until after

Congress had ratified the French treaties. Congress refused to begin any negotiations until American independence was officially recognized in London or British forces withdrawn, neither of which the royal commissioners could promise.

Unbeknownst to the British negotiators, the Crown had already authorized the evacuation of British troops from Philadelphia, a withdrawal that further weakened what little bargaining power the commissioners had. After the stunning British defeat at Saratoga, General Howe resigned his command, and Sir Henry Clinton replaced him. Fearing a blockade by the French fleet that had sailed from France in June 1778, Clinton pulled his troops out of Philadelphia and sent them to New York. As General Clinton's forces marched eastward toward New York City, Washington pursued them across New Jersey before encamping at White Plains, north of the city. From that time on, the northern theater, scene of the major campaigns and battles in the first years of the war, settled into a long stalemate.

ACTIONS ON THE FRONTIER   The one major American success of 1778 occurred far from the New Jersey battlefields. Out to the west, along the Great Lakes, at Forts Niagara and Detroit, the British had incited frontier Tories and Indians to raid western settlements and had offered to pay for American scalps. To end the attacks, young George Rogers Clark took 175 frontiersmen on flatboats down the Ohio River in early 1778. They marched through the woods and on the evening of July 4 surprised the British at Kaskaskia (in present-day Illinois). At the end of the year, Clark marched his men (almost half of them French volunteers) through icy rivers and flooded prairies, sometimes in water neck deep, and captured an astonished British garrison at Vincennes (in present-day Indiana).

Meanwhile, Tories and Iroquois in western Pennsylvania continued to terrorize frontier settlements throughout the summer of 1778. In response, General Washington dispatched an expedition of 4,000 men. At Newton, New York, the American force defeated the only serious opposition on August 29, 1779, and proceeded to carry out Washington's instruction that the Iroquois country be not "merely overrun but destroyed." The American troops burned about forty Indian villages. The destruction broke the power of the Iroquois Confederacy for all time, but sporadic encounters with various tribes of the region continued through the end of the war. By thus decimating the major Indian tribes along the frontier, the American Revolution cleared the way for rapid settlement of the trans-Appalachian West after the war ended.

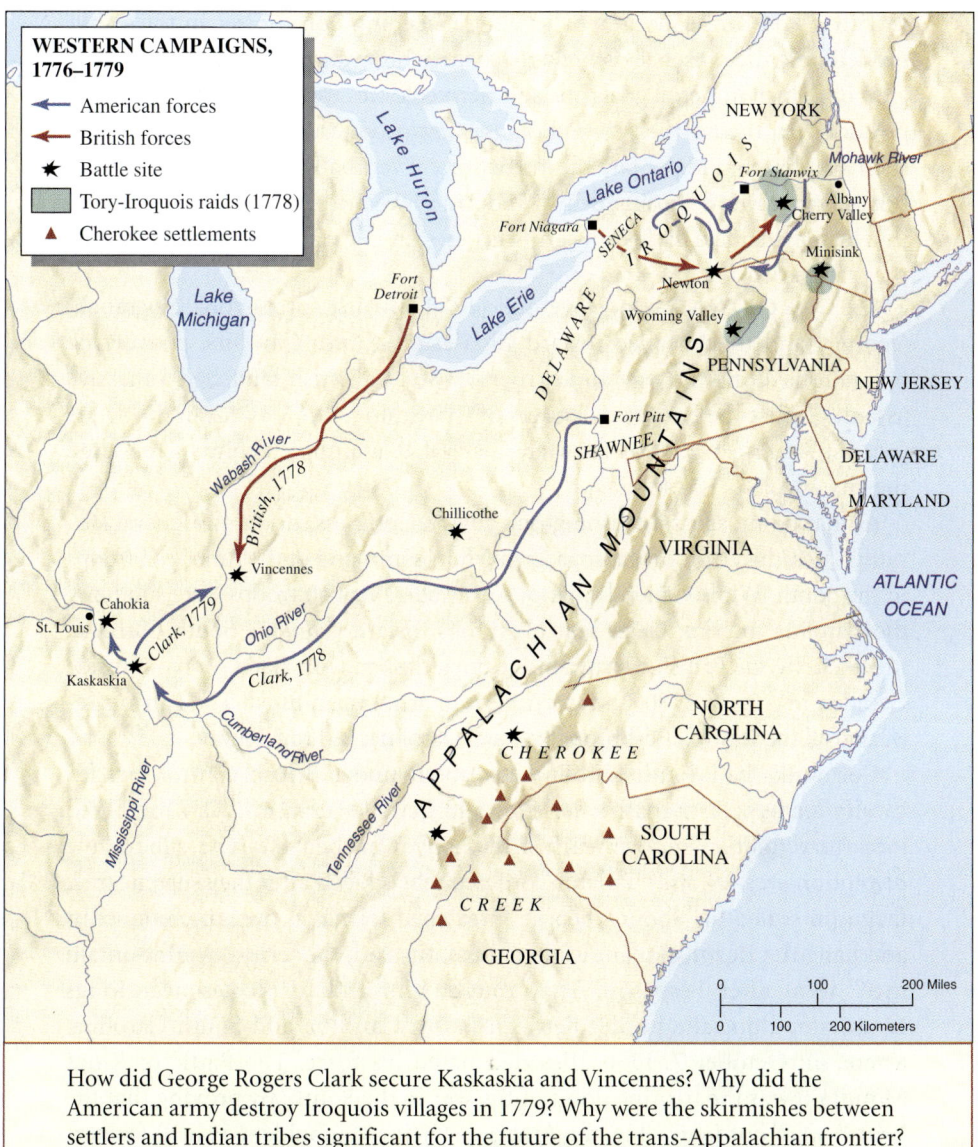

WESTERN CAMPAIGNS, 1776–1779

← American forces
← British forces
★ Battle site
▨ Tory-Iroquois raids (1778)
▲ Cherokee settlements

How did George Rogers Clark secure Kaskaskia and Vincennes? Why did the American army destroy Iroquois villages in 1779? Why were the skirmishes between settlers and Indian tribes significant for the future of the trans-Appalachian frontier?

THE WAR IN THE SOUTH

At the end of 1778, the focus of the British military action shifted suddenly to the South. The whole region from Virginia southward had been free of major action since 1776. Now it would become the focus of the war as the

British tested King George's belief that a sleeping Tory power in the South needed only the presence of a few redcoats to be awakened. From the point of view of British imperial goals, the southern colonies were ultimately more important than the northern ones because they produced valuable staple crops, such as tobacco, indigo, tar, and turpentine. Eventually the war in the South not only involved opposing British and American armies but also degenerated into brutal guerrilla-style civil conflicts between Loyalists and Patriots.

THE CAROLINAS   In November 1778, British forces took Savannah, Georgia, and then headed toward Charleston, South Carolina, plundering plantations along the way. In February 1780 the British launched a massive assault against the Patriot defenders of Charleston. On May 12, in the single greatest American loss of the war, General Benjamin Lincoln surrendered the city and its 5,500 soldiers.

At that point, against Washington's advice, Congress turned to General Horatio Gates, the victor of Saratoga, giving him command of the American troops in the South. While General Charles Cornwallis's British troops were subduing the Carolina interior, Gates sent his troops toward Camden, South Carolina, then held by the British. Cornwallis's troops clashed with Gates's forces outside Camden in August 1780, and the American army was routed. The Patriots retreated all the way to Hillsborough, North Carolina, 160 miles away.

Cornwallis had South Carolina just about under British control, but his cavalry leaders, Sir Banastre Tarleton and Patrick Ferguson, who mobilized local Tory militiamen, overreached themselves in their effort to subdue the revolutionaries. "Bloody Tarleton" ordered rebels killed after they surrendered. Ferguson sealed his doom when he threatened to march over the mountains and hang the Revolutionary leaders there. Instead, the feisty "overmountain men" went after Ferguson. They caught him and his Tories near Kings Mountain, along the border between North Carolina and South Carolina. There, on October 7, 1780, they decimated his force. The Battle of Kings Mountain was the turning point of the war in the South. By proving that the British were not invincible, the American victory emboldened small farmers to join guerrilla bands under such colorful partisan leaders as Francis Marion, "the Swamp Fox," and Thomas Sumter, "the Carolina Gamecock."

While the overmountain men were closing in on Ferguson, Congress chose a new commander for the southern theater, General Nathanael Greene, "the fighting Quaker" of Rhode Island. Greene shrewdly lured Cornwallis, taxing the British troops' energy and supplies as they chased the Americans across the Carolinas. Splitting his army, Greene sent out about 700 men under General Daniel Morgan to engage Tarleton's 1,000 men at

MAJOR CAMPAIGNS IN THE SOUTH, 1778–1781
← American forces
← British forces
★ Battle site

Why did the British suddenly shift their campaign to the South? How did Nathanael Greene undermine British control of the Deep South? Why did Cornwallis march to Virginia and camp at Yorktown? How was the French navy crucial to the American victory? Why was Cornwallis forced to surrender?

Cowpens, South Carolina, on January 17, 1781. The Americans routed the British; Tarleton and a handful of cavalry escaped, but over 100 of his men were killed, and more than 700 were taken prisoner. Morgan and his men then linked up with Greene's main force, and the combined army offered battle at Guilford Courthouse, North Carolina (near what became Greensboro), on March 15, 1781. After inflicting heavy losses, Greene withdrew, and Cornwallis was left in possession of the field, but at a cost of nearly 100 men killed and more than 400 wounded.

Cornwallis's army marched off toward Wilmington, on the North Carolina coast, to take on supplies from British ships. Greene returned to South Carolina, hoping to lure Cornwallis after him or force the British to give up the state. There he joined forces with the local guerrillas and in a series of brilliant actions kept losing battles while winning the war. By September 1781 he had narrowed British control in the Deep South to Charleston and Savannah, although for more than a year longer Whigs and Tories slashed at each other "with savage fury" in the backcountry.

Meanwhile, Cornwallis's army had headed north, away from Greene's forces, reasoning that Virginia must be eliminated as a source of reinforcement before the Carolinas could be subdued. In 1781, Cornwallis met up with the traitor Benedict Arnold, now a *British* general, who had been engaged in a war of maneuver against the American forces. Arnold, from July until September 1780, had been the American commander at West Point, New York. Overweening in ambition, lacking in moral scruples, and a reckless spender on his fashionable wife, he had nursed a grudge against Washington over an official reprimand for his extravagances as commander of reoccupied Philadelphia. Arnold crassly plotted to sell out the American garrison at West Point to the British, even suggesting how they might capture George Washington himself. The American seizure of the British go-between, Major John André, had ended Arnold's plot. Warned that his plan had been discovered, Arnold joined the British in New York, and the Americans hanged André as a spy.

YORKTOWN   When Lord Cornwallis linked up with the now-British general Benedict Arnold at Petersburg, Virginia, their combined forces totaled 7,200, far more than the small American army they faced. The arrival of American reinforcements led Cornwallis to pick Yorktown, Virginia, as a defensible site. There appeared to be little reason to worry about a siege, since General Washington's main army seemed preoccupied with attacking New York, and the British navy controlled American waters.

Then, in 1781, the elements for a combined American-French action suddenly fell into place. As General Cornwallis moved his British army into

Surrender of Lord Cornwallis

By John Trumbull. The artist completed his painting of the pivotal British surrender at Yorktown in 1781.

Virginia in May, Washington persuaded the commander of the French army to join forces for an attack on New York. The two armies linked up in July, but before they could strike at New York, word came from the West Indies that an entire French fleet and some 3,000 soldiers under Admiral de Grasse were bound for Chesapeake Bay. Washington and his troops slipped out of New York and met up with the French army in Philadelphia; the combined American-French forces immediately marched south toward Yorktown. Meanwhile, a second French fleet, which had been blockaded by the British at Newport, evaded the barricade and sailed south toward Chesapeake Bay.

On August 30, 1781, Admiral de Grasse's fleet reached Yorktown, where his troops joined the American force already watching Cornwallis. On September 6, de Grasse forced the British fleet to abandon the effort to relieve Cornwallis, whose fate was quickly sealed. When the siege of Yorktown began, on September 28, Washington commanded 16,000 soldiers, double the size of the British army. Unable to break the siege or escape, Cornwallis was forced to surrender. On October 17, 1781, a red-coated drummer boy climbed atop the British parapet and began beating the call for a truce. On October 19, their colors cased (that is, sheathed in a cloth covering as a sign of surrender), the British force marched out to the tune of "The World Turned Upside Down." Cornwallis himself claimed to be too ill to appear.

NEGOTIATIONS

Whatever lingering hopes of victory the British may have harbored vanished at Yorktown. "Oh God, it is all over," Lord North groaned at news of the surrender. On February 27, 1782, the House of Commons voted against continuing the war and on March 5 authorized the Crown to make peace. Peace negotiations between the American diplomats—Benjamin Franklin, John Jay, and John Adams—and the British began in Paris, but their difficult task was immediately complicated by the French commitment to Spain. Both the United States and Spain were allied with France, but they were not allied with each other. America was bound by its French alliance to fight on until the French made peace, and the French were bound to help the Spanish recover Gibraltar from England. Unable to deliver Gibraltar, or so the tough-minded Jay reasoned, the French might try to bargain off American land west of the Appalachians in its place. Fearful that the French were angling for a separate peace treaty with the British, Jay persuaded Franklin to pursue a peace treaty with the British too. Ignoring their instructions to consult fully with the French, they agreed to further talks with the British. On November 30, 1782, the talks produced a preliminary treaty with Great Britain. If it violated the spirit of the alliance with France, it did not violate the strict letter of the treaty, for the French minister was notified the day before it was signed, and final agreement still depended upon a Franco-British settlement.

THE TREATY OF PARIS   Early in 1783, France and Spain gave up trying to acquire Gibraltar and reached an armistice with Britain. The Treaty of Paris was finally signed on September 3, 1783. In accord with the bargain already struck, Great Britain recognized the independence of the United States and agreed to a Mississippi River boundary to the west. Both the northern and the southern borders left ambiguities that would be disputed for years. Florida, as it turned out, passed back to Spain. The British further granted the Americans the "liberty" of fishing off Newfoundland and in the Gulf of St. Lawrence and the right to dry their catch on the unsettled coast of Canada. On the matter of pre–Revolutionary War debts owed by Americans, the best the British could get was a promise that British merchants should "meet with no legal impediment" in seeking to collect them. And on the tender point of Loyalists whose property had been confiscated, the negotiators agreed that Congress would "earnestly recommend" to the states the restoration of confiscated property. Each of the last two points was little more than a face-saving gesture to the British.

THE POLITICAL REVOLUTION

REPUBLICAN IDEOLOGY   The Americans had won their War of Independence. Had they undergone a political revolution as well? John Adams offered an answer: "The Revolution was effected before the war commenced. The Revolution was in the minds and hearts of the people. . . . This radical change in the principles, opinions, sentiments, and affections of the people, was the real American Revolution."

Yet Adams's observation ignores the fact that the Revolutionary War itself served as the catalyst for a prolonged debate about what forms of government would best serve the new American republic. The conventional British model of mixed government sought to balance the monarchy, the aristocracy, and the common people so as to protect individual liberty. Because of the more fluid and democratic nature of their new society, however, Americans knew that they must develop new political assumptions and institutions. They had no monarchy or aristocracy. Yet how could sovereignty reside in the common people? How could Americans ensure the survival of a republican form of government, long assumed to be the most fragile? The war thus prompted a flurry of state constitution making that remains unique in history. Ideas such as the contract theory of government, the sovereignty of the people, the separation of powers, and natural rights found their way quickly, almost automatically, into the frames of government that were devised while the fight went on—amid other urgent business.

The very idea of republican, or representative, government—a balanced polity animated by civic virtue—was a far more radical departure in that day than it would seem to be to later generations. Through the lens of republican thinking, Americans began to see themselves in a new light. As free citizens of a republic, Americans would cast off the aristocratic corruptions of the Old World and usher in a new reign of individual liberty and public virtue. The new American republic, in other words, would endure as long as the majority of the people were virtuous and willingly placed the good of society above the self-interest of individuals. Herein lay the hope and the danger of the American experiment in popular government: even as leaders enthusiastically fashioned new state constitutions, they feared that their experiments in republicanism would fail because of a lack of civic virtue among the people.

STATE CONSTITUTIONS   Most political experimentation between 1776 and 1787 occurred at the state level. At the onset of the fighting, every colony experienced the departure of its governor and other officials and

NORTH AMERICA, 1783

- England
- United States
- Spain

How did France's treaties with Spain complicate the peace-treaty negotiations with the British? What were the terms of the Treaty of Paris? Why might the ambiguities in the treaty have led to conflicts among the Americans, the Spanish, and the British?

usually the expulsion of Loyalists from its assembly, which then assumed power as a provincial "congress" or "convention." But those legislatures were acting as revolutionary bodies without any legal basis for the exercise of authority. In two states this presented little difficulty. Connecticut and Rhode Island, which as corporate colonies had been virtually little republics, simply purged their charters of any reference to colonial ties. Massachusetts followed their example until 1780.

In the other states the prevailing notions of social contract and popular sovereignty led to written constitutions that specified the framework and powers of government. Constitution making began even before independence. In May 1776, Congress advised the colonies to set up new governments "under the authority of the people." The first state constitutions varied mainly in detail. They formed governments much like the colonial administrations, but with elected governors and senates instead of appointed governors and councils. Generally they embodied, sometimes explicitly, a separation of powers as a safeguard against abuses. Most of them also included a bill of rights that protected the time-honored rights of petition, freedom of speech, trial by jury, freedom from self-incrimination, and the like. Most tended to limit the powers of governors and increase the powers of the legislatures, which had led the people in their quarrels with the colonial governors.

THE ARTICLES OF CONFEDERATION The new national government, like the state governments, grew out of an extralegal revolutionary body. The Continental Congress had exercised power without any constitutional sanction before 1781. Plans for a permanent national government emerged very early, however, when a committee headed by John Dickinson produced a draft constitution, the Articles of Confederation and Perpetual Union, which was adopted in November 1777.

The central government envisaged by the Articles of Confederation had little authority. Congress was intended not as a legislature, nor as a sovereign entity unto itself, but as a collective substitute for the monarch. In essence it was to be a legislative body serving as the nation's chief executive. For all the weaknesses of the central government proposed by the Articles of Confederation, it represented the most appropriate structure for the new nation. After all, the Revolution on the battlefields had yet to be won, and the statesmen did not have the luxury of engaging in prolonged debates over the distribution of power that proposals for other systems would have entailed. There would be time later for modifications.

THE SOCIAL REVOLUTION

Political revolutions often spawn social revolutions. What did the Revolution mean to those workers, servants, farmers, and freed slaves who participated in the Stamp Act demonstrations, supported the boycotts, idolized Tom Paine, and fought with Generals Washington, Gates, and Greene? The more conservative Patriots would have been content to replace royal officials with the rich, the wellborn, and the able and let it go at that. But more radical revolutionaries, in the apt phrase of one historian, raised the question not only of home rule but also of who shall rule at home.

EQUALITY AND ITS LIMITS   This spirit of equality weakened old habits of deference. Participation in the army or militia activated men who had taken little interest in politics. The new political opportunities afforded by the creation of state governments thus led more ordinary citizens to participate than ever before. The social base of the new legislatures was much broader than that of the old assemblies.

Men fighting for their liberty found it difficult to justify denying other white men the rights of suffrage and representation. The property qualifications for voting, which already admitted an overwhelming majority of white men, were lowered still further in some states. In Pennsylvania, Delaware, North Carolina, and Georgia, any male taxpayer could vote, although office-holders had to meet more stringent property requirements. In the state legislatures younger men often replaced older men, some of whom had been Loyalists. More often than not, the newcomers were men with less property and little education. Some states concentrated much power in a legislature chosen by a wide suffrage, but not even Pennsylvania, which adopted the most radical state constitution, went quite so far as to grant universal male suffrage.

New developments in land tenure that grew out of the Revolution extended the democratic trends of suffrage requirements. The state legislatures seized Tory estates. This land was of small consequence, however, in comparison with the unsettled land that had been at the disposal of the Crown and proprietors. Now in the hands of state assemblies, much of this land was distributed as rewards to veterans of the war. Western lands, formerly closed by the Royal Proclamation of 1763 and the Quebec Act of 1774, were soon thrown open to settlers.

THE PARADOX OF SLAVERY   Members of the Revolutionary generation of leaders were the first to consider abolishing slavery. The principles of liberty and equality so crucial to the rebellion against England had clear implications for enslaved Americans. Thomas Jefferson's draft of the Declaration of Independence indicted the king for having violated the "most sacred rights of life and liberty of a distant people" by encouraging the slave trade in the colonies, but Jefferson had deleted the clause "in complaisance to South Carolina and Georgia." After independence all the states except Georgia stopped the importation of African slaves, although South Carolina later reopened it.

Social democracy

In this watercolor by Benjamin Latrobe, a gentleman plays billiards with artisans, suggesting that "the spirit of independence was converted into equality."

African American soldiers or sailors were present at most major Revolutionary battles, from Lexington to Yorktown, most of them serving on the Loyalist side. Slaves who served in the cause of independence got their freedom and in some cases land bounties. But the British army, which freed tens of thousands of slaves during the war, was a greater instrument of emancipation than the American forces. Most of the freed blacks found their way to Canada or to British colonies in the Caribbean. American Patriots had shown no mercy to blacks caught aiding or abetting the British cause. A Charleston mob hanged and then burned Thomas Jeremiah, a free black man who was convicted of telling slaves that the British "were come to help the poor Negroes."

In the northern states, which had fewer slaves than the southern states, the doctrines of liberty led swiftly to emancipation for all, either during the fighting or shortly afterward. South of Pennsylvania the potential consequences of emancipation were so staggering—South Carolina had a black majority—that whites refused to extend the principle of liberty to their slaves. Although some southern slave-holders were troubled, most could not bring themselves to free their own slaves. Anti-slavery sentiment in the southern states went only so far as to relax the manumission laws under which owners might voluntarily free their slaves. Some 10,000 enslaved Virginians were manumitted during the 1780s. By the outbreak of the Civil War, in 1861, approximately half the African Americans living in Maryland were free.

Slaves, especially in the upper South, also earned their freedom through their own actions during the Revolutionary era, frequently by running away.

They often gravitated to the growing number of African American communities in the North. Because of emancipation laws in the northern states, and with the formation of free black neighborhoods in the North and in several southern cities, runaways found refuge and the opportunities for new lives. It is estimated that 80,000 to 100,000 slaves fled to freedom during the Revolution.

THE STATUS OF WOMEN   The logic of liberty applied to the status of women as much as to that of African Americans. Women had remained essentially confined to the domestic sphere during the eighteenth century. They could not vote or preach or hold office. Few had access to formal education. Only rarely could women own property or execute contracts. Divorces were extremely difficult to obtain.

The Revolution offered women new opportunities. Women plowed fields and melted down pots and pans to make shot. Women also served the armies in various roles—by handling supplies and serving as spies or couriers. Wives often followed their husbands to army camps, where they nursed the wounded and sick, cooked and washed for the able, and frequently buried the dead. On occasion, women took their husbands' places in the firing line.

To be sure, most women retained the constricted domestic outlook that had long been imposed upon them, but a few free-spirited reformers demanded equal treatment. In an essay titled "On the Equality of the Sexes," written in 1779 and published in 1790, Judith Sargent Murray of Gloucester, Massachusetts, stressed that women were perfectly capable of excelling outside the domestic sphere.

Early in the Revolutionary struggle, Abigail Adams, one of the most learned women of the time, wrote her husband, John: "In the new Code of Laws which I suppose it will be necessary for you to make I desire you would remember

Elizabeth Freeman

Also known as Mum Bett, Freeman was born around 1742 and sold as a slave to a Massachusetts family. She won her freedom by claiming in court that the Bill of Rights and the new state constitution gave liberty to all, and her case contributed to the eventual abolition of slavery in Massachusetts. One of Freeman's great-grandchildren was the scholar and civil rights leader W. E. B. Du Bois.

the Ladies. . . . Do not put such unlimited power into the hands of the Husbands." Since men were "Naturally Tyrannical," she stressed, "why then, not put it out of the power of the vicious and the Lawless to use us with cruelty and indignity." Otherwise, "the Ladies" would "foment a Rebellion, and will not hold ourselves bound by any Laws in which we have no voice, or Representation."

John Adams expressed surprise that women might be discontented, but he clearly knew the privileges enjoyed by males and was determined to retain them: "Depend upon it, we know better than to repeal our Masculine systems." The supposedly more liberal Thomas Jefferson agreed with John Adams on the matter. When asked about women's voting rights, he replied that "the tender breasts of ladies were not formed for political convulsion." The legal status of women thus did not benefit dramatically from the egalitarian doctrine unleashed by the Revolution. Married women in most states still forfeited control of their own property to their husbands, and women gained no political rights.

INDIANS AND THE REVOLUTION   The war for American independence had profound effects on the Indians in the southern backcountry and in the Old Northwest region west of New York and Pennsylvania. Most tribes sought to remain neutral in the conflict, but both British and American agents lobbied the chiefs to fight on their side. The result was the disintegration of the alliance among the six tribes making up the Iroquois League. The Mohawks, for example, succumbed to British promises to protect them from encroachments by American settlers on their lands. The Oneidas, on the other hand, fought on the side of the American Patriots. The results of such alliances was chaos on the frontier. Indians on both sides attacked villages, burned crops, and killed civilians. The new American government assured its Indian allies that it would respect their lands and their rights. In December 1777 the Continental Congress promised Oneida leaders that "we shall [always] love and respect you. As our trusty friends, we shall protect you; and shall at all times consider your welfare as our own." But once the war ended and independence was secured, the U.S. government turned its back on such pledges. By the end of the eighteenth century, land-hungry American whites were again pushing into Indian territories on the western frontier.

FREEDOM OF RELIGION   The Revolution tested traditional religious loyalties and set in motion a transition from the toleration of religious dissent to a complete freedom of religion as embodied in the principle of separation of church and state. The Anglican Church, established as the official state religion in five colonies and parts of two others, was especially vulnerable

Religious development

The Congregational Church developed a national presence in the early nineteenth century, and Lemuel Haynes, depicted here, was its first African American preacher.

because of its association with the Crown. With the single exception of Virginia, all the states had eliminated tax support for the church before the fighting was over. In 1776 the Virginia Declaration of Rights (a bill of rights) guaranteed the free exercise of religion, and in 1786 the Virginia Statute of Religious Freedom (written by Thomas Jefferson) declared that "no man shall be compelled to frequent or support any religious worship, place or ministry whatsoever" and "that all men shall be free to profess and by argument to maintain, their opinions in matters of religion." These statutes and the Revolutionary ideology that justified them helped shape the course that religion would take in the new United States: pluralistic and voluntary rather than monolithic and state supported.

In churches as in government, the Revolution set off a period of constitution making as some of the first national church bodies emerged. In 1784 the Methodists, who at first were an offshoot of the Anglicans, came together in a general conference at Baltimore. The Anglican Church, rechristened Episcopal, gathered in a series of meetings that by 1789 had united the various dioceses in a federal union; in 1789 the Presbyterians also held their first general assembly in Philadelphia. That same year the Catholic Church got its first higher official in the United States when John Carroll was named bishop of Baltimore.

The Emergence of an American Culture

The Revolution helped excite a sense of common nationality. One of the first ways in which a national consciousness was forged was through the annual celebration of the new nation's independence from Great Britain. On July 2, 1776, when the Second Continental Congress had resolved "that these United Colonies are, and of right ought to be, free and independent states," John Adams had written his wife, Abigail, that future generations would remember that date as their "day of deliverance."

As it turned out, however, Americans fastened not upon July 2 but upon July 4 as their Independence Day. To be sure, it was on the Fourth that Congress formally adopted the Declaration of Independence and ordered it to be printed and distributed throughout the states, but America by then had been officially independent for two days. The celebration of Independence Day became the most important public ritual in the United States. Huge numbers of people from all walks of life suspended their normal routine in order to devote a day to parades, formal orations, and fireworks displays. In the process the infant republic began to create its own myth of national identity that transcended local or regional concerns and forged a sense of national unity.

AMERICA'S "DESTINY"   In a special sense, American nationalism embodied an idea of divine mission. Many people, at least since the time of the Pilgrims, had thought of America as singled out by God for a special identity, a special mission. John Winthrop referred to the Puritan commonwealth as representing a "city upon a hill," and Jonathan Edwards believed that God had singled out America as "the glorious renovator of the world." This sense of mission was neither limited to New England nor rooted solely in Calvinism. From the democratic rhetoric of Thomas Jefferson to the pragmatism of George Washington to heady toasts bellowed in South Carolina taverns, patriots everywhere articulated a special role for American leadership in history. The mission was now a call to lead the way toward liberty and equality. Meanwhile, however, Americans had to address more immediate problems created by their new nationhood. The Philadelphia patriot, doctor, and scientist Benjamin Rush issued a prophetic statement in 1787: "The American war is over: but this is far from being the case with the American Revolution. On the contrary, but the first act of the great drama is closed."

End of Chapter Review

- **Military Strategies** The Americans had to create an army—the Continental army—from scratch and sustain it. To defeat the British, Washington realized that the Americans had to wage a war of attrition, given that the British army was fighting a war thousands of miles from its home base. To defeat the Americans, Britain's initial strategy was to take New York and sever the troublesome New England colonies from the rest.

- **Turning Points** The American victory at Saratoga in 1777 was the first major turning point of the war. Washington's ability to hold his forces together despite daily desertions and two especially difficult winters was a second major turning point. The British lost support in the southern colonies when they executed the rebels they captured in backcountry skirmishing.

- **Loyalists, "Tories"** The American Revolution was a civil war, dividing families and communities. There were at least 100,000 Tories, or Loyalists, in the colonies. They included royal officials, Anglican ministers, wealthy southern planters, and the elite in large seaport cities; they also included many humble people, especially recent immigrants. After the hostilities ended, most Loyalists, including slaves who had fled their plantations to support the British cause, left for Canada, the West Indies, or England.

- **Worldwide Conflict** The French were prospective allies from the beginning of the conflict, because they resented their losses to Britain in the Seven Years' War. After the British defeat at Saratoga, France and the colonies agreed to fight together until independence was won. Further agreements with Spain and the Netherlands helped to make the Revolution a worldwide conflict. French supplies and the presence of the French fleet ensured the Americans' victory at Yorktown.

- **A Social Revolution** The American Revolution disrupted and transformed traditional class and social relationships. More white men gained the vote as property requirements were removed. Northern states began to free slaves, but southerner states were reluctant. Although many women had undertaken non-traditional roles during the war, they remained largely confined to the domestic sphere afterward, with no changes to their legal or political status. The Revolution had catastrophic effects on the Native Americans, regardless of which side they had embraced. American settlers seized Native American land, often in violation of existing treaties.

CHRONOLOGY

1776	General Washington's troops cross the Delaware River; Battle of Trenton
1776–1777	Washington's troops winter at Morristown, New Jersey
1777	Battle of Saratoga; General Burgoyne surrenders
1777–1778	Washington's troops winter at Valley Forge, Pennsylvania
1778	Americans and French form an alliance
1781	Battles of Cowpens and Guildford Courthouse
1781	General Cornwallis surrenders at Yorktown, Virginia
1781	Articles of Confederation are ratified
1783	Treaty of Paris is signed
1786	Virginia adopts the Statute of Religious Freedom

KEY TERMS & NAMES

7

SHAPING A
FEDERAL UNION

FOCUS QUESTIONS

wwnorton.com/studyspace

- What were the achievements of the Confederation government?
- What were the shortcomings of the Articles of Confederation?
- Why did the delegates to the Constitutional Convention draft a completely new constitution?
- How important was the issue of slavery in the Constitution?
- What were the main issues in the debate over ratification of the Constitution?

In an address to fellow graduates at the Harvard commencement ceremony in 1787, young John Quincy Adams, the son of John and Abigail Adams, lamented "this critical period" when the United States was struggling to establish itself as a new nation. Historians thereafter used his phrase to designate the years when the infant republic operated under the Articles of Confederation, from 1781 to 1787. Fear of a British-like centralized government dominated the period and limited the scope and effectiveness of the new government. Yet while the Confederation had its weaknesses, it also generated major achievements during the so-called critical period. Moreover, lessons learned under the Confederation would prompt the formulation of a new national constitution intended to better balance central and local authority.

THE CONFEDERATION

The Confederation Congress had little authority. It could only request money from the states; it could make treaties with foreign countries but could not enforce them; it could borrow money but lacked the means to ensure repayment. Congress was virtually helpless to cope with the postwar problems of international relations and economic depression, problems that would have challenged the resources of a much stronger government. Yet in spite of its handicaps, the Confederation Congress somehow managed to keep the young republic afloat and to lay important foundations. It concluded the Treaty of Paris in 1783, ending the Revolutionary War, created the first federal executive departments, and formulated principles of land distribution and territorial government that would guide westward expansion all the way to the Pacific coast.

THE ARTICLES OF CONFEDERATION When the Articles of Confederation took effect, in 1781, they did little more than legalize the status quo. Congress had responsibility over foreign affairs and questions of war and peace; it could decide disputes between the states; it had authority over coinage, the postal service, Indian affairs and the western territories. But it had no courts and no power to enforce its resolutions and ordinances. It also had no power to levy taxes but had to rely on requests submitted to the states, which state legislatures could ignore—and usually did.

The new state legislatures, after their predecessors' battles with Parliament, were in no mood for a strong central government. Congress could not effectively regulate interstate and foreign commerce, and for certain important acts a "special majority" was required. Nine states had to approve measures dealing with war, treaties, coinage, finances, or the army and navy. Unanimous approval by the states was needed to levy tariffs (often called duties) on foreign imports. Amendments to the Articles also required unanimous ratification by the states.

The Confederation had neither an executive nor a judicial branch; there was no administrative head of government (only the president of the Congress, chosen annually), and there were no federal courts. In 1781, however, anticipating ratification of the Articles of Confederation, Congress set up three executive departments: Foreign Affairs, Finance, and War. Each was to have a single head responsible to Congress. Given time and stability, Congress and the department heads might have evolved into something like the parliamentary cabinet system. As it turned out, these agencies were the forerunners of the government departments to be established under the Constitution.

FINANCE   Since there was neither a president nor a prime minister, but only the presiding officer of Congress and a secretary, the closest thing to an executive head of the Confederation was Robert Morris, who was superintendent of finance in the final years of the war. Morris wanted to make both himself and the Confederation more powerful. He envisioned a coherent program of federal taxation and debt management to make the national government financially stable.

To anchor his plan, Morris secured in 1781 a congressional charter for the Bank of North America, which would hold government cash, lend money to the government, and issue currency. But his program depended ultimately upon the Confederation government's having a secure income, and it proved impossible to win the unanimous approval of the states for amendments to the Articles of Confederation that would have provided for such income. As a consequence the Confederation never did put its finances in order. The Continental currency quickly proved worthless. The government debt, domestic and foreign, grew from $11 million to $28 million as Congress paid off citizens' and soldiers' claims. Each year, Congress ran a deficit in its operating expenses.

LAND POLICY   The Confederation Congress might have drawn an independent income from the sale of western lands, but throughout the Confederation period little acreage was sold. The Confederation nevertheless dealt more effectively with the western lands than with anything else. There Congress had direct authority, at least on paper. Thinly populated by Indians, French settlers, and a growing number of American squatters, the region north of the Ohio River and west of the Appalachian Mountains had long been the site of overlapping claims by colonies and speculators.

Between 1784 and 1787, policies for western development emerged in three major ordinances of the Confederation Congress. These documents, which rank among the Congress's greatest achievements—and among the most important in American history—set precedents that the United States would follow in its future expansion. Under Thomas Jefferson's proposed ordinance of 1784, when a territory's population equaled that of the smallest existing state, the territory would be eligible to achieve full statehood.

In the Land Ordinance of 1785, the delegates outlined a plan of surveys and sales that eventually stamped a rectangular pattern on much of the nation's surface. Wherever Indian titles had been extinguished, the Northwest was to be surveyed and six-mile-square townships established along east-west and north-south lines. Each township was in turn to be divided into thirty-six sections, each one mile square (or 640 acres). The 640-acre sections were to be auctioned for no less than $640. Such terms favored land speculators, of course, since few common folk had that much money or were able to work that much land. In later years new land laws would make smaller lots available at lower prices, but in 1785, Congress confronted an empty Treasury, and delegates believed that this system would raise the needed funds.

THE NORTHWEST ORDINANCE   Spurred by the plans for land sales and settlement, Congress drafted the Northwest Ordinance of 1787. The new plan abandoned the commitment to early self-government in the territories. Because of the trouble that might be expected from squatters who were clamoring for free land, the Northwest Ordinance required a period of colonial transition. At first the territory fell subject to a governor, a secretary, and three judges, all chosen by Congress. When any territory in the region had a population of 5,000 free male adults, it could choose an assembly, and Congress would name a governing council. The governor would have a veto, and so would Congress.

The resemblance of these territorial governments to the old royal colonies is clear, but there were three significant differences. For one, the Northwest Ordinance anticipated statehood when any territory's population reached 60,000 "free inhabitants." At that point a convention could be called to draft a state constitution and apply to Congress for statehood. Ohio was the first territory to gain statehood in this way. For another, it included a bill of rights that guaranteed religious freedom, proportional representation, trial by jury, habeas corpus, and the application of common law. Finally, the ordinance permanently excluded slavery from the Northwest territories. This decision proved fateful. As the progress of emancipation in the existing states gradually freed all slaves in the North, the Ohio River boundary of the Old Northwest extended the line between freedom and slavery all the way to the Mississippi River, encompassing what would become the states of Ohio, Indiana, Illinois, Michigan, and Wisconsin.

The Northwest Ordinance of 1787 had an importance larger than establishing a formal procedure for transforming territories into states. It represented a sharp break with the imperialistic assumption behind European expansion into the Western Hemisphere. The new states were to be admitted to the American republic as equals rather than treated as subordinate colonies.

The federal lands south of the Ohio River followed a different process of development. Title to the western lands remained with Georgia, North

Carolina, and Virginia for the time being, but settlement proceeded at a far more rapid pace during and after the Revolution, with substantial population centers growing up in Kentucky and Tennessee.

The Iroquois and Cherokees, battered during the Revolution, were in no position to resist encroachments. During the mid-1780s the Iroquois were forced to cede land in western New York and Pennsylvania, and the Cherokees gave up all claims in South Carolina, much of western North Carolina, and large portions of present-day Kentucky and Tennessee. At the same time, the major Ohio tribes dropped their claim to most of Ohio, except for a segment bordering the western part of Lake Erie. The Creeks, pressed by Georgia to cede portions of their lands in 1784–1785, went to war in the summer of 1786 with covert aid from Spanish-controlled Florida. When Spanish support lapsed, however, the Creek chief struck a bargain in 1791 that gave the Creeks favorable trade arrangements with the United States but did not restore the lost land.

TRADE AND THE ECONOMY   The American economy after the Revolution went through a turbulent transition. Although farmers enmeshed in local markets maintained their livelihood during the Revolutionary era, commercial agriculture dependent upon trade with foreign markets collapsed during the war. In New England and much of the backcountry, fighting seldom interrupted the tempo of farming, and the producers of foodstuffs for local markets benefited in particular from rising prices and wartime demands. Virginia suffered a loss of enslaved workers, most of them carried off by the British. The British decision to close its West Indian colonies to American trade devastated what had been a thriving commerce in timber, wheat, and various foodstuffs.

British trade with the United States resumed after 1783, however. American ships were allowed to deliver American products and return to the United States with British goods, but they could not carry British goods anywhere else. The pent-up demand for consumer goods created a vigorous market in exports to America, fueled by British credit and the hard money that had come into the new nation with foreign aid, the expenditures of foreign armies, and wartime trade and privateering. The result was a quick cycle of postwar boom and bust, a buying spree followed by a money shortage and economic troubles that lasted several years.

In colonial times the chronic trade deficit with Britain had been offset by the influx of coins from the once lucrative trade with the West Indies. Now American ships found themselves legally excluded from the British

Merchants' counting house

Americans involved in overseas trade, such as the merchants depicted here, had been sharply affected by the dislocations of war.

West Indies. But the islands still needed wheat, fish, and lumber, and American shippers had not lost their talent for smuggling. By 1787, Americans were also trading with the Dutch, the Swedes, the Prussians, the Moroccans, and the Chinese. By 1790 the value of American commerce and exports had far exceeded the trade of the colonies. Although most of the exports were the products of American forests, fields, and fisheries, during and after the war more workers had turned to small-scale manufacturing—shoes, textiles, soap—mainly for domestic markets.

DIPLOMACY Yet while postwar trade flourished, the shortcomings and failures of the Confederation government remained far more apparent—and advocates of a stronger central government grew extremely vocal in demanding changes. In the diplomatic arena there remained the nagging problems of relations with Great Britain and Spain, both of which still kept illegal military posts on American soil and conspired with Indians. Another major irritant to the British was the American confiscation of Loyalist property. The peace treaty with Britain had obligated Congress to end confiscations of Tory property, to guarantee immunity to Loyalists for twelve

months, during which they could return to the United States and wind up
their affairs, and to recommend that the states return confiscated property.
Persecutions, even lynchings, of Loyalists occurred even after the end of the
war. After 1783 some Loyalists returned unmolested, however, and resumed
their lives in their former homes. By the end of 1787, moreover, all the states
had rescinded any laws discriminating against former Tories.

With Spain the chief issues were the disputed southern boundary of the
United States and the right to navigate the Mississippi River. According to
the preliminary treaty with Britain, the United States claimed as its southern
boundary a line running eastward from the mouth of the Yazoo River in
what is now Mississippi. The treaty ending the war with Britain had also
given Americans the right to navigate the Mississippi River to its mouth,
near New Orleans, but the river was entirely within Spanish Louisiana in its
lower reaches. The right to send boats or barges down the Mississippi River
was crucial because of the growing American settlements upriver in Kentucky and Tennessee, but in 1784 Louisiana's Spanish governor closed the
river to American commerce. In 1785 the Spanish government sent to America an ambassador who entered into long but fruitless negotiations with
John Jay, the secretary for foreign affairs, over navigation of the Mississippi
River and the southern border of the United States. The issue of American
access to the lower Mississippi would remain unsettled for nearly another
decade.

THE CONFEDERATION'S PROBLEMS   Of greatest concern to most
Americans after the Revolution were two issues: protection of new industries
from foreign competition and the currency shortage. Merchants and artisans
were frustrated by British policies excluding them from British markets, and
in retaliation they sought from the states tariffs on foreign goods (taxes on imports) that competed with theirs. The infant United States would be on its way
to economic independence, they argued, if only the money that flowed into
the country were invested in domestic manufactures instead of being paid out
for foreign goods. Nearly all the states gave some preference to American
goods, but the lack of consistency in their laws put them at cross-purposes
with one another.

The shortage of cash and other economic difficulties gave rise to more
immediate demands for paper currency, for postponement of tax and debt
payments, and for laws to "stay" (delay) the foreclosure of mortgages. Farmers who had profited during the war found themselves squeezed afterward by
depressed crop prices and mounting debts while merchants sorted out and
opened up new trade routes. Creditors demanded hard money (coins), but it

was in short supply—and paper money was both scarce and virtually worthless after the depreciation of the Continental currency. By 1785 the demand for new paper money became the most divisive issue in state politics. In 1785–1786 seven states (Pennsylvania, New York, New Jersey, South Carolina, Rhode Island, Georgia, and North Carolina) issued paper money. In spite of the cries of calamity, the money served positively as a means of extending credit to hard-pressed farmers through state loans on farm mortgages. It was also used to fund state debts and to pay off the claims of veterans.

Domestic industry

American craftsmen, such as this cabinet-maker, favored tariffs on foreign goods that competed with their own products.

SHAYS'S REBELLION   But many Americans—especially bankers and merchants—were horrified by such inflationary policies. An event in Massachusetts provided the final proof (some said) that the country was on the brink of anarchy: Shays's Rebellion. After 1780, Massachusetts had remained in the grip of a rigidly conservative state government. The state levied high poll and land taxes to pay off a massive war debt, held mainly by wealthy creditors in Boston. The taxes fell most heavily upon beleaguered farmers and the poor in general.

When the legislature adjourned in 1786 without providing paper money or any other relief from taxes and debts, hard-pressed farmers in three western agricultural counties cried foul. They called town meetings and issued resolutions demanding relief from debts and foreclosures. They also submitted petitions, all to no avail. So then they organized an armed uprising. Armed bands of angry farmers closed the courts and prevented farm foreclosures, and a ragtag "army" of some 1,200 rebels led by Captain Daniel Shays, a destitute farmer and war veteran, advanced upon the federal arsenal at Springfield in 1787. Shays and his followers sought a more flexible monetary policy, laws allowing them to use corn and wheat as money, and the right to postpone paying taxes until the postwar agricultural depression lifted.

Shays's Rebellion

Shays and his followers demanded a more flexible monetary
policy and the right to postpone paying taxes until the
postwar agricultural depression lifted.

The state militia responded to the uprising by scattering Shays's men with
a single volley that left four dead. The rebels nevertheless had a victory of
sorts. The new state legislature decided to address the agricultural crisis by
eliminating some taxes on farmers. But a more important consequence was
the impetus the rebellion gave to conservatism and nationalism.

CALLS FOR A STRONGER GOVERNMENT   Shays's Rebellion convinced many political leaders that the Articles of Confederation were inadequate. Self-interest led bankers, merchants, and artisans to promote a stronger
central government as the only alternative to anarchy. Americans were
gradually losing the ingrained fear of a powerful central authority as they
saw evidence that tyranny might come from other quarters, including the
common people themselves.

Such developments led many of the "Founding Fathers" to revise their assessment of the American character. "We have, probably," concluded George
Washington in 1786, "had too good an opinion of human nature in forming
our confederation." People were stretching the meaning of liberty far beyond
what he and others had envisioned. He found a "spirit of *locality*" rampant
in the state legislatures that was destroying the "aggregate interests of the
community." Even worse, he saw people like Daniel Shays taking the law and

other people's property into their own hands. James Madison and other so-called Federalists concluded that the new republic must now depend for its success upon the constant virtue of the few rather than the public spirited-ness of the many.

ADOPTING THE CONSTITUTION

For these reasons, well before Shays's Rebellion, prominent political leaders were demanding a convention to revise the Articles of Confederation to strengthen the national government. After stalling for several months, Congress in 1787 passed a resolution endorsing a national convention "for the sole and express purpose of revising the Articles of Confederation." By then five states had already named delegates; before the meeting six more states had acted. Rhode Island kept aloof throughout, leading critics to label it Rogue Island.

THE CONSTITUTIONAL CONVENTION   Twenty-nine delegates began work in Philadelphia on May 25. Altogether fifty-five attended at one

Drafting the Constitution

George Washington presides over a session of the Constitutional Convention in Philadelphia.

time or another, and after four months thirty-nine signed the Constitution. The document's durability and flexibility testify to the remarkable qualities of its creators. The delegates were surprisingly young: forty-two was the average age. Most were planters, merchants, lawyers, judges, and bankers, many of them widely read in history, law, and political philosophy. At the same time they were practical, experienced, and tested in the fires of the Revolution. Twenty-one had fought in the conflict, seven had been state governors, most had served in the Continental Congress, and eight had signed the Declaration of Independence.

The magisterial George Washington served as presiding officer but participated little in the debates. Eighty-one-year-old Benjamin Franklin, the oldest delegate, also said little from the floor but provided a wealth of experience, wit, and common sense. More active in the debates were the thirty-six-year-old James Madison, the ablest political philosopher in the group; George Mason, the prickly author of the Virginia Declaration of Rights and a slave-holding planter who was burdened by gout, chronic indigestion, and a deep-rooted suspicion of all government; the witty, eloquent, and arrogant New York aristocrat Gouverneur Morris; James Wilson of Pennsylvania, one of the shrewdest lawyers in the new nation and next in importance at the convention only to Washington and Madison; and Roger Sherman of Connecticut, a self-trained lawyer adept at negotiating compromises. John Adams, like Thomas Jefferson, was serving abroad on a diplomatic mission. Also conspicuously absent during most of the convention was Alexander Hamilton, who regretfully went home when the two other New York delegates walked out to protest the loss of states' rights.

The delegates spent four sweltering months fighting flies, the humidity, and one another. However, on certain fundamentals they generally agreed: that government derives its just powers from the consent of the people but that society must be protected from the tyranny of the majority; that the people at large must have a voice in their government but that checks and balances must be provided to keep any one group from dominating; that a stronger central authority was essential but that all power is subject to abuse. Even the best of people are naturally selfish, they believed, and therefore government could not be founded upon a trust in goodwill and virtue. Yet by carefully checking power with countervailing power, the Founding Fathers hoped to devise institutions that could somehow constrain individual sinfulness and channel individual self-interest on behalf of the public good. James Madison proved to be the energizing force at the convention, persuading others by the convincing eloquence of his arguments.

THE VIRGINIA AND NEW JERSEY PLANS   James Madison drafted the proposals that came to be called the Virginia Plan, presented on May 29, 1787. This plan called for separate legislative, executive, and judicial branches and a truly national government whose laws would be binding upon individual citizens as well as states. Congress would be divided into two houses: a lower house to be chosen by popular vote and an upper house of senators elected by the state legislatures. Congress could disallow state laws under the plan and would itself define the extent of its and the states' authority.

On June 15, delegates critical of the Virginia Plan submitted the New Jersey Plan, which kept the existing equal representation of the states in a unicameral Congress but gave the Congress power to levy taxes, regulate commerce, and name a plural executive (with no veto) and a supreme court. The plans presented the convention with two major issues: whether to amend the Articles of Confederation or draft a new document and whether to apportion congressional representation by population or by state.

On the first point the convention voted to design a national government as envisioned by Madison and the other Virginians. Experience had persuaded the delegates that an effective central government, as distinguished from a loose confederation of states, needed the power to levy taxes, regulate commerce, fund an army and navy, and make laws binding upon individual citizens. The painful lessons of the 1780s suggested to them, moreover, that in the interest of order and uniformity the states must be denied certain powers: to issue money, void contracts, make treaties, wage war, and levy tariffs.

But other issues sparked furious disagreements. The first clash in the convention involved representation, and it was solved by the Great Compromise (sometimes called the Connecticut Compromise, as it was proposed by Roger Sherman). In the House of Representatives, apportionment would be by population, which

James Madison

Madison was only thirty-six when he assumed a major role in the drafting of the Constitution. This miniature (1783) is by Charles Willson Peale.

pleased the more populous states; in the Senate there would be equal representation of each state (although the vote would be by individuals, not by states), which appeased the smaller states.

An equally contentious struggle ensued between northern and southern delegates over slavery. Of all the issues that emerged during the Constitutional Convention of 1787, none was more volatile than the question of slavery. During the eighteenth century the economies of Virginia and the Carolinas had become dependent upon enslaved workers, and delegates from those states were determined to protect the future of the institution. Few if any of the Constitution's framers considered the possibility of abolishing slavery in those states—mostly southern—where it was still legal. In this respect they reflected the prevailing attitude of their time. Most agreed with South Carolina's John Rutledge when he asserted, "Religion and humanity [have] nothing to do with this [slavery] question. Interest alone is the governing principle of nations."

The "interest" of southern delegates, with enslaved African Americans so numerous in their states, dictated that slaves be counted as part of the population in determining the number of a state's representatives. Northerners were willing to count slaves when deciding each state's share of taxes but not for purposes of representation in Congress. The delegates, with little dissent, agreed to a compromise whereby a slave would be counted as three fifths of a citizen for the sake of apportioning both representatives and direct taxes to those states with slaves.

A more sensitive issue for the delegates involved an effort to prevent the new central government from stopping the slave trade with Africa. Some state governments had already outlawed the practice, and several delegates demanded that the national government do the same. Southern delegates quickly protested. Eventually it was agreed that Congress would not prohibit the importation of enslaved Africans until 1808 but could levy a tax of $10 a head on imported slaves. In drafting both provisions, a sense of delicacy—and hypocrisy—dictated the use of euphemisms. The Constitution thus spoke of "free persons" and "all other persons." The odious word *slavery* did not appear in the Constitution until the Thirteenth Amendment (1865) abolished the "peculiar institution."

If the delegates found the slavery issue fraught with peril, they considered irrelevant any discussion of the legal or political role of women under the new constitution. The Revolutionary rhetoric of liberty prompted a few women to demand political equality. "The men say we have no business [with politics]," Eliza Wilkinson of South Carolina observed, "but I won't have it thought that because we are the weaker sex as to bodily strength we are capable of nothing more than domestic concerns. They won't even allow us liberty of thought, and that is all I want." Her complaint, however, fell on deaf ears. There was never any formal discussion of women's rights at the convention. The new political framework still defined politics and government as outside the realm of female endeavor.

THE SEPARATION OF POWERS   The details of the government structure generated less debate in Philadelphia than the basic issues pitting the large states against the small and the northern states against the southern. Existing state constitutions, several of which already separated powers among legislative, executive, and judicial branches, set an example that reinforced the convention's resolve to disperse power with checks and balances. Some delegates displayed a thumping disdain for any democratizing of the political system. Hamilton called the people "a great beast," and Elbridge Gerry of Massachusetts asserted that most of the nation's problems "flow from an excess of democracy."

Those elitist views were incorporated into the Constitution's mixed legislative system, which allowed direct popular choice in just one chamber of Congress. The lower house was designed to be closer to the voters, who elected its delegates every two years. The upper house, or Senate, was elected by the state legislatures rather than by the voters themselves. Staggered six-year terms for senators were intended to prevent the choice of a majority in any given year and thereby further isolate senators from the passing fancies of public passion.

The delegates struggled over issues related to the new executive branch. The decision that a single person be made the chief executive caused the delegates "considerable pause," according to James Madison. George Mason protested that this would create a "fetus of monarchy." Indeed, although subject to election every four years, the chief executive would wield powers that would exceed those of the British king. The president could veto acts of Congress, subject to being overridden by a two-thirds vote in each house, was commander in chief of the armed forces, and was responsible for the execution of the laws. The chief executive could make treaties with the advice and consent of two thirds of the Senate and appoint diplomats, judges, and other officers with the consent of a majority of the Senate. The president was instructed to report annually on the state of the nation and was authorized to recommend legislation.

But the president's powers were limited in certain key areas. The chief executive could neither declare war nor make peace; those powers were reserved for Congress. Unlike the British monarch, moreover, the president could be removed from office. The House could impeach (indict) the chief executive—and other civil officers—on charges of treason, bribery, or "other high crimes and misdemeanors"; the president could then be removed by the Senate with a two-thirds vote to convict. The presiding officer at the trial of a president would be the chief justice, since the usual presiding officer of the Senate (the vice president) would have a personal stake in the outcome.

The leading nationalists—men like James Madison, James Wilson, and Alexander Hamilton—wanted to strengthen the independence of the president by entrusting the choice to popular election. But an elected executive was still too far beyond the American experience. Besides, a national election would have created enormous problems of organization and voter qualification. James Wilson suggested instead that the people of each state choose presidential electors equal to the number of their senators and representatives. Others proposed that the legislators make the choice. Finally the convention voted to let the legislature decide the method in each state. Before long nearly all the states were choosing their electors by popular vote, and the electors were acting as agents of the party will, casting their votes as they had pledged them before the election. This method diverged from the original expectation that the electors would deliberate and make their own choices.

The third branch of government, the judiciary, caused surprisingly little debate. Both the Virginia and the New Jersey Plans had called for a supreme court, which the Constitution established, providing specifically for a chief justice of the United States and leaving up to Congress the number of other justices. Although the Constitution nowhere authorizes the courts to declare laws void when they conflict with the Constitution, the power of the Supreme Court to review the legality of congressional actions (judicial review) is implied and was soon exercised in cases involving both state and federal laws. Article VI declares the federal Constitution, federal laws, and treaties to be "the supreme Law of the Land," state laws or constitutions "to the Contrary notwithstanding."

Although the Constitution extended vast new powers to the national government, the delegates' mistrust of unchecked power is apparent in repeated examples of countervailing forces: the separation of the three branches of government, the president's veto, the congressional power of impeachment and removal, the Senate's power to approve treaties and appointments, and the courts' implied right of judicial review. In addition, the new form of government specifically forbade Congress to pass ex post facto laws (laws adopted after an event to criminalize deeds already committed). It also

Signing the Constitution, September 17, 1787
Thomas Pritchard Rossiter's painting shows George Washington presiding over what Thomas Jefferson called "an assembly of demi-gods" in Philadelphia.

reserved to the states large areas of sovereignty—a reservation soon made explicit by the Tenth Amendment. By dividing sovereignty between the people and the government, the framers of the Constitution provided a distinctive contribution to modern political theory. That is, by vesting ultimate authority in the people, they divided sovereignty *within* the government. This constituted a dramatic break with the colonial tradition. The British had always insisted that the sovereignty of the king in Parliament was indivisible.

The most glaring defect of the Articles of Confederation, the rule of state unanimity that defeated every effort to amend them, led the delegates to provide a less forbidding, though still difficult, method of amending the Constitution. Amendments can be proposed either by a two-thirds vote of each house in the Congress or by a national convention specially called by two thirds of the state legislatures. Amendments can be ratified by approval of three fourths of the states acting through their legislatures or in special conventions.

THE FIGHT FOR RATIFICATION The final article of the Constitution provided that it would become effective upon ratification by nine states (not quite the three-fourths majority required for amendment). The Congress submitted the draft Constitution to the states on September 28, 1787. In the ensuing political debate, advocates of the Constitution assumed the name Federalists. Opponents, who favored a more decentralized federal system, became anti-Federalists.

The Federalists were better prepared and better organized. They were usually clustered in or near cities and tended to be more cosmopolitan, more urbane, and better educated. Anti-Federalists tended to be small farmers and frontiersmen who saw little to gain from the promotion of interstate commerce and much to lose from prohibitions on paper money and on "stay" laws, which prevented foreclosure proceedings against farmers. Many of them also feared that an expansive land policy was likely to favor speculators.

THE FEDERALIST   Among the supreme legacies of the debate over the Constitution was a collection of essays called *The Federalist,* originally published in New York newspapers between 1787 and 1788. Initiated by Alexander Hamilton, the eighty-five articles published under the name Publius included about thirty by James Madison, nearly fifty by Hamilton, and five by John Jay. Written to promote state ratification of the Constitution, the essays defended the principle of a supreme national authority but sought to reassure doubters that there was little reason to fear tyranny in the new government.

In perhaps the most famous *Federalist* essay, Number 10, Madison argued that the country's very size and the diversity of the expanding republic would make it impossible for any single faction to form a majority that could dominate the government. This contradicted the prevailing notion that republics could work only in small countries like Switzerland and the Netherlands. In larger countries republican government would descend into anarchy and tyranny through the influence of factions. Quite the contrary, Madison argued. A republic with a balanced federal government could survive in a large and diverse country better than in a smaller country. "Extend the sphere," he wrote, "and you take in a greater variety of parties and interests; you make it less probable that a majority of the whole will have a common motive to invade the rights of other citizens."

Madison and the other Federalists also insisted that the new union would promote prosperity by reducing taxes, paying off the war bonds and state debts, and expanding the money supply. The anti-Federalists, however, highlighted the dangers of power. They especially noted the absence of a bill of rights to protect individuals and states, and they found the ratification process highly irregular, which it was—indeed, it was illegal under the Articles of Confederation. The Anti-Federalist leaders—Patrick Henry and Richard Henry Lee of Virginia, George Clinton of New York, and Samuel Adams and Elbridge Gerry of Massachusetts—were often men whose careers and reputations had been established well before the Revolution. The Federalist leaders, on the other hand, were more likely to be younger men whose careers had begun in the Revolution and who had been "nationalized" in the fires of battle—men like Hamilton, Madison, and Jay.

The two groups disagreed more over means than ends, however. Both sides acknowledged that a stronger national government was needed and that it required an independent income to function properly. Both were convinced that the people must erect safeguards against tyranny, even the tyranny of the majority. Once the new government had become an accomplished fact, few diehards were left who wanted to undo the work of the Philadelphia convention.

THE DECISION OF THE STATES   Ratification of the new federal constitution gained momentum before the end of 1787, and several of the smaller states were among the first to act, apparently satisfied that they had gained all the safeguards they could hope for in equality of representation in the Senate. New Hampshire was the ninth state to ratify the Constitution, on June 21, 1788, enabling it to be put into effect, but the Union could hardly succeed without the approval of Virginia, the most populous state, or New York, which had the third highest population and occupied a key position geographically.

There was strong opposition in both states. In Virginia, Patrick Henry became the chief spokesman for backcountry farmers who feared the powers of the new government, but wavering delegates were won over by a proposal that the convention should recommend a bill of rights. Virginia's convention voted for ratification on June 25, 1788. In New York, Alexander Hamilton and the other Federalists delayed a vote in the hope that action by Virginia would persuade the delegates that the new framework would go into effect with or without New York. On July 26, 1788, they carried the day by the closest margin thus far, 30 to 27. North Carolina stubbornly withheld action until November 1789, when amendments comprising a bill of rights were submitted by Congress. Rhode Island, true to form, did not relent until May 29, 1790, by the closest margin of all—2 votes.

RATIFICATION OF THE CONSTITUTION

Order of Ratification	State	Date of Ratification
1	Delaware	December 7, 1787
2	Pennsylvania	December 12, 1787
3	New Jersey	December 18, 1787
4	Georgia	January 2, 1788
5	Connecticut	January 9, 1788
6	Massachusetts	February 6, 1788
7	Maryland	April 28, 1788
8	South Carolina	May 23, 1788
9	New Hampshire	June 21, 1788
10	Virginia	June 25, 1788
11	New York	July 26, 1788
12	North Carolina	November 21, 1789
13	Rhode Island	May 29, 1790

Upon notification that New Hampshire had become the ninth state to ratify the Constitution, the Confederation Congress began to draft plans for a transfer of power to the new federal government created by the Constitution. On September 13, 1788, it selected New York City as the initial capital of the new government and fixed the date for elections. On October 10, 1788, the Confederation Congress transacted its last business and passed into history. "Our constitution is in actual operation," the elderly Benjamin Franklin wrote to a friend; "everything appears to promise that it will last; but in this world nothing is certain but death and taxes." George Washington was even more uncertain about the future under the new plan of government. He had told a fellow delegate as the convention adjourned, "I do not expect the Constitution to last for more than twenty years."

"A MORE PERFECT UNION"

The Constitution has lasted much longer, of course, and in the process of "creating a more perfect union," it has provided a remarkably creative model of republican government whose features have been repeatedly borrowed by other nations through the years. Yet what makes the U.S. Constitution so distinctive is not its specific provisions but its remarkable harmony with the particular "genius of the people" it governs. The Constitution has provided a flexible system of government that presidents, legislators, judges, and the people have modified to accord with a fallible human nature and changing social, economic, and political circumstances. In this sense the Founding Fathers not only created "a more perfect Union" in 1787, they also engineered a form of government whose resilience has enabled later generations to continue to perfect their republican experiment. But the framers of the Constitution failed in one significant respect: in skirting the issue of slavery so as to cement the new Union, they unknowingly allowed tensions over the "peculiar institution" to reach the point where there would be no political solution—only civil war.

End of Chapter Review

CHAPTER SUMMARY

- **Confederation Government** Despite the weak form of government deliberately crafted under the Articles of Confederation, the Confederation government managed to construct alliances, wage the Revolutionary War to a successful conclusion, and negotiate the Treaty of Paris. It created executive departments and established the way in which western lands would be organized and governments would be formed in the territories.

- **Articles of Confederation** Postwar economic conditions were difficult because British markets were closed to the new nation and the Articles had not provided for a means to raise taxes or stimulate economic recovery. Shays's Rebellion made many Americans fear that anarchy would destroy the new republic and led them to clamor for a stronger national government.

- **Constitutional Convention** Delegates gathered at the convention in Philadelphia to revise the existing government, but almost immediately they proposed scrapping the Articles of Confederation. An entirely new document emerged, delineating separate executive, legislative, and judicial branches. Argument about representation was resolved by establishing a two-house legislature, with equal representation by state in the Senate and by population in the House of Representatives.

- **Slavery and the Constitution** Southern delegates would not support a constitution that failed to protect the institution of slavery and provide for the international slave trade. In determining how enslaved people would be counted for the sake of apportioning direct taxes and representation in the lower house, it was agreed that three-fifths of the enslaved population would be counted. It was also agreed that Congress would not forbid participation in the transatlantic slave trade before 1808. Nevertheless, the framers of the Constitution avoided using the word *slavery* in the Constitution.

- **Ratification of the Constitution** Ratification of the Constitution was difficult, especially in the key states of Virginia and New York. Anti-Federalists such as Virginia's Patrick Henry favored a decentralized federal system and feared that the absence of a bill of rights would lead to a loss of individual and states' rights. To sway New York State toward ratification, Alexander Hamilton, James Madison, and John Jay wrote *The Federalist*, a series of articles defending a strong national authority. Ratification became possible only with the promise of a bill of rights.

CHRONOLOGY

1781	Articles of Confederation take effect
1784	Treaty of Fort Stanwix forces the Iroquois to give up land in New York and Pennsylvania
1785	Land Ordinance outlines a plan for surveying and selling government lands
1786–1787	Shays's Rebellion
1787	Northwest Ordinance outlines a detailed plan for organizing western territories
1787	Constitutional Convention is held in Philadelphia
1787–1788	*The Federalist Papers* are published
1788	Confederation government is phased out
1790	Rhode Island becomes the last state to ratify the Constitution

KEY TERMS & NAMES

8

THE FEDERALIST ERA

FOCUS QUESTIONS

 wwnorton.com/studyspace

- What were the main problems facing Washington's administration?
- What was Hamilton's vision of the new republic?
- How did religious freedom become a reality for the new country?
- How did European affairs complicate the internal political and diplomatic problems of the new country?
- Why did Madison and Jefferson lead the opposition to Hamilton's policies?

The new American republic was a sprawling nation of energetic individuals eager to test the limits of their freedom and exploit the nation's vast natural resources and economic opportunities. The new constitution created a more powerful central government to deal more effectively with the challenges "facing" the vast new nation, but several foreign and domestic crises did not allow for an easy transition.

A NEW NATION

In 1789 the United States and the western territories reached from the Atlantic Ocean to the Mississippi River and hosted almost 4 million people. The new republic harbored distinct regional differences. Although still characterized by small farms and bustling seaports, New England was developing

New beginnings

An engraving from the title page of *The Universal Asylum and Columbian Magazine* (published in Philadelphia in 1790). America is represented as a woman laying down her shield to engage in education, art, commerce, and agriculture.

a manufacturing sector. The middle Atlantic states boasted the most well-balanced economy, the largest cities, and the most diverse collection of ethnic and religious groups. The South, an intensely agricultural region, was increasingly dependent upon enslaved laborers. By 1790 the southern states were exporting as much tobacco as they had been before the Revolution. Most important, however, was the surge in cotton production. Between 1790 and 1815, thanks largely to the invention of the cotton gin, cotton production increased thirtyfold.

The United States in 1790 remained a predominantly rural society. Eighty percent of households were involved in agricultural production. Only a few cities had more than 5,000 residents. The first national census, taken in 1790, counted 750,000 African Americans, almost a fifth of the population. Most of them lived in the five southernmost states; less than 10 percent lived outside the South. Most African Americans, of course, were enslaved, but there were many free blacks as a result of the Revolutionary turmoil. In fact, the proportion of free to enslaved blacks was never higher than in 1790.

The 1790 census did not even count the many Indians still living east of the Mississippi River. There were over eighty tribes numbering perhaps as many as 150,000 people in 1790. In the Old Northwest along the Great Lakes, the British continued to arm the Indians and encouraged them to resist American encroachments on Indian lands. Between 1784 and 1790, Indians killed or captured some 1,500 settlers in Kentucky alone. Such bloodshed generated a ferocious reaction among settlers eager to eradicate the Indians. In the South the five most powerful tribes—the Cherokees, Chickasaws, Choctaws, Creeks, and Seminoles—numbered between 50,000 and 100,000. They steadfastly refused to recognize U.S. authority and used Spanish-supplied weapons to thwart white settlement.

Only about 125,000 whites and blacks lived west of the Appalachian Mountains in 1790. But that was soon to change. Rapid population growth, cheap land, and new economic opportunities fueled the westward migration. The average white woman gave birth to eight children, and the white population doubled approximately every twenty-two years. This made for a very young population on average. In 1790 almost half of all white Americans were under the age of sixteen.

A NEW GOVERNMENT   The new Congress of the United States opened with a whimper rather than a bang. On March 4, 1789, the appointed date of its first session in bustling New York City, only eight senators and thirteen representatives took their seats. A month passed before both chambers could gather a quorum. Only then could the presiding officer of the Senate certify the foregone conclusion that George Washington, with 69 votes, was the unanimous choice of the Electoral College for president. John Adams, with 34 votes, the second-highest number, became vice president. George Washington was a reluctant first president. Yet he agreed to serve because he had been "summoned by my country." A self-made man with little formal education, Washington had a remarkable capacity for moderation and mediation that helped keep the infant republic from disintegrating.

THE GOVERNMENT'S STRUCTURE   The president and the Congress had to create a new government. During the summer of 1789, Congress created executive departments corresponding to those already formed under the Confederation. To head the Department of State, Washington named Thomas Jefferson, recently back from his diplomatic duties in France. Leadership of the Department of the Treasury went to President Washington's wartime aide, Alexander Hamilton, who had since become a prominent lawyer in New York. Tall, graceful Edmund Randolph, former governor of Virginia and owner of a 7,000-acre debt-ridden plantation worked by 200 slaves, assumed the new position of attorney general. Washington routinely called these men to sit as a group to discuss and advise on policy matters. This was the origin of the president's cabinet, an advisory body for which the Constitution made no formal provision.

Washington named John Jay as the first chief justice of the Supreme Court, a post Jay held until 1795. Born in New York City in 1745, Jay had graduated from King's College (now Columbia University). His distinction as a lawyer led New York to send him as its representative to the First and Second Continental Congresses. After serving as president of the Continental Congress in 1778–1779, Jay became the American minister (ambassador) in Spain. While in Europe he helped John Adams and Benjamin Franklin negotiate the Treaty of Paris in 1783. After the Revolution, Jay served as secretary of foreign affairs. He joined Madison and Hamilton as co-author of *The Federalist* and became one of the most effective champions of the Constitution.

THE BILL OF RIGHTS   The ratification of the Constitution did not end the debate about the centralization of power in the federal government. Amid the debates over ratification of the Constitution, four states—Massachusetts,

Debates over ratification

This satirical, eighteenth-century engraving illustrates some of the major issues in Connecticut politics on the eve of ratification.

New York, Virginia, and North Carolina—requested that a "bill of rights" be added to protect individual freedoms, state's rights, and civil liberties. To address such concerns, Congressman James Madison presented to Congress in May 1789 a cluster of constitutional amendments that have since become known as the Bill of Rights. After considerable discussion and debate, Congress approved the amendments in September 1789, and a few days later President George Washington officially transmitted the amendments to the states for ratification. By the end of 1791, the necessary three fourths of the states had approved ten of the twelve proposed amendments.

The Bill of Rights amendments protected certain fundamental individual rights: freedom of religion, press, speech, and assembly; the right to keep and bear firearms; the right to refuse to house soldiers in a private home; protection from unreasonable searches and seizures; the right to refuse to testify against oneself; the right to a speedy public trial, with legal counsel present before an impartial jury; and protection against "cruel and unusual" punishment. The Ninth and Tenth Amendments declare that the enumeration of rights in the Constitution "shall not be construed to deny or disparage others retained by the people" and that "powers not delegated to the United States by the Constitution . . . are reserved to the States respectively, or to the people." The states voted separately on each proposed amendment, and the Bill of Rights became effective on December 15, 1791.

Madison viewed the Bill of Rights as "the most dramatic single gesture of conciliation that could be offered the remaining opponents of the government." Those "opponents" included prominent Virginians George Mason and Richard Henry Lee as well as artisans, small traders, and backcountry farmers who expressed a profound egalitarianism. These "poor and middling" folk doubted that even the "best men" were capable of subordinating self-interest to the good of the Republic. They believed that all people were prone to corruption; no one could be trusted. Therefore, a bill of rights was necessary to protect the liberties of all against the encroachments of a few. Yet the Bill of Rights, it is important to note, provided no rights or legal protection to African Americans or Indians.

RELIGIOUS FREEDOM   The debates over the Constitution and the Bill of Rights generated a religious revolution as well as a political revolution. Unlike the New England Puritans, who sought to ensure that governments explicitly and officially supported their particular religious beliefs, the men who drafted and amended the Constitution made no direct mention of God. They were determined to protect freedom of religion from government interference. The First Amendment declares that "Congress shall make no law respecting an establishment of religion or prohibiting the free exercise thereof." This statement has since become one of the most important—and most disputed—principles of American government. In the late eighteenth century the United States was virtually alone among nations in refusing to establish a single government-mandated and tax-supported religion. In addition, at the time the Bill of Rights was ratified, all but two states—New York and Virginia—still sponsored some form of official religion or maintained a religious requirement for holding political office. In 1789, when the Bill of Rights was created, many people feared that the new national government might impose a particular religious faith on the people. The First Amendment addressed this concern by fostering a pluralistic framework within which people of all religious persuasions could flourish. It prohibits the federal government from endorsing or supporting any particular religion or interfering with the religious choices that people make. As Thomas Jefferson later explained, the First Amendment was intended to erect a "wall of separation between church and State."

HAMILTON'S VISION

Raising revenue to operate its affairs was the new federal government's most critical task, and Congress quickly enacted a tariff (a tax on imported goods) intended to raise money and protect America's new manufacturers from foreign competition by raising prices on imported goods. Yet most of the Americans who bought the now higher priced imported goods were tied to the farm economy. This circumstance raised a basic and perennial question: should rural consumers be forced to subsidize the nation's infant manufacturing sector by supporting tariffs?

The tariff launched the effort to get the country on a sound financial footing. In finance, with all its broad implications for government policy in general, it was the thirty-four-year-old Alexander Hamilton who seized the initiative in 1789. The first secretary of the Treasury was born out of wedlock on a Caribbean island, deserted by his ne'er-do-well Scottish father, and left an orphan at thirteen by the death of his mother. With the help of friends and relatives, he found his way, at seventeen, to New York, attended King's College, and entered the Continental army, where he became Washington's favorite aide. Colonel Hamilton distinguished himself at the siege of Yorktown, and he remained a frustrated military genius, hungry for greater glory on the field of battle. After the war he studied law, passed the bar examination, established a legal practice in New York, and became a self-made

Alexander Hamilton
Secretary of the Treasury from 1789 to 1795.

aristocrat, serving as a collector of revenues and as a member of the Confederation Congress. An early convert to nationalism, he played a crucial part in promoting the new constitution and in defending its provisions in *The Federalist*.

During the Revolutionary War, Hamilton had witnessed the near-fatal weaknesses of the Confederation Congress. Its lack of authority and money almost lost the war. Now, as the nation's first secretary of the Treasury, he was determined to transform an economically weak and fractious cluster of states into a powerful global force. To flourish in a warring world, Hamilton believed, the United States needed to unleash the energy and ambition of its citizens so as to create a vibrant economy driven by the engines of capitalism. He wanted to nurture the hustling, bustling, aspiring spirit that he believed distinguished Americans from others. Just as he had risen from poverty and shame to success, he wanted to ensure that Americans would always have such opportunities. To that end he envisioned a limited but assertive government that encouraged new fields of enterprise and fostered investment and entrepreneurship. Thriving markets and new industries would best ensure the fate of the Republic, and a secure federal debt would give investors a stake in the success of the new national government. The young Hamilton viewed economic growth as the new nation's source of energy and cohesion. He was supremely confident in his ability to shape fiscal policies that would provide economic opportunity and ensure government stability. His success in creating a budget, a funded debt, a federal tax system, a national bank, a customs service, and a coast guard provided the foundations for American capitalism.

ESTABLISHING THE PUBLIC CREDIT The new government needed Hamilton's ambition and brilliance. In a series of reports submitted to Congress in 1790 and 1791, the Treasury secretary outlined his visionary program for government finances and the economic development of the

United States. Hamilton's "Reports on Public Credit" dealt with the vexing issue of war-generated debt. Both the federal government and the individual states had emerged from the Revolution owing substantial debts. France, Spain, and Holland had lent the United States money and supplies to fight the war, and Congress had incurred more debt by printing paper money and selling government bonds to investors. State governments had also accumulated huge debts. After the war some states had started paying off their debts, but the efforts were uneven. Only the federal government could wipe the slate clean. Hamilton insisted that the state debts from the Revolution were a *national* responsibility because all Americans had benefited from independence. He also knew that the federal government's willingness to assume responsibility for paying off the state debts would heighten a sense of nationalism by helping the people see the benefits of a strong central government.

Hamilton's controversial report on public credit made two key recommendations: first, it called for funding the federal debt at face value, which meant that citizens holding government bonds could exchange them for new interest-bearing bonds with the same face value; second, it declared that the federal government should assume state debts from the Revolution. Holders of state bonds could exchange them for new national bonds. The funding scheme was controversial because many farmers and ex-soldiers in need of money after the war had sold their bonds to speculators for a fraction of their value. The original bondholders argued that they should be reimbursed for their losses; otherwise, the speculators would gain a windfall. Hamilton sternly resisted. The speculators, he argued, had "paid what the commodity was worth in the market, and took the risks." Therefore, they should reap the profits. In fact, Hamilton insisted, the government should favor the speculative investors because they represented the bedrock of a successful nation anchored in capitalism.

Payment of the national debt, Hamilton believed, would be not only a point of national honor and sound finance, ensuring the country's credit for the future; it would also be an occasion to assert the new federal power of taxation and thus instill respect for the authority of the national government. It was on this point that Madison, who had been Hamilton's close ally in the movement for a stronger government, broke with him. Madison did not question whether the debt should be paid, but he was troubled that speculators would become the chief beneficiaries. Also disturbing to the Virginian was the fact that northerners held most of the debt. Madison's opposition touched off a vigorous debate that deadlocked the congressional debate over debt funding and assumption through much of 1790.

The stalemate ended in the summer of 1790, when Hamilton, Jefferson, and Madison reached a compromise. In return for northern votes in Congress in favor of locating the permanent national capital on the Potomac River along the Virginia border, Madison pledged to seek enough southern votes to pass the debt-assumption bill, with the further arrangement that those states with smaller debts would get in effect outright grants from the federal government to equalize the difference. These arrangements secured enough votes to carry Hamilton's funding and assumption plans. The national capital would be moved from New York City to Philadelphia for ten years, after which it would be located in a new federal city (Washington, D.C.) bordering northern Virginia. In August 1790, Congress finally passed the legislation for Hamilton's plan. Jefferson later claimed to have been "duped" by Hamilton into agreeing to the "Compromise of 1790" because he did not fully understand the implications of the debt-assumption plan. It is more likely that Jefferson had been outsmarted. He only later realized how relatively insignificant the location of the national capital was when compared with the far-reaching effects of Hamilton's economic program.

A NATIONAL BANK   Alexander Hamilton's ingenious new financial program generated, as if by magic, a great sum of capital for the new republic. Having established the federal government's creditworthiness, the relentless Hamilton moved on to a related measure essential to his vision of national greatness: a central national bank, modeled on the Bank of England, which by issuance of bank notes (paper money) would provide a uniform national currency as well as a source of expanding capital for the developing economy. Government bonds held by the bank would back up the currency. The Bank of the United States, chartered by Congress, would remain under government oversight, but private investors (stockholders) would supply most of the $10 million capital and name twenty of the twenty-five directors; the government would provide the remaining capital and name five directors.

Once again James Madison rose to lead the opposition to Hamilton, arguing that he could find no basis in the Constitution for a national bank. Congress, however, passed the banking bill over Madison's objections. The vote in Congress revealed the growing sectional division in the young United States. Representatives from the northern states voted 33 to 1 in favor of the national bank; southern congressmen opposed the bank 19 to 6. Before signing the bill into law, President Washington sought the advice of his cabinet and found an equal division of opinion. This resulted in the first great debate on constitutional interpretation. Should there be a strict or a broad construction of the Constitution? Were the powers of Congress only those explicitly stated in the document, or were others implied? The argument turned chiefly on Article I, Section 8, which authorizes Congress to "make all Laws which shall be necessary and proper for carrying into execution the foregoing Powers."

Such language fueled disagreement and led to a colossal confrontation between Jefferson and Hamilton. Secretary of State Jefferson pointed to the Tenth Amendment, which reserves to the states and the people powers not delegated to Congress. A bank might be a convenient aid to Congress in collecting taxes and regulating the currency, but it was not, as Article I, Section 8, specified, *necessary*. Hamilton insisted that the power to charter corporations was included in the sovereignty of any government, whether or not expressly stated. George Washington accepted Hamilton's argument and signed the bill. By doing so, in Jefferson's words, the president had opened up "a boundless field of power," which in coming years would lead to a further broadening of implied powers with the approval of the Supreme Court.

ENCOURAGING MANUFACTURES   Alexander Hamilton's audacious plans for the new country were not yet exhausted. At the end of 1790, he submitted the second of his "Reports on Public Credit," which included a proposal for an excise tax on alcoholic beverages to help raise federal revenue to cover the nation's debts. Six weeks later Hamilton proposed a national mint, which was established in 1792 to provide money for the new nation. And on December 5, 1791, as the culmination of his financial program, he proposed, in his "Report on Manufactures," an extensive program of federal aid to promote the development of manufacturing enterprises, a pressing need for the American economy.

In the "Report on Manufactures," Hamilton argued for active government encouragement of manufacturing to provide productive uses for the new capital he had created by his funding, assumption, and banking schemes. Multiple advantages would flow from the aggressive development of manufactures: the diversification of labor in a country given over too exclusively to farming; improved productivity through the greater use of machinery; work for those not ordinarily employed, such as women and children; the promotion of immigration; a greater scope for the diversity of talents in business; and a better domestic market for agricultural products.

To secure his ends, Hamilton advocated protective tariffs, some of which were enacted in 1792, to protect young American industries from foreign competitors. Tariffs were, in essence, taxes on imported goods. The rest of Hamilton's manufacturing program was filed away—but not forgotten: it provided an arsenal of arguments for the manufacturing sector in years to

Certificate of the New York Mechanick Society

An illustration of the growing diversification of labor, by Abraham Godwin (ca. 1785).

come. Hamilton denied that his scheme favored the northern states. If, as seemed likely, the northern and middle Atlantic states should become the chief sites for manufacturing, he claimed, they would create robust markets for agricultural products, some of which the southern states were peculiarly qualified to produce. The nation as a whole would benefit, he argued, as commerce between North and South increased, supplanting the traditional transatlantic trade with Europe.

HAMILTON'S ACHIEVEMENT Largely because of the skillful Hamilton, the Treasury Department during the 1790s began retiring the Revolutionary War debt, enhanced the value of the Continental paper dollar, secured the government's credit, and attracted foreign capital. Prosperity, so elusive in the 1780s, began to flourish at the end of the century.

Hamilton professed a truly nationalist outlook, and he focused his energies on the rising power of commercial capitalism. Tying the government closely to the rich and the wellborn, Hamilton believed, promoted the government's financial stability and guarded the public order against the potential social turbulence that he feared would emerge in a republic. But many Americans then and since have interpreted such views as elitist and self-serving. To be sure, Hamilton never understood the people of the villages and farms, the people of the frontier. They were foreign to his world, despite his own humble beginnings. And they, along with the planters of the South, would be at best only indirect beneficiaries of his programs. There were, in short, vast numbers of people who saw little gain from the Hamiltonian economic program and thus were drawn into opposition against it. Indeed, Jefferson claimed that he and Hamilton were "pitted against each other every day in the cabinet like two fighting-cocks."

THE REPUBLICAN ALTERNATIVE

Debate over Hamilton's economic program spawned the first national political parties. Alexander Hamilton emerged as the embodiment of the Federalists; in opposition, James Madison and Thomas Jefferson led those who took the name Republicans (also called the Democratic Republicans) and thereby implied that the Federalists aimed at a monarchy. Neither side in the disagreement over national policy deliberately set out to create formal political parties. But there were growing differences of both philosophy and self-interest that simply would not subside.

The crux of the debate centered on the relative power of the federal government and the states. At the outset, Madison assumed leadership of Hamilton's opponents in Congress, and he argued that Hamilton was trampling upon states' rights in forging a powerful central government. After the Compromise of 1790, which assured the federal funding of state debts, Jefferson and Madison resolutely opposed Hamilton's policies. They sharply criticized his tax on whiskey, which would especially burden the trans-Appalachian farmers whose livelihood depended upon the sale of the beverage. They also lambasted his proposal for a national bank and his "Report on Manufactures." As these differences developed, the personal hostility between Jefferson and Hamilton festered within the cabinet, much to the distress of President Washington.

JEFFERSON'S AGRARIAN VIEW Thomas Jefferson, twelve years Hamilton's senior, was in most respects his opposite. In contrast to the self-made Hamilton, Jefferson was an agrarian aristocrat, the son of a successful surveyor and land speculator. Jefferson read or spoke seven languages.

Thomas Jefferson

A portrait by Charles Willson Peale (1791).

He was an architect of some distinction (Monticello, the Virginia state capitol, and the University of Virginia are monuments to his talent), a man who understood mathematics and engineering, an inventor, and an agronomist.

Hamilton and Jefferson had contrasting perspectives on America's future. Hamilton was a hardheaded realist who foresaw a diversified capitalist economy, with agriculture balanced by commerce and industry, and was thus the better prophet. Jefferson was an agrarian idealist who feared that the growth of crowded cities would divide society into a capitalist aristocracy on the one hand and a deprived working class on the other. Hamilton feared anarchy and loved order; Jefferson feared tyranny and loved liberty.

Hamilton championed a strong central government run by a wealthy elite actively engaged in encouraging capitalist enterprise. Jefferson wanted to preserve a decentralized agrarian republic. Jefferson's ideal America was one in which small farmers predominated. He did not oppose all forms of manufacturing; he simply feared that the unlimited expansion of commerce and industry would produce a large class of propertyless wage laborers dependent upon others for their livelihood and therefore subject to political manipulation and economic exploitation.

CRISES FOREIGN AND DOMESTIC

As the disputes between Jefferson and Hamilton intensified, George Washington proved ever more adept at transcending party differences and holding things together with his unmatched prestige. In 1792 he won unanimous reelection, and no sooner had his second term begun than problems of foreign relations leaped to center stage, delivered by the consequences of the French Revolution, which had begun in 1789, during the first months of his presidency. Americans supported the popular revolt against the French monarchy, up to a point. By the spring of 1792, however, the idealistic experiment in liberty, equality, and fraternity had turned into a monster that plunged France into war with Austria and Prussia and began devouring its own children, along with its enemies, in the Terror of 1793–1794, during which thousands of French aristocrats were executed.

Secretary of State Thomas Jefferson wholeheartedly endorsed the efforts of French revolutionaries to replace the monarchy with a republican form of government. By contrast, Vice President John Adams decided that the French Revolution had run amok; it had become barbarous and godless. Such conflicting attitudes toward the French Revolution transformed the first decade of American politics into one of the most fractious periods in the nation's history.

The French Revolution also transformed international relations and set in motion a series of complex European alliances and prolonged wars that would frustrate the desire of the young United States to remain neutral in world affairs. After the execution of King Louis XVI, early in 1793, Great Britain joined with the monarchies of Spain and Holland in a war against the French republic. For the next twenty-two years, Britain and France were at war, with only a brief respite, until the final defeat of the French forces under Napoléon in 1815. The war presented George Washington, just beginning his second term in 1793, with an awkward problem. By the 1778 Treaty of Alliance, the United States was a perpetual ally of France, obligated to defend her possessions in the West Indies.

Americans, however, wanted no part of the European war. They were determined to maintain their lucrative trade with both sides. For their part, Hamilton and Jefferson found in the neutrality policy one issue on which they could agree. Where they differed was in how best to implement it. President Washington issued a neutrality proclamation on April 22, 1793, that declared the United States "friendly and impartial toward the belligerent powers."

CITIZEN GENET   At the same time, President Washington had accepted Thomas Jefferson's argument that the United States should recognize the new French government (becoming the first country to do so) and welcome its new ambassador to the United States, Edmond-Charles Édouard Genet. Early in 1793, Genet landed at Charleston, South Carolina, where he received a hero's welcome, and made his way northward to Philadelphia. En route he brazenly engaged in quite nonneutral activities. He outfitted privateers to capture British ships, and he conspired with frontiersmen and land speculators to launch an attack on Spanish Florida and Louisiana in retaliation for the Spanish monarchy's opposition to the French Revolution.

After arriving in Philadelphia, Genet quickly became an embarrassment even to his Republican friends. The cabinet finally agreed unanimously that he had to go, and President Washington demanded his recall. The behavior of the French made it hard even for Republicans to retain sympathy for the French Revolution, but Jefferson and others maintained their support. Jefferson was so disgusted by Washington's refusal to support the French Revolution and by his own ideological warfare with Alexander Hamilton that he would resign as secretary of state at the end of 1793. Nor did the British make it easy for Federalists to rally to their side. Near the end of 1793, they began seizing American ships trading with French islands in the Caribbean. By 1794 a prolonged foreign-policy crisis between the United States and Great Britain threatened to renew warfare between the two old enemies.

JAY'S TREATY   Early in 1794, Republican leaders in Congress were gaining support for commercial retaliation to end British trade abuses when the British gave George Washington a timely opening for a settlement. They stopped seizing American ships, and on April 16, 1794, Washington named Chief Justice John Jay as a special envoy to Great Britain. Jay left with instructions to settle all major issues dividing the United States and Great Britain: to get the British out of their forts along the northwestern frontier, win reparations for the losses of American shippers, secure compensation to planters for southern slaves carried away by British ships at the end of the Revolutionary War in 1783, and negotiate a new commercial treaty that would renew American commerce with the British West Indies.

The pro-British Jay had little leverage with which to wring concessions from the British, however, and after seven months of negotiations he won only two pledges: the British promised to evacuate the northwestern posts by 1796 and to pay damages for the seizure of American ships and cargo in 1793–1794. In exchange for those concessions, Jay agreed to the British definition of neutral rights. He accepted the principles that naval products (tar, pitch, and turpentine), food, and war supplies headed to enemy ports on neutral ships were contraband and that trade with enemy colonies prohibited in peacetime could not be opened in wartime (the "rule of 1756"). Britain also gained most-favored-nation treatment in American commerce and a promise that French privateers would not be outfitted in American ports. Finally, Jay conceded that the British need not compensate U.S. citizens for the enslaved people whom the British had helped to escape during the war, and he promised that the pre-Revolutionary American debts to British merchants would be paid by the U.S. government. Perhaps most important, he failed to gain unrestricted access for American commerce in the British West Indies.

Public outrage greeted the terms of Jay's Treaty. The public debate was so intense that some Americans feared civil war might erupt. Thomas Jefferson and the Democratic Republicans who favored France in its war with Britain were furious; they wanted no concessions to the hated British. They took to the streets, hanged John Jay in effigy, and claimed that the treaty he negotiated was unconstitutional. The heated dispute helped to crystallize the differences between the nation's first competing political parties, the Republicans and the Federalists. Even Federalist shippers, ready for a settlement with the British on almost any terms, criticized Jay's failure to fully open up the British West Indies to American commerce. Much of the outcry, however, came from disappointed Republican partisans who had sought an escalation of the conflict with the hated England. In the end, moderation prevailed. George Washington worried that his opponents were prepared to separate "the Union into Northern & Southern." Once he endorsed Jay's Treaty, there were even calls for his impeachment. Yet the president, while acknowledging that the proposed agreement was imperfect, concluded that adopting it was the only way to avoid a war with Britain that the U.S. was bound to lose. Without a single vote to spare, Jay's Treaty won the necessary two-thirds majority on June 24, 1795. Washington reductantly signed the treaty, deciding it was the best he was likely to get. The major votes in Congress were again aligned by region; 80 percent of the votes for the treaty came from New England or the middle Atlantic states; 74 percent of the votes against the treaty were cast by southerners.

FRONTIER TENSIONS   Other events also had an important bearing on Jay's Treaty, adding force to the importance of resolving the disputed border with Canada. While Jay was haggling in London, frontier conflict with Indians escalated, with U.S. troops twice crushed by northwestern tribes. At last, General Wayne, known as "Mad Anthony," led an expedition into the Northwest Territory in the fall of 1793. The following year, on August 4, Indians representing eight tribes and reinforced by Canadian militias, attacked General Wayne's force south of Detroit at the Battle of Fallen Timbers. The Americans repulsed them, and the Indians suffered substantial losses. Dispersed and decimated, the Indians finally agreed to the Treaty of Greenville, signed in 1795. According to the terms of the treaty, the United States bought from twelve tribes, at the cost of a $10,000 annuity, the rights to the southeastern quarter of the Northwest Territory (now Ohio and Indiana) and enclaves at the sites of Detroit, Chicago, and Vincennes, Indiana.

THE WHISKEY REBELLION   Soon after the Battle of Fallen Timbers, the Washington administration decided on another show of strength in the backcountry, against the so-called Whiskey Rebellion. Treasury Secretary Hamilton's federal tax on liquor, levied in 1791, had angered frontier farmers because it taxed their most profitable commodity. In the areas west of the Appalachian Mountains, the primary cash crop was liquor distilled from grain or fruit. Such emphasis on distilling reflected a practical problem. Many farmers could not afford to transport bulky crops of corn and rye across the mountains or down the Mississippi River to the seaboard markets. Instead, it was much more profitable to distill liquor from corn and rye or apples and peaches. Unlike grain crops, distilled spirits could be easily stored,

Whiskey Rebellion

George Washington as commander in chief reviews the troops mobilized to quell the Whiskey Rebellion in 1794.

shipped, or sold—and at higher profits. Western farmers were also suspicious of the new federal government in Philadelphia and considered the whiskey tax another part of Hamilton's scheme to pick the pockets of the poor to enrich the pockets of urban speculators. All through the backcountry, from Georgia to Pennsylvania and beyond, the whiskey tax aroused resistance and evasion.

In the summer of 1794, discontent over liquor taxes exploded into open rebellion in western Pennsylvania, where vigilantes, mostly of Scottish or Irish descent, terrorized revenue officers. Rebels robbed the mails, stopped court proceedings, and threatened an assault on Pittsburgh. On August 7, 1794, President Washington issued a proclamation ordering the rebels to disperse and go home and calling out militiamen from Virginia, Maryland, Pennsylvania, and New Jersey. Getting no response from the "Whiskey boys," he ordered the army to suppress the rebellion.

Under the command of General Henry Lee, 13,000 soldiers marched out from Harrisburg, Pennsylvania, across the Allegheny Mountains with Alexander Hamilton in their midst, itching to smite the insurgents. The tax-defying rebels, however, disappeared into the woods. The troops finally captured twenty barefoot, ragged rebels, whom they paraded down Market Street in Philadelphia and clapped into prison. Some of the soldiers regretted not having cornered more of the rebels. As one of the militiamen explained, "We all lament that so few of the insurgents fell—such disorders can only be cured by copious bleedings."

There was, in fact, little bleeding of any kind. One of the captured rebels died in prison. Two were convicted of treason and sentenced to be hanged, but Washington pardoned them on the grounds that one was a "simpleton" and the other "insane." Although President Washington had overreacted, the government had made its point in defense of the rule of law and federal authority. It thereby gained "reputation and strength," according to Alexander Hamilton, by suppressing an elusive rebellion that, in Thomas Jefferson's words, "could never be found." The use of such excessive federal force led many who sympathized with the frontiersmen to become Republicans, however, and Jefferson's party scored heavily in the next Pennsylvania elections.

PINCKNEY'S TREATY   While these stirring events were transpiring in Pennsylvania, Spain was suffering setbacks to its schemes to consolidate its control over Florida and the Louisiana territory. Spain had refused to recognize the legitimacy of America's southern boundary established by the Treaty of Paris in 1783, and its agents thereafter sought to thwart American expansion southward. The Spanish encouraged the Creeks, Choctaws,

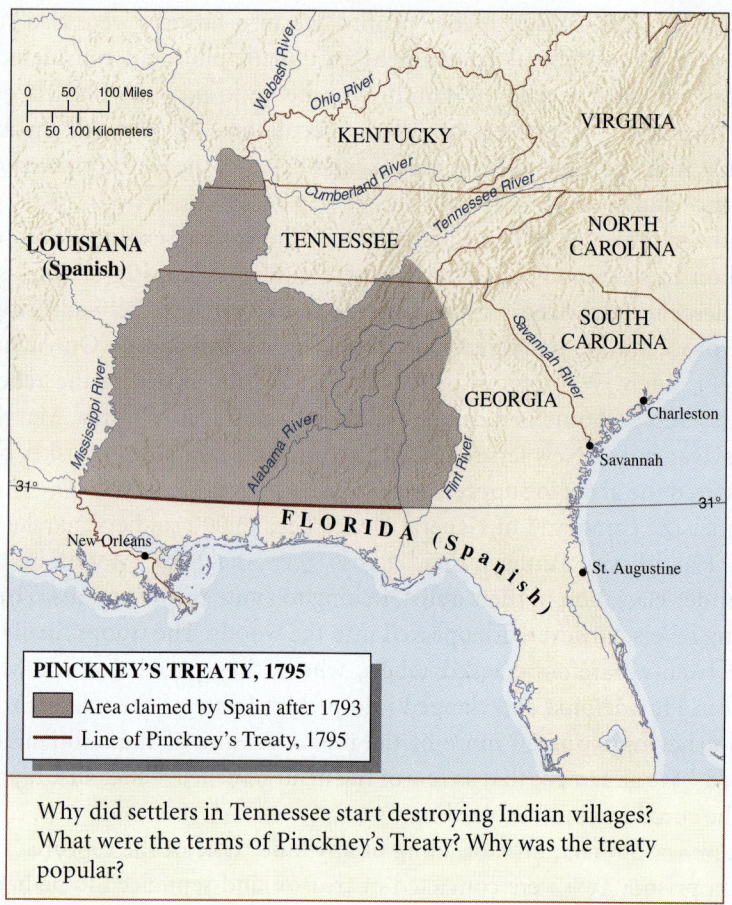

PINCKNEY'S TREATY, 1795

Area claimed by Spain after 1793
Line of Pinckney's Treaty, 1795

Why did settlers in Tennessee start destroying Indian villages? What were the terms of Pinckney's Treaty? Why was the treaty popular?

Chickasaws, and Cherokees to create the same terror and turmoil for American settlers as the British had fomented along the Ohio River.

In the mid-1790s, however, the shifting balance of power in Europe led Spain to end its designs on America. This change of heart resulted in Pinckney's Treaty, by which the U.S. ambassador, Thomas Pinckney, pulled off a diplomatic triumph in 1795 when he won Spanish acceptance of an American boundary at the 31st parallel, open access to the Mississippi River, the right to transport goods to New Orleans without having to pay customs duties for a period of three years (with promise of renewal), a commission to settle American claims against Spain, and a promise on each side to refrain from inciting Indian attacks on the other. Pinckney's Treaty was immensely popular, especially among westerners eager to use the Mississippi River to transport crops to market.

SETTLEMENT OF NEW LAND

Now that John Jay and Thomas Pinckney had settled matters with Britain and Spain and General Anthony Wayne in the Northwest had suppressed Indian resistance, a renewed surge of settlers headed for the West. New lands, ceded by the Indians in the Treaty of Greenville, revealed a Congress once again divided on the issue of federal land policy. There were two basic viewpoints on the matter: that federal lands should serve mainly as a source of revenue and that it was essential to get the western territories settled quickly, an endeavor that required low land prices. Policy would evolve from the first to the second viewpoint, but for the time being the federal government's need for revenue took priority.

LAND POLICY   Opinions on land policy, like opinions on other issues, separated Federalists from Republicans. The more influential Federalists, such as Hamilton and Jay, preferred to build the population of the eastern states first, lest the East lose both political influence and a labor force important to the growth of manufactures. Men of their persuasion favored high federal land prices to enrich the Treasury and the sale of relatively large parcels of land to speculators rather than small tracts to settlers. Jefferson and Madison were reluctantly prepared to go along with such a land policy for the sake of reducing the national debt, but Jefferson yearned for a plan by which the land could be settled more readily by common folk. In any case, he suggested, frontiersmen would do as they had done before: "They will settle the lands in spite of everybody." The pioneers of the West, always moving out beyond the settlers and the surveyors, were already proving him right.

The Federalist land policy prevailed in the Land Act of 1796, which retained the 640-acre minimum size mandated by the Northwest Ordinance of 1787 while doubling the price per acre to $2 and requiring that the full amount be paid within a year. Such terms were well beyond the means of most settlers and even many speculators. As a result, by 1800 federal land offices had sold fewer than 50,000 acres. Continuing demands for cheaper land led to the Land Act of 1800, which reduced the minimum unit to 320 acres and spread payments over four years. The Land Act of 1804 further reduced the minimum parcel to 160 acres, which became the traditional homestead, and lowered the price per acre to $1.64.

THE WILDERNESS ROAD   The lure of western lands led thousands of settlers to follow pathfinder Daniel Boone into the territory known as Kentucky, or Kaintuck, from the Cherokee name Ken-Ta-Ke (Great Meadow). In

The Wilderness Road

Daniel Boone Escorting Settlers through the Cumberland Gap by George Caleb Bingham.

the late eighteenth century the Indian land in Kentucky was a farmer's fantasy and a hunter's paradise, with its fertile soil and abundant forests teeming with buffalo, deer, and wild turkeys.

Boone himself was the product of a pioneer background. Born on a small farm in 1734 in central Pennsylvania, the son of hardworking Quakers, he moved with his family to western North Carolina in 1750. There Boone emerged as the region's greatest hunter, trading animal skins for salt and other household goods. After hearing numerous reports about the territory over the mountains, Boone set out alone in 1769 to find a trail into Kentucky. Armed with a long rifle, tomahawk, and hunting knife, he found what was called the Warriors' Path, a narrow foot trail that buffalo, deer, and Indians had worn along the steep ridges. It took him through the Cumberland Gap, in southwestern Virginia.

In 1773, Boone led the first group of settlers through the Appalachian Mountains at the Cumberland Gap. Two years later he and thirty woodsmen used axes to widen the Warriors' Path into what became known as the Wilderness Road, a passage that more than 300,000 settlers would use over the next twenty-five years. At a point where a branch of the Wilderness Road intersected with the Kentucky River, near what is now Lexington, Boone built a settlement that was named Boonesborough.

A steady stream of settlers, mostly Scotch-Irish from Pennsylvania, Virginia, and North Carolina, poured into Kentucky during the last quarter of the eighteenth century. That they were trespassing on Indian lands did not faze them. The backcountry pioneers came on foot or horseback, often leading a mule or a cow that carried their few tools and other possessions. On a good day they might cover fifteen miles. Near a creek or spring they would buy a parcel or stake out a claim and mark its boundaries by chopping notches into "witness trees." They would then build a lean-to for temporary shelter and clear the land for planting. The pioneers grew melons, beans, turnips, and other vegetables, but corn was the preferred crop because it kept well and had so many uses. Pigs provided pork, and cows supplied milk, butter, and cheese. Many of the frontier families also built crude stills to manufacture a potent whiskey they called corn likker.

TRANSFER OF POWER

By 1796, President Washington had decided that two terms in office were enough. Weary of the increasingly bitter political quarrels and the venom of the partisan press, he was ready to retire to Mount Vernon, his beloved home in northern Virginia. He would leave behind a formidable record of achievement: the organization of a national government with demonstrated power, the establishment of the national credit and a growing economy, the settlement of territory previously held by Britain and Spain, the stabilization of the northwestern frontier, and the admission of three new states: Vermont (1791), Kentucky (1792), and Tennessee (1796).

WASHINGTON'S FAREWELL President George Washington's farewell address to the nation focused on domestic policy and, in particular, on the need for unity among Americans in backing their new government. Washington decried the "baneful effects" of sectionalism and partisanship while acknowledging that parties were "useful checks upon the administration of the government, and serve to keep alive the spirit of liberty."

In foreign relations, he asserted, the United States should display "good faith and justice toward all nations" and avoid either "an habitual hatred or an habitual fondness" for other countries. The young nation should also "steer clear of permanent alliances with any portion of the foreign world." This statement drew little notice at the time, but it proved profoundly important in shaping American attitudes toward foreign policy for generations thereafter. Later spokesmen for an isolationist policy would distort Washington's position by claiming that he had opposed any "entangling alliances." On the contrary, Washington was not preaching isolationism; he was instead warning against any further permanent arrangements like the one with France, still technically in effect. Washington recognized that "we may safely trust to temporary alliances for extraordinary emergencies." The first president's warning against permanent foreign entanglements served as a fundamental principle in U.S. foreign policy until the early twentieth century.

THE ELECTION OF 1796 With George Washington out of the race, the United States in 1796 held its first partisan election for president. The logical choice of the Federalists would have been Washington's protégé, Alexander Hamilton, the chief architect of their programs. But Hamilton's policies had left scars and made enemies. In Philadelphia a caucus of Federalist congressmen chose John Adams of Massachusetts as their heir apparent, with Thomas Pinckney of South Carolina, fresh from his treaty negotiations in Spain, as the nominee for vice president. As expected, the Republicans drafted Thomas Jefferson and added geographic balance to the ticket with Senator Aaron Burr of New York.

The campaign of 1796 was intensely partisan. Republicans caricatured John Adams as "His Rotundity" because of his short, paunchy physique. They also labeled him a pro-British monarchist. The Federalists countered that Jefferson was a French-loving atheist eager to incite another war with Great Britain. They also charged that the philosophical Jefferson was unsuited to executive leadership; he was not decisive enough. The growing strength of the Republicans, fueled by the smoldering resentment of Jay's Treaty, very nearly swept Jefferson into office and perhaps would have but for the French ambassador's public appeals for Jefferson's election—an action that backfired. The Federalists won a majority among the electors, but Alexander Hamilton hatched an impulsive scheme that nearly threw the election away after all. Thomas Pinckney, Hamilton thought, would be easier to influence than would the strong-minded Adams. He therefore sought to have the South Carolina Federalists withhold a few votes for Adams and bring Pinckney in first. The Carolinians cooperated, but New Englanders got wind of the scheme and dropped Pinckney. The upshot of Hamilton's failed scheme was to cut Pinckney out of both the presidency and the vice presidency and elect Jefferson as vice president with 68 electoral votes to Adams's 71.

THE ADAMS YEARS

Vain and cantankerous, John Adams had crafted a distinguished career as a Massachusetts lawyer, as a leader in the Revolutionary movement, as the hardest-working member of the Continental Congress, as a diplomat in France, Holland, and Britain, and as George Washington's vice president. His political philosophy fell somewhere between Jefferson's and Hamilton's. He shared neither the one's faith in the common people nor the other's fondness for an aristocracy of "paper wealth." He favored the classic republican balance of aristocratic, democratic, and monarchical elements in government. A man of powerful intellect and forthright convictions, Adams was haunted by the feeling that he was never properly appreciated—and he may have been right. On the overriding issue of his administration, war and peace, he kept his head when others about him were losing theirs—probably at the cost of his reelection.

THE WAR WITH FRANCE   As the nation's second president, Adams faced the daunting task of succeeding the most popular man in America. He inherited George Washington's divided cabinet—there was as yet no precedent for changing personnel at the start of each new administration. Adams also inherited a menacing quarrel with France, a by-product of Jay's Treaty. When Jay accepted the British demand that food and naval products, as well as war supplies, bound for enemy ports be considered contraband subject to seizure, the French reasoned that American cargo headed for British ports was subject to the same interpretation. The French loosed their corsairs on American ships with an even more devastating effect than the British had in 1793–1794. By the time of Adams's inauguration, in 1797, the French had plundered some 300 American ships and broken diplomatic relations with the United States.

President Adams immediately acted to restore relations with France. In 1797, Charles Cotesworth Pinckney (brother of Thomas) sailed for Paris with John Marshall, a Virginia Federalist, and Elbridge Gerry, a Massachusetts Republican, for further negotiations. After long, nagging delays the three commissioners were accosted by three French officials (whom Adams labeled X, Y, and Z in his report to Congress). The French diplomats said that negotiations could begin only if the Americans paid a bribe of $250,000 to the French government.

Such bribes were common eighteenth-century diplomatic practice, but the American answer, according to the commissioners' report, was "no, no, not a sixpence." When the so-called XYZ affair was reported in Congress and the press, the response was translated into the more stirring slogan "Millions for defense but not one cent for tribute." Even the most partisan

John Adams

Political philosopher and politician, Adams was the first president to take up residence in the White House, in early 1801.

Republicans, except for Thomas Jefferson, were hard put to make any more excuses for the French, and many of them joined the chorus for war. An undeclared naval war in fact raged from 1798 to 1800, but Adams resisted a formal declaration of war. Congress, however, authorized the capture of armed French ships, suspended commerce with France, and renounced the 1778 Treaty of Alliance, which was already defunct.

Adams used the French crisis to strengthen American defenses. In 1798, Congress created a Department of the Navy, and by the end of 1799 the number of naval ships had increased from three to thirty-three. By then American ships had captured eight French vessels and secured America's overseas commerce.

By the fall of 1798, even before the naval war was fully under way, the French foreign minister, Charles-Maurice de Talleyrand, had begun to make peace overtures. Adams named three peace commissioners, who arrived in Paris to find themselves confronting a new government under First Consul Napoléon Bonaparte. They sought two objectives: $20 million to pay for the

Conflict with France

A cartoon indicating the anti-French sentiment generated by the XYZ affair. The three American negotiators (at left) reject the Paris Monster's demand for money.

American ships seized by the French and the formal cancellation of the 1778 Treaty of Alliance. By the Convention of 1800, ratified in 1801, the French agreed only to terminate the alliance and the quasi war.

THE WAR AT HOME   The simmering naval conflict with France mirrored an ideological war at home between Federalists and Republicans. Already-heated partisan politics had begun boiling over during the latter years of Washington's administration. The rhetoric grew so personal that opponents commonly resorted to duels. Federalists and Republicans saw each other as traitors to the principles of the American Revolution. Thomas Jefferson, for example, decided that Alexander Hamilton, George Washington, John Adams, and other Federalists were suppressing individual liberty in order to promote selfish interests. He adamantly opposed Jay's Treaty because it was pro-British and anti-French, and he was disgusted by the army's suppression of the Whiskey Rebellion.

Such volatile issues forced Americans to take sides, and the Revolutionary generation of leaders, a group that John Adams had called the band of brothers, began to fragment into die-hard factions. Long-standing political friendships disintegrated amid the venomous partisan attacks and sectional divisions between North and South. Jefferson observed that a "wall of separation" had come to divide the nation's political leaders. "Politics and party hatreds," he wrote his daughter from the nation's capital, "destroy the happiness of every being here."

Jefferson was no innocent in the matter; his no-holds-barred tactics contributed directly to the partisan tensions. As vice president under Adams, he displayed a gracious deviousness. He led the Republican faction opposed to Adams and schemed to embarrass him. In 1797, Jefferson secretly hired a rogue journalist, James Callender, to produce a scurrilous pamphlet that described President Adams as a deranged monarchist intent upon naming himself king.

For his part the combative Adams refused to align himself completely with the Federalists, preferring instead to mimic George Washington

THE PROVIDENTIAL DETECTION

The partisan divide

The war with France deepened the division between the Federalists and Republicans.

and retain his independence as chief executive. He was too principled and too prickly to toe a party line. Soon after his election he invited Jefferson to join him in creating a bipartisan administration. After all, they had worked well together in the Continental Congress and in France, and they harbored great respect for each other. After consulting with James Madison, however, Jefferson refused to accept the new president's offer. Within a year he and Adams were at each other's throats.

The conflict with France deepened the partisan divide emerging in the young United States. The real purpose of the French crisis all along, the more ardent Republicans suspected, was to provide Federalists with an excuse to suppress their American opponents. The infamous Alien and Sedition Acts of 1798 lent credence to their suspicions. These and two other measures, passed amid the wave of patriotic war fever, limited freedom of speech and the press and the liberty of aliens. Proposed by extreme Federalists in Congress, the legislation did not originate with John Adams but had his blessing. Goaded by his wife, Abigail, his primary counselor, Adams signed the controversial statutes and in doing so made the greatest mistake of his presidency. By succumbing to the partisan hysteria and enacting the vindictive acts, Adams bore out what Benjamin Franklin had said about him years before: he "means well for his country, is always an honest man, often a wise one, but sometimes and in some things, absolutely out of his senses."

Three of the four repressive acts engineered by the Federalists reflected native hostility to foreigners, especially the French and the Irish, a large number of whom had become active Republicans and were suspected of revolutionary intent. The Naturalization Act extended from five to fourteen years the residency requirement for citizenship. The Alien Act empowered the president to deport "dangerous" aliens at his discretion. The Alien Enemies Act authorized the president in time of declared war to expel or imprison enemy aliens at will. Finally, the Sedition Act defined as a high misdemeanor any conspiracy against legal measures of the government, including interference with federal officers and insurrection or rioting. What is more, the law forbade writing, publishing, or speaking anything of "a false, scandalous and malicious" nature against the government.

The purpose of such laws was transparently partisan, designed to punish Republicans. Of the ten convictions under the act, all were directed at Republicans, some for trivial matters. In the very first case a drunk Republican was fined $100 for wishing out loud that the wad of a salute cannon might hit President Adams in his rear. The few convictions under the act only created martyrs to the cause of freedom of speech and the press and exposed the vindictiveness of Federalist judges.

To offset the "reign of witches" unleashed by the Alien and Sedition Acts, Jefferson and Madison drafted the Kentucky and Virginia Resolutions. These passed the legislatures of their respective states in late 1798. The resolutions, much alike in their arguments, denounced the Alien and Sedition Acts as "alarming infractions" of constitutional rights and advanced the state-compact theory: since the Constitution arose as a compact among the states, the resolutions argued, it followed that the states retained the right to say when Congress had exceeded its powers. The states could "interpose" their judgment on acts of Congress and "nullify" them if necessary.

These doctrines of interposition and nullification, reworked by later theorists, were destined to be used for causes unforeseen by their authors. At the time, it seems, both Jefferson and Madison intended the resolutions to serve chiefly as propaganda, the opening guns in the presidential campaign of 1800. Neither Kentucky nor Virginia took steps to nullify or interpose its authority in the enforcement of the Alien and Sedition Acts. Instead, both called upon the other states to help them win a repeal in Congress. In Virginia, citizens talked of armed resistance to the federal government.

REPUBLICAN VICTORY   As the presidential election of 1800 approached, civil unrest boiled over. Grievances mounted against Federalist policies: taxation to support an unneeded army, the Alien and Sedition Acts, the lingering fears of John Adams's affinity for "monarchism," the hostilities aroused by Alexander Hamilton's economic programs, the suppression of the Whiskey Rebellion, and Jay's Treaty. When Adams opted for peace with France in 1800, he probably doomed his one chance for reelection. Only a wave of patriotic war fever with a united party behind him could have gained him victory at the polls. His decision for peace gained him much goodwill among Americans but left the Hamiltonians angry and his party divided.

In 1800 the Federalists summoned enough unity to name Adams and Charles Cotesworth Pinckney as their candidates. But the Hamiltonian Federalists continued to snipe at the president and his policies, and soon after his renomination Adams removed two of them from his cabinet. A furious Hamilton struck back with a pamphlet questioning Adams's fitness to be president, citing his "disgusting egotism." Intended for private distribution among Federalist leaders, the pamphlet reached the hands of Aaron Burr, who circulated it widely.

Jefferson and Burr, as the Republican presidential candidates, once again represented the alliance of Virginia and New York. Jefferson, perhaps even more than Adams, became the target of vitriolic abuse. Opponents labeled him an atheist and a supporter of the excesses of the French Revolution. Jefferson refused to answer the attacks and directed the campaign from his Virginia home at Monticello. He was portrayed as a friend to farmers and a champion of states' rights, frugal government, liberty, and peace.

John Adams proved more popular than his party, whose candidates generally fared worse than the president, but the Republicans edged him out by 73 electoral votes to 65. The decisive states were New York and South Carolina, either of which might have given the victory to Adams. But in New York former senator Aaron Burr's organization won control of the legislature, which cast the electoral votes. In South Carolina, Charles Pinckney (cousin of the Federalist Pinckneys) won over the legislature with well-placed promises of Republican patronage. Still, the result was not final, for Jefferson and Burr had tied with 73 votes each, and the choice of the president was thrown into the House of Representatives, where Federalist diehards tried vainly to give the election to Burr. This was too much for Hamilton, who opposed Jefferson but held a much lower opinion of Burr. The stalemate in the House continued for thirty-five ballots. The deadlock was broken only when a Jefferson supporter assured a Federalist congressman from Delaware that Jefferson, if elected, would refrain from the wholesale removal of Federalists appointed to federal offices and would uphold Hamilton's financial policies. The representative resolved to vote for Jefferson, and several other Federalists agreed simply to cast blank ballots, permitting Jefferson to win without any of them having to vote for him.

Before the Federalists relinquished power to the Jeffersonian Republicans on March 4, 1801, their lame-duck Congress passed the Judiciary Act of 1801. Intended to ensure Federalist control of the judicial system, this act created sixteen federal circuit courts with a new judge for each and increased the number of federal attorneys, clerks, and marshals. Before he left office, Adams named John Marshall to the vacant office of chief justice of the Supreme Court and appointed Federalists to all the new positions in the federal judiciary, including forty-two justices of the peace for the new District of Columbia. The Federalists, defeated and destined never to regain national power, had in the words of Jefferson "retired into the judiciary as a stronghold."

The election of 1800 marked a major turning point in American political history. It was the first time that one political party, however ungracefully, relinquished power to the opposition party. Jefferson's victory signaled the emergence of a new, more democratic political system, dominated by parties, partisanship, and wider public participation—at least among white men. Before and immediately after independence, politics was a popular but undemocratic activity: people took a keen interest in public affairs, but

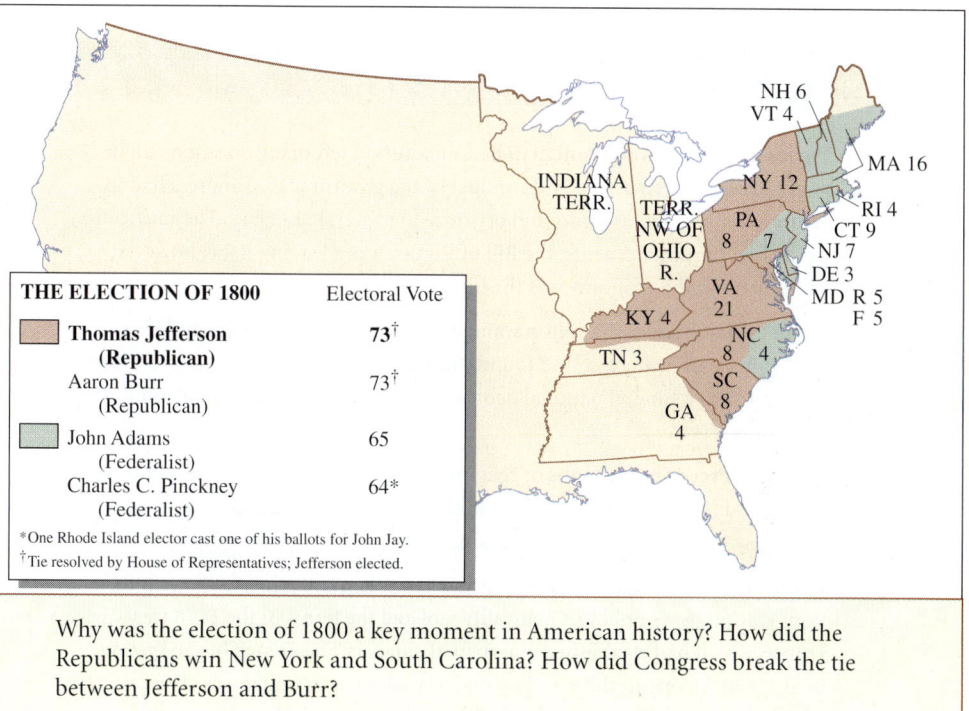

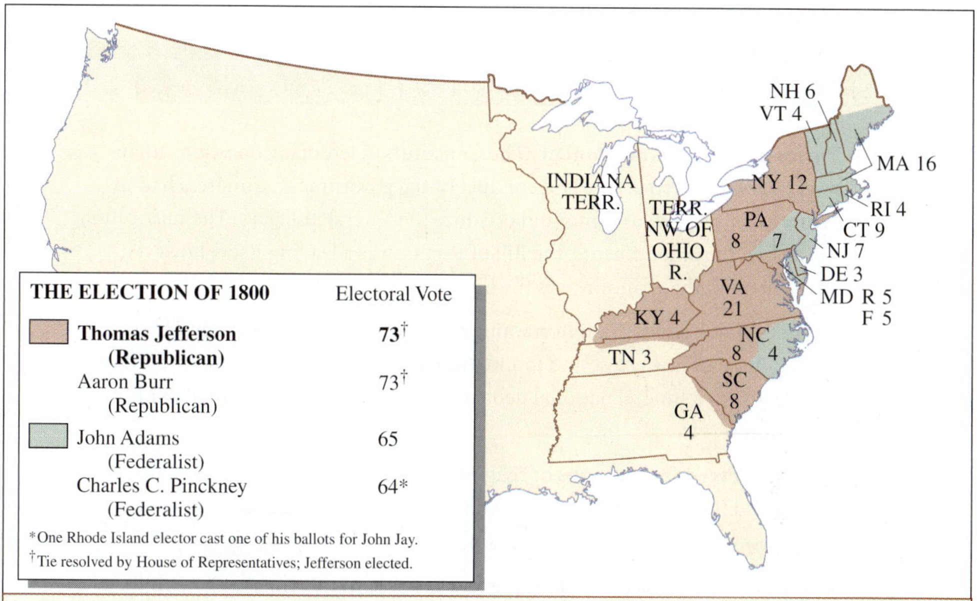
INDIANA TERR.
TERR. NW OF OHIO R.
NH 6
VT 4
MA 16
NY 12
RI 4
CT 9
PA 8 7
NJ 7
DE 3
MD R 5 F 5
VA 21
KY 4
NC 8 4
TN 3
SC 8
GA 4
THE ELECTION OF 1800
Electoral Vote
Thomas Jefferson (Republican) 73†
Aaron Burr (Republican) 73†
John Adams (Federalist) 65
Charles C. Pinckney (Federalist) 64*
*One Rhode Island elector cast one of his ballots for John Jay.
†Tie resolved by House of Representatives; Jefferson elected.

Why was the election of 1800 a key moment in American history? How did the Republicans win New York and South Carolina? How did Congress break the tie between Jefferson and Burr?

socially prominent families, the "rich, the able, and the wellborn," dominated political life. However, the fierce political battles of the late 1790s, culminating in 1800 with Jefferson's election, wrested control of politics from the governing elite and established the right of more people to play an active role in governing the young republic. With the gradual elimination of property qualifications for voting and the proliferation of newspapers, pamphlets, and other publications, the "public sphere" in which political issues were debated and decided expanded enormously in the early nineteenth century.

John Adams regretted the democratization of politics and the rise of fractious partisanship. "Jefferson had a party, Hamilton had a party, but the commonwealth had none," he sighed. The defeated president was so distraught at the turn of events that he decided not to participate in Jefferson's inauguration in the new capital of Washington, D.C. Instead, he boarded a stagecoach for the 500-mile trip to his home in Quincy, Massachusetts. He and Jefferson would not communicate for the next twelve years.

CHAPTER SUMMARY

- **Formation of the Government** The Constitution left many questions unanswered about the structure and conduct of the government. Congress had to create executive departments and organize the federal judiciary. The ratification of the first ten amendments, the Bill of Rights, was a leading issue; however, strengthening the economy was the highest priority.

- **Hamiltonian Vision** Hamilton wanted to create a vibrant economy. He succeeded in establishing a sound foundation for American capitalism by crafting a budget with a funded national debt, a federal tax system, a national bank, and a customs service.

- **Religious Freedom** In terms of religion, the Constitution does not mention a deity and the First Amendment guarantees people the right to worship freely, regardless of their religious persuasion.

- **Neutrality** With the outbreak of European-wide war during the French Revolution, Washington's policy of neutrality violated the terms of the 1778 treaty with France, which had established a perpetual alliance. The French began seizing British and American ships and an undeclared war was under way. The resulting unrest contributed to the creation of the first two political parties: Hamiltonian Federalists and Jeffersonian Republicans.

- **Jeffersonian Vision** James Madison and Thomas Jefferson became increasingly critical of Hamilton's policies, which favored a strong federal government and weaker state governments. Jefferson, on the other hand, championed an agrarian vision, in which independent small farmers were the backbone of American society. He feared that the growth of cities would enrich the aristocracy and widen divisions between the rich and the poor.

CHRONOLOGY

KEY TERMS & NAMES

9

THE EARLY REPUBLIC

FOCUS QUESTIONS

 wwnorton.com/studyspace

- What were the main achievements of Jefferson's administration?
- What was the impact of the Marshall court on the U.S. government?
- How did the Louisiana Purchase change the United States?
- What were the causes of the War of 1812?
- What were the effects of the War of 1812?

The early years of the new American republic laid the foundation for the nation's development as the first society in the world organized around the promise of equal opportunity for all—except African Americans, Native Americans, and women. Americans in the fifty years after independence were on the move and on the make. Their prospects seemed unlimited, their optimism unrestrained. Land sales west of the Appalachian Mountains soared in the early nineteenth century as aspiring farmers shoved Indians aside in order to establish homesteads of their own. Enterprising, mobile, and increasingly diverse in religion and national origin, thousands of ordinary folk uprooted themselves from settled communities and went west in search of personal advancement, occupying more territory in a single generation than had been settled in the 150 years of colonial history. Between 1800 and 1820 the trans-Appalachian population soared from 300,000 to 2 million. By 1840, over 40 percent of Americans lived west of the Appalachians in eight new states.

The migrants flowed westward in three streams between 1780 and 1830. One ran from the Old South—Maryland, Virginia, and the Carolinas—through Georgia into the newer states of Alabama and Mississippi. Another wave traversed the Blue Ridge Mountains from Maryland and Virginia, crossing into Kentucky and Tennessee. The third route was in the North, taking New Englanders westward into upstate New York, Pennsylvania, Ohio, and Michigan. Many of the pioneers stayed only a few years before continuing westward in search of cheaper and more fertile land.

The spirit of opportunistic independence affected free blacks as well as whites, Indians as well as immigrants. Free blacks were the fastest-growing segment of the population during the early nineteenth century. Many slaves had gained their freedom during the Revolutionary War, by escaping, joining British forces, or serving in American military units. Every state except South Carolina and Georgia promised freedom to slaves who fought the British. Afterward state after state in the North outlawed slavery, and antislavery societies blossomed, exerting increasing pressure on the South to end the degrading practice.

Pressure of another sort affected the besieged Indian tribes. The westward migration of whites brought incessant conflict with Native Americans. Indians fiercely resisted but ultimately succumbed to a federal government and a federal army determined to displace if not exterminate them. Most whites, however, were less concerned about Indians and slavery than they were about seizing their own opportunities. Politicians ignored or suppressed the volatile issue of slavery; their priorities were elsewhere. Westward expansion, economic growth, urban development, and the democratization of politics preoccupied a generation of Americans born after 1776—especially outside the South. In 1790 nine out of ten Americans lived on the land and engaged in what is called household production; their sphere of activity was local. But with each passing year, farmers increasingly focused on producing surplus crops and livestock to be sold in regional markets. Cotton prices soared, and in the process the Deep South grew ever more committed to a plantation economy dependent upon slave labor, world markets, and New England shippers and merchants. The burgeoning market economy produced boom-and-bust cycles, but overall the years from 1790 to 1830 were quite prosperous, with young Americans experiencing unprecedented opportunities for economic gain and geographic mobility.

While most Americans after the Revolution continued to work as farmers, a growing number of young adults found employment in new or greatly expanded enterprises: textiles, banking, transportation, publishing, retailing, teaching, preaching, medicine, law, construction, and engineering. Techno-logical innovations (steam power, power tools, and new modes of trans-portation) and their social applications (mass communication turnpikes, the postal service, banks, and corporations) fostered an array of new indus-tries and businesses. The emergence of a factory system transformed the nature of work for many Americans. Proud apprentices, journeymen, and master craftsmen, who controlled their labor and stressed quality rather than quantity, resented the proliferation of mills and factories populated by "half-trained" workers dependent upon an hourly wage and subject to the sharp fluctuations of the larger economy.

Young America was rapidly changing. The decentralized agrarian republic of 1776, nestled along the Atlantic seaboard, had become by 1830 a sprawl-ing commercial nation connected by networks of roads and canals and cemented by economic relationships—all animated by a restless spirit of enterprise, experimentation, and expansion.

JEFFERSONIAN SIMPLICITY

On March 4, 1801, the soft-spoken, brilliant, and charming Thomas Jefferson became the first president to be inaugurated in the new federal city. Washington, District of Columbia, was then an array of undistinguished buildings clustered around two centers, Capitol Hill and the executive man-sion. Congress, having met in eight towns since 1774, had at last found a permanent home but enjoyed few amenities. There were two places of amusement, a racetrack and a theater thick with "tobacco smoke, whiskey breaths, and other stenches." Practically deserted much of the year, the na-tion's new capital came to life only when Congress assembled.

Jefferson's inauguration befitted the simple surroundings. The new presi-dent walked two blocks from his lodgings to the unfinished Capitol, entered the Senate chamber, took the oath administered by the recently appointed Chief Justice John Marshall, read his address in a barely audible voice, and returned to his boardinghouse for dinner. A tone of simplicity and concilia-tion ran through Jefferson's inaugural address. "We are all Republicans—we are all Federalists," he assured the nation. He then presented a ringing affir-mation of republican government: "I know, indeed, that some honest men fear that a republican government cannot be strong; that this government is not strong enough. I believe this, on the contrary, the strongest government on earth. I believe it is the only one where every man . . . would meet inva-sions of the public order as his own personal concern."

JEFFERSON IN OFFICE

The deliberate display of republican simplicity at Jefferson's inauguration set the style of his administration. Although a man of expensive personal tastes, he took pains to avoid the monarchical trappings of his Federalist predecessors. Jefferson, a widower, discarded the coach in which Washington and Adams had traveled to state occasions and rode about the city on horseback, often by himself. He continued to wear plain clothes. White House dinners were held at a circular table so that no one should take precedence. This practice infuriated several European diplomats accustomed to aristocratic formalities, and they boycotted White House affairs.

Jefferson called his election the "revolution of 1800," but the electoral margin had been razor thin, and the policies that he followed were more conciliatory than revolutionary. Jefferson placed in policy-making positions men of his own party, and he was the first president to pursue the role of party leader, cultivating congressional support at his dinner parties and elsewhere. In the cabinet the leading figures were Secretary of State James Madison, a longtime neighbor and political ally, and Swiss-born secretary of the Treasury Albert Gallatin, a Pennsylvania Republican whose financial skills had won him the respect of the Federalists. In an effort to cultivate Federalist New England, Jefferson chose men from that region for the positions of attorney general, secretary of war, and postmaster general.

The executive mansion

A watercolor of the president's house during Jefferson's term in office. Jefferson described it as "big enough for two emperors, one pope, and the grand lama in the bargain."

In lesser offices, Jefferson resisted the wholesale removal of Federalists, preferring to wait until vacancies appeared. But pressure from Republicans often forced him to remove Federalists. In one area, however, he managed to remove the offices rather than the appointees. In 1802, Congress repealed the Judiciary Act of 1801 and so abolished the circuit judgeships and other offices to which John Adams had made his "midnight appointments" before leaving office.

MARBURY V. MADISON   The midnight appointments that President Adams made just before he left office sparked the important case of *Marbury v. Madison* (1803), the first in which the Supreme Court asserted its right to declare an act of Congress unconstitutional. The case involved the appointment of the Maryland Federalist William Marbury as justice of the peace in the District of Columbia. Marbury's official letter of appointment, or commission, signed by President Adams just two days before he left office, remained undelivered when James Madison became secretary of state, and President Jefferson directed him to withhold it. Marbury then sued for a court order (a writ of mandamus) directing Madison to deliver his commission. Chief Justice John Marshall, a Virginia Federalist and a distant cousin of Jefferson, whom he despised, wrote the Court's opinion. He held that Marbury deserved his commission but denied that the Court had jurisdiction in the case. Marshall and the court ruled that Section 13 of the Federal Judiciary Act of 1789, which gave the Court original jurisdiction in mandamus proceedings, was unconstitutional because the Constitution specified that the Court should have original jurisdiction only in cases involving ambassadors or states. The Court, therefore, could issue no order in the case. With one bold stroke, the Federalist Marshall had chastised the Jeffersonians while avoiding an awkward confrontation with an administration that might have defied his order. At the same time he established the stunning precedent of the Court's declaring a federal law invalid on the grounds that it violated provisions of the Constitution.

The bitter feud between Thomas Jefferson and John Marshall over the *Marbury* case revealed fundamental divisions in the new United States over the nature of the new nation. Jefferson and other Republicans remained committed to the idea that the individual states should remain the primary agents of political power. In contrast, Marshall and the Federalists insisted that modern nationhood required a powerful central government capable of creating and enforcing laws for all of the American people. Marshall got the better of the argument. During his long tenure as chief justice (1801–1835), which spanned the administrations of five presidents, he established the foundations for American jurisprudence, the authority of the Supreme Court, and the constitutional supremacy of the national government over the states.

DOMESTIC REFORMS   Jefferson's first term produced a succession of triumphs in both domestic and foreign affairs. The president did not set out to discard Alexander Hamilton's Federalist economic program, despite his strident criticism of it. Under the tutelage of Treasury Secretary Gallatin, he learned to accept the national bank as an essential convenience. Jefferson detested Hamilton's belief that a federal debt was a national "blessing" because it gave the bankers and investors who lent money to the U.S. government a direct stake in the success of the new republic. Jefferson believed that a large federal debt would bring only high taxes and government corruption, so he set about reducing government expenses and paying down the debt. In 1802, Jefferson won the repeal of the whiskey tax, much to the relief of backwoods distillers, drinkers, and grain farmers.

Without the revenue from such taxes, frugality was all the more necessary to a federal government chiefly dependent upon its tariffs and the sale of western lands for revenue. Happily for the Treasury, both trade and land sales flourished. The continuing Napoleonic Wars in Europe increased American shipping traffic, and thus tariff revenues padded the Treasury. At the same time, settlers flocked to the western land purchased from the federal government. Ohio's admission to the Union in 1803 increased the number of states to seventeen.

By "wise and frugal government," Jefferson and Gallatin reasoned, the United States could live within its income, like a prudent farmer. The basic formula was simple: cut back on military expenses. A peacetime army menaced a free society anyway. It therefore should be kept to a minimum, with defense left primarily to state militias. The navy, which the Federalists had already reduced, ought to be reduced further. Coastal defense, Jefferson argued, should rely upon land-based fortifications and a "mosquito fleet" of small gunboats.

In 1807, Jefferson crowned his reforms by signing an act that outlawed the foreign slave trade as of January 1, 1808, the earliest date possible under the Constitution. At the time, South Carolina was the only state that still permitted the trade, but for years to come an illegal traffic in Africans would continue. By one informal estimate perhaps 300,000 enslaved blacks were smuggled into southern states between 1808 and 1861.

THE LOUISIANA PURCHASE   In 1803, events produced the greatest single achievement of Jefferson's administration. The Louisiana Purchase was a brilliant diplomatic coup that more than doubled the territory of the United States by bringing into its borders the entire Mississippi River valley west of the river itself, a region from which would be formed six states in their entirety and most or part of nine more.

The French had settled Louisiana in the early eighteenth century, but after their defeat by England in the Seven Years' War they had ceded the territory to Spain, with Great Britain receiving West Florida in exchange. Soon after taking power in France in 1799, however, the audacious general Napoléon Bonaparte had forced the Spanish to return the territory and expressed his intention of creating a North American empire. In 1797, Napoléon had made his first conquest when his army defeated the Austrians in northern Italy. Thereafter, he would build an empire greater than those of Caesar and Charlemagne. He became the most feared man in Europe—and in America. When word of the transfer of Louisiana from Spain to France reached Washington, D.C., in 1801, Jefferson dispatched the New Yorker Robert R. Livingston, as the new American minister to France. Spain in control of the Mississippi River outlet was bad enough, but the power-hungry Napoléon in control could mean serious trouble.

Livingston engaged the French in a series of long and frustrating negotiations. In April 1803, Napoléon's foreign minister suddenly asked if the United States would like to buy the whole of Louisiana. Livingston snapped up the offer. Napoléon was willing to sell the Louisiana Territory because his French army in Haiti had been decimated not only by a slave revolt but also by yellow fever. Some 24,000 soldiers died on the island. Having failed to conquer the sugar-rich island and eager to renew his struggle against England, Napoléon had apparently decided simply to cut his losses in the New World, turn a quick profit, please the Americans, and go back to reshaping the map of Europe.

By the Treaty of Cession, dated April 30, 1803, the United States paid about $15 million for the huge territory. The surprising turn of events presented President Jefferson with a "noble bargain"—and a constitutional dilemma. Nowhere did the Constitution mention the purchase of territory. Jefferson at first suggested a constitutional amendment, but his advisers argued against delay lest Napoléon change his mind. The power to purchase territory, they reasoned, resided in the power to make treaties. In the end, Jefferson relented, trusting, he said, "that the good sense of our country will correct the evil of loose construction when it shall produce ill effects." Jefferson's bold decision to swallow his constitutional scruples and acquire the vast Louisiana Territory proved to be one of the most important factors shaping America's development. New England Federalists boggled at the prospect of new western

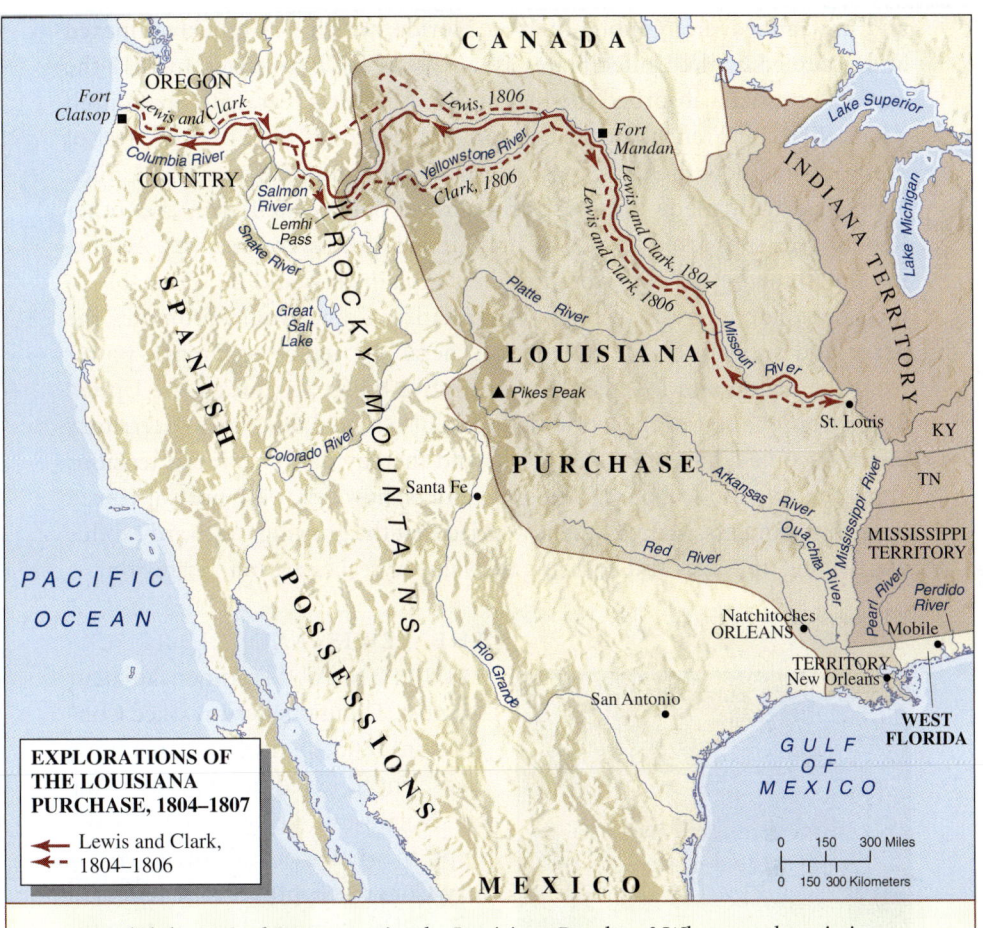

How did the United States acquire the Louisiana Purchase? What was the mission of Lewis and Clark's expedition? What were the consequences of Lewis and Clark's reports about the western territory?

states that would probably strengthen the Jeffersonian party. In a reversal that foreshadowed many similar reversals on constitutional issues, Federalists found themselves arguing for strict construction of the Constitution while Republicans brushed aside such scruples. Gaining some 875,000 square miles of valuable territory trumped any legal concerns. The Senate ratified the treaty by an overwhelming vote of 26 to 6, and on December 20, 1803, U.S. representatives took formal possession of the Louisiana Territory.

The Spanish kept West Florida, but within a decade it would be ripe for the plucking. American settlers in 1810 staged a rebellion in Baton Rouge and proclaimed the republic of West Florida, which was quickly annexed and occupied by the United States as far east as the Pearl River. In 1812 the state of Louisiana absorbed the region. The following year, with Spain itself a battlefield for French and British forces, U.S. troops took over the rest of West Florida, now the Gulf coast of Mississippi and Alabama. The United States had truly made the most of a shrewd bargain. Jefferson and other Republicans supported the Louisiana Purchase for several reasons. Acquiring the immense territory, the president explained, would be "favorable to the immediate interests of our Western citizens" and would promote "the peace and security of the nation in general" by removing French power from the region and by creating a protective buffer separating the United States from the rest of the world. Jefferson also hoped that the new territory might become a haven for free blacks and thereby diminish racial tensions along the Atlantic seaboard. New Englanders, however, were not convinced by such arguments. Many of them worried that the growing westward exodus was driving up wages and lowering the value of real estate in their region.

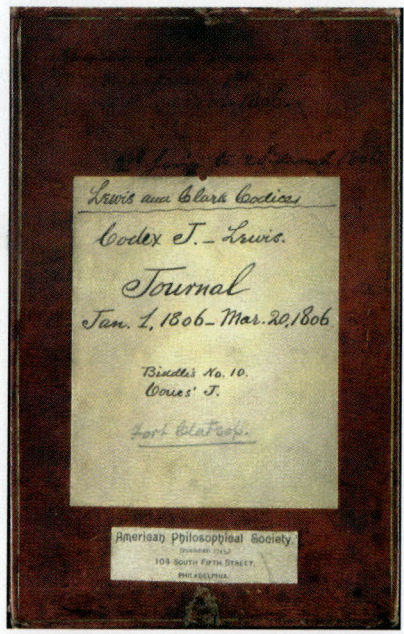

One of Lewis and Clark's journals
Lewis and Clark kept detailed journals during their entire journey.

THE LEWIS AND CLARK EXPEDITION A longtime amateur scientist, Thomas Jefferson asked Congress in 1803 to finance a mapping and scientific expedition to explore the far Northwest, beyond the Mississippi, in what was still foreign territory. Congress approved, and Jefferson assigned as commanders the twenty-nine-year-old Meriwether Lewis, his former private secretary, and another Virginian, a former army officer, William Clark.

In 1804 the "Corps of Discovery," numbering nearly fifty, set out from the small village of St. Louis to ascend the muddy Missouri River. Local Indians introduced them to clothes made from deer hides, taught them hunting techniques, and traded horses. Lewis and Clark kept detailed journals of their travels and drew maps of the unexplored regions. As they moved up the Missouri, the landscape changed from forest to prairie grass. They saw immense herds of bison and other large game animals. The expedition passed trappers and traders headed south with rafts and boats laden with furs. Six months after leaving St. Louis, near the Mandan Sioux villages in what is now North Dakota, they built a fort and wintered in relative comfort, sending back a barge loaded with maps, soil samples, and plant and animal specimens. In the spring they added to their main party a French guide and his remarkable young Shoshone wife, Sacagawea, who provided crucial help as a guide, translator, and negotiator. At the head of the Missouri River, the expedition took the north fork, thenceforth named the Jefferson River, crossed the rugged Rocky Mountains, braved attacks by grizzly bears, and in canoes descended the Snake and Columbia Rivers to the Pacific. The following spring they split into two parties, with Lewis heading back east by almost the same route and Clark going by way of the Yellowstone River. They reunited at the juncture of the Missouri and Yellowstone Rivers, returning together to St. Louis in 1806, having been gone nearly two and a half years and having traversed over 8,000 miles. No longer was the Far West unknown country. Their reports of friendly Indians and abundant beaver

One of Lewis and Clark's maps

In their journals, Lewis and Clark sketched detailed maps of unexplored regions.

pelts attracted traders and trappers to the region and gave the United States a claim to the Oregon Country by right of discovery and exploration.

Exploring the far Northwest

Captain Clark and His Men Shooting Bears, from a book of engravings of the Lewis and Clark expedition (ca. 1810).

POLITICAL SCHEMES President Jefferson's policies, including the Louisiana Purchase, brought him solid support in the South and the West. Even New Englanders were moving to his side. By 1809, John Quincy Adams, the son of the second president, would become a Republican. Other Federalists panicked. The acquisition of vast new territories in the West would reduce New England and the Federalist party to insignificance in political affairs. Under the leadership of Timothy Pickering, secretary of state under Washington and Adams and now a U.S. senator, a group of bitter Massachusetts Federalists, called the Essex Junto, considered seceding from the Union, an idea that would simmer in New England for another decade.

Timothy Pickering and other Federalists also hatched a scheme that involved Vice President Aaron Burr, a prominent New Yorker who had been on the outs with the Jeffersonians. Their plan, which would link New York with New England and depended upon Burr's election as governor of New York, could not win the support of even the extreme Federalists: Alexander Hamilton bitterly opposed it on the grounds that Burr was "a dangerous man, and one who ought not to be trusted with the reins of government."

Those remarks led to Hamilton's famous duel with Burr in July 1804 at Weehawken, New Jersey, across the Hudson River from New York City. Hamilton personally opposed dueling, but his romantic streak and sense of manly honor compelled him to meet the vice president's challenge and demonstrate his courage—he was determined not to kill his opponent. Burr had no such scruples; he shot Hamilton through the heart. Hamilton's death ended both Pickering's scheme and Burr's political career—but not Burr's intrigues. Burr would lose the gubernatorial election.

In the meantime, the presidential campaign of 1804 began when a Republican congressional caucus renominated Jefferson. Opposed by the Federalist Charles C. Pinckney, Jefferson won 162 of the 176 electoral votes. It was the first landslide election in American history.

DIVISIONS IN THE REPUBLICAN PARTY

JOHN RANDOLPH AND THE OLD REPUBLICANS Freed from a strong opposition—Federalists made up only a quarter of the new Congress—the Republican majority began to lose its cohesion as the nineteenth century progressed. The Virginia congressman known as John Randolph of Roanoke, initially a Jefferson supporter, became the most conspicuous of the dissidents. A brilliant, witty, but erratic and unyielding Virginia planter-philosopher, he was a powerful combination of principle, intelligence, wit, arrogance, and rancor.

Randolph became the crusty spokesman for a shifting group of "Old Republicans," whose adherence to party principles had rendered them more Jeffersonian than Jefferson himself. The Old Republicans were mostly southerners who defended states' rights and strict construction of the Constitution. They opposed any compromise with the Federalists and promoted an agrarian way of life. The Jeffersonian, or moderate, Republicans tended to be more pragmatic and nationalist in their orientation. As Thomas Jefferson himself demonstrated, they were willing to go along with tariffs on imports and a national bank. Randolph broke with Jefferson in 1806, when the president sought an appropriation of $2 million for a thinly disguised bribe to win French influence in persuading Spain to give up the Floridas. Thereafter he resisted Jefferson's initiatives almost reflexively. Randolph and his colleagues were sometimes called Quids, or the Tertium Quid (Third Something), and their dissent gave rise to talk of a third party, neither Republican nor Federalist. But they never got together, and their failure would typify the experience of almost all third-party movements thereafter.

THE BURR CONSPIRACY For all of his public popularity, Jefferson in some quarters aroused intense opposition. New Yorker Aaron Burr, for example, hated the president. Sheer brilliance and shrewdness had carried

Aaron Burr to the vice presidency, and he might have become Jefferson's heir apparent but for his taste for conspiracies. Caught up in the dubious schemes of Federalist diehards in 1800 and again in 1804, he ended his political career when he killed Alexander Hamilton. Indicted in New York and New Jersey for murder and heavily in debt, Burr fled first to Spanish-held Florida. Once the furor subsided, the vice president boldly returned to Washington in November to preside over the Senate. As long as he stayed out of New York and New Jersey, he was safe from arrest.

But Burr focused his attention less on the Senate than on a cockeyed scheme to carve out a personal empire for himself in the West. The so-called Burr conspiracy originated when Burr met with General James Wilkinson, an old friend with a tainted Revolutionary War record who was a spy for the Spanish and had a penchant for easy money, a taste for rum, and an eye for intrigue. Just what Wilkinson and Burr were up to will probably never be known. The most likely explanation is that they sought to organize a secession of the Louisiana Territory and set up an independent republic. Wilkinson developed cold feet, however, and sent a letter to President Jefferson warning of "a deep, dark, wicked and wide-spread conspiracy." Traveling south to recruit adventurers, Burr was apprehended and taken to Richmond, Virginia, for a trial that, like the conspiracy, had a stellar cast. Charged with treason, Burr was brought before Chief Justice John Marshall.

The case established two major constitutional precedents. The first came about when Jefferson, on the grounds of executive privilege, ignored a subpoena requiring him to appear in court with certain papers. He believed that the independence of the executive branch would be compromised if the president were subject to a court writ. The second was Marshall's rigid definition of treason. Treason under the Constitution, Marshall concluded, consisted of "levying war against the United States or adhering to their enemies" and required "two witnesses to the same overt act." Since the prosecution failed to produce two witnesses to an overt act of treason by Burr, the jury found him not guilty. To avoid further legal entanglements, Burr left the country for France. He returned unmolested in 1812 to practice law in New York and died at the age of eighty.

WAR IN EUROPE

Oppositionists of whatever stripe were more an annoyance than a threat to Jefferson. The more intractable problems of his disastrous second term involved the renewal of the European war in 1803, which helped resolve the problem of Louisiana but put more strains on Jefferson's desire to avoid "entangling alliances" and the quarrels of Europe. In 1805, Napoléon's defeat of Russian and Austrian forces gave him control of western Europe. That same year the British defeat of the French and Spanish fleets in the Battle of Trafalgar secured Britain's control of the seas. The war then turned into a battle of elephant and whale, Napoléon's army dominant on land, the British navy dominant on the water, neither able to strike a decisive blow at the other and neither restrained by concerns over neutral shipping rights or international law.

Preparation for war to defend commerce

In 1806 and 1807, American shipping was caught in the crossfire of the war between Britain and France.

HARASSMENT BY BRITAIN AND FRANCE For two years after the renewal of European warfare, American shippers reaped the benefits, taking over trade with the French and Spanish West Indies. But in the case of the *Essex* (1805), a British court ruled that the practice of shipping French and Spanish goods through U.S. ports on their way elsewhere did not neutralize enemy goods. The practice violated the British rule of 1756, under which trade closed in time of peace remained closed in time of war. Goods shipped in violation of the rule would be seized. After 1807, British interference with American shipping increased, not just in a desperate effort to keep supplies from Napoléon's continent but also to hobble U.S. competition with British merchant ships.

In 1806 the British ministry set up a paper blockade of Europe. Vessels headed for European ports had to get British licenses and accept British inspection or be liable to seizure. It was a paper blockade because even the powerful British navy was not large enough to monitor every European port. Napoléon retaliated with his "Continental System," proclaimed in the Berlin Decree of 1806 and the Milan Decree of 1807. In the first he declared his own paper blockade of the British Isles; in the second he ruled that neutral ships that complied with British regulations were subject to seizure when they reached Continental ports. The situation presented American shippers with a dilemma: if they complied with the demands of one side, they were subject to seizure by the other.

The prospects for profits were so great, however, that American shippers ran the risk. Seamen faced a more dangerous risk: a renewal of the practice of impressment. The use of press-gangs to kidnap men in British (and colonial) ports was a long-standing method of recruitment used by the British navy. The seizure of British subjects from American vessels became a new source of recruits, justified on the principle that British subjects remained British subjects for life: "Once an Englishman, always an Englishman."

In the summer of 1807, the British frigate *Leopard* accosted a U.S. vessel, the *Chesapeake,* just outside territorial waters off the coast of Virginia. After the *Chesapeake*'s captain refused to allow his ship to be searched, the *Leopard* opened fire, killing three and wounding eighteen. The *Chesapeake,* unready for battle, was forced to strike its colors (that is, to lower its flag as a sign of surrender). A British search party seized four men, one of whom was later hanged for desertion from the British navy. Public wrath was so aroused that Jefferson could have had war on the spot. Like Adams before him, however, he resisted war fever and suffered politically as a result.

THE EMBARGO   Instead of rushing to war, Jefferson resolved to use public indignation at the British to promote "peaceable coercion." In 1807 he persuaded Congress to pass the sweeping Embargo Act, which stopped all exports of American goods and prohibited American ships from leaving for foreign ports. It also effectively ended imports, since it was unprofitable for foreign ships to return from America empty. The constitutional basis of the embargo was the power to regulate commerce, which in this case Republicans interpreted broadly as the power to prohibit commerce.

Jefferson's ill-considered embargo failed from the beginning, however, because few Americans were willing to make the necessary sacrifices. Trade remained profitable despite the risks, and violating the embargo was almost laughably easy. While American ships sat idle in ports, their crews laid off and unpaid, smugglers flourished and the British enjoyed a near monopoly on legitimate trade. Neither France nor Great Britain was significantly hurt by Jefferson's policy.

But Jefferson was injured. The unpopular embargo revived the languishing Federalist party in New England, which renewed the charge that Jefferson was in league with the French. At the same time, agriculture in the South and the West suffered for want of foreign outlets for grain, cotton, and tobacco. After fifteen months, Jefferson accepted failure, and on March 1,

1809, he signed a repeal of the embargo shortly before he relinquished the "splendid misery" of the presidency. In the election of 1808, the presidency passed to another Virginian, Secretary of State James Madison.

THE DRIFT TO WAR   The brilliant Madison proved to be a mediocre chief executive. From the beginning his presidency was entangled in foreign affairs and crippled by his naïveté. Madison and his advisers repeatedly over-estimated the young republic's diplomatic leverage and military strength. The result was humiliation and near defeat. Still insisting on neutral rights and freedom of the seas, Madison continued Jefferson's policy of "peaceful coercion" by different but equally ineffective means. In place of the embargo, Congress had substituted the Nonintercourse Act, which reopened trade with all countries except France and Great Britain and authorized the president to reopen trade with whichever nation gave up its restrictions on American trade. Nonintercourse proved as impotent as the embargo. Madison's policies created an economic recession and brought no change in British policy. In the vain search for an alternative, Congress in 1810 reversed itself and adopted a measure introduced by Nathaniel Macon of North Carolina. Macon's bill re-opened trade with the warring powers but provided that if either dropped its restrictions, nonintercourse would be restored with the other.

Napoléon's foreign minister, the Duke de Cadore, announced that he had withdrawn the Berlin and Milan Decrees, but the carefully worded Cadore letter had strings attached: revocation of the decrees depended upon with-drawal of the British orders in council. The strings were plain to see, but Madison foolishly went along in the hope of putting pressure on the British. The British initially refused to give in, and on June 1, 1812, Madison reluc-tantly asked Congress for a declaration of war. On June 16, however, the British foreign minister, facing economic crisis, revoked the orders in coun-cil. Britain preferred not to risk war with the United States on top of its war with Napoléon. But it was too late. On June 18, Congress, unaware of the British repeal, granted Madison's request for war. With more time or patience, Madison's policy would have been vindicated without resort to war.

The War of 1812

CAUSES   The main cause of the war—the violation of American shipping rights—seems clear enough. Yet the geographic distribution of the congres-sional vote for war raised a troubling question. Most votes for war came from the farm regions that stretched from Pennsylvania southward and westward. The maritime states of New York and New England, the region that bore the brunt of British attacks on U.S. shipping, voted against the war declaration. One explanation for this seeming anomaly is simple enough: the farming regions suffered damage to their markets for grain, cotton, and tobacco while New England shippers made profits from smuggling in spite of the British restrictions.

Other plausible explanations for the sectional vote, however, include frontier Indian attacks that were blamed on British agents, western land hunger, and the American desire for territory in British Canada and Spanish Florida. The constant pressure to open new lands repeatedly forced or persuaded Indians to sign treaties they did not always understand, causing stronger resentment among tribes that were losing more and more of their land. It was an old story, dating from the Jamestown settlement, but one that took a new turn with the rise of a powerful Shawnee leader, Tecumseh.

Tecumseh recognized the consequences of Indian disunity and set out to form a confederation of tribes to defend Indian hunting grounds, insisting that no land cession was valid without the consent of all tribes, since they held the land in common. By 1811, Tecumseh had matured his plans and headed south from the Indiana Territory to win the Creeks, Cherokees, Choctaws, and Chickasaws to his cause. His speeches were filled with emotion and anger. "The white race is a wicked race," he declared. "They seize your land; they corrupt your women." Only by driving them out "upon a trail of blood" would the Indians survive.

General William Henry Harrison, governor of the Indiana Territory, learned of Tecumseh's plans and met with him twice. In the fall of 1811, however, Harrison decided that Tecumseh must be stopped. He gathered 1,000 troops near the Shawnees' capital on the Tippecanoe River while the Indian leader was away. Although Tecumseh had warned the Shawnees against fighting in his absence, they attacked Harrison's encampment. A quarter of Harrison's men died or were wounded, yet the Shawnees lost the Battle of Tippecanoe; their town was burned, their supplies destroyed. Tecumseh's dreams of an Indian confederacy went up in smoke, and the Shawnee leader sought British protection in Canada.

The Battle of Tippecanoe reinforced suspicions that British agents were inciting the Indians. Frontier settlers believed that a U.S. conquest of Canada would end British influence among the Indians and open a new empire for land-hungry Americans. Canada was also one place where the British, in case of war, were vulnerable to an American attack. Madison and others acted on the mistaken assumption that the Canadians were eager to be liberated from

British control. Thomas Jefferson had told Madison that the U.S. "acquisition of Canada" was simply a "matter of marchin'" north with a military force." The British were vulnerable in Florida as well. East Florida, still under Spanish control, also posed a threat to the Americans, since Spain allowed sporadic Indian attacks across the border with Georgia. Moreover, the British were suspected of smuggling goods through Florida and intriguing with the Indians on the southwestern border.

Such concerns helped generate war fever. In the Congress that assembled in 1811, several new members from southern and western districts clamored for war in defense of "national honor" and demanded an invasion of Canada. Among them were Henry Clay and Richard Mentor Johnson of Kentucky, Felix Grundy of Tennessee, and John C. Calhoun of South Carolina. John Randolph of Roanoke christened these "new boys" the "war hawks." The young senator Henry Clay, a tall, rawboned westerner know for his combative temperament and propensity for dueling, yearned for war. "I am for resistance by the *sword*," he vowed. He promised that the Kentucky militia stood ready to march on Canada and acquire its lucrative fur trade.

Tecumseh

The Shawnee leader who tried to unite Indian tribes in defense of their lands. Tecumseh was killed in 1813 at the Battle of the Thames.

PREPARATIONS   As it turned out, the war hawks would get neither Canada nor Florida, for in 1812 James Madison had carried into war a nation that was ill prepared both financially and militarily. The Republican emphasis on small federal budgets and military cutbacks was not an effective way to win a war. And Madison, a studious, soft-spoken man, lacked anything resembling the martial qualities needed to inspire national confidence. He was no George Washington.

Moreover, the national economy was not prepared for war. The year before, despite urgent pleas from Treasury Secretary Albert Gallatin, Congress had let the twenty-year charter of the Bank of the United States expire. Meanwhile, trade had collapsed, and tariff revenues had declined. Loans were needed to cover about two thirds of the war costs, but northeastern opponents of the war were reluctant to lend money.

The military situation was almost as bad. War had become more likely for nearly a decade, but Republican budgetary constraints had prevented preparations. When the War of 1812 began, the army numbered only 6,700 men, ill trained, poorly equipped, and led by aging officers past their prime. The navy, on the other hand, was in comparatively good shape, with able officers and trained men. Its ships were well outfitted and seaworthy—all sixteen of them. In the first year of the war, the navy produced the only U.S. victories, in isolated duels with British vessels, but their effect was mainly an occasional boost to morale. Within a year the British had blockaded the U.S. coast, except for New England, where they hoped to cultivate anti-war feeling, and most of the little American fleet was bottled up in port.

THE WAR IN THE NORTH The only place where the United States could effectively strike at the British was Canada. To that end, the Madison administration opted for a three-pronged assault along the Lake Champlain route toward Montreal, with General Henry Dearborn in command; along the Niagara River, with forces under General Stephen Van Rensselaer; and into Upper Canada (north of Lake Erie and Lake Ontario) from Detroit, with General William Hull and some 2,000 men.

In Detroit the sickly and senile Hull procrastinated while his position worsened and the news arrived that an American fort isolated at the head of Lake Huron had surrendered. The British commander cleverly played upon Hull's worst fears. Gathering what redcoats he could to parade in view of Detroit's defenders, he announced that thousands of Indian allies were at the rear and he would be unable to control them once fighting began. Fearing a massacre, Hull, without consulting his officers and without a shot being fired, surrendered his entire force.

Along the Niagara River front, General Van Rensselaer was more aggressive. An advance party of 600 Americans crossed the river and worked their way up the bluffs on the Canadian side to occupy Queenston Heights. The stage was set for a major victory, but the New York militia refused to reinforce Van Rensselaer's men, claiming that their military service did not obligate them to leave the country. They complacently remained on the New York side and watched their outnumbered countrymen fall to a superior force across the river.

On the third front, the old invasion route via Lake Champlain, the incompetent General Dearborn led his army north from Plattsburgh toward Montreal. He marched his men up to the border, where the state militia once

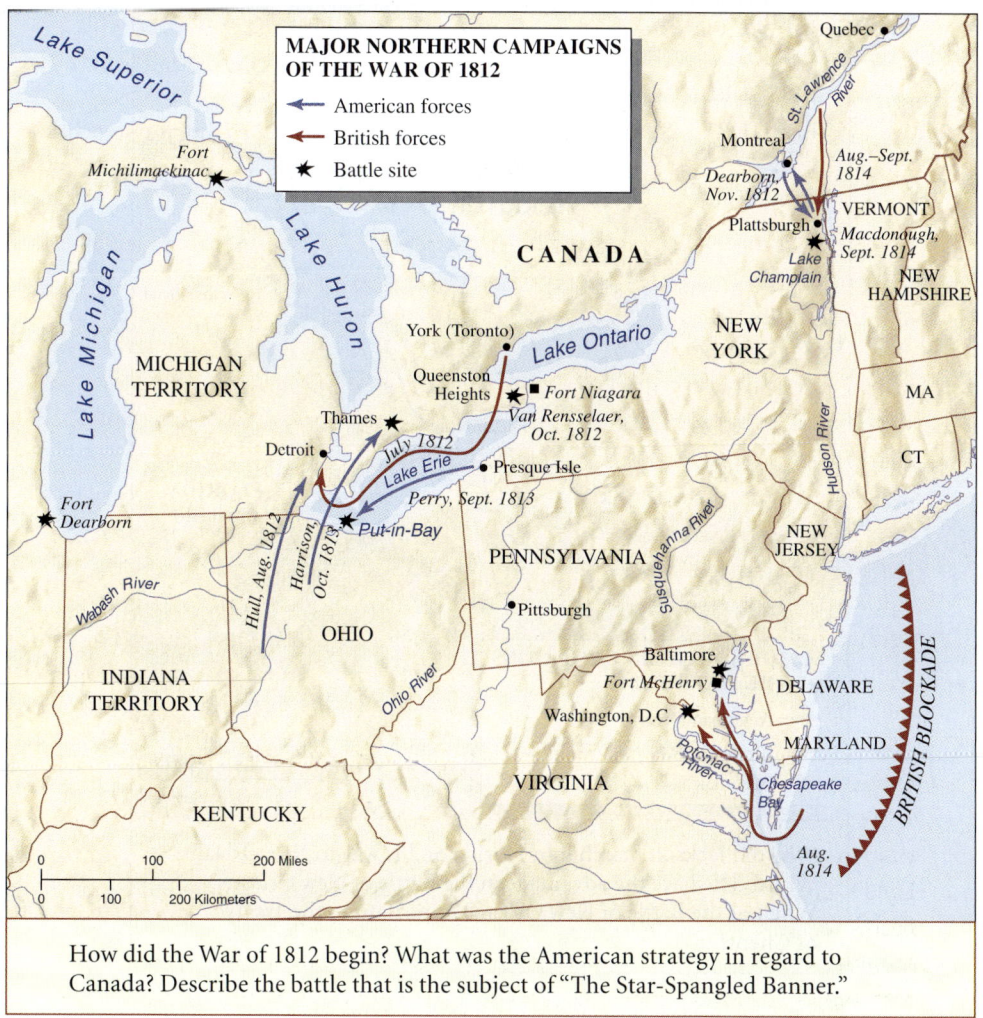

MAJOR NORTHERN CAMPAIGNS OF THE WAR OF 1812

→ American forces
→ British forces
★ Battle site

How did the War of 1812 begin? What was the American strategy in regard to Canada? Describe the battle that is the subject of "The Star-Spangled Banner."

again stood on its alleged constitutional rights and refused to cross, and then marched them back to Plattsburgh.

Madison's navy secretary now pushed vigorously for American control of inland waters. At Presque Isle (near Erie), Pennsylvania, in 1813, the twenty-eight-year-old Oliver Hazard Perry, already a fourteen-year veteran who had seen action against Tripoli, was busy building ships from green timber. At the end of the summer, Commodore Perry set out in search of the British, whom he found at Lake Erie's Put-in-Bay on September 10. After completing the preparations for battle, Perry told an aide, "This is the most important day of my life."

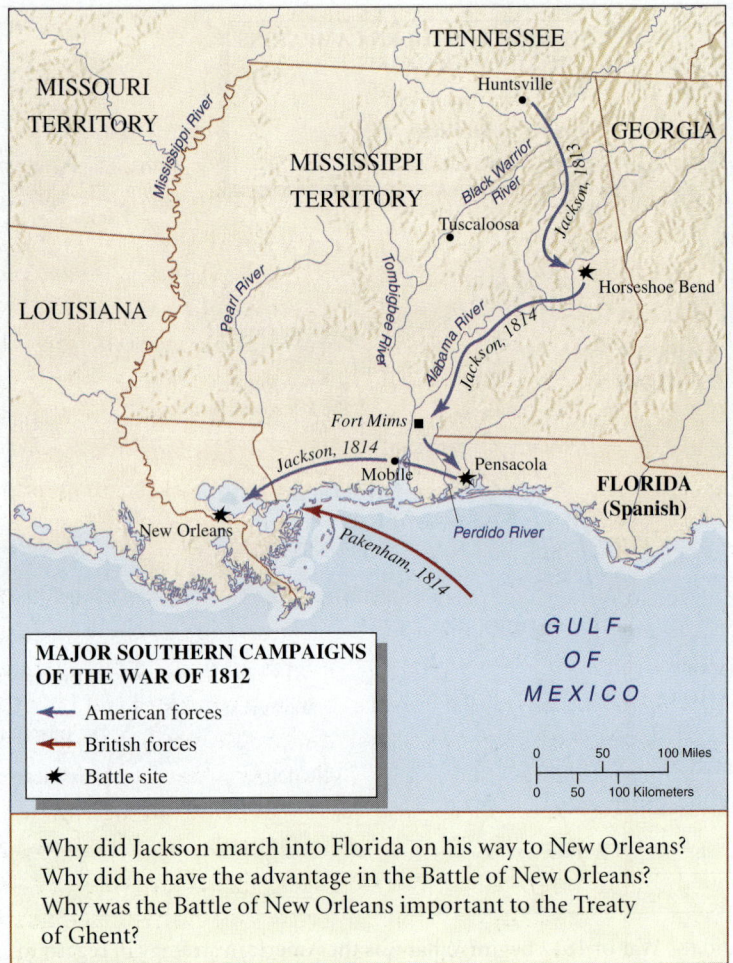

MISSOURI
TERRITORY

TENNESSEE

Huntsville

GEORGIA

Mississippi River

MISSISSIPPI
TERRITORY

Black Warrior River

Jackson, 1813

Tuscaloosa

Pearl River

Tombigbee River

Horseshoe Bend

LOUISIANA

Alabama River

Jackson, 1814

Fort Mims

Jackson, 1814

Pensacola

Mobile

FLORIDA
(Spanish)

New Orleans

Pakenham, 1814

Perdido River

GULF
OF
MEXICO

**MAJOR SOUTHERN CAMPAIGNS
OF THE WAR OF 1812**

← American forces
← British forces
★ Battle site

| 0 | 50 | 100 Miles |
| 0 | 50 | 100 Kilometers |

Why did Jackson march into Florida on his way to New Orleans?
Why did he have the advantage in the Battle of New Orleans?
Why was the Battle of New Orleans important to the Treaty
of Ghent?

Two British warships used their superior weapons to pummel the *Lawrence*, Perry's flagship, from a distance. After four hours of intense shelling, none of the *Lawrence*'s guns was working, and most crew members were dead or wounded. The British expected the Americans to turn tail, but Perry refused to quit. He had himself rowed to another vessel, carried the battle to the enemy, and finally accepted the surrender of the entire British squadron. Hatless, begrimed, and bloodied, Perry sent General William Henry Harrison the long-awaited message: "We have met the enemy and they are ours."

More good news followed. At the Battle of the Thames, in Canadian territory east of Detroit on October 5, General Harrison eliminated British power in Upper Canada and released the Northwest from any further threat.

In the course of the battle, the great Indian leader Tecumseh was killed, his dream of Indian unity dying with him.

THE WAR IN THE SOUTH   In the South, too, the war flared up in 1813. On August 30, Creeks allied with the British attacked Fort Mims, on the Alabama River above Mobile, killing almost half the people in the fort. As major general of the Tennessee militia, Andrew Jackson summoned about 2,000 volunteers and set out on a vengeful campaign that crushed Creek resistance. The decisive battle occurred in eastern Alabama on March 27, 1814, at Horseshoe Bend, on the Tallapoosa River, in the heart of Upper Creek country in east-central Alabama. Jackson's Cherokee allies played a crucial role in the battle. Only 200 of the 1,000 Creek warriors survived the fighting. By contrast, less than 50 of Jackson's soldiers and Indian allies were killed. With the Treaty of Fort Jackson, the Indians ceded two thirds of their land to the United States, including part of Georgia and most of Alabama.

BRITISH STRATEGY   Four days after the Battle of Horseshoe Bend, Napoléon's French Empire collapsed. Now free to deal solely with America, the British developed a threefold plan of operations for 1814: they would launch a two-pronged invasion of America via Fort Niagara and Lake Champlain to increase the clamor for peace in the Northeast; extend the naval blockade to New England, subjecting coastal towns to raids; and seize New Orleans and take control of the Mississippi River, lifeline of the West. Yet after a generation of conflict in Europe and around the world, war-weariness countered the British thirst for revenge against the former colonials. British plans were also stymied by the more resolute young American commanders Madison had placed in charge of strategic areas by the summer of 1814.

The main British effort focused on invading the United States from Canada via Lake Champlain. A land assault might have taken Plattsburgh and forced American troops out of their protected positions nearby, but England's army, led by General George Prevost, governor general of Canada, bogged down while its flotilla engaged a U.S. naval squadron, led by Commodore Thomas Macdonough, on Lake Champlain. The battle ended in September 1814 with the British ships destroyed or captured.

FIGHTING IN THE CHESAPEAKE   Meanwhile, however, American forces suffered the most humiliating experience of the war as the British captured and burned Washington, D.C. On the evening of August 24, 1814, redcoats marched unopposed into Washington and straight to the White House, where officers ate a meal that had been prepared for President

Madison and his wife, Dolley, who had hastily joined other refugees in Virginia. The British then burned the White House, the Capitol, and all other government buildings. A tornado the next day compounded the damage, but a violent thunderstorm dampened both the fires and the enthusiasm of the British forces, who headed north to assault Baltimore.

That attack was a different story. With some 13,000 men, chiefly militia, American units fortified the heights behind the city. About 1,000 men held Fort McHenry, on an island in the harbor. The British fleet bombarded the fort to no avail, and the invaders abandoned their attack. Francis Scott Key, a Washington lawyer, watched the siege from a British vessel in the harbor, where he was pleading for the release of a prisoner. The sight of the battered flag still in place at dawn inspired him to draft the verses of what came to be called "The Star-Spangled Banner." Later revised and set to the tune of an English drinking song, it was immediately popular and eventually became America's national anthem.

THE BATTLE OF NEW ORLEANS The British failure to capture Baltimore followed by three days their defeat on Lake Champlain; their offensive against New Orleans, however, had yet to run its course. Along the Gulf coast, General Andrew Jackson had been shoring up the defenses of Mobile and New Orleans. In late 1814, without authorization, he invaded the

Jackson's army defends New Orleans

Andrew Jackson's defeat of the British at New Orleans, January 1815.

Panhandle region of Spanish Florida and took Pensacola, putting an end to British efforts to organize Indian attacks on American settlements. Back in Louisiana by the end of November, he began to erect defenses around New Orleans. But the British fleet, with some 8,000 soldiers under General Sir Edward Pakenham, cautiously took up positions just south of the city.

Pakenham's painfully careful approach—he waited until all his artillery was available—gave Jackson time to build defensive earthworks bolstered by cotton bales. It was an almost invulnerable position, but Pakenham, contemptuous of Jackson's motley array of frontier militiamen, Creole aristocrats, free blacks, and pirates, ordered a brave but foolish assault at dawn on January 8, 1815. His redcoats emerged out of the morning fog and ran into a murderous hail of artillery shells and deadly rifle fire. Before the British withdrew, about 2,000 had been killed or wounded, including Pakenham himself, whose body, pickled in a barrel of rum, was returned to the ship where his wife awaited news of the battle. A British officer, after watching his battered troops retreat, wrote that there "never was a more complete failure." The Americans suffered only a few dozen casualties.

The slow pace of communication during the early nineteenth century meant that the Battle of New Orleans occurred after a peace treaty had been signed in Europe. But this is not to say that the battle had no effect on the outcome of the war, for the treaty was yet to be ratified by either government, and the British might have exploited to advantage the possession of New Orleans had they won control of it. The battle ensured that both governments acted quickly to ratify the treaty. The unexpected American victory at New Orleans would also generate a wave of patriotic nationalism that would help transform a victorious general, Andrew Jackson, into a dynamic president.

THE TREATY OF GHENT Efforts to negotiate an end to the war had begun in 1812, even before hostilities commenced, but negotiations bogged down after the fighting started. The British were stalling, awaiting news of smashing victories to strengthen their hand. Word of the U.S. victory on Lake Champlain weakened the British resolve. The British will to fight was further eroded by a continuing power struggle in Europe, by the eagerness of British merchants to renew trade with America, and by the war-weariness of a tax-burdened public. The British finally decided that the war was not worth the cost. Envoys from both sides eventually agreed to end the fighting, return prisoners, restore previous boundaries, and settle nothing else. The Treaty of Ghent was signed on Christmas Eve of 1814.

THE HARTFORD CONVENTION   While the diplomats converged on a peace settlement in Europe, an entirely different kind of meeting was taking place in Hartford, Connecticut. The Hartford Convention represented the climax of New England's disaffection with "Mr. Madison's war." New England had managed to keep aloof from the war and extract a profit from illegal trading and privateering. After the fall of Napoléon in 1815, however, the British extended their blockade to New England, occupied part of Maine, and conducted several raids along the coast. Even Boston seemed threatened. Instead of rallying to the American flag, however, Federalists in the Massachusetts legislature voted to convene a meeting of New England states to plan independent action.

On December 15, 1814, the Hartford Convention assembled with delegates from Massachusetts, Rhode Island, Connecticut, Vermont, and New Hampshire. The convention proposed seven constitutional amendments designed to limit Republican influence, including the requirement of a two-thirds vote to declare war or admit new states, a prohibition on embargoes lasting more than sixty days, a one-term limit on the presidency, and a ban on successive presidents from the same state.

The Hartford Convention carried the unmistakable threat of secession if its demands were ignored. Yet the threat quickly evaporated. When messengers from Hartford reached Washington, D.C., they found the battered capital celebrating the good news from Ghent and New Orleans. The consequence was a fatal blow to the Federalist party, which never recovered from the stigma of disloyalty stamped on it by the Hartford Convention.

We Owe Allegiance to No Crown
The War of 1812 generated a renewed spirit of nationalism.

THE AFTERMATH   For all the ineptitude with which the War of 1812 was fought, it generated an intense patriotic feeling. Despite the standoff with which it ended at Ghent, Americans felt victorious, thanks to Andrew Jackson and his men at New Orleans, as well as to the heroic exploits of U.S. frigates in their duels with British ships. However, the war revealed America's desperate need for a more efficient system of internal transportation—roads, bridges, canals. Even more important, the conflict launched the United States toward economic independence as the interruption of trade encouraged the birth of American manufactures. This was a profound development, for the emergence of a factory system would generate far-reaching social effects as well as economic growth. After forty years of fragile independence, it dawned on the world that the new republic might not only survive but flourish.

One of the strangest results of the War of 1812 was a reversal of roles by the Republicans and the Federalists. Out of the wartime experience the Republicans had learned some lessons in nationalism. The necessities of war had "Federalized" Madison or "re-Federalized" the Father of the Constitution. Perhaps, he reasoned, a peacetime army and navy were necessary. He also had come to see the value of a national bank and of higher tariffs to protect infant American industries from foreign competition. But while Madison was embracing such nationalistic measures, the Federalists were borrowing the Jeffersonian theory of states' rights and strict construction in an effort to oppose Madison's policies. It was yet another reversal of roles in constitutional interpretation. It would not be the last.

End of Chapter Review

CHAPTER SUMMARY

- **Jefferson's Administration** Thomas Jefferson did not dismantle much of Hamilton's program, but he did promptly repeal the whiskey tax and cut back on government expenditures. He involved the navy in subduing the Barbary pirates and negotiated with the Spanish and then with the French to ensure that the Mississippi River remained open to American commerce. The purchase of the Louisiana Territory through negotiations with French Emperor Napoleon dramatically expanded the boundaries of the United States.

- **Marshall Court** John Marshall, a Federalist, played influential roles in many crucial decisions during his long tenure as chief justice of the Supreme Court. In *Marbury v. Madison*, the Court declared a federal act unconstitutional for the first time. With that decision, the Court assumed the right of judicial review over acts of Congress. As chief justice, Marshall established the constitutional supremacy of the federal government over the state governments.

- **Louisiana Purchase** The Louisiana Purchase led to a debate on the nature of the Constitution, in which Federalists feared that the addition of new territories and states would change the country and strengthen the Republicans. Jefferson's "Corps of Discovery," led by Meriwether Lewis and William Clark, explored the new region's resources, captured the public imagination, and gave the United States a claim to the Oregon Country.

- **War of 1812** Renewal of the European war in 1803 created conflicts with Britain and France. Neither country wanted its enemy to purchase U.S. goods, so both declared blockades. In retaliation, Jefferson had Congress pass the Embargo Act, which prohibited all foreign trade. James Madison ultimately declared war over the issue of neutral shipping rights and the fear that the British were inciting Native Americans to attack frontier settlements.

- **Aftermath of the War of 1812** The Treaty of Ghent, signed in 1814, ended the War of 1812 without settling any of the disputes. One effect of the conflict over neutral shipping rights was to launch the economic independence of the United States, as goods previously purchased from England were now manufactured at home. Federalists and Republicans seemed to exchange roles: delegates from the waning Federalist party met at the Hartford Convention to consider states' rights and secession, whereas the Republicans embraced nationalism and a broad interpretation of the Constitution.

CHRONOLOGY

1803	*Marbury v. Madison*
1803	Louisiana Purchase
1804–1806	Lewis and Clark expedition
1807	*Chesapeake* affair
1807	Embargo Act is passed
1808	International slave trade is outlawed
1811	Battle of Tippecanoe
1814	Battle of Horseshoe Bend
1814	Treaty of Ghent
1814	Hartford Convention
1815	Battle of New Orleans

KEY TERMS & NAMES

Part Three

AN
EXPANSIVE
NATION

housands of Americans during the early nineteenth century spilled over the Appalachian Mountains, crossed the Mississippi River, and in the 1840s reached the Pacific Ocean. Wagons, canals, flatboats, steamboats, and eventually railroads helped transport them. The feverish expansion of the United States into new western territories brought Americans into more conflict with Native Americans, Mexicans, the British, and the Spanish. Only a few people, however, expressed moral reservations about displacing others. Most Americans believed it was the "manifest destiny" of the United States to spread throughout the continent—at whatever cost and at whomever's expense. Americans generally felt that they enjoyed the blessing of Providence in their efforts to consolidate the continent and bring it under their control.

During the early nineteenth century most people continued to earn their living from the soil, but textile mills and manufacturing plants began to dot the landscape and transform the nature of work and the pace of life. By midcentury the United States was emerging as one of the world's major industrial powers. In addition, the lure of cheap land and plentiful jobs, as well as the promise of political equality and religious freedom, attracted millions of immigrants from Europe. The newcomers, mostly from Germany and Ireland, faced ethnic prejudices, religious persecution, and language barriers that made assimilation into American culture difficult.

These developments gave life in the second quarter of the nineteenth century a dynamic quality. The United States, said the philosopher-poet Ralph Waldo Emerson, was "a country of beginnings, of projects, of designs, of expectations." A restless optimism characterized the period. People of a lowly social status who heretofore had accepted their lot in life now strove to climb the social ladder and enter the political arena. The patrician republic espoused by Jefferson and Madison gave way to the frontier democracy promoted by Andrew Jackson and his supporters. Americans were no longer content to be governed by a small, benevolent aristocracy of talent and wealth. They began to demand—and obtain—government of, by, and for the people.

The fertile economic environment during the antebellum era helped foster the egalitarian idea that individuals (except African Americans,

Native Americans, and women) should have an equal opportunity to better themselves and should be granted political rights and privileges. In America, observed a journalist in 1844, "one has as good a chance as another according to his talents, prudence, and personal exertions."

The exuberant individualism embodied in such mythic expressions of economic equality and political democracy spilled over into the cultural arena during the first half of the century. The so-called Romantic movement applied democratic ideals to philosophy, religion, literature, and the fine arts. In New England, Ralph Waldo Emerson and Henry David Thoreau joined other "transcendentalists" in espousing a radical individualism. Other reformers were motivated more by a sense of spiritual mission than by democratic individualism. Reformers sought to introduce public schools, abolish slavery, promote temperance, and improve the lot of the disabled, the insane, and the imprisoned. Their efforts ameliorated some of the problems created by the frenetic economic growth and territorial expansion. But reformers made little headway against slavery. It would take a brutal civil war to dislodge America's "peculiar institution."

10

NATIONALISM AND SECTIONALISM

FOCUS QUESTIONS

wwnorton.com/studyspace

- How did economic policies after the War of 1812 reflect the nationalism of the period?
- What characterized the Era of Good Feelings?
- What were the various issues that promoted sectionalism?
- How did the Supreme Court under John Marshall strengthen the federal government and the national economy?
- What were the main diplomatic achievements of these years?

A mid the jubilation that followed the War of 1812, Americans began to transform their young republic into a sprawling nation. Hundreds of thousands of people began to stream westward at the same time that the largely local economy was maturing into a national market. The spread of plantation slavery and the cotton culture into the Old Southwest—Alabama, Mississippi, Arkansas, Louisiana, and Texas as well as the frontier areas of Tennessee, Kentucky, and Florida— disrupted family ties and changed social life. In the North and the West, meanwhile, a dynamic urban middle class began to emerge. Such dramatic changes prompted vigorous political debates over economic policies, transportation improvements, and the extension of slavery into the new territories. In the process the nation began to divide into three powerful regional blocs—North, South, and West—whose shifting coalitions would shape the political landscape until the Civil War.

ECONOMIC NATIONALISM

After the War of 1812, a new surge of economic prosperity generated a widespread sense of well-being and enhanced the prestige of the national government. The idea spread that the young nation needed a more balanced "national" economy of farming, commerce, and manufacturing, as well as a more muscular military. President James Madison, in his first annual message to Congress after the war, recommended several steps to strengthen the nation and the economy: better fortifications, a permanent national army and a strong navy, a new national bank, effective protection of the new industries against foreign competition through the use of tariffs, a system of canals and roads for commercial and military use, and to top it off, a great national university. "The Republicans have out-Federalized Federalism," one observer remarked.

THE BANK OF THE UNITED STATES   The trinity of ideas promoting economic nationalism—proposals for a second national bank; for protective tariffs; and for government-financed roads, canals, and eventually railroads, called internal improvements—ignited the greatest controversies. Issues related to money—the reliability and availability of currency, the relative value of paper money and "specie" (silver and gold coins), and the structure and regulation of the banking system—often dominated political debates. After the national bank's charter expired, in 1811, the country fell into a financial muddle. State-chartered local banks mushroomed with little or no regulation, and their bank notes (paper money) flooded the channels of commerce with currency of uncertain value. Because state banks were loosely and poorly regulated, they often issued paper money for loans far in excess of the "hard money" they stored in their vaults. Such loose lending practices led initially to an economic boom, followed by a dramatic inflation fed by the excess of paper money circulating in the economy. Eventually the inherent value of the excess bank notes would plummet and the bubble would burst, causing recession and depression. Because hard money had been in such short supply during the war (because coins were typically required to pay off foreign debts), many state banks suspended specie payments, meaning that they stopped exchanging coins for paper money submitted by depositors. The result was chronic instability and occasional chaos in the banking sector.

In the face of this growing financial turmoil, President Madison and most of the younger generation of Republicans swallowed their constitutional reservations about a powerful national bank. In 1816, Congress created a new Bank of the United States (B.U.S.), to be located in Philadelphia. Modeled on Alexander Hamilton's first national bank, its charter again would run for twenty years, and the government owned a fifth of the stock and named five of the twenty-five directors. The bank served as the depository for government funds, and its bank notes were accepted in payments to the government. In return for its privileges, the Bank of the United States had to handle the government's funds without charge, lend the government up to $5 million upon demand, and pay the government a cash bonus of $1.5 million.

The bitter debate over the B.U.S. set a pattern of regional alignment for most other economic issues. Missouri senator Thomas Hart Benton predicted that the currency-short western towns would be at the mercy of a centralized eastern bank. "They may be devoured by it any moment! They are in the jaws of the monster! A lump of butter in the mouth of a dog! One gulp, one swallow, and all is gone!"

The debate over the national bank was also noteworthy because of the leading roles played by the era's greatest statesmen: John C. Calhoun of South Carolina, Henry Clay of Kentucky, and Daniel Webster of New Hampshire. Calhoun, as an economic nationalist, introduced the bank measure and pushed it through, justifying its constitutionality by citing the congressional power to regulate the currency. Clay, who had long opposed a central national bank, now asserted that new circumstances had made one indispensable. Webster, on the other hand, led the opposition of the New Englanders, who did not want Philadelphia to displace Boston as the nation's banking center. Later, after he had moved from New Hampshire to Massachusetts, Webster would return to Congress as the champion of a much stronger national government, whereas events would steer Calhoun toward a defiant embrace of states' rights.

A PROTECTIVE TARIFF   The shift of investment capital from commerce to manufactures, begun during Thomas Jefferson's embargo of 1807, had accelerated during the war. But new American manufacturers insisted that they needed "protection" from foreign competitors. After the War of 1812 ended, a sudden renewal of cheap British imports generated pleas for tariffs (taxes on imports) to "protect" young American industries. The self-interest of the manufacturers, who as yet had little political power, was reinforced by a patriotic desire for economic independence from Britain.

The Tariff of 1816, the first intended more to protect industry against foreign competition than to raise revenue, easily passed in Congress. New England supported the tariff and the South opposed it, while the middle Atlantic states and the Old Northwest cast only five negative votes altogether.

Led by John Calhoun, the minority of southerners who voted for the tariff had hoped that the South might itself become a manufacturing center. Although in 1810 the southern states had almost as many mills and factories as New England, within a few years New England would move ahead of the South in manufacturing and Calhoun would reverse himself and turn against tariffs. The tariff would then become a sectional issue, with northern manufacturers and food producers favoring higher tariffs while southern cotton and tobacco planters and northern shipping interests would favor lower duties.

INTERNAL IMPROVEMENTS   The third major economic issue of the time involved goverment financing of internal improvements: the building of roads and the development of water transportation. The war had highlighted the shortcomings of the nation's limited transportation network: the movement of troops through the western wilderness had proved very difficult. At the same time, settlers found that unless they located themselves near navigable waters, they were cut off from trade.

The federal government had entered the field of internal improvements under Thomas Jefferson. Jefferson and his successors, Madison and Monroe, wanted the federal government to have undisputed authority to improve the national transportation system. In 1803, when Ohio became a state, Congress decreed that 5 percent of the proceeds from state land sales would go to

The Union Manufactories of Maryland in Patapsco Falls, Baltimore County (ca. 1815)

A textile mill established during the embargo of 1807, the Union Manufactories would employ more than 600 people by 1825.

building a National Road from the Atlantic coast into Ohio and beyond as the territory developed. Construction of the National Road began in 1815. Originally called the Cumberland Road, it was the first federally financed interstate roadway. By 1818 it ran from Cumberland, Maryland, to Wheeling, Virginia, on the Ohio River. By 1838 it extended all the way to Vandalia, Illinois. By reducing transportation costs and opening up western markets, the National Road and privately financed turnpikes accelerated the commercialization of agriculture.

In 1817, John C. Calhoun put through the House a bill to fund internal improvements. Opposition to federal spending on transportation projects centered in New England and the South, regions that expected to gain the least from federal projects designed to spur western development. Support came largely from the West, which urgently needed good roads. On his last day in office, President Madison, bothered by questions about the bill's constitutionality, vetoed the proposed legislation. Internal improvements remained for another hundred years, with few exceptions, the responsibility of states and private enterprise.

Nonetheless, despite disagreements about who would pay for such improvements, better transportation and communication (daily newspapers, express mail service, and the telegraph) during the second quarter of the nineteenth century helped create a national market for goods and services. No longer limited to local or regional markets, farmers and manufacturers rapidly expanded production. Banks offered easy access to capital, and enterprising Americans rushed to take advantage of unprecedented entrepreneurial opportunities. Commercial agriculture and the factory system began to displace subsistence farming and household production during this period. Mills and factories sprouted up across the countryside. New technologies greatly increased productivity and in the process changed the rhythms of work and the relationships between laborers and employers. These first stirrings of an industrial revolution spawned a sustained economic expansion that would transform society and politics.

THE AMERICAN SYSTEM   The national banking system, protective tariffs, and transportation improvements were all intended to spur the development of what historians have called the market revolution that was transforming the young American economy. With each passing year, farmers, merchants, and manufacturers devoted themselves more and more to producing commodities and goods for commercial markets, which often lay far from the sources of production. American capitalism was maturing—rapidly. While many Old Republicans lamented the transition to an increasingly urban-industrial-commercial society, others decided that such democratic capitalism was the wave of the future.

Henry Clay emerged during the first half of the nineteenth century as the foremost spokesman for what he came to call the American System. Born and raised in Virginia, Clay became a successful attorney in Lexington, Kentucky, before launching a political career. He was fond of gambling, liquor, and women, and like his foe Andrew Jackson, he had a brawling temper that led to several duels. During the 1820s, as Speaker of the House, Clay became the chief proponent of economic nationalism. Prosperity, he insisted, depended upon the federal government's assuming an active role in shaping the economy. He scoffed at the old Jeffersonian fear that an urban-industrial society would necessarily grow corrupt. Clay instead promoted the "market revolution" and the rapid development of the new western states and territories. The American System he championed included several measures: (1) high tariffs to impede the import of European products and thereby "protect" fledgling American industries, (2) higher prices for federal lands, the proceeds of which would be distributed to the states to finance internal improvements that would facilitate the movement of goods to markets, and (3) a strong national bank to regulate the nation's money supply and thereby ensure sustained economic growth.

Clay's American System aroused intense support—and opposition. Some critics argued that higher prices for federal lands would discourage western migration. Others believed that tariffs benefited industrialists at the expense of farmers and "common" folk, who paid higher prices for the goods produced by tariff-protected manufacturers. And many feared that the B.U.S. was potentially a tyrannical force, dictating the nation's economic future and in the process centralizing power at the expense of states' rights and individual freedoms. The debates grew in scope and intensity during the first half of the nineteenth century. In the process, they would aggravate sectional tensions to the breaking point.

"GOOD FEELINGS"

JAMES MONROE As James Madison approached the end of a turbulent presidency, he, like Thomas Jefferson, turned to a fellow Virginian, another secretary of state, to be his successor. For Madison that man would be James Monroe. At the outbreak of the Revolution, Monroe was just beginning his studies at the College of William and Mary. He joined the army at sixteen, was wounded at Trenton, and had been made a lieutenant colonel by the time the war ended. Later he studied law with Thomas Jefferson, absorbing Jeffersonian principles in the process.

Monroe had served as a representative in the Virginia assembly, as governor of Virginia, as a representative in the Confederation Congress, as a U.S. senator, and as minister (ambassador) to France, England, and Spain. Under Madison he had been secretary of state and secretary of war. In the 1816 presidential election he overwhelmed his Federalist opponent, Rufus King of New York. Monroe, with his powdered wig, cocked hat, and knee breeches, was the last of the Revolutionary generation to serve in the White House and the last president to dress in the old style.

Firmly grounded in traditional Republican principles, especially the primacy of states' rights, Monroe was never able to keep up with the onrush of the "new nationalism." Monroe accepted as an accomplished fact the Bank of the United States and the protective tariff, but during his tenure there was no further extension of economic nationalism. Indeed, there was a minor setback: he permitted the National Road to be carried forward, but in his veto of the 1822 Cumberland Road bill, he denied the authority of Congress to collect tolls for its repair and maintenance. Instead, he urged a constitutional amendment, as had Jefferson and Madison, to remove all doubt about federal authority in the field of internal improvements.

Monroe surrounded himself with some of the ablest young Republican leaders: John Quincy Adams became secretary of state, William H. Crawford of Georgia continued as secretary of the Treasury, and John C. Calhoun headed the War Department. The new administration took power with America at peace and the economy flourishing. Soon after his inauguration, Monroe embarked on a goodwill tour of New England. In Boston, lately a hotbed of wartime dissent, a Federalist newspaper commented on the president's visit under the heading "Era of Good Feelings." The label became a popular catchphrase for Monroe's administration, one that historians would later seize upon. For two years, harmony in national politics reigned, and even when troubles arose, little of the blame fell on Monroe. In 1820 he was reelected without opposition, as the Federalists were too weak to put up a candidate. Monroe won all the electoral votes except three abstentions and one vote from New Hampshire for John Quincy Adams.

RELATIONS WITH BRITAIN Fueling the contentment after the war was a growing rapprochement with England. American shippers resumed trade with Britain in 1815. The Treaty of Ghent had ended the war, but it left unsettled a number of minor disputes. Two important compacts, the Rush-Bagot Agreement of 1817 and the Convention of 1818, subsequently removed several potential causes of irritation. In the first, resulting from an exchange of letters between Acting Secretary of State Richard Rush and the British minister to the United States, Charles Bagot, the threat of naval competition on the Great Lakes vanished with an arrangement to limit forces there to several U.S. ships collecting customs duties. Although the exchange made no reference to the disputed land boundary between the United States and Canada, its spirit gave rise to the tradition of an unfortified border, the longest in the world.

The Convention of 1818 covered three major points. It settled the northern limit of the Louisiana Purchase by extending the national boundary along the 49th parallel west from Lake of the Woods in what would become Minnesota to the crest of the Rocky Mountains. West of that point the Oregon Country would be open to joint U.S.-British occupation, but the boundary remained unsettled. The right of Americans to fish off Canada's Newfoundland and Labrador, granted in 1783, was acknowledged again. The chief remaining problem was Britain's continuing exclusion of U.S. ships from the British West Indies in order to reserve that lucrative trade for itself. The rapprochement with Britain therefore fell short of perfection.

THE EXTENSION OF BOUNDARIES The year 1819 was one of the more fateful in American history, a time when a whole sequence of developments came into focus. Controversial efforts to expand U.S. territory, an intense financial panic, a combative debate over the extension of slavery, and several landmark Supreme Court cases combined to bring an unsettling end to the Era of Good Feelings.

The aggressive new nationalism reached a climax with the acquisition of Florida. Spanish sovereignty over Florida was more a technicality than an actuality. The tenuously held province had been a thorn in the side of the United States during the War of 1812, when it had served as a center of British intrigue; a haven for Creek refugees, who were beginning to call themselves Seminoles (Runaways, or Separatists); and a harbor for runaway slaves and criminals.

Spain, once the dominant power of the Americas, was now in rapid decline, suffering from both internal decay and colonial revolts and unable to enforce its obligations under Pinckney's Treaty of 1795 to pacify the Florida frontier. In 1816, U.S. forces clashed with a group of escaped slaves who had taken over a British fort on the Apalachicola River in west Florida. Seminoles were soon fighting white settlers in the area, and in 1817 Secretary of War Calhoun authorized the use of federal troops against the Seminoles and summoned General Andrew Jackson from Nashville to take command.

BRITISH POSSESSIONS

Convention of 1818

Lake of the Woods

OREGON COUNTRY

49th parallel

Joint occupation by Britain and U.S. 1818

U.S. TERRITORIES

42nd parallel

Arkansas River

UNITED STATES

Nashville

Adams-Onís Treaty Line, 1819

Red River

SPANISH POSSESSIONS

Mississippi River

ATLANTIC OCEAN

PACIFIC OCEAN

Sabine River

Pensacola St. Marks St. Augustine

FLORIDA Ceded by Spain to U.S., 1819

GULF OF MEXICO

BRITISH

SPANISH

BOUNDARY TREATIES, 1818–1819

0   150   300 Miles

0   150 300 Kilometers

What territorial terms did the Convention of 1818 settle? How did Jackson's actions in Florida help Adams claim the territory from Spain? What were the terms of the treaty with Spain?

Jackson's orders allowed him to pursue Indians into Spanish territory but not to attack any Spanish post. A man of Jackson's tenacity naturally felt hobbled by such a restriction, since when it came to Spaniards or Indians, few white Tennesseans—and certainly not Andrew Jackson—bothered with technicalities. In early 1818, without presidential approval, Jackson ordered his force of 2,000 federal troops, Tennessee volunteers, and Creek allies to cross the border into Spanish Florida from their encampment in south Georgia. In April the Americans assaulted a Spanish fort at St. Marks and destroyed Seminole villages. They also captured and court-martialed two Indian chiefs and two British traders accused of inciting Indian attacks. Jackson ordered their immediate execution, an act that outraged the British government and caused great consternation among President Monroe's cabinet. But the Tennessee general kept moving. In May he captured Pensacola, the Spanish capital of West Florida, established a provisional American government, and then returned to Tennessee. The entire Florida Panhandle was in American hands by the end of May 1818.

Jackson's exploits aroused anger in Madrid and concern in Washington. Spain demanded the return of its territory and the punishment of Jackson, but Spain's impotence was plain for all to see. Monroe's cabinet at first prepared to disavow Jackson's actions, especially his direct attack on Spanish posts. Calhoun, as secretary of war, wanted to discipline Jackson for disregard of orders—a stand that would later cause bad blood between the two men—but privately confessed a certain pleasure at the outcome. In any case a man as popular as Jackson was almost invulnerable. And he had one important friend in Washington, Secretary of State John Quincy Adams, who realized that Jackson's military actions had strengthened his own hand in negotiations already under way with the Spanish. U.S. forces withdrew from Florida, but negotiations resumed with the knowledge that the United States could retake Florida at any time.

With Florida's fate a foregone conclusion, John Quincy Adams cast his eye toward a larger purpose, a final definition of the ambiguous western boundary of the Louisiana Purchase and—his boldest stroke—extension of its boundary to the Pacific coast. In lengthy negotiations with Spain, Adams gradually gave ground on claims to Texas but stuck to his demand for a transcontinental line for the western boundary of the Louisiana Territory, extending it to the Pacific. Agreement on the Transcontinental Treaty came in 1819. Spain ceded all of Florida to the United States in return for the U.S. government's assumption of Spanish debts owed to U.S. merchants. The western boundary of the Louisiana Purchase would run along the Sabine River in Texas and then, in stair-step fashion, up to the Red River, along the Red, and up to the Arkansas River. From the source of the Arkansas, it would go north to the 42nd parallel and thence west to the Pacific coast. Florida became a U.S. territory, and its first governor was Andrew Jackson. In 1845, Florida would finally achieve statehood.

CRISES AND COMPROMISES

THE PANIC OF 1819 John Quincy Adams's Transcontinental Treaty of 1819 (also called the Adams-Onís Treaty) was a diplomatic triumph and the climactic event of America's postwar nationalism. Even before it was signed, however, two thunderclaps signaled the end of the brief Era of Good Feelings and warned of stormy weather ahead: the financial panic of 1819 and the controversy over Missouri statehood. The panic resulted from a sudden collapse of cotton prices in the British market as British textile mills turned from American cotton to cheaper East Indian sources. The price collapse set off a decline in the demand for other American goods and revealed the fragility of the prosperity that had begun after the War of 1812.

By borrowing excessive sums of money to finance their entrepreneurial schemes, businessmen, bankers, farmers, and land speculators had caused a volatile expansion of credit, succumbing to the contagion of a get-rich-quick fever that was sweeping the country. Even the directors of the second Bank of the United States engaged in the same reckless extension of loans that the state banks had pursued. In 1819, just as alert businessmen began to take alarm, a case of extensive fraud and embezzlement in the Baltimore branch of the Bank of the United States came to light. The disclosure led to the resignation of the director of the bank. His replacement, Langdon Cheves, a former congressman from South Carolina, established sounder policies.

Cheves reduced salaries and other costs, postponed the payment of dividends, restrained the extension of credit, and presented for redemption the state bank notes that came in, thereby forcing the state-chartered banks to keep specie (gold and silver) reserves. Cheves rescued the bank from near ruin, but only by putting pressure on the state banks. They in turn put pressure on their debtors, who found it harder to renew old loans or get new ones. In 1822, his job completed, Cheves retired and was succeeded in the following year by Nicholas Biddle of Philadelphia. The Cheves policies were the result rather than the cause of the panic, but they pinched debtors. Hard times lasted about three years, and many people blamed the federal bank for the financial panic. After the panic passed, resentment of the national bank lingered in the South and the West.

THE MISSOURI COMPROMISE Just as the financial panic was spreading across the country, another cloud appeared on the horizon: the onset of a fierce sectional controversy over slavery. By 1819 the country had an equal number of slave states and free states—eleven of each. The line between them was defined by the southern and western boundaries of Pennsylvania and the Ohio River. Although slavery lingered in some places north of the line, it was on its way to extinction there. West of the Mississippi River, however, no move had been made to extend the dividing line across the Louisiana Territory, where slavery had existed from the days when France and Spain had colonized the area. At the time, the Missouri Territory encompassed all of the Louisiana Purchase except the state of Louisiana, which entered the Union in 1812, and the Arkansas Territory, organized in 1819. The old French town of St. Louis became the funnel through which settlers, largely southerners who brought their slaves with them, rushed westward beyond the Mississippi River.

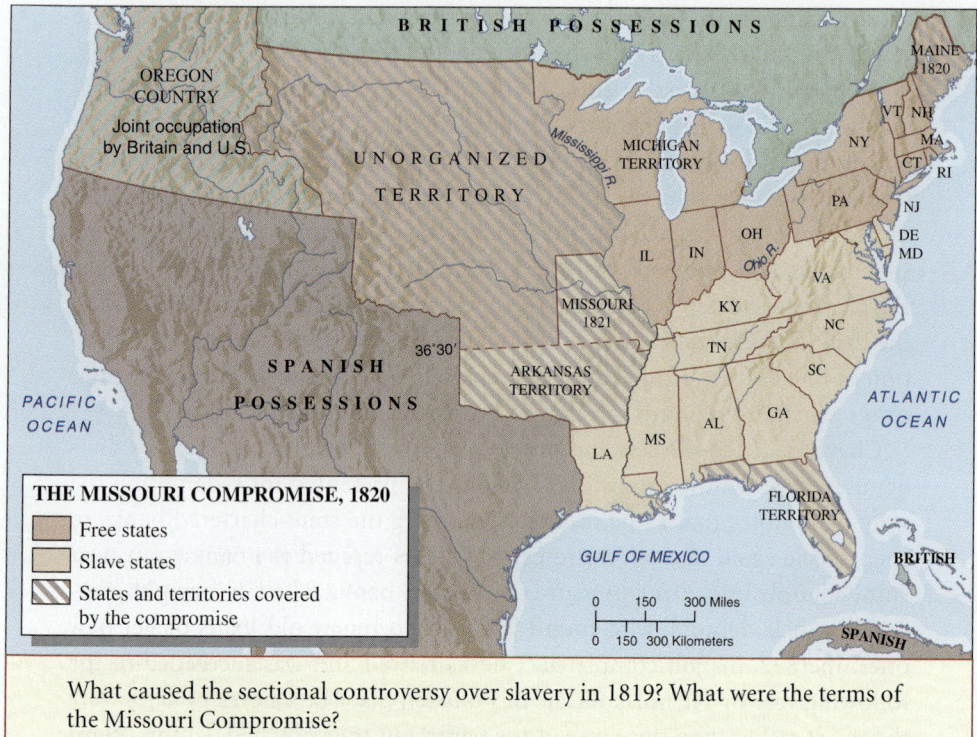

BRITISH POSSESSIONS

MAINE 1820

OREGON COUNTRY

Joint occupation by Britain and U.S.

UNORGANIZED TERRITORY

MICHIGAN TERRITORY

Mississippi R.

Ohio R.

VT NH
NY MA
CT RI
PA NJ
OH DE MD
IL IN
VA
KY
TN NC
SC

MISSOURI 1821

36°30'

SPANISH POSSESSIONS

ARKANSAS TERRITORY

PACIFIC OCEAN

ATLANTIC OCEAN

AL GA
MS
LA

FLORIDA TERRITORY

GULF OF MEXICO

BRITISH

THE MISSOURI COMPROMISE, 1820

Free states

Slave states

States and territories covered by the compromise

0   150   300 Miles

0   150   300 Kilometers

SPANISH

What caused the sectional controversy over slavery in 1819? What were the terms of the Missouri Compromise?

In early 1819 the House of Representatives was asked to approve legislation enabling the Missouri Territory to draft a state constitution, its population having passed the minimum of 60,000. At that point, Representative James Tallmadge Jr., a New York congressman, proposed a resolution prohibiting the transport of more slaves into Missouri, which already had some 10,000, and providing freedom at age twenty-five to those slaves born after the territory's admission as a state. The House passed the amendment on an almost strictly sectional vote, and the Senate rejected it by a similar tally, but with several northerners joining in the opposition. With population growing faster in the North, a political balance between the free states and the slave states could be held only in the Senate, where each state has two senators, regardless of population.

Maine's coincidental application for statehood made it easier to arrive at an agreement. Since colonial times, Maine had been the northern province of Massachusetts. The Senate linked its request for separate statehood with Missouri's and voted to admit Maine as a free state and Missouri as a slave state, thus maintaining the balance between free and slave states in the

Senate. A senator further extended the compromise by an amendment to exclude slavery from the rest of the Louisiana Purchase north of 36°30′, Missouri's southern border. Slavery thus would continue in the Arkansas Territory and in Missouri but would be excluded from the remainder of the area. People at that time presumed that what remained was the Great American Desert, unlikely ever to be settled. Thus the arrangement seemed to be a victory for the slave states. On August 10, 1821, President Monroe proclaimed the admission of Missouri as the twenty-fourth state. For the moment the controversy was settled. "But this momentous question," the aging Thomas Jefferson wrote to a friend, "like a firebell in the night awakened and filled me with terror. I considered it at once as the knell of the Union."

JUDICIAL NATIONALISM

JOHN MARSHALL   During the early nineteenth century many of the nation's leading attorneys and judges were nationalists. They believed that an expanding nation needed a central government with enough power and responsibility to override state and local interests. And they argued that an independent judiciary should have the authority to settle disputes between the states and the federal government. The continuing leader among these judicial nationalists was John Marshall. During Marshall's early years on the Court (he served thirty-four years altogether), he affirmed the principle of judicial review of legislative acts. In *Marbury v. Madison* (1803) and *Fletcher v. Peck* (1810) the Court struck down first a federal law and then a state law as unconstitutional.

STRENGTHENING THE FEDERAL GOVERNMENT   In the fateful year of 1819, John Marshall and the Supreme Court made two decisions of major importance in checking the power of the states and expanding the power of the federal government: *Dartmouth College v. Woodward* and *McCulloch v. Maryland.*

The *Dartmouth College* case involved an attempt by the New Hampshire legislature to alter a charter granted the

John Marshall

Chief justice and pillar of judicial nationalism.

college by King George III in 1769, under which the governing body of trustees became a self-perpetuating board. In 1816 the state's Republican legislature, irritated by this residue of monarchical rule as well as by the fact that Federalists dominated the board of trustees, placed Dartmouth under the control of a board named by the governor. The original trustees sued and lost in the state courts but, with Daniel Webster as their counsel, gained a hearing before the Supreme Court. The original charter, declared Marshall, was a valid contract that the legislature had violated, an action expressly forbidden by the Constitution. This decision implied an enlarged definition of *contract* that seemed to put private corporations beyond the reach of the states that chartered them. "If business is to prosper," Marshall explained, "men must have the assurance that contracts will be enforced."

John Marshall's single most important interpretation of the constitutional system appeared in *McCulloch v. Maryland*. In the unanimous 1819 decision the Court upheld the "implied powers" of Congress to charter the Bank of the United States and denied the state of Maryland's attempt to tax it. In a lengthy opinion, Marshall rejected Maryland's argument that the federal government was the creature of sovereign states. Instead, he insisted, it arose directly from the people acting through the state conventions that had ratified the Constitution ("We, the people of the United States, . . . do ordain and establish"). Whereas sovereignty was divided between the states and the national government, the latter, "though limited in its powers, is supreme within its sphere of action."

The state's effort to tax the national bank conflicted with the supreme law of the land. One great principle that "entirely pervades the Constitution," Marshall wrote, was "that the Constitution and the laws made in pursuance thereof are supreme: . . . they control the Constitution and laws of the respective states, and cannot be controlled by them." Maryland's effort to tax a national bank was therefore unconstitutional, for "the power to tax involves the power to destroy"—which was precisely what the legislatures of Maryland and several other states had in mind with respect to the national bank.

John Marshall's last great decision, *Gibbons v. Ogden* (1824), established national supremacy in regulating interstate commerce and thereby dealt another blow to proponents of states' rights. In 1808 the New York legislature had granted Aaron Ogden the exclusive ferry rights on the Hudson River between New York and New Jersey. A competitor, Thomas Gibbons, protested the state's right to grant such a monopoly. On behalf of a unanimous Court, Marshall ruled that the state's action conflicted with the federal Coasting Act, under which Gibbons operated. Congressional power to regulate commerce among the states, the Court said, "like all others vested in Congress, is complete in itself, may be exercised to its utmost extent, and acknowledges no limitations other than are prescribed in the Constitution." In striking down the monopoly created by the state, the nationalist Marshall opened the way to extensive development of steamboat navigation and, soon afterward, railroads. Such judicial nationalism provided a crucial support for economic expansion.

NATIONALIST DIPLOMACY

THE PACIFIC NORTHWEST In foreign affairs, too, nationalism prevailed. Within a few years of final approval of John Quincy Adams's Transcontinental Treaty in 1819, the secretary of state drew another important transcontinental boundary line. Spain had abandoned its claim to the Oregon Country above the 42nd parallel. Russia, however, had claims along the Pacific coast as well, including trading outposts from Alaska as far south as California. In 1823, Secretary of State Adams contested "the right of Russia to any territorial establishment on this continent." The U.S. government, he informed the Russian minister, assumed "that the American continents are no longer subjects for any new European colonial establishments." The upshot of his protest was a treaty signed in 1824, whereby Russia, which had more pressing concerns in Europe, accepted the latitude line of 548409 as the southern boundary of its claim. The Oregon Territory, to the south of the line, remained subject to joint occupation by the United States and Great Britain under their agreement of 1818.

THE MONROE DOCTRINE Secretary of State Adams's disapproval of further European colonization in the Western Hemisphere had clear implications for Latin America as well. One consequence of the Napoleonic Wars and the French occupation of Spain and Portugal was a series of wars of liberation in Latin America. Within little more than a decade after the flag of rebellion was first raised in 1811, Spain had lost almost its entire empire in the Americas. All that was left were the islands of Cuba and Puerto Rico and the colony of Santo Domingo on the island of Hispaniola.

That Spain could not regain her empire seems clear enough in retrospect. The British navy would not have permitted it because Britain's trade with the area was too important. For a time after Napoléon's final defeat, in 1815, however, European rulers were determined to restore monarchical "legitimacy" everywhere. In 1822, when the major European powers met in the Congress

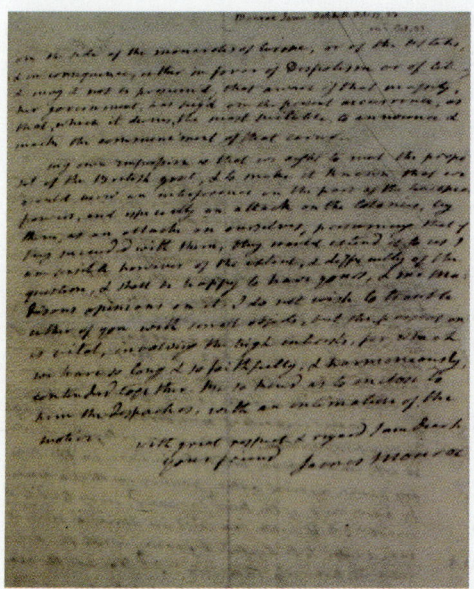

Forefather's advice

In this letter, Monroe asked former president Jefferson for advice on foreign policy.

of Verona, they authorized France to suppress the constitutionalist movement in Spain and restore the authority of the monarchy. In 1823, French troops crossed the Spanish border, put down the rebels, and restored King Ferdinand VII to absolute authority. Rumors began to circulate that France would also try to restore Ferdinand's "legitimate" power over Spain's American empire. President Monroe and Secretary of War Calhoun were alarmed at the possibility, although John Quincy Adams took the more realistic view that any such action was unlikely. The British foreign minister, George Canning, was also worried about French and Spanish intentions, and he urged the United States to protect Latin America. Monroe at first agreed, with the support of his sage advisers Jefferson and Madison.

Adams urged upon Monroe and the cabinet the independent course of proclaiming a unilateral policy against the restoration of Spain's colonies. "It would be more candid," Adams said, "as well as more dignified, to avow our principles explicitly to Russia and France, than to come in as a cockboat in the wake of the British man-of-war." Adams knew that the British navy would stop any action by a European power in Latin America. The British wanted the United States to agree not to acquire any more Spanish territory, including Cuba, Texas, and California, but Adams preferred to avoid such a commitment.

President Monroe incorporated the substance of Adams's views into his annual message to Congress in 1823. The Monroe Doctrine, as it was later called, comprised four major points: (1) that "the American continents . . . are henceforth not to be considered as subjects for future colonization by any European powers"; (2) that the political system of European powers was different from that of the United States, which would "consider any attempt on their part to extend their system to any portion of this hemisphere as dangerous to our peace and safety"; (3) that the United States would not interfere with existing European-controlled colonies; and (4) that the United States would keep out of the internal affairs of European nations and their wars.

At the time the statement drew little attention, either in the United States or abroad. Over the years, however, the Monroe Doctrine, not even so called until 1852, became one of the cherished principles of U.S. foreign policy. For the time being, however, it slipped into obscurity for want of any occasion to invoke it. In spite of Adams's affirmation, the United States came in as a cockboat in the wake of the British man-of-war after all, for the effectiveness of the doctrine depended upon British naval supremacy. The doctrine had no standing in international law. It was merely a statement of intent sent by an American president to Congress and did not even draw enough interest for the European powers to renounce it.

ONE-PARTY POLITICS

Almost from the start of Monroe's second term, in 1821, jockeying for the presidential succession in 1824 began. Three members of Monroe's cabinet were active candidates: Secretary of War John C. Calhoun, Secretary of the Treasury William H. Crawford, and Secretary of State John Quincy Adams. Speaker of the House Henry Clay, an outspoken economic nationalist, also thirsted for the office. And on the fringes of the Washington scene, a new force appeared in the person of former general Andrew Jackson, the scourge of the British, Spanish, and Seminoles, who became a senator from Tennessee in 1823. All were Republicans, for again no Federalist stood a chance, but they were competing in a new political world, complicated by the crosscurrents of nationalism and sectionalism. With only one party there was in effect no party, for there existed no generally accepted method for choosing a "regular" candidate.

State legislatures were free to nominate presidential candidates. Tennessee

Henry Clay

Clay entered the Senate at twenty-eight despite the requirement that senators be at least thirty years old.

and Pennsylvania supported Jackson, and Calhoun agreed to serve as his running mate. (The 1824 election was the first to feature paired presidential and vice-presidential candidates.) Kentucky named Clay, Massachusetts named Adams, and the amiable, hulking Crawford was selected by a poorly attended congressional caucus. Of the four candidates, only two articulated defined programs, and the outcome was an early lesson in the danger of committing oneself on the issues too soon. Crawford's friends emphasized his devotion to states' rights and strict constitutional construction. Clay, on the other hand, took his stand for the "American System": the national bank, the protective tariff, and a national program of government-financed internal improvements to bind the country together and strengthen its economy. Adams was close to Clay, openly dedicated to internal improvements but less strongly committed to the tariff. Jackson, where issues were concerned, carefully avoided commitment. His managers hoped that by being all things to all voters, Jackson could capitalize on his popularity as the hero of New Orleans at the end of the War of 1812.

THE "CORRUPT BARGAIN" The election of 1824 featured squabbling personalities and sectional partisanship more than substantive issues. Adams, the only northern candidate, carried New England, the former bastion of the Federalist party, and won most of New York's electoral votes. Clay took Kentucky, Ohio, and Missouri, while Crawford carried Virginia, Georgia, and Delaware. Jackson swept the Southeast plus Illinois and Indiana and, with Calhoun's support, the Carolinas, Pennsylvania, Maryland, and New Jersey.

The result was inconclusive in both the electoral vote and the popular vote. In the Electoral College, Jackson had 99 votes; Adams, 84; Crawford, 41; and Clay, 37. In the popular vote the proportion ran about the same. Whatever else might have been said about the outcome, it was clearly a defeat for Clay's American System: New England and New York opposed him on internal improvements, the South and the Southwest on the protective tariff. Sectionalism had defeated the national economic program, yet the advocate of the American System now assumed the role of president maker, since the election was thrown into the House of Representatives, where Clay's influence as Speaker was decisive. Clay had little trouble choosing, since he regarded Jackson as unfit for the office. "I cannot believe," he muttered, "that killing 2,500 Englishmen at New Orleans qualifies for the various, difficult and complicated duties of the Chief Magistracy." He eventually threw his support to John Quincy Adams. Clay disliked Adams, and vice versa, but Adams endorsed the high tariffs, internal transportation improvements, and strong national bank that were the centerpieces of Clay's American System.

Clay also expected Adams to name him secretary of state. Whatever the reasons, Clay's decision to support Adams backfired on the Kentuckian's own aspirations for the White House. The final vote in the House, which was by state, carried Adams to victory with 13 votes to Jackson's 7 and Crawford's 4.

It was a costly victory, for it united Adams's foes and crippled his administration before it got under way. Andrew Jackson dismissed Clay as "the Judas of the West," who thereafter would be burdened by the charge that he had entered into a selfishly "corrupt bargain" with Adams to gain the presidency. There is no evidence that Adams entered into any secret bargain with Clay to win his support, but the charge was widely believed after Adams made Clay his secretary of state, the office from which three successive presidents had risen. A campaign to elect Jackson next time crystallized almost immediately after the 1824 decision. "The people have been cheated," Jackson growled. William Crawford's supporters, including Martin Van Buren, "the Little Magician" of New York politics, soon moved into the Jackson camp.

JOHN QUINCY ADAMS   Short, plump, peppery John Quincy Adams was one of the ablest men, hardest workers, and finest intellects ever to enter the White House. But he also was one of the most ineffective presidents. Like his father, the aristocratic, crotchety Adams lacked the common touch and the politician's gift for compromise. A stubborn man who saw two brothers and two sons die from alcoholism, he suffered from chronic bouts of depression that spawned a grim self-righteousness and self-pity, qualities that did not endear him to fellow politicians.

Adams's first message to Congress provided a grandiose blueprint for national development, set forth so bluntly that it became a political disaster. The central government, the president asserted, should finance internal improvements, set up a national university, fund scientific explorations, build astronomical observatories, and create a department of the interior. To refrain from using broad federal powers, Adams maintained, "would be treachery to the most sacred of trusts." In leading the nation, officers of the government should not be "palsied by the will of our constituents."

John Quincy Adams

Adams was known as a brilliant man but an ineffective leader.

Such provocative language obscured whatever grandeur of conception the message to Congress had. For a minority president to demean the sovereignty of the voter was tactless enough, but for the son of John Adams to cite the example "of the nations of Europe and of their rulers" was downright suicidal. At one fell swoop he had revived all the Republican suspicions of the Adamses as closet monarchists.

Adams's presidential message to Congress hastened the emergence of a new party system. The minority who cast their lot with Adams and Clay were turning into National Republicans; the opposition, the growing party of Jacksonians, were the Democratic Republicans, who would eventually drop the name Republican and become Democrats.

Adams's headstrong plunge into nationalism and his refusal to play the game of politics condemned his administration to utter frustration. The popular mood was turning against federal authority. Congress ignored most of Adams's domestic proposals, and in foreign affairs the triumphs he had scored as secretary of state had no sequels.

The central political issue during Adams's presidency was a complex debate over tariff policy. The panic of 1819 had provoked calls in 1820 for a higher tariff, but the effort failed by one vote in the Senate. In 1824 those determined to protect American industry from foreign competition renewed the effort, with greater success. The Tariff of 1824 favored the middle Atlantic and New England manufacturers by raising duties on woolens, cotton, iron, and other finished goods. Henry Clay's Kentucky won a tariff on hemp, a fiber used for making rope, and a tariff on raw wool brought the wool-growing interests to the support of the measure. Additional federal revenues were raised with duties on sugar, molasses, coffee, and salt.

Four years later Andrew Jackson's supporters sought to advance their presidential candidate through an awkward scheme hatched by John Calhoun. The plan was to present an alternative bill with such outrageously high tariffs on imported raw materials that the eastern manufacturers would join the commercial interests there and, with the votes of the agricultural South and Southwest, combine to defeat the measure. In the process, Jacksonians in the Northeast could take credit for supporting the tariff, and other Jacksonians, wherever it fit their interests, could take credit for opposing it—while Jackson himself remained in the background. Virginia's John Randolph saw through the ruse. The tariff bill, he asserted, "referred to manufactures of no sort of kind, but the manufacture of a President of the United States."

The complicated scheme did help elect Jackson in 1828, but in the process John Calhoun became a victim of his own machinations. His tariff bill, to his chagrin, passed, thanks to the growing strength of manufacturing interests in New England and several crucial amendments that exempted certain raw materials needed by American industry. Daniel Webster, now a senator from Massachusetts, explained that he was ready to deny all he had said before against the tariff because New England had built up her manufactures on the understanding that the protective tariff was a settled policy.

When the tariff bill passed in May 1828, it was Calhoun's turn to explain his newfound opposition to the gospel of tariff protection, and nothing so well illustrates the flexibility of constitutional principles as the switch in positions by Webster and Calhoun. Back in South Carolina, Calhoun prepared the *South Carolina Exposition and Protest* (1828), which was issued anonymously along with a series of resolutions by the state legislature. In that document, Calhoun set forth the right of a state to nullify an act of Congress that it found unconstitutional.

THE ELECTION OF ANDREW JACKSON   Thus the stage was set for the contentious election of 1828, which might more truly be called a political revolution than that of 1800. But if the issues of the day had anything to do with the election, they were hardly visible in the campaign, in which politicians on both sides reached depths of scurrilousness that had not been plumbed since 1800. Those campaigning for Adams denounced Jackson as a hot-tempered, ignorant barbarian, a participant in repeated duels and frontier brawls, a man whose fame rested upon his reputation as a killer. In addition, Jackson's enemies dredged up the story that he had lived in adultery with his wife, Rachel, before they were married. In fact they had been married for two years before discovering that her divorce from her former husband had not been finalized. As soon as the divorce was official, Andrew and Rachel had remarried. A furious Jackson blamed Clay for the campaign slurs against his wife's chastity. He bitterly dismissed his longtime enemy as "the basest, meanest scoundrel that ever disgraced the image of his god."

The Jacksonians, however, were also not averse to mudslinging. They lambasted Adams, condemning him as a man corrupted by foreigners in the courts of Europe. They called Adams a gambler and a spendthrift for having bought a billiard table and a chess set for the White House and a puritanical hypocrite for despising the common people and warning Congress to ignore the will of the people. The Jacksonians also attacked Adams for signing the Tariff of 1828 and for winning the 1824 election by backroom deals. Adams had gained the presidency in 1824, the Jacksonians claimed, by the "corrupt bargain" with Clay.

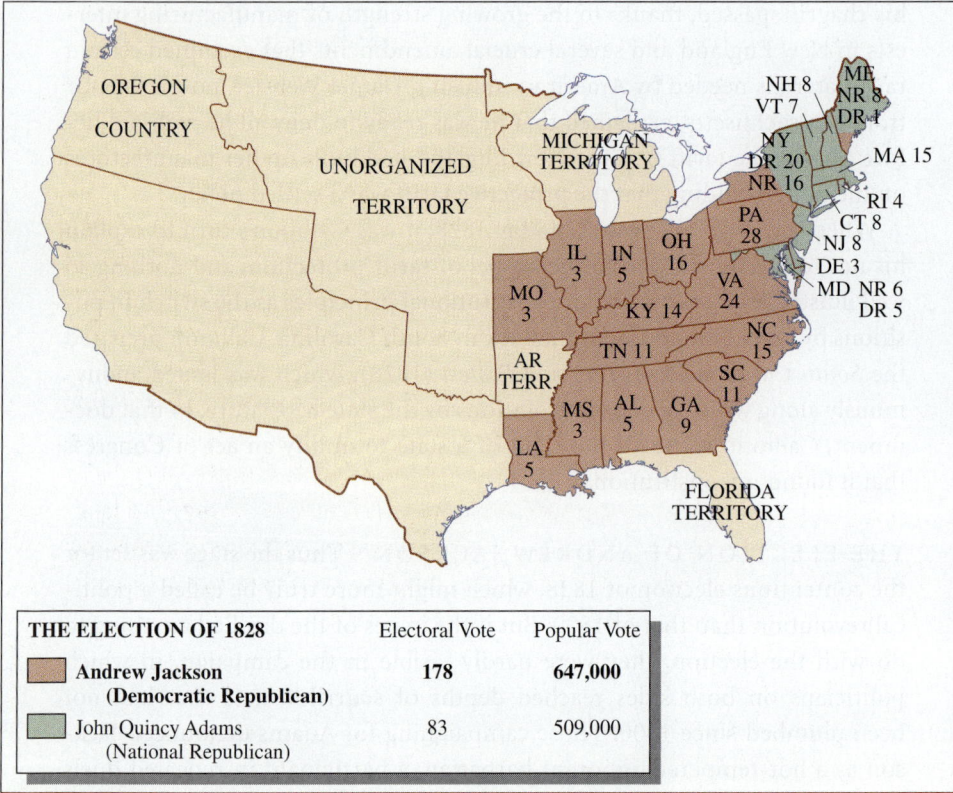

THE ELECTION OF 1828	Electoral Vote	Popular Vote
Andrew Jackson (Democratic Republican)	**178**	**647,000**
John Quincy Adams (National Republican)	83	509,000

How did the two presidential candidates, Adams and Jackson, portray each other? Why did Jackson seem to have the advantage in the election of 1828? How did the broadening of suffrage affect the presidential campaign?

In the campaign of 1828, Jackson held most of the advantages. As a military victor, he stirred the patriotism of voters. As a son of the West and an Indian fighter, he was a hero to voters in the new states along the frontier. As a planter and slaveholder, he had the trust of southern planters. Debtors and local bankers who hated the national bank also turned to Jackson. In addition, his vagueness on the issues protected him from attack by interest groups. Not least of all, Jackson benefited from a growing spirit of democracy in which the common folk were no longer satisfied to look to elites for leadership, as they had done in the past.

Since the Revolution and especially since 1800, more and more states had reduced the property requirements for voting. Some states granted universal male suffrage. After 1815 the new states of the West entered the Union with either white male suffrage or a modest taxpaying requirement, and older states such as Connecticut (in 1818), Massachusetts (in 1821), and New York (in 1821) abolished their property requirements for voting. As more men voted and participated in political activities, the ideal of social equality took on more importance in the political culture.

Jackson embodied this new, more democratic political world. A tall, sinewy frontiersman born in South Carolina, he was a fighter, horse trader, land speculator, and frontier lawyer. A fellow law student described him as a "most roaring, rollicking, game-cocking, horse-racing, card-playing, mischievous fellow." One of his campaign slogans announced, "Adams can write, Jackson can fight."

The 1828 election returns revealed that Jackson had won by a comfortable margin. The electoral vote was 178 to 83. Adams had won New Jersey, Delaware, all of New England (except 1 of Maine's 9 electoral votes) and a scattering of votes in New York and Maryland. All the rest belonged to Jackson. A convulsive era in American politics was about to begin, as the new president was eager to transform the tone and tenor of American politics.

CHAPTER SUMMARY

- **Economic Policies** The Tariff of 1816 protected American manufacturing, and the second Bank of the United States provided a stronger currency, thus strengthening the national economy. Henry Clay's American System anticipated an active economic role for the federal government with its vision of a national bank, a protective tariff, and federally funded internal improvements, such as roads.

- **Era of Good Feelings** James Monroe's term in office was initially dubbed the Era of Good Feelings because it began with peace and prosperity. The demise of the Federalists ended the first party system in America, leaving the Republicans as the only political party in the nation. The seeming unity of the Republicans was shattered by the election of 1824, which Andrew Jackson lost as a result of what he believed was a "corrupt bargain" between John Quincy Adams and Henry Clay.

- **Sectionalism** The growth of the cotton culture transformed life in the South, in part by encouraging the expansion of slavery. As settlers streamed west, the extension of slavery into the new territories became the predominant concern of southern politicians. The Missouri Compromise, a short-term solution, exposed the emotions and turmoil that the problem generated. During this time, the North changed as well—an urban middle class emerged.

- **Strengthening the Federal Government** The Marshall court used the "necessary and proper" clause to endorse the exercise of implied constitutional powers of the federal government. In striking down a federal law and a state law, the Court confirmed the primacy of the national judiciary. Further decisions of the Marshall court protected contract rights against state action and established the federal government's supremacy over interstate commerce.

- **The Monroe Doctrine** The main diplomatic achievements of the period between the end of the War of 1812 and the coming civil war concerned America's boundaries and the resumption of trade with its old enemy, Great Britain. The Monroe Doctrine expressed the idea that America was no longer open to colonization and proclaimed American neutrality in European affairs.

CHRONOLOGY

1810	Supreme Court issues *Fletcher v. Peck* decision
1815	Construction of the National Road begins
1816	Second Bank of the United States is established
	First protective tariff goes into effect
1819	Supreme Court issues *McCulloch v. Maryland* decision
	United States and Spain agree to the Transcontinental (Adams-Onís) Treaty
1821	Florida becomes a territory
	Missouri becomes a state
1823	President Monroe enunciates the principles of the Monroe Doctrine
1824	Supreme Court issues *Gibbons v. Ogden* decision
	John Quincy Adams wins the presidential election by what some critics claim is a "corrupt bargain" with Henry Clay
1828	John C. Calhoun publishes the *South Carolina Exposition and Protest*

KEY TERMS & NAMES

11

THE JACKSONIAN IMPULSE

FOCUS QUESTIONS wwnorton.com/studyspace

- To what extent did Andrew Jackson's election initiate a new era in American politics?

- What was Jackson's attitude toward federal involvement in the economy?

- How did Jackson respond to the nullification controversy?

- What happened to the Indians living east of the Mississippi River by 1840?

- Why did a new party system of Democrats and Whigs emerge?

The election of Andrew Jackson coincided with a distinctive new era in politics, economic development, and social change. Jackson was the first president not to come from a prominent colonial family. As a self-made soldier, politician, and slave-owning land speculator from the backcountry, he symbolized a transformation in the nation's social structure and political temper. The Jacksonian era was supposedly animated by the emergence of the "common man" in political life.

Profound economic and social developments were reshaping the young United States. In 1828 there were twenty-four states and almost 13 million people, many of them recent arrivals from Germany and Ireland. The national population was growing rapidly, doubling every twenty-three years. Surging foreign demand for cotton and other goods helped fuel a transportation revolution and an economic boom. Shoe factories sprouted up across the New England countryside, as did textile mills, their spinning looms fed by cotton grown in the newly cultivated lands of Alabama and Mississippi.

Cities increasingly became the centers of the nation's commerce, industry, finance, and politics. The urban population grew twice as fast as the rural population during the second quarter of the nineteenth century. A more urban society and a more specialized and speculative economy created more instability as people took greater risks to make money. A more stratified social order also emerged, with some people acquiring great wealth while most others worked for wages.

Local life was increasingly connected to regional, national, and even global networks. An agrarian economy that earlier had produced crops and goods for household use or local exchange expanded into a market-oriented economy engaged in national and international commerce. New canals and roads opened up eastern markets to western farmers in the Ohio River valley. The new "market economy" brought with it regional specialization and increasing division of labor. As more land was put into cultivation and commercial farmers came to rely upon banks for credit to buy land and seed, they were subject to greater risks and the volatility of the market. In the midst of periodic financial panics and sharp business depressions, farmers unable to pay their debts lost their farms to "corrupt" banks, which they believed had engaged in reckless speculative ventures and had benefited from government favoritism.

For many people the transition to cash-crop agriculture and capitalist manufacturing was painful and unsettling. A traditional economy of independent artisans and subsistence farmers was giving way to a system of centralized workshops, mills, and factories based upon wage labor. Chartered corporations and commercial banks began to dominate local economies. With the onset of the factory system and urban commerce, people left farms and shops and became dependent upon others for their food, clothing, and livelihood. This transformation called into question the traditional assumption of Thomas Jefferson and others that a republic could survive only if most of its citizens were independent, self-reliant property owners, neither too rich to dominate other people nor too poor to become dependent and subservient.

A New Political Culture

At the same time that the urban population was increasing and more people were engaging in wage labor rather than agriculture, many states, especially those west of the Appalachian Mountains, were reducing or eliminating the property requirement for voting. This enabled white men with little or no property to participate in the political process. The easing of voting restrictions reflected the feeling on the part of workers, artisans, and small merchants, as well as farmers, that a more democratic ballot would help combat the rising influence of commercial and manufacturing interests. By 1830 only six states continued to require voters to own property. The easing of such restrictions meant that four times as many men voted in the 1828 presidential election as had voted in 1824.

By gaining access to the political process as voters, propertyless men encouraged a new type of politician, one who identified with the values and desires of the masses. To have been born in a log cabin and to be a "common" man wearing a coonskin cap rather than a powdered wig became great political advantages during the Jacksonian era. As President Andrew Jackson himself declared, he governed on behalf of "the humble members of society—the farmers, mechanics, and laborers."

The mass-based Democratic party that ushered Jackson into the White House in early 1829 reflected the emergence of a new political culture during the 1820s. Up to that time well-organized national political parties had been virtually nonexistent. The Jacksonian era witnessed the crystallization of formal parties (the Democratic party and the Whig party), which took

The Verdict of the People

George Caleb Bingham's painting depicts the increasingly democratic politics of the mid–nineteenth century.

particular stands on issues, held formal nominating conventions to select presidential and vice-presidential candidates, and had as members congressmen and senators who voted with their party on the issues.

The second quarter of the nineteenth century also witnessed a new style of politicking. It featured fierce polemics, colorful politicians, expensive campaigns, tightly controlled local party "machines," and intense partisan loyalties. Politics during the Jacksonian era was a vibrant public phenomenon that involved mass marches, vigorous debates, and high voter turnout. The local party machines used a partisan network of employers and landlords to help party members find jobs and housing; in return they could expect their members to vote without question for the candidates they designated. Citizens turned to local, state, and federal politicians to help relieve their distress and promote their prosperity. For example, they expected the government to settle the Indian "problem," open up new and cheaper land, and build roads and canals along which they could send their produce and goods.

The new Democratic party was an unstable coalition of northern workers (many of them Irish and German immigrants), owners of small farms, landless laborers, and aspiring entrepreneurs from all sections of the country. Their shared concern was the preservation of a "just" and "virtuous" society in which most people were small property holders jealous of their freedom from monopolists or corrupt politicians. Democrats therefore opposed tariffs and the central national bank, as well as any other efforts to centralize government power. At the same time frontier folk settling in the new states of the Old Northwest (Ohio, Indiana, and Illinois) and the Old Southwest were no longer willing to defer to traditional political and social elites.

Yet to call the Jacksonian era the age of the common man, as many historians have done, is misleading. While political participation increased during the Jacksonian era, the period never produced true economic and social equality. Power and privilege for the most part remained in the hands of an "uncommon" elite. Moreover, many Jacksonians in power proved to be as opportunistic and manipulative as the "corrupt" patrician politicians they displaced. And for all their egalitarian rhetoric, Jacksonian Democrats never embraced the principle of economic equality. "Distinctions in society will always exist under every just government," Andrew Jackson observed. "Equality of talents, or education, or of wealth cannot be produced by human institutions." He and his supporters wanted people to have an equal chance to compete in the economic marketplace and in the political arena, but they never sanctioned equality of income or status. "True republicanism," one commentator declared, "requires that every man shall have an equal chance—that every man shall be free to become as unequal as he can." In the afterglow of Jackson's electoral victory, however, few observers troubled with such distinctions. It was time to celebrate the commoner's ascension to the presidency.

JACKSON TAKES OFFICE

Andrew Jackson's father had died before Andrew was born, and his mother scratched out a meager living as a housekeeper before dying of cholera when her son was fifteen. Jackson grew to be proud, gritty, and short-tempered, and he became a good hater. During the Revolution, when he was a young boy, two of his brothers were killed by British redcoats, and the young Jackson was gashed and scarred by a British officer's saber. He also carried with him the conviction that it was not enough for a man to be right; he had to be tough—even ferocious—as well, qualities that inspired his soldiers to nickname him Old Hickory. During a duel with a man reputed to be the best shot in Tennessee, Jackson nevertheless let his opponent fire first. For his gallantry the future president received a bullet that wedged itself next to his heart. He nevertheless straightened himself, patiently took aim, and killed his foe. "I should have hit him," Jackson claimed, "if he had shot me through the brain."

Andrew Jackson was the most popular politician since George Washington. He was a commanding figure with a cutthroat ambition. "I was born for a storm," he once boasted; "a calm does not suit me." Tall and lean with the bony limbs of a skeleton, he looked gaunt and haggard—as well as intrepid and domineering. His ashen skin, chiseled features, deep-blue eyes, jutting chin, and iron-gray hair accentuated his steely personality. A British visitor said he had a "gamecock look." By nature, Jackson was visceral and combative—a fearless fighter governed by an explosive temper and strong prejudices. "His passions are terrible," said Thomas Jefferson, who deemed the volatile Jackson "dangerous" and "unfit" for the presidency.

As a victorious and wildly popular general, Jackson often behaved as a tyrant. It was not enough for him to win; others must fail—and be killed or humiliated. He not only had deserters and captives executed; he once had a teenager shot for refusing to comply with an officer's order. During and then after the Battle of New Orleans, in 1815, he took control of the chaotic city, declared martial law, and ruled with an iron fist for two months, imposing a nightly curfew, censoring the newspaper, jailing city officials (including judges), and threatening to execute dissenters. After retiring from the army,

All Creation Going to the White House

The scene following Jackson's inauguration as president, according to the satirist Robert Cruikshank.

Jackson became an attorney, a planter, a Tennessee legislator, and a U.S. senator. Now, as the nation's seventh president, he was determined to change the structure and tone of the federal government. The new president curried the support of the masses. Senator Daniel Webster scoffed at the huge, unruly crowd attending Jackson's inauguration: "Persons have come 500 miles to see Genl. Jackson; & they really seem to think that the Country is rescued from some dreadful danger."

Jackson did view himself as a savior of sorts, a crusading president with the courage to restore precious values that had been lost in the rapid growth of the young nation. He earnestly believed that the American political system had strayed from the egalitarian agrarian republic envisioned by Thomas Jefferson. National politics, he had decided, had quickly fallen under the sway of wealthy bankers and entrepreneurs preoccupied with promoting their self-interest at the expense of the public good. The principled, ferocious Jackson vowed to attack and eliminate such corrupting elitism. Like Jefferson, he hated commerce, he hated speculators, and most of all, he hated central bankers, for they symbolized concentrated economic power that necessarily constricted individual freedom. An ardent Jeffersonian whom Jefferson himself distrusted, Jackson insisted that the majority of the people—not the financial elite—should rule. Yet ironies abounded as the audacious new president assumed leadership of a self-conscious democratic revival. Jackson, an owners of slaves and hater of Indians (his "savage enemies"), was determined to restore political equality (for white men), rather than centralized federal power, as the centerpiece of the American republic. He also wanted to lower taxes, reduce government spending, shrink the federal bureaucracy, destroy the national bank, and cleanse politics of what he viewed as the corrosive effects of self-interest. And he was determined to remove the "ill-fated race" of Indians so that white Americans could exploit their lands. In typical fashion, Jackson acted quickly—and decisively.

APPOINTMENTS AND RIVALRIES Andrew Jackson believed that government workers who stayed too long in office became corrupt. So he set about replacing John Quincy Adams's appointees with his own supporters. But his use of the "spoils system" has been exaggerated. During his first year in office, Jackson replaced only about 9 percent of the appointed officials in the federal government, and during his entire term he replaced fewer than 20 percent.

Jackson's administration was from the outset divided between the partisans of Secretary of State Martin Van Buren and those of Vice President John C. Calhoun. Much of the political history of the next few years would turn upon the rivalry between these two statesmen as each jockeyed for position as Jackson's successor. Van Buren held most of the advantages, foremost among them his skill at timing and tactics. Jackson, new to political administration, leaned heavily upon him for advice. Calhoun, a humorless man of towering intellect and apostolic zeal, possessed a demonic sense of duty and a keen interest in political theory. As vice president he was determined to defend southern interests, especially the preservation of slavery, against the advance of northern industrialism and abolitionism.

THE EATON AFFAIR In his battle for political power with Calhoun, Van Buren had luck as well as political skill on his side. Fate handed him a trump card: the succulent scandal known as the Peggy Eaton affair. The daughter of an Irish tavern owner, Margaret "Peggy" O'Neale was a vivacious widow whose husband supposedly had committed suicide upon learning of her affair with the Tennessee senator John Eaton, a close friend of Jackson. Her marriage to Eaton, three months before he entered Jackson's cabinet as secretary of war, had scarcely made a virtuous woman of her in the eyes of

Political scandal

This political cartoon depicts Jackson and his Cabinet welcoming a popular French dancer and actress to the White House. This cartoon has long been associated with the Eaton affair.

the proper ladies of Washington. Floride Calhoun, the vice president's wife, especially objected to Peggy Eaton's lowly origins and unsavory past. She pointedly snubbed her, and the cabinet wives followed suit.

Peggy's plight reminded Jackson of the gossip that had pursued his wife, Rachel, and he pronounced Peggy Eaton "chaste as a virgin." The cabinet members, however, were unable to cure their wives of what Van Buren dubbed "the Eaton Malaria." Van Buren was a widower, free to lavish on poor Peggy all the attention that Jackson thought was her due. Mrs. Eaton herself, however, finally gave in to the chill and withdrew from the Washington social scene. The outraged Jackson linked Calhoun to what he called a conspiracy against her and drew even closer to Van Buren.

INTERNAL IMPROVEMENTS While Washington social life weathered the gossip-filled winter of 1829–1830, Van Buren delivered some additional blows to Calhoun. It was easy to bring Jackson into opposition to federally financed internal improvements and thus to programs with which

Calhoun had long been identified. In 1830 the Maysville Road bill, passed by Congress, offered Jackson a happy chance for a dual thrust at his rivals John Calhoun and Henry Clay. The bill authorized the government to buy stock in a road from Maysville to Clay's hometown of Lexington. The proposed road lay entirely within the state of Kentucky, and though part of a larger scheme to link up with the National Road via Cincinnati, it could be viewed as a purely local undertaking. On that ground, Jackson vetoed the bill, and his decisive action garnered widespread acclaim. Yet while Jackson continued to oppose federal aid to local projects, he supported such projects as the National Road. Even so, Jackson's opposition to the Maysville Road set an important precedent, on the eve of the railroad age, for limiting federal initiative in transportation improvements. The early railroad lines would be built altogether by state funds and private capital until at least 1850.

NULLIFICATION

CALHOUN'S THEORY   There is a fine irony to Vice President John Calhoun's plight in the Jackson administration, for the South Carolinian was now midway between his early phase as an economic nationalist and his later phase as a states' rights sectionalist. Conditions in his home state had brought on the change. Suffering from prolonged agricultural depression, South Carolina lost almost 70,000 residents to emigration during the 1820s and would lose nearly twice that number in the 1830s. Most South Carolinians blamed the protective tariff, which tended to raise the prices of manufactured goods from Britain and Europe. Insofar as tariffs discouraged the sale of foreign goods in the United States, they reduced the ability of British and French traders to buy southern cotton. This situation worsened already existing problems of low cotton prices and farmland exhausted from perennial planting. The South Carolinians' malaise was compounded by the increasing criticism of slavery. Hardly had the nation emerged from the Missouri controversy when the city of Charleston, South Carolina, was thrown into panic by the thwarted Denmark Vesey slave insurrection of 1822.

The unexpected passage of the Tariff of 1828, called the tariff of abominations by its critics, left Calhoun no choice but to join the opposition or give up his base of political support in his home state. Calhoun's *South Carolina Exposition and Protest* (1828), written in opposition to the new tariff, contained a finespun theory of nullification, whereby a state could in effect repeal a federal law. This theory stopped just short of justifying secession from the Union. The unsigned statement accompanied resolutions of the South

Carolina legislature protesting the tariff. Calhoun, however, had not entirely abandoned his earlier nationalism. He wanted to preserve the Union by protecting the minority rights that the agricultural and slaveholding South claimed. The fine balance he struck between states' rights and central authority was actually not far removed from Andrew Jackson's own philosophy, but growing tensions between the two men would complicate the issue. The flinty Jackson, in addition, was determined to prevent any state defiance of federal law.

John C. Calhoun

During the Civil War, the Confederate government printed, but never issued, a one-cent postage stamp bearing this likeness of Calhoun.

THE WEBSTER-HAYNE DEBATE   South Carolina's leaders hated the tariff because it helped northern manufacturers and forced South Carolina planters to pay higher prices for American products. But they had postponed any action against its enforcement, hoping for a new tariff policy from the Jackson administration. There the issue stood until 1830, when the great Webster-Hayne debate sharpened the lines between states' rights and the Union. The immediate occasion for the debate, however, was the question of government land.

The federal government still owned immense tracts of land, and the question of how to dispose of the acreage dominated the sectional debate. Late in 1829 a Connecticut senator, fearing the continued drain of residents from New England, sought to restrict land sales in the West. When the resolution came before the Senate in 1830, Missouri's Thomas Hart Benton, who for years had been calling for lower land prices, denounced it as a sectional attack designed to impede the settlement of the West so that the East might maintain its supply of cheap factory labor and its political leverage.

Robert Y. Hayne of South Carolina took Benton's side. Senator Hayne saw in the public land issue a chance to strengthen the political alliance of South and West reflected in the 1828 presidential vote for Jackson. Perhaps by endorsing a policy of cheap land in the West, southerners could win western support for lower tariffs. The government, said Hayne, endangered the Union by imposing a hardship upon one section to the benefit of another.

Senator Daniel Webster of Massachusetts rose to offer a dramatic defense of the East. Possessed of a thunderous voice and a theatrical flair, Webster was the nation's foremost orator. With the gallery hushed, the "God-like Daniel" denied that the East had ever sought to restrict development of the West. Webster then lured Hayne into defending states' rights and upholding the doctrine of nullification instead of pursuing a coalition with the West.

Hayne took the bait. Young, handsome, and himself an accomplished speaker, he defended Calhoun's *South Carolina Exposition,* arguing that the Union was a compact of the states and that the federal government, which was their agent, could not be the judge of its own powers, else its powers would be unlimited. Rather, the states remained free to judge when the national government had overstepped the bounds of its constitutional authority. The right of state interposition, whereby a state could interpose its authority over a federal law in order to thwart an unjust federal statute, was "as full and complete as it was before the Constitution was formed."

In rebutting the idea that a state could thwart a federal law, Webster offered a nationalistic view of the Constitution. From the beginning, he asserted, the American Revolution had been a crusade of the united colonies rather than one of each separately. True sovereignty resided in the people as a whole, for whom both federal and state governments acted as agents in their respective spheres. If a single state could nullify a law of the federal government, Webster insisted, then the Union would be a "rope of sand," a practical absurdity. A state could neither nullify a federal law nor secede from the Union. The practical outcome of nullification would be a confrontation leading to civil war.

Those sitting in the Senate galleries and much of the nation at large thrilled to Webster's eloquence. His closing statement has become justly famous: "Liberty and Union, now and forever, one and inseparable." In the practical world of coalition politics, Webster also had the better argument, for the Union and majority rule meant more to westerners, including Jackson, than the abstractions of state sovereignty and nullification promoted by Calhoun and other southerners. As for the sale of public lands, the disputed resolution to restrict land sales was soon defeated anyway. And whatever one might argue about the origins of the Union, its evolution would validate Webster's position.

THE RIFT WITH CALHOUN   As yet, however, Jackson had not spoken out on the issue. Like Vice President Calhoun he was a slaveholder, and he might be expected to sympathize with South Carolina, his native state. Soon all doubt was removed, at least on the point of nullification. On April 13, 1830, at the annual Jefferson Day dinner honoring the birthday of the former president, Jackson and Van Buren agreed that the president should present a toast that would indicate his opposition to nullification. When his turn came, Jackson rose, stood erect as a poplar, raised his glass, pointedly stared at Calhoun, and announced, "Our Union—it must be preserved!" Calhoun tried to parry Jackson's challenge with a toast to "the Union, next to our liberty most dear!" But Jackson had set off a bombshell that exploded the plans of the states' righters.

Nearly a month afterward, the final nail was driven into the coffin of Calhoun's presidential ambitions. On May 12, 1830, Jackson saw for the first time a letter confirming reports that in 1818 Calhoun, as secretary of war, had proposed disciplining him for his reckless behavior during the invasion of Spanish-held Florida. This discovery prompted a tense correspon-

The Rats Leaving a Falling House

During his first term, Jackson was beset by dissension within his administration. Here "public confidence in the stability of this administration" is toppling.

dence between President Jackson and Calhoun and ended with a curt note from the president cutting off further communication.

The rift prompted Jackson to take a dramatic step: he removed all Calhoun partisans from the cabinet. He then named Van Buren the U.S. minister to London, pending Senate approval. In the fall of 1831, Jackson announced his readiness for one more term as president, with the idea of returning Van Buren from London in time for the New Yorker to succeed him in 1836. But in 1832, when the Senate reconvened, Van Buren's enemies opposed his appointment as minister to England and gave Calhoun, as vice president, a chance to reject the nomination with a tie-breaking vote. "It will kill him, sir, kill him dead," Calhoun told Senator Thomas Hart Benton. Benton disagreed: "You have broken a minister, and elected a Vice-President." So, it turned out, he had. Calhoun's vote against Van Buren aroused popular sympathy for the New Yorker, who would soon be nominated to succeed Calhoun as vice president.

His own presidential hopes blasted, Calhoun eagerly became the public leader of the South Carolina nullificationists, who believed that despite reductions supported by Jackson, tariff rates remained too high. By the end of 1831, Jackson was calling for further tariff reductions to take the wind out of the nullificationists' sails, and the Tariff of 1832 did cut revenues another $5 million, but mainly on unprotected items. Average tariff rates were about 25 percent, but rates on cottons, woolens, and iron remained around 50 percent. South Carolinians again labeled such high rates an "abomination."

THE SOUTH CAROLINA ORDINANCE White South Carolinians, living in the only state where slaves were a majority, feared that the federal authority to impose tariffs might eventually be used to end slavery. In the state elections of 1832, the advocates of nullification took the initiative in organization and agitation. A state convention overwhelmingly adopted a nullification ordinance repudiating the tariff acts of 1828 and 1832 as unconstitutional. The legislature chose Robert Hayne as governor and elected John Calhoun to succeed him as senator. Calhoun promptly resigned as vice president in order to defend nullification on the Senate floor.

In the crisis, South Carolina found itself standing alone. Other southern states expressed sympathy, but none endorsed nullification. Jackson's response was measured and firm—at least in public. In private he threatened to hang Calhoun and all other traitors—and later expressed regret that he had failed to hang at least Calhoun. In his annual message on December 4, 1832, Jackson announced his firm intention to enforce the tariff, but once again he urged Congress to lower the rates. On December 10 he followed up with his Nullification Proclamation, a document that characterized the doctrine of nullification as an "impractical absurdity." Jackson appealed to the people of his native state not to follow false leaders: "The laws of the United States must be executed. . . . Those who told you that you might peaceably prevent their execution, deceived you. . . . Their object is disunion. But be not deceived by names. Disunion by armed force is treason."

CLAY'S COMPROMISE Jackson then sent federal soldiers and ships to Charleston to enforce the tariff in South Carolina. The nullifiers mobilized the state militia while their local opponents, called Unionists, organized a volunteer force. In 1833 the president requested from Congress a "force bill" authorizing him to use the army to compel compliance with federal law in

South Carolina. At the same time he endorsed a bill in Congress that would have lowered tariff duties.

When the force bill was introduced, Calhoun immediately rose in opposition, denying that either he or his state favored disunion. Calhoun claimed that he did not want the South to leave the Union; he wanted the region to regain its political dominance of the Union. Passage of the bill eventually came to depend upon the support of the shrewd Kentucky senator Henry Clay, who finally yielded to those urging him to save the day. On February 12, 1833, he introduced a plan to reduce the tariff gradually until 1842, by which time no rate would be more than 20 percent. South Carolina would have preferred a greater reduction, but Clay's plan got the nullifiers out of the dilemma they had created.

On March 1, 1833, Congress passed the compromise tariff and the force bill, and Jackson signed both. The South Carolina convention then met and rescinded its nullification ordinance. In a face-saving gesture it nullified the force bill, for which Jackson no longer had any need. Both sides were able to claim victory. The president had upheld the supremacy of the Union, and South Carolina had secured a reduction of the tariff. A sulking Calhoun, worn out by the controversy, returned to his plantation. "The struggle, so far from being over," he ominously wrote, "is not more than fairly commenced."

RACIAL PREJUDICE IN THE JACKSONIAN ERA

The Jacksonian era was rife with contradictions. Many of the same social factors and economic forces that promoted the democratization of the political process during the 1820s also led Democrats, North and South, to justify white supremacy, slavery, and the removal of Indians from their ancestral lands. The same Democrats who demanded political equality for themselves denied social equality and political rights to African Americans, Indians, and women.

What explains such contradictory behavior? By emphasizing the racial inferiority of Indians and blacks, white wage earners could, in a tortuous sense, enhance their own self-esteem and justify their own economic interests. In addition, many northern workers feared that their own jobs would be jeopardized if runaway slaves continued to stream northward or if all the enslaved workers in the South were freed.

ATTITUDES TOWARD BLACKS Roger B. Taney, Andrew Jackson's attorney general, declared in 1831 that blacks were a "separate and degraded people" and therefore could be discriminated against by local and state governments. Free blacks in most northern states during the Jacksonian era were denied basic civil rights and forced to live under segregated conditions. In 1829 government officials in Cincinnati, a haven for runaway southern slaves, ordered all African Americans out of the city within thirty days. A mob of whites decided to hurry them on, destroying most of the city's black neighborhood in their fury.

Anti-black riots occurred in other northern cities as well. Whites who participated in an 1834 riot against African Americans in Philadelphia explained that they were simply defending themselves against the efforts of blacks and abolitionists "to break down the distinctive barrier between the colors [so] that the poor whites may gradually sink into the degraded condition of the Negroes—that, like them, they may be slaves and tools" of economic elites. Four years later the state of Pennsylvania officially disenfranchised blacks. By 1860 almost every state, old and new, had disenfranchised free blacks while easing voting qualifications for white men.

The Democratic coalition that elected Jackson thus depended for its survival upon a widely shared "white racism" and the ability to avoid potentially divisive discussions of slavery. In the South the majority of farmers who supported the slaveholding Jackson and identified with the Democrats did not own slaves, but they still embraced theories of racial superiority.

JACKSON'S INDIAN POLICY   During the 1820s and 1830s the United States was fast becoming a multicultural nation, home to people from many countries. Most whites, however, were as racist in their treatment of Indians as they were in their treatment of blacks. "Next to the case of the black race within our bosom," declared former president James Madison, "that of the red [race] on our borders is the problem most baffling to the policy of our country."

Yet Andrew Jackson saw nothing baffling about Indian policy. His attitude toward Indians was typically western: Native Americans were barbarians and better off out of the way. Jackson and most Americans on the frontier despised and feared Indians—and vice versa. Jackson believed that a "just, humane, liberal policy toward Indians" dictated moving all of them onto the plains west of the Mississippi River, to the Great American Desert, which white settlers would never covet since it was believed to be fit mainly for lizards and rattlesnakes.

Most of the northern tribes were too weak to resist the offers of federal commissioners who, if necessary, used bribery and alcohol to woo the chiefs. Only rarely did tribes rebel. In Illinois and the Wisconsin Territory an armed clash known as the Black Hawk War erupted in 1832. Under Chief Black Hawk, bands of Sauk and Fox sought to reoccupy land they had abandoned the previous year. Facing famine and hostile Sioux west of the Mississippi River, they were simply seeking a place to raise a crop of corn. The Illinois militia mobilized to expel them, chased them into the Wisconsin Territory, and massacred women and children as they tried to escape across the Mississippi River. When Black Hawk surrendered, he confessed that his "heart is dead, and no longer beats quick in his bosom. He is now a prisoner to the white men; they will do with him as they wish. But he can stand torture and is not afraid of death. He is no coward. Black Hawk is an Indian." The Black Hawk War came to be remembered, however, less because of the atrocities inflicted on the Indians than because among the participants were two native Kentuckians later to be pitted against each other: Lieutenant Jefferson Davis of the regular army and Captain Abraham Lincoln of the Illinois volunteers.

In the South two proud Indian nations, the Seminoles and the Cherokees, put up a stubborn resistance to white encroachments. The Seminoles were in fact a group of different tribes that had gravitated to Florida in the eighteenth century. They fought a protracted guerrilla war in the Everglades from 1835 to 1842, but most of the vigor went out of their resistance after 1837, when their leader, Osceola, was seized by treachery under a flag of truce, imprisoned, and left to die. After 1842 only a few hundred Seminoles remained, hiding out in the swamps. Most of the rest had been banished to the West.

THE TRAIL OF TEARS   The Cherokees had, by the end of the eighteenth century, fallen back into the mountains of northern Georgia and western North Carolina, settling on land guaranteed to them in 1791 by a treaty with the U.S. government. In 1827 the Cherokees, relying upon their treaty rights, adopted a constitution in which they pointedly declared that they were not subject to any other state or nation. The next year, Georgia declared that after June 1, 1830, the authority of state law would extend over the Cherokees living within the boundaries of the state.

The discovery of gold in 1829 brought bands of rough white prospectors onto Cherokee land. The Cherokees sought relief in the Supreme Court, but in *Cherokee Nation v. Georgia* (1831) John Marshall ruled that the Court lacked jurisdiction because the Cherokees were a "domestic dependent nation" rather than a foreign state in the meaning of the Constitution. Marshall added, however, that the Cherokees had "an unquestionable right" to their land until they wished to cede it to the United States.

The Trail of Tears and the rush for gold

Native Americans were exiled to territory west of Arkansas and Missouri, largely as a result of the discovery of gold in the Cherokee Nation. Thousands of miners flooded the area by late 1829.

In 1830 a Georgia law had required whites in the Cherokee territory to obtain licenses authorizing their residence there and to take an oath of allegiance to the state. Two New England missionaries among the Indians refused to abide by the law and were sentenced to four years at hard labor. On appeal their case reached the Supreme Court as *Worcester v. Georgia* (1832), and the court held that the Cherokee Nation was "a distinct political community" within which Georgia law had no force. The Georgia law was therefore unconstitutional. Now Georgia faced down the Supreme Court with the tacit consent of the president. Andrew Jackson is supposed to have said privately about the chief justice, "Marshall has made his decision, now let him enforce it!" Whether or not he spoke so bluntly, Jackson did nothing to implement the Court's decision. Under the circumstances there was nothing for the Cherokees to do but give in and sign a treaty, which they did in 1835. They gave up their land in the Southeast in exchange for land in the Indian Territory west of Arkansas, $5 million from the federal government, and expenses for transportation.

Why did Congress exile the Choctaws, Chickasaws, Creeks, Seminoles, and Cherokees to territory west of Arkansas and Missouri? How far did the tribes have to travel, and what were the conditions on the journey? Why were the Indians not forced to move before the 1830s?

By 1838 some 17,000 Cherokees, and some 2,000 African Americans they had enslaved, had departed westward, following other tribes (Choctaws, Chickasaws, Creeks, and Seminoles) on the 800-mile "Trail of Tears." It was a grueling journey that killed many of the exiles. Four thousand Cherokees did not survive the trip. A few who never left their homeland held out in their native mountains and acquired title to land in North Carolina; thenceforth they were the "Eastern Band" of Cherokees.

THE BANK CONTROVERSY

THE BANK'S OPPONENTS The overriding national issue in the presidential campaign of 1832 was neither Andrew Jackson's Indian policy nor South Carolina's obsession with the high tariff. It was the question of rechartering the Bank of the United States, whose legal mandate would soon lapse. Jackson had absorbed the West's hostility toward the bank after the panic of 1819. He believed that "hard" money—gold and silver coins—was the only legitimate medium of exchange. He remained skeptical of all forms of paper currency, and he insisted that the bank was unconstitutional—no matter what Chief Justice John Marshall had said in *McCulloch v. Maryland*. Jackson, suspicious of all banks, especially disliked a central national bank.

Under the management of Nicholas Biddle, the second Bank of the United States had facilitated business expansion and supplied a stable currency by forcing state banks to keep a specie (gold or silver) reserve on hand to back up their paper currency. The bank also acted as the collecting and disbursing agent for the federal government, which held a fifth of the bank's $35 million capital stock. From the start this combination of private and public functions caused problems for the bank. As the government's revenues soared, the bank became the most powerful lending institution in the country, a central bank, in effect, whose huge size enabled it to determine the amount of available credit for the nation. Moreover, by issuing paper money of its own, the bank provided a stable, uniform currency for the expanding economy as well as a mechanism for regulating the pace of growth.

Arrayed against the bank were powerful enemies: some of the state and local banks that had been forced to reduce their volume of paper money, groups of debtors who had suffered from the reduction, and businessmen and speculators on the make, who disliked the bank's tight credit policies. States' rights groups questioned the bank's constitutionality. Financiers on New York's Wall Street resented the supremacy of the bank on Philadelphia's Chestnut Street. Like Jackson, many westerners and workingmen believed that the bank was a powerful monopoly controlled by the wealthy few and was irreconcilable with a democracy. Biddle, born to wealth and social prestige, cultured, witty, and supremely self-confident, was an excellent banker but also a convenient symbol for those who saw the bank as the cozy friend of capitalists.

THE RECHARTER EFFORT The bank's twenty-year charter would run through 1836, but Biddle could not afford the uncertainty of waiting

Rechartering the bank

President Andrew Jackson battling the "Hydra-headed" Bank of the United States.

until then for a renewal. He pondered whether to force the issue of recharter before the election of 1832 or after. On this point, leaders of the National Republicans, especially Henry Clay and Daniel Webster, argued that the time to move was before the election. Clay, already the candidate of the National Republicans, proposed making renewal of the bank charter the central issue of the presidential election. Friends of the bank held a majority in Congress, and Jackson would risk loss of support in the election if he vetoed renewal. But Biddle and his allies failed to grasp the depth of public distaste for the bank and succeeded mainly in handing Jackson a charged issue on the eve of the election. "The Bank," Jackson told Martin Van Buren in May 1832, "is trying to kill me. But I will kill it."

Both houses of Congress passed the recharter by a comfortable margin but without the two-thirds majority needed to override a presidential veto. On July 10, 1832, Jackson vetoed the bill, sending it back to Congress with a ringing denunciation of monopoly and special privilege. An effort to over-rule the veto failed in the Senate. The stage was set for a nationwide financial crisis and a dramatic presidential campaign.

CONTENTIOUS POLITICS

CAMPAIGN INNOVATIONS In the 1832 presidential campaign a third party entered the field for the first time. The Anti-Masonic party had grown out of popular hostility toward the Masonic order, a fraternal organization whose members were suspected of having kidnapped and murdered a New Yorker for revealing the "secrets" of his lodge. Opposition to a fraternal order was hardly the foundation upon which to build a lasting national political organization, but the Anti-Masonic party made three important contributions to national politics: in addition to being the first third party, it was the first party to hold a national nominating convention and the first to announce an official platform, all of which it accomplished in 1831 when it nominated William Wirt of Maryland for president.

The major parties followed its example by holding national conventions of their own. In 1831, delegates of the National Republican party assembled in Baltimore to nominate Henry Clay. Andrew Jackson endorsed the idea of a nominating convention for the Democratic party (the name Republican was now formally dropped) to demonstrate popular support for its candidates. To that purpose the convention first adopted the two-thirds rule for nomination (which prevailed until 1936) and then named Martin Van Buren as Jackson's running mate. The Democrats, unlike the other two parties, adopted no formal platform at their first convention and relied substantially upon hoopla and the president's popularity to carry the election.

The outcome was an overwhelming endorsement of Jackson in the Electoral College, with 219 votes to 49 for Clay, and a less overwhelming but solid victory in the popular vote, 688,000 to 530,000. William Wirt carried only Vermont. South Carolina, preparing for nullification and unable to stomach either Jackson or Clay, delivered its 11 votes to the governor of Virginia.

THE REMOVAL OF GOVERNMENT DEPOSITS Andrew Jackson viewed the 1832 election as a mandate to further weaken the Bank of the United States, and he decided to remove all government deposits and distribute them to state banks. When Secretary of the Treasury Louis McLane balked, Jackson fired him. In the reshuffling, Attorney General Roger Taney moved to the Treasury, where he complied with the president's wishes. Taney continued to draw on government accounts with the national bank but deposited new government receipts in state banks. By the end of 1833, twenty-three state banks—"pet banks," as they came to be called—had the benefit of federal deposits. Transferring the government's deposits was a highly questionable action under the law, and the Senate voted to censure Jackson.

Biddle also rejected Jackson's efforts to cripple the bank. "This worthy President," he declared, "thinks that because he has scalped Indians and imprisoned Judges, he is to have his way with the Bank. He is mistaken." Biddle ordered that the B.U.S. curtail loans throughout the nation and demand the redemption of state bank notes in specie as quickly as possible. By tightening the nation's money supply, he sought to bring the economy to a halt, create a sharp depression, and reveal to the nation the importance of maintaining the bank.

The financial contraction resulting from the bank war quickly gave way to a speculative binge encouraged by the deposit of federal funds in state banks. With the restraint of the Bank of the United States removed, the state banks issued paper money without keeping sufficient gold reserves on hand. New banks proliferated, blissfully printing bank notes to lend to speculators. Sales of public land rose from 4 million acres in 1834 to 15 million in 1835 and 20 million in 1836. At the same time, the states plunged heavily into debt to finance the building of roads and canals, inspired by the success of New York's Erie Canal in opening up the entire state's economy to the markets of the eastern seaboard and Europe. By 1837 the total indebtedness of the states had soared to $170 million.

FISCAL MEASURES   Still, the federal surplus continued to mount as the widespread purchases of public land continued. Many westerners proposed simply to lower the price of land; southerners preferred to lower the tariff, but such action would upset the compromise achieved in the Tariff of 1833. Finally, in 1836, Congress passed the Distribution Act, a compromise that allowed the government to distribute most of the surplus as loans to the states. To satisfy Jackson's concerns, the funds were technically deposits, but the government never required repayment. Distribution of the federal surplus was to be in proportion to each state's representation in Congress.

About a month after passage of the Distribution Act, Jackson's Treasury secretary issued the Specie Circular of July 11, 1836. With that document the president belatedly applied his hard-money convictions to the sale of public land. According to his order, the government after August 15 would accept only gold and silver in payment for land. Doing so would supposedly "repress frauds," withhold support "from the monopoly of the public lands in the hands of speculators and capitalists," and discourage the "ruinous extension" of bank notes and credit.

Irony dogged Jackson to the end on this matter. Since few settlers had gold or silver coins, they were now left all the more at the mercy of speculators for land purchases. Both the Distribution Act and the Specie Circular put many state banks in jeopardy. The distribution of the federal surplus to the state governments entailed the removal of large deposits from state banks. In turn the state banks had to call in many of their loans in order to accumulate enough money to be able to transfer federal funds to the state governments. This situation caused greater dismay in the already chaotic state banking community. At the same time the new requirement that only hard money be accepted for federal land purchases put an added strain on the local supplies of gold and silver.

BOOM AND BUST   The boom-and-bust cycle of the 1830s had causes larger even than Andrew Jackson, causes that were beyond his control. The soaring inflation of mid-decade was rooted not solely in a sudden expansion of bank notes, as it seemed at the time, but also in an increase of gold and silver flowing into the country from England, France, and especially Mexico for investment and for the purchase of American cotton and other products.

Contrary to appearances the gold and silver reserves in U.S. banks actually kept pace with the increase of bank notes despite reckless behavior by some banks. By 1836, however, a tighter economy had caused a decline in both British investments abroad and British demand for American cotton just when the new western lands were creating a rapid increase in the cotton supply. Fortunately for Jackson, the panic of 1837 did not erupt until he was out of the White House. His successor would serve as the scapegoat.

Van Buren and the New Party System

THE WHIG COALITION   Before the depression set in, the Jacksonian Democrats reaped a political bonanza. Jackson had defeated nullification in South Carolina and eliminated the national bank, and the people loved him for it. The hard times following the contraction of the economy turned Americans against Nicholas Biddle and the national bank but not against Jackson, the professed friend of "the people" and foe of the "selfish" interests of financiers and speculators.

By 1834, Jackson's opponents had begun to pull together a new coalition of diverse elements, united chiefly by their hostility to him. The imperious demeanor of the so-called champion of democracy had given rise to the name King Andrew I. Jackson's followers therefore were labeled Tories, supporters of the king, and his opponents Whigs, a name that linked them to the Patriots of the American Revolution. The diverse coalition of Whigs clustered around the National Republican party of John Quincy Adams, Henry Clay, and Daniel Webster. Into the combination streamed remnants of the Anti-Masons and the Democrats, who for one reason or another were alienated by Jackson's stand on the bank, Indian removal, hard money, or internal improvements. Of the forty-one Democrats in Congress who had voted to recharter the bank, twenty-eight had joined the Whigs by 1836.

Whiggery always had about it an atmosphere of social conservatism and elitism. The core Whigs were the supporters of Henry Clay, men who promoted a national economic policy. In the South the Whigs enjoyed the support of the urban banking and commercial interests, as well as their planter associates, holders of most of the slaves in the region. In the West, farmers who valued internal improvements joined the Whig ranks. Most states' rights supporters eventually dropped away, and by the early 1840s the Whigs were becoming the party of economic nationalism, even in the South. Unlike the Democrats, who attracted Catholic immigrants from Germany and Ireland, Whig voters tended to be native-born or British-American Protestants—Presbyterians, Baptists, and Congregationalists—who were active in promoting social reforms such as abolition and temperance.

THE ELECTION OF 1836   By 1836 a two-party system was emerging from the Jackson and anti-Jackson forces, a system that would remain in even balance for twenty years. In 1835, eighteen months before the election, the Democrats held their second national convention, nominating Jackson's handpicked successor, Vice President Martin Van Buren. The Whig coalition, united chiefly in its opposition to Jackson, held no convention but adopted a strategy of multiple candidacies, hoping to throw the election into the House of Representatives. The result was a free-for-all reminiscent of 1824, except this time one candidate stood apart from the rest. It was Van Buren against the field. The Whigs put up three favorite sons: Daniel Webster, named by the Massachusetts legislature; Hugh Lawson White, chosen by anti-Jackson Democrats in the Tennessee legislature; and William Henry Harrison of Indiana, nominated by a predominantly Anti-Masonic convention in Pennsylvania. In the popular vote, Van Buren outdistanced the entire Whig field, with 765,000 votes to 740,000 votes for the Whigs, most of which were cast for Harrison.

Martin Van Buren

Van Buren earned the nickname the "Little Magician."

Martin Van Buren, the eighth president, was the first of Dutch ancestry. The son of a tavern keeper in Kinderhook, New York, he had attended a local academy, read law, and entered politics. Although he kept up a limited legal practice, he had been primarily a professional politician, so skilled in the arts of organization and manipulation that he was dubbed the "Little Magician." Elected governor of New York, Van Buren quickly resigned to join Jackson's cabinet and, because of Jackson's support, became vice president. Short and trim, Van Buren was also called the Red Fox for his long reddish sideburns, dominant forehead, and long, striking nose. His elegant attire, engaging personality, and constant political scheming gave further credence to his nicknames.

THE PANIC OF 1837   President Van Buren inherited a financial panic. An already precarious economy was tipped over by a depression in England, which resulted in a drop in the price of cotton and caused English banks and investors to contract their activities in the United States and refuse extensions of loans. This was a particularly hard blow since much of America's economic expansion depended upon European—and mainly English—investment capital. As creditors hastened to foreclose, the inflationary spiral went into reverse. States curtailed ambitious plans for roads and canals and in many cases felt impelled to repudiate their debts. In the crunch many of the state banks collapsed.

The common folk, as always, were particularly hard hit during the economic slump and largely had to fend for themselves. By the fall of 1837, a third of the workforce was jobless. Those still fortunate enough to have jobs saw their wages cut by 30 to 50 percent within two years. At the same time, prices for food and clothing skyrocketed. As the winter of 1837 approached, a journalist reported that in New York City 200,000 people were "in utter and hopeless distress with no means of surviving the winter but those provided by charity." There was no government aid, only that provided by churches and charitable organizations.

Van Buren's advisers and supporters blamed speculators and bankers for the hard times. At the same time they expected the evildoers to get what they deserved in a healthy shakeout that would restore the economy. Van Buren did not believe that he or the government had any responsibility to rescue hard-pressed farmers or businessmen or to provide assistance to the jobless and homeless. But he did feel obliged to keep the government itself in a healthy financial situation. To that end he called a special session of Congress in 1837, which quickly voted to postpone indefinitely the distribution of the surplus because of a probable upcoming deficit and approved an issue of Treasury notes (currency) to cover immediate expenses.

AN INDEPENDENT TREASURY   Van Buren proposed that the federal government cease risking its deposits in shaky state banks and set up an independent Treasury. Under this plan the federal government would keep its funds in its own vaults and do business entirely in hard money. The Whigs preferred that the federal government promote economic development, perhaps in the form of tariff or currency legislation.

Van Buren's Independent Treasury Act aroused stiff opposition from a combination of Whigs and conservative Democrats who feared deflation,

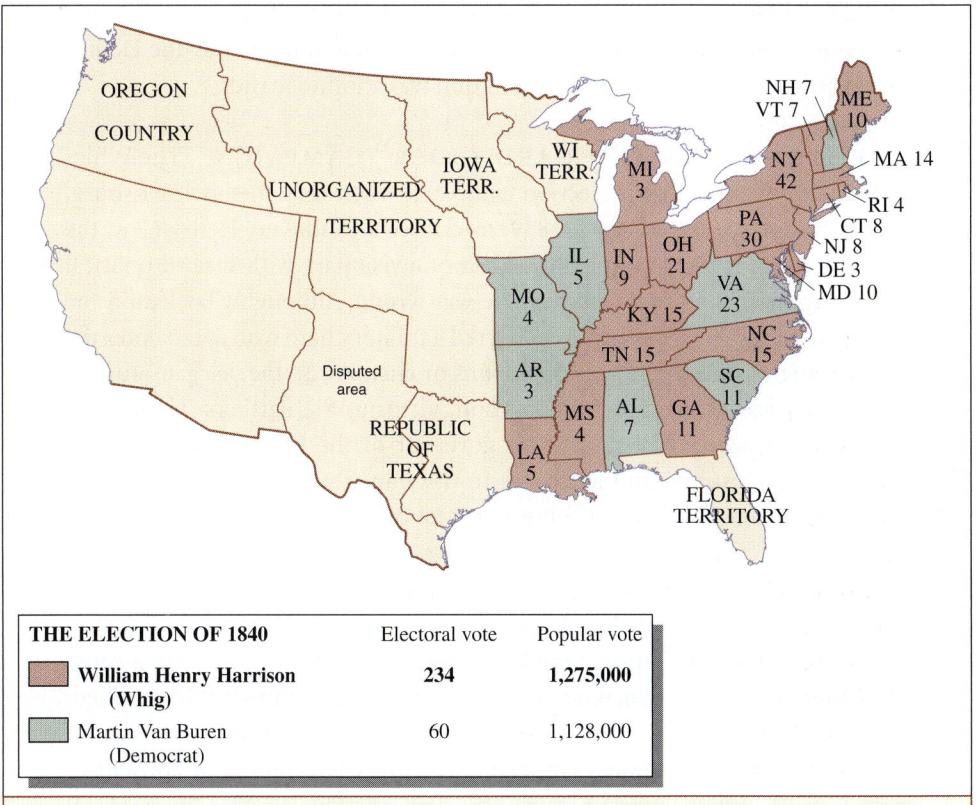

THE ELECTION OF 1840	Electoral vote	Popular vote
William Henry Harrison (Whig)	**234**	**1,275,000**
Martin Van Buren (Democrat)	60	1,128,000

Why did Van Buren carry several western states but few others? How did the Whigs achieve a decisive electoral victory over the Democrats? How was their strategy in 1840 different from their campaign in 1836?

and it took the Red Fox several years of maneuvering to get what he wanted. John Calhoun signaled a return to the Democratic fold, after several years of flirting with the Whigs, when he came out in favor of the independent Treasury. Van Buren gained western support for the plan by backing a more liberal policy of federal land sales. Congress finally passed the Independent Treasury Act on July 4, 1840. Although the Whigs repealed it in 1841, it would be restored in 1846.

The protracted struggle over the Treasury was only one of several issues that occupied politicians' attention during the late 1830s. Petitions asking Congress to abolish slavery and the slave trade in the District of Columbia provoked tumultuous debate, especially in the House of Representatives. A dispute over the Maine boundary kept British-American animosity at a simmer. But basic to the spreading malaise was the depressed condition of the economy, which lasted through Van Buren's term. Fairly or not, the administration became the target of growing discontent. The president won renomination by the Democrats easily enough, but the general election was another matter.

THE "LOG CABIN AND HARD CIDER" CAMPAIGN   The Whigs got an early start on their election campaign when they met at Harrisburg, Pennsylvania, on December 4, 1839, to choose a candidate. Henry Clay, the legislative veteran who coupled the ideas of a visionary with shrewd political savvy, expected 1840 to be his year. He was wrong. Although Clay led on the first ballot, the Whig convention preferred a military hero who could enter the race with few known political convictions or enemies. So the delegates turned to the colorless William Henry Harrison, victor at the Battle of Tippecanoe against the Shawnees in 1811 while governor of the Indiana Territory and briefly a congressman and a senator from Ohio. To rally their states' rights wing, the Whigs chose for vice president John Tyler of Virginia, Clay's close friend.

The Whigs had no platform. Taking stands on issues would have risked dividing a coalition united chiefly by opposition to the Democrats. But they had a catchy slogan, "Tippecanoe and Tyler Too," and they soon had a rousing campaign theme, which a Democratic newspaper unwittingly supplied: it declared sardonically "that upon condition of his receiving a pension of $2,000 and a barrel of cider, General Harrison would no doubt consent to withdraw his pretensions, and spend his days in a log cabin on the banks of the Ohio." The Whigs seized upon the cider and log cabin symbols to depict Harrison as a simple man sprung from the people. Actually, he sprang from one of the first families of Virginia, was a college graduate, and lived in an Ohio farmhouse.

The presidential campaign of 1840 produced the largest turnout of any election up to that time. To the Whigs, Van Buren symbolized the economic slump as well as aristocratic snobbery. "Van! Van! Is a Used-Up Man!" went one of their campaign slogans, and down he went by the thumping margin of 234 electoral votes to 60.

ASSESSING THE JACKSON YEARS

The Whigs may have won in 1840, but the Jacksonian movement had permanently altered American politics. Commoners were now much more involved in the political process. By 1840 both parties were tightly organized down to the precinct level, and the proportion of white men who voted in the presidential election had nearly tripled, from 26 percent in 1824 to 78 percent in 1840. That much is beyond dispute, but the phenomenon of Andrew Jackson, the great symbol for an age, has inspired conflicts of interpretation as spirited as those among his supporters and opponents at the time. Was he the leader of a vast democratic movement that welled up in the West and mobilized a farmer-laborer alliance to sweep the "Monster" bank into the dustbin of history? Or was he essentially a frontier tycoon, an opportunist for whom the ideal of democracy provided effective political rhetoric?

In the Jacksonian view the alliance of government and business always invited special favors and made for an eternal source of corruption. The central bank epitomized such evil. Good government policy, at the national level in particular, avoided the granting of special privileges and let free competition regulate the economy.

In the bustling world of the nineteenth century, Jackson's laissez-faire policies actually opened the way for a host of aspiring entrepreneurs eager to replace the established economic elite with a new order of free-enterprise capitalism. And in fact there was no great conflict in the Jacksonian mentality between the farmer or planter who delved in the soil and the independent speculator and entrepreneur who grew wealthy by other means. Jackson himself was both. The Jacksonian mentality did not foresee the degree to which, in a growing country, unrestrained enterprise could lead to new economic combinations, centers of economic power largely independent of government regulation. But history is forever producing unintended consequences. Here the ultimate irony would be that the laissez-faire rationale for preserving an agrarian republic eventually became the justification for the growth of unregulated corporate powers far greater than any ever wielded by Nicholas Biddle's hated central bank.

CHAPTER SUMMARY

- **Jacksonian Democracy** Jackson's America was very different from the America of 1776. Most white men had gained the vote when states removed property qualifications for voting. The Jacksonians sought to democratize economic opportunity; thus politics changed with the advent of national conventions, at which party leaders chose their party's candidates and platforms. Powerful elites remained in charge of society and politics, however.

- **Jacksonian Policies** Jackson wanted to lower taxes and reduce government spending. He vetoed bills to use federal funds for internal improvements, and his belief that banks were run by corrupt businessmen for their own ends led him to veto a bill for the rechartering of the second Bank of the United States.

- **Nullification Controversy** When a South Carolina convention nullified the Tariffs of 1828 and 1832, Jackson requested that Congress pass a "force bill" authorizing the army to compel compliance with the tariffs. After South Carolina accepted a compromise tariff put forth by Henry Clay, the state convention nullified the force bill. Nullification, an extreme states' rights ideology, had been put into action. The crisis was over, but both sides claimed victory.

- **Indian Removal Act of 1830** The Indian Removal Act of 1830 authorized the relocation of eastern Indians to federal lands west of the Mississippi River. The Cherokees used the federal court system to try to block this relocation, but despite the Marshall court's decision in their favor, federal troops forced them to move; the event and the route they took came to be known as in the Trail of Tears. By 1840 only a few Seminoles and Cherokees remained, hiding in remote areas of the Southeast.

- **Democrats and Whigs** Jackson's arrogant behavior, especially his use of the veto, led many to regard him as "King Andrew." Groups who opposed him coalesced in a new party, known as the Whigs, thus forming the country's second party system. The panic of 1837, during Martin Van Buren's administration, ensured Whig victory in the election of 1840 despite the party's lack of a coherent political program.

CHRONOLOGY

1828	Tariff of abominations goes into effect
1830	Congress passes the Indian Removal Act
	Andrew Jackson vetoes the Maysville Road Bill
1831	Supreme Court issues *Cherokee Nation v. Georgia* decision
1832	Supreme Court issues *Worcester v. Georgia* decision
	South Carolina issues ordinance of nullification
	Andrew Jackson vetoes the Bank Recharter Bill
1833	Congress passes Henry Clay's compromise tariff
1836	Martin Van Buren is elected president
1837	Financial panic follows a drop in the price of cotton
1837–1838	Eastern Indians are forced west on the Trail of Tears
1840	William Henry Harrison, a Whig, is elected president

KEY TERMS & NAMES

12

THE DYNAMICS
OF GROWTH

FOCUS QUESTIONS   wwnorton.com/studyspace

- How did the explosive growth of industry, agriculture, and transportation change America?
- What were some inventions that economically and socially improved the country?
- How had immigration changed by the mid nineteenth century?
- Why did early labor unions emerge?

The Jacksonian-era political debate between democratic ideals and elitist traditions was rooted in a profound transformation of social and economic life. Between 1815 and 1850 the United States became a transcontinental power, expanding all the way to the Pacific coast. An industrial revolution in the Northeast began to reshape the economy and propel an unrelenting process of urbanization. In the West commercial agriculture began to emerge, focused on the surplus production of corn, wheat, and cattle. In the South, cotton became king, and its reign came to depend upon the expanding institution of slavery. At the same time, innovations in transportation—canals, steamboats, and railroads—conquered time and space and knit together an expanding transcontinental market. In sum, an eighteenth-century economy based upon small-scale farming and local commerce matured into a far-flung capitalist marketplace entwined with world trade. These economic developments in turn generated changes in every other area of life, from politics to the legal system, from family dynamics to social values.

AGRICULTURE AND THE NATIONAL ECONOMY

The first stage of industrialization brought with it an expansive commercial and urban outlook that supplanted the agrarian philosophy espoused by Thomas Jefferson and many others. "We are greatly, I was about to say fearfully, growing," South Carolina's John C. Calhoun told his congressional colleagues in 1816, and many other statesmen shared his ambivalent outlook. Would the agrarian Republic retain its virtue and cohesion amid the chaotic commercial development? In the brief Era of Good Feelings after the War of 1812, such a troublesome question was easily brushed aside as economic opportunities seemed available to free Americans everywhere. Nowhere was this more evident than in the cotton-growing states of the South.

COTTON   Cotton has been cultivated since ancient times, but the proliferation of English textile mills during the late eighteenth century created a rapidly growing global market for the fluffy fiber. For many years, cotton clothing had remained rare and expensive because of the need for hand labor to separate the lint from the tenacious green seeds in order to make thread. But that problem was solved in 1793 when Eli Whitney, a Yale graduate who had gone south to teach, devised a mechanism for removing the sticky seeds. The cotton gin (short for "engine") enabled a person to separate fifty times as much cotton as could be done by hand.

By inventing the cotton gin, Eli Whitney spurred a revolution. Cotton production soared during the first half of the nineteenth century, and planters found a profitable new use for slavery. Planters and their enslaved workers migrated westward from the Carolinas and Georgia into Kentucky, Tennessee, Alabama, Mississippi, Louisiana, and Texas, where the cotton culture became a way of life tying the Old Southwest to the coastal Southeast. Cotton became the major export commodity for the United States. After Napoléon's defeat in 1815, European demand for cotton skyrocketed. From 1815 to 1819, cotton averaged 39 percent of the value of all exports, and from the mid-1830s to 1860 it accounted for more than half the total. Cotton precipitated a phenomenal expansion of the national economy.

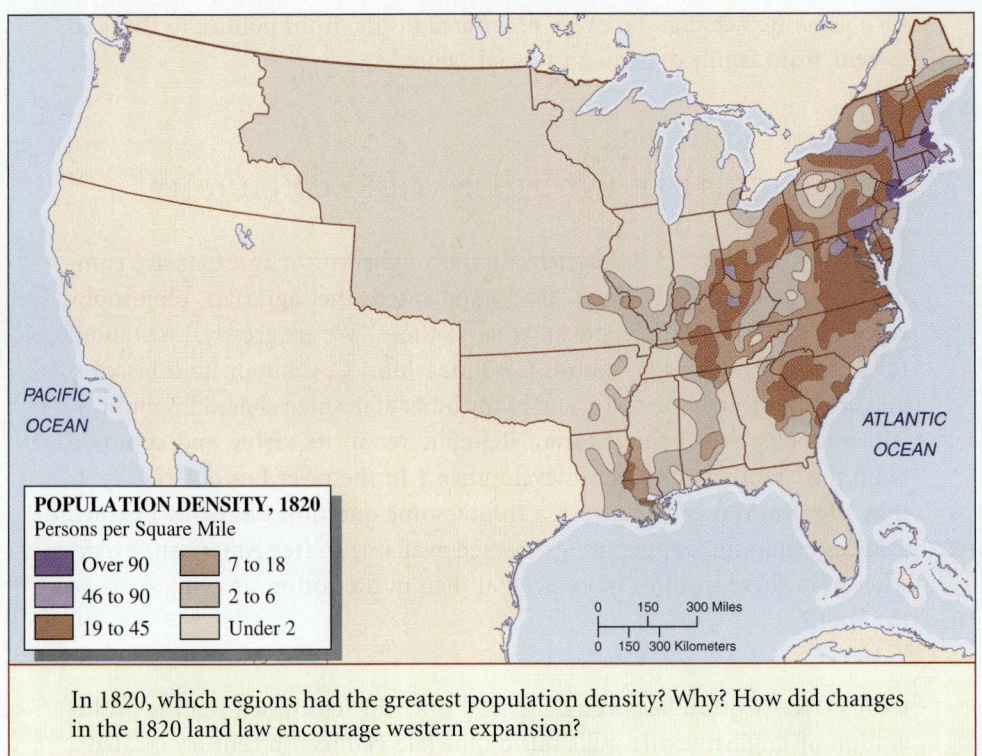

POPULATION DENSITY, 1820
Persons per Square Mile

- Over 90
- 46 to 90
- 19 to 45
- 7 to 18
- 2 to 6
- Under 2

In 1820, which regions had the greatest population density? Why? How did changes in the 1820 land law encourage western expansion?

The South supplied the North with both raw materials and markets for manufactures. Income from the North's role in handling the cotton trade then provided surpluses for capital investment in new enterprises. Cotton thereby became a crucial element of the national economy—and the driving force behind the expansion of slavery.

FARMING THE WEST The westward flow of planters and their slaves to Alabama and Mississippi during these flush times mirrored another migration: through the Ohio River valley and the Great Lakes region, where the Indians had been steadily pushed westward. By 1860 more than half the nation's population resided west of the Appalachians, and restless migrants had long since spilled across the Mississippi River and touched the shores of the Pacific. The fertile woodland soil, riverside bottomlands, and black loam of the midwestern prairies drew farmers from the rocky lands of New England and the exhausted soils of the Southeast. The development

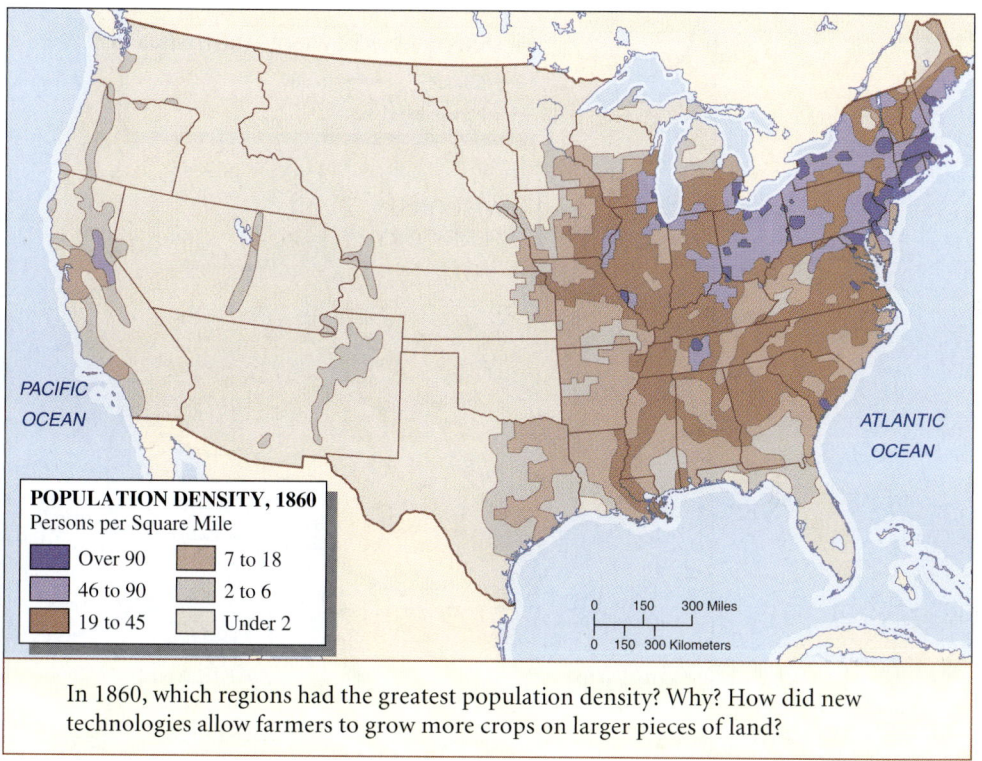

POPULATION DENSITY, 1860
Persons per Square Mile

- Over 90
- 46 to 90
- 19 to 45
- 7 to 18
- 2 to 6
- Under 2

PACIFIC OCEAN

ATLANTIC OCEAN

In 1860, which regions had the greatest population density? Why? How did new technologies allow farmers to grow more crops on larger pieces of land?

of iron plows, called sodbusters, greatly eased the grueling job of breaking the soil.

A new federal land law passed in 1820 reduced the minimum price per acre and reduced the minimum plot from 160 acres to 80. A settler could now buy a farm for as little as $100, and over the years the proliferation of state banks made it possible to continue buying land on credit rather than coming up with cash. Even that was not enough for westerners, however, who began a long—and eventually victorious—agitation for further relaxation of the land laws. They favored "preemption," the right of squatters to purchase land at the minimum price, and graduation, the progressive reduction of the price of land that did not sell immediately.

Congress eventually responded to the land mania with two bills. Under the Preemption Act of 1830, squatters could stake out claims ahead of the land surveys and later get 160 acres at the minimum price of $1.25 per acre. Under the Graduation Act of 1854, the price of unsold land was to be reduced in stages over thirty years.

Why were river towns important commercial centers? What was the impact of the steamboat and the flatboat on travel in the West? How did the Erie Canal transform the economy of New York and the Great Lakes region?

TRANSPORTATION, COMMUNICATION, AND THE MARKET REVOLUTION

NEW ROADS   Transportation improvements helped spur the development of a national market for goods and services. In 1795 the Wilderness Road, which followed the trail blazed by Daniel Boone twenty years before, was opened to wagon and stagecoach traffic, thereby easing the western

CANADA

VERMONT

MAINE

NEW YORK

NEW HAMPSHIRE

St. Lawrence River

Lake Ontario

Erie Canal

Troy

Lowell

Syracuse

Albany

MA

Boston

Buffalo

Mohawk and Genesee Turnpike

Northampton

Lake Erie

Kingston

Hudson River

CT

RI

Cleveland

Delaware and Hudson Canal

New Haven

Akron

PENNSYLVANIA

Delaware and Raritan Canal

Susquehanna R.

Harrisburg

New York

Pittsburgh

Penn. State Canal

New Brunswick

Wheeling

Trenton

Delware River

Forbes Road

Lancaster

Philadelphia

NEW JERSEY

Monongahela R.

Baltimore

Cumberland

Frederick Turnpike

DELAWARE

Washington

MARYLAND

VIRGINIA

Potomac River

Richmond

Buchanan

James River

Lynchburg

Portsmouth

Chesapeake Bay

NORTH CAROLINA

0   100   200 Miles

0   100   200 Kilometers

route through the Cumberland Gap into Kentucky and Tennessee. In the Deep South there were no such major highways. South Carolinians and Georgians pushed westward on whatever trails or rutted roads had appeared. To the northeast, public demand for graded and paved roads packed with crushed stones (called macadam) gathered momentum after completion of the Philadelphia-Lancaster Turnpike in 1794 (the term *turnpike* derives from a pole, or pike, at the tollgate, which was turned to admit the traffic). By 1821 there were some 4,000 miles of turnpikes.

WATER TRANSPORTATION By the early 1820s the turnpike boom was giving way to new developments in water transportation: Flatboats, river steamboats, and canal barges, which carried goods far more cheaply than did Conestoga wagons on the National Road. The first commercially successful steamboat appeared when Robert Fulton and Robert R. Livingston sent the *Clermont* up New York's Hudson River in 1807. After that the use of steamboats spread rapidly to other eastern and western rivers. By 1836, 361 steamboats were navigating the western waters. During the next decade the shallow-draft, steam-powered ships ventured into the far reaches of the Mississippi River valley.

The durable flatboat still carried to market most of the western wheat, corn, flour, meal, port, whiskey, soap and candles (byproducts of slaughterhouses), lead from Missouri, copper from Michigan, lumber from the Rockies, and ironwork from Pittsburgh. But the steamboat, by bringing cheaper and faster two-way traffic to the Mississippi River valley, created a transcontinental market and an agricultural empire that became the new breadbasket of America. Along with the new farmers came promoters, speculators, and retailers. Villages at strategic trading points along the streams evolved into centers of commerce and urban life. The port of New Orleans grew in the 1830s and 1840s to lead all others in exports.

By then, however, the Erie Canal was drawing eastward much of the midwestern trade that had once gone down the Mississippi River to the Gulf of Mexico. In 1817 the New York legislature had endorsed Governor DeWitt Clinton's dream of a canal connecting the Hudson River with Lake Erie. Eight years later, in 1825, the canal, forty feet wide and four feet deep, was open for the entire 363 miles from Albany west to Buffalo; branches soon put most of the state within its reach. The Erie Canal was an engineering marvel. The longest canal in the world, it reduced travel time from New York City to Buffalo from twenty days to six, and the cost of moving a ton of freight plummeted from $100 to $5.

The speedy success of the New York waterways inspired a mania for canals in other states that lasted more than a decade. But no other canal ever matched the spectacular success of the Erie. It rendered the entire Great Lakes region an economic tributary to New York City and had major economic and political consequences, tying together West and East while further isolating the Deep South. The commercial bonanza created by the Erie Canal caused small towns such as Syracuse, Rochester, and Buffalo, New York, as well as Cleveland, Ohio, and, eventually, Chicago, Illinois, to blossom into major metropolises. It virtually revolutionired American economic activity. With the addition of new canals spanning Ohio and Indiana from north to south, much of the upper Ohio River valley was also drawn into New York's economic sphere.

The Erie Canal

Junction of the Northern and Western Canals (1825), an aquatint by John Hill.

RAILROADS   The financial panic of 1837 and the subsequent depression cooled the canal fever. Meanwhile, a more versatile form of transportation was gaining on the canal: the railroad. In 1825, the year the Erie Canal was completed, the world's first commercial steam railway began operation in England, and soon the American port cities of Baltimore, Charleston, and Boston were alive with schemes to connect to the hinterlands by rail. By 1840, American railroads, with a total of 3,328 miles, had outdistanced the canals by just two miles. Over the next twenty years, though, railroads grew nearly tenfold, covering 30,626 miles; more than two thirds of that total was built in the 1850s. But it was not until the eve of the Civil War that railroads surpassed canals in total haulage.

The railroad also gained supremacy over other forms of transportation because of its economy, speed, and reliability. Trains averaged ten miles an hour, doubling the speed of stagecoaches. Railroads also provided indirect benefits, by reducing shipping costs. The railroads' demand for iron and equipment of various kinds also provided an enormous market for many

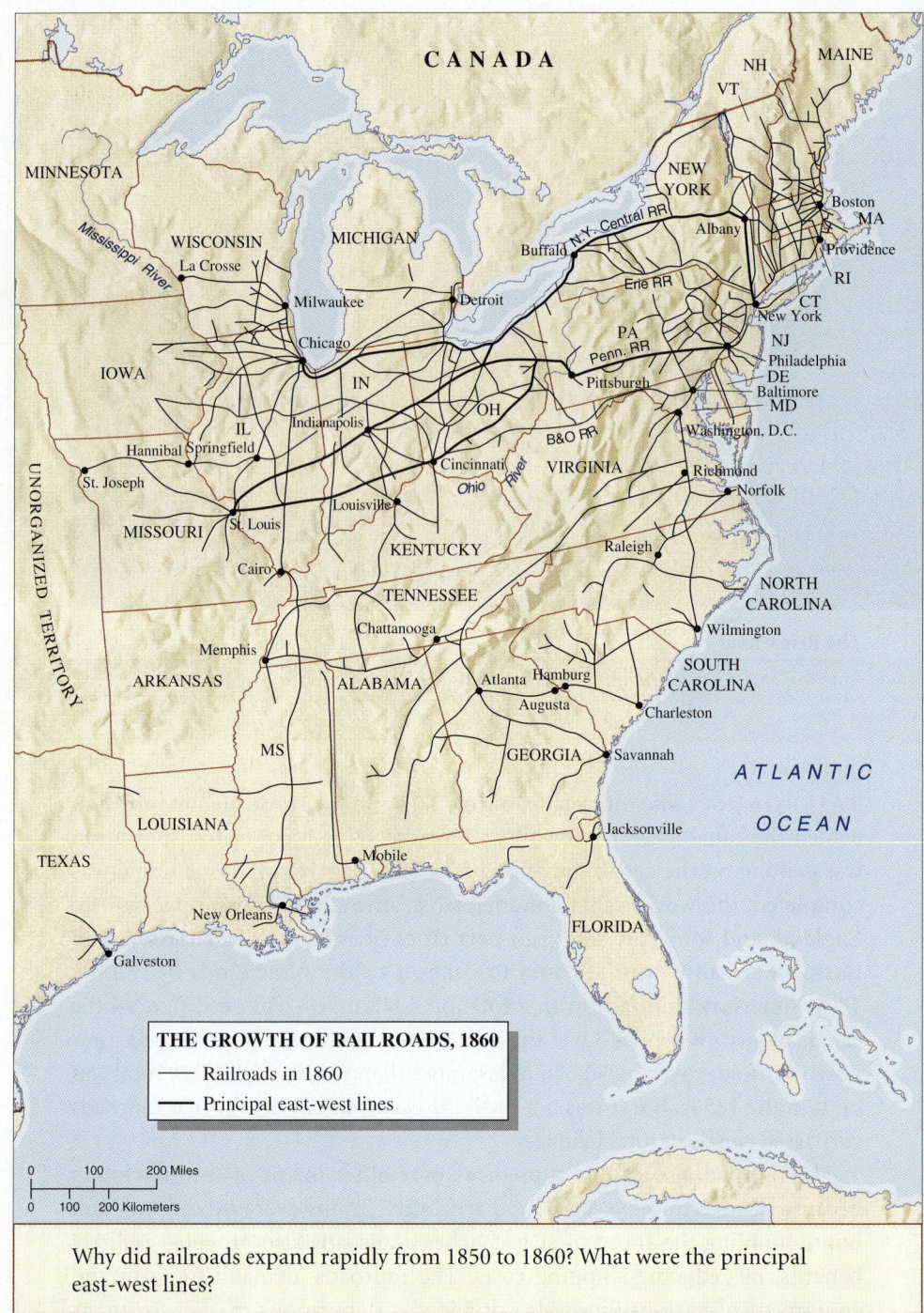

THE GROWTH OF RAILROADS, 1860

— Railroads in 1860

— Principal east-west lines

Why did railroads expand rapidly from 1850 to 1860? What were the principal east-west lines?

other industries. And the ability of railroads to operate year-round in all kinds of weather gave them an advantage in carrying freight.

But the epic railroad boom had negative effects as well. By opening up possibilities for quick and often shady profits, it helped corrupt political life, and by opening up access to the trans-Appalachian West, it helped accelerate the decline of Indian culture. In addition, the railroad dramatically quickened the tempo and mobility of life. The writer Nathaniel Hawthorne spoke for many Americans when he charged that the locomotive "comes down upon you like fate, swift and inevitable." With its unsettling whistle it brought "the noisy world into the midst of our slumbrous peace."

OCEAN TRANSPORTATION The year 1845 witnessed a great innovation in ocean transport with the launching of the first clipper ship, the *Rainbow.* The sleek clippers doubled the speed of the older merchant vessels, and trading companies rushed to purchase them. Long and lean, with tall masts and many sails, the clipper ships cut dashing figures during their brief but colorful career, which lasted less than two decades. What prompted the clipper boom was the lure of Chinese tea, a drink long coveted in America but in scarce supply. Asian tea leaves were a perishable commodity that had to reach the market quickly, and the new clippers made this possible. Even more important, the discovery of California gold in 1848 lured thousands of prospectors and entrepreneurs from the Atlantic seaboard. The new California settlers generated an urgent demand for goods, and the clippers met it. But clippers, while fast, lacked ample cargo space, and after the Civil War they would give way to the larger steamship.

THE ROLE OF THE GOVERNMENT The massive internal improvements of the antebellum era were the product of initiatives by both state governments and private investors or corporations. After the panic of 1837, however, the states left railroad development mainly to private corporations, the source of most investment capital. Still, several southern and western states built their own lines, and most states granted generous tax concessions. The federal government helped too, despite ferocious debates over whether direct involvement in internal improvements was constitutional. The federal government bought stock in turnpike and canal companies and, after the success of the Erie Canal, extended land grants to several western states for the support of canal projects. Congress also provided for railroad surveys by government engineers, granted tracts of land, and reduced the tariff duties on iron used in railroad construction.

A COMMUNICATIONS REVOLUTION   The transportation revolution also helped spark dramatic improvements in communications. At the beginning of the century, it took days or often weeks for news to travel along the Atlantic seaboard. For example, after George Washington died in 1799 in Virginia, the announcement of his death did not appear in New York City newspapers until a week later. Naturally news took even longer to travel to and from Europe. On December 24, 1814, the United States and Great Britain met in Belgium to sign the peace treaty ending the War of 1812. Yet two weeks later, on January 8, 1815, the Battle of New Orleans was fought. Both armies were oblivious to the cease-fire that had been declared. It took forty-nine days for news of the peace treaty ending the War of 1812 to reach New York from Europe.

The speed of communications accelerated greatly as the nineteenth century unfolded. The construction of turnpikes, canals, railroads, and scores of post offices, as well as and the development of steamships and the telegraph, generated a communications revolution. By 1830, Andrew Jackson's inaugural address could be "conveyed" from Washington, D.C., to New York City in sixteen hours, but it reached New Orleans in six days. Mail began to be delivered by "express," a system in which riders could mount fresh horses at relay stations. Still, even with such advances the states and territories west of the Appalachian Mountains struggled to get timely deliveries and news.

THE INDUSTRIAL REVOLUTION

While the South and the West developed the agricultural basis for a national economy, the Northeast was laying the foundation for an industrial revolution. Technology in the form of the cotton gin and the mechanical grain harvester and improvements in transportation had quickened agricultural development. But technology altered the economic landscape even more profoundly, by giving rise to the factory system.

EARLY TEXTILE MANUFACTURES   In the eighteenth century, Great Britain had a long head start over the rest of the world in industrial production. Britain led the way in the development of iron smelting by coke (refined coal), the invention of the steam engine in 1705, its improvement by James Watt in 1765, and a series of inventions that mechanized textile production. Britain carefully guarded its hard-won secrets, forbidding the export of machines and preventing informed mechanics from leaving the country. But the secrets could not be kept. In 1789, Samuel Slater arrived in Rhode Island from England with the plan of a water-powered spinning machine in his head. He contracted with an enterprising merchant-manufacturer to build a mill in Pawtucket, and in that little mill, completed in 1790, nine children turned out a satisfactory cotton yarn.

Still, the progress of textile production faltered until Thomas Jefferson's embargo in 1807 and the War of 1812 restricted imports and encouraged New England merchant capitalists to transfer their resources from shipping to manufacturing. New England, it happened, had one distinct advantage: ample rivers near the coast, where water transportation was readily available. By 1815, New England textile mills numbered in the hundreds. The foundations of textile manufacture were laid, and they spurred the growth of garment trades and a machine-tool industry that built and serviced the mills.

AMERICAN TECHNOLOGY Meanwhile, Americans became famous for their "practical" inventiveness. In 1804, Oliver Evans developed a high-pressure steam engine that was adapted to a variety of uses in ships and factories. Among the other outstanding American originals was Cyrus Hall McCormick of Virginia. McCormick invented a primitive grain reaper in 1831, a development as significant to the agricultural economy of the Old Northwest as the cotton gin was to the South.

After tinkering with his machine for almost a decade, McCormick applied for a patent in 1841. Six years later he moved to Chicago and built a plant for manufacturing his reapers and mowers. Within just a few years he had sold thousands of machines, transforming the scale of agriculture. With a sickle a farmer could harvest half an acre of wheat a day; with a McCormick reaper two people could work twelve acres a day. McCormick's success attracted other manufacturers and inventors, and soon there were mechanical threshers to separate the grains of wheat from the straw. As the volume of agricultural products soared, prices dropped, income rose, and for many farm families in the Old Northwest the standard of living improved.

A spate of inventions in the 1840s generated profound changes. In 1844, Charles Goodyear patented a process for "vulcanizing" rubber, which made the product stronger and more elastic, and in the process created the fabric for rainproof coats. In the same year the first intercity telegraph message was transmitted, from Baltimore to Washington, D.C., on the device Samuel F. B. Morse had invented back in 1832. The telegraph was slow to catch on, but seventeen years after that demonstration, with the completion of connections to San Francisco, an entire continent had been wired for instant communication. In 1846, Elias Howe patented his design of the sewing machine, soon improved upon by Isaac Merrit Singer. The sewing machine, incidentally, was one invention that slowed the progress of the factory. Since it was adapted to use in the home, it gave the "putting-out" system a new life in the clothing industry.

It is hard to exaggerate the importance of science and technology in changing the way people were living by midcentury. Improved transportation and a spreading market economy combined with innovations in canning and refrigeration allowed for a more healthful diet. Fruits and vegetables, heretofore available only during harvest season, could be shipped during much of the year. At the same time, the scientific breeding of cattle helped make meat and milk more abundant.

Technological advances also improved living conditions: houses could be larger, better heated, and better illuminated. Although working-class residences had few creature comforts, the affluent were able to afford indoor plumbing, central heating, gas lighting, bathtubs, iceboxes, and sewing machines. Even the lower classes were able to afford new coal-burning cast-iron cooking stoves, which facilitated more varied meals and improved heating. The first sewer systems helped cities begin to rid streets of human and animal waste, while underground water lines enabled fire companies to use hydrants rather than bucket brigades. Machine-made clothes fit better and were cheaper than clothes sewed by hand from homespun cloth; newspapers and magazines were more abundant and affordable, as were clocks and watches. Technology changed not only how people lived but also how they worked. The factory system would have profound effects on the nineteenth-century economic landscape, particularly in the Northeast.

THE LOWELL SYSTEM   Modern industrialism in America appeared first in New England. At Lowell, Massachusetts, along the Merrimack River, the Merrimack Manufacturing Company in 1822 developed a water-powered plant similar to one in Waltham, Massachusetts, in which spinning and weaving by power machinery had been brought together under one roof for the first time in 1813. Lowell grew dramatically, and it soon provided the model for other mill towns in Massachusetts, New Hampshire, and Maine.

The chief features of the "Lowell system" were a large capital investment, the concentration of all production processes in one plant under unified management, and specialization in a relatively coarse cloth requiring minimally skilled workers. In the public mind, however, the system was associated above all with the conscious attempt by its founders to establish model

***Merrimack Mills and Boarding-Houses* (1848)**

Just one of the textile companies in Lowell, Massachusetts.

mill communities that would enhance rather than corrupt the social fabric. The founders would avoid the drab, crowded, and wretched life of the English mill villages by locating their mill in the countryside and then establishing an ambitious program of paternal supervision of the workers. Initially the employees were mostly young women from New England farm families whose prospects for finding gainful employment or a husband were diminishing. They later were supplanted by young Irish immigrant women. With so many men migrating westward, New England had been left with a surplus of women. Employers also preferred to hire women because of their manual dexterity and their willingness to work for wages lower than those demanded by men. Many women were drawn to the mills by the chance to escape the wearying routine of farm life and earn money to help their family or improve their own circumstances.

To reassure concerned parents, the mill owners promised to provide the "Lowell girls" with good wages, tolerable work, comfortable housing, moral discipline, and a variety of educational and cultural opportunities, such as lectures and evening classes. Initially visitors to Lowell praised the well-designed red-brick mills. The laborers appeared "healthy and happy." The female workers lived in dormitories staffed by matronly supervisors, church attendance was mandatory, and temperance regulations and curfews were rigidly enforced. Despite thirteen-hour days and six-day workweeks, one worker described Lowell's community life as approaching "almost Arcadian simplicity." But with mushrooming growth, Lowell lost its innocence. By 1840 it had thirty-two mills and factories in operation, and the blissful rural town had become a bleak industrial city.

Other factory centers sprouted up across New England, displacing forests and farms and engulfing villages, filling the air with smoke, noise, and stench. Between 1820 and 1840 the number of Americans engaged in manufacturing increased eightfold, and the number of city dwellers more than doubled. During the 1830s, as textile prices and wages dropped, relations between workers and managers deteriorated. A new generation of owners and foremen stressed efficiency and profit margins over community values. The machines were worked at a faster pace, and workers organized strikes to protest conditions.

The "Lowell girls" drew attention less because they were typical than because they were special. Increasingly common was the family system, sometimes called the Rhode Island system or the Fall River system, which prevailed in textile companies outside northern New England. Factories that relied upon water-power often appeared in unpopulated areas, along with tenements or mill villages that increasingly housed newly arrived foreign immigrants. Whole families might be hired, the men for heavy labor, the women and children for the lighter work. The system also promoted paternalism. Employers dominated the life of the mill villages. Employees worked from sunup to sunset and longer in

Mill girls

Massachusetts mill workers of the mid–nineteenth century, photographed holding shuttles. Although mill work initially provided women with an opportunity for independence and education, conditions soon deteriorated as profits took precedence.

winter. Such long hours were common on the farms of the time, but in factories the work was more intense and less varied and offered no seasonal letup.

INDUSTRIALIZATION AND THE ENVIRONMENT Textile mills along New England's rivers provided new jobs but in the process transformed the environment. The mills, fed by waterpower, led to deforestation, air pollution, and a decline in the spring fish runs throughout New England's network of river valleys. They also provoked violent conflicts between farmers and mill owners.

Between 1820 and 1850 some forty textile and flour mills were built along the Merrimack River, which runs from New Hampshire through northeastern Massachusetts. In pre-industrial England and America the common-law tradition required that water be permitted to flow as it had always flowed; the right to use it was reserved to those who owned land adjoining streams and rivers. In other words, running water, by nature, could not be converted into private property. People living along rivers could divert water for

Milling and the environment

A milldam on the Appomattox River near Petersburg, Virginia, in 1865. Milldams were used to produce a head of water for operating a mill.

domestic use or to water livestock but could not use naturally flowing water to irrigate land or drive machinery.

The rise of the water-powered textile industry challenged those long-standing assumptions. Entrepreneurs acquired water rights by purchasing land adjoining rivers and buying the acquiescence of nearby landowners; then, in the 1820s, they began renting the water that flowed to the textile mills. Water suddenly became a commodity independent of the land. It was then fully incorporated into the industrial process. Canals, locks, and dams were built to facilitate the needs of the proliferating mills. Flowing water was transformed from a societal resource to a private commodity.

The changing uses of water transformed the region's ecology. Rivers shape regions far beyond their banks, and the changing patterns of streams now affected marshlands, meadows, vegetation, and the game and other wildlife that depended upon those habitats. The dams built to harness water to turn the mill wheels that ground corn and wheat flooded pastures and decimated fish populations, spawned urban growth that in turn polluted the rivers, and aroused intense local resentment, particularly among the New Hampshire residents far upstream of the big Massachusetts textile factories. In 1859 angry farmers, loggers, and fishermen tried to destroy a massive dam in Lake Village, New Hampshire. But their axes and crowbars caused little damage. By then the Industrial Revolution could not be stopped. The textile system was not only transforming lives and property; it was reshaping nature as well.

INDUSTRY AND CITIES   In 1855 a journalist exclaimed that "the great phenomenon of the Age is the growth of cities." In terms of the census definition of *urban*, as a place with 8,000 inhabitants or more, the proportion of urban to rural populations grew from 3 percent in 1790 to 16 percent in 1860. Because of their strategic locations and their importance as centers of trade and transportation, the Atlantic seaports of New York, Philadelphia, Baltimore, and Boston were the four largest U.S. cities throughout the pre–Civil War period. New York outpaced all its competitors. By 1860 it was the first American city to boast a population of more than 1 million, largely because of its superior harbor and its unique access to commerce afforded by the Erie Canal.

Pittsburgh, at the head of the Ohio River, was already a center of iron production by 1800, and Cincinnati, at the mouth of the Little Miami River, soon surpassed all other meatpacking centers. Louisville, because it stood at the falls of the Ohio River, became an important trade center. On the Great Lakes the leading cities—Buffalo, Cleveland, Detroit, Chicago, and Milwaukee—also stood at important breaking points in water transportation. Chicago was especially well located to become a hub of both water and rail transportation, connecting the Northeast, the South, and the trans-Mississippi West. During the 1830s, St. Louis tripled in size, mainly because most of the trans-Mississippi grain and fur trade was funneled down the Missouri River. By 1860, St. Louis and Chicago were positioned to challenge Baltimore and Boston for third and fourth places on the list of the nation's largest cities.

THE POPULAR CULTURE

During the colonial era, Americans had little time for play or amusement. Most adults worked from dawn to dusk six days a week. In rural areas, people participated in barn raisings and corn-husking parties, shooting matches and footraces, while residents of the seacoast sailed and fished. In colonial cities, people attended balls, went on sleigh rides and picnics, and played "parlor games" at home—billiards, cards, and chess. By the early nineteenth century, however, a more urban society could indulge in more diverse forms of recreation. As more people moved to cities in the first half of the nineteenth century, they began to create a distinctive urban culture. Laborers and shopkeepers sought new forms of leisure and entertainment as pleasant diversions from their long workdays.

URBAN RECREATION Social drinking was pervasive during the first half of the nineteenth century. Barn raisings, corn huskings, quilting parties, militia musters, church socials, court sessions, holidays, and political gatherings—all featured liquor, hard cider, or beer. In Mississippi, recalled Senator Henry Foote, heavy drinking on such social occasions had become so fashionable that "a man of strict sobriety" was considered "a cold-blooded and uncongenial wretch."

The more affluent and educated people viewed leisure time as an opportunity for self-improvement and so attended lectures by prominent figures such as Ralph Waldo Emerson and the minister Henry Ward Beecher. Circuses began touring the country. Footraces, horse races, and boat races began attracting thousands of spectators. Nearly 100,000 people attended a horse race at Union Track on Long Island.

So-called blood sports were also a popular form of amusement. Cockfighting and dogfighting at saloons attracted excited crowds and frenzied betting.

Bare Knuckles

Blood sports emerged as popular urban entertainment for men of all social classes.

Prizefighting, also known as boxing, eventually displaced the animal contests. Imported from Britain, boxing surged into prominence at midcentury and then, as now, proved popular with all social classes. The early contestants tended to be Irish or English immigrants, often sponsored by a neighborhood fire company, fraternal association, or street gang.

THE PERFORMING ARTS   Theaters were the most popular form of indoor entertainment at midcentury. People flocked to opera houses and to watch a wide spectrum of performances: Shakespeare's tragedies, "blood and thunder" melodramas, comedies, minstrel shows, operas, magic shows, performances by acrobatic troupes, and pageants. Audiences were predominantly young and middle-aged men. "Respectable" women rarely attended. Behavior in antebellum theaters was raucous. Audiences cheered the heroes and heroines and hissed at the villains. If an actor did not meet expectations, spectators hurled epithets, nuts, eggs, fruit, shoes, or chairs.

The 1830s witnessed the emergence of the first uniquely American form of mass entertainment: blackface minstrel shows, featuring white performers made up as blacks. "Minstrelsy" drew upon African American subjects and reinforced prevailing racial stereotypes. It featured banjo and fiddle music, "shuffle" dances, and lowbrow humor. Between the 1830s and the 1870s, minstrel shows were immensely popular, especially among northern working-class ethnic groups and southern whites.

Although antebellum minstrel shows usually portrayed slaves as loyal and happy and caricatured northern free blacks as superstitious buffoons who preferred slavery to freedom, minstrelsy represented more than an expression of virulent racism and white exploitation of black culture; it also provided a medium for the expression of authentic African American dance and music.

The Crow Quadrilles

This sheet-music cover, printed in 1837, shows eight vignettes caricaturing African Americans. Minstrel shows enjoyed nationwide popularity while reinforcing racial stereotypes.

IMMIGRATION

Throughout the nineteenth century, land and jobs in America were plentiful. The United States in the nineteenth century thus remained the world's strongest magnet for immigrants, offering them chances to take up farming or urban employment.

During the forty years from the outbreak of the Revolution to the end of the War of 1812, immigration had slowed to a trickle. Wars in Europe restricted travel from Europe until 1815. Within a few years, however, passenger ships had begun to cross the North Atlantic in large numbers. The years from 1845 to 1854 saw the greatest proportional influx of immigrants in U.S. history, 2.4 million, or about 14.5 percent of the total population in 1845. In 1860 the population was 31 million, with more than one of every eight resident foreign-born. The three largest groups were the Irish (1.6 million), the Germans (1.2 million), and the British (588,000).

THE IRISH   What caused so many Irish to flee their homeland in the nineteenth century was the onset of a prolonged depression that brought immense social hardship. The most densely populated country in Europe,

Ireland was so ravaged by its economic collapse that in rural areas the average age at death declined to nineteen. By the 1830s the number of Irish immigrants leaving for America was growing quickly; and after an epidemic of potato rot in 1845, called the Irish potato famine, killed upward of 1 million peasants, the flow of Irish immigrants to Canada and the United States became a flood. By 1850 the Irish constituted 43 percent of the foreign-born population of the United States. Unlike the German immigrants, who were predominantly male, the Irish newcomers were relatively evenly apportioned by sex; in fact a slight majority of them were women, most of whom were single young adults.

Most of the Irish arrivals had been tenant farmers, but their rural sufferings left them with little taste for farmwork and little money with which to buy land in America. Many Irish men hired on with the construction crews building canals and railways—about 3,000 went to work on the Erie Canal as early as 1818. Others labored in iron foundries, steel mills, warehouses, mines, and shipyards. Many Irish women found jobs as domestic servants, laundresses, or workers in New England textile mills. In 1845 the Irish constituted only 8 percent of the workforce in the Lowell mills; by 1860 they made up 50 percent. Relatively few immigrants during the Jacksonian era found their way to the South, where land was expensive and industries scarce. The widespread use of slavery also left few opportunities in the region for immigrant laborers.

Too poor to move inland, most of the destitute Irish congregated in the eastern cities. By the 1850s the Irish made up over half the population of Boston and New York City and were almost as prominent in Philadelphia. Irish newcomers crowded into filthy, poorly ventilated

Irish immigration

In 1847 nearly 214,000 Irish immigrated to the United States and Canada aboard the ships of the White Star Line and other companies. Despite promises of spacious, well-lit, well-ventilated, and heated accommodations on ships, 30 percent of these immigrants died on board such "coffin ships."

buildings plagued by high rates of crime, infectious disease, prostitution, alcoholism, and infant mortality. The archbishop of New York at midcentury described the Irish as "the poorest and most wretched population that can be found in the world."

Many enterprising Irish immigrants forged remarkable careers, however. Twenty years after arriving in New York, Alexander T. Stewart became the owner of the nation's largest department store and thereafter accumulated vast real estate holdings in Manhattan. Michael Cudahy, who began work in a Milwaukee meatpacking business at age fourteen, became head of the Cudahy Packing Company and developed a process for the curing of meats using refrigeration. Dublin-born Victor Herbert emerged as one of America's most revered composers, and Irish dancers and playwrights came to dominate the stage.

These accomplishments, however, did little to quell the anti-Irish sentiments prevalent in nineteenth-century America. Irish immigrants confronted demeaning stereotypes and violent anti-Catholic prejudices. Protestants remained fearful of a "papist plot" to turn America into a Catholic nation. And ethnic prejudice was rampant. Many employers posted signs saying "No Irish Need Apply." But the Irish could be equally contemptuous of other groups, such as free blacks, who competed with them for low-status jobs. In 1850 the *New York Tribune* expressed concern that the Irish, having themselves escaped from "a galling, degrading bondage" in their homeland, typically voted against any proposal for equal rights for African Americans. For their part, many blacks viewed the Irish with equal disdain.

The Irish, after becoming citizens, formed powerful voting blocs. Drawn mainly to the party of Andrew Jackson, they set a crucial example of identification with the Democrats, one that other ethnic groups by and large followed. In Jackson the Irish immigrants found a hero. Himself the son of Scots-Irish colonists, he was also popular for having defeated the hated English at New Orleans. In addition, the Irish immigrants' loathing of aristocracy, which they associated with English rule, attracted them to the party claiming to represent "the common man."

Although property requirements initially kept most Irish Americans from voting, a New York State law extended the franchise in 1821, and five years later the state removed the property qualification altogether. In the 1828 election, Irish voters made the difference between Jackson and John Quincy Adams. With African Americans, women, and Native Americans still years away from gaining voting rights, Irish men became the first "minority group" to exert a remarkable political influence.

Perhaps the greatest collective achievement of the Irish immigrants was their stimulating the growth of the Catholic Church in the United States. Years of persecution had instilled in Irish Catholics a fierce loyalty to the doctrines of the church as the supreme authority over all the affairs of the world. Such passionate attachment to Catholicism generated both community cohesion among Irish Americans and fear among American Protestants.

GERMAN AND OTHER IMMIGRANTS   During the eighteenth century, Germans had responded to William Penn's offer of religious freedom and cheap, fertile land by coming in large numbers to America. As a consequence, when a new wave of German immigration formed in the 1830s, there were still many Germans in Pennsylvania and Ohio who had preserved their language and rural culture.

The new wave of migration took on a markedly different cast. It peaked in 1854, just a few years after the crest of Irish arrivals, when 215,000 Germans disembarked in U.S. ports. These immigrants included a large number of learned, cultured professional people—doctors, lawyers, teachers, engineers—some of them refugees from the failed German revolution of 1848. In addition to an array of political opinions, the Germans brought with them a variety of religious preferences. A third of the new arrivals were Catholic, most were Protestants (usually Lutherans), and a significant number were Jews, freethinking atheists, or agnostics.

Unlike the Irish, many Germans were independent farmers, skilled workers, or shopkeepers who arrived with enough money to establish themselves as skilled laborers or in farm jobs. They often migrated in families and groups rather than individually, and this clannish quality helped them sustain elements of their language and culture in the New World.

Among those who prospered in America were Ferdinand Schumacher, who began peddling flaked oatmeal in Ohio and whose business eventually became the Quaker Oats Company; Heinrich Steinweg, a piano maker who changed his name to Steinway and became famous for the quality of his pianos; and Levi Strauss, a Jewish tailor who followed the gold rushers to California and began making durable work pants that were later dubbed blue jeans, or Levi's. Major centers of German settlement developed in southwestern Illinois and Missouri (around St. Louis), Texas (near San Antonio), Ohio, and Wisconsin (especially around Milwaukee). The larger German communities developed traditions of bounteous food, beer, and music, along with German turnvereins (gymnastic societies), sharpshooter clubs, fire-engine companies, and kindergartens.

Two other groups that began to arrive during the 1840s and 1850s were but the vanguard for greater numbers to come later. Annual arrivals from Scandinavia, most of them religious dissenters, did not exceed 1,000 until 1843, but by 1860 a total of 72,600 Scandinavians were living in the United States. The Norwegians and Swedes gravitated, usually in family groups, to Wisconsin and Minnesota, where the climate and woodlands reminded them of home.

By the 1850s the rapid development of California after the discovery of gold had attracted Chinese, who, like the Irish in the East, did the heavy work of construction. Most of the Chinese immigrants came from Kwang-tung Province,* a region noted for its political turmoil, social violence, and economic hardship. The immigrants to the United States were mostly married, illiterate men desperate for work. Single women did not travel abroad, and married women usually stayed behind to raise their children. During the mid–nineteenth century a laborer in southern China might earn $5 a month; in California he could work for a railroad or a mine and make six times as much. After three or four years of such work, an immigrant could return to China with his savings and become a "big, very big gentleman."

NATIVISM   Many native-born Americans resented those newcomers who brought with them alien languages, mysterious customs, and perhaps worst of all, feared religions. The flood of Irish and German Catholics aroused Protestant hostility to "popery." A militant Protestantism growing out of the early nineteenth-century revivals heated up the climate of suspicion. There were also fears that German communities were fomenting political radicalism and that the Irish were forming voting blocs, but above all hovered the "menace" of unfamiliar religious practices. Catholic authoritarianism was widely perceived as a threat to hard-won American liberties—religious and political.

By the 1830s, nativism was conspicuously on the rise. In 1834 a series of anti-Catholic sermons by the leading New England minister of the era, the revivalist and later abolitionist Lyman Beecher, incited a mob to burn a convent in Charlestown, Massachusetts. In 1844 armed clashes between Protestants and Catholics in Philadelphia caused numerous deaths and injuries.

*The traditional (Wade-Giles) spelling is used here. About a century after these events, the Chinese government adopted pinyin transliterations, which became more widely used after 1976, so that, for example, Peking became Beijing and, in this case, Kwangtung became Guangdong.

A Know-Nothing cartoon

The Catholic Church supposedly attempts to control American religious and political life through Irish immigration.

Sporadically the nativist spirit took organized form in groups that proved their patriotism by hating foreigners and Catholics.

In 1855, delegates from thirteen states gathered to form the American party, which had the trappings of a secret fraternal order. Members pledged never to vote for any foreign-born or Catholic candidate. When asked about the organization, they were to say "I know nothing," and in popular parlance the American party thus became the Know-Nothing party. In state and local campaigns during 1854, Know-Nothings carried one election after another. They swept the Massachusetts legislature, winning all but two seats in the lower house. That fall they elected more than forty congressmen. For a while the Know-Nothings threatened to control New England, New York, and Maryland and showed strength elsewhere, but the movement subsided when slavery became the focal issue of the 1850s.

The Know-Nothings demanded the exclusion of immigrants and Catholics from public office and the extension of the period for naturalization (citizenship) from five to twenty-one years, but the American party never gathered the political strength to effect such legislation. Nor did Congress act during the period to restrict immigration in any way.

IMMIGRANT LABOR   By meeting the need for cheap, unskilled labor, immigrants made a twofold contribution to economic growth: they moved into jobs vacated or bypassed by those who went to work in the factories, and they made up a pool of labor from which factory workers were eventually drawn.

In New England the large number of Irish workers, accustomed to harsh treatment and willing to work for what natives considered low wages, spelled the end of the "Lowell girls." By 1860, immigrants made up more than half the labor force in New England's mills. Even so their pay was generally higher than that of the women and children who worked to supplement family incomes. The flood of immigration never rose fast enough to stem the long-term rise in wages. Factory labor thus continued to draw laborers from the countryside. Work in the cities offered higher real wages than work on the farm. Labor costs encouraged factory owners to seek ever more efficient machines in order to increase production without hiring more workers. In addition, the owners' desire to control the upward pressure on wage rates accelerated the emphasis on mass production. By stressing high production and low prices, owners made it easier for workers to buy the items they made.

ORGANIZED LABOR

Skilled workers in cities before and after the Revolution were called artisans, craftsmen, or mechanics. They made or repaired shoes, hats, saddles, ironware, silverware, jewelry, glass, ropes, furniture, tools, weapons, and an array of wooden products; printers published books, pamphlets, and newspapers. These skilled workers operated within a guild system, a centuries-old economic and social structure developed in medieval Europe to serve the interests of particular crafts.

The daily routine of urban workers engaged in the "finishing trades" in antebellum America was a mixture of labor, recreation, and fellowship. Their workday began at around six in the morning. At eight-thirty they would take a break to eat pastries. At eleven another break would feature a dram of beer or sugared rum. The workers ate lunch around one o'clock and took another break in late afternoon. During their breaks they would engage in animated discussions of political issues, social trends, and an array of other topics and ideas. Workers in several of the skilled trades, especially shoemaking and printing, formed their own professional associations. Like medieval guilds, which were organized by particular trades, these trade associations were

The Shoemaker, from *The Book of Trades* (1807)

When Philadelphia boot makers and shoe-makers went on strike in 1806, a court found them guilty of a "conspiracy to raise their wages."

local societies that promoted the interests of their members. The trade groups pressured politicians for tariffs to protect them from foreign imports, provided insurance benefits, and drafted regulations to improve working conditions, ensure quality control, and provide equitable treatment of apprentices and journeymen. They also sought to control the total number or tradesmen in their profession so as to maintain wage levels. The New York shoe-makers, for instance, complained about employers taking on too many apprentices, insisting that "two was as many as one man can do justice by."

The use of slaves as skilled workers also caused controversy among tradesmen. White journeymen in the South objected to competing with enslaved laborers. Other artisans refused to take advantage of slave labor. The Baltimore Carpenters' Society, for example, admitted as members only those employers who refused to use forced labor.

EARLY UNIONS   Early labor unions faced serious legal obstacles—they were prosecuted as unlawful conspiracies. In 1806, for instance, Philadelphia shoemakers were found guilty of a "combination to raise their wages." The decision broke the union. Such precedents were used for many years to hamstring labor organizations until the Massachusetts Supreme Judicial Court made a landmark ruling in *Commonwealth v. Hunt* (1842). In that case the court ruled that forming a trade union was not in itself illegal, nor was a demand that employers hire only members of the union.

Until the 1820s labor organizations took the form of local trade unions, confined to one city and one craft. From 1827 to 1837, however, organization on a larger scale began to take hold. In 1834 the National Trades' Union was set up to federate the city societies. At the same time, national craft unions were established by the shoemakers, printers, combmakers, carpenters, and handloom weavers, but all the national groups and most of the local ones vanished in the economic collapse of 1837.

LABOR POLITICS   With the widespread removal of property qualifications for voting, working-class politics flourished briefly in the 1830s. Workingmen's parties appeared in New York, Boston, Philadelphia, and about fifteen states. They admitted many who were not workers by any strict definition, and their leaders were mainly reformers and small businessmen. These labor parties faded quickly, for a variety of reasons: the inexperience of labor politicians left the parties prey to manipulation by political professionals; some of their issues were also espoused by the major parties; and they were vulnerable to attack on the grounds of extreme radicalism. In addition, they often splintered into warring factions, thus limiting their effectiveness.

Once the labor parties had faded, many of their supporters found their way into a radical wing of the Jacksonian Democrats, which acquired the name Locofocos in 1835 when their opponents from New York City's regular Democratic organization, Tammany Hall, turned off the gaslights at one of their meetings and they produced candles, lighting them with the new friction matches known as locofocos. The Locofocos soon faded as a separate group but endured as a radical faction within the Democratic party.

Though the working-class parties elected few candidates, they did succeed in drawing notice to their demands, many of which attracted the support of middle-class reformers. Above all they called for free public education for all children and the abolition of imprisonment for debt, causes that won widespread popular support. The labor parties and unions also actively promoted the ten-hour workday. In 1836, President Andrew Jackson established the ten-hour workday at the Naval Shipyard in Philadelphia in response to a strike, and in 1840 President Martin Van Buren extended the limit to all government offices and projects. In private jobs the ten-hour workday became increasingly common, although by no means universal, before 1860.

THE REVIVAL OF UNIONS   During the first half of the nineteenth century, labor unions remained local and weak. Often they came and went with a single strike. The greatest single labor dispute before the Civil War occurred on February 22, 1860, when shoemakers at Lynn and Natick, Massachusetts, walked out after their requests for higher wages were denied. Before the strike ended, it had spread through New England, involving perhaps twenty-five towns and 20,000 workers. The strike stood out not just for its size but also because the workers won. Most of the employers agreed to wage increases, and some also agreed to recognize the union as a bargaining agent.

By the mid–nineteenth century the union movement was maturing. Workers sought union recognition and regular collective-bargaining agreements. They also shared a growing sense of solidarity. In 1852 the National Typographical Union revived the effort to organize skilled crafts on a national scale. Others followed, and by 1860 about twenty such organizations had appeared, although none was yet strong enough to do much more than hold national conventions and pass resolutions.

Symbols of organized labor

A pocket watch with an International Typographical Union insignia.

THE RISE OF THE PROFESSIONS

The dramatic social changes of the first half of the nineteenth century opened up an array of new professions. Bustling new towns required new services—retail stores, printing shops, post offices, newspapers, schools, banks, lawyers, doctors, and others—that created more high-status jobs than had ever existed before. By definition, professional workers are those who have specialized knowledge and skills that ordinary people lack. To be a professional in Jacksonian America, to be a self-governing individual exercising trained judgment in an open society, was the epitome of the democratic ideal, an ideal that rewarded hard work, ambition, and merit.

The rise of the professions resulted in large measure from the expansion of education and the circulation of knowledge. In the half century after the Revolution, Americans became a distinctively literate people. The nation's passion for reading fueled a thirst for education. Teaching was one of the fastest-growing vocations in the antebellum period. Public schools initially preferred men over women as teachers, usually hiring them at age seventeen or eighteen. The pay was so low that few stayed in the profession their entire career, but for many educated, restless young adults, teaching was a convenient first job that offered independence and stature, as well as an alternative to the rural isolation of farming. The New Englander Bronson Alcott remembered being attracted to teaching by "a curiosity to see beyond the limits of my paternal home and become acquainted with the great world."

Teaching was a common stepping-stone for men who became lawyers. In the decades after the Revolution, young men, often hastily or superficially trained, swelled the ranks of the legal profession. They typically would teach

Medical training

This nineteenth-century surgical amphitheater allowed students to observe operations from seats surrounding the operating table.

for a year or two before clerking for a veteran attorney, who would train them in the law in exchange for their labors. The absence of formal standards for legal training and the scarcity of law schools help explain why there were so many attorneys in the antebellum period. In 1820 eleven of the twenty-three states required no specific length or type of study for aspiring lawyers.

Like attorneys, physicians in the early nineteenth century often had little formal academic training. Healers of every stripe and motivation established a medical practice without regulation. Most of them were self-taught or had learned their profession by assisting a doctor for several years, occasionally supplementing such internships with a few classes at the handful of new medical schools, which in 1817 graduated only 225 students. That same year there were almost 10,000 physicians in the nation. By 1860 there were 60,000 self-styled physicians, and quackery was abundant. As a result, the medical profession lost its social stature and the public's confidence.

The industrial expansion of the United States during the first half of the nineteenth century spurred the profession of engineering, a field that has since become the single largest professional occupation for men in the United States. Building canals and railroads, developing machine tools and steam engines, constructing roads and bridges—all required specialized expertise. Beginning in the 1820s, Americans gained access to technical knowledge in mechanics' institutes, scientific libraries, and special schools that sprouted up across the young nation. By the outbreak of the Civil War, engineering had become one of the largest professions in the nation.

WOMEN'S WORK   Women during the first half of the nineteenth century still worked primarily in the home. The prevailing assumption was that women by nature were most suited to marriage, maternal duties, and household management. The only professions readily available to women were nursing (often midwifery, the delivery of babies) and teaching, both of which were extensions of the domestic roles of health care and child care. Teaching and nursing commanded lower status and pay than did the male-dominated professions.

Many middle-class or affluent women focused their time outside the home on religious and benevolent work. They were unstinting volunteers in churches and reform societies. A very few women, however, courageously pursued careers in male-dominated professions. Harriet Hunt of Boston was a teacher who, after nursing her sister through a serious illness, set up shop in 1835 as a self-taught physician and persisted in medical practice although she was twice rejected for admission by the Harvard Medical School. Elizabeth Blackwell of Ohio managed to gain admission to the Geneva Medical College of Western New York, despite the disapproval of the faculty. When she walked into her first class, "a hush fell upon the class as if each member had been struck with paralysis." Blackwell had the last laugh when she finished first in her class in 1849, but thereafter the medical school refused to admit any more women. Blackwell went on to found the New York Infirmary for Women and Children and later had a long career as a professor of gynecology at the London School of Medicine for Women.

JACKSONIAN INEQUALITY

During the years before the Civil War, the American myth of young men rising from rags to riches endured. The legend had just enough basis in fact to make it plausible. John Jacob Astor, the wealthiest man in America (worth more than $20 million at his death in 1848), came of humble if not exactly destitute origins. But his and similar cases were more exceptional than common. Those who started with the handicaps of poverty and ignorance seldom made it to the top. In 1828 the top 1 percent of New York's families (worth $34,000 or more) held 40 percent of the wealth, and the top 4 percent held 76 percent. Similar circumstances prevailed in Philadelphia, Boston, and other cities.

A supreme irony of the times was that the so-called age of the common man, the age of Jacksonian democracy, seems actually to have been an age of growing social and economic inequality. Years before, in the late eighteenth century, slavery aside, American society probably approached equality more closely than any other population of its size anywhere else in the world. During the last half of the 1700s, social mobility was higher than before or since. By the time popular egalitarianism caught up with reality, reality was moving back toward greater inequality.

Why that happened is difficult to say, except that the boundless wealth of the untapped frontier narrowed as the land was occupied and claims on various opportunities were staked out. Such developments had taken place in New England towns even before the end of the seventeenth century. But despite growing social distinctions, it seems likely that the white population of America, at least, was better off than the general run of Europeans. New frontiers, both geographic and technological, raised the level of material well-being for all. And religious as well as political freedoms continued to attract people eager for liberty in a new land.

End of Chapter Review

CHAPTER SUMMARY

- **Transportation and Communication Revolutions** While the cotton culture boomed in the South, with a resultant increase in slavery, commercial agriculture emerged in the West, aided by a demand for corn, wheat, and cattle and by many inventions. The first stages of the Industrial Revolution in the Northeast reshaped the region's economy and led to the explosive growth of cities and factories. The Erie Canal contributed to New York City's status as the nation's economic center and spurred the growth of Chicago and other midwestern cities. The revolution in transportation and communication linked rural communities to a worldwide marketplace.

- **Inventions and the Economy** Inventions in agriculture included the cotton gin, which increased cotton production in the South. Other inventions, such as John Deere's steel plow and Cyrus McCormick's mechanized reaper, helped Americans, especially westerners, farm their land more efficiently and more profitably. Canals and other improvements in transportation allowed goods to reach markets quicker and more cheaply than ever before. The railroads, which expanded rapidly during the 1850s, and the telegraph diminished the isolation of the West and united the country economically and socially.

- **Immigration** The promise of cheap land and good wages drew millions of immigrants to America. Those who arrived in the 1840s came not just from the Protestant regions of Britain and Europe that had supplied most of America's previous immigrants. The devastating potato famine led to an influx of destitute Irish Catholic families. Also, Chinese laborers were drawn to California's goldfields, where nativists objected to their presence because of their poverty and their religion.

- **Workers Organize** The first unions, formed by artisans who feared a loss of status in the face of mechanization, were local and based on individual crafts. An early attempt at a national union collapsed with the panic of 1837. Unions faced serious legal obstacles even after a Massachusetts court ruled in 1842 that the formation of unions was legal. Weak national unions had reappeared by 1860.

CHRONOLOGY

1793	Eli Whitney invents the cotton gin
1794	Philadelphia-Lancaster Turnpike is completed
1795	Wilderness Road opens
1807	*Clermont*, the first successful steamboat, sails to Albany
1825	Erie Canal opens
1831	Cyrus McCormick invents a mechanical reaper
1834	National Trades' Union is organized
1837	John Deere invents the steel plow
1842	Massachusetts Supreme Judicial Court issues *Commonwealth v. Hunt* decision
1845	*Rainbow*, the first clipper ship, is launched
1846	Elias Howe invents the sewing machine
1848	California gold rush begins

KEY TERMS & NAMES

13

AN AMERICAN RENAISSANCE: RELIGION, ROMANTICISM, AND REFORM

FOCUS QUESTIONS wwnorton.com/studyspace

- What were the main changes in the practice of religion in America during the early nineteenth century?
- Which religious sects flourished during this time period?
- What were the distinguishing characteristics of American literature during the antebellum period?
- How did American education change during this period?
- What were the goals of the social-reform movement?
- What was the status of women in this period?

American thought and culture in the early nineteenth century remained rooted in two contrasting perspectives: Puritan piety and Enlightenment rationalism. America, it was widely believed, had a mission to stand as an example of republican virtue to the world. The concept of America's unique mission still carried spiritual overtones, for the religious fervor that quickened in the Great Awakening had reinforced the idea of a providential national destiny and had infused American idealism with an element of moral perfectionism. The combination of widespread religious belief and fervent social idealism brought major reforms and advances in human rights during the first half of the nineteenth century.

RATIONAL RELIGION

DEISM After the Revolution, the currents of the rational Enlightenment and the spiritual Great Awakening, now mingling, now parting, flowed on into the nineteenth century and in different ways eroded the remnants of Calvinist orthodoxy. As time passed, the puritanical image of a stern God promising predestined hellfire and damnation gave way to a more optimistic religious outlook. Enlightened rationalism increasingly stressed humanity's inherent goodness rather than its depravity and encouraged a belief in social progress and the promise of individual perfectibility.

Many leaders of the Revolutionary War era, such as Thomas Jefferson and Benjamin Franklin, were Deists. After the American Revolution and especially during the 1790s, when the French Revolution generated excited attention in the United States, interest in Deism increased. In every major city "deistical societies" were formed, and college students especially took delight in criticizing conventional religion. By the use of reason, Deists believed, people might grasp the natural laws governing the universe. Deists did not believe that every statement in the Bible is literally true. They were skeptical of miracles and questioned the divinity of Jesus. Deists also opposed religious coercion of all sorts.

UNITARIANISM AND UNIVERSALISM Orthodox Christians lumped Deism with atheism, but scientific rationalism soon began to make deep inroads into American Protestantism. The Congregational churches around Boston proved most vulnerable. A strain of rationalism had run through Puritan belief in its stress on literacy and the need for "right reason" to interpret the Scriptures. Moreover, Boston's progress—some would say its degeneration—from Puritanism to prosperity had persuaded many affluent families that they were anything but sinners in the hands of an angry God.

By the end of the eighteenth century, many well-educated New Englanders were embracing Unitarianism, a belief emphasizing the oneness and benevolence of a loving God, the inherent goodness of people, and the primacy of the individual's reason and conscience over established creeds and scriptural literalism. People are not inherently depraved, Unitarianism stressed; they are capable of doing tremendous good, and *all* are eligible for salvation. Boston was the center of the Unitarian movement, and its notion of "rational religion" flourished chiefly within Congregational churches. During the early nineteenth century more and more of these "liberal" churches adopted the name *Unitarian*.

A parallel anti-Calvinist movement, Universalism, attracted a different—and much larger—social group: wage laborers and people of more humble means. Universalists stress the salvation of all men and women, not just the predestined elect of the Calvinist doctrine. God, they teach, is too merciful to condemn anyone to eternal punishment; eventually all souls will come into harmony with God. "Thus, the Unitarians and Universalists were in fundamental agreement," wrote one historian of religion, "the Universalists holding that God was too good to damn man; the Unitarians insisting that man was too good to be damned." Although both religious groups remained relatively small in number, they exercised a powerful influence over intellectual life, especially in New England.

The Second Great Awakening

Despite the inroads of rationalism, most Americans remained a profoundly religious people, as they have been ever since. There was, the perceptive French visitor Alexis de Tocqueville observed in the 1830s, "no country in the world where the Christian religion retains a greater influence over the souls of men than in America." After the Revolution, American religious life witnessed a profound transformation. The established denominations gave way to newer, more democratic sects. Anglicanism was affected the most. It suffered the stigma of being aligned with the Church of England, and it lost its status as the official religion in most states. To diminish their pro-British image, Virginia Anglicans renamed themselves Episcopalians. But even the new name did not prevent the denomination from losing its traditional leadership position in the South.

At the same time that Anglicanism was losing stature and support, a new denomination—Methodism—was experiencing dramatic growth. In 1784, Methodists met in Baltimore and announced that they were abandoning Anglicanism and forming a distinct new denomination committed to the aggressive conversion of all people: men, women, Indians, and African Americans. The restless, energetic reform-minded Methodists, inspired by their founder, the English Anglican priest John Wesley, abandoned the gloomy predestination of Calvinism in favor of a life of unceasing "cheerful activism." Methodists abandoned the Anglican prayer book, loved singing hymns, welcomed the working poor and the oppressed, and emphasized the possibility of Christian perfection in their earthly lives.

Around 1800, fears that secularism was on the march sparked an intense series of revivals that soon grew into the Second Great Awakening. The new wave of evangelical fervor fed upon the spreading notion of social equality. Methodists and Baptists, neither of whom featured an educated clergy, sought to democratize religious practices and congregational structures. Such "populist" tendencies were reinforced by the growing popularity of the concept of free will. Salvation was available to everyone who chose to follow Christ.

Between 1800 and 1840 fiery revivals crisscrossed the United States. By the time the flames died down, the landscape of American religious life had been turned topsy-turvy. The once dominant Congregational and Anglican churches were displaced by newer sects, such as the Baptists and the Methodists. By the mid–nineteenth century, there would be more Methodist churches by far than those of any other denomination. The percentage of Americans who joined Protestant churches increased sixfold between 1800 and 1860.

John Wesley

Wesley's gravestone reads, "Lord let me not live to be useless."

The Second Great Awakening involved two very different centers of activity. One emerged among the elite New England colleges, especially Yale, and then spread west across New York into Pennsylvania and Ohio, Indiana and Illinois. The other center of revivalism coalesced in the backwoods of Tennessee and Kentucky and spread across rural America. What both forms of Protestant revivalism shared was a simple message: salvation is available not just to a select few but to anyone who repents and embraces Christ.

FRONTIER REVIVALS In its frontier phase the Second Great Awakening, like the first, generated great excitement and dramatic behavior. It gave birth, moreover, to two religious phenomena—the backwoods circuit-riding preacher and the camp meeting—that helped keep the fires of revivalism burning in the backwoods. Preachers on horseback found ready audiences among lonely frontier folk hungry for spiritual meaning and a sense of community. Revivals were often unifying events; they bridged many social, economic, political, and even racial divisions. In the backwoods and in small rural hamlets, the traveling revival was as welcome an event as the traveling circus—and equally entertaining.

The Baptists embraced a simplicity of doctrine and organization that appealed especially to rural people. Their theology was grounded in the authority of the Bible and the recognition of a person's innate depravity. But they replaced the Calvinist notion of predestination with the concept of universal redemption and highlighted the ritual of adult baptism. They also stressed the equality of all before God, regardless of wealth, social standing, or education. Since each congregation was its own highest authority, a frontier church would choose a Baptist minister on its own.

The Methodists, who shared with the Baptists an emphasis on salvation by free will, established a much more centralized organization. They also developed the most effective recruiting method of all: the minister on horseback, who sought out converts in the most remote areas with the message of salvation as a gift free for the taking. The "circuit rider" system began with Francis Asbury, a tireless British-born revivalist who scoured the trans-Appalachian frontier for lost souls, preaching some 25,000 sermons during his long career. Asbury's mobile evangelism perfectly suited the frontier environment and the new democratic age. By the 1840s the Methodists had grown into the largest Protestant denomination in the country.

African Americans were especially attracted to the new Methodist and Baptist churches. Richard Allen, who would later help found the African Methodist Episcopal (AME) Church, said in 1787 that "there was no religious sect or denomination that would suit the capacity of the colored people as well as the Methodist." He decided that the "plain and simple gospel suits best for any people; for the unlearned can understand [it]." But even more important, the Methodists actively recruited blacks. They were "the first people," Allen noted, "that brought glad tidings to the colored people." The Baptists did as well. Like the Methodists, they offered a gospel of salvation open to all, regardless of wealth, social standing, gender, or race. As free as well as enslaved African Americans joined white Baptist or Methodist churches, they infused the congregations with exuberant energy and emotional music.

During the early nineteenth century the revival fervor spread through the West and into more settled regions back East. Camp meetings were held in late summer or fall, when farmwork slackened. People converged from far and wide, camping in wagons, tents, or crude shacks. The crowds often numbered in the thousands, and the unrestrained atmosphere made for chaos. If a particular hymn or sermon excited participants, they would shout, dance, or repeat the phrase. Mass excitement swept up even the most skeptical onlookers, and infusions of the spirit elicited strange manifestations. Some participants went into cataleptic trances; others contracted the "jerks," laughed "the holy laugh," babbled in unknown tongues, or got down on all fours and barked like dogs to "tree the devil," as a hound might tree a raccoon.

But dwelling on the bizarre aspects of the camp meetings distorts a social institution that offered a meaningful outlet to isolated rural folk. For women the camp meetings provided an alternative to the rigors and isolation of farm life. Women, in fact, played the predominant role, as they had in earlier revivals. Evangelical ministers repeatedly applauded the spiritual energies of women and affirmed their right to give witness to their faith in public. Camp meetings provided opportunities for women to participate as equals in large public rituals. In addition, the various organizational needs of large revivals offered numerous opportunities for women to exercise leadership roles outside the home, including service as traveling evangelists themselves. Phoebe Worrall Palmer, for example, hosted revival meetings in her New York City home, then traveled across the United States as a camp meeting evangelist. Such opportunities to assume traditional male roles bolstered women's self-confidence and expanded their horizons beyond the domestic sphere. Their religious enthusiasm often inspired them to work on behalf of various social-reform efforts, including expanded educational opportunities for women and the right to vote. So in many ways and on many levels, the energies of the revivals helped spread a more democratic faith among the frontier people. The evangelical impulse also led to an array of interdenominational initiatives intended to ensure that new converts sustained their faith. Various denominations, for example, joined forces to create the American Bible Society and the American Sunday School Union. The Bible Society gave free bibles to new converts, and the Sunday School Union provided weekly educational instruction, including basic literacy, even in backwoods communities.

CHARLES FINNEY AND THE BURNED-OVER DISTRICT   Regions swept by revival fevers have been compared to forests devastated by fire. In 1830–1831 alone the number of churches in New England grew by a third. Western New York from Lake Ontario to the Adirondacks experienced such intense levels of fiery evangelical activity that it was labeled the burned-over district.

The most successful northern evangelist was an energetic former lawyer named Charles Grandison Finney (1792–1875). In the winter of 1830–1831, he preached for six months in upstate New York and helped generate 100,000 conversions. Finney wrestled with an age-old question that had plagued Protestantism: what role can the individual play in earning salvation? Orthodox Calvinists had long argued that grace is a gift of God to a select few, a predetermined decision apart from human understanding or control.

Religious revival

An aquatint of a Methodist camp meeting in 1819.

In contrast, Finney insisted that the individual could choose to be saved. Finney thus transformed revivals into well-organized collective conversions.

Finney believed that conversion offered the opportunity for "perfectionism." By embracing Christ, a convert could thereafter be free of sin, but Christians also had an obligation to improve the larger society. Finney therefore helped found an array of groups designed to reform various social ills: alcoholism, prostitution, war, and slavery. The revivals thus provided one of the most powerful motives for the reform impulse that characterized the age. Lyman Beecher, one of the towering champions of revivalism, stressed that the Second Great Awakening was not focused simply on promoting individual conversions; it was also intended to "reform human society."

THE MORMONS   The burned-over district crackled with spiritual fervor and gave rise to several new religious movements, the most important of which was the Church of Jesus Christ of Latter-day Saints, or the Mormons. Its founder, Joseph Smith, was the barely literate child of wandering Vermont farmers who finally settled in the village of Palmyra in western New York. In 1820 young Smith, then fourteen, declared that he had seen God and Christ, both of whom had forgiven his sins and announced that all religious denominations were false. Three and a half years later, in 1823, Smith, who had become a relentless seeker of buried treasure and an ardent believer in folk magic and the occult, reported that an angel named Moroni had visited him. Moroni was supposedly the son of the prophet Mormon and the last survivor of the Nephites, descendants of ancient Hebrews who had traveled to America 2,000 years before Columbus and had been visited by Jesus after his crucifixion and resurrection. According to Smith, Moroni led him to a hillside near his father's farm, where he unearthed golden tablets on which was etched the Book of Mormon, supposedly a lost "gospel" of the Bible buried some 1,400 years earlier.

On the same September day for each of the next three years, Smith went back to the hill and talked with the angel, who let him view the thin golden plates each time, but it was not until 1827 that Moroni allowed Smith to take them home. There, over the course of a year, Smith used supernatural "seer" stones to decipher the strange hieroglyphic language etched into the plates. (Smith said that Moroni thereafter retrieved the plates, and they have never been seen again.) The resulting 588-page Book of Mormon, published in 1830, includes large portions of the King James Bible but claims that a new prophet will visit the Americas to herald the millennium, during which the human race will be redeemed and the Native American "Lamanites," whose dark skins betray their sinfulness, will be rendered "white and delightsome" people again.

With the remarkable Book of Mormon as his gospel, the charismatic Smith set about forming his own church. He dismissed all Christian denominations as frauds, denied that there was a hell, opposed slavery, and promised that the Second Coming was imminent. Within a few years, Smith, whom the Mormons simply called Joseph, had gathered thousands of devout converts, most of them poor New England farmers who, like Smith's family, had migrated to western New York. These religious seekers, many of them cut off from organized communities and traditional social relationships, found in Mormonism the promise of a pure kingdom of Christ in America. Mormons rejected the notion of original sin staining the human race in favor of an optimistic creed stressing human goodness.

From the outset the Mormon "saints" upset their "gentile" neighbors and the political authorities with their close-knit sense of community, their eerily secret rituals, their assurance of righteousness, and their refusal to abide by local laws and conventions. Joseph Smith denied the legitimacy of civil governments and the federal Constitution. As a result, no community wanted to host him and his "peculiar people." In their search for a refuge from persecution and for the "promised land," the ever-growing contingent of Mormons moved from western New York to Ohio, then to Missouri, and finally, in 1839, to the half-built Mississippi River town of Commerce, Illinois, which they renamed Nauvoo. Within a few years, Nauvoo had become a bustling, well-planned community of 12,000 centered on an impressive neoclassical temple overlooking the river. In the process of developing Nauvoo, Joseph Smith, "the Prophet," became the community's leading entrepreneur and political czar: he owned the hotel and general store, served as mayor and as lieutenant general of the city's militia (the Nauvoo Legion), and was the trustee of the church. Smith's lust for power grew as well. He began excommunicating dissidents and announced his intention to become president of the United States.

Smith also excited outrage by practicing "plural marriage," whereby he accumulated two dozen wives and encouraged other Mormon leaders to do the same. In 1844 a crisis arose when Mormon dissidents, including Smith's first wife, Emma, denounced his polygamy. The upshot was not only a schism in the church but also an attack on Nauvoo by non-Mormons in the neighboring counties. When Smith ordered Mormons to destroy an opposition newspaper, he and his brother Hyrum were arrested and charged with treason. On June 27, 1844, an anti-Mormon mob of masked men stormed the feebly defended Nauvoo jail and killed Joseph and Hyrum Smith.

In Brigham Young (1801–1877), the remarkable successor to Joseph Smith, the Mormons found a stern new leader who was strong-minded, intelligent, and authoritarian (and husband to twelve wives). A Vermont carpenter and an early convert to Mormonism, Young succeeded Smith and promised Illinois officials that the Mormons would leave Illinois. Their new destination was 1,300 miles away, near the Great Salt Lake in Utah, a vast, sparsely populated area owned by Mexico. In early 1846, in wagons and on foot, 12,000 Mormon migrants started their grueling trek to the "promised land" of Utah. The first to arrive at Salt Lake, in July 1847, found only "a broad and barren plain hemmed in by the mountains . . . the paradise of the lizard, the cricket and the rattlesnake." By the end of 1848, however, the Mormons had developed an efficient irrigation system, and over the next decade they brought

Brigham Young

Young was the president of the Mormons for thirty years.

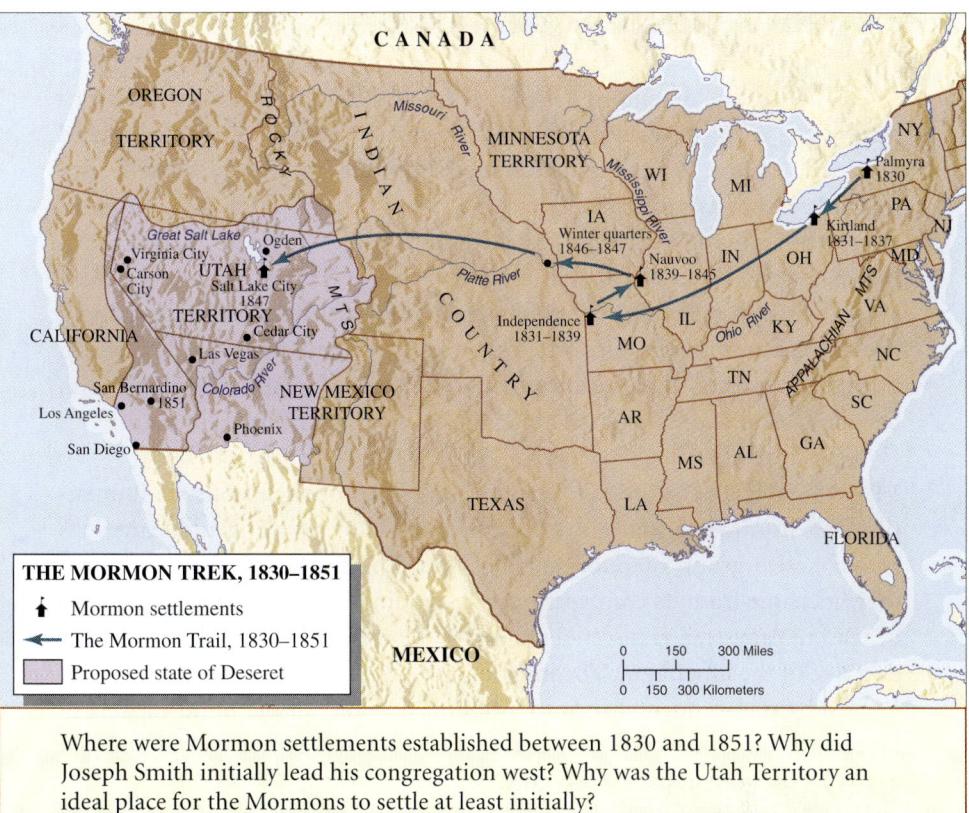

THE MORMON TREK, 1830–1851

- Mormon settlements
- The Mormon Trail, 1830–1851
- Proposed state of Deseret

Where were Mormon settlements established between 1830 and 1851? Why did Joseph Smith initially lead his congregation west? Why was the Utah Territory an ideal place for the Mormons to settle at least initially?

about a spectacular greening of the desert. At first they organized their own state, named Deseret (meaning "Land of the Honeybee," according to Young), but their independence was short-lived. In 1848, having been defeated by American armies, Mexico signed the Treaty of Guadalupe Hidalgo, ceding to the United States what is now California, Nevada, Utah, Texas, and parts of Arizona, New Mexico, Colorado, and Wyoming. Two years later, Congress incorporated the Utah Territory, including the Mormons' Salt Lake settlement, into the United States. Nevertheless, with Brigham Young named the territorial governor, the new arrangement afforded the Mormons virtual independence. For over twenty years, Young successfully defied federal authority. By 1869 some 80,000 Mormons had settled in Utah, and they had developed aggressive efforts to convert the 20,000 Indians in the territory.

Romanticism in America

The revival of emotional piety and the founding of new religions during the early 1800s represented a widespread tendency in the United States and Europe to accentuate the stirrings of the spirit rather than the dry logic of reason. Another great victory of heart over head was the Romantic movement in thought, literature, and the arts. By the 1780s a revolt was brewing in Europe against the well-ordered world of Enlightenment thinkers. Were there not, many wondered, more activities that reason and logic could explain: moods, impressions, feelings; mysterious, unknown, and half-seen things? Americans took readily to the Romantics' emphasis on a realm beyond reason, individual freedom, and the inspiring beauties of nature.

TRANSCENDENTALISM   The most intense proponents of such Romantic ideals in America were the transcendentalists of New England, America's first cohesive group of public intellectuals. The transcendental movement drew its name from its emphasis on transcending (or rising above) the limits of reason. American transcendentalism had a close affinity with the Quaker doctrine of the inner light. The inner light, a gift from God's grace, was transformed by transcendentalists into intuition, a faculty of the mind capable of perceiving things inaccessible to reason. In both cases, adherents believed that everyone contains a spark of divinity.

In 1836 an informal discussion group known as the Transcendental Club began to meet in Boston and Concord, Massachusetts to discuss philosophy, literature, and religion. It was a loose association of freethinkers who shared a rejection of traditional conventions and a relentless intellectual curiosity. Some were focused on individual freedom while others stressed collective efforts to reform society. They were united by their differences. The transcendentalists called themselves the "club of the like-minded," quipped a Boston preacher, "because no two . . . thought alike." A woman who participated in the discussions more tartly noted that the transcendentalists "dove into the infinite, soared into the illimitable, and never paid cash." They asserted the right of individuals to interpret life in their own way. The club included liberal clergymen such as Theodore Parker and George Ripley; writers such as Henry David Thoreau, Bronson Alcott, and Orestes Brownson; and learned women such as Margaret Fuller and Elizabeth Peabody and her sister Sophia, who married Nathaniel Hawthorne in 1842. Fuller edited the group's quarterly review, the *Dial* (1840–1844), before the duty fell to Ralph Waldo Emerson, soon to become the high priest of transcendentalism.

EMERSON AND THOREAU

More than any other person, Emerson embodied and championed the transcendentalist gospel. Sprung from a line of New England ministers, he set out to be a Unitarian parson but quit the "cold and cheerless" denomination because of growing doubts about its emotional vitality. After traveling in Europe, where he met England's great literary Romantics, Emerson settled in Concord to take up the life of an essayist, poet, and popular speaker on the lecture circuit, preaching the sacredness of Nature and the good news of optimism, self-reliance, and the individual's

Ralph Waldo Emerson

Emerson is most remembered for leading the transcendentalist movement.

unlimited potential. Having found reason "cold as a cucumber," he was determined to *transcend* the limitations of inherited conventions and rationalism in order to penetrate the inner recesses of the self.

Emerson's young friend and Concord neighbor Henry David Thoreau practiced the introspective self-reliance that Emerson preached. "I like people who can do things," Emerson stressed, and Thoreau, fourteen years his junior, could do many things well: carpentry, masonry, painting, surveying, sailing, and gardening. Thoreau, Emerson noted, was "as ugly as sin, long-nosed, queer-mouthed," and possessed of "uncouth and somewhat rustic manners." But he displayed a sense of uncompromising integrity, outdoor vigor, and tart individuality that Emerson found captivating.

Thoreau was also a thoroughgoing individualist. "If a man does not keep pace with his companions," he wrote, "perhaps it is because he hears a different drummer." After graduating from Harvard, Thoreau settled down in Concord to eke out a living as a part-time surveyor and maker of pencils. But he yearned to be a writer and a philosophical naturalist, and he took daily saunters in the woods and fields to drink in the beauties of nature and reflect upon the mysteries of life. The scramble for wealth among his neighbors disgusted rather than tempted him. "The mass of men," he wrote, "lead lives of quiet desperation."

Determined to practice "plain living and high thinking," Thoreau embarked on an experiment in self-reliant simplicity. On July 4, 1845, he took to the woods to live in a cabin he had built on Emerson's land beside Walden

Henry David Thoreau

Thoreau was a lifelong abolitionist.

Pond, on the outskirts of Concord. He wanted to free himself from the complexities and hypocrisies of society so as to devote his time to reflection and writing. His purpose was not to lead a hermit's life. He frequently walked the mile or so to Concord to dine with his friends and often welcomed guests at his cabin. "I went to the woods because I wished to live deliberately," he wrote in *Walden, or Life in the Woods* (1854), ". . . and not, when I came to die, discover that I had not lived."

Thoreau saw the Mexican War, which erupted while he was at Walden Pond, as a corrupt attempt to advance the cause of slavery. He refused to pay his poll tax as a gesture of opposition, for which he was put in jail (for only one night; an aunt paid the tax). Out of the incident grew the classic essay "Civil Disobedience" (1849), which would influence the passive-resistance movements of Mahatma Gandhi in India and Martin Luther King Jr. in the American South. "If the law is of such a nature that it requires you to be an agent of injustice to another," Thoreau wrote, "then, I say, break the law."

The influence of Thoreau's ideas more than a century after his death shows the impact that a contemplative individual can have on the world of action. For the most part, Thoreau and the transcendentalists avoided organized reform or political activities. They prized their individual freedom and distrusted all institutions—even those promoting causes they deemed worthy. The transcendentalists taught a powerful lesson: people must follow their conscience. In doing so, they inspired reform movements and were the quickening force for a generation of writers who produced the first age of classic American literature.

THE FLOWERING OF AMERICAN LITERATURE

Ever since gaining independence, the United States had suffered from a cultural inferiority complex. The Old World continued to set the standards in philosophy, literature, and the fine arts. As a British literary critic sneered in 1819, "Americans have no national literature." That may have been true, but during the early nineteenth century American culture began to flower.

A New England renaissance featured four poets who shaped the American imagination in a day when poetry was still read by a wide public: Henry Wadsworth Longfellow, John Greenleaf Whittier, Oliver Wendell Holmes Sr., and James Russell Lowell. Emily Dickinson was the most strikingly original and elusive of the writers contributing to this renaissance, but few of her poems were published during her lifetime. Two New York writers, Washington Irving and James Fenimore Cooper, began to draw wide

Edgar Allan Poe

Poe has had immense influence on poets and prose writers in America and abroad.

notice in Britain as well as in America. Irving's *The Sketch Book* (1819–1820) introduced such captivating stories as "Rip Van Winkle" and "The Legend of Sleepy Hollow." Cooper wrote about the frontiersman Natty Bumppo (also known as Hawkeye) in *The Pioneers* (1823), the first of the five *Leather-Stocking Tales*, novels pitting people against nature in the backwoods. The Virginian Edgar Allan Poe emerged as the master of horrifying stories and profound poetry. Then, in the half decade of 1850–1855, came the publication of such classics as *The Scarlet Letter* and *The House of the Seven Gables* by Nathaniel Hawthorne, *Moby-Dick* by Herman Melville, and *Leaves of Grass* by Walt Whitman. The literary historian F. O. Matthiessen wrote in his book *American Renaissance*, "You might search all the rest of American literature without being able to collect a group of books equal to these in imaginative quality."

The most provocative writer during the antebellum period was Walt Whitman, a remarkably vibrant personality who disdained inherited social conventions and artistic traditions. There was something elemental in Whitman's overflowing character, something bountiful and generous and compelling—even his faults and inconsistencies were ample. Born on a Long Island farm, he moved with his family to Brooklyn and from the age of twelve worked mainly as a handyman and journalist, frequently taking the ferry across the harbor to bustling Manhattan.

Whitman remained relatively obscure until the first edition of his poems, *Leaves of Grass* (1855), caught the eye and aroused the ire of readers. Emerson

***Politics in an Oyster House* (1848) by Richard Caton Woodville**

Newspapers often fueled public discussions and debates.

found it "the most extraordinary piece of wit and wisdom that America has yet contributed," but more conventional critics shuddered at Whitman's explicit sexual references and groused at his indifference to rhyme and meter as well as his buoyant egotism. The jaunty Whitman refused to conform to genteel notions of art, however, and he spent most of his career working on *Leaves of Grass*, enlarging and reshaping it in successive editions. He identified the growth of his gargantuan collection of poems with the growth of the country, which he celebrated in all its variety. Thoreau described Whitman as the "greatest democrat the world has seen."

NEWSPAPERS The flowering of American literature during the first half of the nineteenth century came at a time of massive expansion in newspaper readership. In 1847, Richard Hoe of New York invented the rotary press, which printed 20,000 sheets an hour, and thereby expedited production of cheap newspapers as well as magazines and books. The availability of newspapers costing only a penny apiece transformed daily reading into a form of popular entertainment. Newspaper circulation soared. The "penny dailies," explained one editor, "are to be found in every street, lane, and alley; in every hotel, tavern, countinghouse, [and] shop." The United States had more newspapers than any other nation in the world.

EDUCATION

Literacy in nineteenth-century America was surprisingly widespread. In 1840, according to census data, some 78 percent of the total population and 91 percent of the white population could read and write. Since the colonial period, in fact, Americans had enjoyed the highest literacy rate in the

Western world. Most children were taught to read in church or private schools, by formal tutors, or by their families.

EARLY PUBLIC SCHOOLS   During the 1830s the demand for government-supported public schools peaked. Workers wanted free public schools to give their children an equal chance at economic and social success. Education, it was also argued, would be a means of social reform, by improving manners and reducing crime and poverty.

Horace Mann of Massachusetts led the drive for statewide school systems. Trained as a lawyer, he shepherded through the state legislature in 1837 a bill that created a state board of education, then served as its leader. Mann went on to sponsor many reforms in Massachusetts, including the first state-supported training for teachers, a state association of teachers, and a minimum school year of six months. Mann defended the public-school system as the best conduit to social stability and equal economic opportunity: "Education then, beyond all other devices of human origin, is a great equalizer of the conditions of men—the balance wheel of the social machinery."

While the North had made great strides in public education by 1850, the educational pattern in the South continued to reflect the region's aristocratic pretensions and rural isolation: the South had a higher percentage of college students than any other region but a lower percentage of public-school students. And the South had some 500,000 white illiterates, more than half the total number in the young nation.

Nationwide, most students going beyond the elementary grades went to private academies, often subsidized by church and public funds. Such schools, begun in colonial days, multiplied until there were more than 6,000 of them in 1850. Public high schools became well established in school systems only after the Civil War; in 1860 there were barely 300 in the country.

HIGHER EDUCATION   The post-Revolutionary proliferation of colleges continued after 1800 with the spread of small denominational colleges and state universities. The nine colleges founded in the colonial period survived, but not many of the fifty that had sprung up between 1776 and 1800 lasted. Of the seventy-eight colleges and universities in 1840, thirty-five had been founded after 1830, almost all affiliated with a Christian denomination. A post-Revolutionary movement for state-supported universities flourished in those southern states that had had no colonial university. Federal policy abetted the spread of universities in the West. When Congress

The George Barrell Emerson School, Boston, ca. 1850

Although higher education for women initially met with some resistance, seminaries like this one, started in the 1820s and 1830s, taught women mathematics, physics, and history, as well as music, art, and the social graces.

granted statehood to Ohio in 1803, it set aside two townships for the support of a state university and kept up that policy in other new states.

Colleges and universities during the nineteenth century were tiny when compared with today's institutions of higher learning. Most enrolled 100 students or fewer, and the largest rarely had more than 600. Virtually all of those students were men. Elementary education for girls was generally accepted, but training beyond that level was not. Progress began with the academies, some of which taught boys and girls alike. Good "female seminaries," like those founded by Emma Willard at Troy, New York (1821), and Mary Lyon at South Hadley, Massachusetts (1837), paved the way for women's colleges.

The curricula in female seminaries usually differed from the courses in men's schools, giving more attention to the social amenities and such "embellishments" as music and art. Vassar, opened at Poughkeepsie, New York, in 1861, is usually credited with being the first women's college to give priority to conventional academic subjects and standards. In general, the

West gave the greatest impetus to coeducation, with state universities in the lead. But once admitted, female students remained in a subordinate status. At Oberlin College in Ohio, for instance, women were expected to clean male students' rooms and were not allowed to speak in class or recite at graduation exercises. Coeducation did not mean equality.

ANTEBELLUM REFORM

The United States in the antebellum period was awash in reform movements. The urge to eradicate evil had its roots in the American sense of spiritual zeal and moral mission, which in turn drew upon the rising faith in human perfectibility promoted by both revivalists and Romantic idealists. The revival fever of the Second Great Awakening helped generate a widespread belief that people could eradicate many of the evils afflicting society. Transcendentalism, the spirit of which infected even those unfamiliar with its philosophical roots, offered a Romantic faith in the individual and the belief that human intuition led to right thinking and social reform.

Such a perfectionist bent found outlet in diverse reform movements and activities during the first half of the nineteenth century. Few areas of life escaped the concerns of the reformers: observance of the Sabbath, dueling, crime and punishment, the hours and conditions of work, poverty, vice, care of the handicapped, pacifism, foreign missions, temperance, women's rights, and the abolition of slavery.

While a perfectionist impulse helped excite the reform movements of the Jacksonian era, social and economic changes helped supply the reformers themselves, most of whom were women. The rise of an urban middle class offered affluent women greater time to devote to social concerns. Material prosperity enabled them to hire maids and cooks, often Irish immigrants, who in turn freed them from the performance of household chores. Many women joined charitable organizations, most of which were led by men. Some reformers proposed legislative remedies for social ills; others stressed personal conversion or private philanthropy. Whatever the method or approach, social reformers mobilized in great numbers during the second quarter of the nineteenth century.

TEMPERANCE   The temperance crusade was perhaps the most widespread of the reform movements. The census of 1810 reported some 14,000 distilleries producing 25 million gallons of alcoholic beverages each year. William Cobbett, an English reformer who traveled in the United States, noted in 1819 that one could "go into hardly any man's house without being asked to drink wine or spirits, even *in the morning.*"

The temperance movement during the first half of the nineteenth century rested on a number of arguments. Foremost was the religious demand that "soldiers of the cross" lead blameless lives. Others stressed the economic implications of sottish workers. The dynamic new economy, with factories and railroads moving on strict schedules, made tippling by the labor force a far greater problem than it had been in a simpler agrarian economy. Humanitarians also emphasized the relationship between drinking and poverty. Much of the movement's propaganda focused on the sufferings of innocent mothers and children. "Drink," said a pamphlet from the Sons of Temperance, "is the prolific source (directly or indirectly) of nearly all the ills that afflict the human family."

In 1826 a group of Boston ministers organized the American Society for the Promotion of Temperance, which pursued its objectives through lectures, press campaigns, an essay contest, and the formation of local and state societies. A favorite device was to ask each person who took the pledge to put by his or her signature a T for "total abstinence." With that a new word entered the language: *teetotaler.*

PRISONS AND ASYLUMS   Romantic era's belief that people are innately good and capable of improvement brought about major changes in the treatment of prisoners, the disabled, and dependent children. If removed from society, the theory went, the needy and deviant could be made whole again. Unhappily, this ideal kept running up against the dictates of convenience and economy. The institutions for people with problems had a way of turning into breeding grounds of brutality and neglect.

Gradually the idea of the penitentiary developed. An early model of the new system, widely copied, was the Auburn Penitentiary, commissioned by New York in 1816. The prisoners at Auburn had separate cells and gathered only for meals and group labor. Discipline was severe. The men were marched out in lockstep and never put face-to-face or allowed to talk. But prisoners were at least reasonably secure from abuse by their fellow prisoners. The system, its advocates argued, had a beneficial effect on the prisoners and saved money, since the workshops supplied prison needs and produced goods for sale at a profit. By 1840 there were twelve penitentiaries of the Auburn type scattered across the nation.

The reform impulse also found an outlet in the care of the insane. The charter of the Pennsylvania Hospital, founded in 1751 and one of the first such institutions in the country, provided for the care of "lunaticks," but before 1800 few other hospitals provided care for the mentally ill. There were in fact few hospitals of any kind. The insane were usually confined at home with hired keepers or in jails or almshouses. After 1815, however, public asylums that separated the disturbed from criminals began to appear.

The most important figure in arousing public concern about the plight of the mentally ill was Dorothea Dix. A pious Boston schoolteacher, she was called upon to instruct a Sunday-school class at the East Cambridge House of Correction in 1841. She found there a roomful of insane people completely neglected, fed slop, and without heat on a cold March day. In a report to the Massachusetts legislature in 1843, Dix told of people confined "in *cages, closets, cellars, stalls, pens! Chained, naked, beaten with rods,* and *lashed into obedience.*" Wardens charged Dix with "slanderous lies," but she won the support of leading reformers as well as a large state appropriation for improving the treatment of the insane. From Massachusetts she carried her campaign throughout the country and abroad. By 1860 she had persuaded twenty states to develop programs to improve conditions in prisons and asylums.

WOMEN'S RIGHTS   Whereas Dorothea Dix stood out as an example of the opportunity that social reform activities gave middle-class women to enter public life, Catharine Beecher, a founder of women's schools in Connecticut and Ohio, published a guide prescribing the domestic sphere for women. *A Treatise on Domestic Economy* (1841) became the leading handbook of what historians have labeled the "cult of domesticity." While Beecher upheld high standards in women's education, she also accepted the prevailing view that the "woman's sphere" was the home and argued that young women should be trained primarily in the domestic arts of housework and child rearing.

The official status of women during this period remained much as it had been in the colonial era. Legally a woman was unable to vote, and after marriage she was denied legal control of her property and even of her children. Women could not be ministers or pursue most other professions. Higher education was rarely an option. A wife often could not make a will, sign a contract, or bring suit in court without her husband's permission. Gradually, however, more and more women began to complain about their status. The organized movement for women's rights in the United States had its origins in 1840, when the anti-slavery movement split over the question of

women's right to participate. Women decided then that they needed to organize on behalf of their own emancipation, too.

In 1848 two prominent moral reformers and advocates of women's rights,
Lucretia Mott, a Philadelphia Quaker, and Elizabeth Cady Stanton, a graduate of Troy Female Seminary who refused to be merely "a household
drudge," called a convention to discuss "the social, civil, and religious condition and rights of women." The hastily organized Seneca Falls Convention,
the first of its kind, issued on July 19, 1848, the Declaration of Sentiments.
The document proclaimed the self-evident truth that "all men and women
are created equal," and the attendant resolutions held that all laws placing
women "in a position inferior to that of men, are contrary to the great pre-
cept of nature, and therefore of no force or authority." Such language was
too strong for most of the 1,000 delegates, and only about a third of them
signed the document. Yet the Seneca Falls gathering represented an important first step in the evolving campaign for women's rights.

From 1850 until the Civil War, the leaders of the women's rights movement
held annual conventions and carried on a program of organizing, lecturing,
and petitioning. The movement had to struggle in the face of meager funds
and anti-feminist women and men. It owed its success to the work of a few
courageous women who refused to be intimidated by the odds against
them. Susan B. Anthony, an ardent Quaker already active in temperance and
anti-slavery groups, joined the
crusade in the 1850s. Unlike
Stanton and Mott, she was unmarried and therefore able to
devote most of her attention to
the women's crusade. As one observer put it, Stanton "forged the
thunderbolts and Miss Anthony
hurled them." Both were young
when the movement started, and
both lived into the twentieth
century, focusing after the Civil
War on demands for women's
suffrage. Although women did
not win voting rights until much
later, they did make some legal
gains. The state of Mississippi,
seldom regarded as a hotbed of
reform, was the first to grant

**Elizabeth Cady Stanton and
Susan B. Anthony**

Stanton (left) "forged the thunderbolts and
Miss Anthony hurled them."

married women control over their property, in 1839; by the 1860s eleven more states had such laws.

UTOPIAN COMMUNITIES   The pervasive climate of reform during and after the Jacksonian era also excited a quest for utopia. Plans for ideal communities had long been an American passion, at least since the Puritans set out to build a wilderness Zion in New England. Over 100 utopian communities sprang up between 1800 and 1900. Among the most durable were the Shakers, officially the United Society of Believers in Christ's Second Appearing, founded by Ann Lee (Mother Ann Lee), who arrived in New York State from England with eight followers in 1774. Believing religious fervor to be a sign of inspiration from the Holy Ghost, Shakers had strange fits in which they saw visions and prophesied. These manifestations later evolved into a ritual dance—hence the name Shakers. Mother Ann claimed that God was genderless and that she was the female incarnation, as Jesus had been the male. She preached celibacy to prepare Shakers for the perfection that was promised them in heaven.

Mother Ann died in 1784, but the group found new leaders. From the first community at New Lebanon, New York, the movement spread into New England, Ohio, and Kentucky. By 1830 about twenty groups of Shakers were flourishing. In these communities all property was held in common, and strict celibacy was practiced. Men and women not only slept separately but also worked and ate separately. The superbly managed Shaker farms yielded a surplus for the market. They were among the nation's leading sources of garden seed and medicinal herbs, and many of their manufactures, including clothing, household items, and especially furniture, were prized for their simple beauty.

John Humphrey Noyes, founder of the Oneida Community, developed a quite different ideal community. Educated at Dartmouth and Yale Divinity School, he was converted at one of Charles G. Finney's revivals and entered the ministry. He was forced out, however, when he declared that with true conversion came perfection and a complete release from sin. In 1836 he gathered a group of a dozen or so "Perfectionists" around his home in Putney, Vermont. Ten years later Noyes announced a new doctrine of "complex marriage," which meant that every man in the community was married to every woman and vice versa. "In a holy community," he claimed, "there is no more reason why sexual intercourse should be restrained by law, than why eating and drinking should be." To outsiders such theology smacked of "free love," and Noyes was arrested. He fled to New York State and in 1848 established the Oneida Community, which numbered more than 200 by 1851.

In contrast to these religious-based communities, Robert Owen's New Harmony was based upon a secular principle. A British capitalist who worried about the degrading social effects of the factory system, Owen bought the town of Harmonie, Indiana, promptly christening it New Harmony. In 1825 a varied group of about 900 colonists gathered in New Harmony for a period of transition from Owen's ownership to the new system of cooperation. The high proportion of learned participants generated a certain intellectual electricity about the place. There were frequent lectures and social gatherings with music and dancing. For a time, New Harmony looked like a brilliant success, but it soon fell into discord. The problem, it seems, was one common to most reform groups: every idealist wanted his own plan put into practice. In 1827, Owen returned from a visit to England to find New Harmony insolvent. The following year he dissolved the project.

Brook Farm in Massachusetts was the most celebrated of all the utopian communities because it grew out of the transcendental movement. George Ripley, a Unitarian minister and transcendentalist, conceived of Brook Farm as a combination of high thinking and plain living. In 1841 he and several dozen other like-minded utopians moved to the 175-acre farm eight miles southwest of Boston. Brook Farm became America's first secular utopian community. One of its members, the novelist Nathaniel Hawthorne, called Brook Farm "our beautiful scheme of a noble and unselfish life." The social experiment attracted great attention and hundreds of visitors. Its residents shared the tasks of maintaining the buildings, tending the fields, and preparing the meals. They also organized picnics, dances, lectures, and discussions. Most Brook Farmers found considerable fulfillment in the new community. Said one, "We were happy, contented, well-off and care-free; doing a great work in the world, enthusiastic and faithful, we enjoyed every moment of every day." The place survived financially, however, mainly because of an excellent community school that drew tuition-paying students from outside. But when a new central building burned down on the day of its dedication in 1846, the community spirit expired in the embers.

Like Brook Farm, most of the utopian communities were short-lived. While such social experiments had little effect on the larger society, they did express the deeply ingrained desire for perfectionism inherent in the American character, a desire that would continue to spawn such noble, if frequently naive, experiments thereafter. Among all the targets of the reformers' wrath, however, one great evil would finally take precedence over the others: human bondage. The transcendentalist reformer Theodore Parker declared that slavery was "the blight of this nation, the curse of the

North and the curse of the South." The paradox of American slavery coupled with American freedom, of "the world's fairest hope linked with man's foulest crime," in the novelist Herman Melville's words, would inspire the climactic crusade of the age, abolitionism, one that would ultimately move to the center of the political stage and sweep the nation into an epic—and tragic—civil war.

End of Chapter Review

CHAPTER SUMMARY

- **Second Great Awakening**   The Second Great Awakening, an evangelical movement, generated revivals, especially in the backwoods. The Calvinist doctrine of predestination was often replaced by the concept of salvation by free will. The more democratic sects, such as Baptists and Methodists, gained members. Evangelists preached to enslaved people that everyone is equal in the eyes of God.

- **Religious Movements**   The burned-over district was the birthplace of several religious movements, including the Church of Jesus Christ of Latter-day Saints, whose followers call themselves Mormons. Largely because they engaged in plural marriage, Mormons were persecuted, and their "prophet," Joseph Smith, lost his life. Smith's successor, Brigham Young, led the Mormons on a trek to then-isolated Utah in the hope that they could worship freely there. Another sect of this period, the Shakers, established their own celibate communities and believed that the Second Coming of Christ was imminent.

- **Romanticism**   The transcendentalists embraced the Romantic movement in reaction to scientific rationalism and Calvinist orthodoxy, producing works that transcended reason and the material world. At the same time, improved technology and communication allowed the works of novelists, essayists, and poets to reach a mass market.

- **Social Reform Movements**   America had an astonishingly high literacy rate, and reformers sought to establish statewide school systems. New colleges, most with religious affiliations, also sprang into existence. A few institutions, such as Vassar College, aimed to provide women with an education equal to that available to men at the best colleges. Social reformers sought to eradicate such evils as excessive drinking. They were active in the Sunday-school movement, the establishment of Bible societies, and the reform of prisons and asylums. With the Seneca Falls Convention of 1848, social reformers also launched the women's rights movement.

- **Cult of Domesticity**   The cult of domesticity relegated women to the home. Middle-class women were educated to manage the household, inculcate in their children a strong sense of morality, and please their husbands. Married women had no rights under the law, and women could not vote.

CHRONOLOGY

1826	Ministers organize the American Society for the Promotion of Temperance
1830–1831	Charles G. Finney begins preaching in upstate New York
1830	Joseph Smith reveals the Book of Mormon
1836	Transcendental Club holds its first meeting
1839	Mormons establish the community of Nauvoo, Illinois
1841	Catharine Beecher's *Treatise on Domestic Economy* is published
1846	Mormons, led by Brigham Young, undertake trek to Utah
1848	At Seneca Falls Convention, women issue the Declaration of Sentiments
	John Humphrey Noyes establishes the Oneida Community
1854	Henry David Thoreau's *Walden, or Life in the Woods* is published
1855	Walt Whitman's *Leaves of Grass* is published

KEY TERMS & NAMES

14
MANIFEST DESTINY

FOCUS QUESTIONS wwnorton.com/studyspace

- What were the dominant issues in national politics in the 1840s?
- Why did settlers migrate west, and what conditions did they face?
- Why did Texas declare independence from Mexico in 1836, and why were many Americans reluctant to accept it as a new state in the Union?
- What were the causes of the Mexican War?
- What territories did the United States gain from the Mexican War, and what controversial issue consequently arose?

In the American experience the West has always had a mythical magic and allure. Moving westward was one of the primary sources of energy and hope in the development of the United States. The West—whether, initially, the enticing lands over the Allegheny Mountains that became Ohio and Kentucky or, later, the fertile prairies watered by the Mississippi River or, at last, the spectacular lands on the Pacific coast that became the states of California, Oregon, and Washington—served as a powerful magnet for adventurous people dreaming of freedom and self-fulfillment. During the 1840s the quest for better economic opportunities and more space in the West continued to excite the American imagination. People frustrated by the growing congestion and rising cost of living along the Atlantic seaboard saw in the West a bountiful source of personal freedom, business potential, social democracy, and adventure. "If hell lay to the west," one pioneer declared, "Americans would cross heaven to get there."

Millions of Americans in the nineteenth century crossed the Mississippi River and endured unrelenting hardships in order to fulfill their "providential destiny" to subdue and settle the entire continent. Economic depressions in 1837 and 1841 intensified the appeal of starting anew out West. Texas, Oregon, and Utah were the favored destinations until the discovery of gold in California in 1848 sparked a stampede that threatened to depopulate New England of its young men. Trappers and farmers, miners and merchants, hunters, ranchers, teachers, house servants, and prostitutes, among others, also headed west seeking their fortune. Others sought religious freedom or new converts to Christianity. Whatever the reason, the pioneers formed an unceasing migratory stream flowing across the Great Plains and the Rocky Mountains. Of course, the West was not empty land waiting to be developed by hardy pioneers, trappers, and miners. Others had been there long before the American migration. The Indian and Mexican inhabitants of the region soon found themselves swept aside by successive waves of American settlers.

THE TYLER YEARS

When President William Henry Harrison took office in 1841, elected, like Andrew Jackson, mainly on the strength of his military record and his lack of a public stand on major issues, observers expected him to be a tool in the hands of Whig leaders Daniel Webster and Henry Clay. Webster became secretary of state, and although Clay preferred to stay in the Senate, his friends filled the cabinet. As it turned out, however, Harrison's administration would never prove itself, for Harrison served the shortest term of any president. At the inauguration, held on a chilly, rainy day, he caught cold. On April 4, 1841, exactly one month after the inauguration, he died of pneumonia at age sixty-eight. He was the first president to die in office.

John Tyler, the first vice president to succeed upon the death of a president, served practically all of Harrison's term. At age fifty-one, the Virginia slaveholder was the youngest president to date. He had already had a long career as legislator, governor, congressman, and senator, and his positions on all the important issues had been forcefully stated. Although a

Webster-Ashburton Treaty

A political cartoon of Webster and Ashburton negotiating.

Whig, he favored a strict construction of the Constitution and was a stubborn defender of states' rights. When someone asked if he was a nationalist, Tyler retorted that he had "no such word in my political vocabulary." He opposed Henry Clay's "American System"—protective tariffs, a national bank, and internal improvements at national expense. Originally a Democrat, Tyler had broken with the party over Andrew Jackson's condemnation of South Carolina's effort to nullify a federal law and Jackson's imperious use of executive authority. Thus Tyler, the states-rights-defending Whig, had been chosen to "balance" the ticket by party leaders in 1840; no one expected that he would wield power. After Tyler become president, some critics called him "His Accidency."

DOMESTIC AFFAIRS   Given more finesse by Henry Clay, the powerful senator might have bridged the policy divisions between him and the president. But for once, driven by his own presidential ambition, the Great Compromiser lost his instinct for compromise. When Congress met in a special session in 1841, Clay introduced a series of resolutions designed to supply the platform that the party had evaded in the previous election. The chief points were repeal of the Independent Treasury Act, establishment of a third Bank of the United States, distribution to the states of money from federal land sales, and higher tariffs. The imperious Clay then set out to push his program through Congress. "Tyler dares not resist. I will drive him before me," Clay predicted.

Tyler, it turned out, was not easily driven. Although he agreed to the repeal of the Independent Treasury Act and signed a higher tariff bill in 1842, Tyler vetoed Clay's bill for a new national bank. This shocking action prompted his entire cabinet to resign, with the exception of Secretary of State Daniel Webster. Tyler replaced the defectors with anti-Jackson Democrats who, like him, had become Whigs. Irate congressional Whigs expelled Tyler from the party, and Democrats viewed him as an untrustworthy renegade. Henry Clay assumed leadership of the Whig party, and the stubborn Tyler became a president without a party. Such fractious political turmoil occurred as the economic depression worsened. Bank failures mounted. Unemployment soared.

FOREIGN AFFAIRS   In foreign relations, tensions with Great Britain captured President Tyler's attention. A major issue involved the suppression of the African slave trade, which both countries had outlawed in 1808. In 1841 the British prime minister asserted the right to patrol off the coast of Africa and search American vessels for slaves. Relations were further strained late in 1841, when 135 enslaved Africans on the *Creole*, bound from Hampton Roads, Virginia, to be sold in New Orleans, mutinied and sailed to the Bahamas, where the British set them free. Secretary of State Webster demanded that the slaves be returned as American property, but the British refused (the dispute was not settled until 1853, when England paid $110,000 to the owners of the freed slaves).

At this point a new British government accepted Webster's overtures for negotiations and sent Lord Ashburton to Washington, D.C. Ashburton was widely known to be friendly to Americans, and the talks proceeded smoothly. The negotiations settled the contested Maine boundary as well as other border disputes with Great Britain by accepting the existing line between the Connecticut and St. Lawrence Rivers and compromising on the line between Lake Superior and Lake of the Woods along the border between Canada and the future state of Minnesota. The Webster-Ashburton Treaty (1842) also provided for joint naval patrols off the African coast to suppress the slave trade.

The Western Frontier

In the 1840s most Americans were no more stirred by the quarrels of John Tyler and Henry Clay over such issues as the banking system and tariffs than students of history would be at a later date. What aroused public interest was the ongoing economic depression and the continuing migration westward across the Great American Desert and the Rocky Mountains to the Pacific coast. In 1845 a magazine editor named John L. O'Sullivan labeled this bumptious spirit of expansion. "Our manifest destiny," he wrote, "is to overspread the continent allotted by Providence for the free development of our yearly multiplying millions." God, in other words, deemed that the United States should extend itself from the Atlantic to the Pacific—and beyond. At its best this much-trumpeted notion of Manifest Destiny offered a moral justification for American expansion, a prescription for what an enlarged United States could and should be. At its worst it was a cluster of flimsy rationalizations for naked greed and imperial ambition. Whatever the case, settlers began streaming into the Far West during the 1840s in the aftermath of the panic of 1837 and the prolonged economic depression.

As they crossed the Mississippi River and made their way westward, pioneers entered not only a new environment but a new culture as well. The Great Plains and the Far West were already occupied by Indians and Mexicans, who had lived in the region for centuries and had established their own distinctive customs and ways of life. Now they were joined by Americans of diverse ethnic origins and religious persuasions. It made for a volatile mix.

WESTERN INDIANS   Historians estimate that over 325,000 Indians inhabited the Southwest, the Great Plains, California, and the Pacific Northwest in 1840, when the flood of white settlers began to pour into the region. The Native Americans often warred against one another. They were divided into more than 200 tribes, each with its own language, religion, economic base, kinship practices, and system of governance. Some were primarily farmers; others were nomadic hunters who preyed upon game animals, as well as other Indians.

Many tribes resided on the Great Plains, a vast grassland stretching from the Mississippi River west to the Rocky Mountains and from Canada south to Mexico. Plains Indians such as the Arapaho, Blackfoot, Cheyenne, Kiowa, and Sioux were horse-borne nomads; they migrated across the grasslands with the buffalo herds, carrying their tepees with them. Disputes over buffalo and hunting grounds sparked clashes between rival tribes, events that help explain the cult of the warrior among the Plains Indians. Scalping or killing an enemy would earn praise from elders and feathers for ceremonial headdresses.

Quite different Indian tribes lived to the south and west of the Plains Indians. In the arid region including what is today Arizona, New Mexico, and southern Utah were the peaceful Pueblo tribes: Acoma, Hopi, Laguna, Taos, Zia, Zuni. They were sophisticated farmers who lived in adobe villages along rivers that irrigated their crops of corn, beans, and squash. Their rivals were the Apache and the Navajo, war-loving hunters who roamed the countryside in small bands and preyed upon the Pueblos. They, in turn, were periodically harassed by their powerful enemies, the Comanches.

To the north, in the Great Basin between the Rocky Mountains and the Sierra Nevadas, Paiutes and Gosiutes struggled to survive in the harsh, arid region of what is today Nevada, Utah, and eastern California. They traveled in family groups and subsisted on berries, pine nuts, insects, and rodents. West of the mountains, along the California coast, Indians lived in small villages. They gathered wild plants and acorns and were adept at fishing in the rivers and bays. The Indian tribes living in the Northwest—the Nisqually, Spokane, Yakama, Chinook, Klamath, and Nez Perce (Pierced Nose)—enjoyed the most abundant natural resources and the most temperate climate.

All the Indian tribes eventually felt the unrelenting pressure of white expansion. Because Indian life on the plains depended upon the buffalo, the influx of white settlers and buffalo hunters posed a direct threat to the Indians' cultural survival. In an 1846 petition to President James Polk, the

Buffalo Hunt, Chasing Back (1860s)
This painting by George Catlin shows a hunter outrunning a buffalo.

Sioux protested that "for several years past the Emigrants going over the Mountains from the United States have been the cause that Buffalo in great measure left our hunting grounds, thereby causing us to go into the Country of Our Enemies to hunt, exposing our lives daily for the necessary subsistence of our wives and children and getting killed on several occasions." But the federal government turned a deaf ear to such pleas for assistance. It continued to build a string of frontier forts to protect the advancing settlers, and it sought to use treaties to gain control of more Indian land. When officials of the Bureau of Indian Affairs could not coerce, cajole, or confuse Indian leaders into selling the title to their tribal land, fighting ensued. And after the discovery of gold in California in 1848, the tidal wave of white expansion flowed all the way to the west coast.

THE SPANISH WEST AND MEXICAN INDEPENDENCE As American settlers moved westward, they also encountered Spanish-speaking peoples. Many whites were as contemptuous of Hispanics as they were of Indians. Senator Lewis Cass, an expansionist from Michigan, expressed the sentiment of many Americans during a debate over the annexation of New Mexico. "We do not want the people of Mexico," he declared, "either as citizens or as subjects. All we want is a portion of territory." The vast majority of the Spanish-speaking people in what is today called the American Southwest resided in New Mexico. Most of them were mestizos (of mixed Indian and

Spanish blood), and they were usually poor ranch hands or small farmers and herders.

The centuries-old Spanish efforts at colonization had been less successful in Arizona and Texas than in New Mexico and Florida. The Yuma and Apache Indians in Arizona and the Comanches and Apaches in Texas had thwarted Spanish efforts to establish Catholic missions. In eastern Texas during the first half of the eighteenth century, French traders from Louisiana undermined the authority and influence of the Spanish missions that were established. The French supplied the Indians with guns, ammunition, and promises of protection. Several of the Texas missions were abandoned and reestablished near San Antonio in 1731. By 1750 the Pawnees, Wichitas, Comanches, and Apaches were using Spanish horses and French rifles to raid Spanish settlements in Texas. By 1790 the Latino population in Texas numbered only 2,510, while in New Mexico it exceeded 20,000.

In 1807, French forces had occupied Spain and imprisoned the king, creating chaos throughout Spain's colonial possessions, including Mexico.

"¡Viva El Cura Hidalgo!"

This patriotic broadside celebrating Mexican independence shows Father Miguel Hidalgo in an oval medallion.

Miguel Hidalgo y Costilla, a creole priest (born in the New World of European ancestry), took advantage of the fluid situation to convince Indians and mestizos to revolt against Spanish rule in Mexico. The poorly organized uprising failed miserably. In 1811, Spanish troops captured Hidalgo and executed him. Other Mexicans, however, continued to yearn for independence. In 1820, Mexican creoles again tried to liberate themselves from Spanish authority. By then the Spanish forces in Mexico had lost much of their cohesion and dedication. Facing a growing revolt, the last Spanish officials withdrew in 1821, and Mexico became an independent nation. The infant Mexican republic struggled to develop a stable government, however, and an effective economy. Localism and corruption flourished. And Americans were eager to take advantage of Mexico's instability.

Mexican independence from Spain unleashed tremors throughout the Southwest. American fur traders streamed into New Mexico and Arizona and developed a lucrative commerce in beaver pelts. American entrepreneurs also flooded into the western Mexican province of California and soon became a powerful force for change; by 1848, Americans made up half the non-Indian population. In Texas, American adventurers decided to promote their own independence from a newly independent—and chaotic—Mexican government. Suddenly, it seemed, the Southwest was ripe for a new phase of American exploitation and settlement.

THE ROCKY MOUNTAINS AND OREGON COUNTRY During the early nineteenth century the Northwest frontier consisted of the Nebraska, Washington, and Oregon Territories. Fur traders especially were drawn to the Missouri River, with its many tributaries. During the 1820s and 1830s the fur trade had inspired a reckless breed of "mountain men" who relished life in the wilderness. They were the first whites to find their way around the Rocky Mountains, and they pioneered the trails that settlers by the 1840s were beginning to traverse as they flooded the Oregon Country and trickled across the border into California.

Beyond the mountains the Oregon Country stretched from the 42nd parallel north to 54°40′. In between, Spain and Russia had given up their right of settlement, leaving Great Britain and the United States as the only claimants. By the Convention of 1818, the two countries had agreed to "joint occupation" of the region. Until the 1830s, however, joint occupation had been a legal technicality because the only American presence was the occasional mountain man who wandered across the Sierra Nevadas or the infrequent trading vessel from Boston or New York City. Word of Oregon's fertile soil, plentiful rain, and magnificent forests gradually spread eastward. By the late 1830s a stream of emigrants had begun flowing along the Oregon Trail. Soon "Oregon fever" swept the nation. By 1845 there were about 5,000 settlers in Oregon's Willamette River valley.

THE SETTLEMENT OF CALIFORNIA California was also an alluring attraction for new settlers and entrepreneurs. It first felt the influence of European culture in 1769, when Spain grew concerned about Russian fur traders moving south along the Pacific coast from their base in Alaska. To thwart Russian intentions, Spain sent a naval expedition to explore and settle the region. The Spanish discovered San Francisco Bay and constructed presidios (military garrisons) at San Diego and Monterey. Even more important, Franciscan friars, led by Junípero Serra, established a Catholic mission at San Diego.

Over the next fifty years, Franciscans built twenty more California missions, spaced a day's journey apart along the coast from San Diego to San Francisco. There they converted Indians and established thriving agricultural estates. As they had in Mexico, the Spanish monarchy awarded huge land grants in California to a few ex-soldiers and colonists, who turned the grants into profitable cattle ranches. The Indians were left with the least valuable land, and most of them subsisted as farmers or artisans serving the missions. The mission-centered culture created by the Hispanic settlers who migrated to California from Mexico was quite different from the patterns of conquest and settlement in Texas and New Mexico. In those more settled regions the original missions were converted into secular parishes and the property divided among the Indians. In California the missions were much larger, more influential, and longer lasting.

Franciscan missionaries, aided by Spanish soldiers, gathered most of the coastal Indian population in California under their control: the number of "mission Indians" more than doubled between 1776 and 1784. The Spanish saw the Indians as ignorant, indolent heathens who must be converted to Catholicism and made useful members of the Spanish Empire. Viewing the missions as crucial imperial outposts, the Spanish government provided military support, annual cash grants, and supplies from Mexico. The Franciscan friars enticed the local Indians into the adobe-walled, tile-roofed missions by offering gifts or impressing them with their "magical" religious rituals. Once inside the missions, the Indians were baptized as Catholics, taught the Spanish language, and stripped of their Indian heritage. They were forced to wear Spanish clothes, abandon their native rituals, and obey the friars. Soldiers living in the missions enforced the will of the friars.

The California mission served multiple roles. It was church, fortress, home, town, farm, and imperial agent. The missions were economic as well as religious and cultural institutions; they quickly became substantial agricultural enterprises. Missions produced crops, livestock, clothing, and household goods, both for profit and to supply the neighboring presidios. Indians provided the labor.

The Franciscans used overwhelming force to maintain the labor system in the missions. Rebellious Indians were whipped or imprisoned; soldiers hunted down runaways. Mission Indians died at an alarming rate. One Franciscan friar reported that "of every four Indian children born, three die in their first or second year, while those who survive do not reach the age of twenty-five." Infectious disease was the primary threat, but the intensive labor regimen took a high toll as well. The Indian population along the California coast declined from 72,000 in 1769 to 18,000 by 1821. Saving souls cost many lives.

EARLY DEVELOPMENT OF CALIFORNIA   For all of its rich natural resources, California remained thinly populated by Indians and mission friars well into the nineteenth century. In 1821, when Mexico wrested its independence from Spain, Californians took comfort in the fact that Mexico City was so far away it would exercise little effective control over its most distant state. During the next two decades, Californians, including many recent American arrivals, staged ten revolts against the Mexican governors dispatched to lord over them.

Yet the shift from Spanish to Mexican rule did produce a dramatic change in California history. In 1824, Mexico passed a colonization act that granted hundreds of huge "rancho" estates to Mexican settlers. With free labor extracted from Indians, who were treated like slaves, the rancheros lived a life of self-indulgent luxury, gambling, horse racing, bull baiting, and dancing. They soon cast covetous eyes on the vast estates controlled by the Franciscan missions. In 1833–1834 they persuaded the Mexican government to confiscate the missions, exile the friars, release the Indians from church control, and make the mission lands available to new settlement. Within a few years some 700 new rancho grants of 4,500 to 50,000 acres were issued along the coast from San Diego to San Francisco. Organized like feudal estates, these California ranches resembled southern cotton plantations, but the death rate among Indian workers was twice as high as that of enslaved blacks in the Deep South.

Few accounts of life in California took note of the brutalities inflicted upon the Indians, however. Instead, they portrayed the region as a proverbial land of milk and honey, ripe for development. Such a natural paradise could not long remain a secret, and already Americans had been visiting the Pacific coast in search of profits and land. By the mid-1830s, shippers had begun setting up agents to buy cowhides and store them until a company ship arrived. One of the traders, John A. Sutter, had tried the Santa Fe trade first, then found his way to California. At the juncture of the Sacramento and American Rivers (later the site of Sacramento), he built an enormous enclosure that guarded an entire village of settlers and shops. Completed in 1843, the enclosure became a magnet for Americans bent on settling the Sacramento country. It stood at the end of what became the most traveled route through the Sierra Navadas, the California Trail, which forked off from the

Oregon Trail and ran through the mountains near Lake Tahoe. By 1846 there were perhaps 800 Americans in California, along with 8,000 to 12,000 Californians of Mexican descent.

MOVING WEST

Most of the western pioneers during the second quarter of the nineteenth century were American-born whites from the Upper South and the Midwest. Only a few African Americans joined in the migration. Although some emigrants traveled by sea to California, most went overland. Between 1841 and 1867 some 350,000 men, women, and children made the arduous trek to California or Oregon, while hundreds of thousands of others settled along the way in Colorado, Texas, Arkansas, and other areas.

THE SANTA FE TRAIL After gaining its independence in 1821, the government of Mexico was much more interested in trade with the United States than Spain had been. In Spanish-controlled Santa Fe, in fact, all commerce with the United States had been banned. After 1821, however, trade flourished. Hundreds of entrepreneurs made the 1,000-mile trek from St. Louis to Santa Fe, forging a route that became known as the Santa Fe Trail. Soon Mexican traders began leading caravans east to Missouri. By the 1830s there was so much commercial activity between Mexico and St. Louis that the Mexican silver peso had become the primary medium of exchange in Missouri. The traders pioneered more than a new territory. They also showed that heavy wagons could cross the plains and the mountains, and they developed the technique of organized caravans for common protection.

Wagon-wheel ruts near Guernsey, Wyoming
The wheels of thousands of wagons traveling to Oregon cut into solid rock as oxen strained up hillsides, leaving indentations that are still visible today.

THE OVERLAND TRAILS Like travelers on the Santa Fe Trail, people bound for Oregon and California rode in wagon caravans. But on the Overland Trails to the West Coast, most of them were settlers rather than traders. They traveled mostly in family groups and came from all

WAGON TRAILS WEST

—— Oregon Trail
—— Mormon Trail
- - - California Trail
—— Oxbow Route
···· Santa Fe Trail
—— Continental Divide

What did settlers migrating west hope to find? Describe the experience of a typical settler traveling on the Overland Trails.

over the United States. The wagon trains followed the trail west from Independence, Missouri, along the North Platte River into what is now Wyoming, through South Pass down to Fort Bridger, then down the Snake River to the Columbia River and along the Columbia to their goal in Oregon's fertile Willamette River valley. They usually left Missouri in late spring, completing the grueling 2,000-mile trek in six months. Traveling in ox-drawn canvas-covered wagons nicknamed prairie schooners, they jostled their way across the dusty or muddy trails and traversed rugged mountains. By 1845 some 5,000 people were making the arduous journey annually. The discovery of gold in California in 1848 brought some 30,000 pioneers along the Oregon Trail in 1849. By 1850, the peak year of travel along the trail, the annual count had risen to 55,000.

The journey west was extraordinarily difficult. Cholera claimed many lives. On average there was one grave every eighty yards along the trail between the Missouri River and the Willamette. The trail's grinding routine of chores and physical labor took its toll on once-buoyant spirits. This was especially true for women, who worked throughout the day and into the night. Women cooked, washed, sewed, and monitored the children while men drove the wagons, tended the horses and cattle, and did the heavy labor. But the unique demands of the trail soon dissolved such neat distinctions and posed new tasks. Women found themselves gathering buffalo dung for fuel, pitching in to dislodge a wagon mired in mud, helping to construct an impromptu bridge, or performing a variety of other "unladylike" tasks.

Contrary to the mythology, Native Americans rarely attacked wagon trains. Less than 4 percent of the fatalities associated with the Overland Trails experience resulted from Indian raids. More often, Indians either allowed the settlers to pass through their tribal lands unmolested or demanded payment. Many wagon trains never encountered a single Indian, and others received generous aid from Indians who served as guides, advisers, or traders. The Indians, one female pioneer noted, "proved better than represented." To be sure, as the number of pioneers increased dramatically during the 1850s, clashes between whites and Indians over water and land increased, but never to the degree portrayed in Western novels and films.

THE INDIANS AND GREAT PLAINS ECOLOGY   The massive migrations along the Overland Trail wreaked havoc on the environment of the Great Plains. Hundreds of thousands of settlers and traders brought with them millions of animals—horses, cattle, oxen, and sheep—all of which consumed huge amounts of prairie grass. The wagons and herds trampled vegetation and gouged ruts in the landscape that survive to this day. With the onset of the California gold rush in 1849, Plains Indians, led by Cheyennes, began supplying buffalo meat and skins to the white pioneers. Tracking and killing buffalo required many horses, and the four-legged creatures added to the strain on the prairie grasslands and river bottoms. A major climatic change coincided with the mass migrations sparked by the discovery of gold in California. In 1849 a prolonged drought struck the region west of the Mississippi River and produced widespread suffering. Starving Indians demanded or begged for food from passing wagon trains. Tensions between

Native Americans and white travelers brought additional federal cavalry units to the plains, exacerbating the shortage of forage grasses.

In 1851, U.S. officials invited the Native American tribes from the northern plains to a conference in the grassy valley, along the North Platte River, near Fort Laramie in what is now southeastern Wyoming. Almost 10,000 Indians—men, women, and children—attended the treaty council. What made the huge gathering even more remarkable is that so many of the tribes were at war with one another. After nearly three weeks of heated discussions, during which the chiefs were presented with a mountain of gifts, federal negotiators and tribal leaders agreed to the Fort Laramie Treaty. The government promised to provide an annual cash payment to the Indians as compensation for the damage caused by wagon trains traversing their hunting grounds. In exchange the Indians agreed to stop harassing white caravans, allow federal forts to be built, and confine themselves to a specified area "of limited extent and well-defined boundaries." Specifically, the Indians were restricted to land north and south of a corridor through which the Overland Trails passed.

Indian rendering of the Fort Laramie Treaty

This buffalo-hide robe commemorates the 150th anniversary of the signing of the Fort Laramie Treaty.

Several tribes, however, refused to accept the provisions. The most power-ful, the Lakota Sioux, reluctantly signed the agreement but thereafter failed to abide by its restrictions. "You have split my lands and I don't like it," declared Black Hawk, a Sioux chief at Fort Laramie. "These lands once belonged to the Kiowas and Crows, but we whipped these nations out of them, and in this we did what the white men do when they want the lands of the Indians." Despite the dissension, the agreement was significant, in part because it foreshadowed the "reservation" concept of Indian management that would be instituted after the Civil War.

THE PATHFINDER: JOHN FREMONT The most aggressive cham-pion of American settlement in Mexican California and the Far West was John Charles Frémont, "the Pathfinder." Frémont, born in Savannah, Geor-gia, and raised in the South, became the consummate explorer and romantic adventurer. Possessed of boundless energy and reckless courage, a robust love of the outdoors, and an exuberant, self-promoting personality, he inspired both respect and awe.

Frémont was commissioned a second lieutenant in the U.S. Topographical Corps in 1838. In 1842 he mapped the Oregon Trail beyond South Pass—and met Christopher "Kit" Carson, one of the most knowledgeable of the moun-tain men. Carson became Frémont's frequent associate and the most famous frontiersman after Daniel Boone. In 1843–1844, Frémont, typically clad in a deerskin shirt, blue army trousers, and moccasins, launched a second—and unauthorized—"military" expedition into Mexican-controlled territories. He moved on to Oregon, then swept down the eastern slopes of the Sierra Nevadas, headed southward through the central valley of California, bypassed the mountains in the south, and returned via the Great Salt Lake. His excited reports on both expeditions, published together in 1845, gained a wide national circulation and played a crucial role in prompting the mass migra-tions to Oregon and California.

ANNEXING TEXAS

AMERICAN SETTLEMENTS America's lust for new land focused on the most accessible of all the Mexican borderlands, Texas. By the 1830s, Texas was rapidly turning into a province of the United States, for Mexico in 1823 had begun welcoming American settlers (Anglos) into the region as a means of stabilizing the border.

Foremost among the promoters of the American colonization of Texas was Stephen F. Austin, a Missouri resident who gained from Mexico a huge land grant originally given to his father by Spanish authorities. Before Spain finally granted Mexican independence, the twenty-eight-year-old Austin had started a colony on the lower Brazos River in central Texas, and by 1824 more than 2,000 hardy souls had settled on his land. Most of the newcomers were southern farmers drawn to rich new cotton land selling for only a few cents an acre. By 1830 the coastal region of Texas had approximately 20,000 white settlers and 1,000 African American slaves brought in to work the cotton. The newcomers quickly outnumbered the Mexicans in the area and showed little interest in Catholicism or other aspects of Mexican culture.

The Mexican government, opposed to slavery, grew alarmed at the flood of strangers engulfing its Texas province and in 1830 forbade further immigration. But illegal immigrants from the United States crossed the long border as easily as illegal Mexican immigrants would later cross in the opposite direction. By 1835 the Anglo population in Texas had mushroomed to around 30,000, about ten times the Mexican population. Friction mounted in 1832 and 1833 as Americans demanded greater representation and power from the Mexican government. Instead of granting the request, General Antonio López de Santa Anna, who had seized power in Mexico, dissolved the national congress late in 1834 and became dictator. In the fall of 1835, Texans rebelled against Santa Anna's "despotism." A furious Santa Anna ordered all Americans expelled, all Texans disarmed, and all rebels arrested. As fighting erupted, volunteers from southern states rushed to assist the 30,000 Texans in their revolution against a Mexican nation of 7 million people.

TEXAS INDEPENDENCE   At San Antonio the Mexican army assaulted a small garrison of Texans and American volunteers holed up in an abandoned mission, the Alamo. Among the most celebrated of the volunteers was Davy Crockett, the Tennessee frontiersman who had fought Indians under Andrew Jackson and served as a congressman. He was indeed a colorful character, full of spunk and brag and thoroughly expert at killing with his trusty rifle, Old Betsy.

On February 23, 1836, General Santa Anna demanded that the Alamo's defenders surrender, only to be answered with a defiant cannon shot. Thousands of Mexican soldiers then launched a series of assaults. For twelve days the Mexicans were repulsed and suffered fearful losses. Then, on March 6, the defenders of the Alamo, fewer than 200, were awakened by the sound of Mexican bugles playing the dreaded "Degüello" ("No Mercy to the Defenders").

Soon thereafter Santa Anna's men attacked from every side. They were twice repulsed, but on the third try, as the defenders ran low on ammunition, the Mexicans broke through the battered north wall.

The frontiersmen used their muskets as clubs, but soon most were slain. Santa Anna ordered the wounded Americans hacked to death with swords and their bodies burned with the rest. The only survivors were sixteen women, children, and servants. It was a complete victory for Santa Anna, but a costly one. While Santa Anna dictated a "glorious" victory declaration, his aide wrote in his diary, "One more such 'glorious victory' and we are finished."

On March 2, 1836, while the siege of the Alamo continued, delegates from all fifty-nine Texas towns met at the village of Washington-on-the-Brazos and signed a declaration of independence. Over the next seventeen days the delegates drafted a constitution for the Republic of Texas and established an interim government. The delegates then hastily adjourned as Santa Anna's troops, fresh from their victory at the Alamo, bore down upon them.

The commander in chief of the gathering Texas forces was Sam Houston, a flamboyant Tennessee frontiersman who was born into a military family in Virginia in 1793. His father died when Sam was fourteen, and his mother took the children to live on a farm in eastern Tennessee. As a youth, Houston befriended Cherokee Indians and developed close ties with them, learning their customs and language. He joined the army in 1813, serving under Andrew Jackson in the Creek War. Having received three near-mortal wounds, Houston rose to the rank of first lieutenant before resigning in 1818 to practice law. He later served two terms in Congress and in 1827 was elected governor of Tennessee. In 1835 he moved to Texas and soon thereafter was named commanding general of the revolutionary army.

Sam Houston

Houston was commander in chief of the Texas forces.

After the Mexican victory at the Alamo, Sam Houston beat a strategic retreat eastward from Gonzales, gathering reinforcements as he went, including volunteers from the United States. Just west of the San Jacinto River he paused near the site of the city that would later bear his name, and on April 21, 1836, he surprised a Mexican encampment there. The 800 Texans and American volunteers charged, yelling "Remember the Alamo," and over-whelmed the panic-stricken Mexican force. They killed 630 Mexican soldiers while losing only 9 of their own, and they took Santa Anna prisoner. The Mexican dictator bought his freedom by signing a treaty recognizing the independence of Texas. The Mexican Congress repudiated the treaty and refused to recognize the loss of its northern province, but the war was at an end.

NEGOTIATIONS FOR ANNEXATION   In 1836, residents of the Lone Star Republic drafted a constitution that legalized slavery and banned free blacks. They made Sam Houston their first president and voted for annexation to the United States as soon as the opportunity arose. The U.S. president then was Houston's old friend Andrew Jackson, but even Old Hickory could put politics ahead of friendship and be discreet when delicacy demanded it. The addition of Texas as a new slave state in 1836 threatened to ignite a fractious sectional quarrel that might endanger Martin Van Buren's election as Jackson's successor. Worse than that, it raised the specter of war with Mexico. Concerned about such repercussions, Jackson delayed official recognition of the Republic of Texas until his last day in office, and his successor, Van Buren, avoided the issue of annexation during his term as president.

Rebuffed in Washington, Texans focused on building their separate republic. They began to talk of expanding Texas to the Pacific, creating a new nation rivaling the United States. France and Britain extended official recognition to the nation of Texas and began to develop trade relations with the republic. Meanwhile, thousands of Americans poured into the new republic. The population grew from 40,000 in 1836 to 150,000 in 1845. Many settlers were attracted by low land prices. And most were eager to see Texas join the Union.

Reports of growing British influence in Texas during the early 1840s created anxieties in the U.S. government and among southern slaveholders, who became the chief advocates of annexation. Soon after John Tyler became president, in 1841, he endorsed the idea of annexing Texas. The United States began secret negotiations with Texas in 1843, and in April, John C. Calhoun, then serving as secretary of state, completed an annexation treaty that went to the Senate for ratification.

Calhoun chose this moment to send the British minister (that is, the ambassador) to the United States a letter instructing him on the blessings of slavery and stating that the annexation of Texas was needed to foil the British abolitionists. Publication of the note fostered the claim that Calhoun and Tyler wanted Texas as a means to promote the expansion of slavery. It was so worded, one newspaper editor wrote to Andrew Jackson, as to "drive off every northern man from the support of the measure." Sectional division, plus fear of a war with Mexico, contributed to the Senate's overwhelming rejection of Calhoun's Texas annexation treaty in 1843. Whig opposition contributed more than anything else to its defeat.

POLK'S PRESIDENCY

THE ELECTION OF 1844   Although adding Texas to the Union was a popular idea among the citizenry, prudent leaders in both political parties had hoped to keep the divisive issue out of the 1844 presidential campaign. Whig Henry Clay and Democrat Martin Van Buren, the leading candidates, opposed annexation of pro-slavery Texas on the ground that the debate might spark civil war. Whigs embraced Clay's stance, and the party's convention nominated Clay unanimously. The Whig platform omitted any reference to Texas.

The Democratic Convention was a different story. Former President Van Buren's southern supporters, including Andrew Jackson, abandoned his effort to gain the nomination because of his opposition to Texas annexation. With the convention deadlocked, expansionist forces nominated James Knox Polk of Tennessee. The party platform promoted territorial expansion, and to win support in the North and the West, as well as in the South, it called for "the re-occupation of Oregon and the re-annexation of Texas."

The Democratic combination of southern and western expansionism constituted a winning strategy that forced Whig nominee Henry Clay to hedge his statement on Texas. While he still believed the integrity of the Union to be the chief consideration, he had "no personal objection to the annexation" if it could be achieved "without dishonor, without war, with the common consent of the Union, and upon just and fair terms." His explanation seemed clear enough, but prudence was no match for spread-eagle oratory and the emotional pull of Manifest Destiny. Clay's divisive stand turned more Whig votes to the new Liberty party, an anti-slavery party begun in 1840. In the western counties of New York, the Liberty party drew enough votes from the Whigs to give the state to Polk. Had he carried New York, the overconfident Clay would have won the election by 7 electoral votes. Instead, Polk won a narrow plurality of 38,000 popular votes nationwide but a clear majority of the Electoral College, 170 to 105. At forty-nine, Polk was the youngest president the nation had seen.

POLK'S PRIORITIES   Born near Charlotte, North Carolina, James Polk moved to Tennessee as a young man. After studying at the University of

Polk's Dream (1846)

The devil advises Polk to claim all of disputed Oregon even if "you deluge your country with seas of blood, produce a servile insurrection and dislocate every joint of this happy and prosperous union!!!"

North Carolina, he became a successful lawyer and planter and entered politics early, serving fourteen years in Congress (four as Speaker of the House) and two as governor of Tennessee. "Young Hickory," as his partisans liked to call him, was a short, slender man with a shock of grizzled hair, probing gray eyes, and a seemingly permanent grimace. Humorless and dogmatic, he had none of Andrew Jackson's charisma but shared Jackson's strong prejudices and his stubborn determination. Polk had a penchant for eighteen-hour workdays, which destroyed his health during his four years in the White House. He would die just three months after leaving office in 1849. Yet he died knowing that his strenuous efforts had paid off. Polk was one of the few presidents to accomplish all of his major objectives.

On domestic policies, Polk adhered to Jackson's principles, but he and the new Jacksonians subtly reflected the growing influence of the slaveholding South on the Democratic party. Abolitionism, Polk warned, could destroy the Union, but his pro-slavery stance further fragmented public opinion. Anti-slavery northerners had already begun to drift away from the Democratic party, which was increasingly perceived as representing the slaveholding interest in the South.

Single-mindedly committed to the tasks at hand, Polk was a poor diplomat but a formidable leader. His major objectives were reduction of the tariff, reestablishment of the federal independent Treasury, settlement of the Oregon boundary dispute with Britain, and the acquisition of California from Mexico. He got them all. The Walker Tariff of 1846, in keeping with Democratic tradition, lowered tariff rates, and in the same year, Polk persuaded Congress to restore the independent Treasury, which the Whigs had eliminated. Twice Polk vetoed internal-improvement bills, leading critics to charge that he was determined to further the South's interests at the expense of the national interest.

Polk's chief concern remained geographic expansion. The acquisition of slaveholding Texas was already under way before he took office. President Tyler, taking Polk's election as a mandate to act, had asked Congress to accomplish annexation by joint resolution, which required only a simple majority in each house and avoided the two-thirds Senate vote needed to ratify a treaty. Congress had read the election returns too, and after a bitter debate over slavery, the resolution passed by votes of 27 to 25 in the Senate and 120 to 98 in the House. On March 1, 1845, just three days before Polk was inaugurated, Tyler signed the resolution offering to admit Texas to the Union. Texas voters ratified the action in October, and the new state formally entered the Union on December 29, 1845. A furious Mexico dispatched troops to the Texas border.

OREGON   Meanwhile, the Oregon boundary issue heated up as American expansionists insisted that President Polk abandon previous offers to settle with Britain on the 49th parallel and stand by the Democrats' platform pledge to take all of Oregon. In his inaugural address, President Polk claimed that the American title to Oregon was "clear and unquestionable," but privately he favored a prudent compromise. The British, however, refused his offer to extend the boundary along the 49th parallel. Polk then withdrew the offer and renewed his demand for all of Oregon. In his message to Congress at the end of 1845, he asked permission to give Britain notice that joint occupation of Oregon would end in one year. After a bitter debate, Congress adopted the provocative resolution.

Fortunately for Polk the British government had no enthusiasm for war over a distant territory at the cost of profitable trade relations with the United States. In early June 1846 the British government submitted a draft treaty to extend the Canadian-American border along the 49th parallel and through the main channel south of Vancouver Island. On June 18 the Senate ratified the treaty. Most of the country was satisfied. Southerners cared less about Oregon than Texas, and northern business interests valued British trade more than Oregon. Besides, the country was by then at war with Mexico.

THE MEXICAN WAR

THE OUTBREAK OF WAR   On March 6, 1845, two days after Polk took office, the Mexican government broke off relations with the United States. When an effort at negotiation failed, Polk ordered troops under General Zachary Taylor to take up positions along the Rio Grande. These positions lay in territory that was doubly disputed: Mexico recognized neither the U.S. annexation of Texas nor the Rio Grande boundary between itself and Texas. Polk's intention was clear: he wanted to goad the Mexicans into a conflict in order to secure Texas and also obtain California and New Mexico. Ulysses S. Grant, then a young officer serving under Taylor, later admitted, "We were sent to provoke a fight, but it was essential that Mexico commence it."

Polk resolved that he could achieve his purposes only by force, and he won the cabinet's approval of a war message to Congress. That very evening, May 9, 1846, the news arrived that Mexicans had attacked U.S. soldiers north of the Rio Grande. Eleven Americans were killed, five wounded, and the remainder taken prisoner. Polk's provocative scheme had worked. In his war message the president seized the high ground, declaring that the use of force was a response to Mexican aggression, a recognition that war had been forced upon the United States. Mexico, he claimed, "has invaded our territory, and shed American blood upon the American soil." The House and Senate quickly passed the resolution, and Polk signed the declaration of war on May 13, 1846.

RESPONSES TO THE WAR   In the Mississippi River valley, where expansion fever ran high, the war with Mexico was immensely popular. Polk's aggressive actions in Texas gained widespread support from rabid expansionists. The editor John L. O'Sullivan exclaimed that God wanted Americans to take over the lands owned by the "imbecile and distracted" Mexico because of their racial superiority. "The Anglo-Saxon foot is already on its borders. Already the irresistible army of Anglo-Saxon emigration has begun to pour down upon it, armed with the plow and the rifle." O'Sullivan spoke for many Americans who believed it their duty to redeem the Mexican people from their "backward" civilization and their chaotic government.

Whig opinion in the North, however, ranged from lukewarm to hostile. Massachusetts congressman John Quincy Adams, who voted against participation, called it "a most unrighteous war." An obscure congressman from Illinois named Abraham Lincoln, upon taking his seat in 1847, began introducing "spot resolutions," calling upon President Polk to name the spot where American blood had been shed on American soil, implying that the troops may in fact have been in Mexico when fired upon. Once again, as in 1812, New England was a hotbed of opposition. Some New Englanders were ready to separate from the slave states, and the Massachusetts legislature called the conflict a war of conquest. The fiery abolitionist William Lloyd Garrison charged that the unjust war was one "of aggression, of invasion, of conquest, and rapine—marked by ruffianism, perfidy, and every other feature of national depravity."

PREPARING FOR BATTLE   However flimsy the justification for conflict, both the United States and Mexico were ill prepared for war. The U.S. military was small and inexperienced. At the outset of war, the regular army numbered barely over 7,000, in contrast to the Mexican force of 32,000. Many of the Mexicans, however, had been pressed into service or recruited from prisons and thus made less than enthusiastic fighters. Before the war ended, the American force would grow to 104,000, of whom about 31,000 were regular army troops and marines. The rest were six- and twelve-month volunteers.

Among the volunteers were sons of Henry Clay and Daniel Webster, but most of the soldiers came from coarser backgrounds. Volunteer militia companies, often filled with frontier toughs, lacked uniforms, standard equipment, and discipline. Repeatedly, despite the best efforts of the commanding generals, these undisciplined forces engaged in plunder, rape, and murder. Nevertheless, these rough-and-tumble Americans consistently defeated the larger Mexican forces, which had their own problems with training, discipline, and munitions.

The Mexican War would be fought on four fronts: southern Texas, central Mexico, New Mexico, and California. And it would last two years, from May 1846 to February 1848. The United States entered the war without even a tentative plan of action, and politics complicated the task of devising one. President Polk sought to manage every detail of the conflict. What Polk wanted, Senator Thomas Hart Benton wrote later, was "a small war, just large enough to require a treaty of peace, and not large enough to make military reputations, dangerous for the presidency." Winfield Scott, general in chief of the army, was both a Whig and a politically ambitious officer. Polk nevertheless put him in charge of the southern Texas front, but when Scott quarreled with Polk's secretary of war, the exasperated president withdrew the appointment.

There now seemed a better choice for commander. General Zachary Taylor's men had scored two victories over Mexican forces north of the Rio Grande, and on May 18, 1846, they crossed the river border and occupied Matamoros, which a demoralized and bloodied Mexican army had abandoned. These quick victories brought Taylor instant popularity, and the president responded willingly to the public demand that he be made overall commander for the conquest of Mexico. Old "Rough-and-Ready" Taylor, a bowlegged and none-too-handsome man of sixty-one, seemed unlikely stuff from which to fashion a hero, but he had achieved Polk's main objective, the conquest of Mexico's northern provinces. Taylor became an immediate folk hero to his troops and to Americans back home, so much so that Polk began to see him as a political threat.

THE ANNEXATION OF CALIFORNIA   President Polk had long coveted the valuable Mexican territory along the Pacific coast and had tried buying it, but to no avail. He then sought to engineer a Texas-style revolt against Mexican rule among the American settlers in California. To that purpose, near the end of 1845, John C. Frémont recruited a band of sixty frontiersmen, including Kit Carson, ostensibly for another exploration of California and Oregon. In 1846, Frémont and his men moved into the Sacramento River valley in northern California. Soon thereafter, on June 14, Americans in the area captured Sonoma, proclaimed the independent Republic of California, and hoisted the hastily designed Bear flag, a California grizzly bear and star painted on white cloth, a version of which would become the state flag.

By the end of June, Frémont had endorsed the Bear Flag Republic and set out for Monterey on the coast. Before he arrived, the commander of the U.S. Pacific Fleet, having heard of the outbreak of hostilities, sent a party ashore to raise the U.S. flag and proclaim California part of the United States. The Republic of California had lasted less than a month, and most Californians of whatever origin welcomed a change that promised order and stability instead of the confusion of the unruly Bear Flaggers. Sporadic clashes with Mexicans continued until 1847, when they finally capitulated. Meanwhile, Colonel Stephen Kearny's army, having earlier captured Santa Fe, ousted the Mexican forces from southern California and occupied Los Angeles.

TAYLOR'S BATTLES   Both California and New Mexico had been taken from Mexican control before General Zachary Taylor fought his first major battle in northern Mexico. Having waited for more men and munitions, Taylor and his troops finally headed southward, in September 1846, toward the heart of Mexico. Their first goal was the fortified city of Monterrey, which

Taylor took after a five-day siege. President Polk was growing increasingly unhappy with Taylor's popularity, however, and with what he considered Taylor's excessive passivity. Polk's greatest flaw as commander in chief was that he sought to manage the war for partisan political purposes. Most of the generals he appointed were selected for their political views rather than their military skill. He wanted to defeat both Mexico and the Whigs—at the same time.

But Polk's grand strategy was itself flawed. Having never seen the Mexican desert, the president wrongly assumed that Taylor's men could live off the land and need not depend upon resupply. Polk therefore misunderstood the general's reluctance to strike out across several hundred miles of barren desert north of Mexico City. On another point the president was simply duped. The old Mexican general Santa Anna, forced out of power in 1845, got word to Polk from his exile in Cuba that in return for the right considerations he would bring about a settlement of the war. Polk in turn assured the Mexican leader that Washington would pay well for any territory taken from Mexico. In 1846, Polk ordered U.S. forces to allow Santa Anna to return to his homeland. Soon Santa Anna was again in command of the Mexican army and was named president once more. But instead of carrying out his pledge to Polk to negotiate an end to the war, Santa Anna prepared to fight Taylor's army. Polk's blundering scheme had put the ablest Mexican general back in command.

In October 1846, Polk and his cabinet decided to order an assault on Mexico City from the south by way of Veracruz, which left General Taylor's forces idle. Polk would have preferred a Democratic general to lead the new offensive, but for want of a better choice he named Winfield Scott to the field command. Zachary Taylor, miffed at his reduction to a minor role and harboring a "violent disregard" for Scott's abilities, disobeyed orders and took the offensive himself.

Near the hacienda of Buena Vista, Santa Anna's large but ill-trained army met Taylor's untested volunteers. The Mexican general invited the vastly outnumbered Americans to surrender. "Tell him to go to hell," Taylor replied. In the hard-fought Battle of Buena Vista (February 22–23, 1847), Taylor's son-in-law, Colonel Jefferson Davis, the future president of the Confederacy, led a regiment that broke up a Mexican cavalry charge. Neither side could claim victory. Buena Vista was the last major action on the northern front, and Taylor was granted leave to return home. He returned to the United States with a seething contempt for Polk.

SCOTT'S TRIUMPH   Meanwhile, the long-planned southern assault on Mexico City began on March 9, 1847, when Winfield Scott's army landed on the beaches south of Veracruz. It was the first major amphibious operation by U.S. forces and was carried out without loss. The Mexican commander surrendered on March 27 after a week-long siege. Scott and some 14,000 soldiers then retraced the 260-mile route to Mexico City taken by Cortés and his Spanish troops more than 300 years before. Santa Anna tried to set a trap for the Americans at the mountain pass of Cerro Gordo, but Scott's men did the trapping, taking more than 3,000 Mexican prisoners.

Scott then waited until reinforcements and new supplies arrived from the coast. After three months, with his numbers almost doubled, Scott and his

MAJOR CAMPAIGNS OF
THE MEXICAN WAR

⟵ U.S. forces   ⟵ Mexican forces

★ Battle site

--- Line set by Treaty of
Guadalupe Hidalgo, 1848

How did Polk's fear of Taylor's popularity undermine the Americans' military strategy? What was the significance of Winfield Scott's assault on Mexico City?

army set out on August 7 through the mountain passes into the Valley of Mexico. In September the general directed a brilliant flanking operation around the lakes and marshes that guard the eastern approaches to Mexico City. On September 13, 1847, U.S. forces entered Mexico City. At the national palace a battalion of marines raised the flag and occupied "the halls of Montezuma."

After the fall of the Mexican capital, Santa Anna resigned and fled the country. By the Treaty of Guadalupe Hidalgo, signed on February 2, 1848, Mexico gave up all claims to Texas above the Rio Grande and ceded California and New Mexico to the United States. In return the United States agreed to pay Mexico $15 million and assume the claims of U.S. citizens against Mexico up to $3.25 million. Like the Louisiana Purchase, it was a remarkable bargain. The Senate ratified the treaty on March 10, 1848. By the end of July, the last remaining U.S. soldiers had boarded ship for home.

THE WAR'S LEGACIES The Mexican War cost the United States 1,733 killed, 4,152 wounded, and, as usual, far more—11,550—dead of disease, mostly dysentery and chronic diarrhea ("Montezuma's revenge"). It remains the deadliest war in American history in terms of the percentage of combatants killed. Out of every 1,000 U.S. soldiers in Mexico, some 110 died. The next highest death rate would be in the Civil War, with 65 killed out of every 1,000 participants.

The military and naval expenditures were $98 million. For that price, and payments made under the treaty, the United States acquired more than 500,000 square miles of territory (more than 1 million, counting Texas), including the strategic Pacific harbors of San Diego, Monterey, and San Francisco. Except for a small addition made by the Gadsden Purchase in 1853, these annexations rounded out the continental United States and doubled its size.

The Mexican War was a crushing defeat for Mexico and a defining event for the United States. Several important firsts are associated with the war: the first successful offensive American war, the first major amphibious military operation, and the nation's first war covered by correspondents. It was also the first significant combat experience for a group of junior officers who would serve as leading generals during the Civil War: Robert E. Lee, Ulysses S. Grant, Thomas "Stonewall" Jackson, George B. McClellan, George Pickett, Braxton Bragg, George Meade, and others.

Initially the victory in Mexico unleashed a surge of national pride, but as the years passed, the Mexican War was increasingly seen as a war of conquest. Ulysses S. Grant later called it "one of the most unjust ever waged by a stronger against a weaker nation." America's terrible Civil War fifteen years later, he added, was "our punishment" for the unholy Mexican War. The acquisition of Oregon, Texas, California, and the New Southwest made the United States a transcontinental nation. Extending authority over this vast new land greatly expanded the scope of the federal government. In 1849, for example, Congress created the Department of the Interior to supervise the distribution of land, the creation of new territories and states, and the "protection" of the Indians and their land. President Polk naively assumed that the dramatic expansion of American territory to the Pacific would strengthen "the bonds of Union." He was wrong. No sooner was Texas annexed and gold discovered in California than a violent debate erupted over the extension of slavery into the new territories. That debate would culminate in a war that would nearly destroy the Union.

End of Chapter Review

- **Nationalism** Nationalism and westward expansion were the dominant issues in the 1840s, although President John Tyler, a Whig, vetoed traditional Whig policies, such as a new national bank and higher tariffs. Boundaries with Canada were finally settled. The desire for westward expansion culminated in the Mexican War.

- **Westward Migration** Many Americans believed that the West was divinely ordained to be part of the United States. Although populated by Indians and Latinos, the West was portrayed as an empty land. The lure of cheap, fertile land led to "Oregon fever," and settlers moved along the Overland Trails, enduring great physical hardships.

- **Texas Republic** Many southerners had moved to the Mexican province of Texas to grow cotton, taking their slaves with them. The Mexican government opposed slavery and in 1830 forbade further immigration. American settlers declared Texas independent in 1836, and the slaughter at the Alamo made the independence of Texas a popular cause in the United States. As soon as Mexico recognized the Texas Republic, many Texans clamored for annexation. The notion was unpopular among the growing anti-slavery faction, however, because it meant adding another slave state to the Union; thus, Texas remained independent for nearly a decade.

- **Mexican War** Annexation of Texas, declared by a joint resolution of Congress in 1845, infuriated Mexico. The newly elected president, James K. Polk, sought to acquire California and New Mexico as well as Texas, but negotiations soon failed. When Mexican troops crossed the Rio Grande, Polk urged Congress to declare war.

- **Results of the Mexican War** In 1848, in the Treaty of Guadalupe Hidalgo, Mexico ceded California and New Mexico to the United States and gave up claims to land north of the Rio Grande. The vast acquisition did not strengthen the Union, however, because a fierce debate immediately erupted allowing slavery in the new territories.

CHRONOLOGY

1821	Mexico gains independence from Spain
1836	Americans are defeated at the Alamo
	Texans take Santa Anna prisoner west of the San Jacinto River
1841	John Tyler becomes president
1842	Americans and British agree to the Webster-Ashburton Treaty
1845	United States annexes Texas
	Mexican War begins
1846	Most of the Donner party die en route to California
1848	Treaty of Guadalupe Hidalgo ends the Mexican War
1849	California gold rush begins
1851	Plains Indians agree to the Fort Laramie Treaty

KEY TERMS & NAMES

Part Four

A HOUSE DIVIDED AND REBUILT

O f all the regions of the United States during the first half of the nineteenth century, the South was the most distinctive. Southern society remained rural and agricultural long after the rest of the nation had embraced urban-industrial development. Likewise, the planter elite's tenacious desire to preserve and expand the institution of slavery muted social-reform impulses in the South and ignited a prolonged political controversy that would end in civil war.

The relentless settlement of the western territories set in motion a ferocious competition between North and South for political influence in the burgeoning West. Would the new western states be "slave" or "free"? The issue of allowing slavery into the new territories involved more than humanitarian concern for the plight of enslaved blacks. By the 1840s the North and the South had developed quite different economic interests. The North wanted high tariffs on imported products to "protect" its industries from foreign competition. Southerners, on the other hand, favored free trade because they wanted to import British goods in exchange for the profitable cotton they provided British textile mills.

A series of political compromises glossed over the fundamental differences between the regions during the first half of the nineteenth century. But abolitionists refused to give up their crusade against slavery. Moreover, a new generation of politicians emerged in the 1850s, leaders from both North and South who were less willing to seek political compromises. The continuing debate over allowing slavery into the western territories kept sectional tensions at a fever pitch. By the time Abraham Lincoln was elected president in 1860, many people had decided that the nation could not survive half-slave and half-free; something had to give.

In a last-ditch effort to preserve the institution of slavery, eleven southern states seceded from the Union and created a separate

Confederate nation. That, in turn, prompted northerners such as Lincoln to support a civil war to preserve the Union. No one realized in 1861 how prolonged and costly the War between the States would become. Over 630,000 soldiers and sailors would die of wounds or disease. The colossal carnage caused even the most seasoned observers to blanch in disbelief. As President Lincoln confessed in his second inaugural address, in 1865, no one expected the war to become so "fundamental and astonishing."

Nor did anyone envision how sweeping the war's effects would be upon the future of the country. The northern victory in 1865 restored the Union and in the process helped accelerate America's transformation into a modern nation-state. National power and a national consciousness began to displace the sectional emphases of the antebellum era. A Republican-led Congress enacted federal legislation to foster industrial and commercial development and western expansion. In the process the United States began to leave behind the Jeffersonian dream of a decentralized agrarian republic.

The Civil War also ended slavery, yet the status of the freed African Americans remained precarious. The former slaves found themselves legally free, but few of them had property, a home, education, or training. Although the Fourteenth Amendment (1868) set forth guarantees for the civil rights of African Americans and the Fifteenth Amendment (1870) provided that black men could vote, southern officials found ingenious—and often violent—ways to avoid the spirit and letter of the new laws.

The restoration of the former Confederate states to the Union did not come easily. Bitterness and resistance festered among the vanquished. Although Confederate leaders were initially disenfranchised, they continued to exercise considerable authority in political and economic matters. In 1877, when the last federal troops were removed from the occupied South, former Confederates declared themselves "redeemed" from the stain of military occupation. By the end of the nineteenth century, most states of the former Confederacy had devised a system of legal discrimination against blacks that re-created many aspects of slavery.

15

THE OLD SOUTH

FOCUS QUESTIONS

wwnorton.com/studyspace

- How diverse was the South's economy, and what was its unifying feature?

- How did dependence on agriculture and slavery shape the distinctive culture of the Old South? Why did southern whites who did not hold slaves defend the "peculiar institution"?

- What led to the emergence of the abolitionist movement? How did white southerners respond to it?

- How did enslaved people respond to their bondage during the antebellum period? How did free persons of color fit into southern society?

Southerners, a North Carolina newspaper editor once wrote, are "a mythological people, created half out of dream and half out of slander, who live in a still legendary land." Most Americans, including southerners themselves, have long harbored a cluster of myths and stereotypes about the South. Perhaps the most enduring myths come from the classic movie *Gone with the Wind* (1939). The South portrayed in such romanticized Hollywood productions is a stable agrarian society led by paternalistic white planters and their families, who live in white-columned mansions and represent a "natural" aristocracy of virtue and talent within their community. In these accounts, southerners are kind to their slaves and devoted to the rural values of independence and chivalric honor, values celebrated by Thomas Jefferson.

By contrast, a much darker image of the Old South emerged from abolitionist pamphlets and Harriet Beecher Stowe's best-selling novel, *Uncle*

Tom's Cabin (1852). Those exposés of southern culture portrayed planters as arrogant aristocrats who raped enslaved women, brutalized enslaved workers, and lorded over their community with haughty disdain for the rights and needs of others. They bred slaves like cattle, broke up slave families, and sold slaves "down the river" to certain death in the Louisiana sugar mills and rice plantations.

Such contrasting images die hard, in large part because each one is rooted in reality. Nonetheless, efforts to determine what set the Old South apart from the rest of the nation generally pivot on two lines of thought: the impact of the environment (climate and geography) and the effects of human decisions and actions. The South's warm, humid climate was ideal for the cultivation of commercial crops such as tobacco, cotton, rice, and sugarcane. The growth of those lucrative cash crops helped foster the plantation system and its dependence upon enslaved labor. The lust for profits trumped concerns over the morality of slavery. In the end the profitability of slavery and the racist attitudes it engendered brought about the sectional conflict over the extension of slavery that ignited the Civil War.

THE DISTINCTIVE FEATURES OF THE OLD SOUTH

While geography was a key determinant of the South's economy and culture, many observers have located the origins of southern distinctiveness in the institution of racial slavery. The resolve of whites to maintain and expand such a labor system in turn led to a sense of racial unity that muted class conflict among whites. Yet the biracial character of the population exercised an even greater influence over southern culture, as it has since that time. In shaping patterns of speech, folklore, music, and literature, black southerners immeasurably influenced and enriched the region's culture.

The South differed from other sections of the country in its high proportion of native-born Americans in its population, both white and black. Unlike the North, the South drew few European immigrants after the Revolution. One reason was that the main shipping lines went from Britain to northern ports; another, that the prospect of competing with slave labor deterred immigrants. After the Missouri controversy of 1819–1821, the South increasingly became a consciously minority region, its population growth lagging behind that of other sections of the country and its defiant dependence upon slavery more and more an isolated and odious anachronism. The South's determination to preserve and expand slavery in the face of growing criticism in the North and around the world further isolated and defined the region. A prickly defensiveness increasingly shaped southern attitudes and actions.

RELIGION IN THE OLD SOUTH   The growing defensiveness of the South with respect to slavery was especially evident in the region's religious life. The South was overwhelmingly Protestant. Although there were pockets of Catholicism and Judaism in the large coastal cities—Baltimore, Richmond, Charleston, Savannah, and New Orleans—the vast majority of southerners were Baptist or Methodist. In the eighteenth century the first generation of Baptists and Methodists condemned slavery, welcomed blacks to their congregations, and accorded women important roles in their churches. By the early nineteenth century, however, having grown concerned about the diminishing participation of white men in their churches, the two denominations had changed their stance. Ministers began to mute their opposition to slavery. In 1785 the Methodists formally abandoned their policy of denying church membership to slaveholders. By the 1830s most Protestant preachers in the South had switched from attacking slavery to defending it as a divinely ordained social system evident in the Bible. Most of the ministers who refused to promote slavery left the region.

AGRICULTURAL DIVERSITY   The preponderance of farming was another distinctive southern characteristic, whether pictured as the Jeffersonian yeoman living by the sweat of his brow or the lordly planter dispatching his slave gangs. The focus on King Cotton and other cash crops such as rice and sugarcane has obscured the degree to which the South fed itself from its own fields. In 1860 the South had half the nation's cattle, over 60 percent of the hogs, nearly 45 percent of the horses, 52 percent of the oxen, nearly 90 percent of the mules, and about 33 percent of the sheep, the last mostly in the Upper South.

Yet the story of the antebellum southern economy was hardly one of unbroken prosperity. The South's cash crops, intensively planted year after year, quickly exhausted the soil. Planting cotton or tobacco year after year leached the fertility from the fields. By 1860 much of eastern Virginia had long before abandoned tobacco and in some places had turned to growing wheat for the northern market. The older farmlands had trouble competing with the newer soil farther west, in Alabama, Mississippi, and Louisiana, but these lands, too, began to show wear and tear. So first the Southeast and then the Old Southwest faced a growing sense of economic crisis as the nineteenth century advanced.

Southern agriculture

Planting sweet potatoes on James Hopkinson's plantation, Edisto Island, South Carolina, April 1862.

MANUFACTURING AND TRADE   By 1840 many thoughtful southerners had concluded that the agrarian region desperately needed to diversify its economy by developing its own manufacturing and trade. After the War of 1812, as cotton growing swept everything before it, the South became increasingly dependent upon the northern economy. Cotton and tobacco were exported mainly in northern vessels, and southerners also relied upon connections in the North for goods imported from Europe. The South became a kind of colonial dependency of the North.

Two major explanations were given for the lag in southern industrial development. First, blacks were presumed unsuited to factory work, perhaps because they supposedly could not adjust to the discipline of work by the clock. Second, the ruling elites of the Old South were said to have developed a lordly disdain for industrial activity because a certain aristocratic prestige derived from owning plantations and holding slaves. But any argument that black labor was incompatible with industry flew in the face of the evidence, since factory owners bought or hired enslaved workers for just about every kind of manufacture.

The legendary indifference of aristocratic planters to profits and losses is also a myth. More often than not, by the second quarter of the nineteenth century the successful planter was an acquisitive entrepreneur bent on maximizing profits. Economic historians have concluded that enslaved workers on average supplied a hefty 10 percent return on their cost. By a strictly economic calculation, investment in slaves and land was the most profitable investment available in the antebellum South.

WHITE SOCIETY IN THE SOUTH

If an understanding of the Old South must begin with a knowledge of potent social myths, it must end with a sense of tragedy. Since colonial days white southerners had won short-term economic gains at the cost of both lagging social development and moral isolation in the eyes of the world. The concentration on slave-based agriculture as well as the paucity of cities and immigrants deprived the South of dynamic sources of economic growth and social innovation. The slaveholding South hitched its wagon not to a star but to the growing British demand for cotton. During the late 1850s southern agricultural prosperity seemed endless. Yet end it did. The heyday of expansion in British textiles was over by 1860, but by then the Deep South had become locked into large-scale cotton production that would endure for generations to come.

THE PLANTER ELITE   During the first half of the nineteenth century, wealth in the South was increasingly concentrated in the hands of the planter elite. Although giant plantations were relatively few in number, they set the tone for economic and social life. What distinguished the plantation from the farm, in addition to its size, was the use of a large enslaved labor force, managed by overseers, to grow primarily staple crops (cotton, rice, tobacco, and sugarcane) for profit.

If to be called a planter one had to hold twenty slaves, only 1 out of every 30 whites in the South in 1860 was a planter. Fewer than 11,000 planters held 50 or more slaves, and the owners of over 100 slaves numbered only 2,300. The census listed just 11 planters with 500 slaves and only 1 with as many as 1,000 slaves. Yet this privileged elite tended to think of its class interests as synonymous with the interests of the entire South and to perceive of its members as "natural aristocrats."

The planter group, making up under 4 percent of the adult white men in the South, held more than half the slaves and produced most of the cotton and tobacco and all of the sugar and rice. In a white population numbering just over 8 million in the states and territories that allowed slavery in 1860, the total number of slaveholders was only 383,637. But assuming that each family numbered five people, then whites with some proprietary interest in

King Cotton Captured

This engraving shows cotton being trafficked in Louisiana.

slavery constituted 1.9 million, or roughly a fourth of the South's white population. While most southern whites belonged to the small-farmer class, they often deferred to the planter elite. In part such deference reflected the desire of many small farmers to become planters themselves. Over time, however, land and slave prices soared, thereby narrowing prospects for upward social mobility. Between 1830 and 1860 the cotton belt witnessed a growing concentration of wealth in the hands of a slaveholding elite.

The mistress of the plantation supervised the domestic household in much the same way that the planter took care of the business outdoors. She oversaw the preparation of food and linens, the housecleaning, the care of the sick, and a hundred other details. While plantation wives enjoyed entertaining and being entertained, they owed their genteel circumstances to the domestic services provided by enslaved blacks, often women and girls.

One of the most frustrating realities for the plantation mistress was the lack of personal freedom occasioned by the complex demands of her "separate sphere" of genteel domesticity. White women living in a slaveholding culture confronted a double standard in terms of moral and sexual behavior. While they were expected to be models of Christian piety and sexual discretion, their husbands, brothers, and sons enjoyed greater latitude. Many white planters and their sons viewed slave women not only as sources of labor but also as sources of sexual satisfaction. They often rationalized the rape of a slave woman as no crime at all, for slaves had no rights in their eyes.

THE MIDDLE CLASS   Overseers on the largest plantations generally came from the middle class of small farmers or skilled workers (artisans) or were younger sons of planters. Most wanted to become slaveholders themselves. Occasionally there were black overseers, but the highest management position to which a slave could aspire was usually that of "driver," or leader, placed in charge of a small group of slaves with the duty of getting them to work without creating dissension.

The most numerous white southerners were the yeoman farm families, who lived in simple two-room cabins rather than columned mansions. They raised a few hogs and chickens, grew some corn and cotton, and traded with neighbors more than they bought from stores. The men in the family focused their energies on outdoor labor. Women and children worked in the fields during harvesttime but spent most of their days attending to domestic chores. Many of these "middling" farmers owned a handful of slaves, but most had none. Most of the South's small farms were located in the midst of the plantation economy.

Southern farmers were typically mobile folk, willing to pull up stakes and move west or southwest in pursuit of better land. They tended to be fiercely independent and suspicious of government authority, and they overwhelmingly embraced the Democratic party and evangelical Protestantism. Even though only a minority of the middle-class farmers held slaves, most of them supported the slave system. They feared that the slaves, if freed, would compete with them for land, and they enjoyed the social status that racially based slavery afforded them. Such sentiments pervaded the border states as well as the Deep South. Kentucky, for example, held a referendum on the issue of slavery in 1849, and the voters, most of whom owned no slaves, resoundingly endorsed the slave system.

"POOR WHITES"   Stereotyped views of southern society had prepared many visitors to the Old South to see only planters and "poor whites," and many a yeoman farmer living in crude comfort, his wealth concealed in cattle and swine off foraging in the woods, was mistaken for "white trash," a degraded class relegated to the least desirable land and given over to hunting and fishing, hound dogs and moonshine whiskey. Speculation had it that the "poor whites" were descended from indentured servants or convicts transported to the colonies from Britain. The problem, however, was less heredity than environment, the consequence of a trilogy of "lazy diseases": hookworm, malaria, and pellagra, all of which produced an overpowering lethargy. Around 1900 modern medicine discovered cures for these diseases. By 1930 the regional diseases had practically disappeared, taking with them many of the stereotypes about "poor whites."

HONOR AND VIOLENCE   From colonial times most southern white men had prided themselves on adhering to a moral code centered on a prickly sense of honor that included a combative sensitivity to slights; loyalty to family, locality, state, and region; deference to elders and social "betters"; and an almost theatrical hospitality. Duels constituted the ultimate public expression of personal honor and manly courage. Although not confined to the South, dueling was much more common there than in the rest of the young nation, a fact that gave rise to the observation that southerners will be polite until they are angry enough to kill you. Dueling was outlawed in the northern states after Aaron Burr killed Alexander Hamilton in 1804, and a number of southern states and counties banned the practice as well—but the prohibition was rarely enforced. Many of the most prominent southern leaders—congressmen, senators, governors, newspaper editors, and planters—engaged in duels. The roster of participants included Andrew Jackson, Henry Clay, Sam Houston, and Jefferson Davis.

BLACK SOCIETY IN THE SOUTH

Slavery was one of the fastest growing elements of American life during the first half of the nineteenth century. In 1790 there were fewer than 700,000 enslaved blacks in the United States. By 1830 there were more than 2 million, and by 1860 there were almost 4 million. Slavery was the most important force shaping American history, yet by no means was it monolithic in character, nor was it inescapable.

"FREE PERSONS OF COLOR"   African Americans had diverse experiences in the United States, depending upon their geographic location and the nature of their working and living conditions. In the Old South "free persons of color" occupied an uncertain status, balanced somewhere between slavery and freedom, subject to racist legal restrictions not imposed upon whites. Free blacks gained liberty in several ways. Over the years some slaves were able to purchase their freedom, and some gained it as a reward for wartime military service. Others were freed by conscientious masters.

By 1830 there were 319,000 free blacks in the United States, about 150,000 of whom lived in the South. The "free persons of color" included a large number of mulattoes, people of mixed racial ancestry. The census of 1860 reported 412,000 such people in the United States, or about 10 percent of the black population, probably a drastic undercount. In cities such as Charleston and especially New Orleans, "colored" society became virtually a third caste, made up of people who occupied a status somewhere between that of blacks and that of whites. Some of them built substantial fortunes and even became slaveholders.

Free Blacks

This badge, issued in Charleston, South Carolina, was worn by a free black so that he would not be mistaken for someone's "property."

Black slaveholders were a tiny minority, however. The 1830 census revealed that 3,775 free blacks held 12,760 slaves. Most often black slaveholders were free blacks who bought their own family members with the express purpose of freeing them. But some African Americans engaged in slavery for purely selfish reasons.

Free blacks were often skilled artisans (blacksmiths, carpenters, cobblers), farmers, or common laborers. The increase in their numbers slowed as legislatures put more and more restrictions on the right to free slaves, but by 1860 there were 260,000 free blacks in the slave states, a little over half the national total of 488,000. They were most numerous in the Upper South and tended to live in urban areas.

Free blacks suffered widespread discrimination. All southern states required them to carry a pass. Whites often fraudulently claimed that a free black was in fact one of their runaway slaves, and if the African American did not have an official certificate of freedom, he or she could be enslaved. In many other ways as well, free blacks were not truly free. In North Carolina, blacks could not travel farther than one county away from their home. Most southern states prohibited them from voting. Blacks were not allowed to testify in court against whites, nor could they hold church services without the presence of a white minister.

PLANTATION SLAVERY   Most slaves worked on large plantations. The preferred jobs were household servant and skilled worker, such as blacksmith and carpenter. Field hands were usually housed in one- or two-room wooden shacks with dirt floors. Based on detailed records from eleven plantations in the Lower South (South Carolina, Georgia, Alabama, and Mississippi) scholars have calculated that more than half of all slave babies died in the first year of life, a mortality rate more than twice that of white infants.

Field hands worked from dawn to dusk. The slave codes adopted by the southern states subjected slaves not only to the slaveholder's governance but to surveillance by patrols of county militiamen, who abused slaves found at large. A majority of both planters and small farmers whipped slaves, at least occasionally. The difference between a good owner and a bad one, according to one ex-slave, was the difference between "one who did not whip you too much" and one who "whipped you till he'd bloodied you and blistered you."

Organized slave revolts were difficult in the face of overwhelming white authority and firepower. In the nineteenth century only three major slave insurrections were attemped, two of which were betrayed before they got under way. Only the Nat Turner insurrection of August 1831, in rural Virginia, got beyond the planning stage. Turner, a black overseer, was also a religious exhorter who professed a divine mission in leading the movement. The revolt began when a small group of slaves killed Turner's master's family and set off down the road, repeating the process at other farmhouses, where other slaves joined in. Before it ended, at least fifty-five whites had been killed. Eventually trials resulted in seventeen hangings and seven deportations. The Virginia militia, for its part, indiscriminately killed many slaves in the process of putting down the rebels.

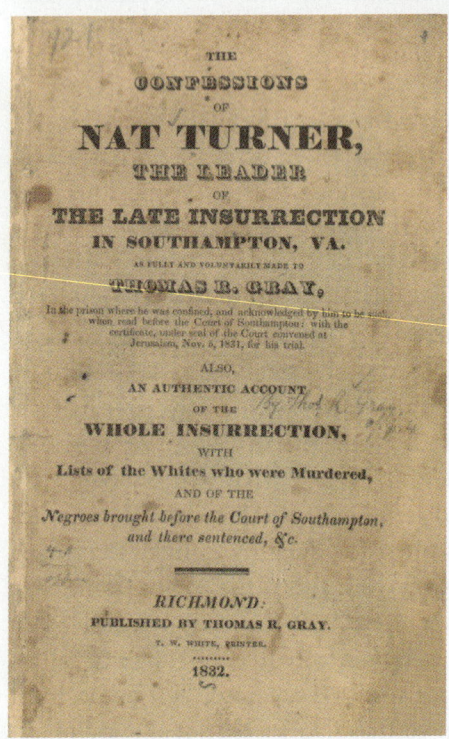

The confessions of Nat Turner

Published account of Turner's rebellion, written by Turner's lawyer, Thomas Gray.

There were very few Nat Turners, however. Slaves more often

retaliated against oppression by malingering or engaging in outright sabotage. Yet slaves also knew that they would likely eat better on a prosperous plantation than on one they had reduced to poverty, and the shrewdest slaveholders knew that they would more likely benefit by holding out rewards than by inflicting pain. Plantations based on the profit motive fostered mutual dependency between slaves and slaveholders, as well as natural antagonism. And in an agrarian society in which personal relations counted for much, blacks could win concessions that moderated the harshness of slavery, permitting them a certain degree of individual and community development.

THE EXPERIENCE OF SLAVE WOMEN Although black men and women often performed similar labors, they did not experience slavery in the same way. During the colonial period male slaves vastly outnumbered females. By the mid–eighteenth century, however, the gender ratio had come into balance. Once slaveholders realized how profitable a fertile female slave could be over time, giving birth every two and a half years to a child who eventually could be sold, they began to encourage reproduction through a variety of incentives. Pregnant slaves were given less work to do and more food. Owners on some plantations rewarded new mothers with dresses and silver dollars.

But if motherhood endowed enslaved women with stature and benefits, it also entailed exhausting demands. Within days after childbirth the mother was put to work spinning, weaving, or sewing. A few weeks thereafter mothers were sent back to the fields; breast-feeding mothers were often forced to take their babies to the fields with them. On larger plantations elderly women, called grannies, kept the children during the day while their mothers worked outside. Once slave women passed their childbearing years, around the age of forty, their workload increased. Slaveholders put middle-aged women to work full-time in the fields or performing other outdoor labor. Enslaved women were expected to do "man's work" outside. They cut trees, hauled logs, plowed fields with mules, dug ditches, spread fertilizer, slaughtered animals, hoed corn, and picked cotton. Slave women of all ages usually worked in sex-segregated gangs, which enabled them to form close bonds with one another. To enslaved African Americans, developing a sense of community and camaraderie meant emotional and psychological survival.

Enslaved women faced the constant threat of sexual abuse. Sometimes a white master or overseer would rape a woman in the fields or cabins. Sometimes the owner would lock a woman in a cabin with a male slave whose task was to impregnate her. Female slaves responded to the sexual abuse in different ways. Often they fiercely resisted the sexual advances—and were usually

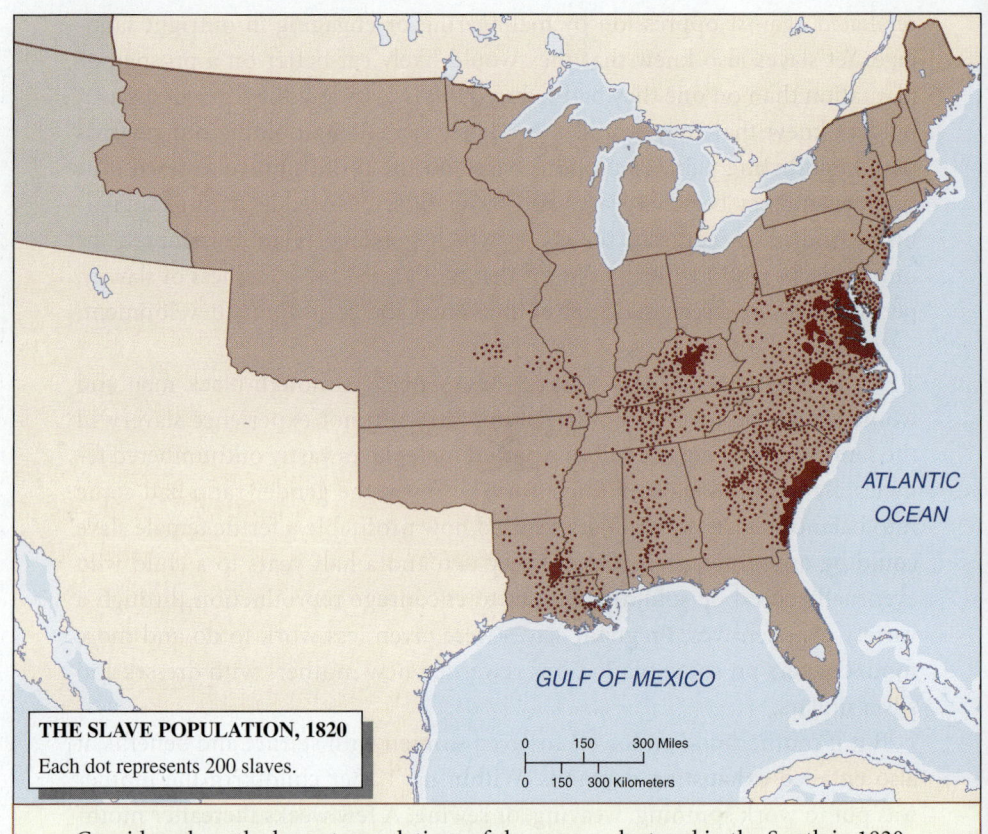

THE SLAVE POPULATION, 1820

Each dot represents 200 slaves.

ATLANTIC OCEAN

GULF OF MEXICO

0   150   300 Miles

0   150   300 Kilometers

Consider where the largest populations of slaves were clustered in the South in 1820. Why were most slaves clustered in these regions of the South and not in others? What were the limitations on the spread of slavery? How was the experience of plantation slavery different for men and women?

whipped or even killed for their disobedience. Some seduced their master away from his wife. Others killed their babies rather than see them grow up in slavery.

FORGING A SLAVE COMMUNITY   To generalize about slavery is to miss elements of diversity from place to place and time to time. The experience was as varied as people are. Enslaved African Americans were victims, but to stop at so obvious a perception would be to miss an important story of endurance and achievement. If ever there was an effective melting pot in American history, it may have been that in which Africans with a variety of ethnic, linguistic, and tribal origins fused to form a new community and a new culture as African Americans. Slave culture incorporated many African

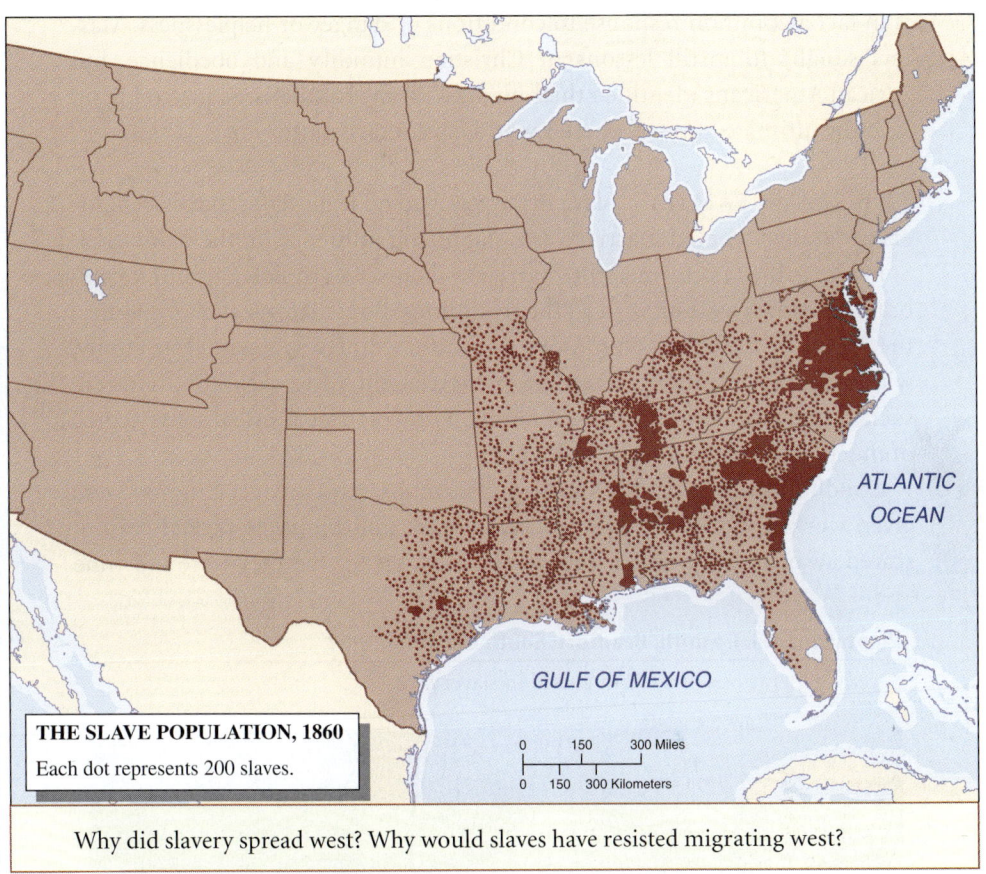

THE SLAVE POPULATION, 1860

Each dot represents 200 slaves.

ATLANTIC OCEAN

GULF OF MEXICO

Why did slavery spread west? Why would slaves have resisted migrating west?

customs, especially in areas with few whites. Among the Gullah of the South Carolina and Georgia coast, for example, a researcher found as late as the 1940s more than 4,000 words still in use from the languages of twenty-one African tribes. Elements of African culture not only have survived but have interacted with those of the other cultures with which they came in contact.

SLAVE RELIGION Among the most important manifestations of slave culture was its dynamic religion, a mixture of African and Christian elements. Most Africans brought with them to the Americas a concept of a Creator, or Supreme God, whom they could recognize in the Christian Jehovah, and lesser gods, whom they might identify with Christ, the Holy Ghost, and the saints, thereby reconciling their African beliefs with Christianity. Alongside the church they retained beliefs in spirits, magic spells and herbs, and conjuring (the practice of healing by warding off evil spirits). Belief in magic is in fact a common response to conditions of danger or helplessness. Masters sought to instill lessons of Christian humility and obedience, but African Americans identified their plight with that of the Israelites in Egypt. And the ultimate hope of a better world gave solace in this one.

THE SLAVE FAMILY   Slave marriages had no legal status, but slaveholders generally accepted marriage as a stabilizing influence on the plantation. Sometimes they performed the marriages themselves or had a minister celebrate a formal wedding with all the trimmings. But whatever the formalities, the norm for the slave community, as for the white, was the nuclear family, with the father regarded as head of the household. Most slave children were socialized by means of the nuclear family, a process that afforded some degree of independence from white influence.

Childhood was short for slaves. At five or six years of age, children were given work assignments: they collected trash and kindling, picked cotton, scared away crows, weeded, and ran errands. By age ten they were full-time

Plantation of J. J. Smith, Beaufort, South Carolina, 1862

Several generations of a family raised in slavery.

field hands. Children were often sold to new masters. In Missouri an enslaved woman saw six of her seven children, aged one to eleven, sold to six separate masters.

THE CULTURE OF THE SOUTHERN FRONTIER

There was substantial social and cultural diversity in the South during the three decades before the Civil War. The region known as the Old Southwest, for example, is perhaps the least well known. It includes the states and territories west of the Georgia-Alabama border—Alabama, Mississippi, Arkansas, Louisiana, and Texas—as well as the frontier areas of Tennessee, Kentucky, and Florida.

Largely unsettled until the 1820s, this region bridged the South and the West, exhibiting characteristics of both areas. Raw and dynamic, marked by dangers, uncertainties, and opportunities, it served as a powerful magnet, luring thousands of settlers from Virginia and the Carolinas. By the 1830s most cotton production was centered in the Lower South. The migrating southerners carved out farms, built churches, established towns, and eventually brought culture and order to a raw frontier. As they took up new lives and occupations, the southern pioneers transplanted many practices and institutions from the coastal states. But they also fashioned a distinctly new set of values and customs.

THE DECISION TO MIGRATE During the 1820s the agricultural economy of the Upper South suffered from falling commodity prices and soil exhaustion. Hard times in the Carolinas and Virginia led many residents of those states to migrate to the Old Southwest. Women were underrepresented among these migrants. Most dreaded the thought of taking up life in such a disease-ridden, violent, and primitive region, one that offered them neither independence nor adventure. Many women feared that life on the frontier would produce a "dissipation" of morals. They heard vivid stories of frontier lawlessness, drunkenness, gambling, and miscegenation.

Enslaved blacks had many of the same reservations about moving west. Almost 1 million captive African Americans were taken to the Old Southwest during the antebellum era, most of them in the 1830s. Like white women, they feared the region's harsh working conditions and torpid heat and humidity. They were also despondent at the breakup of their family ties. As the former slave turned abolitionist Frederick Douglass observed, the "removal" of a slave to the Southwest was considered a form of psychological "death."

A MASCULINE CULTURE   The frontier environment in the Old Southwest prompted important changes in gender roles, and relations between men and women became uncreasingly inequitable. Young men in the Old Southwest indulged in activities that would have generated disapproval in the Carolinas and Virginia. They drank, gambled, fought, and indulged their sexual desires. Alcohol consumption reached new heights along the southwestern frontier. Most plantations had their own stills for manufacturing whiskey, and alcoholism ravaged frontier families. Violence was also commonplace. The frequency of fights, stabbings, shootings, and murders shocked visitors. Equally disturbing was the propensity of white men to take sexual advantage of slave women. An Alabama woman married to a lawyer-politician was outraged by the "beastly passions" of the white men who fathered slave children and then sold them like livestock. She also recorded in her diary instances of men regularly beating their wives with whips and drinking to excess. Wives, it seems, had little choice but to endure the mistreatment because, as one woman wrote about a friend whose husband abused her, she was "wholly dependent upon his care."

ANTI-SLAVERY MOVEMENTS

EARLY OPPOSITION TO SLAVERY   The first organized emancipation movement appeared with the formation, in 1817, of the American Colonization Society, which proposed to resettle freed slaves in Africa. Its supporters included such prominent figures as James Madison, James Monroe, Henry Clay, John Marshall, and Daniel Webster, and its appeal was broad. Some backed it because of their opposition to slavery, while others saw it as a way to uphold slavery, by ridding the country of potentially troublesome free blacks. Articulate elements of the free African American community denounced it from the start. A group of free blacks in Philadelphia, for example, stressed that they had "no wish to separate from our present homes for any purpose whatever." America, they insisted, was their native land.

Nevertheless, in 1821 agents of the Colonization Society acquired a parcel of land in West Africa that became the nucleus of a new country. In 1822 the first freed slaves arrived there from the United States, and twenty-five years later the society relinquished control to the Free and the Independent Republic of Liberia. But given its uncertain purpose, the colonization movement received only meager support from either anti-slavery or pro-slavery elements. By 1860 only about 15,000 blacks had emigrated, approximately

12,000 with the help of the Colonization Society. The number was infinitesimal compared with the number of slave births in the United States.

FROM GRADUALISM TO ABOLITION   Meanwhile, in the early 1830s the anti-slavery movement went in a new direction. In Boston in 1831, William Lloyd Garrison began publication of an anti-slavery newspaper, the *Liberator*. Garrison, who had risen from poverty in Newburyport, Massachusetts, had been apprenticed to a newspaperman and had edited several anti-slavery newspapers, but he had grown impatient with the strategy of moderation. In the first issue of his new paper, he renounced "the popular but pernicious doctrine of gradual emancipation" and vowed: "I *will be* as harsh as truth, and as uncompromising as justice. On this subject, I do not wish to think, to speak, or write, with moderation."

Garrison's combative language outraged slaveholders. Their anger at abolitionists soared after the Nat Turner insurrection in 1831. Garrison, they assumed, bore a large part of the responsibility for the affair, but there is no evidence that Nat Turner had ever heard of him, and Garrison said that his newspaper had not a single subscriber in the South at the time. However violent his language, Garrison was in fact a pacifist, opposed to the use of force.

During the 1830s, Garrison became the nation's most fervent foe of slavery. In 1831 he and his followers set up the New England Anti-Slavery Society. Two years later, with the help of Garrison and other abolitionists, two wealthy New York merchants, Arthur and Lewis Tappan, founded the American Anti-Slavery Society. They hoped to build on the publicity gained by the British anti-slavery movement, which had just induced Parliament to end slavery throughout the British Empire.

The American Anti-Slavery Society stressed "that Slaveholding is a heinous crime in the sight of God, and that the duty, safety, and best interests of all concerned, require its *immediate abandonment*, without expatriation." The society went beyond the issue of emancipation to argue that blacks should "share an equality with the whites, of

William Lloyd Garrison

Vocal abolitionist and advocate of immediate emancipation.

civil and religious privileges." The group issued a barrage of propaganda for its cause, including periodicals, tracts, lecturers, organizers, and fund-raisers.

FRACTIOUS TENSIONS   As the anti-slavery movement spread, debates over tactics intensified. The Garrisonians, mainly New Englanders, were radicals who believed that American society had been corrupted from top to bottom and needed universal reform. Garrison embraced just about every important reform movement of the day: abolition, temperance, pacifism, and women's rights. He broke with the organized church, which to his mind was in league with slavery. The federal government was all the more so. The Constitution, he said, was "a covenant with death and an agreement with hell." Garrison therefore refused to vote.

Other reformers were less dogmatic. They saw American society as fundamentally sound and concentrated on purging it of slavery. Most of these abolitionists were evangelical Christians, and they promoted pragmatic political organization as the best instrument to end slavery. Garrison struck them as an impractical fanatic.

A showdown came in 1840 on the issue of women's rights. Women had joined the abolition movement from the start, but the activities of the

Sarah (left) and Angelina (right) Grimké

After moving away from their slaveholding family, the Grimké sisters devoted themselves to abolitionism and feminism.

Grimké sisters brought the issue of women's rights to center stage. Sarah and Angelina Grimké, daughters of a prominent slaveholding family in South Carolina, had broken with their parents and moved north to embrace Quakerism, abolitionism, and feminism. They set out speaking first to women in New England and eventually to audiences of both men and women.

Male leaders chastised the Grimkés and other female activists for engaging in "unfeminine" activity. The chairman of the Connecticut Anti-Slavery Society declared, "No woman will speak or vote where I am a moderator. It is enough for women to rule at home." He refused to "submit to PETTICOAT GOVERNMENT." Angelina Grimké stoutly rejected the conventional arguments. "It is a woman's right," she insisted, "to have a voice in all laws and regulations by which she is to be governed, whether in church or in state."

The debate over the role of women in the anti-slavery movement crackled and simmered until it finally exploded in 1840. At the American Anti-Slavery Society's annual meeting, the Garrisonians insisted upon the right of women to participate equally in the organization. They did not commit the group to women's rights in any other way, however. Contrary opinion, mainly from the Tappans' New York group, ranged from outright anti-feminism to the simple fear of scattering their energies over too many reforms. The New Yorkers thus broke away to form the American and Foreign Anti-Slavery Society.

BLACK ANTI-SLAVERY ACTIVITY   White male abolitionists also balked at granting full recognition to black abolitionists of either sex. White abolitionists expected free blacks to take a backseat in the movement. Despite the invitation to form separate black groups, black leaders were active in the white societies from the beginning. Three attended the organizational meeting of the American Anti-Slavery Society in 1833, and some, notably former slaves, who could speak from firsthand experience, became outstanding agents for the movement.

One of the most effective black abolitionists was Sojourner Truth. Born to slaves in New York in 1797, she was given the name Isabella, but she renamed herself in 1843 after experiencing a mystical conversation with God, who told her "to travel up and down the land" preaching against the sins of slavery. She did just that, crisscrossing the country during the 1840s and 1850s, exhorting audiences to support abolition and women's rights. Having been a slave until she fled to freedom in 1828, Sojourner Truth spoke with conviction and knowledge about the evils of the "peculiar institution" and the inequality of women. As she reportedly told a gathering of the Ohio Women's Rights Convention in 1851, "I have plowed, and planted, and gathered into barns, and no man could head me—and ar'n't I a woman? I have borne thirteen children,

Frederick Douglass (left) and Sojourner Truth (right)

Both Douglass and Truth were leading abolitionists and captivating orators.

and seen 'em mos' all sold off into slavery, and when I cried out with a mother's grief, none but Jesus heard—and ar'n't I a woman?" Through such compelling testimony, Sojourner Truth demonstrated the powerful intersection of abolitionism and women's rights agitation, and in the process she tapped the distinctive energies that women brought to reformist causes.

An equally gifted black abolitionist was Frederick Douglass, originally of Maryland. Blessed with an imposing appearance and a simple eloquence, he became the best-known black man in America. "I appear before the immense assembly this evening as a thief and a robber," he told a Massachusetts group in 1842. "I stole this head, these limbs, this body from my master, and ran off with them." Fearful of capture after publishing his influential *Narrative of the Life of Frederick Douglass* (1845), he left for an extended lecture tour of the British Isles and returned two years later with enough money to purchase his freedom. He then started an abolitionist newspaper for blacks, the *North Star*, in Rochester, New York.

Douglass's *Narrative* was the best known of hundreds of accounts of enslavement and the escape to freedom, many of which described the Underground Railroad, a network of people who helped runaways escape and start new lives, often over the Canadian border. A few intrepid black refugees ventured back into slave states to organize additional escapes. Harriet Tubman, the most celebrated liberator, was born a slave on a Maryland plantation in about 1820 and escaped when her master died. She fled north, eventually arriving in Philadelphia. There she met William Still, an African American clerk for the Pennsylvania Anti-Slavery Society who served as a "conductor" on the Underground Railroad, a network of escape routes and "safe houses" for runaways. Between 1810 and 1850, tens of thousands of southern slaves ran away and fled north. Tubman soon became a conductor herself, returning nineteen times. Slipping back into the slave states, she would shepherd runaways northward, traveling at night and sleeping by day in the barns or attics of sympathizers along the way. A feisty, determined woman, she threatened to kill any slave who wanted to turn back. Among the 300 slaves Tubman helped liberate were her parents, her sister, and her two children.

REACTIONS TO ABOLITION   Racism was a national problem in the nineteenth century. Even in the North, blacks encountered widespread racial

Abolition under attack

This color engraving depicts the riot at Alton, Illinois, in 1837, in which the abolitionist Elijah Lovejoy was killed.

discrimination and segregation. Garrison, Douglass, and other abolitionists often confronted hostile white crowds who disliked blacks or found anti-slavery agitation bad for business. In 1837 an Illinois mob killed the anti-slavery newspaper editor Elijah P. Lovejoy, giving the movement a martyr to the causes of both abolition and freedom of the press.

In the 1830s, abolition took a political turn, focusing at first on Congress. One shrewd strategy was to deluge Congress with petitions calling for the abolition of slavery in the nation's capital, the District of Columbia. Most such petitions were presented by former president John Quincy Adams, elected to the House from Massachusetts in 1830. In 1836, however, the House adopted a rule to lay abolition petitions automatically on the table, in effect ignoring them. Adams, "Old Man Eloquent," stubbornly fought this "gag rule" as a violation of the First Amendment and hounded its supporters until the rule was repealed in 1844.

Meanwhile, in 1840, the year of the schism in the anti-slavery movement, a small group of abolitionists called a national convention in Albany, New York, and launched the Liberty party, with James G. Birney, a onetime slaveholder in Alabama and Kentucky, as its candidate for president. In the 1840 presidential election, Birney polled only 7,000 votes, but in 1844 he won 60,000, and from that time forth an anti-slavery party contested every national election until Abraham Lincoln won the presidency in 1860.

THE DEFENSE OF SLAVERY   James Birney was but one among a number of southerners propelled north during the 1830s by the South's growing hostility to emancipationist ideas. The anti-slavery movement in the Upper South had its last stand in 1831–1832, when the Virginia legislature rejected a plan of gradual emancipation and African colonization. Thereafter southern partisans worked out an elaborate intellectual defense of slavery, presenting it in a positive light. In 1837, South Carolina's John C. Calhoun told the Senate that slavery was not evil. Instead it was "good—a great good." He brazenly asserted that the Africans brought to America "had never existed in so comfortable, so respectable, or so civilized a condition, as that which is now enjoyed in the Southern states."

The evangelical Christian churches, which had widely condemned slavery at one time, gradually turned pro-slavery, at least in the South. Ministers of all denominations joined in the argument. Had not the patriarchs of the Hebrew Bible held bondsmen? Had not Saint Paul advised servants to obey their masters and told a fugitive servant to return to his master? And had not Jesus remained silent on the subject, at least insofar as the Gospels reported his words? In 1844–1845, disputes over slavery split two great denominations along sectional lines and led to the formation of the Southern Baptist Convention and the Methodist Episcopal Church, South. Presbyterians, the only other major denomination to split, did not do so until the Civil War.

A more fundamental feature of the pro-slavery argument stressed the racial inferiority of blacks. Other arguments took a more "practical" view. Not only was slavery profitable, one argument went, but it was also a matter of social necessity. Thomas Jefferson, for instance, in his *Notes on the State of Virginia* (1785), argued that emancipated slaves and whites could not live together without the risk of a race war growing out of the resentment of past injustices. What is more, it seemed clear to some defenders of slavery that blacks could not be expected to work if freed. They were too shiftless and improvident, the argument went. White workers, on the other hand, feared the competition in the job market if slaves were freed.

In his books *Sociology for the South; or, The Failure of Free Society* (1854) and *Cannibals All! or, Slaves without Masters* (1857), George Fitzhugh of Virginia argued that slavery provided security for African Americans in sickness and old age, whereas workers in the North were exploited for profit and then cast aside. People were not born equal, he insisted. Fitzhugh argued for an organic, hierarchical society, much like the family, in which each member had a place with both rights and obligations.

Within one generation such ideas had triumphed in the white South. Opponents of the faith in slavery as a "positive good" were either silenced or exiled. Freedom of thought in the Old South had become a victim of the region's growing obsession with the preservation and expansion of slavery.

End of Chapter Review

CHAPTER SUMMARY

- **The Southern Economy** Cotton was not the only profitable crop in the South. Parts of the South became increasingly diversified, raising tobacco, indigo, sugar, and subsistence crops. Despite the belief that slaves were unsuited for factory work, some manufacturing ventures in the South employed slaves. Slavery was the unifying element in all southern enterprises.

- **Southern Culture** Throughout the antebellum era the American South became increasingly committed to a cotton economy, which in turn was dependent upon slave labor. Despite efforts to diversify the economy, the wealth and status associated with cotton prompted the westward expansion of the plantation culture. In defense of slavery, evangelical churches declared that it was sanctioned by the Bible; southerners proclaimed it a "positive good" for African Americans. Whereas only a quarter of white southerners held slaves, the planter elite set the standard for southern white culture. Its dominant features were a strict hierarchy based on race, a preoccupation with masculine honor, and the glorification of white women's chastity.

- **Anti-Slavery Movement** Northern opponents of slavery promoted several solutions, including deportation of African Americans to colonies in Africa, gradual emancipation, and immediate abolition. Radical abolitionist efforts in the North provoked a strong reaction among white southerners, stirring fears for their safety and resentment of interference. Yet many northerners shared the belief in the racial inferiority of Africans.

- **Southern Black Culture** The enslaved responded to their oppression in a variety of ways. Although many slaves attempted to run away, only a few openly rebelled. Some survived by relying on their own communities, family ties, and Christian faith. Although nominally free, blacks who won their freedom were not permitted to vote or testify against whites in court.

CHRONOLOGY

1808	Participation in the international slave trade is outlawed
1817	American Colonization Society is founded
1822	Denmark Vesey conspiracy is discovered in Charleston, South Carolina
1831	Nat Turner leads slave insurrection in Virginia
	William Lloyd Garrison begins publication of the *Liberator*
1833	Great Britain abolishes slavery throughout the British Empire
	American Anti-Slavery Society is founded
1837	Abolitionist editor Elijah P. Lovejoy is murdered
1840	Abolitionists form the Liberty party
1845	*Narrative of the Life of Frederick Douglass* is published
1851	Sojourner Truth delivers "Aren't I a Woman Speech"
1852	Harriet Beecher Stowe's *Uncle Tom's Cabin* is published

KEY TERMS & NAMES

16

THE CRISIS OF UNION

FOCUS QUESTIONS wwnorton.com/studyspace

- Who were the members of the free-soil coalition, and what arguments did they use to demand that slavery not spread to the territories?

- Why did the issue of statehood for California precipitate a crisis for the Union?

- What were the major elements of the Compromise of 1850?

- How did the Kansas-Nebraska Act initiate the collapse of the second party system?

- Why did the southern states secede?

W ars have a way of corrupting ideals and breeding new wars, often in unforeseen ways. America's victory over Mexico in 1848 and its acquisition of vast new territories gave rise to heated quarrels over the newly acquired land. Those quarrels set in motion a series of fractious disputes that would culminate in a crisis of union.

SLAVERY IN THE TERRITORIES

THE WILMOT PROVISO   The Mexican War was less than three months old when the seeds of a new conflict began to sprout. On August 8, 1846, a freshman Democrat from Pennsylvania, David Wilmot, stood up in the House of Representatives to discuss President James K. Polk's request for $2 million to support the war against Mexico. Wilmot favored expansion, he explained, even the annexation of Texas as a slave state. But slavery had come to an end in Mexico, and if the United States should acquire Mexican territory, "God forbid that we should be the means of planting this institution [slavery] upon it." If any additional land be acquired from Mexico, Wilmot declared, "neither slavery nor involuntary servitude shall ever exist in any part of said territory."

The proposed Wilmot Proviso ignited the festering debate over slavery. For a generation, since the Missouri controversy of 1819–1821, the issue had been lurking in the wings, kept there most of the time by politicians who feared its disruptive force. For the two decades following Wilmot's proposal, however, the question of extending slavery into new territories dominated political discussion.

The House adopted the Wilmot Proviso, but the Senate balked. When Congress reconvened in December 1846, President Polk persuaded Wilmot to withhold his amendment, but by then others were ready to take up the cause of prohibiting slavery in the new territories. When a New York congressman revived the proviso, the House again approved the amendment; again the Senate refused to endorse it. The House finally gave up, but in one form or another Wilmot's idea was kept alive.

Senator John C. Calhoun of South Carolina at last devised a thesis to counter the Wilmot Proviso, which he set before the Senate in four resolutions on February 19, 1847. The Calhoun resolutions, which never came to a vote, argued that since the territories were the common possession of the states, Congress had no right to prevent any citizen from taking slaves into them. To do so would violate the Fifth Amendment, which forbids Congress to deprive any person of life, liberty, or property without due process of law, and slaves were property. By this clever stroke of logic, Calhoun took the basic guarantee of liberty, the Bill of Rights, and turned it into a basic guarantee of slavery. Calhoun's logic became established southern dogma, echoed by his colleagues and formally endorsed by the Virginia legislature.

POPULAR SOVEREIGNTY   To bypass the brewing conflict over slavery President Polk suggested extending the Missouri Compromise, dividing free and slave territory at the latitude of 36°30′ all the way to the Pacific. Senator Lewis Cass of Michigan, an ardent Whig expansionist, offered a different solution. He argued that the citizens of a territory should "regulate their own internal concerns," like the citizens of a state. Such an approach would take the contentious issue of allowing slavery in the new territories out of the national arena and put it in the hands of those directly affected.

Popular sovereignty, or "squatter sovereignty," as Cass's idea was also called, had much to commend it. Without directly challenging the slave-holders' access to the new territories, it promised to open the territories quickly to nonslaveholding farmers, who would almost surely become the majority. With this tacit understanding the idea prospered in Cass's Old Northwest, where Senator Stephen A. Douglas of Illinois and other promi-nent Democrats soon endorsed it.

In 1848, when the Mexican War ended, the question of slavery in the new territories was no longer hypothetical. Nobody doubted that Oregon would become "free soil," but it, too, was drawn into the growing controversy. Territorial status for Oregon, pending since 1846, was delayed because its provisional government had excluded slavery. To concede that provision would imply an authority drawn from the powers of Congress, since a terri-tory was created by Congress. After much wrangling, an exhausted Congress let Oregon settlers organize their territorial status without slavery but post-poned a decision on the Southwest territories. President Polk signed the bill on the principle that Oregon was north of 36°30′, the Missouri Compromise demarcation.

Polk had promised to serve only one term, and having accomplished his major goals, he refused to run again. At the 1848 Democratic Convention, Michigan senator Lewis Cass, the author of "squatter sovereignty," won the presidential nomination, but the party's platform simply skirted the sover-eignty issue, denying the power of Congress to interfere with slavery in the states and criticizing all efforts to bring the question before Congress. The Democrats hoped that voters would reward their party for winning the war against Mexico. The Whigs devised an even more artful shift. Once again, as in 1840, they passed over Henry Clay, their party leader, this time for a gen-eral, Zachary Taylor, whose popularity had grown since the Battle of Buena Vista. A resident of Louisiana and the holder of more than 100 slaves, Taylor was an apolitical figure who had never voted in a national election. Once again, as in 1840, the party adopted no platform.

THE FREE-SOIL COALITION   The anti-slavery impulse was not easily squelched, however. David Wilmot had raised a standard to which a broad coalition could rally. People who shied away from the militant abolitionism of William Lloyd Garrison could more readily endorse the exclusion of slav-ery from all the territories. By doing so, moreover, they could strike a blow for liberty without caring about slavery itself, or about the slaves. One might simply want free soil for white farmers while keeping the unwelcome blacks far away in the South, where they supposedly belonged. Free soil in the new territories, therefore, rather than abolition in the South itself, became the rallying point for many Americans—and also the name of a new party.

Three major groups entered the new free-soil political coalition: rebellious Democrats, anti-slavery Whigs, and members of the anti-slavery Liberty party. In 1848 they organized the Free-Soil party at a convention in Buffalo, New York. Its presidential nomination went to the former Democratic president Martin Van Buren. The party platform pledged to abolish slavery whenever such action became constitutional, but its main principle was the Wilmot Proviso, and it entered the campaign with the catchy slogan of "free soil, free speech, free labor, and free men."

The impact of the new party on the 1848 election was mixed. The Free-Soilers split the Democratic vote enough to throw New York's 36 electoral votes to Taylor, and they split the Whig vote enough to give Ohio to Lewis Cass, but Van Buren's total of 291,000 votes was far below the totals of 1,361,000 for Taylor and 1,222,000 for Cass. Taylor won with 163 electoral votes to 127 for Cass, and both major parties retained a national following.

Martin Van Buren

Martin Van Buren was nominated as the presidential candidate for the Free-Soil party at the party's convention in Buffalo, New York. In this cartoon, he is shown riding a buffalo past the Democratic and Whig candidates.

THE BUFFALO HUNT.

THE CALIFORNIA GOLD RUSH   Meanwhile, a new dimension had been introduced into the vexing question of slavery in the territories. On January 24, 1848, gold was discovered in the Mexican province of California, which nine days later would be ceded to the United States as a result of the treaty ending the Mexican War. Word spread quickly, and gold fever became a worldwide epidemic. The rush to California became the greatest mass migration in American history—and one of the most significant events in the first half of the nineteenth century. The infusion of California gold into the U.S. economy triggered a surge of prosperity and dramatic economic growth that eventually helped finance the Union military effort in the Civil War. New business enterprises emerged to serve the burgeoning population of miners, including one dedicated to the production of sturdy denim trousers made of sailcloth, their pockets reinforced by copper rivets. The blue jeans, known to this day as Levi's, were developed by the German Jewish immigrant Levi Strauss. The gold rush also shifted the nation's center of gravity westward, spurred the construction of railroads and telegraph lines, and excited dreams of an eventual American empire based in the Pacific.

During 1849 more than 80,000 gold-seeking adventures reached California, with 55,000 traveling overland and the rest going by ship. The massive migration to California had profound effects nationwide. So many men left New England, for instance, it would be years before the region's gender ratio evened out again. The influx of migrants quickly reduced California's 14,000 Mexicans to a minority, and sporadic conflicts with the Indians of the Sierra Nevada foothills decimated the territory's Native Americans.

Of all the frontiers in the American experience, the mining frontier was perhaps the most unstable. Unlike the land-hungry pioneers who traversed the Overland Trails, the miners were mostly unmarried young men with diverse ethnic and cultural backgrounds. Few miners were interested in permanent settlement. They wanted to strike it rich quickly and return home. The mining camps in California's valleys and canyons and along its creek beds thus sprang up like mushrooms and disappeared almost as rapidly.

After touring the gold region, the territorial governor reported that the surge of newcomers had "entirely changed the character of Upper California." The mining camps and shantytowns may have had colorful names—Whiskey Flat, Lousy Ravine, Petticoat Slide, Piety Hill—but the male-dominated communities were in fact dismal, dirty, disorderly, and often lawless. Vigilante justice prevailed in camps speckled with saloons and gambling halls. One newcomer reported that "in the short space of twenty-four days, we have had murders, fearful accidents, bloody deaths, a mob, whippings, a hanging, an attempt at

Gold miners, ca. 1850

Daguerreotype of miners panning for gold at their claim.

suicide, and a fatal duel." Within six months of arriving in California in 1849, one gold seeker in every five was dead. The goldfields and mining towns were so dangerous that nearly everyone carried a weapon—usually a pistol or bowie knife. Suicides were common, and disease was rampant.

Women were as rare in the mining camps as liquor and guns were abundant. In 1850 less than 8 percent of California's total population was female, and even fewer women dared to live in the camps. Racial and ethnic prejudice was another feature of the camps, where white Americans often looked with disdain upon the Hispanics and Chinese, who were most often employed as wage laborers to help in the panning process, separating gold from sand and gravel. But the white Americans focused their contempt on the Indians. In the mining culture it was not a crime to kill Indians or to work them to death. American miners tried several times to outlaw foreigners in the mining country but had to settle for a tax on foreign miners, which was applied to Mexicans in express violation of the treaty ending the Mexican War.

CALIFORNIA STATEHOOD   In 1849 the new president, Zachary Taylor, decided to use California's request for statehood as a lever to end the stalemate in Congress over the slavery issue. Born in Virginia and raised in Kentucky, Taylor had been a soldier most of his adult life. Constantly on the move, he had acquired a home in Louisiana and a plantation in Mississippi. Southern Whigs had rallied to his support, expecting him to uphold the cause of slavery. Instead, he turned out to be a southern man who championed Union principles. Slavery should be upheld where it existed, Taylor believed, but he had little patience with abstract theories about slavery in territories where it probably could not exist. Why not make the California and New Mexico Territories, acquired from Mexico, free states immediately, Taylor reasoned, and bypass the vexing issue of slavery?

But the Californians, in desperate need of organized government, were ahead of him. In December 1849, without consulting Congress, California organized a free-state (no-slavery) government. New Mexico responded more slowly, but by 1850 Americans there had adopted a free-state constitution. In his annual message on December 4, 1849, President Taylor endorsed immediate statehood for California and urged Congress to avoid injecting slavery into the issue. The new Congress, however, was in no mood for simple solutions. By 1850, tensions over the morality and the future of slavery were boiling over. At the same time that tempers were flaring over the issue of allowing slavery into the new western territories, anti-slavery members of the House of Representatives were proposing legislation to ban slavery in the District of Columbia. Further complicating the political debate over slavery was the claim by Texas, a slave state, to half of the New Mexico Territory. These were only a few of the complex dilemmas confronting the nation's statesmen as they assembled in Washington, D.C., for the 1850 legislative session.

THE COMPROMISE OF 1850

The spotlight fell on the Senate, where the Compromise of 1850, one of the great dramas of American politics, was enacted by a stellar cast: the great triumvirate of Henry Clay, John C. Calhoun, and Daniel Webster. As the players took their places, some southern legislators began to talk openly about seceding from the Union if the Congress restricted slavery from the new states. "If, by your legislation, you seek to drive us from the territories of California and New Mexico," thundered Robert Toombs, a Georgia congressman, then "*I am for disunion.*"

THE GREAT DEBATE   In January 1850, the seventy-three-year-old Clay presented a package of eight resolutions designed to solve all the disputed issues. He proposed to (1) admit California as a free state, (2) organize the

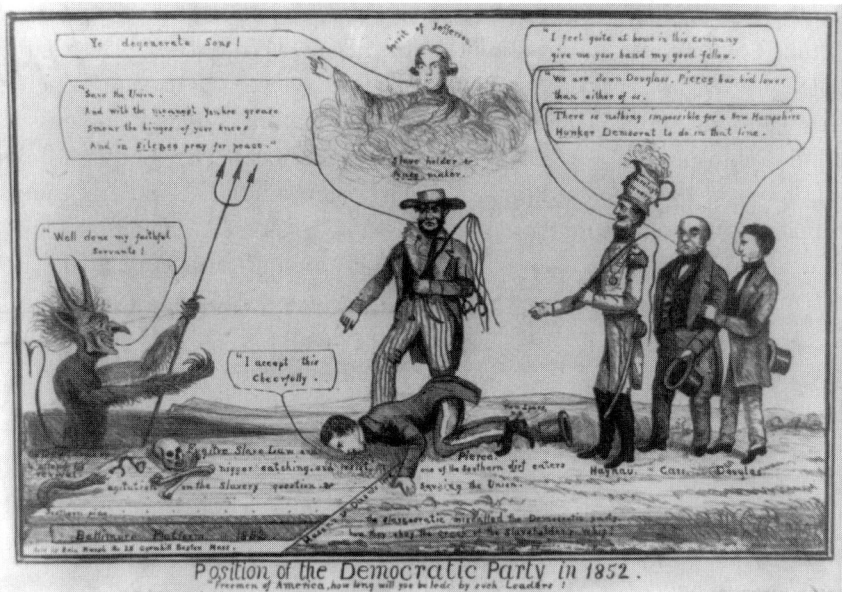

Drama in American politics

This cartoon attacks Democratic presidential candidate Franklin Pierce for his party's endorsement of the Compromise of 1850.

remainder of the Southwest territories without restrictions on slavery, (3) deny Texas its extreme claim to much of New Mexico, (4) compensate Texas by assuming its debt, (5) retain slavery in the District of Columbia, but (6) abolish the slave trade across its boundaries, (7) adopt a more effective fugitive slave act, and (8) deny congressional authority to interfere with the interstate slave trade. His proposals, in substance, became known as the Compromise of 1850, but only after the most celebrated debate in the annals of Congress.

On February 5–6, Clay summoned all his eloquence in defending his proposed settlement. In the interest of "peace, concord and harmony," he called for an end to "passion, passion—party, party—and intemperance." Otherwise, continued sectional bickering would lead to a "furious, bloody, implacable, exterminating" civil war. To avoid that catastrophe, he stressed, California should be admitted on the terms that its own citizens had approved.

The congressional debate continued sporadically through February, with the Texan Sam Houston rising to support Clay's compromise and Mississippi's Jefferson Davis defending the slavery cause on every point. President Taylor, however, believed that slavery in the South could best be protected if southerners avoided injecting the issue into any dispute over new territories. Unlike Calhoun, he did not think that the new western territories were suitable for slave-based agriculture. Because Taylor believed the issue of bringing slaves into the western territories was moot, he continued to urge Congress to admit California and New Mexico without reference to slavery. But few others embraced such a simple solution. In fact, a rising chorus of southern leaders threatened to secede from the Union if slavery were not allowed in California.

Then, in a dramatic move on March 4, Calhoun, desperately ill with tuberculosis, from which he would die in a few weeks, left his sickbed to sit in the Senate chamber. A colleague read his defiant remarks. "I have, Senators, believed from the first that the agitation on the subject of slavery would, if not prevented by some timely and effective measure, end in disunion," wrote Calhoun. Neither Clay's compromise nor Taylor's efforts, he declared, would serve the Union. The South needed simply an acceptance of its rights: to take slaves into the territories, to gain federal assistance in capturing and returning fugitive slaves, and to receive some guarantee of "an equilibrium between the sections." Otherwise, Calhoun warned, the "cords" which bind the Union would be severed.

Three days later Calhoun returned to hear Daniel Webster speak. The "godlike Daniel" no longer possessed the thunderous voice of his youth, nor did his shrinking frame project its once magisterial aura, but he remained a formidable presence. For his address to the Senate, he chose as his central theme the preservation of the Union: "I wish to speak today, not as a Massachusetts man, not as a Northern man, but as an American.... I speak today for the preservation of the Union." The extent of slavery was already determined, he insisted, by the Northwest Ordinance, by the Missouri Compromise, and in the new territories by the law of nature. Both sections, to be sure, had legitimate grievances: on the one hand the excesses of "infernal fanatics and abolitionists" in the North and on the other hand southern efforts to expand slavery. But instead of threatening secession, he declared, let everyone "enjoy the fresh air of liberty and union."

Webster's conciliatory March 7 speech brought down a storm upon his head. New England abolitionists lambasted this "Benedict Arnold" for not aggressively supporting the free-soil cause and for endorsing the new fugitive slave law. On March 11, William H. Seward, the Whig senator from New York, gave the anti-slavery reply to Webster. Compromise with slavery, he argued, was "radically wrong and essentially vicious." Seward insisted that a "higher law than the Constitution" demanded the abolition of slavery.

In mid-April a select committee of thirteen senators bundled Henry Clay's suggestions into one comprehensive bill. Taylor continued to oppose

Clay's compromise, and their feud threatened to split the Whig party. Another crisis loomed when word came that a convention in New Mexico was applying for statehood, with Taylor's support and on the basis of boundaries that conflicted with the Texas claim to the east bank of the Rio Grande.

TOWARD A COMPROMISE   On July 4, 1850, supporters of the Union staged a rally at the base of the unfinished Washington Monument. President Taylor attended the ceremonies in the hot sun. Five days later he died of a gastrointestinal affliction caused by tainted food or water. Taylor's sudden death strengthened the chances of compromise. The soldier in the White House was followed by a politician, Millard Fillmore. The son of a poor farmer in upstate New York, Fillmore had made his way as a lawyer and then as a candidate in the rough-and-tumble world of New York politics. Experience had taught him caution, which some interpreted as indecision, but he had made up his mind to support Henry Clay's compromise and had so informed Taylor. It was a strange switch. Taylor, the Louisiana slaveholder, had stoutly opposed the expansion of slavery and was ready to make war on his native region if it pressed the issue; Fillmore, whom southerners thought to be anti-slavery, was ready to make peace.

At this point the young Senator Stephen A. Douglas of Illinois, a rising star in the Democratic party, rescued Clay's faltering compromise. Short and stocky, brash and brilliant, Douglas adopted the same strategy that Clay had used to pass the Missouri Compromise thirty years before. Reasoning that nearly everybody objected to one or another provision of Clay's proposal, Douglas decided to break it up into six (later five) separate measures. Few members were prepared to vote for all of them, but from different elements Douglas hoped to mobilize a majority for each.

The plan worked. By September 1850, President Fillmore had signed the last of the five measures into law. The Union had muddled through, and the settlement went down in history as the Compromise of 1850. For a time it defused an explosive situation and settled each of the major points at issue.

Millard Fillmore

Fillmore's support of the Compromise of 1850 helped the Union muddle through the crisis.

First, California entered the Union as a free state, ending forever the old balance of free and slave states. Second, the Texas–New Mexico Act made New Mexico a territory and set the Texas boundary at its present location. In return for giving up its land claims, Texas was paid $10 million. Third, the Utah Act set up that future state's territory. The territorial act in each case omitted reference to slavery except to give the territorial legislature authority over "all rightful subjects of legislation" with provision for appeal to the federal courts. For the sake of agreement, the deliberate ambiguity of the statement was its merit. Northern congressmen could assume that territorial legislatures might act to exclude slavery on the unstated principle of popular sovereignty. Southern congressmen assumed that they could not do so.

Fourth, a new Fugitive Slave Act put the matter of retrieving runaways wholly under federal jurisdiction and stacked the cards in favor of slave catchers. Fifth, as a gesture to anti-slavery forces, the slave trade, but not slavery itself, was abolished in the District of Columbia. Millard Fillmore pronounced the five measures making up the Compromise of 1850 "a final settlement" of the issues dividing the nation. Events would soon prove him wrong.

THE FUGITIVE SLAVE ACT   Southern insistence upon the Fugitive Slave Act had presented abolitionists with an emotional new focus for their agitation. The law offered a strong temptation to kidnap free blacks by denying alleged fugitives a jury trial and by providing a reward of $10 for each fugitive delivered to federal authorities. In addition, federal marshals could require citizens to help in its enforcement; violators could be imprisoned for up to six months and fined $1,000. Trouble followed. In Detroit, Michigan, for example, authorities used military force to stop the rescue of an alleged fugitive slave by an outraged mob in October 1850.

There were relatively few such incidents, however. In the first six years of the Fugitive Slave Act, only three runaways were forcibly rescued from slave catchers. On the other hand, probably fewer than 200 were returned to bondage in the South during those years. More than that were rescued by stealth. Still, the Fugitive Slave Act strengthened the anti-slavery impulse in the North.

UNCLE TOM'S CABIN   Anti-slavery forces found their most persuasive appeal not in opposition to the Fugitive Slave Act but in the fictional drama of Harriet Beecher Stowe's best-selling novel, Uncle Tom's Cabin (1852). The daughter, sister, and wife of Congregationalist ministers, Stowe epitomized the powerful religious underpinnings of the abolitionist movement. She had decided to write the novel because of her disgust with the Fugitive Slave Act of 1850. *Uncle Tom's Cabin* depicts a combination of unlikely saints and sinners, social stereotypes, fugitive slaves, and melodramatic escapades. It was a smashing commercial success. Slavery, seen through Stowe's eyes, subjected its victims to callous brutality or, at the hands of indulgent masters, to the indignity of extravagant ineptitude and bankruptcy. Stowe poignantly portrayed the evils of the interstate slave trade, especially the breaking up of slave families, and she highlighted the horrors of the Fugitive Slave Act. It took time for the novel

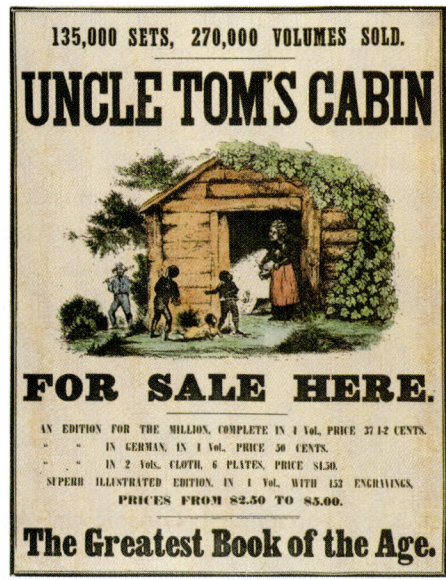

"The Greatest Book of the Age"

Uncle Tom's Cabin, as this advertisement indicates, was a tremendous commercial success.

to work its effect on public opinion, however. The country was enjoying a surge of prosperity, fueled by California gold, and the course of the presidential campaign in 1852 reflected a common desire to lay sectional quarrels to rest.

THE ELECTION OF 1852   The Democrats chose as their presidential candidate Franklin Pierce of New Hampshire, a personable veteran of the Mexican War with little political experience. Soon they had a catchy slogan to aim at the Whigs: "We Polked you in 1844, we shall Pierce you in 1852." The platform pledged the Democrats to "abide by and adhere to a faithful execution of the acts known as the Compromise measures." Pierce rallied both the southern rights' partisans and the Van Burenite Democrats. The Free-Soilers, as a consequence, mustered only half as many votes as they had won in 1848.

The Whigs were less fortunate. They repudiated the lackluster Fillmore in favor of General Winfield Scott, the hero of Mexico City, a Virginia native backed mainly by northern Whigs. The Whig Convention dutifully endorsed the Compromise of 1850, but with some opposition from the North. Scott, an able field commander but an inept politician, had gained a reputation for anti-slavery and nativist sentiments, alienating German-American and Irish-American voters. In the end, Scott carried only four states. The popular vote was closer: 1.6 million to 1.4 million.

Pierce, an undistinguished but sincere, boyishly handsome former congressman, senator, and soldier, was, like James Polk, touted as another Andrew Jackson. But the youngest president yet was unable to unite the warring factions of his party. He was neither a statesman nor a leader. By the end of President Pierce's first year in office, Democratic leaders had decided he was a failure. By trying to be all things to all people, Pierce looked more and more like a "Northern man with Southern principles."

FOREIGN ADVENTURES

CUBA   Foreign diversions now distracted attention from domestic quarrels. Cuba, one of Spain's earliest possessions in the New World, had long been an object of U.S. desire, especially to southerners determined to expand slavery into new areas. In 1854 the Pierce administration offered Spain $130 million for the island, which Spain spurned. The U.S. ministers to Spain, France, and Britain then drafted the Ostend Manifesto, which declared that if Spain, "actuated by stubborn pride and a false sense of honor, refused to sell," the United States must ask itself, "Does Cuba, in the possession of Spain, seriously endanger our internal peace and the existence of our cherished Union?" If so, "we shall be justified in wresting it from Spain." Publication of the supposedly confidential dispatch left the administration no choice but to disavow what northern opinion widely regarded as a "slaveholders' plot" to acquire Cuba.

DIPLOMATIC GAINS IN ASIA   In the Pacific, U.S. diplomacy scored some important achievements. In 1844, China signed an agreement with the United States that opened four ports, including Shanghai, to American trade. A later treaty opened eleven more ports and granted Americans the right to travel and trade throughout China. About fifty Protestant American missionaries were in China by 1855, and for nearly a century China remained the most active site for missionaries.

Japan, meanwhile, had remained closed to U.S. trade for two centuries. Moreover, American whalers wrecked on the shores of Japan had been forbidden to leave the country. Mainly in their interest, President Fillmore entrusted a special Japanese expedition to Commodore Matthew Perry, who arrived in Tokyo in 1853. Perry sought to impress—and intimidate—the Japanese with U.S. military and technological superiority. He demonstrated the cannons on his steamships and presented the Japanese with gifts of rifles, pistols, telegraph instruments, and a working miniature locomotive. For their part the Japanese presented Perry with silk and ornate furnishings. Negotiations followed, and Japan eventually agreed to allow a U.S. consulate, treat castaways cordially, and permit American ships to visit certain ports to take on supplies and make repairs. Broad commercial relations began after the first American envoy, Townsend Harris, negotiated the Harris Convention of 1858, which opened five Japanese ports to U.S. trade. Japan continued to ban emigration but found the law increasingly difficult to enforce, and by the 1880s the Japanese government had abandoned its efforts to prevent Japanese from seeking work abroad.

THE KANSAS-NEBRASKA CRISIS

American commercial interests in Asia helped spark a growing interest in constructing a transcontinental railroad that would link the eastern seaboard to the Pacific coast. Railroad developers and land speculators also promoted this link, as did slaveholders who were eager to see the reach of slavery extended. During the 1850s the idea of building a transcontinental railroad, though a great national goal, reignited sectional rivalries and reopened the slavery issue.

DOUGLAS'S PROPOSAL In 1852 and 1853, Congress debated several proposals for the route of a transcontinental rail line. For various reasons, including terrain, climate, and sectional interests, Secretary of War Jefferson Davis favored a southern route and promoted what became known as the Gadsden Purchase, a barren stretch of land in present-day New Mexico and Arizona. In 1853, at a cost of $10 million, the United States acquired the area from Mexico as a likely route for a railroad to the Pacific coast.

Stephen Douglas, ca. 1852

Author of the Kansas-Nebraska Act.

THE KANSAS-NEBRASKA ACT, 1854

- Free states and territories
- Slave states
- Open to slavery by popular sovereignty, Compromise of 1850
- Open to slavery by popular sovereignty, Kansas-Nebraska Act, 1854
- ★ Battle site

BLEEDING KANSAS

What were the terms of the Kansas-Nebraska Act? How did it lead to the creation of the Republican party?

But midwestern spokesmen had other ideas concerning the path of the railroad. Since 1845, Illinois senator Stephen A. Douglas and others had been pushing for a route through a new territory west of Missouri and Iowa bearing the Indian name Nebraska. In 1854, Douglas, whose capacity for liquor was exceeded only by his capacity for work, put forward a bill dealing with the entire unorganized portion of the Louisiana Purchase to the Canadian border. To grant territorial status to Nebraska required the support of southerners, and to win that support Douglas needed to make some concession on slavery in the new territories. This he did by writing the concept of popular sovereignty into the bill, allowing voters in each territory to decide the issue themselves.

It was a clever dodge since the Missouri Compromise would exclude slaves until a territorial government had made a decision, thereby preventing slaveholders from getting established before the decision was reached. Southerners quickly spotted the barrier, and Douglas just as quickly made two more concessions. He supported an amendment for repeal of the Missouri Compromise insofar as it excluded slavery north of 36°30′, and he agreed to organize two territories: Kansas, west of Missouri, and Nebraska, west of Iowa and Minnesota.

Douglas's motives remain unclear. Railroads were surely foremost in his mind, but he may also have been influenced by the hope that popular sovereignty would quiet the slavery issue and open the Great Plains to development, or by a chance to split the Whigs over the issue. But he had blundered by failing to appreciate the depth of anti-slavery feelings, thus damaging his presidential chances and setting the country on the road to civil war. Douglas himself preferred that slavery not be allowed in the territories. Their climate and geography excluded plantation agriculture, he reasoned, and he could not comprehend how people could get so wrought up over abstract rights to take slaves into the territories. Yet he had in fact opened the possibility that slavery might gain a foothold in Kansas.

Douglas's proposal to repeal the Missouri Compromise was less than a week old when six anti-slavery congressmen published a protest, the "Appeal of the Independent Democrats." Their moral indignation quickly spread among those who opposed Douglas. Across the North, editorials, sermons, speeches, and petitions denounced Douglas's bill as a conspiracy to extend slavery. But Douglas had the votes in Congress for his Kansas-Nebraska Act, and once committed, he forced the issue with tireless energy. The inept President Pierce impulsively added his support, and the bill passed in May 1854 by a vote of 37 to 14 in the Senate and 113 to 100 in the House.

Very well, many in the North reasoned, if the Missouri Compromise was not a sacred pledge and could be scrapped, then they would defy the Fugitive Slave Act. On June 2, 1854, Boston witnessed the most dramatic demonstration against the act. A runaway Virginia slave named Anthony Burns had been taken in by free blacks in Boston when federal marshals arrived to arrest and return him. Incensed by what had happened, a crowd of 2,000 Boston abolitionists led by a minister stormed the jail in an effort to free Burns. In the melee a federal marshal was killed. At Burns's trial, held to determine whether he indeed was a fugitive, a compromise was proposed that would have allowed Bostonians to buy Burns his freedom, but the plan was scuttled by President Pierce, who was determined to enforce the Fugitive Slave Act. On June 2, the day that state militia and federal troops marched Burns through

Boston to a ship waiting to return him to Virginia, some 50,000 people lined the streets. Many of them shouted epithets at the federal officials.

Over the next several weeks, demonstrations against the Fugitive Slave Act grew in scope and intensity. At a July 4 rally in Framingham, Massachusetts, the abolitionist editor William Lloyd Garrison burned copies of the Fugitive Slave Act and the Constitution. Later in the day the transcendentalist Henry David Thoreau delivered a fiery speech in which he charged that the trial of Burns was "really the trial of Massachusetts." Prominent New Englanders despised President Pierce for his handling of the Burns case. In a letter to the White House, one of them wrote: "To the chief slave-catcher of the United States. You damned, infernal scoundrel, if I only had you here in Boston, I would murder you!" As it happened, Anthony Burns was the last fugitive slave to be returned from Boston and was soon freed through purchase by Boston's African American community.

THE EMERGENCE OF THE REPUBLICAN PARTY   The cords that John C. Calhoun had said were binding the Union together were beginning to fray. The national church organizations of Baptists and Methodists, for instance, had split over slavery by 1845 and formed new northern and southern organizations. The national political parties were also beginning to unravel under the strain of slavery. The Democrats managed to postpone disruption for yet a while, but their congressional delegation lost heavily in the North, enhancing the influence of the southern wing.

The strain of the Kansas-Nebraska Act soon destroyed the Whig party. Southern Whigs now tended to abstain from voting, while northern Whigs gravitated toward two new parties. One was the American (Know-Nothing) party, which had raised the banner of nativism and the hope of serving the patriotic cause of Union. More northern Whigs joined with independent Democrats and Free-Soilers in spontaneous anti-slavery coalitions known by a confusing array of names, including the Anti-Nebraska Democratic party, the Fusion party, and the People's party. These coalitions finally converged in 1854, choosing the name Republican.

"BLEEDING KANSAS"   After passage of the Kansas-Nebraska Act, attention swung to the plains of Kansas, where opposing elements gathered to stage what would be a dress rehearsal for civil war. All had agreed that Nebraska would be a free state, but Kansas soon exposed the potential for mischief in Douglas's concept of popular sovereignty. The ambiguity of the law, useful to Douglas in getting it passed, only added to the chaos. The people of Kansas were "perfectly free to form and regulate their domestic institutions in their own way, subject only to the Constitution." That in itself invited conflicting interpretations, but the law failed to specify the time of any decision, adding to each side's sense of urgency in getting control of the territory.

The settlement of Kansas therefore differed from the typical pioneering efforts. Groups sprang up in North and South to hurry right-minded settlers westward, mostly from Missouri and the surrounding states. Although few of them held slaves, they were not sympathetic to abolitionism; racism was prevalent even among nonslaveholding whites. Many of the Kansas settlers wanted to keep all blacks, enslaved or free, out of the territory. By 1860 there were only 627 African Americans in Kansas.

When Kansas's first territorial governor arrived, in 1854, he found several thousand settlers already in place. He ordered that a census be taken and scheduled an election for a territorial legislature in 1855. On election day several thousand "border ruffians" crossed over from Missouri, illegally cast pro-slavery votes, and pledged to kill every "God-damned abolitionist in the Territory." The governor denounced the vote as a fraud but did nothing to alter the results, for fear of being killed. The territorial legislature expelled its few anti-slavery members, adopted a drastic slave code, and made it a capital offense to aid a fugitive slave.

Free-state advocates rejected this "bogus" government and quickly formed their own. In 1855 a constitutional convention, the product of an election of dubious legality, met in Topeka, drafted a state constitution excluding both slavery and free blacks from Kansas, and applied for admission to the Union. By 1856 a free-state "governor" and "legislature" were functioning in Topeka. Thus the territory had two illegal governments vying for recognition and control. The prospect of getting any government to command authority in Kansas seemed dim, and both sides began to arm. Once armed, they began to fight. In May 1856, 700 pro-slavery thugs entered the free-state town of Lawrence and smashed newspaper presses, set fire to the free-state governor's home, stole property, and destroyed the Free-State Hotel.

The "sack of Lawrence" resulted in just one casualty, but the incident aroused a zealous Kansas Free-Soiler named John Brown, who had a history of mental instability. Two days after the sack of Lawrence, Brown, the father of twenty children, set out with four of his sons and three other men toward Pottawatomie, the site of a pro-slavery settlement. There they dragged five men from their houses and hacked them to death in front of their screaming wives and children, ostensibly as revenge for the deaths of free-state men.

The "sack of Lawrence"

This sheet music cover for an anti-slavery song portrays (in the circle) the burning of the Free-State Hotel in Lawrence, Kansas, by a pro-slavery mob in 1856.

The Pottawatomie Massacre (May 24–25, 1856) set off a guerrilla war in the Kansas Territory that lasted through the fall. On August 30, Missouri ruffians raided the free-state settlement at Osawatomie. They looted the houses, burned them to the ground, and shot John Brown's son Frederick through the heart. The elder Brown, who barely escaped, swore to his surviving sons and followers, "I have only a short time to live— only one death to die, and I will die fighting for this cause." Altogether, by the end of 1856, about 200 settlers had been killed in Kansas and $2 million in property destroyed during the territorial civil war.

VIOLENCE IN THE SENATE

The violence in Kansas spilled into Congress itself. On May 22, 1856, the day after the burning of Lawrence and two days before Brown's Pottawatomie Massacre, a flash of savagery on the Senate floor electrified the country. Just two days earlier, Senator Charles Sumner of Massachusetts had finished an inflammatory speech in which he described the treatment of Kansas as "the rape of a virgin territory" and blamed it on the South's "depraved longing for a new slave State." Sumner made the elderly senator Andrew Pickens Butler of South Carolina a target of his censure. He called Butler a liar and implied he kept a slave mistress. Sumner also teased him about a speech impediment, the result of a stroke.

Sumner's indignant rudeness might well have backfired had it not been for Butler's kinsman Preston S. Brooks, a fiery-tempered South Carolina congressman. For two days, Brooks brooded over the insult to his relative, knowing that Sumner would refuse a challenge to a duel. On May 22 a vengeful Brooks confronted Sumner at his Senate desk, accused him of slander against South Carolina and Butler, and began beating him about the head with a cane. Sumner, struggling to rise, wrenched the desk from the floor and collapsed.

Brooks had satisfied his rage but in the process had created a martyr for the anti-slavery cause. Like so many other men in those years, he betrayed the zealot's gift for snatching defeat from the jaws of victory. For two and a half years, Sumner's empty Senate seat was a solemn reminder of the violence done to him. When the House censured Brooks, he resigned, but he was triumphantly reelected. His admirers presented him with new canes. The *Richmond Enquirer* urged Brooks to cane Sumner again: "These vulgar abolitionists in the Senate . . . must be lashed into submission."

SECTIONAL POLITICS   Within the span of five days in May of 1856, "Bleeding Kansas," "Bleeding Sumner," and "Bully Brooks" had fragmented the political landscape. The major parties could no longer evade the slavery issue. Already it had split the hopeful American party wide open. Southern delegates, with help from New York, killed a resolution to restore the Missouri Compromise and nominated Millard Fillmore for president. Later what was left of the Whig party endorsed him as well.

At its first national convention the new Republican party followed the Whig tradition by seeking out a military hero, John C. Frémont, "the Pathfinder," who had led the conquest of Mexican California. The Republican platform also owed much to the Whigs. It favored a transcontinental railroad and, in general, more internal improvements. It condemned the repeal of the Missouri Compromise and the Democratic policy of territorial expansion. The campaign slogan echoed that of the Free-Soilers: "Free soil, free speech, and Frémont." It was the first time a major-party platform had taken a stand against slavery.

The Democrats, meeting two weeks earlier, had rejected Pierce, the hapless victim of so much turmoil. Pierce, who struggled most of his life with alcoholism and self-doubt, may have been the most hated person in the nation by 1852. A Boston newspaper vilified him for promoting sectionalism. "Who but you, Franklin Pierce, have . . . kindled the flames of civil war on the desolated plains of Kansas?" A Philadelphia newspaper was even blunter. The Pierce presidency, it charged, was one of "weakness, indecision, rashness, ignorance, and an entire and utter absence of dignity." Pierce remains the only elected president to be denied renomination by his party. The Democrats also spurned Douglas, because of the damage done by his Kansas-Nebraska Act. The party therefore turned to James Buchanan of Pennsylvania, a former Senator and secretary of state who had long sought the nomination. The Democratic platform endorsed the Kansas-Nebraska Act and urged Congress not to interfere with slavery in either states or territories. The party reached out to its newly acquired Irish Catholic and German Catholic voters by condemning nativism and endorsing religious liberty.

The campaign of 1856 resolved itself as a contest in which the parties vied for northern or southern votes. The Republicans had few southern supporters and only a handful in the border states, where fear of disunion held many Whigs in line. Buchanan thus went into the campaign as the candidate of the only remaining national party. Frémont swept the northernmost states with 114 electoral votes, but Buchanan added five free states to his southern majority for a total of 174.

Buchanan, the first unmarried president, brought to the White House a portfolio of impressive achievements in politics and diplomacy. He had served in Congress, had been ambassador to Russia and Britain, and had been Polk's secretary of state in between. His long quest for the presidency had been built upon a southern alliance, and his political debts reinforced his belief that saving the Union depended upon concessions to the South. Republicans charged that he lacked the backbone to stand up to the southerners who dominated the Democratic majorities in Congress. To them his choice of four slave-state and only three free-state men for his cabinet seemed a bad omen. It was. The new president proved to be a mediocre chief executive.

THE DEEPENING SECTIONAL CRISIS

During James Buchanan's first six months in office in 1857, three major events caused his undoing: the Supreme Court's *Dred Scott* decision, new troubles in Kansas, and a business panic that precipitated a sharp recession.

THE *DRED SCOTT* CASE   On March 6, 1857, two days after Buchanan's inauguration, the Supreme Court rendered a decision in the long-pending case of *Dred Scott v. Sandford*. Dred Scott, born a slave in Virginia in about 1800, had been taken to St. Louis in 1830 and sold to an army surgeon, who took him as his servant to Illinois, then to the Wisconsin Territory (later Minnesota), where slavery was prohibited, and finally returned him to St. Louis in 1842. While in the Wisconsin Territory, Scott had married Harriet Robinson, and they eventually had two daughters.

After his master's death, in 1843, Scott had apparently tried unsuccessfully to buy his freedom. In 1846, Harriet Scott persuaded her husband to file suit in the Missouri courts, claiming that residence in Illinois and the Wisconsin Territory had made them free. A jury decided in their favor, reaffirming the widespread notion that "once free, forever free." But the state supreme court ruled against Scott, arguing that a slave state did not have to honor freedom granted to slaves by free states. When the case rose on appeal to the Supreme

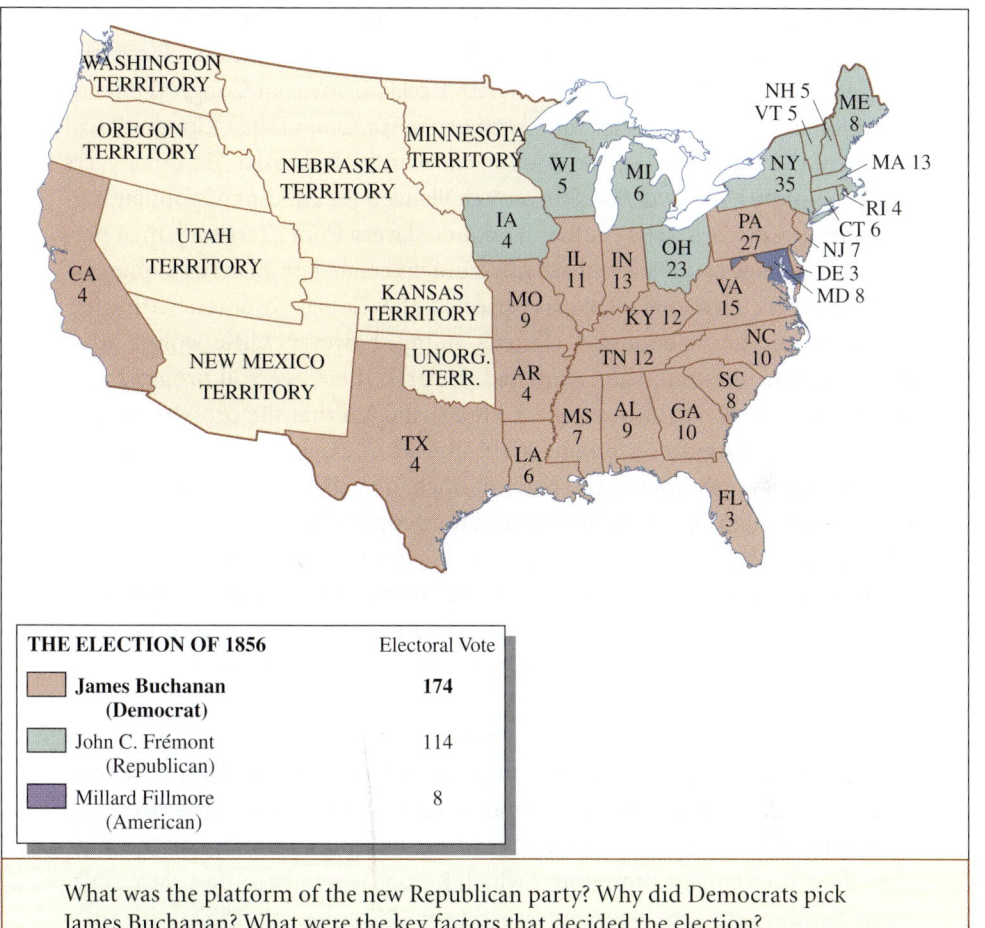

THE ELECTION OF 1856	Electoral Vote
James Buchanan (Democrat)	**174**
John C. Frémont (Republican)	114
Millard Fillmore (American)	8

What was the platform of the new Republican party? Why did Democrats pick James Buchanan? What were the key factors that decided the election?

Court, the nation anxiously awaited its opinion on the issue of whether freedom once granted could be lost by returning to a slave state.

Eight of the justices filed a separate opinion, and one concurred with Chief Justice Roger B. Taney. By different lines of reasoning, seven justices ruled that Scott had reverted to slave status upon his return to Missouri. Taney ruled that Scott lacked standing in the courts because he lacked citizenship. At the time the Constitution was adopted, Taney added, blacks "had for more than a century been regarded as . . . so far inferior, that they had no rights which the white man was bound to respect."

To clarify the definition of Scott's status, Taney moved to a second major question. He argued that the 1820 Missouri Compromise, by ruling that certain new territories were to exclude slaves, had deprived citizens of property by prohibiting slavery, an action "not warranted by the Constitution." Taney and the rest of the Supreme Court had thereby declared an act of Congress unconstitutional for the first time since *Marbury v. Madison* (1803). Congress had repealed the Missouri Compromise in the Kansas-Nebraska Act three years earlier, but the *Dred Scott* decision now challenged the concept of popular sovereignty. If Congress itself could not exclude slavery from a territory, then presumably neither could a territorial government created by an act of Congress.

Pro-slavery elements of course greeted the Court's opinion with glee. Many northerners denounced Taney's ruling, however. Little wonder that Republicans protested: the Court had declared their free-soil program unconstitutional. It had also reinforced the suspicion that the pro-slavery faction was hatching a conspiracy. Were not all but one of the justices who joined Taney southerners? And had not Buchanan chatted with the chief justice at the inauguration and then urged the people to accept the decision as a final settlement?

And what of Dred Scott? Ironically his owner, now a widow, married a prominent Massachusetts abolitionist, who saw to it that Scott and his family were freed in 1857. A year later Dred Scott died of tuberculosis.

THE LECOMPTON CONSTITUTION Out in Kansas, meanwhile, the struggle over slavery continued through the turbulent year of 1857. The contested politics in the territory now resulted in an anti-slavery legislature and a pro-slavery constitutional convention. The convention, meeting at Lecompton, drew up a constitution under which Kansas would become a slave state. A referendum on the document was set for December 21, 1857, with rules and officials chosen by the convention.

Although Kansas had only about 200 slaves at the time, free-state men boycotted the election, claiming that it was rigged. At that point, President Buchanan took a fateful step. Influenced by southern advisers and politically dependent upon southern congressmen, he supported the pro-slavery Lecompton Convention. The election went according to form: 6,226 votes for the constitution with slavery, 569 for the constitution without slavery. Meanwhile, the acting governor had convened the anti-slavery legislature, which called for another election to vote on the Lecompton Constitution. Most of the pro-slavery settlers boycotted this election, and the result, on January 4, 1858, was overwhelming: 10,226 against the constitution, 138 for the constitution with slavery, 24 for the constitution without slavery.

The results suggested a clear majority against slavery, but Buchanan stuck to his support of the Lecompton Constitution, driving another wedge into the

Democratic party. Senator Douglas, up for reelection in Illinois, could not afford to run as a champion of Lecompton. He broke dramatically with the president in a tense confrontation, but Buchanan persisted in trying to drive Lecompton "naked" through Congress. In the Senate, administration forces held firm, and in 1858 the Lecompton Constitution was passed. In the House enough anti-Lecompton Democrats combined to put through an amendment for a new and carefully supervised popular vote in Kansas. Enough senators went along to pass the House bill. Southerners were confident the vote in Kansas would favor slavery because to reject it the voters would have to reject the constitution, an action that would postpone statehood until the population reached 90,000. On August 2, 1858, Kansas voters nevertheless rejected Lecompton, 11,300 to 1,788. With that vote, Kansas, now firmly in the hands of its anti-slavery legislature, largely ended its role in the sectional controversy.

THE PANIC OF 1857 The third crisis of Buchanan's first half year in office, a financial panic, occurred in August 1857. It was brought on by a reduction in Europe's demand for American grain, overly rapid railroad construction, a surge in manufacturing that outran the growth of markets, and the continued weakness and confusion of the state bank-note system. Failure of the Ohio Life Insurance and Trust Company precipitated the panic, which brought on an economic slump from which the country did not emerge until 1859.

Everything in those years seemed to get drawn into the vortex of sectional conflict, and business troubles were no exception. Northern businessmen tended to blame the depression on the Democratic Tariff of 1857, which had put rates at their lowest level since 1816. The agricultural South weathered the crisis better than the North. Cotton prices fell, but slowly, and world markets for cotton quickly recovered. The result was an exalted notion of King Cotton's importance to the world and apparent confirmation of the growing argument that the southern system of slave-based agriculture was superior to the free-labor system of the North.

THE REVIVAL OF 1857–1859 The business panic and depression coincided with a widespread national revival of religious life. In New York City, where over 30,000 people had lost their jobs, Jeremiah Lanphier, a business executive–turned–lay missionary, grew despondent at the suffering in the city as well as an alarming decline in church membership. God, he later claimed, led him to begin a weekly prayer service in the Wall Street financial district so that executives might commune with God. He began on September 23, 1857, with six people attending. Within a few months, though, the number of participants soared. To accommodate the overflow crowds (largely male), nondenominational prayer meetings were offered daily at locations across the city. Soon the daily prayer ritual spread across the nation, especially in the northern tier of states. Women were eventually encouraged to attend the meetings, but they were rarely allowed to speak.

The "prayer-meeting" revivals generated excited discussion; stories about the latest "awakening" dominated big-city newspapers, some of which created regular sections to report the daily progress of the crusade. Between 1857 and 1859 over half a million people joined churches. The revivals of the late 1850s were distinctive in several respects. Unlike the Second Great Awakening of the 1830s and 1840s, the prayer-meeting revivals were largely uninterested in social reform. In fact, prayers about controversial issues, such as slavery, were expressly prohibited at the meetings. The focus of the meetings was personal spiritual renewal, not social transformation. The transcendentalist minister and militant reformer Theodore Parker denounced the revivalists for ignoring the evils of slavery. The Revival of 1857–1859 also differed from earlier awakenings in that it did not feature charismatic ministers or fire-and-brimstone evangelizing. Instead, it was largely a lay movement focused on discreet prayer.

DOUGLAS VERSUS LINCOLN   Amid the recriminations over the *Dred Scott* decision, Kansas, and the deepening economic contraction, the center could not hold. The controversy over slavery in Kansas put severe strains on the most substantial cord of union that was left, the Democratic party. To many, Senator Douglas seemed the best hope for unity and union, one of the few remaining Democratic leaders with support in both the North and the South. But now Douglas was being whipsawed by the extremes. The passage of his Kansas-Nebraska Act had cast him in the role of a doughface, a southern sympathizer. Yet his opposition to the Lecompton Constitution in Kansas, the fraudulent fruit of popular sovereignty, had alienated him from Buchanan's southern junta. For all his flexibility and opportunism, however, Douglas had convinced himself that popular sovereignty was a point of principle, a bulwark of democracy and

Abraham Lincoln

Republican candidate for president, June 1860.

local self-government. In 1858 he faced reelection to the Senate against the opposition of both Buchanan Democrats and Republicans. The year 1860 would give him a chance for the presidency, but first he had to secure his home base in Illinois.

To oppose him, Illinois Republicans named Abraham Lincoln of Springfield, a former Whig state legislator, one-term congressman, and small-town lawyer. Born in a Kentucky log cabin in 1809 and raised on farms in Indiana and Illinois, the young Lincoln had the wit and will to rise above his coarse beginnings. With less than twelve months of sporadic schooling, he learned to read, studied such books as came to hand, and eventually developed a prose style as lean and muscular as the man himself. He worked at various farm tasks, operated a ferry, and made two trips down to New Orleans as a flatboatman. Striking out on his own, he managed a general store in New Salem, Illinois, learned surveying, served in the Black Hawk War in 1832, won election to the legislature in 1834 (at the age of twenty-five), read law, and was admitted to the bar in 1836.

Lincoln abhorred slavery but was no abolitionist. He did not believe the two races could coexist as equals. But he did oppose any further extension of slavery into new territories, assuming that over time it would die a "natural death." Slavery, he said in the 1840s, was a vexing but "minor question on its way to extinction." Lincoln stayed in the Illinois legislature until 1842 and in 1846 won a seat in Congress. After a single term he retired from active politics to cultivate his law practice in Springfield.

In 1854 the Kansas-Nebraska Act drew Lincoln back into the political arena. At first he held back from the rapidly growing Republicans, but in 1856 he joined the new party, and by 1858 he was the obvious Republican choice to oppose Douglas for the Senate. Candidate Lincoln resorted to the classic ploy of the underdog: he challenged the favorite to a debate. Douglas knew he was up against a formidable foe and had little relish for drawing attention to his opponent, but he agreed to meet Lincoln in seven sites around the state. The legendary Lincoln-Douglas debates took place that summer and fall. They attracted

Last Great Discussion.

Let all take notice, that on Friday next, Hon. S. A. Douglas and Hon. A. Lincoln, will hold the seventh and closing joint debate of the canvass at this place. We hope the country will turn out, to a man, to hear these gentlemen.

The following programme for the discussion has been decided upon by the Joint Committee appointed by the People's Party Club and the Democratic Club for that purpose.

Debate announcement

An announcement for the seventh and final Lincoln-Douglas debate.

thousands of spectators and transformed a contest for a Senate seat into a battle for the very future of the Republic.

The two men could not have presented a more striking contrast. Lincoln was well over six feet tall, sinewy and craggy featured with a long neck and deep-set, brooding eyes. Unassuming in manner, dressed in homely, well-worn clothes, and walking with a shambling gait, he lightened his essentially serious demeanor with a refreshing sense of humor. To sympathetic observers, Lincoln conveyed an air of simplicity, sincerity, and common sense. Douglas, on the other hand, was short, rotund, stern, and cocky, attired in the finest custom-tailored suits. A man of considerable abilities and even greater ambition, he strutted to the platform with the pugnacious air of a predestined champion. Douglas traveled to the debate sites in a private railroad car; Lincoln rode alone on his horse.

At the time and since, much attention focused on the second debate, at Freeport, where Lincoln asked Douglas how he could reconcile popular sovereignty with the *Dred Scott* ruling that citizens had the right to carry slaves into any territory. Douglas's answer, thenceforth known as the Freeport Doctrine, was to state the obvious: whatever the Supreme Court might say about slavery, it could not exist anywhere unless supported by local police regulations. Thus, if settlers did not want slavery, they should simply refuse to adopt a local code protecting it.

Douglas then tried to set some traps of his own. He accused Lincoln of advocating racial equality. Lincoln countered by affirming white supremacy. There was, he asserted, a "physical difference between the white and black races," and it would "forever forbid the two races living together on terms of social and political equality." Lincoln did insist that blacks had an "equal" right to freedom and the fruits of their labor. But the basic difference between the two men, Lincoln insisted, lay in Douglas's professed indifference to the moral question of slavery.

If Lincoln had the better of the argument, at least in the long view, Douglas had the better of a close election in traditionally Democratic Illinois. Across the country, however, Democrats did not fare as well in 1858. Most congressional candidates aligned with President Buchanan lost their elections, thus signaling in the North and the West the political shift toward the new Republican party and the politics of anti-slavery. At the same time that the political balance in the North was beginning to shift from the Democrats to the Republicans, political tensions over slavery were becoming more intractable—and violent. In 1858, members of Congress engaged in the largest brawl ever on the floor of the House of Representatives. Harsh words about slavery incited the melee, which involved more than fifty legislators shoving, punching, and wrestling one another as the hapless sergeant at arms tried futilely to restore order. The fracas culminated when John "Bowie Knife" Potter of Wisconsin yanked off the wig of a Mississippi congressman and claimed, "I've scalped him."

JOHN BROWN'S RAID The gradual return of prosperity in 1859 offered hope that the political storms of the 1850s might yet pass. But the sectional issue of slavery still haunted the nation, and like lightning on the horizon it warned that a storm was brewing. In 1859, John Brown surfaced again, this time in the East. Since the Pottawatomie Massacre in 1856, he had led a furtive existence, engaging in fund-raising, recruiting, and occasional bushwhacking. His commitment to abolish the "wicked curse of slavery" had intensified, meanwhile, to a fever pitch.

On October 16, 1859, Brown launched his supreme gesture. From a Maryland farm he crossed the Potomac River with about twenty men, including five blacks, and occupied the federal arsenal in Harpers Ferry, Virginia (now West Virginia). He intended to arm the Maryland slaves he assumed would flock to his cause, set up a black stronghold in the mountains of western Virginia, and provide a nucleus of support for slave insurrections across the South.

What Brown actually did was to take the arsenal by surprise, seize a few hostages, and hole up in the fire-engine house. There he and his band were quickly surrounded by militiamen and town residents. The next morning, Brown sent his son Watson and another supporter out under a white flag, but the enraged crowd shot them both. Intermittent shooting broke out, and another Brown son was wounded.

That night Lieutenant Colonel Robert E. Lee arrived with his aide, Lieutenant J. E. B. Stuart, and a force of U.S. marines. The following morning, October 18, Stuart and his troops broke down the barricaded doors and rushed into the fire-engine house. A young lieutenant found Brown kneeling with his rifle cocked. Before Brown could fire, however, the marine used the hilt of his sword to beat Brown unconscious. By then the siege was over. Altogether, Brown's men had killed four people (including one marine) and wounded nine. Of their own

John Brown

Although his anti-slavery efforts were based in Kansas, Brown was a native of Connecticut.

force, ten died (including two of Brown's sons), five escaped, and seven were captured.

Brown was quickly tried for treason, convicted, and sentenced to be hanged. "Let them hang me," he exulted. "I am worth inconceivably more to hang than for any other purpose." He was never more right. If Brown had failed in his purpose—whatever it was—he had succeeded in becoming a martyr to the anti-slavery cause, and he had set off a panic throughout the slaveholding South. At his sentencing he delivered a powerful speech: "Now, if it is deemed necessary that I should forfeit my life for the furtherance of the ends of justice, and mingle my blood further with the blood of my children and with the blood of millions in this slave country whose rights are disregarded by wicked, cruel, and unjust enactments, I say, let it be done."

When John Brown, still unflinching, met his end, northern sympathizers held solemn observances. "That new saint," Ralph Waldo Emerson predicted, " . . . will make the gallows glorious like the cross." William Lloyd Garrison, the lifelong pacifist, now wished "success to every slave insurrection at the South and in every slave country." By far the gravest effect of Brown's raid was to leave pro-slavery southerners in no mood to distinguish between John Brown and the Republican party. All through the fall and winter of 1859–1860, rumors of slave insurrections swept the region. Every northern visitor, commercial traveler, or schoolteacher came under suspicion, and many were driven out. "We regard every man in our midst an enemy to the institutions of the South," said an Atlanta newspaper editor, "who does not boldly declare that he believes African slavery to be a social, moral, and political blessing."

THE CENTER COMES APART

THE DEMOCRATS DIVIDE Amid the hysteria unleashed by John Brown's assault at Harpers Ferry, the nation approached a presidential election destined to be the most fateful in its history. The Democrats gathered in Charleston, South Carolina, for their 1860 convention. Stephen Douglas's supporters reaffirmed the platform of 1856, which simply promised congressional noninterference with slavery. Southern firebrands, however, now demanded a federal law protecting slavery in the territories. Buchanan supporters, hoping to stop Douglas, encouraged the strategy. When the southern planks lost in the ensuing debate, Alabama's delegation walked out of the convention, followed by delegates representing most of the other southern states. The convention then decided to leave the overwrought atmosphere of

PROGRESSIVE DEMOCRACY—PROSPECT OF A SMASH UP.

"Prospect of a Smash Up" (1860)

This cartoon shows the Democratic party—the last remaining national party—about to be split by sectional differences and the onrush of Republicans, led by Abraham Lincoln.

Charleston and reassemble in Baltimore on June 18. The Baltimore convention finally nominated Douglas. The Charleston seceders met first in Richmond and then in Baltimore, where they adopted the slave-code platform defeated in Charleston and nominated Vice President John C. Breckinridge of Kentucky for president. Another cord of union had snapped: the last remaining national party had fractured.

LINCOLN'S ELECTION   The Republicans, meanwhile, gathered in Chicago in the summer of 1860. There everything suddenly came together for Abraham Lincoln, the uncommon common man. He had emerged on the national scene during his unsuccessful senatorial campaign two years before and had since taken a stance on the containment of slavery strong enough to satisfy the abolitionists yet moderate enough to seem less threatening than they were.

Lincoln won the Republican nomination on the third ballot. The party platform denounced John Brown's raid as "among the gravest of crimes" and affirmed that each state should "control its own domestic institutions." The party repeated its resistance to the extension of slavery and, in an effort to gain broader support, endorsed a higher protective tariff for manufacturers, free homesteads on federal lands, a more liberal naturalization law for immigrants, and internal improvements, including a transcontinental railroad. With this platform, Republicans made a strong appeal to eastern businessmen, western farmers, and the large immigrant population.

Both major party conventions revealed that opinions about slavery tended to become more radical in the Upper North and the Deep South. Attitude seemed to follow latitude. In the border states between North and South—Missouri, Kentucky, Delaware, and Maryland—a sense of moderation aroused the die-hard Whigs there to make one more try at reconciliation. Meeting in Baltimore a week before the Republicans met in Chicago, they organized the Constitutional Union party and named John Bell of Tennessee for president. Their platform simply called for the preservation of the Constitution and the Union.

None of the four candidates generated a national following, and the campaign devolved into a choice between Lincoln and Douglas in the North, Breckinridge and Bell in the South. One consequence of these campaigns was that each section gained a false impression of the other. The South never learned to distinguish Lincoln from the militant abolitionists; the North failed to gauge the force of southern intransigence. Lincoln stubbornly refused to offer the South assurances or to explain his position on slavery, which he insisted was a matter of public record.

The one man who tried to break through the barrier that was falling between the North and the South was Douglas, who attempted to mount a national campaign. Only forty-seven but already weakened by excessive drink, ill health, and disappointments, he wore himself out in one final, glorious campaign. Down through the hostile areas of Tennessee, Georgia, and Alabama, he carried appeals on behalf of the Union.

By midnight on November 6, however, Lincoln's victory was clear. In the final count he had about 39 percent of the total popular vote but a clear electoral majority, with 180 votes in the Electoral College. He carried all eighteen free states by a wide margin. Among all the candidates only Douglas had electoral votes from both slave and free states, but his total of 12 was but a pitiful remnant of Democratic unionism. Bell took Virginia, Kentucky, and Tennessee, and Breckinridge swept the other slave states to come in second with 72 electoral votes.

SECESSION OF THE DEEP SOUTH Lincoln's election panicked southerners. Soon after the election, South Carolina set a special election for December 6 to choose delegates to a state convention. In Charleston on December 20, 1860, the convention unanimously endorsed an Ordinance of Secession, repealed the state's ratification of the Constitution, and severed its ties to the Union. By February 1, 1861, Mississippi, Florida, Alabama, Georgia, Louisiana, and Texas had declared themselves out of the Union. On February 4 a convention of those seven states met in Montgomery, Alabama, where it adopted a provisional constitution for a new nation, the Confederate States

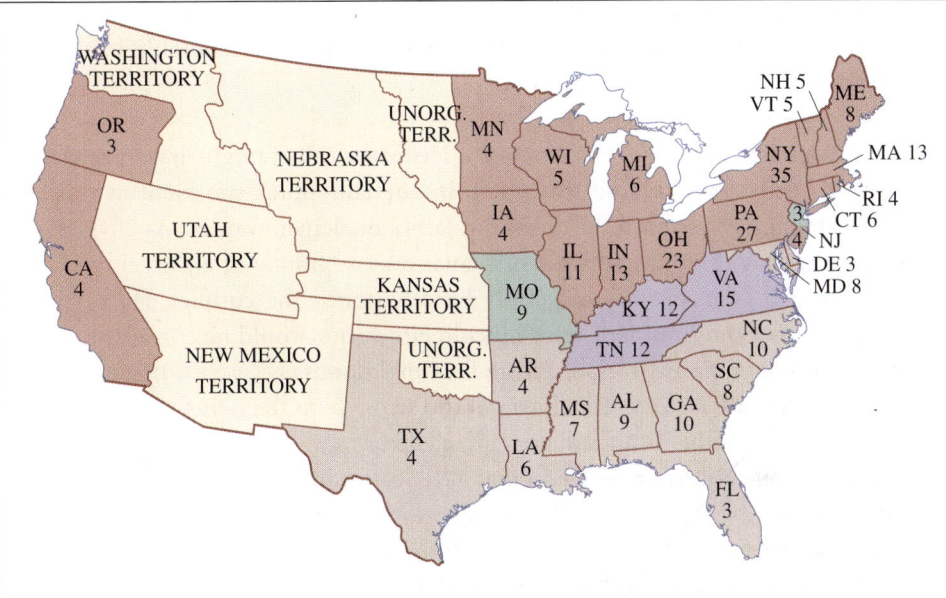

THE ELECTION OF 1860	Electoral Vote	Popular Vote
Abraham Lincoln (Republican)	**180**	**1,866,000**
Stephen A. Douglas (Democrat—northern)	12	1,383,000
John C. Breckinridge (Democrat—southern)	72	848,000
John Bell (Constitutional Union)	39	593,000

What caused the division in the Democratic party? How did Abraham Lincoln position himself to win the Republican nomination? What were the major factors that led to Lincoln's electoral victory?

of America. Two days later the delegates elected Jefferson Davis as its president. He was inaugurated on February 18, with Alexander Stephens of Georgia as vice president.

In all seven states of the southernmost tier, a solid majority had voted for secessionist convention delegates, but their combined vote would not have been a majority of the presidential vote in November. What happened, it seemed, was what often happens in revolutionary situations: a determined and decisive minority acted quickly in an emotionally charged climate and carried its program over the weak objections of a confused and indecisive opposition. Trying to decide whether a majority of southern whites favored secession is probably beside the point—a majority was vulnerable to the decisive action of the secessionists.

BUCHANAN'S WAITING GAME   History is full of might-have-beens. A bold stroke, even a bold statement, by the lame-duck president at this point might have defused the crisis, but James Buchanan waffled. As Ulysses S. Grant recognized, the feckless Buchanan was a "granny of an Executive." Besides, a bold stroke might simply have hastened the conflict. No bold stroke came from president-elect Lincoln either, nor would he consult with the Buchanan administration during the long months before his inauguration on March 4, 1861. He inclined all too strongly to the belief that secession was just another bluff and kept his silence.

In his annual message on December 3, 1860, President Buchanan declared that secession was illegal but that he lacked the constitutional authority to coerce a state to rejoin the Union. "Seldom have we known so strong an argument come to so lame and impotent a conclusion," the *Cincinnati Enquirer* editorialized. There was, however, a hidden weapon in the president's reaffirmation of a duty to "take care that the laws be faithfully executed" insofar as he was able. If the president could enforce the law upon all citizens, he would have no need to "coerce" a state. Indeed, Buchanan's position became the policy of the Lincoln administration, which fought a war on the theory that individuals, but not states, were in rebellion.

Buchanan held firm to his resolve, with some slight stiffening by the end of 1860, when secession became a fact, but he refrained from forceful action. On the day after Christmas, the small federal garrison at Charleston's Fort Moultrie had been moved into the nearly completed Fort Sumter by Major Robert Anderson, a Kentucky Unionist. South Carolina authorities exploded at this provocative act. Commissioners of the newly "independent" state demanded withdrawal of all federal forces, but they had overplayed their hand. Buchanan sharply rejected the South Carolina ultimatum to withdraw and dispatched a steamer, *Star of the West,* to Fort Sumter with reinforcements and provisions. On January 9, as the ship approached Charleston Harbor, Confederate batteries at Fort Moultrie and Morris Island opened fire and drove it away. It was in fact an act of war, but Buchanan chose to ignore the challenge. He decided instead to wait out the remaining weeks of his term, hoping against hope that one of several compromise efforts would yet prove fruitful.

FINAL EFFORTS AT COMPROMISE   Desperate efforts at a compromise that would avoid a civil war continued in Congress until dawn on the day of Lincoln's inauguration. On December 18, 1860, Senator John J. Crittenden of Kentucky had proposed a series of resolutions that recognized slavery in the territories south of 36°30′ and guaranteed the maintenance of slavery where it already existed. The fight for a compromise was carried to the floor of each house of Congress and subjected to intensive but inconclusive debate during January and February.

Meanwhile, a peace conference met in a Washington hotel in February 1861. Twenty-one states sent delegates, and former president John Tyler presided, but the convention's proposal, substantially the same as the Crittenden Compromise, failed to win the support of either house of Congress. The only proposal that met with any success was an amendment guaranteeing slavery where it existed. Many Republicans, including Lincoln, were prepared to go that far to save the Union, but they were unwilling to repudiate their stand against slavery in the territories. As it happened, after passing the House, the amendment passed the Senate without a vote to spare, 24 to 12, on the dawn of inauguration day. It would have become the Thirteenth Amendment, with the first use of the word *slavery* in the Constitution, but the states never ratified it. When a Thirteenth Amendment was ratified, in 1865, it did not guarantee slavery—it abolished it.

End of Chapter Review

CHAPTER SUMMARY

- **Free-Soil Coalition** David Wilmot's declaration that the Mexican territories had been free and therefore should remain so attracted a broad coalition of Americans, including many northern Democrats and anti-slavery Whigs, as well as members of new Liberty party. Like the Wilmot Privoso, the Free-Soil party demanded that slavery not be expanded to the territories.

- **California Statehood** Californians wanted their territory to enter the Union as a free state. Southerners feared that they would loose federal protection of their "peculiar institution" if more free states than slave states emerged. Whereas Senator John C. Calhoun maintained that slavery could not constitutionally be banned in any of the territories, anti-slavery forces demanded that all the territories remain free.

- **Compromise of 1850** It had been agreed that popular sovereignty would settle the status of the territories, but when the territories applied for statehood, the debate over slavery was renewed. The Compromise of 1850 was the result of the impassioned debate over whether to allow slavery in the areas gained from Mexico, which had banned slavery. By the Compromise of 1850, California entered the Union as a free state, the territories of Texas, New Mexico, and Utah were established without direct reference to slavery, the slave trade (but not slavery itself) was banned in Washington, D.C., and a new, stronger fugitive slave act was passed.

- **Kansas-Nebraska Act** The proposal to overturn the Missouri Compromise by opening to slavery the territories north of 36°30′ outraged the nation's growing anti-slavery faction. The Kansas-Nebraska Act destroyed the Whig party, limited the influence of the Democrats, and led to the creation of the Republican party, which absorbed many Free-Soilers and Know-Nothings.

- **Southern Secession** The Democrats' split into northern and southern factions contributed to the success of Abraham Lincoln and the new Republican party in the election of 1860. The Republicans' victory was the immediate cause of secession. Southerners, reeling from John Brown's raid at Harpers Ferry, equated anti-slavery violence with the Republican party. More important, the Republican victory showed that the South no longer had enough votes in Congress to protect its "peculiar institution."

CHRONOLOGY

1848	Free-Soil party is organized
	California gold rush begins
1852	Harriet Beecher Stowe's *Uncle Tom's Cabin* is published
1853	With the Gadsden Purchase, the United States acquires 30,000 square miles from Mexico
1854	President Pierce's administration disavows the Ostend Manifesto, in which the United States declared its intention to seize Cuba from Spain
	Congress passes the Kansas-Nebraska Act
	The Republican party emerges
1856	A pro-slavery mob sacks Lawrence, Kansas; John Brown stages the Pottawatomie Massacre in retaliation
	Charles Sumner of Massachusetts is caned and seriously injured by a pro-slavery congressman in the U.S. Senate
1857	U.S. Supreme Court issues the *Dred Scott* decision
	Lecompton Constitution declares that slavery will be allowed in Kansas
1858	Abraham Lincoln debates Stephen A. Douglas during the 1858 Illinois Senate race
October 1859	John Brown and his followers stage a raid at Harpers Ferry, Virginia, in an attempt to incite a massive slave insurrection
December 1860	South Carolina secedes from the Union
	Crittenden Compromise is proposed

KEY TERMS & NAMES

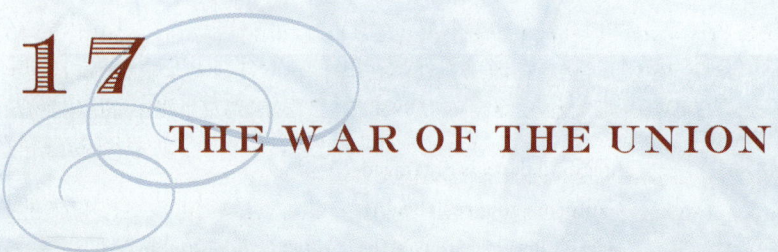

17

THE WAR OF THE UNION

FOCUS QUESTIONS   wwnorton.com/studyspace

- What events led to the firing of the first shots of the Civil War?
- What were the major strategies of the Civil War?
- How did the war affect the home front in both the North and the South?
- What were the reasons for the Emancipation Proclamation?
- How did most enslaved people become free in the United States?

In mid-February 1861, President-elect Abraham Lincoln left Springfield, Illinois, and began a long, roundabout rail trip to Washington, D.C. At the end of the journey, reluctantly yielding to warnings of a plot to assassinate him, he secretly passed through Baltimore in the middle of the night and slipped into Washington before daybreak. As Lincoln prepared to take office and the possibility of civil war captured the attention of a divided nation, no one imagined the horrendous scope and intensity of the conflict that was to come. On both sides, people believed that any fighting would be over quickly and that their daily lives would go on as usual.

END OF THE WAITING GAME

LINCOLN AND SECESSION   In his inaugural address on March 4, 1861, Lincoln reassured southerners that he had no intention of interfering with "slavery in the States where it exists." But secession was another matter.

He insisted that the "Union of these States is perpetual," and he promised to "hold, occupy, and possess" and defend facilities and forts belonging to the federal government. He concluded with an appeal for harmony, saying: "We are not enemies, but friends. We must not be enemies. Though passion may have strained, it must not break our bonds of affection."

The momentum of secession took control of events, however. The day after the inauguration, word arrived from South Carolina that time was running out at the federal garrison at Fort Sumter in Charleston harbor. The commander, Major Robert Anderson, had enough supplies for only a month, and the fort was surrounded by a Confederate "ring of fire." On April 4, Lincoln decided to resupply Anderson's garrison. Hoping to avoid a confrontation, he informed the governor of South Carolina that he was sending provisions but no ammunition or soldiers. The Confederate government wanted a showdown, however, and it ordered the Confederate general Pierre G. T. Beauregard to demand that his former West Point professor surrender Fort Sumter. Anderson refused, and just before dawn on April 12, Confederate cannons opened fire. After thirty-three hours, Anderson, his ammunition exhausted, surrendered.

The attack on Fort Sumter signaled the end of the tense waiting game. On April 15, Lincoln issued a war proclamation calling upon the loyal states to supply 75,000 militiamen to put down the rebellion. Volunteers in both the North and the South crowded into recruiting stations, and huge new armies

War begins

An interior view of the ruins of Fort Sumter.

began to form. On April 19, Lincoln proclaimed a naval blockade of southern ports, which, as the Supreme Court later ruled, confirmed the existence
of a state of war.

TAKING SIDES   Lincoln's war proclamation led four states of the Upper
South to join the Confederacy: Virginia, Arkansas, Tennessee, and North
Carolina. Each had areas (mainly in the mountains) where both slaves and
secessionists were scarce and Union sentiment ran strong. In fact, Unionists
in western Virginia, bolstered by a Union army from Ohio under General
George B. McClellan, formed a new state. In 1863, Congress admitted West
Virginia into the Union with a state constitution that provided for emanci-
pation of the few slaves there.

Of the other slave states, Delaware remained firmly in the Union, but Maryland, Kentucky, and Missouri went through bitter struggles to decide which
side to support. The secession of Maryland would have encircled Washington,
D.C., with Confederate states. To hold on to the crucial state, Lincoln took
drastic measures: he suspended the writ of habeas corpus (under which judges
can require arresting officers to produce their prisoners and justify their arrest) and jailed pro-Confederate leaders. The fall elections ended the threat of
Maryland's secession by returning a solidly Unionist majority in the state.

Kentucky, native state of both Abraham Lincoln and Jefferson Davis, harbored divided loyalties. Its fragile neutrality lasted until September 3, 1861,
when a Confederate force captured several towns. General Ulysses S. Grant
then moved Union troops into Paducah. Thereafter, Kentucky for the most
part remained with the Union. It joined the Confederacy, some have said,
only after the war.

Virginian Robert E. Lee's decision to join the Confederacy epitomized the
agonizing choice facing many Americans in 1861. The son of a Revolutionary
War hero, Lee had graduated second in his class from the U.S. Military Academy at West Point, had fought with distinction during the Mexican War, and
had served in the U.S. Army for thirty years. When Fort Sumter was attacked,
he was summoned by Lincoln's seventy-five-year-old general in chief, Winfield Scott, another Virginian, and offered command of the Union forces. After a sleepless night spent pacing the floor, he told Scott he could not go
against his "country," meaning Virginia. Although Lee failed to "see the good
of secession," he could not "raise my hand against my birthplace, my home,
my children." So Lee resigned his U.S. Army commission, retired to his estate,
and soon answered a call to command the Virginia—later the Confederate—
military forces.

On the other hand, many southerners made great sacrifices to remain loyal to the Union. Some left their native region once the fighting began. Others remained in the South but found ways to support the Union. In every Confederate state except South Carolina, whole regiments were organized to fight for the Union, and at least 100,000 men from the southern states fought against the Confederacy. Many of the southern loyalists were Irish or German immigrants who had no love for slavery or the planter elite. Whatever their motives, they and other southern loyalists played a significant role in helping the Union cause.

NORTHERN AND SOUTHERN ADVANTAGES The South seceded in part out of a growing awareness of its minority status in the nation: a balance sheet of the regions in 1861 shows the accuracy of that perception. The

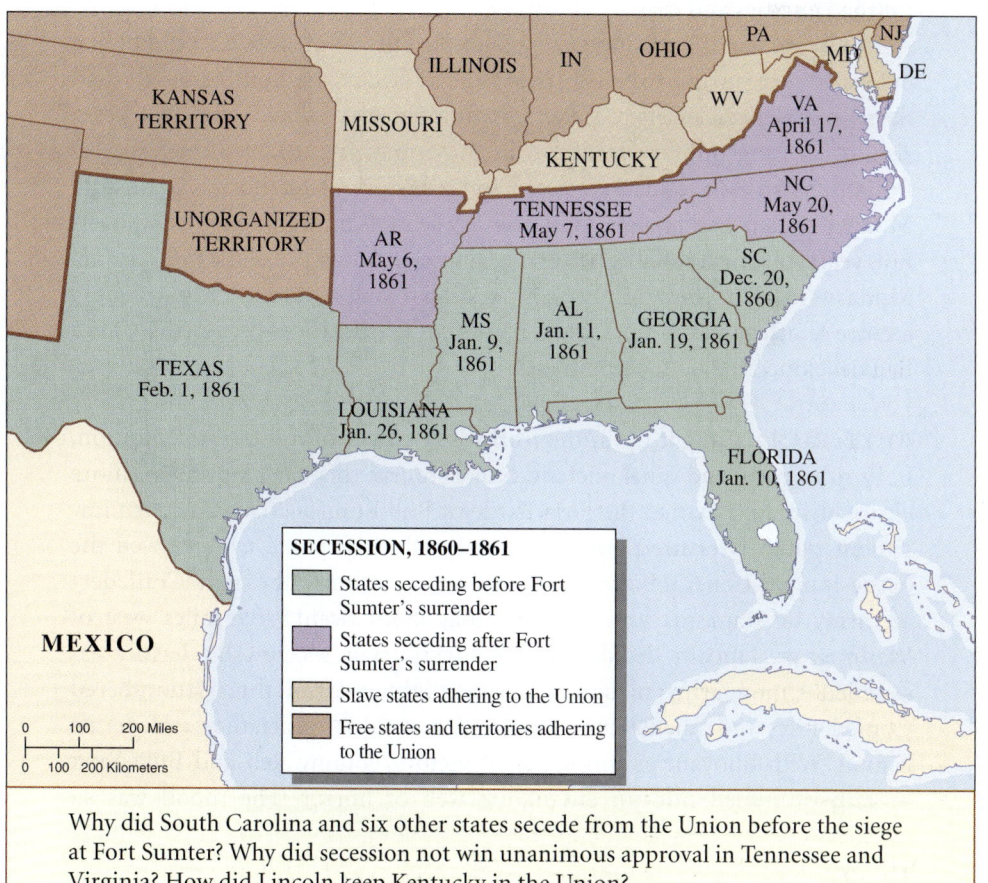

SECESSION, 1860–1861

- States seceding before Fort Sumter's surrender
- States seceding after Fort Sumter's surrender
- Slave states adhering to the Union
- Free states and territories adhering to the Union

Why did South Carolina and six other states secede from the Union before the siege at Fort Sumter? Why did secession not win unanimous approval in Tennessee and Virginia? How did Lincoln keep Kentucky in the Union?

Union held twenty-three states, including four border slave states, while the Confederacy had eleven. The population count was about 22 million in the Union to 9 million in the Confederacy, and about 4 million of the latter were enslaved African Americans. The Union therefore had an edge of about four to one in human resources. To help redress the imbalance, the Confederacy mobilized 80 percent of its military-age white men, a third of whom would die during the prolonged war.

An even greater advantage for the North was its industry. The states that joined the Confederacy produced just 7 percent of the nation's manufactures on the eve of the war. The Union states produced 97 percent of the firearms and 96 percent of the railroad equipment. The North's advantage in transportation weighed heavily as the war went on. The Union had more wagons, horses, and ships than the Confederacy and an impressive edge in railroad engines and cars.

The South had the advantage of geography: the Confederates could fight a defensive war on their own territory. In addition, the South initially had more experienced military leaders. A number of circumstances had given rise to a strong military tradition in the South: frequent skirmishes with Indians, fear of slave insurrections, and a history of territorial expansion. Military careers had prestige, and military schools multiplied in the antebellum years, the most notable being the Citadel in South Carolina and Virginia Military Institute. West Point itself had drawn many southerners, producing a cadre of officers from the region. By the end of the war, however, the Union had developed the better commanders.

BULL RUN   Caught up in the frothy excitement of military preparation, both sides predicted quick victory. Nowhere was this naive optimism more clearly displayed than at the First Battle of Bull Run (or Manassas).*An impatient public pressured both sides to attack. Jefferson Davis allowed the battle-hungry General Pierre G. T. Beauregard to hurry the main Confederate army to Manassas Junction, Virginia, about twenty-five miles west of Washington. Lincoln decided that General Irvin McDowell's hastily assembled Union army of some 37,000 might overrun the outnumbered Confederates and quickly march on to Richmond, Virginia, the Confederate capital. With buoyant assumptions of victory, Johnny Reb and Billy Yank breezily stumbled into an entangling web of horror. The mood was so

---

*The Union most often named battles for natural features; the Confederacy, for nearby towns—thus Bull Run (Manassas), Antietam (Sharpsburg), Stones River (Murfreesboro), and the like.

Union soldiers at Harpers Ferry, Virginia, in 1862

Neither side in the Civil War was prepared for the magnitude of this first "modern" war.

breezy, in fact, that hundreds of civilians had ridden out from Washington to picnic and watch the entertaining spectacle of what they thought would be a one-battle war. Instead, they witnessed a chaotic defeat.

It was a hot, dry day on July 21, 1861, when General McDowell's raw recruits encountered Beauregard's army dug in behind a meandering, log-strewn stream called Bull Run. The two generals, former classmates at West Point, adopted markedly similar plans: each would try to turn the other's left flank. The Union forces almost achieved their purpose early in the afternoon, but Confederate reinforcements, led by General Joseph E. Johnston, poured in to check the Union offensive. Amid the fury a South Carolina general rallied his men by pointing to Thomas Jackson's brigade: "Look! there is Jackson with his Virginians, standing like a stone wall!" The analogy captured Jackson's fortitude, and the general was called "Stonewall" thereafter.

Their attack blunted, the exhausted northern troops eventually broke, and their frantic retreat turned into a panic as fleeing soldiers and terrified civilians clogged the Washington road. Lincoln read a gloomy dispatch from the front: "The day is lost. Save Washington and the remnants of this army. The routed troops will not re-form." Stonewall Jackson had hoped to pursue the fleeing Union troops into Washington. But the Confederates were almost as disorganized and exhausted as the Yankees, and they failed to give chase. The Battle of Bull Run was a sobering experience for both sides. Much of the romance—the splendid uniforms, bright flags, fervent songs—gave way to the agonizing realization that this would be a long, costly struggle.

The War's Early Course

The Battle of Bull Run demonstrated that the war would not be decided with one sudden stroke. General Winfield Scott had predicted as much, and now Lincoln fell back upon the three-pronged "anaconda" strategy that Scott had proposed. It called first for the Union Army of the Potomac to defend Washington D.C., and exert constant pressure on the Confederate capital at Richmond. At the same time the navy would blockade the southern coast and dry up the Confederacy's access to foreign goods and weapons. The final component of the plan would divide the Confederacy by sending navy gunboats and transports to invade the South along the main water routes: the Mississippi, Tennessee, and Cumberland Rivers. Although newspapers derided the anaconda strategy as far too slow, indicative of General Scott's old age and caution, it was intended to entwine and crush the southern resistance, like an anaconda strangling its prey.

The Confederate strategy was simpler. If the Union forces could be stalemated, Jefferson Davis and others hoped, then the British or the French might be persuaded to join their cause, or perhaps public sentiment in the North would force Lincoln to seek a negotiated settlement. So at the same time that armies were forming in the South, Confederate diplomats were seeking assistance in London and Paris, and Confederate sympathizers in the North were urging an end to the North's war effort.

NAVAL ACTIONS   After the Battle of Bull Run and for the rest of 1861 and early 1862, the most important military actions involved naval war and a Union blockade of key southern ports. The Union navy never completely sealed off the South, but it greatly constricted the flow of goods and supplies into the region. The one great threat to the Union navy proved to be short-lived. The Confederates in Norfolk, Virginia, had fashioned an ironclad ship from an abandoned Union steam frigate, the *Merrimack*. Rechristened the *Virginia*, it ventured out on March 8, 1862, and wrought havoc among the Union ships at the entrance to Chesapeake Bay. But as luck would have it, a new Union ironclad, the *Monitor*, arrived from New York in time to engage the *Virginia* the next day. They fought to a draw, and the *Virginia* returned to port, where the Confederates destroyed it when they had to give up Norfolk soon afterward. Thereafter the North tightened its grip on southern ports. The navy extended its bases down the Carolina coast in the late summer and fall of 1862. In the spring of 1862, Admiral David Farragut's ships forced open the lower Mississippi River, captured New Orleans, and took Baton Rouge upriver.

FORMING ARMIES   While the Union navy was blockading southern ports and building new ships, the armies on both sides were recruiting men to form regiments to fight the land battles of the war. After Lincoln's initial call for 75,000 ninety-day militiamen, Congress enlisted 500,000 more men, and after the Battle of Bull Run it added another 500,000. The typical nineteenth-century army often organized its units along community and ethnic lines. The Union army, for example, included a Scandinavian regiment (the 15th Wisconsin Infantry), a Highland Scots unit (the 79th New York Infantry), a French regiment (the 55th New York Infantry), and a mixed unit of Poles, Hungarians, Germans, Spaniards, and Italians (the 39th New York Infantry).

In the Confederacy, Jefferson Davis initially requested 100,000 twelve-month volunteers. Once the fighting started, he was authorized to raise

The U.S. Army recruiting office in City Hall Park, New York City

The sign advertises the money offered to those willing to serve: $677 to new recruits, $777 to veteran soldiers, and $15 to anyone who brought in a recruit.

up to 400,000 three-year volunteers. By early 1862 most of the veteran Confederate soldiers were nearing the end of their enlistment without having encountered much significant action. They were also resisting the bonuses and furloughs offered as incentives for reenlistment. The Confederate government then turned to conscription. On April 16, 1862, all white male citizens aged eighteen to thirty-five were declared members of the army for three years, and those already in service were required to serve out three years. In 1862 the upper age was raised to forty-five, and in 1864 the age limit was further extended from seventeen to fifty, with those under eighteen and over forty-five reserved for state defense.

The conscription law included two loopholes, however. First, a draftee might escape service either by providing an able-bodied substitute who was not of draft age or by paying $500 in cash. Second, exemptions, designed to protect key civilian work, were subject to abuse by men seeking "bomb-proof" jobs. The exemption of one white man for each plantation with twenty or more slaves led to bitter complaints about "a rich man's war and a poor man's fight."

New York Sprouts Violence

picked out, shot, and fell dead in the midst of his imprecations and threats. Some four or five hundred rioters were killed by the military. Victims of the mob numbered eight-

ATTENTION!

By Resolution of a large Meeting of the Merchants and Bankers of New York, held at two o'clock, at the Merchants' Exchange. Merchants are requested to close their Stores, and meet with their Employees on South side of Wall St., for immediate organization.

July 14, 2 P. M.

Call for merchants and clerks to defend their shops during the Draft Riots, 1863.

een, eleven of whom were colored men who were strung up to lamp posts and either shot or strangled to death. About fifty buildings were burned and destroyed, and the property

Draft riots

This broadside called upon storeowners to defend their shops during the New York draft riots of 1863.

The Union took nearly another year to begin drafting men into service. In 1863 the government began to draft men aged twenty to forty-five. Exemptions were granted to specified federal and state officeholders and to others on medical or compassionate grounds. By paying $300, one could avoid service. Conscription spurred men to volunteer, either to collect bounties or to avoid the disgrace of being drafted.

Widespread public opposition to the draft impeded its enforcement in the North and the South. In New York City the announcement of a draft lottery on July 11, 1863, incited a week of rioting in which roving bands of working-class toughs took control of the streets. Although provoked by opposition to the draft, the riots were fueled by racial and ethnic tensions. The mobs, mostly Irish Catholic immigrants, directed their wrath most furiously at African Americans. They blamed blacks for causing the war and for threatening to take their own unskilled jobs. Over 100 people died before soldiers brought from Gettysburg, Pennsylvania, restored order.

CONFEDERATE DIPLOMACY While the Union and Confederate armies mobilized, Confederated diplomacy focused on gaining help from foreign governments in the form of supplies, formal recognition, and perhaps even armed intervention. The first Confederate emissaries to England and France took hope when the British foreign minister received them after their arrival in London in 1861. In Paris, Napoléon III even promised them that he would recognize the Confederacy if Britain would lead the way. When the agents returned to London, however, the government refused to see them, partly because of Union pressure and partly out of British self-interest.

Confederate negotiators were far more successful in getting European supplies than in gaining official recognition as a new nation. The most spectacular feat was the procurement of raiding ships. Although British law prohibited the sale of warships to belligerents, a southern agent was able to have ships built in Britain and then, on trial runs, escape to be outfitted with guns. In all, eighteen such ships were activated and saw action in the Atlantic, Pacific, and Indian Oceans, where they sank hundreds of Union ships and instilled terror in the rest.

THE WEST AND THE CIVIL WAR During the Civil War western settlement continued. New discoveries of gold and silver in eastern California and in Montana and Colorado lured thousands of prospectors and their suppliers. Dakota, Colorado, and Nevada gained territorial status in 1861, Idaho and Arizona in 1863, and Montana in 1864. Silver-rich Nevada gained its statehood in 1864.

With the firing on Fort Sumter, many of the regular army units assigned to frontier outposts in the West began to head east to meet the Confederate threat. Texas was the only western state to join the Confederacy. For the most part, the federal government maintained its control of the western territories during the war.

Many Indian tribes found themselves caught up in the war. Indian regiments fought on both sides, and in the Indian Territory they fought against each other. Indians among the "Five Civilized Tribes" held African American slaves and felt a natural bond with southern whites. Oklahoma's proximity to Texas influenced the Choctaws and Chickasaws to support the Confederacy. The Cherokees, Creeks, and Seminoles were more divided in their loyalties.

ACTIONS IN THE WESTERN THEATER   Little military activity happened in the eastern theater (east of the Appalachian Mountains) before May 1862. The western theater (from the Appalachian Mountains to the Mississippi River), on the other hand, flared up with several clashes and an important penetration of the Confederate states. In western Kentucky the Confederate general Albert Sidney Johnston, a strapping Texan whom Davis considered the South's best general, had perhaps 40,000 men stretched over some 150 miles.

Early in 1862, General Ulysses S. Grant made the first Union thrust against the weak center of Johnston's overextended lines. Grant had graduated from West Point in the lower half of his class and in 1854 had resigned from the army in disgrace for drunkenness. Volunteering to serve in the Union army in 1861, he was assigned as an officer in the western theater. Moving out of Cairo, Illinois, and Paducah, Kentucky, with a gunboat flotilla, Grant swung southward up the Tennessee River and captured Fort Henry in northern Tennessee on February 6. He then moved overland to attack Fort Donelson and on February 16 captured its 12,000 men. Grant's blunt demand of "immediate and unconditional surrender" and his quick success sent a thrill through the dispirited North. The short, slouching, disheveled Grant was now a national hero—but would not be for long.

SHILOH   After defeats in Kentucky and Tennessee, Confederate forces gathered in Corinth, Mississippi, in hopes of retaking control of the Mississippi River valley. As Grant moved his forces southward along the Tennessee River during the early spring of 1862, he made a costly mistake. While planning his attack on Corinth, he clumsily placed his troops on a rolling plateau between two creeks and failed to dig defensive trenches. General Albert Johnston shrewdly recognized Grant's oversight, and on the morning of April 6 the Confederate leader ordered an attack on the vulnerable Union soldiers.

The 44,000 Confederates struck suddenly at Shiloh, the site of a log church in the center of the Union camp in southwestern Tennessee. They found most of Grant's troops still sleeping or eating breakfast. Some died in their bedrolls. After a day of bloody carnage and confusion, Grant's men were pinned against the river. They may well have been annihilated had General Johnston not been mortally wounded at the peak of the battle; his second in command called off the attack. Grant and a brilliant general from Ohio, William Tecumseh Sherman, rallied their troops. Reinforcements arrived that night during a torrential rainstorm, and the next day Grant took the offensive. The Confederates glumly withdrew to Corinth, leaving the Union

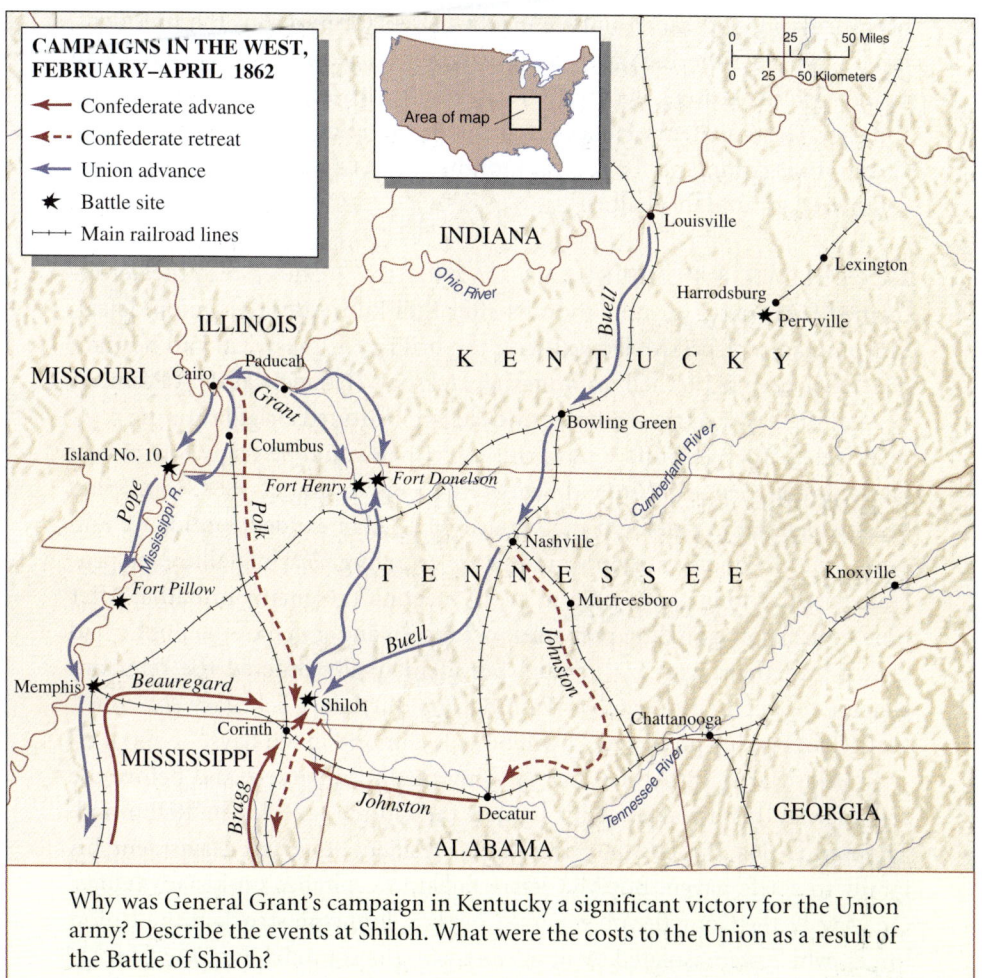

CAMPAIGNS IN THE WEST, FEBRUARY–APRIL 1862

Confederate advance
Confederate retreat
Union advance
Battle site
Main railroad lines

Area of map

0 25 50 Miles
0 25 50 Kilometers

INDIANA

Louisville
Lexington
Harrodsburg
Perryville

ILLINOIS

MISSOURI   Cairo   Paducah

K   E   N   T   U   C   K   Y

Grant

Island No. 10   Columbus

Bowling Green

Ohio River   Buell   Cumberland River

Pope

Fort Henry   Fort Donelson

Mississippi R.   Polk

Nashville

Fort Pillow

T   E   N   N   E   S   S   E   E   Knoxville

Murfreesboro

Memphis   Beauregard   Buell   Johnston

Shiloh
Corinth   Chattanooga

MISSISSIPPI   Bragg

Johnston   Decatur   Tennessee River   GEORGIA

ALABAMA

Why was General Grant's campaign in Kentucky a significant victory for the Union army? Describe the events at Shiloh. What were the costs to the Union as a result of the Battle of Shiloh?

army too battered to pursue. Throughout the Civil War, winning armies would fail to pursue their retreating foe, thus allowing the wounded opponent to slip away and fight again.

Shiloh, a Hebrew word meaning "Place of Peace," was the costliest battle in American history up to that point, although worse was to come. Combined casualties of nearly 20,000 exceeded the total dead and wounded of the Revolution, the War of 1812, and the Mexican War. After Shiloh, Confederate and Union leaders realized there would not be a quick end to the war. Moreover, after this battle the Union lost for a while the leadership of its finest general. Grant had blundered badly. Some critics charged that he had been drinking and called upon Lincoln to replace him. But the president, faced with the dithering of his other generals (especially George McClellan in the eastern theater), declined: "I can't spare this man; he fights." Grant's superior, General Henry Halleck, was not as forgiving, however. He relieved Grant of his command for several months, and as a result the Union thrust southward ground to a halt.

MCCLELLAN'S PENINSULAR CAMPAIGN   The eastern theater remained fairly quiet for nine months after Bull Run. After the Union defeat, Lincoln had replaced McDowell with the brilliant if theatrical and hesitant general George B. McClellan, Stonewall Jackson's classmate at West Point. As head of the Army of the Potomac, McClellan instituted a rigid training regimen, determined to build a powerful force that would be ready for its next battle. When General Winfield Scott retired in November 1861, McClellan became general in chief. On the surface, McClellan exuded confidence and poise, but his innate caution would prove crippling. Fearing failure, he procrastinated as long as possible to avoid meeting the enemy in battle. After nine months of agonizing preparation, Lincoln and much of the public had grown impatient. The exasperated president finally ordered the reluctant general to begin moving by Washington's Birthday, February 22, 1862. McClellan brashly predicted, "I will be in Richmond in ten days."

In mid-March 1862, McClellan's army finally embarked, and before the end of May his advance units sighted the church steeples in Richmond. Thousands fled the city in panic, and President Jefferson Davis sent his family to a safe haven. But McClellan failed to capitalize on his advantage. On May 31 the Confederate general Joseph E. Johnston struck at the Union forces, which were isolated by floodwaters on the south bank of the Chickahominy River. In the Battle of Seven Pines (Fair Oaks), only the arrival of reinforcements prevented a disastrous Union defeat. Both sides took heavy casualties, and Johnston was severely wounded.

At this point the fifty-five-year-old Robert E. Lee assumed command of the Army of Northern Virginia, changing the course of the war. Tall, erect, and broad shouldered, Lee was a dashing, daring leader. Unlike Johnston he enjoyed Jefferson Davis's trust, and he assembled a galaxy of superb field commanders: Stonewall Jackson, James Longstreet, D. H. Hill, Ambrose P. Hill, and J. E. B. Stuart.

Once in command, Lee assaulted the Union forces east of Richmond on June 26, 1862. But heavy losses prevented the Confederates from sustaining their momentum. Lee launched a final desperate attack at Malvern Hill

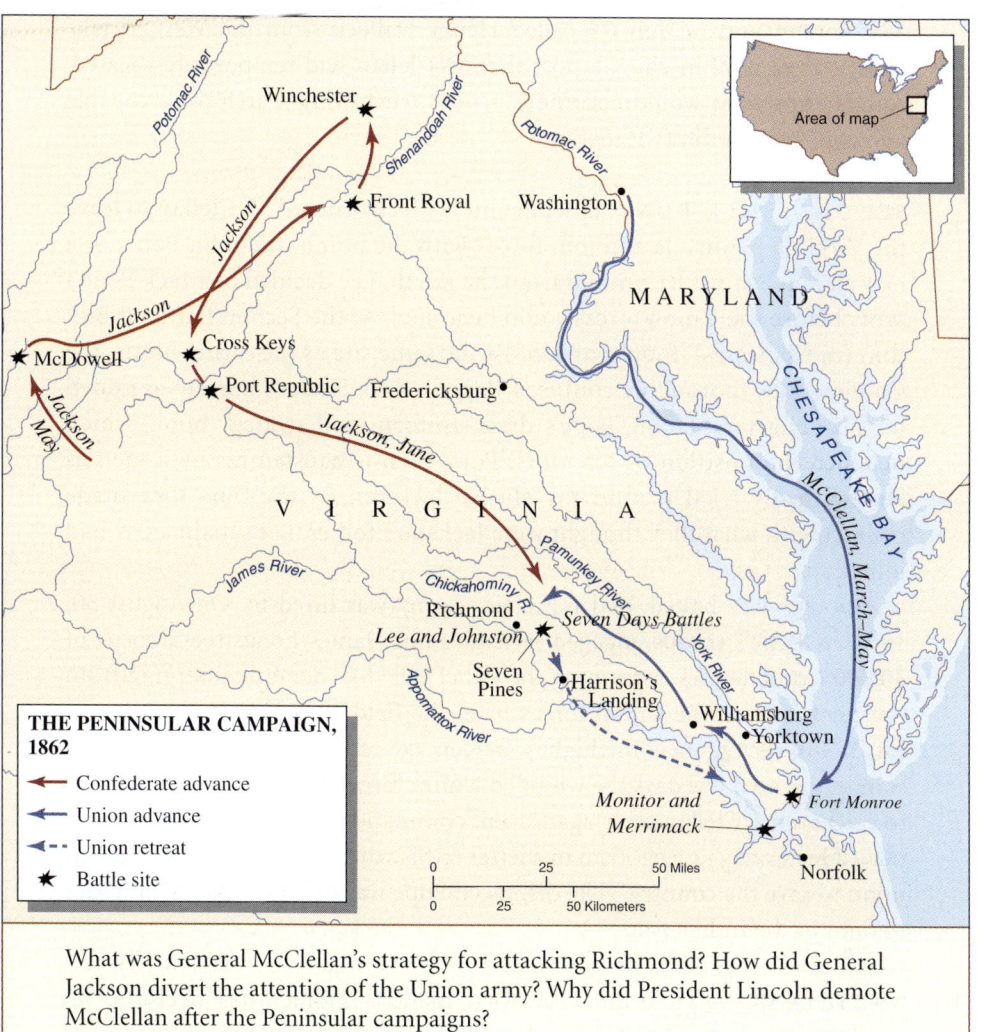

THE PENINSULAR CAMPAIGN, 1862

← Confederate advance
← Union advance
◄-- Union retreat
★ Battle site

What was General McClellan's strategy for attacking Richmond? How did General Jackson divert the attention of the Union army? Why did President Lincoln demote McClellan after the Peninsular campaigns?

(July 1), where the Confederates were riddled by artillery. As D. H. Hill observed, "It was not war, it was murder." This week of intense fighting, lumped together as the Seven Days Battles, failed to dislodge the Union forces.

On July 9 Lincoln visited the front, where McClellan lectured him on the correct strategy. Such insubordination was ample reason to remove the cocky general, but Lincoln recognized that doing so would demoralize the soldiers, who were still intensely loyal to McClellan. Instead, Lincoln returned to

Washington and on July 11 called Henry Halleck from the West to take charge as general in chief, a post that McClellan had temporarily vacated. Thus began what would become Lincoln's frustrating search for a capable and consistent military leader.

SECOND BULL RUN   Lincoln and Halleck ordered McClellan to leave the Virginia peninsula and join forces with the bombastic John Pope for a new assault against Richmond from the north. Lee decided to attack Pope's army before the Union forces could be joined. At the Second Battle of Bull Run (or Manassas), fought on almost the same site as the earlier battle, the Confederates thoroughly confused Pope. J. E. B. Stuart's horsemen raided his headquarters, taking Pope's dress uniform and strategy book, which outlined the position of his units. Pope then exhausted his own men as he frantically tried to find the elusive Jackson. By the time they made contact with what they thought were Jackson's forces, Lee's main army had joined in.

The trap was baited, and the Union army was lured in. On August 30, 1862, as Pope's troops engaged Jackson's line, James Longstreet's corps of 30,000 Confederates, screaming the Rebel yell "like demons emerging from the earth," drove the Union forces from the field. One New York regiment lost 124 of its 490 men, the highest percentage of deaths in any battle of the war. In the next few days the whipped Union forces pulled back to Washington, where McClellan once again took command and reorganized. He displayed his unflagging egotism in a letter to his wife: "Again I have been called upon to save the country." The disgraced Pope was dispatched to Minnesota to fight in the Indian wars.

ANTIETAM   A victorious Lee then made a momentous decision: he would move the battlefield out of the South and perhaps thereby gain foreign recognition of the Confederacy as a new nation. In September 1862 he led his troops into western Maryland and headed for Pennsylvania. As luck would have it, however, a Union soldier picked up a bundle of cigars and discovered a secret order from Lee wrapped around them. The paper revealed Lee's bold strategy: he had again divided his army, sending Jackson off to take Harpers Ferry, Virginia.

McClellan boasted upon seeing the captured document, "Here is a paper with which, if I cannot whip Bobby Lee, I will be willing to go home." But instead of leaping at his unexpected opportunity, he delayed for sixteen crucial hours, still worried—as always—about enemy strength. Lee was thereby able to reassemble most of his tired army behind Antietam Creek. Still,

McClellan was optimistic, and Lincoln, too, relished the chance for a truly decisive blow. "God bless you and all with you," he wired McClellan. "Destroy the rebel army if possible."

On September 17, 1862, McClellan's army attacked Confederate forces near Sharpsburg, Maryland, along Antietam Creek, and the furious Battle of Antietam (Sharpsburg) began. Outnumbered more than two to one, the Confederates forced a standoff in the most costly day of the Civil War, a day participants thought would never end.

In the late afternoon, McClellan backed off, letting Lee's army slip south across the Potomac River. Lincoln was disgusted by McClellan's failure to follow up and gain a truly decisive victory, and he fired off a tart message to the general: "I have just read your dispatch about sore-tongued and fatigued horses. Will you pardon me for asking what the horses of your army have done . . . that fatigues anything?" Later the president sent his commander a one-sentence letter: "If you don't want to use the army, I should like to borrow it for a while." Failing to receive a satisfactory answer, Lincoln removed McClellan from command.

FREDERICKSBURG   The Battle of Antietam was the turning point in the war. It revived sagging northern morale, emboldened Abraham Lincoln to issue the Emancipation Proclamation, freeing all slaves in the Confederate states, and dashed the Confederacy's hopes of foreign recognition and aid. But the war was far from over. In his search for a fighting general, Lincoln now made the worst choice of all. He turned to Ambrose E. Burnside, a handsome, personable, modest figure who had twice before turned down the job on the grounds that he felt unfit for so large a command.

Yet if the White House wanted him to fight, Burnside would fight, even in the face of the oncoming winter. On a cold December 13, 1862, he sent his men across the icy Rappahannock River to face Lee's forces, who were well entrenched behind a stone wall and on high ground just west of Fredericksburg, Virginia between Washington and Richmond. Blessed with a clear field of fire, Confederate artillery and muskets chewed up the valorous blue ranks as they crossed a mile of open bottomland outside the town. Six times the courageous but suicidal Union assaults melted under the murderous fire coming from protected Confederate positions above and below them. It was, as a Union general said, "a great slaughter-pen." The scene was both awful and awe inspiring, prompting Lee to remark, "It is well that war is so terrible—we should grow too fond of it." After seeing his men suffer more than 12,000 casualties, twice as many as the Confederates, Burnside wept as he gave the order to withdraw.

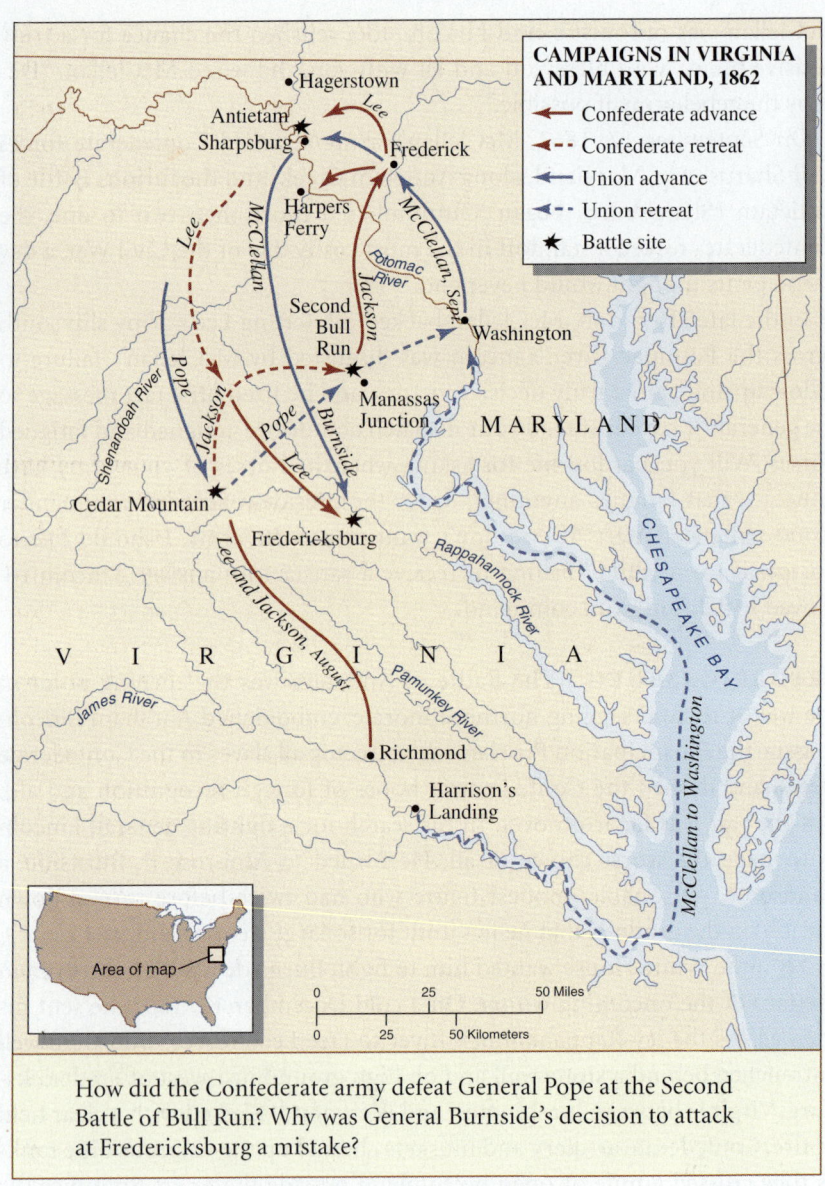

CAMPAIGNS IN VIRGINIA AND MARYLAND, 1862

- ← Confederate advance
- ◄--- Confederate retreat
- ← Union advance
- ◄--- Union retreat
- ★ Battle site

How did the Confederate army defeat General Pope at the Second Battle of Bull Run? Why was General Burnside's decision to attack at Fredericksburg a mistake?

The year 1862 ended with forces in the East deadlocked and the Union advance in the West stalled since midyear. Union morale plummeted: northern Democrats were calling for a negotiated peace, while the so-called Radical Republicans were pushing Lincoln to prosecute the war even more forcefully. Several questioned the president's competence.

In the midst of this second-guessing and carping, the deeper currents of the war were in fact turning in favor of the Union: in the lengthening war the Union's superior resources began to tell on the morale of the Confederacy. In both the eastern and the western theaters the Confederate counterattack had been repulsed. And while the armies clashed, Lincoln, by the stroke of a pen, changed the conflict from a war to restore the Union into a revolutionary struggle for the abolition of slavery: on January 1, 1863, he signed the Emancipation Proclamation.

EMANCIPATION

The Emancipation Proclamation was the product of long and painful deliberation, as opinion was divided even in the North as to whether all slaves should be freed. A deep-seated racial prejudice in the North had prevented the formation of a unified position. While most abolitionists favored both complete emancipation and social integration of the races, many antislavery activists wanted to prohibit slavery only in new territories and states. They were willing to allow slavery to continue in the South in order to avoid racial integration.

Lincoln had insisted that the purpose of the conflict was to restore the Union and that he did not have the authority to free the slaves. Yet the expanding war forced the issue. Fugitive slaves had begun to turn up in Union army camps, and generals did not know whether to declare them free. Some generals put the "contrabands" to work building fortifications; others liberated those slaves who had been held by Confederate owners, thus running the risk of upsetting border-state slaveholders. Lincoln himself edged toward emancipation. The expanding war forced the issue.

As the war continued, Lincoln eventually concluded that emancipation was required for several reasons: slave labor was bolstering the Confederate cause, sagging morale in the North needed the boost of a transcendent moral ideal, and public opinion was swinging that way. Proclaiming a war on slavery, moreover, would end forever any chance that France or Britain would support the Confederacy.

The time to act came after the Battle of Antietam. On September 22, 1862, five days after the Confederates had been forced to retreat from Maryland, Lincoln issued an Emancipation Proclamation. It warned that on January 1, 1863, all slaves in areas still under active rebellion would be "thenceforward and forever free." The Emancipation Proclamation, with few exceptions, freed only those slaves still under Confederate control, but many slaves in

Two views of the Emancipation Proclamation

The Union view (top) shows a thoughtful Lincoln composing the proclamation, the Constitution and the Holy Bible in his lap. The Confederate view (bottom) shows a demented Lincoln, his foot on the Constitution and his inkwell held by the devil.

border states did not bother with such technicalities. The African American abolitionist leader Frederick Douglass was overjoyed at Lincoln's "righteous decree." By contrast, the Democratic newspapers in the North savagely attacked the proclamation, calling it dictatorial, unconstitutional, and catastrophic.

BLACKS IN THE MILITARY Lincoln's Emancipation Proclamation reaffirmed the policy that African Americans could enroll in the armed services and sparked efforts to organize all-black military units. The War Department authorized general recruitment of African Americans all over the country, thus making more concrete Lincoln's transformation of the war from one to preserve the Union into a revolution to overthrow the social, economic, and racial status quo in the South. The first challenge for black troops, however, was to overcome embedded racial fears of northern whites and to prove themselves in battle. By mid-1863, African American soldiers were finally involved in significant combat in the eastern and the western theaters. Lincoln reported that several of his commanders believed that "the use of colored troops constitutes the heaviest blow yet dealt to the rebels."

Altogether, almost 180,000 African Americans served in the Union army, around 10 percent of the total. Some 38,000 gave their lives. Blacks

The 107th U.S. Colored Infantry

From early in the war, Union commanders found "contrabands" useful as informants and guides to unfamiliar terrain.

accounted for about a fourth of all enlistments in the navy, and of those almost 3,000 died. As the war entered its final months, freedom emerged more fully as a legal reality. The Thirteenth Amendment, which abolished slavery in every state, was ratified by three fourths of the reunited states and became part of the Constitution on December 18, 1865, thus removing any lingering doubts about the legality of emancipation. By then, in fact, slavery remained only in the border states of Kentucky and Delaware.

THE WAR BEHIND THE LINES

The scale and scope of the Civil War affected everyone—not simply the combatants. Feeding, clothing, and supplying the vast armies required tremendous sacrifices on the home fronts. The fighting knew no boundaries, as farms and villages were transformed into battlefields and churches became makeshift hospitals. Gender roles were transformed, as women assumed new duties managing households and farms, raising funds, and volunteering as nurses by the thousands. At the same time, federal and state governments assumed expansive new powers in an effort to support a war effort that turned out to be much longer and more expensive than anyone anticipated.

WOMEN AND THE WAR   While breaking the bonds of slavery, the Civil War also loosened traditional restraints on female activity. Women on both sides played prominent roles in the conflict. Initially the call to arms revived heroic images of female self-sacrifice and domesticity. Women in the North and the South sewed uniforms, composed patriotic poems and songs, and raised money and supplies. Thousands of northern women worked with the U.S. Sanitary Commission, which organized medical relief and other services for soldiers. Others supported the freedmen's aid movement to help impoverished freed slaves.

In the North alone, some 20,000 women served as nurses or other medical volunteers. The most famous nurses were Dorothea Dix and Clara Barton, both untiring volunteers in service to the wounded and the dying. Dix, the earnest reformer of the nation's insane asylums, became the Union army's first superintendent of women nurses. Barton was a schoolteacher and then one of the nation's first female patent clerks, but she remained frustrated by her desire to find "something to do that *was* something." She discovered fulfilling work at last as a nurse in the Civil War. Instead of accepting an assignment to a general hospital, she followed the troops on her own, working in makeshift field hospitals. At Antietam she came so close to the fighting that as she worked on a wounded soldier, a Confederate bullet ripped through the sleeve of her dress and killed the man.

The departure of hundreds of thousands of men for the battlefield forced women to assume the public and private roles the men left behind. In many southern towns and counties the home front became a world of white women and children and African American slaves. But not all women willingly accepted the new roles required by the war. Many among the slaveholding elite found themselves woefully unprepared: they could not cook, sew, or knit, and they balked at the idea of daily chores.

Nursing and the war

Clara Barton oversaw the distribution of medicines to Union troops. She later helped found the American Red Cross of which she remained president until the age of 83.

Women in the North and the South found themselves farmers or plantation managers, clerks, munitions-plant workers, and schoolteachers. Some 400 women disguised themselves as men and fought in the war; dozens served as spies; others traveled with the armies, cooking meals, writing letters, and assisting with amputations. The number of widows, spinsters, and orphans mushroomed. Many bereaved women on both sides came to look on the war with what the poet Emily Dickinson called a "chastened stare."

RELIGION AND THE CIVIL WAR   Wars intensify religious convictions (and vice versa), and this was certainly true of the Civil War. Religious concerns pervaded the conflict. Both sides believed they were fighting a holy war with God's divine favor. The Confederate constitution, unlike the U.S. Constitution, explicitly invoked the guidance of Almighty God. Southern leaders thus asserted that the Confederacy was the only truly Christian nation. Clergymen in the North and the South—Protestant, Catholic, and Jewish—saw the war as a righteous crusade. They were among the most partisan advocates of the war, in part because they were so certain that God was on their side and would ensure victory.

During the war both President Lincoln and President Davis proclaimed numerous official days of fasting and prayer in the aftermath of important battles. Such national rituals were a means of mourning the "martyrs" who had given their lives for the righteous cause. Salmon P. Chase, the U.S. secretary of the Treasury, added the motto "In God We Trust" to American coins as a means of expressing the nation's religious zeal. Many soldiers were armed with piety as well as muskets. William Pendleton, the chief artillery officer under Robert E. Lee, named his favorite four cannons after the four Gospels of the Christian scriptures: Matthew, Mark, Luke, and John. His orders revealed his faith: "While we will kill their bodies, may the Lord have mercy on their sinful souls—FIRE!"

Every regiment on both sides had an ordained chaplain, and devotional services in military camps were regularly held and widely attended. More than 1,300 clergymen served in the military camps, with the Methodists providing the largest number. By late 1862, Christian religious revivals were

Religion in the army

The 69th New York State Militia having a religious service in 1861.

sweeping through both northern and southern armies. To facilitate such battlefield conversions, religious organizations distributed millions of Bibles and religious tracts to soldiers and sailors. During the winter of 1863–1864 the widespread conversions among the Union army camped in northern Virginia led one reporter to claim that the soldiers' martial piety might "win the whole nation to Christ." The revivals in the Confederate camps were even larger. Mary Jones, the wife of a Confederate minister in Georgia whose son was a soldier, reported the good news that "revivals in our army are certainly the highest proofs we can possible desire or receive of the divine favor" shrouding the Confederacy. Abraham Lincoln took keen interest in the religious fervor among Confederate soldiers. He expressed concern that "rebel soldiers are praying with a great deal more earnestness" than Union soldiers.

With so many ministers away at the front, lay people, especially women, assumed even greater responsibility for religious activities in churches and synagogues. The war also transformed the religious life of African Americans, who saw the war as a recapitulation of the biblical Exodus: God's miraculous intervention in history on behalf of a chosen people. In those areas of the South taken over by Union armies, freed slaves were able to create their own churches for the first time.

Of course, as the war continued, it became evident that God would not bring victory to both sides. In the South, many Christians were deeply perplexed by the shifting tide of battle. What had happened to God's righteous providence? Seventeen-year-old Emma LeConte of South Carolina anguished in her diary over God's seeming desertion of the Confederacy: "They say *right* always triumphs, but what cause could have been more just than ours?" Religious leaders explained military defeats as God's way of chastening and purifying southerners. The editors of a southern Presbyterian newspaper insisted that God "chastens" only "those he loves."

In the end the war revealed how much religion mattered in American life. It also showed how problematic it is to claim that God is on any particular side. Abraham Lincoln was never sure whose side God was on when he reflected on the transcendent meaning of the horrible war. Yes, he observed, both sides claimed providential sanction. In this regard, he said, "Both *may* be, and one *must* be wrong. God cannot be *for* and *against* the same thing at the same time." After all, Lincoln noted, God could give victory to either side at any moment. "Yet the contest proceeds." Thus Lincoln was one of the few Americans to suggest that God's divine purpose might be something different from simple victory or defeat.

GOVERNMENT DURING THE WAR

Freeing 4 million slaves and loosening the restraints on female activity constituted a monumental social and economic revolution. But an even broader revolution developed as political power shifted from South to North during the Civil War. Before the war, southern congressmen exercised disproportionate influence. Once the secessionists had abandoned Congress to the Republicans, however, dramatic change occurred. Without congressional opposition from the South, Republicans passed a higher tariff, approved a transcontinental railroad that would run through Omaha, Nebraska, to Sacramento, California, and enacted a Homestead Act, which granted free homesteads of 160 acres to settlers who occupied the land for five years—all acts that had been stalled by sectional controversy and were adopted before the end of 1862. That year also saw the passage of the Morrill Land Grant Act, which provided federal aid to state colleges focused on teaching the "agricultural and mechanic arts." The National Banking Act, which created a uniform system of banking and bank-note currency, followed in 1863 and helped the Union address a critical problem: how to finance the war.

UNION FINANCES   Congress had three options for financing the war: raising taxes, printing paper money, and borrowing. The taxes came chiefly in the form of the Morrill Tariff and taxes on manufacturers and nearly every profession. A butcher, for example, had to pay 30¢ for every head of beef he slaughtered, 10¢ for every hog, 5¢ for every sheep. An income tax rounded out the revenue measures.

But federal tax revenues trickled in so slowly that Congress in 1862 ordered the printing of $450 million in "greenbacks," enough to pay the bills without unleashing the kind of runaway inflation that burdened the Confederacy after Jefferson Davis allowed the unlimited issue of paper money. The congressional decision to allow the Treasury to print paper money was a profoundly important development for the U.S. economy, then and since. Unlike previous paper currencies issued by local banks, the federal greenbacks could not be exchanged for gold or silver. Instead, their value relied upon public trust in the government. Many bankers were outraged by the advent of the greenbacks. "Gold and silver are the only true measure of value," one financier declared. "These metals were prepared by the Almighty." But the crisis of the Union and the desperate need to finance the expanding war demanded such a solution.

Still, paper money and taxes provided only about two thirds of the money that financed the war. The rest came chiefly from the sale of government

Union bank note

Bank notes were promissory notes. Generally, the better the art on the note, the more it was trusted.

bonds. A Philadelphia banker named Jay Cooke mobilized a nationwide network of agents to sell government war bonds. It worked well, and over $2 billion was raised in the process.

CONFEDERATE FINANCES Confederate finances were a disaster from the start. Tariffs were tried, but imports were low and therefore raised little revenue. In 1863 the Confederate Congress passed a measure that taxed nearly everything. A 10 percent tax on all agricultural products did more to outrage farmers and planters than to supply the army. Enforcement was so lax and evasion so easy that the taxes produced only negligible income. The last resort, printing paper money, was in fact resorted to early. Beginning in 1861, the new Confederate government began an extended inflationary binge. Altogether, the Confederacy turned out more than $1 billion in paper money, creating a dramatic spike in prices. By 1864 a wild turkey sold in a Richmond market for $100, flour went for $425 a barrel, and bacon for $10 a pound. Those living on a fixed income were caught in a merciless inflationary squeeze.

UNION POLITICS AND CIVIL LIBERTIES On the home front during the Civil War, there was no moratorium on partisan politics, northern or southern. Within his own party, Lincoln faced a Radical wing composed mainly of prewar abolitionists. The so-called Radical Republicans in Congress formed a Joint Committee on the Conduct of the War, which increasingly pressured Lincoln to emancipate the slaves, confiscate southern plantations, and prosecute the war more vigorously. The majority of Republicans, however, supported the president, and the party was virtually united on economic matters.

The Democratic party suffered the loss of its southern wing as well as the death of its leader, Stephen A. Douglas, in June 1861. By and large, northern Democrats supported a war for "the Union as it was" before 1860, giving reluctant support to Lincoln's policies but opposing wartime constraints on civil liberties and the new economic legislation. "War Democrats," such as Senator Andrew Johnson from Tennessee and Secretary of War Edwin Stanton, fully supported Lincoln's policies, while a peace wing of the party preferred a negotiated end to the fighting, even if that meant risking the Union. An extreme fringe among the peace Democrats flirted with outright disloyalty. The Copperheads, as they were called, were strongest in Ohio, Indiana, and Illinois, states with many transplanted southerners, some of whom were pro-Confederate.

Such open sympathy for the enemy led Lincoln to crack down hard. Early in the war he assumed certain emergency powers, such as the suspension of the writ of habeas corpus, which guarantees arrested citizens a speedy hearing. When critics charged that this violated the Constitution, Lincoln's congressional supporters pushed through the Habeas Corpus Act of 1863, which authorized the suspension of the writ. Some 14,000 Confederate sympathizers were arrested under the terms of the act.

In the midterm elections of 1862, the Democrats exploited growing war-weariness and resentment of Lincoln's war measures to gain a startling recovery, though not control of Congress. When asked his reaction to the election results, Lincoln replied that he felt somewhat "like the boy in Kentucky who stubbed his toe while running to see his sweetheart. The boy said he was too big to cry, and far too badly hurt to laugh." In fact the fractious political climate left Lincoln increasingly perplexed as time passed.

At their 1864 national convention the Democrats called for an immediate armistice and named General George McClellan as their candidate, but he distanced himself from the peace platform by declaring that the two sides must agree on the terms of reunion before the fighting could stop. Radical Republicans, who still regarded Lincoln as too soft on the traitorous southerners, tried to thwart his renomination, but Lincoln outmaneuvered them at every turn. In a shrewd move he named as his vice-presidential running mate Andrew Johnson, a "war Democrat" from Tennessee, and called the two of them the National Union ticket to minimize partisanship. As the war ground on through 1864, with Grant's army taking heavy losses in Virginia, Lincoln fully expected to lose the election, but key military victories in

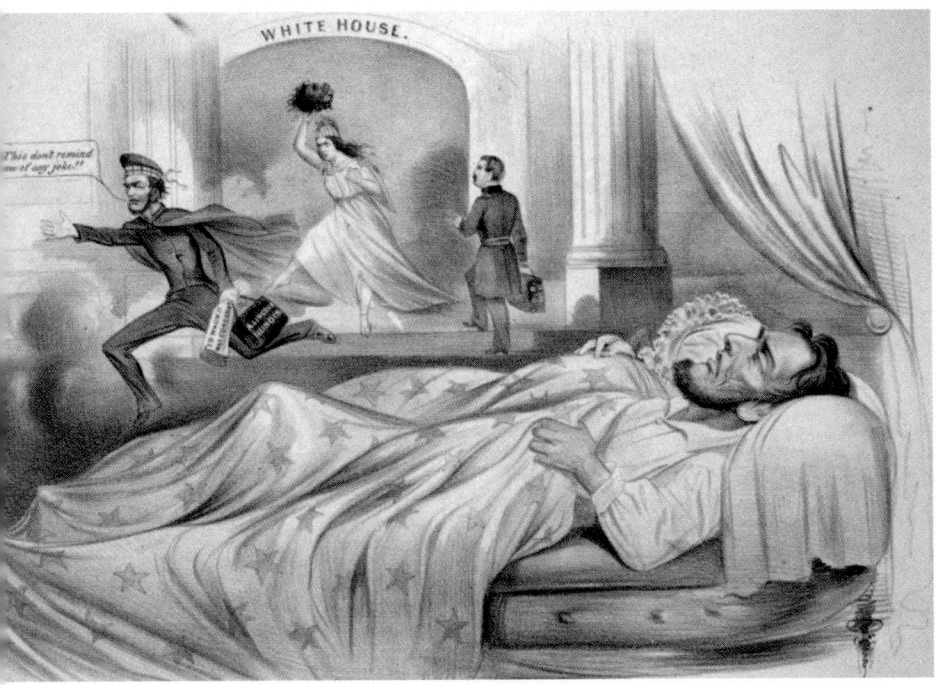

"Abraham's Dream!"

This cartoon depicts President Lincoln having a nightmare about the election of 1864. Lady Liberty brandishes the severed head of a black man at the door of the White House as General McClellan mounts the steps and Lincoln runs away.

August and September turned the tide. McClellan carried only New Jersey, Delaware, and Kentucky.

CONFEDERATE POLITICS   Unlike Lincoln, Jefferson Davis never had to face a presidential contest. He and his vice president, Alexander Stephens, were elected for a six-year term. But discontent flourished in the South as food grew scarce and prices skyrocketed. Starving women incited riots from Richmond to Mobile. A bread riot in Richmond in 1863, for example, ended only when Jefferson Davis threatened to shoot the demonstrators. After the Confederate congressional elections of 1863, about a third of the legislators were openly hostile to the Davis administration. Although parties as such did not figure in the elections, it was noteworthy that many ex-Whigs and other opponents of secession were chosen.

Davis, like Lincoln, had to contend with dissenters. Especially troublesome were supporters of states' rights and secession who steadfastly opposed

Jefferson Davis
President of the Confederacy.

the centralizing tendencies of the Confederate government in Richmond. Georgia and North Carolina were strongholds of such sentiment. The states' rights champions challenged, among other things, the legality of conscription, taxes on farm produce, and above all the suspension of habeas corpus. Vice President Alexander Stephens himself carried on a running battle with Davis, accusing the president of trying to establish a "military despotism."

The internal bickering did not alone cause the Confederacy's defeat, but it certainly contributed to it. Whereas Lincoln was the consummate pragmatist, Davis was a brittle dogmatist with a waspish temper. Once he made a decision, nothing could change his mind. Nor could Davis ever admit a mistake. Such a personality was ill suited to serve as the chief executive of an infant nation.

THE ENVIRONMENT AND THE CIVIL WAR   Wars not only kill and maim people; they also transform the environment. While well over half a million soldiers died of wounds, disease, or accidents, equally appalling numbers of animals, especially horses and mules but also cattle and pigs, were killed in battle or for food. During the final year of the war, nearly 500 horses a day died of shell fire, starvation, overwork, or disease. Fighting during the Civil War also destroyed much of the southern landscape. In 1864 a Confederate major wrote that near Chickamauga, Georgia, just south of Chattanooga, Tennessee, the road was "covered with the skeletons of horses, and every tree bears the mark of battle. Many strong trunks were broken down by artillery fire." Hundreds of bridges and levees were also destroyed during the war, as were endless miles of fences, which foraging soldiers used for firewood. The loss of levees caused massive flooding; the loss of fencing meant that much of the postwar South would revert to open-range grazing. Craters gouged out by cannonballs pockmarked the landscape and provided breeding grounds for mosquitoes. The loss of so many animals meant that the mosquitoes focused on humans for their blood meal, thus increasing the spread of malaria. Hundreds of miles of trenches dug for military defense scarred the land and accelerated erosion. All told, the environment was as much a victim of the warfare as were the soldiers, and it would take years to heal nature's wounds across the South.

THE FALTERING CONFEDERACY

After the Union disaster at Fredericksburg, Lincoln's frustrating search for a capable general turned to one of Burnside's disgruntled lieutenants, Joseph Hooker, a handsome, ruddy-faced, hard-drinking character whose pugnacity had earned him the nickname Fighting Joe. But he soon failed his test of generalship.

CHANCELLORSVILLE With a force of 130,000 men, the largest Union army yet gathered, and a brilliant plan, Hooker chose to do battle at Chancellorsville, Virginia, on May 1–5, 1863. Robert E. Lee, with perhaps half that number of troops, staged a textbook classic of daring and maneuver that took advantage of Hooker's failure of nerve. On May 2 the Confederates slammed into the Union lines with such furor that the defenders panicked and ran. The next day Lee's troops forced Hooker's army to retreat. It was the peak of Lee's career, but Chancellorsville was his last significant victory—and his costliest: the South lost 1,600 soldiers, among them General Stonewall Jackson, mistakenly shot by his own men in the confused fighting. "I have lost my right arm," lamented Lee.

Stonewall Jackson

Jackson was mortally wounded by his own men.

VICKSBURG While Lee's army held the Union forces at bay in the East, Ulysses Grant, his appointment as field commander now restored, had been moving his army down the Mississippi River toward the Confederate stronghold at Vicksburg, in western Mississippi. If Union forces could gain control of the Mississippi River, they could split the Confederacy in two. For months, Grant tried to discover a way to penetrate Vicksburg's heavily fortified defenses. The terrain complicated his task: Vicksburg was surrounded by bayous and marshes that made travel and resupply almost impossible. Torrential rains and widespread disease also hampered the Union army's movements. So in the spring of 1863, Grant finally decided to leave his supply base and live off the land. His soldiers crossed over to Louisiana, took a roundabout route to Jackson, Mississippi, where they routed the Confederates, and headed back to Vicksburg. The Union army pinned down 30,000 Confederates in Vicksburg, and Grant resolved to starve them out.

GETTYSBURG   The plight of besieged Vicksburg put the Confederate high command in a quandary, in response to which Robert E. Lee proposed a diversion. Once again he sought a great victory on northern soil, this time

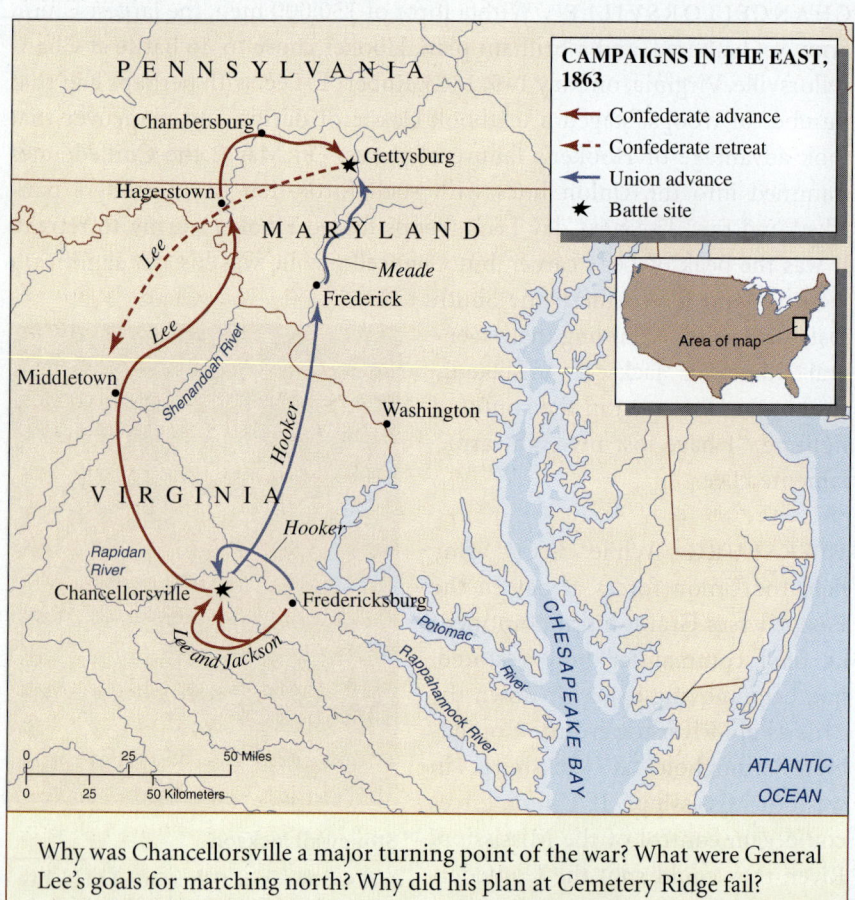

Why was Chancellorsville a major turning point of the war? What were General Lee's goals for marching north? Why did his plan at Cemetery Ridge fail?

in the hope of not just relieving the pressure on Vicksburg but also bringing an end to the war. In June 1863, therefore, he moved his forces into the Shenandoah River valley of western Virginia and again headed north across Maryland. Neither side chose Gettysburg, Pennsylvania, as the site for the war's climactic battle. A Confederate foraging party entered the town in search of shoes and accidentally encountered units of Union cavalry on June 30, 1863. The main forces then quickly converged there.

On July 1, a hot, steamy day, the Confederates pushed the Union soldiers out of the town, but into stronger positions on high ground to the south. The new Union commander, George Meade, hastened reinforcements to the new lines along the heights. On July 2, Confederates launched furious assaults against Meade's army. The Union forces, who outnumbered their attackers almost two to one, fought just as bravely—and the assaults were repulsed.

The next day, Lee staked everything on a final attack on the Union center at Cemetery Ridge. At about two in the afternoon, General George Pickett's 15,000 Confederate troops emerged from the woods west of Cemetery Ridge and began their brave but suicidal advance across rising open ground commanded by Union artillery. "Pickett's charge" was hopeless. At a distance of 700 yards, the Union artillery homed in on the advancing Virginians. Those who avoided the artillery barrage were devastated by a wall of musket fire. At the head of Pickett's division were the University Greys, thirty-one college students from Mississippi. Within an hour of their assault, every one of them had been killed or wounded. As he watched the few survivors returning from the bloody field, General Lee muttered, "All this has been my fault."

With nothing left to do but retreat, Lee's mangled army began to slog south in a driving rain that "washed the blood from the grass." They left a third of their number behind on the ground, having had failed in all their purposes, not the least being to relieve the pressure on Vicksburg. On that same day, July 4, the entire Confederate garrison at Vicksburg surrendered after a forty-seven-day siege. The Confederacy was now irrevocably split. Had Meade aggressively pursued Lee's retreating army, he might have ended the war, but again an army failed to capitalize on its advantage.

After the furious fighting at Gettysburg had ended, a group of northern states funded a military cemetery for the 6,000 soldiers killed in the battle. On November 19, 1863, the new cemetery was officially dedicated. In his brief remarks, since known as the Gettysburg Address, President Lincoln eloquently expressed the pain and sorrow of the brutal civil war. The prolonged conflict was testing whether a nation "dedicated to the proposition that all men are created equal . . . can long endure." Lincoln declared that all

"A Harvest of Death"

Timothy H. O'Sullivan's grim photograph of the dead at Gettysburg.

Americans must ensure that the "honored dead" had not "died in vain." In stirring words that continue to inspire, Lincoln predicted that "this nation, under God, shall have a new birth of freedom—and that government of the people, by the people, and for the people, shall not perish from the earth."

CHATTANOOGA The third great Union victory of 1863 occurred in fighting around Chattanooga, the railhead of eastern Tennessee and gateway to northern Georgia. On September 9 a Union army led by General William Rosecrans took Chattanooga and then rashly pursued General Braxton Bragg's forces into Georgia, where the two sides clashed at Chickamauga (an old Cherokee word presciently meaning "River of Death"). The battle (September 19–20) had the makings of a Union disaster because it was one of the few times the Confederates had a numerical advantage (about 70,000 to 56,000). On the second day, Bragg smashed the Union's right flank, and only the stubborn defence by soldiers under the Virginia Unionist George H. Thomas (thenceforth known as the Rock of Chickamauga) prevented a rout. The battered Union forces fell back to Chattanooga while Bragg cut the railroad and held the city virtually under siege.

Rosecrans seemed stunned and immobilized, but Lincoln urged him to hang on: "If we can hold Chattanooga, and East Tennessee, I think rebellion must dwindle and die." The president then dispatched reinforcements.

General Grant, given overall command of the western theater on October 16, replaced Rosecrans with George Thomas. On November 24 the Union forces broke out of the city and captured Lookout Mountain in what was mainly a feat of mountaineering. The next day, Grant ordered Thomas's troops forward to positions at the foot of Missionary Ridge. But the men did not stop there. Still fuming because the Confederates had jeered them at Chickamauga, they charged toward the crest without orders. One of Thomas's aides explained to Grant, "When those fellows get started all hell can't stop them." The attackers could have been decimated, but the Confederates were unable to lower their cannons enough to hit the scrambling Yankees, and despite Bragg's "cursing like a sailor," his men fled as Thomas's troops reached the summit.

After the Confederate defeat, as the Union forces consolidated their control of East Tennessee, already full of Unionist sympathizers, Jefferson Davis reluctantly replaced Bragg with Joseph Johnston. Lincoln, on the other hand, had finally found the general for whom he had been searching for almost three years. In March 1864, Ulysses S. Grant was brought to Washington and made general in chief.

THE CONFEDERACY'S DEFEAT

During the winter of 1863–1864, Confederates began to despair of victory. A War Department official in Richmond reported in his diary a spreading "sense of hopelessness." The Union's main targets now were Lee's army in Virginia and General Joseph Johnston's forces in Georgia. Grant personally would accompany George Meade, who retained direct command over the Army of the Potomac; operations in the West were entrusted to Grant's longtime lieutenant, William T. Sherman. Grant brought with him a new strategy against Lee. Where his predecessors had hoped for the climactic single battle, he opted for an aggressive war of attrition. He would attack, attack, attack, keeping the pressure on the Confederates, grinding down their numbers and taking away their initiative and their will to fight. Victory, he had decided, would come to the side "which never counted its dead." Grant ordered his commanders to wage total war, confiscating or destroying civilian property of use to the Confederate war effort. It was a brutal, costly, but effective plan.

GRANT'S PURSUIT OF LEE In May 1864, the Union's Army of the Potomac, numbering about 115,000 to Lee's 65,000, moved south across the Rappahannock River into the Wilderness of eastern Virginia, where Hooker had come to grief in the Battle of Chancellorsville. In the nightmarish Battle of the Wilderness (May 5–6), the armies fought blindly through the tangled brush and vines, the horror and agony of the wounded heightened by crackling brushfires. Grant's men suffered heavier casualties than Lee's, but the Confederates were running out of replacements.

Many of the officers in the Army of the Potomac were in awe of Lee. They especially feared another decisive counterattack on their flanks. When one of Grant's officers expressed concern about what Lee might do, Grant exploded:

> Oh, I am heartily tired of hearing what Lee is going to do. Some of you always seem to think he is suddenly going to turn a double somersault, and land in our rear and on both our flanks at the same time. Go back to your command, and try to think what we are going to do ourselves, instead of what Lee is going to do.

Always before, Lee's adversaries had retreated to lick their wounds, but Grant slid off to the left and continued his relentless advance southward, now toward Spotsylvania Court House. "Whatever happens," he assured Lincoln, "we will not retreat."

Ulysses S. Grant

At his headquarters in City Point (now Hopewell), Virginia.

Along the Chickahominy River the two sides clashed at Cold Harbor (June 1–3). In twenty minutes, almost 7,000 attacking Union soldiers were killed or wounded. Many of them had predicted as much. After the failed assault, Confederates retrieved a diary from a dead Massachusetts soldier. The final entry read: "June 3, 1864, Cold Harbor, Virginia. I was killed." Battered and again repulsed, Grant soon had his men moving again, headed for Petersburg, the junction of railroads running into Richmond from the south. "I shall take no backward steps," he declared.

Lee's army dug in around the town while Grant's forces laid

siege. For nine months the two armies faced each other down while Grant kept trying to break the railroad arteries that were Lee's lifeline. Grant's men were generously supplied by vessels moving up the James River, while Lee's forces, beset by hunger, cold, and desertion, wasted away in their muddy trenches. Petersburg had become Lee's prison while disasters piled up elsewhere in the Confederacy. "From the summer of 1862," wrote a Confederate veteran, "the war became a war of wholesale devastation. From the spring of 1864, it seemed to have become nearly a war of extermination."

SHERMAN'S MARCH   While Grant was besieging Lee in Virginia, General William T. Sherman was doggedly pursuing Joseph Johnston's Rebel

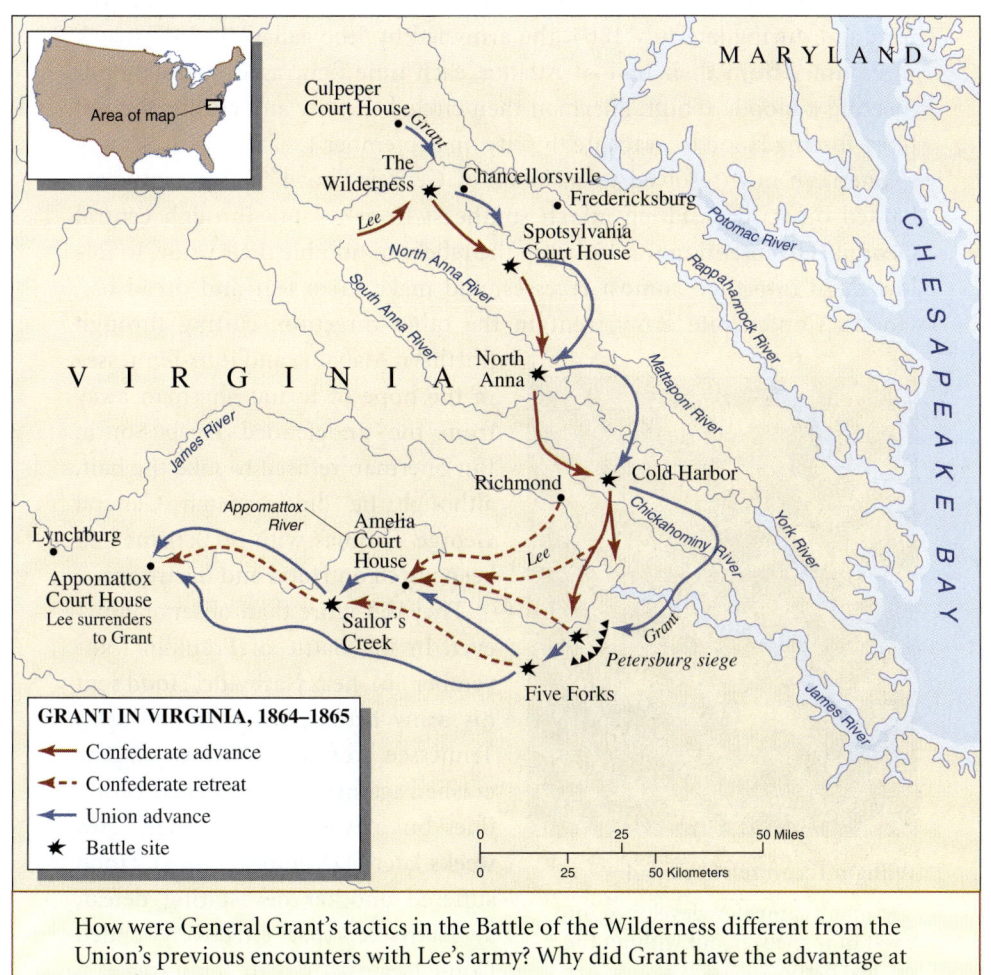

GRANT IN VIRGINIA, 1864–1865

- ◄— Confederate advance
- ◄- - Confederate retreat
- ◄— Union advance
- ★ Battle site

How were General Grant's tactics in the Battle of the Wilderness different from the Union's previous encounters with Lee's army? Why did Grant have the advantage at Petersburg?

army through northern Georgia, toward Atlanta. Tightly strung, profane, and plagued by fits of depression, Sherman was one of the few generals to appreciate the concept of total war. He wanted to destroy Confederate morale as well as Confederate armies. Where Sherman loved a toe-to-toe fight, his opponent Johnston preferred retreat and evasion, determined not to risk a single life until the perfect conditions for fighting were obtained.

An impatient Jefferson Davis finally exploded at Johnston and replaced him with the towering, blond-bearded Texan John B. Hood, who did not know the meaning of retreat or evasion. As Lee once noted, Hood was "all lion, none of the fox." Having had an arm crippled by a bullet at Gettysburg and most of one leg shot off at Chickamauga, Hood had to be strapped to his horse. He was one of the most tenacious—and impetuous—fighters in the war; and during late July 1864, the army led by "the gallant Hood" struck three times from their base at Atlanta, each time fighting desperately but meeting a bloody rebuff. Sherman then circled the city and cut off the rail lines, forcing Hood to evacuate the city on September 1.

Sherman now resolved to make all of Georgia "howl" as his army embarked on its devastating march southeast from Atlanta through central Georgia. His intention was to "whip the rebels, to humble their pride, to follow them into their inmost recesses, and make them fear and dread us." Hood's Confederate army went in the other direction, cutting through

William Tecumseh Sherman

Sherman's campaign developed into a war of maneuver, but without the pitched battles of Grant's campaign.

northern Alabama and into Tennessee in the hope of luring Sherman away from the undefended Deep South. But Sherman refused to take the bait, although he did dispatch General George Thomas with 30,000 men to keep watch on Hood and his troops.

They did more than observe, however. In the Battle of Franklin (November 30), near Nashville, Hood sent his army across two miles of open Tennessee ground. Six waves of gray crashed against the entrenched Union lines but never broke through. Two weeks later (December 15–16), Hood suffered another devastating defeat, at Nashville, that effectively ended Confederate activity in Tennessee.

Meanwhile, Sherman and the main Union force were marching triumphantly through Georgia, waging war against the enemy's resources and will to resist. "War is war," Sherman bluntly declared, "not a popularity contest." On November 15, 1864, his men burned much of Atlanta and then spread out over a front twenty to sixty miles wide and headed southeast, living off the land and destroying any crops, livestock, or supplies that might serve Confederate forces. Bands of stragglers and deserters from both armies joined in looting along the flanks.

When Sherman's army approached Savannah, Georgia, a month later, a swath of desolation 250 miles long lay behind them. Sherman's purpose was clear: he would keep the pressure on the Confederates "until they are not only ruined, exhausted, but humbled in pride and spirit." On December 21, Sherman rode into Savannah, and three days later he offered the city as a Christmas gift to Lincoln. But Sherman paused only long enough to resupply his forces, who then moved on to that "hell-hole of secession," South Carolina. There his men wrought even greater destruction. More than a dozen

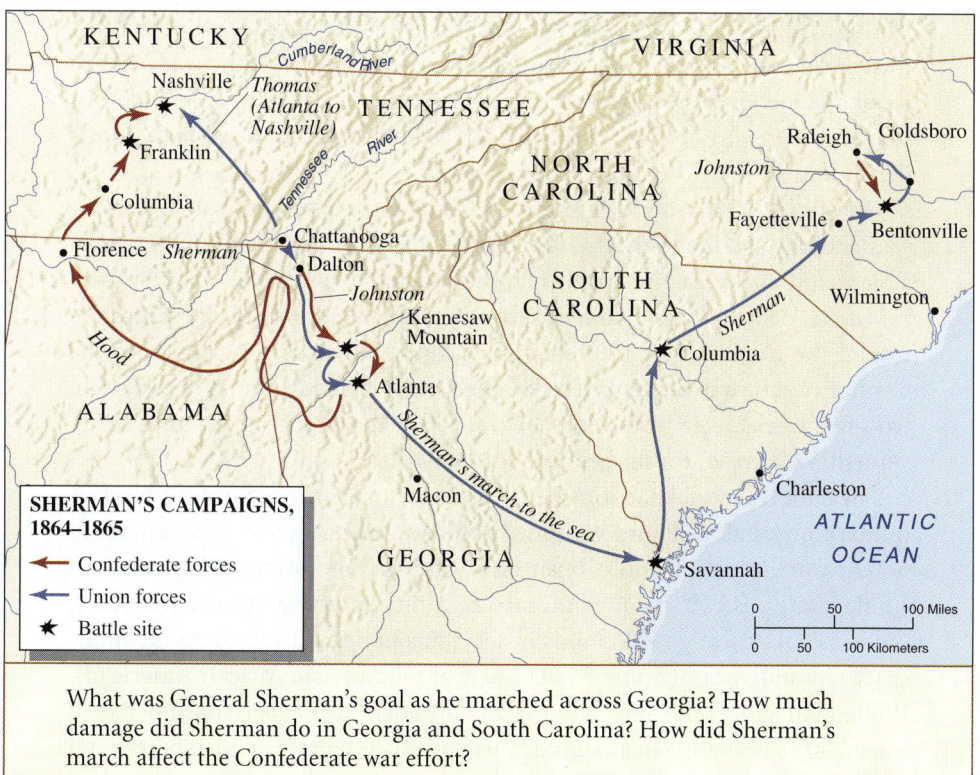

SHERMAN'S CAMPAIGNS, 1864–1865

⟵ Confederate forces
⟵ Union forces
★ Battle site

What was General Sherman's goal as he marched across Georgia? How much damage did Sherman do in Georgia and South Carolina? How did Sherman's march affect the Confederate war effort?

towns were torched, including the state capital of Columbia, which was captured on February 17, 1865. That same day the Confederates abandoned Charleston and headed north to join an army that Joseph Johnston was desperately trying to form.

During the late winter and early spring of 1865, the Confederacy found itself besieged. Defeat was in the air. Some Rebel leaders wanted to negotiate a peace settlement. Confederate secretary of war John C. Breckinridge, the Kentuckian who had served as vice president under James Buchanan and had run for president in 1860, urged Robert E. Lee to negotiate an honorable end to the war. "This has been a magnificent epic," he said. "In God's name, let it not terminate in a farce." But Jefferson Davis dismissed any talk of surrender. If the Confederate armies should be defeated, he wanted the soldiers to disperse and fight a guerrilla war. "The war came and now it must go on," he stubbornly insisted, "till the last man of this generation falls in his tracks, and his children seize his musket and fight our battle."

While Confederate forces made their last stands, Abraham Lincoln prepared for his second term as president. He was the first president since Andrew Jackson to have been reelected. The weary commander in chief had weathered constant criticism during his first term, but with the war nearing its end, Lincoln now garnered deserved praise. The *Chicago Tribune* observed that the president "has slowly and steadily risen in the respect, confidence, and admiration of the people."

On March 4, 1865, amid rumors of a Confederate attempt to abduct or assassinate the president, the six-foot-four-inch rawboned Lincoln, dressed in a black suit and stovepipe hat, his face weathered by prairie wind and political worry, delivered his eloquent second inaugural address on the East Portico of the Capitol. Not 100 feet away, looking down on Lincoln from the Capitol porch, was a twenty-six-year-old actor named John Wilkes Booth, who five weeks later would kill the president in a desperate attempt to do something "heroic" for his beloved South.

The nation's capital had long before become an armed camp and a massive military hospital. Sick and wounded soldiers were scattered everywhere: in hotels, warehouses, schools, businesses, and private homes. Thousands of Confederate deserters roamed the streets. After a morning of torrential rains, the sun broke through the clouds just as Lincoln began to speak to the mudspattered audience of some 35,000, half of whom were African Americans. While managing a terrible civil war, the president had experienced personal tragedy (the loss of a second child, a wife plagued by mental instability) and chronic depression. What had kept him from unraveling were a principled pragmatism and a godly foundation that endowed his life with purpose.

Lincoln's second inaugural address was more sermon than speech, the reflections of a somber statesman still struggling to understand the relation between divine will and human endeavor. Rather than detailing the progress of the war effort or indulging in self-congratulatory celebration, Lincoln focused on the origins and paradoxes of the war. Slavery, he said, had "somehow" caused the war, and everyone bore some guilt for the national shame of racial injustice and its bloody expiation. Both sides had known before the fighting began that war was to be avoided at all costs, but "one of them would *make* war rather than let the nation survive; and the other would *accept* war rather than let it perish."

The weary but resolute commander in chief longed for peace. "Fondly do we hope—fervently do we pray—that this mighty scourge of war may speedily pass away." He wondered aloud why the war had lasted so long and had been so brutal. "The Almighty," he acknowledged, "has His own purposes." Lincoln noted the paradoxical irony of both sides in this civil war reading the same Bible, praying to the same God, and appealing for divine support in its fight against the other. The God of Judgment, however, would not be misled or denied. If God willed that the war continue until "every drop of blood drawn with the lash, shall be paid with another drawn by the sword, as was said three thousand years ago, so still it must be said 'the judgments of the Lord are true and righteous altogether.'" After four years of escalating combat, the war had grown "incomprehensible" in its scope and horrors. Now the president, looking gaunt and tired, urged the Union forces "to finish the work we are in," bolstered with "firmness in the right insofar as God gives us to see the right."

As Lincoln looked ahead to the end of the fighting and a "just and lasting peace," he stressed the need to "bind up the nation's wounds" by exercising the Christian virtues of forgiveness and mercy. Vengeance must be avoided at all costs. Reconciliation must be pursued "with malice toward none; with charity for all." Those eight words marvelously captured Lincoln's hopes for a restored Union. Redemption was his goal; victory was less important than peace. The sublime majesty of Lincoln's brief speech revealed how the rigors of war had transformed and elevated him from the obscure congressman who had entered the White House in 1861. The abolitionist leader Frederick Douglass proclaimed Lincoln's second inaugural address "a sacred effort."

APPOMATTOX   During this final season of the Confederacy, Ulysses Grant's forces kept pushing, probing, and battering General Lee's defenses around Petersburg, twenty miles south of Richmond. The Confederates were slowly starving, their trenches filled with rats and lice. Scurvy and dysentery were rampant. News of Sherman's devastating sweep through Dixie only

Robert E. Lee

Mathew Brady took this photograph in Richmond eleven days after Lee's surrender at Appomattox.

added to the Confederates' gloom and the impulse to desert.

Under siege for almost ten months, the Confederate lines around Petersburg were becoming woefully thin, and Lee decided to abandon Richmond and join Johnston's forces in North Carolina. In Richmond, President Davis, exhausted but still defiant, gathered what valuables he could carry and escaped by train. Torching everything of military and industrial value in Richmond, the retreating Confederate forces left the city on April 2, and the Union army entered, accompanied by Abraham Lincoln himself. Jefferson Davis would be captured in Georgia on May 10 by Union cavalry, but by then the Confederacy was already dead.

As Richmond lay burning, Lee pulled his shrunken army out of the trenches around nearby Petersburg, with Grant's men in hot pursuit. Lee soon found his escape route cut by Union cavalry. Outnumbered six to one, surrounded, and out of food, Lee dismissed proposals to scatter his forces to wage guerrilla warfare. He instead told Grant he was prepared to surrender. Although his men shouted their willingness to keep fighting, Lee decided it was senseless to waste any more lives.

On April 9 (Palm Sunday), 1865, Lee donned a dress uniform and met the mud-spattered Grant in the parlor of Wilmer McLean's home at Appomattox Court House to tender his surrender. Grant, at Lee's request, let the Confederate officers keep their sidearms and permitted soldiers to keep their own horses and mules. Three days later the Confederate troops formed ranks for the last time as they prepared for the formal surrender. Deeply moved by the solemn splendor, Joshua Chamberlain, the Union general in charge, ordered his men to salute their foes as they paraded past. His Confederate counterpart signaled his troops to do likewise. General Chamberlain remembered that there was not a sound—no trumpets or drums, no cheers or jeers, simply "an awed stillness . . . as if it were the passing of the dead." On April 18, Johnston surrendered his forces to Sherman near Durham, North Carolina. The remaining Confederate forces surrendered during May. The brutal war was at last over.

A MODERN WAR

The Civil War was in many respects the first modern war. Its scope was unprecedented. One out of every twelve men served in the war, and few families were unaffected by the event. Over 630,000 men died in the conflict from wounds or disease, 50 percent more than in World War II. Of the survivors, 50,000 returned home with one or more limbs amputated. Disease, however, was the greatest threat to soldiers, killing twice as many as were lost in battle.

The Civil War was also modern in that much of the killing was distant, impersonal, and mechanical. Men were killed without knowing who had fired the shot that felled them. The opposing forces used an array of new weapons and instruments of war: artillery with "rifled," or grooved, barrels for greater accuracy, repeating rifles, ironclad ships, observation balloons, and wire entanglements.

Historians have provided conflicting assessments of the reasons for the Union victory. Some have focused on the inherent weaknesses of the Confederacy: its lack of industry, the fractious relations between the states and the central government in Richmond, poor political and military leadership, faulty coordination and communication, the burden of slavery, and the disparities in population and resources compared with those of the North. Still others have highlighted the erosion of Confederate morale in the face of chronic food shortages and horrific human losses. The debate over why the North won and the South lost the Civil War will probably never end, but as in other modern wars, firepower and manpower were essential factors. Robert E. Lee's own explanation of the Confederate defeat retains an enduring legitimacy: "After four years of arduous service marked by unsurpassed courage and fortitude, the Army of Northern Virginia has been compelled to yield to overwhelming numbers and resources."

End of Chapter Review

- **Civil War Begins** In his inaugural address, Abraham Lincoln made it clear that secession was unconstitutional but that the North would not invade the South. War came when the federal government attempted to resupply forts in the South. When South Carolinians shelled Fort Sumter, in Charleston Harbor, Lincoln issued his call to arms. Other southern states seceded at that point, and the American Civil War was under way.

- **Civil War Strategies** The Confederates had a geographic advantage in that they were fighting to defend their own soil. They expected support from Britain and France because of those nations' dependence on southern cotton for their textile industries. The Union quickly launched a campaign to seize the Confederate capital, Richmond, Virginia. Initial hopes for a rapid victory died at the First Battle of Bull Run. The Union then adopted the "anaconda plan," which involved imposing a naval blockade on southern ports and slowly crushing resistance on all fronts. The Union's industrial might was the deciding feature in a long war of attrition.

- **Wartime Home Fronts** Both sides passed conscription laws. Most of the fighting took place in the South; thus, although the North had more casualties, the impact on the South was greater. Its population was smaller, and its civilians directly experienced local violence and food shortages. The landscape, food supply, and wildlife were destroyed in many areas. In both the North and the South, women played nontraditional roles on farms and even at the battlefront.

- **Emancipation Proclamation** Initially, President Lincoln declared that the war's aim was to restore the Union and that slavery would be maintained where it existed. Gradually he came to see that the Emancipation Proclamation was justified as a military necessity because it would deprive the South of its labor force. He hoped that southern states would return to the Union before his January 1863 deadline, when all slaves under Confederate control would be declared free.

- **Freedom from Slavery** Many slaves freed themselves by escaping to Union camps. Although the Emancipation Proclamation announced the war aim of abolishing slavery, it freed only those people enslaved in areas still under Confederate control. The Thirteenth Amendment freed all enslaved people throughout the United States.

CHRONOLOGY

March 4, 1861	Abraham Lincoln is inaugurated president
April 1861	Fort Sumter falls to Confederate forces; Lincoln issues call to arms
July 1861	First Battle of Bull Run (Manassas)
March 1862	Battle of the *Merrimack* (the *Virginia*) and the *Monitor*
March–July 1862	Peninsular campaign
April, August, September 1862	Battles of Shiloh, Second Bull Run, and Antietam
January 1, 1863	Lincoln signs the Emancipation Proclamation
May–July, November 1863	Siege of Vicksburg, Battles of Gettysburg and Chattanooga
April 9, 1865	Robert E. Lee surrenders at Appomattox Court House
1865	Thirteenth Amendment is ratified

KEY TERMS & NAMES

18

RECONSTRUCTION: NORTH AND SOUTH

FOCUS QUESTIONS

 wwnorton.com/studyspace

- What were the different approaches to Reconstruction?
- How did white southerners respond to the end of the old order in the South?
- To what extent did blacks function as citizens in the reconstructed South?
- What were the main issues in national politics in the 1870s?
- Why did Reconstruction end in 1877?

In the spring of 1865, the wearying war was finally over. At a frightful cost of over 630,000 lives and the destruction of the southern economy and much of its landscape, the Union had emerged triumphant, and some 4 million enslaved African Americans were freed. Now the nation faced the imposing task of reuniting, providing for the freed slaves, and "reconstructing" a ravaged and resentful South.

THE WAR'S AFTERMATH

In the war's aftermath the victors faced difficult questions: Should the Confederate leaders be tried for treason? How should new governments be formed? How and at whose expense was the South's economy to be rebuilt? Should debts incurred by the Confederate state governments be honored? Who should pay to rebuild the South's railroads and public buildings, dredge the clogged southern harbors, and restore damaged levees? What was to be done for the freed slaves? Were they to be given land? social equality? education? voting rights? Such complex questions required sober reflection and careful planning, but policy makers did not have the luxury of time or the benefit of consensus. Some northerners wanted the former Confederate states returned to the Union with little or no changes in the region's social, political, and economic life. Others wanted southern society punished and transformed. At the end of 1865, the editors of the nation's foremost magazine, *Harper's Weekly*, expressed this vengeful attitude when they declared that "the forgive-and-forget policy . . . is mere political insanity and suicide."

DEVELOPMENT IN THE NORTH To some Americans the Civil War was more truly a social revolution than the War of Independence, for it reduced the once-dominant influence of the South's planter elite in national politics and elevated that of the northern "captains of industry." Government, both federal and state, grew more friendly to business leaders and more unfriendly to those who would probe into their activities. The wartime Congress had delivered on the party's major platform promises of the 1860 campaign, which had cemented the allegiance of northeastern businessmen and western farmers to the Republican party.

In the absence of southern members, the wartime Congress had centralized national power and enacted the Republican economic agenda. It passed the Morrill Tariff, which doubled the average level of import duties. The National Banking Act created a uniform system of banking and bank-note currency and helped finance the war. Congress also decided that the first transcontinental railroad would run along a north-central route, from Omaha to Sacramento, and donated public land and sold bonds to ensure its financing. In the Homestead Act of 1862, moreover, Congress provided free federal homesteads of 160 acres to settlers, who had only to occupy the land for five years to gain title. The Morrill Land Grant Act of the same year conveyed to each state 30,000 acres of federal land per member of Congress from the state, the proceeds from the sale of which went to create colleges of "agriculture and mechanic arts." Such measures helped stimulate the North's economy in the years after the Civil War.

DEVASTATION IN THE SOUTH The postwar South offered a sharp contrast to the victorious North. Along the path of General William T. Sherman's Union army, one observer reported in 1866, the countryside of Georgia and South Carolina "looked for many miles like a broad black streak of ruin and desolation." Columbia, South Carolina, said another witness, was "a wilderness of ruins"; Charleston, a place of "vacant houses, of widowed

A street in the "burned district"

Ruins of Richmond, Virginia, in the spring of 1865.

women, of rotting wharves, of deserted warehouses, of weed-wild gardens, of miles of grass-grown streets, of acres of pitiful and voiceless barrenness."

Throughout the South, property values had collapsed. Confederate bonds and paper money were worthless; most railroads were damaged or destroyed. Cotton that had escaped destruction was seized as Confederate property or in forfeit of federal taxes. Emancipation wiped out $4 billion invested in human flesh and left the labor system in disarray. The great age of expansion in the cotton market was over. Not until 1879 would the cotton crop again equal the record harvest of 1860; tobacco production did not regain its prewar level until 1880; the sugar crop of Louisiana did not recover until 1893; and the old rice industry of the Tidewater and the hemp industry of the Kentucky Bluegrass never regained their prewar status.

A TRANSFORMED SOUTH   The defeat of the Confederacy transformed much of southern society. The liberation of slaves, the destruction of property, and the free fall in land values left many planters destitute and homeless. After the Civil War many former Confederates were so embittered that they abandoned their native region rather than submit to "Yankee rule." Some migrated to Canada, Europe, Mexico, South America, or Asia. Others preferred the western territories and states. Still others moved to northern and midwestern cities on the assumption that their educational and economic opportunities would be better among the victors.

Most of those who remained in the South found their farms, homes, and communities transformed. One Confederate army captain reported that on his father's plantation "our negroes are living in great comfort. They were delighted to see me with overflowing affection. They waited on me as before, gave me breakfast, splendid dinners, etc. But they firmly and respectfully informed me: 'We own this land now. Put it out of your head that it will ever be yours again.'"

LEGALLY FREE, SOCIALLY BOUND   In the former Confederate states the newly freed slaves suffered most of all. A few northerners argued that what the ex-slaves needed most was their own land. In 1865, Representative George Washington Julian of Indiana and Senator Charles Sumner of Massachusetts proposed to give freed slaves forty-acre homesteads carved out of Confederate lands taken under the Confiscation Act of 1862. But their plan for outright grants was replaced by a program of rentals, since confiscation was effective under the law only for the lifetime of the Confederate property owner. Discussions of land distribution fueled rumors, however, that freed slaves would get "forty acres and a mule," a slogan that swept the South at the end of the war. But even abolitionists shrank from taking land

Freed slaves in Richmond, Virginia

According to a former Confederate general, freed slaves had "nothing but freedom."

from whites to give to the freed slaves. Citizenship and legal rights were one thing, wholesale confiscation of property and land redistribution quite another. Instead of land or material help, the freed slaves more often got advice about proper behavior.

THE FREEDMEN'S BUREAU   On March 3, 1865, while the war was still raging, Congress set up within the War Department the Bureau of Refugees, Freedmen, and Abandoned Lands to provide "provisions, clothing, and fuel" to relieve "destitute and suffering refugees and freedmen and their wives and children." It was the first federal experiment in social welfare, albeit temporary. Agents of what came to be called the Freedmen's Bureau negotiated labor contracts (a new practice for both African Americans and planters), provided medical care, and set up schools. The bureau had its own courts to deal with labor disputes and land titles, and its agents were authorized to supervise trials involving blacks in other courts. White intransigence and racial prejudice thwarted the efforts of Freedmen's Bureau agents to protect and assist the former slaves, however.

THE BATTLE OVER RECONSTRUCTION

The question of how to reconstruct the South's political structure centered on deciding which governments would constitute authority in the defeated states. As Union forces advanced into the South, President Lincoln in 1862 named military governors for conquered Tennessee, Arkansas, and Louisiana. By the end of the following year, he had formulated a plan for regular civilian governments in those states and any others that might be liberated from Confederate rule.

LINCOLN'S PLAN AND CONGRESS'S RESPONSE   In late 1863, President Lincoln had issued a Proclamation of Amnesty and Reconstruction, under which any former Confederate state could form a Union government whenever a number equal to 10 percent of those who had voted in 1860 took an oath of allegiance to the Constitution and the Union and had received a presidential pardon. Participants also had to swear support for laws and proclamations dealing with emancipation. Excluded from the pardon, however, were certain groups: Confederate officials and officers; judges, congressmen, and military officers of the United States who had left their federal posts to aid the rebellion; and those accused of failure to treat captured African American soldiers and their officers as prisoners of war.

Under this plan, governments loyal to the Union appeared in Tennessee, Arkansas, and Louisiana, but Congress refused to recognize them. In the absence of specific provisions for Reconstruction in the Constitution, politicians disagreed as to where authority to restore Rebel states properly rested. A few conservative and most moderate Republicans supported Lincoln's program of immediate restoration. A small but influential group, known as Radical Republicans, demanded a sweeping transformation of southern society that would include making the freed slaves full-fledged citizens. The Radicals hoped to reconstruct southern society so as to dismantle the planter elite and the Democratic party.

The Radical Republicans were talented, earnest leaders who maintained that Congress, not the president, should supervise the Reconstruction program. To this end in 1864 they helped pass the Wade-Davis Bill, sponsored by Senator Benjamin Franklin Wade of Ohio and Representative Henry Winter Davis of Maryland. In contrast to Lincoln's 10 percent plan, the Wade-Davis Bill required that a *majority* of white male citizens declare their allegiance and that only those who swore an "ironclad" oath that they had always remained loyal to the Union could vote or serve in the state constitutional conventions. The conventions, moreover, would have to abolish slavery, deny political rights to high-ranking civil and military officers of the Confederacy, and repudiate Confederate war debts. Passed during the closing days of the 1864 session, the bill was vetoed by Lincoln. The bill's sponsors then issued the Wade-Davis Manifesto, a blistering statement accusing the president of usurping power and attempting to use readmitted states to ensure his reelection.

Lincoln made his final statement on Reconstruction in his last public address, on April 11, 1865. Speaking from the White House balcony, he dismissed the theoretical question of whether the Confederate states had technically remained in the Union as "good for nothing at all—a mere pernicious abstraction." Those states were simply "out of their proper practical relation with the Union," and the object was to get them back "into their proper practical relation" as quickly as possible. Lincoln hoped to get new southern state governments in operation before Congress met in December. He worried that Congress might push through a harsher Reconstruction program. Lincoln wanted "no persecution, no bloody work," no dramatic restructuring of southern social and economic life.

On the evening of April 14, 1865, Lincoln went to Ford's Theatre and his rendezvous with death. Shot in the head by John Wilkes Booth, a crazed actor and Confederate zealot, the president died the next morning. Pursued into Virginia, Booth was trapped and shot in a burning barn. His last words were "Tell mother I die for my country. I thought I did for the best." Three collaborators were tried and hanged, along with Mary Surratt, at whose boardinghouse they had plotted. Three other conspirators received life sentences, including a Maryland doctor who set the leg Booth had broken when he jumped from Lincoln's box onto the stage.

JOHNSON'S PLAN Lincoln's death elevated to the White House Vice President Andrew Johnson of Tennessee, a combative man who lacked most presidential virtues. Essentially illiterate, Johnson was provincial and bigoted, short-tempered and impetuous. At the inaugural ceremonies in early 1865, he had drunkenly slurred his vice-presidential address, embarrassing Lincoln and the nation. Johnson was a war (pro-Union) Democrat who had been put on the National Union ticket in 1864 as a gesture of unity. Of origins as humble as Lincoln's, Johnson had moved as a youth from his birthplace in Raleigh, North Carolina, to Greeneville, Tennessee, where he became the proprietor of a tailor shop. Self-educated with the help of his wife, Johnson grew prosperous, acquiring several slaves in the process.

Beginning in the 1830s, Johnson emerged as a leading Jacksonian Democrat. A bitter critic of the "swaggering" planter aristocracy "who are too lazy and proud to work," he promoted free land for the poor, defended slavery, and championed white supremacy. A notoriously stubborn man, he became a self-righteous, hot-tempered orator who enjoyed strong drink and employed abusive language to belittle his opponents. His fiery speeches and firm principles helped him win election as mayor, congressman, governor, and senator.

Like many other whites living in mountainous eastern Tennessee, Johnson ardently believed in the Union. In 1861 he was the only southern senator from a Confederate state to vote against secession, leading critics to denounce him as a "traitor" to the region. Yet his devotion to the Union did not include opposition to slavery. He hated the Confederacy because he hated the planter elite. "Damn the Negroes," Johnson bellowed to a friend during the war, "I am fighting those traitorous aristocrats, their masters."

Some Radical Republicans at first thought President Johnson, unlike Lincoln, was one of them. Johnson had, for example, asserted that treason "must be made infamous and traitors must be impoverished." But the Radicals would soon find Johnson to be as unsympathetic as Lincoln had been to their sweeping agenda, if for different reasons. Johnson's loyalty to the Union sprang from a strict adherence to the Constitution and a fervent belief in limited government. He held that the rebellious states should be quickly brought back into their proper relation to the Union because the states and the Union were indestructible. In 1865, Johnson declared that "there is no such thing as Reconstruction. Those states have not gone out of the Union. Therefore Reconstruction is unnecessary."

Johnson's plan to restore the Union thus closely resembled Lincoln's. A new Proclamation of Amnesty, issued on May 29, 1865, excluded from pardon not only those Lincoln had excluded but also everybody with taxable property worth more than $20,000. Those wealthy planters and merchants were the people Johnson believed had led the South to secede. Those in the excluded groups might make special applications for presidential pardon, and before the year was out Johnson had issued some 13,000 pardons.

Andrew Johnson

A pro-Union Democrat from Tennessee.

In each of the Rebel states not already organized by Lincoln, Johnson named a native Unionist provisional governor with authority to call a convention of men elected by loyal voters. Lincoln's 10 percent requirement was omitted. Johnson called upon the conventions to invalidate the secession ordinances, abolish slavery, and repudiate all debts incurred to aid the Confederacy. Each state, moreover, was to ratify the Thirteenth Amendment, which ended slavery. Like Lincoln, Johnson endorsed limited voting rights for blacks. The state conventions for the most part met Johnson's requirements. Emboldened by the president's indulgence, however, southern whites ignored his advice to move cautiously in restoring their political and social traditions. Suggestions of black suffrage were scarcely raised in the state conventions and promptly squelched when they were.

SOUTHERN INTRANSIGENCE   When Congress met in December 1865, for the first time since the end of the war it faced the fact that the new state governments in the former Confederacy were remarkably like the old ones. Among the new members presenting themselves to Congress were Georgia's Alexander Stephens, former vice president of the Confederacy, four Confederate generals, eight colonels, and six cabinet members. The Congress forthwith denied seats to all such officials. It was too much to expect, after four bloody years, that the Unionists in Congress would welcome back ex-Confederate leaders.

Furthermore, the new southern state legislatures, in passing repressive "black codes" restricting the freedom of African Americans, baldly revealed that they intended to preserve the trappings of slavery as nearly as possible. As one southerner stressed, the "ex-slave was not a free man; he was a free Negro," and the black codes were intended to highlight the distinction.

The black codes varied from state to state, but some provisions were common. Existing black marriages, including common-law marriages, were recognized (although interracial marriages were prohibited), and testimony by blacks was accepted in legal cases involving them—and in six states in all cases. Blacks could own property. They could sue and be sued in the courts. On the other hand, in Mississippi they could not own farmland, and in South Carolina they could not own city lots. Blacks who worked for whites were required to enter into labor contracts with their employers, with provision for punishment in case of violation. Their dependent children were subject to compulsory apprenticeship and corporal punishment by the employer. "Vagrant" (unemployed) blacks were punished with severe fines, and if unable to pay they were forced to work in the fields of whites who paid the courts for their cheap labor. Slavery was thus revived in another guise.

THE RADICAL REPUBLICANS Faced with such southern intransigence, moderate Republicans drifted more and more toward the Radical camp. The new Congress set up a Joint Committee on Reconstruction, with nine members from the House and six from the Senate, to gather evidence and submit proposals for reconstructing the southern states. As a parade of witnesses testified to the Rebels' impenitence, initiative on the committee fell to determined Radicals: Benjamin Wade of Ohio, George Julian of Indiana, Henry Wilson of Massachusetts, and most conspicuously of all, Thaddeus Stevens of Pennsylvania and Charles Sumner of Massachusetts.

Stevens, a crusty old bachelor with a chiseled face, thin, stern lips, and brooding eyes, was the domineering floor leader in the House. Driven by a genuine if at times fanatic idealism, he angrily insisted that the "whole fabric of southern society *must* be changed." Sumner, Stevens's counterpart in the Senate, agreed. Now recovered from "Bully" Brooks's 1856 assault, Sumner strove to see the South *reconstructed* rather than simply restored. This aim put him at odds with President Johnson. After visiting the White House, Sumner found the president "harsh, petulant, and unreasonable." He was especially disheartened by President Johnson's "prejudice, ignorance, and perversity" regarding the treatment of African Americans. Sumner, along with other Radicals, now grew determined to take matters into their own hands. He argued that "Massachusetts could govern Georgia better than Georgia could govern herself." The southern plantations, seedbeds of aristocratic pretension and secession, he later added, "must be broken up, and the freedmen must have the pieces."

Most of the Radical Republicans had long been abolitionists, and they approached the question of African American rights with a sincere humanitarian impulse. Yet the Republicans also had political reasons for promoting civil rights. They needed black votes to maintain their control of Congress and the White House. They also needed to disenfranchise former Confederates to keep them from helping to elect Democrats who would restore the old ruling class to power. In public, however, the Radical Republicans rarely disclosed such partisan self-interest. Instead, they asserted that the Republicans, the party of Union and freedom, could best guarantee the fruits of victory and that extending voting rights to African Americans would be the best way to promote their welfare.

The growing conflict of opinion over Reconstruction policy brought about an inversion in constitutional reasoning. Secessionists—and Andrew Johnson—were now arguing that the Confederate states had in fact technically remained in the Union, and some Radical Republicans were contriving arguments that they had left the Union after all. Thaddeus Stevens argued that the Confederate states had indeed seceded and were now conquered provinces, subject to the absolute will of the victors. He added that the "whole fabric of southern society must be changed." Most congressmen, however, held that the Rebel states continued to exist but by the acts of secession and war had forfeited "all civil and political rights under the Constitution." And Congress, not the president, was the proper authority to determine how and when such rights might be restored.

JOHNSON'S BATTLE WITH CONGRESS   A long year of political battling remained, however, before this idea triumphed. By the end of 1865, the Radical Republicans' views had gained only a slight majority in Congress, insufficient to override presidential vetoes. The critical year of 1866 saw the gradual waning of Andrew Johnson's power, much of which was self-induced. Johnson first challenged Congress in February, when he vetoed a bill to extend the life of the Freedmen's Bureau. The measure, he said, violated the Constitution. For the moment, Johnson's prestige remained sufficiently intact that the Senate upheld his veto.

Three days after the veto, however, on George Washington's Birthday, Johnson undermined his authority by launching an intemperate assault

"The Cruel Uncle and the Vetoed Babes in the Wood"

A cartoon depicting Andrew Johnson leading two children, "Civil Rights" and "Bureau," into the "Veto Wood."

upon the Radical Republican leaders during an impromptu speech. From that point, moderate Republicans abandoned the president, and Radical Republicans went on the offensive.

In mid-March 1866 the Radical-led Congress passed the Civil Rights Act. A direct response to the black codes created by unrepentant state legislatures in the South, it declared that "all persons born in the United States ... excluding Indians not taxed" were citizens entitled to "full and equal benefit of all laws." The granting of citizenship to native-born blacks, Johnson claimed, exceeded the scope of federal power. It would, moreover, "foment discord among the races." He vetoed the measure, but this time, in April, Congress overrode his veto. Then in July it enacted a revised Freedmen's Bureau Bill, again overturning a veto. From that point on, Johnson's public and political support steadily eroded.

THE FOURTEENTH AMENDMENT To remove all doubt about the validity of the new Civil Rights Act, the joint committee recommended a new constitutional amendment, which passed Congress in 1866 and was ratified by the states in 1868. The Fourteenth Amendment went far beyond the Civil Rights Act, however. The first section asserts four principles: it reaffirms the state and federal citizenship of all persons—regardless of race—born or naturalized in the United States, and it forbids any state (the word *state* would be important in later litigation) to "abridge the privileges or immunities of citizens," to deprive any *person* (again an important term) "of life, liberty, or property, without due process of law," or to "deny any person . . . the equal protection of the laws."

These clauses have been the subject of lawsuits resulting in applications not foreseen at the time. The "due-process clause" has come to mean that state as well as federal power is subject to the Bill of Rights, and it has been used to protect corporations, as legal "persons," from "unreasonable" regulation by the states. Other provisions of the amendment had less far-reaching effects. One section specified that the debt of the United States "shall not be questioned" but declared "illegal and void" all debts contracted in aid of the Confederate rebellion. The final sentence specified the power of Congress to pass laws enforcing the amendment.

Johnson's home state was among the first to ratify the Fourteenth Amendment. In Tennessee, which had harbored more Unionists than any other Confederate state, the government had fallen under Radical Republican control. The rest of the South, however, steadfastly resisted the Radical challenge to Andrew Johnson's lenient program. In 1866 bloody race riots in Memphis and New Orleans added fuel to the flames. Both incidents sparked indiscriminate massacres of blacks by local police and white mobs. The rioting, Radical Republicans argued, was the natural fruit of Johnson's foolish policy.

RECONSTRUCTING THE SOUTH

THE TRIUMPH OF CONGRESSIONAL RECONSTRUCTION As 1866 drew to an end, the November congressional elections promised to be a referendum on the growing split between Johnson and the Radical Republicans. The president embarked on a speaking tour of the Midwest, a "swing around the circle," which sparked undignified shouting contests between the president and his audiences. In Cleveland he described the Radical Republicans as "factious, domineering, tyrannical" men. Various incidents tended to confirm his image as a "ludicrous boor," which Radical Republican newspapers eagerly promoted. When the election returns came in, the Republicans had more than a two-thirds majority in each house, a comfortable margin with which to override presidential vetoes.

Congress actually enacted a Reconstruction program even before the new members took office. On March 2, 1867, two days before the old Congress expired, it passed three basic laws of congressional Reconstruction over Johnson's vetoes: the Military Reconstruction Act, the Command of the Army Act, and the Tenure of Office Act.

The first of these acts prescribed conditions under which new southern state governments should be formed. The other two sought to block any effort by the president to obstruct the process. The Command of the Army Act required that all orders from the president as commander in chief go through the headquarters of the general of the army, then Ulysses Grant. The Tenure of Office Act required the Senate's permission for the president to remove any federal officeholder whose appointment the Senate had confirmed. In large measure it was intended to retain Secretary of War Edwin

Stanton, the one Radical Republican sympathizer in Johnson's cabinet. But an ambiguity had crept into the wording of the act. Cabinet officers, it said, should serve during the term of the president who appointed them—and Lincoln had appointed Stanton, although, to be sure, Johnson was serving out Lincoln's term.

The Military Reconstruction Act was hailed—or denounced—as the triumphant victory of Radical Reconstruction. Originally intended by the Radical Republicans to give military commanders in the South ultimate control over law enforcement and to leave open indefinitely the terms of restoration, it was diluted by moderate Republicans until it boiled down to little more than a requirement that southern states accept African American suffrage and ratify the Fourteenth Amendment.

Tennessee, which had already ratified the Fourteenth Amendment, was exempted from the application of the act. The other ten states were divided into five military districts, and the commanding officer of each was authorized to keep order and protect the "rights of persons and property." The Johnson governments remained intact for the time being, but new constitutions were to be framed "in conformity with the Constitution of the United States," in conventions elected by male citizens aged twenty-one and older "of whatever race, color, or previous condition." Each state constitution had to provide the same universal male suffrage. Then, once the constitution was ratified by a majority of voters and accepted by Congress, the state legislature had ratified the Fourteenth Amendment, and the amendment had become part of the Constitution, any given state would be entitled to renewed representation in Congress. Persons excluded from officeholding by the proposed amendment were also excluded from participation in the process. Before the end of 1867, new elections had been held in all the states but Texas.

Having clipped the president's wings, the Republican Congress moved a year later to safeguard its Reconstruction program from possible interference by the Supreme Court. On March 27, 1868, Congress simply removed the power of the Supreme Court to review cases arising under the Military Reconstruction Act, which Congress clearly had the constitutional right to do under its power to define the Court's appellate jurisdiction. The Court accepted this curtailment of its authority on the same day it affirmed the notion of an "indestructible Union" in *Texas v. White* (1869). In that case the Court also acknowledged the right of Congress to reframe state governments, thus endorsing the Radical Republican point of view.

THE IMPEACHMENT AND TRIAL OF JOHNSON By 1868, Radical Republicans were convinced not only that the power of the Supreme

Court and the president needed to be curtailed but also that Andrew Johnson himself had to be removed from office. Johnson, though hostile to the congressional Reconstruction program, had gone through the motions required of him. He continued to pardon former Confederates, however, and transferred several of the district military commanders who had displayed Radical Republican sympathies. Johnson lacked Lincoln's resilience and pragmatism, and he allowed his temper to get the better of his judgment. He castigated the Radical Republicans as "a gang of cormorants and bloodsuckers who have been fattening upon the country." During 1867, newspapers reported that the differences between Johnson and the Republicans had grown irreconcilable.

The Radical Republicans unsuccessfully tried to impeach Johnson early in 1867, alleging a variety of flimsy charges, none of which represented an indictable crime. Then Johnson himself provided the occasion for impeachment when he deliberately violated the Tenure of Office Act in order to test its constitutionality. Secretary of War Edwin Stanton had become a thorn in Johnson's side, refusing to resign despite his disagreements with the president's Reconstruction policy. On August 12, 1867, during a congressional recess, Johnson suspended Stanton and named General Ulysses Grant in his place. When the Senate refused to confirm Johnson's action, however, Grant returned the office to Stanton.

The Radical Republicans now saw their chance to remove the president. On February 24, 1868, the House passed eleven articles of impeachment by a party-line vote of 126 to 47. Eight of the articles focused on the charge that Johnson had unlawfully removed Secretary of War Stanton. Article 9 accused the president of issuing orders in violation of the Command of the Army Act. The last two articles in effect charged him with criticizing Congress by "inflammatory and scandalous harangues." Article 11 also accused him of "unlawfully devising and contriving" to violate the Reconstruction Acts, contrary to his obligation to execute the laws. At the very least, it stated, Johnson had tried to obstruct Congress's will while observing the letter of the law.

The Senate trial began on March 5, 1868, and continued until May 26, with Chief Justice Salmon P. Chase presiding. Debate eventually focused on Stanton's removal, the most substantive impeachment charge. Johnson's lawyers argued that Lincoln, not Johnson, had appointed Stanton, so the Tenure of Office Act did not apply to him. At the same time they claimed (correctly, as it turned out) that the law was unconstitutional.

As the five-week trial ended and the voting began in May 1868, seven moderate Republicans and all twelve Democrats voted to acquit. The final tally was 35 to 19 for conviction, one vote short of the two thirds needed for removal from office.

Although the Senate failed to remove Johnson, the trial crippled his already weak presidency. During the remaining ten months of his term, he initiated no other clashes with Congress. In 1868, Johnson sought the Democratic presidential nomination but lost to New York governor Horatio Seymour, who then lost to the Republican, Ulysses Grant, in the general election. The impeachment of Johnson was in the end a great political mistake, for the failure to remove the president damaged Radical Republican morale and support. Nevertheless, the Radical cause did gain something: Johnson's agreement not to obstruct the process of Reconstruction. Thereafter Radical Reconstruction began in earnest.

REPUBLICAN RULE IN THE SOUTH   In June 1868, Congress agreed that seven southern states, all but Virginia, Mississippi, and Texas, had met the more stringent conditions for readmission to the Union. Congress rescinded Georgia's admission, however, when the state legislature expelled twenty-eight African American members and seated former Confederate leaders. The federal military commander in Georgia then forced the legislature to reseat the black members and remove the Confederates, and the state was compelled to ratify the Fifteenth Amendment before being readmitted in July 1870. Mississippi, Texas, and Virginia had returned earlier in 1870, under the added requirement that they, too, ratify the Fifteenth Amendment. That amendment, ratified in 1870, forbids the states to deny any citizen the right to vote on grounds of "race, color, or previous condition of servitude."

Long before the new governments were established, partisan Republican groups had begun to spring up in the South, promoted by the Union League, an organization founded in 1862 to rally support for the federal government. Its representatives enrolled blacks and loyal whites as members, initiated them into the secrets and rituals of the order, and instructed them "in their rights and duties." The Union Leagues became a powerful source of Republican political strength in the South and as a result drew the ire of unreconstructed whites.

THE RECONSTRUCTED SOUTH

Throughout the South during Reconstruction, many former Confederates continued to harbor deeply ingrained racial prejudices. They adopted a militant stance against federally imposed changes in southern society.

Whites used terror, intimidation, and violence to suppress black efforts to gain social and economic equality. In July 1866, for instance, a black woman in Clinch County, Georgia, was arrested and given sixty-five lashes for "using abusive language" in an encounter with a white woman. A month later another black woman suffered the same punishment. The Civil War had brought freedom to the enslaved, but it did not bring protection against exploitation or abuse.

THE FREED SLAVES   Southern blacks were active agents in affecting the course of Reconstruction. Many former slaves found themselves liberated but destitute after the fighting ended. The mere promise of freedom, however, had raised their hopes for biracial democracy, equal justice, and economic opportunity. "Most anyone ought to know that a man is better off free than as a slave, even if he did not have anything," said the Reverend E. P. Holmes, a black Georgia preacher and former domestic servant. "I would rather be free and have my liberty."

Participation in the Union army or navy had provided many freedmen with training in leadership. Black military veterans would form the core of the first generation of African American political leaders in the postwar South. Military service provided many former slaves with the first opportunities to learn to read and write. Army life also alerted them to alternative social choices and to new opportunities for economic advancement and social respectability. Fighting for the Union cause also instilled a fervent sense of nationalism. A Virginia freedman explained that the United States was "now *our* country—made emphatically so by the blood of our brethren."

Former slaves established independent churches after the war, which quickly formed the foundation of African American community life. Blacks preferred Baptist churches over other denominations, in part because its decentralized structure allowed each congregation to worship in its own way. By 1890 over 1.3 million African Americans were worshipping in Baptist churches in the South, nearly three times as many as had joined any other denomination. In addition to forming viable new congregations, freed African Americans organized thousands of fraternal, benevolent, and mutual-aid societies, as well as clubs, lodges, and associations. Memphis, for example, had over 200 such organizations; Richmond boasted twice that number.

Freed slaves also hastened to reestablish and reaffirm their families. Marriages that had been prohibited were now legitimized through the assistance of the Freedmen's Bureau. By 1870 most former slaves were living in two-parent households.

Former slaves had little money or technical training and were thus faced with the prospect of becoming wage laborers to support themselves. To avoid this alternative and retain as much autonomy as possible over their productive energy and that of their children, many freed slaves chose to become sharecroppers, tenant farmers who gained access to separate plots of land owned by whites. In payment for the use of the land and a cabin, and sometimes even the tools, seed, and fertilizer needed to farm the land, they were required to give between one half and two thirds of the harvested crops to the landowner. This arrangement gave them higher status than they would have had as wage laborers. It also gave them the freedom to set their own hours and work as much or as little as they pleased, and it enabled mothers and wives to devote time to domestic responsibilities while contributing to the family's income.

African American communities in the postwar South also sought to establish schools. The antebellum planter elite had denied education to blacks because they feared that literate slaves would organize uprisings. After the war the white elite worried that formal education would encourage poor whites and poor blacks to leave the South in search of better social and economic opportunities. Economic leaders wanted to protect the competitive advantage afforded by the region's low-wage labor market. Yet white opposition to education for blacks made education all the more important to African Americans. South Carolina's Mary McLeod Bethune, the seventeenth child of former slaves and one of the first children in the household born after the Civil War, reveled in the opportunity to gain an education: "The whole world opened to me when I learned to read." She walked five miles to school as a child, earned a scholarship to college, and went on to become the first black woman to found a school that became a four-year college, Bethune-Cookman, in Daytona Beach, Florida.

AFRICAN AMERICANS IN SOUTHERN POLITICS   In the postwar South the new role of African Americans in politics caused the most controversy. If largely illiterate and inexperienced in the rudiments of politics, southern blacks were little different from the millions of whites enfranchised in the age of Jackson or immigrants herded to the polls by political bosses in New York and other cities after the war. Some freedmen frankly confessed their disadvantages. Beverly Nash, a black delegate to the South Carolina convention of 1868, told his colleagues: "I believe, my friends and fellow-citizens, we are not prepared for this suffrage. But we can learn. Give a man tools and let him commence to use them, and in time he will learn a trade. So it is with voting."

Several hundred African American delegates participated in the statewide political conventions. Most had been selected by local political meetings or churches, fraternal societies, Union Leagues, or black Federal army units, although a few simply appointed themselves. The African American delegates "ranged all colors and apparently all conditions," but free mulattoes from the cities played the most prominent roles. At Louisiana's Republican state convention, for instance, nineteen of the twenty black delegates had been born free.

By 1867 former slaves had begun to gain political influence and vote in large numbers, and this development revealed emerging tensions within the African American community. Some southern blacks resented the presence of northern brethren who moved south after the war, while others complained that few ex-slaves were represented in leadership positions. Northern blacks and the southern black elite, most of whom were urban dwellers, opposed efforts to redistribute land to the rural freedmen, and many insisted that political equality did not mean social equality. As a black Alabama leader stressed, "We do not ask that the ignorant and degraded shall be put on a social equality with the refined and intelligent." In general, however,

Freedmen voting in New Orleans

The Fifteenth Amendment, ratified in 1870, guaranteed at the federal level the right of citizens to vote regardless of "race, color, or previous condition of servitude." But former slaves had been registering to vote—and voting in large numbers—in state elections since 1867, as in this scene.

unity rather than dissension prevailed, and African Americans focused on common concerns such as full equality under the law.

Brought suddenly into politics in times that tried the most skilled of statesmen, many African Americans served with distinction. Nonetheless, the derisive label "black Reconstruction," used by later critics, exaggerates African American political influence, which was limited mainly to voting, and overlooks the political clout of the large number of white Republicans, especially in the mountain areas of the Upper South, who supported the congressional plan for Reconstruction. Only one of the new state conventions, South Carolina's, had a black majority, seventy-six to forty-one. Louisiana's was evenly divided racially, and in only two other conventions were more than 20 percent of the members black: Florida's, with 40 percent, and Virginia's, with 24 percent.

In the new state governments any African American participation was a novelty. Although some 600 blacks—most of them former slaves—served as state legislators, no black was ever elected governor, and few served as judges. In Louisiana, however, Pinckney Pinchback, a northern black and former Union soldier, won the office of lieutenant governor and served as acting governor when the white governor was indicted for corruption. Several African Americans were elected lieutenant governor, state treasurer, or secretary of state. There were two black senators in Congress during Reconstruction, Hiram Revels and Blanche K. Bruce, both from Mississippi, and fourteen black members of the House. Among them were some of the ablest congressmen of the time.

CARPETBAGGERS AND SCALAWAGS   The top positions in postwar southern state governments went for the most part to white Republicans whom the opposition labeled carpetbaggers and scalawags, depending upon their place of birth. Northerners who allegedly rushed south with all their belongings in carpetbags to reap political spoils were more often than not Union veterans who had arrived as early as 1865 or 1866, drawn south by the hope of economic opportunity. Others were lawyers, businessmen, editors, teachers, social workers, or preachers who came on sincere missionary endeavors.

The scalawags, or southern white Republicans, were even more reviled and misrepresented. A Nashville newspaper editor called them the "merest trash." Most scalawags had opposed secession, forming a Unionist majority in mountain counties as far south as Georgia and Alabama and especially in the hills of eastern Tennessee. Though many were indeed crass opportunists who indulged in corruption at the public's expense, several were distinguished figures. They included the former Confederate general James Longstreet, who decided after Appomattox that the Old South must change its ways. To that end he became a successful cotton broker in New Orleans, joined the Republican party, and supported the Radical Reconstruction program. Others were former Whigs who supported the Republican party's expansive industrial and commercial program in keeping with Henry Clay's earlier efforts to use the government to promote economic growth and industrial development.

THE RADICAL REPUBLICAN RECORD Former Confederates not only resented carpetbaggers and scalawags, but they also objected to the new state constitutions, primarily because of their provisions allowing for black voting and civil rights. Nonetheless, most of those state constitutions remained in effect for some years after the end of Radical Republican control, and later constitutions incorporated many of their features. Conspicuous among the Radical innovations were steps toward greater democracy, such as requiring universal male suffrage, reapportioning legislatures more nearly according to population, and making more state offices elective.

Given the hostile circumstances under which the Radical Republican governments operated, their achievements were remarkable. They established the first state-supported public school systems, in which some 600,000 black pupils were enrolled by 1877. State governments under the Radical Republicans also paid more attention to the poor and to orphanages, asylums, and institutions for the disabled of both races. Public roads, bridges, railroads, and buildings were repaired or rebuilt. African Americans achieved rights and opportunities that would never again be taken away, at least in principle: equality before the law and the right to own property, carry on business, enter professions, attend schools, and learn to read and write.

Yet several of the Republican state regimes also engaged in systematic corruption. Public money and public credit were often awarded to privately owned corporations, notably railroads, under conditions that invited influence peddling. Still, corruption was not invented by the Radical Republican regimes, nor did it die with them. In Mississippi the Republican Reconstruction governments were quite honest compared with those of their Democratic successors.

RELIGION AND RECONSTRUCTION The religious community played a critical role in the implementation and ultimate failure of Radical Reconstruction. And religious commentators offered quite different interpretations of what should be done with the defeated South. Thaddeus

Stevens and many other Radical Republican leaders who had spent their careers promoting the abolition of slavery and racial equality were motivated primarily by religious ideals and moral fervor. They wanted no compromise with racism. Likewise, most of the Christian missionaries who headed south after the Civil War brought with them a progressive vision of a biracial "beloved community" emerging in the reconstructed South, and they strove to promote social and political equality for freed slaves. For these crusaders, civil rights was a sacred cause. They used Christian principles to challenge the prevailing theological and "scientific" justifications for racial inferiority. They also promoted Christian solidarity across racial and regional lines.

At the same time, the Protestant denominations, all of which had split into northern and southern branches over the issues of slavery and secession, struggled to reunite after the war. A growing number of northern ministers promoted reconciliation between the warring regions after the Civil War. These "apostles of forgiveness" prized white unity over racial equality. For example, the Reverend Henry Ward Beecher, the powerful New York minister whose sister Harriet Beecher Stowe wrote *Uncle Tom's Cabin*, wanted white southern planters—rather than federal officials or African Americans themselves—to oversee Reconstruction. Not surprisingly, Beecher's views gained widespread support among evangelical ministers in the South.

The "white republic"

This cartoon illustrates white unity over racial equality.

The collapse of the Confederacy did not prompt southern whites to abandon their belief that God was on their side. In the wake of defeat and emancipation, white southern ministers reassured their congregations that they had no reason to question the moral foundations of their region or their defense of white racial superiority. For African Americans, the Civil War and emancipation demonstrated that God was on their side. Emancipation was in their view a redemptive act through which God wrought national regeneration. African American ministers were convinced that the United States was indeed a divinely inspired nation and that blacks had a providential role to play in its future. Yet neither black nor idealistic white northern ministers could stem the growing chorus of whites who were willing to abandon goals of racial equality in exchange for national religious reconciliation. By the end of the nineteenth century, mainstream American Protestantism promoted the image of a "white republic" that conflated whiteness, godliness, and nationalism.

THE GRANT YEARS

THE ELECTION OF 1868 Ulysses S. Grant, who served as president during the collapse of Republican rule in the South, brought to the White House little political experience. But in 1868 northern voters supported the Lion of Vicksburg because of his brilliant record as a war leader. Both parties wooed Grant, but his falling-out with President Johnson had pushed him toward the Republicans and had built trust in him among the Radicals.

The Republican party platform of 1868 endorsed Radical Reconstruction, cautiously defending black suffrage as a necessity in the South but a matter that each northern state should settle for itself. It also urged payment of the nation's war debt in gold rather than in the new "greenback" paper currency printed during the war. More important than the platform were the great expectations of a soldier-president, whose slogan was "Let us have peace."

The Democrats opposed the Republicans on both Reconstruction and the debt. The Republican Congress, the Democratic platform charged, had subjected ten states, "in the time of profound peace, to military despotism and Negro supremacy." As for the public debt, the party endorsed the "Ohio idea" of Representative George H. Pendleton: since most war bonds had been bought with depreciated greenbacks, they should be paid off in greenbacks rather than in gold. With no conspicuously available candidate in sight, the convention turned to Horatio Seymour, wartime governor of New York. The Democrats ran a closer race than expected, attesting to the strength of traditional party loyalties. Although Grant swept the Electoral College by 214 to 80, his popular majority was only 307,000 out of 5.7 million votes. Over 500,000 African American voters accounted for Grant's margin of victory.

Grant had proved himself a great military leader, but in the White House he was often blind to the political forces and influence peddlers around him. Shy and withdrawn, he was uncomfortable around intellectuals and impatient with idealists. Grant preferred watching horse races to reading about complex issues. Although personally honest, he was dazzled by men of wealth and unaccountably loyal to greedy subordinates who betrayed his trust. In the formulation of policy, he passively followed the lead of Congress. This approach initially endeared him to Republican party leaders, but it left him ineffective and caused others to grow disillusioned with his leadership. At the outset, Grant consulted nobody on his cabinet appointments. Some of his choices indulged personal whims; others simply reflected bad judgment. Secretary of State Hamilton Fish of New York turned out to be a fortunate exception; he was a master in guiding foreign policy throughout the Grant presidency. Other than Fish, however, Grant's cabinet overflowed with incompetents.

THE GOVERNMENT DEBT   Financial issues dominated Grant's presidency. After the war the Treasury had assumed that the $432 million in greenbacks issued during the conflict would be retired from circulation and that the nation would revert to a "hard-money" currency—gold coins. Congress in 1866 granted the Treasury discretion to do so gradually. Many agrarian and debtor groups resisted this contraction of the money supply, believing that it would mean lower farm prices and harder-to-pay debts. They were joined by a large number of Radical Republicans who thought that a combination of high tariffs and inflation would generate more rapid economic growth. In 1868 "soft-money" supporters in Congress halted the retirement of greenbacks, leaving $356 million outstanding. There matters stood when Grant took office.

The "sound-money" (or hard-money) advocates, mostly bankers, merchants, and other creditors, claimed that Grant's election was a mandate to save the country from the Democrats' "Ohio idea" of using greenbacks to repay government bonds. Quite influential in Republican circles, the hard-money advocates also had the benefit of agreeing with the deeply ingrained popular assumption that gold coins were morally preferable to paper currency. Grant agreed as well, and in his inaugural address he endorsed payment of the national debt in gold as a point of national honor.

SCANDALS   Within less than a year of his election, Grant had fallen into a cesspool of scandal. In the summer of 1869, two unscrupulous financial buccaneers, Jay Gould and James Fisk, connived with the president's brother-in-law to corner the nation's gold market. That is, they would create a public craze for gold by purchasing massive quantities of the precious metal and convincing traders that the price would keep climbing. As more buyers joined the frenzy, the value of gold would soar. The only danger lay in the federal Treasury's selling large amounts of gold.

Grant apparently smelled a rat from the start, but he was seen in public with the speculators. As the rumor spread on Wall Street, gold rose from $132 to $163 an ounce. Finally, on Black Friday, September 24, 1869, Grant ordered the Treasury to sell a large quantity of gold, and the bubble burst. Fisk got out by repudiating his agreements and hiring thugs to intimidate his creditors. "Nothing is lost save honor," he said.

The plot to corner the gold market was only the first of several scandals that rocked the Grant administration. In 1872 the public learned about the financial crookery of the Crédit Mobilier, a construction company that had milked the Union Pacific Railroad for exorbitant fees to line the pockets of insiders who controlled both firms. Union Pacific shareholders were left holding the bag. This chicanery had transpired before Grant's election in 1868, but it now touched a number of prominent Republicans who had been given shares of Crédit Mobilier stock in exchange for favorable votes. Of the thirteen congressmen involved, only two were censured.

Even more odious disclosures soon followed, some involving the president's cabinet. Grant's secretary of war, it turned out, had accepted bribes from merchants who traded with Indians at army posts in the West. He was impeached, but he resigned in time to elude trial. Post-office contracts, it was revealed, went to carriers who offered the highest kickbacks. In St. Louis a "whiskey ring" bribed tax collectors to bilk the government of millions of dollars in revenue. Grant's private secretary was enmeshed in that scheme, taking large sums of money and other valuables in return for inside information. There is no evidence that Grant himself participated in any of the scandals, but his poor choice of associates and his gullibility earned him widespread censure.

WHITE TERROR President Grant initially fought hard to enforce the federal efforts to reconstruct the postwar South. By the time he became president, southern resistance to "Radical rule" had turned violent as unrepentant whites organized vigilante groups to terrorize blacks. Most white southerners remained so conditioned by the social prejudices embedded in the institution of slavery that they were unable to conceive of blacks as citizens. In some places, hostility to the new regimes turned violent. Said one unreconstructed Mississippian in 1875, "Carry the election peaceably if we can, forcibly if we must."

The prototype of all the terrorist groups was the Ku Klux Klan (KKK), organized in 1866 by some young men of Pulaski, Tennessee, as a social club, with the costumes and secret rituals common to fraternal groups. At first a

"Worse Than Slavery"

This Thomas Nast cartoon chides the Ku Klux Klan and the White League for promoting conditions "worse than slavery" for southern blacks after the Civil War.

group of pranksters, its members soon began to intimidate blacks and white Republicans, and the KKK spread rapidly across the South in answer to the Republican party's Union League. Klansmen rode about the countryside, hiding behind masks and under robes, spreading horrendous rumors, harassing blacks, and wreaking violence and destruction. "We are going to kill all the Negroes," a white supremacist declared during one massacre.

At the urging of President Grant, Congress struck back with three Enforcement Acts (1870–1871) to protect black voters. The first of these measures levied penalties on anyone who interfered with any citizen's right to vote. A second placed the election of congressmen under surveillance by federal election supervisors and marshals. The third (the Ku Klux Klan Act) outlawed the characteristic activities of the Klan—forming conspiracies, wearing disguises, resisting law officers, and intimidating government officials. In 1871 the federal government singled out nine counties in up-country South Carolina and pursued mass prosecutions that brought an abrupt halt to Klan terrorism. In general, however, the federal acts designed to protect African Americans suffered from weak and inconsistent enforcement. Moreover, the South's strong tradition of states' rights and local autonomy, as well as racial prejudice, resisted federal force. The unrelenting efforts of white racists to use violence to thwart Reconstruction continued into the 1870s. On Easter Sunday in 1873 in Colfax, Louisiana, a mob of white vigilantes attacked a group of black Republicans, slaughtering eighty-one. White southerners had lost the war, but during the 1870s they were winning the peace with their reactionary behavior. In the process, the goals of racial justice and civil rights were blunted.

REFORM AND THE ELECTION OF 1872 Long before President Grant's first term ended, Republicans broke ranks with the administration.

"What I Know about Raising the Devil"

With the tail and cloven hoof of the devil, Horace Greeley (center) leads a small band of Liberal Republicans in pursuit of incumbent president Ulysses S. Grant and his supporters in this 1872 cartoon.

Their alienation was a reaction to Radical Reconstruction and the incompetence and corruption in the administration. A new faction, called Liberal Republicans, favored free trade, the redemption of greenbacks with gold, the removal federal troops from the South, the restoration of the rights of former Confederates, and civil service reform.

In 1872 the Liberal Republicans held their own national convention, which produced a compromise platform condemning the Republican party's "vindictive" southern policy and favoring civil service reform but remaining silent on the protective tariff. The delegates stampeded to endorse an anomalous presidential candidate: Horace Greeley, editor of the *New York Tribune* and an enthusiastic reformer. During his long career in journalism, Greeley had promoted vegetarianism, freethinking, socialism, and spiritualism. His image as a visionary eccentric was complemented by his open hostility to the Democrats, whose support the Liberals needed. The Democrats gave the nomination to Greeley as the only hope of beating Grant and the Radical Republicans. Greeley's promise to end Radical Reconstruction and restore "self-government" to the South won over Democrats who otherwise despised the man and his beliefs.

The 1872 election results surprised no one. Republican regulars duly endorsed Grant, Radical Reconstruction, and the protective tariff. Grant still had seven southern states in his pocket, generous aid from business and banking interests, and the stalwart support of the Radical Republicans. Above all he still evoked the glory of military heroism. Greeley carried only six southern and border states, none in the North. Devastated by his crushing defeat and the death of his wife, Greeley entered a sanatorium and died three weeks later.

CONSERVATIVE RESURGENCE   The Klan in fact could not take credit for the overthrow of Republican control in any state. Perhaps its most important effect was to weaken the morale of African Americans and Republicans in the South and strengthen in the North a growing weariness

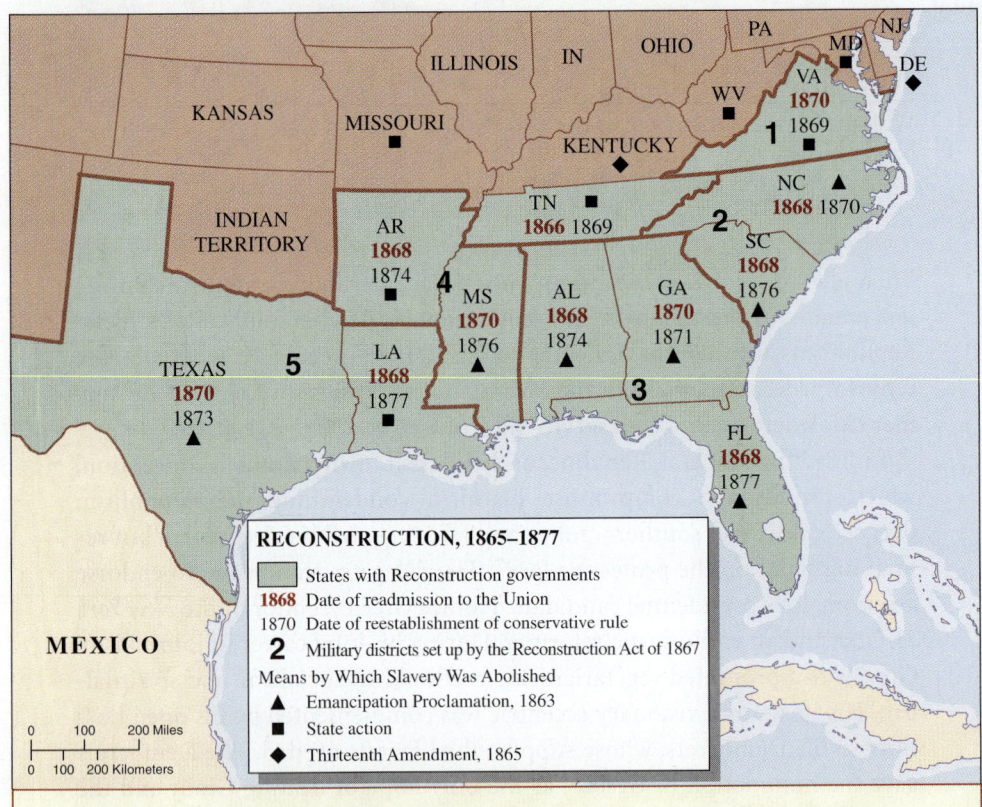

RECONSTRUCTION, 1865–1877

- States with Reconstruction governments
- **1868** Date of readmission to the Union
- 1870 Date of reestablishment of conservative rule
- **2** Military districts set up by the Reconstruction Act of 1867

Means by Which Slavery Was Abolished
- ▲ Emancipation Proclamation, 1863
- ■ State action
- ◆ Thirteenth Amendment, 1865

How did the Military Reconstruction Act reorganize governments in the South in the late 1860s and 1870s? What did the former Confederate states have to do to be readmitted to the Union? How did "Conservative" parties gradually regain control of the South from the Republicans in the 1870s?

with the whole "southern question." Republican control in the South gradually loosened as "Conservative" parties—a name used by Democrats to
mollify former Whigs—mobilized the white vote. Scalawags and many carpetbaggers drifted away from the Radical Republican ranks under pressure
from their white neighbors. Few of them had joined the Republicans out of
concern for African American rights in the first place. And where persuasion
failed to work, Democrats were willing to use chicanery. As one enthusiastic
Democrat boasted, "The white and black Republicans may outvote us, but
we can outcount them."

Such factors led to the collapse of Republican control in Virginia and Tennessee as early as 1869 and in Georgia and North Carolina in 1870. Reconstruction lasted longest in states with the largest black population, where
whites abandoned Klan hoods for barefaced intimidation in paramilitary
groups like the Mississippi Rifle Club and the South Carolina Red Shirts. In
the 1873 elections in Yazoo County, Mississippi, the Republicans cast 2,449
votes and the Democrats 638; two years later the Democrats polled 4,049
votes, the Republicans 7. By 1876, Radical Republican regimes survived only
in Louisiana, South Carolina, and Florida, and those collapsed after the elections of that year.

The erosion of northern interest in promoting civil rights in the postwar
South reflected weariness as well as interest in other activities. Western expansion, Indian wars, new economic opportunities, and political debates
over the tariff and the currency distracted attention from southern outrages.
In addition, a business panic in 1873 led to a sharp depression and created
both social problems and new racial tensions in the North and the South
that helped undermine already inconsistent federal efforts to promote racial
justice in the former Confederacy.

PANIC AND REDEMPTION A paralyzing economic panic followed
closely upon the public scandals besetting the Grant administration. A contraction of the nation's money supply resulting from the Treasury's postwar
withdrawal of greenbacks and the reckless overexpansion of the railroads
into sparsely settled areas helped precipitate a financial panic. During 1873
some twenty-five strapped railroads defaulted on their interest payments. A
financial panic in Europe forced many financiers to unload American stocks
and bonds. Caught short of cash, the prominent investment bank of Jay
Cooke and Company went bankrupt on September 18, 1873. The event so
frightened investors that the New York Stock Exchange had to close for ten
days. The panic of 1873 set off a depression that lasted six years. It was the
longest and most severe contraction that Americans had yet suffered, marked

by widespread bankruptcies, chronic unemployment, and a drastic slowdown in railroad building.

Hard times and political scandals hurt Republicans in the midterm elections of 1874, allowing the Democrats to win control of the House of Representatives and gain seats in the Senate. The new Democratic House launched inquiries into the Grant scandals and unearthed further evidence of corruption in high places. The financial panic, meanwhile, focused attention once more on greenback currency. Since the value of greenbacks was lower than that of gold, paper money had become the chief circulating medium. Most people spent greenbacks first and held their gold or used it to settle foreign accounts, thereby draining much gold out of the country. To relieve this deflationary spiral and stimulate business expansion, the Treasury issued more greenbacks.

For a time the advocates of paper money were riding high. But Grant vetoed an attempt to issue more greenbacks in 1874, and in his annual message he called for the redemption of greenbacks in gold. Congress obliged the president by passing the Specie Resumption Act of 1875. The resumption of payments in gold to customers who turned in greenbacks began on January 1, 1879, after the Treasury had built a gold reserve for the purpose and reduced the value of the greenbacks in circulation. This act infuriated those promoting an inflationary monetary policy and led to the formation of the Greenback party. The much debated and very complex "money question" would remain one of the most divisive issues in American politics through the end of the century.

THE COMPROMISE OF 1877 Grant yearned to run for a third term in 1876, but his scandal-ridden administration cost him Republican support. James Gillespie Blaine of Maine, a former Speaker of the House, emerged as the Republican front-runner, but he, too, bore the taint of scandal. Letters in the possession of James Mulligan of Boston linked Blaine to dubious railroad dealings. Newspapers soon published the "Mulligan letters," and Blaine's candidacy was dealt a hefty blow.

The Republican Convention therefore eliminated Blaine and several other hopefuls in favor of Ohio's favorite son, Rutherford B. Hayes. Three-time governor of Ohio and an advocate of hard money, Hayes had a sterling reputation and had been a civil service reformer. But his chief virtue, as a journalist put it, was that "he is obnoxious to no one."

The Democratic Convention was abnormally harmonious from the start. The nomination went on the second ballot to Samuel J. Tilden, a millionaire

The Compromise of 1877

This illustration represents the compromise between Republicans and southern Democrats that ended Radical Reconstruction.

corporation lawyer and reform governor of New York who had directed a campaign to overthrow the corrupt Tweed ring that controlled New York City politics.

The 1876 election campaign generated no burning issues. Both candidates favored the trend toward relaxing federal authority and restoring white conservative rule in the South. In the absence of strong differences, Democrats aired the Republicans' dirty linen. In response, Republicans waved "the bloody shirt," which is to say that they linked the Democratic party to secession and the outrages committed against Republicans in the South.

Early election returns pointed to a Tilden victory. Tilden had a 254,000-vote edge in the popular vote and won 184 electoral votes, just one short of a majority. Hayes had only 165 electoral votes, but Republicans also claimed 19 disputed votes from Florida, Louisiana, and South Carolina. The Democrats laid a counterclaim to 1 of Oregon's 3 votes. The Republicans had clearly carried Oregon, but the outcome in the South was less certain, and given the fraud and intimidation perpetrated on both sides, nobody will ever know the truth of the matter. In all three of the disputed southern states, rival canvasing boards sent in different returns. The Constitution offered no guidance in this unprecedented situation. Even if Congress had been empowered to sort things out, the Democratic House and the Republican Senate would have proved unable to reach an agreement.

The impasse dragged on for months, and there was even talk of partisan violence. Finally, on January 29, 1877, Congress set up a special Electoral Commission to investigate and report its findings. Its fifteen members, five each from the House, the Senate, and the Supreme Court, were chosen such that there were seven from each major party, with Justice David Davis of Illinois as the swing vote. Davis, though appointed to the Court by Lincoln, was no party regular and in fact was thought to be leaning toward the Democrats. Thus the panel appeared to be stacked in favor of Tilden.

As it turned out, however, the panel got restacked the other way. Shortsighted Democrats in the Illinois legislature teamed up with minority Greenbackers to name Davis their senator. Davis accepted, no doubt with a sense of relief. From the remaining justices, all Republicans, the panel chose Joseph P. Bradley to fill the vacancy. The decision on each disputed state then went by a vote of 8 to 7 along party lines, in favor of Hayes. After much bluster and the threat of a filibuster by the Democrats, the House voted on March 2 to accept the report and declared Hayes elected by an electoral vote of 185 to 184.

Critical to this outcome was the defection of southern Democrats, who had made several informal agreements with the Republicans. On February 26, 1877, a bargain was struck at Wormley's Hotel in Washington, D.C., between prominent Ohio Republicans (including James A. Garfield) and powerful southern Democrats. The Republicans promised that if elected, Hayes would withdraw federal troops from Louisiana and South Carolina, letting the Republican governments there collapse. In return, the Democrats pledged to withdraw their opposition to Hayes, accept in good faith the Reconstruction amendments, and refrain from partisan reprisals against Republicans in the South.

Southern Democrats could now justify deserting Tilden. This so-called Compromise of 1877 brought a final "redemption" from the Radicals and a return to "home rule," which meant rule by white Democrats. As a former slave observed in 1877, "The whole South—every state in the south—has got [back] into the hands of the very men that held us as slaves." Other, more informal promises, bolstered the secret agreement. Hayes's friends pledged more support for rebuilding Mississippi River levees and other internal improvements, including a federal subsidy for a transcontinental railroad along a southern route. Southerners extracted a further promise that Hayes would name a white southerner as postmaster general, the cabinet position with the most patronage jobs to distribute. In return, southerners would let the Republicans make James Garfield the Speaker of the new House. Such a deal illustrates the relative weakness of the presidency compared with Congress during the postwar era.

THE END OF RECONSTRUCTION   In 1877 the new president withdrew federal troops from Louisiana and South Carolina, and the Republican governments there soon collapsed—along with Hayes's claim to legitimacy. Hayes chose a Tennessean as postmaster general. But most of the other promises made at Wormley's Hotel were renounced or forgotten. As for southern promises to protect the civil rights of African Americans, only a few Democratic leaders remembered them for long. Over the next three decades the federal protection of civil rights crumbled under the pressure of restored white rule in the South and the force of Supreme Court decisions narrowing the application of the Fourteenth and Fifteenth Amendments.

Radical Reconstruction never offered more than an uncertain commitment to racial equality. Yet it left an enduring legacy—the Thirteenth, Fourteenth, and Fifteenth Amendments—not dead but dormant, waiting to be revived. If Reconstruction did not provide social equality or substantial economic opportunities for African Americans, it did create the opportunity for future transformation. It was a revolution, sighed former North Carolina governor Jonathan Worth, and "nobody can anticipate the action of revolutions."

CHAPTER SUMMARY

- **Reconstruction** Abraham Lincoln and his successor, the southerner Andrew Johnson, wanted a lenient and quick plan for Reconstruction. Lincoln's assassination made many northerners favor the Radical Republicans, who wanted to end the grasp of the old planter class on the South's society and economy. Congressional Reconstruction included the stipulation that in order to reenter the Union, former Confederate states had to ratify the Fourteenth and Fifteenth Amendments. Congress also passed the Military Reconstruction Act, which attempted to protect the voting rights and civil rights of African Americans.

- **Southern Violence** Many white southerners blamed their poverty on freed slaves and Yankees. White mobs attacked blacks in 1866 in Memphis and New Orleans. That year the Ku Klux Klan was formed as a social club; its members soon began to intimidate freedmen and white Republicans. Despite government action, violence continued and even escalated in the South.

- **Freed Slaves** Newly freed slaves suffered economically. Most did not have the resources to succeed in the aftermath of the war's devastation. There was no redistribution of land; former slaves were given their freedom but nothing else. The Freedmen's Bureau attempted to educate and aid freed slaves and reunite families. Many former slaves found comfort in their families and the independent churches they established. Some took part in state and local governments under the last, radical phase of Reconstruction.

- **Grant Administration** During Ulysses Grant's administration fiscal issues dominated politics. Paper money (greenbacks) was regarded as inflationary; and agrarian and debtor groups opposed its withdrawal from circulation. Many members of Grant's administration were corrupt; scandals involved an attempt to corner the gold market, construction of the intercontinental railroad, and the whiskey ring's plan to steal millions of dollars in tax revenue.

- **End of Reconstruction** Most southern states had completed the requirements of Reconstruction by 1876. The presidential election returns of that year were so close that a special commission was established to count contested electoral votes. A decision hammered out at a secret meeting gave the presidency to the Republican, Rutherford B. Hayes; in return, the Democrats were promised that the last federal troops would be withdrawn from Louisiana and South Carolina, putting an end to the Radical Republican administrations in the southern states.

CHRONOLOGY

1862	Congress passes the Morrill Land Grant Act
	Congress guarantees the construction of a transcontinental railroad
	Congress passes the Homestead Act
1864	Lincoln refuses to sign the Wade-Davis Bill
1865	Congress sets up the Freedmen's Bureau
April 14, 1865	Lincoln is assassinated
1866	Ku Klux Klan is organized
	Congress passes the Civil Rights Act
1867	Congress passes the Military Reconstruction Act
	Congress passes the Tenure of Office Act
1868	Fourteenth Amendment is ratified
	Congress impeaches President Andrew Johnson; the Senate fails to convict him
1877	Compromise of 1877 ends Reconstruction

KEY TERMS & NAMES

Part Five

GROWING

PAINS

T he Federal victory in 1865 restored the Union and in the process helped accelerate America's transformation into a modern nation-state. A distinctly national consciousness began to displace the sectional emphases of the antebellum era. During and after the Civil War the Republican-led Congress pushed through legislation to foster industrial and commercial development and western expansion. In the process the United States abandoned the Jeffersonian dream of a decentralized agrarian republic and began to forge a dynamic new industrial economy generated by an increasingly national market.

After 1865 many Americans turned their attention to the unfinished business of settling a continent and completing an urban-industrial revolution begun before the war. Huge corporations based upon mass production and mass marketing began to dominate the economy. As the prominent social theorist William Graham Sumner remarked, the process of industrial development "controls us all because we are all in it. It creates the conditions of our own existence, sets the limits of our social activity, and regulates the bonds of our social relations."

The Industrial Revolution was not only an urban phenomenon; it transformed rural life as well. Those who got in the way of the new emphasis on large-scale, highly mechanized commercial agriculture and ranching were brusquely pushed aside. The friction between new market forces and traditional folkways generated political revolts and social unrest during the last quarter of the nineteenth century.

The clash between tradition and modernity peaked during the 1890s, one of the most strife-ridden decades in American history. A deep depression, agrarian unrest, and labor violence provoked fears of class warfare. This turbulent situation transformed the presidential election campaign of 1896 into a clash between rival visions of America's future. The Republican candidate, William McKinley, campaigned on behalf of modern urban-industrial values. By contrast, William Jennings Bryan, the nominee of the Democratic and Populist parties, was an eloquent defender of America's rural past. McKinley's victory proved to be a watershed in political and social history. By 1900 the United States would emerge as one of the world's greatest industrial powers, and it would thereafter assume a new leadership role in world affairs.

19

THE SOUTH AND THE WEST TRANSFORMED

FOCUS QUESTIONS

 wwnorton.com/studyspace

- How did life in the South change for blacks and whites politically, economically, and socially after the Civil War?
- What happened to Native Americans as whites settled the West?
- What were the experiences of farmers, cowboys, and miners in the West?
- How did mining affect the development of the West?
- How important was the concept of the frontier to America's political and diplomatic development?

After the Civil War the South and the West provided enticing opportunities for pioneers and entrepreneurs. The two regions were ripe for development. The devastated South had to be rebuilt; the trans-Mississippi West beckoned entrepreneurs and farmers. In both cases, undeveloped regions would prove to be fertile catalysts for urbanization and industrialization. This was particularly true of the West, where before 1860 most Americans had viewed the region between the Mississippi River and California as a barren landscape unfit for human habitation or cultivation, an uninviting land suitable only for Indians and animals. Half the state of Texas, for instance, was still not settled at the end of the Civil War. After 1865, however, the federal government encouraged western settlement and economic development. The construction of transcontinental railroads, the military conquest of the Indians, and a liberal land-distribution policy combined to help lure thousands of pioneers and expectant capitalists westward.

Although the first great wave of railroad building occurred in the 1850s, the most spectacular growth took place during the quarter century after the Civil War. From about 35,000 miles of track in 1865, the national rail network grew to nearly 200,000 miles by 1897. The transcontinental rail lines led the way, and they helped populate the plains and the Far West. Meanwhile, southern rail lines were rebuilt and supplemented with new branches. The defeated South, although not a frontier in the literal sense of the term, attracted investment and industrial development. After 1865, proponents of a "New South" argued that the region must abandon its single-minded preoccupation with agriculture and pursue industrial and commercial development. As a result, the South also West experienced dramatic social and economic changes during the last third of the nineteenth century. By 1900 the South and the West had been transformed in ways that few could have predicted, and twelve new states were created out of the western territories.

THE NEW SOUTH

A FRESH VISION   After the Civil War many southerners looked wistfully to the plantation life that had characterized their region before the firing on Fort Sumter in 1861. A few prominent leaders, however, insisted that the postwar South must liberate itself from nostalgia and create a new society of small farms, thriving industries, and bustling cities. The major prophet of this New South was Henry W. Grady, the young editor of the *Atlanta Constitution*. Grady's compelling vision of a New South attracted many supporters, who preached the gospel of industry with evangelical fervor. The Confederacy, they reasoned, had lost because it had relied too much upon King Cotton. In the future the South must follow the North's example and industrialize. From that central belief flowed certain implications: that a more diversified and a more efficient agriculture would be a foundation for economic growth and that more widespread education, especially vocational training, would promote material success. By the late 1870s, with Reconstruction over and the panic of 1873 forgotten, a mood of progress permeated the editorials and speeches of the day.

ECONOMIC GROWTH   The chief accomplishment of the New South movement was a dramatic expansion of the region's textile production. From

1880 to 1900, the number of cotton mills in the South grew from 161 to 400, and the number of mill workers (among whom women and children outnumbered men) increased fivefold. By 1900 the South had surpassed New England as the nation's largest producer of cotton cloth.

Tobacco growing also increased significantly after the Civil War. Essential to the rise of the tobacco industry was the Duke family of Durham, North Carolina. At the end of the Civil War, the story goes, Washington Duke took a load of tobacco and, with the help of his two sons, beat it out with hickory sticks, stuffed it into bags, hitched two mules to his wagon, and set out across the state, selling tobacco in small pouches as he went. By 1872 the Dukes had a factory producing 125,000 pounds of tobacco annually, and Washington Duke prepared to settle down and enjoy success.

His son Buck (James Buchanan Duke) wanted even greater success, however. He recognized that the tobacco industry was "half smoke and half ballyhoo," so he poured large sums into advertising schemes and perfected the mechanized mass production of cigarettes. Duke also undersold competitors in their own market and cornered the supply of ingredients. In 1890, Duke brought most of his competitors into the American Tobacco Company, which controlled nine tenths of the nation's cigarette production. In 1911 the Supreme Court ruled that the massive company was in violation of the anti-trust laws and ordered it broken up, but by then Duke had found new worlds to conquer, in hydroelectric power and aluminum.

Systematic use of other natural resources helped revitalize the region along the Appalachian Mountain chain from West Virginia to Alabama. Coal production in the South grew from 5 million tons in 1875 to 49 million tons by 1900. At the southern end of the mountains, Birmingham, Alabama, sprang up during the 1870s as a major steel-producing center and soon tagged itself the Pittsburgh of the South.

Industrial growth created a need for wood-framed housing, and after 1870 lumbering became a thriving industry in the South. By the turn of the century, it had surpassed textiles in value. Tree cutting seemed to know no bounds, despite the resulting ecological devastation. In time the industry would be saved only by the warm climate, which fostered quick growth of replanted forests, and the rise of scientific forestry.

Two forces that would impel an even greater industrial revolution were already on the southern horizon at the turn of the century: petroleum in the Southwest and hydroelectric power in the Southeast. In 1901 the Spindletop oil gusher in Texas brought a huge bonanza. Electric power proved equally profitable, and local power plants dotted the South by the 1890s. Richmond, Virginia, developed the nation's first electric streetcar system in 1888, and

Columbia, South Carolina, boasted the first electrically powered cotton mill in 1894. The greatest advance would begin in 1905, when Buck Duke's Southern Power Company set out to electrify entire river valleys in the Carolinas.

AGRICULTURE OLD AND NEW   At the start of the twentieth century, however, most of the South remained undeveloped, at least by northeastern standards. Despite the optimistic rhetoric of Henry Grady and other New South spokesmen, the typical southerner was less apt to be tending a textile loom than, as the saying went, facing the eastern end of a westbound mule. King Cotton survived the Civil War and expanded over new acreage even as its export markets leveled off. Louisiana cane sugar, probably the most war-devastated of all crops, was flourishing again by the 1890s.

The majority of southern farmers were not flourishing, however. A prolonged deflation in crop prices affected the entire Western world during the last third of the nineteenth century. Sagging prices for farm crops made it more difficult than ever to own land. Sharecropping and tenancy among poor blacks and whites became the norm. By 1890 most southern farms were worked by people who did not own the land.

How did the system work? Sharecroppers, who had nothing to offer the landowner but their labor, worked the owner's land in return for supplies and a share of the crop, generally about half. Tenant farmers, hardly better off, might have their own mule, a plow, and credit with the country store. They were entitled to claim a larger share of the crops. The sharecropper-tenant system was horribly inefficient; it was essentially a form of land slavery, and tenants and owners developed an intense suspicion of each other. The folklore of the rural South was replete with tales of tenants who remained stubbornly shiftless and scheming landlords who swindled farmworkers by not giving them a fair share of the crops.

The postwar South suffered an acute shortage of capital; people had to devise ways to operate without cash. One innovation was the crop-lien system: merchants furnished supplies in return for liens (or mortgages) on farmers' crops. To a few tenants and small farmers who seized the chance, such credit offered a way out of dependency, but to most it offered only a hopeless cycle of perennial debt. The merchant, who assumed great risks, generally charged interest that ranged, according to one journalist, "from 24 percent to grand larceny." The merchant required his farmer clients to grow a cash crop, which could be readily sold at harvesttime. Thus the routines of tenancy and sharecropping were geared to a staple crop, usually cotton. The resulting stagnation of rural life held millions, white and black, in bondage to privation and ignorance.

TENANCY AND THE ENVIRONMENT   The pervasive use of tenancy and sharecropping unwittingly caused profound environmental damage. Growing commercial row crops like cotton on the same land year after year leached the nutrients from the soil. Tenants had no incentive to take care of farmland by manuring fields or rotating crops because it was not their own. They used fertilizer to accelerate the growing cycle, but the extensive use of phosphate fertilizers only accelerated soil depletion, by enabling multiple plantings each year. Fertilizer, said an observer, seduced southern farmers into believing that there was a "short cut to prosperity, a royal road to good crops of cotton year after year. The result has been that their lands have been cultivated clean year after year, and their fertility has been exhausted."

Once the soil had lost its fertility, the tenants moved on to another farm, leaving behind rutted fields whose topsoil washed away with each rain. The

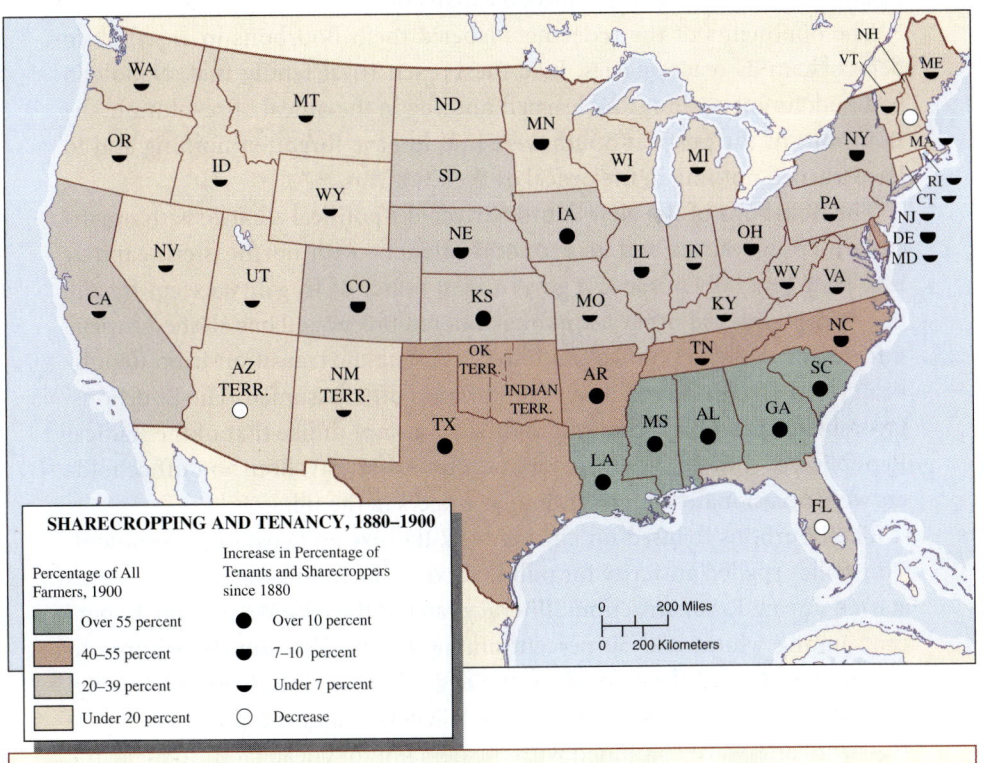

SHARECROPPING AND TENANCY, 1880–1900

Percentage of All Farmers, 1900

- Over 55 percent
- 40–55 percent
- 20–39 percent
- Under 20 percent

Increase in Percentage of Tenants and Sharecroppers since 1880

- ● Over 10 percent
- ◗ 7–10 percent
- ◡ Under 7 percent
- ○ Decrease

Why was there a dramatic increase in sharecropping and tenancy in the late nineteenth century? Why did the South have more sharecroppers than other parts of the country? Why, in your opinion, was the rate of sharecropping low in the western territories of New Mexico and Arizona?

silt and mud flowed into creeks and rivers, swamping many lowland fields and filling millponds and lakes. By the early twentieth century much of the rural South resembled a ravaged land: deep gullies sliced through, bare eroded hillsides, and streams and deep lakes were clogged with silt. As far as the eye could see, red clay devoid of nutrients dominated the landscape.

THE BOURBONS AND THE REDEEMERS   In post-Civil War southern politics, habits of social deference and elitism still prevailed. After Reconstruction ended, in 1877, an elite group of planters, lawyers, merchants, and entrepreneurs dominated southern politics. The supporters of these postwar Democratic leaders referred to them as redeemers because they supposedly saved the South from Yankee domination, as well as from the limitations of a purely rural economy. The redeemers included a rising class of entrepreneurs eager to promote a more diversified economy based upon industrial development and railroad expansion.

The opponents of the redeemers labeled them Bourbons in an effort to depict them as reactionaries. Like the French royal family that, Napoléon had said, forgot nothing and learned nothing in the ordeal of revolution, the Bourbons of the postwar South were said to have forgotten nothing and to have learned nothing in the ordeal of the Civil War.

The Bourbons of the New South perfected a political alliance with northeastern conservatives and an economic alliance with northeastern capitalists. They generally pursued a government policy of frugality, except for the tax exemptions and other favors they offered business. They slashed expenditures and avoided political initiatives, making the transition from Republican rule to Bourbon rule less abrupt than is often assumed. The Bourbons' favorable disposition toward the railroads was not unlike that of the Radical Republicans. And despite their reputation for honesty, Bourbon officeholders were occasionally caught with their fingers in the till.

The Bourbons focused on cutting back the size and cost of government. This policy spelled austerity for public services, including the school systems started during Reconstruction. Illiteracy rates at the time were about 12 percent among whites and 50 percent among blacks. The Bourbons' urge to economize also led them to adopt the degrading system of convict leasing. The destruction of prisons during the Civil War and the poverty of state treasuries afterward combined with the demand for cheap labor to make the leasing of convict workers a way for southern states to avoid penitentiary expenses and generate revenue.

The Bourbons reduced not only state expenditures but also a vast amount of government debt. The corruption and extravagance of Radical Republican rule were commonly advanced as justification for the process, but repudiation of debts was not limited to those incurred during Reconstruction. Altogether, nine states repudiated more than half of what they owed bondholders and other creditors.

The penny-pinching Bourbon regimes did respond to the demand for commissions to regulate the rates charged by railroads for commercial transport. They also established boards of agriculture and public health, agricultural and mechanical colleges, teacher-training schools and women's colleges, and even state colleges for African Americans. Nor can any simplistic interpretation encompass the variety of Bourbon leaders. The Democratic party was then a mongrel coalition that threw old Whigs, Unionists, secessionists, businessmen, small farmers, hillbillies, planters, and even some Republicans together in an alliance against the Reconstruction Radicals. Democrats, therefore, even those who bore the Bourbon label, often marched to different drummers, and the Bourbon regimes never achieved complete unity in philosophy or government.

Perhaps the ultimate paradox of the Bourbons' rule was that these paragons of white supremacy tolerated a lingering black voice in politics and showed no haste to raise legal barriers of racial separation in public places. African

The effects of Radical and Bourbon rule in the South

This 1880 cartoon shows the South staggering under the oppressive weight of military Reconstruction (left) and flourishing under the "Let 'Em Alone Policy" of President Rutherford B. Hayes and the Bourbons (right).

Americans sat in Virginia's state legislature until 1890, in South Carolina's until 1900, and in Georgia's until 1908; some of them were Democrats. The South sent black congressmen to Washington in every election except one until 1900, though they always represented gerrymandered districts into which most of a state's black voters had been thrown. Under the Bourbons the disenfranchisement of black voters remained inconsistent, a local matter brought about mainly by fraud and intimidation, although it occurred often enough to ensure white control of the southern states.

A like flexibility applied in other aspects of race relations. The color line was drawn less strictly immediately after the Civil War than it would be in the twentieth-century South. In some places, to be sure, racial segregation appeared before the end of Reconstruction, especially in schools, churches, hotels, and rooming houses and in private social relations. In other public places, such as trains, depots, theaters, and diners, however, segregation was more sporadic.

DISENFRANCHISING AFRICAN AMERICANS   During the 1890s the attitudes that had permitted moderation in race relations evaporated. A violent "Negrophobia" swept across the South and much of the nation at the end of the century. Many whites had come to resent signs of black success and social influence. An Alabama newspaper editor declared that "our blood boils when the educated Negro asserts himself politically."

Education did bring enlightenment—as it was supposed to do. A new generation of young African Americans born and educated since the end of the Civil War was determined to gain true equality. This generation was more assertive and less patient than their parents. A growing number of young white adults, however, were equally determined to keep "Negroes in their place."

Racial violence and repression surged to the fore during the last decade of the nineteenth century and the first two decades of the twentieth. By the end of the nineteenth century, the so-called New South had come to resemble the racially segregated Old South. Ruling whites ruthlessly imposed their will over all areas of African American life. They prevented blacks from voting and enacted "Jim Crow" laws mandating public separation of the races. This development was not the logical culmination of the Civil War and emancipation but rather the result of a calculated campaign by white elites and racist thugs to limit African American political, economic, and social life.

The political dynamics of the 1890s exacerbated racial tensions. The rise of Populism, a farm-based protest movement that culminated in the creation of a third political party in the 1890s, divided the white vote to such an extent that in some places the African American vote became the balance of power. Some Populists courted black votes. In response the Bourbons revived the

race issue, which they exploited with seasoned finesse, all the while controlling for their ticket a good part of the black vote in plantation areas. Nevertheless, during the 1890s the Bourbons began to insist that the black vote be
eliminated completely from southern elections. Some farm leaders hoped that
the disenfranchisement of African Americans would make it possible for
whites to divide politically without raising the specter of "Negro domination."

But since the Fifteenth Amendment made it illegal simply to deny blacks
the vote, racists accomplished their purpose indirectly, through such devices
as poll taxes (or head taxes) and literacy tests. Mississippi led the way to near-
total disenfranchisement of blacks—and many poor whites as well. The state
called a constitutional convention in 1890 to change the suffrage provisions
of the Radical Republican constitution of 1868. The resulting Mississippi
plan set the pattern that seven more states would follow over the next twenty
years. First, a residence requirement—two years in the state, one year in an
election district—struck at those black tenant farmers who were in the habit
of moving yearly in search of better opportunities. Second, voters were dis-
qualified if convicted of certain crimes, many of them petty. Third, all taxes,
including a poll tax, had to be paid by February 1 of each year. This proviso
fell most heavily on the poor, most of whom were black. Finally, all voters had

"Jim Crow" laws

In this wood engraving, African Americans are depicted leaving Mississippi from
the wharves of Vicksburg.

to be literate. The alternative, designed as a loophole for otherwise-disqualified whites, was an "understanding" clause. The voter, if unable to read the Constitution, could qualify by "understanding" it—to the satisfaction of the registrar. Fraud was thus institutionalized by "legal" disenfranchisement.

Other states added variations on the Mississippi plan. In 1898, Louisiana invented the "grandfather clause," which allowed illiterates to register to vote if their fathers or grandfathers had been eligible to vote on January 1, 1867, when African Americans were still disenfranchised. By 1910, Georgia, North Carolina, Virginia, Alabama, and Oklahoma had adopted the grandfather clause. Every southern state, moreover, adopted a statewide Democratic primary, which became the only meaningful election outside isolated areas of Republican strength. With minor exceptions the Democratic primaries excluded African American voters altogether. The effectiveness of these measures can be seen in a few sample figures: Louisiana in 1896 had 130,000 registered black voters and in 1900, 5,320. In Alabama in 1900, 121,159 black men over twenty-one were literate, according to the census, but only 3,742 were registered to vote.

THE SPREAD OF SEGREGATION   What came to be called Jim Crow social segregation followed disenfranchisement and in some states came first. From 1875 to 1883, in fact, any racial segregation violated a federal Civil Rights Act, which forbade discrimination in places of public accommodation. But in 1883 the Supreme Court ruled on seven civil rights cases involving discrimination against blacks by corporations or individuals. The Court held, with only one dissent, that the force of federal law could not extend to individual action because the Fourteenth Amendment, which provided that "no State" could deny citizens equal protection of the law, stood as a prohibition only against state action; individuals were free to discriminate as they saw fit.

This interpretation left as an open question the validity of state laws *requiring* separate public facilities under the rubric of "separate but equal," a slogan popular with the New South prophets. In 1888, Mississippi required railway passengers to occupy the car set aside for their race. When Louisiana followed suit in 1890, the law was challenged in the case of *Plessy v. Ferguson,* which the Supreme Court decided in 1896.

The test case originated in New Orleans when Homer Plessy, an octoroon (a person of one-eighth African ancestry), refused to leave a whites-only railroad car when asked to do so. He was convicted of violating the segregation statute, and the case rose on appeal to the Supreme Court. The Court ruled in 1896 that segregation laws "have been generally, if not universally recognized as within the competency of state legislatures in the exercise of their police power." Soon the principle of statutory racial segregation extended to every area of southern life, including streetcars, hotels, restaurants, hospitals, parks, and places of employment.

Violence accompanied the Jim Crow laws. From 1890 to 1899, lynchings in the United States averaged 188 per year, 82 percent of which occurred in the South; from 1900 to 1909, they averaged 93 per year, of which 92 percent occurred in the South. Whites constituted 32 percent of the victims during the former period but only 11 percent in the latter. By the end of the nineteenth century, legalized racial discrimination—segregation of public facilities, political disenfranchisement, and vigilante justice punctuated by brutal public lynchings and race riots—had elevated government-sanctioned bigotry to an official way of life in the South. South Carolina senator Benjamin Tillman, an outspoken racist, declared in 1892 that blacks "must remain subordinate or be exterminated."

How did African Americans respond to the resurgence of racism and statutory segregation? Some left the South in search of equality and opportunity, but the vast majority stayed in their native region. In the face of overwhelming force and prejudicial justice, survival in the South required blacks to wear a mask of deference and apply discretion. "Had to walk a quiet life," explained James Plunkett, a Virginia black. "The least little thing you would do, they [whites] would kill ya."

Yet accommodation did not mean total submission. Excluded from the dominant white world and eager to avoid confrontations, black southerners after the 1890s increasingly turned inward and constructed their own culture and nurtured their own pride. A young white visitor to Mississippi in 1910 noticed that nearly every black person he met had "two distinct social selves, the one he reveals to his own people, the other he assumes among the whites."

African American churches continued to serve as the hub for black community life. Often the only public buildings available for blacks, churches were used not only for worship but also for activities that had nothing to do with religion: social gatherings, club meetings, and political rallies. For men especially, churches offered leadership roles and political status. Serving as a deacon was often one of the most prestigious roles an African American man could achieve. Churches enabled African Americans of all classes to interact and exercise roles denied them in the larger society. Religious life provided great comfort to people worn down by the daily hardships and abuses associated with segregation.

One irony of state-enforced segregation is that it opened up new economic opportunities for blacks. A new class of African American entrepreneurs emerged to provide services—insurance, banking, funeral, barbering—to the black community in the segregated South. At the same time, African

Americans formed their own social organizations, all of which helped bolster black pride and provide fellowship and opportunities for service.

Middle-class black women formed a network of thousands of racial-uplift-organizations around the nation. The women's clubs were engines of social service in their communities. Members cared for the aged and the infirm, the orphaned and the abandoned. They created homes for single mothers and provided nurseries for working mothers. They sponsored health clinics and classes in home economics for women. In 1896 the leaders of such women's clubs converged to form the National Association of Colored Women, an organization meant to combat racism and segregation.

IDA B. WELLS One of the most outspoken African American activists of the time was Ida B. Wells. Born into slavery in 1862 in Mississippi, she attended a school staffed by white missionaries. In 1878 yellow fever killed her parents and infant brother. At age sixteen, Wells assumed responsibility for her five younger siblings. In search of economic security and opportunity, Wells moved to nearby Memphis.

In 1883 after being denied a seat on a railroad car because she was black, she became the first African American to file suit against such discrimination. The circuit court decided in her favor and fined the railroad, but the Tennessee Supreme Court overturned the ruling. Wells thereafter discovered "[my] first and [it] might be said, my only love"—journalism—and, through it, a weapon with which to promote civil rights. She became a prominent editor of *Memphis Free Speech*, a newspaper focusing on African American issues.

Ida B. Wells

While raising four children, Wells sustained her commitment to ending racial and gender discrimination.

In 1892, when three of her friends were lynched by a white mob, Wells launched a lifelong crusade against lynching. Angry whites responded by destroying her newspaper office and threatening to lynch her. She moved to New York and continued to use her fiery journalistic talent to criticize Jim Crow laws and demand that African Americans have their voting rights restored. Wells helped found the National Association for the Advancement of Colored People (NAACP) in 1909 and promoted women's suffrage.

WASHINGTON AND DU BOIS
Booker T. Washington, born in Virginia of a slave mother and a white father, fought extreme adversity to get an education at Hampton Institute, one of the postwar missionary schools, and went on to build at Tuskegee, Alabama, a leading college for African Americans. By 1890, Washington had become the nation's foremost black educator.

Washington argued that blacks should not antagonize whites by demanding social or political equality; instead, they should concentrate on establishing an economic base for their advancement. In a speech at the Cotton States and International Exposi-

Booker T. Washington

Founder of the Tuskegee Institute.

tion in Atlanta in 1895 that propelled him to fame, Washington advised African Americans: "Cast down your bucket where you are—cast it down in making friends . . . of the people of all races by whom we are surrounded. Cast it down in agriculture, mechanics, in commerce, in domestic service, and in the professions." He conspicuously omitted politics from, that list and implied an endorsement of segregation: "In all things that are purely social we can be as separate as the five fingers, yet one as the hand in all things essential to mutual progress."

Some people bitterly criticized Washington, in his lifetime and after, for making a bad bargain: the sacrifice of broad educational and civil rights for the dubious acceptance of white conservatives and the creation of economic opportunities for blacks. W. E. B. Du Bois led this criticism. A native of Great Barrington, Massachusetts, and the son of free blacks, Du Bois first experienced southern racial practices as an undergraduate at Fisk University in Nashville. Later he was the first African American to earn a doctoral degree from Harvard (in history) and afterward attended the University of Berlin. In addition to an active career in racial protest, he left a distinguished record as a teacher and scholar. Trim and dapper in appearance, sporting a goatee, carrying a cane, and often wearing gloves, he possessed a combative, fiery spirit. Not long after he began his teaching career, at Atlanta University in 1897, he began to assault Booker T. Washington's accommodationist philosophy and put forward his own program of "ceaseless agitation." He became the architect of the twentieth-century civil rights movement.

W. E. B. Du Bois

A fierce advocate for black education.

Washington, Du Bois argued, preached "a gospel 'of Work and Money to such an extent . . . as to over shadow the higher aims of life." The education of African Americans, Du Bois maintained, should not be merely vocational but should nurture bold leaders willing to challenge segregation and discrimination through political action. He demanded that disenfranchisement and legalized segregation cease and that the laws of the land be enforced. Du Bois castigated Washington's "Atlanta Compromise" philosophy: "We refuse to surrender the leadership of this race to cowards."

THE NEW WEST

Like the South, the vast region west of the Mississippi River has become wrapped in myths and constricting stereotypes. It is a diverse land of extremes—majestic mountains, roaring rivers, searing deserts, dense forests, sprawling grasslands, and fertile plains. For vast reaches of western America, the great epics of the Civil War and Reconstruction were remote events hardly touching the lives of Indians, Mexicans, Asians, and white trappers, miners, cowboys, traders, and Mormons scattered through the plains and mountains. There the march of settlement and exploitation continued, propelled by a lust for land and a passion for profit. Between 1870 and 1900, Americans settled more land in the West than had been occupied by all Americans up to 1870. On one level the settlement of the West beyond the Mississippi River constitutes a colorful drama of determined pioneers and cowboys overcoming all obstacles to secure their vision of freedom and opportunity amid the region's awesome vastness. On another level, however, the colonization of the Far West involved shortsighted greed and irresponsible behavior, a story of reckless exploitation that scarred the land, decimated its wildlife, and nearly exterminated the culture of Native Americans.

In the second tier of trans-Mississippi states—Iowa, Kansas, Nebraska—and in western Minnesota, farmers began spreading out onto the Great Plains after the Civil War. From California, miners spread east through the mountains as scattered enclaves sprang up at one new strike after another. From

Texas nomadic cowboys migrated northward onto the plains and across the Rocky Mountains into the Great Basin. As settlers moved west, they encountered climates and landscapes markedly different from those they had left behind. The scarcity of water and timber on the Great Plains rendered obsolete the ax, the log cabin, the rail fence, and the usual methods of tilling the soil. For a long time the region had been called the Great American Desert; it was thought of only as a barren barrier to cross on the way to the Pacific, unfit for human habitation and therefore, to white Americans, the perfect refuge for Indians. But that view changed in the last half of the nineteenth century as a result of newly discovered deposits of gold, silver, and other minerals, the completion of the transcontinental railroads, the destruction of the buffalo, the rise of the range-cattle industry, and the dawning realization that the arid region need not be a sterile desert. With the use of what water was available, techniques of dry farming and irrigation could make the land fruitful after all.

THE MIGRATORY STREAM   During the second half of the nineteenth century, an unrelenting stream of migrants flowed into the largely Indian and Hispanic West. Millions of Anglo-Americans, African Americans, Mexicans, and European and Chinese immigrants transformed the patterns of western society and culture. Because of the expense of transportation, land, and supplies, the very poor could not afford to relocate. Three quarters of the western migrants were men. The largest number of foreign immigrants came from northern Europe and Canada. In the northern plains, Germans, Scandinavians, and Irish were especially numerous.

AFRICAN AMERICAN MIGRATION   In the aftermath of the collapse of Radical Republican rule in the South, thousands of African Americans began migrating west from Kentucky, Tennessee, Louisiana, Arkansas, Mississippi, and Texas. Some 6,000 southern blacks arrived in Kansas in 1879 alone, and as many as 20,000 may have come the following year. These migrants came to be known as Exodusters, because they were making their exodus from the South—in search of a haven from racism and poverty.

The foremost promoter of African American migration to the West was Benjamin "Pap" Singleton. Born a slave in Tennessee in 1809, he escaped to Detroit. After the Civil War he returned to Tennessee, convinced that God was calling him to rescue his brethren. When Singleton learned that land in Kansas could be had for $1.25 an acre, he began distributing a recruiting pamphlet, *The Advantage of Living in a Free State,* to former slaves. In 1878, Singleton led his first party of 200 colonists to Kansas, bought 7,500 acres that had been an Indian reservation, and established the Dunlop community.

Nicodemus, Kansas

A colony founded by southern blacks in the 1860s.

Over the next several years, thousands of African Americans followed Single-ton into Kansas, causing many southern leaders to worry about the loss of black laborers. In 1879 white Mississippians closed access to the river and threatened to sink all boats carrying black colonists from the South to the West.

The African American exodus to the West died out by the early 1880s. Many of the settlers were unprepared for life on the plains. Their Kansas homesteads were not large enough to allow self-sufficiency, and most of the farmers were forced to supplement their income by hiring themselves out to white ranchers. Drought, grasshoppers, prairie fires, and dust storms led to crop failures. The sudden influx of so many people taxed resources and patience. Many of the black pioneers in Kansas soon abandoned their land and moved to the few cities in the state. Life on the frontier was not always the "promised land" that setters had been led to expect. Nonetheless, by 1890 some 520,000 African Americans lived west of the Mississippi River. As many as 25 percent of the cowboys who participated in the Texas cattle drives were African Americans.

In 1866, Congress passed legislation establishing two "colored" cavalry units and dispatched them to the western frontier. Nicknamed buffalo sol-diers by the Indians, the men were mostly Civil War veterans from Louisiana and Kentucky. They built and maintained forts, mapped vast areas of the Southwest, strung hundreds of miles of telegraph lines, protected railroad construction crews, subdued hostile Indians, and captured outlaws and rustlers. For this they were paid $13 a month. Eighteen of the buffalo soldiers won Congressional Medals of Honor for their service.

MINING THE WEST   Valuable mineral deposits continued to lure people to the West after the Civil War. The mass migration of miners to California in 1849 (the forty-niners) set the typical pattern, in which the disorderly rush of prospectors was quickly joined by camp followers, a motley array of saloon keepers, prostitutes, cardsharps, hustlers, and assorted desperadoes eager to mine the miners. An era of lawlessness eventually gave way to vigilante rule and, finally, to a stable community.

The drama of the 1849 gold rush was reenacted time and again in the following three decades. While nearly 100,000 early rushers were crowding around Pikes Peak in Colorado in 1859, miners discovered the Comstock Lode at Gold Hill, Nevada. The lode produced gold and silver and within twenty years had yielded more than $300 million from shafts that reached hundreds of feet into the mountainside. Yet in Arizona and Montana the most important mineral proved to be neither gold nor silver but copper.

The growing demand for orderly government in the West led to the hasty creation of new territories and eventually the admission of a host of new states. In 1861, Nevada became a territory, and in 1864 it was admitted to the Union in time to give two electoral votes to Abraham Lincoln (their third electoral voter got caught in a snowstorm). After Colorado's admission in 1876, however, no new states entered the union for over a decade because of party divisions in Congress: Democrats were reluctant to create states out of territories that were heavily Republican. After the sweeping Republican victory in the 1888 legislative races, however, Congress admitted the Dakotas, Montana, and Washington in 1889 and Idaho and Wyoming in 1890, completing a tier of states from coast to coast. Utah entered the union in 1896 (after the Mormons abandoned the practice of polygamy) and Oklahoma in 1907, and in 1912 Arizona and New Mexico rounded out the forty-eight continental states.

MINING AND THE ENVIRONMENT   During the second half of the nineteenth century, the nature of mining changed drastically. It became a mass-production industry as individual prospectors gave way to large companies. The first wave of miners who rushed to California in 1849 sifted gold dust and nuggets out of riverbeds by means of "placer" mining, or "panning." But once the placer deposits were exhausted, efficient mining required large-scale operations and huge investments. Companies shifted from surface digging to hydraulic mining, dredging, or deep-shaft "hard-rock" mining. Hydraulic mining used a powerful jet of water to excavate whole hillsides, washing the gravel through sluices that caught gold nuggets and disposed of the tailings (dirt and gravel debris). Dredging carved out whole riverbeds in order to sift gold from the surrounding sand and gravel.

Hydraulicking, dredging, and shaft mining transformed vast areas of vegetation and landscape. Huge hydraulic cannons shot enormous streams of water under high pressure, stripping the topsoil and gravel from the bedrock and creating steep-sloped barren canyons that could not sustain plant life. The tons of dirt and debris unearthed by the water cannons covered rich farmland downstream and created sandbars that clogged rivers and killed fish. All told, some 12 billion tons of earth were blasted out of the Sierra Nevadas and washed into local rivers.

Irate California farmers in the fertile Central Valley bitterly protested the damage done downstream by the industrial mining operations. In 1878 they formed the Anti-Debris Association, with its own militia, to challenge the powerful mining companies. Efforts to pass state legislation restricting hydraulic mining repeatedly failed because mining companies controlled the votes. The Anti-Debris Association then turned to the courts. On January 7, 1884, the farmers won their case when federal judge Lorenzo Sawyer, a former miner, outlawed the dumping of mining debris where it could reach farmland or navigable rivers. Thus *Woodruff v. North Bloomfield Gravel Mining Company* became the first major environmental ruling in the nation. As a result of the ruling, hydraulic mining dried up, leaving a legacy of abandoned equipment, ugly ravines, ditches, gullies, and mountains of discarded rock and gravel.

THE INDIAN WARS   As settlers pressed in from east and west, the Native Americans were forced into what was supposed to be their last refuge. Perhaps 250,000 Indians on the Great Plains and in the mountain regions lived mainly off the buffalo herds, which provided food and, from their hides, clothing and shelter. The 1851 Fort Laramie Treaty, in which the chiefs of the Plains tribes agreed to accept definite tribal borders and allow white settlers to travel on their trails unmolested, worked for a while, with wagon trains passing safely through Indian lands and the army building roads and forts without resistance. Fighting resumed, however, as the emigrants began to encroach upon Indian lands rather than merely pass through them. From 1850 to 1860, for example, 150,000 whites moved into Sioux territory in violation of treaty agreements.

From the early 1860s until the late 1870s, the frontier raged with Indian wars. In 1864, Colonel John Chivington's poorly trained militia assaulted an Indian camp along Sand Creek in Colorado Territory. Although the Indian

What was the Great Sioux War? What happened at Little Bighorn, and what were the consequences? Why were hundreds of Indians killed at Wounded Knee?

camp displayed a white flag of truce, the soldiers slaughtered 200 Indians—men, women, and children. One general called the Sand Creek Massacre the "foulest and most unjustifiable crime in the annals of America."

With other scattered battles erupting, a congressional committee gathered evidence on the grisly Indian wars and massacres. Its 1867 "Report on the Condition of the Indian Tribes" led to an act to establish an Indian Peace Commission charged with removing the causes of Indian wars in general. Congress decided that this would be best accomplished at the expense of the Indians, by persuading them to take up life on out-of-the-way reservations, a solution that perpetuated the encroachment on Indian hunting grounds. In 1870, Indians outnumbered whites in the Dakota territory by two to one; in 1880, whites outnumbered Indians by more than six to one.

In 1867 a conference at Medicine Lodge, Kansas, ended with the Kiowas, Comanches, Arapahos, and Cheyennes reluctantly accepting land m western Oklahoma. The following spring the Sioux agreed to settle within the Black Hills Reservation in Dakota Territory. But Indian resistance on the southern plains continued until the Red River War of 1874-1875, when soldiers led by General Philip Sheridan, a hard-charging Civil War cavalryman, forced the Indians to disband in the spring of 1875. Seventy-two Indian chiefs were imprisoned for three years.

Meanwhile, trouble was brewing again in the north. In 1874, Lieutenant Colonel George A. Custer, a reckless, glory-seeking officer, led an exploratory expedition into the Black Hills. Miners were soon filtering onto the Sioux hunting grounds despite promises that the army would keep them out. The army had done little to protect Indian land, but when ordered to move against wandering bands of Sioux hunting on the range according to their treaty rights, it moved vigorously.

What became the Great Sioux War was the largest military event since the end of the Civil War. It lasted fifteen months and entailed some fifteen battles in present-day Wyoming, Montana, South Dakota, and Nebraska. The Sioux were ably led by chief Sitting Bull. After several indecisive encounters, Custer found the main encampment of Sioux and their Northern Cheyenne allies on the Little Bighorn River. Separated from the main body of his men and surrounded by 2,500 warriors, Custer and 210 soldiers were annihilated.

Instead of following up their victory, the Indians threw away their advantage in celebration and renewed hunting. The army quickly regained the offensive, and the Sioux were forced to give up their hunting grounds and the goldfields in return for payments. Forced onto reservations situated on the least valuable lands in the region, the Indians soon found themselves struggling to subsist under harsh conditions. Many died of starvation or disease.

In the Rocky Mountains and to the west, the same story of hopeless resistance was repeated. Indians were the last obstacle to white expansion, and they suffered as a result. In Idaho the peaceful Nez Perce bands refused to surrender land along the Salmon River, and prolonged fighting erupted there and in eastern Oregon. In 1886 a generation of Indian wars virtually ended with the capture of Geronimo, a chief of the Chiricahua Apaches, who had fought encroachments in the Southwest for fifteen years.

The epilogue, too, would be tragic. Late in 1888, Wovoka (or Jack Wilson), a Paiute in western Nevada, fell ill and in a delirium imagined he had visited the spirit world, where he learned of a deliverer coming to rescue the Indians

The Battle of Little Bighorn, 1876

A painting by Amos Bad Heart Bull, an Oglala Sioux.

and restore their lands. To hasten their deliverance, he said, they had to take up a ceremonial dance at each new moon. The Ghost Dance craze fed upon old legends of a coming messiah and spread rapidly. In 1890 the Lakota Sioux adopted it with such fervor that it alarmed white authorities. They banned the Ghost Dance on Lakota reservations, but the Indians defied the order, and a crisis erupted. On December 29, 1890, a bloodbath occurred at Wounded Knee, South Dakota. An accidental rifle discharge led nervous soldiers to fire into a group of Indians who had come to surrender. Nearly 200 Indians and 25 soldiers died in the Battle of Wounded Knee. The Indian wars had ended with characteristic brutality and misunderstanding.

THE DEMISE OF THE BUFFALO Over the long run the collapse of Indian resistance in the face of white settlement on the Great Plains resulted as much from the decimation of the buffalo herds as from the actions of federal troops. In 1750 there were an estimated 30 million buffalo on the plains; by 1850 there were less than 10 million; by 1900 only a few hundred were left. What happened to them? The conventional story focuses on intensive harvesting of buffalo by white hunters after the Civil War. Americans east of the Mississippi River developed a voracious demand for buffalo robes and buffalo leather. The average white hunter killed 100 animals a day, and the hides and bones (to be ground into fertilizer) were shipped east on railroad cars. Some army officers encouraged the slaughter. "Kill every buffalo you can!" Colonel Richard Dodge told a sport hunter in 1867. "Every buffalo dead is an Indian gone."

This conventional explanation tells only part of a more complicated story, however. The buffalo disappeared from the western plains for a variety of environmental reasons, including a significant change in climate; competition with other grazing animals; and cattle-borne disease. A prolonged drought on the Great Plains during the late 1880s and 1890s, the same drought that would help spur the agrarian revolt and the rise of populism, also devastated the buffalo herds by reducing the grasslands upon which the animals depended. At the same time, the buffalo had to compete for forage with an ever-increasing number of horses, cattle, and sheep. By the 1880s over 2 million horses were grazing on buffalo lands. In addition, the Plains Indians themselves, empowered by horses and guns and spurred by the profits reaped from selling hides and meat to white traders, accounted for much of the devastation of the buffalo herds after 1840. White hunters who killed buffalo by the millions in the 1870s and 1880s played a major role in the animals' demise, but only as the final catalyst. If there had been no white hunters, the buffalo would probably have lasted only another thirty years because their numbers had been so greatly reduced by other factors.

INDIAN POLICY   Most white westerners had little tolerance for moralizing on the Indian question, but many easterners decried the slaughter and mistreatment of Indians. Well-intentioned reformers sought to "Americanize" Indians by dealing with them as individuals rather than tribes. The Dawes Severalty Act of 1887 proposed to introduce the communal Indians to individual land ownership and agriculture. Sponsored by Senator Henry Dawes of Massachusetts, the act permitted the president to divide the land of any tribe and grant 160 acres to each head of a family and lesser amounts to others. To protect the Indians' property, the government held it in trust for twenty-five years, after which the owner won full title and became a U.S. citizen. In 1901, citizenship was extended to the Five Civilized Tribes of Oklahoma and, in 1924, to all Indians.

But the more it changed, the more Indian policy remained the same. Although well intended, the Dawes Act created new chances for more plundering of Indian land and disrupted what remained of the traditional culture. The Dawes Act broke up reservations and often led to the loss of Indian land to whites. Land not distributed to Indian families was sold, and some of the land the Indians did receive was lost to speculators because of the Indians' inexperience with private ownership or simply because of their powerlessness in the face of fraud. Between 1887 and 1934, Indians lost an estimated 86 million of their 130 million acres. Most of what remained was unsuited for agriculture.

CATTLE AND COWBOYS   While the West was being taken from the Indians, cattle entered the grasslands where the buffalo had roamed. Much of the romance of the open-range cattle industry derived from its Mexican roots. The Texas longhorns and the cowboys' horses had in large part descended from stock brought to America by the Spaniards, and many of the industry's trappings had been worked out in Mexico first: the cowboy's saddle, chaps *(chaparreras)* to protect the legs, spurs, and lariat.

For many years wild cattle competed with the buffalo in the Spanish borderlands. Natural selection and contact with Anglo-American cattle produced the Texas longhorns: lean and rangy, they were noted more for speed and endurance than for yielding a choice steak. They had little value, moreover, because the largest markets for beef were too far away. At the end of the Civil War, as many as 5 million longhorns roamed the grasslands of Texas, still neglected—but not for long. In the upper Mississippi Valley, where herds had been depleted by the war, cattle were in great demand, and the Texas cattle could be had just for the effort of rounding them up.

New opportunities arose as railroads pushed farther west, where cattle could be driven through relatively vacant lands. Joseph G. McCoy, an Illinois livestock dealer, encouraged railroad executives to run a line from the prairies to Chicago, the meatpacking center. The Kansas Pacific Railroad liked McCoy's vision, and with its help he made Abilene, Kansas, the western terminus of a new line. In 1867 the first shipment of Texas cattle went to Chicago.

During the twenty years after the Civil War, some 40,000 cowboys roamed the Great Plains. They were young—the average age was twenty-four—and from diverse backgrounds. Some 30 percent were Mexican or African American, and hundreds were Indians. Many others were Civil War veterans from the North and the South, and still others were immigrants from Europe. The life of a cowboy, for the most part, was rarely as exciting as has been depicted by motion pictures and television shows. Working as a ranch hand involved grueling wage labor interspersed with drudgery and boredom.

The thriving cattle industry spurred rapid growth, however. The population of Kansas increased from 107,000 in 1860 to 365,000 ten years later and reached almost 1 million by 1880. Nebraska witnessed similar increases. During the 1860s, cattle would be delivered to rail depots, loaded onto freight cars, and shipped east. By the time the animals arrived in New York

The cowboy era

Cowboys herd cattle near Cimarron, Colorado, 1905.

or Massachusetts, some would be dead or dying, and all would have lost significant weight. The secret to higher profits for the cattle industry was to devise a way to slaughter the cattle in the Midwest and ship the dressed carcasses east and west. That process required refrigeration to keep the meat from spoiling. In 1869, G. H. Hammond, a Chicago meat packer, shipped the first refrigerated beef in an air-cooled railcar from Chicago to Boston. Eight years later Gustavus Swift developed a more efficient system of mechanical refrigeration, an innovation that earned him a fortune and provided the cattle industry with a major stimulus.

The flush times of the cowtowns soon faded, however. The long cattle drives played out because they were economically unsound. The dangers of the trail, the wear and tear on men and cattle, the charges levied on drives that crossed Indian territory, and the advance of farms across the trails combined to persuade cattlemen that they could function best near railroads. As railroads spread out into Texas and across the plains, the cattle business spread with them as far as Montana and on into Canada.

In the absence of laws governing the open range, cattle ranchers at first worked out their own arrangements when rights and uses conflicted. As cattle wandered onto other ranchers' property, cowboys would "ride the line" to keep the strays off the adjoining ranches. In the spring they would "round up" the herds and sort out ownership by identifying the distinctive mark "branded" into the cattle. All that changed in 1873, when Joseph Glidden, an Illinois farmer, invented the first effective barbed wire, which ranchers used to fence off their claims at relatively low cost. Orders for the new fence poured in, and soon the open range was no more.

THE END OF THE OPEN RANGE   Yet a combination of factors put an end to the open range. Farmers kept crowding in and laying out homesteads. The boundless range was being overstocked by 1883, and expenses mounted as stock breeders formed associations to keep intruders off overstocked ranges, establish and protect land titles, deal with railroads and buyers, fight prairie fires, and cope with rustlers and wolves. The rise of sheepherding by 1880 caused still another conflict with the ranchers. A final blow to the open-range industry came with two unusually severe winters, in 1886 and 1887, followed by ten long years of drought.

Surviving the hazards of the range required ranchers to establish legal title, fence in the land, limit the herds to a reasonable size, and provide shelter and hay during the rigors of winter. Moreover, as the long cattle drives gave way to more rail lines and refrigerated railcars, the cowboy settled into a more sedentary existence. Within merely two decades, from 1866 to 1886, the era of the cowboy had come and gone.

RANGE WARS   Conflicting claims over land and water rights triggered violent disputes between ranchers and farmers. Ranchers often tried to drive off neighboring farmers, and farmers in turn tried to sabotage the cattle barons, cutting their fences and spooking their herds. The cattle ranchers also clashed with sheepherders over access to grassland. A strain of ethnic and religious prejudice heightened the tension between ranchers and. herders. In the Southwest, shepherds were typically Mexican Americans; in Idaho and Nevada, they were from the Basque region of Spain, or they were Mormons. Many Anglo-American cattlemen and cowboys viewed those ethnic and religious groups as un-American and inferior, an attitude that helped them rationalize the use of violence against sheepherders. Conflict faded, however, as the sheep for the most part found refuge in the high pastures of the mountains, leaving the grasslands of the plains to the ranchers.

Yet there also developed a perennial tension between large and small cattle ranchers. The large ranchers fenced in huge tracts of public land, leaving the smaller ranchers with too little pasture. To survive, the smaller ranchers cut the fences. In central Texas this practice sparked the Fence-Cutters' War of 1883-1884. Several ranchers were killed and dozens wounded before the state ended the conflict by passing legislation outlawing fence cutting.

FARMERS AND THE LAND   Among the legendary figures of the West, farmers projected an unromantic image in contrast to that of the cowboys, cavalrymen, and Indians. Yet farmers were the mainstay of the western economy. After 1865, on paper at least, the federal land laws offered farmers favorable terms. Under the Homestead Act of 1862, a farmer could gain title to federal land either by simply staking out a claim and living on it for five years or by buying the land at $1.25 an acre after six months.

As so often happens, however, environmental forces more than government policy shaped development. The unchangeable fact of aridity, rather than land laws, influenced institutions in the West after the Civil War. Where farming was impossible, ranchers simply established dominance by control of the water, regardless of the law. Belated legislative efforts to develop irrigable land finally achieved a major success when the 1901 Newlands Reclamation Act (after the aptly named Senator Francis G. Newlands of Nevada) set up the Bureau of Reclamation. The proceeds of public land sales in sixteen states created a fund for irrigation works, and the Reclamation Bureau set about building such major projects as the Boulder (later the Hoover) Dam on the Nevada-Arizona line, the Roosevelt Dam in Arizona, and the Elephant Butte Dam in New Mexico.

The lands of the New West, like those on previous frontiers, passed to their ultimate owners more often from private hands than directly from the government. Many of the 274 million acres claimed under the Homestead Act passed quickly to cattle ranchers or speculators and thence to settlers. The land-grant railroads got some 200 million acres of the public domain between 1851 and 1871 and sold much of it to build towns along the lines. The West of ranchers and fanners was in fact largely the product of the railroads.

The first arrivals on the sod-house frontier of the Plains faced a grim struggle against danger, adversity, and monotony. Though land was relatively cheap, horses, livestock, wagons, wells, fencing, seed, and fertilizer were not. Freight rates and interest rates on loans seemed criminally high. As in the South, declining crop prices produced chronic indebtedness, leading strapped western farmers to embrace virtually any plan to inflate the money

The construction of Hoover Dam

When completed in 1936, Hoover Dam was the world's largest concrete structure.

supply. The land itself, although fertile, resisted planting; the heavy sod broke many a plow. Since wood was almost nonexistent on the prairie, pioneer families used buffalo chips (dried dung) for fuel.

Farmers and their families also fought a constant battle with the elements: tornadoes, hailstorms, droughts, prairie fires, blizzards, and pests. Swarms of locusts would often cloud the horizon, occasionally covering the ground six inches deep and consuming everything in their path. A Wichita newspaper reported in 1878 that the grasshoppers devoured "everything green, stripping the foliage off the bark and from the tender twigs of the fruit trees, destroying every plant that is good for food or pleasant to the eyes, that man has planted."

As time passed and farmers were able to lay aside some money from their labor, farm families could leave their sod houses and build frame houses with lumber carried from Chicago by the railroads. New machinery also provided fresh opportunities for farmers. In 1868, James Oliver, a Scottish immigrant living in Indiana, made a successful chilled-iron plow. With further improvements his "sodbuster" plow greatly eased the task of breaking the shallow but tough grass roots of the Plains. Improvements and new inventions lightened the burden of labor but added to the farmers' capital outlay.

While the overall value of farmland and farm products increased in the late nineteenth century, small farmers did not keep up with the march of progress. Their numbers grew but decreased in proportion to the population at large. The wheat produced on the eastern plains from Minnesota and North Dakota down to Texas, like cotton in the antebellum period, was the great export crop that evened America's balance of payments and spurred economic growth. For a variety of reasons, however, few small farmers prospered. And by the 1890s many were in open revolt against "greedy" bankers, railroads, and grain processors who seemed to thwart their efforts and deny their dreams.

PIONEER WOMEN   The West remained a largely male society throughout the nineteenth century. Women were not only a minority; they also continued to face traditional legal barriers and social prejudice. A wife could not sell property without her husband's approval for example. Texas women could not sue except for divorce, nor could they serve on juries, act as lawyers, or witness a will. But the fight for survival in the West often made husbands and wives more equal partners in everyday life than were their eastern counterparts. Prairie life also allowed women more independence than could be had by leading a domestic life back East.

"THE FRONTIER HAS GONE"   American life reached an important juncture in the last decade of the nineteenth century. After the 1890 population count the superintendent of the national census noted that he could no longer locate a continuous frontier line beyond which population thinned out to fewer than two people per square mile. This fact inspired the historian Frederick Jackson Turner to develop the influential frontier thesis, first outlined in "The Significance of the Frontier in American History," a paper delivered to the American Historical Association in 1893. "The existence of an area of free land," Turner wrote, "its continuous recession, and the advance of American settlement westward, explain American development." The frontier, he added, had shaped the national character in striking ways. It was

> to the frontier [that] the American intellect owes its striking characteristics. That coarseness and strength combined with acuteness and acquisitiveness; that practical, inventive turn of mind, quick to find expedients; that masterful grasp of material things, lacking in the artistic but powerful to effect great ends; that restless, nervous energy; that dominant individualism, working for good and for evil, and with all that buoyancy and exuberance which comes with freedom—these are traits of the frontier, or traits called out elsewhere because of the existence of the frontier.

Women of the frontier

A woman and her family in front of their sod house. The difficult life on the prairie led to more egalitarian marriages than were found in most other regions of the country.

But, Turner ominously concluded in 1893, "the frontier has gone and with its going has closed the first period of American history."

Turner's "frontier thesis" guided several generations of scholars and students in their understanding of the distinctive characteristics of American history. His view of the frontier as the westward-moving source of the nation's democratic politics, open society, unfettered economy, and rugged individualism, far removed from the corruptions of urban life, gripped the popular imagination as well. But it left out much of the story. Turner's description of the frontier experience exaggerated the homogenizing effect of the environment and virtually ignored the role of women, African Americans, Indians, Mormons, Hispanics, and Asians in shaping the diverse human geography of the western United States. Turner also implied that the West would be fundamentally different after 1890 because the frontier experience was essentially over. In many respects, however, that region has retained the qualities associated, with the rush for land, gold, timber, and water rights during the post-Civil War decades. The mining frontier, as one historian has recently written, "set a mood that has never disappeared from the West: the attitude of extractive industry—get in, get rich, get out."

CHAPTER SUMMARY

- **Southern Segregation** By 1900 elite southern whites had regained control of state governments; prominent black Republicans had been squeezed out of political positions; and black men were being kept from exercising their right to vote. Segregation became the social norm. Some African American leaders, most prominently Booker T. Washington, believed that by showing deference to whites, blacks could avoid violence while quietly acquiring an education and property. Others, like Ida B. Wells and W. E. B. Du Bois, wanted to fight segregation and lynching through the courts.

- **Indian Wars and Policies** By 1900, Native Americans in the West were no longer free to roam the plains. Disease and the influx of farmers and miners reduced their numbers and curtailed their way of life. Instances of resistance, such as the Great Sioux War, were dealt with harshly. Initially, Indian tribes were forced to sign treaties and were confined to reservations. From 1887 the American government's Indian policy was aimed at forcing Indians to relinquish their traditional culture and adopt individual land ownership, settled agriculture, and Christianity.

- **Life in the West** Life in the West was harsh and violent, but the promise of cheap land or wealth from mining drew settlers from the East. Most cowboys and miners did not acquire wealth, however, because raising cattle and mining became large-scale enterprises that enriched only a few. Although most westerners were white Protestant Americans or northern European immigrants, Mexicans, African Americans, and Chinese contributed to the West's diversity. As a consequence of the region's rugged isolation, women achieved greater equality in everyday life than did most women elsewhere in the country.

- **Growth of Mining** Mining lured settlers to largely uninhabited regions, thereby hastening the creation of new territories and the admission of new states into the Union. By the 1880s, when mining became a big business employing large-scale equipment, its environmental impact could be seen in the blighted landscape.

- **The American Frontier** The historian Frederick Jackson Turner believed that the enduring presence of the frontier was responsible for making Americans individualistic, materialistic, practical, democratic, and energetic. In 1893 he declared that the closing of the frontier had ended the first stage of America's history.

CHRONOLOGY

1859	Comstock Lode is discovered
1862	Congress passes the Homestead Act
1864	Sand Creek Massacre
1873	Joseph Glidden invents barbed wire
1876	Battle of Little Bighorn
1877	With the Compromise of 1877, Rutherford B. Hayes becomes president and Reconstruction comes to an end
1886	Surrender of Geronimo marks the end of the Indian wars
1887	Congress passes the Dawes Severalty Act
1890	Battle of Wounded Knee
1890	Mississippi plan
1895	Booker T. Washington delivers his Atlanta Compromise speech
1896	Supreme Court issues *Plessy v. Ferguson* decision
1909	National Association for the Advancement of Color People is created

KEY TERMS & NAMES

2 0

BIG BUSINESS AND
ORGANIZED LABOR

wwnorton.com/studyspace

FOCUS QUESTIONS

- What fueled the growth of the post–Civil War economy?
- What roles were played by leading entrepreneurs like John D. Rockefeller, Andrew Carnegie, and J. Pierpont Morgan?
- Who composed the labor force of the period, and what were labor's main grievances?
- What led to the rise of labor unions?

America emerged as an industrial and agricultural giant in the late nineteenth century. Between 1869 and 1899 the nation's population nearly tripled, farm production more than doubled, and the value of manufactures grew sixfold. Within three generations after the Civil War, the predominantly rural nation had became an urban-industrial society buffeted by the imperatives of mass production, mass consumption, and time-clock efficiency. Bigness became the prevailing standard of corporate life, and social tensions worsened with the rising scale of business enterprise.

THE RISE OF BIG BUSINESS

The Industrial Revolution created huge corporations that came to dominate the economy—as well as political and social life—during the late nineteenth century. As businesses grew, their owners sought to integrate all the processes of production and distribution into single companies, thus producing even larger firms. Others grew by mergers, joining forces with their competitors in "pools" or "trusts" in an effort to dominate entire industries. This process of industrial combination and concentration transformed the nation's social order. It also aroused widespread dissent and the emergence of an organized labor movement.

Many factors converged to help launch the dramatic economic growth after the Civil War. The nation's unparalleled natural resources—forests, mineral wealth, rivers—along with a rapidly expanding population, were crucial ingredients. At the same time, inventors and business owners developed more efficient, labor-saving machinery and mass-production techniques that spurred dramatic advances in productivity and efficiency. As the volume and efficiency of production increased, the larger businesses and industries expanded into numerous states and in the process developed standardized machinery and parts, which became available nationwide. Innovative, bold leadership was crucial. A group of shrewd, determined, and energetic entrepreneurs took advantage of fertile business opportunities to create huge enterprises. Federal and state officials after the Civil War actively encouraged the growth of big business by imposing high tariffs on foreign manufacturers as a means of blunting foreign competition and by providing government land and cash to finance railroads and other internal improvements. At the same time that the federal government was issuing massive land grants to railroads and speculators, it was also distributing land to farmers through the Homestead Act of 1862.

The American agricultural sector, by 1870 the world's leader, fueled the rest of the economy by providing wheat and corn to be milled into flour and meal. With the advent of the cattle industry, the processes of slaughtering and packing meat themselves became major industries. So the farm sector directly stimulated the industrial sector of the economy. A national government-subsidized network of railroads connecting the East and West Coasts played a crucial role in the development of related industries and in the evolution of a national market for goods and services. Industry in the United States also benefited from an abundance of power sources—water, wood, coal, oil, and electricity—that were inexpensive compared with those of the other nations of the world.

THE SECOND INDUSTRIAL REVOLUTION   The Industrial Revolution "controls us all," said Yale sociologist William Graham Sumner, "because we are all in it." Sumner and other Americans living during the second half of the nineteenth century experienced what economic historians have termed the Second Industrial Revolution. The First Industrial Revolution began in Britain during the late eighteenth century. It was propelled by the convergence of three new technologies: the coal-powered steam engine, textile machines for spinning thread and weaving cloth, and blast furnaces to produce iron.

The Second Industrial Revolution began in the mid–nineteenth century and was centered in the United States and Germany. It was sparked by three related developments. The first was the creation of an interconnected national transportation and communication network, which facilitated the emergence of new national and even international markets for American goods and services. Contributing to this development were the completion of the national telegraph and railroad systems, the emergence of steamships, and the laying of the undersea telegraph cable, which spanned the Atlantic Ocean and connected the United States with Europe.

During the 1880s a second major breakthrough—the use of electric power—accelerated the pace of industrial change. Electricity created dramatic advances in the power and efficiency of industrial machinery. It also spurred urban growth through the addition of electric trolleys and subways, and it greatly enhanced the production of steel and chemicals.

The third major aspect of the Second Industrial Revolution was the systematic application of scientific research to industrial processes. Laboratories staffed by graduates of new research universities sprouted up across the country, and scientists and engineers discovered dramatic new ways to

"The Hand of Man" (1902)

Photogravure by Alfred Stieglitz.

improve industrial processes. Researchers figured out, for example, how to refine kerosene and gasoline from crude oil and how to improve steel production. Inventors developed new products—telephones, typewriters, adding machines, sewing machines, cameras, elevators, and farm machinery—that resulted in lower consumer prices. These advances in turn expanded the scope and scale of industrial organizations. Capital-intensive industries such as steel and oil, as well as processed food and tobacco, took advantage of new technologies to gain economies of scale that emphasized maximum production and national as well as international marketing and distribution.

BUILDING THE TRANSCONTINENTAL RAILROADS Railroads were the first big business, the first magnet for the great financial markets, and the first industry to develop a large-scale management bureaucracy. The railroads opened the trans-Mississippi West to economic development and transported raw materials to factories, and in so doing they created an interconnected national market for the country's goods and produce. At the same time, the railroads were themselves gigantic consumers of iron, steel, lumber, and other capital goods.

Transcontinental railroads

Using picks, shovels, wheelbarrows, and horse-drawn carts, Chinese laborers largely helped to construct the Central Pacific track.

The renewal of railroad building after the Civil War filled out the railway network east of the Mississippi River, but the most spectacular exploits were the transcontinental lines built across the Great Plains and the Rocky Mountains. Running through sparsely settled land, they served the purpose of binding the country together. The buccaneering executives and financiers directing the transcontinental railroads were shrewd entrepreneurs so driven by dreams of great wealth that they often cut corners and bribed legislators. They also ruthlessly used federal troops to suppress the Plains Indians. But their shenanigans do not diminish the heroic efforts of the workers and engineers who built the rail lines, erected the bridges, and gouged out the tunnels under terrible conditions. Building the transcontinental railroads was an epic feat of daring engineering that tied a nation together, changed the economic and political landscape, and enabled the United States to emerge as a world power.

Before the Civil War, sectional differences over routes had delayed the start of a transcontinental line. Secession and the departure of southerners from Congress finally permitted passage of the Pacific Railroads Act, which Abraham Lincoln signed into law in 1862, authorizing a 2,000-mile line along a north-central route, to be built jointly by the Union Pacific Railroad westward from Omaha, Nebraska, and by the Central Pacific Railroad eastward from Sacramento, California.

Both railroads began construction during the war, but most of the work was done after 1865. The Union Pacific pushed across the plains at a rapid pace, avoiding the Rocky Mountains by going through Evans Pass in Wyoming. The work crews, including large numbers of ex-soldiers and Irish immigrants, had to cope with bad roads, water shortages, rugged weather, Indian attacks, and frequent accidents and injuries.

The Central Pacific construction crews were mainly composed of Chinese workers lured to America first by the California gold rush and then by railroad jobs. Thousands of Chinese had emigrated, raising their numbers in the United States from 7,500 in 1850 to 105,000 in 1880. Most of these "coolie" laborers were single men intent upon accumulating money and returning to their homeland, where they could then afford to marry and buy a parcel of land. Their temporary status and dream of a good life back in China apparently made them more willing than American laborers to endure the dangerous working conditions and low pay of railroad work. By 1867 the Central Pacific Railroad's 12,000 Chinese laborers represented 90 percent of its workforce.

Clearing trees, handling explosives, operating power drills, and working in snowdrifts were dangerous activities, and many Chinese died on the job. Fifty-seven miles east of Sacramento the construction crews encountered

The Union Pacific meets the Central Pacific

The celebration of the completion of the first transcontinental railroad, Promontory, Utah, May 10, 1869.

the towering Sierra Nevadas, through which they had to cut before reaching more level country in Nevada. The Union Pacific had built 1,086 miles to the Central Pacific's 689 when the race ended on the salt plains of Promontory, Utah, near Ogden. There, on May 10, 1869, Leland Stanford, former governor of California and one of the organizers of the Central Pacific, drove a gold spike symbolizing the railroad's completion.

The next transcontinental line, completed in 1881, linked the Atchison, Topeka, and Santa Fe Railroad with the Southern Pacific Railroad in southern California. The transcontinentals soon sprouted numerous trunk lines, which in turn encouraged the building of other transcontinentals. The result was a massive railroad-building boom that lasted into the 1890s and stimulated the rest of the economy.

FINANCING THE RAILROADS   The railroads were built by private companies that raised money for construction primarily by selling bonds to U.S. and foreign investors. While constitutional scruples over state sovereignty initially constrained the granting of federal aid for internal improvements, many states had subsidized the building of railroads within their borders. Finally, in 1850, Illinois senator Stephen Douglas secured from Congress a federal grant of public lands to subsidize a north-south railroad connecting Chicago and Mobile, Alabama. Over the next twenty years, transcontinental railroad companies received generous government aid in the form of federal land grants, as well as loans and tax breaks from federal, state, and local governments.

In the long run, the federal government recovered much if not all of its investment. As farms, ranches, and towns sprouted up around the rail lines, the value of the government land along the tracks skyrocketed. The railroads also hauled government freight, military personnel and equipment, and the mail. Moreover, by helping to accelerate the creation of a national market,

TRANSCONTINENTAL RAILROAD LINES, 1880s

What was the route of the first transcontinental railroad, and why was it not in the South? Who built the railroads? How were they financed?

the railroads spurred economic growth and thereby increased government tax revenues.

But that is only part of the story. The vast sums of money used to finance the building of the transcontinental lines generated shameless profiteering. Prince of the railroad robber barons was Jay Gould, a secretive trickster who mastered the art of buying rundown railroads, making cosmetic improvements, and selling out at a profit while using corporate funds for personal gain and bribes for politicians and judges. Nearly every enterprise he touched was compromised or ruined; Gould, meanwhile, built a fortune that amounted to $100 million upon his death.

Few railroad fortunes were amassed in those freewheeling times by purely ethical methods, but compared with opportunistic rogues such as Gould, most railroad entrepreneurs were giants of honesty. They at least took some interest in the welfare of their companies, if not always in that of the public. Cornelius Vanderbilt, called Commodore by virtue of his early exploits in steamboating, stands out among the railroad barons. Already rich before the Civil War, he decided to give up the hazards of wartime shipping and move his money into land transport. His great achievement was consolidating separate trunk lines into a single powerful rail network led by the New York Central. After the Commodore's death, in 1877, his son William Henry extended the Vanderbilt lines to include more than 13,000 miles in the Northeast. The consolidation trend was nationwide: about two thirds of the nation's railroad mileage were under the control of only seven major groups by 1900.

INVENTIONS SPUR MANUFACTURING   Like the railroad industry, the story of manufacturing after the Civil War shows much the same pattern of expansion and merger in old and new industries. Technological innovations spurred phenomenal increases in productivity. The U.S. Patent Office, which had recorded only 276 inventions during its first decade of existence, the 1790s, registered 234,956 in the 1890s. The list of innovations after the Civil War can be extended nearly indefinitely: barbed wire, farm implements, the air brake for trains (1868), steam turbines, gas distribution and electrical devices, the typewriter (1867), the vacuum cleaner (1869), and countless others. Before the end of the century, the internal-combustion engine and the motion picture were spawning new industries that would blossom in the twentieth century.

These technological advances transformed daily life. In no field was this truer than in the application of electricity to communications and power. Few if any inventions of the time could rival the importance of the telephone, which Alexander Graham Bell patented in 1876. To promote the new device, the inventor and his supporters formed the Bell Telephone Association, out of which grew in 1877 the Bell Telephone Company. In 1885 the Bell interests organized the American Telephone and Telegraph Company, which by 1899 was a huge holding company controlling forty-nine licensed subsidiaries and an operating company for long-distance lines.

In the development of electrical industries, the name Thomas Alva Edison stands above those of other inventors. Edison invented the phonograph in 1877 and the first lightbulb in 1879. At his laboratories in Menlo Park, New Jersey, he created or perfected hundreds of new devices and processes, including the storage battery, Dictaphone, mimeograph, electric motor, electric transmission, and the motion picture.

Until 1880 or so the world was lit by flickering oil or gas lamps. In 1882, with the backing of the financier J. P. Morgan, the Edison Electric Illuminating Company began to supply current to eighty-five customers in New York City, beginning the great electric utility industry. A number of companies making lightbulbs merged into the Edison General Electric Company in 1888. But the use of direct current limited Edison's lighting system to a radius of about two miles. To cover greater distances required an alternating current, which could be transmitted at high voltage and then stepped down by transformers. George Westinghouse, inventor of the air brake for railroads, developed the first alternating-current electric system in 1886 and set up the Westinghouse Electric Company to manufacture the equipment. Edison considered the new method too dangerous, but just as Edison's instrument supplanted Bell's first telephone, the Westinghouse system won the "battle of the currents," and the Edison companies had to switch over. After the invention of the alternating-current motor in 1888, Westinghouse improved upon it. This invention enabled factories to locate wherever they wished. Capable now of using electricity as a power source, they no longer had to cluster around waterfalls and coal deposits for a ready supply of energy.

Entrepreneurs

Thomas Edison and George Westinghouse were rare examples of inventors with the luck and foresight to get rich from the industries they created. Most of the architects of industrial growth—the great captains of industry—were not inventors but pure entrepreneurs, men skilled mainly in organizing and promoting industry. Called robber barons by critics because of their greed and ruthlessness, they helped create thousands of new jobs and supplied the nation with an array of new goods and services. Three post–Civil War business titans stand out for their enterprise: John D. Rockefeller, Andrew Carnegie, and J. Pierpont Morgan. Each of them in different ways replaced the small-scale economy of the early republic with vast new industries that forever altered the size and scope of the nation's business. Two other entrepreneurs, Richard Sears and Alvah Roebuck, perfected mail-order retailing.

ROCKEFELLER AND THE OIL TRUST   Born in New York State, the son of a flamboyant con-man father and a devout Baptist mother, John D. Rockefeller moved as a youth to Cleveland, Ohio. Soon thereafter his father abandoned the family and started a new life under an assumed name with a second wife. Raised by his mother, John Rockefeller developed a passion for systematic organization and self-discipline. He was obsessed with precision, order, and tidiness. And early on he decided to bring order and rationality to the chaotic oil industry.

Cleveland's railroad and shipping connections made that city a strategic location for servicing the oil fields of western Pennsylvania. In economic importance the Pennsylvania oil rush of the 1860s far outweighed the California gold rush of just ten years earlier. Well before the end of the Civil War, derricks checkered the area around Titusville, Pennsylvania, where the first oil well had been struck, and refineries sprang up in Pittsburgh and Cleveland.

Of the two cities, Cleveland had the edge in transportation, and John Rockefeller made the most of the fast-growing commercial city's advantages. A man of icy efficiency and tenacious daring, Rockefeller moved aggressively into the oil business. In 1870 he incorporated his various interests, naming his enterprise the Standard Oil Company of Ohio. His goal was to eliminate all of his competitors. To do that, he hatched an ingenious scheme. In the early 1870s, Rockefeller created the South Improvement Company, which he made the marketing agent for a large percentage of his oil shipments. By controlling this traffic, he gained clout with the railroads, which in turn gave him large rebates (or secret refunds) on the standard freight rates in order to keep his high-volume business. In some cases they even gave

John D. Rockefeller
His Standard Oil Company dominated the oil industry.

him information on competitors' shipments. Rockefeller then approached his Cleveland competitors and pressured them to sell out at his price. Most of them complied. Those who resisted were forced out. In less than six weeks, Rockefeller had taken over twenty-two of his twenty-six rivals. By 1879, Standard Oil was controlling 90 to 95 percent of the oil refined throughout the country.

Much of Rockefeller's success reflected his determination to "pay nobody a profit." Instead of depending upon the products or services of other firms, known as middlemen, Standard Oil started making its own barrels, cans, and whatever else it needed—in economic terms this is called vertical integration. The company kept large cash reserves to make it independent of banks in case of a crisis. Rockefeller also set out to control his transportation needs. With Standard Oil owning most of the pipelines leading to railroads, as well as the railroad tank cars and the oil-storage facilities, it was able to dissuade the railroads from serving its eastern competitors. Those rivals that had insisted upon holding out then faced a giant marketing organization capable of driving them to the wall with price wars.

To consolidate their scattered business interests under more efficient control, Rockefeller and his advisers resorted to the new legal device of the trust. In 1882, Rockefeller organized the Standard Oil Trust. All thirty-seven stockholders in various Standard Oil enterprises conveyed their stock to nine trustees, getting "trust certificates" in return. The nine trustees thereby controlled all the varied Standard Oil companies.

But the trust device, widely copied by other corporations in the 1880s, proved legally vulnerable to prosecution under state laws against monopoly or restraint of trade. In 1892, Ohio's supreme court ordered the Standard Oil Trust dissolved. For a while the company managed to unify control by the simple device of interlocking directorates, through which the board of directors of one company was made identical or nearly so to the boards of the others. Gradually, however, Rockefeller perfected the idea of the holding company: a company that controlled other companies by holding all or at least a majority of their stock. In 1899, Rockefeller brought his empire under the direction of the Standard Oil Company of New Jersey, a holding company. Though less vulnerable to prosecution under state law, some holding companies were broken up by the Sherman Anti-Trust Act of 1890.

Rockefeller not only made a colossal fortune, but he also gave much of it away, mainly to support advances in education and medicine. A man of simple tastes who opposed the use of tobacco and alcohol and believed his fortune was a public trust awarded by God, Rockefeller became the world's leading philanthropist. He donated more than $500 million during his ninety-eight-year lifetime. "I have always regarded it as a religious duty," Rockefeller said late in life, "to get all I could honorably and to give all I could."

CARNEGIE AND THE STEEL INDUSTRY   Andrew Carnegie, like Rockefeller, experienced the atypical rise from poverty to riches that came to be known in those days as the typical American success story. Born in Scotland, he migrated with his family to Allegheny County, Pennsylvania, in 1848. Then thirteen, he started work in a textile mill at wages of $1.20 per week. Quick-witted, shrewd, and brilliant, he worked hard, and in 1853 he became personal secretary and telegrapher to the district superintendent of the Pennsylvania Railroad. When the superintendent became president of the line, Carnegie took his place, and the pace of his career accelerated. During the Civil War, Carnegie went to Washington, D.C., where he developed a military telegraph system.

Carnegie kept on moving—from telegraphy to railroading to bridge building, then to iron- and steelmaking and investments. In 1872 he netted $150,000 on a trip to Great Britain, during which he met Sir Henry Bessemer, who in 1855 had invented what became known as the Bessemer converter, a process by which steel could be produced directly and quickly from pig iron (crude iron made in a blast furnace) by using forced air to heat the metal. The next year, 1873, Carnegie resolved to concentrate on steel, the miracle material of the post–Civil War era, not because it was new but because Bessemer's process had made it suddenly cheap. As more steel was produced, its price dropped and uses soared. In 1860 the United States had produced only 13,000 tons of steel. By 1880, production had reached 1.4 million tons.

Carnegie was never a technical expert on steel. He was a promoter, salesman, and organizer with a gift for hiring men of expert ability. Fiercely competitive and obsessed with efficiency and innovation, he insisted on up-to-date machinery and equipment. Carnegie retained a large portion of his annual profits during good times. During business depressions,

Andrew Carnegie

Steel magnate and business icon.

when construction costs were low and competitors were forced to the wall, he used his surplus capital to buy out competitors and expand. He preached to his employees a philosophy of continual innovation in order to reduce operating costs.

Carnegie stood out from other business titans as a thinker who publicized a philosophy of big business, a conservative rationale that became deeply ingrained in the conventional wisdom of some Americans. Carnegie argued that the captains of industry were on the whole public benefactors. He believed that the best way to dispense a fortune was to donate it during one's lifetime to causes promoting the public good: "The man who dies rich dies disgraced." Carnegie insisted that by supporting universities, libraries, hospitals, parks, halls for meetings and concerts, and church buildings, the wealthy should provide means for the less fortunate to help themselves. Carnegie spent some $60 million on public libraries and another $60 million on higher education.

J. P. MORGAN, FINANCIER Unlike Carnegie and Rockefeller, J. Pierpont Morgan was born to wealth, in Hartford, Connecticut, and increased it enormously through his bold financial innovations. Morgan's father was a partner in a London banking house, and his wealth enabled him to send young Pierpont to schools in Switzerland and Germany. After a brief apprenticeship, Morgan in 1857 began work in a New York firm that represented his father's London bank, and in 1860 he set himself up as its New York agent under the name J. Pierpont Morgan and Company. This firm, under various names, channeled European capital into the United States and grew into a financial power in its own right.

J. Pierpont Morgan

A famous portrait by Edward Steichen (1903).

As an investment banker, Morgan bought corporate stocks and bonds wholesale and sold them at a profit. The growth of large corporations put investment firms such as Morgan's in an increasingly strategic position in the economy. Since the investment business depended upon the health of client companies, investment bankers became involved in the operation of their clients' firms, demanding seats on boards of directors so as to influence company policies.

Like John Rockefeller, J. P. Morgan sought to consolidate rival firms into giant trusts. Morgan realized that railroads were the key to the times, so he bought and reorganized one rail line after another. After the panic of 1893, when hard times gutted the net worth of many railroads, Morgan bought many of them. By the 1890s he controlled a sixth of America's railway system.

Yet Morgan's crowning triumph was the consolidation of the steel industry. In 1901 he bought out Andrew Carnegie's huge steel and iron holdings. Carnegie set the price, nearly $500 million, of which Carnegie's personal share was nearly $300 million. After closing the deal, Morgan told the steel king, "Mr. Carnegie, I want to congratulate you on being the richest man in the world." Morgan's new United States Steel Corporation, a holding company for various steel interests, was a marvel of the new century, the first billion-dollar corporation, the climactic event in the age of relentless corporate consolidation.

SEARS AND ROEBUCK

American inventors helped manufacturers after the Civil War produce a vast number of new products, but the most important challenge was extending the reach of modern commerce to the millions of people who lived on isolated farms and in small towns. In the aftermath of the Civil War, a traveling salesman from Chicago named Aaron Montgomery Ward decided that he could reach more people by mail than on foot and in the process could eliminate the middlemen whose services increased the retail price of goods. Beginning in the early 1870s, Montgomery Ward and Company began selling goods at a 40 percent discount through mail-order catalogs.

Cover of the 1897 Sears, Roebuck and Company catalog

Sears, Roebuck's extensive mail-order business and discounted prices allowed its many products to reach customers in cities and in the backcountry.

By the end of the century, a new retailer had come to dominate the mail-order industry: Sears, Roebuck and Company, founded by two young midwestern entrepreneurs, Richard Sears and Alvah Roebuck, who began offering a cornucopia of goods by mail in the early 1890s. The Sears, Roebuck catalog in 1897 was 786 pages long and was published in German and Swedish as well as English. It included groceries, drugs, tools, bells, furniture, iceboxes, stoves, household utensils, musical instruments, farm implements, boots and shoes, clothes, books, and sporting goods.

The Sears catalog helped create a truly national market and in the process transformed the lives of millions of people. With the advent of free rural mail delivery in 1898 and the widespread distribution of Sears catalogs, families on farms and in small towns and villages could purchase by mail the products that heretofore were either prohibitively expensive or available only to city dwellers. By the turn of the century, 6 million Sears catalogs were being distributed each year, and the catalog had become the single most widely read book in the nation after the Bible.

LABOR CONDITIONS AND ORGANIZATION

SOCIAL TRENDS   Accompanying the spread of giant corporations during the Gilded Age was a rising standard of living for most people. If the rich were still getting richer, a lot of other people were at least better off. The continuing demand for workers, meanwhile, was filled by new groups entering the workforce at the bottom: immigrants above all, but also growing numbers of women and children. Because of a long-term decline in prices and the cost of living, real wages and earnings in manufacturing went up about 50 percent between 1860 and 1890 and another 37 percent from 1890 to 1914. By latter-day standards, however, working conditions were dreary—and dangerous. At the turn of the century, the average hourly wage in manufacturing was about $3.50 in 2009 dollars. The average workweek was fifty-nine hours, which amounted to nearly six ten-hour workdays, but that was only an average. Most steelworkers put in a twelve-hour workday, and as late as the 1920s a great many worked a seven-day, eighty-four-hour workweek.

CHILD LABOR   A growing number of wage laborers in the late nineteenth century were children—boys and girls who worked full-time for meager wages under unhealthy conditions. Young people had always worked in America: farms required everyone to pitch in. After the Civil War, however, many children took up work outside the home, operating machines, sorting coal, stitching clothes, shucking oysters, peeling shrimp, canning food, blowing glass, and tending looms. Parents desperate for income believed they had no choice but to put their children to work. By 1880 one out of every six children was working full-time. By 1900 there were almost 2 million child laborers in the United States. In southern cotton mills, where few African Americans were hired, a fourth of the employees were below the age of fifteen, with half of the children below age twelve. Children as young as eight were laboring alongside adults twelve hours a day, six days a week. This meant they received little or no education and had little time for play or parental nurturance.

Factories, mills, mines, and canneries were dangerous places, especially for children. Throughout Appalachia, soot-smeared boys worked deep in the coal mines. In New England and the South, thousands of young girls worked in dusty textile mills. Children suffered three times as many accidents as adult workers, and respiratory diseases were common in the unventilated buildings. A child working in a textile mill was only half as likely to reach age twenty as a child outside a mill. Although some states passed laws limiting the number of hours children could work and establishing minimum-age requirements, they were rarely enforced and often ignored. By 1881 only seven states, mostly in New England, had laws requiring children to be at least twelve before they worked for wages. Yet the only proof required by employers in such states was a statement from a child's parents. Working-class and immigrant parents were often so desperate for income that they forged work permits for their children or taught them to lie about their age to keep a job.

DISORGANIZED PROTEST   Under these circumstances it was difficult for workers to organize unions. Civic officials and business leaders respected property rights more than the rights of labor. Among workers recently removed from an agrarian world of independent farmers, the idea of permanent labor unions was slow to take hold. And much of the workforce was made up of immigrant workers from a variety of cultures. They spoke different languages and harbored ethnic animosities. Nonetheless, with or without unions, workers often staged impromptu strikes protesting long working hours and wage cuts. During the 1870s, however, such action often led to violent incidents, which colored much of the public's view of labor unions thereafter.

The decade's early years saw a reign of terror in the eastern Pennsylvania coalfields, attributed to an Irish group called the Molly Maguires. The Mollies took their name from an Irish patriot who had directed violent resistance against the British. They were motivated by the dangerous working conditions in the mines and the owners' brutal efforts to suppress union activity. Convinced of the justness of their cause, the Mollies aimed to right perceived wrongs against Irish workers by such methods as intimidation, beatings, and killings. Their terrorism reached its peak in 1874–1875. At trials in 1876, twenty-four of the Molly Maguires were convicted, and ten of them were hanged. The trials also resulted in a wage reduction in the mines.

THE RAILROAD STRIKE OF 1877   A more widespread labor incident was the Great Railroad Strike of 1877, the first major interstate strike in American history. After the financial panic of 1873 and the ensuing depression, the major rail lines in the East had cut wages. In 1877 they made another 10 percent cut, which provoked most of the railroad workers at Martinsburg, West Virginia, to walk off the job and block the tracks. Without organized direction, however, the group of picketers degenerated into a mob that burned and plundered railroad property.

Walkouts and sympathy demonstrations spread spontaneously from Maryland to San Francisco. The railroad strike engulfed hundreds of cities and towns, leaving in its wake over 100 people dead and millions of dollars in property destroyed. Public sympathy for the strikers was so great at first that local militiamen, called out to suppress them, joined the workers instead. Militiamen from Philadelphia managed to disperse one crowd at the cost of twenty-six lives but then found themselves besieged in the railroad's roundhouse, where they disbanded and shot their way out. Federal troops finally quelled the violence, but the looting, rioting, and burning went on for another day until the frenzy wore itself out. A reporter described the scene as "the most horrible ever witnessed, except in the carnage of war." Eventually the strikers, lacking organized bargaining power, had no choice but to drift back to work. Everywhere, the strikes failed.

For many Americans the Great Railroad Strike raised the specter of a worker-based social revolution. As a Pittsburgh newspaper warned, "This may be the beginning of a great civil war in this country between labor and capital." From the point of view of organized labor, however, the Great Railroad Strike demonstrated potential union strength and the need for tighter organization.

THE SAND-LOT INCIDENT   In California the railroad strike indirectly gave rise to a working-class political movement. At a San Francisco sand lot, a meeting to express sympathy for the railroad strikers ended with attacks on some passing Chinese. Within a few days sporadic anti-Chinese riots had led to a mob attack on Chinatown. The depression of the 1870s had hit the West

The rise of oil
Wooden derricks crowd the farm of John Benninghoff in Oil Creek, Pennsylvania, in the 1860s.

Coast especially hard, and the Chinese were handy scapegoats for white laborers' frustrations.

Soon an Irish immigrant, Denis Kearney, had organized the Workingmen's Party of California, whose platform called for an end to further Chinese immigration. A gifted agitator, himself only recently naturalized, Kearney harangued the "sand lotters" about the "foreign peril" and assaulted the rich railroad barons for exploiting the poor. In 1878 his new party won a hefty number of seats to a state constitutional convention. The Workingmen's movement peaked in 1879, when it elected many members to the state legislature and the mayor of San Francisco. Kearney lacked the gift for building a durable movement, but as his party went to pieces, his anti-Chinese theme became a national issue—in 1882, Congress voted to prohibit Chinese immigration for ten years.

TOWARD PERMANENT UNIONS   Meanwhile, efforts to build a permanent labor-union movement were gaining momentum. Earlier efforts, in the 1830s and 1840s, had largely been dominated by reformers with schemes that ranged from free homesteads to utopian socialism. But the 1850s witnessed the beginning of "job-conscious" unions in selected skilled trades.

By 1860 there were about twenty such unions, and during the Civil War, because of the demand for labor, those craft unions grew in strength and number.

There was no overall federation of such groups until 1866, when the National Labor Union convened in Baltimore. The NLU comprised delegates from labor and reform groups more interested in political and social change than in bargaining with employers. The groups espoused such ideas as the eight-hour workday, workers' cooperatives, paper money, and equal rights for women and African Americans. But the organization lost momentum after the death of its president in 1869, and by 1872 it had entirely collapsed. The NLU was not a total failure, however. It was influential in persuading Congress to enact an eight-hour workday for federal employees and to repeal the 1864 Contract Labor Act, which allowed employers to bind immigrant (contract) laborers by paying for their passage from Europe. That those immigrants were willing to work for low wages made them unpopular with American workers.

THE KNIGHTS OF LABOR   Before the National Labor Union collapsed, another labor group of national standing had emerged: the Noble Order of the Knights of Labor, a name that evoked the aura of medieval guilds. The founder of the Knights of Labor, Uriah S. Stephens, a Philadelphia tailor, was a habitual joiner involved with several secret orders, including the Masons. Secrecy, he felt, along with a semireligious ritual, would protect members from retaliation by employers and create a sense of solidarity.

The Knights of Labor, started in 1869, grew slowly, but during the years of depression after 1873, as other unions collapsed, it spread more rapidly. Throughout its existence the Knights emphasized reform measures and preferred boycotts to strikes as a way to put pressure on employers. It also had a liberal membership policy, welcoming all who had ever worked for wages, except lawyers, doctors, bankers, and those who sold liquor. Theoretically it was one big union of all workers, skilled and unskilled, regardless of race, color, creed, or sex. In the 1880s membership in the Knights grew rapidly, from about 100,000 to more than 700,000 in 1886. But the organization peaked in 1886 and went into rapid decline after the failure of a railroad strike.

ANARCHISM   The tensions between labor and management during the late nineteenth century in the United States and Europe helped generate interest in the doctrine of anarchism. Anarchists believed that government—any government—was in itself an abusive device used by the rich and powerful to oppress and exploit the working poor. Anarchists dreamed of the eventual

Members of the Knights of Labor

This national union was more egalitarian than most of its contemporaries.

disappearance of government altogether, and many of them believed that the transition to this stateless society could be hurried along by promoting revolutionary action among the masses. One favored tactic was the use of dramatic acts of violence against representatives of the government. A number of European anarchists emigrated to the United States during the last quarter of the nineteenth century, bringing with them their belief in the impact of "propaganda of the deed."

THE HAYMARKET AFFAIR   Labor-related violence had been increasing during the 1880s, and on May 3, 1886, Chicago's International Harvester plant was the site of a clash between strikers and policemen in which one striker was killed. Leaders of a minuscule anarchist movement in Chicago scheduled an open meeting the following night at Haymarket Square to protest the killing. Under a light drizzle the crowd listened to long speeches promoting socialism and anarchism and was beginning to break up when a group of policemen arrived and called upon the activists to disperse. At that point someone threw a bomb at the police, killing one officer and wounding others. The police fired on the demonstrators, killing four. Six more policemen were also killed. Subsequently, in a trial marked by prejudice and hysteria, seven anarchist leaders were sentenced to death despite the lack of any evidence linking them to the bomb thrower, whose identity was never established. Of the seven, two were reprieved, one committed suicide in prison, and four were hanged. All but one of the group were German speaking, and that one held a membership card in the Knights of Labor.

By the turn of the century, the Knights were but a memory. Several factors accounted for their decline: a leadership devoted more to ideas than to pragmatic organization, the failure of the Knights' cooperative enterprises, and a preoccupation with politics rather than negotiations with management. The Knights nevertheless attained some lasting achievements, among them the creation of the federal Bureau of Labor Statistics and the Foran Act of 1885, which penalized employers who imported contract laborers from abroad. The Knights also spread the idea of unionism and initiated a new type of union organization: the industrial union, an industrywide union of skilled and unskilled workers.

GOMPERS AND THE AFL   The craft unions (skilled workers) opposed the industrial unionism of the Knights. Leaders of the crafts unions feared that joining with unskilled laborers would mean a loss of their craft's identity and a loss of the skilled workers' greater bargaining power. Thus in the summer of 1886, delegates from craft unions met at Columbus, Ohio, and organized the American Federation of Labor (AFL). In structure it differed from that of the Knights in that it was a federation of national craft organizations, each of which retained a large degree of autonomy and exercised greater leverage against management.

Samuel Gompers served as president of the AFL from its start until his death, in 1924, with only one year's interruption. Born in England of Dutch Jewish ancestry, Gompers came to the United States as a teenager, joined the Cigarmakers' Union in 1864, and became president of his New York local in 1877. Gompers and other leaders of the union focused on concrete economic gains—higher wages, shorter hours, better working conditions—and avoided involvement with utopian ideas or politics.

Gompers had a thick hide, liked to talk and drink with workers in the back room, and advocated the strike to achieve labor's objectives. His preference, though, was to achieve those objectives through agreements with management that included provisos for union recognition in the form of closed shops (which could hire only union members) or union-preference shops (which could hire others only if no union members were available).

The AFL at first grew slowly, but by 1890 it had already surpassed the Knights of Labor in membership. By the turn of the century, it claimed 500,000 members in affiliated unions; in 1914, on the eve of World War I, it had 2 million; and in 1920 it reached a peak of 4 million. But even then the AFL embraced less than 15 percent of the nation's nonagricultural workers. All unions, including the unaffiliated railroad brotherhoods, accounted for little more than 18 percent of those workers. Organized labor's strongholds were in transportation and the building trades. Most of the larger manufacturing industries—including textiles, tobacco, and packinghouses—remained almost untouched.

THE HOMESTEAD STRIKE   Two violent labor incidents in the 1890s scarred the emerging industrial-union movement and set it back for forty years: the Homestead steel strike of 1892 and the Pullman strike of 1894. Those dramatic labor conflicts in several respects represented the culminating events of the Gilded Age, a bewildering era during which huge corporations came to exercise overweening influence over American life. Both events pitted organized labor in a bitter contest against two of the nation's largest and most influential corporations. In both cases the stakes were enormous. The two strikes not only represented a test of strength for the organized labor movement but also served to reshape the political landscape at the end of the nineteenth century.

The Amalgamated Association of Iron and Steel Workers, founded in 1876, had by 1891 a membership of more than 24,000 and was probably the largest craft union at the time. But it excluded unskilled steelworkers and had failed to organize the larger steel plants. The massive Homestead Works near Pittsburgh was an important exception. There the union, which included a fourth of Homestead's 3,800 workers, had enjoyed friendly relations with Andrew Carnegie's company until Henry Clay Frick became its president in 1889. A showdown was delayed until 1892, however, when the union contract came up for renewal. Carnegie, who had expressed sympathy for unions in the past, had gone on a lengthy hunting trip to his native Scotland and left matters in Frick's hands. Yet Carnegie knew what was afoot: a cost-cutting reduction in the number of higher-paid skilled workers and a deliberate attempt to smash the union. "Am with you to the end," he wrote to Frick.

As negotiations dragged on, the company announced on June 25 that it would deal with workers as individuals unless an agreement with the union was reached by June 29. A strike—or, more properly, a lockout of unionists—began on that date. Even before the negotiations ended, Frick had begun barricading the plant and had hired as plant guards 300 Pinkerton detectives whose specialty was union busting. On July 6, 1892, a fourteen-hour battle erupted, in which seven workers and three Pinkertons died. In the end the Pinkertons surrendered and marched away, taunted and beaten by crowds in the street. Six days later 8,500 state militiamen appeared at the plant to protect the strikebreakers hired to restore production. The strike dragged on until

November, but by then the union was dead, its leaders charged with murder and treason. Its cause was not helped when an anarchist, a Lithuanian immigrant, tried to assassinate Frick, shooting him twice and stabbing him four times. Much of the local sympathy for the strikers evaporated.

Penniless and demoralized, the defeated workers ended their walkout on November 20 and accepted the company's terms. Only a fifth of the strikers were hired back. Carnegie and Frick, with the support of local, state, and national government officials, had eliminated the union. Across the nation in 1892, state militias intervened to quash twenty-three labor disputes. In the ongoing struggles between workers and owners, big business held sway—in the workplace and in state governments. The Homestead strike was symptomatic of the overweening power of industrial capitalism. By 1899, Andrew Carnegie could report to a friend: "Ashamed to tell you [of my] profits these days. Prodigious!"

THE PULLMAN STRIKE Even more than Homestead, the Pullman strike of 1894 was a notable walkout in American history. It paralyzed the economies of the twenty-seven states and territories making up the western half of the nation. It grew out of a dispute at Pullman, Illinois, a model corporate town built on 4,000 acres outside Chicago, where workers of the Pullman Palace Car Company were housed in neat brick homes nestled on grassy lots along shaded streets. The town's idyllic appearance was deceptive, however. Employees were required to live there, pay rents and utility costs that were higher than those in nearby towns, and buy their goods from company stores. With the onset of the depression of 1893, George Pullman laid off 3,000 of his 5,800 employees and cut wages 25 to 40 percent, but not his rents and other charges. After Pullman fired three members of a workers' grievance committee, a strike began on May 11, 1894.

During this tense period, Pullman workers had been joining the new American Railway Union, founded the previous year by Eugene V. Debs. A charismatic man who led by example and the electric force of his convictions, Debs was a tireless spokesman for labor radicalism who strove to organize *all* railway workers—skilled and unskilled—into the American Railway Union. His earnest appeal generated a tremendous response, and soon he was in charge of a powerful new labor organization. He quickly turned his attention to the controversy in Pullman, Illinois.

In June 1894, after George Pullman refused Debs's plea for arbitration, the union workers stopped handling Pullman railcars. By the end of July they had tied up most of the railroads in the Midwest. The rail owners hired strikebreakers ("scabs") to connect mail cars to Pullman cars so that interference

Eugene V. Debs

Founder of the American Railway Union and later candidate for president as head of the Socialist Party of America.

with Pullman cars would entail interference with the federal mail. U.S. Attorney General Richard Olney, a former railroad attorney, swore in 3,400 special deputies to keep the trains running. When clashes occurred between the deputies and some of the strikers, lawless elements ignored Debs's plea for an orderly boycott and repeated some of the violent scenes of the 1877 strike.

Finally, on July 3, 1894, President Grover Cleveland answered an appeal from the railroads to send federal troops into the Chicago area, where the strike was centered. Illinois governor John Peter Altgeld issued a vigorous protest, insisting that the state could keep order, but Cleveland claimed authority and a duty to ensure delivery of the mail. "If it takes every dollar in the Treasury and every soldier in the United States to deliver a postal card in Chicago," he vowed, "that postal card should be delivered."

As strikers clashed with troops and burned hundreds of railcars, the federal district court granted an injunction forbidding any interference with the mail or any effort to restrain interstate commerce. On July 13 the union called off the strike, and a few days later the district court cited Debs for violating the injunction, and he served six months in jail. The Supreme Court upheld the decree in the case of *In re Debs* (1895) on broad grounds of national sovereignty. Debs served his term, during which he read deeply in socialist literature, and he emerged to devote the rest of his life to socialism.

SOCIALISM AND THE UNIONS   The major American unions for the most part never allied themselves with socialists, as many European labor movements did. Although socialist ideas had been circulating in the United States at least since the 1820s, the movement gained little notice before the rise of Daniel De Leon in the 1890s as the dominant figure in the Socialist Labor party. De Leon proposed to organize industrial unions with a socialist purpose and to build a political party that would abolish the state once it gained power. His ideas seem to have influenced Vladimir Lenin, leader of Russia's Bolshevik revolution of 1917, but De Leon preached revolution at the ballot box, not by violence.

To many, De Leon seemed doctrinaire and inflexible. Eugene Debs was therefore more successful at building a socialist movement in America. In 1897, Debs announced that he was a socialist and organized the Social Democratic party from the remnants of the American Railway Union; he received over 96,000 votes as its candidate for president in 1900. In 1901 his followers joined a number of secessionists from De Leon's party, led by Morris Hillquit of New York, to set up the Socialist Party of America. Debs polled over 400,000 votes as the party's candidate for president in 1904 and more than doubled that, to more than 900,000 votes, or 6 percent of the popular vote, in 1912.

By 1912 the Socialist party seemed well on the way to becoming a permanent fixture in American politics. Thirty-three cities had Socialist mayors. The party sponsored five English-language daily newspapers, eight foreign-language dailies, and a number of weeklies and monthlies. In the Southwest the party built a sizable grassroots following among farmers and tenants. But it reached its peak in 1912. It would be racked by disagreements over America's participation in World War I and was split thereafter.

THE WOBBLIES   During the years of Socialist party growth, a parallel effort to revive industrial unionism emerged, led by the Industrial Workers of the World (IWW), nicknamed the Wobblies. The chief base for this group was the Western Federation of Miners, organized at Butte, Montana, in 1893. Like the Knights of Labor, it was designed to include all workers, skilled or unskilled. Its roots were in the mining and lumber camps of the West, where unstable conditions of employment created a large number of nomadic workers, to whom neither the AFL's pragmatic approach nor the socialists' political appeal held much attraction. The revolutionary goal of the Wobblies was an idea labeled syndicalism by its French supporters: the ultimate destruction of the state and its replacement by one big union. How that union would govern remained vague.

The Wobblies reached out to the fringe elements with the least power and influence, chiefly the migratory workers of the West and the ethnic groups of the East. Always ambivalent about diluting their revolutionary principles, Wobblies scorned the usual labor agreements even when they participated in them. They engaged in spectacular battles with employers but scored few victories. The largest was a textile strike at Lawrence, Massachusetts, in 1912; the strikers won wage raises, overtime pay, and other benefits. But the next year a strike of silk workers at Paterson, New Jersey, ended in disaster, and the IWW entered a rapid decline.

The fading of the movement was accelerated by the hysterical opposition the Wobblies aroused. Its members branded as anarchists, bums, and criminals, the IWW was effectively destroyed during World War I, when most of its leaders were jailed for their militant opposition to the war. Nonetheless, the Wobblies left behind a rich folklore of nomadic working folk and a gallery of heroic agitators.

A NATION TRANSFORMED

By the end of the nineteenth century, the accelerating Industrial Revolution had transformed the nature of work and social life, generated a new urban consciousness and culture, and unleashed rising class tensions. With each passing year, more and more people jettisoned traditional rural folkways in favor of urban environs and enticing economic and social opportunities. As centers of production and consumption, the new industrial cities controlled the pace of national life.

The Industrial Revolution occurred at different rates and produced different effects across the expanding nation. Despite the energetic efforts of New South boosters, the states of the former Confederacy, burdened by a chronic shortage of capital and a poorly educated populace, lagged well behind the rest of the nation in industrial development, urban expansion, and per capita income.

The recurring theme of American life after the Civil War was an acute sense of accelerated social and intellectual change. The velocity and scope of change at midcentury and after was bewildering. Some believed that the United States had lost much of its stability and cohesion as a result of urban-industrial development and western expansion. It had become a loose aggregate of competing individuals, separated from one another by economic differences and ethnic, racial, and class prejudices. How to restore a sense of community and cohesion would become the collective challenge of all Americans.

End of Chapter Review

- **Second Industrial Revolution** The postwar economy was characterized by large-scale industrial development and a burgeoning agriculture sector. The Second Industrial Revolution was fueled by the creation of national transportation and communications systems, the use of electric power, and the application of scientific research to industrial processes. The federal government encouraged growth by imposing high tariffs and granting the railroad companies public land.

- **Rising Big Business** The leading entrepreneurs were extraordinarily skilled at organizing and controlling industry. John D. Rockefeller eventually controlled nearly every facet of the oil industry, consolidating that control through trusts and holding companies. Andrew Carnegie, who believed that competition benefited both society and business, came to dominate the steel industry by buying struggling companies. J. Pierpont Morgan, an investment banker, not only controlled most of the nation's railroads but also bought Carnegie's steel interests in 1901, thereby creating the nation's first billion-dollar company.

- **Labor Conditions and Organizations** The labor force was largely composed of unskilled workers, including recent immigrants and growing numbers of women and children. Some children as young as eight years of age worked twelve hours a day in coal mines and southern mills. In hard times, business owners cut wages without discounting the rents they charged for company housing or the prices they charged in company stores.

- **Rising Labor Unions** It was difficult for unskilled workers to organize effectively. Strikebreakers were plentiful because new immigrants were desperate for work. Business owners often had recourse to state and local militias, which would be mobilized against strikers in the face of perceived anarchy. Craft unions became more successful at organizing as the American Federation of Labor focused on concrete economic gains and better working conditions and avoided involvement in politics.

CHRONOLOGY

1855	Bessemer converter process allows steel to be made quickly and inexpensively
1859	First oil well is struck, in Titusville, Pennsylvania
1869	First transcontinental railroad is completed, at Promontory, Utah
1876	Alexander Graham Bell patents his telephone
1876	Thomas A. Edison makes the first successful incandescent lightbulb
1877	Great Railroad Strike
1882	John D. Rockefeller organizes the Standard Oil Trust
1886	In the Haymarket incident, a bomb set off at a Chicago labor rally kills and wounds police officers
1886	American Federation of Labor is organized
1892	Homestead Strike
1894	Pullman Strike
1901	J. Pierpont Morgan creates the U.S. Steel Corporation

KEY TERMS & NAMES

21

THE EMERGENCE OF URBAN AMERICA

FOCUS QUESTIONS

 wwnorton.com/studyspace

- What accounted for the rise of cities in America?
- How did the "new immigration" change America at the end of the nineteenth century?
- What new forms of mass entertainment had emerged by 1900?
- What was the impact of Darwinian thought on social sciences?
- What were some of the literary and philosophical trends of the late nineteenth century?

Cities are humanity's greatest creation. And in America during the second half of the nineteenth century, cities grew at a rate unparalleled in world history. The late nineteenth century, declared an economist in 1899, was "not only the age of cities, but the age of great cities." Between 1860 and 1910 the urban population of the United States mushroomed from 6 million to 44 million. By 1920 more than half the nation's population lived in urban areas. The rise of big cities created a distinctive urban culture. People from different ethnic and religious backgrounds and every walk of life poured into the high-rise apartment buildings and congested tenements springing up in every major city. They came in search of jobs, wealth, and excitement.

Not surprisingly, the rise of metropolitan America created an array of social problems. Rapid urban development produced widespread poverty and political corruption. It also produced dirt and disease, crowded housing, and unsafe working conditions in factories, mines, mills, and slaughterhouses.

People needed basic services, such as education, transportation, sewers, fresh water, inoculations against disease, and factory inspections to prevent unsafe working conditions. Broadened access to public education and to public health services would eventually improve literacy and lower infant mortality rates. Breakthroughs in medical science would bring cures for tuberculosis, typhoid, and diphtheria—although those infectious diseases would remain the century's leading killers. But in the meantime, the question of how to feed, clothe, shelter, and educate the new arrivals taxed the imagination and patience of many urban leaders.

AMERICA'S MOVE TO TOWN

The prospect of good jobs and social excitement lured people to the cities from the countryside and overseas. City people became recognizably urban in demeanor and outlook. The contrasts between farm and city life grew more vivid with each passing year.

EXPLOSIVE URBAN GROWTH The frontier was a safety valve for urban unrest, the historian Frederick Jackson Turner said in his influential thesis on American development. Its cheap lands afforded a release for the population pressures mounting in the cities. If there were such a thing as a safety valve in his own time, however, he had it exactly backward. The flow of population toward cities was greater than the flow toward the West. Much of the westward migration in fact was itself an urban movement, spawning new towns near the mining digs or at the railheads. On the Pacific coast a greater proportion of the population was urbanized than anywhere else; its major concentrations were first around San Francisco Bay and then in Los Angeles, which became a boomtown after the arrival of the Southern Pacific and Santa Fe Railroads in the 1880s. In the Northwest, Seattle also grew quickly, first as the terminus of three transcontinental railroad lines and, by the end of the century, as the staging area for the Yukon gold rush. Minneapolis, St. Paul, Omaha, Kansas City, and Denver were no longer the mere villages they had been in 1860. The South, too, produced new cities: Durham, North Carolina, and Birmingham, Alabama, which were centers of tobacco and iron production, and Houston, Texas, which handled cotton and cattle and, later, oil. The industrial explosion powered the growth of new cities during this period.

Several technological innovations enabled cities to expand vertically to accommodate their surging populations. In the 1870s, innovations in heating,

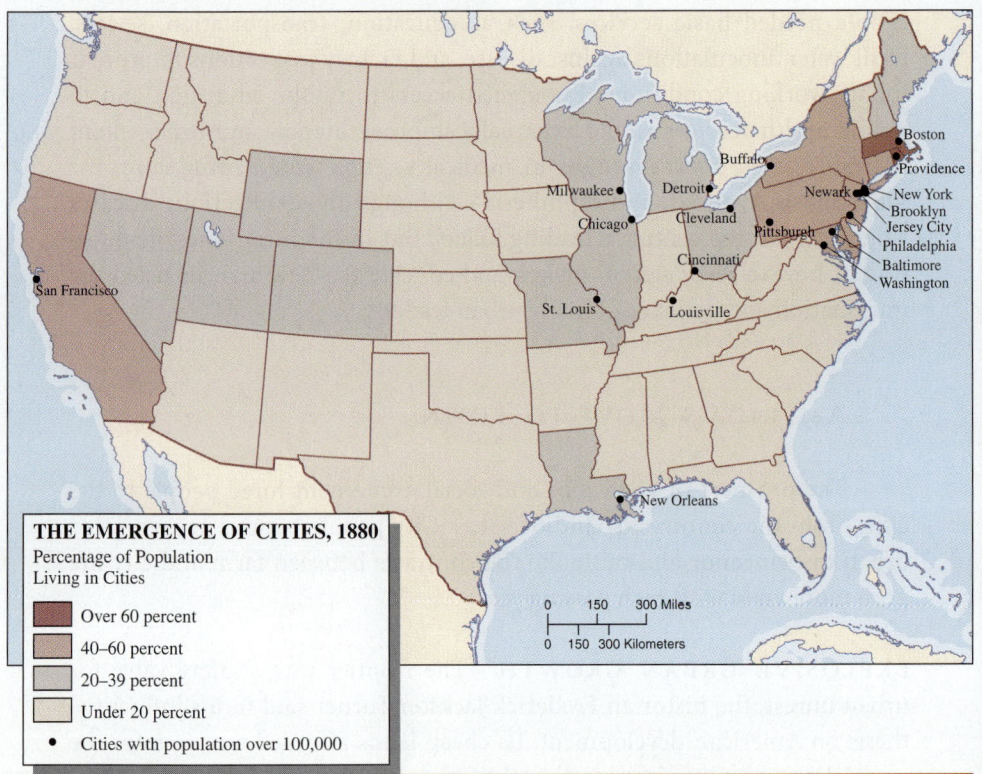

THE EMERGENCE OF CITIES, 1880

Percentage of Population
Living in Cities

- Over 60 percent
- 40–60 percent
- 20–39 percent
- Under 20 percent
- • Cities with population over 100,000

Which states had the largest urban population in 1880? What drove the growth of western cities? How were western cities different from eastern cities?

such as steam circulating through pipes and radiators, contributed to the building of multiple-apartment dwellings, since fireplaces were no longer needed. In 1889 the Otis Elevator Company installed the first electric elevator, which made possible the erection of taller buildings—before the Civil War few structures had risen higher than three or four stories. During the 1880s, engineers developed cast-iron and steel-frame structures, which were stronger than brick and thereby enabled the construction of "skyscrapers," which depend on steel frames and girders.

Cities also expanded horizontally after the introduction of important transportation innovations. Before the 1890s the chief power sources of urban transport were either animals or steam. Horse- and mule-drawn streetcars had appeared in antebellum cities, but they were slow and cumbersome, and cleaning up manure from the streets added to their cost. In 1873, San

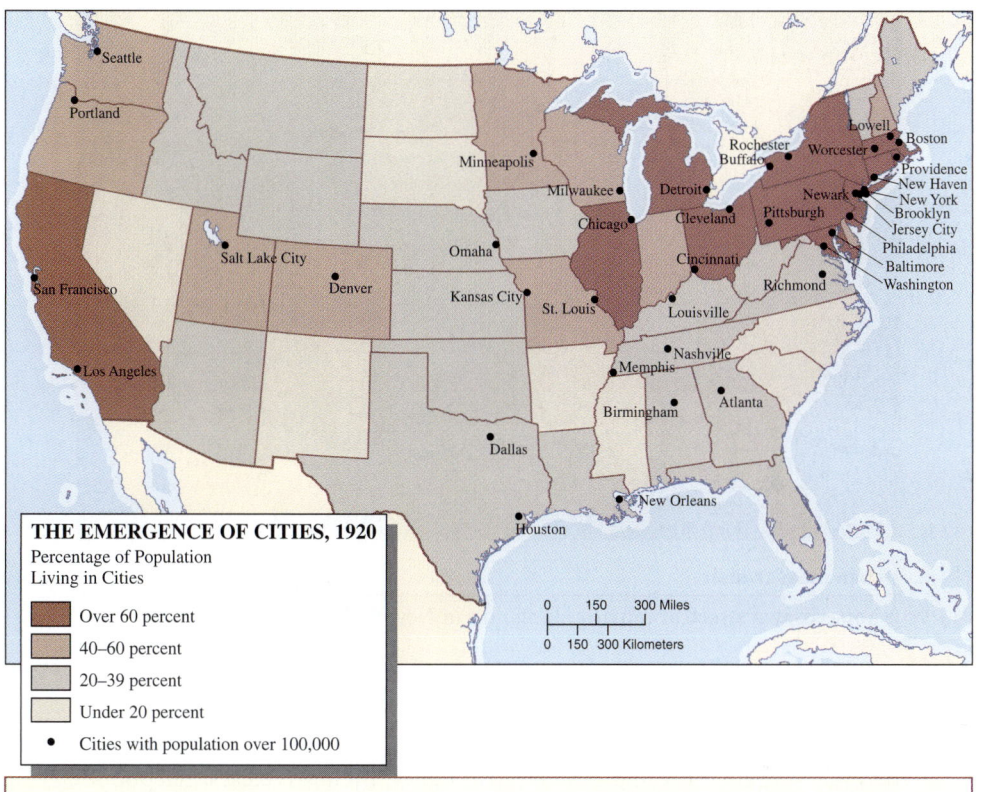

THE EMERGENCE OF CITIES, 1920

Percentage of Population
Living in Cities

- Over 60 percent
- 40–60 percent
- 20–39 percent
- Under 20 percent
- • Cities with population over 100,000

How did technology change urban life in the early twentieth century? What was the role of mass transit in expanding the urban population? How did the demographics of the new cities change between 1880 and 1920?

Francisco became the first city to use cars pulled by steam-driven cables. Some cities used steam-powered commuter trains on elevated tracks, but by the 1890s electric trolleys were preferred. Mass transportation received an added boost around the turn of the century, when subway systems began to operate in Boston, New York, and Philadelphia.

The spread of mass transit allowed large numbers of people to become commuters, and a growing middle class retreated from downtown to live in quieter tree-lined "streetcar suburbs," whence they could travel into the central city for business or entertainment (though laborers generally stayed put, unable to afford even the nickel fare). Urban growth often became a sprawl, since it usually took place without plan, in the interest of a fast buck, and without thought to the need for parks and public services.

Urban mass transit

A horse-drawn streetcar moving along rails in New York City.

THE ALLURE AND PROBLEMS OF THE CITIES   The wonders of
the cities—their glittering new electric lights, their streetcars, telephones,
department stores, vaudeville shows and other amusements, newspapers
and magazines, and a thousand other attractions—cast a magnetic lure on
rural youth. The new cities threw into stark contrast the frustration of unending toil and the isolation of country life. In times of rural depression,
thousands left farms for the cities in search of opportunity and personal
freedom. Yet those who moved to the city often traded one set of problems
for another. Workers in the big cities often had no choice but to live in
crowded apartments, most of which were poorly designed. In 1900, Manhattan's 42,700 tenements housed almost 1.6 million people. Such unregulated
urban growth created immense problems of health and morale.

During the last quarter of the nineteenth century, cities became so
cramped and land so scarce that architects were forced to build upward. In
New York City this resulted in tenement houses. These structures, usually six
to eight stories tall and jammed tightly against one another, housed twenty-
four to thirty-two families. Some city blocks housed almost 4,000 people.
The early tenements were poorly heated and had communal toilets outside
in a yard or alley. Shoehorned into their quarters, families had no privacy,

Urbanization and the environment

A garbage cart retrieves trash in New York City, ca. 1890

free space, or sunshine; children had few places to play except in the streets; infectious diseases and noxious odors were rampant. Not surprisingly, the mortality rate among the urban poor was much higher than that of the general population. In one poor Chicago district at the end of the century, three out of five babies died before their first birthday.

CITY POLITICS   The sheer size of the cities helped create a new form of politics to coordinate citywide services such as public transportation, sanitation, and utilities. Urban political machines thus developed, consisting of local committeemen, district captains, and ultimately a political boss. While the bosses granted patronage favors (awarding city jobs to supporters) and engaged in graft, buying votes and taking kickbacks, they also provided needed services. They distributed food, coal, and money to the poor; found jobs for those who were out of work; sponsored English-language classes for immigrants; organized sports teams, social clubs, and neighborhood gatherings; fixed problems at city hall; and generally helped newcomers adjust to their new life. In return the political professionals felt entitled to some reward for having done the grubby work of the local organization.

CITIES AND THE ENVIRONMENT   Nineteenth-century cities were filthy and disease ridden, noisy and smelly. They overflowed with garbage, contaminated water, horse manure, roaming pigs, and untreated sewage. Providing clean water was a chronic problem, and raw sewage was dumped into streets and waterways. Epidemics of water-related diseases such as cholera, typhoid fever, and yellow fever ravaged populations. Animal waste was pervasive. In 1900, for example, there were over 3.5 million horses in American cities, each of which generated 20 pounds of manure and several gallons of urine daily. In Chicago alone, 82,000 horses produced 300,000 tons of manure each year. The life expectancy of urban draft horses was only two years, which meant that thousands of horse carcasses had to be disposed of each year. In New York City, 15,000 dead horses were removed annually.

During the late nineteenth century, municipal reformers organized to clean up the cities. The "sanitary reformers"—public health officials and municipal engineers—persuaded city governments to banish hogs and cattle, mount cleanup campaigns, establish water and sewage systems, institute trash collection, and replace horses with electric streetcars. By 1900, 94 percent of American cities had developed regular trash-collection services.

Yet such improvements in public health involved important social and ecological trade-offs and caused unanticipated problems. Waste that once had been put into the land was now dumped into waterways. Similarly, solving the horse-manure problem involved trade-offs. The manure dropped on city streets caused stench and bred countless flies, many of which carried diseases such as typhoid fever. But urban horse manure also had benefits. Farmers living on the outskirts of cities used it to fertilize hay and vegetable crops. City-generated manure was the agricultural lifeblood of the vegetable farms outside New York, Baltimore, Philadelphia, and Boston.

Ultimately, however, the development of public water and sewer systems and flush toilets separated urban dwellers and their waste from the agricultural cycle at the same time that the emergence of refrigerated railcars and massive meatpacking plants separated most people from their sources of food. While the advances provided great benefits, a flush-and-forget-it mentality emerged. Well into the twentieth century, people presumed that running water purified itself, so they dumped massive amounts of untreated waste into rivers and bays. The high phosphorous content of bodily waste dumped into streams led to algae blooms that sucked the oxygen out of the water and unleashed a string of environmental reactions that suffocated fish and affected marine ecology.

THE NEW IMMIGRATION

The Industrial Revolution during the second half of the nineteenth century brought to American shores waves of immigrants from every part of the globe. By 1900 nearly 30 percent of the residents of major cities were foreign-born. These newcomers provided much-needed labor, but their arrival also generated ugly racial and ethnic tensions.

AMERICA'S PULL   The migration of foreigners to the United States has been one of the most powerful forces shaping American history, and this was especially true after the Civil War. The tide of immigration rose from just under 3 million in the 1870s to more than 5 million in the 1880s, then fell to a little over 3.5 million in the depression decade of the 1890s and rose to its high-water mark of 8.8 million in the first decade of the new century. Immigrants moved from the agricultural areas of eastern and southern Europe directly to the cities of America. Once in the United States, they wanted to live with others of like language, customs, and religion, and they lacked the means to go west and settle on farms.

This nation of immigrants continued to draw new inhabitants for much the same reasons as before and from much the same segments of society. Immigrants took flight from famine, cholera, or the lack of economic opportunity in their native lands. They fled racial, religious, and political persecution and compulsory military service.

Yet more immigrants were probably pulled by America's opportunities than were pushed out by conditions at home. American industries, seeking cheap labor, sent recruiters abroad. Railroads, eager to sell land and build up the traffic on their lines, distributed tempting propaganda in a medley of languages. Under the Contract Labor Act of 1864, the federal government itself encouraged immigration: it allowed companies to recruit foreign workers by paying for their passage and then recouping the money from the immigrants' wages. The law was repealed in 1868, but not until 1885 did the government forbid companies to import contract labor, a practice that put immigrants under the control of their employers.

A NEW WAVE   Before 1880 immigrants were mainly from northern and western Europe. By the 1870s, however, that pattern had begun to change. The proportion of immigrants from southern and eastern Europe rose sharply. After 1890 they made up a majority of the newcomers, and by the first decade of the new century they formed 70 percent of the immigrants to the United

States. Among these new immigrants were Italians, Hungarians, Czechs, Slovaks, Poles, Serbs, Croats, Russians, Romanians, and Greeks—all people whose culture and language were markedly different from those of western Europe and whose religion for the most part was Judaism or Catholicism.

ELLIS ISLAND   Most immigrants arriving in America passed through a reception center on a tiny island off the New Jersey coast, a mile south of Manhattan, near the Statue of Liberty. In 1892, Ellis Island opened its doors to the "huddled masses" of the world. In 1907, the reception center's busiest year, more than 1 million new arrivals passed through the receiving center, an average of about 5,000 per day; in one day alone, immigration officials processed some 11,750.

MAKING THEIR WAY   Once on American soil, immigrants felt exhilaration, exhaustion, and usually a desperate need for work. Many were greeted by family and friends who had arrived earlier, others by representatives of the many immigrant-aid societies or by agents offering the men jobs

Steerage deck of the S.S. *Pennland*, 1893

These immigrants are about to arrive at Ellis Island in New York Harbor. Many newcomers to America settled in cities because they lacked the means to take up farming.

in mines, mills, or sweatshops. Since most immigrants knew little if any English and nothing about American employment practices, they were easy subjects for exploitation. In exchange for some whiskey and a job, obliging recruiters claimed a healthy percentage of their wages. Among Italians and Greeks these agents were known as padrones, and they came to dominate the labor market in New York. Other contractors provided train tickets to cities such as Buffalo, Pittsburgh, Cleveland, Chicago, Milwaukee, Cincinnati, and St. Louis.

Strangers in a new land, most of the immigrants gravitated to neighborhoods populated by their own kind. The immigrant enclaves—nicknamed Little Italy, Little Hungary, Chinatown, and so on—served as crucial transitional communities between the newcomers' Old World past and their New World future. In such kinship communities, immigrants practiced their religion, clung to their native customs, and conversed in their native tongue. But they paid a price for such community solidarity. When the "new immigrants" moved into an area, older residents typically moved out, taking with them whatever social prestige and political influence they had achieved. The

The Registry Room at Ellis Island

Inspectors asked arriving passengers twenty-nine probing questions, including "Are you a polygamist?"

quality of life quickly deteriorated as housing and sanitation codes then went unenforced.

THE NATIVIST RESPONSE   Then, as now, many native-born Americans saw the wave of new immigration as a threat, and the undercurrent of nativism so often present in American culture surfaced during the late nineteenth century, mainly expressed in anti-Catholic and anti-Semitic sentiments. But more than religious prejudice underlay hostility toward the latest newcomers. Cultural differences confirmed in the minds of nativists the assumption that the Nordic peoples of the old immigration were superior to the Slavic, Italian, Greek, and Jewish peoples of the new immigration. Many of the new immigrants were illiterate, and more appeared so because they could not speak English. Some resorted to crime, and political and social radicals turned up in sufficient numbers to encourage nativists to blame labor disputes on alien elements.

Nativism led to a movement to restrict immigration, but it had mixed success beyond the exclusion of certain individuals deemed undesirable. In 1891, Congressman Henry Cabot Lodge of Massachusetts took up the cause of excluding illiterates, a measure that would have affected much of the new wave of immigrants even though literacy in English was not required. Bills embodying the restriction passed Congress several times during the next twenty-five years but were vetoed by Presidents Grover Cleveland, William H. Taft, and Woodrow Wilson. In 1917, however, Congress overrode Wilson's veto.

Advocates of immigration restriction during the late nineteenth century did succeed in excluding the Chinese, who were victims of every act of discrimination that the new European immigrants suffered and more. They were not white; they were not Christian; many were not literate. By 1880 there were some 75,000 Chinese in California, about a ninth of the state's population. Railroad owners found them hardworking. Many white workers, however, resented them for accepting lower wages, but their greater sin, a New York newspaper editor stressed, was perpetuating "those disgusting habits of thrift, industry, and self-denial."

Exclusion of the Chinese began in 1880, when the urgent need for railway labor had ebbed. A new treaty with China permitted the United States to "regulate, limit, and suspend" Chinese immigration, and in 1882 Congress passed a bill authorizing a ten-year suspension of Chinese immigration. The legislation closing the doors to Chinese immigrants received overwhelming support. The Chinese Exclusion Act was periodically renewed before being extended indefinitely in 1902. Not until 1943 were barriers to Chinese immigration finally removed.

Although the Chinese Exclusion Act sharply reduced the flow of Chinese immigrants, it did not stop the influx completely. In 1910 the West Coast counterpart to Ellis Island opened on rugged Angel Island, six miles offshore from San Francisco, to process tens of thousands of Asian immigrants, most of them Chinese. Those arrivals from China, who could claim a Chinese-American parent were allowed to enter, as were certain officials, teachers, merchants, and students. The powerful prejudice the Chinese immigrants encountered helps explain why over 30 percent of the arrivals at Angel Island were denied entry.

POPULAR CULTURE

The sprawling new cities created new patterns of recreation and leisure. Popular culture took on new or greatly expanded dimensions that endowed life with a more cosmopolitan quality. For example, traveling circuses brought entertainment to small towns as well as large cities. Creative promoters such as Phineas T. Barnum and James A. Bailey made the circus the most eclectic form of entertainment. In the congested metropolitan areas, politics became as much a form of public entertainment as it was a means of providing civic representation and public services. People flocked to hear visiting candidates give speeches in cavernous halls, on outdoor plazas, or from railway cars. In cities such as New York, Philadelphia, Boston, and Chicago, membership in a political party was akin to belonging to a social club. In addition, labor unions provided activities that were more social than economic in nature, and members often visited the union hall as much to socialize as to discuss working conditions. The sheer number of people congregated in cities also helped generate a market for new forms of mass entertainment, such as traveling Wild West shows, vaudeville shows, and spectator sports.

VAUDEVILLE Growing family incomes and innovations in urban transportation—cable cars, subways, electric streetcars and streetlights—enabled more people to take advantage of urban cultural life. By far the most popular—and most diverse—form of theatrical entertainment in the late nineteenth century was vaudeville. The term derives from a French word for a play accompanied by music. It emerged in the United States in seedy beer halls whose owners sought to attract more customers by offering a free show.

Early "variety" shows featured comedians, singers, musicians, blackface minstrels, farcical plays, animal acts, jugglers, gymnasts, dancers, mimes, and magicians. Vaudeville houses became popular gathering places for all social

Vaudeville

For as little as one cent, Vaudeville offered entertainment to customers.

classes and types—men, women, and children—all of whom were expected to behave according to middle-class standards of gentility and decorum.

SALOON CULTURE   The most popular destinations for working-class Americans with free time were saloons and dance halls. The saloon was the poor-man's social club during the late nineteenth century. By 1900 there were more saloons in the United States than there were grocery stores and meat markets. New York City alone had 10,000, or one for every 500 residents. Chicago had one saloon for every 335 people; Houston, one for every 300; San Francisco, one for every 215. Often sponsored by beer brewers and frequented by local politicians, saloons offered a free lunch to encourage patrons to visit and buy 5¢ beer or 15¢ whiskey.

Saloons provided much more than food and drink, however; they were in effect public homes, offering haven and fellowship to people who often worked ten hours a day, six days a week. Saloons were especially popular among male immigrants seeking friends and companionship in a new land. Saloons served as busy social hubs and were often aligned with local political machines. In New York City in the 1880s, most of the primary elections and local political caucuses were conducted in saloons. Saloons were defiantly male enclaves. Although women and children occasionally entered a saloon—through a side door—in order to carry home a pail of beer (called "rushing the growler") or to drink at a backroom party, the main bar at the front was for men only. Some saloons provided "snugs," small separate rooms for female patrons.

Saloons aroused intense criticism. Anti-liquor societies such as the Women's Christian Temperance Union and the Anti-Saloon League charged that saloons contributed to alcoholism, divorce, crime, and absenteeism from work. The reformers demanded that saloons be closed down. Yet drunkenness in saloons was the exception rather than the rule. Most patrons of working-class saloons had little money to waste, and recent studies have revealed that the average amount of money spent on liquor was no more than 5 percent of a man's annual income. Saloons were the primary locus of the workingman's leisure time and political activity. As a journalist observed, "The saloon is, in short, the social and intellectual center of the neighborhood."

OUTDOOR RECREATION The congestion and disease associated with city life led many people to participate in forms of outdoor recreation intended to restore their vitality and improve their health. People sought places within the city to escape the tenements and the factories and offices. New York City in the 1850s set up a park commission, which hired Frederick Law Olmsted to design and plan Central Park. Olmsted went on to design parks for Boston, Brooklyn, Chicago, Philadelphia, and San Francisco. Although originally intended as places where people could walk and commune with nature, parks soon offered more vigorous forms of exercise and recreation. Croquet lawns and tennis courts were among the first additions because they took up little space and required little maintenance.

Even more popular than croquet or tennis was cycling, or "wheeling." In the 1870s, bicycles began to be manufactured in the United States, and by the end of the century a bicycle craze had swept the country. Bicycles were especially popular with women who chafed at the restricting conventions of the Victorian era. The new vehicles offered exercise, freedom, and access to the countryside.

The urban working poor could not afford to acquire a bicycle or join a croquet club, however. Nor did they have as much free time as the affluent. They toiled long hours six days a week, and at the end of their long days and on Sundays they sought recreation and fellowship on street corners or on the front stoops of their apartment buildings. Organ grinders and other musicians would perform on the sidewalks among the food vendors. Many ethnic groups, especially the Germans and the Irish, formed male singing,

Tandem tricycle

In spite of the danger and discomfort of early bicycles, "wheeling" became a popular form of recreation and mode of transportation.

drinking, or gymnastic clubs. Working folk also attended bare-knuckle boxing matches or baseball games and on Sundays would gather for picnics. By the end of the century, large-scale amusement parks such as the one at Brooklyn's Coney Island provided entertainment for the entire family. Yet many inner-city youth could not afford the trolley fare, so the crowded streets and dangerous alleys remained their playgrounds.

WORKINGWOMEN AND LEISURE In contrast to the male public culture centered in saloons, the leisure activities of working-class women, many of them immigrants, were more limited at the end of the nineteenth century. Married women were so encumbered by housework and maternal responsibilities that they had little free time. Married working-class women often used the streets as their public space. Washing clothes, supervising children, or shopping at the local market provided opportunities for fellowship with other women.

Steeplechase Park, Coney Island, Brooklyn, New York

Members of the working class could afford the inexpensive rides at this popular amusement park.

Single women had more opportunities for leisure and recreation than did working mothers. They flocked to dance halls, theaters, amusement parks, and picnic grounds. On hot summer days many working-class folk went to public beaches. With the advent of movie theaters during the second decade of the twentieth century, the cinema became the most popular form of entertainment for women.

Young single women participated in urban amusements for a variety of reasons: escape, pleasure, companionship, and autonomy. As a promotional flyer for a movie theater promised, "If you are tired of life, go to the movies. If you are sick of troubles rife, go to the picture show. You will forget your unpaid bills, rheumatism and other ills, if you stow your pills and go to the picture show." Although some parents and social reformers tried to restrict young single women's freedom to engage in urban recreation and entertainment, many young women followed their own wishes and in so doing helped carve out their own social sphere.

SPECTATOR SPORTS   In the last quarter of the nineteenth century, new spectator sports such as college football and basketball and professional baseball gained mass appeal, reflecting the growing urbanization of life. People could gather easily for sporting events in the large cities. And news of the games could be conveyed quickly by newspapers and specialized sports magazines that relied upon telegraph reports. Saloons also posted the scores. Athletic rivalries between distant cities were made possible by the network of railroads spanning the continent. Spectator sports became urban extravaganzas, unifying the diverse ethnic groups in the large cities and attracting people with the leisure time and ready cash to spend on watching others perform—or bet on the outcome.

Football emerged as a modified form of soccer and rugby. The College of New Jersey (Princeton) and Rutgers played the first college football game in 1869. Some 200 students and other spectators saw Rutgers win, 6 to 4. By the end of the century, dozens of colleges and high schools had football teams, and some college games attracted more than 50,000 spectators.

Baseball card, 1887

The excitement of rooting for the home team united all classes.

Basketball was invented in 1891, when Dr. James Naismith, a physical education instructor, nailed two peach baskets to the walls of the Young Men's Christian Association training school in Springfield, Massachusetts. Naismith wanted to create an indoor winter game that could be played between the fall football and spring baseball seasons. Basketball quickly grew in popularity among boys and girls. All-female Vassar and Smith Colleges added the sport in 1892. In 1893, Vanderbilt University in Tennessee became the first college to field a men's team.

Baseball laid claim to being America's national pastime at midcentury. Contrary to popular opinion, Abner Doubleday did not invent the game. Instead, Alexander Cartwright, a New York bank clerk and sportsman, is recognized as the father of organized baseball. In 1845 he gathered a group of merchants, stockbrokers, and physicians to form the Knickerbocker Base Ball Club of New York.

The first professional baseball team was the Cincinnati Red Stockings, which made its appearance in 1869. In 1900 the American League was organized, and two years later the first World Series was held. Baseball became the national pastime and the most democratic sport in America. People from all social classes (mostly men) attended the games, and ethnic immigrants were among the most faithful fans. Cheering for a city baseball team gave uprooted people a common loyalty and a sense of belonging. Only white players were allowed in the major leagues, however. African Americans played on "minor league" teams or in all-black Negro leagues.

By the end of the nineteenth century, sports of all kinds had become a major cultural phenomenon in the United States. A writer for *Harper's Weekly* announced in 1895 that "ball matches, football games, tennis tournaments, bicycle races, [and] regattas, have become part of our national life." They "are watched with eagerness and discussed with enthusiasm and understanding by all manner of people, from the day-laborer to the millionaire."

EDUCATION AND THE PROFESSIONS

THE SPREAD OF PUBLIC EDUCATION   The growth of public education, spurred partly by the determination to "Americanize" immigrant children, helped quicken the emergence of a new urban society after the Civil War. In 1870 there were 7 million pupils in public schools; by 1920 the number had more than tripled. Despite such progress, leaders in education struggled to overcome a pattern of political appointments, corruption, and incompetence in the public schools.

The spread of secondary schools accounted for much of the increased enrollment. In antebellum America private academies had prepared those who intended to enter college. At the beginning of the Civil War, there were only about 100 public high schools in the whole country, but their number grew to about 800 in 1880 and to 6,000 at the turn of the century.

HIGHER EDUCATION   Colleges at this time sought to instill discipline and morality, with a curriculum heavy on mathematics and the classics (and, in church-related schools, theology), along with ethics and rhetoric. History, modern languages and literature, and some science courses were tolerated, although laboratory work was usually limited to a professor's demonstration in class.

The college-student population rose from 52,000 in 1870 to 157,000 in 1890 and 600,000 in 1920. During those years the number of institutions

Women as students

An astronomy class at Vassar College, 1880.

rose from 563 to about 1,000. To accommodate the diverse needs of these growing numbers, colleges moved from rigidly prescribed courses toward an elective system. The new approach allowed students to favor their strong points and colleges to expand their scope. But as the prominent Massachusetts politician Henry Cabot Lodge complained, it also allowed students to "escape without learning anything at all by a judicious selection of unrelated subjects taken up only because they were easy or because the burden imposed by those who taught them was light."

Colleges remained largely male enclaves, but women's access to higher education did improve markedly in the late nineteenth century. Before the Civil War a few colleges had already become coeducational, and state universities in the West were commonly open to women from the start. But colleges in the South and the East fell in line very slowly. Vassar, opened in 1865, was the first women's college to teach by the same standards as the best of the men's colleges. In the 1870s two more excellent women's schools appeared in Massachusetts: Wellesley and Smith, the latter being the first to set the same admission requirements as men's colleges. Thereafter the older women's colleges rushed to upgrade their standards in the same way.

The dominant new trend in American higher education after the Civil War was the rise of the graduate school. Heretofore most professors had a knowledge more broad than deep. With some notable exceptions they engaged in little research, nor were they expected to advance the frontiers of knowledge. Gradually, however, more and more American scholars studied at German universities, where training was more systematic and focused. After the Civil War the German system became the basis for the modern American graduate university. By the 1890s the doctorate degree was fast becoming a requirement for a professorship.

REALISM IN THOUGHT, CULTURE, AND LITERATURE

Much as popular culture was transformed as a result of the urban-industrial revolution, intellectual life adapted to new social realities. Before the Civil War various forms of idealism dominated American thought. Although quite diverse in motive and method, idealists shared a basic conviction that fundamental truths rested in the unseen world of ideas and spirit or in the distant past rather than in the tangible world of fact and contemporary experience. The most prominent writers, artists, and philosophers were more concerned with Romantic or biblical themes than with common aspects of "real" life.

At midcentury and after, however, a more realistic sensibility began to challenge this idealistic tradition. This realistic movement matured into a full-fledged cultural force during the second half of the nineteenth century. More and more thinkers, writers, and artists focused on the emerging realities of scientific research and technology, factories and railroads, cities and immigrants, wage labor and social tensions.

The rise of realism resulted from a transformed social, intellectual, and moral landscape. The horrors of the Civil War led many people to adopt a more realistic outlook, as did the growing influence of a modern scientific belief that empirical evidence constituted the only admissible basis for knowledge.

The prestige of empirical science increased enormously during the second half of the nineteenth century as researchers explored electromagnetic induction, the conservation of matter, the laws of thermodynamics, and the relationship between heat and energy. Breakthroughs in chemistry led to new understandings about the formation of compounds and the nature of reactions. Discoveries of fossils opened up new horizons in geology and paleontology, and greatly improved microscopes enabled zoologists to decipher cell structures.

Charles Darwin

Darwin's theories influenced more than a century of political debate.

DARWINISM AND SOCIAL DARWINISM

Every field of thought in the post–Civil War years felt the impact of Charles Darwin's *On the Origin of Species* (1859). In that seminal work, Darwin argued that existing species, including humanity itself, had evolved through a long process of "natural selection" from less complex forms of life: those species that adapted to survival by reason of quickness, shrewdness, or other advantages reproduced their kind, while others died away. This idea of evolution shocked people who held conventional religious views in that it contradicted a literal interpretation of the creation stories in the biblical book of Genesis. Heated arguments arose between scientists and clergymen. Some of the faithful rejected Darwin's doctrine while others found their faith severely shaken. Many people, however, eventually came to reconcile science and religion, viewing evolution as a natural process created by God.

The temptation to apply evolutionary theory to the social (human) world proved irresistible. Darwin's fellow Englishman Herbert Spencer became the first major prophet of what came to be called social Darwinism, and he exerted an important influence on American thought. Spencer argued that human society and institutions, like plant and animal species, passed through the process of natural selection, which resulted in what he called the "survival of the fittest."

If, as Spencer believed, society naturally evolved for the better, then individual freedom was inviolable, and any government interference with the competitive process of social evolution was a serious mistake. Social Darwinism thus endorsed a hands-off government policy, then known as laissez-faire; it decried the government regulation of business, the proposals for a graduated income tax, sanitation and housing regulations, and even protection of consumers against medical quacks. Such initiatives, no matter how well intended, would only help the "unfit" survive and thereby impede progress. The only acceptable charity for social Darwinists was voluntary, and even that was of dubious value. Spencer warned that "fostering the good-for-nothing at the expense of the good, is an extreme cruelty."

For Spencer and his many supporters, successful businessmen and corporations were the engines of social progress. If small businesses were crowded out by trusts and monopolies, that too was part of the evolutionary process. Corporate titan John D. Rockefeller told his Baptist Sunday-school class that the "growth of a large business is merely a survival of the fittest."

REFORM DARWINISM   Herbert Spencer's use of Darwin to promote "rugged individualism" did not go without challenge. Reform found its major philosopher in an obscure civil servant, Lester Frank Ward, who fought his way up from poverty and never lost his empathy for the underdog. Ward's book *Dynamic Sociology* (1883) singled out one product of evolution that Spencer and others had neglected: the human brain. Humans, unlike animals, had a mind that could plan for and shape the future. Far from being the helpless pawn of powerful evolutionary forces, Ward argued, humanity could actively shape the process of societal improvement. The competition extolled by Spencer and other social Darwinists was in fact highly wasteful, as was the natural competitive process: plant or cattle breeding, for instance, could actually improve upon the results of natural selection.

Ward's so-called reform Darwinism held that cooperation, not competition, would best promote progress. Government could become the agency of progress by striving first to ameliorate poverty, which impeded the development of the mind, and then to promote the education of the masses. "Intelligence, far more than necessity," Ward wrote, "is the mother of invention," and "the influence of knowledge as a social factor, like that of wealth, is proportional to the extent of its distribution." Intellect, rightly informed by science, could plan successfully. In the benevolent "sociocracy" of the future, Ward argued, legislatures would function mainly to sanction decisions worked out in the sociological laboratory.

PRAGMATISM   Around the turn of the century, the concept of evolutionary human and social development found expression in a philosophical principle set forth in mature form by the Harvard professor William James in his book *Pragmatism: A New Name for Some Old Ways of Thinking* (1907). James shared Lester Frank Ward's concern with the role of ideas in the process of evolution. Pragmatists, said James, believed that ideas gain their validity not from their inherent truth but from their social consequences and practical applications. Thus scientists could test the validity of their ideas in the laboratory and judge their import by their applications. Pragmatism reflected a quality often looked upon as genuinely American: the inventive, experimental spirit that recognized that science—and society—are characterized by change rather than fixity.

John Dewey, who would become the chief philosopher of pragmatism after James, preferred the term *instrumentalism,* by which he meant that ideas were instruments for action, especially for promoting social reform. Dewey, unlike James, threw himself into movements for the rights of labor and women, the promotion of peace, and the reform of education. He believed that education was the process through which society would gradually progress toward greater social equality and harmony.

REALISM IN FICTION AND NONFICTION

Literature also felt the impact of new scientific ideas and the modern urban scene. A rebellious group of young writers discarded the Romanticism and sentimentalism of antebellum culture in favor of fiction and poetry that depicted contemporary reality without moralizing.

CLEMENS Samuel Langhorne Clemens (Mark Twain) was a transitional figure between Romanticism and realism. A native of Missouri, he was impelled to work at age twelve, becoming first a printer and then a Mississippi riverboat pilot. When the Civil War shut down the river traffic, he briefly joined a Confederate militia company, then left with his brother for Nevada, where he wrote for a local newspaper. He moved on to California in 1864 and first gained widespread notice with his tall tale of the gold country, "The Celebrated Jumping Frog of Calaveras County" (1865). With the success of *Roughing It* (1872), an account of his western years, he moved to Hartford, Connecticut, and was able to set himself up as a full-time author and hilarious lecturer.

A Tramp Abroad (1880)

Mark Twain in the frontispiece to his travel narrative.

Clemens was the first significant writer born and raised west of the Appalachian Mountains. His early writings accentuate his western background, but for his greatest books he drew heavily upon his boyhood in the border slave state of Missouri and the tall-tale tradition of southwestern humor. In *The Adventures of Tom Sawyer* (1876), he evoked the prewar Hannibal, Missouri, where his own boyhood was cut so short. Clemens's masterpiece, *The Adventures of Huckleberry Finn* (1884), created unforgettable characters in Huck Finn, his shiftless father, the runaway slave Jim, the Widow Douglas, "the King," and "the Duke." Huck Finn embodied the instinct of every red-blooded boy to "light out for the territory" whenever polite society set out to civilize him. Huck's effort to help his friend Jim escape bondage expressed well the moral dilemmas imposed by slavery on everyone.

LITERARY NATURALISM Realism grew into a powerful literary movement during the 1880s, but during the 1890s it took on a new character in the writings of the so-called naturalists. This group of young literary rebels imported scientific determinism into literature, viewing people as prey to natural forces and internal drives without control or full understanding of them. Frank Norris thus pictured in *McTeague* (1899) the descent into madness of a San Francisco dentist and his wife, driven by greed, violence, and lust. Stephen Crane in *Maggie: A Girl of the Streets* (1893) and *The Red Badge of Courage* (1895) portrayed people caught up in environments that were beyond their control. *Maggie* depicts a tenement girl driven to prostitution and death amid scenes so grim and controversial that Crane had to finance the book's publication himself. *The Red Badge of Courage,* his masterpiece, evokes fear, nobility, and courage amid the carnage of the Civil War.

Two naturalists, Jack London and Theodore Dreiser, achieved a degree of popular success. London was both a professed socialist and a believer in the German philosopher Friedrich Nietzsche's doctrine of the superman. In adventure stories such as *The Call of the Wild* (1903) and *The Sea Wolf* (1904), London celebrated the triumph of brute force and the will to survive.

Theodore Dreiser did not celebrate the overwhelming power of social and biological forces; he dissected them for the reader. The result was powerfully disturbing to readers accustomed to more genteel fare. Dreiser shocked the public probably more than the others with protagonists who sinned without remorse and without punishment. *Sister Carrie* (1900), for example, shows Carrie Meeber surviving illicit loves and going on to success on the stage.

SOCIAL CRITICISM Behind their dogma of determinism, several of the naturalists harbored intense outrage at human misery and social injustice. Their indignation was shared by an increasing number of journalists and social critics who addressed themselves more directly to protest and reform. One of the most influential of these reformers was Henry George, a journalist who vowed to seek out the cause of poverty in the midst of the industrial progress he saw around him. The basic social problem, George reasoned, was the "unearned increment" in wealth that came to those who owned land. He published the fruit of his thought in *Progress and Poverty* (1879), a thick, rambling, and difficult book whose earnest moralism and sympathetic tone helped it sell 2 million copies in several languages.

George held that everyone had a basic right to the use of the land, since it was provided by nature to all. Nobody had a right to the increasing value that accrued from it, however, since that was created by the community, not by its owner. He proposed simply to tax the "unearned" increment in the value of the land, or the rent. George's "single-tax" idea generated much discussion, but his influence centered on the paradox he posed in his title, *Progress and Poverty,* and his plea for social cooperation and equality.

Another prominent social critic, Thorstein Veblen, brought to his work a background of formal training in economics and the purpose of making that subject into an evolutionary or historical science. In his best-known work, *The Theory of the Leisure Class* (1899), he examined the pecuniary values of the affluent and introduced phrases that have since become commonplace in our language: *conspicuous consumption* and *conspicuous leisure.* With the advent of industrial society, Veblen argued, the showy display of money and property became the conventional basis of social status. For the upper classes, moreover, it became necessary to spend time nonproductively as evidence of the ability to afford a life of leisure.

THE SOCIAL GOSPEL

While novelists, journalists, and commentators were writing about the rising social tensions and injustices of late-nineteenth-century America, more and more people were addressing these problems through social action. Some reformers focused on legislative solutions to social problems; others stressed philanthropy or organized charity. A few militants promoted socialism or anarchism. Whatever the method or approach, however, social reformers were on the march at the turn of the century, and their activities gave American life a new urgency and energy.

THE RISE OF THE INSTITUTIONAL CHURCH Churches responded slowly to the mounting social concerns, for American Protestantism had become one of the main props of the established order. The Reverend Henry Ward Beecher, for instance, pastor of the fashionable Plymouth Congregational Church in Brooklyn, preached material success, social Darwinism, and the unworthiness of the poor.

As the middle classes moved out to the streetcar suburbs, their churches followed. From 1868 to 1888, for instance, seventeen Protestant churches abandoned the area south of Fourteenth Street in Manhattan. In the center of Chicago, 60,000 residents had no church, Protestant or Catholic. Where churches became prosperous, they fell under the spell of complacent respectability and do-nothing social Darwinism. Some prominent clergymen expressed open disdain for the lower classes. Not surprisingly, more and more working-class people felt out of place in churches where affluence was both worshipped and flaunted.

Gradually, however, some religious leaders realized that Protestantism was in danger of losing its working-class constituency unless it reached out to the urban poor. Two organizations were created expressly for that purpose: the Young Men's Christian Association (YMCA) entered the United States from England in the 1850s and grew rapidly after 1870, and the Salvation Army, founded in London in 1878, entered the United States a year later. Individual urban churches also began to develop institutional features that were more social than strictly religious in function. Church leaders

A Salvation Army group

Flint, Michigan, 1894.

acquired gymnasiums, libraries, lecture rooms, and other facilities in an effort to draw working-class people back to organized religion.

RELIGIOUS REFORMERS   Church reformers who feared that Christianity was becoming irrelevant to the needs and aspirations of the working poor began preaching what came to be called the social gospel. Washington Gladden of Columbus, Ohio, maintained that true Christianity resided not in rituals, dogmas, or even the mystical experience of God but in the principle that "thou shalt love thy neighbor as thyself." Christian law should therefore govern the workplace, with laborer and employer united in serving each other's interests. The "law of greed and strife," he insisted, "is not a natural law; it is unnatural; it is a crime against nature; the law of brotherhood is the only natural law." In attacking the premises of social Darwinism, Gladden thus argued for labor's right to organize, supported maximum-hours laws and factory inspections, and endorsed anti-trust legislation.

EARLY EFFORTS AT URBAN REFORM

THE SETTLEMENT HOUSE MOVEMENT   While preachers of the social gospel dispensed inspiration, other dedicated reformers attacked the problems of the slums from residential community centers called settlement houses. By 1900 perhaps 100 settlement houses existed in America, some of the best known being Jane Addams and Ellen Starr's Hull-House in Chicago and Lillian Wald's Henry Street Settlement in New York City.

The settlement houses were staffed mainly by young middle-class idealists, a majority of them college-trained women who had few other outlets for meaningful work. Settlement workers sought to broaden the horizons and improve the lives of slum dwellers in diverse ways. At Hull-House, for instance, staff members recruited the neighborhood children for clubs and kindergarten and set up

Jane Addams

One of the heroic leaders of the settlement house movement.

a nursery for the infant children of working mothers. Settlement houses were also meant to provide workingmen with an alternative to the saloon as a place of recreation and an alternative to the neighborhood political boss as a source of social services. Their programs gradually expanded to include health clinics, lectures, music and art studios, employment bureaus, men's clubs, gymnasiums, and savings banks.

Settlement house leaders realized, however, that the spreading slums made their work as effective as bailing out the ocean with a teaspoon. They therefore organized political support for tenement laws, public playgrounds, juvenile courts, mothers' pensions, workers' compensation laws, and legislation prohibiting child labor.

WOMEN'S EMPLOYMENT AND ACTIVISM   Settlement house workers, insofar as they were paid, made up but a fraction of all gainfully employed women. With the rapid population growth in the late nineteenth century, the number of employed women steadily increased, as did the percentage of women in the labor force. These changes in occupational status had little connection to the women's rights movement, however, which increasingly focused on the issue of suffrage. Immediately after the Civil War, Susan B. Anthony, a seasoned veteran of the movement, demanded that the Fifteenth Amendment guarantee the vote for women as well as black men. But she made little impression on those who insisted that women belonged solely in the home.

In 1869 the unity of the women's movement disintegrated in a manner reminiscent of the anti-slavery rift three decades before. The question once again was whether the movement should concentrate on one overriding issue or broaden its focus. Susan B. Anthony and Elizabeth Cady Stanton founded the National Woman Suffrage Association to promote a women's suffrage amendment to the Constitution, but they looked upon suffrage as but one among many feminist causes to be promoted. Later that same year, Lucy Stone, Julia Ward Howe, and other leaders formed the American Woman Suffrage Association, which focused single-mindedly on the vote as the first and most basic reform.

In 1890, after three years of negotiation, the rival groups united as the National American Woman Suffrage Association, with Elizabeth Cady Stanton as president for two years, followed by Susan B. Anthony until 1900. The work thereafter was carried on by a new generation of activists, led by Anna Howard Shaw and Carrie Chapman Catt. Over the years the movement achieved some local and partial victories as a few states granted women suffrage in school board or municipal elections. In 1869 the territory of

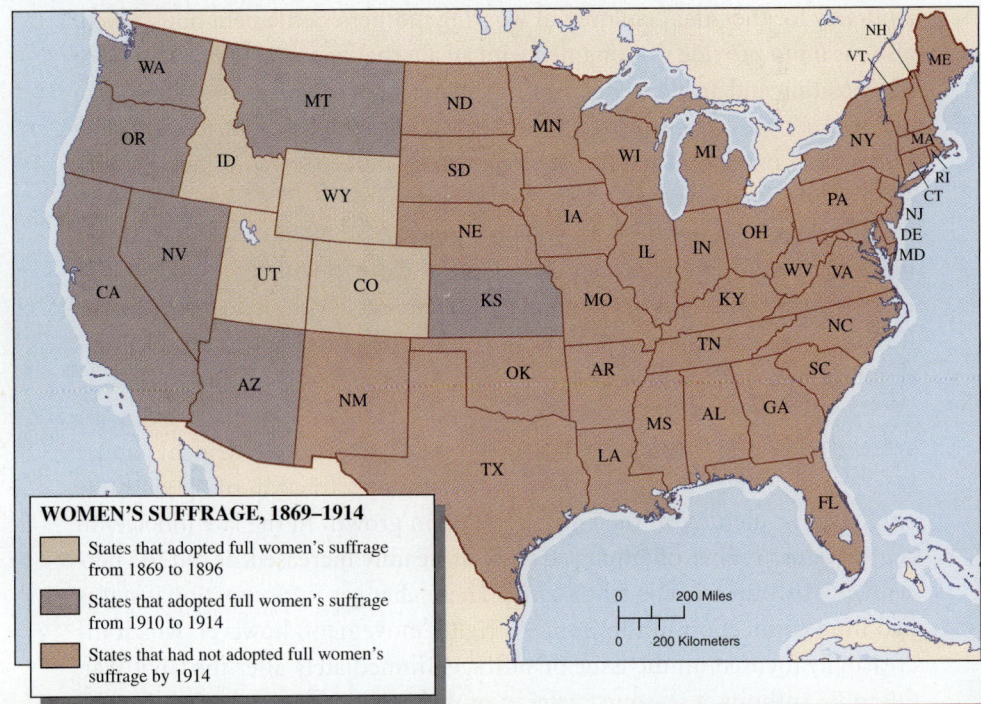

WOMEN'S SUFFRAGE, 1869–1914

- States that adopted full women's suffrage from 1869 to 1896
- States that adopted full women's suffrage from 1910 to 1914
- States that had not adopted full women's suffrage by 1914

Which states first gave women the right to vote? Why did it take fifty-one years, from Wyoming's grant of full suffrage to women until ratification of the Nineteenth Amendment, for women to receive the right to vote? How was suffrage part of a larger women's reform movement?

Wyoming provided full suffrage to women and after 1890 retained women's suffrage when it became a state. Three other western states soon followed suit, but not until New York acted in 1917 did a state east of the Mississippi River adopt universal suffrage.

Despite the focus on the vote, women did not confine their public activism to that issue. In 1866 the Young Women's Christian Association, a parallel to the YMCA, appeared in Boston and spread elsewhere. The New England Women's Club, started in 1868 by Julia Ward Howe and others, was an early example of the women's clubs that proliferated to such an extent that a General Federation of Women's Clubs was established in 1890 to tie them together nationally. Many women's clubs confined themselves to "literary" and social activities, but others became deeply involved in charities and reform. The New York Consumers' League, formed in 1890, and the National

Consumers' League, established nine years later, sought to make the buying public, chiefly women, more aware of degrading labor conditions.

TOWARD A WELFARE STATE Even without the support of voting women in most places, many states adopted rudimentary measures to regulate big business and labor conditions in the public interest. They passed laws to regulate railroads and working conditions, but the laws were generally poorly enforced or overturned by the courts. In the meantime, it was often the local political machines that stepped in to help those who were suffering. While local and federal governments lacked a bureaucracy to assist those who had fallen on hard times, the political machines in the cities supplied temporary jobs, food, or other necessities. The machines, then, were the precursor to the modern welfare state.

At the end of the nineteenth century, opinion in the country stood poised between conservative rigidities and a growing sense that new conditions imposed new personal and government responsibilities. The last two decades of the nineteenth century had already seen a slow erosion of free-market values, which had found their most secure home in the courts. There emerged instead a concept of the general-welfare state, which called upon the government to act on behalf of the whole society rather than allow rugged individualism to run rampant. The conflict between government intervention and laissez-faire values spilled over into the new century, but by the mid–twentieth century, after the Progressive movement and the New Deal, the nation would be firmly committed to the premises of the general-welfare state.

CHAPTER SUMMARY

- **Rise of Cities** America's cities grew in all directions. Electric elevators and new steel-frame construction allowed architects to extend buildings upward. Mass transit allowed the middle class to retreat to suburbs. Crowded tenements bred disease and crime and created an opportunity for urban political bosses to accrue power, in part by distributing to the poor the only relief that existed.

- **New Immigration** By 1900, 30 percent of Americans were foreign-born, with many immigrants coming from eastern and southern Europe rather than western and northern Europe, like most immigrants of generations past. Thus their languages and culture were vastly different from those of native-born Americans. They tended to be Catholic or Jewish rather than Protestant. Beginning in the 1880s, nativists advocated immigration laws to exclude the Chinese and the poor and demanded that immigrants pass a literacy test. A federal immigration station on Ellis Island, in New York Harbor, opened in 1892 to process immigrants arriving by ship from across the Atlantic.

- **Mass Entertainment** Cities began to create urban parks, like New York's Central Park, as places for all citizens to stroll, ride bicycles, or play games such as tennis. Vaudeville shows emerged as a popular form of entertainment. Saloons served as local social and political clubs for men. It was in this era that football, baseball, and basketball emerged as spectator sports.

- **Social Darwinism** Charles Darwin's *On the Origin of Species* shocked people who believed in a literal interpretation of the Bible's account of creation. Darwin's scientific theory was applied to human society and social institutions by Herbert Spencer and William Graham Sumner, who equated economic and social success with "survival of the fittest" and advanced the idea that government should not interfere to promote equality.

- **Rise of Realism** American literature responded to the changes in society at this time. Samuel L. Clemens (Mark Twain) wrote humorously about his experiences and observations and later created masterpieces that playfully comment on social issues. The movement known as naturalism shocked many readers in the 1890s by depicting individuals as victims of a brutal world. Social critics such as Henry George were shocked by the vast disparities between rich and poor. The social gospel movement, in which the religious community reached out to the poor, was another response to America's poverty.

CHRONOLOGY

1858	Construction of New York's Central Park begins
1859	Darwin's *On the Origin of Species* is published
1882	Congress passes the Chinese Exclusion Act
1889	Hull-House, a settlement house, opens in Chicago
1889	Otis Elevator Company installs the first electric elevator
1890	National American Woman Suffrage Association is formed
1891	Basketball is invented
1892	Ellis Island, a federal center for processing immigrants, opens
1900	Baseball's National League is formed

KEY TERMS & NAMES

22

GILDED AGE POLITICS AND AGRARIAN REVOLT

FOCUS QUESTIONS wwnorton.com/studyspace

- What were the major features of American politics during the Gilded Age?
- What were the major issues in politics during this period?
- What were the main problems facing farmers in the South and the Midwest after the Civil War?
- How and why did farmers become politicized?
- What was significant about the election of 1896?

In 1873 the writers Mark Twain and Charles Dudley Warner created an enduring label for the post–Civil War era when they collaborated on a novel titled *The Gilded Age*. The book depicts an age of widespread political corruption, corporate greed, and social vulgarity. Generations of political scientists and historians have since reinforced the two novelists' judgment. As a young college graduate in 1879, future president Woodrow Wilson described the state of the post–Civil War political system: "No leaders, no principles; no principles, no parties."

PARADOXICAL POLITICS

Political life in the Gilded Age, the thirty-five years between the end of the Civil War and the end of the nineteenth century, had several distinctive elements. Local politics, especially in cities crowded with waves of new immigrants, was usually controlled by "rings"—small groups of political insiders who managed the nomination and election of candidates, ran primaries, and influenced policy. Each ring typically had a powerful "boss" who ran things, using his "machine"—a network of neighborhood activists and officials—to govern the town or city. Bosses organized neighborhoods (precincts), mediated disputes, picked candidates, helped the needy, and distributed patronage (municipal jobs and contracts) to loyal followers and corporate contributors. The various city rings and bosses were usually corrupt and rarely efficient, but they did bring structure, stability, and services to rapidly growing and often chaotic inner-city communities. Colorful figures such as New York City's William "Boss" Tweed shamelessly ruled, plundered, and occasionally improved municipal government, often through dishonest means and frequent bribes. Until his arrest in 1871 and his conviction in 1873, Tweed used the Tammany Hall ring to dominate the nation's largest city.

National political parties during the Gilded Age were much more dominant forces than they are today. Party loyalty was powerful, often extending over many generations. Parties also were the nexus of political activity. They controlled access to political offices, dominated elections, and shaped policy making. Throughout the last third of the nineteenth century, a close balance between Republicans and Democrats in Congress created the sense of a stalemate. Neither party was willing to embrace controversial issues or take bold initiatives because neither had a commanding advantage with the electorate. Timidity prevailed. The Gilded Age has long been viewed as a time of political mediocrity, in which the parties refused to confront "real issues" such as the runaway growth of an unregulated economy and its attendant social injustices.

Voters of the time nonetheless thought politics was very important. Voter turnout during the Gilded Age was commonly about 70 to 80 percent, even in the South, where the disfranchisement of African Americans was not yet complete. (By contrast, the turnout for the 2008 presidential election was almost 57 percent.) The paradox of such a high rate of voter participation in the face of the inertia at the national political level raises an obvious question: how was it that leaders who failed to address

William "Boss" Tweed

Tweed is represented here as having a money-bag face and a $15,500 diamond stickpin.

the "real issues" of the day presided over the most highly organized and politically active electorate in U.S. history?

The answer is partly that the politicians and the voters believed that they *were* dealing with crucial issues: tariff rates, the initial efforts to regulate corporations, monetary policy, Indian disputes, civil service reform, and immigration. But the answer also reflects the extreme partisanship of the times and the essentially local nature of political culture during the Gilded Age.

PARTISAN POLITICS Most Americans after the Civil War were intensely loyal to the Democratic or Republican party. Political parties gave people an anchor for their activity and their loyalty in an unstable world. Local party officials took care of those who voted their way and distributed appointive public offices and other favors to party loyalists. These "city machines" used patronage and favoritism to retain the loyalty of business supporters while providing jobs, food, or fuel to working-class voters who had fallen on hard times. The party faithful eagerly took part in rallies and picnics, deriving from them a sense of camaraderie as well as an opportunity for recreation that offered a welcome relief from their usual workday routine.

Party loyalties and voter turnout in the late nineteenth century reflected religious and ethnic divisions as well as geographic differences. The Republican party attracted mainly Protestants of British descent. Its base was New England, and its other strongholds were New York and the Upper Midwest. The Republicans, the party of Abraham Lincoln, could rely upon the votes of African Americans and Union veterans of the Civil War.

The Democrats, by contrast, tended to be a heterogeneous, often unruly coalition embracing southern whites, immigrants and Catholics of any origin in the northern states, Jews, freethinkers, skeptics, and all those repelled by the "party of morality." As one Chicago Democrat explained, "A Republican is a man who wants you t' go t' church every Sunday. A Democrat says if a man wants to have a glass of beer on Sunday he can have it."

Republicans pressed nativist policies, calling for restrictions on both immigration and the employment of foreigners. They also promoted the teaching of the "American" language in the schools. The cause of banning alcoholic beverages revived along with nativism in the 1880s. Among the immigrants who crowded into the growing cities were many Irish, Germans, and Italians, who tended to enjoy alcoholic beverages. Republicans increasingly saw saloons as the central social evil around which all others revolved, including vice, crime, political corruption, and neglect of families, and they associated these problems with the ethnic groups that frequented saloons.

POLITICAL STALEMATE AT THE NATIONAL LEVEL   Between 1869 and 1913, from the presidency of Ulysses S. Grant through that of William Howard Taft, Republicans monopolized the White House except for the two nonconsecutive terms of the New York Democrat Grover Cleveland, but Republican domination was more apparent than real. Between 1872 and 1896 no president won a majority of the popular vote. In each of those presidential elections, sixteen states invariably voted Republican and fourteen voted Democratic, leaving a pivotal six states whose results might change. The important swing-vote role played by two of those states, New York and Ohio, helps explain the election of eight presidents from those states from 1872 to 1908.

Lackluster presidents also contributed to the political stalemate. No chief executive between Abraham Lincoln and Theodore Roosevelt exercised "strong" leadership. None challenged the prevailing view that Congress, not the White House, should formulate policy. Senator John Sherman of Ohio expressed the widely held notion that the legislative branch should predominate in a republic: "The President should merely obey and enforce the law."

Republicans controlled the Senate and Democrats controlled the House during the Gilded Age. Only during 1881 to 1883 and 1889 to 1891 did a Republican president coincide with a Republican Congress, and only between 1893 and 1895 did a Democratic president enjoy a Democratic majority in Congress. The counterbalancing strength of the parties in Congress and the fear in each party of alienating key factions deterred any vigorous initiatives in Congress. Because most bills required bipartisan support to pass both houses and because legislators tended to vote along party lines, the Democrats and the Republicans pursued a policy of evasion on the national issues of the day. Only the tariff provoked clear-cut divisions, between protectionist Republicians and low-tariff Democrats, but there were individual exceptions even on that. On the important questions of the money supply, regulation of big business, farm problems, civil service reform, and immigration, the parties differed very little. As a result, they primarily became vehicles for seeking office and dispensing patronage in the form of government jobs and contracts.

STATE AND LOCAL INITIATIVES   Unlike those of today, Americans during the Gilded Age expected little direct support from the federal government; most significant political activity occurred at the state and local levels. Residents of the western territories were largely forced to fend for themselves rather than rely upon federal authorities. They formed towns, practiced vigilante justice, and made laws on their own. Once incorporated into the Union, the former territories retained much of their autonomy.

Thus state governments after the Civil War were the primary centers of political activity and innovation. Over 60 percent of the nation's spending and taxing was exercised by state and local authorities. Then, unlike today, the large cities spent far more on local services than did the federal government. And three fourths of all public employees worked for state and local governments. Local issues such as prohibition, Sunday closing laws, and parochial-school funding often generated more excitement than complex debates over tariffs and monetary policies. It was the state and local governments that first sought to curb the power and restrain the abuses of corporate interests.

CORRUPTION AND REFORM: HAYES TO HARRISON

During the Gilded Age, states attempted to regulate big business; most of those efforts were overturned by the courts, however. A close alliance thus developed between business owners and political leaders at every level. Railroad passes, free entertainment, and a host of other favors were freely provided to politicians, newspaper editors, and other leaders in positions to influence public opinion or affect legislation.

Both Republican and Democratic leaders also squabbled over the "spoils" of office, the appointive offices at the local and national levels. After each election it was expected that the victorious party would throw out the defeated party's appointees and appoint its own men to office. The patronage system of awarding government jobs to supporters invited corruption. It also was so time-consuming that it distracted elected officials from more important issues. Yet George Washington Plunkitt, a Democratic boss in New York City, spoke for many Gilded Age politicians when he explained that "You can't keep an organization together without patronage. Men ain't in politics for nothin'. They want to get somethin' out of it." Each party had its share of corrupt officials willing to buy and sell government appointments or congressional votes, yet each also witnessed the emergence of factions promoting honesty in government. The struggle for "cleaner" government soon became one of the foremost issues of the day.

HAYES AND CIVIL SERVICE REFORM   In the aftermath of Reconstruction, President Rutherford B. Hayes embodied the "party of morality." Hayes brought to the White House in 1877 a new style of uprightness, in

"The Bosses of the Senate"

This 1875 cartoon bitingly portrays the period's alliance between big business and politics.

sharp contrast to the graft and corruption practiced by members of the Grant administration. The son of an Ohio farmer, Hayes had been wounded four times in the Civil War and had been promoted to the rank of major general. Elected governor of Ohio in 1867, he served three terms.

Hayes's presidency suffered from the supposedly secret deal that awarded him victory over the New York Democrat Samuel Tilden in the 1876 election. Snide references to Hayes as "His Fraudulence" denied him any chance at a second term, which he renounced from the beginning. Hayes's Republican party was split between so-called Stalwarts and Half-Breeds, led respectively by Senators Roscoe Conkling of New York and James G. Blaine of Maine. The difference between these Republican factions was even murkier than that between the two major parties. The Stalwarts had been stalwart in their support of President Grant during the furor over the misbehavior of his cabinet members. They also promoted Radical Reconstruction of the South and the "spoils system" of distributing federal political jobs to party loyalists. The Half-Breeds acquired their name because they were only half-loyal to Grant and half-committed to reform of the spoils system.

Hayes aligned himself with the growing public discontent over political corruption in the Grant administration. In promoting civil service reform, he issued an executive order in 1877 declaring that those already in office (for the most part Grant's appointees) would be dismissed only for the good of the government and not for political reasons. For all of Hayes's efforts to clean house, he retained a limited vision of government's role in society. On the economic issues of the day, he held to a conservative line that would guide his successors for the rest of the century. His solution to labor troubles, demonstrated during the Great Railroad Strike of 1877, was to send in federal troops and break the strike. His answer to the demands of farmers and debtors that he expand the currency was to veto the Bland-Allison Act, which provided for a limited expansion of silver currency through the government's purchase of $2 million to $4 million in silver coins per month. (The bill was passed when Congress overrode Hayes's veto.)

GARFIELD AND ARTHUR   With Hayes out of the running for a second term, the Stalwarts, led by Conkling, brought Ulysses S. Grant forward for a third time, still a strong contender despite the tarnish of his administration's scandals. For two days the Republican Convention in Chicago was deadlocked, with Grant holding a slight lead over James G. Blaine and John Sherman. When Wisconsin's delegates suddenly switched their votes to former House Speaker (now Senator-elect) James A. Garfield, the convention stampeded to the dark-horse candidate from Ohio. As a sop to the Stalwarts, the convention tapped Chester A. Arthur, of customhouse notoriety, for vice president.

The Democrats named Winfield Scott Hancock, a Union general during the Civil War, to counterbalance the Republicans' "bloody-shirt" attacks on their party as the vehicle of secession. In the close election, Garfield eked out a plurality of only 39,000 votes, or 48.5 percent of the vote, but with a comfortable margin of 214 to 155 in the Electoral College.

On July 2, 1881, after only four months in office, President Garfield was walking through the Washington, D.C., railroad station when a deranged man, Charles Guiteau, shot him in the back. "I am a Stalwart," Guiteau shouted to the arresting officers. "Arthur is now President of the United States." Two months later, Garfield died of complications resulting from the shooting.

Chester Arthur, one of the chief henchmen of Stalwart leader Roscoe Conkling, was now president. Little in his past suggested that he would rise above spoils politics. But Arthur, a wealthy, handsome widower who loved fine wines and sported a lavish wardrobe and billowing sideburns, demonstrated surprising leadership qualities. He distanced himself from Conkling and the Stalwarts and established a genuine independence.

Most startling of all was Arthur's emergence as something of a civil service and tariff reformer. The assassin Guiteau had unwittingly galvanized public support of political reform. A civil service reform bill sponsored by "Gentleman George" Pendleton, a Democratic senator from Ohio, passed in 1883, setting up a three-member Civil Service Commission independent of the cabinet departments, the first such federal agency established on a permanent basis. About 14 percent of all government jobs would now be filled on the basis of competitive examinations rather than political connections. What was more, the president could enlarge the class of jobs based on merit at his discretion, as many presidents later did.

Meanwhile, the tariff continued to be the most controversial national political issue. The high tariff, a heritage of the Civil War, had by the early 1880s raised federal revenues to a point where the government was enjoying a surplus that drew money into the Treasury and out of circulation, thus impeding economic growth. Some argued that lower tariff rates would reduce consumer prices by enabling foreign competition and at the same time leave more money in circulation. In 1882, Arthur named a special tariff commission, which recommended a 20 to 25 percent rate reduction, but Congress's effort to enact the proposal was marred by logrolling (the trading of votes to benefit different legislators' local interests). The result was the "mongrel tariff" of 1883, so called because of its different rates for different commodities. Overall, the new tariff provided for a slight rate reduction, but it also raised the duty on some products.

THE SCURRILOUS CAMPAIGN   As the 1884 presidential election neared, Chester Arthur's record as an unexpected reformer might have attracted voters, but it did not please the leaders of his party. The Republicans dumped Arthur and turned to the majestic senator James G. Blaine of Maine, leader of the Half-Breed Republicans. Blaine was the consummate politician. He inspired the party faithful with his oratory, and at the same time he knew how to wheel and deal in the backrooms.

During the campaign, however, letters surfaced that linked Blaine to efforts to exchange his influence for selfish gain. For the reform element of the Republican party, this was too much, and many bolted the ticket. Party regulars scorned the idealists as "goo-goos"—the good-government crowd who ignored partisan realities—and one newspaper editor jokingly tagged them Mugwumps, after an Algonquian word for a self-important chieftain.

Senator James G. Blaine of Maine

The Republican candidate in 1884.

The rise of the Mugwumps influenced the Democrats to nominate the New Yorker Stephen Grover Cleveland as a reform candidate. Elected mayor of Buffalo in 1881, Cleveland first attracted national attention for battling corruption in that city. In 1882 he was elected governor of New York, and he continued to build a reform record by fighting New York City's corrupt Tammany Hall ring. As mayor and as governor, he repeatedly vetoed what he considered special-privilege bills serving selfish interests. Cleveland possessed little charisma but impressed the public with his stubborn integrity. He was a crusader against corruption, and as such he drew many of those making up the growing chorus of political reformers.

But a scandal erupted when the *Buffalo Evening Telegraph* revealed that as a bachelor, Cleveland had had an affair with an attractive Buffalo widow, Maria Halpin. Mrs. Halpin had named Cleveland as the father of a boy born to her in 1874. Cleveland had responded by providing financial support when the child was placed in an orphanage. The respective personal escapades of Blaine and Cleveland provided the 1884 campaign with some of the most colorful battle cries in political history: "Blaine, Blaine, James G. Blaine, the continental liar from the state of Maine," Democrats chanted; Republicans countered with "Ma, ma, where's my pa? Gone to the White House, ha, ha, ha!"

Near the end of the mudslinging campaign, Blaine and his supporters committed two fateful blunders. The first occurred at New York's fashionable Delmonico's restaurant, where Blaine attended a lavish fund-raising dinner with a clutch of millionaire bigwigs. Cartoons and accounts of this "Belshazzar's feast" festooned the opposition press for days.

The second fiasco occurred when a Protestant minister visiting the Republican headquarters in New York City insolently referred to the Democrats as the party of "rum, Romanism, and rebellion." Blaine let pass the implied insult to Irish Catholics—a fatal oversight, since he had always cultivated Irish American support with his anti-English talk and public reminders that his mother was Catholic. Democrats spread the word that Blaine was anti-Irish and anti-Catholic. The two incidents may have tipped the election. The electoral vote, in Cleveland's favor, stood at 219 to 182, although the popular vote ran far closer: Cleveland's plurality nationwide was fewer than 30,000 votes.

CLEVELAND AND THE SPECIAL INTERESTS   For all of Cleveland's hostility to the spoils system and politics as usual, he represented no sharp break with the conservative public policies of his Republican predecessors, except in opposing government favors to business. He held to a strictly limited view of government's role in both economic and social matters, a rigid philosophy illustrated by his 1887 veto of a bill to aid drought-stricken farmers. Back to Congress it went, with a lecture on the need to limit the powers and functions of government. "Though the people support the government, the government should not support the people," Cleveland asserted.

Cleveland also incurred the wrath of many Union war veterans with his firm stand against expanded pensions. Congress had passed the first Civil War pension law in 1862 to provide for Union veterans disabled in service and for the widows, orphans, and dependents of veterans. By 1882 the Grand Army of the Republic, an organization of Union veterans and a powerful pressure group, was trying to get pensions paid for any disability, no matter how it was incurred. Meanwhile, many veterans succeeded in getting legislators to pass private pension bills. Insofar as time permitted, Cleveland examined the bills critically and vetoed the dubious ones. The issue reached a climax in 1887 when Cleveland vetoed a new dependents pension bill containing more liberal benefits for veterans and their families. Cleveland argued that it would become a refuge for frauds rather than a "roll of honor."

In about the middle of his term, Cleveland advocated an important new policy: railroad regulation. Since the late 1860s, states had adopted laws regulating railroads, and from the early 1870s Congress had debated federal legislation. In 1886 a Supreme Court decision spurred action. Reacting to the case of *Wabash, St. Louis, and Pacific Railroad Company v. Illinois*, in which the Court had ruled that a state could not regulate rates on interstate traffic, Cleveland urged that since this "important field of control and regulation [has] thus been left entirely unoccupied," Congress should act.

It did, and in 1887 Cleveland signed into law an act creating the Interstate Commerce Commission (ICC), the first independent federal regulatory commission. The law required that all freight and passenger railroad rates be "reasonable and just," and it empowered the ICC to investigate railroads and prosecute violators of its regulations. Railroads were also forbidden to grant secret rebates to preferred shippers or enter into pools (agreements among

Grover Cleveland

As president, Cleveland made the issue of tariff reform central to the politics of the late 1880s.

competing companies to fix rates). The commission's actual powers proved to be weak, however, when first tested in the courts.

THE TARIFF Cleveland's most dramatic challenge to the power of special interests focused on tariff reform. Why was the tariff such an important and controversial issue? During the late nineteenth century, Republican party officials and business leaders assumed that national prosperity and high tariffs were closely linked. Others disagreed. Many observers concluded that the formation of huge corporate "trusts" was not a natural development of a maturing capitalist system. Instead, critics charged that government tariff policies had fostered big business at the expense of small producers and retailers by effectively shutting out foreign imports, thereby enabling American corporations to dominate their markets and charge higher prices for their products. By shielding manufacturers from foreign competition, critics argued, the tariff made it easier for them to combine and form ever-larger entities.

Cleveland agreed. Having decided that the rates were too high and too often inequitable, he devoted his entire annual message to Congress in 1887 to the subject. Cleveland noted that tariff revenues had bolstered the federal surplus, making the Treasury "a hoarding place for money needlessly withdrawn from trade and the people's use." The high tariff, he added, pushed up prices for everybody and benefited only a few politically powerful manufacturing interests. The wise solution was to spur Congress to look at the items on the tariff list, more than 4,000 of them, with an eye to eliminating as many as possible and lowering all the remaining duties. Cleveland's tariff proposal accomplished his purpose of drawing party lines more firmly. For the first time in years, the upcoming presidential election would provide a sharp difference between the major parties on an issue of substance—the tariff.

THE ELECTION OF 1888 Cleveland was the obvious nominee of his party for reelection in 1888. The Republicans, now calling themselves the GOP (Grand Old Party), turned to the obscure Benjamin Harrison. The grandson of a former president, Harrison boasted a good war record, and little in his political record would offend any voter. The Republican platform accepted Cleveland's challenge to make the tariff the chief issue. To ensure against tariff reduction, manufacturers obligingly filled up Harrison's campaign fund, which was used to denounce Cleveland's un-American "free-trade" stance and his vetoes of bills providing for veterans' pensions.

On the eve of the election, Cleveland suffered a devastating blow from a dirty campaign trick. Posing as an English immigrant and using the false name Charles F. Murchison, a California Republican had written the British ambassador, Sir Lionel Sackville-West, asking his advice on how to vote. Sackville-West hinted in reply that the man should vote for Cleveland. Published two weeks before the election, the "Murchison letter" aroused a storm of protest against foreign intervention and suggested a link between Cleveland and British free traders.

Still, the outcome in the election was very close. Cleveland won the popular vote by 5,538,000 to 5,447,000, but that was little comfort. The distribution of votes was such that Harrison, with the key states of Indiana and New York on his side, carried the Electoral College by 233 to 168.

REPUBLICAN REFORM UNDER HARRISON As president, Benjamin Harrison was a competent figurehead overshadowed by his flamboyant secretary of state, James G. Blaine. Harrison's first step was to reward those responsible for his victory. He owed a heavy debt to the Union war veterans, which he discharged by naming the head of the veterans' group to the office of federal pension commissioner. The new commissioner proceeded to approve veterans' pensions with such abandon that the secretary of the interior removed him from office six months later. In 1890, Harrison signed the Dependent Pension Act, substantially the same measure that Cleveland had vetoed three years earlier. Any war veteran unable to make a living by manual labor for whatever reason was granted a monthly pension. The pension rolls would almost double by 1893.

During the first two years of Harrison's term, the Republicans controlled the presidency and both houses of Congress for the second time since 1875. They made the most of their clout. During 1890 several significant pieces of legislation made their way to the White House for Harrison's signature. In addition to the Dependent Pension Act, the president approved the Sherman Anti-Trust Act, the Sherman Silver Purchase Act, the McKinley Tariff Act, and the admission of Idaho and Wyoming as new states, following the admission of the Dakotas, Montana, and Washington in 1889.

"King of the World"

Republican reform targeted the growing power of monopolies, such as that of Rockefeller's Standard Oil.

Both parties had pledged during the campaign to address the growing power of trusts and monopolies. The Sherman Anti-Trust Act, named for Ohio senator John Sherman, chairman of the committee that drafted it, forbade contracts, combinations, or conspiracies in restraint of trade or in the effort to establish monopolies in interstate or foreign commerce. A broad consensus put the vague law through, but its passage turned out to be largely symbolic. During the next decade successive administrations rarely enforced the new law, in part because of confusion about what constituted "restraint of trade." From 1890 to 1901, the Justice Department instituted only eighteen anti-trust suits, and four of those were against labor unions.

Congress, meanwhile, debated currency legislation against the backdrop of growing distress in the farm regions of the West and the South. Hard-pressed farmers demanded increased coinage of silver to inflate the currency supply and raise commodity prices, making it easier for them to earn the money they needed to pay their debts. The silverite forces were also strengthened, especially in the Senate, by members from new western states with silver-mining interests. Congress thus passed the Sherman Silver Purchase Act, replacing the Bland-Allison Act of 1878. The new act required the Treasury to purchase 4.5 million ounces of silver each month and to issue in payment paper money redeemable in gold or silver. Although it doubled the amount of silver purchased, that was still too little to inflate the nation's overall money supply. The stage was thus set for the currency issue to eclipse all others during the financial panic that would sweep the country three years later.

Republicans viewed their victory over Cleveland in 1888 as a mandate not just to maintain the protective tariff but to raise it. Piloted through Congress by the prominent Ohio representative William McKinley, the McKinley Tariff of 1890 raised duties on manufactured goods to the highest level ever. The absence of a public consensus for higher tariffs became clearly visible in the 1890 midterm elections: voters repudiated the Republican-sponsored McKinley Tariff with a landslide of Democratic votes. In the new House, Democrats outnumbered Republicans by almost three to one; in the Senate the Republican majority was reduced to eight. One of the election casualties was Congressman McKinley himself. But there was more to the election than the tariff. Voters also reacted to the baldly partisan measures of the Harrison administration and to its extravagant expenditures on military pensions and other programs.

The large Democratic vote in 1890 may also have been a reaction to Republican efforts to legislate on a local level against government-supported Catholic (parochial) schools. In many districts with a high percentage of Catholic constituents, Democratic legislators had defied the principle of separation of church and state by allocating local tax revenues to help support those schools. In 1889, Wisconsin Republicans pushed through a law that struck at parochial schools and turned large numbers of outraged Catholic immigrants into Democratic activists. Protestant Republicans also sought to ban alcoholic beverages. Between 1880 and 1890 sixteen out of twenty-one states outside the South held referenda on a constitutional prohibition of alcohol, although only six states actually voted for prohibition. With this assault on drinking, Republicans were playing a losing game, arousing anti-prohibitionists on the Democratic side. In 1890 the Democrats swept state after state.

THE FARM PROBLEM AND AGRARIAN PROTEST MOVEMENTS

The 1890 election reflected more than a reaction against the Republican tariff, patronage politics, extravagant spending, and moralizing. The Democratic victory revealed a deep-seated unrest in the farming communities of the South and the western Midwest, as well as in the mining towns of the Rocky Mountains. As the congressional Democrats took power, the beginnings of an acute economic crisis appeared on the horizon: farmers' debts mounted as crop prices plummeted.

Frustrated by the unwillingness of Congress to meet their demands and ease their plight, disgruntled farmers focused on political efforts. Like so many of their counterparts laboring in urban factories, they realized that social change required demonstrations of power, and power lay in numbers—and organization. Unlike labor unions, however, the farm organizations faced a complex array of economic variables affecting their livelihood. They had to deal with more than just management. Bankers, food processors, railroad and grain-elevator operators, as well as the world commodities market, all affected the agricultural sector. So, too, did unpredictable forces of nature: droughts, blizzards, insects, and erosion.

There were also important obstacles to collective action by farmers. Farmers' rugged individualism and physical isolation made communication and organization especially difficult. Another hurdle was that agricultural interests had diverged after the Civil War and in some cases conflicted with one another. On the Great Plains, for example, the railroads were the largest landowners. In addition, there were large absentee landowners, some foreign, who leased out vast tracts of land. There were also huge "bonanza" farms that employed hundreds of seasonal workers. Yet the majority of farmers were simple rural folk in the South and West who were moderate-size landowners, small land speculators, tenant farmers, sharecroppers, and hourly wage workers. It was the middle-size landowners who were most affected by rapidly rising land values and rising indebtedness. Those farmers were concerned with land values and crop prices, while tenants, sharecroppers, and farmhands supported land-distribution schemes that would give them access to their own land.

Given such a diversity of interests within the agricultural sector, farm activists discovered that it was often difficult to develop and maintain a cohesive political organization. Yet for all the difficulties, they persevered, and the results were dramatic, if not completely successful. Thus, for example, the deep-seated unrest in the farming communities of the South and the West began to find voice in the Granger movement, the Farmers' Alliances, and the new People's party (also known as the Populist party), agrarian movements of considerable political and social significance.

ECONOMIC CONDITIONS   Since the end of the Civil War, many farmers in the South and Midwest suffered worsening economic and social conditions. The source of their problems was a long decline in commodity prices, from 1870 to 1898, the result of domestic increases in production and growing international competition for world markets. Considerations of abstract economic forces puzzled many farmers, however. How could one speak of overproduction when so many remained in need? Instead, many farmers assumed, there must be a screw loose somewhere in the system.

The railroads and the food processors who handled the farmers' products were seen as the villains. Farmers resented the high railroad freight rates that

"I Feed You All!"

This 1875 poster shows the farmer at the center of society.

prevailed in farm regions with no alternative forms of transportation. High tariffs also operated to the farmers' disadvantage, because they protected manufacturers from foreign competition, allowing them to raise the prices of factory goods upon which farmers depended. Farmers, however, had to sell their wheat, cotton, and other staples in foreign markets, where competition lowered prices. Tariffs inflicted a double blow on farmers because, insofar as they hampered imports, they indirectly hampered exports, by making it harder for foreign buyers to get the currency or exchange necessary to purchase American crops.

Debt, too, had been a perennial agricultural problem. After the Civil War, farmers had grown ever more enmeshed in debt: western farmers incurred mortgages to cover the costs of land and machinery, while southern farmers were forced to pledge their crops to the local merchant in exchange for food and supplies. As commodity prices dropped, the debt burden grew because farmers had to cultivate more wheat or cotton to raise the same amount of money. By growing more, they furthered the vicious cycle of surpluses and price declines.

THE GRANGER MOVEMENT   When the Department of Agriculture sent Oliver H. Kelley, a former Minnesota farmer and post-office clerk, on a tour of the South in 1866, it was the farmers' isolation that most impressed him. To address the problem, Kelley in 1867 founded the National Grange of the Patrons of Husbandry, better known as the Grange (an old word for granary). In the next few years the Grange mushroomed, reaching a membership as high as 1.5 million by 1874. While the Grange started out as a social and educational response to the isolation of farm folk, as it grew, it began to promote farmer-owned cooperatives for the buying and selling of crops. The Grangers' goal was to free farmers from the conventional "middlemen" to whom they were forced to pay high fees.

The Grange soon became indirectly involved in politics, through independent third parties, especially in the Midwest during the early 1870s. The Grangers' chief political goal was state regulation of the rates charged by railroads and crop warehouses. In five states they brought about the passage of "Granger laws," which were soon challenged in the courts. In a key case involving warehouse regulation, *Munn v. Illinois* (1877), the Supreme Court affirmed that the state, according to its "police powers," had the right to regulate property that was clothed in a public interest.

"Gift for the Grangers"

A promotional print for Grange members showing scenes of farming and farm life.

Although such legal victories bolstered the Granger cause, the movement gradually declined as members' energies were drawn off into cooperatives, whereby farmers would make collective agreements about the storage and sale of their crops. Other former Grange members focused on political action. In 1875, out of the independent political movements, grew the Greenback party, which favored expanding of the money supply by means of more paper money. In the 1878 midterm elections the

Greenbacks polled over 1 million votes and elected fifteen congressmen. But in 1880 the party's fortunes declined, and it disintegrated after 1884.

FARMERS' ALLIANCES   As the Grange lost energy, another consortium of farm organizations grew in size and significance: the Farmers' Alliances. Like the Grange, the Farmers' Alliances offered social and recreational activities for their members, but they also emphasized political action. Struggling farmers throughout the South and Midwest, where tenancy rates were highest, rushed to join the Alliance movement. They saw in collective action a way to seek relief from the hardships created by chronic indebtedness, declining crop prices, and devastating droughts. Yet unlike the Grange, which was a national organization that tended to attract larger and more prosperous farmers, the Alliance was a grassroots organization representing marginal farmers. It would become the largest and most dynamic farmers' movement in American history.

The Alliance movement swept across the southern cotton belt and established strong positions in Kansas and the Dakotas. In 1886 a white minister in Texas, which had one of the largest and most influential Alliance movements, responded to the appeals of African American farmers by organizing the Colored Farmers' National Alliance. The white leadership of the Alliance movement in Texas endorsed this development because the Colored Alliance stressed that its objective was economic justice, not social equality. By 1890 the Alliance movement had members from New York to California, numbering about 1.5 million, and the Colored Farmers' National Alliance claimed over 1 million members.

A powerful attraction for many isolated, struggling farmers and their families was the sense of community provided by the Alliance network. The Alliance movement welcomed rural women and men over sixteen years of age who displayed a "good moral character," believed in God, and demonstrated "industrious habits." Lawyers and blacks were excluded. Women embraced the opportunity to engage in economic and political issues. An Alliance publication made the point explicitly: "The Alliance has come to redeem woman from her enslaved condition, and place her in her proper sphere." The number of women in the movement grew rapidly, and many assumed key leadership roles in the "grand army of reform."

The Alliance movement sponsored some 1,000 rural newspapers to spread the word about the farm problem. It also recruited 40,000 lecturers, who fanned out across the countryside to help people understand the tyrannical forces arrayed against the farm sector: bankers and creditors, Wall Street, railroads, and corporate giants who controlled both the markets and the political process. Unlike the Grange, however, the Alliance proposed an elaborate economic program. In 1890, Alliance agencies and exchanges in some eighteen states claimed a business of $10 million, but they soon went the way of the Granger cooperatives, victims of both discrimination by wholesalers, manufacturers, railroads, and bankers and their own inexperienced management and overextended credit.

In 1887, Charles W. Macune, the new Alliance president, proposed that Texas farmers create their own Alliance Exchange in an effort to free themselves from their dependence upon grain processors and banks. Members of the exchange would sign joint notes (to be exchanged for cash), borrow money from banks, and purchase their goods and supplies from a new corporation created by the Alliance in Dallas. The exchange would also build its own warehouses to store and market members crops. While their crops were being stored, member farmers would be able to obtain credit from the warehouse cooperative so that they could buy household goods and supplies.

This grand cooperative scheme collapsed when Texas banks refused to accept the paper money from Alliance members. Macune and others then focused their energies on what Macune called a "subtreasury plan." Under this scheme, farmers would be able to store their crops in new government warehouses and obtain government loans for up to 80 percent of the value of their crops at 1 percent interest. Besides providing immediate credit, the plan would allow the farmer the leeway to hold a crop for a better price later, since he would not have to sell it immediately at harvesttime to pay off debts. The plan would also promote inflation because the loans to farmers would be made in new legal-tender notes.

The subtreasury plan went before Congress in 1890 but was never adopted. Its defeat, as well as setbacks to other Alliance proposals, convinced many farm leaders that they needed more political power in order to secure railroad regulation, currency inflation, state departments of agriculture, anti-trust laws, and farm credit.

FARM POLITICS   In the farm states west of the Mississippi River, where hard times had descended after the blizzards of 1887, farmers demanded third-party political action to address their concerns. In the South, however, white Alliance members hesitated to bolt the Democratic party, seeking instead to influence or control it. Both approaches gained startling success, with independent parties under various names upsetting the political balance in western states.

The farm protest movement produced colorful leaders, especially in Kansas, where Mary Elizabeth Lease emerged as a fiery speaker. Born in Pennsylvania, Lease migrated to Kansas, taught school, raised a family, and failed at farming in the mid-1880s. She then studied law and became one of the state's first female attorneys. At the same time, she took up public speaking on behalf of various causes, including freedom from English rule for her ancestral Ireland, prohibition of alcoholic beverages, and women's right to vote. By the end of the 1880s, Lease had joined the Alliance as well as the Knights of Labor, and she soon ap-

Mary Elizabeth Lease, 1890

A charismatic leader in the farm protest movement.

plied her oratorical gifts to the cause of free silver. A tall, proud, imposing woman, Lease drew attentive audiences. "The people are at bay," she warned in 1894; "let the bloodhounds of money beware." She urged angry farmers to obtain their goals "with the ballot if possible, but if not that way then with the bayonet." Like so many of the Populists, Lease viewed the urban-industrial East as the enemy of the working classes. "The great common people of this country," she shouted, "are slaves, and monopoly is the master. The West and South are bound and prostrate before the manufacturing East."

In the South the Alliance forced the Democrats to nominate candidates pledged to their program. In 1890 the southern states elected four pro-Alliance governors, seven pro-Alliance legislatures, forty-four pro-Alliance congressmen, and several senators. Among the most respected of the southern Alliance leaders was Thomas E. Watson of Georgia. The son of prosperous slaveholders who had lost everything after the Civil War, Watson became a successful lawyer and colorful orator on behalf of the Alliance cause. He took the lead in urging African American tenant farmers and sharecroppers to join with their white counterparts in ousting the white political elite. "You are kept apart," he told black and white farmers, "that you may be separately fleeced of your earnings."

THE POPULIST PARTY AND THE ELECTION OF 1892 As economic conditions worsened, agrarian activists decided to form a new national political party. In 1891 delegates from farm, labor, and reform organizations met in Cincinnati to discuss the creation of the People's party. Few southerners attended, but many delegates endorsed the third-party idea after their failure to win over the Democratic party to the subtreasury plan. In 1891, William Peffer of Kansas and Tom Watson of Georgia were the first People's party candidates elected to the Senate. In 1892 a larger meeting in St. Louis proposed a national convention of the People's party at Omaha to adopt a platform and choose national candidates.

The 1892 Populist platform focused on issues of finance, transportation, and land. Its financial program demanded implementation of the subtreasury plan, unlimited coinage of silver, an increase in the money supply, and a graduated income tax, whose rates would rise with personal levels of income. As for transportation, the party called for the government to nationalize the railroads, as well as the telephone and telegraph systems. It also called for the government to reclaim from railroads and other corporations lands "in excess of their actual needs" and to forbid land ownership by immigrants who were not citizens. Finally, the platform endorsed the eight-hour workday and laws restricting immigration, taking these positions to win support from urban workers, whom Populists looked upon as fellow "producers." The party's platform turned out to be more exciting than its candidate, Iowa's James B. Weaver. Though an able, prudent man, Weaver carried the stigma of his defeat on the Greenback ticket twelve years before. To attract southern voters who might be distracted by Weaver's service as a Union general, the party named a former Confederate general for vice president.

The Populist party was the startling new feature of the 1892 campaign. The Democrats renominated Grover Cleveland, and Republicans turned again to Benjamin Harrison. The tariff remained the chief issue between them. The outcome, however, was different. Both major candidates polled over 5 million votes, but Cleveland carried a plurality of the popular vote and a majority of the Electoral College. Weaver gained over 1 million votes, 10 percent of the total, and carried Colorado, Kansas, Nevada, and Idaho, for a total of twenty-two electoral votes. In Kansas the Populists won the governor's office, four congressional seats, and control of the state senate. In neighboring Nebraska they won control of both statehouses.

POPULISM AND RELIGION   Religion played a crucial role in the rise of Populism. At the new party's 1892 convention, one of the delegates said the gathering was like "a religious revival, a crusade, a Pentecost of politics in which a tongue of flame sat upon every man, and each spoke as the spirit gave him utterance." Populists believed that God was on their side in the fight to "save our republican institutions and common Christianity from decay and death." A Populist flyer promoting the new political party declared that "we are men that fear God and love his commands." Alliance meetings and Populist rallies often occurred in evangelical Protestant churches. They began with prayers and included the singing of hymns, the passing of an offering plate, and a period of instruction, or "exhortation." Speakers promoted the "conversion" of voters to the sacred cause. Evangelical ministers and lay leaders were in the vanguard of the agrarian social and political organizations. A leading evangelical Populist, the Reverend Thomas Dixon, argued that the farm revolt was "the result of divine inspiration." It constituted "a great social and moral revolution" that "would elevate mankind" and "purify politics."

The Economy and the Silver Solution

INADEQUATE CURRENCY While agitated farmers were funneling their discontent into politics and businessmen were consolidating their holdings, a fundamental weakness in the economy was about to manifest itself in a major economic collapse. The nation's money supply in the late nineteenth century lacked the flexibility to grow along with the expanding economy. From 1865 to 1890, the amount of currency in circulation per capita decreased about 10 percent. Currency deflation raised the cost of borrowing money, as a tight money supply caused bankers to hike interest rates on loans.

Metallic currency dated from the Mint Act of 1792, which authorized free and unlimited coinage of silver and gold at a ratio of 15 to 1, meaning that the amount of precious metal in a silver dollar weighed fifteen times as much as that in a gold dollar, a reflection of the relative value of gold and silver at the time. "Free and unlimited coinage" simply meant that owners of precious metals could have any quantity of their gold or silver coined free, except for a nominal fee to cover costs.

A fixed ratio of the values of gold and silver did not reflect fluctuations in the market value of the metals, however. When gold rose to a market value higher than that reflected in the official ratio, owners ceased to present it for coinage. The country was actually on a silver standard until 1837, when Congress changed the ratio to 16 to 1, which soon reversed the situation. Silver became more valuable in the open market than in coinage, and the country drifted to a gold standard. This state of affairs prevailed until 1873, when Congress passed a general revision of the coinage laws and dropped the then-unused provision for the coinage of silver.

This occurred just when silver production in the western states began to increase, however, reducing its market value through the growth in supply. Soon advocates of currency inflation began to denounce the "crime of '73," which they had scarcely noticed at the time. Gradually suspicion grew that bankers and merchants had conspired in 1873 to ensure a scarcity of money. But the pro-silver forces had little more legislative success than the advocates of greenback inflation. The Bland-Allison Act of 1878 and the Sherman Silver Purchase Act of 1890 provided for some silver coinage, but too little in each case to offset the overall contraction of the nation's money supply.

THE DEPRESSION OF 1893   Just ten days before Grover Cleveland started his second presidential term in 1893 (the only nonconsecutive second term of a president in U.S. history), the Philadelphia and Reading Railroad declared bankruptcy, setting off a national financial panic. Not only was business affected, but entire farm regions were also devastated by the spreading depression. A quarter of the cities' unskilled workers lost their

National panic

The New York Stock Exchange on the morning of Friday, May 5, 1893.

jobs, and by the fall of 1893 over 600 banks had closed and 15,000 businesses had failed. Farm foreclosures soared. By 1894 the economy had reached bottom. The catastrophic depression lasted another four years, with unemployment hovering at 20 percent. In New York some 35 percent were unemployed, and 20,000 homeless people camped out at police stations and other makeshift shelters. Violent labor strikes at Pullman, Illinois, and at the Homestead Works steel-making plant outside Pittsburgh symbolized the fracturing of the social order. In 1894 some 750,000 workers went on strike, millions found themselves unemployed, and railroad construction workers, laid off in the West, began tramping east and talked of marching on Washington, D.C.

One protest group that reached Washington was "Coxey's Army," led by Jacob S. Coxey, a wealthy Ohio quarry owner turned Populist who demanded that the federal government provide the unemployed with meaningful work. Coxey, his wife, and their son, Legal Tender Coxey, rode in a carriage ahead of some 400 hardy protesters who finally straggled into Washington. There Coxey was arrested for walking on the grass. Although his ragtag army dispersed peacefully, the march on Washington, as well as the growing political strength of Populism, struck fear into the hearts of many Americans. Critics portrayed Populists as "hayseed socialists" whose election would endanger property rights and the entire capitalist system.

The 1894 congressional elections, taking place amid this climate of mushrooming anxiety, represented a severe setback for the Democrats, who paid politically for the economic downturn, and the Republicans were the chief beneficiaries. The third-party Populists emerged with six senators and seven representatives. They had polled 1.5 million votes for their congressional candidates and expected the festering discontent to carry them to national power in 1896.

SILVERITES VERSUS GOLDBUGS   The course of events would dash that hope, however. In the mid-1890s national attention focused on the currency issue. One of the causes of the 1893 depression was the failure of a major British bank, which had led many British investors to sell their American stocks and bonds in return for gold. Soon after Grover Cleveland's inauguration, the U.S. gold reserve had fallen below $100 million. To plug the drain on the Treasury, by stopping the issuance of silver notes redeemable in gold, the president sought repeal of the Sherman Silver Purchase Act. Cleveland won the repeal in 1893, but at the cost of an irreparable division in his own party. One embittered pro-silver Democrat labeled the president a traitor.

Western silver interests now escalated their demands for silver coinage, presenting a strategic dilemma for Populists: should the party promote the long list of varied reforms it had originally advocated, or should it try to ride the silver issue into power? The latter seemed the practical choice. As a consequence, the Populist leaders decided, over the protests of more radical members, to hold their 1896 nominating convention last, confident that the two major parties would at best straddle the silver issue and they would then reap a harvest of bolting silverite Republicans and Democrats.

THE ELECTION OF 1896   Contrary to those expectations, the major parties took opposing positions on the currency issue. The Republicans, as expected, chose Ohioan William McKinley on a gold-standard platform. On

William Jennings Bryan

His "cross of gold" speech at the 1896 Democratic Convention roused the delegates and secured him the party's presidential nomination.

the Democratic side the pro-silver forces gathered to wrest control of the party from Cleveland and the fiscal conservatives. In William Jennings Bryan the silver Democrats found a crusading, charismatic leader. A fervent Baptist and advocate of the free coinage of silver, Bryan was a two-term congressman from Nebraska who had been defeated in the senate race in 1894. At the 1896 convention the self-assured Bryan delivered a speech that had most of the 20,000 delegates on their feet and many in tears. Like a revivalist at a camp meeting, he galvanized the audience with the emotion of his appeal. Bryan spoke for silver and the New West, for the "hardy pioneers" and against the "financial magnates" of the urban East as well as Cleveland's "do-nothing" response to the depression. He directly challenged Republicans as well as Cleveland and the gold Democrats with a compelling Christian metaphor: "You shall not press down upon the brow of labor this crown of thorns. You shall not crucify mankind upon a cross of gold!"

The next day the theatrical Bryan was nominated on the fifth ballot, and in the process the Democratic party was fractured beyond repair—for the time being. Disappointed pro-gold Cleveland Democrats were so disgusted by Bryan's inflationary program and Populist rhetoric that they walked out of the convention and nominated their own candidate, who then announced, "Fellow Democrats, I will not consider it any great fault if you decide to cast your vote for [the Republican] William McKinley."

When the Populists met in St. Louis two weeks later, they faced an impossible choice. "If we fuse [with the Democrats]," one Populist admitted, "all the silver men we have will leave us for the more powerful Democrats." But if the Populists named their own candidate, they would divide the silver vote with Bryan and give the election to McKinley. In the end the delegates backed Bryan but chose their own vice-presidential candidate, Georgia's Thomas Watson, and invited the Democrats to drop their vice-presidential nominee, an action Bryan refused to countenance.

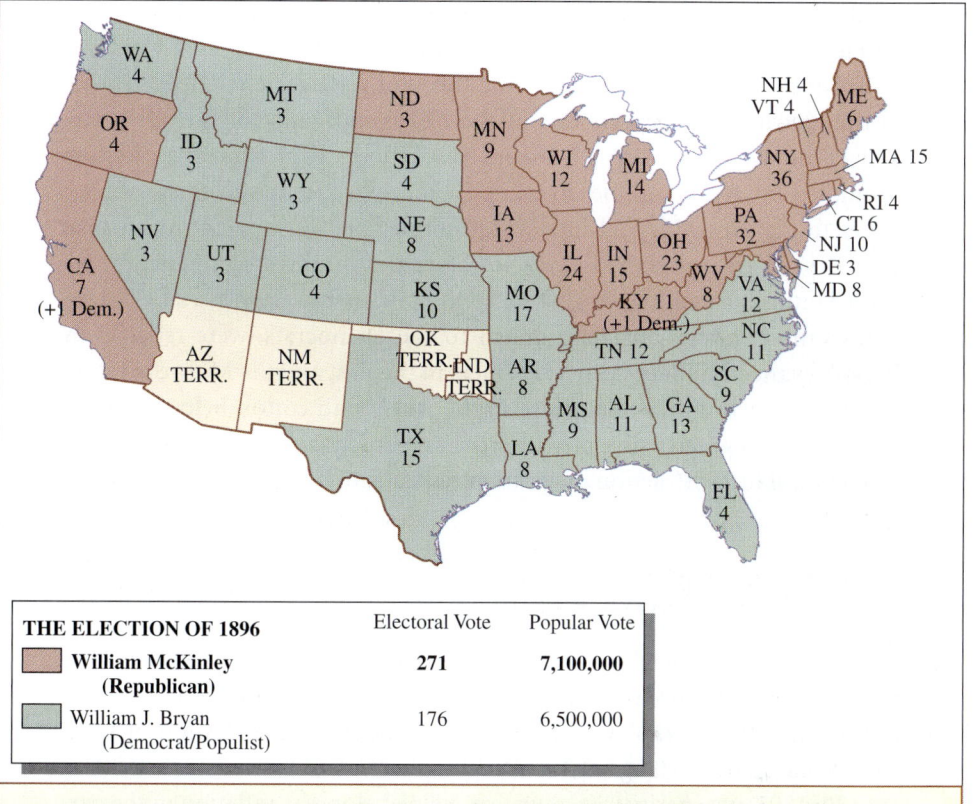

THE ELECTION OF 1896	Electoral Vote	Popular Vote
William McKinley **(Republican)**	**271**	**7,100,000**
William J. Bryan (Democrat/Populist)	176	6,500,000

How did Bryan's "cross of gold" speech divide the Democratic party? How was McKinley's strategy different from Bryan's? Why was Bryan able to carry the West and the South but unable to win in cities and the Northeast?

During the 1896 campaign the thirty-six-year-old Bryan crisscrossed the country, using his spellbinding eloquence to support "the struggling masses" of workers, farmers, and small-business owners and promising the panacea of the unlimited coinage of silver. By contrast, McKinley conducted a "front-porch campaign," receiving select delegations of supporters at his home in Canton, Ohio, and giving only prepared responses. His campaign manager, Mark Hanna, shrewdly portrayed Bryan as a radical whose "communistic spirit" would ruin the capitalist system. Many observers agreed with the portrait.

By preying upon such fears, the McKinley campaign raised vast sums of money to finance an army of 1,400 Republican speakers who stumped the country in his support. In the end the Democratic-Populist-silverite candidates were overwhelmed. McKinley won the popular vote by 7.1 million to 6.5 million and the Electoral College vote by 271 to 176.

Bryan carried most of the West and the South but garnered little support in the metropolitan centers east of the Mississippi and north of the Ohio and Potomac Rivers. Urban workers saw little to gain from the inflation promoted by Bryan and the silverites. Factory workers in the cities found it easier to identify with McKinley's "full dinner pail" campaign slogan than with Bryan's free silver. Moreover, in the critical midwestern battleground, from Minnesota and Iowa eastward to Ohio, Bryan carried not a single state. Many ethnic voters, normally drawn to the Democrats, were repelled by Bryan's evangelical Baptist style. Farmers in the East and the Midwest, moreover, were hurting less than those in the wheat and cotton belts. With less tenancy and a greater diversity of crops in those farm regions, prospering farmers saw little attraction in agrarian radicalism.

A NEW ERA

The election of 1896 was a climactic political struggle between rural and metropolitan America, and metropolitan America won. As its first important act, the McKinley administration called a special session of Congress to raise the tariff again. The Dingley Tariff of 1897 became the highest ever. By 1897, prosperity was returning, helped along by inflation of the currency, which bore out the arguments of the Greenbackers and silverites. But the inflation came, in one of history's many ironies, not from silver but from a new flood of gold onto the market and into the mints. During the 1880s and 1890s, discoveries of gold in South Africa, Canada, and Alaska led to spectacular new gold rushes, a return to the gold standard, and an end to the free-silver movement.

At the close of the nineteenth century, the old issues of tariff and currency policy, which had dominated national politics since the Civil War, gave way to global concerns: the outbreak of the War of 1898 and the acquisition of territories outside the Western Hemisphere. At the same time, the advent of a new century brought new social and political developments. Although the Populist movement faded with William Jennings Bryan's defeat, most of the progressive policies promoted by Bryan Democrats and Populists, dismissed as too radical and controversial in 1896, would be implemented over the next two decades. Bryan's impassioned candidacy helped transform the Democratic party into a vigorous instrument of "progressive" reform during the early twentieth century. Democrats began to promote anti-trust prosecutions, state laws to limit the working hours of women and children, the establishment of a minimum wage, and measures to support farmers and protect labor union organizers. As the United States looked ahead to a new century, it began to place more emphasis on the role of the national government in society and the economy.

End of Chapter Review

CHAPTER SUMMARY

- **Gilded Age Politics** Americans were intensely loyal to the two major parties, which operated on a local scale by distributing favors. "City machines" also provided working-class men with jobs and gave relief (money or necessities) to the poor, thereby winning votes. New York's Tammany Hall ring under the boss William Marcy Tweed best exemplifies the corruption resulting from this system. The major political parties shared power nearly equally during the Gilded Age, and neither party was willing to embrace bold initiatives.

- **National Politics** Politicians focused on tariff reform, the regulation of corporations, Indian wars and Indian policy, civil service reform, and immigration. In the 1884 presidential election, Republicans favoring reform, dubbed Mugwumps, bolted their party to support the Democrat, Grover Cleveland, a reformer.

- **Farm Problems** Farmers had serious grievances at the end of the nineteenth century. Commodity prices were falling because of domestic overproduction and international competition, and many farmers had gone into debt: they had bought new machinery on credit at high interest rates and were paying the railroads exorbitant rates to ship their goods to market without receiving the rebates that large corporations had the leverage to demand. In addition, high tariffs allowed manufacturers to raise the price of goods that farmers needed.

- **Farm Movements** Despite farmers' traditional reluctance to organize, many reacted to their difficulties by joining the Granger movement, which promoted farmer-owned cooperatives, and, subsequently, Farmers' Alliances, grassroots social organizations that also promoted political action. The Alliances became a major force in the Midwest and the South. Influenced by their success, delegates from farm, labor, and reform organizations in 1892 established the People's party, also known as the Populist party. Populists sought greater regulation of business by the federal government and the free coinage of silver (because they hoped that the ensuing inflation would make it easier for them to repay their debts). To appeal to urban voters, they endorsed the eight-hour workday and restrictions on immigration.

- **Rise of Populism** The Populists did well in 1892 and, with the depression of 1893, had high hopes for the next presidential election. But the Democrat, William Jennings Bryan stole the silver issue from the Populists. The Populists thus fused with the Democrats, but Bryan lost the election to the Republicans, who in a well-organized, well-financed campaign won the urban northeastern vote by portraying the Democratic candidate as a dangerous radical. The People's party did not recover from the blow.

CHRONOLOGY

1877	Rutherford B. Hayes is inaugurated president
1877	Supreme Court issues *Munn v. Illinois* decision
1881	President James A. Garfield is assassinated
1881	Chester Arthur becomes president
1883	Congress passes the Pendleton Civil Service Reform Act
1885	Grover Cleveland, a Democrat, begins his first term as president
1886	Supreme Court issues *Wabash, St. Louis, and Pacific Railroad Company v. Illinois* decision
1887	Interstate Commerce Commission is created
1888	Grover Cleveland loses the presidency to Benjamin Harrison
1890	Congress passes the Sherman Anti-Trust Act, the Sherman Silver Purchase Act; and the McKinley Tariff
1892	People's party drafts the Omaha platform
1892	Grover Cleveland wins a second term as president
1893	Economic depression affects a substantial proportion of the population
1896	In the presidential election, Republicans defeat the Democrats, who have the support of the Populists

KEY TERMS & NAMES

Part Six

MODERN

AMERICA

he United States entered the twentieth century on a wave of unrelenting change. In 1800 the nation was a rural, agrarian society largely detached from the concerns of international affairs. By 1900 the United States had become a highly industrialized urban culture with a growing involvement in world politics and commerce. In other words, the nation was on the threshold of modernity.

The prospect of modernity both excited and scared Americans. Old truths and beliefs clashed with unsettling scientific discoveries and social practices. People debated the legitimacy of Darwinism, the existence of God, the dangers of jazz, and the federal effort to prohibit the sale of alcoholic beverages. The automobile and airplane helped shrink distances, and communications innovations such as radio and film contributed to a national consciousness. In the process the United States began to emerge from its isolationist shell.

Noninvolvement in foreign wars and nonintervention in the internal affairs of foreign governments formed the pillars of foreign policy until the end of the century. During the 1890s, however, expanding commercial interests around the world led Americans to extend the horizons of their concerns. Imperialism was the order of the day among the great European powers, and a growing number of American expansionists demanded that the United States also adopt a global ambition and join in the hunt for new territories and markets. Such mixed motives helped spark the War of 1898 and helped justify the resulting acquisition of colonies outside the continental United States. Entangling alliances with European powers soon followed.

The outbreak of the Great War in Europe in 1914 posed an even greater challenge to the American tradition of isolation and nonintervention. The prospect of a German victory over the French and the British threatened the European balance of power, which had long ensured the security of the United States. By 1917 it appeared that Germany might emerge triumphant and begin to menace the Western Hemisphere. Woodrow Wilson's crusade to use American intervention in World War I to transform the world order in accordance with his idealistic principles severed U.S. foreign policy from its isolationist moorings. It also spawned a prolonged debate about the role of the United States in world affairs, a debate that World War II would resolve for a time on the side of internationalism.

While the United States was entering the world stage as a formidable military power, it was also settling into its role as a great industrial power.

Cities and factories sprouted across the landscape. An abundance of new jobs served as a magnet attracting millions of immigrants. They were not always welcomed, nor were they readily assimilated. Ethnic and racial strife, as well as labor agitation, increased after 1900. In the midst of such social turmoil and unparalleled economic development, reformers made their first sustained attempt to adapt their political and social institutions to the realities of the industrial age. The worst excesses and injustices of urban-industrial development—corporate monopolies, child labor, political corruption, hazardous working conditions, urban ghettos—were finally addressed in a comprehensive way. During the Progressive Era (1890–1917) local, state, and federal governments sought to rein in the excesses of industrial capitalism and develop a more efficient public policy.

A conservative Republican resurgence challenged the notion of the new regulatory state during the 1920s. Free enterprise and corporate capitalism witnessed a dramatic revival. But the stock market crash of 1929 helped propel the United States and the world into the worst economic downturn in history. The unprecedented severity of the Great Depression renewed public demands for federal programs to protect the general welfare. "This nation asks for action," declared President Franklin D. Roosevelt in his 1933 inaugural address. The many New Deal initiatives and agencies instituted by Roosevelt and his Democratic administration created the framework for a welfare state that has since served as the basis for American public policy.

The New Deal helped revive public confidence and put people back to work, but it did not end the Great Depression. It took a world war to restore full employment. The necessity of mobilizing the nation in support of the Second World War also accelerated the growth of the federal government. And the incredible scope of the war helped catapult the United States into a leadership role in world politics. The creation and use of nuclear bombs ush-ered in a new era of atomic diplomacy that held the fate of the world in the balance. For all of the new creature comforts associated with modern life, Americans in 1945 found themselves living amid an array of new anxieties, not the least of which was a global "cold war" against communism.

23

AN AMERICAN EMPIRE

FOCUS QUESTIONS wwnorton.com/studyspace

- What motivated America's "new imperialism"?
- What was the role of religion as a motive for American territorial expansion?
- What were the causes of the War of 1898?
- What did America gain from the War of 1898?
- What were the main achievements of Theodore Roosevelt's foreign policy?

Throughout the nineteenth century most Americans displayed what one senator called "only a languid interest" in foreign affairs. The overriding priorities of the time were industrial development, western settlement, and domestic politics. Foreign relations simply were not important to the vast majority of people. After the Civil War an isolationist mood swept across the United States as the country basked in its geographic advantages: wide oceans as buffers, the British navy situated between America and the powers of Europe, and militarily weak neighbors in the Western Hemisphere.

Yet the notion of America's having a Manifest Destiny ordained by God to expand its territory and its influence remained alive in the decades after the Civil War. Several prominent political and business leaders argued that the rapid industrial development of the United States required the acquisition—or conquest—of foreign territories in order to gain easier access to vital materials. In addition, as their exports grew, American companies and farmers became increasingly intertwined in the world economy. This involvement, in turn, required an expanded naval force to protect the global shipping lanes. And a modern steam-powered navy needed bases where its ships could replenish their supplies of coal and water. For these reasons and others the United States during the last quarter of the nineteenth century began to expand its military presence beyond the Western Hemisphere, often at the expense of other nations' sovereignty.

Toward the New Imperialism

By the late nineteenth century, European powers had already unleashed a new surge of imperialism in Africa and Asia, where they had seized territory, established colonies, and promoted economic exploitation, racial superiority, and Christian evangelism. Writing in 1902, the British economist J. A. Hobson declared that imperialism was "the most powerful factor in the current politics of the Western world."

IMPERIALISM IN A GLOBAL CONTEXT   Western imperialism had economic roots; it was above all a quest for new markets and sources of raw materials. The Second Industrial Revolution generated such dramatic increases in production that business leaders felt compelled to find new markets for their burgeoning supply of goods and new sources of investment for their growing supply of capital. Manufacturers, on the other hand, were eager to find new sources of raw materials to supply their expanding needs. At the same time, the aggressive nationalism and bitter rivalries of the European powers made all of them compete with one another as they expanded their far-flung empires.

The result was a widespread process of imperial expansion into Africa and Asia. Beginning in the 1880s, the British, French, Belgians, Italians, Dutch, Spanish, and Germans used military force and political guile to conquer those continents. Each of the imperial nations, including the United States, dispatched Christian missionaries to convert native peoples. By 1900 some 18,000 Christian missionaries were scattered around the world. Often the conversion to Christianity was the first step in the loss of a culture's indigenous traditions. Western religious activities also influenced the colonial power structure. As a British nationalist explained such global ambitions, "Today, power and domination rather than freedom and independence are the ideas that appeal to the imagination of the masses—and the national ideal has given way to the imperial." This imperial outlook triggered clashes among the Western powers that would lead to unprecedented conflict in the twentieth century.

AMERICAN IMPERIALISM   As the European nations expanded their control over much of the rest of the world, the United States also began to acquire territories outside the North American continent. Most Americans became increasingly aware of world markets as developments in transportation and communication quickened the pace of commerce and diplomacy. From the first, agricultural exports had been the basis of economic growth. Now the conviction grew that American manufacturers had matured to the point where they could outsell foreign competitors in the world market. But should the expansion of markets lead to territorial expansion as well—or to intervention in the internal affairs of other countries? On such points, Americans disagreed, but a small yet influential group of public officials embraced the idea of acquiring overseas possessions, regardless of the implications. These expansionists included Senators Albert J. Beveridge of Indiana and Henry Cabot Lodge of Massachusetts, Theodore Roosevelt, and not least of all, naval captain Alfred Thayer Mahan.

During the 1880s, Captain Mahan had become a leading advocate of sea power and Western imperialism. In 1890 he published *The Influence of Sea Power upon History, 1660–1783*, in which he argued that national greatness and prosperity flowed from sea power. Modern economic development called for a powerful navy, a strong merchant marine, foreign commerce, colonies, and naval bases. Mahan championed America's "destiny" to control the Caribbean, build an isthmian canal, and spread Western civilization in the Pacific. His ideas were widely circulated in popular journals and within the U.S. government.

Yet even before Mahan's writings became influential, a gradual expansion of the navy had begun. In 1880 the nation had fewer than 100 seagoing vessels, many of them rusting or rotting at the docks. By 1896 eleven powerful new battleships had been built or authorized.

IMPERIALIST THEORY   Claims of racial superiority bolstered the new imperialist spirit. Spokesmen in each Western country, including the United States, used the arguments of social Darwinism to justify economic exploitation and territorial conquest. Among nations as among individuals, expansionists claimed, the fittest survive and prevail. John Fiske, a historian and popular lecturer on Darwinism, developed racial corollaries from Darwin's ideas. In *American Political Ideas Viewed from the Standpoint of*

Universal History (1885), he stressed the superior character of "Anglo-Saxon" institutions and peoples. The English-speaking "race," he argued, was destined to dominate the globe and transform the institutions, traditions, language—even the blood—of the world's peoples. Josiah Strong, a Congregationalist minister, added the sanction of religion to theories of racial and national superiority. In his book *Our Country: Its Possible Future and Its Present Crisis* (1885), Strong asserted that the "Anglo-Saxons" embodied two great ideas: civil liberty and "a pure spiritual Christianity." The Anglo-Saxon was "divinely commissioned to be, in a peculiar sense, his brother's keeper."

EXPANSION IN THE PACIFIC

For Josiah Strong and other expansionists, Asia offered an especially alluring target for American imperialism. President Andrew Johnson's secretary of state, William H. Seward, believed that the United States must inevitably exercise commercial domination "on the Pacific Ocean, and its islands and continents." Eager for American manufacturers to exploit Asian markets, Seward believed the United States first had to remove all foreign interests from the northern Pacific coast and gain access to that region's valuable ports. To that end, Seward cast covetous eyes on the British colony of British Columbia, sandwiched between Russia's possessions in Alaska and the Washington Territory.

Late in 1866, while encouraging British Columbians to consider making their colony a U.S. territory, Seward learned of Russia's desire to sell Alaska. He leaped at the opportunity, and in 1867 the United States bought Alaska for $7.2 million, less than 2¢ an acre. "Seward's folly" of buying the Alaskan "icebox" proved to be the biggest bargain since the Louisiana Purchase.

SAMOA AND HAWAII Seward's successors at the State Department sustained his expansionist vision. During the post–Civil War years the United States sought coaling stations and trading posts in the Pacific Ocean, and it laid claim to various small islands and atolls. Two of those island groups were especially strategic: Samoa and Hawaii (also known as the Sandwich Islands). In 1878 the Samoans signed a treaty granting the United States a naval base on one of its islands. The following year the German and British governments worked out similar arrangements on other Samoan islands. In Hawaii the Americans had a clearer field to exploit. The islands, a united kingdom since 1795, hosted a sizable settlement of American missionaries and planters. The Hawaiian Islands were strategically more important to the United States than Samoa was, since their occupation by another major power might have posed a threat to American sugar interests and even to defense of the continent.

In 1875 the Hawaiians signed a reciprocal trade agreement, according to which their sugar entered the United States duty-free. Twelve years later they granted the United States a naval base at Pearl Harbor, near Honolulu. Those agreements prompted a boom in sugar growing, and American settlers in Hawaii came to dominate the economy. In 1887 the Americans forced Hawaii's king to create a constitutional government, which they controlled.

Queen Liliuokalani

The Hawaiian queen sought to preserve her nation's independence.

Hawaii's political climate changed sharply when the king's sister, Queen Liliuokalani, ascended the throne in 1891 and tried to reclaim power. Shortly before that, the McKinley Tariff had destroyed Hawaii's favored position in the sugar trade by putting the sugar of all countries on the duty-free list and granting growers in the United States a 2¢ subsidy per pound of sugar. The resultant economic crisis and discontent in Hawaii led the white population to revolt early in 1893 and seize power. U.S. Marines supported the coup. Within a month the new American-dominated government sent a delegation to Washington and signed a treaty annexing Hawaii to the United States.

These events occurred just weeks before President Benjamin Harrison left office, however, and Democratic senators blocked the treaty's ratification. President Cleveland withdrew the treaty and sent a special commissioner to Hawaii to investigate. The commissioner ordered the marines home and reported that Americans on the islands had acted improperly. Most Hawaiians opposed annexation, said the commissioner, who thought the revolution had been engineered mainly by U.S. sugar planters hoping for annexation in order to be eligible for the new subsidy for sugar grown in the United States. Cleveland therefore proposed to restore the queen in return for amnesty to the revolutionists. The provisional government refused to step down, however, and on July 4, 1894, it proclaimed the islands the Republic of Hawaii, which included in its constitution a standing provision for annexation to the United States.

In 1897, when William McKinley became president, he was looking for an excuse to annex the Hawaiian Islands. This excuse was found when the Japanese, also hoping to take over the islands, sent warships to Hawaii. McKinley responded by sending U.S. warships and asking the Senate to annex the territory. When the Senate could not muster the two-thirds majority needed to approve the treaty, McKinley used a joint resolution of the House and the Senate to achieve his aims. The resolution passed by simple majorities in both houses, and the United States annexed Hawaii in the summer of 1898.

THE WAR OF 1898

Until the 1890s a nagging ambivalence about acquiring overseas territories had checked America's drive to expand. Suddenly, in 1898 and 1899, inhibitions collapsed, and the United States embarked on an aggressive program of global expansion.

"CUBA LIBRE"   Throughout the second half of the nineteenth century, Cubans had repeatedly revolted against Spanish rule, only to be ruthlessly put down. Cuba was one of Spain's oldest colonies and had become a major export market for the mother country. Yet American investments in Cuba, mainly in sugar and mining, were steadily increasing—the United States in fact traded more with Cuba than Spain did—and the growing economic interest in their island neighbor made Americans sympathetic to the idea of Cuban independence. So when Cubans revolted against Spanish rule on February 24, 1895, public feeling in the United States was with the rebels.

Events in Cuba supplied exciting copy for the press. William Randolph Hearst's *New York Journal* and Joseph Pulitzer's *New York World* were at the time locked in a monumental competition for readers. "It was a battle of gigantic proportions," one journalist wrote, "in which the sufferings of Cuba merely chanced to furnish some of the most convenient ammunition." The sensationalism in covering events in Cuba came to be called yellow journalism, and Hearst emerged as its undisputed champion.

PRESSURE FOR WAR   American neutrality in the Cuban struggle for independence changed sharply when William McKinley entered office in 1897. His platform had endorsed Cuban independence as well as U.S. control of

Hawaii and the construction of an isthmian canal. Knowing that the Cuban rebels enjoyed American support, Spain offered autonomy (self-government without formal independence) in return for peace. The Cubans rejected the offer. Spain was thus impaled on the horns of a dilemma, unable to end the rebellion and unready to give up Cuba.

Early in 1898, events moved rapidly to arouse American opinion against Spain. On February 9 Hearst's *New York Journal* released the text of a letter from a Spanish official, Depuy de Lôme, to a friend in Havana. In the letter, which had been stolen from the post office by a Cuban spy, de Lôme called President McKinley "weak and a bidder for the admiration of the crowd." The breach in diplomatic etiquette was such that de Lôme resigned to prevent further embarrassment to his government.

Six days later, during the night of February 15, 1898, the U.S. battleship *Maine* exploded and sank in Havana Harbor, with a terrible loss of 260 men. The ship's captain, one of only 84 survivors, scribbled a telegram to Washington: "*Maine* blown up in Havana Harbor at nine forty tonight and destroyed. Many wounded and doubtless more killed or drowned. . . . Public opinion should be suspended until further report." But those eager for a war with Spain saw no need to withhold judgment; they demanded an immediate declaration of war. Theodore Roosevelt, then serving as the assistant secretary of the navy, called the sinking "an act of dirty treachery on the part of the Spaniards." The United States, he declared, "needs a war."

A naval court of inquiry reported that an external mine had sunk the ship. Lacking hard evidence, the court made no effort to fix the blame, but the yellow press had no need of evidence. The *New York Journal* gleefully reported: "The Whole Country Thrills with War Fever." The outcry against Spain rose in a crescendo with the words "Remember the *Maine!* To Hell with Spain!" Few of those promoting war wrestled with the obvious fact that the Spanish government was determined to avoid a confrontation with the United States and therefore had nothing to gain from sinking the *Maine*. (A comprehensive study in 1976 concluded that the sinking of the *Maine* was an accident, the result of an internal explosion triggered by a fire in its coal bunker.)

The weight of outraged public opinion and the influence of militant Republicans such as Theodore Roosevelt and Henry Cabot Lodge eroded President McKinley's neutrality. On March 9, the president pushed through Congress a $50 million defense appropriation. The Spanish government, sensing the growing militancy in the United States, announced a unilateral cease-fire in early April. On April 10 the Spanish ambassador gave the U.S. State Department a message that amounted to a surrender. But the message came too late. The following day, McKinley sent Congress his war message.

The sinking of the *Maine* in Havana Harbor

The uproar created by the incident and its coverage in the "yellow press" helped to push President William McKinley to declare war.

He asked for the power to use armed forces in Cuba to protect U.S. property and trade. On April 20 a joint resolution of Congress declared Cuba independent and demanded withdrawal of Spanish forces. The Teller Amendment, added on the Senate floor, disclaimed any U.S. designs on Cuban territory. McKinley signed the resolution and sent a copy to the Spanish government. On April 22 the president announced a blockade of Cuba, an act of war under international law. Rather than give in to an ultimatum, the Spanish government declared war on April 24. Determined to be first, Congress declared war the next day, making the declaration retroactive to April 21, 1898.

Why such a rush to war after the message from Spain had indicated that it was ready for an armistice? No one knows for sure, but it seems apparent that too much momentum and popular pressure had built up for a confidential message to change the course of events. Also, leaders of the business

News announcements, 1898

A crowd watches men post news announcements outside the New York Tribune building, during the War of 1898.

community were demanding a quick resolution of the problem. Many of them lacked faith in the willingness or ability of the Spanish government to resolve the crisis. Still, it is fair to ask why McKinley did not take a stronger stand for peace. He might have defied Congress and public opinion, but in the end he deemed the political risk too high. The ultimate blame for war, if blame must be levied, belongs to the American people for letting themselves be whipped into such a hostile frenzy.

MANILA   The war itself lasted only 114 days. The American victory marked the end of Spain's once-great New World empire and the emergence of the United States as a world power. But if war with Spain saved many lives by ending the insurrection in Cuba, it also led to brutal U.S. efforts to suppress another insurrection, in the Philippines, and it created a host of commitments in the Caribbean and the Pacific that would haunt American policy makers throughout the twentieth century.

The War of 1898 was barely under way before the U.S. Navy produced a spectacular victory in an unexpected quarter: Manila Bay. While public attention centered on Cuba, young Theodore Roosevelt focused on the Spanish-controlled Philippines in the western Pacific Ocean: the assistant secretary of the navy had ordered Commodore George Dewey to engage Spain's ships in the Philippines in case of war. President McKinley had approved the orders. Arriving late on April 30, 1898, Dewey's squadron destroyed or captured all the Spanish warships in Manila Bay. While Dewey waited for reinforcements, Emilio Aguinaldo, whom he had brought out of exile to make trouble for the Spanish, declared the Philippines independent on June 12. Once Dewey's reinforcements arrived, the American forces, with the help of Filipino insurrectionists under Aguinaldo, liberated Manila from Spanish control on August 13.

THE CUBAN CAMPAIGN   While these events transpired halfway around the world, the fighting in Cuba reached a surprisingly quick climax. The U.S. Navy blockaded the Spanish fleet at Santiago while an invasion force of some 17,000 American troops was hastily assembled at Tampa, Florida. One significant unit was the First Volunteer Cavalry, better known as the Rough Riders and best remembered because Lieutenant Colonel Theodore Roosevelt was second in command. Eager to get "in on the fun" and "to act up to my preachings," Roosevelt had quit the Navy Department after war was declared. He ordered a custom-fitted blue uniform with yellow trim, grabbed a dozen pairs of spectacles, and rushed to help organize a colorful volunteer regiment of Ivy League athletes, leathery ex-convicts, Indians, and southwestern sharpshooters.

The major land action of the Cuban campaign occurred on July 1. While a much larger American force attacked Spanish positions at San Juan Hill, a smaller unit, including the dismounted Rough Riders—most of whose horses were still in Florida—and two African American regiments, seized the enemy position atop nearby Kettle Hill. Theodore Roosevelt later claimed that he "would rather have led that charge than [have] served three terms in the U.S. Senate." A friend wrote to Roosevelt's wife that her husband was "revelling in victory and gore."

On July 3, Spain's ships made a gallant run for it, but the aging vessels were little match for the newer American fleet. The casualties were one-sided: 474 Spanish were killed or wounded and 1,750 taken prisoner, while only one American was killed and one wounded. Spanish officials in Santiago surrendered on July 17. On July 25 an American force moved onto the Spanish-held island of Puerto Rico.

The next day the Spanish government in Madrid sued for peace. After discussions lasting two weeks, negotiators signed an armistice on August 12, 1898, less than four months after the war's start and the day before American troops entered Manila. The peace protocol specified that Spain should give up Cuba and that the United States should annex Puerto Rico and occupy the city, bay, and harbor of Manila pending the transfer of power in the Philippines.

And so the "splendid little war," as the future secretary of state John Hay called it in a letter to Roosevelt, officially ended. It was splendid only in the sense that its cost was relatively slight. Of the more than 274,000 Americans who served during the war and the ensuing demobilization, 5,462 died, but only 379 in battle. Most succumbed to malaria, typhoid, dysentery, or yellow fever. At such a cost the United States was launched onto the world stage as a great power, with all the benefits—and burdens—of that new status.

THE DEBATE OVER ANNEXATION   The United States and Spain signed the Treaty of Paris on December 10, 1898, but the status of the Philippines remained in limbo. President McKinley, who claimed at first that he could not locate the Philippines on a map, gave ambiguous signals to the peace commission, which itself was divided. There had been no demand for annexation of the Philippines or other Spanish possessions before the war, but Commodore Dewey's victory at Manila Bay quickly aroused expansionist fever. Business leaders began thinking of the commercial possibilities in the nearby continent of Asia, such as oil for the lamps of China and textiles for its millions of inhabitants. Missionary societies yearned to convert "the little brown brother" to Christianity. Although most of these Filipino candidates for conversion were already Catholic, the word went forth that the Philippines should be taken for the sake of their souls. Spanish negotiators raised the delicate point that U.S. forces had no claim by right of conquest and had even taken Manila after the armistice. American negotiators finally offered the Spanish $20 million as compensation for possession of the Philippines, as well as Puerto Rico in the Caribbean and Guam in the Pacific.

Meanwhile, Americans had taken other giant steps in the Pacific. Congress had annexed Hawaii in the midst of the war. In 1899, after another outbreak of fighting over the royal succession in Samoa, Germany and the United States agreed to partition the Samoa Islands. The United States annexed the easternmost islands; Germany took the rest.

The Treaty of Paris was opposed by most Democrats and Populists and some Republicans. Anti-imperialists argued that the unprecedented acquisition of the Philippines would undermine democracy. They appealed to

"Well, I Hardly Know Which to Take First!"

At the end of the nineteenth century, it seemed that Uncle Sam had developed a considerable appetite for foreign territory.

traditional isolationism, American principles of self-government, the inconsistency of liberating Cuba and annexing the Philippines, involvement in foreign entanglements that would undermine the logic of the Monroe Doctrine, and the danger that the Philippines would be expensive if not impossible to defend. The prospect of incorporating into the United States so many alien peoples was also troubling. Some critics insisted that the former Spanish colonies were not capable of establishing self-sustaining democracies. "Bananas and self-government cannot grow on the same piece of land," one senator claimed.

The opposition might have been strong enough to kill the treaty had not William Jennings Bryan influenced the vote for approval. A formal end to the war, he argued, would open the way for the future independence of Cuba and the Philippines. Ratification finally came on February 6, 1899. But President McKinley had no intention of granting the Philippines their independence. He insisted that the United States take control of the islands as an act of "benevolent assimilation." In February 1899 an American soldier outside Manila fired on Filipino nationalists, and the United States found itself in a new war.

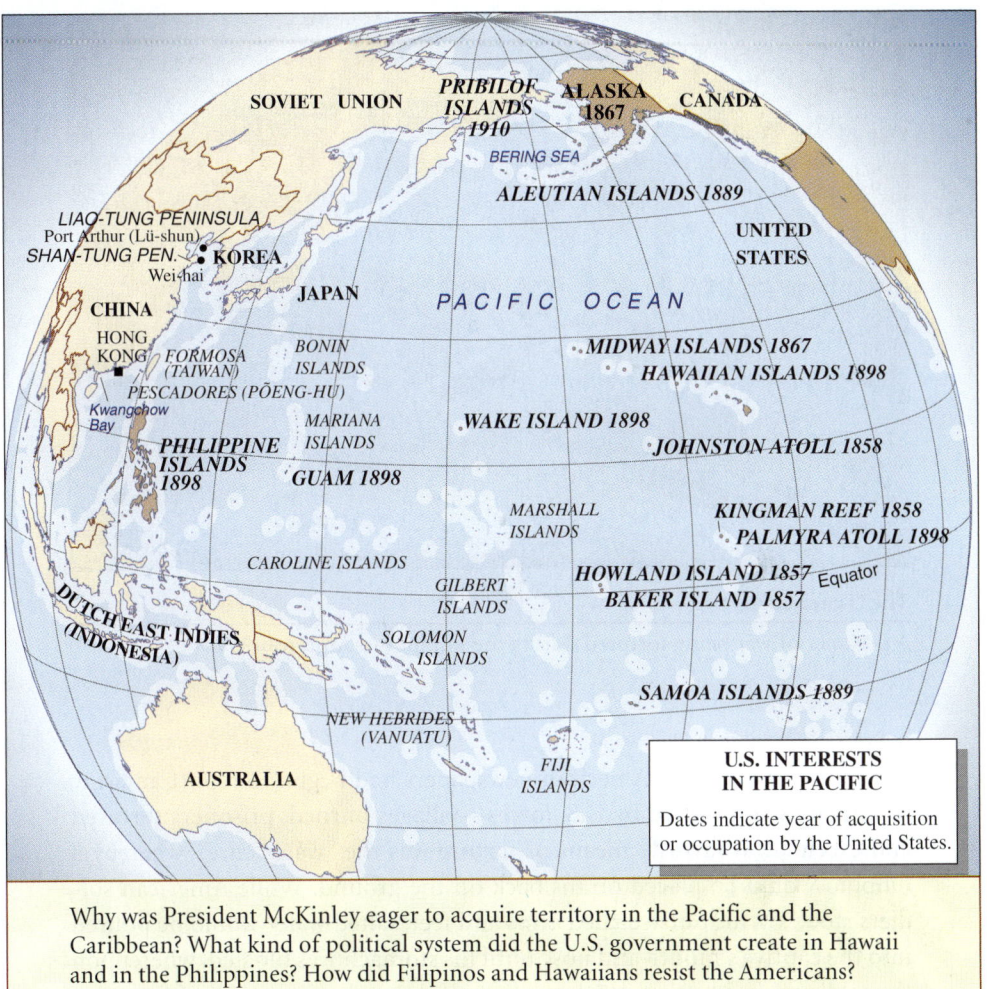

SOVIET UNION

PRIBILOF ISLANDS 1910

ALASKA 1867

CANADA

BERING SEA

ALEUTIAN ISLANDS 1889

LIAO-TUNG PENINSULA
Port Arthur (Lü-shun)
SHAN-TUNG PEN.
Wei-hai
KOREA

UNITED STATES

CHINA

JAPAN

PACIFIC OCEAN

HONG KONG

FORMOSA (TAIWAN)

BONIN ISLANDS

PESCADORES (PÕENG-HU)

MIDWAY ISLANDS 1867

HAWAIIAN ISLANDS 1898

Kwangchow Bay

PHILIPPINE ISLANDS 1898

MARIANA ISLANDS

WAKE ISLAND 1898

JOHNSTON ATOLL 1858

GUAM 1898

MARSHALL ISLANDS

KINGMAN REEF 1858

PALMYRA ATOLL 1898

CAROLINE ISLANDS

GILBERT ISLANDS

HOWLAND ISLAND 1857

BAKER ISLAND 1857

Equator

DUTCH EAST INDIES (INDONESIA)

SOLOMON ISLANDS

NEW HEBRIDES (VANUATU)

SAMOA ISLANDS 1889

AUSTRALIA

FIJI ISLANDS

U.S. INTERESTS IN THE PACIFIC

Dates indicate year of acquisition or occupation by the United States.

Why was President McKinley eager to acquire territory in the Pacific and the Caribbean? What kind of political system did the U.S. government create in Hawaii and in the Philippines? How did Filipinos and Hawaiians resist the Americans?

Since Aguinaldo's forces were more or less in control of the islands outside Manila, what followed over the next two years was largely an American war of conquest.

THE PHILIPPINE-AMERICAN WAR The American effort to suppress Filipino nationalism lasted three years, eventually involved some 126,000 U.S. troops, and took the lives of hundreds of thousands of Filipinos (most of them civilians) and 4,234 American soldiers. The nature of the war also cost the United States much of its professed benevolence. It was a sordid conflict, with massacres committed by both sides. Within the first year of the

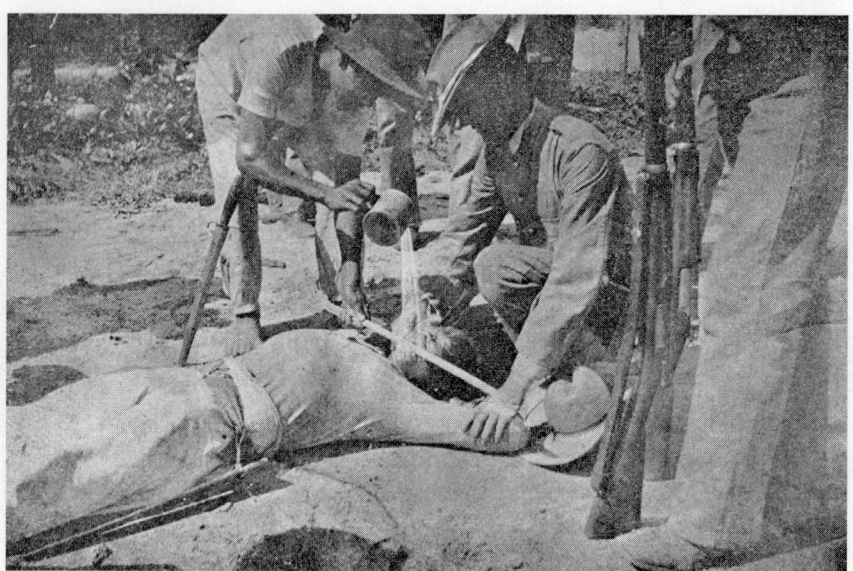

The "water cure"

A prisoner of war being tortured during the Philippine-American War.

war in the Philippines, American newspapers had begun to report an array of atrocities committed by U.S. forces—villages burned, prisoners tortured and executed. A favorite means of torture was the "water cure," whereby a Filipino would be placed on his back on the ground. While American soldiers stood on his outstretched arms and feet, salted water would be poured into the captive's mouth and nose until his stomach was bloated, whereupon the soldiers would stomp on the prisoner's abdomen, forcing all of the water out. This process would be repeated until the captive told the soldiers what they wanted to know—or he died. A Senate investigation revealed the scope of such atrocities, but in the end the senators did nothing. Their attitude resembled that of President Theodore Roosevelt, who was convinced that "nobody was seriously damaged" by the "water cure," whereas "Filipinos had inflicted terrible tortures upon our own people." Still, he wrote, "torture is not a thing that we can tolerate." Yet he did tolerate such torture, in large part because he believed that the American army was bringing peace and order and freedom to the Philippines. The "dark abuses" were the price Americans paid for the "progress of humanity." Thus did the United States alienate and destroy a Filipino independence movement modeled after America's own struggle for independence from Great Britain. Organized Filipino

Turmoil in the Philippines

Emilio Aguinaldo (seated third from right) and other leaders of the Filipino insurgence.

resistance had collapsed by the end of 1899, but even after the American capture of Aguinaldo in 1901, sporadic guerrilla action lasted until mid-1902.

Against the backdrop of this nasty guerrilla war, the great debate over annexation continued in the United States. In 1899 several anti-imperialist groups united to form the American Anti-Imperialist League. The league attracted members representing many shades of opinion. The industrialist Andrew Carnegie footed the bills; on imperialism, at least, the union leader Samuel Gompers agreed with the steel king. The usually soft-spoken philosopher William James exploded in voicing his opposition to the expansionists: "God damn the United States for its vile conduct in the Philippine Isles!" The selfish proponents of imperialism, he declared, had caused the nation to "puke up its ancient soul."

RELIGION AND EMPIRE   Among those supporting the war against Spain and the imperial conquest of Spain's Caribbean and Pacific colonies were many religious leaders. In Boston, for example, the *Herald* reported that Protestant ministers were the most rabid supporters of America's new imperialism. The time was ripe for "evangelization of the world." Foreign missionary activity had soared after the Civil War as Protestants asserted that Christianity was the "highest and purest form of religion in the world" and evangelicals eagerly spread the blessings of Christianity around the globe.

Protestant missionaries and their supporting organizations unabashedly promoted the global superiority of the Anglo-Saxon "race" and the Christian religion, and they were often virulently anti-Catholic. The *California Christian Advocate*, for example, cheered the declaration of war with Catholic Spain: "The war is the Kingdom of God coming!" Another Protestant magazine, the *Pacific Advocate*, announced that "the cross will follow the flag" as "righteous" American soldiers prepared to liberate Cuba from Spanish control. Another evangelical declared that missionary activity was itself "a war of conquest." For Catholic Americans, however, the war against Spain, one of the oldest and most intensely Catholic nations in the world, was more problematic. They objected to Protestant plans to evangelize the Catholic Cubans. A Catholic official warned that efforts to convert the Catholics of Cuba, Puerto Rico, and the Philippines "would be the speediest and most effective way to make the inhabitants of those islands discontented and opposed to America."

In the debate over America's annexing the Spanish colonies, religious arguments held sway. Senator Albert Beveridge, an ardent imperialist, declared that "we are God's chosen people." The United States, he added, had a "sacred duty" to bring the blessings of American Christianity to the lands acquired from Spain. Others shared this notion of providential responsibility for the "backward" peoples of the world. Lyman Abbott, a prominent Protestant clergyman and editor, said that America was a divine instrument of Christian imperialism. It was, he said, "the function of the Anglo-Saxon race to confer these gifts of civilization, through law, commerce, and education, on the uncivilized people of the world." Abbott lambasted the anti-imperialists:

> It is said that we have no right to go to a land occupied by barbaric people and interfere with their life. It is said that if they prefer barbarism they have a right to be barbarians. I deny the right of a barbaric people to retain possession of any quarter of the globe. What I have already said I reaffirm: barbarism has no rights which civilization is bound to respect. Barbarians have rights which civilized people are bound to respect, but they have no right to their barbarism.

Abbott and others insisted that the United States could not shirk its providential duty to "save" the former Spanish colonies from barbarism.

ORGANIZING THE ACQUISITIONS   In the end the imperialists won the debate. President McKinley quickly moved to set up a civil government in the Philippines. On July 4, 1901, the U.S. military government came to an end, and under an act of Congress, Judge William Howard Taft became the civil governor. The Philippine Government Act, passed by Congress on July 1, 1902, declared the Philippine Islands an "unorganized territory." The Tydings-McDuffie Act, in 1934, offered independence after ten more years, and independence finally took effect on July 4, 1946.

Closer to home, Puerto Rico had been acquired in part to serve as a U.S. outpost guarding the approach to the Caribbean and any future isthmian canal. In 1900 the Foraker Act established a civil government on the island. Residents of the island were declared citizens of Puerto Rico; they were not made citizens of the United States until 1917. In 1952, Puerto Rico became a commonwealth with its own constitution and elected officials, a unique status. Like a state, Puerto Rico is free to change its constitution insofar as it does not conflict with the U.S. Constitution.

Liberated Cuba, American authorities soon learned, posed problems at least as irksome as those in the new possessions. After the American occupation forces had restored order, started schools, and improved sanitary conditions, they began handing the reins of power to the Cubans. The Platt Amendment, added to an army appropriations bill passed by Congress in 1901, sharply restricted the new government's independence, however. The amendment required that Cuba never impair its independence by signing a treaty with a third power, that it keep its debt within the government's power to repay it out of ordinary revenues, and that it acknowledge the right of the United States to intervene in Cuba for the preservation of Cuban independence and the maintenance of "a government adequate for the protection of life, property, and individual liberty." Finally, Cuba had to sell or lease to the United States lands to be used for coaling or naval stations, a proviso that led to a U.S. naval base at Guantánamo Bay.

IMPERIAL RIVALRIES IN EAST ASIA

THE "OPEN DOOR"   During the 1890s the United States was not the only nation to emerge as a world power. Another was Japan. Commodore Matthew Perry's voyage of 1853–1854 had opened Japan to Western ways, and the island nation had expanded in earnest after the 1860s. Flexing its new muscles, Japan defeated China's stagnant empire in the First Sino-Japanese War (1894–1895) and as a result acquired the island of Formosa (modern-day Taiwan). China's weakness, demonstrated in the war, led Russia, England, France, and Germany to renew their scramble for "spheres of influence" on that remaining frontier of imperialist expansion.

"The Open Door"

Cartoon depicting Uncle Sam propping open a door for China with a brick labeled "U.S. Army and Navy Prestige," as colonial powers look on.

The possibility that those competing powers would carve up China and erect tariff barriers in their own spheres of influence dimmed the bright prospect of American trade with China. Yet the British had much to lose in a tariff war, for they already enjoyed substantial trade with China, so in 1899 they suggested that the United States join them in preserving China's commercial and territorial integrity. The State Department agreed that something must be done, but Secretary of State John Hay preferred to act alone rather than in concert with the British.

What came to be known as the Open Door policy was outlined in Hay's Open Door Note, dispatched in 1899 to London, Berlin, and St. Petersburg and a little later to Tokyo, Rome, and Paris. It proposed to keep China open to trade with all countries on an equal basis. None except Britain accepted Hay's principles, but none rejected them either, so Hay simply announced that all powers had accepted the policy.

The Open Door policy was rooted in the self-interest of American businesses eager to exploit Chinese markets. Yet it also tapped the deep-seated sympathies of those who opposed imperialism, especially as it pledged to protect China's territorial integrity. But it had little legal standing. When the Japanese, concerned about Russian pressure in Manchuria, asked how the United States intended to enforce the Open Door policy, Hay replied that the United States was "not prepared" to do so. So it would remain for forty years, a hollow but dangerous commitment, until continued Japanese expansion would bring about war with America in 1941.

THE BOXER REBELLION   A new Asian crisis arose in 1900 when a group of Chinese nationalists known to the Western world as Boxers (Fists of Righteous Harmony) rebelled against foreign involvement in China, surrounding the foreign embassies in Peking. The British, Germans, Russians, Japanese, and Americans quickly mounted a military expedition to relieve the embassy compound. Hay, fearful that the intervention might become an excuse to dismember China, seized the chance to further refine his Open Door policy. The United States, he declared in a circular letter of July 3, 1900, sought a solution that would "preserve Chinese territorial and administrative integrity" as well as "equal and impartial trade with all parts of the Chinese Empire." Six weeks later the expedition reached Peking and broke the Boxer Rebellion.

BIG-STICK DIPLOMACY

More than any other American political leader of his time, Theodore Roosevelt transformed the role of the United States in world affairs. The nation had emerged from the War of 1898 a world power, and he insisted that this status entailed major new responsibilities. To ensure that the United States accepted its international obligations, Roosevelt stretched both the Constitution and executive power to the limit. In the process he pushed a reluctant nation onto the center stage of world affairs.

ROOSEVELT'S RISE   In the fall elections of 1898, Republicans benefited from the euphoria of military victory, increasing their majority in Congress. That hardly amounted to a mandate for imperialism, however, since the election preceded most of the debates on the issue. But in 1900 the Democrats turned once again to William Jennings Bryan, who sought to make imperialism the "paramount issue" of the campaign. The Democratic platform condemned the Philippine conflict as "an unnecessary war" that had "placed the United States, previously known . . . throughout the world as the champion of freedom, in the false and un-American position of crushing with military force the efforts of our former allies to achieve liberty and self-government." The Republicans welcomed the opportunity to disagree. They renominated William McKinley and named as his running mate Theodore Roosevelt, who had been elected governor of New York after his self-inflated role in the War of 1898.

The trouble with Bryan's idea of a solemn referendum on imperialism was the near impossibility of making any presidential contest so simple. Bryan himself complicated his message by insisting once again on the free coinage of silver, and the tariff became an issue again as well. The Republicans' biggest advantage was probably the return to national prosperity, which they were fully ready to take credit for. Those who opposed imperialism but also opposed free silver or tariff reduction faced a bewildering choice.

The outcome was a victory for McKinley greater than his last, 7.2 million to 6.4 million popular votes and 292 to 155 electoral votes. There had been no clear-cut referendum on annexations, but the question was settled nonetheless, although it would take another year and a half to subdue the Filipino rebels. The job would be finished under the direction of another president, however.

On September 6, 1901, at a reception at the Pan-American Exposition in Buffalo, an anarchist named Leon Czolgosz (pronounced chole-gosh) approached McKinley, a pistol concealed in his bandaged hand, and fired at point-blank range. McKinley died eight days later, thereby elevating Theodore Roosevelt to the White House. "Now look," erupted Republican senator Mark Hanna, "that damned cowboy is President of the United States!"

Six weeks short of his forty-third birthday, Roosevelt was the youngest man ever to take charge of the White House, but he had more experience in public affairs than most and more vitality than any. Born in 1858, the son of a wealthy New York merchant and a Georgia belle, Roosevelt had grown up in Manhattan in cultured comfort, had visited Europe as a child, spoke German fluently, and had graduated from Harvard Phi Beta Kappa in 1880. Roosevelt loved rigorous exercise and outdoor adventure. Boxer, wrestler, and outdoorsman, he was also a voracious reader, a renowned historian and essayist, and a zealous moralist.

Roosevelt studied law briefly and within two years of graduation from college won election to the New York legislature. That same year he published *The Naval War of 1812*, the first of numerous historical, biographical, and other works to flow from his pen. He seemingly had the world at his feet—and then disaster struck. In 1884 his beloved mother, only forty-eight years old, died. Eleven hours later, in the same house, his twenty-two-year-old wife struggled with kidney failure before dying in his arms, having recently given birth to their only child. Roosevelt was distraught and bewildered. "The light has gone out of my life," he wrote in his diary. The double funeral was so wrenching that the officiating minister wept throughout his prayer. In an attempt to recover from this "strange and terrible fate," Roosevelt turned his baby daughter over to his sister, quit his political career, sold the family house, and moved west to take up the cattle business in the Dakota Territory. The blue-blooded New Yorker relished hunting, leading roundups, capturing outlaws, fighting Indians—and reading novels by the campfire. Although his western career lasted only two years, he never got over being a cowboy.

Back in New York City, Roosevelt remarried and ran unsuccessfully for mayor; he later served six years as civil service commissioner in Washington, D.C., and two years as New York City's police commissioner. After President

U.S. INTERESTS IN THE CARIBBEAN

▨	United States and its possessions
☐	Occupied by or a protectorate of the United States

UNITED STATES

GULF
OF
MEXICO

BAHAMA
ISLANDS

ATLANTIC
OCEAN

Havana

Veracruz
Occupied 1914

MEXICO

CUBA
Occupied
1898–1902,
1906–1909, 1912,
1917, 1922
Protectorate
1898–1934

Guantánamo
(U.S. naval base)

DOMINICAN
REPUBLIC
Occupied 1916–1924
Protectorate 1905–1941

BRITISH
HONDURAS

GUATEMALA

HONDURAS

JAMAICA

HAITI
Occupied 1915–1934
Protectorate 1915–1936

PUERTO
RICO
Annexed 1898

EL SALVADOR

NICARAGUA
Occupied 1912–1925,
1926–1933

COSTA RICA

Proposed route for
Nicaraguan canal

PANAMA
CANAL ZONE
Leased from
Panama 1903

CARIBBEAN
SEA

VIRGIN ISLANDS
Acquired from
Denmark 1917

VENEZUELA

PANAMA
Protectorate 1903–1939

COLOMBIA

0	150	300 Miles
0	150	300 Kilometers

Why did America want to build the Panama Canal? How did the U.S. government interfere with Colombian politics in an effort to gain control of the canal? What was the Roosevelt Corollary?

McKinley appointed him assistant secretary of the navy in 1897, Roosevelt did all he could to promote the war with Spain over Cuba. "A just war," he insisted, "is in the long run far better for a man's soul than the most prosperous peace."

Roosevelt combined his boundless energy with an unshakable righteousness that led him to cast every issue in moral and patriotic terms. He saw the presidency as his "bully pulpit," and he was eager to preach fist-smacking sermons on the virtues of honesty, civic duty, and the strenuous life to his national flock. But appearances were deceiving. His energy left a false impression of impulsiveness, and the talk of morality cloaked a cautious pragmatism. Roosevelt could get carried away, but as he said of his foreign-policy actions, that was likely to happen only when "I am assured that I shall be able eventually to carry out my will by force."

THE PANAMA CANAL   After the War of 1898, the United States became more deeply involved than ever in the Caribbean, where one issue overshadowed every other: the Panama Canal. The narrow isthmus of Panama had long excited dreams of an interoceanic canal. After America's victory over Spain, Secretary of State John Hay commenced talks with the British ambassador about revising the Clayton-Bulwer Treaty of 1850, which prohibited either nation from constructing a transoceanic canal. The negotiations led to the Hay-Pauncefote Treaty of 1901, in which Britain gave its consent to the American plan for a canal across Panama.

Other obstacles remained, however. From 1881 to 1887, a French company had spent nearly $300 million and had sacrificed some 20,000 lives to dig less than a third of a canal through Panama. The company now offered to sell its holdings to the United States. Meanwhile, Secretary of State Hay had opened negotiations with Ambassador Tomás Herrán of Colombia on the subject of a canal across Panama, which was then a reluctant province of Colombia. In return for a canal zone six miles wide, the United States agreed to pay $10 million in cash and a rental fee of $250,000 a year. The U.S. Senate ratified the Hay-Herrán Treaty in 1903, but the Colombian senate held out for $25 million in cash.

Colombia's rejection of the treaty heightened the desire of Panamanian rebels for independence. An employee of the French canal company then hatched a plot in collusion with the company's representative, Philippe Bunau-Varilla. Bunau-Varilla visited Roosevelt and Hay and then, apparently with inside information, informed the Panamanian rebels that the U.S.S. *Nashville* would arrive at Colón, Panama, on November 2, 1903.

Digging the canal

President Theodore Roosevelt operating a steam shovel during his 1906 visit to the Panama Canal.

An army of some 500 Panamanians revolted against Colombian rule the next day. Colombian troops, who could not penetrate the overland jungle, found U.S. ships blocking the sea-lanes. On November 13 the Roosevelt administration made good on its collusion with the revolutionaries by recognizing Panama's independence, and on November 18 Roosevelt and the new Panamanian ambassador, who happened to be Bunau-Varilla, signed a treaty extending the Canal Zone from six to ten miles in width. For $10 million down and $250,000 a year, the United States received "in perpetuity the use, occupation and control" of the Canal Zone. Colombia eventually got its $25 million, in 1921, but only after America's interest in Colombian oil had lubricated the wheels of diplomacy. There was no apology, but the payment was made to remove "all misunderstandings growing out of the political events in Panama, November, 1903." The strategic canal opened on August 15, 1914, two weeks after the outbreak of World War I in Europe. It was a tribute to American engineering and a boon to American commerce and the Panamanian economy.

THE ROOSEVELT COROLLARY   Even without the canal the United States would have been concerned with the stability of the Caribbean region, and particularly with the activities of any hostile power there. A prime excuse for intervention in those days was to force the collection of debts owed to foreigners. In 1904 a crisis over the Dominican Republic's debts prompted Roosevelt to formulate U.S. policy. In his annual address to Congress in 1904, he outlined what came to be known as the Roosevelt Corollary to the Monroe Doctrine: the principle, in short, that since the Monroe Doctrine prohibited European intervention in the region, the United States was justified in intervening first to forestall involvement by European nations. Roosevelt suggested that the United States could exercise an "international police power" in its own sphere of influence. As put into practice by mutual agreement with the

The world's constable

President Theodore Roosevelt wields "the big stick," symbolizing his aggressive diplomacy.

Dominican Republic in 1905, the Roosevelt Corollary called for the United States to appoint a collector of customs, who would apply a portion of the nation's revenues to debt payments owed American companies. The principle, applied peaceably in 1905, became the basis for military interventions later on.

THE RUSSO-JAPANESE WAR   In east Asia, meanwhile, the principle of equal trading rights embodied in the Open Door policy was tested when tensions between Russia and Japan flared into a fight over China and Korea. On February 8, 1904, war broke out when Japanese warships devastated the Russian fleet. The Japanese then occupied Korea and drove the Russians back across the Yalu River into Manchuria. But neither side could score a knockout blow, and neither relished a prolonged war. When the Japanese signaled President Roosevelt that they would welcome a negotiated settlement, he sponsored a peace conference, held in Portsmouth, New Hampshire. With the Treaty of Portsmouth (1905), the concessions all went to the Japanese. Russia acknowledged Japan's "predominant political, military, and economic interests in Korea" (Japan would annex the kingdom in 1910), and both powers agreed to evacuate Manchuria.

RELATIONS WITH JAPAN   Japan's show of strength in the war with Russia raised doubts about the security of the Philippines. During the Portsmouth talks, Roosevelt sent Secretary of War William Howard Taft to meet with the Japanese foreign minister in Tokyo. The two men arrived at the Taft-Katsura Agreement of July 29, 1905, in which the United States accepted Japanese control of Korea, and Japan disavowed any designs on the Philippines. Three years later the Root-Takahira Agreement, negotiated by Secretary of State Elihu Root and the Japanese ambassador, promised to respect each other's possessions and reinforced the Open Door policy by supporting "the independence and integrity of China" and "the principle of equal opportunity for commerce and industry in China."

Behind the diplomatic facade of goodwill, however, lay simmering mutual distrust. For many Americans the Russian threat in east Asia now gave way to distrust of Japan's "yellow peril" (a term apparently coined by Germany's kaiser Wilhelm II). Racial animosities on the West Coast helped sour relations with Japan. In 1906, San Francisco's school board ordered students of Chinese, Japanese, and Korean descent to attend a separate public school. The Japanese government sharply protested the show of ethnic prejudice, and President Roosevelt managed to talk the school board into changing its policy. For its part, Japan agreed to limit sharply its issuance of visas to the

United States. This "Gentleman's Agreement" of 1907, the precise terms of which have never been revealed, halted the influx of Japanese immigrants and brought some respite to racial agitation in California.

THE UNITED STATES AND EUROPE   At the same time that the United States was expanding into Asia and the Caribbean, events in Europe also required attention. While Roosevelt was mediating the Russo-Japanese War in 1905, another crisis was brewing in Morocco, where the Germans and French fought for control. Roosevelt felt that the United States had something at stake in preventing the outbreak of a major war. At the behest of Germany, he talked the French and the British into attending an international conference at Algeciras, Spain, with American delegates present. Roosevelt then maneuvered the Germans into accepting his compromise proposal. The Act of Algeciras, signed in 1906, affirmed the independence of Morocco and guaranteed an open door for trade there. Roosevelt received the Nobel Peace Prize in 1906 for his work at Portsmouth and Algeciras. Despite all his bellicosity on other occasions, he had earned it.

Before Roosevelt left the White House, in March 1909, he celebrated America's rise to the status of a world power with one great flourish. In late 1907 he sent the entire U.S. Navy, by then second in strength only to the British fleet, on a grand tour around the world. It was the first such display of American naval might in the Pacific, and many feared the reaction of the Japanese, for whose benefit Roosevelt had in fact staged the show. They need not have worried, for in Japan the flotilla received the greatest welcome of all. Thousands of schoolchildren turned out, waving tiny American flags and singing "The Star-Spangled Banner" in English. The triumphal procession continued home by way of the Mediterranean and steamed back into American waters in early 1909, just in time to close out Roosevelt's presidency on a note of success.

Yet it was a success that would have mixed consequences. Roosevelt's ability to deploy American power abroad was burdened by a racist ideology shared by many prominent political figures of the time. He once told the graduates of the Naval War College that all "the great masterful races have been fighting races, and the minute that a race loses the hard fighting virtues . . . it has lost the right to stand as equal to the best." On another occasion he called war the best way to promote "the clear instinct for race selfishness" and insisted that "the most ultimately righteous of all wars is a war with savages." Such a belligerent and bigoted attitude would come back to haunt the United States in world affairs—and at home.

CHAPTER SUMMARY

- **New Imperialism** By the beginning of the twentieth century, the idea of a manifest destiny and American industrialists' need for new markets for their goods fueled America's "new imperialism." The ideology of social Darwinism was used to justify the colonization of less industrially developed nations as white Americans held that their own industrial superiority proved their racial superiority and, therefore, the theory of the survival of the fittest. White Americans rationalized further that they had a duty to Christianize and uplift "backward" peoples.

- **Religion and Imperialism** Protestant missionaries felt impelled to take Christianity to native peoples throughout the world. The evangelical missionaries were anti-Catholic and in the Philippines refused to distinguish between Catholic Filipinos and non-Christians. An indigenous people's acceptance of Christianity was the first step toward the loss of their indigenous culture.

- **War of 1898** Spain still had an extensive empire, and Cuba was one of its oldest colonies. When Cubans revolted against Spain in 1895, many Americans were sympathetic to their demand for independence. The insurrection was harshly suppressed, and sensational coverage in certain New York newspapers further aroused Americans' sympathy. Early in 1898, the publication of a letter by Spain's minister to the United States, Depuy de Lôme, which criticized President McKinley, and then the explosion of the U.S. battleship *Maine* in Havana Harbor propelled America into a war with Spain despite the reluctance of President McKinley and many business interests.

- **Results of the War of 1898** Although the Teller Amendment declared that the United States had no intention of annexing Cuba, America curtailed Cuba's freedom and annexed other territories taken from Spain in the War of 1898. Insurrection followed in the Philippines when insurgents saw that the islands would be administered by the United States. In the treaty that ended the war, America gained Puerto Rico as well as Guam and other islands in the Pacific. Meanwhile, Hawaii had been annexed during the war.

- **Big-Stick Diplomacy** As president, Theodore Roosevelt actively pursued an imperialist foreign policy, confirming the United States' new role as a world power. He arbitrated the treaty that ended the Russo-Japanese War, proclaimed the Open Door policy with China; allowed his administration to engage in dealings that made possible American control over the Panama Canal, and sent the navy's entire fleet around the world as a symbol of American might. He articulated an extension of the Monroe Doctrine whereby the United States might intervene in disputes between North and South America and other world powers.

CHRONOLOGY

1894	Republic of Hawaii is proclaimed
1895	Cuban insurrection breaks out against Spanish rule
1898	U.S. battleship *Maine* explodes in Havana Harbor
1898	War of 1898
1898	United States annexes Hawaii
1899	U.S. Senate ratifies the Treaty of Paris, ending the War of 1898
1899–1902	Filipino insurgents resist U.S. domination
1900	International alliance quells the Boxer Rebellion
1903	Panamanians revolt against Colombia
1904	Russo-Japanese War
1907	Great White Fleet circumnavigates the globe in a demonstration of America's rise to world-power status
1914	Panama Canal opens

KEY TERMS & NAMES

24

THE PROGRESSIVE ERA

FOCUS QUESTIONS

 wwnorton.com/studyspace

- Who were the progressives, and what were some of their major causes?
- Who were the muckrakers, and what impact did they have?
- What were Theodore Roosevelt's and William Taft's progressive programs, and what were those programs' goals?
- Why was the election of 1912 significant?
- How was Woodrow Wilson's progressivism different from Roosevelt's?

Theodore Roosevelt's emergence as a national leader coincided with the onset of what historians have labeled the Progressive Era (1890–1917). Progressivism was very diverse in its motives and methods. It was less an organized movement than a multifaceted response to the problems created by unregulated industrialization, unplanned urbanization, and unrelenting immigration. Progressives believed that American life was threatened by social instability, economic injustice, and political corruption. But progressives were not despondent. They were convinced that society could be improved through creative initiatives and concerted action. By working together in a spirit of community, individuals, organizations, and governments could ensure the "progress" of American society. And in fact they did so through an array of reforms and initiatives, some of which conflicted with one another. By the 1920s, progressives had implemented significant changes in all levels of government and across all levels of society.

The progressive impulse arose in response to many societal changes, the most powerful of which were the devastating depression of the 1890s and its attendant social unrest. The depression brought hard times to the cities, worsened already-dreadful factory conditions, deepened distress in rural areas, and provoked both the fears and the conscience of the rapidly growing middle and upper-middle classes. Although the United States boasted the highest per capita income in the world, it also harbored some of the poorest people. In 1900 an estimated 10 million of the 82 million Americans lived in desperate poverty. Most of the destitute were immigrants living in the major cities.

By the turn of the century, so many outraged activists were at work seeking to improve social conditions and political abuses that people began to speak of a Progressive Era, a time of fermenting idealism, moral and religious fervor, and constructive social, economic, and political change. The scope of the social crisis was so vast and complex that new remedies were needed. Old prejudices toward the poor and needy had to be changed. Reform needed to become more pragmatic and scientific. "The conditions of life forced by our civilization upon the poor in our great cities are undemocratic, unchristian, and unrighteous," said Vida Scudder, a settlement house leader. But the efforts to address widespread poverty had to be "wholly free from the spirit of social dogmatism and doctrinaire assertion. . . . As we become more practical, we also become better idealists."

ELEMENTS OF REFORM

Political progressives crusaded against the abuses of urban political bosses and corporate robber barons. Their goals were greater democracy, honest and efficient government, more effective regulation of big business and "special interests," and greater social justice for working people.

The progressive movement represented the animating spirit of the times rather than a single organized group or party. What reformers shared was a common assumption that the complex social ills and tensions generated by the urban-industrial revolution required expanding the scope of local, state, and federal government authority so as to elevate the public interest over private greed. Many progressives were motivated by religious beliefs that led some of them to concentrate on moral reforms such as the prohibition of alcoholic beverages and Sunday closing laws.

The "real heart of the movement," declared one reformer, was "to use the government as an agency of human welfare." Governments were now called upon to provide a broad range of direct public services: schools, good roads (a movement propelled first by cyclists and then by automobilists), conservation of natural resources, public health and welfare, care of the disabled, and farm loans and farm demonstration agents (county workers who visited farms to demonstrate new technology), among others. Such initiatives represented the first tentative steps toward what would become known during the 1930s and thereafter as the welfare state.

THE ANTECEDENTS OF PROGRESSIVISM   The progressive impulse began at the local level in the 1880s as a response to problems caused by industrialization and urbanization and only gradually emerged on the national level. Beginning in the large cities of the East and the Midwest, private citizens worked to improve basic public services such as sewerage, housing, and transportation. Reformers of local government believed in greater efficiency, less favoritism, and more expertise. They wanted to reorder government itself through detailed budgets, audits, and a more rationalized structure of government offices. Early efforts to improve public health, education, and factory conditions grew out of a desire to improve the administration and enforcement of local and state laws.

Another significant force in fostering the spirit of progressivism was the growing prominence of socialist critiques of living and working conditions. The Socialist party of the time, small but earnest and vocal, served as the left wing of progressivism. Most progressives found socialist remedies unacceptable, and the main progressive reform impulse grew in part from a desire to counter the growing appeal of socialist doctrines by promoting more mainstream reforms. More important in spurring progressive reform were social critics who dramatized the need for action through investigative journalism.

THE MUCKRAKERS   Chronic urban poverty, unsafe working conditions, infectious diseases, and child labor in unhealthy factories were complex social issues; remedying them would take more than an idealistic desire to effect change in government, public health, and working conditions. The public's consciousness needed to be raised, a process that required publicizing both scandals and festering social ills. A group of investigative journalists dubbed "muckrakers" rose to the challenge. These writers, who thrived on exposing corruption and social injustice, got their name when Theodore Roosevelt compared them to a character in John Bunyan's *Pilgrim's Progress:* "A man that could look no way but downwards with a muckrake in his hands." "Muckrakers are often indispensable to . . . society," Roosevelt said, "but only if they know when to stop raking the muck."

Henry Demarest Lloyd was one of the first muckrakers. His book *Wealth against Commonwealth* (1894) provided a critical examination of the Standard

Oil Company and other monopolies. Lloyd exposed the growth of corporate giants responsible to none but themselves, able to corrupt if not control governments. Lincoln Steffens, in a series of articles later collected into a book, *The Shame of the Cities* (1904), similarly revealed the prevalence of municipal corruption. Another early muckraker was Jacob Riis, a Danish immigrant who exposed slum conditions in *How the Other Half Lives* (1890). The chief outlets for these social critics were the popular middle-class magazines that began to flourish in the 1890s, such as the *Arena* and *McClure's.*

Cover of McClure's Magazine, 1902

This cover features Ida Tarbell's muckracking series on the Standard Oil Company.

Without the muckrakers, progressivism would never have achieved widespread popular support. In feeding a growing public appetite for facts about modern social problems, the muckrakers demonstrated one of the salient features of the progressive movement, and one of its central failures. The progressives were stronger on diagnosis than on remedy. They harbored a naive faith in the power of democracy. Reveal the facts, expose corruption, arouse public indignation, and bring government closer to the people, they assumed, and the correction of evils would follow automatically. The cure for the ills of democracy was, to progressive reformers, a more enlightened and engaged democracy.

FEATURES OF PROGRESSIVISM

DEMOCRACY   The most important progressive reform intended to democratize government and foster greater grassroots political participation was the direct primary, in which candidates would be nominated by the vote of all party members rather than by a few political bosses who selected candidates for the parties. After South Carolina adopted the first statewide primary in 1896, the concept spread within two decades to nearly every other state.

The primary was but one expression of a broad progressive movement for greater public participation in the political process. In 1898, South Dakota became the first state to adopt the initiative and referendum, procedures that allow voters to enact laws directly. If a designated number of voters petitioned to have a measure put on the ballot (the initiative), the electorate could then vote it up or down (the referendum). Oregon also adopted a spectrum of reform measures, including a voter-registration law (1899), the initiative and referendum (1902), the direct primary (1904), a sweeping corrupt-practices act (1908), and the recall (1910), whereby public officials could be removed by a public petition and vote. By 1920 nearly twenty states had adopted the initiative and referendum, and nearly a dozen had adopted the recall. The direct election of U.S. senators by the people, rather than by the state legislatures, was another progressive political reform. The popular election of senators required a constitutional amendment, and by 1912 the Senate finally agreed to the Seventeenth Amendment, which was ratified by the states in 1913.

EFFICIENCY   A second major theme of progressivism was the "gospel of efficiency." In the business world during the early twentieth century, Frederick W. Taylor, the original "efficiency expert," developed an array of scientific industrial management techniques designed to cut manufacturing costs and enhance productivity. Taylorism, as scientific management came to be known, promised to reduce waste through the detailed analysis of labor processes. By meticulously studying the time it took each worker to perform a task, Taylor prescribed the optimal technique for the average worker and established detailed performance standards for each job classification. The promise of higher wages, he believed, would motivate workers to exceed "average" expectations.

Instead, many workers resented Taylor's innovations. They saw in scientific management a tool to make employees work faster than was healthy or fair. Yet Taylor's controversial efficiency system brought concrete improvements in productivity, especially among those industries whose production processes were highly standardized and whose jobs were precisely defined.

In government the efficiency movement called for nonpartisan "experts" to replace bureaucrats and demanded the reorganization of agencies to prevent redundancy, establish clear lines of authority, and assign accountability to specific officials. The most ardent disciple of the principle of "scientific" government by experts was Wisconsin governor Robert M. La Follette, "Fighting Bob," who established a Legislative Reference Bureau staffed by professors and specialists to provide research, advice, and help in the drafting of legislation designed to curb the power of special interests and promote social justice. This "Wisconsin idea" of efficient government was widely publicized and copied by other states.

Two progressive ideas for making municipal government more efficient gained headway in the first decade of the new century. One, the commission system, was first adopted by Galveston, Texas, in 1901, when local government collapsed in the aftermath of a devastating hurricane that killed 6,000 people and destroyed half the town. The system placed ultimate authority in a board composed of elected administrative heads of city departments—commissioners of sanitation, police, utilities, and so on. By 1914 more than 400 towns and small cities across the country had adopted the commission system. The more durable idea, however, was the city-manager plan, under which a professional administrator ran the municipal government in accordance with policies set by the elected council and mayor. Staunton, Virginia, first adopted the plan in 1908. By 1914 the National Association of City Managers had heralded the arrival of a new profession.

Robert M. La Follette

A progressive proponent of expertise in government.

REGULATION   Of all the problems facing American society at the turn of the century, one engaged a greater diversity of reformers and elicited more solutions than any other: the regulation of giant corporations, which became a third major theme of progressivism. Beginning in the 1870s, states had tried to regulate the freight rates of railroads and the working conditions in other businesses, only to be thwarted by Supreme Court rulings. The judges declared that only the federal government could regulate companies involved in interstate commerce. By the 1890s the growth of monopolistic corporations had spurred reformers to act on a national level. Some progressives believed that the problems of concentrated economic power and its abuses should be left to business to work out for itself, a policy known as laissez-faire. Others advocated an active government policy of trust-busting in the belief that restoring old-fashioned competition was the best way to prevent economic abuses.

Efforts to restore the competitiveness of small firms proved unworkable, however, in part because breaking up large corporations was a very complicated endeavor. As a consequence, the main thrust of progressive reform over the years was toward regulation, rather than dissolution, of big businesses. To some extent, regulation and "stabilization" won acceptance among business leaders because whatever respect they paid to competition in principle, they preferred not to face it in practice. As time passed, however, regulatory agencies often came under the influence or control of those they were supposed to regulate.

SOCIAL JUSTICE   A fourth important feature of the progressive spirit was the impulse toward social justice, which manifested itself in an array of activities: the promotion of private charities; efforts by sanitation reformers to clean up cities through personal hygiene, municipal sewers, and public-awareness campaigns; and campaigns aimed at regulating child labor and the consumption of alcohol. Led by women, the settlement house movement of the late nineteenth century had spawned a corps of social workers and genteel reformers animated by religious ideals and devoted to the uplift of slum dwellers. By 1910 there were over 400 settlement houses in cities across the country.

Child labor

A young girl working as a spinner in a cotton mill in Vermont, 1910.

The settlement house movement, led by Jane Addams, Ellen Gates Starr, and Lillian Wald, manifested an important aspect of progressivism: women, mostly middle-class married women, were the driving force behind the grassroots progressive movement. In massive numbers they fanned out to address social ills. The Women's Christian Temperance Union (WCTU), founded in 1874, was the largest women's group in the nation at the end of the nineteenth century, boasting 300,000 members. Frances Willard, the dynamic president of the WCTU between 1879 and 1898, adopted the motto "do everything" to emphasize that all social problems

were interconnected. Members of
the WCTU strove to close saloons,
improve prison conditions, shelter
prostitutes and abused women and
children, support female labor unions,
and champion women's suffrage. The
WCTU also lobbied for the eight-
hour workday, the regulation of child
labor, better nutrition, the federal
inspection of food processors and
drug manufacturers, free kindergartens and public playgrounds, and
uniform marriage and divorce laws
across the states.

But with time it became apparent
that social evils extended beyond
the reach of private charities and
demanded government intervention.
Labor legislation was perhaps the
most significant reform to emerge
from the drive for social justice. It
emerged first at the state level. The

Frances Elizabeth Willard

Willard founded the WCTU and lobbied
for women's suffrage.

National Child Labor Committee, organized in 1904, led a movement for
state laws banning the still-widespread employment of young children.
Within ten years the committee helped foster in most states new laws
banning the labor of underage children (the minimum age varying from
twelve to sixteen) and limiting the hours older children might work.

Closely linked to the child-labor reform movement was a concerted effort to regulate the hours of work for women. Spearheaded by Florence
Kelley, the head of the National Consumers' League, this progressive crusade
promoted the passage of state laws addressing the long working hours imposed on women who were wives and mothers.

The Supreme Court pursued a curiously erratic course in ruling on
new state labor laws. In *Lochner v. New York* (1905), the Court voided a ten-
hour-workday law because it violated workers' "liberty of contract" to accept
any terms they chose. Then in *Muller v. Oregon* (1908), the high court
upheld a ten-hour-workday law for women. The justices relied largely on
sociological data that attorney Louis D. Brandeis presented regarding
the adverse effects of long hours on the health and morals of women. In

Bunting v. Oregon (1917), the Court accepted a ten-hour workday for both men and women but for twenty more years held out against state minimum-wage laws.

Legislation to protect workers against avoidable accidents gained momentum from disasters such as the 1911 fire at the Triangle Shirtwaist Company in New York City, in which 146 workers died, mostly Jewish and Italian immigrants, most of them women and many of them in their teens, because the owner kept the stairway doors locked to prevent theft. Workers trapped on the three upper floors of the ten-story building died in the fire or leaped to their death. Stricter building codes and factory-inspection acts followed.

PROGRESSIVISM AND RELIGION   Religion was a crucial source of energy for progressive reformers. Christians and Jews embraced the social gospel, seeking to express their faith through aid to the less fortunate. Jane Addams called the impulse to found settlement houses for the waves of immigrants arriving in American cities "Christian humanitarianism." She and others often used the phrase "social righteousness" to explain the connection between social activism and religious belief. Protestants, Catholics, and Jews worked closely together to promote state laws providing for minimum-wage levels and shorter workdays. Some of the reformers applied their crusade for social justice to organized religion itself. Frances Willard, who spent time as a traveling evangelist, lobbied church organizations to allow women to become ministers. As she said, "If women can organize missionary societies, temperance societies, and every kind of charitable organization . . . why not permit them to be ordained to preach the Gospel and administer the sacraments of the Church?"

PROHIBITION   For many progressive activists with strong religious convictions, the cause of liquor prohibition was the foremost societal concern. The WCTU had been battling the sale of alcoholic beverages since 1874, but the most successful political action followed the formation in 1893 of the Anti-Saloon League, an organization that pioneered the strategy of the single-issue pressure group. In 1913 the league endorsed an amendment to the Constitution prohibiting the sale of all alcoholic beverages, which was adopted by Congress in 1917. By the time it was ratified, two years later, state and local action had already dried up areas occupied by nearly three fourths of the nation's population.

ROOSEVELT'S PROGRESSIVISM

While most progressive initiatives originated at the state and local levels, national reform efforts began to appear around 1900. Theodore Roosevelt brought to the White House in 1901 an expansive vision of the presidency that well suited the cause of progressive reform. In one of his first addresses to Congress, he stressed the need for a new political approach. When the Constitution was first drafted in 1787, he explained, the nation's social and economic conditions were quite unlike those at the dawn of the twentieth century. Modern urban-industrial society required more active government involvement.

More than any other president since Abraham Lincoln, Roosevelt possessed an activist bent. Still, his initial approach to reform was cautious. He sought to avoid the extremes of socialism on the one hand and laissez-faire individualism on the other. A skilled political maneuverer, he broke the tradition of the Gilded Age presidents by serving as a very active chief executive. Roosevelt greatly expanded the role and visibility of the presidency, as well as the authority and scope of the federal government. He cultivated party leaders in Congress and steered away from such divisive issues as the tariff and regulation of the banks. And when he did approach the explosive issue of the trusts, he took care to reassure the business community. For him politics was the art of the possible. Unlike the more radical progressives and the doctrinaire "lunatic fringe," as he called it, he would take half a loaf rather than none at all.

THE TRUSTS On the issue of huge business trusts, Roosevelt endorsed the "sincere conviction that combination and concentration should be, not prohibited, but supervised and within reasonable limits controlled." In 1902 he proposed a "Square Deal" for all, calling for enforcement of existing anti-trust laws and stricter controls on big business. Effective regulation, he insisted, was better than a futile effort to restore small business by breaking up all giant corporations, which might be achieved only at a cost to the efficiencies of scale gained in larger operations.

Because Congress balked at regulatory legislation, Roosevelt forced the issue by a more vigorous federal prosecution of the Sherman Anti-Trust Act of 1890. He chose his target carefully. In the case against the sugar trust (*United States v. E. C. Knight and Company*, 1895), the Supreme Court had declared manufacturing strictly an *intrastate* activity. Most railroads, however, were beyond question engaged in *interstate* commerce and thus subject to federal

Roosevelt's duality

Theodore Roosevelt as an "apostle of prosperity" (top) and as a Roman tyrant (bottom). Roosevelt's energy, spirit, self-righteousness, and impulsiveness elicited sharp reactions.

authority. Consequently, in 1902, Roosevelt moved against the Northern Securities Company, a holding company merging the competing Great Northern and Northern Pacific Railroads. Roosevelt attacked the trust for essentially forming a monopoly, and in 1904, in *United States v. Northern Securities Company*, the Supreme Court ordered the combination dissolved. Roosevelt continued to use his executive powers to enforce the Sherman Anti-Trust Act, but he avoided conflict in Congress by proposing no further anti-trust legislation. Altogether, his administration brought about twenty-five anti-trust suits.

THE 1902 COAL STRIKE   Roosevelt also used the "big stick" against corporations in the coal strike of 1902. On May 12 some 150,000 members of the United Mine Workers (UMW) walked off the job in West Virginia and Pennsylvania. They demanded a 20 percent wage increase, a reduction in daily working hours from ten to nine, and formal recognition of their union by management. The operators dug in their heels and shut down the mines in an effort to starve out the miners, many of whom were immigrants from eastern Europe. One mine owner revealed the social prejudices of the era when he asserted, "The miners don't suffer—why, they can't even speak English."

Previous presidents such as Rutherford Hayes and Grover Cleveland had responded to labor unrest by dispatching federal troops. But the coal strike had not become violent when Roosevelt aggressively intervened. He was concerned about the approach of winter amid a nationwide coal shortage and the effects of the strike on the fall congressional elections—he told a friend that the public would blame the Republicans if coal were in short supply. By October 1902 the strike had caused the price of coal to soar, and hospitals and schools reported empty coal bins. Roosevelt thus decided upon a bold move: he invited leaders of both sides to a conference in Washington, where he appealed to their "patriotism, to the spirit that sinks personal considerations and makes individual sacrifices for the public good." The mine owners attended the conference but refused even to speak to the UMW leaders. The "extraordinary stupidity and temper" of the "wooden-headed" owners infuriated Roosevelt. With the conference deadlocked, the president threatened to take over the mines and send in the army to run them. Militarizing the mines would have been an act of dubious legality, but the owners feared that Roosevelt might do it and that public opinion would support him.

The coal strike ended on October 23 with an agreement to submit the issues to an arbitration commission named by the president. The agreement enhanced the prestige of both Roosevelt and the union's leader, although it produced only a partial victory for the miners. By the arbitrators' decision in 1903, the miners won a nine-hour workday but only a 10 percent wage increase and no union recognition by the owners.

AN EXPANDING GOVERNMENT   In 1903, Congress strengthened both anti-trust enforcement and government regulation by creating a new federal agency, the Department of Commerce and Labor, and passing the Elkins Act, which made it illegal for corporations to take, as well as to give, secret rebates to their preferred customers. The newly established Bureau of Corporations had no direct regulatory powers, but it did have a mandate to report on the activities of interstate corporations. Its findings could lead to anti-trust suits, but its purpose was rather to help corporations correct malpractices and avoid the need for lawsuits. Many companies cooperated, but others held back. When Standard Oil refused to turn over its records, the government brought an anti-trust suit that resulted in the company's dissolution in 1911. The Supreme Court ordered the American Tobacco Company broken up at the same time.

ROOSEVELT'S SECOND TERM

Roosevelt's energy and policies built a coalition of progressive- and conservative-minded voters who assured his election in his own right in 1904. The Democrats, having twice lost with William Jennings Bryan, turned to Alton B. Parker, who as chief justice of New York's supreme court, had upheld labor's right to the closed shop (requiring that all employees be union members) and the state's right to limit hours of work. Despite Parker's liberal record, party leaders presented him as a safe conservative. Yet the effort to portray their Democratic candidate as more conservative than Roosevelt proved a futile gesture for the party that had twice nominated Bryan. Despite Roosevelt's trust-busting, most business leaders, according to the *New York Sun,* preferred the "impulsive candidate of the party of conservatism to the conservative candidate of the party which the business interests regard as permanently and dangerously impulsive."

Roosevelt's invincible popularity and the sheer force of his personality swept him to an impressive victory of 7.6 million votes to Parker's 5.1 million, with 336 electoral votes for Roosevelt and 140 for Parker. The Democratic nominee Parker carried only the Solid South of the former Confederacy and two border states, Kentucky and Maryland. On election night, Roosevelt announced that he would not run again, a statement he later would regret.

LEGISLATIVE LEADERSHIP   Elected in his own right, Roosevelt approached his second term with heightened confidence and a stronger commitment to progressive reform. In 1905 he devoted most of his annual message to the need for greater regulation and control of big business. The independent Roosevelt took aim at the railroads first.

Roosevelt asked Congress to extend the authority of the Interstate Commerce Commission to give it more effective control over railroad freight rates. He had to mobilize all the pressure and influence at his disposal to push through the bill introduced by Representative Peter Hepburn of Iowa. Enacted in 1906, the Hepburn Act gave the ICC the power to set maximum freight rates. The commission no longer had to go to court to enforce its decisions. The Hepburn Act also extended the ICC's regulatory reach beyond railroads, to pipelines, freight companies, sleeping-car companies, bridges, and ferries.

On the very day after passage of the Hepburn Act, a growing movement for the regulation of meat packers, food processors, and makers of drugs and patent medicines reached fruition. Discontent with abuses in the processing of food and drugs had grown rapidly as a result of muckrakers' disclosures. The chief chemist of the Agriculture Department, for example, supplied telling evidence of harmful additives used in the preparation of "embalmed meat" and other food products. Others reported on dangerous ingredients in some patent medicines.

Perhaps the most telling blow against such abuses was struck by Upton Sinclair's novel *The Jungle* (1906), which graphically portrays the filthy conditions in Chicago's meatpacking industry. Roosevelt read *The Jungle*—and reacted quickly. He sent two federal agents to Chicago to investigate, and their report confirmed all that Sinclair had said. Soon Roosevelt and Congress were hammering out a bill to address the problems.

The meat industry

Pigs strung up along the hog-scraping rail at Armour's packing plant in Chicago, ca. 1909.

The Meat Inspection Act of 1906 required federal inspection of meats destined for interstate commerce and empowered officials in the Agriculture Department to impose sanitary standards. The Pure Food and Drug Act, enacted the same day, placed restrictions on the makers of prepared foods and patent medicines and forbade the manufacture, sale, or transportation of adulterated, misbranded, or harmful foods, drugs, and liquors.

With the achievements of 1903 and 1906, Theodore Roosevelt's campaign for regulatory legislation reached its chief goals and in the process moved the federal government a great distance from the laissez-faire policies that had prevailed before the turn of the century.

CONSERVATION   One of the most enduring legacies of Roosevelt's leadership was his energetic support for the emerging environmental conservation movement. Roosevelt was the first president to challenge the long-standing myth of America's having inexhaustible natural resources. In fact, Roosevelt declared that conservation of natural resources was the "great material question of the day." He and other early conservationists were convinced that the tradition of freewheeling individual and corporate exploitation of the environment must be supplanted by the scientific management of the nation's natural resources for the long-term public benefit. "The things that will destroy America," he said, "are prosperity at any price, peace at any price, safety first instead of duty first, the love of soft living and the get-rich-quick theory of life."

After the Civil War a growing number of conservation organizations and individual activists had begun to oppose the unregulated exploitation of natural resources and sought to preserve wilderness areas. Just as reformers promoted the regulation of business and industry for the public welfare, conservationists championed efforts to manage and preserve the natural environment for future generations. Among the first promoters of resource conservation were ardent sportsmen among the social elite (including Theodore Roosevelt), who worried that rapacious commercial hunters and trappers were killing game animals to the point of extermination. In 1886, for example, the sportsman-naturalist George Bird Grinnell, editor of *Forest and Stream*, founded the Audubon Society to protect wild birds from being decimated for their plumage. Two years later Grinnell, Roosevelt, and a dozen other recreational hunters formed the Boone and Crockett Club, named in honor of Daniel Boone and Davy Crockett, the legendary frontiersmen. The club's goal was to ensure that big-game animals and fish were protected for posterity, a goal shared by national monthly newspapers such as *American Sportsman*, *Forest and Stream*, and *Field and Stream*. By 1900 most states had enacted laws regulating game hunting and had created game refuges and wardens to enforce the new rules, much to the chagrin of local hunters, including Indians, who now were forced to abide by state laws designed to protect the interests of wealthy recreational hunters.

Along with industrialists concerned about water quality, Roosevelt and the sportsmen conservationists formed a powerful coalition promoting the rational government management of natural resources: rivers and streams, forests, minerals, and natural wonders. Those concerns, as well as the desire of railroad companies to transport tourists to destinations featuring majestic scenery, led the federal government to displace Native Americans in order to establish the 2-million-acre Yellowstone National Park in 1872 at the junction of the Montana, Wyoming, and Idaho Territories (the National Park Service would be created in 1916 after other parks had been established). In 1881, Congress created a Division of Forestry (now the U.S. Forest Service) within the Department of the Interior. At the same time, New York State officials established a Forest Commission in 1885 to manage timber in the vast state-owned acreage of the Adirondack Mountains. Seven years later the legislature created the 5-million-acre Adirondack Park. The legislature also imposed restrictions on hunting in state forests and created a "forest police" to enforce the new regulations. As president, Theodore Roosevelt created fifty federal wildlife refuges, approved five new national parks, and designated as national monuments unfit for economic use such natural treasures as the Grand Canyon.

In 1898, while serving as vice president, Roosevelt had endorsed the appointment of Gifford Pinchot, a close friend and the nation's first professional forester, as the head of the Division of Forestry. Pinchot and Roosevelt believed that conservation entailed the scientific management of natural resources to serve the public interest. Pinchot explained that the conservation movement sought to promote the "greatest good for the greatest number for the longest time."

Roosevelt and Pinchot championed the progressive notion of efficiency and government regulation. They were not romantics about nature, nor were they ecologists; they did not understand the complex interdependence of trees, plants, insects, and animals, nor did they appreciate the environmental benefits of natural fires. Instead, they were utilitarian progressives determined to ensure that entrepreneurs and industrialists exploited nature in appropriate ways. As Pinchot insisted, "The first principle of conservation is development." He sought to ensure the wisest "use of the natural resources now existing on this continent for the benefit of the people who live here now."

The president and Pinchot were especially concerned about the millions of acres of public land still owned by the government. Over the years vast

Roosevelt's western tour

Roosevelt visited Yellowstone National Park in 1903.

tracts of federal land had been given away or sold at discount prices to large business enterprises. Roosevelt and Pinchot were determined to end such carelessness. They championed the systematic management of natural resources by government experts trained to promote the most efficient public use of the environment. "Forestry," Pinchot explained, "is handling trees so that one crop follows another." He and Roosevelt opposed the mindless clear-cutting of entire forests for short-term profit and sought to restrict particular forests from any economic development. In fact, Roosevelt as president used the Forest Reserve Act (1891) to exclude from settlement or harvest some 172 million acres of federal timberland. Lumber companies were furious, but Roosevelt held firm. As he bristled, "I hate a man who skins the land."

From Roosevelt to Taft

Toward the end of his second term, Roosevelt crowed: "I have had a great time as president." But he was ready to move on, and he held to his 1904 decision not to run again. Instead, he sought to have his secretary of war, William Howard Taft, replace him, and the Republican Convention ratified the choice on its first ballot in 1908. The Democrats, whose conservative strategy had backfired in 1904, decided to give William Jennings Bryan one more chance. Still vigorous at forty-eight, Bryan retained a faithful following, but once again it was not enough. In the end, voters opted for Roosevelt's chosen successor, leaving Bryan only the southern states plus Nebraska, Colorado, and Nevada. The real surprise of the election was the strong showing of the Socialist party candidate, labor hero Eugene V. Debs, who attracted 421,000 votes, illustrating the mounting intensity of working-class unrest.

Born to a prominent Cincinnati family, Taft boasted more experience in public service than any other president since Martin Van Buren. After graduating second in his class at Yale, he had progressed through appointive

William Howard Taft

Speaking at Manassas, Virginia, in 1911.

offices, from assistant prosecutor, tax collector, and judge in Ohio to solicitor in the Justice Department, federal judge, governor general in the Philippines, and secretary of war. The presidency was the only elective office he ever held. Later he would be appointed chief justice of the Supreme Court (1921–1930), a job more suited to his temperament.

Taft never felt comfortable in the White House. He once observed that whenever someone said "Mr. President," he looked around for Roosevelt. The political dynamo in the family was his wife, Helen, who had wanted the presidency more than he. One of the major tragedies of Taft's presidency was that Helen Taft suffered a debilitating stroke soon after they entered the White House, and for most of his term she remained unable to serve as his political adviser.

TARIFF REFORM   A former student of the social Darwinist William Graham Sumner, Taft had absorbed the laissez-faire views of his mentor and therefore differed with orthodox Republican protectionism. Against Roosevelt's advice he had promised a tariff reduction during the campaign, and true to his word he called a special session of Congress to consider his proposal eleven days after his inauguration. But if Taft seemed bolder in pressing an issue that Roosevelt had skirted, he proved less adroit in shepherding legislation through Congress.

A reduced tariff passed the House with surprising ease. Before the Senate passed the bill, however, it made more than 800 changes, most of which raised tariff rates. Outraged by the obvious catering to special state and local interests, a group of ten progressive Republicans joined the Democrats in an unsuccessful effort to defeat the bill. Taft at first agreed with them but then, fearful of a party split, backed the Republican majority and agreed to an imperfect bill. Temperamentally conservative, inhibited by scruples about interfering too much with the legislative process, Taft drifted into the orbit of the Republican Old Guard and quickly alienated the progressive wing of his party, whom he tagged "assistant Democrats."

BALLINGER AND PINCHOT   In 1910, President Taft's policies drove the wedge deeper between the conservative and progressive Republican factions. What came to be known as the Ballinger-Pinchot controversy made Taft appear to be a less reliable custodian of Roosevelt's conservation policies than he actually was. The controversy arose after Taft's secretary of the interior, Richard A. Ballinger, turned over coal-rich federal lands in Alaska to a group of investor friends. Apparently without Ballinger's knowledge, this group had already agreed to sell part of the land to a mining syndicate. When Gifford Pinchot, chief of forestry, revealed the scam, Taft fired Pinchot for insubordination. A joint congressional investigation later exonerated Ballinger of all charges of fraud or corruption, but conservationist suspicions created such pressure that he resigned in 1911.

Joseph Cannon

Caricature of Cannon enjoying too much decision-making power as House Speaker.

In firing Pinchot, Taft had acted according to the strictly legal view that his training had taught him to value. But the unsavory circumstances surrounding the incident tarnished Taft's public image. Events had conspired to cast the president in a conservative role at a time when progressive sentiment was riding high. The result was a sharp setback in the congressional elections of 1910, first by the widespread defeat of pro-Taft candidates in the Republican primaries and then by the election of a Democratic majority in the House and enough Democrats in the Senate to allow progressive Republicans to wield the balance of power.

TAFT AND ROOSEVELT In 1910, Theodore Roosevelt returned from extended travels abroad. With news accounts highlighting Taft's "betrayal" of Roosevelt's programs, the former president's followers urged him to take action. After hesitating for several months, Roosevelt again entered the political arena. At a speech in Kansas, he issued a stirring call for an array of new federal regulatory laws, a federal social-welfare program, and new measures of direct democracy, including the old Populist demands for the initiative, recall, and referendum on a nationwide basis. Thereafter, Roosevelt intensified his criticism of the Taft administration.

Equally critical of Taft was Senator Robert La Follette of Wisconsin, who in 1911 helped organize the National Progressive Republican League and soon became its leading candidate for the Republican party nomination. A militant reformer fiercely committed to greater government regulation of business and civil rights for all Americans, La Follette was more of a crusader than a politician. Complicating matters for the Republicans, Roosevelt officially threw his hat into the ring in 1912. Even though many of La Follette's supporters rushed to embrace the ex-president, the Wisconsin idealist stubbornly refused to give way. He felt that Roosevelt was not genuinely committed to the sweeping reforms necessary for a truly progressive America.

The rebuke implicit in Roosevelt's decision to run against Taft, his chosen successor, was in many ways undeserved. During Taft's first year in office, one political tempest after another had left his image irreparably damaged. The three years of solid achievement that followed could not restore its luster or reunite his divided party. Taft had at least attempted tariff reform, which Roosevelt had never dared. And in the end his administration set aside more public land for conservation in four years than

The Bull Moose candidate in 1912

A skeptical view of Theodore Roosevelt.

Roosevelt's had in nearly eight, and it brought more anti-trust suits, by a score of eighty to twenty-five. Taft also established the Bureau of Mines and the federal Children's Bureau (1912). He supported both the Sixteenth Amendment (1913), which authorized a federal income tax, and the Seventeenth (1913), which provided for the popular election of senators instead of their appointment by state legislatures.

Despite Taft's progressive record, Roosevelt turned against his former friend and lieutenant. Brusquely pushing aside La Follette's claim to the progressive Republican mantle, Roosevelt won most of the Republican primaries in 1912, even in Taft's Ohio. But such popular support was no match for Taft's advantages as president and party leader. The Taft forces nominated their man at the national convention by the same steamroller tactics that had nominated Roosevelt in 1904. Outraged at such "naked theft," the Roosevelt delegates issued a call for a Progressive party convention, which assembled in Chicago on August 5. The new third-party supporters were a curious mixture of social gospel clergymen and laymen, college presidents, professors, journalists, businessmen, and social workers. Roosevelt told the group he felt "fit as a bull moose" in accepting their nomination. Now it was the Democrats' turn.

WILSON'S PROGRESSIVISM

WILSON'S RISE The emergence of Thomas Woodrow Wilson as the Democratic nominee in 1912 climaxed a political rise even more rapid than that of Grover Cleveland. In 1910, before his entering the race for election as governor of New Jersey, Wilson had been president of Princeton University but had never run for public office. Born in Staunton, Virginia, in 1856, the son of a stern Presbyterian minister, he had grown up in Georgia and the Carolinas during the Civil War and Reconstruction.

Driven by a sense of destiny and duty, Wilson was resolute, humane, rigid, and self-exacting to a fault. He nurtured a righteous commitment to principle, and his fits of tenacious inflexibility would prove to be his greatest weakness. Running as a reform candidate, Wilson was elected governor of New Jersey. After his election he pressured New Jersey lawmakers to enact a workers' compensation law, a corrupt-practices law, measures to regulate public utilities, and ballot reforms. Such strong leadership in a state known as the home of the trusts because of its lenient incorporation laws brought Wilson to national attention.

In the spring of 1911, a group of southern Democrats in New York opened a Wilson presidential campaign headquarters, and Wilson set forth on strenuous tours to all regions of the country, denouncing special privilege and political bossism. Wilson believed that the president of the country should be as active in directing legislation as in steering the administration and guiding the enforcement of laws. In calling for a stronger presidency, Wilson expressed views closer to Roosevelt's than to Taft's. He likewise shared Roosevelt's belief that politicians should promote the general welfare rather than narrow special interests. And like Roosevelt he was critical of big business, organized labor, socialism, and agrarian radicalism.

Despite a fast start the Wilson campaign seemed headed for defeat by convention time, and House Speaker Champ Clark of Missouri seemed destined to win the nomination. On the fourteenth ballot, however, William Jennings Bryan, having decided that party conservatives were behind Clark, went over to Wilson; others followed, and Wilson captured the nomination.

THE ELECTION OF 1912   The 1912 presidential election involved four candidates: Wilson and Taft represented the two major parties, while Eugene Debs ran as a Socialist, and Roosevelt headed the Progressive party ticket. They all shared a basic progessive assumption that the old notion of do-nothing government was bankrupt; modern conditions required active intervention to promote the general welfare of American society.

No sooner did the campaign open than Roosevelt's candidacy almost ended. While stepping into a car in Milwaukee, he was shot by a crazed man. The bullet went through his overcoat, spectacles case, and fifty-page speech, then fractured a rib before lodging just below his right lung. Roosevelt demanded that he be driven to the auditorium to deliver his speech. In a dramatic gesture he showed the audience his bloodstained shirt and punctured text and vowed, "It takes more than this to kill a bull moose."

With Taft and Debs trailing, the campaign settled down to a debate over the competing ideologies of the two front-runners: Roosevelt's New Nationalism and Wilson's New Freedom. The fuzzy ideas that Roosevelt fashioned into his New Nationalism had first been presented systematically in *The Promise of American Life* (1909), a widely influential book by Herbert Croly, a New York journalist. Its central point was that progressives must give up Jeffersonian prejudices against big government and use the power of government to achieve democratic ends in the public interest.

Roosevelt's New Nationalism would enable government to promote social justice and enact such reforms as graduated income and inheritance taxes, workers' compensation for disabling injuries or illnesses, regulations to improve the working conditions of women and children, and a stronger Bureau of Corporations. These ideas and more went into the platform of his

Progressive party, which called for a federal trade commission with sweeping authority over business and a tariff commission to set rates on a "scientific basis."

Before the end of his administration, Wilson would be swept into the current of such New Nationalism, too, but initially he adhered to the decentralizing anti-trust traditions of his party. Wilson relied heavily for his political stances on Louis D. Brandeis, the progressive lawyer from Boston, who focused Wilson's thought much as Croly had focused Roosevelt's. Brandeis's design for Wilson's New Freedom program differed from Roosevelt's New Nationalism in its belief that the federal government should restore competition rather than regulate monopolies. It required eliminating all trusts, lowering tariffs, and breaking up the concentration of financial power on Wall Street. Brandeis and Wilson also dreamed of turning over most federal social programs to the states and cities. In this sense they saw the vigorous expansion of federal power as a temporary necessity, not a permanent condition. Having restored competition and diffused power and programs, the national government would revert to its aloof heritage. Roosevelt, who was convinced that both corporate concentration and an expanding federal government were permanent developments, dismissed the New Freedom as mere nostalgia.

The Republican schism between Taft and Roosevelt opened the way for Woodrow Wilson to win by 435 electoral votes to 88 for Roosevelt and 8 for Taft. The 1912 election was significant in a number of respects. First, it was a high-water mark for progressivism. The candidates debated the basic issues in a campaign unique in its focus on vital alternatives and its highly philosophical tone. And the Socialist party, the left wing of progressivism, polled over 900,000 votes for Eugene V. Debs, about 6 percent of the total vote, its highest proportion ever.

Wilson's reforms

Woodrow Wilson campaigning from a railroad car.

Second, the election gave the Democrats effective national power for the first time since the Civil War. For two years during the second administration of Grover Cleveland, from 1893 to 1895, they had held the White House and majorities in both houses of Congress, but they had quickly fallen out of power during the severe economic depression of the 1890s. Now, under

Wilson, the Democrats again held the presidency and enjoyed majorities in the House and Senate.

Third, Wilson's election brought southerners back into the orbit of national and international affairs in a significant way for the first time since the Civil War. Five of Wilson's ten cabinet members were born in the South, and pious William Jennings Bryan, the secretary of state, was an idol of the southern masses. At the president's right hand, and one of the most influential members of the Wilson circle, was "Colonel" Edward M. House of Texas. Wilson described House as "my second personality." Southern legislators, by virtue of their seniority, held most committee chairmanships. As a result,

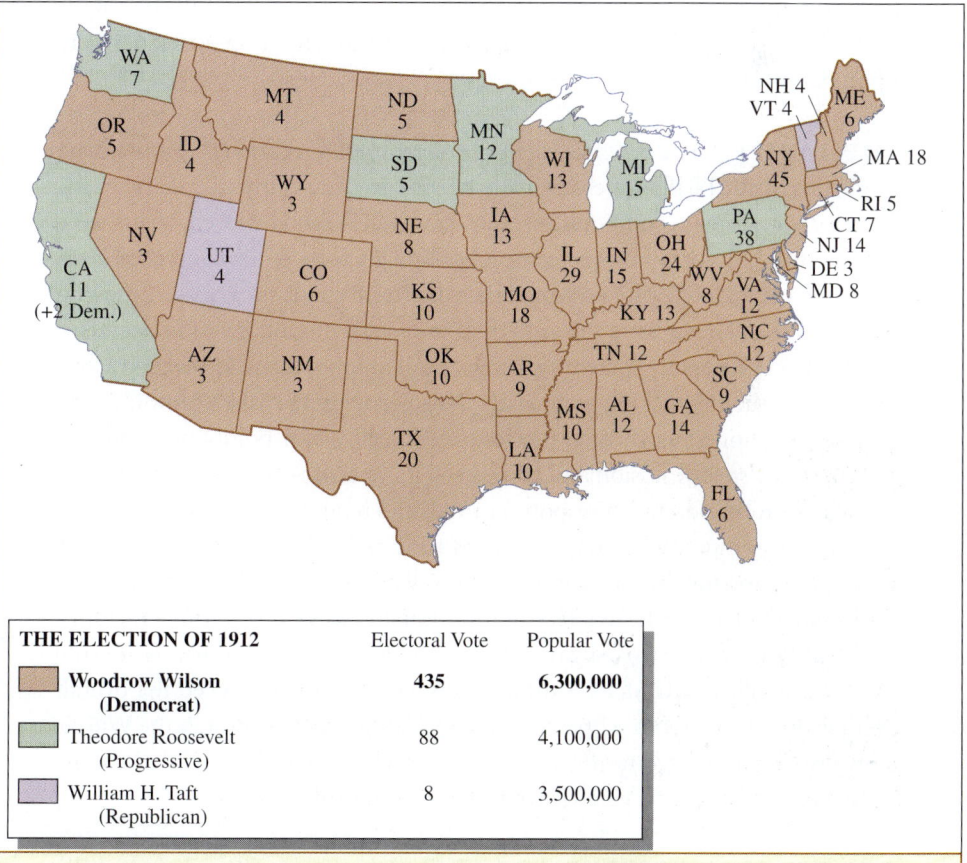

THE ELECTION OF 1912	Electoral Vote	Popular Vote
Woodrow Wilson (Democrat)	**435**	**6,300,000**
Theodore Roosevelt (Progressive)	88	4,100,000
William H. Taft (Republican)	8	3,500,000

Why was Taft so unpopular? How did the division between Roosevelt and Taft give Wilson the victory? Why was Wilson's victory in 1912 significant?

much of the progressive legislation of the Wilson era would bear the names of the southern Democrats who guided the bills through Congress.

WILSONIAN REFORM   Wilson's 1913 inaugural address vividly expressed the ideals of economic reform that inspired many progressives. "We have been proud of our industrial achievements," he observed, "but we have not hitherto stopped thoughtfully enough to count the human cost." He promised a lower tariff and a new nationally regulated banking system. Whereas Roosevelt had been a strong president by force of personality, Wilson became a strong president by force of conviction. The president, he argued, must become the dynamic voice in national affairs. Wilson courted popular support, but he also courted members of Congress through personal contacts, invitations to the White House, and speeches to Congress. He used patronage power to reward friends and punish enemies. Though he might have acted through a bipartisan progressive coalition, he chose instead to rely upon party loyalty.

THE TARIFF   The new president's leadership met its first test on the issue of tariff reform. Tariffs were originally needed to protect infant American industries from foreign competition. Now, however, Wilson believed, tariffs were being abused by corporations to suppress foreign competition and keep consumer prices high. He often claimed that the "tariff made the trusts," believing that tariffs had encouraged the growth of industrial monopolies and degraded the political process by spawning armies of paid lobbyists who invaded Congress each year. In attacking high tariffs, Wilson sought to strike a blow for consumers and honest government. He acted quickly and boldly, summoning Congress to a special session and addressing it in person—the first president to do so since John Adams. In response to Wilson's request for lower tariff duties to promote competition, Congress voted for tariff reductions, with only four Democrats crossing the party line, and the bill passed the House easily. The opposition centered in the Senate, the traditional graveyard of tariff reform. In the end, Louisiana's two "sugar senators" were the only Democrats to vote against the bill. The Underwood-Simmons Tariff of 1913 reduced the overall average duty from about 37 percent to about 29 percent. Although the Wilson administration lowered tariff rates, it raised revenues with the first federal income tax levied under the newly ratified Sixteenth Amendment.

THE FEDERAL RESERVE ACT   Before the new tariff had cleared the Senate, the administration proposed the first major banking and currency reform since the Civil War. Ever since Andrew Jackson had killed the second

Bank of the United States in the 1830s, the nation had been without a central bank. Instead, the country's money supply was administered by hundreds of private banks. Such a decentralized system fostered instability and inefficiency. It also gave disproportionate influence to banks centered in New York City. By 1913 virtually everyone had agreed that the banking system needed restructuring. Wilson told Congress that a federal banking system was needed to ensure that "the banks may be the instruments, not the masters, of business and of individual enterprise and initiative."

The Federal Reserve Act of 1913 created a new national banking system with twelve regional Federal Reserve banks, each owned by member banks in its district. All national banks became members of the new Federal Reserve System; state banks could join if they wished. Each member bank had to subscribe 6 percent of its capital to the Federal Reserve bank and deposit a portion of its reserve there.

This arrangement made it possible to expand both the money supply and bank credit in times of high business activity or as the level of borrowing increased. A Federal Reserve Board exercised general supervision over the activities of the member banks and adjusted interest rates to fight inflation or stimulate business. It is hard to exaggerate the significance of the passage of the Federal Reserve Act. Through Wilson's skillful leadership, Congress took a major step in providing the nation with a sound yet flexible currency system and at the same time helped decentralize the money supply.

ANTI-TRUST LAWS Wilson made trust-busting the central focus of the New Freedom because the concentration of economic power had continued to grow despite the Sherman Anti-Trust Act and the federal watchdog agency, the Bureau of Corporations. During the summer of 1914, Wilson decided to make a strong Federal Trade Commission (FTC) the cornerstone of his anti-trust program. Created in 1914, the

"Reading the Death Warrant"

Woodrow Wilson's plan for banking and currency reform spells the death of the "money trust," according to this cartoon.

five-member commission replaced Roosevelt's Bureau of Corporations and assumed new powers to define "unfair trade practices" and issue "cease-and-desist" orders when it found evidence of unfair competition.

Henry D. Clayton, an Alabama Democrat, drafted an anti-trust bill, passed in 1914, that outlawed practices such as price discrimination (charging different customers different prices for the same goods); "tying" agreements, which limited the right of dealers to handle the products of competing manufacturers; and corporations' acquisition of stock in competing corporations. In every case, however, conservative forces in the Senate qualified these provisions by tacking on the weakening phrase "where the effect may be to substantially lessen competition" or words of similar effect. And conservative southern Democrats and northern Republicans amended the Clayton Anti-Trust Act to allow for broad judicial review of the FTC's decisions, further weakening its freedom of action. In accordance with the president's recommendation, however, corporate officials were made personally responsible for any violations.

Agrarian reformers allied with organized labor won a stipulation in the Clayton Act declaring that farm and labor organizations were not per se unlawful combinations in restraint of trade. Injunctions in labor disputes, moreover, were not to be handed down by federal courts unless "necessary to prevent irreparable injury to property." President Wilson himself admitted that the act did little more than affirm the right of unions to exist by forbidding their dissolution for being in restraint of trade.

Administration of the anti-trust laws generally proved disappointing to the more vehement progressives under Wilson. The Justice Department offered advice to business owners interested in arranging matters so as to avoid anti-trust prosecutions. The appointment of conservatives to the Interstate Commerce Commission and the Federal Reserve Board won plaudits from the business world and profoundly disappointed progressives.

SOCIAL JUSTICE Wilson's political agenda focused on restoring economic opportunity and competition. He had in fact never been a strong progressive of the social-justice persuasion. He carried out his promises to lower the tariff, reorganize the banking system, and strengthen the anti-trust laws, but he was not inclined to go much further. The New Freedom was now complete, he wrote late in 1914; the future would be "a time of healing because [it would be] a time of just dealing."

The sweep of events and the pressures of more far-reaching progressives pushed Wilson beyond where he intended to go on some points. Yet Wilson retained several social blind spots. Although he endorsed state action for women's suffrage, he declined to support a federal suffrage amendment because his party platform had not done so. He withheld support from federal child-labor legislation because he regarded it as a state matter, and he opposed a bill providing federal loans for strapped farmers on the grounds that it was "unwise and unjustifiable to extend the credit of the government to a single class of the community."

PROGRESSIVISM FOR WHITES ONLY Like many other progressives, Woodrow Wilson showed little interest in the plight of African Americans. In fact, he shared many of the racist attitudes prevalent at the time. Although Wilson never joined the Ku Klux Klan and he denounced its "reign of terror," he sympathized with its motives of restoring white rule in the postwar South and relieving whites of the "ignorant and hostile" power of the black vote. As a student at Princeton, Wilson had detested the enfranchisement of blacks, arguing that Americans of Anglo-Saxon origin would always resist domination by "an ignorant and inferior race."

Later, as a politician, Wilson courted black voters, but he rarely consulted African American leaders and repeatedly avoided opportunities to associate with them in public. Many of the southerners he appointed to his cabinet

The privileged elite

President Wilson and the First Lady ride in a carriage.

were uncompromising racists who systematically segregated the employees in their agencies. When black leaders protested these actions, Wilson replied that such racial segregation was intended to eliminate "the possibility of friction" in the federal workplace.

PROGRESSIVE RESURGENCE   The need to weld a winning political coalition in 1916 pushed Wilson back on the road of reform. Progressive Democrats were restless, and after war broke out in Europe in 1914, further divisions in the party arose over defense preparedness and foreign policy. At the same time the Republicans were repairing their own rift. The Progressive party showed little staying power in the 1914 midterm election, and Roosevelt showed little will to preserve it. Most observers recognized that Wilson could gain reelection only by courting progressives of all parties. In 1916 the president scored points with them when he nominated Louis D. Brandeis to the Supreme Court. Conservatives waged a vigorous battle against Brandeis, but Senate progressives rallied to win confirmation of the social-justice champion as the first Jewish member of the Supreme Court.

Wilson, meanwhile, began to embrace the broad program of farm and labor reforms he had earlier spurned. The agricultural sector continued to suffer from a shortage of capital. To address the problem, Wilson supported a proposal to set up special rural banks to sponsor farm loans. With this boost the Federal Farm Loan Act became law in 1916. It created twelve Federal Land banks, which paralleled the Federal Reserve banks and offered low-interest loans to farmers.

Farmers with the newfangled automobiles had more than a passing interest as well in the Federal Highways Act of 1916, which provided dollar-matching contributions to states with highway departments that met certain federal standards. The measure authorized the distribution of $75 million over five years and marked a sharp departure from Jacksonian opposition to internal improvements at federal expense, just as the Federal Reserve System departed from Jacksonian banking principles. Although the argument that highways were one of the nation's defense needs had weakened constitutional scruples against the act, the Highways Act still restricted support to "post roads" used for the delivery of mail. A renewal act in 1921 would mark the beginning of a systematic network of numbered U.S. highways.

The progressive resurgence of 1916 broke the logjam on workplace reforms as well. Advocates of child-labor legislation persuaded Wilson to overcome doubts about its constitutionality and sign the Keating-Owen Act, which excluded from interstate commerce goods manufactured by children under the age of fourteen. But the Supreme Court soon ruled it unconstitutional on the grounds that regulation of interstate commerce could not extend to the conditions of labor. On the other hand, the Supreme Court upheld the Adamson Act of 1916, which mandated the eight-hour workday for railroad workers.

In Wilson's first term, progressive government reached its zenith. Progressivism had conquered the old premise that the government is best that governs least. Progressivism, a loose amalgam of agrarian, business, government, and social reform, amounted in the end to a movement for active government on behalf of the public interest.

LIMITS OF PROGRESSIVISM

Like all great historic movements, progressivism contained elements of paradox and irony. Despite all the talk of greater democracy at the turn of the century, it was also the age of disenfranchisement of African Americans in the South and xenophobic reactions to "new" immigrants. The initiative and referendum, supposedly democratic reforms, proved subject to manipulation by well-financed publicity campaigns. And much of the public policy of the time came to be formulated by experts and members of appointed boards, not by broad segments of the population. There is a fine irony in the fact that the drive to increase the political role of ordinary people paralleled efforts to strengthen executive leadership and exalt professional expertise. This much-ballyhooed Progressive Era of efficiency and expertise, in business as well as government, generated a situation in which more and more key decisions were made by unelected policy makers.

Progressivism was largely a middle-class movement in which the poor and unorganized had little influence. It is surprising that a movement so dedicated to democratic rhetoric should experience so steady a decline in voter participation. In 1912, the year of Roosevelt's Bull Moose campaign, voting dropped off by between 6 and 7 percent. The new politics of issues and charismatic leaders proved to be less effective in turning out voters than traditional party organizations and bosses had been. And by 1916 the optimism of an age that looked to infinite progress was already confronted by a vast slaughter. Europe had stumbled into a horrific war, and America would soon be drawn in. The twentieth century, which had dawned with such bright hopes, held in store episodes of unparalleled carnage.

End of Chapter Review

- **Progressivism** Progressives believed that industrialization and urbanization were negatively affecting American life. They were middle-class idealists in both political parties who sought reform and regulation in order to ensure social justice. Many progressives wished to curb the powers of local political machines and establish honest and efficient government. They also called for an end to child labor, laws promoting safety in the workplace; a ban on the sale of alcoholic beverages, legislation curbing trusts, and women's suffrage.

- **Muckrakers** Theodore Roosevelt named the journalists whose works exposed social ills "muckrakers." New inexpensive popular magazines, such as *McClure's*, published articles about municipal corruption, horrendous conditions in meat-packing plants and urban slums, and predatory business practices. By raising public awareness of these issues, muckrakers contributed to major changes in the workplace and in governance.

- **Square Deal Program** President Roosevelt used his executive position to endorse his Square Deal program, which included regulating trusts, arbitrating the 1902 coal strike, regulating the railroads, and cleaning up the meat and drug industries. Taft continued to bust trusts and reform the tariff, but Republican party bosses, reflecting their big business interests, ensured that the tariff reductions were too few to satisfy the progressives in the party. Roosevelt decided to seek the Republican presidential nomination in 1912 because of progressives' disillusionment with Taft.

- **Presidential Election of 1912** In 1912, after the Republicans renominated Taft, Roosevelt's supporters bolted the convention, formed the Progressive party, and nominated Roosevelt. Although some Democratic progressives supported Roosevelt, the split in the Republican party led to Woodrow Wilson's success. Having won a majority in both houses of Congress as well as the presidential election, the Democrats effectively held national power for the first time since the Civil War.

- **Wilsonian Progressivism** Although Wilson was a progressive, his approach was different from Roosevelt's. His New Freedom program promised less federal intervention in business and a return to such traditional Democratic policies as a low tariff. Wilson began a rigorous anti-trust program and oversaw the establishment of the Federal Reserve System. He opposed federal programs promoting social justice and initially withheld support for federal regulation of child labor and a constitutional amendment guaranteeing women's suffrage. A southerner, he believed blacks were inferior and supported segregation.

CHRONOLOGY

1902	Theodore Roosevelt attempts to arbitrate the coal strike
1902	Justice Department breaks up Northern Securities Company
1903	Congress passes the Elkins Act
1906	Upton Sinclair's *The Jungle* is published
1906	Congress passes the Meat Inspection Act and the Pure Food and Drug Act
1908	Supreme Court issues *Muller v. Oregon* decision
1909	William Taft is inaugurated president
1911	Triangle Shirtwaist Company fire
1913	Congress passes the Federal Reserve Act
1914	Congress passes the Clayton Anti-Trust Act
1916	Louis Brandeis is nominated to fill a seat on the Supreme Court

KEY TERMS & NAMES

25

AMERICA AND
THE GREAT WAR

FOCUS QUESTIONS wwnorton.com/studyspace

- Why did Woodrow Wilson involve the United States in Mexico's affairs?
- What were the causes of World War I in Europe?
- Why did the United States enter the Great War in Europe?
- How did Wilson promote his peace plan?
- Why did the United States fail to ratify the Treaty of Versailles?
- What were the consequences of the war at home and abroad?

Throughout the nineteenth century the United States reaped the benefits of its geographic distance from the wars that plagued Europe. The Atlantic Ocean provided a welcome buffer. During the early twentieth century, however, the nation's comfortable isolation ended. Expanding world trade entwined American interests with the fate of Europe. In addition, the development of steam-powered ships and submarines meant that foreign navies could threaten American security. At the same time, the election of Woodrow Wilson in 1912 brought to the White House a stern and often self-righteous moralist determined to impose his standards for right conduct on renegade nations. This combination of circumstances made the outbreak of war in Europe in 1914 a profound crisis for the United States, a crisis that would transform the nation's role in international affairs.

WILSON AND FOREIGN AFFAIRS

President Woodrow Wilson had no experience or expertise in foreign relations. The former college professor admitted before taking office, "It would be an irony of fate if my administration had to deal chiefly with foreign affairs." But events in Latin America and Europe were to make the irony all too real. From the summer of 1914, when a catastrophic world war erupted in Europe, foreign relations increasingly preoccupied Wilson's attention.

Although lacking in international experience, Wilson did not lack ideas or convictions about global issues. He saw himself as a man of destiny who would help create a new world order governed by morality and idealism rather than crass national interests. Both he and Secretary of State William Jennings Bryan believed that America had a religious duty to promote democracy around the world. How to foster such democratic idealism and self-determination abroad, however, remained a thorny issue, as Wilson soon discovered in responding to rapidly changing events on his own continent.

INTERVENTION IN MEXICO Wilson's first challenge emerged within American's southern neighbor, Mexico. Between 1876 and 1910, Porfirio Díaz had dominated Mexico. As military dictator he had suppressed opposition and showered favors upon wealthy allies and foreign investors. Eventually, however, the dictator's grip slipped, and in 1910 popular resentment boiled over in revolt. Revolutionary armies occupied Mexico City, and in 1911 Díaz fled.

The leader of the rebellion, Francisco Madero, proved unable to manage the tough customers attracted to the revolt by the scramble for power. In 1913, Madero's chief of staff, General Victoriano Huerta, assumed power, and Madero was murdered soon afterward. President Wilson challenged the legitimacy of Huerta's violent coup but expressed sympathy with a revolutionary faction led by Venustiano Carranza and began to put diplomatic pressure on Huerta. "I am going to teach the South American republics to elect good men," he vowed to a British diplomat.

Early in 1914, Wilson removed an arms embargo against Mexico in order to help Carranza's forces, and he stationed U.S. warships off Veracruz to halt foreign arms shipments to Huerta. On April 9, 1914, several American sailors gathering supplies in Tampico strayed into a restricted area and were arrested. The Mexican officials quickly released them and apologized to the U.S. naval commander. There the incident might have ended, but the naval officer demanded that the Mexicans salute the American flag. Wilson backed him up and won from Congress authority to use force to bring Huerta to

Pancho Villa

Villa (center) and his followers rebelled against the president of Mexico and antagonized the United States with violent attacks against "gringos."

terms. Before the Tampico incident could be resolved, Wilson sent a naval force to Veracruz. U.S. marines and sailors went ashore on April 21, 1914, occupying the city at a cost of 19 American lives; at least 200 Mexicans were killed.

In Mexico the U.S. occupation aroused the opposition of all factions, and Huerta rallied support against a foreign invasion. At this juncture, Wilson accepted a mediation offer by the ABC (Argentina, Brazil, and Chile) powers, which proposed the withdrawal of U.S. forces, the removal of Huerta, and the installation of a provisional government. Huerta refused to step down, but the moral effect of the proposal, his isolation abroad, and the growing strength of his foes soon forced him to leave office. The Carranzistas entered Mexico City, and the Americans left Veracruz. Wilson's "missionary diplomacy" seemed to have worked. In 1915 the United States and several Latin American governments recognized Carranza as president of Mexico.

But no sooner had the Carranzistas taken power than they began to squabble among themselves for the spoils of office. The most incendiary confrontation occurred between Carranza and his foremost general, the popular Pancho Villa, a charismatic former bandit who shrewdly claimed to represent "the people" behind the revolution. Enraged by America's recognition of Carranza as the de facto leader of Mexico, Villa, in early 1916, led an attack that murdered sixteen American mining engineers. It was a deliberate attempt to provoke U.S. intervention, discredit Carranza, and build up Villa as an opponent of the "gringos." Two months later Villa's band of renegades entered Columbus, New Mexico, burned the town, and killed seventeen Americans.

A furious Woodrow Wilson sent General John J. Pershing and a force of 11,000 soldiers deep inside Mexico. For nearly a year, Pershing's troops chased Villa through northern Mexico, but missing their quarry, they returned home in 1917. Carranza then pressed his own war against the bandits and in 1917 put through a new liberal constitution. Mexico was establishing a more orderly government, almost in spite of Wilson's actions rather than because of them.

PROBLEMS IN LATIN AMERICA   In the Caribbean, Wilson found it as hard to act on his democratic ideals as it was in Mexico. During President Taft's term, from 1909 to 1913, the United States had practiced "dollar diplomacy." The policy had its origin in 1909, when Taft had personally cabled the Chinese government on behalf of American investors interested in forming an international consortium to finance railroad lines in China. In Latin America, dollar diplomacy worked differently and with somewhat more success. The idea was to encourage American bankers to help prop up the finances of shaky Caribbean governments.

One of the first applications of Wilsonian idealism to foreign policy came when the president renounced dollar diplomacy. The government, he declared, was not supporting any "special groups or interests." Despite Wilson's public stand against using military force to back up American investments, however, he kept U.S. marines in Nicaragua, where they had been sent by President Taft in 1912 to prevent renewed civil war. There they would stay almost continuously until 1933. In 1915, Wilson dispatched more marines, this time to Haiti, after the country experienced two successive revolutions and subsequent government disarray. The U.S. forces stayed until 1934. Turmoil in the Dominican Republic brought U.S. marines to that country in 1916, where they remained until 1924. The presence of U.S. military force in the region only worsened the already prevalent irritation at "Yankee imperialism."

AN UNEASY NEUTRALITY

During the summer of 1914, problems in Mexico and Central America loomed larger in Wilson's thinking than the gathering storm in Europe. When the thunderbolt of war struck Europe in August 1914, Americans were

How did the European system of alliances spread conflict across all of Europe? How was World War I different from previous wars? How did the war in Europe lead to ethnic tensions in the United States?

stunned. Whatever the troubles in Mexico, whatever disorders and interventions agitated other countries, it seemed unreal that civilized Europe could descend into such an orgy of destruction. At the beginning of the twentieth century, Europe had been peaceful and prosperous. The great powers had worked out what seemed to be a balance of power among themselves. No one imagined a new—and unnecessary—industrialized form of war erupting that would assume such horrible proportions and involve such unprecedented ruthlessness. Between 1914 and 1921 the war was directly responsible for the deaths of over 9 million combatants and the horrible wounding of 15 million more; it would produce at least 3 million widows and 6 million orphans. The war's horror and destructiveness, its obscene butchery and ravaged landscapes, defied belief.

World War I erupted when the Austrian archduke Franz Ferdinand was assassinated by a Serbian nationalist. Austria-Hungary's determination to punish Serbia, and Russia's military mobilization in sympathy with Slavic Serbia, triggered a conflict between the two major European systems of alliances: the Triple Alliance, or Central Powers (Germany, Austria-Hungary, and Italy), and the Triple Entente, or Allied Powers (France, Great Britain, and Russia). The sequence of decisions leading to World War I had unfolded with little thought to their consequences. When Russia refused to stop its army's mobilization, Germany, which backed Austria-Hungary, declared war on Russia on August 1, 1914, and on Russia's ally France two days later. Germany then invaded Belgium to get at France, an action that brought Great Britain into the war on August 4. Japan, eager to seize German holdings in the Pacific, declared war on August 23, and Turkey entered on the side of the

Verdun

A landscape image from Verdun, taken immediately after the battle, shows how the firepower ravaged the land.

Central Powers on October 29. Although allied with the Central Powers, Italy initially stayed out of the war and in 1915 struck a bargain by which it joined the Allied Powers.

The First World War proved to be unlike any previous conflict in its scope and carnage. Machine guns, high-velocity rifles, aerial bombing, poison gas, flame throwers, land mines, long-range artillery, and armored tanks changed the nature of warfare and produced massive casualties and widespread destruction. Over 65 million men served in the armed forces on both sides, and over 9 million combatants were killed in action. Another 19 million were wounded. During the Battle of Verdun, in France, which lasted from February to December 1916, some 32 million artillery shells were fired—1,500 shells for every square meter of the battlefield. Such devastating firepower ravaged the landscape, turning farmland and forests into wasteland.

Trench warfare gave the First World War its lasting character. Most of the great battles involved hundreds of thousands of men crawling out of their muddy, rat-infested trenches and crossing a no-man's-land to attack enemy positions, only to be pushed back a day or a week later. In addition to the dangers of enemy fire, soldiers were forced to deal with flooded trenches and

Fighting on the western front

A gun crew firing on entrenched German positions, 1918.

terrible diseases such as trench fever and trench foot, which could lead to amputation. Lice and rats were constant companions. The stench was unbearable. Soldiers on both sides ate, slept, and fought among the dead and amid the reek of death.

INITIAL REACTIONS   As the trench war along the western front in Belgium and France stalemated, casualties soared and pressure for U.S. intervention increased. On July 1, 1916, the first day of the Battle of the Somme, 20,000 British soldiers were killed and 40,000 others were wounded—in less than twenty-four hours. Shock in the United States over the sudden outbreak of war in Europe gave way to gratitude that an ocean stood between America and the killing fields. President Wilson repeatedly urged Americans to remain "neutral in thought as well as in action."

That was more easily said than done. More than a third of Americans were first- or second-generation immigrants who retained strong ties to their old country. Among the 13 million immigrants from the countries at war, the 8 million German Americans were by far the largest group, and the 4 million Irish Americans harbored a deep-rooted enmity toward England. These groups instinctively leaned toward the Central Powers.

Old-line Americans, largely of British origin, supported the Allied Powers. Those Americans also identified with France, which had contributed to American culture and ideas and to independence itself. Britain and France, if not their ally Russia, seemed the custodians of democracy, while Germany seemed the embodiment of autocracy and militarism. If not a direct threat to the United States, Germany would pose at least a potential threat if it destroyed the balance of power in Europe. High officers of the U.S. government were pro-British in thought from the outset of the war.

A STRAINED NEUTRALITY   At first the war in Europe brought a slump in American exports and the threat of a depression, but by the spring of 1915 the Allies' demand for food and military supplies generated an economic boom. France and Britain bought so much from the United States that they soon needed loans to continue making purchases. Early in the war, Secretary of State William Jennings Bryan, a strict pacifist, declared that loans to any warring nation were "inconsistent with the true spirit of neutrality." Technically he was correct, but Wilson, for all his public professions of neutrality, was in fact determined to aid Great Britain. He quietly began approving credit to sustain trade with the Allies. American investors would advance over $2 billion to the Allies, mostly Britain and France, before the United States entered the war, and only $27 million to Germany.

The administration nevertheless clung to its official stance of neutrality through two and a half years of warfare in Europe and tried to uphold the traditions of "freedom of the seas," which had guided American policy since the Napoleonic Wars of the early nineteenth century. Transatlantic trade assumed a new importance as the German army's advance through Belgium toward Paris bogged down into the stalemate of trench warfare. In a war of attrition, survival depended upon access to supplies, and in such a war British naval power counted for a great deal. In November 1914 the British declared the whole North Sea a war zone and sowed it with mines. Four months later they announced that they would seize ships carrying goods produced by or intended for their enemies.

NEUTRAL RIGHTS AND SUBMARINES British actions, including the blacklisting of companies that traded with the enemy and censoring the mail, raised old issues of neutral rights, but the German reaction introduced an entirely new question. In the face of the British blockade, whereby only submarines could venture out to harass the enemy, the German government proclaimed a war zone around the British Isles. Enemy ships in those waters would be sunk by submarines, the Germans declared. As the chief advantage of U-boat (*Unterseeboot*) warfare was in surprise, the German decision violated the established international procedure of stopping an enemy vessel and providing for the safety of passengers and crew before sinking it. Since the British sometimes flew neutral flags as a ruse, neutral ships in this war zone would also be in danger.

The United States pronounced the new German submarine policy "an indefensible violation of neutral rights" and warned that Germany would be held to "strict accountability" for any destruction of American lives and property. Then, on May 7, 1915, a German U-boat torpedoed the passenger liner *Lusitania,* which exploded and sank within eighteen minutes. Before the ship's departure from New York, bound for Liverpool, the German embassy had published warnings in American newspapers against travel to the war zone, but 128 Americans were nonetheless among the 1,198 persons lost.

Americans were outraged. To quiet the uproar over the *Lusitania,* Wilson urged patience: "There is such a thing as a man being too proud to fight. There is such a thing as a nation being so right that it does not need to convince others by force that it is right." But his previous demand for "strict accountability" forced him to make a stronger response. On May 13, Secretary of State Bryan reluctantly demanded that the Germans abandon unrestricted submarine warfare, disavow the sinking of the *Lusitania,* and pay reparations to the victims' families. The Germans responded that the passenger ship was armed

THE LOST CUNARD STEAMSHIP LUSITANIA

The *Lusitania*

Americans were outraged when a German torpedo sank the *Lusitania* on May 7, 1915.

(which it was not) and carried a secret cargo of small arms and ammunition (which it did). A second State Department message, on June 9, repeated American demands in stronger terms. Bryan, unwilling to risk war over the issue, resigned in protest. His successor, Robert Lansing, signed the note.

In response to the uproar over the *Lusitania,* the German government had secretly ordered U-boat captains to avoid sinking large passenger vessels. When, despite the order, two American lives were lost in the sinking of the New York–bound British liner *Arabic,* the German government declared on September 1, 1915, "Liners will not be sunk by our submarines without warning and without safety of the lives of noncombatants, provided that the liners do not try to escape or offer resistance." With this so-called Arabic Pledge, Wilson's resolute stand seemed to have won a victory for his policy.

THE DEBATE OVER PREPAREDNESS   The *Lusitania* incident and, more generally, the quarrels over protecting neutral commerce during wartime contributed to a growing demand in the United States for a stronger army and navy. After the *Lusitania* sinking the outcry from preparedness advocates grew into a clamor. In his annual message in 1915, Wilson alerted Congress to his plans for war preparedness. The response was far from unanimous. Progressives and pacifists, especially in the rural South and the West, opposed military expansion.

Wilson eventually accepted a compromise between advocates of an expanded force under federal control and advocates of a traditional citizen army. The National Defense Act of 1916 expanded the regular army from 90,000 to 175,000 and permitted a gradual enlargement to 223,000. It also increased the National Guard to 440,000. The Naval Construction Act of 1916 authorized between $500 million and $600 million for a three-year shipbuilding program.

Forced to relent on military preparedness, progressive opponents of a buildup insisted that the financial burden should rest upon the wealthy executives of companies trading with Great Britain they held responsible for pushing the nation toward war. The income tax became their weapon. Supported by a groundswell of popular support, legislators wrote into the Revenue Act of 1916 changes that doubled the basic income tax rate from 1 to 2 percent, lifted the surtax on income over $2 million to 13 percent, added an estate tax graduated up to a maximum of 10 percent, levied a 12.5 percent tax on gross receipts of munitions makers, and added a new tax on corporations. The new taxes amounted to the most clear-cut victory for radical progressives in the entire Wilson period, a victory that Wilson supported in preparation for the upcoming presidential election.

THE ELECTION OF 1916 As the 1916 election approached, Republicans hoped to regain their normal electoral majority, and Theodore Roosevelt hoped to be their leader again. But in 1912 he had committed the deadly sin of bolting his party. His eagerness for the United States to enter the war also scared many voters. Needing somebody who would draw Bull Moose Progressives back into the fold, the Republican regulars turned to Justice Charles Evans Hughes, a progressive governor of New York from 1907 to 1910. On the Supreme Court since 1910, he had neither endorsed a candidate in 1912 nor spoken out on foreign policy.

The Democrats, as expected, chose Woodrow Wilson once again. Their platform endorsed a program of social-welfare legislation and a reasonable degree of military preparedness. The party further endorsed women's suffrage and pledged support for a postwar league of nations to enforce peace with collective-security measures against aggressors. The Democrats' most popular issue was a pledge to keep the nation out of the war in Europe. The peace theme, refined in the slogan "He kept us out of war," became the rallying cry of the Wilson campaign.

The candidates in the 1916 presidential election were remarkably similar. Both Wilson and Hughes were the sons of preachers; both were attorneys and former professors; both had been progressive governors; both were

Peace with honor

Woodrow Wilson's policies of neutrality proved popular in the 1916 campaign.

known for their pristine integrity. Theodore Roosevelt highlighted the similarities between them when he called the bearded Hughes a "whiskered Wilson." Wilson, however, proved to be the better campaigner. In the end, Wilson's twin pledges of peace and progressivism, brought victory. The final vote showed a Democratic sweep of the Far West and the South, enough for narrow victories in the Electoral College, by 277 to 254, and in the popular vote, by 9 million to 8.5 million. Wilson also carried many social-justice progressives who in 1912 had supported Roosevelt's Bull Moose campaign.

LAST EFFORTS FOR PEACE   Immediately after the election, Wilson offered to mediate an end to the European war, but neither side was willing to abandon its major war aims. Wilson then made one more appeal, in the hope that public opinion would force the hands of the warring governments. Speaking before the Senate, he asserted that this would have to be a "peace without victory," for only a "peace among equals" could endure.

Although Wilson did not know it, he was already too late. Exactly two weeks before he spoke, German military leaders had decided to wage unrestricted submarine warfare on all shipping in the Atlantic. Faced with weakening resources in a war of attrition, the Germans took the calculated risk of provoking American anger in the hope of scoring a quick knockout.

On January 31, 1917, Germany announced the new policy, effective the next day: all vessels would be sunk without warning.

On February 3, 1917, Wilson informed a joint session of Congress that the United States had broken diplomatic relations with the German government. He added that he still did not believe the Germans would do what they said they felt at liberty to do—only overt acts would persuade him that they intended to sink neutral ships. In case of such acts, he would take measures to protect American seamen and citizens.

Then, on March 1, Wilson learned that the British had intercepted an important message from the German foreign minister Arthur Zimmermann to his ambassador in Mexico. The note offered an alliance and financial aid to Mexico in case of war between the United States and Germany. In return for attacking the United States, Mexico would recover "the lost territory in Texas, New Mexico, and Arizona." All this was contingent on war with the United States, but an electrified public read in it an aggressive intent. Later in March, on the other side of the world, another bombshell burst when a revolution overthrew Russia's czarist government and established the provisional government of a Russian republic. The fall of the czarist autocracy gave Americans the illusion that all the major Allied powers were now fighting for constitutional democracy—an illusion that was shattered in November 1917, when the Bolsheviks, led by Vladimir Lenin, seized power in Russia and established a Communist dictatorship.

AMERICA'S ENTRY INTO THE WAR

In March 1917, German submarines did the unthinkable: they sank five American merchant vessels. On April 2, Wilson asked Congress to recognize that imperial Germany and the United States were at war. As he insisted, "The world must be made safe for democracy." The war resolution passed the Senate by a vote of 82 to 6 on April 4. The House concurred, 373 to 50, and Wilson signed the measure on April 6, 1917.

How had matters come to this, less than three years after Wilson's proclamation of neutrality? Prominent among the various explanations of America's entrance into the war were the effects of British propaganda and America's substantial trade with the Allies, which some observers credited to self-interested munitions makers. Some Americans thought German domination of Europe would be a threat to U.S. security, especially if it meant the destruction or capture of the British navy. Such factors, however, would not have been decisive without the issue of submarine warfare. That issue need not have become decisive either, since such neutrals as Norway, Sweden, and Denmark took relatively heavier losses yet stayed out of the war. But once Wilson had taken a stand for the traditional rights of neutral nations and noncombatants, he was to some extent at the mercy of decisions by the German high command.

AMERICA'S EARLY ROLE   The scope of America's role in the European war remained unclear for a time. Few on either side of the Atlantic expected more than a token U.S. military effort. Despite Congress's preparedness measures, the army remained small and untested. The navy also was largely undeveloped. But the U.S. Navy made a major contribution when it persuaded the Allies to adopt a system of escorting merchant ships in group convoys, which resulted in an impressive decrease in Allied shipping losses to German submarines.

Within a month of America's declaration of war, the British and French requested money for more supplies, a request Congress had anticipated in the Liberty Loan Act, which added $5 billion to the national debt in "liberty bonds." Of this amount, $3 billion could be lent to the Allied Powers. The United States was also willing to furnish naval support, financial credits, supplies, and munitions. But to train a large army, equip it, and send it across a submarine-infested ocean seemed out of the question.

The thrill of American liberty

This Liberty Loan poster urges immigrants to do their duty for their new country by buying government bonds.

The United States agreed to send a token military force to bolster Anglo-French morale, and on June 26, 1917, the first American contingent, about 14,500 men commanded by General John J. Pershing, began to disembark on the French coast. After reaching Paris, Pershing decided that the war-weary Allies would be unable to mount an offensive by themselves. He therefore requested that

Wilson send 1 million American troops by the following spring, and the president obliged.

When the United States entered the war, the combined strength of the regular army and National Guard was only 379,000; at the end it would be 3.7 million. The need for such large numbers of troops forced Wilson to authorize conscription. Under the Selective Service Act of May 18, 1917, all men aged twenty-one to thirty (later, eighteen to forty-five) had to register for the draft and could be drafted for military service. In the course of the war, about 2 million American men crossed the Atlantic, and about 1.4 million of them saw combat.

MOBILIZING A NATION   One of the most obvious effects of American entry into the war was a dramatic increase in the size and power of the federal government. Complete economic mobilization on the home front was necessary to conduct the war efficiently. In 1916, Congress had created a Council of National Defense, which in turn set up other wartime agencies. The U.S. Shipping Board, organized in 1917, within two years was constructing more than forty steel and ninety wooden ships monthly. In 1917, Congress created a Food Administration, headed by Herbert Hoover, a future president, who sought to raise crop production while reducing civilian consumption of foodstuffs. "Food will win the war" was the slogan. Hoover directed a conservation campaign that "Hooverized" the country with "meatless Tuesdays," "wheatless Wednesdays," "porkless Saturdays," the planting of victory gardens, and the creative use of leftovers. The Fuel Administration introduced the country to daylight saving time and "heatless Mondays" to save fuel.

The War Industries Board (WIB), established in 1917, soon became the most important of all the mobilization agencies. Wilson summoned Bernard Baruch, a brilliant Wall Street investor, to head the board, giving him a virtual dictatorship over the economy. The WIB could allocate raw materials, tell manufacturers what to produce, order construction of new plants, and with presidential approval, fix prices. Despite such efforts, however, the unprecedented mobilization process was often chaotic. Men were drafted only to discover there were no uniforms, weapons, or housing for them. Most of the artillery used by the American army in France had to be acquired from the Allies.

A NEW LABOR FORCE   The closing off of immigration from Europe during the war and the movement of almost 4 million men into the armed services created a labor shortage. To meet it, women, African Americans, and other ethnic minorities were encouraged to enter industries and engage in agricultural activities heretofore dominated by white men. Northern businesses sent recruiting agents into the Deep South to find workers for their factories and mills, and over 400,000 southern blacks began the Great Migration northward during the war years, a mass movement that continued unabated through the 1920s and changed the political dynamics of northern cities. Mexican Americans followed the same migratory pattern. Recruiting agents and newspaper editors portrayed the North as the "land of promise" for southern blacks suffering from their region's depressed agricultural economy and rising racial intimidation and violence. By 1930 the number of African Americans living in the North was triple that of 1910.

But the newcomers were not always welcomed above the Mason-Dixon line. Many white workers resented the new arrivals, and racial tensions sparked clashes across the country. In 1917 over forty African Americans and nine whites were killed during a riot over employment in a defense plant in East St. Louis, Illinois. Two years later the toll of a Chicago race riot was nearly as high, with twenty-three African Americans and fifteen whites left dead. In these and other incidents of racial violence, the pattern was the same: whites angered by the influx of southern blacks into their communities would seize upon an incident as an excuse to rampage through black neighborhoods, killing, burning, and looting while white policemen looked the other way or encouraged the mobs.

For women, American intervention in World War I had more positive effects. Initially women supported the war effort in traditional ways. They helped organize war-bond and war-relief drives, conserved foodstuffs and war-related materials, supported the Red Cross, and joined the army nurse corps. But as the scope of the war widened, both government and industry sought to mobilize women workers for service on farms, loading docks, and railway crews, as well as in the armaments industry, machine shops, steel and lumber mills, and chemical plants. Many women leaders saw such opportunities as a breakthrough. "At last, after centuries of disabilities and discrimination," said a speaker at a Women's Trade Union League meeting in 1917, "women are coming into the labor [force] and festival of life on equal terms with men."

In fact, however, war-generated changes in female employment were limited and brief. About 1 million women participated in "war work," but they usually were young, single, and already working outside the home. Most returned to their previous jobs once the war ended. In fact, male-dominated unions encouraged women to revert to their stereotypical domestic roles after the war. The Central Federated Union of New York baldly insisted that "the same patriotism which induced women to enter industry during the war should induce them to vacate their positions after the war." The anticipated gains of women in the workforce failed to materialize. In 1920 the 8.5 million working women made up a smaller percentage of the labor force than had working women in 1910. Still, one tangible result of women's contributions to the war effort was Woodrow Wilson's decision to endorse women's suffrage. In the fall of 1918, he told the Senate that giving women the vote was "vital to the winning of the war."

WAR PROPAGANDA War needs also led the government to mobilize public opinion. On April 14, 1917, eight days after the declaration of war, President Wilson established the Committee on Public Information. Its executive director, George Creel, a Denver journalist, sold Wilson on the idea that the best approach to influencing public opinion was "expression, not repression"—propaganda instead of censorship. Creel organized a propaganda machine to convey the Allies' war aims to the people and, above all, to the enemy, where it might encourage public pressure to end the fighting.

The Beast of Berlin

A scene from the movie *The Beast of Berlin*, which gave audiences a propagandistic view of World War I.

CIVIL LIBERTIES   By arousing public opinion to a frenzy, the war effort spawned grotesque campaigns of "Americanism" and witch-hunting. Wilson had foreseen these consequences. "Once lead this people into war," he told a newspaper editor, "and they'll forget there ever was such a thing as tolerance." Popular prejudice equated anything German with disloyalty. Schools even dropped German-language courses.

While mobs hunted spies and chased rumors, the federal government stalked bigger game, with often absurd results. The Espionage and Sedition Acts of 1917 and 1918 suppressed criticism of government leaders and war policies. These laws led to more than 1,500 prosecutions and 1,000 convictions. Such repression disillusioned many progressives. Senator Robert La Follette declared that those engaged in such a "witch-hunt" were trying "to throw the country into a state of terror, to coerce public opinion, stifle criticism, suppress discussion of the issues of the war, and put a quietus on all opposition. It is time for the American people to assert and maintain their rights."

These acts targeted radicals. Eugene V. Debs, who had polled over 900,000 votes as the Socialist candidate for president in 1912, was arrested and sentenced to ten years in prison for encouraging draft resistance. In 1920, still in jail, he polled nearly 1 million votes for president.

In an important decision just after the war, the Supreme Court upheld the Espionage and Sedition Acts. *Schenck v. United States* (1919) sustained the conviction of a man for circulating anti-draft leaflets among members of the armed forces. In this case, Justice Oliver Wendell Holmes observed, "Free speech would not protect a man in falsely shouting fire in a theater, and causing a panic." The Sedition Act applied where there was "a clear and present danger" that free speech in wartime might create evils Congress had a right to prevent.

AMERICA AT WAR

American troops played little more than a token role in the European fighting until early 1918, by which time the Allied position had turned desperate. In October the Italian lines collapsed in the face of the Austrian offensive. In November, having suffered millions of casualties and widespread food and ammunition shortages, the provisional government of the Russian republic succumbed to a revolution led by Vladimir Lenin and his Bolshevik party, which promised the Russian people "peace, land, and bread." With German troops deep in Russian territory and armies of "White" Russians organizing to resist the Bolsheviks, Lenin concluded a separate peace with the Germans, the Treaty of Brest-Litovsk, on March 3, 1918. The Central Powers were then free to concentrate their forces on the western front, and the American war effort thus became a "race for France," to restore the balance of strength in that arena. The French premier Georges Clemenceau appealed to the Americans to accelerate their mobilization. "A terrible blow is imminent," he predicted to an American journalist. "Tell your Americans to come quickly."

THE WESTERN FRONT   On March 21, 1918, Clemenceau's prediction came true when the Germans began the first of several offensives in France and Belgium to try to end the war before the Americans arrived in force. By May 1918 there were 1 million fresh U.S. troops in Europe, and for the first time they made a difference. During early June a marine brigade blocked the Germans at Belleau Wood, and army troops took Vaux and opposed the Germans at Château-Thierry. Though these relatively modest actions had limited military significance, their effect on Allied morale was immense.

The turning point in France, the Second Battle of the Marne, erupted on July 15, 1918. The Germans assaulted the French lines, but within three days they had stalled, and the Allies began to roll the German front back into

The Meuse-Argonne offensive

U.S. soldiers fire an artillery gun in Argonne, France.

ENGLAND

NORTH
SEA

NETHERLANDS

Rotterdam

Oostende
Dieppe
Ghent
Antwerp

Calais
Ypres
Armentières
Lille
Brussels

BELGIUM

Cologne

GERMANY

Scheldt River

Koblenz

Boulogne

Strait of Dover

Mons

Meuse River

Rhine River

Arras
Cambrai

Somme River
Oise River

Amiens
Cantigny

Sedan

Aisne River

LUXEMBOURG

Compiègne
Soissons
BELLEAU WOOD
Château-Thierry
Reims
Vesle R.
Épernay

ARGONNE FOREST

Étain
Verdun
Metz

Paris
Versailles

Marne River

FRANCE

Seine River

St.-Mihiel
Nancy

Strasbourg

Moselle River

**WORLD WAR I,
THE WESTERN FRONT, 1918**

- - - Western front, March 1918
——— German offensive, spring 1918
———▶ Allied counteroffensive
——— Western front, November 1918

| 0 | | 50 Miles |
| 0 | | 50 Kilometers |

SWITZERLAND

Why was the war on the western front a stalemate for most of World War I? What was the effect of the arrival of the American troops? Why was the Second Battle of the Marne the turning point of the war?

Belgium. On September 12 an army of more than 500,000 staged the first strictly American offensive of the war, aimed at German forces at St.-Mihiel. Within three days the Germans had pulled back. Two weeks later the massive Meuse-Argonne offensive employed U.S. divisions in a drive toward the rail center at Sedan, which supplied the entire German front. The largest U.S. action of the war resulted in 117,000 American casualties, including 26,000 dead. All along the front from Sedan to Flanders, the Germans were in retreat. "America," wrote a German commander, "thus became the decisive power in the war."

Meanwhile, in an effort to prevent Allied supplies stockpiled in Russia from falling into German hands and to encourage the counter-revolutionary Russian "Whites" in their civil war against the "Reds," fourteen Allied nations sent troops into eastern Russia. On August 2, 1918, some 8,000 Americans joined the expedition and remained on Russian soil until April 1920. But the Allied intervention in Russia was a colossal failure. The Bolsheviks were able to consolidate their power and defeat the Whites. Lenin and the Soviets never forgave the West for attempting to thwart their revolution.

THE FOURTEEN POINTS   As the conflict in Europe was ending, neither the Allies nor the Central Powers, despite Wilson's prodding, had stated openly what they hoped to gain from the bloodletting. Wilson insisted that the Americans had no selfish war aims. "We desire no conquest, no dominion," he stressed in his war message. Unfortunately for his idealistic purpose, the Bolsheviks later published copies of secret treaties in which the British and French had promised territorial gains in order to win Italy, Romania, and Greece to their side. When an Interallied Conference in Paris late in 1917 failed to agree on a statement of aims, Wilson formulated his own.

With advice from a panel of experts, Wilson drew up a peace plan that would be labeled the Fourteen Points. These he presented to a joint session of Congress on January 8, 1918, "as the only possible program" for peace. The first five points called for open diplomacy, freedom of the seas, removal of trade barriers, armaments reduction, and an impartial adjustment of colonial claims based upon the interests of the populations involved. Most of the remaining points called upon the Central Powers to evacuate occupied lands and allow political self-determination for various nationalities, a crucial principle for Wilson. Point 14, the capstone in Wilson's thinking, called for the formation of a "league" of nations to protect global peace. When the Fourteen Points were made public, African American leaders asked the president to add a fifteenth point: an end to racial discrimination. Wilson did not respond.

Wilson sincerely believed in the Fourteen Points, but they also served important political purposes. One of their aims was to keep Russia in the war by stating a more progressive purpose—a vain hope, as it turned out. Another was to reassure the citizens of the Allied Powers that they were involved in a noble cause. A third was to drive a wedge between the governments of the Central Powers and their people by offering a reasonable peace. But the chaos into which Central Europe descended in 1918 as Germany and Austria-Hungary verged on starvation and experienced socialist uprisings took matters out of Wilson's hands.

THE END OF THE WAR   On October 3 a new German chancellor made the overtures for peace on the basis of the Fourteen Points. The Allies accepted the Fourteen Points as a basis of a peace treaty but with two significant reservations: the right to discuss freedom of the seas further and the demand for reparations (financial compensation to the victors) for war damages.

Meanwhile, German morale plummeted, culminating in a naval mutiny. Germany's allies, Bulgaria, Turkey, and Austria-Hungary, dropped out of the war during the early fall of 1918. On November 9 the kaiser, head of the German Empire, abdicated, and a German republic was proclaimed. Two days later, on November 11, 1918, an armistice was signed, ceasing the hostilities. Under the armistice the Germans agreed to evacuate occupied territories, pull their troops back behind the Rhine River, and surrender their navy, railroad equipment, and other matériel. The Germans were assured that Wilson's Fourteen Points would be the basis of the peace conference.

During its nineteen months of participation in the war, the United States saw 126,000 of its servicemen killed. Germany's war dead totaled over 2 million, including civilians; France lost nearly 1.4 million combatants, the United Kingdom lost 703,000 soldiers, and Russia lost 1.7 million. The new Europe emerging from the conflagration would be much different: more violent, more polarized, more cynical, less sure of itself, and less capable of decisive action. The United States, for good or ill, would be sucked into the vacuum of power created by the destructiveness of the Great War.

THE FIGHT FOR PEACE

DOMESTIC UNREST   Woodrow Wilson made a fateful decision to attend the Paris Peace Conference, which convened on January 18, 1919, and would last almost six months. No U.S. president had ever left the country while in office, and doing so dramatized all the more Wilson's messianic vision and his goal of a lasting peace. From one viewpoint it was a shrewd move, for his prestige and determination made a difference at the Paris peace talks. But during his prolonged trip abroad, he lost touch with political developments at home, where his political coalition was already unraveling under the pressures of wartime discontent. Western farmers complained about the government's control of wheat prices while eastern business leaders chafed at federal revenue policies designed, according to the *New York Sun,* "to pay for the war out of taxes raised north of the Mason and Dixon Line." Organized labor, despite real gains during the war, groused about inflation and the problems of reconversion to a peacetime economy.

In the midterm elections of 1918, Wilson defied his advisers and urged voters to elect a Democratic Congress to support his foreign policies. Republicans, who for the most part had supported Wilson's war measures, took affront. So, too, did many voters. In elections held a week before the armistice, the Democrats lost control of both houses of Congress. With an opposition majority in the new Congress, Wilson further weakened his standing by failing to appoint a prominent Republican to the American delegation headed for Paris and the treaty negotiations. Former President Taft suggested that Wilson's real intention in going to Paris was "to hog the whole show."

When Wilson reached Paris in December 1918, enthusiastic demonstrations greeted him. At the conference table, however, he had to deal with some tough-minded statesmen who did not share his utopian zeal. The Paris Peace Conference lasted from January to June 1919. It included delegates from all countries that had declared war or broken diplomatic relations with Germany. But it was dominated by the Big Four: the prime ministers of Britain, France, and Italy and the president of the United States. The British prime minister David Lloyd George was a gifted politician fresh from electoral

The Paris Peace Conference

Woodrow Wilson (second from left) with Georges Clemenceau of France (center) and Arthur Balfour of Great Britain (second from right) during the Paris Peace Conference.

victory following a campaign whose slogan declared, "Hang the kaiser." Italy's prime minister, Vittorio Orlando, was there to pick up the spoils promised his country in the secret 1915 Treaty of London. The French premier Georges Clemenceau, a stern realist, demanded severe measures to weaken Germany and guarantee French security.

THE LEAGUE OF NATIONS   Woodrow Wilson insisted that his cherished League of Nations come first at the conference and in the treaty. Whatever compromises he might have to make regarding territorial boundaries and financial claims, whatever mistakes might result, Wilson believed that a league of nations committed to collective security would maintain international stability. Wilson presided over the commission to draft a league charter. Article X of the charter, which he called "the heart of the League," pledged member nations to consult on military and economic sanctions against aggressors. The use of armed force would be a last resort. The League structure would allow each member an equal voice in the Assembly; the Big Five (Britain, France, Italy, Japan, and the United States) and four rotating members would make up the Council; the administrative staff, in Geneva, Switzerland, would make up the Secretariat; and a Permanent Court of International Justice (set up in 1921 and usually called the World Court) could "hear and determine any dispute of an international character."

On February 14, 1919, Wilson delivered the finished draft of the League charter to the Allies and departed the next day for a visit home. Already he faced opposition. The Republican Henry Cabot Lodge, the powerful chairman of the Senate Foreign Relations Committee, claimed that the League's covenant was unacceptable. His statement of March 4 bore the signatures of thirty-nine Republican senators or senators-elect, more than enough to block ratification.

TERRITORY AND REPARATIONS   Back in Paris in the spring of 1919, Wilson grudgingly acceded to French demands for territorial concessions and reparations payments by Germany. The Allied statesmen also agreed that the Allies would occupy a demilitarized German Rhineland for fifteen years and that the League of Nations would administer Germany's coal-rich Saar Basin. France could use the Saar mines for fifteen years, after which the region's voters would determine whether to join Germany or France.

In other territorial matters, Wilson had to compromise his unrealistic principle of national self-determination. As a result of the Great War, four long-standing multinational empires had disintegrated: the Russian, Austro-Hungarian, German, and Ottoman (Turkish). Hundreds of millions of people

EUROPE AFTER THE TREATY
OF VERSAILLES, 1918

········ 1914 boundaries

New nations

Plebiscite areas

Occupied area

Why was self-determination difficult for states in Central Europe? How did territorial concessions weaken Germany?

had to be reorganized into new nations. There was in fact no way to make
Europe's boundaries correspond to its tangled ethnic groupings because
mixed populations were scattered throughout Central Europe. In some areas,
moreover, national self-determination yielded to other interests, such as
trade and defense. The result was a reorganized map of Central Europe in
which portions of the former Austro-Hungarian Empire became independent,
most notably Czechoslovakia and Yugoslavia, and portions were attached to
Poland, Romania, and Italy. Ethnic and nationalist tensions continued and
would contribute to the crisis that culminated in World War II.

The discussion of reparations was among the longest and most bitter at the conference. Despite a pre-armistice agreement that Germany would be liable only for civilian damages, Clemenceau and Lloyd George proposed that Germany pay reparations for the entire cost of the war. On this point, Wilson made perhaps his most fateful concessions. He agreed to a clause in the treaty in which Germany accepted responsibility for starting the war and thus for its entire financial cost. The "war guilt" clause offended Germans and provided a source of persistent bitterness upon which Adolf Hitler would later capitalize.

On May 7, 1919, the victorious powers presented the treaty to the German delegates, who returned three weeks later with 443 pages of criticism. A few small changes were made, but when the Germans still refused to sign, the French prepared to move their army across the Rhine River. Finally, on June 28, 1919, the Germans gave up and signed the treaty at Versailles.

WILSON'S LOSS AT HOME   On July 8, 1919, Woodrow Wilson returned home with the Versailles Treaty amid a great clamor of popular support. A third of the state legislatures had endorsed the League of Nations, as had thirty-three of the nation's forty-eight governors. Wilson called upon the Senate to accept the "great duty" of ratifying the treaty. Senator Henry Cabot Lodge, however, doubted that the Paris negotiators could make "mankind suddenly virtuous by a statute or a written constitution." Lodge relished a fight. He knew the undercurrents already stirring up opposition to the treaty: the resentment felt by German, Italian, and Irish groups, the disappointment of many progressives with Wilson's compromises on reparations and boundaries, the distractions of demobilization and resulting domestic problems, and the revival of isolationism.

Others agreed. In the Senate a group of "irreconcilables," fourteen Republicans and two Democrats, opposed U.S. participation in the League on any terms. They

"The League of Nations Argument in a Nutshell"

Jay N. "Ding" Darling's summation of the League controversy.

were mainly western and midwestern progressives who feared that new foreign commitments would threaten domestic programs and reforms. The irreconcilables would be useful to Lodge's purpose, but he belonged to a larger group, "reservationists," who insisted upon limiting U.S. involvement in the League. Wilson said that he had already amended the covenant to these ends, pointing out that with a veto in the League Council, the United States could not be obligated by the League to do anything against its will.

Lodge, who set more store by the old balance of power than by Wilson's idea of collective security, offered a set of amendments—his reservations. Wilson responded by agreeing to interpretive reservations but to nothing that would reopen the negotiations with Germany and the Allies. He especially opposed the amendments weakening Article X of the League of Nations covenant, which provided for collective action by the signatory governments against aggression.

By September 1919, with momentum for the treaty slackening, Wilson decided to go directly to the people. Against the advice of doctors and friends, he set forth on a grueling railroad tour through the Midwest to the West Coast, pounding out speeches on his typewriter between stops. In all he traveled 8,000 miles in twenty-two days, giving thirty-two major addresses, which included dire warnings of the consequences the nation and the world would face if the treaty were not approved.

For a while, Wilson seemed to be regaining the initiative, but on October 2, 1919, he suffered a severe stroke that left him paralyzed on his left side and an invalid for the rest of his life. For seventeen months his protective wife, Edith, kept him isolated from all but the most essential business. The illness intensified Wilson's stubbornness. He might have done better to have secured the best compromise possible, but he refused to yield and continued to be needlessly confrontational. As he scoffed to an aide, "Let Lodge compromise."

Lodge resolved to amend the treaty before it was ratified. Between November 7 and 19, the Senate adopted fourteen of Lodge's reservations to the Versailles Treaty, most having to do with the League of Nations. Wilson refused to make any compromises or concessions. As a result, his supporters found themselves thrown into an unlikely combination with the irreconcilables, who opposed the treaty under any circumstances. The Senate vote on the treaty with Lodge's reservations was 39 for and 55 against. On the question of taking the original treaty without reservations, irreconcilables and reservationists combined to defeat ratification again, with 38 for and 53 against.

In the face of strong public criticism, however, the Senate voted to reconsider. On March 19, 1920, twenty-one intransigent Democrats deserted Wilson and joined the reservationists, but the treaty once again fell short of the required two-thirds majority. The real winners were the smallest of the three groups in the Senate, neither the Wilsonians nor the reservationists but the irreconcilables.

When Congress declared the war at an end by a joint congressional resolution on May 20, 1920, Wilson vetoed the action; it was not until after he left office that a joint congressional resolution officially ended the state of war with Germany and Austria-Hungary, on July 2, 1921. Peace treaties with Germany, Austria, and Hungary were ratified on October 18, 1921, but by then Warren Gamaliel Harding was president of the United States.

Lurching from War to Peace

The Versailles Treaty, for all the time it spent in the Senate before being defeated, was but one issue clamoring for public attention in the turbulent period after the war. The year 1919 began with ecstatic victory parades that soon gave way to widespread labor unrest, race riots, domestic terror, and government tyranny. Demobilization of the armed forces and the government's war effort proceeded in haphazard fashion. The War Industries Board closed shop on January 1, 1919, and the sudden cancellation of war-related contracts left workers and business leaders to cope with reconversion to a peacetime economy on their own. Wilson's leadership was missing. He had been preoccupied by the war and the League, and once bedridden by his illness, he became grim and peevish. His rudderless administration floundered through rough waters during its last two years.

THE SPANISH FLU   Amid the initial confusion of postwar life, many Americans confronted a virulent menace that produced far more casualties than the war itself. It became known as the Spanish flu, and its contagion spread around the globe. Erupting in the spring of 1918 and lasting a year, the pandemic killed more than 22 million people worldwide, twice as many as died in World War I. In the United States alone it accounted for over 675,000 deaths, nearly seven times the number of combat deaths in France.

American servicemen returning from France brought the flu with them, and it raced through the congested army camps and naval bases. By September 1918 the epidemic had spread to the civilian population. In that month 10,000 Americans died from the disease. Municipal health officers fined people for spitting on the sidewalks or sneezing without a handkerchief. Millions of people wore surgical masks to work. Still the death toll rose. From September 1918 to June 1919, a quarter of the population contracted the illness.

By the spring of 1919, the pandemic had finally run its course. It ended as suddenly—and as inexplicably—as it had begun. Although another outbreak occurred in the winter of 1920, the population had grown more resistant to its assaults. No plague, war, famine, or natural catastrophe in world history had killed so many people in such a short time.

THE ECONOMIC TRANSITION   Disease was only one of many challenges confronting postwar America. Consumer prices continued to rise steeply after the war, and discontented workers, released from wartime constraints, were more willing to strike for their demands. In 1919 more than 4 million workers walked out in thousands of disputes with management. After a general strike in Seattle, public opinion of militant workers began to turn hostile.

The most celebrated postwar labor confrontation was the Boston police strike, which inadvertently launched a presidential career. On September 9, 1919, most of Boston's police force went out on strike, demanding recognition of their union. Massachusetts governor Calvin Coolidge was furious; he mobilized the National Guard to arrest looters and restore order. After four days the strikers were ready to return, but the police commissioner fired them all. When labor leader Samuel Gompers appealed for their reinstatement, Coolidge responded in words that suddenly turned him into a national figure: "There is no right to strike against the public safety by anybody, anywhere, anytime."

RACIAL FRICTION   The summer of 1919 also sparked a season of deadly race riots across the nation. Whites invaded the black section of Longview, Texas, in search of a teacher who had allegedly accused a white woman of a liaison with a black man. They burned shops and houses and ran several African Americans out of town. A week later in Washington, D.C., reports of black assaults on white women aroused white mobs, and for four days gangs of white and black rioters waged a race war in the streets until soldiers and driving rains ended the fighting.

These were but preliminaries to the Chicago riot of late July, in which 38 people were killed, 537 injured, and 1,000 left homeless. It all started on the shores of Lake Michigan when a black youth's raft drifted into the whites' beach area and whites started stoning him. The climactic disorders of the summer occurred in the rural area around Elaine, Arkansas, where African American tenant farmers tried to organize a union. According to official reports, 5 whites and 25 blacks were killed in the violence, but whites told one reporter that in fact more than 100 blacks had died. Altogether, twenty-five race riots erupted in 1919, and there were eighty racial lynchings.

THE RED SCARE   Public reaction to the wave of labor strikes and race riots reflected the impact of Russia's Bolshevik Revolution. Some radicals thought America's domestic turbulence, like that in Russia, was the first scene in a drama of world revolution. Many Americans decided that they might be right. After all, Lenin's tiny Bolshevik faction in Russia had exploited confusion to impose its will on the entire nation. Wartime hysteria against all things German was thus readily transformed into a postwar Red Scare.

Fears of revolution in America were fueled by the actions of militants. In April 1919 the postal service intercepted nearly forty homemade mail bombs addressed to prominent citizens. One slipped through and blew off the hands of a Georgia senator's maid. In June another bomb destroyed the front of Attorney General A. Mitchell Palmer's house in Washington.

In June 1919 the Justice Department decided to deport radical aliens, and Attorney General Palmer set up as the head of the department's new General Intelligence Division the young J. Edgar Hoover, who began to collect files on radicals. Raids began on November 7, 1919, when federal agents swooped down on offices of the Union of Russian Workers in twelve cities. Many of those arrested were deported without a court hearing. On January 2, 1920, police raids in dozens of cities swept up some 5,000 suspects, many taken from their homes without search warrants. That same month the New York State legislature expelled five duly elected Socialist members.

Basking in popular approval, Palmer continued to warn of the Red menace, but like other fads and alarms, the ugly mood of intolerance passed. By the summer of 1920, the Red Scare had begun to evaporate. Communist revolutions in Europe died out, leaving Bolshevism isolated in Russia. Bombings in the United States tapered off; the wave of strikes and race riots receded. The reactionary attorney general began to seem more threatening to civil liberties than the handful of radicals he uncovered. By September 1920, when a bomb explosion at the corner of Broad and Wall Streets in New York City killed thirty-eight people, Americans were ready to take it for what it was: the work of a crazed mind and not the start of a revolution.

The Red Scare nonetheless left a lasting mark on American life. Part of its legacy was the continuing crusade for "100 percent Americanism" and restrictions on immigration. It also left a stigma on labor unions (already weakened by their internal ethnic and racial tensions) and contributed to the anti-union open-shop campaign—the American plan, its sponsors called it. But for many thoughtful Americans the chief residue of the Great War, President Wilson's physical collapse, and its chaotic aftermath was a profound disillusionment.

End of Chapter Review

CHAPTER SUMMARY

- **Wilson and Mexico** Woodrow Wilson wanted to foster democratic governments in Latin America; he got the United States involved in Mexican politics after Mexico experienced several military coups. The popular Pancho Villa tried to gain power in Mexico by promoting an anti-American program, even making raids across the border into New Mexico.

- **Causes of WWI** Europe had developed a system of alliances that divided the continent in two. Democratic Britain and France, along with the Russian Empire, had formed the Triple Entente. Central Powers were comprised of the new German empire, Austria-Hungary, and Italy. The assassination of the heir to the Austro-Hungarian throne by a Serbian nationalist triggered the world war.

- **U.S. Enters WWI** Most Americans supported the Triple Entente, or Allied Powers, at the outbreak of World War I. The Wilson administration declared the nation neutral but allowed businesses to extend credit to the Allies to purchase food and military supplies. Americans were outraged by the Germans' use of unlimited submarine warfare, especially the 1915 sinking of the British liner *Lusitania*. In 1917 unrestricted submarine activity and the revelation of the Zimmermann telegram, in which the Germans sought to incite the Mexicans to wage war against the United States, led the United States to enter the Great War.

- **Wilson's Peace Plan** Wilson insisted that the United States wanted no selfish gains from the war, only a new, democratic Europe to emerge from the old empires. His famous Fourteen Points speech outlined his ideas for the establishment of continent-wide democratic nation-states and a league of nations.

- **Treaty of Versailles** The United States did not ratify the Treaty of Versailles because Wilson had alienated the Republican senators whose support he needed for ratification. A coalition of "irreconcilables" formed in the Senate: midwestern and western progressives who feared that involvement in a league of nations would stifle domestic reforms and that ratification would necessitate involvement in future wars. The irreconcilables were joined by "reservationists," who would accept the treaty with certain limitations on America's involvement in the League of Nations. Wilson's illness and his refusal to compromise ensured failure of ratification.

- **Consequences of WWI** As a result of the war, four European empires were dismantled, replaced by small nation-states. The reparations imposed on Germany and the "war guilt" clause laid the foundations for German bitterness and led to the rise of Adolf Hitler and the Nazi party. The presence of a Communist regime in the old Russian Empire had major consequences in America. Fear of communism at home, which first manifested itself in the Red Scare of 1919, became a major theme in the twentieth century.

CHRONOLOGY

1914	United States intervenes in Mexico
1914	World War I begins in Europe
1915	British liner *Lusitania,* with Americans aboard, is torpedoed without warning by a German submarine
1916	Congress passes the National Defense Act
March 1917	Zimmermann telegram reveals that Germany is attempting to incite Mexico to enter the war against the United States
April 1917	United States enters the Great War
January 1918	Woodrow Wilson delivers his Fourteen Points speech
November 11, 1918	Representatives of warring nations sign armistice
1919	Supreme Court issues *Schenck v. United States* decision
May 1919	Treaty of Versailles is presented to the Germans
1919	Race riots break out in Chicago
1919	U.S. attorney general launches Red Scare
July 1921	Joint resolution of Congress officially ends the war among the United States, Germany, and Austro-Hungary

KEY TERMS & NAMES

26

THE MODERN TEMPER

FOCUS QUESTIONS wwnorton.com/studyspace

- What accounted for the nativism of the 1920s?
- What was meant by the Jazz Age?
- How did the new social trends of the 1920s challenge traditional attitudes?
- What was modernism, and how did it influence American culture?

The horrors of World War I dealt a shattering blow to the widespread belief that Western civilization was steadily progressing, an assumption that had been a powerful stimulus of progressivism. The editors of *Presbyterian* magazine announced in 1919 that the "world has been convulsed" by the terrible war, and "every field of thought and action has been disturbed."

The war's colossal carnage disillusioned young intellectuals and spurred a new "modernist" sensibility among artists and writers. At once a mood and a movement, as well as a label for a historical era and a cultural style, modernism appeared first in Europe at the end of the nineteenth century and had become a pervasive international force by 1920. It arose out of a widespread recognition that Western civilization had entered an era of bewildering change. New technologies, new modes of transportation and communication, and new scientific discoveries such as quantum mechanics, relativity theory, and Freudian psychology, combined to rupture traditional perceptions of reality and generate new forms of artistic expression. Modernism manifested itself in a cluster of diverse intellectual and artistic movements: impressionism, futurism, dadaism, surrealism, Freudianism. As the French painter Paul Gauguin acknowledged, the upheavals of modernism produced "an epoch of confusion."

At the same time that the war provided an accelerant for modernism, it stimulated volatile social tensions and political radicalism. The postwar wave of strikes, bombings, anti-Communist hysteria, and race riots convinced many Americans that the country had entered a frightening new era of turmoil and turbulence. Conflict abounded. Defenders of tradition located the germs of radicalism in the polyglot cities teeming with immigrants and foreign ideas. The reactionary mood of the 1920s fed on a growing tendency to connect American nationalism with nativism, Anglo-Saxon racism, and militant Protestantism. In sum, postwar America was a fractured society animated by violent contrasts and seething social tensions.

REACTION IN THE TWENTIES

NATIVISM   That so many political radicals in the United States were immigrants strengthened the suspicion that the seeds of sedition were foreign-born. In the early 1920s over half the white men and a third of the white women working in industry were foreign-born, most of them from central or eastern Europe. That socialism and anarchism were prevalent in those regions made such immigrant workers especially suspicious in the eyes of "old stock" Americans.

The most celebrated case of nativist prejudice involved two Italian immigrant anarchists: shoemaker Nicola Sacco and fish peddler Bartolomeo Vanzetti. They were arrested on May 5, 1920, for stealing $16,000 and killing a paymaster and his guard. Both were armed when arrested, both lied to police about their activities, and both were identified by eyewitnesses. The Sacco and Vanzetti case occurred at the height of Italian immigration to the United States and against the backdrop of numerous terror attacks by anarchists, including the 1920 bombing that killed thirty-eight people on Wall Street in New York City. At the trial of Sacco and Vanzetti the judge was openly prejudicial. He privately referred to the defendants as "anarchist bastards." Sacco and Vanzetti were convicted and ordered executed, but appeals of the verdict lasted seven years. People then and since have insisted that Sacco and Vanzetti were sentenced more for their political beliefs and their ethnic origin than for any crime they had committed. The case became a great radical and liberal cause of the 1920s, but despite pleas for mercy and worldwide demonstrations on behalf of the two men, Sacco and Vanzetti were executed in 1927. Recent investigations have pointed to their likely guilt.

The surging postwar nativism generated new efforts to restrict immigration. Congress, alarmed at the influx of foreigners after 1919, passed the Emergency Immigration Act of 1921, which restricted European arrivals each year to 3 percent of the foreign-born of any nationality as shown in the 1910 census. The Immigration Act of 1924 reduced the number to 2 percent based on the 1890 census, which included fewer of the "new" immigrants from southern and eastern Europe. This law set a permanent limitation, which became effective in 1929, of slightly over 150,000 immigrants per year based on the "national origins" of the U.S. population as of 1920. In signing the law, President Calvin Coolidge pledged, "America must be kept American."

However inexact the quotas, their purpose was clear: to tilt the balance in favor of the old immigration from northern and western Europe, which was assigned about 85 percent of the total. The law completely excluded people from east Asia. Yet it left the gate open to immigrants from Western Hemisphere countries, so that an ironic consequence was a substantial increase in the Hispanic Catholic population. People of Latin American descent (chiefly Mexicans, Puerto Ricans, and Cubans) became the fastest-growing ethnic minority in the country.

Klan rally

In 1925, 40,000 Klan members paraded down Pennsylvania Avenue in Washington, D.C.

THE KLAN During the postwar years the tradition of nativist prejudice against "foreigners" took on a new form: a revived Ku Klux Klan modeled on the vigilante group founded in the South after the Civil War. The new Klan was devoted to "100 percent Americanism" rather than to the old Confederacy, and it restricted its membership to native-born white Protestants. It was determined to protect its warped notion of the American way of life not only from blacks but also from Roman Catholics, Jews, and immigrants. In going nativist, the new Klan spread far outside the South. It thrived in small towns and cities in the North and especially in the Midwest. And it was preoccupied with the defense of white ("native") women and Christian morals.

The Klan represented a vicious reflex against the modern and the alien, against shifting moral standards, the declining influence of churches, and the social permissiveness of cities and colleges. In the Southwest the Klan became more than anything else a moral crusade. "It is going to drive the bootleggers forever out of this land," declared a Texan. "It is going to bring clean moving pictures . . . clean literature . . . break up roadside parking . . . enforce the laws . . . protect homes." Instead, the Klan terrorized and assaulted blacks and immigrants. Although the Klan was very successful at raising money and electing Klan-backed local politicians, it rarely succeeded in its goal of coercing African Americans and immigrants to leave its members' communities. In the mid-1920s the Klan's peak membership may have been as high as 4 million, but its influence diminished as quickly as its numbers grew. Nativist excitement declined after passage of the 1924 immigration law. The Klan also suffered from recurrent factional quarrels and schisms. And its willing use of violence tarnished its moral pretensions.

FUNDAMENTALISM   While the Klan saw a threat mainly in the "alien menace," many adherents of the old-time religion saw threats from modernism in the churches: new ideas that the Bible should be studied in the light of modern scholarship (the "higher criticism") or that it could be reconciled with scientific theories of evolution. When such modernist notions surfaced in schools and even pulpits, fundamentalism, grounded in a literal interpretation of the Bible, took on a new militancy.

Among the rural fundamentalist leaders only William Jennings Bryan, the former presidential candidate and secretary of state, had the following, prestige, and eloquence to make the movement a popular crusade. By 1920, Bryan was showing signs of age, but he remained as silver-tongued as ever in his espousal of a unique blend of progressive populism and religious fundamentalism. In 1921 he promoted laws prohibiting the teaching of Darwinian evolution in the public schools. Anti-evolution bills emerged in legislatures, but the only victories came in the South—and there were few of those.

The climax of the crusade came in Tennessee, where in 1925 the state legislature outlawed the teaching of evolution in public schools and colleges. A young science teacher at a high school in Dayton, Tennessee, John T. Scopes,

Courtroom scene during the Scopes trial

The media, food vendors, and others flocked to Dayton, Tennessee, for the case against John Scopes, the teacher who taught evolution.

accepted an offer from the American Civil Liberties Union to defend a test case. It soon was a case heard round the world. Before the opening of the twelve-day "monkey trial" in July 1925, the streets of Dayton swarmed with publicity hounds, curiosity seekers, evangelists and atheists, hucksters, and a mob of reporters.

The two stars of the show were Bryan, who led the prosecution of Scopes for teaching evolution in violation of Tennessee law, and Clarence Darrow, a renowned Chicago trial lawyer and articulate agnostic, who defended Scopes by challenging the anti-evolution law. The trial quickly became a debate between fundamentalism and modernism. When the judge (a practicing evangelist) damaged Darrow's case by ruling out scientific testimony on evolution, most observers assumed the trial was over.

But the defense rebounded by calling Bryan as an expert witness on biblical interpretation. Darrow, who had once supported Bryan as a presidential candidate, now relentlessly entrapped the statesman in literal-minded interpretations and exposed his ignorance of biblical history and scholarship. Bryan insisted that a "great fish" had swallowed Jonah and that Joshua had made the sun stand still—both, according to Darrow, "fool ideas that no intelligent Christian on earth believes." It was a bitter scene. At one point the two men, their patience exhausted in the broiling summer heat, lunged at each other, shaking their fists, leading the judge to adjourn the court.

The next day the testimony ended. The only issue before the court, the judge ruled, was whether Scopes had in fact taught evolution. He was found guilty, but the Tennessee Supreme Court, while upholding the law, overruled the $100 fine on a legal technicality. The chief prosecutor accepted the higher court's advice against "prolonging the life of this bizarre case" and dropped the issue. With more prescience than he knew, Bryan had described the trial as a "duel to the death." Five days after it closed, he died of a heart condition aggravated by heat and fatigue.

PROHIBITION   The reaction against modern social attitudes took many forms. Prohibition of alcoholic beverages offered another example of reforming zeal channeled into a drive for moral righteousness and conformity. Moralists had been campaigning against excessive drink since the eighteenth century. Around 1900, however, the leading temperance organizations, the Women's Christian Temperance Union and the Anti-Saloon League, shifted their efforts from reforming individuals to campaigning for a national prohibition law. The Anti-Saloon League became one of the most effective pressure groups in history, mobilizing Protestant churches behind its single-minded battle to elect "dry" candidates. Proponents of prohibition often displayed blatant ethnic and social prejudices. The head of the Anti-Saloon League castigated German Americans because they "eat like gluttons and drink like swine." For many anti-alcohol crusaders, the primary goal of eliminating alcoholic beverages seemed to be policing the behavior of the poor, the foreign-born, and the working class. One prohibitionist referred to Italian immigrants as "Dagos, who drink excessively [and] live in a state of filth."

The 1916 elections produced in both houses of Congress two-thirds majorities supporting an amendment to the Constitution prohibiting alcoholic beverages. Soon the wartime spirit of sacrifice, the need to use grain for food rather than booze, and wartime hostility to German American brewers transformed the cause into a virtual test of patriotism. On December 18, 1917, Congress sent to the states the Eighteenth Amendment, which one

Prohibition

A 1926 police raid on a speakeasy, where illegal "bootleg" liquor was sold.

year after ratification, on January 16, 1919, banned the manufacture, sale, and transportation of intoxicating liquors nationwide.

The new amendment did not keep people from drinking, however. Congress never supplied adequate enforcement, if such were even possible given the public thirst, the spotty support of local officials, and the profits to be made in bootlegging. In Detroit, across the river from Ontario, Canada, where booze was legal, the liquor industry during Prohibition was second in size only to the auto industry. Speakeasies, hip flasks, and cocktail parties were among the social innovations of the era, along with increased drinking by women. As the popular humorist Will Rogers quipped, "Prohibition is better than no liquor at all."

It would be too much to say that Prohibition gave rise to organized crime, for systematic vice, gambling, and extortion had long been practiced and were often tied in with saloons. But Prohibition supplied ruthless, flamboyant criminals, such as "Scarface" Al Capone, with an enormous source of income, while the automobile and the submachine gun provided criminals with greater mobility and greater firepower. Organized crime bosses showed remarkable gifts for exploiting loopholes in the law when they did not simply bribe policemen and politicians.

Capone was by far the most celebrated criminal of the 1920s. In 1927 he pocketed $60 million from his bootlegging, prostitution, and gambling empire, and he flaunted his wealth as well as his open disregard for legal authorities. He bludgeoned to death several police lieutenants and ordered the execution of dozens of his criminal competitors. Law-enforcement officials began to smash his bootlegging operations in 1929, but they were unable to pin anything on him until a Treasury agent infiltrated his gang and uncovered evidence that was used to convict him later that year of tax evasion. He was sentenced to eleven years in prison.

In the light of the illegal activities of Capone and other members of organized-crime syndicates, it came as opposing no great surprise when a national commission in 1931 reported that enforcement of Prohibition had broken down. Still, the commission voted to extend Prohibition, and President Herbert Hoover chose to stand by what he called the "experiment, noble in motive and far-reaching in purpose."

THE ROARING TWENTIES

In many ways the reactionary temper of the 1920s and the repressive movements to which it gave rise seemed the dominant trends of the decade. But they arose in part as opposing reactions to disruptive social and intellectual currents. During those years a new cosmopolitan, urban America confronted provincial small-town and rural America, and cultural conflict reached new levels of tension.

Young urban intellectuals dismissed the old-fashioned values of the hinterlands. Sinclair Lewis's novel *Main Street* (1920) caricatured the stifling life of a prairie town, depicting a "savorless people, gulping tasteless food, and sitting afterward, coatless and thoughtless, in rocking chairs prickly with inane decorations, listening to mechanical music, saying mechanical things about the excellence of Ford automobiles, and viewing themselves as the greatest race in the world." The banality of small-town life became a pervasive theme in much of the literature of the time, and the heartland responded to such criticisms of rural folkways with counterimages of cities infested with vice, crime, corruption, and foreigners.

THE JAZZ AGE The writer F. Scott Fitzgerald dubbed the postwar era the Jazz Age because young people were willing to experiment with new forms of recreation and sexuality. The new jazz music bubbling up in New Orleans, Kansas City, Memphis, New York City, and Chicago blended African

Frankie "Half Pint" Jackson and his band at the Sunset Cafe, Chicago, in the 1920s

Jazz emerged in the 1920s as an especially American expression of the modernist spirit. African American artists bent musical conventions to give fuller rein to improvisation and sensuality.

and European traditions to form a distinctive sound. The syncopated rhythms of jazz were immensely popular among rebellious young adults and helped spawn carefree new dance steps such as the Charleston and the black bottom, whose gyrations shocked guardians of morality.

If people were not listening to ragtime or jazz or to the family radio shows that became the rage in the 1920s, they were frequenting movie theaters. By 1930 there were more than 23,000 theaters around the country, and they drew more than 95 million customers each week. In Muncie, Indiana, a small city of 35,000, nine movie theaters were operating seven days a week. Films became even more popular after the introduction of sound in 1927.

THE NEW MORALITY   Much of the shock to traditionalists during the Jazz Age came from the changes in manners and morals evidenced first among young people and especially on college campuses. In *This Side* *of Paradise* (1920), a novel of student life at Princeton, F. Scott Fitzgerald wrote of "the great current American phenomenon, the 'petting party.'" None of the Victorian mothers, he said, "had any idea how casually their daughters were accustomed to be kissed." From such novels and from magazines and movies, many Americans learned about the cities' wild parties, illegal drinking, promiscuity, and speakeasies.

Sex came to be discussed with surprising frankness during the 1920s. Much of the talk derived from a spreading awareness of Dr. Sigmund Freud, the Viennese father of psychoanalysis. By the 1920s his ideas had begun to infiltrate popular culture. Books and magazines now included discussions of of libido, Oedipus complexes, sublimation, and repression.

Fashion also reflected the rebellion against prudishness and a loosening of inhibitions. In 1919 women's skirts were typically six inches above the ground; by 1927 they were at the knee, and the "flapper," with her bobbed hair, rolled stockings, cigarettes, lipstick, and sensuous dancing, was providing a shocking model of the new feminism. The name *flapper* derived from the way young female rebels allowed their galoshes to flap around their ankles. Conservative moralists saw the flappers as just another sign of a degenerating society. Others saw in the "new woman" an expression of American individualism.

By 1930, however, the thrill of rebellion was waning; the revolution against Victorian morality had run its course—for a while. Its extreme expressions in time aroused doubts that the indulgence of lust equaled liberation. And the much-discussed revolution in morals was also greatly exaggerated. The twenties roared for only a small proportion of the population. F. Scott Fitzgerald reminded Americans in 1931 that the Jazz Age was jazzy for only the "upper tenth" of the population. Still, some new folkways had come to stay. In the late

The "new woman" of the 1920s

Two flappers dance atop the Hotel Sherman in Chicago, 1926.

1930s a survey disclosed that among college women almost half had had sexual relations before marriage.

THE WOMEN'S MOVEMENT   At the same time that many women were embracing new sexual mores, all women were being liberated politically. The suffrage movement, which had been in the doldrums since 1896, sprang back to life in the second decade of the new century. In 1912, Alice Paul, a Quaker social worker, returned from an apprenticeship with the militant suffragists of England to chair the Congressional Committee of the National American Woman Suffrage Association (NAWSA). Paul instructed female activists to be more aggressive and confrontational: to picket state legislatures, target and "punish" politicians who failed to endorse suffrage, chain themselves to public buildings, provoke police to arrest them, and

Votes for women

Suffragettes march in New York City in 1912, their children by their side.

undertake hunger strikes. By 1917, Paul and her followers were picketing the White House and deliberately inviting arrest, after which they went on hunger strikes in prison.

In 1915 the more moderate but equally persistent Carrie Chapman Catt had once again become head of NAWSA. For several years, President Woodrow Wilson had evaded the issue of a suffrage amendment, but he supported a plank in the 1916 Democratic platform encouraging states to embrace women's suffrage. He addressed NAWSA that year and thereafter worked closely with its leaders. For several years, President Woodrow Wilson had evaded the issue of a suffrage amendment, but he supported a plank in the 1916 Democratic platform encouraging states to embrace women's suffrage. In 1916 he also addressed NAWSA, which by then was once again headed by Carrie Chapman Catt, a more moderate feminist than Paul but equally persistent. Thereafter Wilson worked closely with NAWSA's leaders.

The courageous proponents of women's suffrage put forth several arguments in favor of voting rights. Many assumed that the right to vote and hold office was a matter of simple justice: women were just as capable as men in exercising the rights and responsibilities of citizenship. Others insisted that women were morally superior to men and therefore would raise the quality of the political process by their participation in it. They also would be less prone to use warfare as a solution to international disputes and national differences. Women voters, advocates argued, would also promote the welfare of society rather than partisan or selfish gains. Allowing women to vote would create a great engine for progressive social change. One activist explicitly linked women's suffrage with the social gospel, declaring that women embraced Christ more readily than men and if they were elected to public office, they would "far more effectively guard the morals of society and the sanitary conditions of cities."

Yet the women's suffrage movement was not immune from the prevailing social, ethnic, and racial prejudices of the day. Carrie Chapman Catt echoed the fears of many middle- and upper-class urban dwellers when she warned of the danger that "lies in the votes possessed by the males in the slums of the cities, and the ignorant foreign [immigrant] vote." She added that the nation, with "ill-advised haste" had enfranchised "the foreigner, the Negro and the Indian" but still balked at women voting. In the South, suffragists catered to generations of deeply embedded racism. One of them declared in 1903 that giving white women the vote "would insure immediate and durable white supremacy."

Whatever the motives, President Wilson finally endorsed the "Susan B. Anthony amendment" in speeches to the House and Senate in 1918. In a speech on September 18, he said, "We have made partners of the women in this war. Shall we admit them only to a partnership of suffering and sacrifice and toil and not to a partnership of right?" After six months of delay, debate, and failed votes, the Congress passed the Nineteenth Amendment in the spring of 1919 and sent it to the states for ratification. Tennessee's legislature was the last of thirty-six state assemblies to approve the amendment, and it did so in dramatic fashion. The initial vote was deadlocked 48–48. Then a twenty-four-year-old legislator named Harry Burn changed his vote to yes at the insistence of his mother. The Nineteenth Amendment was ratified on August 18, 1920. It was the climactic achievement of the Progressive Era.

Women thereafter entered politics in growing numbers, but they did not have the transformative effect that boosters had predicted. As it turned out, women tended to vote like men on most issues. One group, however, wanted something more. Alice Paul set a new goal: an equal rights amendment that would eliminate any remaining legal distinctions between the sexes, including the special legislation for the protection of working women that had been put on the books during the previous fifty or so years. Alice Paul saw the equal rights amendment introduced in Congress in 1923; forty-nine years later she would see her amendment adopted. After her death, however, it would fall short of ratification.

Although the sharp increase in the number of women in the workforce during World War I proved short-lived, in the longer view a steady increase in the number of employed women occurred in the 1920s and 1930s. Still, women remained concentrated in traditional occupations, finding employment primarily as domestics, office workers, teachers, clerks, salespeople, dressmakers, milliners, and seamstresses. On the eve of World War II, women's work was little more diversified than it had been at the beginning of the century, but by 1940 it would be on the brink of a major transformation.

THE "NEW NEGRO"   The discrimination experienced by both African Americans and women displayed many parallels, and their struggles for equality have frequently coincided. The most significant development in African American life during the early twentieth century was the Great Migration northward from the South. A massive movement of blacks from the South to the North began in 1915–1916, when rapidly expanding war industries were experiencing a labor shortage, leaving openings in the

North that were filled by African Americans. Altogether between 1910 and 1920 the Southeast lost some 323,000 blacks, or 5 percent of the 1920 native black population, and by 1930 it had lost another 615,000, or 8 percent of the 1920 African American population. The migration led to a slow but steady growth in black political influence in northern cities. African Americans were freer to speak and act in a northern setting, and they gained political leverage by settling in large cities in states with many electoral votes.

Along with political activity came a bristling spirit of protest, a spirit that received cultural expression in a literary and artistic movement labeled the Harlem Renaissance. Claude McKay, a Jamaican immigrant, was the first significant writer of the movement, which sought to rediscover black folk culture. Poems collected in McKay's *Harlem Shadows* (1922) expressed defiance in such titles as "If We Must Die" and "To the White Fiends." Other emergent black writers included Langston Hughes, Zora Neale Hurston, Countee Cullen, Alain Locke, Jean Toomer, and James Weldon Johnson.

The spirit of the "new Negro" also found an outlet in what came to be called Negro nationalism, which exalted blackness, black cultural expression, and at its most extreme, black exclusiveness. The leading spokesman for such views was the flamboyant Marcus Garvey. Racial bias, Garvey said, was so ingrained in whites that it was futile to appeal to their sense of justice. He advised blacks to liberate themselves from the surrounding white culture. "We have outgrown slavery," he declared, "but our minds are still enslaved to the thinking of the Master Race."

Garvey endorsed the "social and political separation of all peoples to the extent that they promote their own ideals and civilization." Such a separatist message appalled other African American leaders. W. E. B. Du Bois, for example, labeled Garvey "the most dangerous enemy of the Negro race. . . . He is either a lunatic or a traitor." Garvey and his aides created

Marcus Garvey

Garvey was the founder of the Universal Negro Improvement Association and a leading spokesman for "Negro nationalism" in the 1920s.

their own black version of Christianity, organized their own fraternal lodges and community cultural centers, started their own businesses, and published their own newspaper. Garvey's message of racial pride and self-reliance appealed to many blacks who had arrived in the northern cities during the Great Migration and had grown embittered with the hypocrisy of American democracy during the postwar economic slump. Garvey declared that the only lasting hope for blacks was for them to flee America and build their own republic in Africa.

In 1916, Garvey brought to New York City the Universal Negro Improvement Association, which he had started in his native Jamaica two years before. He quickly enlisted 500,000 members, and claimed as many as 6 million by 1923. At the peak of his popularity, however, Garvey was convicted of mail fraud. He was imprisoned from 1925 until 1927, when he was pardoned and deported to Jamaica by President Calvin Coolidge. Garvey died in obscurity in London in 1940, but the memory of his movement kept alive an undercurrent of racial pride that would reemerge later under the slogan of black power.

Even more influential in promoting black rights was the National Association for the Advancement of Colored People (NAACP). Founded in 1910, it was led by northern white liberals and black leaders such as Du Bois. Its main strategy was getting the federal government to enforce the Fourteenth and Fifteenth Amendments. In 1919 the NAACP launched a campaign against lynching, still a common atrocity in many parts of the country and most of whose victims were black. An anti-lynching bill making mob murder a federal offense passed the House in 1922 but lost to a filibuster by southern senators. Nonetheless, the bill stayed before the House until 1925, and continuing agitation on the issue helped to reduce lynchings, which declined to a third of what they had been the previous decade. But one lynching was too many for a so-called progressive society.

THE CULTURE OF MODERNISM

After 1920 changes in the realms of science and social thought were perhaps even more dramatic than those affecting women and African Americans. As the twentieth century advanced, the faith in progress and reform expressed by progressives fell victim to a series of frustrations and disasters, including the Great War, the failure of the League of Nations to win approval in the United States, Woodrow Wilson's physical and political collapse, and the failure of Prohibition. On a grander scale, startling new findings in physics further shook prevailing assumptions.

SCIENCE AND SOCIAL THOUGHT   Physicists of the early twentieth century altered the image of the cosmos in bewildering ways. Since Isaac Newton's research in the late seventeenth century, conventional wisdom had held that the universe was governed by laws that the scientific method could ultimately uncover. A world of such certain order and rationality had bolstered hopes of infinite progress in human knowledge.

This rational world of order and certainty disintegrated at the beginning of the new century when Albert Einstein, a young German physicist, announced his theory of relativity, which maintained that space, time, and mass were not absolutes but instead were relative to the location and motion of the observer. Newton's eighteenth-century mechanics, according to Einstein's relativity theory, worked well enough at relatively slow speeds, but the more nearly one approached the velocity of light (about 186,000 miles per second), the more all measuring devices would change accordingly, so that yardsticks would become shorter, clocks and heartbeats would slow down, even the aging process would ebb.

Relativity was not the only disconcerting concept that Einstein discovered. The farther one reached out into the universe and the farther one reached down into the minute world of the atom, the more certainty dissolved. The discovery of radioactivity in the 1890s showed that atoms were not irreducible units of matter and that some of them emitted particles of energy. This meant, Einstein noted, that mass and energy were not separate phenomena but interchangeable. By 1921, when Einstein was awarded the Nobel Prize, his abstract concept of relativity had become internationally recognized—and popularized. Hundreds of books about relativity had been published. His theories also had consequences that Einstein had not foreseen. Younger physicists built upon them to further transform notions of reality and the universe.

The pace of theoretical physics quickened as the twentieth century unfolded. The German physicist Max Planck discovered that electromagnetic emissions of energy, whether as electricity or light, came in little bundles that he called quanta. The development of quantum theory suggested that atoms were far more complex than once believed. In 1927 the pioneering German physicist Werner Heisenberg announced that the activities within an atom were ultimately indescribable. One could never know both the position and the velocity of an electron, Heisenberg concluded, because the very process of observation would affect the behavior of the particle, altering its position or its velocity.

Heisenberg's simple, yet startling "uncertainty principle" meant that human knowledge had limits. Just as Enlightenment thinkers had drawn on Isaac Newton's principles of gravitation two centuries before to formulate their views on the laws governing society, the ideas of relativity and uncertainty in the twentieth century persuaded some people to deny the relevance of absolute values in any sphere of society, thus undermining the concepts of personal responsibility and absolute standards. Anthropologists aided the process by transforming the word *culture*, which had before meant "refinement," into a term for the whole system of ideas, folkways, and institutions within which any group lives. Even the most primitive societies had a culture, and all things being relative, one culture should not impose its value judgments upon another. Two anthropologists, Ruth Benedict and Margaret Mead, were especially effective in spreading this viewpoint.

MODERNIST ART AND LITERATURE   The cluster of scientific ideas associated with Charles Darwin, Sigmund Freud, and Albert Einstein helped inspire a modernist revolution in the minds of many intellectuals and creative artists during the early twentieth century. The modernist world was one in which, as Karl Marx said, "all that is solid melts into air." Modernism arose out of a widespread recognition that Western civilization was entering an era of bewildering change. New technologies, new modes of transportation and communication, and new scientific discoveries combined to transform the nature of everyday life and to generate dramatic new forms of artistic expression and architectural design.

Whereas nineteenth-century writers and artists took for granted an accessible world that could be readily observed and accurately represented, self-willed modernists viewed reality as something to be created rather than copied, expressed rather than reproduced. As a consequence, they concluded that the subconscious regions of the psyche were more interesting and more potent than reason, common sense, and logic.

In the various arts such concerns spawned abstract painting, atonal music, free verse, stream-of-consciousness narrative, and interior monologues in stories and novels. Writers showed an intense concern with new forms of expression in an effort to violate expectations and shock their audiences.

The chief American prophets of modernism were living in Europe: Ezra Pound and T. S. Eliot in London and Gertrude Stein in Paris. All were deeply concerned with creating new and often difficult styles of modernist expression. Pound, as foreign editor of *Poetry,* served as the conduit through which many American poets achieved publication in the leading journals and magazines promoting experimentalism. At the same time he became the leader of the imagist movement, a revolt against the ornamental verbosity of Victorian poetry in favor of the concrete image.

Ezra Pound's brilliant protégé was the St. Louis–born Harvard graduate T. S. Eliot, who in 1915 contributed to *Poetry* his first major poem, "The Love Song of J. Alfred Prufrock," the musings of an ineffectual man who "after tea and cakes and ices" could never find "the strength to force the moment to its crisis." Eliot went to Oxford in 1913 and soon decided to make England his home and poetry his career. He rejected the nineteenth century's "cheerfulness, optimism, and hopefulness," as well as the traditional notion of poetry as the literal representation of a beautiful world. The modern poet, he insisted, must "be able to see beneath both beauty and ugliness; to see the boredom, and the horror and the glory." Eliot's *The Waste Land* (1922) made few concessions to readers in its obscure allusions, its juxtaposition of unexpected metaphors, its deep sense of postwar disillusionment and melancholy, and its suggestion of a burned-out civilization. The poem became for an alienated younger generation almost the touchstone of the modern temper.

Gertrude Stein, another voluntary exile, settled in Paris in 1903 and became an early champion of experimentalism and a collector of modern art. Long regarded as no more than the literary eccentric who wrote, "Rose is a rose is a rose is a rose," she would later be recognized as one of the chief promoters of the modernist prose style. At the time she was known chiefly through her influence on such literary expatriates of the 1920s as Sherwood Anderson and Ernest Hemingway, whom she told, "All of you young people who served in the war, you are the lost generation."

The earliest chronicler of that "lost" generation, F. Scott Fitzgerald, blazed up brilliantly and then quickly flickered out like the tinseled, carefree, sad young characters in his novels. Successful and famous at age twenty-four, having published *This Side of Paradise* in 1920, he, along with his wife, Zelda, experienced and depicted the "greatest, gaudiest spree in history." What gave depth to the best of Fitzgerald's work was what a character in *The Great Gatsby* (1925), his finest novel, called "a sense of the fundamental decencies" amid all the surface gaiety—and almost always a sense of impending doom.

Ernest Hemingway suffered even more from a psychic wound inflicted by an uncaring world. For him literature was a means of defense, a way to strike back, and in the process find a meaning for himself rather than accept one imposed by society. Hemingway's novels *The Sun Also Rises* (1926) and *A Farewell to Arms* (1929) depict a desperate search for "real" life and the doomed, war-tainted love affairs of Americans of the "lost" generation. Hundreds of writers tried to imitate Hemingway's terse style, but few had his gift, which lay less in what he had to say than in the way he said it.

THE SOUTHERN RENAISSANCE   As modernist literature arose in response to the changes taking place in the United States and Europe, so southern literature of the 1920s reflected a regional world in the midst of rebirth. A southern renaissance in writing emerged from the conflict between the dying world of tradition and the modern commercial world struggling to come to life in the aftermath of the Great War. While in the South the conflict of values aroused the Ku Klux Klan and fundamentalist furies that tried desperately to bring back the world of tradition, it also inspired the creativity of the South's young writers.

Two of the most notable of the new southern writers were Thomas Wolfe and William Faulkner. Fame rushed in first on Wolfe and his native Asheville, North Carolina, which he wrote about in his first novel, *Look Homeward, Angel.* "Against the Victorian morality and the Bourbon aristocracy of the South," Wolfe had "turned in all his fury," wrote newspaper editor Jonathan Daniels, a former classmate. Despite his lust for experience and knowledge, his demonic drive to escape the encircling hills for the "fabled" world outside, and his agonized search for some "lost lane-end into heaven," Wolfe never completely severed his roots in the South.

William Faulkner's achievement, more than Wolfe's, was rooted in the coarsely textured social world that produced him. Born near Oxford, Mississippi, he grew up there and transmuted his hometown into the fictional Jefferson, in Yoknapatawpha County. In writing *Sartoris* (1929), he began to discover that his "own little postage stamp of native soil was worth writing about" and that he "would never live long enough to exhaust it." With *Sartoris* and the creation of his mythical land of Yoknapatawpha, Faulkner kindled a blaze of creative energy. Next, as he put it, he wrote his gut into *The Sound and the Fury* (1929). It was one of the triumphs of the modernist style, but most early readers, taking their cue from the title instead of the critics, believed that its complex prose and themes signified nothing.

Modernism and the southern literary renaissance, both of which emerged from the crucible of the Great War and its aftermath, were products of the

1920s. But the widespread alienation felt by the writers and artists of the 1920s did not survive the decade. The onset of the Great Depression in 1929 sparked a renewed sense of commitment and affirmation in the arts, as if people could no longer afford the art-for-art's-sake emphasis of the 1920s. Alienation would give way to social engagement in the decade to come.

End of Chapter Review

- **Nativism** With the end of the Great War, race riots and the fear of communism ushered in a wave of virulent nativism. With many "old stock" Americans fearing that many immigrants were socialists, Communists, or anarchists, Congress passed laws to restrict immigration. The revived Ku Klux Klan was devoted to "100 percent Americanism" and regarded Catholics, Jews, immigrants, and African Americans as threats to America.

- **Jazz Age** The fads and attitudes of the 1920s, perhaps best represented by the frantic rhythms of jazz music and the fast-paced, sexy movies from Hollywood, led F. Scott Fitzgerald to dub the decade the Jazz Age. The hemlines of women's dresses rose, and sex was openly discussed. The Harlem Renaissance gave voice to black literature and music, and African Americans in northern cities felt freer to speak out against racial injustice and express pride in their race.

- **Reactionary Mood** Many white Americans felt that their religion and way of life were under attack by modern trends. They feared that women's newly earned right to vote might destabilize the family and that scientific scholarship would undermine biblical truth. These modern and traditional forces openly clashed at the Scopes trial in Dayton, Tennessee, in 1925, where the right to teach evolution in public schools was tested in court.

- **Modernism** The carnage of the Great War shattered Americans' belief in the progress of Western civilization. In the movement known as modernism, young artists and intellectuals reflected this disillusionment. For modernists, no longer could the world be easily observed through reason, common sense, and logic; instead, reality was something to be created and expressed through new artistic and literary forms, like abstract painting, atonal music, free verse in poetry, and stream-of-conscious narrative and interior monologues in stories and novels.

CHRONOLOGY

1910	National Association for the Advancement of Colored People is founded
1916	Marcus Garvey brings to New York the Universal Negro Improvement Association
1920	Prohibition begins
1920	Nineteenth Amendment, guaranteeing women's suffrage, is ratified
1920	F. Scott Fitzgerald's *This Side of Paradise* is published
1921	Albert Einstein receives the Nobel Prize in physics
1921	Congress passes the Emergency Immigration Act
1922	T. S. Eliot's *The Waste Land* is published
1923	Alice Paul's equal rights amendment is introduced in Congress
1924	Congress passes the Immigration Act
1925	Scopes "monkey trial" tests the teaching of evolution in Tennessee public schools

KEY TERMS & NAMES

27

REPUBLICAN RESURGENCE AND DECLINE

FOCUS QUESTIONS wwnorton.com/studyspace

- To what extent were the policies of the 1920s a rejection of progressivism?
- Why were the 1920s an era of conservatism?
- What drove the growth of the American economy in the 1920s?
- What were the causes of the stock market crash and the Great Depression?

The progressive political coalition that elected Theodore Roosevelt in 1904 and reelected Woodrow Wilson in 1916 had fragmented by 1920. It began to show signs of fissure during the war, when radicals and other reformers were disaffected by America's involvement. After the war, in 1919, Roosevelt died at age sixty, just as he was beginning a campaign for the 1920 Republican presidential nomination. On the Democratic side, Wilson's support continued to erode as his health problems incapacitated him. Beyond Washington, organized labor resented the administration's unsympathetic attitude toward the strikes of 1919–1920, and western farmers complained that wartime price controls on commodities had discriminated against them. While prominent intellectuals grew disillusioned with the popular support for Prohibition, the Ku Klux Klan, and religious fundamentalism, many among the middle class lost interest in political activism. They instead channeled their energies into building a new business civilization based upon mass production and mass consumption, greater leisure, and the introduction of labor-saving electrical appliances in the home. Moreover, progressivism's final triumphs at the national level crystallized before the war's end: the Eighteenth Amendment, which outlawed alcoholic beverages, was ratified in 1919, and the Nineteenth Amendment, which extended women's suffrage to the entire country, became law a year later.

Progressivism did not completely disappear in the 1920s, however. Although smaller in number, reformers remained active in Congress during much of the decade even while the White House was in conservative Republican hands. The progressive impulse for "good government" and extended public services remained strong, especially at the state and local levels, where movements for better roads, education, public health, and social welfare gained momentum during the decade. At the same time, however, the reactionary temper of the times gave rise to the grassroots drive for moral righteousness and conformity animating the Ku Klux Klan and the fundamentalist and prohibitionist movements.

"Normalcy"

THE ELECTION OF 1920 After World War I most Americans grew weary of Wilson's crusading idealism and suspicious of leaders promoting reform. Wilson himself recognized the shifting public mood. "It is only once in a generation," he remarked, "that a people can be lifted above material things. That is why conservative government is in the saddle two-thirds of the time."

At the Republican Convention in 1920, the three strongest presidential contenders canceled each other out in the balloting. The party leaders then turned to a stunning mediocrity, the affable Ohio senator Warren G. Harding, who set the tone of his campaign when he told a Boston audience; "America's present need is not heroics, but healing; not nostrums, but normalcy; not revolution, but restoration; not agitation, but adjustment; not surgery, but serenity; not the dramatic, but the dispassionate; not experiment, but equipoise; not submergence in internationality, but sustainment in triumphant nationality." Harding caught the mood of the times—a longing for "normalcy" and contentment with the status quo.

Harding's promise of a "return to normalcy" reflected his own conservative values and folksy personality. The son of an Ohio farmer, he described himself not as an intellectual or a crusader but "just a plain fellow" who was "old-fashioned and even reactionary in matters of faith and morals." Such a description, however, suggests a certain puritan regimen that Harding never practiced. Far from being an old-fashioned moralist in his personal life, he drank bootleg liquor in the midst of Prohibition, smoked and chewed tobacco, relished weekly poker games, and had numerous liaisons and several children with women other than his austere wife, whom he called "the Duchess." The general public, however, remained unaware of Harding's escapades. Instead, voters saw him as a handsome, charming, gregarious, and lovable politician. A man of self-confessed limitations in vision, leadership, and intellectual power, he once admitted that "I cannot hope to be one of the great presidents, but perhaps I may be remembered as one of the best loved." He got his wish.

The Democrats in 1920 hoped that Harding would not be president at all. James Cox, a former newsman and former governor of Ohio, won the presidential nomination of a fragmented Democratic party on the forty-fourth ballot. For vice president the convention named New Yorker Franklin D. Roosevelt, who as assistant secretary of the navy occupied the same position his Republican cousin Theodore Roosevelt had once held.

The Democrats suffered from the breakup of the Wilsonian coalition and the conservative postwar mood. In the words of the progressive journalist William Allen White, Americans in 1920 were "tired of issues, sick at heart of ideals, and weary of being noble." The country voted overwhelmingly for Harding's promised "return to normalcy." Harding polled 16 million votes to 9 million for Cox, who carried no state outside the Democratic Solid South.

EARLY APPOINTMENTS AND POLICY Harding in office had much in common with Ulysses Grant. His cabinet, like Grant's, mixed some of the best men in the party with some of the worst. Charles Evans Hughes became a distinguished secretary of state. Herbert Hoover in the Commerce Department, Andrew W. Mellon in the Treasury Department, and Henry C. Wallace in the Agriculture Department were also efficient, forceful figures. Of the others, Secretary of the Interior Albert B. Fall landed in prison and Attorney General Harry M. Daugherty only narrowly escaped prosecution. Many lesser offices went to members of the soon notorious "Ohio gang," a group of Harding's Ohio friends, headed

ALUMINUM TRUST TARIFF

MR. MELLON GETS THE PAN
—Fitzpatrick in the St. Louis *Post-Dispatch*

Andrew Mellon

Mellon was accused of allowing his Aluminium Company of America to become a monopoly.

by Daugherty, with whom the president met regularly for poker games lubricated with illegal liquor.

Harding and his friends set about dismantling or neutralizing as many components of progressivism as they could. Harding's four appointments to the Supreme Court were all conservatives, including Chief Justice William Howard Taft, who announced that he had been "appointed to reverse a few decisions." During the 1920s the Taft court struck down a federal child-labor law and a minimum-wage law for women, issued numerous injunctions against striking unions, and made rulings limiting the powers of federal regulatory agencies.

The Harding administration established a pro-business tone reminiscent of the McKinley White House of the 1890s. To sustain economic growth, Secretary of the Treasury Mellon promoted government spending cuts and federal tax reductions. As Ronald Reagan would argue sixty years later, Mellon insisted that tax cuts should go mainly to the rich, on the assumption that wealth in the hands of the few would spur economic growth through increased capital investment.

At Mellon's behest, Congress first repealed the wartime excess-profits tax and lowered the maximum rate on personal income from 65 percent to 50 percent. Subsequent revenue acts eventually lowered the maximum tax rate to 20 percent. The Revenue Act of 1926 extended further benefits to high-income individuals by lowering estate taxes and repealing the gift tax. Much of the tax money released to the wealthy by these acts seems to have fueled the speculative excess of the late 1920s as much as it boosted consumer spending and entrepreneurial activity. Mellon, however, did balance the federal budget for a time. Government expenditures fell, as did the national debt.

In addition to tax cuts, Mellon favored the time-honored Republican policy of high tariffs on imported goods. So, too, did spokesmen for several emerging industries. Wartime innovations in chemical and metal processing revived the argument for protection of infant American industries from foreign competition. The Fordney-McCumber Tariff of 1922 dramatically increased rates on chemical and metal products as a safeguard against the revival of German industries that had previously commanded the field. To please the farmers, the new act further extended the duties on imported farm products.

Higher tariffs had unexpected consequences, however. During the war the United States had been transformed from a debtor nation to a creditor nation. Foreign capital had long flowed into the United States, playing an important role in fueling economic expansion. But the private and public credits given the Allies to purchase American supplies during the war had reversed the pattern. Mellon now insisted that the European powers repay all that they had borrowed during the war, but the American tariff walls erected against imports made it all the harder for other nations to sell their products in the United States and thereby acquire dollars with which to repay their war debts. For nearly a decade further extensions of U.S. loans and investments sent more dollars abroad, postponing the settling of accounts.

Rounding out the Republican economic program was a more lenient attitude toward government regulation of corporations. Neither Harding nor his successor, Calvin Coolidge, could dissolve the regulatory agencies created by progressivism, but they named commissioners who promoted "friendly" government regulation. Harding appointed conservatives to the Interstate Commerce Commission, the Federal Reserve Board, and the Federal Trade Commission. One senator characterized the new appointments as "the nullification of federal law by a process of boring from within." Republican senator Henry Cabot Lodge agreed, noting, "We have torn up Wilsonism by the roots."

ADMINISTRATIVE CORRUPTION Republican conservatives such as Lodge, Mellon, Coolidge, and Hoover were operating out of a sincere philosophical conviction intended to benefit the nation. By contrast, the crass members of Harding's Ohio gang used their White House connections to line their own pockets. In 1923, Harding learned that the head of the Veterans Bureau was systematically looting the government's medical and hospital supplies. The corrupt administrator resigned and fled to Europe, and Harding's general counsel committed suicide.

Not long afterward a close crony of Attorney General Harry Daugherty's also shot himself. The man held no federal appointment, but he had set up an office in the Justice Department from which he peddled influence for a fee. Daugherty himself was implicated in the fraudulent handling of German assets seized after the war. When investigated, he refused to testify on the grounds that he might incriminate himself. Twice brought to court, he was never indicted; possibly the lack of evidence was a result of his destruction of pertinent records. These were but the most visible of the many scandals that touched the Justice Department, the Prohibition Bureau, and other federal agencies under Harding.

But one major scandal rose above all others. Teapot Dome, like the Watergate break-in fifty years later, became the catchword for an era of government corruption. A government-owned oil deposit on federal land in Wyoming,

Teapot Dome had been set aside to be administered by the Interior Department under Albert Fall. Fall let private companies exploit the oil deposits, arguing that such contracts were in the government's interest. Yet he acted in secret, without allowing competitive bids.

Suspicion grew when Fall's personal standard of living suddenly skyrocketed. It turned out that he had taken "loans" of about $400,000 (which came in "a little black bag") from oil executives. For the rest of his life, Fall insisted that the loans were unrelated to the oil leases and that he had contrived a good deal for the government, but at best the questionable circumstances revealed his fatal blindness to propriety.

Harding himself avoided public disgrace. How much he knew of the scandals swirling around him remains unclear, but he knew enough to give the appearance of being troubled. "My God, this is a hell of a job!" he confided to a journalist. "I have no trouble with my enemies, I can take care of my enemies all right. But my damn friends, my God-damn friends. . . . They're the ones that keep me walking the floor nights!" In 1923, Harding left on what

"Juggernaut" of corruption

This 1924 cartoon alludes to the dimensions of the Teapot Dome scandal.

would be his last journey, a speaking tour to the West Coast and a trip to the Alaska Territory. In Seattle he suffered an attack of food poisoning, recovered briefly, then died in a San Francisco hotel.

Not since the death of Lincoln had there been such an outpouring of grief for a "beloved president," for the kindly, ordinary man who found it in his heart (as Wilson had not) to pardon Eugene Debs, the former Socialist candidate who had been jailed for opposing U.S. intervention in World War I. As Harding's funeral train moved toward Washington, D.C., then back to Ohio, millions stood by the tracks to honor their lost leader.

Eventually, however, grief yielded to scorn and contempt. For nearly a decade after Harding's death, scandalous revelations concerning his administrative officials were paraded before congressional committees and then the courts. Harding's extramarital affairs also came to light. As a result of the amorous detours and corrupt associates, Harding's foreshortened administration came to be viewed as one of the worst in history. More recently, however, scholars have credited Harding with leading the nation out of the turmoil of the postwar years and creating the foundation for the decade's remarkable economic boom. They also stress that he was a hardworking president who played a far more forceful role in shaping economic and foreign policies than was previously believed. Harding also promoted diversity and civil rights. He appointed Jews to key federal positions. No previous president had promoted women's rights as forcefully as Harding did. Still, even Harding's foremost scholarly defender admits that he lacked good judgment and "probably should never have been president."

"SILENT CAL"   The news of Harding's death came when Vice President Calvin Coolidge was visiting his father in the mountain village of Plymouth, Vermont, his birthplace. There, at 2:47 A.M. on August 3, 1923, by the light of a kerosene lamp, Colonel John Coolidge administered the oath of office to his son. The rustic simplicity of Plymouth, the very name itself, evoked just the image of traditional values and solid integrity that the country would long for amid the wake of the Harding scandals.

Coolidge brought to the White House a clear conviction that the presidency should revert to its passive stance of the Gilded Age and defer to the leadership of Congress. Americans embraced the unflappability and unstained integrity of Silent Cal and his conservatism. Even more than Harding, Coolidge identified the nation's welfare with the success of big business. "The chief business of the American people is business," he intoned. "The man who works there worships there." Where Harding had sought to balance the interests of labor, agriculture, and industry, Coolidge focused on

Conservatives in the White House

Warren Harding (left) and Calvin Coolidge (right).

industrial development at the expense of the other two areas. He sought to unleash the free-enterprise system, and even more than Harding, he strove to end government regulation and reduce taxes.

THE ELECTION OF 1924   In filling out Harding's unexpired term, Calvin Coolidge distanced himself from the scandals and put two lawyers of undoubted integrity in charge of the prosecutions. A man of honesty and ability, a good administrator who delegated well and managed Republican factions adroitly, Coolidge quietly took control of the Republican party machinery and seized the initiative in the campaign for the 1924 nomination, which he won with only token opposition.

The Coolidge luck held as the Democrats again fell victim to internal dissension, prompting humorist Will Rogers's classic statement that "I am a member of no organized political party. I am a Democrat." The party's divisions reflected the deep rift between the new urban culture of the twenties and the more traditional hinterland, a gap that the party could not bridge. It took 103 ballots to bestow a tarnished nomination on John W. Davis, a prominent New York City lawyer from West Virginia who could nearly outdo Coolidge in conservatism.

While the Democrats bickered, a new farm-labor coalition was mobilizing a third-party effort. Meeting in Cleveland, Ohio, on July 4, 1924, farm and labor groups reorganized the Progressive party and nominated Wisconsin senator Robert M. La Follette for president. La Follette also won the support of the Socialist party and the American Federation of Labor.

In the campaign, Coolidge focused on La Follette, whom he called a dangerous radical who would turn America into a "communistic and socialistic state." The country preferred to "keep cool with Coolidge," who swept both the popular and the electoral votes by decisive majorities. Davis took only the solidly Democratic South, and La Follette carried only his native Wisconsin.

THE NEW ERA

Business executives interpreted the 1924 Republican victory as a vindication of their leadership, and Coolidge saw in the decade's surging prosperity a confirmation of his pro-business philosophy. In fact, the prosperity and technological achievements of the time had much to do with Coolidge's victory over the Democrats and Progressives. Many middle-class voters who had formed an important part of the Progressive coalition were now absorbed instead into the new corporate and consumer world created by advances in communications, transportation, and business organization. As more and more commentators stressed, the United States was entering a "new era" of advanced capitalism. The 1920s were years of extraordinary innovation and inventiveness.

THE CONSUMER CULTURE The economy was changing markedly during the 1920s. Dramatic increases in efficiency meant that the marketplace was flooded with new consumer delights. Goods once available only to the wealthy were now accessible to the general public. Middle-class consumers could own cameras, wristwatches, cigarette lighters, vacuum cleaners, and washing machines. But the production of those enticing new goods would produce economic havoc if people did not abandon their traditional notions of frugality and go on a buying spree. Hence, business leaders, salespersons, and public relations experts began a concerted effort to eradicate what was left of the original Protestant ethic's emphasis on plain living.

The public had to be taught the joys of carefree consumerism, and the new industry of mass advertising obliged. By portraying impulse buying as a therapeutic measure to bolster self-esteem, advertisers shrewdly helped undermine notions of frugality. In his popular novel *Babbitt*, Sinclair Lewis

The rise of radio

The radio brought this farm family together and connected them to the outside world. By the end of the 1930s, millions would tune in to newscasts, soap operas, sports events, and church services.

recognized advertising's impact upon middle-class life: "These standard advertised wares—toothpastes, socks, tires, cameras, instantaneous hot water heaters—were the symbols and proofs of excellence."

Inventions in communications, such as motion pictures, radio, and telephones, were transforming social life and creating a more homogeneous national culture. In 1905 the first movie house opened, in Philadelphia, and within three years there were nearly 10,000 movie theaters nationwide. During the next decade, Hollywood, California, became the center of movie production, spinning out Westerns and the timeless comedies of Mack Sennett's Keystone Company, where slapstick comedians, most notably Charlie Chaplin, perfected their art, transforming it into a powerful form of social criticism. By the mid-1930s every large city and most small towns had movie theaters, and films replaced oratory as the chief mass entertainment, growing into a multimillion-dollar industry that catered to the working poor as well as to the affluent. In the mid-1920s motion pictures were attracting 50 million people weekly, or half the national population.

Radio broadcasting had an even more spectacular growth. The first radio commercial aired in 1922. By the end of that year, there were over 500 stations and some 3 million receivers in action. In 1927, Congress established a Federal Radio Commission to regulate the industry; in 1934 it became the Federal Communications Commission, with authority over other forms of communication as well. Calvin Coolidge was the first president to address the nation by radio, and he did so each month, paving the way for Franklin Roosevelt's popular and influential "fireside chats."

A nationwide mass culture replaced the local and regional economies of the nineteenth century. The leading advertising agency explained in 1926 that the advent of nationally circulated magazines, chain stores, syndicated news features, motion pictures, national brand names, and radio programs was creating "a nation which lives to [the same] pattern everywhere." Nonetheless, even though working-class folk could buy brand goods, phonographs, and radios, as well as movie tickets, the new consumer culture did not erase social distinctions. "Participating in mass culture," as one historian stressed, "made them feel no more mainstream or middle class, no less ethnic, religious, or working class than they already felt."

AIRPLANES, AUTOMOBILES, AND THE ECONOMY Advances in transportation were equally startling. Wilbur and Orville Wright, owners of a Dayton, Ohio, bicycle shop, built the first airplane, which they flew on a beach near Kitty Hawk, North Carolina, in 1903. The use of planes advanced slowly until the outbreak of war in Europe in 1914. An American aircraft industry developed during the war but foundered in the postwar demobilization. In 1925 the government began to subsidize the industry through airmail contracts, and the following year it started a program of federal aid to air transport and navigation, making available funds for the construction of airports.

Aviation received a psychological boost in 1927 when Charles A. Lindbergh Jr. flew the first transatlantic solo flight, traveling from New York to Paris in thirty-three and a half hours. The scope of the New York City parade honoring Lindbergh surpassed even the celebration of victory in World War I. The accomplishments of Lindbergh and other aviators helped catapult the aviation industry into prominence. By 1930 there were forty-three airline companies in operation in the United States.

Nonetheless, by far the most significant transportation development of the twentieth century was the automobile. The first motor car had been manufactured for sale in 1895, but the founding of the Ford Motor Company in 1903 revolutionized the industry. Ford's reliable Model T appeared in 1908 at a price of $850 (in 1924 it would sell for $290). Henry Ford aimed "to democratize the

Ford Motor Company's Highland Park plant, 1913

Gravity slides and chain conveyors contributed to the mass production of automobiles.

automobile. When I'm through everybody will be able to afford one, and about everyone will have one." He was right. In 1916 the number of cars manufactured passed 1 million; by 1920 more than 8 million were registered, and in 1929 there were more than 23 million. The production of automobiles stimulated the whole economy by consuming large amounts of steel, rubber, glass, and textiles. It gave rise to a gigantic market for oil products just as the Spindletop gusher in Texas heralded the opening of vast southwestern oil fields. The automotive revolution also quickened the movement for good roads, introduced efficient mass-production assembly-line techniques to other industries, speeded transportation and tourism, encouraged the sprawl of suburbs, and sparked real estate booms in California and Florida.

STABILIZING THE ECONOMY   During the 1920s the efficiency craze, which had been a prominent feature of the progressive impulse, powered the wheels of mass production and consumption and became a cardinal belief of Republican leaders. As Harding's and Coolidge's dynamic secretary of commerce, Herbert Hoover transformed the trifling Commerce Department into the most active agency of those two Republican administrations. During a period of government retrenchment, Hoover promoted expansion. He sought out new markets for business and sponsored more than 1,000 conferences on product design, production, and distribution. He also extended the wartime emphasis on standardization to include, for example, automobile tires and paving bricks, bedsprings and toilet paper.

Most of all, Hoover endorsed the burgeoning trade-association movement. The organization of business trade associations became his favorite instrument for "stabilization," to avoid the waste inherent in competition. Through such associations, executives in a given field shared information on sales, purchases, shipments, production, and prices. That information allowed them to plan with more confidence and thereby more accurately predict costs, set prices, and assess markets while maintaining a more stable workforce and paying steadier wages. Sometimes abuses crept in as the associations skirted the edge of legality by engaging in price-fixing and other monopolistic practices, but the Supreme Court in 1925 held the practice of sharing information as such to be within the law.

THE BUSINESS OF FARMING   During the Harding and Coolidge administrations, agriculture remained the weakest sector in the economy, in many ways as weak as it had been during the 1890s, when cities flourished and much of rural America languished. For a brief time after World War I, farmers' hopes soared on wings of prosperity. The wartime boom lasted into 1920, and then commodity prices collapsed as European farmers resumed high levels of production. Low prices persisted into 1923, especially in the wheat and corn belts. A bumper cotton crop in 1926 resulted in a price collapse and an early taste of depression in much of the South, where foreclosures and bankruptcies spread.

In some ways, farmers shared the business outlook of the so-called New Era. Many commercial farms, like many corporations, were getting larger, more efficient, and more mechanized. By 1930 about 13 percent of all farmers had tractors, and the proportion was even higher on the western plains. Better plows and other new machines were part of the mechanization process that accompanied improved crop yields, fertilizers, and methods of animal breeding.

Farm organizations of the 1920s moved from the attempted alliance with urban labor that had marked the Populist era toward a new view of farmers as profit-conscious business owners. During the postwar farm depression, farm groups formed regional commodity-marketing associations, which enabled them to negotiate ironclad contracts with producers for the delivery of their crops over a period of years. These associations also brought order to the marketing of farm products, requiring uniform standards and grades, efficient handling and advertising, and a business-like organization with professional technicians and executives.

But if concern with marketing co-ops and other business-like approaches drew farmers further from populist traditions, nagging problems still invited political solutions. The most effective political response to the collapse of farm prices in the early 1920s was the formation of the farm bloc, a congressional coalition of western Republicans and southern Democrats that put through a program of agricultural legislation from 1921 to 1923. During that period the farm bloc passed bills exempting farm cooperatives from anti-trust laws and creating new credit banks that could lend to cooperative producing and marketing associations.

In the spring of 1924, Senator Charles L. McNary of Oregon and Representative Gilbert N. Haugen of Iowa introduced a bill to secure "equality for agriculture in the benefits of the protective tariff." Their plan sought to dump American farm surpluses on the world market in order to raise commodity prices in the home market. The goal was to achieve "parity"—that is, to raise domestic farm prices to a point where farmers would have the same purchasing power relative to other commodity prices that they had enjoyed between 1909 and 1914, a time viewed in retrospect as a golden age of American agriculture. A McNary-Haugen bill finally passed both houses of Congress in 1927 and again a year later, only to be vetoed both times by President Coolidge, who criticized the measure as an unsound effort at price-fixing and un-American and unconstitutional to boot. Nonetheless, the bill catapulted the farm problem into the arena of national debate, defined it as a problem of crop surpluses, and revived the political alliance between the South and the West.

SETBACKS FOR UNIONS   Urban workers more than farmers shared in the affluence of the 1920s. "A workman is far better paid in America than anywhere else in the world," a French visitor wrote in 1927, "and his standard of living is enormously higher." Nonfarm workers gained about 20 percent in real wages between 1921 and 1928, while farm income rose only 10 percent. The benefits of this rise were distributed unevenly, however. Miners and textile workers suffered a decline in real wages. In these and other trades, technological unemployment followed the introduction of new production methods and more efficient machines, because technology eliminated some jobs at the same time that it created others.

Organized labor did no better than organized agriculture in the 1920s. Even though President Harding had supported the practice of collective bargaining and tried to reduce the twelve-hour workday and the six-day workweek so that laborers "may have time for leisure and family life," he ran into stiff opposition in Congress. Overall, unions suffered a setback after the growth years of the war as the Red Scare and the strikes of 1919 created concerns that unions practiced political subversion. The brief postwar depression of 1921 further weakened the unions, as did the popularity of open-shop

The Gastonia strike

These female textile workers pit their strength against that of a national guardsman during the strike at the Loray Mill in Gastonia, North Carolina, in 1929.

associations. While the open shop in theory implied only the employer's right to hire anyone, in practice it often meant discrimination against unionists and the refusal to recognize unions even in shops where most of the workers belonged to one. Prosperity, propaganda, welfare capitalism, and active hostility combined to cause union membership to drop from about 5 million in 1920 to 3.5 million in 1929.

PRESIDENT HOOVER, ENGINEER

HOOVER VERSUS SMITH   On August 2, 1927, while on vacation in the Black Hills of South Dakota, President Coolidge passed to reporters slips of paper with the curious statement "I do not choose to run for President in 1928." Exactly what he meant puzzled observers and has since perplexed historians. Apparently he at least half hoped to be drafted at the convention, but his statement cleared the way for Herbert Hoover to mount an active campaign for the Republican nomination. Well before the 1928 Republican Convention in Kansas City, Hoover was too far in the lead to be stopped. The party platform took credit for postwar prosperity, debt and tax reduction, and the high protective tariff that had been in operation since 1922 ("as vital to American agriculture as it is to manufacturing"). It rejected the McNary-Haugen program but promised to create a farm board to manage crop surpluses more efficiently.

The Democratic nomination went to Governor Alfred E. Smith of New York. The Democratic party had had its fill of factionalism in 1924, and all remained fairly harmonious until Smith revealed in his acceptance speech a desire to liberalize Prohibition. Hoover, by contrast, had pronounced the outlawing of alcoholic beverages "a great social and economic experiment, noble in motive and far-reaching in purpose," and he called for improved enforcement.

The two candidates projected sharply different images. Hoover was the Quaker son of middle America, the successful engineer and businessman from rural Iowa, the brilliant architect of Republican prosperity, a simple man who dressed plainly, spoke tersely, and followed his strong conscience. Smith was the prototype of those things that rural and small-town America distrusted: the son of Irish immigrants, Catholic, and a critic of Prohibition.

Campaign sheet music

The sheet music for the Democratic nominee, Alfred Smith (left) and the Republican nominee, Herbert Hoover (right) drew on popular tunes and motifs of the time.

Outside the large cities such qualities were handicaps that Smith could scarcely surmount, for all his affability and wit. Protestant fundamentalists launched a furious attack on him. The Klan mailed out thousands of postcards proclaiming that the Catholic New Yorker was the Antichrist.

In the third consecutive Republican landslide, Hoover won 21 million popular votes to Smith's 15 million and an even more top-heavy electoral majority of 444 to 87. Hoover even cracked the Solid South, leaving Smith only six Deep South states plus Massachusetts and Rhode Island. The election was above all a vindication of Republican prosperity, but the shattering defeat of the Democrats concealed a major political realignment in the making. Smith had nearly doubled the vote for the Democratic candidate of four years before. Smith's image, though a handicap in the hinterlands, swung big northern cities back into the Democratic column. In the agricultural states of the West, there were signs that some disgruntled farmers had switched over to the Democrats. A coalition of urban workers and unhappy farmers was in the making, and the Great Depression of the 1930s would solidify it.

HOOVER IN CONTROL   The milestone year of 1929 dawned with high hopes. The economy seemed solid, income was rising, and the chief architect of Republican prosperity was about to enter the White House. "I have no fears for the future of our country," Hoover told his inauguration audience. "It is bright with hope."

Herbert Hoover

"I have no fears for the future of our country," Hoover told the nation at his inauguration in 1929.

Forgotten in the rush of later events would be Hoover's credentials as a progressive, humanitarian president. Over the objection of Treasury Secretary Mellon, he announced a plan for tax reductions in the low-income brackets. He shunned corrupt patronage practices, and he refused to countenance "Red hunts" or interference with peaceful picketing of the White House. He also defended his wife's right to invite prominent African Americans to the White House, and he sought more money for all-black Howard University.

Hoover showed greater sympathy than Coolidge for the struggling agricultural sector. In 1929 he pushed through Congress the Agricultural Marketing Act, which established both a Federal Farm Board with a revolving loan fund of $500 million to help farm cooperatives market commodities and a program enabling the Farm Board to set up "stabilization corporations" empowered to buy surpluses. To open up glutted markets, he also proposed higher tariffs on imported farm products. After a fourteen-month struggle with competing interests, however, Hoover settled for a generally upward revision of tariffs on manufactures as well as farm goods. The Hawley-Smoot Tariff of 1930 carried duties to a new high. Average rates went from about 32 to 40 percent. More than 1,000 economists petitioned Hoover to veto the bill because, they predicted, it would raise prices paid by consumers, damage the export trade and thus hurt farmers, promote inefficiency, and provoke foreign reprisals. Events proved them right, but Hoover felt that he had to go along with his party in an election year. That proved to be a disastrous mistake, for it only exacerbated the growing economic depression.

THE ECONOMY OUT OF CONTROL   Depression? Most Americans during the 1920s had come to assume that there would never be another depression. Their misguided optimism proved to be an important factor in generating the economic free fall after 1929. After 1921 the idea that American business had entered a new era of *permanent* growth had taken hold. Such naive talk helped promote an array of get-rich-quick schemes.

Until 1927 stock values had risen with profits, but then they began to soar on wings of fanciful speculation. Treasury secretary Mellon's tax reductions had released money that, with the help of aggressive brokerage houses, found its way to Wall Street. One could now buy stock on margin—that is, make a small down payment (usually 10 percent) and borrow the rest from a broker, who held the stock as security against a down market. If the stock price fell and the buyer failed to provide more cash, the broker could sell the stock to cover his loan.

Gamblers in the market ignored warning signs. By 1927 residential construction and automobile sales were catching up to demand, business inventories had risen, and the rate of consumer spending had slowed. By mid-1929, production, employment, and other gauges of economic activity were declining. Still the stock market rose, driven by excessive confidence and perennial greed. By 1929 the stock market had become a fantasy world. Conservative financiers and brokers who counseled caution went unheeded. Hoover worried, too, and he sought to discourage speculation, but to no avail. On September 4 stock prices wavered, and the next day they dropped. The great bull market staggered on into October, trending downward but with enough good days to keep hope alive. On October 22 a leading bank president told reporters, "I know of nothing fundamentally wrong with the stock market or with the underlying business and credit structure."

THE CRASH AND ITS CAUSES   The next day, stock values tumbled, and the day after that a wild scramble to unload stocks lasted until word arrived that leading bankers had formed a pool to buy stocks and halt the slide. For the rest of the week, stock prices steadied, but after a weekend to think the situation over, people began to sell their stocks. On Tuesday, October 29, the most devastating single day in the market's history to that point, the index dropped almost 13 percent. The plunge in prices fed on itself as brokers sold the shares they held for buyers who failed to come up with more cash. During October the value of stocks on the New York Stock Exchange fell by an average of 37 percent.

Business and government leaders initially expressed hope. According to President Hoover, "the fundamental business of the country" was sound. Some speculators who got out of the market went back in for bargains but found themselves caught in a slow erosion of values. By 1933 the value of stocks on the New York Stock Exchange was less than 20 percent of the value at the market's 1929 peak.

Caution was now the watchword for consumers and business leaders. Buyers held out for lower prices, orders fell off, wages fell or ceased altogether, and the decline in purchasing power brought further cutbacks in business activity. From 1929 to 1932, personal income declined by more than half. Unemployment continued to rise dramatically, from 1.6 million in 1929 to 12.8 million in 1933, from 3 percent to 25 percent of the labor force. Farmers, already in trouble, faced catastrophe as commodity prices were cut in half. More than 9,000 banks closed during this period, hundreds of factories and mines shut down, entire towns were abandoned, and thousands of farms were sold to pay debts. A cloud of gloom spread across the nation.

The stock market crash alone did not cause the Great Depression, but it did reveal major structural flaws in the economy and in government policies. Too many businesses during the 1920s had maintained prices and taken profits while holding down wages. As a result, about a third of the nation's personal income went to only 5 percent of the population. By plowing profits back into expansion rather than raising wages, business brought on a growing imbalance between rising productivity and declining purchasing power. As the demand for goods declined, the rate of investment in new plants and equipment also began to decline. For a time the softness of purchasing power was concealed by an increase in installment buying, and the deflationary effects of high tariffs were concealed by the volume of foreign loans and investments, which supported foreign demand for American goods. But the flow of American capital abroad began to dry up when the stock market became a more attractive investment. Swollen profits and dividends enticed the rich into market speculation. When trouble came, the bloated corporate structure collapsed.

Government policies also contributed to the debacle. The domineering secretary of the Treasury in the 1920s, Andrew Mellon, displayed a supreme confidence in market capitalism. He himself was one of the wealthiest men in the world. To him the appropriate role of government was to promote free enterprise by cutting taxes, reducing regulation, and balancing the budget. Mellon's tax reductions led to oversaving by the consuming public, which helped diminish the demand for consumer goods. The growing money supply fed the fever of speculation by lowering interest rates. Hostility toward unions discouraged collective bargaining and may have worsened the prevalent imbalances in income. High tariffs discouraged foreign trade. Lax enforcement of anti-trust laws encouraged concentration, monopolies, and high prices.

Another culprit was the gold standard. The world monetary system remained fragile throughout the 1920s. When economic output, prices, and savings began dropping in 1929, policy makers—certain that they had to keep their currencies tied to gold at all costs—either did nothing or tightened money supplies, thus exacerbating the downward spiral. The only way to restore economic stability within the constraints of the gold standard was to let prices and wages continue to fall. The best policy, Andrew Mellon advised, would be to "liquidate labor, liquidate stocks, liquidate the farmers, liquidate real estate," allowing the downturn to "purge the rottenness out of the system." Such passivity helped turn a recession into the world's worst depression.

THE HUMAN TOLL OF THE DEPRESSION   The devastating collapse of the economy caused immense social hardships across the nation. By 1933, 13 million people were out of work, and many more found themselves working fewer hours. African Americans and Mexicans were usually the first laid off. Factories shut down, banks closed, and farms went bankrupt; millions of people found themselves not only jobless but also homeless and penniless. Hungry people lined up at soup kitchens; others rummaged through trash cans behind restaurants. Local welfare agencies were swamped with appeals for charity and quickly ran out of funds. Many of the destitute slept on park benches or in alleys. Others congregated in makeshift shelters in vacant lots. Thousands of desperate men in search of jobs rode the rails. These hobos, or tramps, as they were derisively called, sneaked onto empty railway cars and rode from town to town looking for work. During the winter homeless people wrapped themselves in newspapers to keep warm, sarcastically referring to their coverings as Hoover blankets. Some grew weary of their grim fate and ended their lives. Suicide rates soared during the 1930s. America had never before experienced social distress on such a scale.

HOOVER'S EFFORTS AT RECOVERY   Although the policies of public officials helped bring on economic collapse, few political or economic leaders acknowledged the severity of the crisis: all that was needed, they thought, was a slight correction of the market. Those who held to the theory of limited government, such as Andrew Mellon, thought the economy would cure itself. Government should do nothing; the depression should be allowed to run its course until the economy had purged itself of its excesses. Hoover, however, was unwilling to sit by and let events take their course. In fact, he did more than any previous president had done in such dire economic circumstances. Still, his own philosophy, now hardened into dogma, set strict limits on action by the federal government, and he refused to set his philosophy aside even to meet the unprecedented emergency.

Hoover believed that the country's main need was confidence. In speech after speech, he exhorted the public to keep up hope. He asked business and labor leaders to keep the mills and shops open, maintain wage levels, and spread out the work to avoid layoffs—in short, to let the shock fall on corporate profits rather than on purchasing power. In return, union leaders, who had little choice, agreed to refrain from making wage demands and staging strikes.

While reassuring the public, however, Hoover also accelerated the start of government construction projects in order to provide jobs, but state and local cutbacks more than offset the new federal spending. At Hoover's demand, the Federal Reserve returned to an easier credit policy, and Congress passed a modest tax reduction to put more purchasing power into people's pockets. The high Hawley-Smoot Tariff, proposed at first to help farmers, brought reprisals abroad, devastating foreign trade.

As always, depression hurt the political party and president in power. Near the city dumps and along railroad tracks, the dispossessed huddled in shacks of tar paper and galvanized iron, in old packing boxes and abandoned cars. These squalid settlements were labeled Hoovervilles; a Hoover flag was an empty pocket turned inside out. Such scornful labels reflected the quick erosion of Hoover's political support. In 1930 the Democrats gained their first national victory since 1916, winning a majority in the House and enough gains in the Senate to control it in coalition with farm-state Republicans in the West.

CONGRESSIONAL INITIATIVES   With a new Congress in session, demands for federal action impelled Hoover to stretch his philosophy of government to its limits. He was ready now to use government resources to at least shore up the financial institutions. In early 1932 the new Congress responded to pleas from the desperate banking sector by setting up the Reconstruction Finance Corporation (RFC) to provide emergency loans to banks, life-insurance companies, building-and-loan societies, farm-mortgage associations, and railroads. The RFC staved off some bankruptcies, but Hoover's critics charged that it favored business at the expense of workers. The RFC nonetheless remained a key federal agency throughout the decade and during World War II.

Further help to the financial structure came with the Glass-Steagall Act of 1932, which increased the availability of commercial loans. It also released about $750 million in gold formerly used to back Federal Reserve notes, countering the effect of foreign withdrawals and domestic hoarding of gold at the same time that it enlarged the supply of credit. For homeowners the Federal Home Loan Bank Act of 1932 created with Hoover's blessing a series of discount banks for home mortgages. They provided to savings-and-loan

Impact of the Depression

Two children set up shop in a Hooverville in Washington, D.C.

associations a service much like the one that the Federal Reserve System provided to commercial banks.

Hoover's critics argued that all these measures reflected a dubious "trickle-down" theory. If government could help banks and railroads, asked New York senator Robert F. Wagner, "is there any reason why we should not likewise extend a helping hand to that forlorn American, in every village and every city of the United States, who has been without wages since 1929?" The contraction of credit devastated such debtors as farmers and those who made purchases on the installment plan or held balloon mortgages, whose monthly payments increased over time.

By 1932, members of Congress were filling the hoppers with bills to provide federal relief directly to distressed people. At that point, Hoover might have pleaded "dire necessity," taken the leadership of the relief movement, and salvaged his political fortunes. Instead, he held back and only grudgingly edged toward federal humanitarian relief. On July 21, 1932, he signed the Emergency Relief Act, which avoided a federal dole (direct cash payments to individuals) but gave the RFC $300 million for relief loans to the states, authorized loans of up to $1.5 billion for state and local construction projects, and appropriated $322 million for federal construction.

FARMERS AND VETERANS IN PROTEST Government relief for farmers had long since been abandoned. Faced with total loss, some farmers defied the law. Angry mobs stopped foreclosures and threatened to lynch bankers and judges. In Nebraska, farmers burned corn to keep warm; dairy farmers dumped milk into roadside ditches in an effort to raise prices. Like voluntary efforts to reduce the number of acres cultivated, these strikes generally failed, but they vividly dramatized the farmers' frustration and anger.

Fears of organized revolt arose when unemployed World War I veterans converged on Washington, D.C., in the spring of 1932. The "Bonus Expeditionary Force" grew quickly to more than 20,000. Their purpose was to get immediate payment of the cash bonus to 4 million war veterans that Congress had voted in 1924 in the form of life insurance payable in 1945 (earlier to heirs of deceased veterans). The House approved a bonus bill, but when the Senate voted it down, most of the veterans went home. The rest, along with their wives and children, having no place to go, camped in vacant government buildings and in a shantytown within sight of the Capitol. The chief of the Washington police gave the squatters a friendly welcome and won their trust, but a fearful White House fretted. Eager to disperse the destitute veterans, Hoover persuaded Congress to vote funds to buy their tickets home. More left, but others stayed even after Congress adjourned, hoping at least to meet with the embattled president.

Anger and frustration

Unemployed veterans, members of the Bonus Expeditionary Force, clash with
Washington, D.C. police at Anacostia Flats in July 1932.

Late in July the administration ordered the shantytown razed. In the ensuing melee a policeman panicked, fired into the crowd, and killed two veterans. The secretary of war then dispatched about 700 soldiers under General
Douglas MacArthur, who was aided by junior officers Dwight D. Eisenhower
and George S. Patton. The soldiers easily drove out the unarmed veterans and
their families and burned the shacks. General MacArthur self-righteously
explained in his report that when dealing with "riotous elements," a show of
"obvious strength gains a moral ascendancy." MacArthur hysterically claimed
that the "mob," spurred by "the essence of revolution," was about to seize
control of the government. To most Americans the Bonus Army was more
pathetic than threatening. The spectacle of army troops using tanks to dislodge unarmed veterans did not help Hoover's eroding image.

The stress took its toll on Hoover's health and morale. "I am so tired," he
sometimes sighed, "that every bone in my body aches." As the months
passed, presidential news conferences grew more strained and less frequent.
When friends urged Hoover to seize the reins of leadership, he replied, "I
can't be a Theodore Roosevelt" or "I have no Wilsonian qualities." His gloom
and growing sense of futility were apparent to the country. In a mood more
despairing than rebellious, Americans waited impatiently to see what the
next presidential campaign would bring.

End of Chapter Review

- **"Return to Normalcy"** Although progressivism lost its appeal after the Great War, the Eighteenth Amendment (paving the way for Prohibition) and the Nineteenth Amendment (guaranteeing women's suffrage) marked the culmination of that movement at the national level. Reformers still actively worked for good and efficient government at the local level, but overall the drive was for a "return to normalcy"—conformity and moral righteousness.

- **Era of Conservatism** Many Americans, particularly people in rural areas and members of the middle class, wanted a return to a quieter, more conservative way of life after World War I, and Warren Harding's landslide Republican victory allowed just that. The policies of Harding's pro-business cabinet were reminiscent of those of the McKinley White House more than two decades earlier. Union membership declined in the 1920s as workers' rights were rolled back by a conservative Supreme Court and in response to fears of Communist subversion. Workers, however, shared in the affluence of the 1920s, thereby contributing to the rise of a mass culture.

- **Growth of Economy** The budget was balanced through reductions in spending and taxes, while tariffs were raised to protect domestic industries, setting the tone for a prosperous decade. Harding's successor, Calvin Coolidge, actively promoted the interests of big business. The public responded enthusiastically to the mass marketing of new consumer goods such as radios and affordable automobiles. Agriculture, however, lagged after the wartime boom evaporated.

- **The Great Depression** The stock market crash revealed the structural flaws in the economy, but it did not cause the Great Depression. Government policies throughout the twenties—high tariffs, lax enforcement of anti-trust laws, an absence of checks on speculation, and adherence to the gold standard—contributed to the onset of the Depression. Hoover's attempts to remedy the problems were too few and too late. Banks failed, businesses closed, homes and jobs were lost.

CHRONOLOGY

1903	Wright Brothers fly the first airplane
1903	Ford Motor Company is founded
1922	First radio commercial is aired
1923	President Warren Harding dies in office
1927	Charles Lindbergh Jr. makes first solo transatlantic flight
1928	Herbert Hoover is elected president
October 29, 1929	Stock market crashes
1930	Congress passes Hawley-Smoot Tariff
1932	Congress sets up the Reconstruction Finance Corporation
1932	Congress passes the Glass-Steagall Act
1933	Bonus Expeditionary Force converges on Washington to demand payment of bonuses promised to war veterans

KEY TERMS & NAMES

28

NEW DEAL AMERICA

FOCUS QUESTIONS wwnorton.com/studyspace

- What were the immediate challenges facing Franklin Roosevelt in March 1933?
- What were the lasting social effects of the New Deal legislation?
- Why did the New Deal draw criticism from conservatives and liberals?
- How did the New Deal expand the federal government's authority?
- What were the major cultural changes of the 1930s?

Upon arriving in the White House in March 1933, Franklin Delano Roosevelt (FDR) inherited a nation mired in the third year of an unprecedented depression. No other business slump had been so deep, so long, so baffling, or so painful. One out of every four Americans was unemployed, and in many large cities nearly half the adults were out of work. Some 500,000 Americans had lost homes or farms because they could not make their mortgage payments. Thousands of banks had failed; millions of depositors had lost their life savings. The global depression had also helped accelerate the rise of fascism and communism. Totalitarianism was on the march in Europe and Asia—and democratic capitalism was on the defensive. President Roosevelt and a supportive Congress immediately adopted bold measures to relieve the human suffering, restore confidence, and promote economic recovery. Such initiatives provided the foundation for what came to be called welfare capitalism.

FROM HOOVERISM TO THE NEW DEAL

On June 14, 1932, while the ragtag Bonus Army was still encamped in Washington, D.C., Republicans gathered in Chicago to renominate Herbert Hoover. The delegates went through the motions in a mood of defeat. The Democrats, in contrast, converged on Chicago later in the month confident that they would nominate the next president. New York governor Franklin D. Roosevelt had already lined up most of the delegates, and he won the nomination on the fourth ballot.

In a dramatic gesture, Roosevelt appeared in person to accept the nomination instead of awaiting formal notification. He told the expectant delegates, "I pledge you, I pledge myself to a new deal for the American people." What the New Deal would be in practice Roosevelt had little idea as yet, but he was much more flexible and willing to experiment than Hoover. What was more, his upbeat personality communicated joy and hope, as did his campaign song, "Happy Days Are Here Again."

FRANKLIN ROOSEVELT   Born in 1882 into a wealthy family, educated by governesses and tutors at his father's Hudson River estate, Franklin Roosevelt led the cosmopolitan life of a young patrician. After attending an elite Massachusetts boarding school, he earned degrees from Harvard College and Columbia University Law School. While a law student, he married Anna Eleanor Roosevelt, a niece of President Theodore Roosevelt, his own distant cousin.

In 1910, Franklin Roosevelt won a Democratic seat in the New York State Senate. As a freshman legislator he displayed the contradictory qualities that would characterize his political career: he was an aristocrat who empathized with common folk, a traditionalist with a penchant for experimentation, an affable charmer with an infectious smile and upturned chin who harbored profound convictions, and a skilled political tactician with a shrewd sense of timing and a distinctive willingness to listen to and learn from others.

In 1912, Roosevelt had backed Woodrow Wilson, and for both of Wilson's terms he served as his assistant secretary of the navy. Then, in 1920, largely on the strength of his name, he gained the Democratic vice-presidential nomination. Political defeat was followed by personal crisis when in 1921, at the age of thirty-nine, Roosevelt contracted polio, which left him permanently crippled, unable to stand or walk without braces. But his prolonged struggle with this disability transformed the snobbish young aristocrat. A friend recalled that Roosevelt emerged from his struggle with polio "completely warm-hearted, with a new humility of spirit" that led him to identify with the poor and the suffering. For seven years, aided by his talented wife, Roosevelt strengthened his body, and in 1928 he ran for governor of New York and won. Reelected by a whopping majority of 700,000 in 1930, he became the Democratic front-runner for the presidency in 1932.

Behind the public facade of a cheery and self-confident politician, Roosevelt was at times a crass manipulator of people and power. Obsessed with gaining the highest office in the land, he was willing to sacrifice all else in his life—marriage, health, staff, friends—to that end. Roosevelt occasionally inflated his own accomplishments and took credit for those of others, but his own strengths and achievements were considerable. A born leader, he had a talent for surrounding himself with capable people and getting the most out of them. Most important, however, was his bulldog determination to succeed, to overcome all obstacles, to triumph over despair and adversity, and in the process to achieve greatness.

THE 1932 CAMPAIGN   Partly to dispel doubts about his health, Roosevelt set forth on a grueling campaign tour in 1932. He blamed the Depression on Hoover and the Republicans, and he began to define what he meant by the New Deal. Like Hoover, Roosevelt pledged to balance the budget, but he left open the loophole that he would incur short-term deficits to prevent starvation. He was evasive on the tariff, and on farm policy he offered several options pleasing to farmers but ambiguous enough not to alarm city dwellers. He came out unequivocally for strict regulation of electric companies, and he consistently stood by his party's pledge to repeal the Prohibition amendment. Perhaps most important, he recognized that a mature economy would require imaginative national planning: "The country needs, and, unless I mistake its temper, the country demands bold, persistent experimentation." What came across to voters, however, was less the content of his speeches than his irrepressible confidence.

The dour Hoover, by contrast, had no confidence. Democrats, he argued, ignored the international causes of the Depression. Roosevelt's reckless proposals, Hoover warned, "would destroy the very foundations of our American system." But few were listening. Frustrated by the persistent Depression, the country wanted a new course, a new leadership, a new deal.

Some voters took a dim view of both major candidates. Those who believed that only a radical departure would suffice supported the Socialist party candidate, Norman Thomas, who polled 882,000 votes, and a few went on to support the Communist party candidate, who won 103,000 votes. The wonder is that a desperate people did not turn in greater numbers to such radical alternatives. Instead, they swept Roosevelt into office by a whopping margin.

The "New Deal" Candidate

Governor Franklin D. Roosevelt, the Democratic nominee for president in 1932, campaigning in Topeka, Kansas. Roosevelt's confidence inspired voters.

THE INAUGURATION   For the last time the country waited four months, until March 4, for a new president and Congress to take office. The Twentieth Amendment, ratified on January 23, 1933, provided that the president would thereafter take office on January 20 and the newly elected Congress on January 3.

Amid spreading destitution and misery, unemployment continued to rise during the bleak winter of 1932–1933, and panic struck the banking system. As bank after bank collapsed, frantic people rushed to their own banks to remove their savings. The run on the banks exacerbated the crisis and paralyzed the economy. When the Hoover administration left office, four fifths of the nation's banks were closed, and the country was on the brink of economic paralysis.

The profound crisis of confidence that greeted Roosevelt when he took office on March 4, 1933, gave way to a mood of expectancy. The new president promised vigorous action. He asserted "that the only thing we have to fear is fear itself." He would not merely exhort, he promised: "This nation asks for action, and action now!" He called for "broad executive power to

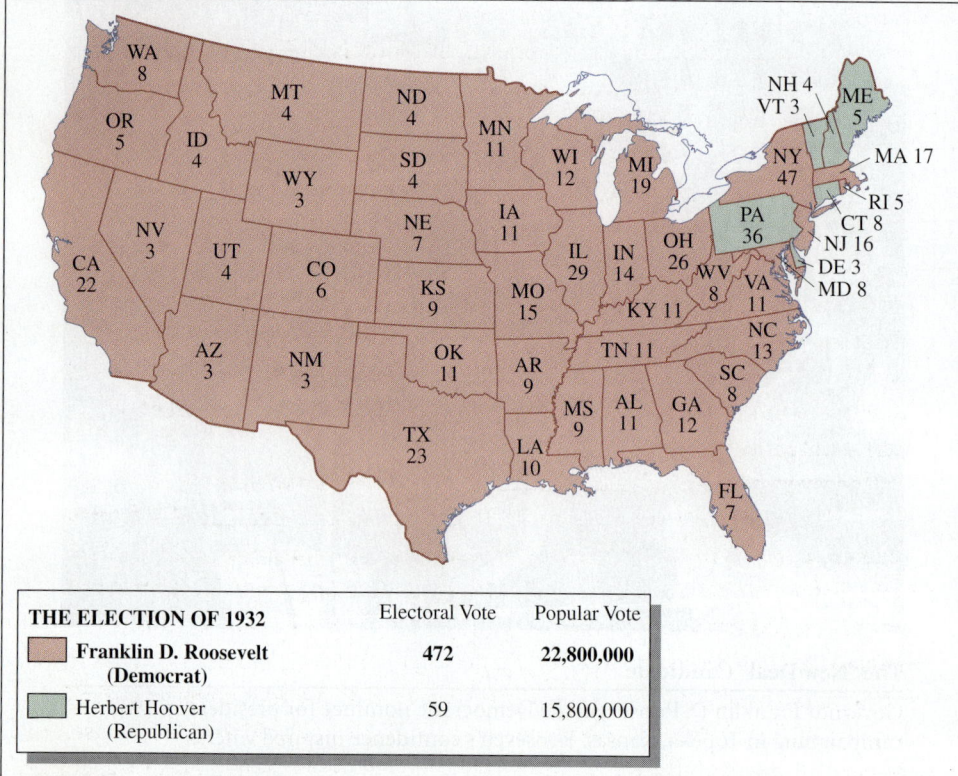

THE ELECTION OF 1932	Electoral Vote	Popular Vote
Franklin D. Roosevelt (Democrat)	472	22,800,000
Herbert Hoover (Republican)	59	15,800,000

Why did Roosevelt appeal to voters struggling during the Depression? What were Hoover's criticisms of Roosevelt's "New Deal"? What policies defined Roosevelt's New Deal during the presidential campaign?

wage a war" against the economic crisis. It was exactly what a distraught nation wanted to hear. One citizen wrote Roosevelt that the speech was "the finest thing this side of heaven. It seemed to give the people, as well as myself, a new hold on life."

COMPETING SOLUTIONS When Roosevelt and the New Dealers arrived in Washington, they were confronted by three major challenges: reviving the devastated economy, relieving the human misery brought on by the Great Depression, and alleviating the desperate plight of farmers and their families. Roosevelt's "brain trust" of advisers developed conflicting opinions about how best to turn the economy around. Some promoted vigorous enforcement of the anti-trust laws as a means of restoring business competition; others argued for the opposite, saying that anti-trust laws should be suspended so as to enable large corporations to collaborate with the federal government in "managing" the economy. Still others called for a massive expansion of welfare programs and a prolonged infusion of government spending to address the profound human crisis and revive the economy.

For his part, Roosevelt vacillated among these three schools of thought. In part his approach reflected the political reality that conservative southern Democrats controlled the Congress and the president could not risk alienating these powerful proponents of balanced budgets and limited government. Roosevelt's inconsistencies also reflected his own outlook. He was a pragmatist rather than an ideologue. As he once explained, "Take a method and try it. If it fails admit it frankly and try another." Roosevelt's New Deal would therefore take the form of a series of trial-and-error actions, several of which were misguided failures.

Roosevelt and his advisers initially settled on a three-pronged strategy. First, they sought to remedy the financial crisis and provide short-term emergency relief for the jobless. Second, they tried to promote industrial recovery by dramatically increasing federal spending and by facilitating cooperative agreements between management and organized labor. Third, they attempted to raise commodity prices (and thereby farm income) by paying farmers to reduce the size of their crops and herds. By reducing the overall supply of farm products, prices for grain and meat would eventually rise. None of these initiatives worked perfectly, but their combined effect was to restore hope and energy to a nation paralyzed by fear and uncertainty.

STRENGTHENING THE MONETARY SYSTEM   On his second day in office, Roosevelt followed through on his pledge to act decisively: he called a special session of Congress and declared a four-day bank holiday to halt hysteria and restore confidence in the financial system. It took the Democratic-controlled Congress only seven hours to pass the Emergency Banking Relief Act, which permitted sound banks to reopen and provided managers for those still in trouble. On March 12, 1933, in the first of his radio-broadcast "fireside chats," the president insisted that it was safer to "keep your money in a reopened bank than under the mattress." The following day, deposits in reopened banks exceeded withdrawals. Having ended the bank panic, Roosevelt slashed military pensions and government payrolls and then urged Congress to pass the Twenty-first Amendment, which ended Prohibition.

Those measures were but the beginning of an avalanche of executive and legislative action. Between March 9 and June 16, 1933, the so-called Hundred Days, Congress passed more than a dozen of Roosevelt's major proposals, a body of legislation whose scope was unprecedented in American history.

The galloping snail

A vigorous Roosevelt drives Congress to action in this *Detroit News* cartoon from March 1933.

With the banking crisis over, an acute debt problem continued to paralyze farmers and homeowners, along with a lingering distrust of the banks. By early 1933, banks were foreclosing on farm mortgages at the rate of 20,000 per month. By executive decree, Roosevelt reorganized all farm credit agencies into the Farm Credit Administration. Congress then authorized the extensive refinancing of farm mortgages at lower interest rates to stem the tide of foreclosures. The Home Owners' Loan Act provided a similar service to city dwellers through the Home Owners' Loan Corporation, which refinanced mortgage loans at lower monthly payments for strapped homeowners. The Banking Act further shored up confidence in the banking system, by creating the Federal Deposit Insurance Corporation to insure personal bank deposits up to $5,000. It also required commercial banks to separate themselves from investment-brokerage operations.

Roosevelt and Congress also tightened the regulation of Wall Street. The Federal Securities Act required that new stock and bond issues register with the Federal Trade Commission and, later, with the Securities and Exchange Commission, a new agency that regulated the chaotic stock and bond markets.

RELIEF MEASURES   Another urgent priority in 1933 was relieving the widespread personal distress caused by the Depression. Hoover had steadfastly resisted using federal funds to provide direct assistance to the unemployed. Roosevelt had fewer qualms.

Congress took a first step toward relief with the creation of the Civilian Conservation Corps (CCC), which provided useful jobs to working-class men aged eighteen to twenty-five. Nearly 3 million CCC workers thereafter performed a variety of jobs in forests, parks, and recreational areas and on soil-conservation projects. They built roads, bridges, campgrounds, and fish hatcheries; planted trees; taught farmers how to control soil erosion; and fought fires. Directed by army officers and foresters, they worked under military discipline and were perhaps the most direct analogue of an army at war in the whole New Deal. Like the military at the time, CCC camps were racially segregated.

The Federal Emergency Relief Administration (FERA) addressed the broader problems of human distress. Designed as a shared undertaking of the federal government and state and city governments, it was in fact shaped and directed by the Roosevelt administration. Harry L. Hopkins, a tireless social worker from Iowa who had directed Roosevelt's relief program in New York State, headed the new effort and became the second most powerful figure in the administration. He pushed the FERA with a boundless energy, spending $5 million within two hours of taking office. FERA funds created jobs by financing state construction of over 5,000 public buildings and 7,000 bridges, organized adult literacy programs, financed college education for poor students, and set up day-care centers for low-income families. The FERA also helped local agencies dispense food and clothing to the needy.

The first large-scale experiment with *federal* work relief, which put people directly on the government payroll at competitive wages, came with the formation of the Civil Works Administration (CWA). Created in November 1933, when it had become apparent that the state-sponsored programs funded by the FERA were inadequate, the CWA provided federal jobs and wages to those unable to find work that winter. It was hastily conceived and implemented but during its four-month existence put to work over 4 million people. The agency organized a variety of useful projects: making highway repairs and laying sewer lines, constructing or improving more than 1,000 airports and 40,000 schools, and providing 50,000 teaching jobs that helped keep rural schools open. As the number of people employed by the CWA soared, the program's costs skyrocketed to over $1 billion. Roosevelt balked at the expenditures and worried that people would become dependent upon federal jobs. So in the spring of 1934, he ordered the CWA dissolved. By April some 4 million workers were again unemployed.

Roosevelt nevertheless continued to favor providing jobs over doling out cash to the unemployed. In 1935, therefore, he asked, for an array of new federal job programs, and Congress responded by passing a $4.8-billion bill providing work relief for the jobless. To manage these programs, Roosevelt created the Works Progress Administration (WPA), headed by Harry Hopkins. Hopkins was told to provide millions of jobs quickly, and as a result some of the new jobs appeared to be make-work or mere "leaning on shovels." But by the time the WPA died, during World War II, it had left permanent monuments on the landscape in the form of buildings, bridges, hard-surfaced roads, airports, and schools.

The WPA also employed a wide range of talented Americans in the Federal Theatre Project, the Federal Art Project, the Federal Music Project, and the Federal Writers' Project. Talented writers such as Ralph Ellison, John Cheever, and Saul Bellow found work writing travel guides to the United States, and Orson Welles directed Federal Theatre Project productions. Critics charged that these programs were frivolous, but Hopkins replied that writers and artists needed "to eat just like other people." The National Youth Administration (NYA), also under the WPA, provided part-time employment to students, set up technical training programs, and aided jobless youths. Twenty-seven-year-old Lyndon Johnson was director of an NYA program in Texas, and Richard Nixon, a penniless Duke University law student, found work through the NYA at 35¢ an hour. Although the WPA took care of only about 3 million out of some 10 million jobless at any one time, in all it helped some 9 million Americans weather desperate times before it expired in 1943.

RECOVERY THROUGH REGULATION

In addition to rescuing the banks and providing immediate relief for the unemployed, Roosevelt and his advisers promoted the recovery of the agricultural and industrial sectors. Roosevelt's brain trust of university-trained experts, lawyers, and professors initially believed that the trend toward economic concentration was inevitable: big businesses were not going to disappear. The brain trust also believed that the mistakes of the 1920s showed that the only way to operate an integrated economy at full capacity and in the public interest was through stringent federal regulation and organized central planning in cooperation with big business, not by breaking up huge corporations. The success of government-led economic planning during World War I reinforced such ideas. New recovery programs sprang from those beliefs.

AGRICULTURAL RECOVERY   The sharp decline in crop prices after 1929 meant that many farmers could not afford to plant or harvest their crops. The Agricultural Adjustment Act of 1933 created the Agricultural Adjustment Administration (AAA), which sought to help raise commodity prices by paying farmers to cut back production. The money for the benefit payments made to farmers would be raised from a "processing tax" levied on the businesses that processed farm products (such as cotton gins, flour mills, and meatpacking plants).

As a complement to the AAA, Roosevelt created the Commodity Credit Corporation. This CCC extended loans to farmers above the market price of their crops, which were kept off the market in federal warehouses. If crop prices rose over time, a farmer could repay the loan, retrieve the crops, and sell them. If prices did not rise, the government kept the crops in storage, and the farmer kept the loaned money.

By the time Congress acted on the farm bills in 1933, the growing season was already under way, and the prospect of another bumper cotton crop created an urgent problem. The AAA reluctantly sponsored a plow-under program. To destroy a growing crop was a "shocking commentary on our civilization," Agriculture Secretary Henry A. Wallace lamented. "I could tolerate it only as a cleaning up of the wreckage from the old days of unbalanced production." In addition to plowing under ripening crops, the AAA encouraged farmers to destroy young livestock in order to reduce their supply and thereby raise prices.

For a while these farm measures worked. By the end of 1934, Wallace could report significant declines in wheat, cotton, and corn production and a simultaneous increase in commodity prices. Farm income increased by 58 percent between 1932 and 1935. The AAA was only partially responsible for the gains, however. The devastating drought that settled over the Great Plains between 1932 and 1935 played a major role in reducing production and creating the epic "dust bowl" migrations so poignantly evoked in John Steinbeck's novel *The Grapes of Wrath*. Many migrant families had actually been driven off the land by AAA benefit programs that encouraged large farmers to take land worked by tenants and sharecroppers out of cultivation.

Although it created unexpected problems, the AAA achieved successes in boosting the overall farm economy. Many conservatives, however, opposed its sweeping powers, and on January 6, 1936, the Supreme Court, in *United States v. Butler,* ruled the AAA's tax on food processors unconstitutional. The administration hastily devised a new plan to achieve crop reduction indirectly, with the Soil Conservation and Domestic Allotment Act (1936), which it pushed through Congress in six weeks. The new act omitted processing taxes and acreage quotas but provided benefit payments to farmers who engaged in soil-conservation practices and cut back on soil-depleting staple crops. Since the money to pay benefits came out of general funds and not from taxes, the approach was not vulnerable to lawsuits.

The act was an almost unqualified success as an engineering and educational project because it helped heal the scars of erosion and the plague of dust storms. But soil conservation nevertheless failed as a device for limiting production. With their worst lands taken out of production, farmers cultivated their fertile acres more intensively. In response, Congress passed the Agricultural Adjustment Act of 1938, which reestablished the earlier programs but left out the processing taxes. Benefit payments to farmers would come from general federal funds. Increasingly, federal farm programs came to dominate the nation's agricultural economy.

INDUSTRIAL RECOVERY   The industrial counterpart to the AAA was the National Industrial Recovery Act (NIRA), passed in 1933. The NIRA had two major components. One created the Public Works Administration (PWA), granting $3.3 billion for public buildings, highway programs, flood control, bridges, tunnels, and aircraft carriers. Under the direction of Interior Secretary Harold L. Ickes, the PWA indirectly served the purpose of work relief. Ickes focused on well-planned permanent improvements, and he used private contractors rather than workers on the government payroll. PWA workers built Virginia's Skyline Drive, New York's Triborough Bridge, the Overseas Highway from Miami to Key West, and Chicago's subway system.

The more controversial and ambitious part of the NIRA created the National Recovery Administration (NRA), headed by the colorful former army general Hugh S. Johnson. Modeled on the War Industries Board of 1917–1918, its purpose was twofold: to stabilize the business sector by reducing chaotic competition through the implementation of codes that set wages and prices and to generate more purchasing power for consumers by providing jobs, defining labor standards, and raising wages. The NRA raised trade union hopes for the protection of basic hour and wage standards and liberal hopes for comprehensive government planning for the economy.

In each industry, committees representing management, labor, and government drew up fair-practice codes. The labor standards were quite progressive. Every code set a forty-hour workweek and minimum weekly wages of $13 ($12 in the South, where living costs were considered lower), which more than doubled earnings in some cases. Labor by children under the age of sixteen was prohibited.

Labor unions, already hard-pressed by the economic downturn and a loss of members, were understandably concerned about the NRA's efforts to reduce competition by allowing businesses to cooperate in fixing wages and prices as well as production levels. To gain their support, the NRA included a provision that guaranteed the right of workers to organize unions. While prohibiting employers from interfering with union-organizing efforts, however, the NRA did not create adequate enforcement measures, nor did it require employers to bargain in good faith with labor representatives.

For a time the NRA worked, and an air of confidence began to replace the depression blues as the downward spiral of wages and prices subsided. But as soon as economic recovery began, critics charged that the larger companies were dominating the code negotiations, that they were using the codes to stifle competition by dividing up markets and entrenching their own positions, and that price-fixing among industry giants was robbing small producers of the chance to compete. The NRA wage codes also excluded agricultural and domestic workers—three out of every four employed African Americans.

A sharecropper's family affected by the Oklahoma dust bowl

When the drought and dust storms showed no signs of relenting, many people headed west toward California.

The effort to develop detailed codes for every industry in the nation proved an administrative nightmare, and the daily annoyances of code enforcement inspired growing hostility among business executives.

By 1935 the NRA had developed more critics than friends, and a full economic recovery was nowhere in sight. In 1935, when the Supreme Court declared the NRA unconstitutional, few mourned. Yet the NRA experiment left an enduring mark. With dramatic suddenness the industry codes had set important new workplace standards, such as the forty-hour workweek and the abolition of child labor. The NRA's endorsement of collective bargaining also spurred union growth.

REGIONAL PLANNING The wide-ranging scope of the New Deal embraced more than the centralized planning approaches of the NRA. The creation of the Tennessee Valley Authority (TVA) was a truly bold venture to revitalize one of the most underdeveloped and poverty-stricken regions of the country, where disease and illiteracy were rampant.

In May 1933, Congress created the TVA as a multipurpose public corporation. The TVA sought to bring cheap electricity to the Tennessee Valley, build fertilizer plants, provide jobs and recreation, and educate rural folk in the ways of modern life. By 1936 the TVA had six dams completed or under way, and the agency had developed a plan to build nine high dams on the Tennessee River, which would create the "Great Lakes of the South." The TVA, moreover, opened the rivers to boat and barge traffic, fostered soil conservation and forestry, experimented with fertilizers, and drew new industry to the region.

The TVA's success at generating greater power consumption and lower electricity rates awakened private utilities to the mass consumer markets. It also transported farmers of the valley from the age of kerosene to the age of electricity. Although 90 percent of urban dwellers had electricity by 1930, only 10 percent of rural Americans did. Through loans of more than $321 million to rural cooperatives, the Rural Electrification Administration paved the way for the electrification of 288,000 rural households in the Tennessee Valley and across the nation.

THE SOCIAL COST OF THE DEPRESSION

Although New Deal programs helped ease the devastation wrought by the Depression, they did not restore prosperity or end the widespread human suffering. Throughout the 1930s the Depression continued to take a toll on ordinary Americans who remained in the throes of a shattered economy that was only slowly working its way back to health during the 1930s.

CONTINUING HARDSHIPS   As late as 1939, some 9.5 million workers (17 percent of the labor force) remained unemployed. Prolonged economic hardship continued to create personal tragedies and tremendous social strains. Poverty led desperate people to do desperate things. Petty theft soared during the 1930s, as did street-corner begging, homelessness, and prostitution. Although the divorce rate dropped, in part because couples could not afford to live separately or pay the legal fees to obtain a divorce, all too often husbands down on their luck simply deserted their wives and children. A 1940 survey revealed that 1.5 million husbands had left home.

With their future uncertain, married couples often decided not to have children; the birthrate plummeted. Couples with children sometimes could not support them. In 1933 the Children's Bureau reported that one out of every five children was not getting enough to eat. Struggling parents often sent children to live with relatives or friends. Some 900,000 children left home and joined the army of homeless "tramps."

DUST BOWL MIGRANTS   In the southern plains of the Midwest and the Mississippi Valley, a decade-long drought spawned an environmental and human catastrophe known as the dust bowl. Colorado, New Mexico, Kansas, Nebraska, Texas, and Oklahoma were the hardest hit. As crops withered, income plummeted. Unrelenting winds swept across the treeless plains, scooping up millions of tons of parched topsoil into billowing dark clouds that floated east across entire states, engulfing farms and towns in what were called black blizzards. A massive dust storm in May 1934 darkened skies from Colorado to the Atlantic seaboard, depositing silt on porches and rooftops as well as on ships in the Atlantic Ocean. In 1937 there were seventy-two major dust storms. The worst of them killed livestock and people and caused railroads to derail and automobiles to careen off roads. By 1938 over 25 million acres of prairie land had lost most of its topsoil.

What made these dust storms worse than normal was the transition during the early twentieth century from scattered subsistence farming to widespread industrial agriculture. Huge "factory farms" used dry-farming techniques to plant vast acres of wheat, corn, and cotton. The advent of powerful tractors, deep-furrow plows, and mechanical harvesters greatly increased the scale and intensity of farming—and the indebtedness of farmers. The mercurial cycle of falling crop prices and rising indebtedness led farmers to plant as much and as often as they could. Overfarming and overgrazing

Dust storm approaching, 1930s

When a dust storm blew in, it brought utter darkness, as well as the sand and grit that soon covered every surface, both indoors and out.

disrupted the fragile ecology of the plains by decimating the native prairie grasses that stabilized the nutrient-rich topsoil. Constant plowing loosened vast amounts of dirt, which were easily swept up by powerful winds during the devastating drought of the 1930s. Hordes of grasshoppers followed the gigantic dust storms and devoured what meager crops were left standing. Human misery paralleled the environmental devastation. Parched farmers could not pay mortgages, and banks foreclosed on their property. Suicides and divorces soared in the dust bowl states. With each year, millions of people abandoned their farms.

Uprooted farmers and their families formed a migratory stream flowing from the blighted South and Midwest toward California, buoyed by currents of hope and desperation. The West Coast was rumored to have plenty of jobs. So off they went on a cross-country trek in search of new opportunities. Although frequently lumped together as "Okies," most of the dust bowl refugees were from cotton belt communities in Arkansas, Texas, and Missouri, as well as Oklahoma. During the 1930s and 1940s, some 800,000 people left those four states and headed to the Far West. Not all were farmers; many were white-collar workers and retailers whose jobs had been tied to the health of the agriculture sector. Most of the dust bowl migrants were white, and most were adults in their twenties and thirties who relocated with spouses and children. Some traveled on trains or buses; others hopped a freight train or hitched a ride; most rode in their own cars, the trip taking four to five days on average.

The dust bowl migrants who had come from cities gravitated to California's urban areas—Los Angeles, San Diego, or San Francisco. Many of the newcomers, however, moved into the San Joaquin Valley, the agricultural heartland of the state. There they discovered that California was no paradise. Only a few of the migrants could afford to buy land. Most found themselves competing with local Latinos and Asians for seasonal work as pickers in the cotton fields or orchards of large corporate farms. Living in tents or crude cabins and frequently on the move, they suffered from exposure and poor sanitation.

They also felt the sting of social prejudice. The writer John Steinbeck explained that "Okie us'ta mean you was from Oklahoma. Now it means you're a dirty son-of-a-bitch. Okie means you're scum. Don't mean nothing in itself, it's the way they say it." Such hostility toward the migrants drove a third of them to return to their home states. Most of the farmworkers who stayed tended to fall back upon their old folkways rather than assimilate into their new surroundings. These gritty "plain folk" had brought with them their own prejudices against blacks and ethnic minorities, as well as a potent tradition of evangelical Protestantism and a distinctive style of music variously labeled country, hillbilly, or cowboy. This "Okie" subculture remains a vivid part of California society.

MINORITIES AND THE NEW DEAL   The Great Depression was especially traumatic for the most disadvantaged groups. However progressive Franklin Roosevelt was on social issues, he failed to assault long-standing patterns of racism and segregation for fear of alienating conservative southern Democrats in Congress. As a result, many of the New Deal programs were for whites only. The Federal Housing Administration, for example, refused to guarantee mortgages on houses purchased by blacks in white neighborhoods. In addition, both the CCC and the TVA practiced racial segregation.

The efforts of the Roosevelt administration to raise crop prices by reducing production proved especially devastating for African Americans and Mexican Americans. To earn the federal payments for reducing crops as provided by the AAA and other New Deal agriculture programs, many farm owners would first take out of cultivation the marginal lands worked by tenants and sharecroppers, many of whom were blacks or Latinos. The effect

Migratory Mexican field worker at home

On the edge of a frozen pea field in Imperial Valley, California, this home to a migratory Mexican family reflects both poverty and impermanence.

was to drive the landless off farms and eliminate the jobs of many migrant workers. Over 200,000 African American tenant farmers nationwide were displaced by the AAA.

Mexican Americans suffered as well. Thousands of Mexicans had migrated to the United States during the 1920s, most of them settling in California, New Mexico, Arizona, Colorado, Texas, and the midwestern states. But because many of them Americans were unable to prove their citizenship, either because they were ignorant of the regulations or because their migratory work hampered their ability to meet residency requirements, they were denied access to the new federal relief programs under the New Deal. As economic conditions worsened, government officials called for the deportation of Mexican-born Americans to avoid the cost of providing them with public services. By 1935 over 500,000 Mexican Americans and their American-born children had returned to Mexico. The state of Texas alone returned over 250,000 people.

Native Americans were also devastated by the Great Depression. They initially were encouraged by Roosevelt's appointment of John Collier as the commissioner of the Bureau of Indian Affairs (BIA). Collier steadily increased the number of Native Americans employed by the BIA and strove to ensure that Indians gained access to the various New Deal relief programs. Collier's primary objective, however, was passage of the Indian Reorganization Act. He wanted the new legislation to replace the provisions of the 1887 Dawes Act, which had sought to "Americanize" Indians by breaking up their tribal land and allocating it to individuals. Collier insisted that the Dawes Act had produced only widespread poverty and demoralization. He hoped to reinvigorate Indian cultural traditions by restoring land to tribes, granting Indians the right to charter business enterprises and establish self-governing constitutions, and providing federal funds for vocational training and economic development. The act that Congress finally passed was a much-diluted version of Collier's original proposal, however.

CULTURE IN THE THIRTIES

In view of the celebrated—if exaggerated—alienation of writers, artists, and intellectuals rebelling against the materialism of the 1920s, one might have expected the onset of the Great Depression to have deepened their despair. Instead, it brought a renewed sense of militancy and affirmation, as if society could no longer afford the art-for-art's-sake outlook of the 1920s. By the summer of 1932, even the "golden boy" of the lost generation, the writer F. Scott Fitzgerald, had declared that "to bring on the revolution, it may be necessary to work within the Communist party." But few Americans remained Communists for long. Being a notoriously independent lot, most left-wing writers rebelled at demands to hew to a shifting party line. And many abandoned communism upon learning that the Soviet leader Joseph Stalin practiced a tyranny more horrible than anything under the czars.

LITERATURE AND THE DEPRESSION   Among the Depression-era writers who addressed themes of immediate social significance, two novelists deserve special notice: John Steinbeck and Richard Wright. The single piece of fiction that best captured the ordeal of the Depression, Steinbeck's

The Grapes of Wrath (1939), treats workers as people rather than ideological tools. Steinbeck had traveled with displaced "Okies" fleeing the Oklahoma dust bowl to pursue jobs in the fields of California's Central Valley. This firsthand experience allowed him to create a vivid tale of the Joad family's painful journey west from Oklahoma.

Among the most talented of the young novelists emerging in the 1930s was Richard Wright, an African American born near Natchez, Mississippi. The grandson of former slaves and the son of a sharecropper who deserted his family, Wright ended his formal schooling in the ninth grade (as valedictorian of his class). He then worked in Memphis and greedily devoured books he borrowed on a white friend's library card, all the while saving up to go north to escape the racism of the segregated South. In Chicago the Federal Writers' Project gave him a chance to develop his talent. His period as a Communist, from 1934 to 1944, gave him an intellectual framework that did not overpower his fierce independence. *Native Son* (1940), Wright's masterpiece tells the story of Bigger Thomas, a product of the ghetto, a man hemmed in, and finally impelled to murder, by forces beyond his control.

POPULAR CULTURE While many writers and artists dealt directly with the human suffering and social tensions spawned by the Great Depression, the more popular cultural outlets, such as radio programs and movies, provided patrons with a welcome escape from the decade's grim realities.

By the 1930s, radio had become a major source of family entertainment. More than 10 million families owned a radio, and by the end of the decade the number had tripled. Millions of housewives listened to radio "soap operas," ongoing dramas that were broadcast daily in fifteen-minute episodes and derived their name from their sponsors, soap manufacturers.

Late-afternoon radio programs were directed at children home from school. In the evening after supper, families would gather around the radio to listen to newscasts; comedies such as *Amos 'n' Andy* and the husband-and-wife team of George Burns and Gracie Allen; adventure dramas such as *Jack Armstrong, The Lone Ranger, Dick Tracy*, and *The Green Hornet;* and big-band musical programs, all interspersed with commercials. On Sundays most radio stations broadcast church services. Fans could also listen to baseball and football games or boxing matches. Franklin Roosevelt was the first president to take full advantage of the popularity of radio broadcasting. He hosted sixteen "fireside chats" to generate public support for his New Deal initiatives.

Movies were even more popular than radio shows. In the late 1920s what had been silent films were transformed by the introduction of sound. The "talkies" made movies the most popular form of entertainment during

The Marx Brothers

In addition to their vaudeville antics, the Marx Brothers satirized social issues such as Prohibition.

the 1930s—much more popular than they are today. The introduction of double features in 1931 and the construction of outdoor drive-in theaters in 1933 also boosted interest and attendance. More than 60 percent of the population—70 million people—saw at least one movie each week.

The movies of the 1930s rarely dealt directly with hard times. Exceptions were the film versions of *Gone with the Wind* (1939) and *The Grapes of Wrath* (1940). Much more common were movies intended for pure entertainment; they transported viewers into the realm of adventure, spectacle, humor, and fantasy. People relished shoot-'em-up gangster films, animated cartoons, spectacular musicals, "screwball" comedies, and horror films such as *Dracula* (1931), *Frankenstein* (1931), *The Mummy* (1932), and *Werewolf of London* (1935).

The best way to escape the daily troubles of the Depression was to watch one of the zany comedies of the Marx Brothers, former vaudeville performers. As one Hollywood insider explained, the movies of the 1930s were intended to "laugh the big bad wolf of the depression out of the public mind." *The Cocoanuts* (1929), *Animal Crackers* (1930), and *Monkey Business* (1931) introduced Americans to the anarchic antics of Chico, Groucho, Harpo, and Zeppo

Marx, who combined slapstick humor with verbal wit to create plotless masterpieces of irreverent satire.

THE SECOND NEW DEAL

During Roosevelt's first year in office, his programs and his personal charms generated massive support. The president's travels and speeches, his twice-weekly press conferences, and his radio-broadcast fireside chats brought vitality and warmth in contrast to Hoover's aloof coldness. In the congressional elections of 1934, the Democrats increased their strength in both the House and the Senate, an almost unprecedented midterm victory for a party in power. Only seven Republican governors remained in office throughout the country.

ELEANOR ROOSEVELT One of the reasons for Roosevelt's popularity was his wife, Eleanor, who became an enormous political asset and would prove to be one of the most influential and revered leaders of the time. From an early age, Eleanor Roosevelt had embraced social service. Her compassion resulted in part from the loneliness she experienced as she was growing up and in part from the sense of betrayal she felt upon learning in 1918 that her husband was engaged in an extramarital affair with Lucy Mercer, her secretary. In the face of personal troubles, Eleanor Roosevelt "lived to be kind." Compassionate without being maudlin, more stoic than sentimental, she exuded warmth and sincerity, and she challenged the complacency of the comfortable and the affluent.

The First Lady

An intelligent, principled, and candid woman, Eleanor Roosevelt became a political figure in her own right. Here she is serving as guest host for a radio program, ca. 1935.

Eleanor Roosevelt redefined the role of the presidential spouse. She was the first woman to address a national political convention, to write a nationally syndicated column, and to hold regular press conferences.

A tireless advocate and agitator, Eleanor crisscrossed the nation, representing the president and the New Deal, defying local segregation ordinances to meet with African American leaders, supporting women's causes and organized labor, highlighting the plight of unemployed youth, and imploring Americans to live up to their egalitarian and humanitarian ideals.

CRITICISM   Public criticism of the New Deal during Franklin Roosevelt's first year in office was muted. But not for long. The Depression's downward slide had been halted, but unemployment remained high (10 million were out of work in 1935, more than 20 percent of the workforce), and prosperity remained elusive. "We have been patient and long suffering," said a farm leader in October 1933. "We were promised a New Deal. . . . Instead we have the same old stacked deck." Even more unsettling to some was the dramatic growth of executive power and the emergence of welfare capitalism, whereby workers developed a sense of entitlement to federal support programs. In 1934 a group of conservative businessmen and politicians, including Alfred E. Smith and John W. Davis, two former Democratic presidential candidates, formed the American Liberty League to oppose New Deal measures as violations of personal and property rights.

More potent threats to Roosevelt came from the hucksters of social panaceas. The most flamboyant of the group was Louisiana's "Kingfish," Senator Huey P. Long. A short, strutting man, Long sported pink suits and pastel shirts, red ties, and two-toned shoes. He was a brilliant but unscrupulous reformer driven by a relentless urge for power and attention. First as Louisiana's governor, then as political boss of the state, Long had delivered tax favors, roads, schools, free textbooks, charity hospitals, and better public services. That he had become a sort of state dictator in the process, using bribery, physical intimidation, and blackmail to achieve his ends, seemed irrelevant to many of his ardent supporters.

"The Kingfish"

In 1933, Long joined Roosevelt in Washington as a Democratic senator. He initially supported the New Deal but quickly grew suspicious of the

Huey Long, governor of Louisiana. Although he often led people to believe he was a country bumpkin, Long was a shrewd lawyer and consummate politician.

NRA's collusion with big business. He had also grown jealous of Roosevelt's mushrooming popularity, having developed his own aspirations for the Oval Office. Promoting himself as a true if self-indulgent friend of the people, Long devised his own plan for dealing with the Great Depression.

Long's Share-the-Wealth program proposed to confiscate large personal fortunes, guarantee every family a cash grant of $5,000 and every worker an annual income of $2,500, provide pensions to the aged, reduce working hours, pay veterans' bonuses, and ensure a college education for every qualified student. It did not matter to him that his projected budgets failed to add up or that his program offered little to promote an economic recovery. Whether he had a workable plan or not, by early 1935 the charismatic Long was claiming 7.5 million supporters across the country.

Another popular social scheme was hatched by a gray-haired California doctor, Francis E. Townsend. Outraged by the sight of three elderly women

Promoters of welfare capitalism

Dr. Francis E. Townsend, Rev. Gerald L. K. Smith, and Rev. Charles E. Coughlin (left to right) attended the Townsend Recovery Plan convention in Cleveland, Ohio.

raking through garbage cans in Long Beach, Townsend called for government pensions for the aged. In 1934 he began promoting the Townsend Recovery Plan, which would pay $200 a month to every citizen over sixty who retired from employment and promised to spend the money within each month. The plan had the lure of providing financial security for the aged and stimulating economic growth. Critics noted that the cost of his program, which would benefit 9 percent of the population, would be more than half the national income. Yet Townsend was indifferent to details. "I'm not in the least interested in the cost of the plan," he blandly told a House committee.

A third huckster of panaceas, Father Charles E. Coughlin, the Roman Catholic "radio priest," founded the National Union for Social Justice in 1935. In broadcasts over the CBS radio network, he promoted schemes for the coinage of silver and made attacks on bankers that increasingly hinted at anti-Semitism.

Coughlin, Townsend, and Long drew support largely from desperate lower-middle-class Americans. Of the three, Long had the widest following. A 1935 survey showed that he could draw over 5 million votes as a third-party candidate for president in 1936, perhaps enough to undermine Roosevelt's chances of reelection. Beset by pressures from both ends of the political spectrum, Roosevelt hesitated for months before deciding to "steal the thunder" from the left by instituting an array of new programs. "I'm fighting Communism, Huey Longism, Coughlinism, Townsendism," Roosevelt told a reporter in early 1935. He needed "to save our system, the capitalist system," from such "crackpot ideas." Political pressures impelled Roosevelt to move to the left, but so did the growing influence within the administration from Supreme Court justices Louis Brandeis and Felix Frankfurter. These powerful advisers urged Roosevelt to be less cozy with big business and to push for restored competition and heavy taxes on large corporations.

OPPOSITION FROM THE COURT A series of Supreme Court decisions finally spurred the president to act. On May 27, 1935, the Court killed the National Industrial Recovery Act by a unanimous vote. The defendants in *Schechter Poultry Corporation v. United States*, quickly tagged the "sick-chicken" case, had been convicted of selling an "unfit chicken" and violating other NRA code provisions. The high court ruled that Congress had delegated too much power to the executive branch when it granted the code-making authority to the NRA. Congress had also exceeded its power under the commerce clause by regulating intrastate commerce. The poultry in question, the Court decided, had "come to permanent rest within the state," although earlier it had been moved across state lines. In a press conference soon afterward, Roosevelt fumed: "We have been relegated to the horse-and-buggy definition of interstate commerce." The same line of conservative judicial reasoning, he warned, might endanger other New Deal programs.

LEGISLATIVE ACHIEVEMENTS OF THE SECOND NEW DEAL

To rescue his legislative program from such judicial and political challenges, Roosevelt in 1935 ended the stalemate in Congress and launched the second phase of the New Deal. He demanded several pieces of "must" legislation, most of which Congress passed within a few months.

The National Labor Relations Act, often called the Wagner Act for its sponsor, New York senator Robert Wagner, gave workers the right to bargain with employers through unions of their own choice and prohibited employers from interfering with union activities. The Wagner Act also created a National Labor Relations Board to supervise plant elections and certify unions as bargaining agents where a majority of the workers approved. The board could also investigate the actions of employers and issue "cease-and-desist" orders against specified unfair practices.

Social Security

A poster distributed by the government to educate the public about the new Social Security Act.

The Social Security Act of 1935, Roosevelt announced, was the New Deal's "cornerstone" and "supreme achievement." Indeed, it has proved to be the most significant and far-reaching of all the New Deal initiatives. The concept was by no means new. Progressives during the early 1900s had proposed a federal system of social security for the aged, indigent, disabled, and unemployed. Other nations had already enacted such programs, but the United States remained steadfast in its tradition of individual self-reliance. The Great Depression revived the idea, however, and Roosevelt masterfully guided the legislation through Congress.

The Social Security Act included three major provisions. Its centerpiece was a federally administered pension fund for retired people over the age of sixty-five and their survivors. Beginning in 1937, workers and employers contributed payroll taxes to establish the fund. Benefit payments started in 1940 and averaged $22 per month, a modest sum even for those depressed times. Roosevelt stressed that the pension program was not intended to guarantee a comfortable retirement; it was designed to supplement other sources of income and protect the elderly from some of the "hazards and vicissitudes of life." Only later did Americans come to perceive of Social Security as the *primary* source of retirement income for most of the aged.

The Social Security Act also set up a shared federal-state unemployment-insurance program, financed by a payroll tax on employers. In addition, the new legislation committed the national government to a broad range of social-welfare activities based upon the assumption that "unemployables"—people who were unable to work—would remain a state responsibility while the national government would provide work relief for the able-bodied. To that end the law inaugurated federal grants-in-aid for three state-administered public-assistance programs—old-age assistance, aid to dependent children, and aid to the blind—and further aid for maternal, child-welfare, and public health services.

When compared with similar programs in Europe, the Social Security system was quite conservative. It was the only government pension program in the world financed by taxes on the earnings of workers: most other countries funded such programs out of general revenues. The Social Security payroll tax was also a regressive tax: it entailed a single fixed rate for all, regardless of income level. It thus hurt the poor more than the rich, and it also impeded Roosevelt's efforts to revive the economy because it removed from circulation a significant amount of money: the new Social Security tax took money out of workers' pockets and placed it in a pension trust fund, exacerbating the shrinking money supply that was one of the main causes of the Depression. By taking discretionary income away from workers, the government blunted the sharp increase in public consumption needed to restore the health of the economy. In addition, the Social Security system initially excluded 9.5 million workers who most needed the new program: farm laborers, domestic workers, and the self-employed, a disproportionate percentage of whom were African Americans.

Roosevelt regretted the limitations of the Social Security Act, but he knew that they were necessary compromises in order to see it through Congress and enable it to withstand court challenges. As he replied to an aide who criticized funding the pension program through employee contributions:

> I guess you're right on the economics, but those taxes were never a problem of economics. They are politics all the way through. We put those payroll contributions there so as to give the contributors a moral, legal, and political right to collect their pensions and their unemployment benefits. With those taxes in there, no damn politician can ever scrap my Social Security program.

The last of the major bills making up the second phase of the New Deal was the Revenue Act of 1935, sometimes called the Wealth-Tax Act but popularly known as the soak-the-rich tax. The Revenue Act raised tax rates on income above $50,000. Estate and gift taxes also rose, as did the corporate tax on all but small corporations (those with an annual income below $50,000).

Business leaders fumed over Roosevelt's tax and spending policies. The wealthy resented their loss of status and the growing power of government and labor. They railed against the New Deal and Roosevelt, whom they called a traitor to his own class. Visitors at the home of J. P. Morgan Jr. were cautioned not to mention Roosevelt's name lest it raise Morgan's blood pressure. By "soaking" the rich, Roosevelt stole much of the thunder from the political left, although the results of his tax policy fell short of the promise. The new soak-the-rich tax failed to increase federal revenue significantly, nor did it result in a significant redistribution of income. Still, the prevailing view was that the president had moved in a dangerously radical direction. Roosevelt countered by stressing his basic conservatism and asserting that he had no love for socialism: "I am fighting communism. . . . I want to save our system, the capitalistic system." Yet he added that to save it from revolutionary turmoil required a more equal "distribution of wealth."

ROOSEVELT'S SECOND TERM

On June 27, 1936, Roosevelt accepted the Democratic party's nomination for a second term. He promised to continue to promote a government motivated by a "spirit of charity" rather than a government "frozen in the ice of its own indifference."

THE ELECTION OF 1936   The popularity of Roosevelt and the New Deal impelled the Republican Convention in 1936 to avoid candidates too closely identified with the "hate-Roosevelt" contingent. The party chose

Governor Alfred M. Landon of Kansas, a former Bull Moose Progressive who had endorsed many New Deal programs. He was probably more liberal than most of his backers and clearly more so than the party's platform, which lambasted the New Deal for usurping power.

The Republicans hoped that the followers of Huey Long, Charles Coughlin, Francis Townsend, and other dissidents would combine to draw enough votes away from Roosevelt to throw the election to them. But that possibility faded when an assassin, the son-in-law of a Louisiana judge whom Long had sought to remove, gunned down the Kingfish in 1935. Coughlin, Townsend, and a remnant of the Long movement supported Representative William Lemke of North Dakota on a Union party ticket, but it was a forlorn effort, polling only 882,000 votes.

In 1936, Roosevelt forged a new electoral coalition that would affect national politics for years to come. While holding the support of most traditional Democrats in the North and the South, the president made strong gains among beneficiaries of New Deal farm programs in the West. In the

Campaigning for a second term

Roosevelt campaigning with labor leader John L. Lewis (to the right of Roosevelt) and Martin McIntyre (far right) in Wilkes-Barre, Pennsylvania.

northern cities he held on to the ethnic groups helped by New Deal welfare measures. Many middle-class voters whose property had been saved by New Deal initiatives flocked to support him, as did intellectuals stirred by the ferment of new ideas coming from the government. The revived labor union movement threw its support to Roosevelt, and in the most profound departure of all African American voters for the first time cast the majority of their ballots for a Democratic president. "My friends, go home and turn Lincoln's picture to the wall," a Pittsburgh journalist told black Republicans. "That debt has been paid in full." The final tally revealed that 81 percent of those with an income under $1,000 a year opted for Roosevelt, as did 79 percent of those earning between $1,000 and $2,000. By contrast, only 46 percent of those earning over $5,000 voted for FDR.

In his acceptance speech to the Democratic Convention, Roosevelt abandoned efforts to reassure corporate leaders. As the Americans of 1776 had sought freedom from political autocracy, he noted, the Americans of 1936 sought freedom from the "economic royalists." He later claimed that never before had business leaders been "so united against one candidate." They were "unanimous in their hate for me—and I welcome their hatred." Roosevelt campaigned with tremendous buoyancy, and he wound up carrying every state except Maine and Vermont, with a popular vote of 27.7 million to Landon's 16.7 million. Democrats would also dominate Republicans in the new Congress, by 77 to 19 in the Senate and 328 to 107 in the House. After the lopsided victory, Roosevelt rode a wave of popularity into his second term.

THE COURT-PACKING PLAN   Soon after his landslide reelection, however, Roosevelt found himself deluged in a sea of troubles. His second inaugural address, delivered on January 20, 1937, promised even greater reforms. The challenge to American democracy, he maintained, was that millions of citizens "at this very moment are denied the greater part of what the very lowest standards of today call the necessities of life. . . . I see one-third of a nation ill-housed, ill-clad, ill-nourished." He viewed the election of 1936 as a mandate for even more extensive government action, and the overwhelming Democratic majorities in Congress ensured the passage of new legislation to buttress the Second New Deal. But one major roadblock stood in the way: the Supreme Court.

By the end of its 1936 term, the Court had ruled against New Deal programs in seven of the nine major cases it reviewed. Suits against the Social Security and Wagner Acts were pending. Given the conservative bent of the

Court, the Second New Deal seemed in danger of being nullified, just as much of the original New Deal had been.

For that reason, Roosevelt resolved to change the Court's conservative stance by enlarging the Court, a move for which there was ample precedent and power. Congress, not the Constitution, determines the size of the Court, which at different times has numbered six, seven, eight, nine, and ten justices and in 1937 numbered nine. On February 5, 1937, Roosevelt sent his plan to enlarge the Court to Congress, without having consulted congressional leaders. He wanted to create up to fifty new federal judges, including six new Supreme Court justices, and diminish the power of the judges who had served ten or more years or had reached the age of seventy.

But the "Court-packing" maneuver, as opponents quickly tagged the president's scheme, backfired. It was a shade too contrived, much too brazen, and far too political. By implying that some judges were impaired by senility, Roosevelt affronted the elder statesmen of Congress and the Court, especially Justice Louis D. Brandeis, who was both the oldest and the most liberal of the Supreme Court judges. Roosevelt's scheme also ran headlong into a deep-rooted public veneration of the courts and aroused fears that a future president might use the precedent for quite different purposes.

As it turned out, unforeseen events derailed Roosevelt's drive to change the Court. A sequence of Court decisions during the spring of 1937 reversed previous judgments in order to uphold the Wagner and Social Security Acts. In addition, a conservative justice resigned, and Roosevelt named to the vacancy one of the most consistent New Dealers, Senator Hugo Black of Alabama.

Roosevelt later claimed he had lost the battle but won the war. The Court had reversed itself on important New Deal legislation, and the president was able to appoint justices in harmony with the New Deal. But the episode fractured the Democratic party and blighted Roosevelt's prestige. For the first time, Democrats in large numbers deserted the president, and the Republican opposition found a powerful issue to use against the administration. During the first eight months of 1937, the momentum of Roosevelt's 1936 landslide victory ebbed. As Secretary of Agriculture Henry Wallace later remarked, "The whole New Deal really went up in smoke as a result of the Supreme Court fight."

A NEW DIRECTION FOR UNIONS Rebellions meanwhile erupted on other fronts while the Court-packing bill pended. Under the impetus of the New Deal, the labor union movement stirred anew. John L. Lewis, head of the United Mine Workers, increased membership in the UMW from 150,000 to

500,000 within a year. Spurred by Lewis's example, Sidney Hillman of the Amalgamated Clothing Workers and David Dubinsky of the International Ladies Garment Workers joined him in promoting a campaign to organize workers in the mass-production industries. As leaders of industrial unions (composed of all types of workers in a particular industry), which were in the minority by far, they found the smaller, more restrictive craft unions (composed of skilled male workers only, with each union serving just one trade) to be obstacles to organizing the country's basic industries.

In 1935, with the passage of the Wagner Act, the industrial unionists formed a Committee for Industrial Organization (CIO), and craft unionists (in the AFL) began to fear submergence by the mass unions of mostly unskilled workers. Jurisdictional disputes spread among the unions, and in 1936 the AFL expelled the CIO unions, which then formed a permanent structure, called after 1938 the Congress of Industrial Organizations (also known by the initials CIO). The rivalry spurred both groups to greater unionizing efforts.

The CIO's major organizing drives in the automobile and steel industries began in 1936, but they were thwarted by management's use of blacklisting, private detectives, labor spies, vigilante groups, and other forms of intimidation to suppress the unions. Early in 1937 automobile workers spontaneously adopted a new technique, the "sit-down strike," in which workers refused to leave a plant until employers had granted collective-bargaining rights to their union.

Led by the fiery young autoworker and union organizer Walter Reuther, thousands of employees at the General Motors assembly plants in Flint, Michigan, occupied the factories and stopped all production. Yet management refused to recognize the union efforts, and the standoff lasted over a month before the company finally relented and signed a contract recognizing the United Automobile Workers. Other automobile manufacturers soon followed suit. And the following month, U.S. Steel capitulated to the Steel Workers Organizing Committee (later the United Steelworkers of America), granting the union recognition and its members a 10 percent wage hike and a forty-hour workweek.

Having captured two giants of heavy industry, the CIO went on in the next few years to organize much of industrial America: the rubber, oil, and electronics industries and a good part of the textile industry, in which unionists had to fight protracted struggles to organize scattered plants. The slow pace of labor organizing in textiles denied the CIO a major victory in the South comparable to its swift conquest of automobiles and steel in the North, but even down South a labor movement gained a foothold. Union membership in the United States grew from under 3 million in 1933 to 8.5 million in 1940. Wages rose and working conditions improved because of their efforts. Whether by design or accident, union members became solidly Democratic.

A SLUMPING ECONOMY   During the years 1935 and 1936 the economy finally showed signs of recovery. By the spring of 1937, economic output had moved above the 1929 level. But worried about deficits and rising inflation, Roosevelt ordered sharp cuts in federal spending. At the same time the Treasury began to reduce disposable income by collecting $2 billion in Social Security from employee paychecks. Private spending could not fill the gap left by reductions in government spending, and big business still lacked the faith to risk large capital investments. The result was the slump of 1937, which was sharper than that of 1929 but was called by the press a recession, to distinguish it from a depression. By the end of 1937, an additional 4 million people had been thrown out of work; grim scenes of the earlier depression reappeared. The 1937 recession ignited a fierce debate within the administration. One group, led by Treasury Secretary Henry Morgenthau, favored less federal spending and a balanced budget. The other group, which included Harry Hopkins and Harold Ickes, argued for renewed government spending and stricter enforcement of anti-trust laws.

ECONOMIC POLICY AND LATER REFORMS   Roosevelt seemed bewildered by the recession, but he eventually endorsed the ideas of the spenders. In the spring of 1938, he asked Congress to adopt a large-scale spending program intended to increase mass purchasing power, and Congress voted almost $3.3 billion, mainly for public-works projects. In a short time the increase in spending reversed the economy's decline, but the recession and Roosevelt's reluctance to adopt massive, sustained government spending forestalled the achievement of full recovery. Only the massive crisis of World War II would return the U.S. economy to full production and full employment.

The 1937 recession further eroded Roosevelt's prestige and dissipated the mandate of the 1936 elections. The only major reforms enacted in Roosevelt's second term were the Wagner-Steagall National Housing Act, the Bankhead-Jones Farm Tenant Act, and the Fair Labor Standards Act. The Housing Act of 1937 set up the U.S. Housing Authority in the Department of the Interior, which extended long-term loans to local agencies willing to assume part of the cost of slum clearance and public housing. The agency also subsidized rents for low-income residents.

"A Prop against Human Erosion"

Editorial cartoonist Daniel Fitzpatrick comments on the passing of the Minimum Wage and Hour Law.

The Farm Tenant Act, passed in 1937, was to be administered by a new agency, the Farm Security Administration (FSA). The program offered loans to prevent marginally profitable farm owners from sinking into tenancy. It also offered loans to help tenants purchase their own farms. But by the late 1930s the idea of small homesteads was doomed to failure. American mythology still exalted the family farm, but in reality the ever-larger agricultural unit predominated. In the end the FSA proved to be little more than another relief operation that tided a few farmers over during difficult times. Sadly, a more effective answer to the problem awaited national mobilization for war, which moved many tenants into military service or the defense industry, broadened their horizons, and taught them skills that enabled them to leave the farm altogether.

The Fair Labor Standards Act of 1938 applied only to employees in enterprises that operated in or affected interstate commerce. It set a minimum wage of 40¢ an hour and a maximum workweek of forty hours, to be put into effect over several years. The act also prohibited the employment of children under the age of sixteen. Southern congressmen howled in opposition to the bill because it raised wages in their region and thus increased employers' expenses.

THE LEGACY OF THE NEW DEAL

SETBACKS FOR THE PRESIDENT Although critics were unable to defeat the Fair Labor Standards Act, their stiff resistance revealed that an effective opposition to the New Deal was emerging within the president's own party, especially in the conservative southern wing. Southern Democrats were at best uneasy bedfellows of organized labor and African Americans, and more and more of them began cooperating with conservative Republicans. By the end of 1937, a formidable anti–New Deal bloc had developed in Congress.

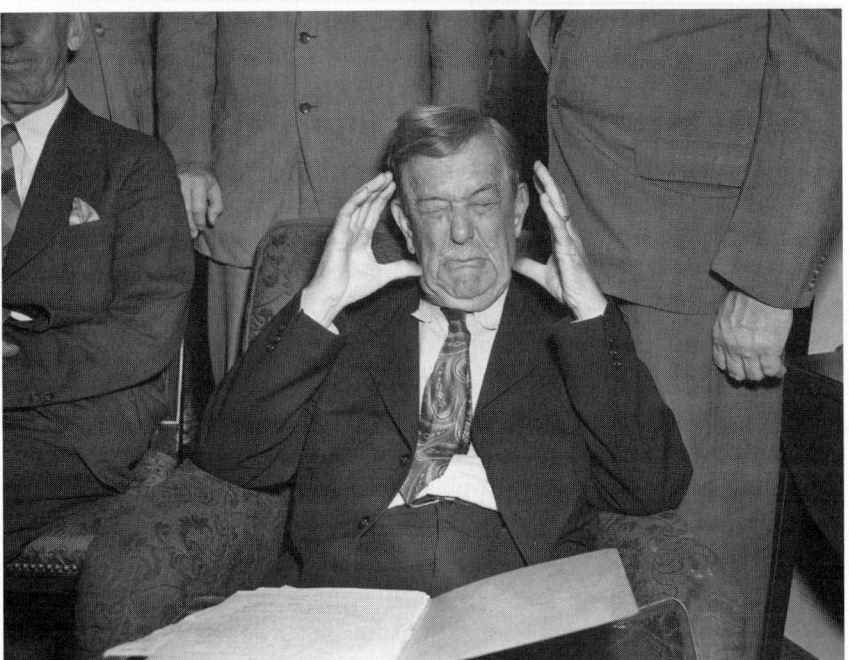

Meeting of the anti–New Dealers

Senator Ellison D. "Cotton Ed" Smith of South Carolina cringes at the thought of a fourth term for Roosevelt, while meeting with fellow anti–New Dealers at the Mayflower Hotel in Washington.

As the political season of 1938 advanced, Roosevelt unfolded a new idea as momentous as his Court-packing plan: a proposal to reshape the Democratic party in the image of the New Deal. He announced his plan to campaign in Democratic primaries as the party leader with the goal of seeing his own supporters nominated. Instead of succeeding, however, the effort to shape the state elections backfired and broke the spell of presidential invincibility, or what was left of it. As in the Court-packing fight, Roosevelt had risked his prestige while handing his adversaries a combustible issue to use against him. His opponents tagged his intervention in the primaries an attempt to "purge" the Democratic party of its southern conservatives; the word evoked visions of Adolf Hitler and Joseph Stalin, tyrants who had purged their Nazi and Communist parties with blood.

The elections of November 1938 resulted in another setback for the administration, caused in part by the friction among the Democrats. FDR had failed in his efforts to liberalize the party by ousting southern conservatives. The Democratic dominance in the House fell from 229 to 93, in the Senate from 56 to 42. The margins remained large, but the president now headed an increasingly divided party. In his State of the Union message in 1939, Roosevelt for the first time proposed no new reforms. He did manage, however, to put through his plan to streamline the executive branch. Under the Administrative Reorganization Act of 1939, the president could "reduce, coordinate, consolidate, and reorganize" the agencies of government. With that, Roosevelt's domestic innovations feebly ended.

A HALFWAY REVOLUTION   The New Deal had petered out as war was erupting in Asia and Europe, but it had wrought several enduring changes. By the end of the 1930s, the power of the national government was vastly larger than it had been in 1932, and hope had been restored to people who had grown disconsolate. But the New Deal entailed more than just bigger government and revived public confidence. It also constituted a significant change from the older liberalism embodied in the progressivism of Theodore Roosevelt and Woodrow Wilson. Those reformers, despite their sharp differences, had assumed that the function of progressive government was to use aggressive regulation to ensure that the people had an equal opportunity to pursue their notions of happiness.

Franklin Roosevelt and the New Dealers went beyond the concept of regulated capitalism by insisting that the government not simply *respond* to social crises but also take positive steps to *avoid* them. To this end, the New Deal's various benefit programs sought to ensure a minimum level of well-being for all Americans. The New Deal had established minimum qualitative standards for labor conditions and public welfare and helped middle-class Americans hold on to their savings, their homes, and their farms. The protection afforded by bank-deposit insurance, unemployment pay, and Social Security pensions would come to be universally accepted as a safeguard against future depressions.

In implementing his domestic program, Roosevelt steered a zigzag course between the extremes of laissez-faire capitalism and socialism. The first New Deal experimented for a time with a managed economy under the NRA but abandoned that experiment for a turn toward enforcing competition through regulation and increased government spending. This tactic finally produced full employment during World War II.

Roosevelt himself, impatient with political theory, was flexible in developing policy: he kept what worked and discarded what did not. The result was, paradoxically, both profoundly revolutionary and profoundly conservative. Roosevelt sharply increased the regulatory functions of the federal government and laid the foundation for what would become an expanding welfare system. Despite what his critics charged, however, his initiatives fell far short of socialism; they left the basic capitalist structure in place. In the process of such bold experimentation and dynamic preservation, the New Deal represented a "halfway revolution" that permanently altered the nation's social and political landscape.

End of Chapter Review

CHAPTER SUMMARY

- **Stabilizing the Economy** In March 1933 the economy, including the farm sector, was shattered; millions of Americans were without jobs and the most basic necessities of life. FDR and his "brain trust" of advisers set out to restore confidence in the economy by supporting the banking industry and providing short-term emergency relief for the unemployed, promoting industrial recovery, and reducing the size of crops by raising commodity prices.

- **The New Deal** Initially most of the New Deal programs were conceived as temporary relief and recovery efforts. They eased hardships but did not restore prosperity. It was during the Second New Deal that reform measures, such as Social Security and the Wagner Act, reshaped the nation's social structure.

- **New Deal Criticisms** Some conservatives criticized the New Deal for violating personal and property rights and steering the nation toward socialism. Some liberals believed that the measures did not tax the wealthy enough to provide the aged and disadvantaged with adequate financial security.

- **Federal Expansion** The New Deal expanded the powers of the national government by establishing regulatory bodies and laying the foundation of a social welfare system. The federal government would in the future regulate business to some extent to avoid social and economic problems.

- **Culture of the 1930s** The literature of the 1930s turned away from the alienation from materialism that characterized the literary works of the previous decade's "lost generation." John Steinbeck and Richard Wright, for example, realistically depicted ordinary people living in, and suffering through, extraordinary times. Radio comedies and the new "talking" movies allowed people to escape their daily troubles.

29

FROM ISOLATION
TO GLOBAL WAR

FOCUS QUESTIONS

 wwnorton.com/studyspace

- What was the effect of isolationism and the peace movement on American politics between the two world wars?
- What events in Europe seemed to herald another international conflict in the 1930s?
- How did the United States respond to German aggression in Europe in the late 1930s?
- How did events in Asia lead to Japan's attack on Pearl Harbor?

In the late 1930s the winds of war swept across Asia and Europe, abruptly shifting the focus of American politics from domestic to foreign affairs. Roosevelt, like Woodrow Wilson before him, had to turn his attention from social and economic reform to military preparedness and war. And the public again had to wrestle with a painful choice: involve the country in volatile world affairs or remain aloof and officially neutral.

POSTWAR ISOLATIONISM

THE LEAGUE AND THE UNITED STATES Between Woodrow Wilson and Franklin Roosevelt lay two decades of relative isolation from foreign entanglements. The post–World War I mood of indifference to global affairs set the pattern. The voters in 1920 expressed their resistance to international commitments, and President-elect Harding lost little time in disposing of American membership in the League of Nations. The spirit of isolation found other expressions as well: higher tariffs, the Red Scare, and the restrictive immigration laws with which the nation all but shut the door to newcomers.

The United States may have felt the urge to insulate itself from a wicked world, but it could hardly ignore its substantial global interests. American business had expanding worldwide connections. Investments and loans abroad put in circulation the dollars that enabled foreigners to purchase American exports. America's overseas possessions, moreover, directly involved the country in world affairs, especially in the Pacific. Even the League of Nations was too great an organization to ignore. After 1924 the United States gradually entered into joint efforts with the League in such tasks as policing the international trade in drugs and arms, and American diplomats took part in a variety of economic, cultural, and technical conferences.

WAR DEBTS AND REPARATIONS   Probably nothing did more to heighten American isolationism during the 1920s and 1930s—or anti-American feeling in Europe—than the war-debt tangle. When in 1917 the Allies had begun to exhaust their sources of private credit in the United States, the U.S. government advanced them millions of dollars, first for the war effort and then for postwar reconstruction.

To Americans the repayment of the war debts seemed a simple matter of obligation, but Europeans commonly had a different perception. The French and the British had insisted that they could repay their war-related debts to the United States only as they collected reparations from defeated Germany. Twice during the 1920s the resulting strain on Germany brought the structure of international payments to the verge of collapse, and both times the Reparations Commission called in American bankers to work out rescue plans.

The whole structure finally did collapse during the Great Depression. In 1931, President Hoover negotiated a moratorium on both German reparations and Allied payment of war debts. At the end of 1932, after Hoover's debt moratorium ended, most European countries defaulted on their war debts to the United States. In retaliation, Congress passed the Johnson Debt Default Act of 1934, which prohibited private loans to any defaulting government.

ATTEMPTS AT DISARMAMENT   After World War I many Americans decided that the armaments race had caused the war and that arms limitations treaties would bring lasting peace. The United States had no intention of maintaining a large army, but under the shipbuilding program begun in

1916, it had constructed a fleet second only to that of Britain. Neither the British nor the Americans relished a naval armaments race, but both were alarmed by the growth of Japanese military power.

Since 1914, Japanese-American relations had grown increasingly strained. During World War I, Japan had taken China's Shan-tung Peninsula and the islands of Micronesia from Germany. In 1917, after the United States entered the war, Viscount Kikujiro Ishii visited Washington to secure American recognition of Japan's expanded position in Asia, dropping hints that Germany had several times tried to get Japan to quit the war. To forestall the loss of an ally in the war, Secretary of State Robert Lansing had signed an ambiguous agreement saying that "Japan has special interests in China." Americans were unhappy with the Lansing-Ishii Agreement, but it was viewed as the only way to keep Japan in the war.

After the war ended, Japanese-American relations deteriorated. To address the problem, President Warren Harding invited eight key countries to the Washington Naval Conference of 1921. It opened with a surprise announcement by the U.S. secretary of state, Charles Evans Hughes, who laid out a plan to destroy most of the world's navies. Delegates from the United States, Britain, Japan, France, and Italy signed the Five-Power Treaty (1922), incorporating

The Washington Conference, 1921

The Big Five at the conference were (from left) Iyesato Tokugawa (Japan), Arthur Balfour (Great Britain), Charles Evans Hughes (United States), Aristide Briand (France), and Carlo Schanzer (Italy).

Hughes's plan for tonnage limits on their navies and a moratorium of ten years during which no battleships would be built. The five powers also agreed to refrain from further fortification of their Pacific possessions. The agreement in effect partitioned the world: U.S. naval power became supreme in the Western Hemisphere, Japanese power in the western Pacific, and British power from the North Sea to Singapore.

Two other major agreements emerged from the Washington Conference. With the Four-Power Treaty, the United States, Britain, Japan, and France agreed to respect one another's possessions in the Pacific. The Nine-Power Treaty for the first time pledged the signers to support the principle of the Open Door enunciated by Secretary of State John Hay in 1899. The Open Door enabled all nations to compete for trade and investment opportunities in China on an equal footing rather than allow individual nations to create economic monopolies in particular regions of that country. The signers of the Nine-Power Treaty also promised to respect the territorial integrity of China. The powers, in addition to those signing the Five-Power Treaty, were China, Belgium, Portugal, and the Netherlands.

With these agreements in hand, President Harding could boast of a brilliant diplomatic stroke that relieved citizens of the need to pay for an enlarged navy and defused potential conflicts in the Pacific. Yet the agreements were without obligation and without teeth. The signers of the Four-Power Treaty agreed only to consult, not to help one another. The formal endorsement of the Open Door in the Nine-Power Treaty was just as ineffective, for the United States remained unwilling to use force to uphold the principle. Moreover, the naval-disarmament treaty set tonnage limits only on battleships and aircraft carriers; the race to build cruisers, destroyers, submarines, and other smaller craft continued.

THE KELLOGG-BRIAND PACT   During and after World War I the fanciful ideal of simply abolishing war seized the American imagination. Peace societies thrived, and the glorious vision of ending war by the stroke of a pen culminated in the Kellogg-Briand Pact of 1928. This unique treaty originated when the French foreign minister Aristide Briand proposed to President Calvin Coolidge's secretary of state, Frank B. Kellogg, an agreement whereby the two countries would never go to war with each other. Kellogg countered with a scheme to have all nations sign the pact, an idea all the more acceptable to the many peace organizations of the day.

The Pact of Paris (its official name), signed on August 27, 1928, declared that the signatories "condemn recourse to war . . . and renounce it as an instrument of national policy." Eventually sixty-two nations joined the pact, but all reserved "self-defense" as an escape hatch. The U.S. Senate included a reservation declaring the Monroe Doctrine necessary to America's self-defense and then ratified the agreement by a vote of 85 to 1. A Virginia senator who voted for "this worthless, but perfectly harmless peace treaty" wrote a friend that he feared it would "confuse the minds of many good people who think that peace may be secured by polite professions of neighborly and brotherly love."

THE "GOOD NEIGHBOR" POLICY   In Latin America the spirit of peace and noninvolvement helped allay long-festering resentments against the United States, which had freely intervened in the Caribbean during the first two decades of the century. In 1924, American marines left the Dominican Republic after an eight-year occupation. U.S. troops left Nicaragua a year later but returned in 1926 with the outbreak of disorder and civil war. In 1927 the Coolidge administration negotiated an agreement for U.S.-supervised elections, but one rebel leader, César Augusto Sandino, held out, and the marines stayed until 1933.

In 1930, President Hoover improved America's image in Latin America by permitting publication of a memorandum that denied that the Monroe Doctrine justified U.S. intervention in Latin America. It stopped short of repudiating intervention on any grounds, but that fine point hardly blunted the celebration in Latin America. Although Hoover never endorsed this so-called Clark Memorandum, named for American diplomat Reuben Clark, he never ordered military intervention in the region. Before he left office, steps had been taken to withdraw American forces from Nicaragua and Haiti.

Franklin D. Roosevelt likewise embraced the policy of the "good neighbor" and soon advanced it in practice. In 1933, at the Seventh Pan-American Conference, the United States supported a resolution declaring that no nation "has the right to intervene in the internal or external affairs of another." Under President Roosevelt the marines completed their withdrawal from Nicaragua and Haiti, and in 1934 the president negotiated with Cuba a treaty that abrogated the Platt Amendment of 1901, which had given the United States a formal right to intervene in Cuba.

War Clouds

JAPANESE INCURSIONS INTO CHINA   Improving U.S. relations in the Western Hemisphere during the 1930s proved an exception in an otherwise dismal world scene as war clouds darkened over Europe and Asia. Actual conflict erupted in Asia first, where unsettled social and political conditions in China had attracted foreign encroachments since before the beginning of the century. Chinese nationalist aspirations in 1929 and China's subsequent clashes with Russia convinced the Japanese that their own extensive investments in Manchuria, including the South Manchurian Railway, were in danger.

Japanese military occupation of Manchuria began with the Mukden incident of 1931, when an explosion destroyed a section of railroad track near that city. The Japanese army based in Manchuria to guard the railway blamed the incident on the Chinese and used it as a pretext to occupy all of Manchuria. In 1932 the Japanese converted Manchuria into the puppet empire of Manchukuo.

The Manchuria incident, as the Japanese called their undeclared war, flagrantly violated the Nine-Power Treaty, the Kellogg-Briand Pact, and Japan's pledges as a member of the League of Nations. But when China asked the League and the United States for help, neither obliged. President Herbert Hoover refused to invoke military or economic sanctions.

In early 1932, Japan's indiscriminate bombing of civilians in Shanghai, China's great port city, aroused Western indignation but no action. When the League of Nations condemned Japanese aggression in 1933, Japan withdrew from the League. Thereafter, hostilities in Manchuria gradually subsided and ended with a truce. An uneasy peace settled upon east Asia for four years, during which time Japan's military leaders extended their political sway in Tokyo.

ITALY AND GERMANY   The rise of the Japanese militarists paralleled the rise of totalitarian dictators in Italy and Germany. In 1922, Benito Mussolini had seized power in Italy after organizing the Fascist movement, a composite of superheated nationalism and socialism. The party's program, and above all Mussolini's promise to restore order and pride in a country fragmented by dissension and self-doubts, enjoyed a wide appeal. Once in power, Mussolini largely abandoned the socialist part of his platform and gradually suppressed all opposition. By 1925 he was wielding dictatorial power as Il Duce (the Leader).

There was always something ludicrous about the strutting, bombastic Mussolini. Italy, after all, was a minor European power. But Germany was another matter, and most Americans were not amused, even at the beginning, by Il Duce's German counterpart, Adolf Hitler. Hitler's National Socialist German Workers' (Nazi) party duplicated the major features of Italian fascism, including the ancient Roman salute. Hitler capitalized on the weakness of Germany's postwar government, the poverty and despair caused by a severe economic depression, and festering German resentment toward the Versailles Treaty.

Named chancellor on January 30, 1933, Hitler swiftly won dictatorial powers and in 1934 assumed the title Führer (national leader). The Nazi police state cranked up the engines of tyranny, persecuting Jews, whom Hitler blamed for Germany's troubles, and re-arming in defiance of the Versailles Treaty. Hitler flouted international agreements, pulled Germany out of the League of Nations in 1933, and threatened to extend control over all German-speaking peoples. Despite Hitler's provocations, the European democracies lacked the will to resist.

RUSSIAN RECOGNITION Isolationist sentiment in the United States grew even more potent during the early 1930s, but one significant exception to American insularity was Roosevelt's decision to favor official recognition

Axis leaders

Mussolini and Hitler in Munich, June 1940.

of Soviet Russia. By 1933 the reasons for America's refusal to recognize the Bolshevik regime had grown stale. Seen as an expansive market for U.S. goods, the Soviet Union stirred fantasies of an American trade boom, much as China had at the beginning of the century. Japanese expansionism in Asia, moreover, gave the Soviet Union and the United States a common foreign-policy concern. Given an opening by the shift of opinion, Roosevelt invited the Soviet commissar for foreign affairs to visit Washington, D.C. After nine days of talks, a formal exchange of notes on November 16, 1933, signaled the renewal of diplomatic relations. The Soviet commissar promised that his country would abstain from promoting Communist propaganda in the United States, extend religious freedom to Americans in the Soviet Union, and reopen the question of unpaid Russian debts to the United States.

THE MARCH OF AGGRESSION   After 1932 a catastrophic chain of events in Asia and Europe sent the world hurtling toward disaster. In 1934, Japan renounced the Five-Power Treaty. The next year, Mussolini commenced Italy's conquest of Ethiopia. That same year a referendum in Germany's Saar Basin, held in accordance with the Versailles Treaty, delivered the coal-rich region into the hands of Hitler. In 1936, Hitler's armed forces reoccupied the Rhineland, a direct violation of the Versailles Treaty. The French did nothing to oust the German force, however.

The year 1936 also brought the Spanish Civil War, which began with an uprising of the Spanish armed forces in Morocco, led by General Francisco Franco, against the democratically elected Spanish republic. Over the next three years, Franco established a fascist dictatorship with help from Hitler and Mussolini while the European democracies left the Spanish republic to its fate.

On July 7, 1937, Japanese and Chinese troops clashed at the Marco Polo Bridge, west of Peking, and the incident quickly developed into a full-scale war. World War II had begun in Asia two years before it would erupt in Europe. That same year, Japan and Italy joined Germany in establishing an alliance known as the Rome-Berlin-Tokyo "Axis."

By 1938 the peace of Europe trembled in the balance. Having rebuilt German military power, Hitler forced the *Anschluss* (union) of Austria with Germany in March 1938. Six months later British and French leaders, recognizing the situation's severity but failing to comprehend Hitler's ruthlessness, sought to appease the German leader by agreeing to abandon the Sudetenland

Keeping in mind the terms of the Treaty of Versailles, explain why Hitler began his campaign of expansion by invading the Rhineland and the Sudetenland. Why would Hitler have wanted to retake the Polish Corridor? Why did the attack on Poland begin World War II, whereas Hitler's previous invasions of his European neighbors did not?

in Czechoslovakia, a country that probably had the second-strongest army in central Europe. Germany promptly took the mountainous Sudetenland, largely German in population, which had been given to Czechoslovakia at the Paris Peace Conference in 1919 because of its strategic importance to that new nation's defense.

After promising that the Sudetenland would be his last territorial demand, Hitler brazenly broke his pledge in 1939: he occupied the remainder of Czechoslovakia and seized former German territory from Lithuania. In quick succession the Spanish republic collapsed on March 28, and Mussolini seized the kingdom of Albania on April 7. On September 1, 1939, Hitler launched his conquest of Poland. A few days before, he had signed a non-aggression pact with Soviet Russia. Having deserted Czechoslovakia, Britain and France now honored their commitment to go to war if Poland was invaded.

DEGREES OF NEUTRALITY   During these years of deepening crisis, the Western democracies seemed paralyzed, hoping in vain that each concession would appease the appetites of fascist dictators. Americans retreated more deeply into isolation. The neutrality laws of the 1930s sought to keep the United States insulated from the quarrels of Europe. But while Americans wanted to steer clear of war altogether, their sympathies were more strongly than ever with the Western democracies, and the triumph of fascist aggression in Europe aroused fears for national security. The Neutrality Act of 1935 forbade the sale of arms and munitions to all belligerents (warring nations) whenever the president proclaimed that a state of war existed. It also declared that Americans who traveled on belligerents' ships did so at their own risk. Roosevelt would have preferred discretionary authority to levy an embargo only against aggressors, but he reluctantly accepted the act because it was to be effective for only six months.

Yet on October 3, 1935, just weeks after Roosevelt signed it, Italy invaded Ethiopia, and Roosevelt invoked the Neutrality Act. When Congress reconvened in 1936, it extended the arms embargo and added a provision forbidding loans to belligerents. It was in July 1936, while Italian troops were mopping up the last resistance in Ethiopia, that the Spanish Civil War broke out. Roosevelt then became more isolationist than some of the most extreme isolationists. Although the Spanish Civil War involved a fascist uprising against a recognized democratic government, Roosevelt accepted the French and British position that only their nonintervention would keep the fight from spreading to the rest of Europe.

The conflict in Spain led Roosevelt to seek a "moral embargo" on the arms trade, and he encouraged Congress to extend the neutrality laws to instances of civil war. Congress did so in 1937 with only one dissenting vote. The Western democracies then stood by as German and Italian soldiers, planes, and armaments supported Franco's overthrow of Spanish democracy.

In the spring of 1937, Congress passed another neutrality law, which continued restraints on arms sales and loans, forbade Americans to travel on the ships of nations at war, and prohibited the arming of American merchant ships trading with warring nations. The new law also empowered the president to require that goods other than arms or munitions exported to belligerents be sold on a cash-and-carry basis (that is, the nation purchasing the goods would have to pay cash and transport the cargo in its own ships). This was an ingenious scheme to preserve a profitable trade without running the risk of war.

The new law had its first test in July 1937, when Japanese and Chinese forces clashed at the Marco Polo Bridge. Since neither side declared war, Roosevelt was able to avoid invoking the neutrality law, which would have favored the Japanese, since China had greater need of American arms but few means to get supplies past the Japanese navy. A flourishing international trade in munitions evolved as ships carried American military equipment across the Atlantic to England, where it was reloaded onto British ships bound for Hong Kong. Roosevelt, by his refusal to invoke the neutrality laws, had challenged strict isolationism.

Neutrality

A 1938 cartoon shows U.S. foreign policy entangled by the serpent of isolationism.

Roosevelt soon ventured a step further. In Chicago on October 5, 1937, he denounced the "reign of terror and international lawlessness" whereby 10 percent of the world's population threatened the peace of the other 90 percent. He called for a "quarantine" against those nations "creating a state of international anarchy and instability from which there is no escape through mere isolation or neutrality." Public reaction to the speech was mixed, but the president nevertheless quickly backed off from its implications and refused to spell out any program for dealing with aggression.

After the German occupation of Czechoslovakia in 1939, Roosevelt began to abandon his neutral stance. He could no longer pretend impartiality in the deepening European struggle. He began to educate the public about the menace of unchecked fascism. He urged Congress to repeal the munitions embargo and permit the United States to sell arms on a cash-and-carry basis to Britain and France, but to no avail. "You haven't got the votes," Vice President John Nance Garner told him, "and that's all there is to it." When the Germans attacked Poland on September 1, Roosevelt proclaimed official neutrality but in a radio talk stressed that he would not, like Woodrow Wilson in 1914, ask Americans to remain neutral in thought because "even a neutral has a right to take account of the facts."

Roosevelt summoned Congress into special session and asked again for amendments to the Neutrality Act. "I regret the Congress passed the Act," he confessed. "I regret equally that I signed the Act." Under the Neutrality Act of 1939, Britain and France could buy supplies with cash and in their own ships take away weapons or anything else they wanted. American ships, on the other hand, were excluded from the ports of warring nations and from specified war zones. Roosevelt then designated as a war zone the Baltic Sea, the waters around Great Britain and Ireland, and the waters from Norway south to the coast of Spain. One unexpected effect of this move was to relieve Hitler of any inhibitions about using unrestricted submarine warfare to blockade Britain.

Once the great democracies of western Europe faced war, American public opinion, appalled at Hitler's expansive tyranny, rallied to aid its allies without being drawn into the war itself. For a time it seemed that the Western Hemisphere could remain insulated. After the Nazis overran Poland in less than a month, the war settled into a stalemate in early 1940 that began to be called the phony war. What lay ahead, it seemed, was a long war of attrition—much like World War I—in which Britain and France would have the resources to outlast Hitler. That illusion lasted from October 1939 until the spring of 1940.

THE STORM IN EUROPE

BLITZKRIEG   In the spring of 1940, the long winter lull in the European fighting suddenly erupted into *blitzkrieg* (lightning war). At dawn on April 9, without warning, Nazi troops occupied Denmark and landed along the Norwegian coast. Denmark fell in a day, Norway within a few weeks. On May 10, Hitler unleashed dive bombers and tank divisions on neutral Belgium and the Netherlands. On May 21, German troops moving down the valley of the Somme River reached the English Channel, cutting off a British force sent to help the Belgians and the French. A desperate evacuation from the French beaches at Dunkirk enlisted every available boat, from warship to tug. Amid the chaos some 338,000 soldiers, about a third of them French, escaped to England.

Having outflanked France's heavily fortified defense perimeter, the Maginot Line, the German forces rushed ahead, cutting the French armies to pieces and spreading panic by strafing refugees. On June 14 the Nazi swastika flew over Paris.

The Blitz

In London, St. Paul's Cathedral looms above the destruction wrought by German bombs during the Blitz. Churchill's response: "We shall never surrender."

AMERICA'S GROWING INVOLVEMENT   Britain now stood alone, but its new prime minister, Winston Churchill, breathed defiance. "We shall go on to the end," he pledged; "we shall never surrender." Nevertheless, America seemed suddenly vulnerable as Hitler unleashed his air force against Britain. President Roosevelt called for a military buildup and the production of 50,000 combat planes a year. In 1940, Congress voted more than $17 billion for defense. In response to Churchill's appeal for military supplies, the War and Navy Departments began releasing stocks of arms, planes, and munitions to the British.

The world crisis transformed Roosevelt. Having been stalemated for much of his second term by congressional opposition to his domestic program, he was revitalized by the war in Europe. Nervous cabinet officers, military leaders, and diplomats now encountered a decisive president willing to exert executive authority on behalf of Britain, which in the summer of 1940, in the desperate Battle of Britain, finally forced the Germans to give up plans to invade the British Isles. Submarine warfare, meanwhile, strained the resources of the battered Royal Navy. Churchill urgently requested the transfer of American destroyers to help protect convoys from submarines.

"The Only Way We Can Save Her [Democracy]"

Political cartoon suggesting the U.S. not intervene in European wars.

Secret negotiations led to an executive agreement under which fifty "overaged" U.S. destroyers went to the British in return for ninety-nine-year American leases on naval and air bases in Newfoundland, Bermuda, and islands in the Caribbean. Roosevelt disguised the action as necessary for defense of the hemisphere. Two weeks later, on September 14, 1940, Congress adopted the first peacetime conscription in American history. All 16 million men aged twenty-one to thirty-five were required to register, those chosen in a lottery and found fit were required to fulfill a year's military service within the United States.

The new state of affairs prompted vigorous debate between "internationalists," who believed national security demanded aid to Britain, and isolationists, who charged that Roosevelt was drawing the United States into an unnecessary war. In 1940, internationalists organized the nonpartisan Committee to Defend America by Aiding the Allies, drawing its strongest support from the East and West Coasts and the South. Two months later isolationists formed the America First Committee. The isolationists argued that a Nazi victory over Great Britain, while distasteful, would pose no threat to American national security.

FDR'S THIRD TERM   In the midst of these profound global crises, the quadrennial presidential campaign came due. Isolationist sentiment was strongest in the Republican party, yet its nominee took a different stance.

Wendell L. Willkie was a former Democrat who had voted for Roosevelt in 1932. An Indiana farm boy whose disheveled charm inspired strong loyalty, he openly supported aid to the Allies.

The Nazi victory in France ensured that Roosevelt would decide to run for an unprecedented third term. The president cultivated party unity with his foreign policy and kept a sphinxlike silence about his intentions. The world crisis reconciled southern conservatives to the man whose foreign policy, at least, they supported. At the convention in Chicago, Roosevelt won the nomination for a third term with only token opposition. For his new running mate, he tapped his secretary of agriculture, Henry A. Wallace, a devoted supporter who would appeal to farm voters.

Throughout the summer, Roosevelt assumed the role of a man above the political fray, busy rather with urgent matters of defense and diplomacy. Because Willkie's foreign-policy ideas mirrored Roosevelt's, the Republican nominee was reduced to attacking New Deal red tape and promising to run the programs better. Roosevelt won the election by a comfortable margin of 27 million votes to Willkie's 22 million and by a wider margin, 449 to 82, in the Electoral College. Though the popular vote was closer than it had been in any presidential election since 1916, the dangerous world situation had persuaded a majority of voters to back the Democrats' slogan: "Don't switch horses in the middle of the stream."

THE "ARSENAL OF DEMOCRACY" Bolstered by the mandate for a third term, Roosevelt moved quickly to provide greater aid to besieged Britain, whose cash was running out. Since direct government loans would arouse memories of earlier war-debt defaults—the Johnson Debt Default Act of 1934 forbade such loans anyway—the president created an ingenious device to bypass that issue and yet supply British needs: the "lend-lease" program. In a fireside chat, Roosevelt told the nation that America must become "the great arsenal of democracy" to help prevent Britain's fall, and to do so it must make new efforts to help the British purchase American supplies. The lend-lease bill, introduced in Congress on January 10, 1941, authorized the president to sell, lend, or lease arms and other equipment and supplies to "any country whose defense the President deems vital to the defense of the United States."

For two months a bitter debate over the lend-lease bill raged in Congress and around the country. Isolationists saw it as the point of no return. Administration supporters denied that lend-lease would lead to American involvement in the war, but they knew that it did increase the risk. Lend-lease became law in early 1941, and Britain and China were the first beneficiaries.

While the nation debated, the war intensified. Italy had officially entered the European war as Hitler's ally in June 1940. In late 1940, as the American presidential campaign approached its climax, Mussolini launched attacks on Greece and, from Italian-controlled Libya, assaulted the British in Egypt. But his troops had to fall back in both cases, and in the spring of 1941 German forces under General Erwin Rommel joined the Italians in Libya, forcing the British to withdraw to Egypt, their resources having been drained to help Greece. In April 1941, Nazi armored divisions overwhelmed Yugoslavia and Greece, and by the end of May airborne forces had subdued the Greek island of Crete, putting Hitler in a position to menace the entire Middle East.

With Hungary, Romania, and Bulgaria forced into the Axis fold, Hitler controlled nearly all of Europe, but his ambition was unbounded. On June 22, 1941, Nazi troops suddenly fell upon the Soviet Union, their ally, hoping to use another lightning stroke to eliminate the potential threat on Germany's eastern front. The Nazis massed 3.6 million soldiers on a 2,000-mile front from the Arctic Ocean to the Black Sea. After retreating for four months, however, Russian soldiers and civilians rallied to defend Leningrad, Moscow, and Sevastopol. During the winter of 1941–1942, a ferocious Soviet counterattack proved to be the most important development of the war in Europe. Still, in the summer of 1941 the Nazi juggernaut appeared unstoppable.

Winston Churchill had already decided to provide British support to the Soviet Union in case of such an attack. Roosevelt adopted the same policy, offering American aid to Russia two days after the German invasion in late June 1941. Stalinist Russia, so long as it held out against the Germans, ensured Britain's survival. American aid was now indispensable to Europe's defense, and the logic of lend-lease led to deeper American involvement. To deliver aid to Britain, supply ships had to maneuver through the German submarine "wolf packs" in the North Atlantic. So in April 1941, Roosevelt informed Churchill that the U.S. Navy would extend its patrol areas in the North Atlantic nearly to Iceland.

In August 1941, Roosevelt and Churchill held a secret meeting off the coast of Newfoundland. There they drew up a statement of international principles known as the Atlantic Charter. Their joint statement called for the self-determination of all peoples, economic cooperation, freedom of the seas, and a new international system of collective security. The Soviet Union later endorsed the charter.

Having entered into a joint statement of war aims with the anti-Axis powers, the United States soon became involved in shooting incidents in the North Atlantic. After a German submarine attacked a U.S. battleship, the president ordered American ships to "shoot on sight" any German or Italian raiders ("rattlesnakes of the Atlantic") that ventured into American waters. Five days later the U.S. Navy announced that it would convoy British-bound merchant ships all the way to Iceland.

Further attacks prompted Congress to make more changes in the 1939 Neutrality Act requested by the president. On November 17, Congress removed the bans on arming merchant vessels and allowed them to enter combat zones and belligerent ports. Step-by-step the United States was giving up neutrality and embarking on naval warfare against Germany. Still, Americans hoped to avoid the final step of all-out war. The decision to go to war would be made in response to aggression in an unexpected quarter—Hawaii.

Repercussions of rising tension between the U.S. and Japan

A sign reading "No Japs served here" appeared on a cafe window near the Boston fish pier, December 1941.

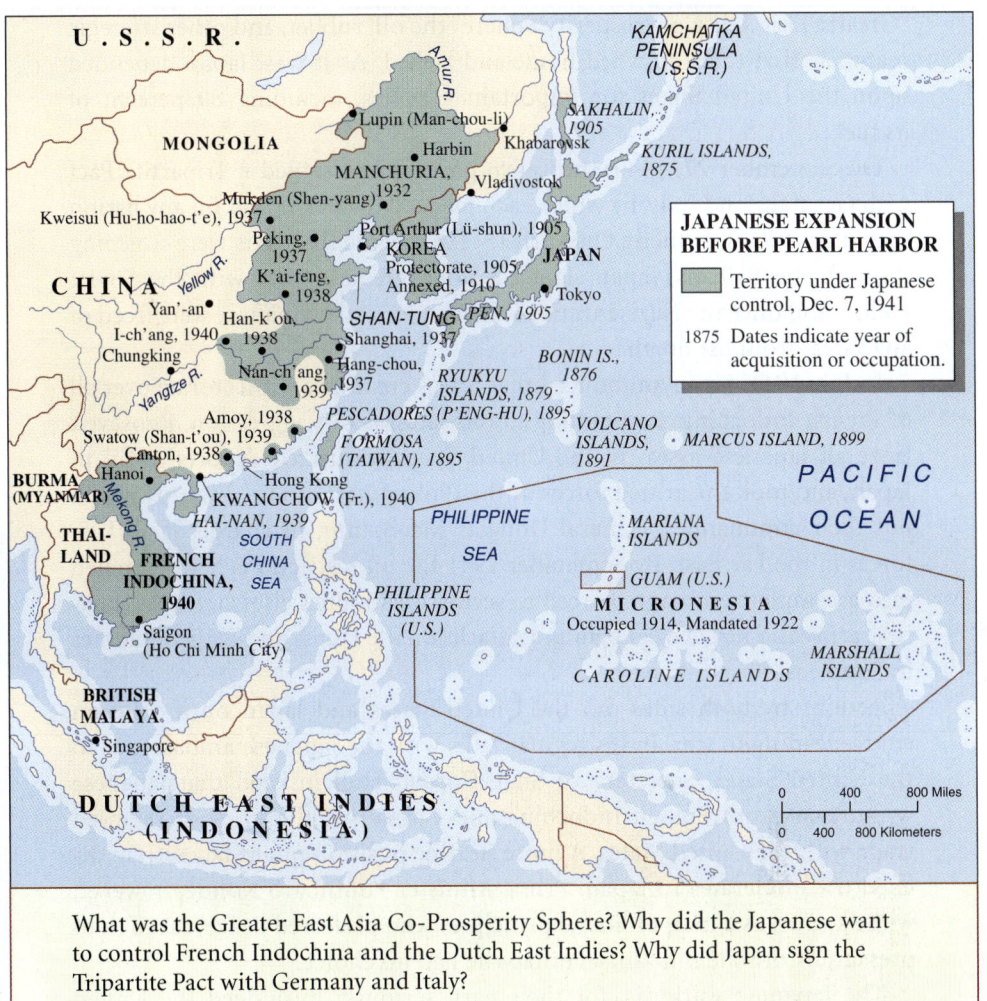

JAPANESE EXPANSION BEFORE PEARL HARBOR

Territory under Japanese control, Dec. 7, 1941

1875 Dates indicate year of acquisition or occupation.

What was the Greater East Asia Co-Prosperity Sphere? Why did the Japanese want to control French Indochina and the Dutch East Indies? Why did Japan sign the Tripartite Pact with Germany and Italy?

THE STORM IN THE PACIFIC

JAPANESE AGGRESSION After the Nazi victories in Europe during the spring of 1940, America's relations with Japan took a turn for the worse. Japanese militarists, bogged down in the vastness of China, now eyed new temptations in Southeast Asia. They wanted to incorporate into their

"Greater East Asia Co-Prosperity Sphere" the oil, rubber, and other strategic materials that their crowded homeland lacked. As it was, Japan depended upon the United States for important supplies, including 80 percent of its fuel.

On September 27, 1940, the Tokyo government signed a Tripartite Pact with Germany and Italy, by which each pledged to declare war on any nation that attacked any of them. On April 13, 1941, while the Nazis were sweeping through the Balkans, Japan signed a nonaggression pact with the Soviet Union, and once the Nazis invaded Russia in June, the Japanese were freed of any threat from the north.

In July 1941, Japan announced that it was creating a protectorate over all of French Indochina. Responding to this latest act of aggression, Roosevelt froze all Japanese assets in the United States, restricted exports of oil to Japan, and took the armed forces of the Philippines into the U.S. Army and put their commander, General Douglas MacArthur, in charge of all U.S. forces in the Far East. By September 1941 the oil restrictions had tightened into a complete embargo. Forced to secure oil supplies elsewhere, the Japanese army and navy began planning attacks on the Dutch and British colonies in Southeast Asia.

Actions by both sides put the United States and Japan on a collision course leading to war. In his regular talks with the Japanese ambassador to the United States, Secretary of State Cordell Hull insisted that Japanese withdrawal from French Indochina and China was the price of renewed trade with the United States. A more flexible position might have strengthened the moderates in Japan. Prime Minister Fumimaro Konoe, however, while known as a man of liberal principles who preferred peace, caved in to pressures from the militants. Perhaps he had no choice.

The Japanese warlords, for their part, seriously misjudged the United States. The desperate wish of the Americans to stay out of the war might still have enabled the Japanese to conquer the British and Dutch colonies in the Pacific. But the warlords decided that they dared not leave the U.S. Navy intact and the Philippines untouched on the flank of their new lifeline to the south.

TRAGEDY AT PEARL HARBOR   Thus a tragedy began to unfold with a fatal certainty, mostly out of sight of the American people, whose attention was focused on the Nazi submarine threat in the Atlantic. Late in August 1941, Prime Minister Konoe proposed a meeting with President Roosevelt.

Secretary of State Hull urged the president not to meet unless agreement on fundamental issues could be reached in advance. On September 6 the Japanese government approved a surprise attack on Hawaii and gave Konoe six more weeks in which to reach a settlement.

The Japanese emperor's concern about the risk of an attack afforded the prime minister one last chance to pursue a compromise, but the presence of Japanese troops in China remained a stumbling block to any American agreement. In October, Konoe urged War Minister Hideki Tōjō to consider withdrawing Japanese forces while saving face by keeping some troops in north China. Instead, the inflexible Tōjō forced Konoe to resign in October. Tōjō himself became prime minister the next day. The war party was now in complete control of the Japanese government.

By late November, Washington officials knew that war was imminent. Reports of Japanese troop transports moving south from Formosa prompted U.S. officials to send warnings to Pearl Harbor and Manila and to the British government. The massive Japanese movements southward clearly signaled attacks on the British and the Dutch. American leaders had every reason to expect war in the southwest Pacific, but none expected that Japan would commit most of its aircraft carriers to another attack 5,000 miles away, at Pearl Harbor, the major American base in the Pacific.

On the morning of December 7, 1941, American servicemen decoded the last part of a secret Japanese message breaking off the diplomatic negotiations in Washington. Tōjō instructed Japan's ambassador to deliver the message at 1 P.M. (7:30 A.M. in Honolulu), about a half hour before the attack was to begin, but delays held up delivery by more than an hour. The War Department sent out an alert at noon that something was about to happen, but the message, which went by commercial wire because radio contacts were broken, arrived in Hawaii eight and a half hours later. Even so, the decoded Japanese message did not mention Pearl Harbor specifically, and U.S. military leaders there would probably have assumed the attack was to come in Southeast Asia.

It was still a sleepy Sunday morning in Hawaii when the first Japanese planes roared down the west coast and the central valley of Oahu to begin their assault. For nearly two hours the Japanese planes kept up their fierce attack. Of the eight U.S. battleships in Pearl Harbor, three were sunk, and the others were badly battered. Altogether, nineteen ships were sunk or disabled. At the airfields on the island, the Japanese destroyed about 180 planes. Before it was over, the raid had killed more than 2,400 American military personnel and civilians.

The attack on Pearl Harbor

This view from an army airfield shows the destruction brought on by the surprise attack.

The surprise attack fulfilled the dreams of its planners, but it fell short of total success in two ways. The Japanese ignored oil-storage tanks in Hawaii, without which the surviving U.S. ships might have been forced back to the West Coast, and they missed the American aircraft carriers that had fortuitously left port a few days earlier. In the naval war to come, those aircraft carriers would be decisive.

Later that day (December 8 in the western Pacific), Japanese forces invaded the Philippines, Guam, Midway, Hong Kong, and the Malay Peninsula. With one stroke the Japanese had silenced America's debate on neutrality—a suddenly unified and vengeful nation resolutely prepared for the struggle.

The day after the attack on Pearl Harbor, President Roosevelt told Congress that December 7 was "a date which will live in infamy," and he asked for a declaration of war. It was approved with only one dissenting vote, by

Representative Jeanette Rankin of Montana, a pacifist who was unable in good conscience to vote for war in 1917 or 1941. On December 11, Germany and Italy impetuously declared war on the United States. The separate wars in Asia and Europe had become one global conflict—and American isolationism was cast aside.

CHAPTER SUMMARY

- **Isolationism** America distanced itself from global affairs—a stance reflected in the Red Scare, laws limiting immigration, and high tariffs. Yet America could not ignore the international events because its business interests became increasingly global. Although the United States never joined the League of Nations, it sent unofficial observers to Geneva. The widespread belief that arms limitations would reduce the chance of future wars led America to participate in the Washington Naval Conference of 1921 and the Kellogg-Briand Pact of 1928.

- **Totalitarianism** Totalitarian dictators came to power in Europe in the 1920s and 1930s. In Italy, Benito Mussolini assumed control by promising law and order. Adolf Hitler's National Socialist German Workers' party succeeded in part by responding to the humiliation that many Germans felt after Germany's defeat in the Great War. Hitler rearmed Germany in defiance of the Treaty of Versailles and aimed to unite all German speakers in a new German empire. Civil war in Spain and the growth of the Soviet Union under Joseph Stalin contributed to a precarious balance of power in Europe between the major nations.

- **American Neutrality** By 1938, Hitler had annexed Austria and seized the German-dominated areas of Czechoslovakia. By March 1939, Hitler seized the rest of Czechoslovakia. He faced no opposition until he sent troops to invade Poland in September of 1939, after signing a nonaggression pact with the Soviet Union. At last, the British and French governments believed that they had no option but to declare war. The United States issued declarations of neutrality, but with the fall of France, President Roosevelt's administration accelerated American aid to France and Britain.

- **Japanese Threat** The bombing of an American gunboat in China by Japanese planes in 1937 alienated Americans. Further Japanese aggression in Asia contributed to the deterioration of U.S.-Japanese relations. After Japan allied itself with Germany and Italy and announced its intention to take control of French Indochina, President Roosevelt froze Japanese assets in the United States and restricted oil exports to Japan. The Japanese leadership, fearing that the U.S. Navy might challenge its conquests, decided to bomb the Pacific Fleet at Pearl Harbor, Hawaii. The attack was a surprise, carried out without a declaration of war.

CHRONOLOGY

1921	Representatives of the United States, Great Britain, France, Italy, and Japan attend the Washington Naval Conference
1922	United States begins sending observers to the League of Nations
1922	Benito Mussolini comes to power in Italy
1928	More than sixty nations sign the Kellogg-Briand Pact pledging not to go to war with one another, except in matters of self-defense
1933	Adolf Hitler becomes chancellor of Germany
1939	Soviet Union agrees to a nonaggression pact with Germany
September 1939	German troops invade Poland
1940	Battle of Britain
September 1940	Germany, Italy, and Japan sign the Tripartite Pact
December 7, 1941	Japanese launch surprise attack on U.S. military base at Pearl Harbor, Hawaii

KEY TERMS & NAMES

30

THE SECOND
WORLD WAR

FOCUS QUESTIONS wwnorton.com/studyspace

- What effect did World War II have on American society?
- How did the Allied forces win the war in Europe?
- How did the United States gain the upper hand in the Pacific sphere?
- What efforts did the Allies make to shape the postwar world?

The Japanese attack on Pearl Harbor ended a period of uneasy neutrality for the United States, and it plunged the nation into a global conflict that would cost the lives of over 400,000 Americans. The war would also transform social and economic life, as well as international affairs. The Second World War would become the most destructive and far-reaching conflict in history. It was so terrible in its intensity and obscene in its cruelties that it altered the image of war itself. Devilish new instruments of destruction were invented—plastic explosives, proximity fuses, rockets, jet airplanes, and atomic weapons—and systematic genocide emerged as an explicit war aim of the Nazis. The scorching passions of such a total war blanched many moral scruples. Racist propaganda flourished on both sides, and intense hatred of the enemy caused many military and civilian prisoners to be executed. Over 50 million deaths resulted from the war, two thirds of them civilians. The physical destruction was incalculable. Whole cities were leveled, nations dismembered, and societies transformed. The world is still coping with the consequences.

AMERICA'S EARLY BATTLES

At the end of 1941, the United States was woefully unprepared to wage a world war on multiple fronts. The army and navy were understaffed and underequipped. And it would take months for the economy make the transition to full-scale military production. Yet time was of the essence. Japanese and German forces had seized the initiative and were on the move. Momentum was on their side.

SETBACKS IN THE PACIFIC   For months after Pearl Harbor, the news from the Pacific was "all bad," as President Roosevelt confessed. The well-armed and well-led Japanese captured a string of Allied outposts in the three months before the end of December 1941: Guam, Wake Island, the Gilbert Islands, Hong Kong, Singapore, and Java. Other British and American territories toppled like dominoes. The Japanese capture of Rangoon, in Burma (Yangon in present-day Myanmar), in March 1942 cut off the Burma Road, the main supply route to China. By May the Japanese had ousted U.S. forces from the Philippines, and they controlled a new empire that stretched from Burma eastward through the Dutch East Indies and extended to Wake Island and the Gilbert Islands.

The Japanese might have consolidated an almost impregnable empire with the resources they had seized. But leaders of the Japanese navy succumbed to what one of its admirals later called victory disease: intoxicated with easy victories, they decided to push farther into the South Pacific, isolate Australia, and strike again at Hawaii. Japanese planners hoped to destroy the American navy before the productive power of the United States could be brought to bear on the war effort.

CORAL SEA AND MIDWAY   During the spring of 1942, American forces finally halted the Japanese advance toward Australia in two key naval clashes. The Battle of the Coral Sea (May 7–8, 1942) stopped a fleet convoying Japanese troop transports toward New Guinea. Planes from the *Lexington* and the *Yorktown* sank one Japanese aircraft carrier, damaged another, and destroyed smaller ships. American losses were greater, but the Japanese designs on Australia were thwarted.

Less than a month after the Coral Sea conflict, Admiral Isoroku Yamamoto, the Japanese naval commander, led his fleet toward Midway, the westernmost of Hawaii's inhabited islands, from which he hoped to render Pearl Harbor helpless. This time it was the Japanese who were the victims of surprise. American cryptanalysts had by then broken the Japanese

Early defeats

U.S. prisoners of war, captured by the Japanese in the Philippines, 1942.

naval code, and Admiral Chester Nimitz, commander of the central Pacific, knew their plan of attack. He reinforced Midway with planes and the aircraft carriers *Enterprise, Hornet,* and *Yorktown.*

The first Japanese foray against Midway, on June 4, 1942, severely damaged the American installations on the island, but at the cost of about a third of the Japanese planes. Meanwhile, American dive bombers caught three of the four Japanese carriers in the process of servicing their planes. The decks of the Japanese ships were cluttered with bombs, gasoline, and planes. Dive bombers sank three of them during the first assault. Later the Japanese lost another carrier, but not before its planes had disabled the *Yorktown.* The only other major American loss was a destroyer. The Japanese defeat at Midway was the turning point of the Pacific war. It demonstrated that aircraft carriers, not battleships, would decide the naval conflict.

SETBACKS IN THE ATLANTIC Early Allied setbacks in the Pacific were matched by losses in the Atlantic. Since the blitzkrieg of 1940, German submarine "wolf packs" had wreaked havoc in the North Atlantic. In 1942, German U-boats appeared off American shores and began to attack coastal ships, most of them tankers. Nearly 400 ships were lost in American waters before effective countermeasures brought the problem under control. The naval command hastened the building of small escort vessels, meanwhile pressing into patrol service all kinds of surface craft and planes, some of them civilian. During the second half of 1942, these efforts sharply reduced American losses.

MOBILIZATION AT HOME

Roosevelt's declaration of war ended not only the long public debate on isolation and intervention but also the long economic depression that had ravaged the country during the 1930s. The war effort required all of America's immense productive capacity and full employment of the workforce. For 1942 alone the government ordered 60,000 planes, 45,000 tanks, and 8 million tons of merchant shipping. The next year's goals were even higher. Mobilization was in fact already further along than preparedness had been in 1916–1917. The draft had been in effect for more than a year, and the army had grown to more than 1.4 million men by July 1941. Congress quickly extended the term of military service to six months after the war's end. Men between the ages of eighteen and forty-five were now drafted. Altogether, more than 15 million American men and women would serve in the armed forces during the war. The average soldier or sailor was twenty-six years old, stood five feet eight inches, and weighed 144 pounds, an inch taller and eight pounds heavier than the average recruit in World War I. Less than half the servicemen had finished high school.

ECONOMIC CONVERSION   The economy, too, was already partially mobilized for war, by lend-lease and the defense buildup. Congress had authorized the president to reshuffle government agencies and to allot materials and facilities as needed for defense, with penalties for any agency that failed to comply. The War Production Board, created in 1942, directed the conversion of manufacturing to war production. The Office of Scientific Research and Development mobilized thousands of scientists to design the many technologies and devices that contributed to the war effort, which would include radar, sonar, the proximity fuse, and the bazooka.

The pressure of wartime needs and the stimulus of government spending more than doubled the gross national product between 1940 and 1945. Government expenditures during the war years soared. The total was about 10 times what America spent in World War I and 100 times the expenditures during the Civil War. The massive infusion of government capital into the economy also encouraged greater centralization and consolidation in private industry. Larger companies tended to win the most government contracts, and the more they won, the larger they became. Conversely, those without government contracts withered and died. In 1942 alone, 300,000 businesses shut down.

USE IT UP – WEAR IT OUT – MAKE IT DO!

OUR LABOR AND OUR GOODS ARE FIGHTING

War-effort advertisement

The Office of War Information created the ad's slogan in 1943.

America's basic economic problem during the war years was no longer creating jobs but finding workers for the booming shipyards, aircraft factories, and munitions plants. Millions of people who had lived on the margins of the economic system, especially women, were now brought fully into the workforce. Pockets of stubborn poverty did not disappear, but for most civilians the war spelled neither severe hardship nor suffering but a better life than ever before, despite shortages and the rationing of consumer goods. Labor unions benefited directly from the dramatic growth of the civilian workforce. Union membership increased significantly during the war years, from about 11 million to 15 million.

ECONOMIC CONTROLS Increased family income and government spending during the war raised fears of inflation. Some of the available money went into taxes and war bonds, but even so, more purchasing power was sent chasing scarce consumer goods just as industrial production was converting to war needs. Consumer durables such as cars, washing machines, and nondefense housing in fact ceased to be produced at all. In the face of such wartime shortages, only strict restraints would keep prices from soaring out of sight. In 1941, Roosevelt created the Office of Price Administration, and the following year Congress authorized it to set price ceilings. With prices frozen, basic consumer goods had to be allocated through rationing, which began with tires and was gradually extended to other scarce items such as sugar, coffee, meat, and gasoline.

At first, however, wages and farm prices were not tightened, and this complicated matters. War prosperity offered farmers a chance to recover from two decades of distress, and farm-state legislators raised both floors and ceilings on farm prices. Higher food prices reinforced workers' demands for higher wages. To relieve this inflationary pressure, the president won new authority to control wages and farm prices. Businesses and workers chafed at the new controls, and on occasion the government was forced to seize industries threatened by strikes. The coal mines and railroads were nationalized for a short time in 1943. Despite these problems the government's program to stabilize the war economy succeeded. By the end of the war, consumer prices had risen only about 31 percent, a far better record than the World War I rise of 62 percent.

To make the economic controls work, the government launched a program to encourage the conservation of resources. As one popular slogan had it, "Use it up, wear it out, make it do or do without." People collected scrap metal and grew their own food in backyard "victory gardens." In 1942, when the war plants faced a rubber shortage, President Roosevelt asked citizens to turn in "old tires, old rubber raincoats, old garden hoses, rubber shoes, bathing caps, gloves—whatever you have that is made of rubber."

DOMESTIC CONSERVATISM Despite the government's efforts to encourage sacrifices for the war effort, Americans expressed their discontent with price controls, labor shortages, rationing, and a hundred other petty vexations. They manifested those concerns against Roosevelt liberalism at the polls in a reaction that indicated a growing political conservatism. In 1942 the congressional elections registered a national swing away from the New Deal. Republicans gained forty-six seats in the House and nine in the Senate, chiefly in the farm areas of the midwestern states. Democratic losses outside the South strengthened the southern delegation's position within the party, and the delegation itself reflected conservative victories in southern primaries. A coalition of conservatives dismantled "nonessential" New Deal agencies, including the National Youth Adminstration, the Civilian Conservation Corps, and the Farm Security Administration.

Organized labor, despite substantial gains during the war, felt the impact of the conservative trend. In the spring of 1943, when John L. Lewis led the coal miners out on strike, Congress passed the Smith-Connally War Labor Disputes Act, which authorized the government to seize plants useful to the war effort. In 1943 a dozen states adopted laws restricting picketing and other union activities, and in 1944 Arkansas and Florida set in motion a wave of "right-to-work" legislation that outlawed the closed shop (requiring that all employees be union members).

SOCIAL EFFECTS OF THE WAR

MOBILIZATION AND THE DEVELOPMENT OF THE WEST The dramatic expansion of defense production after 1940 and the mobilization of millions of people in the armed forces accelerated economic development and a population boom in the western states. Nearly 8 million people moved into the states west of the Mississippi River between 1940 and 1950. The Far West experienced the fastest rate of urban growth in the country. Small cities such as Phoenix and Albuquerque mushroomed while Seattle, San Francisco, Los Angeles, and San Diego witnessed dizzying growth. San Diego's population, for example, increased by 147 percent between 1941 and 1945. The migration of workers to new defense jobs in the West had significant demographic effects. Lured by news of job openings and higher wages, African Americans from Texas, Oklahoma, Arkansas, and Louisiana headed west. During the war years, Seattle's African American population jumped from 4,000 to 40,000, Portland's from 2,000 to 15,000.

CHANGING ROLES FOR WOMEN The war marked an important watershed in the status of women. With millions of men going into military service, the demand for labor shook up old prejudices about sex roles in the workplace—and in the military. Nearly 200,000 women served in the Women's Army Corps (WAC) and the navy's equivalent, Women Accepted for Volunteer Emergency Service (WAVES). Lesser numbers joined the Marine Corps, the Coast Guard, and the Army Air Force.

Over 6 million women entered the workforce during the war, an increase of more than 50 percent and in manufacturing alone an increase of some 110 percent. By 1944 over a third of all American women were in the labor force. Old barriers fell overnight as women became toolmakers machinists, riveters, crane operators, lumberjacks, stevedores, blacksmiths, and railroad workers. Desperate for laborers, the government launched an intense publicity campaign to draw women into traditional

Women in the military

This navy recruiting poster urged women to join the WAVES (Women Accepted for Volunteer Emergency Service).

male jobs. "Rosie the Riveter," an attractive woman depicted in overalls, served as the cover girl for the recruiting campaign.

One striking feature of the wartime economy was the proportion of older, married women in the workforce. In 1940 about 15 percent of married women were employed outside the home; by 1945, 24 percent were. In the workforce as a whole, married women for the first time outnumbered single women. Many women were eager to get away from the grinding routine of domestic life. One female welder remembered that her wartime job "was the first time I had a chance to get out of the kitchen and work in industry and make a few bucks. This was something I had never dreamed would happen." And it was something that many women did not want to relinquish after the war.

AFRICAN AMERICANS IN WORLD WAR II The most volatile social issue ignited by the war was African American participation in the defense effort. From the start, black leaders demanded equality in the armed forces and defense industries. Eventually about 1 million African Americans served in the armed forces, but most were assigned to segregated units. The most important departure from this pattern came with a 1940 decision to integrate officer-candidate schools, except those for air force cadets. A separate military flight school at Tuskegee, Alabama, trained about 600 African American pilots, many of whom distinguished themselves in combat.

Tuskegee Airmen, 1942

One of the last segregated military training schools, the flight school at Tuskegee trained African American men for combat during World War II.

War industries were even less hospitable to integration. "We will not employ Negroes," said the president of North American Aviation. In 1941, A. Philip Randolph, the brilliant head of the Brotherhood of Sleeping Car Porters, organized a march on Washington to demand an end to racial discrimination in defense industries. The Roosevelt administration, alarmed at the prospect of a mass descent on the capital, struck a bargain. Randolph called off the march in return for an executive order prohibiting racial discrimination in companies that received federal defense contracts.

African American leaders quickly challenged all kinds of discrimination, including racial segregation itself. Membership in the NAACP soared during the war, from 50,000 to 450,000. African Americans could look forward to greater political participation after the Supreme Court, in *Smith v. Allwright* (1944), struck down Texas's whites-only primary on the grounds that political primaries were part of the election process and thus subject to the Fifteenth Amendment's guarantee of the right to vote.

LATINOS IN THE LABOR FORCE   As rural folk moved to the western cities, many farm counties across the nation experienced a labor shortage. In an ironic about-face, local and federal government authorities who before the war had forced undocumented Mexican laborers back across the border now recruited them to harvest crops. Before it would assist in providing the needed workers, the Mexican government insisted that the United States ensure minimum working and living conditions. The result was the creation of the bracero program in 1942, whereby Mexico agreed to provide seasonal farmworkers in exchange for a promise by the U.S. government not to draft them into military service. The workers were hired on year long contracts, and American officials provided transportation from the border to their job sites. Under the bracero program some 200,000 Mexican farmworkers entered the western United States. At least that many more crossed the border as undocumented workers.

The rising tide of Mexican Americans in Los Angeles provoked a growing stream of anti-Latino editorials and incidents. Even though Mexican Americans fought in the war with great valor, earning seventeen Congressional Medals of Honor, there was constant conflict between servicemen and Mexican American gang members and teenage "zoot-suiters" in southern California. In 1943 several thousand off-duty sailors and soldiers, joined by hundreds of local white civilians, rampaged through downtown Los Angeles streets, assaulting Latinos, African Americans, and Filipinos. The weeklong violence came to be labeled the zoot-suit riots. (Zoot suits were the flamboyant suits popular in the 1940s and worn by some young Mexican American men.)

NATIVE AMERICANS AND THE WAR EFFORT Indians supported the war effort more fully than any other group in American society. Almost a third of eligible Native American men, over 25,000 people, served in the armed forces. Another one fourth worked in defense-related industries. Thousands of Indian women volunteered as nurses or joined the WAVES. As was the case with African Americans, Indians benefited from the experiences afforded by the war. Those who left reservations to work in defense plants or to join the military gained new vocational skills as well as a greater awareness of opportunities available in the larger American society.

Marine Navajo "code talkers"

The Japanese were never able to break the Native Americans' codes used by signalmen, such as those shown here during the Battle of Bougainville in 1943.

Why did so many Native Americans fight in such high numbers for a nation that had stripped them of their land and decimated their heritage? Some felt that they had no choice. Mobilization for the war effort ended many New Deal programs that had provided Indians with jobs. Reservation Indians thus faced the necessity of finding new jobs elsewhere. Others viewed the Nazis and the Japanese warlords as threats to their own homeland. The most common sentiment animating Indian involvement in the war effort, however, seems to have been a genuine sense of patriotism.

Whatever the reasons, Indians distinguished themselves in the military. Unlike their African American counterparts, Indian servicemen were integrated into regular units. Perhaps the most distinctive activity performed by Indians was their service as "code talkers": every military branch used Indians to encode and decipher messages using their native languages.

INTERNMENT OF JAPANESE AMERICANS   The record on civil liberties during World War II was on the whole better than that during World War I, if only because there was virtually no domestic opposition to the war effort after the attack on Pearl Harbor. Neither German Americans nor Italian Americans faced the harassments meted out to their counterparts in the previous war; few had much sympathy for Hitler or Mussolini. The shameful exception to an otherwise improved record was the treatment accorded to Americans of Japanese descent in the months following the attack on Pearl Harbor. One California barbershop offered "free shaves for Japs" but noted that it was "not responsible for accidents." Others were even blunter. Idaho's governor declared: "A good solution to the Jap problem would be to send them all back to Japan, then sink the island. They live like rats, breed like rats, and act like rats." Such attitudes were widespread, and the government finally succumbed to demands that it force all Japanese, citizens or not, into "war relocation camps" in the interior of the country.

Caught up in the war hysteria and racial prejudice unleashed by the attack on Pearl Harbor, President Roosevelt initiated the removal and confinement of Japanese Americans when he issued Executive Order 9066 on February 19, 1942. More than 60 percent of the internees were U.S. citizens; a third were under the age of nineteen. More than 100,000 people were eventually removed from their homes and businesses. Forced to sell their farms and businesses at great losses, the internees lost both their liberty and their property. Not until 1983 did the government acknowledge the injustice of the internment policy. Five years later Congress voted to give $20,000 and an apology to each of the 60,000 former internees who were still living.

THE ALLIED DRIVE TOWARD BERLIN

By mid-1942 the "home front" had begun to get news from the war fronts that some of the lines were holding at last. By midyear a fleet of American air and sea subchasers was suppressing German U-boats off the Atlantic coast. This event was all the more important because Allied war plans called for the defeat of Germany first.

WAR AIMS AND STRATEGY   There were good reasons for giving top priority to defeating Hitler: Nazi forces in western Europe and the Atlantic posed a more direct threat to the Western Hemisphere than did Japan, and Germany's war potential exceeded Japan's. Yet Japanese attacks involved Americans directly in the Pacific war from the start, and as a consequence more Americans went to the Pacific than crossed the Atlantic during the first year of fighting.

The Pearl Harbor attack brought British prime minister Winston Churchill to Washington, D.C., for talks about a joint war plan. Thus began a successful but not always harmonious wartime alliance between the United States and Great Britain. The meetings in Washington in 1942 affirmed the priority of winning the war against Germany. Agreement on war aims did not bring agreement on strategy, however. When Roosevelt and Churchill met at the White House a second time in 1942, they could not agree on the location of the first attack against the Nazis. American strategists wanted to strike German-held France directly across the English Channel before the end of 1942. With vivid memories of the last war, the British feared a mass bloodletting in trench warfare if they struck prematurely. In eastern Europe two totalitarian regimes—the Germans and the Soviets—waged a colossal war while managing mass death camps. Stalin's henchmen killed more captive peoples than Hitler's. The Soviets, while quietly victimizing their own, were also bearing the brunt of the German attack in the east. Thus they insisted that the Western Allies do something to relieve the pressure along the Russian front. Finally, the Americans accepted Churchill's proposal to invade French North Africa, now allied with Germany.

THE NORTH AFRICAN CAMPAIGN   On November 8, 1942, British and American units commanded by General Dwight D. Eisenhower landed in Morocco and Algeria. Completely surprised, French forces under the Vichy government (which collaborated with the Germans) had little will to resist. Farther east, British forces were pushing German armies back across

Libya. Before spring the Germans were caught in a gigantic pair of pincers. By April the British had linked up with American forces. Hammered from all sides and unable to retreat across the Mediterranean, an army of more than 200,000 Germans surrendered on May 12, 1943, leaving all of North Africa in Allied hands.

While the Battle of Tunisia was still unfolding, Roosevelt and Churchill met at Casablanca, Morocco. It was a historic occasion. No U.S. president had ever flown while in office, and none had ever visited Africa. But the absence of precedent did not deter Roosevelt. Stalin declined to leave the beleaguered Soviet Union for the meeting, but he continued to press for the opening of a second front in western Europe. Since the German invasion of Russia in 1941, over 90 percent of German military casualties had occurred on the eastern front. The British and American engagements with German forces in North Africa were minuscule in comparison with the scope and fury of the fighting in Russia.

Churchill and Roosevelt spent eight days at Casablanca hammering out key strategic decisions. The Americans wanted to launch a massive Allied invasion of German-occupied France as soon as possible, but the British still insisted that such a major assault was premature. They convinced the Americans that they should follow up a victory in North Africa with an assault on Sicily and Italy. Roosevelt and Churchill also decided to step up the bombing of Germany and to increase shipments of military supplies to the Soviet Union and the Nationalist Chinese forces fighting the Japanese.

Before leaving Casablanca, Roosevelt announced, with Churchill's endorsement, that the war would end only with the "unconditional surrender" of all enemies. This demand was designed to reassure Stalin that the Western Allies would not negotiate separately with the Germans. The West desperately needed Soviet cooperation in defeating Germany, and Roosevelt and Churchill were eager to reassure Stalin of their good intentions.

THE BATTLE OF THE ATLANTIC While fighting raged in North Africa, the more crucial Battle of the Atlantic reached its climax on the high seas. Several factors contributed to the success of the Allied effort. Scientists had perfected a variety of detection devices: radar, which the British had already used to advantage in the Battle of Britain, bounced radio waves off objects and registered their position on a screen; sonar detected sound waves from submerged U-boats; sonobuoys, dropped from planes, radioed back their findings; and advanced magnetic equipment enabled aircraft to detect objects underwater.

By early 1943 in the western portion of the North Atlantic, there were at any given time an average of 31 convoys with 145 escorts and 673 merchant ships, as well as a number of heavily escorted troopships. None of the troopships going to Britain or the Mediterranean was lost. The U-boats kept up the Battle of the Atlantic until the war's end, but their commander later admitted that the battle had been lost by the end of May 1943. He credited the difference largely to radar. What he did not know then was that the Allies had a secret weapon: by early 1943 their cryptanalysts were routinely decoding German messages and telling their subchasers where to look for German U-boats.

SICILY AND ITALY   On July 10, 1943, after the Allied victory in the North African campaign, about 250,000 British and American troops landed on the Italian island of Sicily, scoring a complete surprise. The German-Italian collapse in Sicily ended Mussolini's twenty years of Fascist rule. On July 25, 1943, Italy's king notified the dictator of his dismissal as prime minister. A new Italian government startled the Allies when it offered not only to surrender but also to switch sides in the war. Unfortunately, mutual suspicions prolonged talks until September 3, while the Germans poured reinforcements into Italy. Mussolini, plucked from imprisonment by a daring German airborne raid, became head of a puppet Fascist government in northern Italy.

Therefore the Allied assault on the Italian mainland did not turn into an easy victory. The main landing at Salerno on September 9 encountered heavy German resistance, as the steep terrain favored the defenders. The Americans, joined by British troops, nevertheless secured beachheads within a week and captured Naples. After a five-month siege of Rome, the Americans finally took the fabled city on June 4, 1944. Yet they enjoyed only a brief moment of glory, for the long-awaited cross-Channel landing in France, begun two days later, quickly became the focus of attention.

THE STRATEGIC BOMBING OF EUROPE   Behind the long-postponed landings on the Normandy beaches lay months of preparation. While waiting, the U.S. Army Air Force and the Royal Air Force (RAF) had attacked the installations and troops making up what Hitler called "Fortress Europe." By 1943, American strategic bombers were full-fledged partners of the RAF in the effort to pound Germany into submission. Yet despite the widespread damage it caused, the strategic air offensive ultimately failed to dismantle German production or, as later studies found, break civilian

WORLD WAR II IN EUROPE AND AFRICA, 1942–1945

★ Major battle

◼ Axis Powers at outbreak of the war

◻ Maximum extent of Axis military power

◄— Allied offensives

◄- - Heaviest Allied aerial bombing

⋯⋯ Inside limit of German U-boat operations

What was the Allies' strategy in North Africa, and why was it important for the invasion of Italy? Why did Eisenhower's plan on D-day succeed? What was the Battle of the Bulge? What was the role of strategic bombing in the war? Was it effective?

morale. By the end of 1943, however, new jettisonable gas tanks permitted Allied escort fighters to fly as far as Berlin and back, protecting the bomber groups. Thereafter, heavy losses of both planes and pilots forced the German Luftwaffe to conserve its strength and cease challenging every Allied mission.

With air supremacy assured, the Allies were free to concentrate on their primary urban and industrial targets and, when the time came, provide cover for the Normandy landings. On April 14, 1944, General Eisenhower assumed control of the strategic air forces for the invasion of German-controlled France. On D-day, June 6, 1944, he told the troops, "If you see fighting aircraft over you, they will be ours."

THE TEHRAN MEETING   Late in November 1943, Churchill and Roosevelt had met with Stalin in Tehran, Iran, to coordinate plans for the invasion of France and a Soviet offensive from the east. After Churchill and Roosevelt assured Stalin that a cross-Channel invasion was finally coming, the Soviet premier in return promised to enter the war against Japan after Germany's defeat. The Allied leaders also agreed to begin plans for a new international peacekeeping organization and for the occupation of postwar Germany. Politics continued to complicate military strategy.

Earlier in November, while on the way to the Tehran meeting, Churchill and Roosevelt had met with China's general Chiang Kai-shek in Cairo. The resulting Declaration of Cairo affirmed that war against Japan would continue until Japan's unconditional surrender, that all Chinese territories taken by Japan would be restored to China, and that "in due course Korea shall become free and independent."

D-DAY AND AFTER   In early 1944, General Dwight D. Eisenhower, smart, efficient, and well organized, arrived in London to take command at the Supreme Headquarters of the Allied Expeditionary Force and prepare for the cross-Channel assault on German-controlled France. Within a few months, over 1 million American soldiers were training along England's southern coast for the invasion.

The daring cross-Channel invasion of France, called Operation Overlord, surprised the Germans. Eisenhower fooled Hitler's generals into believing that the invasion would come at Pas-de-Calais, on the French-Belgian border. Instead, the landings occurred in Normandy, about 200 miles south. Airborne forces dropped behind the beaches during the night while planes and battleships pounded the coastal defenses.

At dawn on June 6, 1944, D-day, the invasion fleet of some 5,300 ships carrying 370,000 soldiers and sailors filled the horizon off the Normandy

Operation Overlord

General Dwight D. Eisenhower instructing paratroopers before they board their airplanes to launch the D-day assault.

coast. Overhead, thousands of Allied planes supported the invasion force. Sleepy German soldiers awoke to see the vast armada arrayed before them. Despite Eisenhower's meticulous planning and the imposing array of Allied troops and firepower, the D-day invasion almost failed. Cloud cover and German anti-aircraft fire caused many of the paratroopers and glider pilots to miss their landing zones. Oceangoing landing craft delivered their troops to the wrong locations. Low clouds led the Allied planes to drop their bombs too far inland. The naval bombardment was equally ineffective. In addition, rough seas made many soldiers seasick and capsized dozens of landing craft. Over 1,000 men drowned. Waterlogged radios failed to work, and the deafening noise of the artillery and gunfire made oral communication impossible.

On Utah Beach the American troops made it in against relatively light opposition, but farther east, on a four-mile segment designated Omaha Beach, bombardment failed to take out the German defenders, and the Americans were caught in heavily mined water. In just ten minutes, 197 of the 205 men in one rifle company were killed or wounded. By nightfall the bodies of some 5,000 killed or wounded Allied soldiers were strewn across Normandy's

The landing at Normandy

D-day, June 6, 1944. Before they could huddle under a seawall and begin to root out the region's Nazi defenders, soldiers on Omaha Beach had to cross a fifty-yard stretch that exposed them to bullets fired from machine guns housed in concrete bunkers.

beaches. German losses were even heavier; entire units were decimated or captured. Operation Overlord was the greatest amphibious invasion in the annals of warfare. It was also a climactic battle of World War II, but it was small when compared with the offensive launched by the Russians a few weeks after D-day. Between June and August 1944 the Red Army killed, wounded, or captured more German soldiers than were stationed in all of western Europe. Still, the Normandy invasion was a turning point in the war—and a pivotal point in America's rise to global power. With the beachhead secured, the Allied leaders knew that victory was now in their grasp.

Within two weeks after D-day, the Allies had landed 1 million troops, 556,000 tons of supplies, and 170,000 vehicles. They had seized a beachhead sixty miles wide and five to fifteen miles deep. They continued to pour men and supplies onto the beaches and to edge inland through the marshes and hedgerows. A stubborn Hitler issued disastrous orders to contest every inch of land. Field Marshal Erwin Rommel, convinced that all was lost, began to intrigue for a separate peace. Other like-minded German officers, sure that the war was hopeless, tried to kill Hitler at his headquarters on July 20, 1944, but the Führer survived the bomb blast, and hundreds of conspirators and suspects were tortured to death. Rommel was granted the option of suicide, which he took.

Meanwhile, Hitler's tactics brought calamity to the German forces in western France. On July 25, American units broke out westward into Brittany and eastward toward Paris. On August 15 a joint American-French invasion force landed on the French Mediterranean coast and raced up the Rhone Valley. German resistance in France collapsed. A division of the Free French Resistance, aided by American forces, had the honor of liberating Paris on August 25. Hitler's forces retreated toward the German border, and by mid-September most of France and Belgium had been cleared of enemy troops.

LEAPFROGGING TO TOKYO

Even in the Pacific, relegated to a lower priority, Allied forces had brought the war within reach of the enemy's homeland by the end of 1944. The war's first American offensive, in fact, had been in the southwest Pacific. There the Japanese, stopped at the Battles of Coral Sea and Midway, had thrust into the southern Solomon Islands and were building an airstrip on Guadalcanal, from which they would be able to attack Allied transportation routes to Australia. On August 7, 1942, two months before the North Africa landings, the First Marine Division landed on Guadalcanal and seized the airstrip.

MACARTHUR IN NEW GUINEA Meanwhile, American and Australian forces under General Douglas MacArthur had begun to push the Japanese out of their positions on New Guinea's northern coast. These costly battles, fought through some of the hottest, most humid, and most mosquito-infested swamps in the world, secured the eastern tip of New Guinea by the end of January 1943.

At this stage, American war planners were confronted with two propositions by the leaders of rival branches of the armed service, the army and the navy. The vainglorious MacArthur, sometimes accused of being a legend in his own mind, proposed to move his forces westward along the northern coast of New Guinea toward the Philippines and ultimately to Tokyo. Naval admiral Chester Nimitz argued for a sweep through the islands of the central

SEA OF OKHOTSK

SOVIET UNION

Russians 1944–1945

SAKHALIN

KUR
ISL

MONGOLIA

MANCHURIA

Peking

SEA OF
JAPAN

KOREA

JAPAN

Hiroshima

Tokyo

C H I N A

YELLOW
SEA

Nanking

Nagasaki

Shanghai

BONIN
ISLANDS

HIMALAYAS

Chungking

Stilwell
Road

EAST
CHINA
SEA

OKINAWA

Iwo Jima

Ledo

1943

Burma
Road

FORMOSA
(TAIWAN)

1945

INDIA

K'un-ming

1945

MARIA
ISLAN

Lashio

BURMA
(MYANMAR)

HONG
KONG

PHILIPPINE

Rangoon
(Yangon)

THAILAND

Corregidor
1942

Luzon

SEA

Saip

Manila

FRENCH
INDOCHINA

BATAAN PENINSULA

SOUTH
CHINA
SEA

PHILIPPINES

Gua

Leyte

Mindanao

PALAU

CAROLIN

BRITISH
NORTH
BORNEO

BRUNEI

ADMIRA
ISLAN

BRITISH
MALAYA

SARAWAK

1944–1945

SUMATRA

Singapore

BORNEO

1943

Equator

CELEBES
(SULAWESI)

MOLUCCAS

BISMA
SE

DUTCH EAST INDIES

Java Sea

NEW GUINEA

JAVA

TIMOR

Port
More

INDIAN

OCEAN

AUSTRALIA

| 0 | 400 | 800 | 1,200 Miles |
| 0 | 400 | 800 | 1,200 Kilometers |

What was "leapfrogging"? Why were the battles in the Marianas a major turning point in the war? What was the significance of the Battle of Leyte Gulf? How did the battle at Okinawa affect the way both sides proceeded in the war? Why did President Truman decide to drop atomic bombs on Hiroshima and Nagasaki?

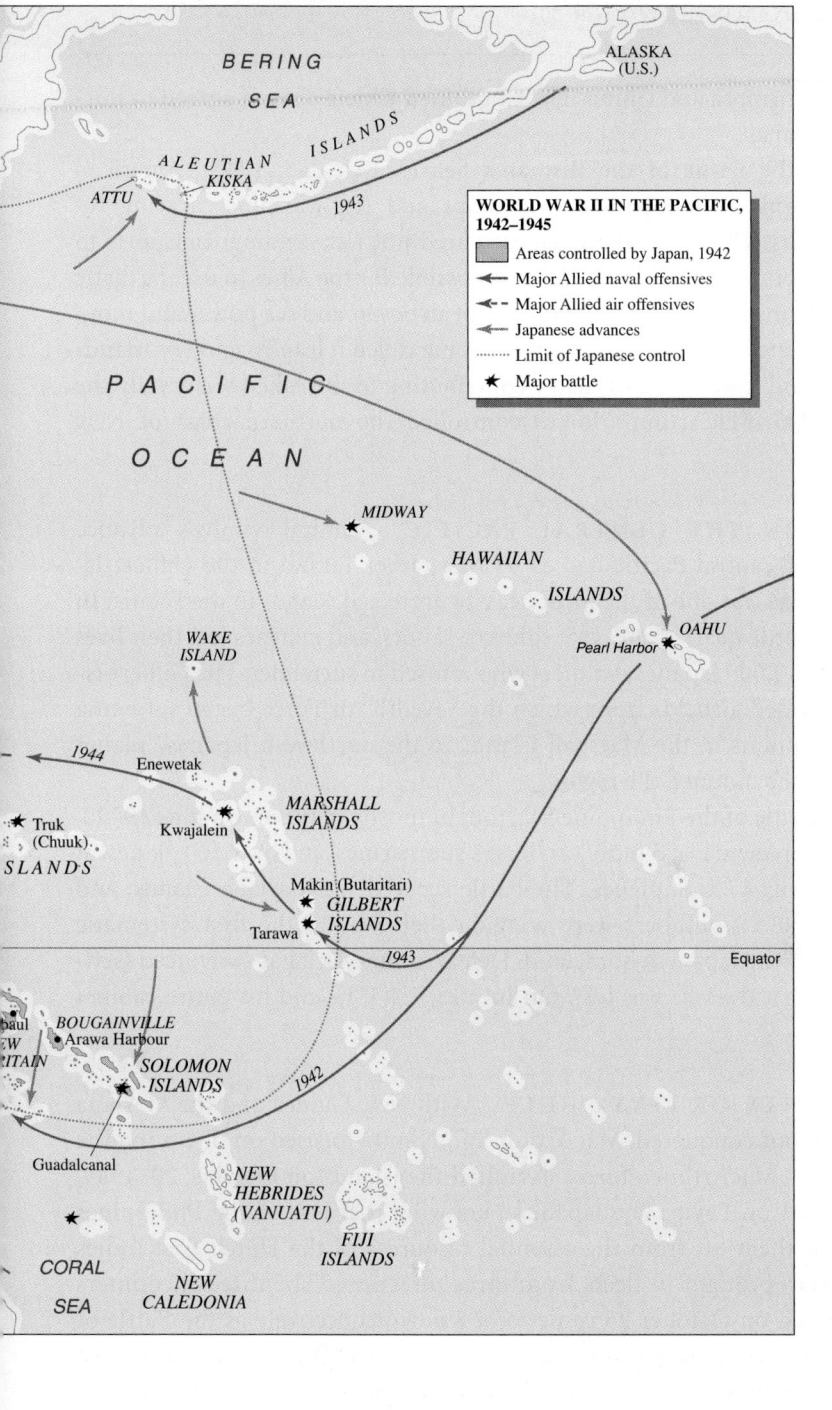

BERING
SEA

ALASKA
(U.S.)

ALEUTIAN   ISLANDS
KISKA
ATTU   1943

PACIFIC

OCEAN

MIDWAY

HAWAIIAN

ISLANDS

OAHU
Pearl Harbor

WAKE
ISLAND

1944
Enewetak

Truk
(Chuuk)
SLANDS

MARSHALL
ISLANDS

Kwajalein

Makin (Butaritari)
GILBERT
ISLANDS
Tarawa

1943   Equator

aul   BOUGAINVILLE
W   Arawa Harbour
ITAIN   SOLOMON
ISLANDS   1942

Guadalcanal

NEW
HEBRIDES
(VANUATU)

FIJI
ISLANDS

CORAL   NEW

SEA   CALEDONIA

**WORLD WAR II IN THE PACIFIC,
1942–1945**

Areas controlled by Japan, 1942
Major Allied naval offensives
Major Allied air offensives
Japanese advances
Limit of Japanese control
★ Major battle

Pacific to Formosa and China. The Combined Chiefs of Staff agreed to pursue both plans.

During the Battle of the Bismarck Sea (March 2–3, 1943), American bombers sank eight Japanese troopships and ten warships carrying reinforcements. Thereafter the Japanese dared not risk sending transports to reinforce points under siege, making it possible for the Allies to use the tactic of neutralizing Japanese strongholds with airpower and sea power and moving on, leaving them to die on the vine. Some called it leapfrogging or island-hopping, and it was a major factor contributing to the Allied victory. By the end of 1943, MacArthur's forces controlled the northern coast of New Guinea.

NIMITZ IN THE CENTRAL PACIFIC   Admiral Nimitz's advance through the central Pacific had as its first target Tarawa in the Gilbert Islands. Tarawa was one of the most heavily protected islands in the Pacific. In a pitched battle nearly 1,000 U.S. soldiers, sailors, and marines lost their lives rooting out 4,000 Japanese soldiers who refused to surrender. The Gilbert Islands provided airfields from which the Seventh Air Force began softening up strong points in the Marshall Islands to the northwest. Japanese planes completely abandoned the region.

In the Battle of the Philippine Sea, fought mostly in the air on June 19–20, 1944, the Japanese lost 3 more carriers, 2 submarines, and over 300 planes, at a cost of only 17 U.S. planes. The battle secured the Mariana Islands, and soon large B-29 bombers were winging their way to the first systematic bombing of the Japanese homeland. Defeat in the Marianas convinced General Tōjō that the war was lost. On July 18, 1944, he and his entire cabinet resigned.

THE BATTLE OF LEYTE GULF   With New Guinea and the Mariana Islands all but conquered, MacArthur and Nimitz focused on liberating the Philippines. MacArthur's forces assaulted the islands on October 20, 1944, landing first on Leyte. The Japanese, knowing that loss of the Philippines would cut them off from the essential resources of the Dutch East Indies (Indonesia), brought in fleets from three directions. The three encounters that resulted on October 25 came to be known collectively as the Battle of Leyte Gulf, the largest naval engagement in history. The Japanese lost most of their remaining sea power and the ability to defend the Philippines. Also remarkable was the first use of suicide attacks as Japanese pilots crash-dived into American ships, killing themselves in the process. Called kamikazes (a reference to the "divine wind" that centuries before was believed to have saved Japan from a Mongol invasion) by the Allies and *tokkotai* (meaning "special attack force") by the Japanese, most of the pilots were not fanatical volunteers. The majority of the thousand or so who died were very young student draftees (between the ages of seventeen and twenty-four) who had been ordered to steer their planes into Allied ships. Whatever their motives, the *tokkotai* caused substantial damage.

A NEW AGE IS BORN

ROOSEVELT'S FOURTH TERM   In 1944, war or no war, the calendar dictated another presidential election. This time the Republicans turned to a former crime fighter and New York governor, Thomas E. Dewey, as their candidate. No Democrat challenged Roosevelt, but a fight did develop over the second spot on the ticket. Vice President Henry Wallace had aggravated southern conservatives and northern city bosses, who feared his ties with labor unions, so Roosevelt finally chose the relatively unknown Missouri senator Harry S. Truman.

Dewey ran under the same handicap as Alf Landon and Wendell Willkie had before him. He did not propose to dismantle Roosevelt's programs; rather, he argued that it was time for younger men to replace the "tired" old leaders of the New Deal. The problem was that even though he was considerably younger than Roosevelt, Dewey showed few signs of vitality. Although blessed with a silky voice and a stylish wardrobe, he was ill at ease in public, stiff, formal, seemingly arrogant, and worst of all—dull. Roosevelt showed signs of illness and exhaustion, but nevertheless, on November 7, 1944, he was once again elected, this time by a popular vote of 25.6 million to 22 million and an electoral vote of 432 to 99.

CONVERGING MILITARY FRONTS   Meanwhile, Allied forces were mired in war in Europe; complete victory remained elusive. After the quick sweep across France, the Allies lost momentum in the fall of 1944 and settled down to slugging it out along the border of Germany. The armies would fight along this line all winter, but first, on December 16, 1944, the Germans sprang a surprise in the rugged Ardennes Forest, where the Allied line was thinnest. The Nazis advanced along a fifty-mile bulge in the Allied lines in Belgium and Luxembourg (hence the name the Battle of the Bulge) before they stalled at Bastogne. Reinforced by the Allies just before it was surrounded,

Bastogne held out for six days against relentless attacks. The American situation remained desperate until December 23, when the weather improved, allowing Allied airpower to drop supplies and attack the Germans. On December 26, the besieged American army at Bastogne was relieved.

Germany's sudden counterattack upset Eisenhower's timetable and made continued coordination with the Soviet army even more crucial. Having poured resources into the battle at Bastogne, the Nazis were unable to hold the eastern front when the Soviets began their final offensive in January 1945. The destruction of Hitler's last reserve units at the Battle of the Bulge also left open the door to Germany's heartland. The western offensives began in February, and by early March Allied forces were crossing the Rhine River into Germany. By that time the Soviet offensive on the eastern front had also reached the German border.

YALTA AND THE POSTWAR WORLD   As the final offensives against Germany got under way, the Big Three leaders met again, in early February 1945 at Yalta, a resort in southern Russia. While the focus at Tehran in 1943

The Yalta Conference

Churchill, Roosevelt, and Stalin confer on the shape of the postwar world in February 1945.

had been on wartime strategy, the leaders now discussed the shape of the postwar world. Stalin was self-confident, demanding, and sarcastic. He knew that the Soviet forces' control of key areas ensured that his demands would be met. Two aims loomed large in Roosevelt's thinking. One was the need to ensure that the Soviet Union would join the war against Japan. The other was based upon the lessons he had drawn from the previous world war. Chief among the mistakes to be remedied were the failures of the United States to join the League of Nations and of the Allies to maintain a united front in negotiations with the German aggressors after the war.

The Yalta meeting thus began by calling for a conference to create a new world organization, called the United Nations. The conferees also decided that substantive decisions in the new organization's Security Council would require the agreement of its five permanent members: the United States, Britain, the Soviet Union, France, and China.

GERMANY AND EASTERN EUROPE   With Hitler's Third Reich empire stumbling to its doom, the leaders at Yalta had to make arrangements for the postwar governance of Germany. The war map dictated the basic pattern of occupation zones: the Soviet Union would control eastern Germany, and the Western Allies would control the rich industrial areas of the west. The national capital of Berlin, isolated within the Soviet zone, would be jointly occupied. Churchill and Roosevelt insisted that liberated France receive a zone along its border with Germany and one in Berlin. Austria was similarly divided, with Vienna, like Berlin, under joint occupation within the Soviet zone. Russian demands for reparations of $20 billion to the Allies, half of which would go to the Soviet Union, were referred to a reparations commission. That commission never reached agreement, although the Soviets took untold amounts of German machinery and equipment from their occupation zone.

With respect to Eastern Europe, where Soviet forces were advancing on a broad front, there was little the Western Allies could do to influence events. Poland became the main focus of Western concern. Britain and France had gone to war in 1939 to defend it, and now, six years later, the course of the war had ironically left Poland's fate in the hands of the Soviets. Events had long foreshadowed the outcome. When they entered Poland in 1944, the Soviets allowed a puppet regime in Lublin to take control of civil administration. The Soviets refused to recognize the legitimacy of Poland's government-in-exile in London, formed by officials who had fled the country following Hitler's invasion in 1939. With Soviet troops at the gates of Warsaw, the underground resistance in the city rose up against the Nazi occupiers. But because the Polish underground supported the Polish government-in-exile, the Soviet armies idled for two months while the Nazis killed thousands of Poles in Warsaw, potential rivals of the Soviets' Lublin puppet government.

At Yalta the Big Three promised to sponsor free elections, democratic governments, and constitutional safeguards of freedom throughout Europe. The Yalta Declaration of Liberated Europe reaffirmed faith in the principles of the Atlantic Charter and the Declaration of the United Nations, but in the end it made little difference. It may have postponed Communist takeovers in Eastern Europe for a few years, but before long Communist members of coalition governments had purged the opposition. Russia, twice invaded by Germany in the twentieth century, was determined to create compliant buffer states between it and the German state.

YALTA'S LEGACY   Critics later attacked the Yalta agreements for "giving" Eastern Europe over to Soviet domination. Some argued that Roosevelt's declining health allowed him to buckle under Stalin's insistent demands. Yet the course of the war, not personal diplomacy, shaped the actions at Yalta. The Soviets had the upper hand in Eastern Europe. Perhaps the most bitterly criticized of the Yalta accords was a secret agreement on the Far East, made public after the war. The Combined Chiefs of Staff estimated that Japan could hold out for eighteen months after the defeat of Germany. Costly campaigns thus lay ahead, and the atomic bomb was still an expensive and untested gamble.

Roosevelt thus believed he had no choice but to accept Stalin's demands on postwar arrangements in the Far East, subject technically to agreement later by China's general Chiang Kai-shek. Stalin wanted continued Soviet control of Outer Mongolia through its puppet People's Republic, acquisition of the Kuril Islands from Japan, and recovery of rights and territory lost after the Russo-Japanese War of 1905. Stalin in return promised to enter the war against Japan two or three months after the German defeat, recognize Chinese sovereignty over Manchuria, and conclude a treaty of friendship and alliance with the Chinese Nationalists. Roosevelt's concessions would later appear in a different light, but given their geographic advantages in Asia, as in Eastern Europe, the Soviets were in a position to get what they wanted in any case.

THE COLLAPSE OF THE THIRD REICH   By 1945 the collapse of Nazi resistance was imminent, but President Roosevelt did not live to join the celebrations. Throughout 1944 his health had been declining, and on April 12, 1945, while drafting a speech, he died from a cerebral hemorrhage.

Hitler's Germany collapsed less than a month later. The Allied armies rolled up almost unopposed to the Elbe River, where they met advance detachments of Soviets on April 25. Three days later Italian partisans killed Mussolini as he tried to flee. In Berlin, which was under siege by the Soviets, Hitler married his mistress, Eva Braun, in an underground bunker on April 30, just before killing her and himself. On May 2, Berlin fell to the Soviets. That day, German forces in Italy surrendered. On May 7, the Germans signed an unconditional surrender treaty in the Allied headquarters at Reims, France.

Massive victory celebrations on V-E day, May 8, 1945, were tempered by the tragedies that had engulfed the world: mourning for the lost president and the death and mutilation of untold millions. Most shocking was the Allied armies' confirmation of the existence of the death camps in which Nazis had sought to apply their "final solution" to the "Jewish problem": the wholesale extermination of some 6 million Jews, along with more than 1 million others from occupied countries.

May 8, 1945

The celebration in New York City's Times Square on V-E day.

During the war, reports from Red Cross and underground sources had amassed growing evidence of Germany's systematic genocide of European Jews. Stories appeared in major American newspapers as early as 1942, but they were nearly always buried on inside pages. Reports of such horror seemed beyond belief. In addition, American government officials, even some Jewish leaders, dragged their feet on the question for fear that relief efforts for Jewish refugees might stir latent anti-Semitism at home. Finally Roosevelt had set up a War Refugee Board in 1944. It managed to rescue about 200,000 European Jews and some 20,000 others. But more might have been done. The Allies rejected a plan to bomb the rail lines leading to Auschwitz the largest death camp in Poland, although American planes hit industries five miles away. Moreover, few refugees were accepted by the United States. The Allied handling of the Holocaust was inept at best and disgraceful at worst.

A GRINDING WAR AGAINST JAPAN   The sobering thought that Japan must still be defeated cast a further pall over the victory celebrations. American forces continued to assault the Japanese Empire in the early months of 1945, but at a heavy cost. On February 19, 1945, U.S. marines invaded Iwo Jima, a volcanic island 760 miles from Tokyo that was needed in order to provide a fighter escort for bombers over Japan and a landing strip for disabled B-29 bombers. It took nearly six weeks to secure the site from Japanese defenders hiding in caves, and the cost was high: more than 20,000 American casualties, including nearly 7,000 deaths.

The fight for Okinawa, beginning on Easter Sunday, April 1, was even bloodier. The island was large enough to afford a staging area for the planned invasion of the Japanese islands, and its capture required the largest amphibious operation of the Pacific war, involving some 300,000 troops. The fight raged until late June, incurring nearly 50,000 American casualties. The Japanese lost an estimated 140,000, including about 42,000 Okinawans. When resistance on Okinawa collapsed, the Japanese emperor instructed his new prime minister to seek peace, but he included conditions unacceptable to the Allies.

THE ATOMIC BOMB   In 1939 the physicist Albert Einstein had alerted President Roosevelt to German research on nuclear fission. In response the president in 1940 had launched the $2-billion top-secret Manhattan Project, involving over 120,000 scientists and technicians in several locations. In a laboratory in Los Alamos, New Mexico, under the direction of J. Robert

The American Chemical Society exhibit on atomic energy

J. R. Oppenheimer points to a photograph of the huge column of smoke and flame caused by the bomb upon Hiroshima.

Oppenheimer, a group of physicists worked out the scientific and technical problems of the bomb's construction. On July 16, 1945, the first atomic fireball rose from the desert. Oppenheimer said later that in the bunker where observers watched the test blast, "a few people laughed, a few people cried, most people were silent." President Harry S. Truman, thrust into the presidency upon Roosevelt's death in April, wrote in his diary, "We have discovered the most terrible bomb in the history of the world."

Word of the new weapon changed all strategic calculations. How to use this awful weapon posed profound problems. Some scientists favored a demonstration explosion for the Japanese in a remote area, but that idea was vetoed because only two bombs were available, and even those might misfire.

The choice of targets received more consideration. After deciding against Kyōto, Japan's ancient capital and repository of national and religious treasures, priority went to Hiroshima, a port city of 400,000 people in southern Japan, which was a center of war industries, headquarters of the Japanese Second General Army, and command center for the homeland's defenses.

On July 25, 1945, President Truman ordered the atomic bomb dropped if Japan did not surrender before August 3. Although an intense scholarly debate has emerged over the decision to drop the bomb, it is clear that Truman believed that the atomic bomb would save lives by avoiding an American invasion against defenders who would fight like "savages, ruthless, merciless, and fanatic."

The ferocious Japanese defense of Okinawa had convinced military planners that an amphibious invasion of Japan itself, scheduled to begin on November 1, 1945, could cost as many as 250,000 Allied casualties and even more Japanese losses. Moreover, some 100,000 Allied prisoners of war being held in Japan would most likely be executed when an invasion began. It is important to remember as well that the bombing of cities and the consequent killing of civilians had become accepted military practice during 1945. Once the Japanese navy was destroyed, American ships had roamed the Japanese coastline, shelling targets onshore. American planes had bombed at will and mined the waters of the Inland Sea. Tokyo, Nagoya, and other major cities had been devastated by firestorms created by incendiary bombs. The firebomb raids on Tokyo on a single night in March 1945 killed 100,000 civilians and left over 1 million people homeless. The use of atomic bombs on Japanese cities was thus seen as a logical next step to end the war without an invasion of Japan. As it turned out, American scientists greatly underestimated the physical effects of the atomic bomb. They predicted that 20,000 people would be killed. The number would be much higher.

On July 26, the heads of the American, British, and Chinese governments issued the Potsdam Declaration, demanding that Japan surrender or face "prompt and utter destruction." The deadline passed, and at 8:15 A.M. on August 6, flying at 31,600 feet, a B-29 bomber named *Enola Gay* released the five-ton uranium bomb nicknamed Little Boy. Forty-three seconds later, as the *Enola Gay* turned sharply to avoid the blast, the bomb tumbled to an altitude of 1,900 feet, where it exploded as planned with the force of 20,000 tons of TNT. A blinding flash of light was followed by a fireball towering to 40,000 feet. The tail gunner on the *Enola Gay* described the scene: "It's like bubbling molasses down there . . . the mushroom is spreading out . . . fires are springing up everywhere . . . it's like a peep into hell."

The aftermath of "Little Boy"

This image shows the wasteland that remained after the atomic bomb "Little Boy" decimated Hiroshima in 1945.

The shock wave, firestorm, cyclonic winds, and radioactive rain killed some 80,000 people. By the end of the year, the death toll had reached 140,000 as the effects of radiation burns and infection took their toll. In addition, 70,000 buildings were destroyed, and four square miles of the city turned to rubble.

Two days after the Hiroshima bombing an opportunistic Soviet Union, eager to share the spoils of victory, hastened to enter the war in Asia. The Allies had long been urging Stalin to join their fight against the Japanese, but the Soviet dictator had delayed as long as possible so as to conserve economic and human resources. Now, however, with the Japanese on the verge of capitulation, he rushed to engage the Japanese in order to share in the spoils of victory. Truman and his aides, frustrated by the stubborn refusal of Japanese military and political leaders to surrender and fearful that the Soviet Union's entry into the war would complicate negotiations, ordered the second atomic bomb dropped. On August 9, a B-29 aircraft named *Bockscar*, carrying a bomb dubbed Fat Man, flew over its primary target, Kokura. The city was so shrouded in haze and smoke from an earlier air raid, however, that *Bockscar* turned to its secondary target, Nagasaki, where at 11:02 A.M. it dropped its terrifying bomb, killing 36,000 people. That night the Japanese emperor urged his cabinet to surrender on the sole condition that he remain as sovereign. The next day the U.S. government announced its willingness to let the emperor keep his throne, but under the authority of an Allied supreme commander. Frantic exchanges ended with Japanese acceptance of the terms on August 14, 1945, when the emperor himself delivered a radio message announcing the surrender to his people. On September 2, 1945, General MacArthur and other Allied representatives accepted Japan's formal surrender on board the battleship *Missouri*.

THE FINAL LEDGER

Thus ended the most deadly conflict in human history. One estimate has it that 70 million fought in the war, at a cost of some 50 million military and civilian dead, including those murdered in Nazi concentration camps. The Soviet Union suffered the greatest losses of all: over 13 million military deaths, more than 7 million civilian deaths, and at least 25 million left homeless. World War II was more costly for the United States than any other foreign war: 292,000 battle deaths and 114,000 other deaths. But in proportion to its population, the United States suffered a loss far smaller than that of any of the other major Allies or their enemies, and American territory escaped the devastation inflicted on so many other parts of the world.

World War II transformed American life. Mobilization for the war stimulated a phenomenal increase in productivity and brought full employment, thus ending the Great Depression and laying the foundation for an era of unprecedented prosperity. New technologies and products developed for military purposes—radar, computers, electronics, plastics and synthetics, jet engines, rockets, atomic energy—began to transform the private sector as well. And new opportunities for African Americans and other minorities as well as for women set in motion changes that would culminate in the civil rights movement of the 1960s and the feminist movement of the 1970s.

The Democratic party benefited from the war effort by solidifying its control of both the White House and Congress. The dramatic expansion of the federal government occasioned by the war continued after 1945. Presidential authority and prestige increased enormously at the expense of congressional and state power. The isolationist sentiment in foreign relations that had been so powerful in the 1920s and 1930s disintegrated as the United States emerged from the war with far-flung global responsibilities and interests. Thus the war's end opened a new era for the United States in the world arena. It accelerated the growth of American power while devastating all other world powers, leaving the United States economically and militarily the strongest nation on earth.

CHAPTER SUMMARY

- **WWII and American Society**   White and black Americans migrated to states West of the Mississippi, and especially to the Far West, to take jobs in factories; unemployment was soon a thing of the past. Farmers, too, recovered from hard times. Many women took nontraditional jobs, some in the military. About 1 million African Americans served in the military, in segregated units. Among the most famous were some 600 pilots trained in Tuskegee, Alabama. Japanese Americans, however, lost their civil rights; they were interned in "war relocation camps" in the interior, far from the West Coast, where most of them had lived and worked.

- **Road to Allied Victory**   The immediate war aim was to defeat Adolf Hitler in Europe. In 1942, British and American troops were engaging German and Italian troops in North Africa; and by 1943, all of North Africa was controlled by the Allies. From there they launched attacks on Sicily and then Italy. Joseph Stalin, meanwhile, demanded a full-scale Allied attack on the Atlantic coast to ease pressure on the eastern front, but D-day was delayed until June 6, 1944. Meanwhile, areas under Axis control were heavily bombed in an unsuccessful attempt to pound Germany into submission.

- **The Pacific War**   The Japanese advance was halted as early as June 1942 with the Battle of Midway. Then began the process of regaining territory island by island. The American army fought slow, costly battles in New Guinea, then, in 1943, headed toward the Philippines. Fierce resistance at Iwo Jima and Okinawa and Japan's refusal to surrender after the firebombing of Tokyo led the new president, Harry Truman, to order the use of the newly developed atomic bomb.

- **Postwar World**   In January 1942, twenty-six nations at was with the Axis Powers, seeing the need for a permanent peacekeeping force, signed the Declaration of the United Nations. The Big Three—Franklin Roosevelt, Winston Churchill, and Joseph Stalin—meeting in Yalta, on the Crimean Sea, in February 1945, decided that Europe would be divided into occupation zones, in which the Allies would sponsor free elections and democratic governments. It soon became clear, however, that Stalin would not honor that agreement.

CHRONOLOGY

May 1942	Battle of the Coral Sea
June 1942	Battle of Midway
January 1943	Roosevelt, Churchill, and the Combined Chiefs of Staff meet at Casablanca
July 1943	Allied forces land on Sicily
November–December 1943	Roosevelt and Churchill meet Stalin for the first time, in Tehran
June 6, 1944	D-day
February 1945	At the Yalta Conference, Roosevelt, Churchill, and Stalin plan the shape of the postwar world
February 1945	U.S. Marines capture Iwo Jima
April 12, 1945	Franklin Roosevelt dies
April 30, 1945	Hitler commits suicide
May 8, 1945	V-E day
August 6, 1945	Atomic bomb is dropped on Hiroshima
August 9, 1945	Atomic bomb is dropped on Nagasaki
September 2, 1945	Japanese surrender

KEY TERMS & NAMES

Part Seven

THE
AMERICAN
AGE

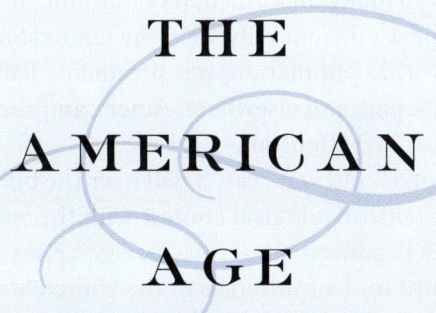

The United States emerged from World War II the preeminent military and economic power in the world. While much of Europe and Asia struggled to recover from the physical devastation of the war, the United States was virtually unscathed, its economic infrastructure intact and operating at peak efficiency. By 1955 the United States, with only 6 percent of the world's population, was producing half of the world's goods. In Europe, Japan, and elsewhere, American products and popular culture attracted excited attention.

Yet the specter of a "cold war" cast a pall over the buoyant revival of the economy. The tense ideological contest with the Soviet Union and Communist China produced numerous foreign crises and sparked a domestic witch hunt for Communists in the United States that far surpassed earlier episodes of political and social repression in the nation's history. Both major political parties accepted the geopolitical assumptions embedded in the ideological cold war with international communism. Both Republican and Democratic presidents affirmed the need to "contain" the spread of Communist influence around the world.

This bedrock assumption eventually embroiled the United States in a costly war in Southeast Asia, which destroyed Lyndon Johnson's presidency and revived isolationist sentiments. The Vietnam War was also the catalyst for a countercultural movement in which young idealists of the "baby boom" generation promoted many overdue social reforms, including the reforms that were the focus of the civil rights, feminist, and environmental movements. But the youth revolt also contributed to an array of social ills, from street riots to drug abuse to sexual promiscuity. The social upheavals of the 1960s and early 1970s provoked a conservative backlash as well. Richard Nixon's paranoid reaction to his critics led to the Watergate affair and the destruction of his presidency.

Through all of this turmoil, however, the basic premises of welfare-state capitalism that Franklin Roosevelt had instituted with his New Deal programs remained essentially intact. With only a few exceptions, both Republicans and Democrats after 1945 came to accept the notion that the federal government must assume greater responsibility for the welfare of individuals than had heretofore been the case. Even Ronald Reagan, a sharp critic of liberal social-welfare programs, recognized the need for the federal government to provide a "safety net" for those who could not help themselves.

This fragile consensus on public policy began to disintegrate in the late 1980s amid stunning international events and less visible domestic changes. The internal collapse of the Soviet Union and the disintegration of European communism surprised observers and sent policy makers scurrying to respond to a post–cold war world in which the United States remained the only legitimate superpower. After forty-five years, American foreign policy was no longer centered on a single adversary, and world politics lost its bipolar quality. During the early 1990s the two Germanys reunited, apartheid in South Africa ended, and Israel and the Palestinians signed a treaty providing peace—for a while.

At the same time, U.S. foreign policy began to focus less on military power and more on economic competition and technological development. In those arenas, Japan and a reunited Germany challenged the United States for preeminence. By reducing the public's fear of nuclear annihilation, the end of the cold war also reduced American interest in foreign affairs. The presidential election of 1992 was the first since 1936 in which foreign-policy issues played virtually no role. This was an unfortunate development, for post–cold war world affairs remained volatile and dangerous. The implosion of Soviet communism after 1989 unleashed a series of ethnic, nationalist, and separatist conflicts. Responding to pleas for assistance, the United States found itself drawn into crises in faraway locations, such as Bosnia, Somalia, Kosovo, Afghanistan, and Iraq.

As the new multipolar world careened toward the end of a century and the start of a new millennium, fault lines began to appear in the American social and economic landscape. A gargantuan federal debt and rising annual deficits threatened to bankrupt a nation that was becoming top-heavy with retirees. Without fully realizing it, much less appreciating its cascading consequences, the American population was becoming disproportionately old. The number of people aged ninety-five to ninety-nine doubled between 1980 and 1990, and the number of centenarians increased 77 percent. The proportion of the population aged sixty-five and older rose steadily during the 1990s. By the year 2010, over half of the elderly population was over seventy-five. This demographic fact harbored profound social and political implications. It exerted increasing stress on health-care costs, nursing-home facilities, and the very survival of the Social Security system.

At the same time that the gap between young and old was increasing, so, too, was the disparity between rich and poor. This trend threatened to stratify a society already experiencing rising levels of racial and ethnic tension. Between 1960 and 1990 the gap between the richest 20 percent of the population and the poorest 20 percent doubled. Over 20 percent of all American children in 1990 lived in poverty, and the infant-mortality rate rose. The infant-death rate in Japan was less than half that in the United States. Despite the much-ballyhooed "war-on-poverty" programs initiated by Lyndon Johnson and continued in one form or another by all of his successors, the chronically poor at the start of the twenty-first century were more numerous and more bereft of hope than in 1964.

31

THE FAIR DEAL AND CONTAINMENT

FOCUS QUESTIONS wwnorton.com/studyspace

- How did the cold war emerge?
- How did Harry Truman respond to the Soviet occupation of Eastern Europe?
- What was Truman's Fair Deal?
- What was the background of the Korean War, and how did the United States become involved?
- What were the roots of McCarthyism?

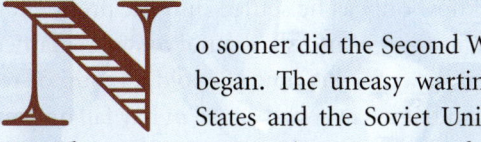

No sooner did the Second World War end than a "cold war" began. The uneasy wartime alliance between the United States and the Soviet Union had collapsed by the fall of 1945. The two strongest nations to emerge from the carnage of World War II could not bridge their ideological differences over such basic issues as human rights, individual liberties, economic freedom, and religious beliefs. Mutual suspicion and a race to gain influence and control over the so-called third world countries further polarized the two nations. The defeat of Japan and Germany had created power vacuums that sucked the United States and the Soviet Union into an unrelenting war of words fed by clashing geopolitical interests. At the same time, the devastation wrought by the war in western Europe and the exhaustion of its peoples led to anti-colonial uprisings in Asia and Africa that threatened to strip Britain and France of their empires. The postwar world was thus an unstable one in which international tensions shaped the contours of domestic politics and culture as well as foreign relations.

DEMOBILIZATION UNDER TRUMAN

TRUMAN'S UNEASY START   "Who the hell is Harry Truman?" Roosevelt's chief of staff asked the president in the summer of 1944. The question was on more lips when, after less than twelve weeks as vice president, Harry Truman took the presidential oath on April 12, 1945. Clearly he was not as charismatic or as magisterial as Franklin Roosevelt, and that was one of the burdens he would bear. Roosevelt and Truman came from quite different backgrounds. For Truman there had been no inherited wealth, no early contact with the great and near great, no European travel, no Harvard—indeed, no college at all. Born in 1884 in western Missouri, Truman grew up in Independence, outside Kansas City. Too nearsighted to join in the activities of other boys, Truman became bookish and introverted. After high school, however, he spent a few years working in Kansas City banks and grew into an outgoing young man.

During World War I, Truman served in France as captain of an artillery battery. Afterward he opened a clothing business, but it failed during the recession of 1922, and Truman then entered politics. In 1934, Missouri sent him to the U.S. Senate, where he remained fairly obscure until he chaired a committee investigating corruption in defense industries during World War II.

Harry Truman was a plain, decent man who evoked the spirit of Andrew Jackson: his decisiveness, his feistiness, his family loyalty. But that was a side of the man the people came to know only as he settled into the presidency. On his first full day as president, as the war in Asia ground on, he remained awestruck. "Boys, if you ever pray, pray for me now," he told a group of reporters. "I don't know whether you fellows ever had a load of hay fall on you, but when they told me yesterday what had happened, I felt like the moon, the stars and all the planets had fallen on me."

Truman favored much of the New Deal and was even prepared to extend its scope, but he was uneasy with many of the most ardent New Deal reformers. Within ninety days of taking office, he had replaced much of the Roosevelt cabinet with his own choices. On the whole his cabinet was more conservative in outlook and included several mediocrities. Truman suffered the further handicap of seeming to be a caretaker for the remainder of Roosevelt's term. Few expected him to run on his own in 1948.

The new president gave a significant clue to his domestic policies on September 6, 1945, when he sent Congress a comprehensive peacetime program

The Eldridge General Store, Fayette County, Illinois

Postwar America quickly demobilized, turning its attention to the pursuit of abundance.

that proposed to enlarge the New Deal. Its twenty-one points included expansion of unemployment insurance to cover more workers, a higher minimum wage, a permanent Fair Employment Practices Committee, slum clearance and low-rent housing, regional development of the nation's river valleys, and a public-works program. "Not even President Roosevelt asked for so much at one sitting," charged the House Republican leader. "It's just a plain case of out-dealing the New Deal." But Truman did not have the same success as Roosevelt in getting his legislation through Congress. Beset by other problems, Truman soon saw his new domestic proposals mired in disputes over the transition to a peacetime economy.

CONVERTING TO PEACE   The raucous celebrations that greeted Japan's surrender signaled a rapid demobilization of the armed forces and a return to domestic pursuits. The public demanded that the president and Congress bring the troops home as soon as possible. By 1947 the total armed forces had shrunk to 1.5 million from a wartime high of 12 million. By early 1950 the army had been reduced to 600,000 troops.

The military veterans returned to colleges, jobs, wives, and babies. Population growth, which had dropped off sharply in the Depression decade, now soared. Americans born during this postwar period composed what came to be known as the baby boom generation, an oversize population cohort that would become a dominant force shaping the nation's social and economic life.

The end of the war, with its sudden demobilization and conversion to a peacetime economy, generated labor unrest and strikes but not the postwar depression that many had feared. Several shock absorbers cushioned the economic impact of demobilization: unemployment insurance and other Social Security benefits; the Servicemen's Readjustment Act of 1944, known as the GI Bill of Rights, under which the federal government spent $13 billion on military veterans for education, vocational training, medical treatment, unemployment insurance, and loans for building houses and going into business; and most important, the pent-up demand for consumer goods that was fueled by wartime shortages. Instead of sinking into depression after the war, the economy enjoyed a spurt of private investment in new production facilities and equipment.

CONTROLLING INFLATION   The most acute economic problem facing postwar America was not depression but inflation. During the war, America was essentially fully employed. The government also froze wages and prices—and prohibited labor strikes. When wartime controls were removed, prices shot up. Prices of farm commodities soared 14 percent in one month and by the end of 1945 were 30 percent higher than they had been in August. As prices rose, so, too, did corporate profits. Labor unions increasingly demanded that they receive their share of the postwar bounty.

Within six weeks of the war's end, corporations confronted union demands for higher wages and better benefits. A series of strikes followed. By January 1946 more workers were on strike than ever before in U.S. history. In response to a threatened rail strike, President Truman, miffed at what he considered to be excessive union demands, threatened to draft striking railroad workers into the armed forces. The strike ended a few weeks later.

The wartime Office of Price Administration maintained some restraint on price increases while gradually ending the rationing of most goods. After the 1946 congressional elections, Truman gave up the battle to control consumer prices.

PARTISAN CONFLICT   Before the 1946 congressional elections, public discontent ran high, with most of it directed against the administration. Labor union supporters tagged Truman "the No. 1 strikebreaker," while much of the public, angry at striking unions, blamed the White House for the strikes. Critics of the administration had a field day coining campaign slogans. The most effective was the simple "Had enough?" attributed to a

Boston ad agency: the message was that the Democrats had simply been in power too long. In the end, Republicans won majorities in both houses of Congress for the first time since 1928.

Taft-Hartley Act cartoon

Taft and Hartley look for John Lewis, the head of the Mine Workers Union.

The rising public criticism of organized labor spurred the new Republican Congress to pass the Taft-Hartley Labor Act of 1947 to curb the power of the unions. It banned the closed shop (in which nonunion workers could not be hired) but permitted a union shop (in which workers newly hired were required to join the union) except where banned by state law. The anti-union legislation included provisions forbidding "unfair" union practices such as "featherbedding" (paying for work not done), refusing to bargain in good faith, and contributing to political campaigns. Furthermore, union leaders had to take oaths declaring that they were not members of the Communist party. The act also forbade strikes by federal employees and imposed a "cooling-off" period of eighty days on any strike that the president found to be dangerous to the national health or safety.

Truman's veto of the "shocking" Taft-Hartley bill, which unions called "the slave-labor act," restored his credit with labor and brought many unionists who had voted Republican in 1946 back to the Democratic fold. But the bill passed over the president's veto. Its most severe impact was probably on the CIO's Operation Dixie, a drive to win unions a more secure foothold in the South. By 1954 fifteen states, mainly in the South, had used the Taft-Hartley Act's authority to pass "right-to-work" laws forbidding union shops. Those laws also eroded union strength in the North as many firms began to migrate to right-to-work southern states.

Yet the conflicts between Truman and Congress obscured the high degree of bipartisan cooperation in matters of government reorganization and foreign policy. In 1947 a bipartisan majority in Congress passed the National Security Act, which created a National Military Establishment, headed by the secretary of defense with subcabinet Departments of the Army, the Navy, and the Air Force, and the National Security Council, which included the president, the secretary of defense and the heads of the new subcabinet departments, and the secretary of state, among others. The act made permanent the Joint Chiefs of Staff, a wartime innovation, and established the Central Intelligence Agency (CIA) to coordinate global intelligence gathering.

THE COLD WAR

BUILDING THE UNITED NATIONS The wartime military alliance against Nazism disintegrated after 1945, and the United States entered into a "cold war" with the Soviet Union. The pragmatic Roosevelt had expected that the great powers in the postwar world would have separate geographic spheres of influence but believed he had to temper such realpolitik with an organization "which would satisfy widespread demand in the United States for new idealistic or universalist arrangements for assuring the peace."

On April 25, 1945, two weeks after Roosevelt's death and two weeks before the German surrender, delegates from fifty nations at war with the Axis met in San Francisco to draw up the Charter of the United Nations. Additional members would be admitted by a two-thirds vote of the General Assembly. This body, one of the two major agencies set up by the charter, included delegates from all member nations and was to meet annually in regular session to approve the budget, receive annual reports from UN agencies, and choose members of the Security Council and other bodies.

The Security Council, the other major charter agency, would remain in permanent session and would have "primary responsibility for the maintenance of international peace and security." Its eleven members (fifteen after 1965) included six (later ten) members elected for two-year terms and five permanent members: the United States, the Soviet Union, Britain, France, and China. Each permanent member could veto any question of substance. The Security Council might investigate any dispute, recommend settlement or reference to another UN body—the International Court of Justice at The Hague, in the Netherlands—and take measures, including the use of military force. The U.S. Senate, in sharp contrast to the reception it gave the League of Nations, ratified the UN charter by a vote of 89 to 2.

DIFFERENCES WITH THE SOVIETS There were signs of trouble in the wartime alliance linking Britain, the Soviet Union, and the United States as early as the spring of 1945 as the Soviet Union set up compliant governments in the nations of Eastern Europe, violating the Yalta promises of democratic elections. Protests against such actions led to Soviet counterprotests that the British and the Americans were negotiating a German surrender in Italy "behind the back of the Soviet Union."

Such was the atmosphere when Truman entered the White House. A few days before the San Francisco conference to organize the United Nations, the president gave Soviet foreign minister Vyacheslav Molotov a tongue-lashing in Washington on the Polish situation. "I have never been talked to like that in my life," Molotov protested. "Carry out your agreements," Truman snapped, "and you won't get talked to like that."

On May 12, 1945, four days after victory in Europe, Winston Churchill sent Truman a telegram: "What is to happen about Europe? An iron curtain is drawn down upon [the Russian] front. We do not know what is going on behind [it]. . . . Surely it is vital now to come to an understanding with Russia, or see where we are with her, before we weaken our armies mortally." Nevertheless, as a gesture of goodwill, and over Churchill's protest, the U.S. forces withdrew from the occupation zone in Germany that had been assigned to the Soviet Union at Yalta. Americans still hoped that the Yalta agreements would be carried out, and they were even more eager to have Soviet help in defeating Japan.

Although the Soviets admitted British and American observers to their sectors of Eastern Europe, there was little the Western powers could have done to prevent Soviet control of the region even if they had kept up their military strength. The presence of Soviet armed forces frustrated the efforts of non-Communists to gain political influence in Eastern European countries. Opposition leaders were exiled, silenced, executed, or imprisoned.

Secretary of State James F. Byrnes, who took office in 1945, struggled through 1946 with the problems of postwar treaties. In early 1947 the Council of Foreign Ministers finally produced treaties for Italy, Hungary, Romania, Bulgaria, and Finland that confirmed Soviet control over Eastern Europe, which in Russian eyes seemed but a parallel to American control over Japan and Western control over most of Germany and all of Italy. The Yalta Conference's guarantees of democracy in Eastern Europe had turned out much like the Open Door policy in China, little more than pious rhetoric sugarcoating the realities of power and national interest. The Soviet Union controlled Eastern Europe and refused to budge.

CONTAINMENT   By the beginning of 1947, relations with the Soviet Union had become even more troubled. The year before, Stalin had pronounced international peace impossible "under the present capitalist development of the world economy." His statement impelled George F. Kennan, counselor of the U.S. embassy in Moscow, to send an 8,000-word dispatch to the State Department, in which he sketched the roots of Soviet policy.

More than a year later, Kennan, back at the State Department in Washington, spelled out his ideas for a proper response to the Soviets. In a 1947 article published anonymously in *Foreign Affairs*, he provided a brilliant historical and psychological analysis of Soviet insecurity and postwar intentions. He predicted that the Soviets would try to fill "every nook and cranny available . . . in the basin of world power." Therefore, he insisted, the United States must pursue "a long-term, patient but firm and vigilant *containment* of Russian expansive tendencies."

Kennan's "containment" concept dovetailed with the outlook of Truman and his advisers. They all harbored a growing fear that the Soviet lust for power reached beyond Eastern Europe, posing dangers in the eastern Mediterranean, the Middle East, and western Europe itself. The Soviet Union especially sought access to the Mediterranean region, long important to Russia for purposes of trade and defense. After the war the Soviet Union pressed Turkey for territorial concessions and the right to build naval bases on the Bosporus, an important gateway between the Black Sea and the Mediterranean. In 1946, civil war broke out in neighboring Greece between a British-backed government and a Communist-led faction that held the northern part of the country. In 1947 the British ambassador informed the U.S. government that the British could no longer bear the economic and military burden of aiding Greece and suggested that the United States assume the responsibility.

THE TRUMAN DOCTRINE AND THE MARSHALL PLAN On March 12, 1947, Truman asked Congress for $400 million in economic and military aid to Greece and Turkey. In his speech to Congress, the president announced what quickly became known as the Truman Doctrine. Although intended as a response to a specific crisis, its rhetoric was universal. "I believe," Truman declared, "that it must be the policy of the United States to support free peoples who are resisting attempted subjugation by armed minorities or by outside pressures." In 1947, Congress passed the Greek-Turkish aid bill and by 1950 had spent $659 million on the program. Turkey achieved economic stability, and Greece defeated a Communist insurrection in 1949.

Such immediate gains created long-term problems, however. The Truman Doctrine marked the beginning of a contest that people began to call a cold war. Greece and Turkey were but the front lines in an ideological struggle between East and West for world power and influence. That struggle quickly focused on western Europe, where wartime damage had devastated factory production and a severe drought in 1947, followed by a harsh winter, had destroyed crops. Coal shortages in London left only enough fuel to heat and light homes for a few hours each day. In Berlin, people were freezing or starving to death. The transportation system in Europe was in shambles: bridges were out, canals clogged, and rail networks destroyed. Amid the chaos the Communist parties of France and Italy were flourishing.

In the spring of 1947, former general George C. Marshall, who had replaced James Byrnes as secretary of state, called for massive aid to rescue western Europe from disaster and possible Communist subversion. "Our policy," he pledged, "is directed not against country or doctrine, but against hunger, poverty, desperation, and chaos." Marshall offered aid to all European countries, including the Soviet Union, but Moscow refused to participate in the "imperialist" scheme.

In late 1947, Truman submitted his proposal for the European Recovery Program to Congress. Soon thereafter a Communist coup d'état in Czechoslovakia

"It's the Same Thing"

The Marshall Plan, which distributed aid throughout Europe, is represented in this 1949 cartoon as a modern tractor driven by a prosperous farmer. In the foreground a poor, overworked man is yoked to an old-fashioned "Soviet" plow, forced to go over the ground of the "Marshal Stalin Plan," while Stalin himself tries to persuade others that "it's the same thing without mechanical problems."

ended the last remaining coalition government in Eastern Europe. The Communist seizure of power in Prague assured congressional passage of the Marshall Plan, which from 1948 until 1951 provided $13 billion to promote European economic recovery.

DIVIDING GERMANY   The Marshall Plan drew the nations of western Europe closer together, but the breakdown of the wartime alliance with the Soviet Union left the problem of postwar Germany unsettled. The German economy had stagnated, requiring the U.S. Army to carry a staggering burden of relief to prevent civilians from starving. Slowly occupation zones evolved into functioning governments. In 1948 the British, French, and Americans merged their zones, and the "West Germans" elected delegates to a federal constitutional convention.

THE OCCUPATION OF GERMANY AND AUSTRIA

- French zone
- British zone
- U.S. zone
- Soviet zone

How did the Allies divide Germany and Austria at the Yalta Conference? What was the "iron curtain"? Why did Truman airlift supplies to Berlin?

Soviet resentment of the Marshall Plan and the political unification of West Germany led the Soviets, in April 1948, to restrict road and rail traffic into West Berlin; on June 23 they stopped all traffic. The next day the Soviets cut off electricity to the western sector of the divided city. The Soviets hoped the blockade would force the Allies to give up either Berlin or the plan to unify Germany. It was war by starvation and intimidation, but Truman stood firm. After considering the use of armed convoys to supply West Berlin, he opted for a massive airlift. At the time it seemed like an impossible task. But the Allied air forces quickly brought in planes from around the world, and soon they were flying in up to 13,000 tons of food, coal, and other supplies a day.

The massive airlift went on for months. Finally, on May 12, 1949, after extended talks, the Soviets lifted the blockade. Before the end of the year, the Federal Republic of Germany had a functioning government. At the end of May 1949, an independent German Democratic Republic arose in the Soviet-dominated eastern zone, thus dividing Germany into two independent states.

ALLIANCES As relations between the Soviets and western Europe chilled, transatlantic unity ripened into a formal military alliance. On April 4, 1949, diplomats signed the North Atlantic Treaty. Twelve nations were represented: the United States, Britain, France, Belgium, the Netherlands, Luxembourg, Canada, Denmark, Iceland, Italy, Norway, and Portugal. Greece and Turkey joined the alliance in 1952, West Germany in 1955, and Spain in 1982. The treaty pledged that an attack against any one of the members would be considered an attack against all. A council of the North Atlantic Treaty Organization (NATO) would govern the alliance. In 1950 the council voted to create an integrated defense force for western Europe. Five years later the Warsaw Treaty Organization appeared as the Eastern European counterpoint to NATO.

The eventful year of 1948 produced another foreign-policy decision with long-term consequences. Late in 1947 the UN General Assembly voted to partition Palestine into Jewish and Arab states. Despite fierce Arab opposition, Jewish leaders proclaimed the independence of the new State of Israel on May 14, 1948. President Truman, who had been in close touch with Jewish leaders at home and abroad, ordered immediate recognition of the new state; the United States was the first nation to do so.

The neighboring Arab states thereupon attacked Israel, which held its own. UN mediators gradually worked out truce agreements with Israel's Arab neighbors, restoring an uneasy peace by May 11, 1949, when Israel joined the United Nations. But the mutual hatred and intermittent warfare between Israel and the Arab states have festered ever since, complicating

NATO

NATO is depicted as a symbol of renewed strength for a battered Europe.

U.S. foreign policy, which has aimed to maintain friendship with both sides while insisting on the legitimacy of the Israeli nation.

CIVIL RIGHTS DURING THE 1940S

The social tremors triggered by World War II and the onset of the cold war transformed America's racial landscape. The government-sponsored racism of the German Nazis, the Italian Fascists, and the Japanese imperialists focused attention on the need for the United States to improve its own race relations and to provide for equal rights under the law.

For most of his political career, Harry Truman had shown little concern for the plight of African Americans. He had grown up in western Missouri assuming that blacks and whites preferred to be segregated from one another. As president, however, he began to reassess his convictions. In the fall of 1946, Truman hosted a delegation of civil rights activists who urged him to condemn the resurgence of the Ku Klux Klan and the lynching of African Americans. Truman soon appointed a Committee on Civil Rights to investigate racist violence and recommend preventive measures. In its report the committee urged the renewal of the Fair Employment Practices Committee and the creation of a permanent civil rights commission to investigate abuses. It also argued that federal aid be denied to any state that mandated segregated schools and public facilities.

On July 26, 1948, Truman banned racial discrimination in the hiring of federal employees. Four days later he issued an executive order ending racial segregation in the armed forces. The air force and navy quickly complied, but the army dragged its feet until the early 1950s. By 1960 the armed forces were the most racially integrated of all national organizations.

JACKIE ROBINSON　Meanwhile, racial segregation was being confronted in a much more public field of endeavor: professional baseball. In April 1947, as the baseball season opened, the National League's Brooklyn Dodgers included the first black player to cross the color line in major league baseball: Jackie Robinson. Born in Georgia and raised in California, Robinson was an army veteran and baseball player in the Negro leagues. Branch Rickey, president of the Dodgers, selected Robinson to integrate professional baseball not only because of his athletic potential but also because of his willingness to control his temper in the face of virulent racism. During his first season with the Dodgers, teammates and opposing players viciously baited Robinson, pitchers threw at him, base runners spiked him, and spectators booed and taunted him in every city. Hotels refused him rooms, and restaurants denied him service. Hate mail arrived by the bucket load. On the other hand, black spectators were electrified by Robinson's courageous example; they turned out in droves to see him play.

As time passed, Robinson won over many racist fans and players with his quiet courage, self-deprecating wit, and determined performance. Soon other teams signed black players. Baseball's pathbreaking efforts stimulated the integration of football and basketball teams. Jackie Robinson vividly demonstrated that racism, not inferiority, impeded African American advancement in the postwar era and that segregation need not be a permanent condition of American life.

Jackie Robinson

Racial discrimination remained widespread throughout the postwar period. In 1947, Jackie Robinson of the Brooklyn Dodgers became the first black player in major league baseball.

SHAPING THE FAIR DEAL As the 1948 election approached, the issue of civil rights presented daunting political challenges. While some Americans applauded Truman's efforts to desegregate the federal workforce, others were appalled. Liberals thought that his efforts were not bold enough. Southern conservative Democrats found him too radical. Truman's chances for winning the election of 1948 seemed bleak.

The president had a game plan for 1948, however. His advisers knew that to win another presidential term, he needed the midwestern and western farm belts. In metropolitan areas he needed to carry the union and African American vote, which Truman wooed by working closely with unions and pressing the cause of civil rights. Truman's advisers counted on the Solid South to stay in the Democratic column. With the South and the West, Truman could afford to lose some New Deal strongholds in the East and still win. This strategy erred chiefly in underrating the rebellion that would take four Deep South states out of Truman's camp because of his support for civil rights.

Truman used his State of the Union message to set the agenda for an election year. The 1948 speech offered something to nearly every group the

Democrats hoped to win over. The first goal, Truman remarked, was "to secure fully the essential human rights of our citizens," and he promised a special message later on civil rights. "To protect human resources," he proposed federal aid to education, increased and extended unemployment and retirement benefits, a comprehensive system of health insurance, more federal support for public housing, and the extension of rent controls. As one senator put it, the speech "raised all the ghosts of the old New Deal."

THE ELECTION OF 1948   The Republican majority in Congress for the most part spurned the Truman program, an action it would later regret. Scenting victory in November, Republican delegates again nominated Thomas Dewey, the former New York governor. The platform endorsed most of the New Deal reforms as an accomplished fact and approved the administration's bipartisan foreign policy; Dewey promised to run things more efficiently, however.

In July a glum Democratic Convention gathered in Philadelphia expecting to do little more than go through the motions but found itself surprised by a fierce debate over civil rights. To keep from stirring southern hostility, the administration sought a platform plank that opposed racial discrimination only in general terms. Activists, however, sponsored a plank that called on Congress to take action. Thirty-seven-year-old Minneapolis mayor Hubert H. Humphrey electrified the delegates and set off a ten-minute demonstration when he declared, "The time has arrived for the Democratic party to get out of the shadow of states' rights and walk forthrightly into the bright sunshine of human rights." Segregationist delegates from Alabama and Mississippi instead walked out of the convention.

"I Stand Pat!"

Truman's support of civil rights for African Americans had its political costs, as this 1948 cartoon suggests.

A group of rebellious southern Democrats, miffed by Truman's progressive civil rights plank, met later in Birmingham, Alabama. There, while

"Dewey Defeats Truman"

Truman's victory in 1948 was a huge upset, so much so that even the early edition of the *Chicago Daily Tribune* was caught off guard, running this premature headline.

waving Confederate flags and singing "Dixie," they nominated South Carolina governor Strom Thurmond on a States' Rights ticket, which was quickly dubbed the Dixiecrat party. The Dixiecrats denounced Truman's civil rights initiatives and defended states' rights against federal actions. They sought to draw enough electoral votes to preclude a majority for either major party, throwing the election into the House of Representatives, where they might strike a sectional bargain. A few days later the left wing of the Democratic party gathered in Philadelphia to name Henry A. Wallace on a Progressive party ticket. These splits in the Democratic ranks seemed to spell the final blow to Truman.

But Truman, undaunted, set out on a 31,000-mile "whistle-stop" train tour, during which he castigated the "do-nothing" Eightieth Congress, provoking cries from his audiences to "pour it on, Harry!" and "give 'em hell, Harry." Truman responded, "I don't give 'em hell. I just tell the truth and they think it's hell." Dewey, in contrast, ran a restrained campaign designed to avoid controversy. By so doing, he may have snatched defeat from the jaws of victory.

The polls and the pundits predicted a sure win for Dewey, but on election day Truman chalked up the biggest upset in history, taking 24.2 million votes (49.5 percent) to Dewey's 22 million (45.1 percent) and winning by a

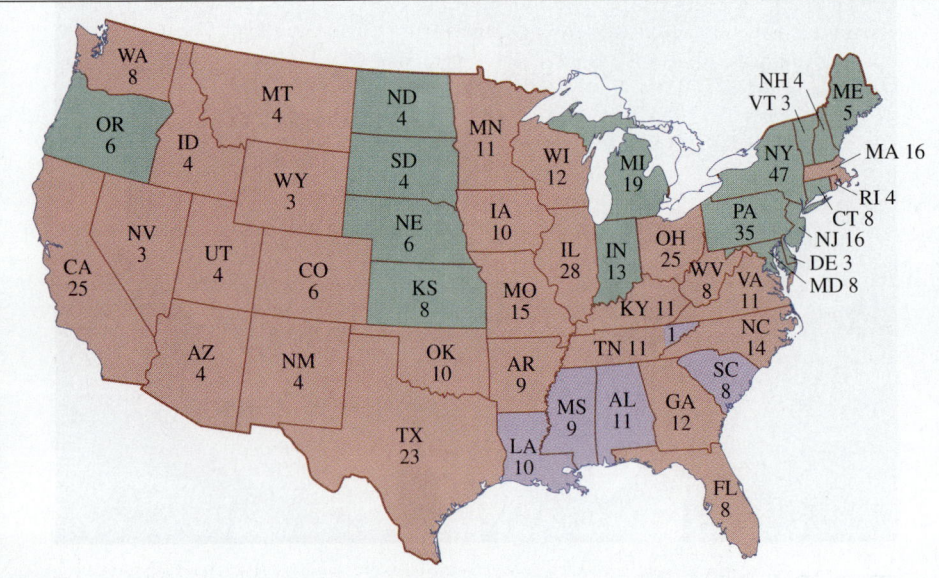

THE ELECTION OF 1948	Electoral Vote	Popular Vote
Harry S. Truman (Democrat)	**303**	**24,200,000**
Thomas E. Dewey (Republican)	189	22,000,000
J. Strom Thurmond (States' Rights Democrat)	39	1,200,000

Why did the political pundits predict a Dewey victory? Why was civil rights a divisive issue at the Democratic Convention? How did the candidacies of Thurmond and Wallace help Truman?

thumping margin of 303 to 189 in the Electoral College. Thurmond and Wallace each got more than 1 million votes, but the revolt of right and left had worked to Truman's advantage. The Dixiecrat rebellion backfired by angering black voters, while the Progressive party's radicalism made it hard to tag Truman soft on communism. Thurmond carried four Deep South states, and his success hastened a momentous disruption of the Democratic Solid South. But Truman's victory carried Democratic majorities into Congress.

Truman viewed his upset victory as a vindication for the New Deal and a mandate for moderate liberalism. His 1949 State of the Union message repeated the agenda he had set forth the year before. "Every segment of our population and every individual," he stressed, "has a right to expect from his government a fair deal." Whether deliberately or not, he had invented a tag, the Fair Deal, to distinguish his program from the New Deal.

Some of Truman's Fair Deal proposals became law, but most of them were extensions or enlargements of New Deal programs already in place: a higher minimum wage, expansion of Social Security coverage, extension of rent controls, increased farm subsidies, and a sizable slum-clearance and public-housing program. Despite Democratic majorities in Congress, however, the conservative coalition of southern Democrats and Republicans disdained any drastic departures in domestic policy. Congress balked at civil rights bills, national health insurance, federal aid to education, and a plan to provide subsidies that would support farm income rather than farm prices. Congress also turned down Truman's demand for repeal of the Taft-Hartley Act.

THE COLD WAR HEATS UP

Global concerns, never far from center stage in the postwar world, plagued Truman's second term, as they had his first. Now some Americans began to fear that Communists were infiltrating their society. In his inaugural address, Truman called for an anti-Communist foreign policy resting on four pillars: the United Nations, the Marshall Plan, NATO, and a "bold new plan" for technical assistance to underdeveloped parts of the world, a program that came to be known as Point Four. This program to aid the postwar world never accomplished its goals, in part because other international problems soon diverted Truman's attention.

"LOSING" CHINA One of the most intractable problems, the China tangle, was fast unraveling in 1949. The Chinese Nationalists, led by Chiang Kai-shek, had been fighting Mao Tse-tung (Mao Zedong)* and the Communists since the 1920s. The outbreak of war with Japan in 1937 halted the civil war, and both Roosevelt and Stalin believed that the Nationalists would control China after the war.

The commanders of U.S. forces in China during World War II, however, concluded that Chiang's government had become hopelessly corrupt, tyrannical, and inefficient. U.S. policy during and immediately after the war promoted peace between the factions in China. But when the civil war resumed

---

*The traditional (Wade-Giles) transliteration of Chinese, with pinyin transliterations in parentheses, is used in this text up to 1976. After Mao's death the Chinese government adopted the pinyin translations that are widely used today: Mao Tse-tung became Mao Zedong; Peking became Beijing.

in 1945, American forces ferried Nationalist armies back into the eastern and northern provinces as the Japanese withdrew.

It soon became a losing fight for the Nationalists as the Communists won over the land-hungry peasantry. By late 1949 the Nationalist government had fled to the island of Formosa, which it renamed Taiwan. Truman's critics asked bitterly, "Who lost China?" and a State Department report blamed Chiang for his failure to hold on to the support of the Chinese people. In fact it is hard to imagine how the U.S. government could have prevented a Communist victory short of undertaking a massive military intervention, which would have been risky, costly, and unpopular. After 1949 the United States continued to recognize the Nationalist government on Taiwan as the rightful government of China, delaying formal relations with Communist China for thirty years. In an effort to shore up friendly governments in Asia, the United States in 1950 recognized the French-supported government of Emperor Bao Dai in Vietnam and shortly afterward extended aid to the French in their battle against Ho Chi Minh's Vietnamese guerrillas.

As the Communists were securing control in China, U.S. intelligence discovered that the Soviets had set off an atomic explosion. News of the Soviet bomb in 1949 provoked an intense reappraisal of the strategic balance of power in the world, causing Truman in 1950 to order the construction of a hydrogen bomb, a weapon far more powerful than the atomic bomb, lest the Soviets make one first. In addition, the National Security Council recommended rebuilding conventional military forces to provide options other than nuclear war. Such a plan represented a major departure from America's time-honored aversion to keeping large standing armies in peacetime. It was also an expensive proposition. But the American public was growing more receptive to the nation's role as world leader, and an invasion of South Korea by Communist forces from the north clinched the issue for most Americans.

WAR IN KOREA   The Japanese had occupied Korea since 1910, and after their defeat and withdrawal in 1945 the victorious Allies faced the difficult task of creating a new Korean nation. Complicating that task was the fact that Soviet troops had advanced into northern Korea and accepted the surrender of Japanese forces above the 38th parallel, while U.S. forces had done the same south of that line. The Soviets quickly organized a Korean government along Stalinist lines, while the Americans set up a Western-style regime in the south.

Like the postwar division of Germany, the victors' decision to divide Korea began as a temporary expedient and ended as a permanent fact. With the onset of the cold war, it became clear that Soviet-American agreement on unification was no more likely in Korea than in Germany. By the end of 1948, separate Korean regimes had appeared in the two sectors, and occupation forces had withdrawn. The weakened state of the demobilizing American military contributed to the impression that South Korea was vulnerable to a Communist assault. Evidence in Soviet archives reveals that Stalin encouraged the North Koreans to use force to unify their country and oust the Americans from the peninsula. The Soviets helped design a war plan that called for North Korean forces to seize Seoul within three days and all of South Korea within a week. Stalin apparently assumed the United States would not intervene.

On June 25, 1950, over 80,000 North Korean soldiers crossed the boundary and swept down the peninsula. President Truman responded decisively. He and his advisers assumed that the North Korean attack was directed by Moscow and was a brazen indication of the aggressive designs of Soviet communism. Truman made two critical decisions. First, he decided to wage war under the auspices of the United Nations rather than unilaterally. Second, he decided to send troops without asking Congress for a formal declaration of war.

An emergency meeting of the UN Security Council quickly censured the North Korean "breach of peace." The Soviet delegate, who held veto power, was at the time boycotting the council because it would not seat Communist China in place of Nationalist China. On June 27, its first resolution having been ignored, the Security Council called on UN members to "furnish such assistance to the Republic of Korea as may be necessary to repel the armed attack and to restore international peace and security in the area."

Truman ordered American air, naval, and ground forces into action. Eventually, U.S. units numbered over 350,000, while the South Koreans contributed 500,000. In all, some fourteen other nations sent another 50,000 men. Later the UN authorized a unified command and put General Douglas MacArthur in charge. The defense of South Korea remained chiefly an American affair and one that set a precedent of profound consequence: war by order of a president rather than by vote of Congress. Yet it had the sanction of the UN Security Council and could technically be considered a "police action," not a war. Other presidents had ordered U.S. troops into action without a declaration of war, but never on such a scale.

Truman's conviction that the invasion of South Korea was orchestrated by Stalin led to two other decisions that had far-reaching consequences. First, Truman decided that the Korean conflict was actually a diversion for a Soviet invasion of western Europe, so he began a major expansion of American forces in NATO. Second, while dispatching U.S. military units to Korea and Europe, Truman increased assistance to the French troops in Indochina, creating the Military Assistance Advisory Group for Indochina—the start of America's deepening military involvement in Vietnam.

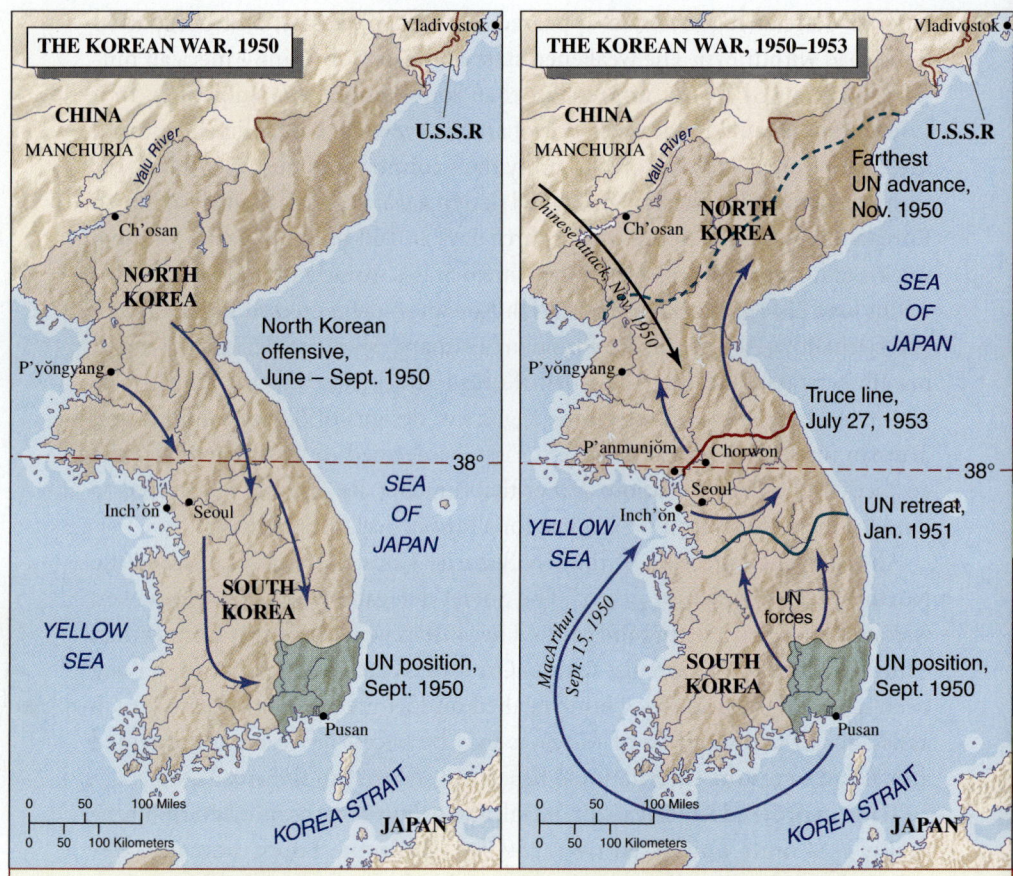

How did the surrender of the Japanese in Korea set up the conflict between Soviet-influenced North Korea and U.S.-influenced South Korea? What was General MacArthur's strategy for retaking Korea? Why did President Truman remove MacArthur from command?

For three months the fighting went badly for the South Korean and UN forces. By September they were barely hanging on to the Pusan perimeter in the southeast corner of Korea. Then, in a brilliant maneuver on September 15, 1950, General MacArthur landed a new force to the North Korean rear at Inch'ŏn. Synchronized with a breakout from Pusan, the sudden blow stampeded the enemy back across the border.

At that point, MacArthur persuaded Truman to allow him to push north and seek to reunify Korea. The Soviet delegate was now back in the Security Council, wielding his veto, so on October 7 the United States got approval for this course from the UN General Assembly, where the veto did not apply.

U.S. forces had crossed the North Korean boundary by October 1 and continued northward. President Truman, concerned about broad hints of Communist Chinese intervention, flew 7,000 miles to Wake Island for a conference with General MacArthur on October 15. There the general discounted chances that the Chinese Red Army would act, but if it did, he confidently predicted, "there would be the greatest slaughter."

That same day, Peking announced that Communist China "cannot stand idly by." On October 26, UN units reached the Yalu River, Korea's border with China. MacArthur predicted total victory by Christmas, but on the night of November 25, several hundred thousand Chinese "volunteers" counterattacked. Massive "human-wave" attacks, with the support of tanks and planes, turned the tables on the UN forces, sending them into a desperate retreat just at the onset of winter. It had become "an entirely new war," MacArthur concluded. Soon he was reporting that the war was dragging on because the administration refused to let him blockade the Chinese mainland.

Truman opposed leading the United States into the "gigantic booby trap" of a ground war with China, and the UN forces soon rallied. By January 1951 over 900,000 UN troops under General Matthew Ridgway finally secured their lines below Seoul and then launched a counterattack that in some places carried them back across the 38th parallel in March. When Truman seized the chance and offered negotiations to restore the boundary and end the war, General MacArthur undermined the move by issuing an ultimatum for China to make peace or suffer an attack. Truman decided then that he had no choice but to accept MacArthur's aggressive policy or fire him. Civilian control of the military was at stake, Truman later asserted. On April 11, 1951, the president removed MacArthur, whom he called Mr. Prima Donna, from all his commands and replaced him with Ridgway.

Truman's action set off an uproar across the country, and a tumultuous reception greeted MacArthur upon his first return home since 1937. MacArthur's dramatic speech to a joint session of Congress provided the climactic event. A Senate investigation showcased the administration's arguments, best summarized by General Omar Bradley, chairman of the Joint Chiefs of Staff. The MacArthur strategy, he said, "would involve us in the wrong war at the wrong place at the wrong time and with the wrong enemy." Most Americans found Bradley's logic persuasive.

On June 24, 1951, the Soviet representative at the United Nations proposed a cease-fire in Korea along the 38th parallel, which Secretary of State Dean Acheson accepted in principle a few days later. China and North Korea responded favorably—at the time, General Ridgway's "meat-grinder" offensive was inflicting severe losses. Truce talks started in July, only to drag on for

September 1950

American soldiers engaged in the recapture of Seoul from the North Koreans.

two years while the fighting continued. The chief snags were exchanges of prisoners and the South Korean president's insistence on unification.

By the time a truce was reached, on July 27, 1953, Truman had relinquished the White House to Dwight D. Eisenhower. The truce line followed the front at that time, mostly a little north of the 38th parallel, with a demilitarized zone separating the forces; repatriation of prisoners would be voluntary, supervised by a neutral commission. No peace conference ever took place, and Korea, like Germany, remained divided. The war had cost the United States more than 33,000 battle deaths and 103,000 wounded or missing. South Korean casualties, all told, were about 1 million, and North Korean and Chinese casualties an estimated 1.5 million.

ANOTHER RED SCARE The costs of the Korean War included the far-reaching consequences of a second Red Scare, which had grown since 1945 as the domestic counterpart to the cold war abroad and reached a climax during the Korean conflict. Since 1938 the House Un-American Activities Committee (HUAC) had kept up a barrage of accusations about supposed subversives in the federal government.

In 1947 the HUAC subpoenaed nineteen prominent Hollywood writers, producers, and actors, intending to prove that Communist party members dominated the Screen Writers Guild, that they injected subversive propaganda into motion pictures, and that President Roosevelt had brought improper pressure to bear upon the industry to produce pro-Soviet films during the war. Ten of the witnesses, the so-called Hollywood Ten, jointly decided to use the First Amendment as a defense, and each of them refused to answer the question "Are you now or have you ever been a member of the Communist party?" All ten had been members of the party, but they would not answer the question as a matter of principle, claiming that party identification was their business, especially since membership in the Communist party at that time was not illegal in the United States. They were all judged to be in contempt and were sentenced to up to a year in prison. But greater punishment awaited them. The movie industry blacklisted the Hollywood Ten, denying them further work.

In the highly charged atmosphere of the postwar years, Truman decided that he, too, must become more vigilant in rooting out Communists from the government. On March 21, 1947, therefore, just nine days after he announced the Truman Doctrine, the president signed an executive order setting up procedures for an employee loyalty program in the federal government. Designed partly to protect the president's political flank, it failed to do so mainly because of disclosures of earlier Communist penetrations of the government that were few in number but sensational in character.

The case most embarrassing to the administration involved Alger Hiss, president of the Carnegie Endowment for International Peace, who had served in several government departments, including the State Department. Whittaker Chambers, a former Soviet agent and later an editor of *Time* magazine, told the HUAC in 1948 that Hiss had given him secret documents ten years earlier, when Chambers was spying for the Soviets. Hiss sued for libel, and Chambers produced microfilms of the State Department documents that he claimed Hiss had passed to him. Hiss denied the accusation, whereupon he was indicted and, after one mistrial, convicted in 1950. The charge was perjury, but he was convicted of lying about espionage, for which he could not be tried because the statute of limitations on that crime had expired.

President Truman, taking at face value the many testimonials to Hiss's integrity, had called the charges against him a "red herring." Secretary of State Dean Acheson compounded the damage when, meaning to express compassion, he pledged not "to turn my back on Alger Hiss." The Hiss affair had another political consequence: it raised to national prominence a young California congressman, Richard M. Nixon, who doggedly insisted on pursuing the case and then exploited an anti-Communist stance to win election to the Senate in 1950.

More cases of Communist infiltration surfaced. In 1950 the government disclosed the existence of a British-American spy network that had fed information about the development of the atomic bomb to the Soviet Union. These disclosures led to the arrest of, among others, Julius and Ethel Rosenberg.

JOSEPH McCARTHY'S WITCH HUNT Revelations of Soviet spying encouraged politicians in both parties to exploit the public's fears. If a man of such respectability as Hiss was guilty, many wondered, who could be trusted? Early in 1950 a little-known Republican senator from Wisconsin, Joseph R. McCarthy, surfaced as the shrewdest and most ruthless exploiter of the nation's anxieties. He took up the cause of anti-communism with a vengeance, claiming that the State Department was infested with Communists and that he had a list of their names. Later there was confusion as to whether he had said there were 205, 81, 57, or "a lot" of names on the list and even whether the sheet of paper he brandished contained any such list. Confusion would typically surround McCarthy's charges.

McCarthy never uncovered a single Communist agent in the government. But with the United States at war with Korean Communists in mid-1950, he continued to arouse public fears. Republicans encouraged him to keep up

Joseph McCarthy

Senator McCarthy (left) and his aide Roy Cohn (right) exchange comments during testimony.

the game. In 1951 he listed Generals George Marshall and Dwight Eisenhower among the disloyal. He kept up his outrageous campaign without successful challenge until the end of the Korean War.

Fears of Communist espionage led Congress in 1950 to pass the McCarran Internal Security Act over President Truman's veto, requiring Communist and Communist-front organizations to register with the attorney general. Aliens who had belonged to totalitarian parties were barred from admission to the United States. Documents recently uncovered in Russian archives and U.S. security agencies reveal that the Soviets did indeed operate an extensive espionage ring in the United States after World War II. Russian agents recruited several hundred American spies to ferret out secrets regarding atomic weapons, defense systems, and military intelligence.

ASSESSING THE COLD WAR   In retrospect the onset of the cold war takes on an appearance of terrible inevitability. America's preference for international principles such as self-determination, free trade, and democracy conflicted with the Soviet Union's preference for international spheres of influence and totalitarian control. Russia, after all, had suffered two German invasions in the first half of the twentieth century, and Soviet leaders wanted tame buffer states on their borders for protection.

The people of Eastern Europe were again caught in the middle. But the Communists themselves held to a universal principle: world revolution. And since the time of President James Monroe, Americans had bristled at the thought of foreign intervention in their sphere of influence, the Western Hemisphere. Thus, to create a defensive shield against the spread of communism, the United States signed mutual defense treaties. Under a 1947 treaty signed at Rio de Janeiro, the nations of the Western Hemisphere agreed to aid any country in the region that was attacked. In 1951 the United States and Japan signed a treaty that permitted the United States to maintain military forces in Japan. That same year, American negotiators signed other mutual defense treaties with the Philippines, Australia, and New Zealand.

The policy initiatives of the Truman years led the country to abandon its long-standing aversion to peacetime alliances. It was a far cry from the world of 1796, when George Washington in his farewell address warned against "those overgrown military establishments which . . . are inauspicious to liberty" and advised his country "to steer clear of permanent alliances with any portion of the foreign world." But then Washington had warned only against participation in the "ordinary" combinations and collusions of Europe, and surely the postwar years had seen extraordinary events and unprecedented new alliances.

End of Chapter Review

CHAPTER SUMMARY

- **The Cold War** The cold war was an ideological contest between the democracies of the Western Hemisphere (especially the United States) and the Communist countries of the Eastern Hemisphere (especially the Soviet Union and China) that emerged after World War II. Immediately after the war, the Soviet Union established puppet governments in Eastern Europe, violating promises made at the Yalta Conference. The United States and the Soviet Union, former allies, differed on issues of human rights, individual liberties, and self-determination.

- **Containment** President Truman responded to the Soviet occupation of Eastern Europe with the policy of containment, the aim of which was to halt the spread of communism. Truman proposed giving economic aid to countries in danger of Communist control, such as Greece and Turkey; and with the Marshall Plan, he offered such aid to all European nations. In a defensive move, the United States in 1949 became a founding member of the North Atlantic Treaty Organization (NATO), a military alliance of Western democracies.

- **Truman's Fair Deal** Truman proposed not only to preserve the New Deal but also to expand it. He vetoed a Republican attempt to curb unions. He oversaw the expansion of Social Security and through executive orders ended segregation in the military and banned racial discrimination in the hiring of federal employees.

- **The Korean War** After a Communist government came to power in China in 1949, Korea became a "hot spot." The peninsula had been divided at the 38th parallel after World War II, with a Communist regime in the north and a Western-style regime in the south. After North Koreans crossed the dividing line in June 1950, Truman decided to go to war under the auspices of the United Nations and without asking Congress to declare war. The war was thus waged by the United States with the participation of more than a dozen member nations of the United Nations. A truce, concluded in July 1953, established a demilitarized zone on either side of the 38th parallel.

- **McCarthyism** The onset of the cold war inflamed another Red Scare. During the Korean War, investigations by the House Committee on Un-American Affairs (known as HUAC) sought to find "subversives" within the federal government. Senator Joseph R. McCarthy of Wisconsin exploited Americans' fears of Soviet spies' infiltrating the highest levels of the U.S. government. McCarthy was successful in the short term because, with most Eastern European nations being held as buffer states by the Soviet Union and the war in Korea being indirectly fought against Communist China, the threat of a world dominated by Communist governments seemed real to many Americans.

CHRONOLOGY

1944	Congress passes the Servicemen's Readjustment Act (GI Bill of Rights)
April 1945	Fifty nations at war with the Axis Powers sign the United Nations Charter
1947	Congress passes the Taft-Hartley Labor Act
1947	National Security Council is established
May 1948	Israel is proclaimed an independent nation
July 1948	Truman issues an executive order ending segregation in the U.S. armed forces
October 1948	Allied forces begin airlifting supplies to West Berlin
November 1948	Truman defeats Dewey in the presidential election
1949	North Atlantic Treaty Organization is created
1949	China "falls" to communism
1950	United States and other UN members go to war in Korea

KEY TERMS & NAMES

32

THROUGH THE PICTURE WINDOW: SOCIETY AND CULTURE, 1945–1960

FOCUS QUESTIONS

 wwnorton.com/studyspace

- Why did the U.S. economy grow rapidly in the postwar period?
- To what extent was conformity the main characteristic of society in the 1950s?
- What was the image of the family in this period, and what was the reality?
- What were the characteristics of the Beat generation?

Americans emerged from World War II elated, proud of their military strength and industrial might, and eager to enjoy peacetime prosperity. As the editors of *Fortune* magazine proclaimed in 1946, "This is a dream era, this is what everyone was waiting through the blackouts for. The Great American Boom is on." So it was. An American public that had known deprivation and sacrifice for a decade and a half began to enjoy unprecedented economic growth, access to a cornucopia of new consumer products, and social contentment—at least on the surface. By 1957 the editors of *U.S. News and World Report* had proclaimed that "never have so many people, anywhere, been so well off."

Amid the rising affluence and optimism, however, many social critics, writers, and artists expressed a growing sense of unease with what they deemed the vulgarity and superficiality of middle-class culture. Was postwar society becoming too complacent, too conformist, too materialistic? These questions reflected the perennial tension in American life between idealism and materialism, a tension that arrived with the first settlers and remains with us today. Americans have always struggled to accumulate goods and cultivate goodness. During the postwar era the nation tried to do both. For a while, at least, it appeared to succeed.

PEOPLE OF PLENTY

The dominant feature of post–World War II society was its remarkable prosperity. After a surprisingly brief postwar recession, businesses shifted from wartime production the peacetime manufacture of an array of consumer goods. The economy soared to record heights. The gross national product nearly doubled between 1945 and 1960, and the 1960s witnessed an even more spectacular expansion of the economy. By 1970 the gap between the living standard in the United States and that in the rest of the world had become a chasm: with 6 percent of the world's population, Americans produced and consumed nearly two thirds of its goods. Poverty remained a chronic condition for many among the rural poor and for the minorities living in urban ghettos, but their plight was largely ignored amid the wave of boosterism and consumerism.

Several factors contributed to this sustained economic surge. The massive federal expenditures to meet military needs during the war had catapulted the economy out of the Depression. High government spending continued to drive the postwar economy, thanks to the tensions generated by the cold war. Military-related research also helped spawn the new glamour industries of the postwar era: chemicals, electronics, and aviation.

Most of the other major industrial nations of the world—England, France, Germany, Japan, the Soviet Union—had been physically devastated during the war, leaving American manufacturers with a virtual monopoly on international trade. In addition, the widespread use of new and more efficient machinery and computers led to a 35 percent jump in the productivity of American workers between 1945 and 1955.

The major catalyst in promoting economic expansion after 1945, however, was the unleashing of pent-up consumer demand. During the war, civilians had postponed purchases of major items such as cars and houses and in the process had saved over $150 billion. Now they were eager to buy. The United States after World War II experienced a purchasing frenzy.

THE GI BILL OF RIGHTS   Part of that frenzy was indirectly financed by the federal government. People feared that a sharp postwar drop in military

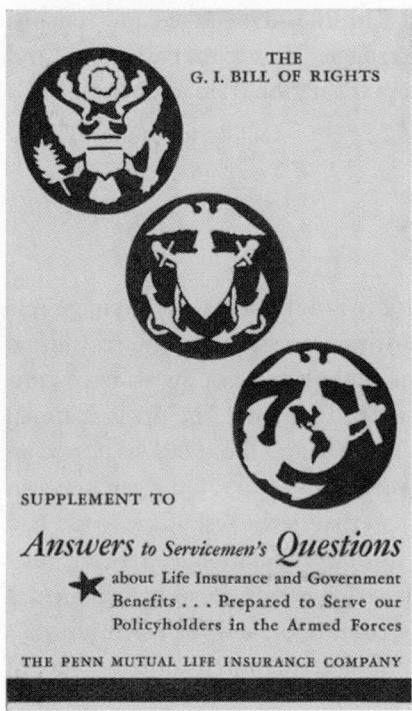

THE
G. I. BILL OF RIGHTS

SUPPLEMENT TO

Answers to Servicemen's Questions

★ about Life Insurance and Government
Benefits . . . Prepared to Serve our
Policyholders in the Armed Forces

THE PENN MUTUAL LIFE INSURANCE COMPANY

GI Bill of Rights supplement

This booklet informed servicemen about the new legislation.

spending and the sudden influx of veterans into the civilian workforce would send the economy into a downward spiral and produce widespread unemployment. Those concerns led Congress to pass the Servicemen's Readjustment Act of 1944. Popularly known as the GI Bill of Rights (*GI* meaning "government issue," a phrase that was stamped on military uniforms and was slang for "serviceman"), it led to the creation of a new government agency, the Veterans Administration. The GI Bill also provided unemployment pay for veterans for one year, preference for veterans seeking government jobs, loans for home construction, access to government hospitals, and generous subsidies for postsecondary education. Between 1944 and 1956 almost 8 million veterans took advantage of $14.5 billion in GI Bill subsidies to attend college or enroll in job-training programs. Some 5 million veterans bought new homes using GI Bill benefits. These two provisions of the GI Bill combined to produce a social revolution.

Before World War II approximately 160,000 Americans graduated from college each year. By 1950 the figure had more than tripled. In 1949, veterans accounted for 40 percent of all college enrollments. For the first time in the nation's history, a significant number of working-class men had the opportunity to earn a college degree. In turn a college education or vocational training served as a lever into the middle class and fostered economic security. The United States could boast the world's best-educated workforce.

But while the GI Bill helped erode class barriers, it was less successful in dismantling racial barriers. Many African American veterans could not take equal advantage of the education benefits. Most colleges and universities after the war remained racially segregated, by regulation or by practice. In 1946 only a fifth of the 100,000 African Americans who had applied for education benefits had enrolled in a program.

THE BABY BOOM The return of some 12 million veterans to private life also helped generate the postwar baby boom, which peaked in 1957. Between 1946 and 1964, 76 million Americans were born, reversing a century-long decline in the nation's birthrate and creating a massive demographic upheaval whose repercussions are still being felt. Such a dramatic growth rate had a host of reverberating effects. Indeed, much of America's social history since the 1940s has been the story of the unusually large baby boom generation and its progress through the stages of life. The postwar surge in births created a massive demand for diapers, baby food, toys, medicine, schools, books, teachers, furniture, and housing. The baby boomers were raised during the 1950s and 1960s, a period of unprecedented prosperity and American omnipotence abroad, but they entered adulthood during the 1970s, a period of energy crises, inflationary pressures, and diminished national prestige. They inherited a nation flush with affluence and will bequeath a nation mired in debt. During their childhood the baby boomers lived amid a child-obsessed culture; in their youth the nation was youth obsessed. The iconoclastic Columbia University historian Richard Hofstadter worried that America was being overrun by the "overvalued child." The baby boomer novelist Benjamin Cheever confessed that "we were spoiled. No denying that. And we have spoiled our children."

AN EXPANDING CONSUMER CULTURE The baby boom was accompanied by a postwar construction boom. The proportion of homeowners in the population increased by 50 percent between 1945 and 1960. And those new homes featured the latest electrical appliances: refrigerators, washing machines, sewing machines, vacuum cleaners, freezers, electric mixers, and television sets. By far the most popular new household product was the TV set. In 1946 there were 7,000 primitive black-and-white TV sets in the country; by 1960 there were 50 million high-quality sets. Nine out of ten homes had one, and by 1970, 38 percent of homes had the new color sets. What differentiated the affluence of the post–World War II era from earlier periods of prosperity was its ever-widening dispersion. In 1955, union leader George Meany proclaimed that "American labor never had it so good."

On the surface many African Americans were also beneficiaries of the wave of prosperity that swept over postwar society. By 1950, blacks were earning on average more than four times their 1940 wages. While gains had been made, however, African Americans and other minority groups lagged behind whites in their rate of improvement. Indeed, the gap between the average yearly income of whites and blacks widened during the 1950s. Yet the

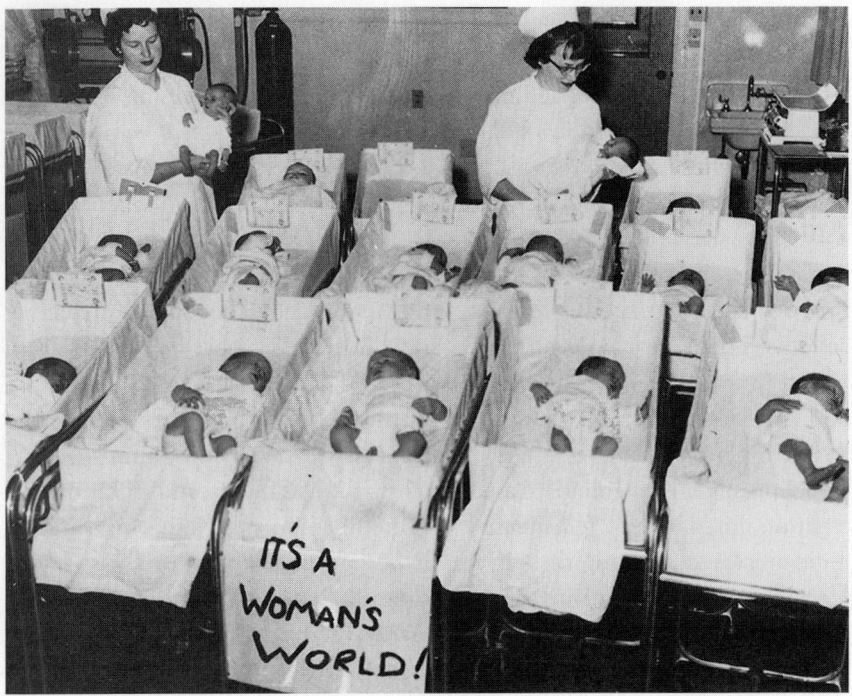

The baby boom

Much of America's social history since the 1940s has been the story of the baby boom generation.

desire to present a united front against communism led commentators to ignore issues of racial and economic injustice. Such corrosive neglect would fester and explode during the 1960s, but for now the emphasis was on consensus, conformity, and economic growth.

To perpetuate the postwar prosperity, economists repeated the basic marketing strategy of the 1920s: the public must be taught to consume more and expect more. Economists knew that Americans had more money than ever before. The average adult had twice as much *real* income in 1955 as in the rosy days of the late 1920s before the crash. Still, many people who had undergone the severities of the Depression and the rationing required for the war effort had to be weaned from a decade and a half of imposed frugality in order to nourish the growing consumer culture.

Advertising became a more crucial component of the consumer culture than ever before. Expenditures for TV ads increased 1,000 percent during the 1950s. Such startling growth rates led the president of NBC to claim in 1956 that the primary reason for the postwar economic boom was that "advertising has created an American frame of mind that makes people want more things, better things and newer things." Paying for such "things" was no problem. Between 1945 and 1957 consumer credit soared 800 percent. Whereas families in other industrialized nations were typically saving 10 to 20 percent of their income, American families by the 1960s were saving only 5 percent.

Young Americans in particular participated in the consumer culture. By the late 1950s the baby boom generation was entering its teens, and the disproportionate number of affluent adolescents generated a vast new specialized market for youth-oriented goods ranging from transistor radios,

Black cotillion dance

Presentation of the debutantes of 1954.

Hula-hoops, and rock-and-roll records to cameras, surfboards, *Seventeen* magazine, and Pat Boone movies. Most teenagers had far more discretionary income and free time than those of previous generations had had. Teens in the postwar era knew nothing of depressions or rationing; they were immersed in abundance from an early age and took for granted the notion of carefree consumption.

THE SUBURBAN FRONTIER   The population increase of the 1950s and 1960s was an urban as well as a suburban phenomenon. Dramatic new technological advances in agricultural production reduced the need for manual laborers. Almost 20 million Americans left the land for the city between 1940 and 1970. Much of the urban population growth occurred in the South, the Southwest, and the West, in an arc that stretched from the Carolinas to California, regions that by the 1970s were being lumped together and called the sunbelt. The dispersion of air-conditioning throughout these warm regions dramatically enhanced their attractiveness to northerners. But the Northeast remained the most densely populated area; by the early 1960s, 20 percent of the nation's population lived in the corridor that stretched south from Boston to Norfolk, Virginia.

While more people concentrated in cities, Americans after World War II were spreading out within the metropolitan areas. During the 1950s, suburbs grew six times faster than cities. By 1970 more people lived in suburbs

Suburban life

A woman vacuums her living room in Queens, New York, 1953, illustrating the 1950s ideal of domestic contentment facilitated by electrical appliances.

(76 million) than in central cities (64 million). Suburban development required cars, highways, and government-backed home mortgages. It also required bold entrepreneurs.

William Levitt, a brassy New York developer, led the suburban revolution. In 1947, on 1,200 acres of Long Island farmland, he built 10,600 houses that were inhabited by more than 40,000 people, mostly adults under thirty-five and their children. Other developers soon mimicked Levitt's suburbs around the country. Expanded automobile production and highway construction facilitated the rush to the suburbs as people were able to commute longer distances to work. Car production soared, and a car-dependent culture soon emerged. Widespread car ownership necessitated an improved road network. Local and state governments built many new roads, but the guiding force was the federal government. In 1947, Congress authorized the construction of 37,000 miles of federal highways, and nine years later it funded 42,000 additional miles of interstate expressways.

The federal government also fostered the suburban revolution through loans to developers and consumers. By insuring loans for up to 95 percent of the value of a house, the Federal Housing Administration made it easy for a builder to borrow money to construct low-cost homes. In addition, military veterans were given substantial assistance with home ownership. A veteran could buy a Levitt house with no down payment and monthly installments of $56. African Americans and other racial minorities, however, were often discriminated against. Contracts for homes in Levittown, Long Island, for example, specifically excluded "members of other than the Caucasian race." Such discrimination, whether explicit or implicit, was widespread; the nation's suburban population in 1970 was 95 percent white.

THE GREAT BLACK MIGRATION World War II, like World War I, spurred a mass migration of rural southern blacks to the cities of other regions. This second migration was much larger in scope than the first, and its social consequences were much more dramatic. After 1945 more than 5 million southern blacks, mostly farm folk, left their native regions in search of better jobs, higher wages, decent housing, and greater social equality. During the 1950s, for example, the African American population of Chicago more than doubled. The South Side of Chicago soon became known as the capital of black America. It remains the neighborhood with the largest concentration of African Americans in the nation.

Many southern blacks streamed northward in search of a new promised land only to see their dreams dashed. In northern cities such as Chicago, Philadelphia, Newark, Detroit, New York, Boston, and Washington, D.C., African Americans from the rural South confronted harsh new realities.

Family on relief

Black families who migrated from the South became a part of a marginalized population in Chicago, dependent on public housing.

Slumlords often gouged them for rent, employers refused to hire them, and some union bosses denied them membership. Soon the promised land had become an ugly nightmare of slum housing, joblessness, illiteracy, dysfunctional families, welfare dependency, street gangs, pervasive crime, and racism.

The unexpected tidal wave of African American migrants severely taxed the resources of urban governments and the tolerance of white racists. Throughout the North angry whites attacked blacks who dared move into their neighborhoods. Northern cities sought to deal with the migrants and alleviate racial stress by constructing massive public-housing projects to accommodate the newcomers. These overcrowded all-black enclaves were essentially segregated prisons. To be sure, many African American migrants and their children did manage through extraordinary determination and ingenuity to "clear"—to climb out of the teeming ghettos and into the middle class. But most did not. As a consequence the great black migration produced a web of complex social problems in northern cities that in the 1960s would erupt into a crisis.

A CONFORMING CULTURE

In the 1950s, social commentators mostly ignored people and cultures outside the mainstream. As evidenced in many of the new look-alike suburbs sprouting up across the land, much of white middle-class social life during the two decades after World War II exhibited an increasingly homogenized character. Suburban life encouraged uniformity. People felt a need for companionship and a sense of belonging as they moved into communities of strangers. "Conformity," predicted a journalist in 1954, "may very well become the central social problem of this age."

CORPORATE LIFE   During World War II, big business had grown bigger. The government had relaxed its anti-trust activity, and huge defense contracts promoted corporate concentration and consolidation. In 1940, for example, the 100 largest companies were responsible for 30 percent of all manufacturing output; three years later they were producing 70 percent. After the war fewer and fewer people were self-employed; many now worked for large corporations, with manual labor giving way to mental labor for a large part of the workforce. In the huge companies as well as in similarly large government agencies and universities, the working atmosphere promoted conformity and regimentation rather than individualism.

WOMEN'S "PLACE" Increasing conformity in middle-class business and corporate life was mirrored in the middle-class home. A special issue of *Life* magazine in 1956 featured the "ideal" middle-class woman, a thirty-two-year-old "pretty and popular" white suburban housewife, mother of four, who had married at age sixteen. Described as an excellent wife, mother, volunteer, and "home manager," she hosted dozens of dinner parties each year, sang in her church choir, worked with the PTA and the Campfire Girls, and was devoted to her husband. "In her daily round," *Life* reported, "she attends club or charity meetings, drives the children to school, does the weekly grocery shopping, makes ceramics, and is planning to study French." *Life*'s ideal of the middle-class woman reflected a veritable cult of feminine domesticity that witnessed a dramatic revival in the postwar era. The soaring birthrate reinforced the deeply embedded notion that a woman's place was in the home. "Of all the accomplishments of the American woman," the *Life* cover story proclaimed, "the one she brings off with the most spectacular success is having babies."

Even though millions of women had responded to wartime appeals and joined the traditionally male workforce, afterward they were encouraged—and

The new household

A Tupperware party in a middle-class suburban home.

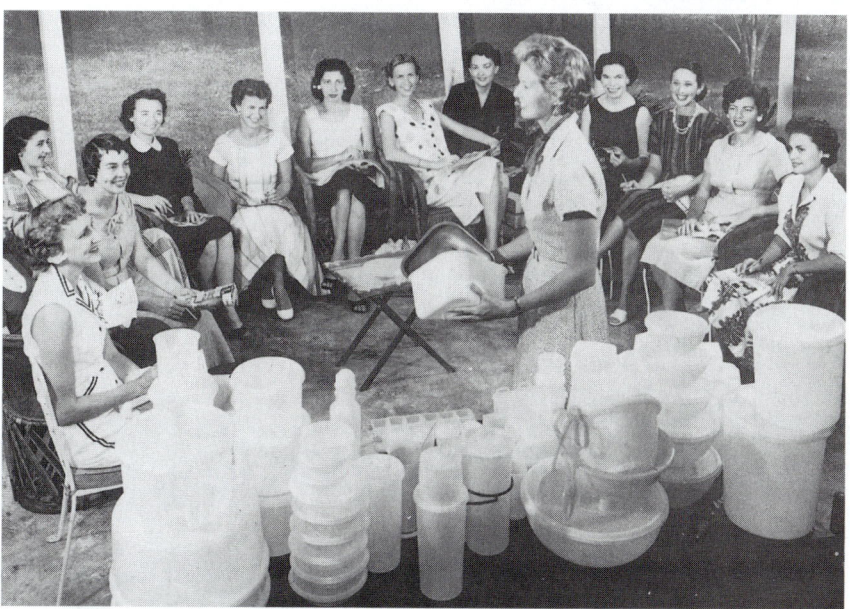

even forced—to turn their jobs over to the returning veterans and resume their full-time commitment to home and family. Throughout the postwar era, educators, politicians, ministers, advertisers, and other commentators exalted the cult of domesticity and castigated the few feminists who were encouraging women to broaden their horizons beyond crib and kitchen. Women were to dismiss any thoughts of continuing their own career in the workplace and were to return to their traditional domestic roles. Nonetheless, despite the ideal of women remaining in the home and the stigma associated with violating this norm, the percentage of women working outside the home increased overall during the 1950s.

THE SEARCH FOR COMMUNITY   Americans were on the move after World War II. Some 20 percent of the population changed their place of residence each year. One cause of the mobility was the largest corporations' standard policy of relocating their sales and managerial employees. As they moved from central city to suburb, from suburb to suburb, from farm to city, from state to state, people searched for a sense of community and rootedness.

Billy Graham preaches to thousands, 1955

The Baptist evangelist used radio and television to promote his huge crusades, as droves of Americans, encouraged by the president, Congress, and billboard advertising, joined churches and attended revival meetings.

Hence Americans, even more than usual, became joiners: they joined civic clubs, garden clubs, car pools, and babysitting groups.

RELIGIOUS REVIVAL   Americans also joined churches and synagogues in record numbers. The postwar era witnessed a massive renewal of religious participation. In 1940 less than half the adult population belonged to a church; by 1960 over 65 percent were official communicants. Bible sales soared, and books, movies, and songs with religious themes were stunning commercial successes. Conservative Protestants found willing allies among Republican leaders in their effort to reaffirm America's Christian commitment. President Eisenhower repeatedly promoted a patriotic crusade to bring Americans back to God. "Recognition of the Supreme Being," he declared, "is the first, the most basic, expression of Americanism. Without God, there could be no form of American government, nor an American way of life." The president had himself joined a church for the first time only in 1953, but he characterized himself as the "most intensely religious man I know." Not to be outdone, Congress in 1954 added the phrase "under God" to the Pledge of Allegiance and in 1956 made the statement "In God We Trust" mandatory on all coins and currency. In 1956, Congress also made "In God We Trust" the national motto.

The prevailing tone of the popular religious revival of the 1950s was upbeat and soothing. Most ministers assumed that people were not interested in "fire-and-brimstone" harangues from the pulpit; congregants did not want their conscience overburdened with a sense of personal sin or social guilt about issues such as segregation and inner-city poverty. Instead, they wanted to be reassured that their own comfortable way of life was indeed God's will.

CRACKS IN THE PICTURE WINDOW

Yet despite widespread prosperity, all was not well in postwar America. The widely publicized affluence masked festering poverty in rural areas and urban ghettos. People were also profoundly anxious about the meaning of their lives and of life in general in the nuclear age. That tranquilizers were the fastest-growing medication suggested that considerable anxiety accompanied the nation's much-trumpeted affluence. Thus one of the most striking aspects of postwar American life was the sharp contrast between the prevailing sentiment that everything was fine and for the best as long as people believed in God, the "American way," and themselves and the increasingly bitter criticism of social life coming from artists, intellectuals, and other commentators.

THE LONELY CROWD   The criticism of postwar life and values began in the early 1950s and quickly gathered momentum. In *The Affluent Society* (1958), for example, the economist John Kenneth Galbraith warned that sustained economic growth would not necessarily solve chronic social problems. He reminded readers that for all of America's vaunted postwar prosperity, the nation had yet to confront, much less eradicate, the chronic poverty plaguing the nation's inner cities and rural hamlets. Postwar cultural critics also questioned the supposed bliss offered by middle-class suburban life. John Keats, in *The Crack in the Picture Window* (1956), launched a savage assault on life in the huge new suburban developments. Suburbanites, he concluded, were locked into a deadly routine, hounded by financial insecurity, engulfed by mass mediocrity, and living, in short, in a "homogeneous, postwar Hell."

Social critics in the 1950s repeatedly cited the huge modern corporation as an important source of regimentation in American life. The most provocative analysis of the docile new corporate character was David Riesman's *The Lonely Crowd* (1950). Riesman, a social psychologist, detected a fundamental

Suburban pastimes

A suburban family enjoys playing with Hula-hoops in their backyard.

shift in the dominant American personality from what he called the "inner-directed" type to the "other-directed" type. Inner-directed people, Riesman argued, possess a deeply internalized set of basic values implanted by strong-minded parents or other elders. Such an assured, self-reliant personality, Riesman claimed, had prevailed in nineteenth-century life. But during the mid–twentieth century a new, other-directed personality had displaced it. In the huge hierarchical corporations that abounded in postwar America, employees who could win friends and influence people thrived; rugged individualists indifferent to personal popularity did not. The other-directed people who adapted to the corporate culture had few internal convictions and standards; they did not follow their conscience so much as adapt to the prevailing standards of the moment. They were concerned more with being well liked than with being independent.

Riesman amassed considerable evidence to show that the other-directed personality was not just an aspect of the business world; its characteristics were widely dispersed throughout middle-class life. One of its sources, Riesman suggested, may have been Dr. Benjamin Spock's influential advice on raising children. Spock's popular manual, *The Common Sense Book of Baby and Child Care*, sold 1 million copies a year between its first appearance in 1946 and 1960. Spock stressed that parents should foster in their children qualities and skills that would enhance their chances in what Riesman called the "popularity market."

YOUTH CULTURE AND DELINQUENCY   Heeding Dr. Spock's advice, most parents of the 1950s tended to be permissive with their children, who occupied a distinctive place in postwar life. One commentator described the American family in 1957 as a "child-centered anarchy." As the baby boomers were reaching adolescence during the 1950s, a distinctive teen subculture began to emerge. And as most adults in postwar society were striving to get along and to conform to the values of the club or civic group or corporation, so, too, were most young people embracing the values of their parents and the capitalist system.

Yet such conformity and striving for popularity masked a great deal of turbulence. During the 1950s a wave of juvenile delinquency swept across middle-class society. By 1956 over 1 million teens a year were being arrested. Car theft was the leading offense, but larceny, rape, and murder were not uncommon. A Boston judge announced that the entire city was being "terrorized" by juvenile gangs. What was causing the delinquency? J. Edgar Hoover, head of the Federal Bureau of Investigation, insisted that the root of

Youth culture

A drugstore soda fountain, a popular outlet for teenagers' consumerism in the 1950s.

the problem was a lack of religious training in more and more households. Others pointed to the growing number of urban slums, whose "brutish" environment could lead to criminality. Yet those factors failed to explain why so many middle-class kids from God-fearing families were becoming delinquents. One explanation may have been the unprecedented mobility of young people. Access to automobiles enabled teens to escape parental control, and in the words of one journalist, cars provided "a private lounge for drinking and for petting or sex episodes."

ROCK AND ROLL   Many concerned observers blamed the delinquency on a new form of music that emerged during the postwar era: rock and roll. In 1955, *Life* magazine published a long article about a mysterious new "frenzied teenage music craze" that was creating "a big fuss." Alan Freed, a Cleveland disc jockey, had coined the term *rock and roll* in 1951. At a record store he had noticed white teenagers buying rhythm and blues (R&B) records that had heretofore been purchased only by African Americans and Hispanic Americans. Freed began playing R&B records on the air but labeled the music rock and roll (a phrase used in African American communities to refer to dancing and sex) to surmount the racial barrier.

Freed's radio program was an immediate success, and its popularity helped bridge the gap between "white" and "black" music. African American singers such as Chuck Berry, Little Richard, and Ray Charles and Hispanic American performers such as Ritchie Valens (Richard Valenzuela) were suddenly the rage among young white middle-class audiences eager to claim their own cultural style and message.

At the same time, Elvis Presley, a young white truck driver and aspiring singer from Memphis, Tennessee, began experimenting with "rockabilly" music, his unique blend of gospel, country-and-western, and R&B rhythms and lyrics. In 1956 the twenty-one-year-old Presley released "Heartbreak Hotel," and over the next two years the sensual baritone won fourteen gold records and emerged as the most popular entertainer in history. His sexually suggestive stage performances, featuring twisting hips and a gyrating pelvis, drove teenagers wild.

Such hysterics prompted cultural conservatives to urge parents to confiscate and destroy Presley's records because they promoted "a pagan concept of life." A Catholic cardinal denounced Presley as a vile symptom of a new teen "creed of dishonesty, violence, lust and degeneration." Patriotic groups claimed that rock-and-roll music was a tool of Communist insurgents designed to corrupt American youth.

Yet rock and roll survived the assaults and in the process gave adolescents a self-conscious sense of belonging to a unique social

Elvis Presley, 1956

The teenage children of middle-class America made rock and roll a thriving industry in the 1950s and Elvis its first star. The strong beat of the music combined with the electric guitar, its signature instrument, produced a distinctive new sound.

group with distinctive characteristics and tastes. It also represented an unprecedented intermingling of racial, ethnic, and class identities.

ALIENATION IN THE ARTS Dissatisfaction with the conventions and conformity of American society surfaced not only in rock and roll; it was manifested also in literature as well as in some of the artwork of the times. Many of the best novels and plays of the postwar period reinforced David Riesman's image of modern American society as a "lonely crowd" of individuals, hollow at the core, groping for a sense of belonging and affection. Arthur Miller's much-celebrated play *Death of a Salesman* (1949) explored this theme powerfully. Willy Loman, an aging, confused traveling salesman in decline, centers his life and that of his family on the notion of material success through personal popularity, only to be abruptly told by his boss that he is in fact a failure. Willy, for all his puffery about being well liked, admits that he is "terribly lonely." He has no real friends; even his relations with his family are neither honest nor intimate. When Willy finally realizes that he has been leading a counterfeit existence, he yearns for a life in which "a man is not a piece of fruit," but eventually he is so dumbfounded by his predicament that he decides he can endow his life with meaning only by ending it.

Nor are there many happy endings in the best novels of the postwar period. A brooding sense of resigned alienation dominated literary fiction in the two decades after 1945. The characters in novels such as James Jones's *From Here to Eternity* (1951), Ralph Ellison's *Invisible Man* (1952), Saul Bellow's *Dangling Man* (1944) and *Seize the Day* (1956), William Styron's *Lie Down in Darkness* (1951), and John Updike's *Rabbit, Run* (1961), among many others, tend to be like Willy Loman: restless, tormented, impotent individuals who are unable to fasten on a satisfying self-image and therefore can find neither contentment nor respect in an overpowering or impersonal world.

Many visual artists also explored the theme of desolate loneliness in urban-industrial American life. Virtually all of Edward Hopper's paintings, for example, depict isolated individuals, melancholy, anonymous, and motionless. The silence of his scenes is deafening, the monotony striking, the alienation absorbing.

A group of younger painters in New York City felt that postwar society was so chaotic that it denied any attempt at literal representation. Their anarchic technique came to be called abstract expressionism, and during the late 1940s and 1950s it dominated not only the American art scene but the international field as well. Abstract expressionists included Jackson Pollock, Robert Motherwell, Willem de Kooning, Arshile Gorky, Clyfford Still, Adolph Gottlieb, and Mark Rothko. "Abstract art," Motherwell declared, "is an effort to close the void that modern men feel."

In practice this meant that the *act* of painting was as important as the result and that art no longer had to represent one's visual surroundings. Instead, it could unapologetically represent the painter's personal thoughts and actions. Wyoming-born Pollock, for example, placed his huge canvases flat on the floor and then walked around each side, pouring and dripping his paint in an effort to "literally be *in* the painting." Such action paintings, with their commanding size, bold form, powerful color contrasts, and rough texture, were vibrant, frenzied, meditative, disorienting, and provocative.

THE BEATS The desire to liberate self-expression and reject middle-class conventions also animated a small but highly visible and controversial group of young writers, poets, painters, and musicians known as the Beats. These young men—Jack Kerouac, Allen Ginsberg, Gary Snyder, William Burroughs, and Gregory Corso, among others—rebelled against the mundane horrors

Allen Ginsberg

Ginsberg, considered the poet laureate of the Beat generation, reads his uncensored poetry to a crowd in Washington Square Park in New York City.

of middle-class life. The Beats were not lost in despair, however; they strenuously embraced life. But it was life on their own terms, and their terms were shocking to most observers.

The self-described Beats grew out of the bohemian underground in New York's Greenwich Village. Essentially apolitical throughout the 1950s, the Beats sought personal rather than social solutions to their hopes and anxieties. As Jack Kerouac insisted, his friends were not beat in the sense of beaten; they were "mad to live, mad to talk, mad to be saved." Their road to salvation lay in hallucinogenic drugs and alcohol, sex, a penchant for jazz and the street life of urban ghettos, an affinity for Buddhism, and a restless, vagabond spirit that took them speeding back and forth across the country between San Francisco and New York.

This existential mania for intense experience and frantic motion provided the subject matter for the Beats' writing. Ginsberg's long prose poem *Howl*, published in 1956, features an explicit sensuality as well as an impressionistic attempt to catch the color, movement, and dynamism of modern life. Kerouac published his autobiographical novel *On the Road* a year later. In frenzied prose it portrays the Beats' life of "bursting ecstasies" and maniacal traveling. *Howl* and *On the Road* elicited angry sarcasm from many reviewers, but the books enjoyed brisk sales, especially among young people. *On the Road* made the best-seller list, and soon the term *Beat generation* or *beatnik* referred to almost any young rebel who openly dissented from middle-class life.

A Paradoxical Era

For all their eccentricities and vitality the Beats had little impact on the prevailing patterns of postwar social and cultural life. The same held true for most of the critics who attacked the smug conformity and excessive materialism they saw pervading their society. The public had become weary of larger social or political concerns in the aftermath of the Depression and the war. Instead, Americans eagerly focused on personal and family goals and material achievements.

Yet those achievements, considerable as they were, eventually created a new set of problems. The benefits of abundance were by no means equally distributed during the 1950s, and millions of people still lived in poverty. For those more fortunate, unprecedented affluence and security fostered greater leisure and independence, which in turn provided opportunities for pursuing more diverse notions of what the good life entailed. Yet the conformist mentality of the cold war era discouraged experimentation. By the mid-1960s, tensions between innovation and convention would erupt into open conflict. Many members of the baby boom generation would become the leaders of the 1960s rebellion against corporate conformity and consumerism. Ironically, the person who would warn Americans of the 1960s of the mounting dangers of the burgeoning "military-industrial complex" was the president who had long symbolized its growth: Dwight D. Eisenhower.

CHAPTER SUMMARY

- **Growth of U.S. Economy** High levels of government spending, begun before the war, continued during the postwar period. The GI Bill of Rights gave a boost to home buying and helped many veterans attend college and thereby enter the middle class. Unemployment was virtually nonexistent, and consumer demand for homes, cars, and the household goods that had been unavailable during the war fueled the economy, as did buying on credit.

- **Conformity in American Society** After World War II, with the growth of suburbs, corporations, and advertising, society appeared highly uniform, yet pockets of poverty persisted, and minorities did not prosper to the extent that white Americans did. Most white mothers did not work outside the home and were expected to find pleasure in housework. Attendance at worship services soared. The semblance of uniformity was perhaps a reaction to the feeling that society was threatened by an atheistic communism. Although popular culture reflected the affluence of the white middle class, the art and literature of the period hinted at an underlying alienation.

- **The American Family** Conformity extended to the image of the family as depicted on television and in magazines. Typically a family consisted of a father who worked in a city and a mother who stayed at home in the suburbs, devoting herself to home, husband, and children. This image did not reflect everyone's reality, however. A wave of juvenile delinquency swept middle-class society, and millions of Americans, especially minorities, lived in poverty during this era of affluence. The great black migration allowed some black families to climb into the middle class, but left many stuck in the teeming ghettos in northern cities.

- **The Beat Generation** Dissatisfaction with conformity was reflected in the literature and art of the Beat generation. Artists such as Edward Hopper dwelled on the desolate loneliness of urban settings, and a group of younger painters turned from realism to abstract expressionism in the belief that modern society was too chaotic to be represented in a literal manner. The Beats were a small yet highly visible group of writers and artists who rebelled against the regimented horrors of war and the mundane horrors of middle-class life. They sought their salvation through the use of hallucinogenic drugs, alcohol, sex, and music in their attempts to capture the vitality of modern life.

CHRONOLOGY

1944	Congress passes the Servicemen's Readjustment Act (GI Bill of Rights)
1949	Arthur Miller's *Death of a Salesman* is produced
1950	David Riesman's *The Lonely Crowd* is published
1952	Ralph Ellison's *Invisible Man* is published
1956	Elvis Presley's "Heartbreak Hotel" is released
1956	Allen Ginsberg's *Howl* is published
1957	Jack Kerouac's *On the Road* is published
1957	Baby boom peaks
1958	John Kenneth Galbraith's *The Affluent Society* is published

KEY TERMS & NAMES

33

CONFLICT AND DEADLOCK: THE EISENHOWER YEARS

FOCUS QUESTIONS · · · S · wwnorton.com/studyspace

- What were the main characteristics of Eisenhower's "dynamic conservatism"?
- What shaped American foreign policy in the 1950s?
- What events in Southeast Asia led to America's involvement in Vietnam?
- Why did the civil rights movement emerge in the 1950s?

The New Deal political coalition established by Franklin Roosevelt and sustained by Harry Truman posed a formidable challenge to Republicans after World War II. To counter the potent combination of Solid South white Democrats, African Americans, members of other minority groups, and organized labor, the Grand Old Party turned in 1952 to General Dwight David Eisenhower, a military hero capable of attracting independent voters as well as some Democrats. Eisenhower's commitment to a "moderate Republicanism" promised to slow the rate of government expansion while retaining many of the cherished social programs established by Roosevelt and Truman. Eisenhower promised to restore the authority of state and local governments and restrain the executive branch from political and social "engineering." In the process, the former general sought to reinforce traditional virtues and inspire Americans with a vision of a brighter future amid a continuing "cold war."

"TIME FOR A CHANGE"

By 1952 the Truman administration had piled up a heavy burden of political liabilities: a bloody stalemate in Korea, renewed wage and price controls at home, reckless charges of subversion and disloyalty among federal employees, and the exposure of corrupt lobbyists and influence peddlers who rigged favors in Washington. The disclosure of government corruption led Truman to fire nearly 250 employees of the Internal Revenue Service. Doubts lingered that he would ever finish the housecleaning.

THE POLITICAL RISE OF EISENHOWER It was, in a slogan of the day, "time for a change," and Republicans saw public sentiment turning their way as the 1952 election approached. Republican leaders recruited General Dwight D. Eisenhower to be their candidate. Despite his roots in Kansas Republican conservatism, Eisenhower had initially supported Roosevelt and the New Deal, and he admired Roosevelt's wartime leadership. During the Truman years, however, Eisenhower reverted to the political party of his youth. In early 1952 he affirmed that he was a Republican and permitted his name to be entered in party primaries. He won the nomination on the first ballot, then balanced the ticket by selecting as his running mate a youthful Californian, the thirty-nine-year-old senator Richard M. Nixon, who had built a career on strenuous opposition to domestic "subversives."

THE ELECTION OF 1952 The Twenty-second Amendment, ratified in 1951, forbade any president from serving more than two terms. The amendment exempted the current incumbent, Harry Truman. But he had no desire to run again. Weary of the war in Korea and harassed by charges of subversion and corruption in his administration, Truman withdrew and gave his support to Illinois governor Adlai E. Stevenson, who roused the delegates to the Democratic Convention with an eloquent speech welcoming them to Chicago.

The 1952 campaign matched two contrasting personalities. Eisenhower, though a political novice, was a world military hero who had been in the public eye for a decade. Stevenson was hardly known outside Illinois. The genial Eisenhower, who disliked politics and politicians, pledged to clean up "the mess in Washington." To this he added a promise, late in the campaign, that as president-elect he would secure "an early and honorable" peace in Korea.

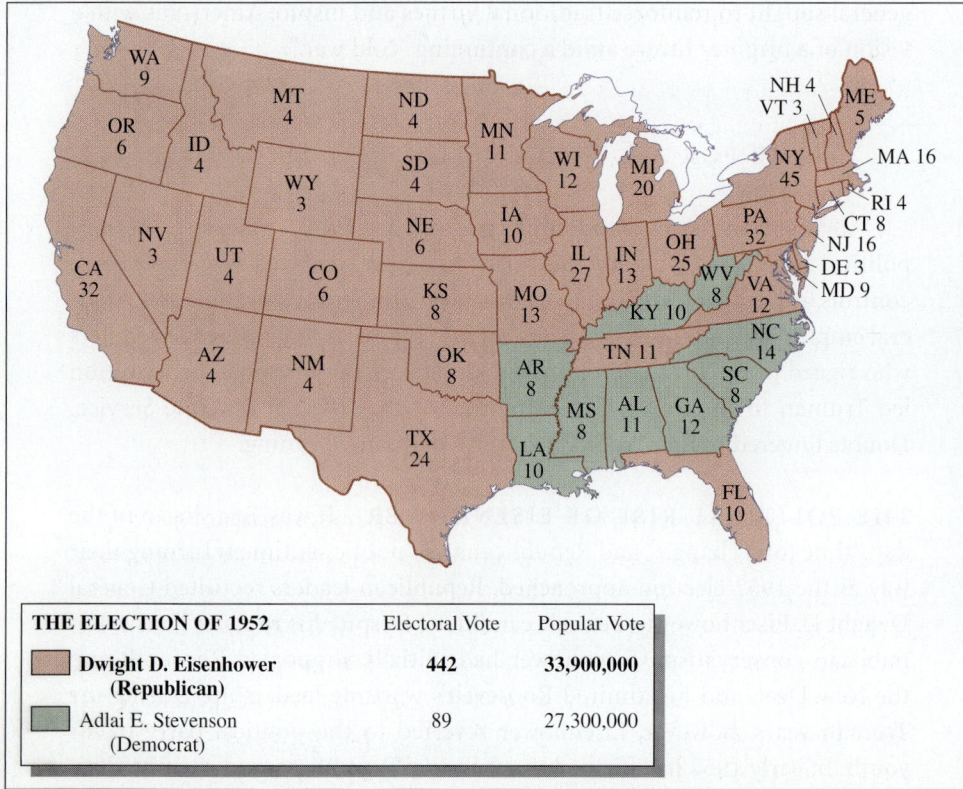

THE ELECTION OF 1952	Electoral Vote	Popular Vote
Dwight D. Eisenhower (Republican)	**442**	**33,900,000**
Adlai E. Stevenson (Democrat)	89	27,300,000

Why was the contest between Adlai Stevenson and Dwight Eisenhower so lopsided? Why was Eisenhower's victory in the South remarkable? Did Eisenhower's broad appeal help congressional Republicans win more seats?

Stevenson offered a keen intellect spiced with a quick wit, but his resolve to "talk sense" and "tell the truth to the American people" came across as too aloof, a shade too intellectual. The Republicans labeled him an egghead in contrast to Eisenhower, the folksy man of the people, the man of decisive action.

In the end, Stevenson's humor and intellect were no match for Eisenhower's popularity. The war hero triumphed in a landslide of nearly 34 million votes to a little over 27 million for Stevenson. The election marked a turning point in Republican fortunes in the South: for the first time since the 1850s, the South was moving toward a two-party system. Stevenson carried only eight southern states plus West Virginia; Eisenhower picked up five states on the periphery of the Deep South: Florida, Oklahoma, Tennessee, Texas, and Virginia. The "nonpolitical" Eisenhower had made it respectable, even fashionable, to vote Republican in the South. Elsewhere, too, the general made inroads into the Democrats' New Deal coalition, attracting supporters among the ethnic and religious minorities in the major cities who had long identified with the Democratic party.

The voters, it turned out, liked Eisenhower better than they liked his party. In the 1952 election, Democrats retained most of the governorships, lost control of the House by only eight seats, and broke even in the Senate. The congressional elections two years later would weaken the Republican grip on Congress, and Eisenhower would have to work with a Democratic Congress throughout his term in office.

EISENHOWER'S "HIDDEN-HAND" PRESIDENCY

IKE   Born in Denison, Texas, in 1890, Dwight David Eisenhower grew up in Abilene, Kansas, and attended the U.S. Military Academy at West Point, New York. As a general during World War II, he took command of American forces in the European theater and directed the invasion of North Africa in 1942. In 1944 he assumed command of Allied forces in preparation for the invasion of German-controlled Europe. After the war, by then the five-star general of the army, Eisenhower became chief of staff and supreme commander of NATO forces, with a brief interlude as president of Columbia University.

Far from being a "do-nothing" president, as some have charged, Eisenhower was an effective leader. The art of leadership, he once explained, required "persuasion—and conciliation—and education—and patience. That's the only kind of leadership I know—or believe in—or will practice." The public image of Ike was warm, sincere, and unpretentious, a man who rose above partisan politics. Those who were close to him have presented another side, however. When provoked, the genial general could unleash a fiery temper and release a stream of scalding profanity. One student of Eisenhower's leadership techniques has spoken of a "hidden-hand" presidency, in which Ike deliberately cultivated a public image of passivity to cloak his active involvement in policy decisions.

"DYNAMIC CONSERVATISM" AT HOME   Eisenhower called his domestic program dynamic conservatism, which meant being "conservative when it comes to money and liberal when it comes to human beings." Budget cutting was a high priority. Eisenhower warned repeatedly against the dangers of "creeping socialism," "huge bureaucracies," and budget deficits. His administration ended wage and price controls and reduced federal farm-price subsidies.

But although Eisenhower chipped away at New Deal programs, his presidency in the end served rather to legitimate the New Deal by keeping its basic structure and premises intact during an era of prosperity. In some ways the administration expanded the New Deal, especially after 1954, when it had the help of Democratic Congresses. Amendments to the Social Security Act in 1954 and 1956 brought coverage to millions in categories formerly excluded: professional people, domestic and clerical workers, farmworkers, and members of the armed forces. The federal minimum wage rose in 1955 from 75¢ to $1 an hour. Federal expenditures for public health rose steadily in the Eisenhower years, and low-income housing continued to be built, although on a much-reduced scale. Some farm-related aid programs were actually expanded.

Despite Eisenhower's disapproval of federal electric-power programs, he continued to support government public-works projects that served the national interest. Two such programs left major monuments to his presidency: the St. Lawrence Seaway and the interstate highways. The St. Lawrence Seaway, opened in 1959 as a joint venture with Canada, allowed oceangoing ships to reach the Great Lakes. The Federal-Aid Highway Act of 1956 authorized the federal government to contribute 90 percent of the cost of building 42,500 miles of limited-access interstate highways to serve the needs of commerce and defense, as well as the convenience of private citizens. The states provided the remaining 10 percent.

CONCLUDING AN ARMISTICE   America's new global responsibilities absorbed much of Eisenhower's attention. The most pressing problem when he entered office was the painful deadlock in the Korean peace talks. To break the stalemate, Eisenhower took a bold stand. In mid-May 1953 he stepped up aerial bombardment of Communist North Korea, then had Secretary of State John Foster Dulles warn the Chinese of his willingness to use atomic bombs. Whether for that reason or others, negotiations moved quickly toward an armistice along the established border just above the 38th parallel and toward a complicated arrangement for an exchange of prisoners that allowed captives to decide whether to accept or refuse repatriation.

On July 26, 1953, Eisenhower announced the conclusion of the Korean armistice agreement. No one knows if he actually would have forced the issue with atomic weapons. Perhaps the more decisive factors in bringing about a settlement were the mounting Chinese losses and the spirit of uncertainty and caution felt by the Russian Communists after the death of Joseph Stalin on March 5, 1953, six weeks after Ike's inauguration.

COMMUNIST PARTY ORGANIZATION U.S.A-FEB. 9, 1950

The Army-McCarthy hearings, June 1954

The attorney Joseph Welch (hand on head) listening incredulously to Senator McCarthy's claims of Communist infiltration of the U.S. Army.

CONCLUDING A WITCH HUNT   The Korean armistice helped to end the meteoric career of Senator Joseph McCarthy. The Wisconsin senator had launched a one-man crusade to root out Communists and spies. Eventually the logic of McCarthy's unscrupulous tactics led to his self-destruction, but not before he had left many careers and reputations in ruins. The Eisenhower Republicans thought their victory in 1952 would curb McCarthy's recklessness, but the senator grew more outlandish in both his charges and his investigative methods.

McCarthy finally overreached himself in the spring of 1954, when as chairman of the Senate's Government Operations Committee he made the absurd charge that the U.S. Army itself was "soft" on communism. The televised Army-McCarthy hearings displayed McCarthy at his worst, scowling at critics, bullying witnesses, repeatedly calling "point of order." He became the perfect foil for the army's gentle but unflappable legal counsel, Joseph Welch, whose rapier wit repeatedly drew blood. On December 2, 1954, the Senate voted 67 to 22 to "condemn" McCarthy for contempt of the Senate. McCarthy's political career collapsed. For all his attacks and inquiries he had never uncovered one Communist in the government. McCarthyism, Eisenhower joked, had become McCarthywasm. To the end, Eisenhower refused to "get down in the gutter with that guy" and sully the dignity of the presidency. He did work resolutely against McCarthy behind the scenes, but some scholars consider his "hidden-hand" approach to have been ineffective at best and cowardly at worst.

Chief Justice Earl Warren

One of the most influential Supreme Court justices of the twentieth century.

Eisenhower believed that espionage posed a real danger to national security. He denied clemency to Julius and Ethel Rosenberg, who had been convicted of passing atomic secrets to the Russians, on the grounds that they "may have condemned to death tens of millions of innocent people." The Rosenbergs were electrocuted in 1953.

INTERNAL SECURITY The anti-Communist crusade survived McCarthy's downfall. Even before 1954, Eisenhower stiffened the government security program that Truman had set up in 1947. In 1953 he issued an executive order broadening the basis for firing subversive government workers, replacing Truman's criterion of "disloyalty" with the new category of "security risk." Under the new edict, federal workers could lose their jobs because of dubious political associations or personal behavior that might make them careless or vulnerable to blackmail. The Supreme Court, however, modified some of the more extreme expressions of this continuation of the Red Scare.

In 1953, Eisenhower appointed as chief justice of the Supreme Court former Republican governor Earl Warren of California, a decision he later pronounced the "biggest damnfool mistake I ever made." Warren, who had seemed safely conservative while in electoral politics, led an active Court on issues of civil rights and liberties. The Warren Court (1953–1969), under the chief justice's influence, became an important force for social and political change in the 1960s. In connection with security programs and loyalty requirements, the Court veered back in the direction of individual rights.

FOREIGN INTERVENTION

DULLES AND FOREIGN POLICY The Eisenhower administration promised new foreign-policy departures under the direction of Secretary of State John Foster Dulles. Grandson of one secretary of state and nephew of another, Dulles pursued a lifetime career as an international lawyer and sometime diplomat. Son of a minister and himself an earnest Presbyterian, Dulles, in the words of the British ambassador, resembled those old zealots of the wars of religion who "saw the world as an arena in which the forces of good and evil were continuously at war." But he was also a man of immense energy, intelligence, and experience.

The foreign-policy planks of the 1952 Republican platform, which Dulles wrote, showed both the moralist and the tactician at work. Truman's policy of "containing" communism was needlessly defensive, Dulles thought. Americans instead should promote the "liberation" of sovereign nations from Soviet domination. Eisenhower was quick to explain, however, that liberating Eastern Europe from Soviet control would not involve military force. He would promote independence "by every peaceful means, but only by peaceful means."

Yet for all his talk of liberating Eastern Europe, Dulles made no significant departure from the containment strategy created under Truman. Instead, he institutionalized containment in the rigid mold of his cold war rhetoric and extended it to the military strategy of deterrence. Dulles's endorsement of "massive retaliation" was an effort to get, in the slogan soon current, "more bang for the buck." By this time both the United States and the Soviet Union had exploded hydrogen bombs. With the new policy of deterrence, what Winston Churchill called a "balance of terror" had replaced the old balance of power. The threat of nuclear holocaust was terrifying, but the notion that the United States would risk such a disaster in response to local wars had little credibility.

Dulles's policy of "brinkmanship" depended for its strategic effect upon those very fears of nuclear disaster. Dulles argued in 1956 that in following a tough policy of confronting communism, a nation sometimes had to "go to the brink" of nuclear war. Such a firm stand had halted aggression in Korea in 1953 when America threatened to use

"Don't Be Afraid—I Can Always Pull You Back."

Secretary of State John Foster Dulles pushes a reluctant America to the brink of war.

atomic weapons. Dulles also employed brinkmanship in Indochina in 1954, when U.S. aircraft carriers moved into the South China Sea "both to deter any Red Chinese attack against Indochina and to provide weapons for instant retaliation."

INDOCHINA: THE BACKGROUND TO WAR   Like the rest of the old colonial world of Asia and Africa, French Indochina experienced a wave of nationalism after World War II, damaging both the power and the prestige of France. By the early 1950s most of British Asia was independent or on its way to independence: India, Pakistan, Ceylon (now Sri Lanka), Burma (now Myanmar), and the Malay States (now Malaysia). The Dutch and the French, however, were less willing to give up their colonies, a situation that created a dilemma for U.S. policy makers. Americans sympathized with the colonial nationalists but wanted Dutch and French help fending off the spread of communism. The Dutch and the French concentrated on maintaining control of their colonial empires, which meant that they had to reconquer areas that had passed from Japanese occupation into the hands of local patriots. The Truman administration had felt obliged to comply with Dutch and French pleas for aid.

Ho Chi Minh

A seasoned revolutionary, Ho Chi Minh cultivated a humble, proletarian image of himself as Uncle Ho, a man of the people.

French Indochina, created in the nineteenth century out of the old kingdoms of Cambodia, Laos, and Vietnam, offered a variation on colonial nationalism. During World War II, opposition to the Japanese occupation of Indochina was led by the Viet Minh (League for the Independence of Vietnam), whose members were nationalists who had fallen under the influence of Communists led by the magnetic rebel Ho Chi Minh. At the end of the war, the Viet Minh controlled part of northern Vietnam, and on September 2, 1945, Ho Chi Minh proclaimed a Democratic Republic of Vietnam, with its capital in Hanoi. Ho had secretly received American help against the Japanese during the war, but his bids for further aid after the war went unanswered. Vietnam was a low priority in U.S. diplomatic concerns, which at the time were focused on restoring western Europe and containing the spread of communism there.

In 1946 the French government recognized Ho's new government as a "free state" within the French-Indochinese union. Before the year was out, however, Ho had opposed French efforts to establish another regime in the southern provinces, and his clash with the French soon expanded into the First Indochina War. This was a troubling development for the U.S. government. On the one hand, the United States resented France's determination to restore colonial rule. On the other hand, Truman was determined to see France become a bulwark against communism in Europe. As a result, the U.S. government acquiesced in France's efforts to crush Vietnamese nationalism.

The Viet Minh movement thereafter became more dependent upon the Soviet Union and Communist China for help. In 1950, with the outbreak of fighting in Korea, the struggle in Vietnam took on the appearance of a battleground in the cold war. When the Korean War ended, American aid to the French in Vietnam, begun by the Truman administration, escalated dramatically. By the end of 1953, the Eisenhower administration was paying about two thirds of the cost of the French war effort in Indochina.

Dien Bien Phu

Captured French soldiers march through the battlefield after their surrender.

But even with lavish U.S. aid the French were unable to suppress the well-organized and tenacious Viet Minh. In 1954 a major French force had been sent to Dien Bien Phu, in the northwest corner of Vietnam, near the Laotian border, in the hope of luring Viet Minh guerrillas into the open and overwhelming them with superior firepower. The French instead found themselves surrounded by a superior force that laid siege to their stronghold.

In March 1954 the French government requested an American air strike to relieve the pressure on Dien Bien Phu. Eisenhower seemed to endorse forceful action when he advanced his "domino theory" at a news conference on April 7. He implied that if Indochina fell to the Communists, the rest of Asia would be next. Eisenhower, however, opposed direct U.S. military action unless the British lent support. When they refused, the president backed away from unilateral action, explaining that it would be a "tragic error to go in alone as a partner of France."

America's decision not to intervene sealed the fate of the besieged French garrison at Dien Bien Phu. On May 7, 1954, the Viet Minh overwhelmed the courageous but vastly outnumbered French resistance. It was the very eve of the day on which an international conference at Geneva took up the question of Indochina. Six weeks later, as French forces continued to suffer defeats in Vietnam, a new French government promised an early settlement. On July 20, representatives of France, Britain, the Soviet Union, the People's Republic of China, and the Viet Minh signed the Geneva Accords and the next day produced their Final Declaration, which proposed to make Laos and Cambodia independent and divide Vietnam at the 17th parallel. The Viet Minh would take power in the north, and the French would remain south of the line until elections in 1956 would reunify Vietnam. American and South Vietnamese representatives refused to join in the accords or sign the Final Declaration.

Eisenhower announced that although the United States "had not itself been party to or bound by the decision taken at the Conference," any renewal of Communist aggression in Vietnam "would be viewed by us as a matter of grave concern." (He failed to note that the United States had agreed at Geneva to "refrain from the threat or use of force to disturb" the agreements that the U.S. refused to sign.) Ho Chi Minh and his government in Hanoi quickly sought to consolidate control throughout the north. In the hinterlands local Communists held kangaroo courts, trying and then executing landowners and confiscating their land. Residents of the north who wished to leave for the south did so with American aid. Over 900,000 refugees, most of them Catholics, relocated in the south, causing staggering logistical problems for the struggling new government there.

Power in the south gravitated to a new premier, Ngo Dinh Diem, a Catholic nationalist who had opposed both the French and the Viet Minh. Diem took office during the Geneva talks, after returning from exile in a New Jersey seminary. In 1954, Eisenhower offered to assist Diem if he would enact democratic reforms and distribute land to the peasants. U.S. aid took the form of training Diem's armed forces and police. Eisenhower remained opposed to the use of U.S. combat troops. He was convinced that such military intervention would bog down into a costly stalemate—as it eventually did.

Instead of instituting comprehensive reforms, however, Diem suppressed his political opponents on both the right and the left, offering little or no land distribution and permitting widespread corruption. In 1956 he refused to join in the elections to reunify Vietnam, and the United States endorsed his decision. But Diem's efforts to eliminate all opposition only played into the hands of the Communists, who found more and more recruits among the discontented peasantry. By 1957 guerrilla forces in the south, known as the Viet Cong, had begun attacks on the Diem government, and in 1960 the resistance formed its own political arm, the National Liberation Front. As guerrilla warfare gradually disrupted South Vietnam, Eisenhower was helpless to do anything but "sink or swim with Ngo Dinh Diem."

REELECTION AND FOREIGN CRISES

As the United States continued to forge postwar alliances and bring pressure to bear on foreign governments by practicing brinkmanship, a new presidential campaign unfolded. Despite having suffered a coronary seizure in the fall of 1955 and undergoing an operation for ileitis (an intestinal inflammation) in early 1956, Eisenhower decided to run for reelection. He retained widespread public support although the Democrats controlled Congress. Meanwhile, new crises required him to take decisive action.

A LANDSLIDE FOR IKE   In 1956 the Republican Convention renominated Eisenhower by acclamation and again named Nixon the vice-presidential candidate. The party platform endorsed Eisenhower's "modern Republicanism." The Democrats turned again to Adlai Stevenson, with a platform that revived party issues: less "favoritism" to big business, repeal of the Taft-Hartley Act, increased aid to farmers, and tax relief for those in low-income brackets.

Neither candidate generated much excitement. The Democrats focused their fire on the heir apparent, Richard Nixon, a "man of many masks." Stevenson roused little enthusiasm for two controversial proposals: to replace military conscription with an all-volunteer army and to ban hydrogen-bomb tests by international agreement. Both involved military questions that put Stevenson at a disadvantage by pitting his judgment against that of a successful former general. Voters handed Eisenhower a landslide victory. In carrying Louisiana, Eisenhower became the first Republican to win a Deep South state since Reconstruction; nationally, he carried all but seven states.

CRISIS IN THE MIDDLE EAST   To forestall Soviet penetration in the Middle East, the Eisenhower-Dulles foreign policy cultivated Arab friendship, and in 1955 Dulles had completed his line of alliances across the northern tier of the Middle East. Under American sponsorship, Britain had joined Turkey, Iraq, Iran, and Pakistan in the Middle East Treaty Organization (METO), or the Baghdad Pact Organization, as the treaty was commonly called. But after Iraq, the only Arab member, withdrew in 1959, the alliance lost its cohesion and credibility. The Arab states remained aloof from the organization. These were the states of the Arab League (Egypt, Jordan, Lebanon, Syria, Iraq, Saudi Arabia, and Yemen), which had warred on Israel in 1948–1949 and remained committed to its destruction.

The most fateful developments in the Middle East turned on the rise of the Egyptian general Gamal Abdel Nasser, who overthrew King Farouk in 1952. Nasser's nationalist regime soon pressed for the withdrawal of British forces guarding the Suez Canal, the crucial link between the Mediterranean Sea and the Indian Ocean. Eisenhower and Dulles supported Nasser's demand, and in 1954 an Anglo-Egyptian treaty provided for British withdrawal within twenty months. Ownership of the canal remained with the Anglo-French Suez Canal Company, however.

Nasser, like other leaders of the third world, remained unaligned in the cold war and sought to play both sides off against each other. The United States in turn courted Egyptian support by offering a loan to build a huge hydroelectric plant at Aswān on the Nile River. From the outset the administration's proposal was opposed by Jewish constituencies concerned with Egyptian threats to Israel and by southern congressmen who feared the competition from Egyptian cotton. In 1956, when Nasser increased trade with the Soviet bloc and recognized Communist China, Dulles abruptly canceled the loan offer.

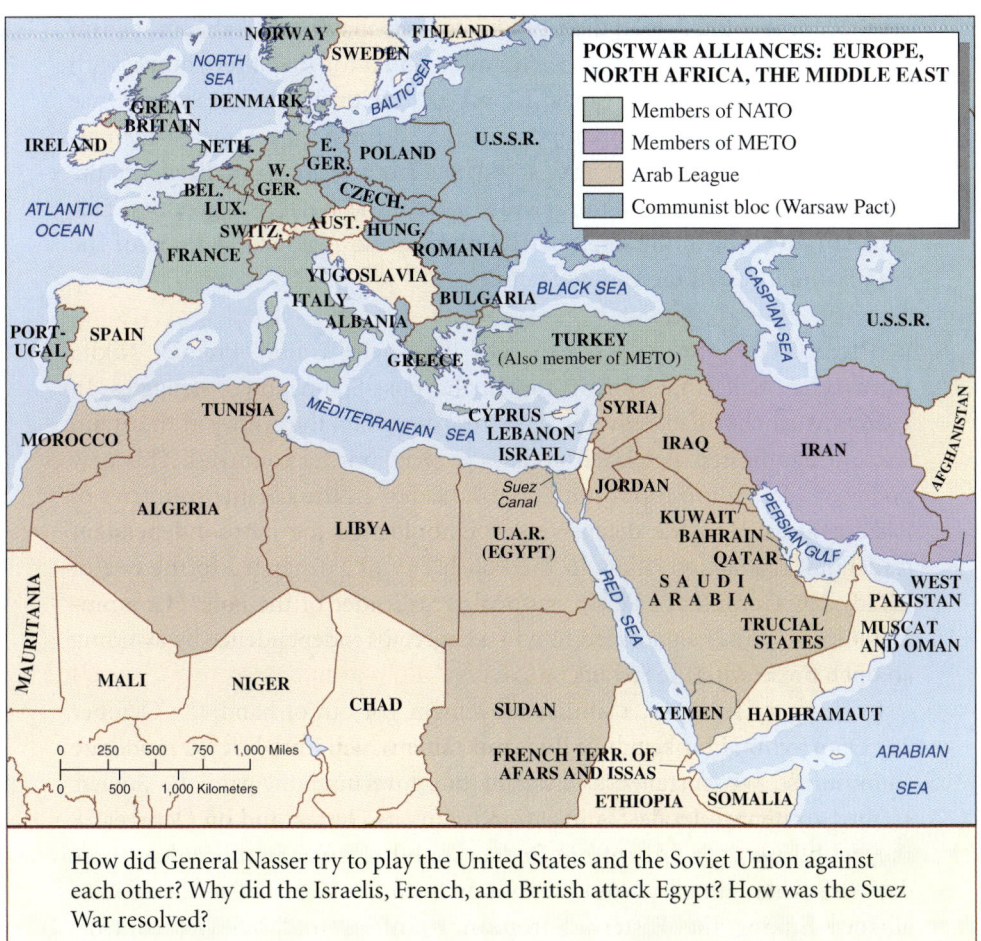

POSTWAR ALLIANCES: EUROPE, NORTH AFRICA, THE MIDDLE EAST

- Members of NATO
- Members of METO
- Arab League
- Communist bloc (Warsaw Pact)

How did General Nasser try to play the United States and the Soviet Union against each other? Why did the Israelis, French, and British attack Egypt? How was the Suez War resolved?

The outcome was far from a triumph of American diplomacy. The chief victims, it turned out, were Anglo-French interests in the Suez. Unable to retaliate against the United States, Nasser took control of the Suez Canal Company. The British and the French were furious. While negotiations dragged on, Israeli forces invaded the Gaza Strip and the Sinai Peninsula. Ostensibly their aim was to root out Arab guerrillas, but actually it was to synchronize with the British and the French, who began bombing Egyptian air bases and occupied Port Said, at the northern end of the canal.

The Suez War put the United States in a quandary. Either the administration could support its Western allies and see the troublesome Nasser crushed, or it could defend the UN Charter and champion Arab nationalism against imperialist aggression. Eisenhower opted for the latter course, with the unusual result that the Soviet Union sided with the United States. Once the threat of American embargoes had forced the Anglo-French-Israeli alliance to halt its advance against Egypt, the Soviets capitalized on the situation by threatening to use missiles against the Western aggressors. This belated bravado won for the Soviet Union in the Arab world some of the credit actually owed the United States.

REPRESSION IN HUNGARY   In the Soviet Union, Premier Nikita Khrushchev had come out on top in the post-Stalin power struggles. In 1956, Khrushchev had delivered a "secret" speech on the crimes of the Stalin era and had hinted at relaxed policies in neighboring countries. This new policy of "de-Stalinization" put Stalinist leaders in the satellite countries of Eastern Europe on the defensive and emboldened the more independent leaders to take action. Riots in the Polish city of Poznań led to the rise of Władysław Gomułka, a Polish nationalist, as leader of the Polish Communist party. Gomułka managed to win a degree of independence by avoiding an open break with the Soviets.

In Hungary, however, a similar movement got out of hand. On October 23, 1956, fighting broke out in Budapest, after which Imre Nagy, a moderate Communist, was installed as head of the government. Again the Soviets seemed content to let de-Stalinization follow its course, and on October 28 they withdrew their forces from Budapest. But Nagy's announcement three days later that Hungary would withdraw from the Warsaw Pact (a military alliance linking the Eastern European countries under Soviet control) brought Soviet tanks back into Budapest. Although Khrushchev was willing to relax relations with the Eastern European satellites, he refused to allow them to break with the Soviet Union or abandon their mutual defense obligations. The Soviets installed a more compliant leader in Hungary, János Kádár, and hauled Nagy off to Moscow, where a firing squad executed him in 1958. It was a tragic ending to an independence movement that at the outset promised the sort of moderation that might have vindicated George Kennan's policy of containment, if not Dulles's notion of liberation.

REACTIONS TO SPUTNIK   On October 4, 1957, the Soviets launched the first satellite, called *Sputnik 1*. Americans, until then complacent about their technical superiority, suddenly discovered an apparent "missile gap." If the Soviets were so advanced in rocketry, then perhaps they could hit American cities with missiles. All along, Eisenhower had known that the "missile gap" was more illusory than real, but he could not reveal the fact that high-altitude American U-2 spy planes were gathering that information.

Soviet success with its Sputnik program prompted the United States to increase defense spending, offer NATO allies intermediate-range ballistic missiles pending development of long-range intercontinental ballistic missiles (ICBMs), set up a new agency to coordinate space efforts, and establish a crash program in science education and military research. In 1958, Congress created the National Aeronautics and Space Administration (NASA) to coordinate research and development in the space program. Before the end of the year, NASA had unveiled a program to put people in orbit, but the first manned U.S. flight, by Commander Alan B. Shepard Jr., did not take place until May 5, 1961. Finally, in 1958, Congress enacted the National Defense Education Act, which authorized federal grants for training, especially in mathematics, science, and modern languages, as well as for student loans and fellowships.

FESTERING PROBLEMS ABROAD

Once the Suez and Hungary crises had faded from the front pages, Eisenhower enjoyed eighteen months of smooth sailing in foreign affairs. Nonetheless, a brief flurry of media attention occurred in 1958 when hostile demonstrations were held in Peru and Venezuela against Vice President Richard Nixon, who was on a goodwill tour of eight Latin American countries. Meanwhile, problems in the Middle East and Europe continued to fester, only to reemerge with new force in 1958. The cold war would again be played out in the Middle East and in Eastern Europe, as well as at America's back door, in Cuba.

THE MIDDLE EAST   By 1958, Congress had approved what came to be called the Eisenhower Doctrine, a resolution that promised to extend economic and military aid to Middle East nations and to use armed force if necessary to assist any such nation against military aggression by any Communist country.

Egypt's president Nasser, meanwhile, had emerged from the Suez crisis with heightened prestige, and in 1958 he created the United Arab Republic by a (short-lived) merger with Syria. Then a leftist coup in Iraq, supposedly inspired by Nasser and the Soviets, threw out the pro-Western government there. Lebanon, already unsettled by internal conflict, appealed to the United States for support to fend off a similar fate. Eisenhower immediately ordered 5,000 marines into Lebanon, limiting them to the capital, Beirut, and its airfield. He proposed to go no farther because, he said later, if the government was not strong enough to hold out with such protection, then "we probably should not be there." In October 1958, once the situation had stabilized and the Lebanese factions had reached a compromise, the U.S. forces withdrew.

BERLIN   The problem of Berlin, an urban island of Western capitalism deep in Soviet-controlled East Germany, continued to fester with little chance of a resolution. Soviet premier Nikita Khrushchev called it a "bone in his throat." West Berlin served as a "showplace" of Western democracy and prosperity in the middle of Communist East Germany, a listening post for Western intelligence gathering, and a funnel through which news and propaganda from the West penetrated what the British leader Winston Churchill had called the iron curtain. Although East Germany had sealed its western frontiers, refugees could still pass from East to West Berlin. On November 10, 1958, however, Khrushchev threatened to give East Germany control of East Berlin and the air lanes into West Berlin. After the deadline he set, May 27, 1959, Western occupation authorities would have to deal with the East German government, in effect recognizing it, or face the possibility of another blockade.

Eisenhower refused to budge from his position on Berlin. At the same time, he refused to engage in saber rattling or even to cancel existing plans to reduce the overall size of the army. Khrushchev, it turned out, was no more eager for confrontation than Eisenhower. Khrushchev's deadline passed almost unnoticed. In September 1959 the Soviet premier visited the United States, stopping in New York, Washington, D.C., Los Angeles, San Francisco, and Iowa. In talks with Eisenhower, he endorsed "peaceful coexistence," and Eisenhower admitted that the Berlin situation was "abnormal." They agreed to discuss the problem at a summit meeting in the spring.

THE U-2 SUMMIT   The planned summit meeting blew up in Eisenhower's face, however. On May 1, 1960, a Soviet rocket brought down an American U-2 spy plane over the Soviet Union. After a period of international jousting with Khrushchev, Eisenhower took personal responsibility for the incident—an unprecedented action for a head of state—and justified it on grounds of national security. At a summit meeting in Paris five days later, Khrushchev called upon the president to repudiate the U-2 flights, which had been going on for more than three years, and "pass severe judgment on those responsible." When Eisenhower refused, Khrushchev left the meeting.

Fidel Castro

Castro (center) became Cuba's Communist premier in 1959, following years of guerrilla warfare against the regime of Fulgencio Batista.
He planned a social and agrarian revolution and opposed foreign
control of the Cuban economy.

CASTRO'S CUBA   Among all of Eisenhower's foreign troubles, the
greatest thorn in his side was the Communist regime of Fidel Castro, which
took power in Cuba on January 1, 1959, after two years of guerrilla warfare
against a right-wing dictator. Castro's forces had the support of many Americans who hoped for a new day of democratic government in Cuba. But
those hopes were dashed when American television reported unfair trials
and summary executions conducted by the victorious leader. When Castro
instituted programs of land reform and nationalization of foreign-owned
property, relations with the United States worsened. Some observers believed, however, that by rejecting Castro's requests for loans and other help,
the U.S. government lost a chance to influence the direction of the Cuban
revolution. Some thought, too, that by acting upon the assumption that
Communists had the upper hand in his movement, the administration may
have ensured that fact.

Castro, on the other hand, eagerly accepted Soviet support. In 1960 he entered a trade agreement to swap Cuban sugar for Soviet oil and machinery.
One of Eisenhower's last acts as president, on January 3, 1961, was to suspend

diplomatic relations with Cuba. The president also secretly authorized the CIA to begin training a force of Cuban refugees for a new revolution. The final decision on the use of that force would rest with the next president, John F. Kennedy.

THE EARLY YEARS OF THE CIVIL RIGHTS MOVEMENT

While the cold war had produced a tense stalemate by the mid-1950s, race relations in the United States threatened to destroy the domestic tranquility masking years of injustice. Eisenhower entered office committed to civil rights in principle. During his first three years, public facilities in Washington, D.C., were desegregated. Beyond that, however, two aspects of the president's philosophy inhibited vigorous action in enforcing the principle of civil rights: his preference for state or local action over federal involvement and his doubt that laws could change deeply embedded racial attitudes. "I don't believe you can change the hearts of men with laws or decisions," he said. Eisenhower's passive stance meant that government leadership in the civil rights field came from the judiciary more than the executive or legislative branch of the government.

In the mid-1930s the NAACP had resolved to test the separate-but-equal doctrine that had upheld racial segregation since the *Plessy* decision in 1896. Charles H. Houston, vice dean of the Howard University Law School, laid the plans, and his former student Thurgood Marshall served as chief NAACP lawyer. They decided to begin their efforts to integrate society by focusing on higher education. But it took almost fifteen years to convince the courts that segregated schooling must end. In *Sweatt v. Painter* (1950), the Supreme Court ruled that a separate black law school in Texas was not equal in quality to the state's whites-only schools. The Court ordered the state to remedy the situation.

THE *BROWN* DECISION   By the early 1950s, challenges to state laws mandating segregation in the public schools were rising through the appellate courts. Five such cases, from Kansas, Delaware, South Carolina, Virgina, and the District of Columbia—usually cited by reference to the first, *Brown v. Board of Education of Topeka, Kansas*—came to the Supreme Court for joint argument by NAACP attorneys in 1952. Chief Justice Earl Warren wrote the opinion, handed down on May 17, 1954, in which a unanimous Court declared that "in the field of public education the doctrine of 'separate but

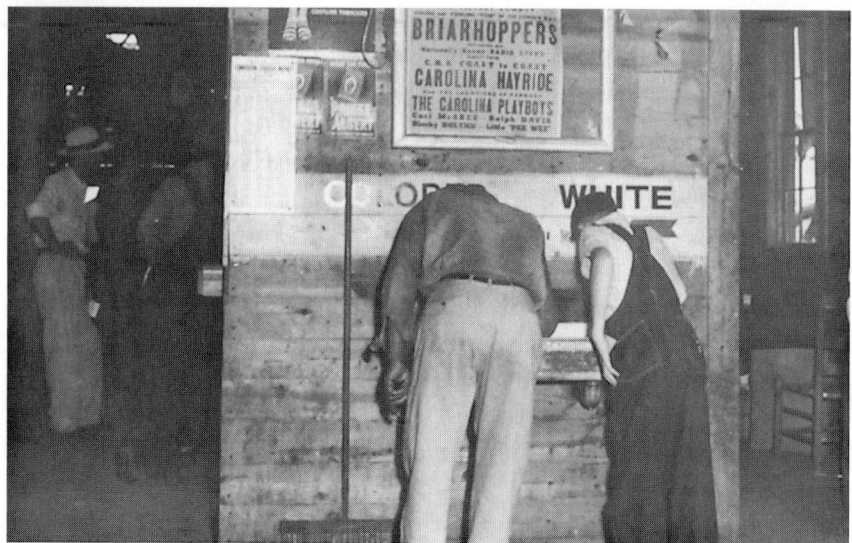

Civil rights stirrings

In the late 1930s the NAACP began to test the constitutionality of racial segregation.

equal' has no place." In support of its opinion, the Court cited sociological and psychological findings demonstrating that even if separate facilities were equal in quality, the mere fact of separating people by race engendered feelings of inferiority. A year later, after further argument, the Court directed that the process of racial integration should move "with all deliberate speed."

But Eisenhower refused to force states to comply with the Court's decisions. Privately he maintained "that the Supreme Court decision *set back* progress in the South *at least fifteen years.* The fellow who tries to tell me you can do these things by *force* is just plain *nuts.*" While token integration began as early as 1954 in the border states, hostility mounted in the Deep South and Virginia, led by the newly formed Citizens' Councils. The Citizens' Councils were middle- and upper-class versions of the Ku Klux Klan that spread quickly across the region and eventually included 250,000 members. Instead of physical violence and intimidation, the Councils used economic coercion against blacks who crossed racial boundaries. African Americans who defied white supremacy would lose their jobs, have their insurance policies canceled, or be denied personal loans or home mortgages. The Citizens' Councils grew so powerful in many communities that membership became almost a prerequisite for an aspiring white politician.

Before the end of 1955, opponents of court-ordered integration grew dangerously belligerent. Virginia senator Harry F. Byrd supplied a rallying cry: "Massive Resistance." In 1956, 101 members of Congress signed a "Southern Manifesto" denouncing the Supreme Court's decision in the *Brown* case as "a clear abuse of judicial power." In six southern states at the end of 1956, not a single black child attended school with whites.

THE MONTGOMERY BUS BOYCOTT   The essential role played by the NAACP and the courts in providing a legal lever for the civil rights movement often overshadows the courageous contributions of individual African Americans who took great personal risks to challenge segregation. In Montgomery, Alabama, for example, on December 1, 1955, Rosa Parks, a black seamstress committed to gaining equal rights, was arrested for refusing to give up her seat on a city bus to a white man. (As was the case in many southern communities, Montgomery had a local ordinance that required blacks to give up a bus or train seat to a white when asked.) The next night, black community leaders met in the Dexter Avenue Baptist Church to organize a massive bus boycott.

In Dexter Avenue's twenty-six-year-old pastor, Martin Luther King Jr., the movement found a charismatic leader. Born in Atlanta, the grandson of a slave and the son of a minister, King possessed intelligence, courage, and eloquence. After graduating from Morehouse College in Atlanta, he attended divinity school and earned a doctorate in philosophy from Boston University before accepting a call to preach in Montgomery. He inspired the civil rights movement with a compelling plea for nonviolent disobedience based upon the Gospels, the writings of Henry David Thoreau, and the example of Mahatma Gandhi in India. To his antagonists he said, "We will soon wear you down by our capacity to suffer, and in winning our freedom we will so appeal to your heart and conscience that we will win you in the process."

The Montgomery bus boycott achieved a remarkable solidarity. For more than a year, blacks used car pools, hitchhiked, or simply walked. But the white civic leaders held out against the boycott and against the pleas of a bus company tired of losing money. The boycotters finally won a federal case they had initiated against bus segregation, and in 1956 the Supreme Court affirmed that "the separate but equal doctrine can no longer be safely followed as a correct statement of the law." The next day, King and other African Americans boarded the buses.

To keep alive the spirit of the boycott, King and a group of associates in 1957 organized the Southern Christian Leadership Conference. Several days

Montgomery, Alabama

Martin Luther King Jr., here facing arrest for leading a civil rights march, advocated nonviolent resistance to racial segregation.

later King found an unexploded dynamite bomb on his front porch. Two hours afterward he addressed his congregation:

> I'm not afraid of anybody this morning. Tell Montgomery they can keep shooting and I'm going to stand up to them; tell Montgomery they can keep bombing and I'm going to stand up to them. If I had to die tomorrow morning I would die happy because I've been to the mountain top and I've seen the promised land and it's going to be here in Montgomery.

THE ROLE OF RELIGION The African American leaders of the civil rights movement were animated by powerful religious beliefs. Ministers were in the vanguard of the movement for racial equality and social justice. As the Reverend Andrew Young, one of King's lieutenants, said, "Ours was an evangelical freedom movement that identified salvation with not just one's personal relationship with God, but a new relationship between people black and white." African American congregations were the seedbed for civil rights

"Freedom" songs

Church congregation singing during the early civil rights movement.

protesters and volunteers. A deep religious faith bolstered those who risked life and freedom by marching, picketing, and protesting racial injustice. Numerous black churches were bombed by white racists who viewed them as the primary source of African American activism. The evangelical tradition in the African American community also provided many of the gospel "freedom" songs that enlivened civil rights marches and protests and gave solace and encouragement to those arrested. "We Shall Overcome," derived from an old gospel hymn, became the anthem of the civil rights movement.

An Atlanta newspaper reporter highlighted the courageous role of black churches in the movement when he asked, "Have they not provided the meeting-places, theme-song, and leaders for the center of non-violent protest?" The contrast with the indifferent attitude of southern white churches was vivid. White churches were "doing nothing at all," said the editor of the *Atlanta Constitution*. He explained that it was "strikingly clear that Christianity and the [black] churches have never been more relevant (taken as a whole)—or less on the sidelines."

THE CIVIL RIGHTS ACT Despite President Eisenhower's reluctance to take the lead in desegregating schools, he supported the right of African Americans to vote. In 1956, hoping to exploit divisions between northern and southern Democrats and to reclaim some of the black vote for the Republicans, Eisenhower proposed legislation that became the Civil Rights Act of 1957, the first civil rights law passed since Reconstruction. It finally got through the Senate, after a year's delay, with the help of majority leader Lyndon B. Johnson, a Texas Democrat who won southern acceptance by watering it down. The Civil Rights Act established the Civil Rights Commission and a new Civil Rights Division in the Justice Department, which could seek injunctions to prevent interference with the right to vote. Yet by 1959 the Civil Rights Act had not added a single southern black to the voting rolls. Neither did the Civil Rights Act of 1960, which provided for federal court referees to register African Americans where a court found a "pattern and practice" of discrimination. This act, too, lacked teeth and depended upon vigorous presidential enforcement to achieve any real results.

DESEGREGATION IN LITTLE ROCK A few weeks after passage of the Civil Rights Act of 1957, Arkansas governor Orval Faubus called out the National Guard to prevent nine African American students from entering Little Rock's Central High School under a federal court order. A conference between the president and the governor proved fruitless, but on court order Governor Faubus withdrew the National Guard. When the students tried to enter the school, a hysterical white mob forced local authorities to remove them. At that point, Eisenhower, who had said two months before that he could not "imagine any set of circumstances that would ever induce me to send federal troops," ordered 1,000 U.S. paratroopers to Little Rock to protect the black students, and he placed the Arkansas National Guard on federal service. The soldiers stayed through the school year.

In the summer of 1958, Faubus decided to close the high schools of Little Rock rather than allow integration, and court proceedings dragged on into 1959 before the schools could be reopened. In that year, massive resistance to integration in Virginia collapsed when both state and federal courts struck down state laws that had cut off funds to integrated schools. Thereafter, massive resistance for the most part was confined to the Deep South, where five states—from South Carolina west through Louisiana—still opposed even token integration.

ASSESSING THE EISENHOWER PRESIDENCY

Dwight Eisenhower entered office in 1953 after being elected in a landslide and held high approval ratings for ending the Korean War and handling foreign crises. He won a second landslide election in 1956. Yet support for the president did not translate into support for his party. Eisenhower's decisive win failed to swing a congressional majority for Republicans in either house, leaving the country in the hands of a Republican president and a Democratic Congress. Eisenhower was thus the first president to face three successive Congresses controlled by the opposition party. This meant that he could manage few initiatives in domestic policy, although he did oversee the admission of the first states that are not contiguous to the continental forty-eight: Alaska became the forty-ninth state on January 3, 1959, and Hawaii became the fiftieth on August 21, 1959.

During Eisenhower's second term the country experienced an economic slump, a drop in tax revenues, and a large federal deficit. The country also suffered the embarrassments of the U-2 spy-plane incident and Cuba's falling into the Communist orbit. Emotional issues such as civil rights, defense policy, and corrupt aides compounded Eisenhower's troubles. The president's reluctance to enforce civil rights rulings and his unwillingness to speak out on behalf of racial equality undermined his efforts to promote the general welfare. One observer called the Eisenhower years "the time of the great postponement," during which the president left domestic and foreign policies "about where he found them in 1953."

Yet opinion of Eisenhower's presidency has improved with time. Even critics now grant that Eisenhower succeeded in ending the war in Korea and settling the dust raised by Senator Joseph McCarthy. Although Eisenhower failed to end the cold war and in fact institutionalized global confrontation, he did sense the limits of American power and kept its application to low-risk situations. He also tried to restrain the arms race. Although he took few initiatives in addressing social and racial issues, he did sustain the major innovations of the New Deal. Although he tolerated unemployment of as much as 7 percent, he saw to it that inflation remained minimal during his two terms.

Eisenhower's January 17, 1961, farewell address to the American people showed his remarkable foresight in his own area of expertise, the military. He highlighted, perhaps better than anyone else could have, the dangers of a huge military establishment in a time of peace: "In the councils of government we must guard against the acquisition of unwarranted influence, whether sought or unsought, by the military-industrial complex. The potential for the disastrous rise of misplaced power exists and will persist." Eisenhower confessed that his great disappointment was that he could affirm only that "war has been avoided," not that "a lasting peace is in sight."

End of Chapter Review

CHAPTER SUMMARY

- **Eisenhower's Dynamic Conservatism** As president, Eisenhower accepted most of the New Deal's social legislation. He expanded Social Security coverage and launched ambitious public works programs, such as the construction of the interstate highway system and the St. Lawrence Seaway. He opposed massive government spending and large budget deficits, however, so he cut spending on an array of domestic programs and on national defense.

- **American Foreign Policy in the 1950s** Eisenhower continued the policy of containment to stem the spread of communism. His first major foreign-policy accomplishment in this respect was to end the fighting in Korea. To confront Soviet aggression, Eisenhower relied on nuclear deterrence, which allowed for reductions in conventional military forces and thus led to budgetary savings.

- **Communism in S.E. Asia** After World War II, Truman and then Eisenhower believed that the French should regain control of Indochina so that the country could serve as a barrier against the spread of communism in Southeast Asia. Ho Chi Minh, a nationalist and a Communist, led the Viet Minh movement, which in 1954 defeated the French at the Battle of Dien Bien Phu. The Geneva Accords, adopted in 1954, temporarily divided the country in half, with the Viet Minh ruling in the north and the dictator Ngo Dinh Diem ruling in the south. Communist guerrilla forces, known as the Viet Cong, found recruits among discontented South Vietnamese and attacked the Diem government. By 1957 the Eisenhower administration had no option but to "sink or swim with Ngo Dinh Diem."

- **Civil Rights Movement** In the 1930s the National Association for the Advancement of Colored People began laying the foundation for challenging the "separate but equal" doctrine, through a series of test cases in federal courts. By the early 1950s, the NAACP was targeting state-mandated segregation in public schools. In the most significant case, *Brown v. Board of Education*, the Court nullified the "separate but equal" doctrine. Whereas white southerners defended their old way of life, rallying to a call for "massive resistance," African Americans and other proponents of desegregation sought to achieve integration through nonviolent means. The Montgomery, Alabama, bus boycott was significant because it was the first large-scale—and ultimately successful—instance of nonviolent resistance and because it galvanized the civil rights movement under the leadership of Dr. Martin Luther King Jr. The desegregation of a public high school in Little Rock, Arkansas, marked another turning point when President Eisenhower reluctantly threw the support of the federal government behind the integrationists.

CHRONOLOGY

March 1953	Joseph Stalin dies
June 1953	Ethel and Julius Rosenberg are executed
July 1953	Armistice is reached in Korea
April–July 1954	Army-McCarthy hearings are televised
1954	Supreme Court issues ruling in *Brown v. Board of Education of Topeka, Kansas*
July 1954	Geneva Accords propose a settlement to the war in Indochina
December 1955	Montgomery, Alabama, bus boycott begins
1956	In Suez War, Israel, Britain, and France attack Egypt
1956	Hungarian revolt against the Warsaw Pact is quickly suppressed
1957	Federal troops are ordered to guarantee the safety of students attempting to integrate Central High School in Little Rock, Arkansas
1957	Soviet Union launches *Sputnik 1*
1960	U-2 incident reveals that the United States is flying spy planes over the Soviet Union

KEY TERMS & NAMES

34

NEW FRONTIERS: POLITICS AND SOCIAL CHANGE IN THE 1960s

FOCUS QUESTIONS wwnorton.com/studyspace

- What were the goals of John F. Kennedy's New Frontier program, and how successful was it?
- What was the aim of Lyndon Johnson's Great Society program, and how successful was it?
- What were the achievements of the civil rights movement by 1968?
- Why did the United States become increasingly involved in Vietnam?
- Why and how did Kennedy attempt to combat communism in Cuba?

For those pundits who considered the social and political climate of the 1950s dull, the following decade would provide a striking contrast. The 1960s were years of extraordinary turbulence and innovation in public affairs—as well as tragedy and trauma. Many social ills that had been simmering for decades suddenly forced their way onto the national agenda. At the same time, the deeply entrenched assumptions of the cold war ideology directed against communism led the country into the longest, most controversial, and least successful war in its history.

THE NEW FRONTIER

KENNEDY VERSUS NIXON In 1960 there was little sense of dramatic change on the horizon. The presidential election that year featured two candidates—Richard M. Nixon and John F. Kennedy—with very different personalities and backgrounds. Though better known than Kennedy because of his eight years as Eisenhower's vice president, Nixon had developed the reputation of a cunning chameleon, the "Tricky Dick" who concealed his duplicity behind a series of masks.

Nixon possessed great ability, however, as well as tenacious energy and a compulsive love for combative politics. Born in suburban Los Angeles in 1913, he grew up in a Quaker family that struggled to make ends meet. After law school and military service in the Pacific during World War II, Nixon jumped into the political arena in 1946 as a Republican and surprised observers by unseating a popular congressman in southern California. He arrived in Washington eager to reverse the tide of New Deal liberalism. Four years later he won election to the Senate. In his campaigns, Nixon unleashed scurrilous personal attacks on his opponents, shrewdly manipulating the growing anti-Communist hysteria. Yet Nixon became a respected, effective legislator, and by 1950 he was the most requested Republican speaker in the country. His rapid rise to political stardom led to his being offered the vice-presidential nomination in 1952 and 1956. He was an active, highly visible vice president.

Although Kennedy lacked such experience and exposure, he boasted an abundance of assets, including a widely publicized record of heroism in World War II, a glamorous wife, a Harvard education, and a large, wealthy, Roman Catholic family. Yet the handsome forty-three-year-old candidate lacked national prominence and political distinction. Kennedy's record in the Senate was mediocre.

During his campaign for the 1960 Democratic presidential nomination, however, Kennedy had shown that he had energy, grace, and ambition. As the first Catholic to run for the presidency since Al Smith in 1928, he strove to dispel the impression that his religion was a major political liability. In his acceptance speech at the Democratic Convention, Kennedy found the stirring rhetoric that would stamp the rest of his campaign and his presidency: "We stand today on the edge of a New Frontier—the frontier of unknown opportunities and perils—a frontier of unfulfilled hopes and threats."

The turning point in the presidential campaign came when Richard Nixon agreed to debate his less prominent opponent on television. During the first of four debates, some 70 million viewers saw Nixon, still weak from a recent illness, perspiring heavily and looking haggard, uneasy, and even sinister before the camera. Kennedy, on the other hand, projected a cool poise that made him seem equal, if not superior, in his fitness for the office. Kennedy's popularity immediately shot up in the polls.

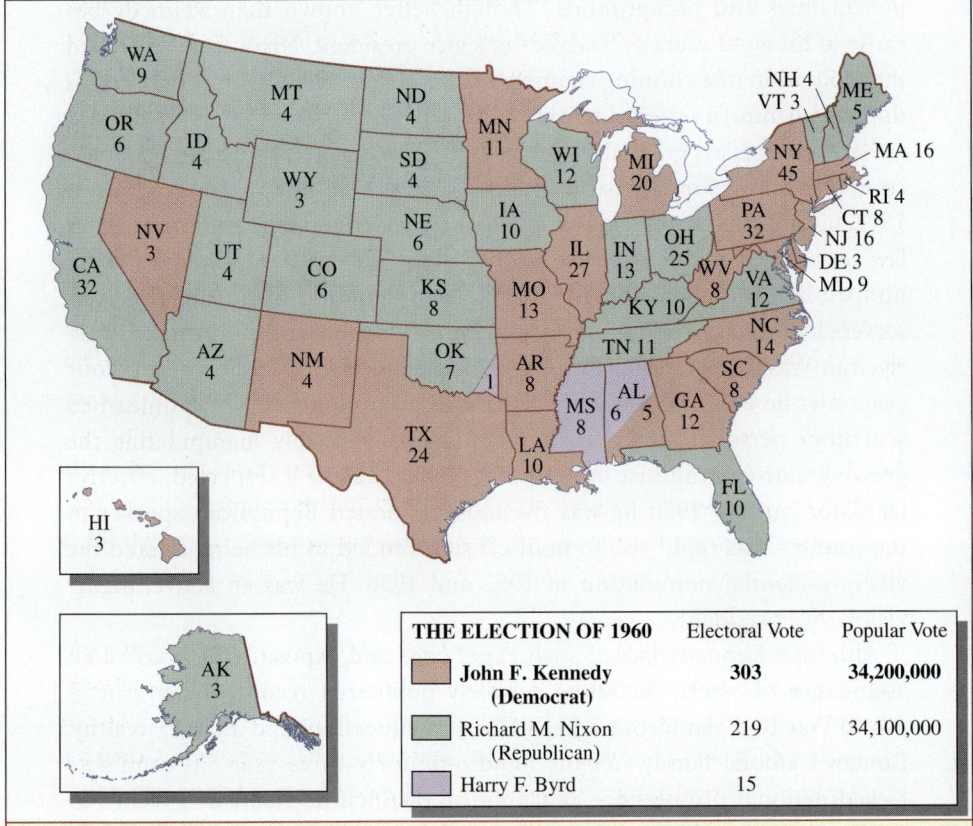

THE ELECTION OF 1960	Electoral Vote	Popular Vote
John F. Kennedy (Democrat)	303	34,200,000
Richard M. Nixon (Republican)	219	34,100,000
Harry F. Byrd	15	

How did the election of 1960 represent a sea change in American presidential politics? What event was the turning point in the campaign? How did John F. Kennedy win the election in spite of winning fewer states than Richard M. Nixon?

When the votes were counted, Kennedy and his running mate, Lyndon Johnson of Texas, had won the closest presidential election since 1888. The winning margin was only 118,574 votes out of more than 68 million cast. Kennedy's wide lead in the electoral vote, 303 to 219, belied the paper-thin margin in several key states.

THE NEW ADMINISTRATION   John F. Kennedy was the youngest person ever elected president, and he sought to attract to his cabinet the "best and the brightest" minds, men who would inject a tough, dispassionate, pragmatic, and vigorous outlook into government affairs. To that end he asked Robert McNamara, one of the whiz kids who had reorganized the Ford Motor Company, to bring his managerial magic to bear on the Department of Defense. Kennedy appointed Harvard professor McGeorge Bundy, whom he called "the second smartest man I know," as special assistant for national security affairs and chose as his secretary of state Dean Rusk, a career diplomat and former Rhodes scholar. When critics attacked the appointment of Kennedy's thirty-five-year-old brother Robert as attorney general, the president quipped, "I don't see what's wrong with giving Bobby a little experience before he goes into law practice."

The inaugural ceremonies set the tone of elegance and youthful vigor that would come to be called the Kennedy style. After the poet Robert Frost paid tribute to the administration in verse, Kennedy dazzled listeners with his uplifting rhetoric. "Let every nation know," he proclaimed, ". . . that we shall pay any price, bear any burden, meet any hardship, support any friend, oppose any foe, to assure the survival and success of liberty. And so, my fellow Americans: ask not what your country can do for you—ask what you can do for your country." Spines tingled; the glittering atmosphere and inspiring language of the inauguration seemed to herald an era of fresh promise and youthful energy.

THE KENNEDY RECORD Despite his idealistic rhetoric, however, Kennedy had a difficult time launching his New Frontier domestic program. Elected by a razor-thin margin, he did not have a popular mandate. Nor did he show much skill in dealing with a Democratic majority in a Congress controlled by conservative southerners. Congress blocked his efforts to increase federal aid to education, provide health insurance for the aged, and create a department of urban affairs.

Administration proposals did nevertheless win some notable victories in Congress. They included a new Housing Act that appropriated nearly $5 billion for urban renewal over four years, an increase in the minimum wage, and enhanced Social Security benefits. Just two months into his administration, Kennedy launched the celebrated Peace Corps to supply volunteers for educational and technical service in underdeveloped countries. Kennedy also won support for an accelerated space program to land astronauts on the moon before the end of the decade. Congress readily approved a series of broad foreign-aid programs to help Latin American nations, dubbed the Alliance for Progress. Another important initiative was a bold tax-reduction bill intended to accelerate economic growth. Passed in 1964, after Kennedy's death, it provided a surprisingly potent boost to the economy. Perhaps Kennedy's most significant legislative accomplishment was the Trade Expansion Act of 1962, which eventually led to tariff cuts averaging 35 percent on goods traded between the United States and the European Economic Community (the Common Market).

Kennedy-Nixon debates

John Kennedy's poise and precision in the debates with Richard Nixon impressed viewers and voters.

THE WARREN COURT Under Chief Justice Earl Warren the Supreme Court continued to be a decisive influence on domestic life during the 1960s. In *Gideon v. Wainwright* (1963), the Court required that every felony defendant be provided a lawyer regardless of the defendant's ability to pay. In 1964 the Court ruled in *Escobedo v. Illinois* that a person accused of a crime must also be allowed to consult a lawyer before being interrogated by police. Two years later, in *Miranda v. Arizona,* the Court issued perhaps its most bitterly criticized ruling when it ordered that an accused person in police custody be informed of certain basic rights: the right to remain silent; the right to know that anything said can be used against the individual in court; and the right to have a defense attorney present during interrogation. In addition, the Court established rules for police to follow in informing suspects of their legal rights before questioning could begin.

EXPANSION OF THE CIVIL RIGHTS MOVEMENT

The most important developments in domestic life during the 1960s occurred in civil rights. John F. Kennedy was initially reluctant to challenge conservative southern Democrats on the race issue. Nor was he as personally committed to civil rights as his younger brother Robert, the attorney general. Despite a few dramatic gestures of support for African American leaders, President Kennedy only belatedly grasped the moral and emotional significance of what would become the most widespread reform movement of the decade. Eventually, however, his conscience was pricked by the grassroots civil rights movement led by Martin Luther King Jr., a movement that would profoundly change the contours of American life.

SIT-INS AND FREEDOM RIDES   After the Montgomery bus boycott of 1955–1956, King's philosophy of "militant nonviolence" inspired thousands to challenge segregation and discrimination with direct action. At the same time, lawsuits to desegregate the schools activated thousands of parents and young people. The momentum generated a genuine mass movement when four black college students courageously sat down and demanded service at a "whites-only" Woolworth's lunch counter in Greensboro, North Carolina, on February 1, 1960. Within a week the "sit-in" movement had spread to six more towns in the state, and within two months demonstrations had occurred in fifty-four cities in nine states.

In 1960, student activists, black and white, formed the Student Nonviolent Coordinating Committee (SNCC), which worked with King's Southern Christian Leadership Conference (SCLC) to spread the civil rights movement. The sit-ins became "kneel-ins" at churches and "wade-ins" at segregated public swimming pools. During the year after the Greensboro sit-ins, over 3,600 black and white activists spent time in jail. In many communities they were struck with clubs, poked with cattle prods, pelted with rocks, burned with cigarettes, and subjected to unending verbal abuse. Nonetheless, the protesters refused to retaliate.

In May 1961 the Congress of Racial Equality (CORE) sent a group of black and white "freedom riders" on buses to test a federal ruling that had banned segregation on buses and trains and in their depots. In Alabama, mobs attacked the young travelers with fists and pipes, burned one of the buses, and assaulted Justice Department observers, but the demonstrators persisted, drawing national attention and generating new support for their cause. Yet President Kennedy was not inspired by the courageous freedom riders. Preoccupied with a crisis in Berlin, he ordered an aide to tell them to "call it off." Former president Harry Truman dismissed the bus activists northern "busybodies." It fell to Attorney General Robert Kennedy to use federal marshals to protect the freedom riders during the summer of 1961.

FEDERAL INTERVENTION In 1962, the racist Governor Ross Barnett of Mississippi, a rabid racist who believed that God made "the Negro different to punish him," defied a court order by refusing to allow James Meredith, an African American student, to enroll at the University of Mississippi. Attorney General Robert Kennedy sent federal marshals to enforce the law. Federal troops then intervened, and Meredith was registered at Ole Miss, but only after two deaths and many injuries.

Everywhere, it seemed, African American activists and white supporters were challenging deeply entrenched patterns of segregation and prejudice. In 1963, Martin Luther King launched a series of demonstrations in Birmingham, Alabama, where Police Commissioner Eugene "Bull" Connor proved the perfect foil for King's tactic of nonviolent civil disobedience. Connor's policemen used dogs, tear gas, electric cattle prods, and fire hoses on the protesters while millions of Americans watched the confrontations on television.

King, who was arrested and jailed during the demonstrations, wrote his now-famous Letter from a Birmingham City Jail, a stirring defense of his nonviolent strategy that became a classic of the civil rights movement. "One who breaks an unjust law," he stressed, "must do so openly, lovingly, and

Birmingham, Alabama, May 1963

Eugene "Bull" Connor's police unleash dogs on civil rights demonstrators.

with a willingness to accept the penalty." In his letter, King signaled a shift in his strategy for social change. Heretofore he had emphasized the need to educate southern whites about the injustice of segregation and other patterns of discrimination. Now he focused more on gaining federal enforcement of the law and new legislation by provoking racists to display their violent hatred in public.

Southern traditionalists defied efforts to promote racial integration. In 1963, Alabama Governor George Wallace dramatically stood in the doorway of a building at the University of Alabama to block the enrollment of African American students, but he stepped aside in the face of insistent federal marshals. Later that night, NAACP official Medgar Evers was shot to death as he returned to his home in Jackson, Mississippi.

The high point of the integrationist phase of the civil rights movement occurred on August 28, 1963, when over 200,000 blacks and whites marched down the Mall in Washington, D.C., toward the Lincoln Memorial, singing "We Shall Overcome." The March on Washington for Jobs and Freedom was the largest civil rights demonstration in American history. Standing in front of Lincoln's statue, Martin Luther King delivered one of the century's memorable speeches: "Even though we face the difficulties of today and tomorrow, I still have a dream. It is a dream chiefly rooted in the American dream . . . one day . . . the sons of former slaves and the sons of former slaveowners will be able to sit together at the table of brotherhood." Such racial harmony had not yet arrived, however. Two weeks later a bomb exploded in a Birmingham church, killing four African American girls who had arrived early for Sunday school.

Yet King's dream—shared and promoted by thousands of other activists—survived. The intransigence and violence that civil rights workers encountered won converts to their cause across the country and forced whites nationwide to confront the myths of their own virtue and innocence with the brutal facts of racial hatred. Persuaded by his brother Robert, a man of greater conviction, compassion, and vision, and by the pressure of events, President Kennedy finally decided that enforcement of existing statutes was not enough; new legislation was needed to deal with the race question. In 1963 he told the nation that racial discrimination "has no place in American life or law," and he endorsed an ambitious civil rights bill intended to end discrimination in public facilities, desegregate public schools, and protect black voters. Southern conservatives, however, quickly blocked the bill in Congress. The backlash that had surfaced in the South in the 1930s in response to the expansion of Franklin Roosevelt's New Deal continued to shape Democratic politics in the region.

"I Have a Dream," August 28, 1963

Protesters in the March on Washington make their way to the Lincoln Memorial, where Martin Luther King Jr. delivered his now-famous speech.

Although Kennedy saw his support among southern voters plummet, he remained committed to the bill. As he told Martin Luther King: "This is a very serious fight. We're in this up to the neck. The worst trouble would be to lose the fight in Congress. . . . A good many programs I care about may go down the drain as a result of this [bill]—We may all go down the drain . . . so we are putting a lot on the line."

FOREIGN FRONTIERS

EARLY SETBACKS John F. Kennedy's record in foreign affairs was mixed, more spectacularly so than his domestic record. Upon taking office, he discovered that the CIA had in the works a secret operation designed to prepare 1,500 anti-Castro Cubans for an invasion of their homeland. The Joint Chiefs of Staff endorsed the plan; analysts reported that the invasion would inspire Cubans on the island to rebel against Castro. But the scheme, poorly conceived and poorly executed, had little chance of succeeding. When the invasion force landed at Cuba's Bay of Pigs on April 17, 1961, it was brutally subdued in two days, and over 1,100 men were captured.

Two months after the Bay of Pigs disaster, Kennedy met Soviet premier Nikita Khrushchev in Vienna. The volatile Khrushchev tried to bully the inexperienced Kennedy. He threatened to limit Western access to Berlin, the divided city located 100 miles within Communist East Germany. Kennedy was shaken by the aggressive Soviet stand. Upon his return home, he demonstrated his resolve by mobilizing Army Reserve and National Guard units. The Soviets responded by erecting the Berlin Wall, isolating West Berlin and preventing all movement between the two parts of the city.

THE CUBAN MISSILE CRISIS A year later, in the fall of 1962, Khrushchev and the Soviets posed another serious challenge, this time just ninety miles south of Florida. Khrushchev granted Fidel Castro's request for nuclear missiles in Cuba to protect the island from future American-sponsored invasions and to redress the strategic imbalance caused by the presence of U.S. missiles in Turkey aimed at the Soviet Union. While such missiles would hardly alter the worldwide military balance, they would be placed in areas not covered by American radar systems and, if launched, would go undetected, arriving without warning. More important to Kennedy was the psychological effect of American acquiescence to a Soviet presence on its doorstep. Khrushchev's apparent purpose was to demonstrate his toughness to Chinese and Soviet critics of his earlier advocacy of peaceful coexistence. But he misjudged the American response.

On October 14, 1962, U.S. intelligence flights discovered Soviet missile sites under construction in Cuba. Although the Soviet actions violated no law or treaty, the administration immediately decided that the missiles had to be removed; the only question was how. In a series of secret meetings, the Executive Committee of the National Security Council debated whether to launch a "surgical" air strike or a naval blockade of Cuba. President Kennedy wisely opted for a blockade, but since that would technically represent an act of war, it was called a quarantine. It offered the advantage of forcing the Soviets to shoot first, if matters came to that, and left open options of stronger action. Thus, Monday, October 22, began the most perilous week in world history. On that day the president announced the discovery of the missile sites in Cuba and the U.S. naval quarantine of the island nation.

Tensions grew as Khrushchev blustered that Kennedy had pushed humankind "toward the abyss of a world nuclear-missile war." Soviet ships, he declared, would ignore the quarantine. But on Wednesday, October 24, five

Soviet supply ships stopped short of the quarantine line. Two days later the Soviets offered to withdraw the missiles in return for a public pledge by the United States not to invade Cuba.

In the aftermath of the crisis, the United States took several symbolic steps to relax tensions: it agreed to sell surplus wheat to the Soviets; it installed a "hot-line" telephone between Washington and Moscow to provide instant contact between the heads of government; and it removed obsolete missiles from Turkey, Italy, and Britain. The United States also negotiated a treaty with Soviet and British representatives to end nuclear testing in the atmosphere. The treaty, ratified in September 1963, was an important move toward greater international cooperation on nuclear proliferation.

KENNEDY AND VIETNAM   As tensions with the Soviet Union were easing, a crisis was developing in Southeast Asia. Events there would lead to the greatest American foreign-policy debacle of the century. During John Kennedy's "Thousand Days" in office, the turmoil of Indochina never preoccupied public attention for any extended period, but it dominated international diplomatic debates from the time the administration entered office.

In South Vietnam, Premier Ngo Dinh Diem had failed to deliver promised social and economic reforms. His repressive tactics, directed not only against Communists but also against the Buddhist majority and other critics, played into the hands of his enemies. In 1961, White House assistant Walt Rostow and General Maxwell Taylor, the first in a long line of presidential emissaries to South Vietnam's capital, Saigon, proposed a major increase in the U.S. military presence, but Kennedy instead dispatched more military "advisers." When he took office, there had been 2,000 U.S. troops in South Vietnam; by the end of 1963, there were 16,000, none of whom had been officially committed to battle.

But the American-supported Diem regime continued to be its own worst enemy. By mid-1963 growing Buddhist demonstrations against Diem ignited the public discontent in South Vietnam and created consternation abroad. The spectacle of Buddhist monks setting themselves on fire on Saigon streets in protest of Diem's iron-fisted rule shocked Americans but brought from the Diem regime only a sarcastic comment by the premier's sister-in-law about "barbecued monks."

By the fall of 1963, the Kennedy administration had decided that Diem was a lost cause. When dissident Vietnamese generals proposed a coup d'état, the U.S. ambassador assured them that the Kennedy administration would not stand in the way. On November 1 the insurgent military leaders seized the government and murdered Diem. Yet the generals provided no more stability than had earlier regimes, and successive coups set South Vietnam's government spinning from one military leader to another.

KENNEDY'S ASSASSINATION   By the fall of 1963, President Kennedy had come to acknowledge the intractability of the situation in Vietnam. Some of his aides later argued that Kennedy would never have allowed a dramatic escalation of U.S. military involvement in Vietnam. Others strongly disagreed. The question is endless because it is unanswerable, and it is unanswerable because on November 22, 1963, while visiting Dallas, Texas, Kennedy was shot twice in the throat and head and died almost immediately. A few hours later Dallas police arrested Lee Harvey Oswald, a twenty-four-year-old ex-marine drifter who had worked in the Texas School Book Depository, from which the shots were fired at Kennedy. Yet before Oswald could be thoroughly interrogated, he, too, was killed. Two days after his arrest, as television cameras covered his transfer from one jail to another, Jack Ruby, a Dallas nightclub owner, stepped from the crowd of onlookers and fatally shot Oswald in the abdomen.

Oswald's death ignited a controversy over the assassination that still simmers. In December 1963, President Johnson appointed a commission to investigate Kennedy's murder. Headed by Chief Justice Earl Warren, it concluded that Oswald had acted alone. Yet many people were (and are) not convinced, and since 1963 dozens of conspiracy theories have been proposed. Some blame the CIA or the Mafia; others point to Fidel Castro, whom the CIA had once tried to assassinate. Still others insist that Cuban exiles in Miami, angered by Kennedy's failure to rescue their comrades during the Bay of Pigs fiasco, were behind the assassination. Whatever the actual story of the assassination, Kennedy's tragic death enshrined him in the public imagination as a martyred leader cut down in the prime of his life.

LYNDON JOHNSON AND THE GREAT SOCIETY

Lyndon Johnson took the presidential oath of office on board the plane that brought John F. Kennedy's body back to Washington from Dallas. Fifty-five years old, Johnson had spent twenty-six years on the Washington scene and had served nearly a decade as Senate Democratic leader, where he had displayed the greatest gift for compromise since Henry Clay. Johnson brought to the White House a marked change of style from his predecessor. A self-made and self-centered man, he had used gritty determination and shrewd manipulation to work his way out of a hardscrabble rural Texas homeland to become one of Washington's most powerful figures. He had none of Kennedy's elegance. He was a bundle of conflicting elements: earthy, idealistic, domineering, insecure, gregarious, ruthless, and compassionate. His ego was as huge as his ambition.

Those who viewed Johnson as a stereotypical southern conservative ignored his long-standing admiration for Franklin Roosevelt, the depth of his concern for the poor, and his heartfelt commitment to the cause of civil rights. Though a novice in foreign affairs, in the domestic arena during the 1950s Johnson had been unsurpassed in his ability to shepherd legislation through the gauntlet of special-interest lobbyists and Congress. He had once bragged that "Ike couldn't pass the Lord's Prayer in Congress without me." Johnson wanted to be the greatest president, the one who did the most good for the most people. And he would let nothing stand in the way of his grand ambition. He ended up promising far more than he could accomplish, raising false hopes and stoking fiery resentments.

POLITICS AND POVERTY Domestic policy was Johnson's first priority. He exploited the nation's grief after the assassination by declaring that Kennedy's legislative program, stymied in congressional committees,

The Johnson treatment

Lyndon Johnson used powerful body language to intimidate and manipulate anyone who dared disagree with him.

would be passed. Johnson loved the political infighting and legislative detail that Kennedy had loathed. The logjam in Congress that had blocked Kennedy's program broke under Johnson's forceful leadership, and a torrent of legislation poured through. At the top of Johnson's agenda were the stalled measures for a tax reduction and civil rights. In 1962, Kennedy had announced a then-unusual plan to jump-start the sluggish economy: a tax cut to stimulate consumer spending. Congressional Republicans opposed the idea because it would increase the federal budget deficit. And polls showed that public opinion was also skeptical. So

Kennedy had postponed the proposed tax cut for a year; it was still bogged down in Congress when the president was assassinated. Johnson broke the logjam, and the Revenue Act of 1964 provided a needed boost to the economy.

Likewise, the Civil Rights Act that Kennedy had presented to Congress in 1963 became law in 1964 through Johnson's forceful leadership. The bill prohibited racial segregation in public facilities such as bus terminals, restaurants, theaters, and hotels. And it outlawed long-standing racial discrimination in the registration of voters and the hiring of employees. President Johnson revived bipartisan efforts on its behalf, and the bill passed the House in February 1964. In the Senate, however, southern legislators launched a filibuster that lasted two months. Johnson finally prevailed, and the civil rights bill became law on July 2. But the new president knew that it had come at a political price. On the night after signing it, Johnson told an aide that "we have just delivered the South to the Republican Party for a long time to come."

The Civil Rights Act of 1964

President Johnson reaches to shake hands with Dr. Martin Luther King Jr. after presenting the civil rights leader with one of the pens used to sign the Civil Rights Act of 1964.

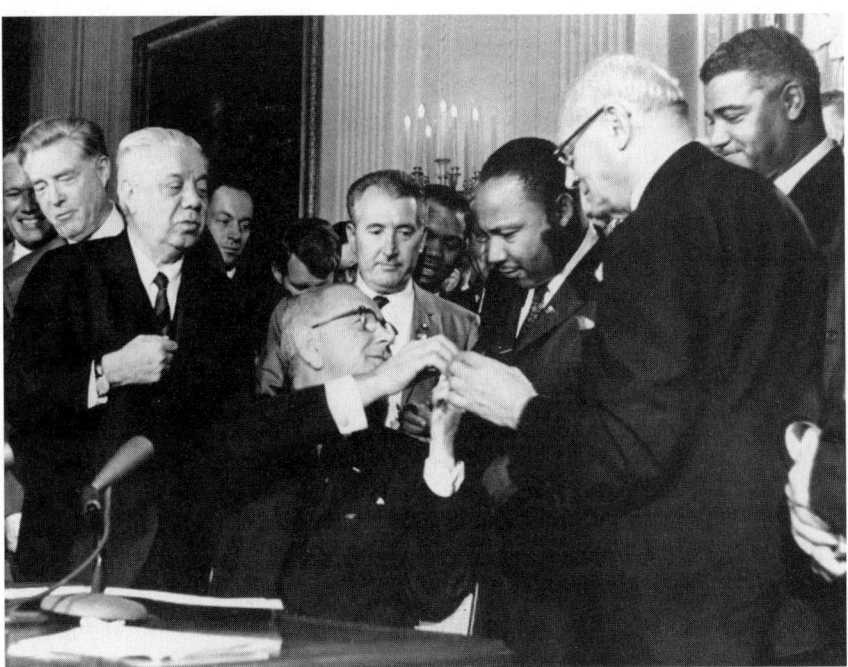

In addition to fulfilling Kennedy's major promises, Johnson launched an ambitious legislative program of his own. In his 1964 State of the Union address, he added to his must-do list a bold new idea that bore the Johnson brand: "This Administration today, here and now, declares unconditional war on poverty in America." The particulars of this "war on poverty" were to come later, the product of a task force at work before Johnson took office.

Americans had "rediscovered" poverty in 1962, when the social critic Michael Harrington published a powerful exposé titled *The Other America*. Harrington argued that more than 40 million people were mired in a "culture of poverty." Unlike the upwardly mobile immigrant poor at the beginning of the century, the modern poor were impervious to hope. President Kennedy had learned of *The Other America* in 1963 and asked his advisers to investigate the problem and suggest solutions. Upon taking office, Lyndon Johnson announced that he wanted an anti-poverty package that was "big and bold, that would hit the nation with real impact." Money for the program would come from the economic growth expected from the tax reduction of more than $10 billion that had passed in 1964.

The administration's war on poverty was embodied in an economic-opportunity bill that incorporated a wide range of programs: a Job Corps for inner-city youths, a Head Start program for disadvantaged preschoolers, work-study programs for college students, grants to farmers and rural businesses, loans to employers willing to hire the chronically unemployed, the Volunteers in Service to America (a domestic Peace Corps), and the Community Action Program, which would allow the poor "maximum feasible participation" in directing neighborhood programs designed for their benefit. Speaking at Ann Arbor, Michigan, Johnson called for a "Great Society" resting on "abundance and liberty for all. The Great Society demands an end to poverty and racial injustice, to which we are fully committed in our time." In theory it was liberalism triumphant; in practice its considerable achievements were accompanied by administrative bungling, corruption, and misguided idealism.

THE ELECTION OF 1964   As the 1964 election approached, Johnson was conceded the Democratic nomination from the start. He chose as his running mate Hubert H. Humphrey of Minnesota, the prominent liberal senator with the seemingly permanent smile and inexhaustible supply of optimism and energy.

The Republicans, meeting in San Francisco, were determined to offer an alternative to Johnson's liberalism. By 1960, Arizona senator Barry Goldwater, a millionaire department-store owner, had emerged as the leader of the party's conservative wing. A movement to nominate Goldwater had begun as early as 1961, mobilizing conservative activists to capture party caucuses and contest primaries. In 1964 they took an early lead, and Goldwater swept the all-important California primary. Thus his forces controlled the Republican Convention.

Goldwater displayed an unusual gift for frightening voters. Accusing the administration of waging a "no-win" war in Vietnam, he urged wholesale bombing of North Vietnam and left the impression of being trigger-happy. He also savaged Johnson's war on poverty and the New Deal tradition. At times he was foolishly candid. In Tennessee he proposed the sale of the Tennessee Valley Authority; in St. Petersburg, Florida, a major retirement community, he questioned the value of Social Security. He had voted against both the nuclear test ban and the 1964 Civil Rights Act. Republican campaign buttons claimed "In your heart, you know he's right." Democrats responded, "In your guts, you know he's nuts."

Johnson, on the other hand, appealed to the middle of the political spectrum. In contrast to Goldwater's bellicose rhetoric on Vietnam, he made a pledge that won great applause at the time and much comment later: "We are not about to send American boys nine or ten thousand miles from home to do what Asian boys ought to be doing for themselves."

The election was a landslide. Johnson polled 61 percent of the total vote; Goldwater carried only Arizona and five states in the Deep South. Johnson won the electoral vote by a whopping 486 to 52. In the Senate the Democrats increased their majority by two (68 to 32) and in the House by thirty-seven (295 to 140).

LANDMARK LEGISLATION In 1965, Johnson took advantage of his electoral mandate to launch his ambitious Great Society program. It would, he promised, end poverty, renovate decaying central cities, provide every young American with the chance to attend college, protect the health of the elderly, enhance cultural life, clean up the air and water, and make the highways safer and prettier.

To accomplish those goals, the Johnson administration pushed legislation through Congress at a pace unseen since Franklin Roosevelt's Hundred Days. Priority went to health insurance and aid to education, proposals that had languished since President Truman had proposed them in 1945. The proposal for a comprehensive medical-insurance plan had long been stalled by the American Medical Association's ardent opposition. But now that Johnson had the votes, the AMA joined Republicans in supporting a bill serving those over age sixty-five. The act not only created the Medicare insurance program for the aged but also included another program, Medicaid, which provided states with federal grants to help cover medical payments for the indigent.

Five days after Johnson submitted his Medicare program, he sent to Congress his proposal for a massive increase in federal aid to elementary and secondary schools. Such proposals had been ignored since the 1940s, blocked alternately by issues of segregation and issues of separation of church and state. Now Johnson and congressional leaders devised a means of extending aid to "poverty-impacted" school districts regardless of their public or religious character.

The momentum generated by these measures had already begun to carry others along, and it continued through the following year. Altogether, the tide of Great Society legislation carried 435 bills through the Congress. Among them was the Appalachian Regional Development Act of 1966, which allocated federal funds for programs to enhance the standard of living in remote mountain areas that had long been pockets of desperate poverty. The Housing and Urban Development Act of 1965 provided for construction of 240,000 housing units. Rent supplements for low-income families followed in 1966, and in that year there began a new Department of Housing and Urban Development, headed by Robert C. Weaver, the first African American cabinet member.

THE IMMIGRATION ACT   Little noticed among the legislation flowing from Congress was a major new immigration bill that had originated in the Kennedy White House. President Johnson signed the Immigration and Nationality Services Act of 1965 in a ceremony held on Liberty Island in New York Harbor. In his speech, Johnson stressed that the new law would redress the wrong done to those "from southern and eastern Europe" and the "developing continents" of Asia, Africa, and Latin America. It would do so by abolishing the discriminatory quotas based upon national origins that had governed immigration policy since the 1920s.

The new law treated all nationalities and races equally. In place of national quotas, it created hemispheric ceilings on visas issued: 170,000 for persons from outside the Western Hemisphere, 120,000 for persons from within. It also stipulated that no more than 20,000 people could come from any one country each year. The new act allowed the entry of immediate family members of American residents without limit. During the 1960s, Asians and Latin Americans became the largest contingent of new Americans.

ASSESSING THE GREAT SOCIETY   The Great Society programs included several successes. The Highway Safety Act and the National Traffic and Motor Vehicle Safety Act established safety standards for automobile manufacturers and highway design, and the scholarships provided for college students under the Higher Education Act were quite popular. Many Great Society initiatives aimed at improving the health, nutrition, and education of poor Americans, young and old, made headway. So, too, did efforts to clean up air and water pollution. Some of Johnson's programs were hastily designed or mismanaged, however, and others were vastly underfunded. Medicare, for example, removed incentives for hospitals to control costs, so medical bills skyrocketed. The Great Society helped reduce the number of people living in poverty, but it did so largely by providing federal welfare payments, not by finding people productive jobs. The war on poverty ended up being as disappointing as the war in Vietnam. Often funds appropriated

Great Society initiatives

President Johnson listens to Tom Fletcher, a father of eight children, describe some of the economic problems in his hometown.

for a program never made it through the tangled bureaucracy to the needy. Widely publicized cases of welfare fraud placed a powerful weapon in the hands of those opposed to liberal social programs. By 1966 middle-class resentment over the cost and waste of the Great Society programs had generated a strong conservative backlash that fueled a Republican resurgence at the polls.

From Civil Rights to Black Power

CIVIL RIGHTS LEGISLATION   Among the successes of the Great Society was a landmark piece of civil rights legislation: the Civil Rights Act of 1964, the most far-reaching civil rights measure ever enacted. It outlawed racial discrimination in hotels, restaurants, and other public accommodations. In addition, its provisions enabled the attorney general to bring suits to end school desegregation, relieving parents of that painful burden. Federally assisted programs and private employers alike were required to eliminate discrimination. An Equal Employment Opportunity Commission administered a ban on job discrimination by race, religion, national origin, or sex.

The Civil Rights Act increased the momentum of the movement. Early in 1965, Martin Luther King Jr. organized a voter-registration drive aimed at the 3 million unregistered African Americans in the South. On March 7 civil rights protesters began a march for voting rights from Selma, Alabama, to Montgomery, only to be violently dispersed by state troopers. A federal judge then agreed to allow the march, and President Johnson provided federal troops for protection. By March 25, when the demonstrators reached Montgomery, they numbered 35,000, and King delivered a rousing address from the steps of the state capitol.

Several days earlier, President Johnson had gone before Congress with a moving plea for voting-rights legislation. The resulting Voting Rights Act of 1965 ensured all citizens the right to vote. It authorized the attorney general to dispatch federal examiners to register voters. In states or counties where fewer than half the adults had voted in 1964, the act suspended literacy tests and other devices commonly used to defraud citizens of the vote. By the end of the year, some 250,000 African Americans were newly registered.

BLACK POWER   Amid this success, however, the civil rights movement began to fragment. On August 11, 1965, less than a week after the passage of the Voting Rights Act, Watts, a predominantly black and poor neighborhood in Los Angeles, exploded in a frenzy of rioting and looting. When the uprising ended, 34 were dead, almost 4,000 rioters were in jail, and property damage exceeded $35 million. The Watts upheaval marked the beginning of four long hot summers of racial conflagration. Riots in 1966 erupted in Chicago and Cleveland and in forty other American cities. The following summer, Newark and Detroit burst into flames. Detroit provided the most graphic instance of urban violence as tanks rolled through the streets to restore order.

In retrospect, it was understandable that the civil rights movement would shift its focus from the rural South to the plight of urban blacks. By the mid-1960s about 70 percent of African Americans lived in metropolitan areas, most of them in central-city ghettos that the postwar prosperity had bypassed. It also seems clear in retrospect that the nonviolent tactics that had worked in the South would not work in the large cities across the nation. In the North racial problems resulted from segregated residential patterns not amenable to changes in the law. Moreover, northern white ethnic groups did not have the cultural heritage that southern whites shared with blacks by virtue of their having lived together for so many generations. A special Commission on Civil Disorders noted that, unlike earlier race riots, which had been started by whites, the urban upheavals of the middle 1960s were initiated by African Americans themselves in an effort to destroy what they could not stomach and what civil rights legislation seemed unable to change.

In the midst of the violence, a new philosophy of racial separatism began to emerge. By 1966, "black power" had become the rallying cry of young activists. Radical members of SNCC had become estranged from Martin Luther King's theories of nonviolence. When Stokely Carmichael, a twenty-five-year-old graduate of Howard University, became head of SNCC in 1966, he adopted a separatist philosophy of black power and ousted whites from the organization. "We reject an American dream defined by white people and must work to construct an American reality defined by Afro-Americans," said a SNCC position paper. H. Rap Brown, who succeeded Carmichael as head of SNCC in 1967, even urged blacks to "get you some guns" and "kill the honkies." Meanwhile, Carmichael had moved on to the Black Panther party, founded in Oakland, California, in 1966. Headed by Huey P. Newton, Bobby Seale, and Eldridge Cleaver, the self-professed urban revolutionaries terrified the public. Eventually the Panthers fragmented in spasms of violence, much of which the FBI and local police officials helped to provoke.

The most articulate spokesman for black power was one of the earliest, Malcolm X (formerly Malcolm Little, the X denoting his lost African surname). Malcolm had risen from a ghetto childhood involving narcotics

Malcolm X

Malcolm X was the black power movement's most influential spokesman.

dealing and other crimes to become the chief disciple of Elijah Muhammad, a Black Muslim prophet who rejected Christianity as "the religion of white devils" and encouraged black culture and black pride. By 1964, Malcolm had broken with Elijah Muhammad and founded an organization committed to fostering alliances between African Americans and the nonwhite peoples of the world. He had also begun to abandon his earlier separatist agenda and violent tactics. But Malcolm was gunned down in Harlem by Black Muslim assassins in early 1965. With him went the most effective voice for urban black militancy. What made the assassination especially tragic was that Malcolm had just months before begun to abandon his strident anti-white rhetoric and preach a biracial message of social change.

Although widely publicized and highly visible, the black power movement never attracted more than a small minority of African Americans. Only about 15 percent of American blacks labeled themselves separatists. The preponderant majority continued to identify with the philosophy of nonviolent integration promoted by Martin Luther King and organizations such as the NAACP.

Despite its strident language and violence, the black power movement had two positive effects upon the civil rights movement. First, it prompted African Americans to take greater pride in their racial heritage. As Malcolm X often pointed out, prolonged slavery and institutionalized racism had eroded the self-esteem of many blacks in the United States. "The worst crime the white man has committed," he declared, "has been to teach us to hate ourselves." He and others helped blacks appreciate their African roots and their American accomplishments. It was Malcolm X who insisted that blacks call themselves African Americans as a symbol of pride in their roots and as a spur to learn more about their history as a people.

Second, the black power phenomenon forced King and other mainstream African American leaders and organizations to focus attention on the economic plight of poor inner-city blacks. Legal access to restaurants, schools, and other public accommodations, King pointed out, meant little to people mired in a culture of urban poverty. They needed jobs and decent housing as much as they needed legal rights. The time had come for radical measures "to provide jobs and income for the poor." Yet as King and others sought to escalate the war on poverty at home, the war in Vietnam was consuming more and more of America's resources and energies.

THE TRAGEDY OF VIETNAM

As domestic violence was escalating in America's inner cities, the war in Vietnam was reaching new levels of intensity and destruction. At the time of President Kennedy's death, there were 16,000 U.S. military advisers in Vietnam. Lyndon Johnson inherited from Kennedy and Eisenhower a long-standing commitment to prevent a Communist takeover in South Vietnam, along with a reluctance to assume the military burden for fighting the war. One president after another had done just enough to avoid being charged with having lost Vietnam. Johnson did the same, fearing that any other course would undermine his influence and endanger his Great Society programs in Congress. But this path took the United States deeper into an expanding military commitment in Southeast Asia. Early on, Johnson doubted that Vietnam was worth a deepening American military involvement. In May 1964 he told his national security adviser, McGeorge Bundy, that he had spent a sleepless night worrying about Vietnam: "It looks to me like we are getting into another Korea. . . . I don't think we can fight them 10,000 miles away from home. . . . I don't think it's worth fighting for. And I don't think we can get out. It's just the biggest damned mess that I ever saw."

ESCALATION   The official sanction for America's "escalation"—a Defense Department term favored in the Vietnam era—was the Tonkin Gulf resolution, approved by Congress on August 7, 1964. On that day, Johnson reported in a national television address that two American destroyers had been attacked by North Vietnamese vessels on August 2 and 4 in the Gulf of Tonkin, off the coast of North Vietnam. Johnson described the attacks, called the Gulf of Tonkin incident, as unprovoked. In truth the destroyers had been monitoring South Vietnamese raids against two North Vietnamese islands— raids planned by American advisers. The Tonkin Gulf resolution authorized the president to "take all necessary measures to repel any armed attack against the forces of the United States and to prevent further aggression."

VIETNAM, 1966

■ Major U.S. military bases

Why was there an American military presence in Vietnam?
What was the Ho Chi Minh Trail? What was the Tet
offensive?

Three months after his landslide victory over Goldwater in November
1964, Johnson made the crucial decisions that would shape American policy
in Vietnam for the next four years. Viet Cong guerrilla attacks on American
forces in February 1965 led Johnson to launch Operation Rolling Thunder,
the first sustained bombing of North Vietnam, which was intended to stop

the flow of soldiers and supplies into the south. Six months later analysts concluded that the bombing had had little effect on the supplies pouring down the Ho Chi Minh Trail from North Vietnam through Laos and into South Vietnam. Still, the bombing continued.

In March 1965 the new U.S. army commander in Vietnam, General William C. Westmoreland, requested and got the first installment of combat troops, ostensibly to defend American airfields. By the end of 1965, there were 184,000 U.S. troops in Vietnam; in 1966 there were 385,000. As combat operations increased throughout South Vietnam, so did American casualties, announced on the nightly television news, along with the "body count" of alleged enemy dead.

THE CONTEXT FOR POLICY Lyndon Johnson's decision to "Americanize" the Vietnam War, so ill-starred in retrospect, was entirely consistent with the foreign-policy principles pursued by all presidents after World War II.

The Tet offensive

Many Vietnamese were driven from their homes during the bloody street battles of the 1968 Tet offensive. Here, following a lull in the fighting, civilians carrying a white flag approach U.S. Marines.

The version of the theory to "contain" communism articulated in the Truman Doctrine, endorsed by Dwight Eisenhower and reaffirmed by John Kennedy, pledged opposition to the advance of communism anywhere in the world. Secretary of State Dean Rusk frequently warned that Thailand, Burma, and the rest of Southeast Asia would fall "like dominoes" to communism if American forces withdrew from Vietnam. Military intervention was thus a logical culmination of the assumptions widely shared by the foreign-policy establishment and leaders of both political parties since the early days of the cold war.

Nor did the United States blindly "stumble into a quagmire" in Vietnam, as some commentators maintained. Johnson insisted from the start that military involvement must not reach levels that would provoke the Chinese or Soviets to intervene with their own forces. He therefore exercised a tight rein over the bombing campaign, once boasting that "they can't even bomb an outhouse without my approval." Such a restrictive policy meant, in effect, that military victory was never possible. America's goal was not to win the war in a conventional sense by capturing enemy territory but to prevent the North Vietnamese and the Viet Cong from winning and, eventually, to force a negotiated settlement with the North Vietnamese. This meant that America would have to maintain a military presence as long as the enemy retained the will to fight.

"How Deep Do You Figure We'll Get Involved, Sir?"

Although U.S. soldiers were first sent to Vietnam as noncombatant advisers, they soon found themselves involved in a quagmire of fighting.

As it turned out, American public support for the war eroded faster than the will of the North Vietnamese leaders to tolerate devastating casualties and destruction. Systematic opposition to the war broke out on college campuses with the escalation of 1965. By 1967 antiwar demonstrations in New York City and at the Pentagon were attracting massive support. Nightly television accounts of the fighting—Vietnam was the first war to receive extended television coverage and hence was dubbed the living-room war—contradicted the official optimism.

In a war of political will, North Vietnam had the advantage. Johnson and his advisers grievously underestimated the tenacity of North Vietnam's commitment to unify Vietnam and expel the United States. While the United States fought a limited war for limited objectives, the Vietnamese Communists fought a total war for their survival. Just as General Westmoreland in early 1968 was assuring Johnson and the American public that his forces were on the verge of gaining the upper hand, the Communists were organizing widespread attacks that jolted American confidence and resolve.

THE TURNING POINT On January 31, 1968, the first day of the Vietnamese New Year (Tet), the Viet Cong and the North Vietnamese defied a holiday truce to launch a wave of surprise assaults on American and South Vietnamese forces throughout South Vietnam. The old capital city of Hue fell to the Communists, and Viet Cong units temporarily occupied the grounds of the U.S. embassy in Saigon. Within a few days, however, American and South Vietnamese forces organized a devastating counterattack. General Westmoreland justifiably proclaimed the Tet offensive a major defeat for the Viet Cong. But while Viet Cong casualties were enormous, the psychological impact of the surprise attacks on the American public was more telling. The scope and intensity of the offensive contradicted upbeat claims by commanders that the war was going well. *Time* and *Newsweek* soon ran anti-war editorials urging American withdrawal. Polls showed that Johnson's popularity had declined to 35 percent. In 1968 the United States was spending $322,000 on every enemy soldier killed in Vietnam; the poverty programs at home received only $53 per person.

During 1968, Lyndon Johnson grew increasingly isolated. He suffered from depression and bouts of paranoia. The secretary of defense reported that a task force of prominent soldiers and civilians saw no prospect for a military victory; the stalemated war was undermining the Great Society programs. The Democratic party was also fragmenting. Robert Kennedy, now a senator from New York, was considering a run for the presidency in order to challenge Johnson's Vietnam policy. Senator Eugene McCarthy of Minnesota had already decided to oppose Johnson in the Democratic primaries. With anti-war students rallying to his candidacy, McCarthy polled a stunning 42 percent of the vote to Johnson's 48 percent in New Hampshire's March primary. It was a remarkable showing for a little-known senator. Each presidential primary now promised to become a referendum on Johnson's Vietnam policy.

On March 31, Johnson made a dramatic decision. He announced a limited halt to the bombing of North Vietnam and fresh initiatives for a negotiated cease-fire. Then he added a stunning postscript: "I shall not seek, and I will not accept, the nomination of my party for another term as your President." Although American combat troops would remain in Vietnam for five more years and the casualties would mount, the quest for military victory had ended. Now the question was how the most powerful nation in the world could extricate itself from Vietnam with a minimum of damage to its prestige and its South Vietnamese allies. It would not be easy. When direct negotiations with the North Vietnamese finally began in Paris in May 1968, they immediately bogged down over North Vietnam's demand for a halt to the bombing by the United States as a precondition for further discussion.

Sixties Crescendo

A TRAUMATIC YEAR   Change moved at a fearful pace throughout the 1960s, but 1968 was the most turbulent and the most traumatic year of all. On April 4, only four days after Johnson's withdrawal from the presidential race, Martin Luther King Jr. was gunned down in Memphis, Tennessee. The assassin, James Earl Ray, had expressed hostility toward African Americans, but Americans continue to debate whether he was a pawn in an organized conspiracy. King's death set off an outpouring of grief among whites and blacks. It also set off riots in over sixty American cities.

Two months later, on June 5, Robert Kennedy was shot in the head by a young Palestinian who resented Kennedy's strong support of Israel. Kennedy died on the day after he had convincingly defeated Eugene McCarthy in the California Democratic primary, thereby momentarily assuming leadership of the anti-war forces in the race for the nomination for president.

CHICAGO AND MIAMI   In August 1968, Democratic delegates gathered inside a Chicago convention hall to nominate Vice President Hubert Humphrey, while almost 20,000 police and national guardsmen and a small army of television reporters stood watch over several thousand diverse protesters herded together miles away in a public park. Chicago mayor Richard J. Daley, who had given "shoot-to-kill" orders to police during the April riots

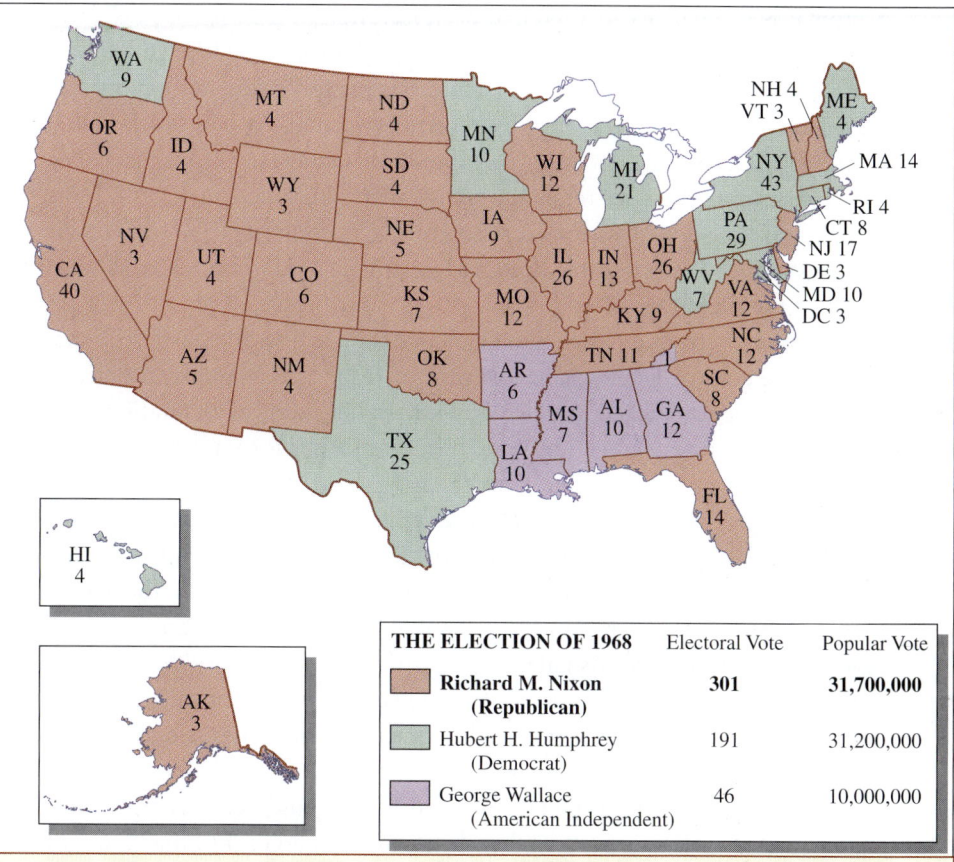

THE ELECTION OF 1968	Electoral Vote	Popular Vote
Richard M. Nixon (Republican)	**301**	**31,700,000**
Hubert H. Humphrey (Democrat)	191	31,200,000
George Wallace (American Independent)	46	10,000,000

How did the riots at the Chicago Democratic Convention affect the 1968 presidential campaign? What does the electoral map reveal about the support base for each of the three major candidates? How was Nixon able to win enough electoral votes in such a close, three-way presidential race? What was Wallace's appeal to over 10 million voters?

following King's assassination, warned that he would not tolerate disruptions. Nonetheless, riots broke out and were televised nationwide. As demonstrators chanted "The whole world is watching," police attacked the crowds with tear gas and billy clubs.

The Democratic party's liberal tradition was clearly in disarray, a fact that gave heart to the Republicans, who gathered in Miami Beach to nominate Richard Nixon and celebrate a remarkable political comeback. Nixon's narrow loss to Kennedy in 1960 had been followed by a disastrous defeat in the California gubernatorial race two years later. In what he labeled his "last press conference," he vowed never again to run for office. Yet Nixon displayed his remarkable resilience by returning to national politics in 1964, when he crisscrossed the nation in support of Goldwater's candidacy. For the next several years he remained active in politics, and in 1968 he was ready to take advantage of Johnson's crumbling popularity. He offered a vision of stability and order that appealed to a majority of Americans, soon to be called the silent majority.

But others were ready as well to challenge the Democratic party regulars. George Wallace, the Democratic governor of Alabama, ran on the American Independent party ticket. Wallace had made his political reputation as a brazen defender of segregation, but in his campaign for national office in 1968 he moderated his position on the race issue. And he appealed even more candidly than Nixon to the fears generated by rioting anti-war protesters, the welfare system, and the growth of the federal government. Wallace's platform was compelling in its simplicity: rioters would be shot, the war in Vietnam won, states' rights and law and order restored, open-housing laws repealed, and welfare cheats jailed.

Wallace's reactionary candidacy generated considerable appeal outside his native South, especially in white working-class communities, where resentment of Johnson's Great Society liberalism was rife. Although never a possible winner, Wallace had to be taken seriously: he could deny Humphrey or Nixon an electoral majority and thereby throw the choice into the House of Representatives, providing an appropriate climax to a chaotic year.

NIXON AGAIN   It did not happen that way. Richard Nixon enjoyed an enormous early lead in the polls, which narrowed as the 1968 election approached. George Wallace's campaign was hurt by his outspoken running mate, retired air force general Curtis LeMay, who suggested that nuclear weapons be used in Vietnam. In October 1968, Hubert Humphrey infuriated Johnson and the party bosses when he announced that, if elected, he would stop bombing North Vietnam "as an acceptable risk for peace."

In the end, Nixon and his running mate, Governor Spiro Agnew of Maryland, eked out a narrow victory of about 500,000 votes, a margin of about 1 percentage point. The electoral vote was more decisive, 301 to 191. Wallace won 10 million votes, 13.5 percent of the total, the best showing by a third-party candidate since Robert La Follette headed the Progressive ticket in 1924. All but one of Wallace's 46 electoral votes were from the Deep South.

Nixon swept all but four of the states west of the Mississippi, while Humphrey's support came almost exclusively from the Northeast.

So at the end of a turbulent year, near the end of a traumatic decade, a nation on the verge of violent chaos looked to Richard Nixon to provide what he had promised in the campaign: "peace with honor" in Vietnam and a middle ground on which a majority of Americans, silent or otherwise, could come together.

End of Chapter Review

CHAPTER SUMMARY

- **Kennedy's New Frontier** President Kennedy promised "new frontiers" in domestic policy, but without a clear Democratic majority in Congress he was unable to increase federal aid to education, provide health insurance for the aged, create a cabinet-level department of urban affairs, or expand civil rights. He championed tariff cuts, however, and an expanded space program.

- **Johnson's Great Society** President Johnson was committed to social reform. He forced the Civil Rights Act through Congress in 1964 and declared "a war" on poverty. Under the Great Society, welfare was expanded, Medicare and Medicaid were created, more grants for college students were established, and racial quotas for immigration were abolished. These programs were expensive and, coupled with the soaring costs of the war in Vietnam, necessitated tax increases, which were unpopular.

- **Civil Rights' Achievements** By the 1960s significant numbers of African Americans and whites were staging non-violent sit-ins. In 1961, "freedom riders" attempted to integrate buses, trains, and bus and train stations in the South. The high point of the early phase of the civil rights movement was the 1963 March on Washington for Jobs and Freedom, at which Martin Luther King Jr. delivered his famous "I Have a Dream" speech. In 1964, President Johnson signed the far-reaching Civil Rights Act. In 1965, King set in motion a massive drive to enroll the 3 million southern African Americans who were not registered to vote. Later that year, Johnson persuaded Congress to pass the Voting Rights Act. The legislation did little to ameliorate the poverty of inner-city blacks or stem the violence that swept northern cities in the hot summers of the late 1960s. By 1968, nonviolent resistance had given way to the more militant black power movement.

- **Escalation in Vietnam** The United States supported the government of South Vietnam even though it failed to deliver promised reforms, win the support of its citizens, or defeat the Communist insurgents, the Viet Cong. Kennedy increased America's commitment by sending advisers, and Johnson went further, deploying combat troops. A turning point in the war was the Viet Cong's Tet offensive, which served to rally anti-war sentiment.

- **Communist Cuba** In early 1961, Kennedy inherited a CIA plot to topple the regime of Fidel Castro, the premier of Cuba. Kennedy naïvely agreed to the plot, whereby some 1,500 anti-Castro Cubans landed at Cuba's Bay of Pigs. The plotters failed to inspire a revolution, and most were quickly captured. Kennedy's seeming weakness in the face of Soviet aggression led the Russian premier, Nikita Khrushchev, to believe that the Soviets could install ballistic missiles in Cuba without American opposition. In October 1962 in a tense standoff, Kennedy ordered a blockage of Cuba and succeeded in forcing Khrushchev to withdraw the missiles.

CHRONOLOGY

1961	Bay of Pigs fiasco
1961	Soviets erect the Berlin Wall
October 1962	Cuban missile crisis
August 1963	March on Washington for Jobs and Freedom
November 1963	John F. Kennedy is assassinated in Dallas, Texas
1964	Congress passes the Civil Rights Act
August 1964	Congress passes the Tonkin Gulf resolution
1965	Malcolm X is assassinated by a rival group of black Muslims
1965	Riots break out in the African American community of Watts, California
January 1968	Viet Cong stage the Tet offensive
April 1968	Martin Luther King Jr. is assassinated
June 1968	Robert Kennedy is assassinated

KEY TERMS & NAMES

35

REBELLION AND REACTION IN THE 1960s AND 1970s

FOCUS QUESTIONS wwnorton.com/studyspace

- What characterized the social rebellion and struggles for civil rights in the 1960s and 1970s?
- How did the war in Vietnam end?
- What was Watergate, and why did it lead to Nixon's resignation?
- Why had the Middle East become an area of concern by the 1970s, and how did the Carter administration deal with crises in the area?

As Richard Nixon entered the White House in early 1969, he faced a nation whose social fabric was in tatters. Everywhere, it seemed, traditional institutions and notions of authority were under attack. The traumatic events of 1968 revealed how deeply divided American society had become and how difficult a task Nixon faced in carrying out his pledge to restore social harmony. The stability he promised proved elusive. His policies and his combative temperament heightened rather than reduced societal tensions. Those tensions reflected profound fissures in the post–World War II consensus promoted by Eisenhower and inherited by Kennedy and Johnson. Ironically, many of the same forces that had promoted the flush times of the Eisenhower years—the baby boom, the containment doctrine of anti-communism, and the superficial focus on the consumer culture—helped generate the social upheaval of the 1960s and 1970s.

THE ROOTS OF REBELLION

YOUTH REVOLT By the early 1960s the postwar baby boomers were maturing. Now young adults, they differed from their elders in that they had experienced neither economic depression nor a major war. In record numbers they were attending colleges and universities: enrollment quadrupled between 1945 and 1970. Many universities had become sprawling institutions increasingly dependent upon research contracts from giant corporations and the federal government. As these "multiversities" grew more bureaucratic and hierarchical, they unwittingly invited resistance from students wary of involvement in what President Eisenhower had called the military-industrial complex.

The Greensboro student sit-ins in 1960 not only precipitated a decade of civil rights activism but also signaled an end to the supposed apathy that had enveloped college campuses and social life during the 1950s. Although primarily concerned with the rights and status of black people, the sit-ins, marches, protests, ideals, and sacrifices associated with the civil rights movement provided inspiring models and rhetoric for other groups demanding justice, freedom, and equality.

The free-speech movement

Mario Savio, a founder of the free-speech movement, speaks at a rally at the University of California at Berkeley.

During 1960–1961 a small but significant number of white students joined the sit-in movement. They and many others were also inspired by President Kennedy's direct appeals to their youthful idealism. Soon, however, it became clear that politics was mixed with principle in the president's position on civil rights. Later, as criticism of escalating American involvement in Vietnam mounted, more and more young people grew disillusioned with the government, corporations, and parental authority. Cynicism bred activism. By the mid-1960s a full-fledged youth revolt had erupted across the country, and rebels began to flow into two distinct yet frequently overlapping movements: the New Left and the counterculture.

THE NEW LEFT   The explicitly political strain of the youth revolt coalesced when Tom Hayden and Al Haber, two student radicals at the University of Michigan, formed Students for a Democratic Society (SDS) in 1960. Two years later Hayden drafted what became known as the Port Huron Statement. It begins: "We are the people of this generation, bred in at least moderate comfort, housed in universities, looking uncomfortably to the world we inherit."

Hayden's manifesto focused on the absence of individual freedom in modern life. The country, he insisted, was dominated by huge organizational structures—governments, corporations, universities—all of which conspired to oppress and alienate the individual. Inspired by the example of African American activism in the South, Hayden declared that students had the power to restore "participatory democracy" to American life by wresting "control of the educational process from the administrative bureaucracy" and then forging links with other dissident movements. He and others adopted the term New Left to distinguish their efforts at grassroots democracy from those of the Old Left of the 1930s, which had espoused an orthodox version of Marxism.

In the fall of 1964, students at the University of California at Berkeley took Hayden's program to heart. When the university's chancellor announced that sidewalk solicitations for political causes would no longer be allowed, several hundred students staged a sit-in. Over 2,000 more joined in, and after a tense standoff the administration relented.

The program and tactics of the SDS spread to universities across the country, but the focus changed as escalating involvement in Vietnam brought a dramatic expansion of the military draft and millions of young men faced the grim prospect of participating in an increasingly unpopular war. In fact, however, Vietnam, like virtually every other war, was a poor man's fight. In 1965–1966, thanks to deferments and exemptions, college students made up only 2 percent of all military inductees. Yet several thousand male collegians would flee to Canada or Sweden to escape the draft, while hundreds of thousands engaged in various protests against a war they considered immoral.

During the eventful spring of 1968—when Lyndon Johnson announced he would not run for reelection and Martin Luther King Jr. was assassinated—campus unrest reached a climax with the disruption of Columbia University in New York City. Mark Rudd, an SDS leader, and a small group of radicals protested the university's insensitive decision to disrupt a neighboring African American community in order to build a new gymnasium. The students occupied some campus buildings, and the protest quickly spread. During the following week more buildings were occupied, faculty and administrative offices were ransacked, and classes were canceled. University officials finally called in the New York City police. While arresting the protesters, officers injured innocent bystanders. Such excessive force angered many unaligned students, who then joined militants in staging a strike that shut down the university for the remainder of the semester. That spring similar clashes among students, administrators, and police occurred at Harvard, Cornell, and San Francisco State.

At the 1968 Democratic Convention in Chicago, the polarization of American society reached a bizarre climax. Inside the tightly guarded convention hall, Democrats were nominating Lyndon Johnson's faithful vice president, Hubert Humphrey, while Chicago's streets roiled with anti-war dissenters. The outlandish behavior of the anarchic protesters provoked an equally outlandish response from Chicago's Mayor Richard J. Daley and his army of police. As a national television audience watched, many police officers went berserk, clubbing and gassing demonstrators as well as bystanders caught up in the chaos. The televised spectacle lasted three days and generated a wave of anger among many middle-class Americans,

Upheaval in Chicago

The violence that accompanied the 1968 Democratic National Convention in Chicago seared the nation.

which Richard Nixon and the Republicans shrewdly exploited at their 1968 nominating convention in Miami Beach. At the same time, the Chicago riots fragmented the anti-war movement.

During 1968 the SDS fractured into rival factions, the most extreme of which called itself the Weathermen, a name derived from a lyric by Bob Dylan: "You don't need a weather man to know which way the wind blows." These hardened young activists launched a campaign of violence and disruption, firebombing university and government buildings and killing innocent people, as well as several of their own. Government forces arrested most of them, and the rest went into hiding. By 1971 the New Left was dead as a political movement. In large measure it had committed suicide by abandoning the pacifist principles that had inspired participants and given the movement its moral legitimacy. The larger anti-war movement also began to fade. There would be a wave of student protests against the Nixon administration in 1970–1971, but thereafter campus unrest virtually disappeared as American troops returned home from Vietnam and the draft ended.

If the social mood was changing during Richard Nixon's presidency, a large segment of the public persisted in the quest for social justice. A *New York Times* survey of college campuses in 1969 revealed that many students were refocusing their attention on the environment. This new ecological awareness would blossom in the 1970s into one of the most compelling items on the nation's social agenda.

THE COUNTERCULTURE   The numbing events of 1968 led other disaffected activists away from radical politics altogether, toward another manifestation of the sixties youth revolt: the counterculture. Long hair, blue jeans, tie-dyed shirts, sandals, mind-altering drugs, rock music, and group living arrangements were more important than revolutionary ideology or mass protest to the hippies, the direct descendants of the Beats of the 1950s. Advocates of the counterculture were, like their New Left peers, primarily young whites alienated by the Vietnam War, racism, political corruption and parental demands, runaway technology, and a crass corporate mentality that equated the good life with material goods. Disillusioned with organized political action, they embraced the credo announced by the zany Harvard professor Timothy Leary: "Tune in, turn on, drop out."

For some the counterculture entailed the embrace of Asian religions such as Buddhism. For others it centered on the frequent use of hallucinogenic drugs such as LSD. Collective living in urban enclaves such as San Francisco's Haight-Ashbury district and New York's East Village was the rage for a while, until conditions grew so crowded and violent that residents migrated elsewhere. Rural communes also attracted bourgeois rebels. During the 1960s and early 1970s, thousands of inexperienced romantics flocked to the countryside, eager to liberate themselves from parental and institutional restraints, live in harmony with nature, and coexist in an atmosphere of love and openness. Only a handful of their utopian homesteads survived more than a few months, however.

Huge outdoor rock concerts were a popular source of community for hippies. The largest of these was the Woodstock Music and Art Fair, held in 1969 on a 600-acre farm near the tiny rural town of Bethel, New York. For three days some 500,000 "flower children" reveled in good music and cheap marijuana. But the carefree spirit of the Woodstock festival was short-lived. When concert promoters tried to replicate the scene four months later, this time at a Rolling Stones concert at the Altamont Speedway near San Francisco, members of the Hells Angels motorcycle gang beat a man to death in front of the stage.

Woodstock

The Woodstock music festival drew nearly half a million people to a farm in Bethel, New York. The concert was billed as three days of "peace, music, . . . and love."

Just as the 1968 Democratic Convention in Chicago marked the end of the New Left as a vital political force, the violence at Altamont sharply diminished the appeal of the counterculture. Moreover, many of the flower children grew tired of their riches-to-rags existence and returned to college to become lawyers, doctors, politicians, or accountants. The search on the part of alienated youth for a better society and a good life was strewn with irony, hypocrisy, disillusionment, and tragedy.

FEMINISM   The ideal of liberation spawned during the 1960s helped accelerate a powerful women's rights crusade. Like the New Left, the new feminism drew much of its inspiration and many of its initial tactics from the civil rights movement. Its aim was to challenge the conventional cult of domesticity that had been touted as the ideal during the 1950s.

The mainstream women's movement was led by Betty Friedan. Her influential book, *The Feminine Mystique* (1963), launched a new phase of female protest on a national level. Women, Friedan wrote, had actually lost ground during the years after World War II, when many left wartime jobs and settled down in suburbia to care for their children. Advertisers and women's magazines promoted the "feminine mystique" of blissful domesticity. In Friedan's view the middle-class home had become "a comfortable concentration camp" where women saw their individual potential suffocated in an atmosphere of mindless materialism, daytime TV, and neighborhood gossip.

Feminist awakenings

In 1967, Syracuse University student Kathy Switzer challenged the Boston Marathon's tradition of excluding women. Officials tried to pull Switzer from the course, but with the aid of fellow runners she completed the race. Women did not become official entrants until 1971.

The Feminine Mystique inspired many women who felt trapped in their domestic doldrums. In 1966, Friedan and other activists founded the National Organization for Women (NOW), whose membership grew rapidly. NOW spearheaded efforts to end job discrimination on the basis of sex, legalize abortion, and obtain federal and state support for child-care centers.

Pressured by NOW, Congress and the Supreme Court in the early 1970s advanced the cause of sexual equality. Under Title IX of the Education Amendments of 1972, colleges were required to institute "affirmative-action" programs to ensure equal opportunities for women in such areas as admissions, faculty and staff hiring, and athletics. Also in 1972, Congress overwhelmingly approved the equal-rights amendment to the Constitution. And in 1973 the Supreme Court, in *Roe v. Wade*, struck down state laws forbidding abortions during the first three months of pregnancy, a ruling based on the constitutional right to privacy. Meanwhile, many bastions of male education, including Yale and Princeton, led a new movement for coeducation that swept the nation.

By the end of the 1970s, however, sharp disputes between moderate and radical feminists had fragmented the women's movement. The movement's failure to broaden its appeal much beyond the confines of the white middle class caused reform efforts to stagnate. In 1982 the equal-rights amendment died, several states short of ratification. The very success of NOW's efforts to liberalize state abortion laws helped generate a powerful backlash, especially among Catholics and fundamentalist Protestants, who mounted a "right-to-life" crusade that helped ignite the conservative political insurgence in the 1970s and thereafter.

Yet the success of the women's movement endured despite setbacks. The growing political power of women and their expanding presence in the workforce combined to become one of the most significant developments of the era. By 1976 over half the married women in America and nine out of ten female college graduates were employed outside the home, a development that one economist called "the single most outstanding phenomenon of this century." Many career women, however, did not regard themselves as feminists; they took jobs because they and their families needed the money to achieve higher levels of material comfort. Whatever their motives, women were changing traditional sex roles and child-rearing practices to accommodate the two-career family, which had replaced the established pattern of male breadwinner and female housekeeper as the new American norm.

HISPANIC RIGHTS The activism that animated the crusade for women's rights also spread to various ethnic minority groups. The labor shortages during World War II had led defense industries to offer Hispanic Americans their first significant access to skilled-labor jobs. As was the case with African Americans, service in the military during the war years helped to heighten an American identity among Hispanic Americans and increase their desire for equal rights and opportunities.

But equality was elusive. After World War II, Hispanic Americans still faced widespread discrimination in hiring, housing, and education. Poverty was widespread. In 1960, for example, the median income of a Mexican American family was only 62 percent of that of a family in the general population. Hispanic American activists during the 1950s and 1960s mirrored the efforts of black civil rights leaders. They, too, denounced segregation, promoted efforts to improve the quality of public education, and struggled to increase Hispanic American political influence and economic opportunities.

One of the most popular initiatives was the use of the term *Chicano* as an inclusive label for all Mexican immigrants, Spanish Americans in New Mexico, old Californios (descendants of the inhabitants of California before it was seized by the United States, most of whom were Indians or of mixed ancestry), and Tejanos (descendants of the inhabitants of Texas before it became independent).* In southern California, members of Young Citizens for Community Action re-formed as Young Chicanos for Community Action, or the Brown Berets, a social-service group designed to promote self-reliance and local involvement within Mexican American neighborhoods. They protested the disproportionate number of Hispanics being killed in the Vietnam War and demanded improvements in their neighborhood schools.

Unlike their African American counterparts, however, Hispanic American leaders faced an awkward dilemma: what should they do about the continuing stream of undocumented Mexicans flowing across the border? Many Mexican Americans argued that their hopes for economic advancement and social equality were put at risk by the daily influx of Mexican laborers willing to accept low-paying jobs in the United States. Mexican American leaders thus helped end the bracero program in 1964 (which trucked in day laborers from Mexico) and in 1962 formed the United Farm Workers (UFW, originally the National Farm Workers Association) to represent Mexican American migrant workers.

The founder of the UFW was the charismatic Cesar Chavez. Born in 1927 in Yuma, Arizona, to Mexican immigrants, Chavez moved with his family to

---

Hispanic, a term used in the United States to refer to people who are from, or trace their ancestry to, Spanish-speaking Latin America or Spain, came to be used increasingly after 1945 in conjunction with growing efforts to promote economic and social justice for those people. (Although frequently used as a synonym for *Hispanic*, the term *Latino* technically refers only to people of Latin American descent.)

California in 1939. There they joined thousands of other migrant farmworkers, moving from job to job, living in tents, cars, or ramshackle cabins. In 1944, at age seventeen, Chavez joined the navy. After the war he married and found work, first as a sharecropper raising strawberries and then as a migrant laborer in apricot orchards. In 1952, Chavez joined the Community Service Organization (CSO), a social-service group that sought to educate and organize the migrant poor so that they could become self-reliant. He founded new CSO chapters and was named general director in 1958.

Chavez left the organization in 1962 when it refused to back his proposal to establish a union for farmworkers. Other CSO leaders believed that it was impossible to organize migrant workers into an effective union. They thought the migrant workers were too mobile, too poor, too illiterate, too ethnically diverse, and too easily replaced by braceros. Moreover, farmworkers did not enjoy protected status under the National Labor Relations Act of 1935 (the Wagner Act). Unlike industrial laborers they were not guaranteed the right to organize or the right to receive a minimum wage. Nor did federal regulations govern the safety of their workplace.

Despite such obstacles, Chavez resolved to organize migrant farmworkers. His fledgling National Farm Workers Association gained national attention in 1965 when it joined a strike by Filipino farmworkers against the corporate grape farmers in California's San Joaquin Valley. Chavez's courage and Catholic piety, his insistence upon nonviolent tactics, his reliance upon college-student volunteers, his skillful alliance with organized labor and religious groups—all combined to attract media interest and popular support.

United Farm Workers

Cesar Chavez (center) with organizers of the grape boycott. In 1968, Chavez ended a three-week fast by taking Communion and breaking bread with Senator Robert Kennedy.

Still, the grape strike itself brought no tangible gains. So Chavez organized a nationwide consumer boycott of grapes. In

1970 the grape strike and the consumer boycott finally succeeded in bringing twenty-six grape growers to the bargaining table. They signed formal contracts recognizing the UFW, and soon migrant workers throughout the West were benefiting from Chavez's strenuous efforts on their behalf. Wages increased, and working conditions improved. In 1975 the California state legislature passed a bill that required growers to bargain collectively with the elected representatives of the farmworkers.

The chief strength of the Hispanic movement lay less in the duplication of the civil rights strategies than in the rapid growth of the Hispanic population. In 1960, Hispanics in the United States numbered slightly more than 3 million; by 1970 their numbers had increased to 9 million; and by 2006 they numbered over 40 million, making them the largest minority in the country.

NATIVE AMERICAN RIGHTS American Indians—many of whom had begun calling themselves Native Americans—also emerged as a political force in the late 1960s. Two conditions combined to make Indian rights a priority: first, white Americans felt a persistent sense of guilt for the destructive policies of their ancestors toward a people who had, after all, first settled the continent; second, the plight of the Native American minority was more desperate than that of any other group in the country. Indian unemployment was 10 times the national rate, life expectancy was 20 years lower than the national average, and the suicide rate was 100 times higher than that for whites.

Although President Lyndon Johnson recognized the poverty of the Native Americans and attempted to funnel federal anti-poverty-program funds into reservations, militants within the Indian community grew impatient with the pace of change. They organized protests and demonstrations against local, state, and federal agencies. In 1963 two Chippewas (Ojibwas) living in Minneapolis, George Mitchell and Dennis Banks, founded the American Indian Movement (AIM) to promote "red power." The leaders of AIM occupied Alcatraz Island in San Francisco Bay in 1969, claiming the site "by right of discovery." And in 1972 a sit-in at the Department of the Interior's Bureau of Indian Affairs (BIA) in Washington attracted national attention to their cause. The BIA was then—and still is—widely viewed as the worst-managed federal agency. Instead of finding creative ways to promote tribal autonomy and economic self-sufficiency, the BIA has served as a classic example of government paternalism gone awry.

Indian protesters subsequently discovered a more effective tactic than direct action and sit-ins: they went into federal courts armed with copies of old treaties and demanded that those documents become the basis for restitution.

In Alaska, Maine, South Carolina, and Massachusetts they won significant settlements that provided legal recognition of their tribal rights and financial compensation at levels that upgraded the standard of living on several reservations.

GAY RIGHTS   The liberationist impulses of the 1960s also encouraged homosexuals to organize and assert their right to equal treatment. On June 27, 1969, New York City police raided the Stonewall Inn, a Greenwich Village bar popular with gay men. The patrons fought back, and the struggle spilled into the streets. Hundreds of other gays and their supporters joined the fracas against the police. Rioting lasted throughout the weekend. When it ended, homosexuals had forged a new sense of solidarity and a new organization, the Gay Liberation Front.

As news of the Stonewall riots spread across the country, the gay rights movement assumed national proportions. One of its main tactics was to encourage people to "come out," to make public their homosexuality. This was by no means an easy decision. By professing their homosexuality, gays faced social ostracism, physical assault, exclusion from the military and civil service, and discrimination in the workplace. Yet despite the risks, thousands of homosexuals did come out. By 1973 almost 800 gay organizations had been formed across the country, and every major city had a visible gay community and cultural life.

Like the civil rights crusade and the women's movement, however, the campaign for gay rights soon suffered from internal divisions and aroused a conservative backlash. Gay activists engaged in fractious disputes over tactics and objectives, and in a nationwide counterattack, conservative moralists and Christian fundamentalists succeeded in repealing new local laws banning discrimination against homosexuals. By the end of the 1970s, the gay movement had lost its initial momentum and was struggling to salvage many of its hard-won gains.

NIXON AND VIETNAM

The numerous liberation movements of the 1960s transformed the tone and texture of American social life. By the early 1970s, however, the national mood was swinging back toward conservatism. The election of Richard Nixon in 1968 and the rise of George Wallace as a national political force on the right reflected the emergence of the "silent majority," those white working-class and middle-class citizens who were determined to regain control of a society they feared was awash in permissiveness. Large as the gap was between the "silent majority" and the varied forces of dissent, the two sides agreed upon one thing: that the Vietnam War remained the dominant event of the time. Until the war ended and all American troops had returned home, the nation would find it difficult to achieve the equilibrium that the new president had promised.

GRADUAL WITHDRAWAL   Nixon and his special assistant for national security, Dr. Henry Kissinger, claimed to have a plan to achieve "peace with honor" in Vietnam. Peace, however, was long in coming and not very honorable when it arrived. The Nixon administration, even while withdrawing U.S. forces, held to a policy of refusing to let the North Vietnamese dominate Indochina. By the time a settlement was reached, in 1973, another 20,000 Americans had died, the morale of the American army had been shattered, millions of Asians had been killed or wounded, and fighting was continuing in Southeast Asia. In the end, Nixon's policy gained little that the president could not have accomplished in 1969.

The administration's new strategy in Vietnam moved along three fronts. The first front was the deadlocked Paris peace talks, where American negotiators demanded the withdrawal of North Vietnamese forces from South Vietnam and the preservation of the U.S.-supported regime of President Nguyen Van Thieu. The North Vietnamese and Viet Cong negotiators insisted on retaining a Communist military presence in the south, however, and on reunifying the Vietnamese people under a Communist-dominated government. There was no common ground on which to come together. Hidden from public awareness and from America's South Vietnamese allies were secret meetings between Henry Kissinger and the North Vietnamese.

On the second front, Nixon tried to defuse domestic unrest generated by the war. To this end he sought to "Vietnamize" the conflict by turning over most of the combat missions to Vietnamese units and sharply reducing the number of U.S. ground forces. To assuage the South Vietnamese, he provided more equipment and training for their army. From a peak of 560,000 in 1969, U.S. combat troops were withdrawn at a steady pace. By 1973 only 50,000 troops remained in Vietnam. In late 1969, Nixon also established a lottery system that clarified the likelihood of being drafted: only those with low lottery numbers would have to go. Nixon was more successful in reducing anti-war activity than in forcing concessions from the North Vietnamese negotiators in Paris.

On the third front, while reducing the number of troops in Vietnam, Nixon and Kissinger secretly expanded the air war to persuade the enemy to come to terms. On March 18, 1969, U.S. planes began Operation Menu, a fourteen-month-long bombing of Communist forces in Cambodia. Over 100,000 tons of bombs were dropped, four times the tonnage dropped on Japan during World War II. Congress did not learn of those raids until 1970, when Nixon announced what he called an "incursion" by U.S. troops into supposedly neutral Cambodia to "clean out" North Vietnamese staging areas.

DIVISIONS AT HOME   News of the Cambodia "incursion" came on the heels of another incident that rekindled public indignation against the war. Late in 1969 the story of the My Lai Massacre broke. During the next two years the public learned the gruesome tale of Lieutenant William Calley, who in 1968 had ordered the murder of over 300 Vietnamese civilians in the village of My Lai. Twenty-five officers were charged with complicity in the massacre and subsequent cover-up, but only Calley was convicted of murder. Nixon then granted him parole.

The loudest public outcry against Nixon's Indochina policy occurred in the wake of the Cambodian "incursion," in the spring of 1970. Campuses across the country witnessed a new wave of protests that closed hundreds of colleges and universities. At Kent State University, the Ohio National Guard was called in to quell rioting, during which the building housing the campus Reserve Officers' Training Corps (ROTC) was burned down by anti-war protesters. Pelted by rocks and verbal taunts, the poorly trained guardsmen panicked and opened fire on the demonstrators, killing four bystanders. Eleven days later, on May 15, Mississippi highway patrolmen riddled a dormitory at Jackson State College with bullets, killing two African American students. Although an official investigation of the Kent State episode condemned the "casual and indiscriminate shooting," polls indicated that the public supported the National Guard; students had "got what they were asking for."

The following year, 1971, the *New York Times* began publishing excerpts from a secret Defense Department study on the Vietnam War. The so-called Pentagon Papers, leaked to the press by a former Pentagon official, Daniel Ellsberg, confirmed what many critics of the war had long suspected: Congress and the public had not received the full story on the Gulf of Tonkin incident of 1964. Contingency plans for American entry into the war were being drawn up even while President Johnson was promising that combat troops would never be sent to Vietnam. The Nixon administration blocked publication of the Pentagon Papers, arguing that it would endanger national security and prolong the war. By a vote of 6 to 3, the Supreme Court ruled

Kent State University

National guardsmen shot and killed four bystanders during anti-war demonstrations on the campus of Kent State University in Ohio.

against the government. Newspapers throughout the country began publication the next day.

WAR WITHOUT END   Although Nixon's decision in the spring of 1970 to use American forces to root out Communist bases in Cambodia did bring a tactical victory, it also served to widen a war he had promised to end. Moreover, his hopes that the South Vietnamese units replacing U.S. forces could hold their own against the North Vietnamese were dashed when they suffered repeated defeats in 1971 and 1972. Disorganized, poorly led, and lacking tenacity, the South Vietnamese soldiers had to call upon U.S. airpower to fend off North Vietnamese offensives.

The deteriorating ground war along with mounting divisions at home and the approach of the 1972 presidential elections combined to produce a shift in the American negotiating position in Paris. In the summer of 1972, Henry Kissinger dropped his insistence upon the removal of all North Vietnamese troops from the south before the withdrawal of the remaining U.S. troops. On October 26, only a week before the presidential election, he announced, "Peace is at hand." But the Thieu regime in South Vietnam objected to the plan for a cease-fire, fearful that the continued presence of North Vietnamese troops in the south virtually guaranteed an eventual Communist victory. Hanoi then stiffened its position by demanding that Thieu resign.

The Paris peace talks broke off on December 16, 1972, and Nixon told his military advisers that only a massive show of American airpower would make the North Vietnamese more cooperative at the negotiating table. Two days later the newly reelected Nixon unleashed furious B-52 raids on Hanoi and Haiphong. The so-called Christmas bombings aroused worldwide protest, but Kissinger claimed Nixon's "jugular diplomacy" worked, for the talks in Paris soon resumed.

On January 27, 1973, the United States, North and South Vietnam, and the Viet Cong signed an "agreement on ending the war and restoring peace in Vietnam." The agreement showed that despite the Christmas bombings, the North Vietnamese never altered their basic stance: they kept 150,000 troops in the south and remained committed to the reunification of Vietnam under one government. What had changed since the previous fall was the willingness of the South Vietnamese, who were never allowed to participate in the negotiations, to accept these terms, albeit reluctantly, on the basis of Nixon's promise that the United States would respond "with full force" to any Communist violation of the agreement.

On March 29, 1973, the last U.S. combat troops left Vietnam. On that same day, almost 600 American prisoners of war, most of them downed pilots, were released from Hanoi. Within months, however, the war between north and south resumed, and the Communist forces gained the advantage. In Cambodia and Laos, where fighting had been more sporadic, a Communist victory also seemed inevitable.

In 1975 the North Vietnamese launched a full-scale armored invasion against the south. President Thieu appealed to Washington for assistance, but the Democratic majority in Congress refused, and on April 30, 1975, Americans watched on television as North Vietnamese tanks rolled into Saigon, soon to be renamed Ho Chi Minh City. The scene at the U.S. embassy in Saigon, where thousands of terrified Vietnamese fought to board the last departing helicopters, was a poignant, tragic ending to America's greatest foreign-policy disaster.

The longest war in U.S. history was finally over, leaving in its wake a bitter legacy. The Vietnam War, described as a noble crusade on behalf of democratic ideals, instead suggested that democracy was not easily transferable to third world regions lacking experience with civil liberties and representative government. The war eroded respect for the military so thoroughly that many young Americans came to regard military service as inherently corrupting and ignoble. The war, fought to show the world that the United States was united in its anti-Communist convictions, divided Americans more drastically than any event since the Civil War. The Vietnam War cost the nation some 58,000 deaths and $150 billion. Little wonder the dominant public reaction to the war's end was the urge to put Vietnam behind us and revert to a noninterventionist foreign policy.

NIXON AND MIDDLE AMERICA

Richard Nixon had been elected in 1968 as the representative of middle America, those middle-class citizens fed up with the liberal politics and radical culture of the 1960s. Nixon selected men for his cabinet and White House staff who would restore conservative values and carry out his orders with blind obedience. John Mitchell, the gruff attorney general who had been a senior partner in Nixon's New York law firm, was the new president's closest confidant. H. R. (Bob) Haldeman, an imperious former advertising executive, served as Nixon's chief of staff. As Haldeman explained, "Every President needs a son of a bitch, and I'm Nixon's. I'm his buffer, I'm his bastard." He was succeeded in 1973 by General Alexander Haig, whom Nixon described as "the meanest, toughest, most ambitious son of a bitch I ever knew." John Ehrlichman, a Seattle attorney and college schoolmate of Haldeman's, served as chief domestic-policy adviser. As secretary of state, Nixon tapped his old friend William Rogers, who had served as attorney general under Eisenhower. Rogers's control over foreign policy was quickly preempted by Henry Kissinger, a distinguished Harvard political scientist who served as national security adviser before becoming secretary of state in 1973. Kissinger came to dominate the Nixon administration's diplomatic planning and emerged as one of the most respected and internationally famous members of the staff. Nixon often had to mediate the tensions between Rogers and Kissinger, noting that the secretary of state considered the German-born Kissinger "Machiavellian, deceitful, egotistical, arrogant, and insulting," while Kissinger viewed Rogers as "vain, emotional, unable to keep a secret, and hopelessly dominated by the State Department bureaucracy."

DOMESTIC AFFAIRS A major reason for Richard Nixon's election in 1968 was the effective "southern strategy" fashioned by his campaign staffers. To garner support among Republican delegates from the South and then win over southern voters in the election, Nixon had assured conservatives that he would slow federal enforcement of civil rights laws and appoint pro-southern justices to the Supreme Court. Once in office, Nixon followed through on his pledges. He appointed no African Americans to his cabinet and refused to meet with the Congressional Black Caucus. In 1970 he launched a concerted effort to block congressional renewal of the Voting Rights Act of 1965 and delay implementation of court orders requiring the desegregation of school districts in Mississippi. The Democratic-controlled Congress then extended the Voting Rights Act over Nixon's veto. The Supreme Court, in the first decision made under the new chief justice, Warren Burger—a Nixon appointee—ordered the integration of the Mississippi public schools. During Nixon's first term, and despite his wishes, affirmative action made major inroads, and more schools were desegregated than in all the Kennedy-Johnson years combined.

Nixon also failed in his attempts to block desegregation efforts in urban areas. The Burger Court ruled unanimously in *Swann v. Charlotte-Mecklenburg Board of Education* (1971) that school systems must bus students out of their neighborhood if necessary to achieve racial integration. Protests over desegregation now occurred more in the North and the West than in the South as white families in Boston, Denver, and other cities denounced the destruction of "the neighborhood school." Busing opponents won a limited victory when the Supreme Court ruled in 1974 that requiring the transfer of students from the inner city to the suburbs was unconstitutional. That ruling, along with the *Regents of the University of California v. Bakke* (1978) decision, which restricted the use of quotas to achieve racial balance in university classrooms, marked the transition of desegregation from an issue of simple justice to a more tangled thicket of conflicting group and individual rights.

It also reflected the growing conservatism of the Supreme Court, a trend encouraged by Nixon. The litany of liberal decisions during the 1960s had made the Warren Court a target for conservatives who resented what they regarded as the government's excessive protection of the "undeserving." Fate and the aging of the justices on the Warren Court gave Nixon the chance to make four new appointments. Only one, William Rehnquist, would consistently support Nixon's conservative interpretation of the Constitution, but overall the tenor of the Court did shift toward a more moderate stance.

Nixon also fervently desired to reverse the welfare-state policies of his Democratic predecessors. But the administration never succeeded in developing a comprehensive domestic agenda acceptable to Congress. Meanwhile, the Democratic Congress moved forward with new legislation: the right of eighteen-year-olds to vote in national elections (1970) and, under the Twenty-sixth Amendment (1971), in state and local elections as well; increases in Social Security benefits tied to the inflation rate; a rise in food-stamp funding; the Occupational Safety and Health Act (1970); and the Federal Election Campaign Act (1971). Moreover, in response to Nixon's proposal to decentralize responsibility for various programs, Congress passed a five-year revenue-sharing plan in 1972 that would distribute $30 billion of federal revenues to the states for use as they saw fit.

During Nixon's first term, Americans in large numbers began to lobby for government action to protect and improve the natural environment. In 1970, hundreds of thousands of activists rallied across the country in support of the first Earth Day. In response, Congress established new programs to control water pollution and passed the Clean Air Act (1970) over Nixon's veto. Congress also created the Environmental Protection Agency (EPA) to oversee federal guidelines for controlling air pollution, toxic wastes, and water quality. The EPA began requiring developers to perform environmental-impact studies before new construction could begin. The agency also set fuel-efficiency standards for automobiles and required manufacturers to reduce the level of carbon monoxide emissions from car engines.

ECONOMIC MALAISE The major domestic development during the Nixon years was a floundering economy. Exacerbated by the expense of the Vietnam War, the annual inflation rate began to rise in 1967, when it was at 3 percent. By 1973 it had reached 9 percent; a year later it was at 12 percent, and it remained in double digits for most of the 1970s. Unemployment, at a low of 3.3 percent when Nixon took office, climbed to 6 percent by the end of 1970 and threatened to keep rising. Somehow the American economy was undergoing a recession and an inflation at the same time. Economists coined the term *stagflation* to describe the syndrome that defied the orthodox laws of economics.

The economic malaise had at least three deep-rooted causes. First, the Johnson administration had attempted to pay for both the Great Society's social-welfare programs and the war in Vietnam without a major tax increase, thereby generating larger federal deficits, a major expansion of the money supply, and rapid price inflation. Second and more important, by the late 1960s American goods faced stiff competition in international markets from West Germany, Japan, and other emerging industrial powers. This development sharply reduced the export of American goods and generated a growing trade deficit. Third, the economy had grown heavily dependent upon cheap sources of energy.

Oil crisis, 1973

The scarcity of oil was dealt with by the rationing of gasoline. Gas stations, such as this one in Colorado, closed on Sundays to conserve supplies.

Just as domestic petroleum reserves began to dwindle and dependence upon foreign sources increased, the nations in the Organization of Petroleum Exporting Countries (OPEC), centered in the Middle East, resolved to use their oil as a political and economic weapon. In 1973, after the United States sent massive aid to Israel during the Yom Kippur War, OPEC announced that it would not sell oil to nations supporting Israel and that it was raising its prices by 400 percent. American motorists thereafter faced long lines at gas stations, schools and offices closed temporarily, factories cut production, and the inflation rate soared.

Another condition leading to stagflation was the flood of new workers—mainly baby boomers and women—entering the labor market. From 1965 to 1980, the workforce grew by 40 percent, almost 30 million workers, a figure greater than the total labor force of France or West Germany. The number of new jobs created could not keep up, leaving many unemployed. At the same time, worker productivity declined, further increasing prices in the face of rising demand.

Stagflation posed a new set of economic problems, but the Nixon administration responded with old remedies. First it tried to reduce the federal deficit by raising taxes and cutting the budget. When the Democratic Congress refused to cooperate with that approach, the White House encouraged the Federal Reserve Board to reduce the money supply by raising interest rates. But that move backfired when the stock market quickly collapsed, plunging the economy into the "Nixon recession." A sense of desperation seized the White House. In 1969, when asked about government restrictions on wages and prices, Nixon had been adamant: "Controls. Oh, my God, no! . . . We'll never go to controls." On August 15, 1971, however, he reversed himself. He froze all wages and prices for ninety days, yet the economy still floundered. By 1973 the wage and price guidelines were made voluntary and were therefore almost entirely ineffective. Stagflation continued to plague the economy for the rest of the decade.

NIXON TRIUMPHANT

Confronting a Congress controlled by Democrats, Richard Nixon focused his energies on foreign policy, where presidential initiatives were less restricted. In tandem with Henry Kissinger, he achieved several major breakthroughs. He also continued to support the efforts to beat the Soviets to the moon. In July 1969 the astronaut Neil Armstrong became the first person to walk on the moon. This extraordinary achievement buoyed American spirits at a time when troops were still mired in Vietnam, cities were boiling over

Race to the moon

In July 1969 a program begun by President Kennedy reached its goal: putting a man on the moon.

with racial unrest, and the economy was languishing. Similarly, Nixon's foreign-policy successes gave Americans new confidence in their government. His administration managed to improve U.S. relations with the major powers of the Communist world—China and the Soviet Union—and fundamentally shift the pattern of the cold war.

By 1969, Nixon had perceived that a new multipolar world order was emerging to replace the conventional cold war confrontation between the United States and the Soviet Union. Since 1945 the United States had lost its monopoly on nuclear weapons and its overwhelming economic dominance and

The United States and China

With President Richard Nixon's visit to China in 1972, the United States formally recognized China's Communist government. Here Nixon and Chinese premier Chou En-lai drink a toast.

geopolitical influence. The rapid rise of competing power centers in Europe, China, and Japan complicated international relations—China had replaced the United States as the Soviet Union's most threatening competitor—but also provided strategic opportunities, which Nixon and Kissinger seized.

In early 1970, Nixon announced a significant alteration in American foreign policy. The United States could no longer be the world's policeman against communism; the long-standing containment policy developed by President Truman must be revised: "America cannot—and will not—conceive *all* the plans, design *all* the programs, execute *all* the decisions, and undertake *all* the defense of the free nations of the world." In explaining what became known as the Nixon Doctrine, the president declared that "our interests must shape our commitments, rather than the other way around." The United States, he and Kissinger stressed, must become more strategic and more realistic in its commitments, and it would begin to establish selected partnerships with Communist countries in areas of mutual interest.

CHINA   In 1971, Henry Kissinger made a secret trip to Peking to explore the possibility of U.S. recognition of China. In 1972, Nixon himself arrived in Peking and made recognition an official and public fact. The irony of the

Henry Kissinger's "shuttle diplomacy"

President Sadat of Egypt and Secretary of State Henry Kissinger, during one of Kissinger's many visits to the Middle East, talk with reporters in an effort to bring peace.

event was overwhelming. Richard Nixon, the former anti-Communist crusader who had condemned the State Department for "losing" China in 1949, had accomplished a diplomatic feat that his Democratic predecessors could not. Yet it was because Nixon had been such an ardent anti-Communist that he could pull off the recognition of China: he could not be accused of going soft on communism.

DÉTENTE China sought the breakthrough in relations with the United States because its festering rivalry with the Soviet Union, with which it shares a long border, had become increasingly bitter. Soviet leaders, troubled by the Sino-American agreements, were also eager to ease tensions with the United States now that they had, as the result of a huge arms buildup following the Cuban missile crisis, achieved virtual parity with the United States in nuclear weapons. Once again Nixon surprised the world, announcing that he would visit Moscow in 1972 for discussions with Leonid Brezhnev, the Soviet premier.

What became known as détente with the Soviets offered the promise of a more orderly and restrained competition between the two superpowers. Nixon and Brezhnev signed the Strategic Arms Limitation Talks (SALT) agreement, which set ceilings on the number of long-range nuclear missiles each nation could possess and limited the construction of antiballistic missile systems. In effect the Soviets were allowed to retain a greater number of missiles with greater destructive power while the United States retained a lead in the total number of warheads. No limitations were placed on new weapons systems, though each side agreed to work toward a permanent freeze on all nuclear weapons.

SHUTTLE DIPLOMACY   The Nixon-Kissinger initiatives in the Middle East were less dramatic and less conclusive than the agreements with China and the Soviet Union, but they did show that the United States recognized Arab power in the region and its own dependence upon oil from Islamic states, which were fundamentally opposed to the existence of Israel. After Israel recovered from the initial shock of the Arab attacks that triggered the Yom Kippur War of 1973, it recaptured the Golan Heights and seized additional Syrian territory. Henry Kissinger, now secretary of state, initiated negotiations that led to a cease-fire and exerted pressure to prevent Israel from taking more Arab territory. American reliance upon Arab oil led to closer ties with Egypt and its president, Anwar el-Sadat, and more restrained support for Israel. Although Kissinger's "shuttle diplomacy," involving numerous visits to the capitals of the Middle East, won acclaim from all sides, it failed to find a comprehensive peace formula for the troubled region. It also ignored the problem of establishing a homeland for Palestinian refugees. But Kissinger's efforts did lay groundwork for the accord between Israel and Egypt in 1977.

THE ELECTION OF 1972   Nixon's foreign-policy achievements allowed him to stage the presidential campaign of 1972 as a triumphal procession. The first threat to his reelection came from the Democratic governor of Alabama, George Wallace, who had the potential to deprive the Republicans of conservative votes. But on May 15, 1972, Wallace was shot by a deranged man. Paralyzed below the waist, the governor was forced to withdraw from the campaign. Meanwhile, the Democrats were further ensuring Nixon's victory by nominating Senator George S. McGovern of South Dakota, a steadfast liberal who embodied anti-war principles and embraced progressive social-welfare policies. At the Democratic Convention, party reforms contributed to McGovern's nomination by increasing the representation of women, African Americans, and other minorities, but those reforms alienated the party regulars.

In 1972, Nixon won the greatest victory of any Republican presidential candidate in history, capturing 520 electoral votes to only 17 for McGovern. During the course of the campaign, McGovern had complained about the "dirty tricks" of the Nixon administration, most especially a curious incident during the summer of 1972 when burglars were caught breaking into the headquarters of the Democratic National Committee in the Watergate apartment complex in Washington, D.C. McGovern's accusations seemed shrill and biased at the time. Nixon and his staff made plans for "four more years" as the investigation of the fateful Watergate break-in unfolded.

WATERGATE

During the trial of the accused Watergate burglars in January 1973, the relentless prodding of Judge John J. Sirica led one of the accused to tell the full story of the Nixon administration's complicity in the episode. James Mc-Cord, security chief of the Committee to Re-elect the President (CREEP), was the first of many informers in a melodrama that unfolded over two years. It ended in the first resignation of a president in American history, the conviction and imprisonment of twenty-five officials of the Nixon administration, including four cabinet members, and the most serious constitutional crisis since the impeachment trial of President Andrew Johnson in 1868.

UNCOVERING THE COVER-UP The trail of evidence pursued by Judge John Sirica, a grand jury, several special prosecutors, and a Senate committee headed by Democrat Samuel J. Ervin Jr. of North Carolina led directly to the White House. No evidence surfaced linking Nixon to the order to commit the break-in or suggesting that he had been aware of plans to burglarize the headquarters of the Democratic National Committee. From the start, however, Nixon participated in the cover-up, using his presidential powers to discredit and block the investigation. Perhaps most alarming was that the Watergate burglary proved to be just one small part of a larger pattern of corruption and criminality sanctioned by the Nixon White House. Having developed a compulsive view of his presidency as being above the law, Nixon had ordered intelligence agencies to spy on his most outspoken opponents, open their mail, and even burglarize their homes in an effort to uncover compromising information.

The Watergate cover-up began to unravel as various people, including John Dean, legal counsel to the president, began to cooperate with prosecuters. It unraveled further in 1973 when L. Patrick Gray, acting director of the FBI, resigned after confessing that he had destroyed several incriminating documents. On April 30 top Nixon aides John Ehrlichman and Bob Haldeman resigned, together with Attorney General Richard Kleindienst.

A few days later Nixon nervously assured the public in a television address, "I am not a crook." New evidence suggested otherwise. John Dean, whom Nixon had dismissed, testified before the Ervin committee and a rapt television audience that Nixon had approved the cover-up. In another bombshell disclosure, a White House aide told the committee that Nixon had installed a taping system in the White House and that many of the conversations about Watergate had been recorded.

A yearlong legal battle for the "Nixon tapes" began. Pleading "executive privilege," Nixon refused to release them. On July 24, 1974, in *United States v. Richard M. Nixon*, the Supreme Court ruled unanimously that the president must surrender all of the tapes. A few days later the House Judiciary Committee voted to recommend three articles of impeachment: obstruction of justice through the payment of "hush money" to witnesses and the withholding of evidence, abuse of power through the use of federal agencies to deprive citizens of their constitutional rights, and defiance of Congress by withholding the tapes. Before the House of Representatives could meet to vote on impeachment, however, Nixon handed over the complete set of White House tapes. On August 9, 1974, fully aware that the evidence on the tapes implicated him in the cover-up, Richard Nixon resigned from office, the only president ever to do so.

THE EFFECTS OF WATER-GATE Vice President Spiro Agnew did not succeed Nixon because Agnew himself had been forced to resign in October 1973 for accepting bribes from contractors before and during his term as vice president. The vice president at the time of Nixon's resignation was Gerald Ford, the former Michigan congressman and House minority leader, whom Nixon had appointed, with congressional approval, under the provisions of the Twenty-fifth Amendment (ratified in 1967). President Ford insisted that he had no intention of pardoning Nixon,

Nixon's resignation

Having resigned his office, Richard Nixon waves farewell outside the White House on August 9, 1974.

who was still liable for criminal prosecution. But a month after Nixon's resignation, on September 8, the new president issued the pardon, explaining that it was necessary to end the national obsession with the Watergate scandal. Many Americans suspected that Nixon and Ford had made a deal, though there was no evidence to confirm the speculation.

If there was a silver lining in Watergate's dark cloud, it was the vigor and resilience of the institutions that had brought a rogue president to justice: the press, Congress, the courts, and an aroused public opinion. The Watergate revelations led Congress to pass several pieces of legislation designed to curb executive power in the future. The War Powers Act (1973) requires a president to inform Congress within forty-eight hours if U.S. troops are deployed in combat abroad and to withdraw troops after sixty days unless Congress specifically approves their stay. In an effort to correct abuses of campaign funds, Congress enacted legislation in 1974 that set new ceilings on political contributions and expenditures. In reaction to the Nixon claim of "executive privilege" as a means of withholding evidence, Congress strengthened the 1966 Freedom of Information Act to require prompt responses to requests for information from government files and to place on government agencies the burden of proof for classifying information as confidential.

An Unelected President

The Watergate crisis so dominated the Washington scene that major domestic and foreign problems received little executive attention. Stagflation, the perplexing combination of inflation and recession, worsened, as did the oil crisis. At the same time, Secretary of State Henry Kissinger, who assumed control over the management of foreign policy, watched helplessly as the South Vietnamese forces crumbled before North Vietnamese attacks, attempted with limited success to establish a framework for peace in the Middle East, and supported a CIA role in the overthrow of the popularly elected Marxist president of Chile.

THE FORD YEARS Gerald Ford inherited those simmering problems, as well as the burden of being an unelected president. An amiable, honest man, Ford enjoyed widespread popular support for only a short time. "I am a Ford, not a Lincoln," he candidly recognized upon becoming vice president. His pardon of Nixon generated a storm of criticism. The *New York Times* called it "an unconscionable act."

Meeting at Vladivostok, in Siberia

President Gerald Ford shakes hands with Soviet Communist Party Chief Leonid Brezhnev.

As president, Ford adopted the posture he had developed as a conservative minority leader in the House: a nay-saying leader of the opposition who believed that the federal government exercised too much power over domestic affairs. In his fifteen months as president, Ford vetoed thirty-nine bills, outstripping Herbert Hoover's record in less than half the time. By resisting congressional pressure to reduce taxes and increase federal spending, he succeeded in plummeting the economy into the deepest recession since the Great Depression. Unemployment jumped to 9 percent in 1975, and the federal deficit hit a record the next year. Ford rejected wage and price controls to curb inflation, preferring voluntary restraints.

In foreign policy, Ford retained Henry Kissinger as secretary of state and pursued Nixon's goals of stability in the Middle East, rapprochement with China, and détente with the Soviet Union. Late in 1974, Ford met with Soviet leader Leonid Brezhnev and accepted the framework for another arms-control agreement that was to serve as the basis for SALT II. Meanwhile, Kissinger's tireless shuttling between Cairo and Tel Aviv produced an agreement: Israel promised to return to Egypt most of the Sinai territory captured in the 1967 War, and the two nations agreed to rely upon negotiations rather than force to settle future disagreements.

These limited but significant achievements should have enhanced Ford's image, but they were drowned in the sea of criticism and carping that followed the loss of South Vietnam to North Vietnam in the spring of 1975. Not only had a decade of American effort in Vietnam proved futile, but the Khmer Rouge, the Cambodian Communist movement, had also won a resounding victory, plunging Cambodia into a fanatic bloodbath. And the OPEC oil cartel was threatening another worldwide boycott while other third world nations denounced the United States as a depraved imperialistic power.

THE ELECTION OF 1976 Amid such turmoil, the Democrats could hardly wait for the 1976 election. At the Republican Convention, Ford thwarted a powerful challenge for the nomination from Ronald Reagan, a former California governor and Hollywood actor. The Democrats chose Jimmy Carter, a former naval officer and engineer turned peanut farmer who had served one term as governor of Georgia. Carter capitalized on the post-Watergate cynicism by promising never to "tell a lie to the American people" and by citing his independence from traditional Washington power politics.

To the surprise of many pundits, the little-known Carter revived the New Deal coalition of southern whites, blacks, urban labor, and ethnic groups to win the election, with 41 million votes to Ford's 39 million. Polls showed that the Carter victory benefited from a heavy turnout of African Americans in the South, where Carter swept every state but Virginia. Minnesota senator Walter F. Mondale, Carter's liberal running mate and a favorite among blue-collar workers and the urban poor, also gave the ticket a big boost. The real story of the election, however, was the low voter turnout. Almost half of America's eligible voters, apparently alienated by Watergate and the lackluster candidates, chose to sit out the election.

THE CARTER INTERREGNUM

EARLY SUCCESSES During the first two years of his term, Jimmy Carter enjoyed several successes. His administration included more African Americans, Hispanics, and women than any before. He offered amnesty to the thousands of young men who had fled the country rather than serve in Vietnam, closing one of the remaining open wounds of that traumatic event. He reformed the civil service to provide rewards for meritorious performance, and he created new cabinet-level Departments of Energy and Education. Carter also pushed through Congress significant environmental initiatives, including a bill to regulate strip mining and a "superfund" to clean up chemical-waste sites.

His success was short-lived, however. In the summer of 1979, when renewed violence in the Middle East produced a second fuel shortage, motorists were again forced to wait in long lines for limited supplies of gasoline that they regarded as excessively expensive. Soon they directed their frustration at the White House. Opinion polls showed Carter with an approval rating of only 26 percent, lower than Nixon's during the worst moments of the Watergate crisis.

Several of Carter's early foreign-policy initiatives also got caught in political crossfires. Soon after his inauguration, Carter vowed that "the soul of our foreign policy" should be the defense of human rights abroad. But the human rights campaign aroused opposition from two sides: those who feared that it sacrificed a detached appraisal of national interest for high-level moralizing and those who believed that human rights were important but that the administration was applying the standard inconsistently.

THE CAMP DAVID ACCORDS   Carter's crowning diplomatic achievement was brokering a peace agreement between Israel and Egypt. In 1978, Carter invited Egypt's president Anwar el-Sadat and Israel's prime minister Menachem Begin to Camp David, the presidential retreat in Maryland, for two weeks of difficult negotiations. The first part of the eventual agreement required Israel to return all land in the Sinai Peninsula in exchange for Egyptian recognition of Israel's sovereignty. This agreement was successfully implemented in 1982, when the last Israeli settler vacated the peninsula. But the second part of the agreement, calling for Israel to negotiate with Sadat to resolve the Palestinian refugee dilemma, began to unravel soon after the Camp David summit. Still, Carter and Secretary of State Cyrus Vance had orchestrated a dramatic display of high-level diplomacy that, whatever its limitations, made an all-out war between Israel and the Arab world less likely. It also represented a significant first step toward a comprehensive settlement of the region's volatile tensions.

MOUNTING TROUBLES   Carter's crowning failure was his mismanagement of the economy. In effect he inherited a bad situation and let it worsen. Carter employed the same economic policies as Nixon and Ford to fight stagflation, but he reversed the order of the federal "cure," preferring to fight unemployment first with a tax cut and increased public spending. Unemployment declined slightly, from 8 to 7 percent in 1977, but inflation soared;

The Camp David Accords

Egyptian president Anwar el-Sadat (left), Jimmy Carter (center), and Israeli prime minister Menachem Begin (right) at the announcement of the Camp David Accords, September 1978.

at 5 percent when he took office, it reached 10 percent in 1978 and kept rising. During one month in 1980, it measured 18 percent. Like previous presidents, Carter then reversed himself to fight the other side of the economic malaise. By midterm he was delaying tax reductions and vetoing government spending programs that he had proposed in his first year. The result was the worst of all possible worlds—a deepened recession and inflation averaging between 12 and 13 percent per year.

IRAN Then the Iranian crisis exploded, producing a yearlong barrage of unwelcome events that epitomized the inability of the United States to control world affairs. The crisis began in 1979 with the overthrow of the shah of Iran, long a staunch American ally and right-wing dictator. The revolutionaries who toppled the shah's government rallied around Ayatollah Ruhollah Khomeini, a fundamentalist Muslim leader who symbolized the militant Islamic values the shah had tried to replace with Western ways. Khomeini's hatred of the United States dated back to 1953, when the CIA had sponsored the overthrow of Iran's prime minister, Mohammed Mossadegh, an ardent nationalist who sought to rid his country of Western influence and interests. The 1953 coup had restored the shah's regime to power.

Late in 1979, Carter allowed the exiled shah to enter the United States to undergo cancer treatment. A few days later, on November 4, a frenzied Iranian mob stormed the U.S. embassy in Tehran and seized the staff. Khomeini applauded the mob action and demanded the shah's return, along with all his wealth, in exchange for the release of the fifty-two American hostages still held captive.

Carter was furious, but his options were limited. He appealed to the United Nations, but Khomeini scoffed at UN requests for the release of the hostages. Carter then froze all Iranian assets in the United States and appealed to American allies to organize a trade embargo of Iran. The trade restrictions were only partially effective—even America's most loyal European allies did not want to lose access to Iranian oil.

So a frustrated Carter, hounded by a public and press demanding "action," authorized a rescue attempt by U.S. commandos in April 1980. The raid was aborted in the Iranian desert because of helicopter malfunctions, however, and it ended with eight fatalities when a U.S. helicopter collided with a transport plane. Carter's presidency died with the failed raid. Secretary of State Cyrus Vance resigned in protest against the risky venture. Meanwhile, nightly television coverage of the taunting Iranian rebels generated a near obsession with the seeming impotence of the United States and the fate of the hostages. On January 20, 1981, the crisis ended after 444 days when Carter released several billion dollars of Iranian assets to ransom the kidnapped hostages. By then, however, Ronald Reagan had been elected president, and Carter was headed into retirement.

The turbulent and often tragic events of the 1970s—the Communist conquest of South Vietnam, the Watergate scandal and Nixon's resignation, the energy shortage and stagflation, and the Iranian hostage crisis—provoked among Americans what Carter labeled a "crisis of confidence." By 1980, U.S. power and prestige seemed to be declining, the economy remained in a shambles, and the social revolution launched in the 1960s, with the questions it raised for the family and other basic social and political institutions, had sparked a backlash of resentment in middle America. With theatrical timing, Ronald Reagan emerged to tap the growing reservoir of public frustration and transform his political career into a crusade to make America "stand tall again." He told his supporters that there was "a hunger in this land for a spiritual revival, a return to a belief in moral absolutes." The United States, he declared, remained the "greatest country in the world. We have the talent, we have the drive, we have the imagination. Now all we need is the leadership."

End of Chapter Review

- **Rebellion and Reaction** Civil rights activism was the catalyst for the heightened interest in social causes, especially among the young. Students for a Democratic Society launched the New Left. Other prominent causes of the era included the anti-war movement, the women's liberation movement, Native American rights, Hispanic rights, and gay rights. By 1970 a counterculture had emerged, featuring young people who used mind-altering drugs, lived on communes, and in other ways "dropped out" of the conventional world, which they viewed as corrupt.

- **End of the Vietnam War** Richard Nixon campaigned for the presidency pledging to secure a "peace with honor" in Vietnam, but years would pass before the war ended. His delays prompted an acceleration of anti-war protests. After the Kent State University shootings, the divisions between supporters and opponents of the war became especially contentious. The publication of the Pentagon Papers in 1971 and the heavy bombing of North Vietnam by the United States in December 1972 aroused intense worldwide protests. A month later North and South Vietnam agreed to end the war. The last U.S. troops left Vietnam in March 1973; two years later the government of South Vietnam collapsed, and the country was reunited under a Communist government.

- **Watergate** In an incident in 1972, burglars were caught breaking into the Democratic campaign headquarters at the Watergate complex in Washington, D.C. Eventually the Committee to Re-elect the President (CREEP) was implicated, and investigators probed the question of President Nixon's involvement. Nixon tried to block the judicial process, which led the public to call for the president to be impeached for obstruction of justice. In 1974, in *United States v. Richard M. Nixon*, the Supreme Court ruled that the president had to surrender the so-called Watergate tapes. Nixon resigned to avoid being impeached and removed from office.

- **Middle East Crisis** After the 1973 Yom Kippur War in the Middle East, the Organization of Petroleum Exporting Countries (OPEC) declined to sell oil to states supporting Israel until a cease-fire was reached. President Carter brokered the Camp David Accords of 1978, which laid the groundwork for a peace treaty between Israel and Egypt. The next year an Islamic revolution took place in Iran. Enraged militants stormed the U.S. embassy in Tehran and seized American diplomats and staff. In retaliation, President Carter froze all Iranian assets in the United States. Carter at last released several billlion dollars in Iranian assets to ransom the hostages. The Iranians released the hostages—but not until Ronald Reagan was in office.

CHRONOLOGY

1960	Students in Greensboro, North Carolina, stage a sit-in to demand service at a "whites-only" lunch counter
1960	Food and Drug Administration approves the birth-control pill
1963	Betty Friedan's *The Feminine Mystique* is published
March 1969	U.S. planes begin a fourteen-month-long bombing campaign aimed at Communist sanctuaries in Cambodia
July 1969	Neil Armstrong becomes the first person to walk on the moon
1971	Ratification of the Twenty-sixth Amendment gives eighteen-year-olds the right to vote in all elections
January 1973	In Paris, the United States, North and South Vietnam, and the Viet Cong agree to restore peace in Vietnam
1973	Congress passes the War Powers Act
April 1975	Saigon falls to the North Vietnamese
1978	Jimmy Carter brokers the Camp David Accords, an agreement between Israel and Egypt
1978	Supreme Court issues the *Bakke* decision
November 1979	Islamic militants storm the U.S. embassy in Tehran and take more than fifty Americans hostage

KEY TERMS & NAMES

Richard Nixon p. 1036

Students for a Democratic Society (SDS) p. 1038

the counterculture p. 1040

Woodstock p. 1041

Cesar Chavez p. 1044

American Indian Movement (AIM) p. 1046

Henry Kissinger p. 1048

Vietnamization p. 1048

Kent State p. 1049

My Lai Massacre p. 1049

Pentagon Papers p. 1049

southern strategy p. 1052

stagflation p. 1054

détente p. 1058

Committee to Re-elect the President (CREEP) p. 1060

Watergate p. 1060

Gerald Ford p. 1061

Jimmy Carter p. 1064

Camp David Accords p. 1065

Iranian hostage crisis p. 1067

36

A CONSERVATIVE INSURGENCY

FOCUS QUESTIONS

 wwnorton.com/studyspace

- What explains the rise of Ronald Reagan and Republican conservatism?
- What was the Iran-Contra incident, and what did it show about the nature of the executive branch of the government, even after Watergate?
- What factors led to the end of the cold war?
- What characterized the economy and society in the 1980s?
- What were the causes of the Gulf War?

President Jimmy Carter and his embattled Democratic administration hobbled through 1979. The economy remained sluggish, double-digit inflation continued unabated, and failed efforts to free the hostages in Iran made the administration appear indecisive. Carter's inability to persuade the nation to embrace his energy-conservation program revealed mortal flaws in his reading of the public mood and his understanding of legislative politics.

While the lackluster Carter administration was foundering, Republican conservatives were forging an aggressive plan to win the White House in 1980 and to assault "liberalism" in Washington. Those plans centered on the popularity and charisma of Ronald Reagan, the Hollywood actor turned California governor and prominent political commentator. Reagan was not a deep thinker, but he was a superb analyst of the public mood, an unabashed patriot, and a committed champion of conservative principles. He was also charming and cheerful, a likable politician renowned for his folksy anecdotes and optimistic outlook. Where the dour Carter denounced the evils of free-enterprise capitalism and scolded Americans to revive long-forgotten virtues of frugality, a sunny Reagan promised a "revolution of ideas" designed to unleash the capitalist spirit, restore national pride, and regain international respect.

Reagan promised to increase military spending, dismantle the "bloated" federal bureaucracy, reduce taxes and regulations, and in general shrink the role of the government. He also wanted to affirm old-time morality by banning abortions and re-instituting prayer in public schools. Reagan's appeal derived from his re-markable skill as a public speaker and his dogmatic commitment to a few overarching ideas and simple themes.

"The Great Communicator"

Ronald Reagan in 1980, shortly before his election.

As a true believer and an able compromiser, he combined the fervor of a revolutionary with the pragmatism of a diplomat.

Such attributes won Reagan two presidential terms, in 1980 and 1984, and ensured the election of his successor, George H. W. Bush, in 1988. Just how revolutionary the Reagan era was remains a subject of intense debate. What cannot be denied, however, is that Reagan's actions and beliefs set the tone for the decade's political and economic life.

THE REAGAN REVOLUTION

THE MAKING OF A PRESIDENT   Born in Illinois in 1911, Reagan graduated from Eureka College and then worked as a radio announcer and sportscaster before heading to Hollywood in 1937. In 1964 he entered the political limelight when he delivered a rousing speech on behalf of Barry Goldwater at the Republican Convention. During two terms as governor of California (1967–1975), he displayed a commitment to conservative principles as well as a political realism and an openness to compromise.

Nevertheless, by the middle 1970s Reagan's brand of free-enterprise conservatism still appeared too extreme for a national audience.

THE MOVE TO REAGAN   By the eve of the 1980 election, however, Reagan had become the beneficiary of three developments that made his conservative vision of America much more viable. First, the 1980 census revealed that the population was aging, and large numbers of retirees were moving from the liberal Northeast to the conservative sunbelt states of the South and the West. This development meant that demographic forces were carrying the electorate toward Reagan's conservative position.

Second, in the 1970s the country experienced a massive revival of evangelical religion. No longer simply a local or provincial phenomenon, Catholic conservatives and Protestant evangelicals had bought television and radio stations and were operating schools and universities. The Reverend Jerry Falwell's grassroots organization, the Moral Majority, expressed the major political and social goals of the religious right wing: free enterprise should remain free, big government should be shrunk, abortion should be outlawed, prayer in public schools should be reinstated, Darwinian evolution should be

Anti-abortion movement

Anti-abortion demonstrators pass the Washington Monument on their way to the Capitol.

replaced in schoolbooks by the biblical story of creation, and Soviet communism should be opposed as a form of pagan totalitarianism. The moralistic zeal and financial resources of the religious right made its adherents effective opponents of liberal political candidates and programs. They rallied to Reagan's call for strengthening traditional values and local government.

A third factor contributing to the conservative resurgence was a well-organized and well-financed backlash against the feminist movement. During the 1970s, women who opposed the social goals of feminism formed counterorganizations with names like Women Who Want to Be Women and Females Opposed to Equality. Spearheading those efforts was Phyllis Schlafly, a right-wing Republican activist from Illinois. Schlafly orchestrated the campaign to defeat the equal-rights amendment and thereafter served as the galvanizing force behind a growing anti-feminist movement. She characterized feminists as a "bunch of bitter women seeking a constitutional cure for their personal problems," and she urged women to embrace their "God-given" roles as wives and mothers. Feminists, she charged, were "anti-family, anti-children, and pro-abortion."

Many of Schlafly's supporters also participated in a mushrooming anti-abortion, or "pro-life," movement. By 1980 the National Right to Life Committee, supported by the National Conference of Catholic Bishops, boasted 11 million members representing most religious denominations. The intensity of its members' commitment made it a powerful political force in its own right, and the Reagan campaign was quick to highlight its own support for traditional "family values," gender roles, and the "rights" of the unborn. Such hot-button cultural issues helped persuade many northern Democrats to support Reagan. Whites alienated by the increasingly liberal social agenda of the Democratic party became a crucial element in Reagan's electoral strategy.

THE ELECTION OF 1980 By 1980, voters were flocking to Reagan's cheery promises of less government, lower taxes, renewed prosperity, waning inflation, and revived military strength and national pride. His "supply-side" economics proposals, soon dubbed Reaganomics by supporters and voodoo economics by critics, suggested that the stagflation of the 1970s had resulted from excessive taxes, which weakened the incentive to work, save, and reinvest. The solution was to slash tax rates. For a long-suffering nation it was, in theory, an alluring economic panacea.

On election day, Reagan swept to a decisive victory, with 489 electoral votes to 49 for Carter, who carried only six states. The popular vote proved equally lopsided: 44 million (51 percent) to 35 million (41 percent), with

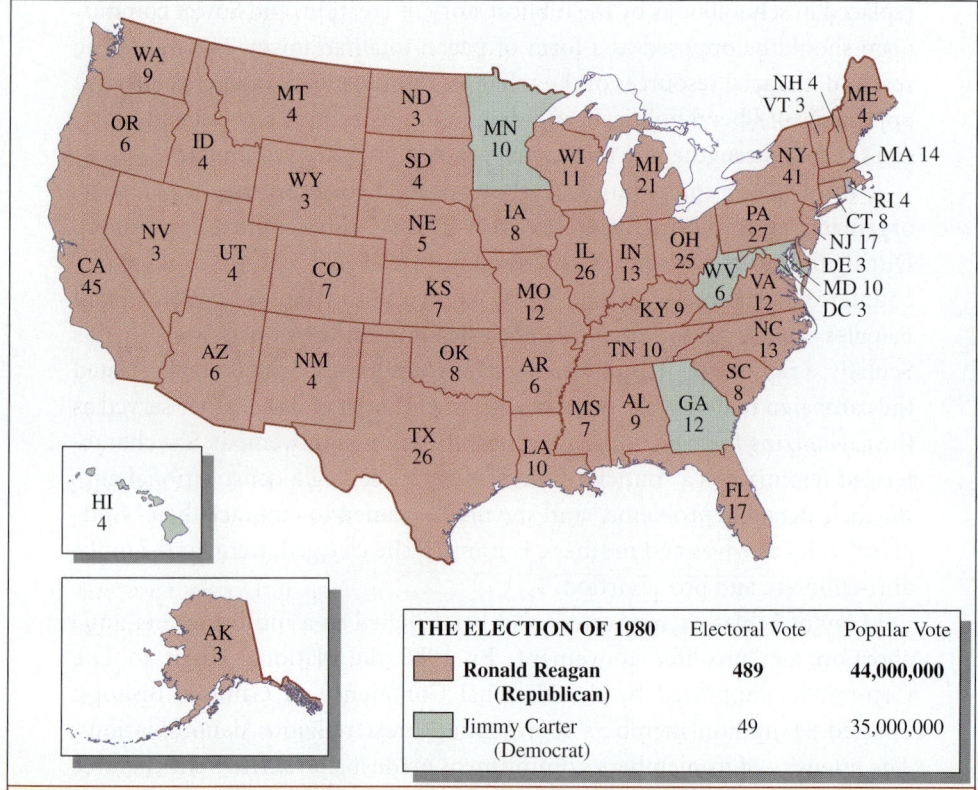

THE ELECTION OF 1980	Electoral Vote	Popular Vote
Ronald Reagan (Republican)	489	44,000,000
Jimmy Carter (Democrat)	49	35,000,000

Why was Ronald Reagan such an appealing candidate in 1980? What was the impact of "nonvoting"? Why was there so much voter apathy?

7 percent going to John Anderson, a moderate Republican who bolted the party after Reagan's nomination and ran on an independent ticket.

In addition to affirming Reagan's conservative agenda, the 1980 election reflected the triumph of what one political scientist called the "largest mass movement of our time": nonvoting. Almost as striking as Reagan's one-sided victory was the fact that his total votes represented only 28 percent of registered voters. Only 53 percent of eligible voters cast ballots in the 1980 election. There were various explanations for the high level of voter apathy among working-class Americans. Some observers stressed the disillusionment with government that grew out of the Watergate affair. Others believed that the Democratic party had alienated its traditional blocs of support. Democratic leaders no longer spoke eloquently on behalf of those at the bottom of America's social scale. By embracing a fiscal conservatism indistinguishable from that of the Republicans, as Carter had done, Democrats had lost their appeal among blue-collar workers and the urban poor. When viewed in this light, Reagan's lopsided triumph represented both a resounding victory for conservative Republicans and a self-inflicted defeat by a fractured Democratic party. Flush with a sense of power and destiny, President-elect Ronald Reagan headed toward Washington with a blueprint for dismantling the welfare state.

REAGAN'S FIRST TERM

REAGANOMICS   Ronald Reagan brought to Washington a cheerful conservative philosophy with a simple premise. "Government is not the solution to our problem," he insisted; "government is the problem." Reagan credited Calvin Coolidge and Coolidge's Treasury secretary, Andrew Mellon, with demonstrating that by reducing taxes and easing government regulation of business, free-market capitalism would revive the economy. By cutting taxes and domestic federal spending and by following a supply-side economic program, he claimed, a surging economy would produce *more* government revenues, which in turn would help reduce the budget deficit.

Early on, Reagan focused on implementing his major campaign pledges: increased defense spending, reduced social spending, and a sweeping tax-reform package. Enough Democrats—mostly sympathetic southern conservatives dubbed boll weevils—supported the measures to pass them by overwhelming majorities. On August 1, 1981, Reagan signed the Economic Recovery Tax Act, which cut personal income taxes by 25 percent, lowered the maximum rate from 70 to 50 percent for 1982, cut the capital gains tax by a third, and offered a broad array of other tax concessions.

The new legislation embodied an idea that went back to Alexander Hamilton, George Washington's Treasury secretary: more money in the hands of the affluent would benefit society at large, since the wealthy would engage in productive consumption and investment. A closer parallel, as Reagan had pointed out, was Treasury Secretary Andrew Mellon's tax-reduction program of the 1920s. The difference was that the Reagan tax cuts were accompanied by massive increases in defense spending, which generated ever-mounting federal deficits. Reagan's advisers insisted that the unbalanced budgets were only temporary; the new tax plan would fuel economic growth and thereby boost tax revenues as personal income and corporate profits skyrocketed. But it did not work out that way. By the summer of 1983, a major economic recovery was under way, but the federal deficits had grown ever larger, so much so that the president, who in 1980 had pledged to balance the federal budget by 1983, had in fact run up debts larger than those of all his predecessors combined.

Bankers and investors feared that the rising federal debt would send interest rates soaring, a fear expressed in sagging bond and stock markets. A business slump and rising unemployment continued through most of 1982. That year the federal deficit doubled. Aides finally convinced Reagan that to reassure the public about deficits and the threat of inflation, the government needed "revenue enhancements," a euphemism for tax increases. With Reagan's support, Congress passed a new tax bill in 1982 that would raise almost $100 billion. During the midterm elections of 1982, Reagan urged voters to "stay the course" and appealed for more time to let his economic program take effect. Meanwhile, the economic slump persisted through that year, with unemployment standing at 10.4 percent, and the congressional Republicans experienced moderate losses in the elections.

THE DEFENSE BUILDUP   Reagan's conduct of foreign policy reflected his belief that trouble in the world stemmed mainly from Moscow. He charged that the Soviets were "prepared to commit any crime, to lie, to cheat" and do anything necessary to promote world communism. To thwart the advance of communism, Reagan and Secretary of Defense Caspar Weinberger embarked upon a major buildup of nuclear and conventional weapons to close the gap that they claimed had developed between Soviet and U.S. military forces.

In 1983, Reagan escalated the nuclear arms race by authorizing the Defense Department to develop a Strategic Defense Initiative, a complex defense system meant to destroy enemy missiles in outer space well before they reached their targets. Despite skepticism among the media and many scientists that such a "Star Wars" defense system could be built, the new initiative forced the Soviets to launch an expensive research and development program of their own to keep pace.

Reagan borrowed the rhetoric of Harry Truman, John Foster Dulles, and John F. Kennedy's inaugural address to express American resolve in the face of "Communist aggression anywhere in the world." Détente deteriorated even further when the Soviets imposed martial law in Poland during the winter of 1981. The crackdown came after Polish workers, united under the banner of an independent union called Solidarity, challenged the Communist monopoly of power. As with the Soviet interventions in Hungary in 1956 and Czechoslovakia in 1968, there was little the United States could do except register protest and impose economic sanctions against Poland's Communist government.

Strategic Defense Initiative

President Reagan addresses the nation on March 23, 1983, about the development of a space-age shield to intercept Soviet missiles.

THE AMERICAS   Reagan's foremost international concern, however, was in Central America, where he detected the most serious Communist threat. The tiny nation of El Salvador, caught up since 1980 in a brutal struggle between Communist-supported revolutionaries and right-wing extremists, received U.S. economic and military assistance. Reagan stopped short of sending troops, but he did increase the number of military advisers and the amount of financial aid sent to the Salvadoran government.

Even more troubling was the situation in Nicaragua. The State Department claimed that the Cuban-sponsored Sandinista government, which had only recently taken control of the country after ousting a corrupt dictator, was funneling Soviet and Cuban arms to leftist Salvadoran rebels. In response the Reagan administration ordered the CIA to train and supply guerrilla bands of disgruntled Nicaraguans, tagged Contras, who staged attacks on Sandinista bases and officials from sanctuaries in Honduras. In supporting these "freedom fighters," Reagan sought not only to impede the traffic in arms to Salvadoran rebels but also to overthrow the Communist Sandinistas.

Critics of Reagan's anti-Sandinista policy accused the Contras of being mostly right-wing fanatics who indiscriminately killed civilians as well as Sandinista soldiers. They also feared that the United States might eventually commit its own combat forces in a Vietnam-like intervention.

"Shhhhhh. It's Top Secret."

A comment on the Reagan administration's covert operations in Nicaragua.

THE MIDDLE EAST The Middle East remained a tinderbox of geopolitical conflict throughout the 1980s. No peaceable end seemed possible in the bloody Iran-Iraq War, which had erupted in 1980, entangled as it was with the passions of Islamic fundamentalism. In 1984 both sides began to attack tankers in the Persian Gulf, a major source of the world's oil. Although the Reagan administration harbored no affection for either nation, it viewed Iranian fundamentalism as the greater threat and funneled aid to Iraq, a policy with unforeseen and grave consequences.

American diplomats continued to see Israel as the strongest ally in the volatile region, all the while seeking to encourage moderate Arab groups and anti-Communist governments. Continuing chaos in Lebanon, where ethnic and religious tensions erupted in near anarchy, threatened both Israel's borders and America's goals for the region. The capital, Beirut, became a battleground for rival Muslim and Christian factions, the army of the Palestine Liberation Organization (PLO), Syrian invaders cast as peacekeepers, and Israelis responding to PLO attacks.

French, Italian, and U.S. forces moved into Beirut as "peacekeepers," but in such small numbers as to become targets themselves. On October 23,

1983, an Islamic suicide bomber drove a truck laden with explosives into the U.S. Marine headquarters at the Beirut airport. The explosion left 241 Americans dead. On February 7, 1984, Reagan announced that the marines would be redeployed on warships offshore. The Israeli forces pulled back to southern Lebanon, while the Syrians remained in eastern Lebanon and imposed a tenuous peace upon the faction-ridden country.

GRENADA   In a fortunate turn for the Reagan administration, an easy military triumph closer to home eclipsed news of the debacle in Lebanon. On the tiny Caribbean island of Grenada, a leftist government had admitted Cuban workers to build a new airfield and had signed military agreements with several Communist-bloc countries. Appeals from the governments of neighboring islands led Reagan in 1983 to order 1,900 soldiers to invade the island, depose the radical regime, and evacuate a group of American students at Grenada's medical school. The UN General Assembly condemned the action, but most Grenadans and their neighbors applauded it, and the intervention was immensely popular in the United States.

REAGAN'S SECOND TERM

By 1983, prosperity had returned, and inflation had subsided; the Reagan "supply-side" economic program seemed to be working as touted. A dramatic fall in oil prices following the fragmentation of the OPEC cartel and Reagan's decision to remove price controls on oil and natural gas produced an economic expansion.

THE ELECTION OF 1984   By 1984, Reagan had restored strength and vitality to the White House and the nation. Reporters began to describe a "Reagan Revolution" in Washington. The president's prospects for reelection were bright. The Democratic nominee, former Minnesota senator and vice president Walter Mondale, faced an uphill struggle. Mondale won a lot of media attention by choosing as his running mate a woman, New York representative Geraldine Ferraro. Attention soon turned to Ferraro's husband's dubious business dealings, however. In any case, Reagan's skill and confidence at campaigning outshone Mondale, and the economic recovery made it difficult for the Democratic nominee to attract interest, much less generate enthusiasm. In the end, Reagan won almost 59 percent of the popular vote and lost only Minnesota and the District of Columbia. His coattails were not as long as they had been in 1980, however. Republicans gained only fifteen seats in the House, leaving them still greatly outnumbered by Democrats, 253 to 182. They also lost two Senate seats, creating a margin of only 53 to 47.

THE REAGAN DOCTRINE   In his 1985 State of the Union message, the reelected president clarified what had come to be called the Reagan Doctrine in foreign affairs. The United States, he proclaimed, would support anti-Communist forces around the world seeking to "defy Soviet-supported aggression." In effect, he was challenging the isolationism that followed the nation's humbling experience in Vietnam. America, he promised, would not hesitate to intervene in the world's hot spots.

Yet for all his stern talk about the Soviet Union's being "an evil empire," Reagan was determined to reach an arms-control agreement with the Soviets. In Geneva in 1985, he met with Mikhail Gorbachev, the innovative new leader of the Soviet Union. The two signed several cultural and scientific agreements and issued a statement on arms-limitations talks, but no treaty was in the offing. Nearly a year after the Geneva summit, on sudden notice and with limited preparation, Gorbachev and Reagan met in Iceland for two days to discuss arms reductions. Early reports predicted a major breakthrough, including a total ban on nuclear weapons, but the talks collapsed over disagreement on

Foreign relations

A light moment at a meeting between U.S. president Ronald Reagan (left) and Soviet premier Mikhail Gorbachev (right).

Reagan's commitment to the Strategic Defense Initiative. After the Iceland meeting the two nations reduced the scope of their discussions in order to break the impasse.

The logjam impeding the arms negotiations suddenly broke when Gorbachev announced that he was willing to deal separately on a medium-range missile treaty. After nine months of strenuous negotiations, Reagan and Gorbachev met amid much fanfare in Washington on December 9, 1987, and signed a treaty to eliminate intermediate-range (300- to 3,000-mile) nuclear missiles. It was an epochal event, not only because it marked the first time that the two nations had agreed to destroy a whole class of weapons systems but also because it represented a key first step toward the eventual end of the arms race altogether. Under the terms of the treaty, the United States would destroy 859 missiles, and the Soviets would eliminate 1,752. Provision was also made for on-site inspections by each side to verify compliance. Still, this winnowing of weapons represented only 4 percent of the total number of nuclear missiles on both sides. Arms-control advocates thus looked toward a second and more comprehensive treaty that would eliminate long-range strategic missiles.

THE IRAN-CONTRA AFFAIR   During the fall of 1986, the Reagan administration suffered a double blow. In the midterm elections, Democrats regained control of the Senate by 55 to 45. For his final two years in office, Reagan would face an opposition Congress. What was worse, on election day reports surfaced that the United States, with Israeli assistance, had been secretly selling arms to Iran in the hope of securing the release of American hostages held in Lebanon by extremist Islamic groups with close ties to Iran. Such action contradicted Reagan's repeated public insistence that his administration would never negotiate with terrorists.

There was more to the story. Over the next several months, revelations reminiscent of the Watergate affair disclosed a more complicated series of covert activities carried out by administration officials. At the center of what came to be dubbed the Iran-Contra affair was the much-decorated marine lieutenant colonel Oliver North. An aide to the National Security Council who specialized in counterterrorism, North had been scheming to use the profits from the secret sale of military weapons to Iran to subsidize the Contra rebels fighting in Nicaragua even though Congress had voted to ban such aid.

Oliver North's activities, it turned out, had been approved by national security adviser Robert McFarlane; McFarlane's successor, Admiral John Poindexter; and CIA director William Casey. Both Secretary of State George Shultz and Secretary of Defense Caspar Weinberger criticized the arms sale

The Iran-Contra affair

National security adviser Robert McFarlane (left) tells reporters about his resignation. Vice Admiral John Poindexter (far right) succeeds him in the post.

to Iran, but their objections were ignored, and they were thereafter kept in the dark about what was going on. Later, on three occasions, Shultz threatened to resign over the continuing operation of the "pathetic" scheme. After information about the secret (and illegal) dealings surfaced in the press, McFarlane attempted suicide, Poindexter resigned, and North was fired Casey, who denied any connection, left the CIA for health reasons and died shortly thereafter from a brain tumor.

Under increasing criticism and amid growing doubts about his credibility and his ability, Reagan appointed both an independent counsel and a three-man commission, led by former Republican senator John Tower, to investigate the scandal. The Tower Commission issued a report early in 1987 that placed much of the responsibility for the bungled Iran-Contra affair on Reagan's loose management style. The president seemed unaware of what his staffers were doing.

The investigations of the independent counsel led to six indictments in 1988. A Washington jury found Oliver North guilty of three relatively minor charges but innocent of nine more serious counts, apparently reflecting the jury's reasoning that he had acted as an agent of higher-ups. His conviction was later overturned on appeal. The Iran-Contra affair left support for the

Nicaraguan Contras badly eroded in Congress, and it undermined much of Reagan's popularity.

THE POOR, THE HOMELESS, AND THE VICTIMS OF AIDS The 1980s were years of vivid contrast. Despite unprecedented affluence, there were countless beggars in the streets and homeless people sleeping in doorways, in cardboard boxes, and on ventilation grates. A variety of factors caused the shortage of low-cost housing: the government had given up on building public housing, urban-renewal programs had demolished blighted areas but provided no housing for those they displaced, and owners had abandoned unprofitable buildings in poor neighborhoods or converted them into expensive condominiums, a process called gentrification.

In addition, after new medications enabled the deinstitutionalization of the mentally ill, many individuals ended up on the streets because the promised community mental-health services failed to materialize. By the summer of 1988, the *New York Times* estimated, more than 45 percent of New York's adults were living in poverty, totally outside the labor force, because of a lack of skills, drug use, and other problems.

Still another group cast aside was composed of people suffering from the frightening newly identified malady that had been named AIDS (acquired immunodeficiency syndrome). At the beginning of the decade, public health officials had begun to report that gay men and intravenous drug users were especially at risk for contracting AIDS. Those infected with the virus that causes AIDS showed signs of fatigue, developed a strange combination of infections, and soon died; people contracted the virus, HIV, by coming into contact with the blood or body fluids of an infected person.

The Reagan administration showed little interest in AIDS in part because it initially was viewed as a "gay" disease. Patrick Buchanan, the conservative spokesman who served as White House director of communications, said that homosexuals had "declared war on nature, and now nature is extracting an awful retribution."

THE REAGAN LEGACY Although Ronald Reagan had declared in 1981 his intention to "curb the size and influence of the federal establishment," the welfare state remained intact when Reagan left office. Neither the Social Security system nor Medicare had been dismantled or overhauled, nor had any other major welfare programs. And the federal agencies that Reagan had threatened to abolish, such as the Department of Education, not only remained in place in 1989 but had seen their budgets grow. The federal budget as a percentage of the gross domestic product was higher when Reagan left office than when he had entered. Moreover, he did not try to push through Congress the incendiary social issues championed by the religious right, such as allowing prayer in public schools and a ban on abortions.

Yet Ronald Reagan succeeded in redefining the national political agenda and accelerated the conservative insurgency that had been developing for over twenty years. His greatest successes were in renewing America's soaring sense of possibilities, bringing inflation under control, stimulating the longest sustained period of peacetime prosperity in history, and helping to light the fuse of democratic freedom in Eastern Europe.

THE ELECTION OF 1988 As a new presidential election unfolded, eight Democratic presidential candidates engaged in a wild scramble for their party's nomination. As the primary season progressed, however, it soon

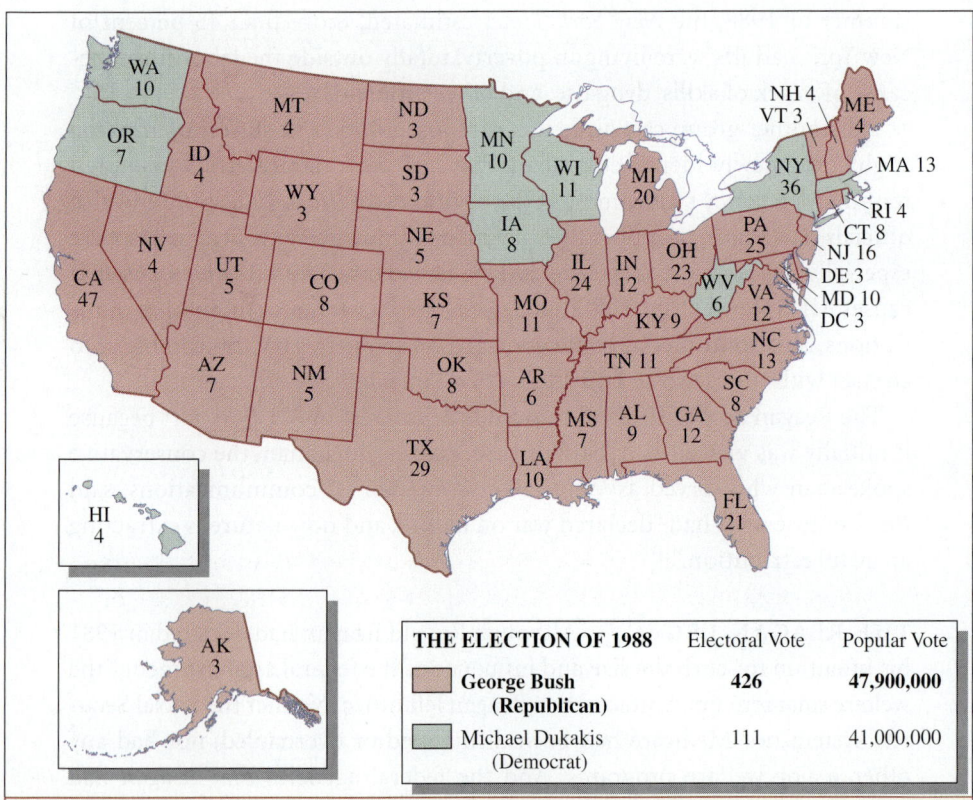

THE ELECTION OF 1988	Electoral Vote	Popular Vote
George Bush (Republican)	426	47,900,000
Michael Dukakis (Democrat)	111	41,000,000

How did George H. W. Bush overtake Michael Dukakis's lead in the polls? What was the role of race and class in the election results?

became a two-man race between Massachusetts governor Michael Dukakis and Jesse Jackson, an African American civil rights activist who had been one of Martin Luther King's chief lieutenants. Dukakis eventually won out and managed a difficult reconciliation with the Jackson forces that left the Democrats unified and confident as the fall campaign began.

The Republicans nominated Reagan's two-term vice president, George H. W. Bush, who after a bumpy start had easily cast aside his rivals in the primaries. As Reagan's handpicked heir, Bush claimed credit for the administration's successes, but like all vice presidents he also faced the challenge of defining his own political identity. Yet at the Republican Convention, Bush delivered a forceful address that sharply enhanced his stature. The most memorable line was a defiant statement on taxes: "Congress will push me to raise taxes, and I'll say no, and they'll push, and I'll say no, and they'll push again. And I'll say to them: Read my lips. No new taxes."

In a campaign given over to mudslinging, the Bush partisans attacked Dukakis as a camouflaged liberal who would increase federal spending, raise taxes, gut the defense budget, and refuse to intervene to prevent Communist aggression abroad. The Republican onslaught took its toll against the less organized, less focused Dukakis campaign. Moreover, the Republicans continued to benefit from the population growth in the sunbelt states, the shift of population from the Democratic cities to the Republican suburbs, and from the votes of many moderate and conservative Democrats and independents. Dukakis captured only ten states plus the District of Columbia, with clusters of support in the Northeast, Midwest, and Northwest. Bush carried the rest, with a margin of about 54 percent to 46 percent in the popular vote and 426 to 111 in the Electoral College.

THE BUSH ADMINISTRATION

George H. W. Bush viewed himself as a guardian president rather than an activist. He lacked Reagan's visionary outlook and skill as a speaker. Bush was a pragmatic caretaker eager to avoid "stupid mistakes" and find a way to get along with the Democratic majority in Congress. "We don't need to remake society," he announced. Bush therefore sought to consolidate the programs that Reagan had put in place rather than launch his own array of programs and policies.

THE DEMOCRACY MOVEMENT ABROAD   Bush entered the White House with more foreign-policy experience than most presidents, and he found the spotlight of the world stage more congenial than wrestling with the intractable problems of the inner cities and the deficit. Within two years of his inauguration, George Bush would lead the United States into two wars. Throughout most of 1989, however, he merely had to sit back and observe the dissolution of one totalitarian or authoritarian regime after another. For the first time in years, global democracy was on the march in a sequence of mostly bloodless revolutions that took the world by surprise.

Although in China a democracy movement came to a tragic end in 1989 when government forces mounted a deadly assault on demonstrators in Beijing's Tiananmen Square, Eastern Europe had an entirely different experience. Mikhail Gorbachev set events in motion by responding to Soviet economic problems with policies of perestroika (restructuring) and glasnost (openness), a loosening of centralized economic planning and censorship. His foreign policy sought rapprochement and trade with the West, and he aimed to relieve the Soviet economy of burdensome military costs.

Gorbachev backed off from Soviet imperial ambitions. Early in 1989, Soviet troops left Afghanistan after spending nine years bogged down in civil war there. Then in July in Paris, Gorbachev repudiated the Brezhnev Doctrine, which asserted the right of the Soviet Union to intervene in the internal affairs of other Communist countries. The days when Soviet tanks would roll through Warsaw and Prague were over, and leaders in the Eastern-bloc countries found themselves beset by demands for democratic reform. With opposition strength building, the old regimes fell with surprisingly little bloodshed. Communist party rule ended first in Poland and Hungary, then in Czechoslovakia and Bulgaria. In Romania the year of peaceful revolution ended in a bloodbath when the Romanian people were joined by the army in a bloody uprising against the brutal dictator Nicolae Ceaușescu. He and his wife were captured, tried, and then executed on Christmas Day.

The most spectacular event in the collapse of the Soviet Empire came on November 9, 1989, when the chief symbol of the cold war—the Berlin Wall—was torn down by Germans, and the East German government succumbed to popular pressures for change. With the borders to the West fully open, the Communist government of East Germany collapsed, a freely elected government came to power, and on October 3, 1990, the five states of East Germany were united with West Germany. The reunified German nation remained in NATO, and the Warsaw Pact alliance was dissolved.

The reform impulse that Gorbachev helped unleash in the Eastern-bloc countries careened out of control within the Soviet Union, however. Gorbachev proved unusually adept at political restructuring. While yielding to the Communist monopoly of government, he built a new presidential system that

Dissolution of the Soviet Empire

West Germans hacking away at the Berlin Wall on November 11, 1989, two days after all crossings between East Germany and West Germany were opened.

gave him, if anything, increased powers. His skills did not extend to an antiquated economy that resisted change, however. The revival of ethnic allegiances added to the instability. Although Russia proper included slightly more than half the Soviet Union's population, it was only one of fifteen constituent republics, most of which began to seek autonomy, if not independence.

Gorbachev's popularity in the Soviet Union shrank as it grew abroad. It especially eroded among the Communist hard-liners, who saw in his reforms the unraveling of their bureaucratic and political empire. On August 18, 1991, a cabal of political and military leaders tried to seize the reins of power in Russia. They accosted Gorbachev at his vacation retreat in the Crimea and demanded that he sign a decree proclaiming a state of emergency and transferring his powers to them. He replied, "Go to hell," whereupon he was placed under house arrest. Twelve hours later the Soviet news agency reported to the world that Gorbachev was "ill" and had temporarily transferred his powers to his vice president and an eight-member emergency committee. Political parties were suspended, newspapers were silenced, a

Action against Gorbachev

In August 1991, one day after Mikhail Gorbachev was placed under house arrest by Communists planning a coup, Russian president Boris Yeltsin (holding papers) makes a speech criticizing the plotters.

curfew was announced, and street demonstrations were banned. Tanks and armored vehicles surrounded government buildings in Moscow. The new leaders promised to end the "chaos and anarchy" they claimed were bedeviling the country.

But the coup was doomed from the start. Poorly planned and clumsily implemented, it lacked effective coordination. The plotters failed to arrest popular leaders such as Boris Yeltsin, the president of the Russian republic, and they neglected to close the airports or cut off telephone and television communications. Most important, the plotters failed to recognize the strength of the democratic idealism unleashed by Gorbachev's reforms.

As the political drama unfolded in the Soviet Union, foreign leaders denounced the coup. On August 20, President Bush responded favorably to Yeltsin's request for support and persuaded other leaders to join him in refusing to recognize the legitimacy of the new Soviet government. The next day, word began to seep out that the plotters had given up and were fleeing. Several committed suicide, and a newly released Gorbachev ordered the others arrested. But Gorbachev's freedom did not bring a restoration of his power. Boris Yeltsin emerged as the most popular political figure in the country. Gorbachev reclaimed the title of president of the Soviet Union, but he was forced to resign as head of the Communist party and admit that he had made a grave mistake in appointing the men who had turned against him.

So what had begun as a reactionary coup turned into a powerful accelerant for stunning changes in the Soviet Union. Most of the fifteen republics proclaimed their independence, with the Baltic republics of Latvia, Lithuania, and Estonia regaining the status of independent nations. The Communist party apparatus was dismantled, prompting celebrating crowds to topple statues of Lenin and other Communist heroes.

The aborted coup accelerated Soviet and American efforts to reduce the stockpiles of nuclear weapons. In 1991, President Bush announced that the United States would destroy all its tactical nuclear weapons on land and at sea in Europe and Asia, take its long-range bombers off twenty-four-hour-alert status, and initiate discussions with the Soviet Union for the purpose of instituting sharp cuts in nuclear missiles with multiple warheads. Bush explained that the prospect of a Soviet invasion of western Europe was "no longer a realistic threat," and this transformation presented an unprecedented opportunity for reducing the threat of nuclear holocaust. The Soviets responded by announcing reciprocal cutbacks. As Colin Powell, chairman of the Joint Chiefs of Staff, remarked, the cold war "has vaporized before our eyes."

By the end of 1991, the Soviet Union had dissolved into a new—and fragile—Commonwealth of Independent States made up of eleven autonomous republics (Georgia joined in 1993). Held together by little other than historic ties and contiguous borders, the federated republics soon suffered outbreaks of ethnic tensions and separatist movements. With the Communist party dissolved, the Soviet Union dismantled, and continuing economic woes creating obstacles to his leadership, Mikhail Gorbachev resigned as president at the end of 1991. Boris Yeltsin, now a national hero, replaced him.

The dilution of the Soviet military threat led the U.S. Defense Department in 1992 to withdraw large numbers of personnel from military bases in Asia and Europe. The Pentagon also announced a plan to shrink the armed forces by 500,000 troops over the next five years. In 1992, Bush and Yeltsin declared their intention to reduce their combined arsenals of nuclear weapons from about 22,500 to no more than 7,000 by 2003. All land-based multiple-warhead missiles were to be destroyed.

PANAMA   The end of the cold war did not spell the end of international tensions and conflicts, however. Indeed, in some respects the world became more unstable. Before the end of 1989, American troops were engaged in battle in Panama, where General Manuel Noriega, as chief of the

Panamanian Defense Forces since 1983, was head of the government in fact if not in title. Years earlier Noriega had worked secretly with the CIA, providing information about developments in Central America. At the same time, he got involved in the lucrative—and illegal—drug trade. In 1988 federal grand juries in Miami and Tampa indicted Noriega and fifteen others on charges of international drug smuggling, gunrunning, and laundering the profits through Panamanian banks.

In 1989, Panama's National Assembly named Noriega head of the government and proclaimed that Panama "is declared to be in a state of war" with the United States. The next day, December 16, 1989, a U.S. marine in Panama was killed. President Bush ordered an invasion of Panama in order to capture Noriega, bring him to the United States so that he could face the charges against him, and install a government headed by opposition leaders.

The 12,000 U.S. military personnel already in Panama were quickly joined by 12,000 more, and in the early morning of December 20 five military task forces struck at strategic targets in the country. Twenty-three U.S. servicemen were killed in the action, and estimates of Panamanians killed and wounded, including many civilians, were as high as 4,000. Noriega was captured, and he was detained in a U.S. federal prison for well over a year before his trial began in late 1991. He was convicted in 1992 on eight counts of racketeering and drug distribution.

THE GULF WAR   Months after Panama had moved to the background of public attention, Saddam Hussein, dictator of Iraq, focused attention on the Middle East when his army suddenly invaded neighboring Kuwait on August 2, 1990. Kuwait had raised its production of oil, contrary to agreements with OPEC. The resulting drop in global oil prices offended the Iraqi regime, deep in debt and heavily dependent upon oil revenues. Saddam Hussein did not expect the firestorm of world indignation that his assault on Kuwait ignited. The UN Security Council unanimously condemned the invasion and demanded withdrawal. American secretary of state James Baker and Soviet foreign minister Eduard Shevardnadze issued a joint statement of condemnation. The Security Council then endorsed Resolution 661, an embargo on trade with Iraq.

President Bush condemned Iraq's "naked aggression" and dispatched planes and troops to Saudi Arabia on a "wholly defensive" mission: to protect Saudi Arabia. British forces soon joined in, as did troops from a half dozen Arab nations. On August 22, Bush ordered the mobilization of American reserve forces for the operation, now dubbed Operation Desert Shield. A flurry of peace efforts failed. Iraq refused to yield. On January 10, Congress began to

The Gulf War

U.S. soldiers adapt to desert conditions during Operation Desert Shield, December 1990.

debate whether to authorize the use of U.S. armed forces. The outcome was uncertain to the end, but on January 12 a resolution for the use of force passed in the House, by a vote of 250 to 183, and in the Senate, by 52 to 47.

An allied force of over thirty nations was committed to Operation Desert Storm by January 1991. The first missiles began to hit Iraq at about 2:30 A.M. Baghdad time on January 17. Saddam Hussein, expecting an allied attack northward into Kuwait, concentrated his forces in that country. But the Iraqis were outflanked when 200,000 allied troops, largely American, British, and French, turned up on the undefended Iraqi border with Saudi Arabia, far to the west. The swift-moving allied ground assault began on February 24 and lasted only four days. Thousands of Iraqi soldiers surrendered, and there was a quick breakthrough into Kuwait.

On February 28, six weeks after the fighting began, President Bush called for a cease-fire, the Iraqis accepted, and the shooting ended. There were 137 American fatalities. The lowest estimate of Iraqi fatalities, civilian and military, was 100,000. The coalition forces occupied about a fifth of Iraq. The consequences of the brief but intense Persian Gulf War, the "mother of all battles" in Saddam Hussein's words, would be played out in the future in ways no one predicted.

End of Chapter Review

- **Rise of Conservatism** Ronald Reagan's charm, coupled with disillusionment over Jimmy Carter's presidency and the Republicans' call for a return to traditional values, won Reagan the presidency in 1980. The Republican insurgency was characterized by a cultural backlash against the feminist movement, and it was supported by Christian evangelicals and people who wanted lower taxes and a smaller, less intrusive federal government.

- **Iran-Contra Scandal** Members of Reagan's administration secretly sold arms to Iran in the hopes of securing the release of American hostages held in Lebanon by extremists sympathetic to Iran. The deal contradicted the president's public claims that he would never deal with terrorists. Furthermore, profits from the arms sales were used to fund right-wing rebels in Nicaragua, known as Contras, despite Congress's having voted to ban any aid to the Contras. An independent commission appointed by the president determined that Reagan's loose management style was responsible for the illegal activities, and Reagan admitted that he had lied to the American people.

- **End of the Cold War** Toward the end of the century, democratic movements exploded in China, where they failed, and in Eastern Europe, where they largely succeeded. In the Soviet Union, Mikhail Gorbachev's steps to restructure the economy and promote more open policies led to demands for further reform. Communist party rule collapsed in the Soviet satellite states. In November 1989, the Berlin Wall was torn down, and a year later Germany was reunified. Russia itself survived a coup by hard-liners, and by 1991 the cold war had ended.

- **Reaganomics** Americans in the 1980s experienced unprecedented prosperity, yet beggars and homeless people were visible in most cities. The prevailing atmosphere was conservative, and AIDS was condemned as a "gay" disease. "Reaganomics" failed to reduce public spending, but the president nevertheless championed tax cuts for the rich. The result was massive public debt and the stock market collapse of 1987.

- **The Gulf War** Saddam Hussein of Iraq invaded Kuwait in 1990. The United Nations condemned Hussein's action and authorized the use of force to dislodge Iraq from Kuwait, and over thirty nations committed themselves to Operation Desert Shield. When Hussein did not withdraw, the allied forces launched Operation Desert Storm, and the Iraqis surrendered within six weeks.

CHRONOLOGY

1982	Israeli troops invade Lebanon
1983	U.S. marines are killed in a suicide bombing in Beirut
1987	Tower Commission issues its report on the Iran-Contra affair
1987	Reagan delivers a speech at the Berlin Wall challenging the Soviet Union to tear down the wall
October 1987	Stock market experiences Black Monday
1989	China's government crushes the democracy movement at Tiananmen Square
November 1989	Berlin Wall is torn down
December 1989	U.S. troops invade Panama and capture Manuel Noriega
August 1991	Failure of a reactionary coup in Russia leads to the emergence of Boris Yeltsin
August 1990	Saddam Hussein invades Kuwait

KEY TERMS & NAMES

37

TRIUMPH AND TRAGEDY: AMERICA AT THE TURN OF THE CENTURY

FOCUS QUESTIONS wwnorton.com/studyspace

- How did the demographics of the United States change between 1980 and 2000?

- What led to the Democratic resurgence of the early 1990s and the surprising Republican landslide of 1994?

- What caused the surge and decline of the stock and financial markets in the 1990s and the early years of the twenty-first century?

- What were the consequences of the rise of global terrorism in the early twenty-first century?

- In what ways was the 2008 presidential election historic?

The United States entered the final decade of the twentieth century triumphant. American vigilance in the cold war had fueled the shocking collapse of the Soviet Union and the birth of democratic capitalism in eastern Europe. The United States was now the world's only superpower. By the mid-1990s the American economy would become the marvel of the world as remarkable gains in productivity afforded by new technologies created the greatest period of prosperity in modern history. Yet no sooner did the century come to an end than America's comfortable sense of physical and material security was shattered by a shocking terrorist assault that would kill thousands, plummet the economy into recession, and call into question conventional notions of national security and personal safety.

AMERICA'S CHANGING MOSAIC

DEMOGRAPHIC SHIFTS   The nation's population had grown to over 306 million by 2010. During the last quarter of the twentieth century, the sunbelt states of the South and the West continued to lure residents from the Midwest and the Northeast. Fully 90 percent of the nation's total population growth during the 1980s occurred in southern or western states. These population shifts forced a massive redistricting of the House of Representatives, with Florida, California, and Texas gaining seats and states such as New York losing them.

Women continued to enter the workforce in large numbers. In 1970, 38 percent of the workforce was female; in 2000 the figure was almost 50 percent. Women made up over a third of the new doctors (up from 4 percent in 1970), 40 percent of the new lawyers (up from 8 percent in 1970), and 23 percent of the new dentists (up from less than 1 percent in 1970).

The decline of the traditional family unit continued. In 2006 less than 65 percent of children lived with two parents, down from 85 percent in 1970. And more people were living alone than ever before, largely as a result of high divorce rates or a growing practice among young people of delaying marriage until well into their twenties. The number of single mothers increased 35 percent during the decade. The rate was much higher for African Americans: in 2000 fewer than 32 percent of African American children lived with both parents, down from 67 percent in 1960.

Young African Americans in particular faced shrinking economic opportunities at the start of the twenty-first century. The urban poor more than others were victimized by high rates of crime and violence, with young black men suffering the most. In 2000 the leading cause of death among African American men between the ages of fifteen and twenty-four was homicide. Over 25 percent of African American men aged twenty to twenty-nine were in prison, on parole, or on probation, while only 4 percent were enrolled in college. Nearly 40 percent of African American men were functionally illiterate.

THE NEW IMMIGRANTS   The racial and ethnic composition of the country was also changing rapidly during the early twenty-first century. By 2010 the United States had more foreign-born and first-generation residents than ever before. Over 30 percent of Americans claimed African, Asian, Hispanic, or American Indian ancestry. Hispanics represented 16 percent of the total population, African Americans 11 percent, Asians about 4 percent,

Illegal immigration

Increasing numbers of Chinese risked their savings and their lives to gain entry to the United States. These illegal immigrants are trying to keep warm after being forced to swim ashore when the freighter carrying them to the United States ran aground near Rockaway Beach in New York City in June 1993.

and American Indians almost 1 percent. The rate of increase among those four groups was twice as fast as it had been during the 1970s.

The primary cause of this dramatic change in the nation's ethnic mix was a surge of immigration. In 2000 the United States welcomed more than twice as many immigrants as all other countries in the world combined. For the first time in the nation's history, the majority of immigrants came not from Europe but from other parts of the world: Asia, Latin America, and Africa. Among the legal immigrants, Mexicans made up the largest share, averaging over 100,000 a year.

THE COMPUTER REVOLUTION   While demographic shifts and immigration were changing the nation's appearance, technological changes were transforming its behavior. A dramatic revolution in information technology produced a surge in productivity and prosperity during the 1980s and 1990s. Cellular phones, laser printers, VCRs and then DVDs, fax machines, personal computers, and iPods became commonplace. The computer age had arrived.

The idea of a programmable machine that would rapidly perform mental tasks had been around since the eighteenth century, but it took the crisis of World War II to gather the intellectual and financial resources needed to develop such a "computer." In 1946 a team of engineers at the University of Pennsylvania created ENIAC (electronic numerical integrator and computer), the first all-purpose, all-electronic digital computer.

With the invention in 1971 of the microprocessor—a computer on a silicon chip—the functions that had once been performed by computers taking up an entire room could be performed by a microchip circuit the size of a postage stamp. Engineers soon incorporated microchips into television sets, wristwatches, automobiles, kitchen appliances, and spacecraft.

The invention of the microchip made possible the personal computer. In 1975 an engineer named Ed Roberts developed the prototype of the so-called personal computer. The Altair 8800 was imperfect and cumbersome, with no display, no keyboard, and not enough memory to do anything useful. But its potential excited a Harvard sophomore named Bill Gates.

The computer age

Beginning with the cumbersome electronic numerical integrator and computer (ENIAC), pictured here in 1946, computer technology flourished, leading to the development of personal computers in the 1980s and the popularization of the Internet in the 1990s.

Gates improved the software of the Altair 8800, dropped out of college, and formed a company called Microsoft to market the new system. By 1977, Gates and others had helped transform the personal computer from a machine for hobbyists into a mass consumer product.

Cultural Conservatism

Cultural conservatives helped elect Ronald Reagan and George Bush in the 1980s, but they were disappointed with the results. Once in office, neither president had, in the eyes of those conservatives, adequately addressed their moral agenda, including a complete ban on abortions and the restoration of prayer in public schools. By the 1990s a new generation of young conservative activists, mostly political independents or Republicans, had emerged as a major force in national affairs. They were more ideological, more libertarian, more partisan, and more impatient than their predecessors.

THE RELIGIOUS RIGHT Although quite diverse, cultural conservatives tended to be evangelical Christians or orthodox Catholics, and they joined together to exert increasing religious pressure on the political process. In 1989 the television evangelist Pat Robertson organized the Christian Coalition to replace Jerry Falwell's Moral Majority as the flagship organization of the resurgent religious right. The Christian Coalition chose the Republican party as the best vehicle for promoting its pro–school prayer, anti-abortion, anti–gay rights positions. In addition to celebrating "traditional family values," it urged politicians to "radically downsize and delimit government." In many respects the religious right took control of the political and social agendas in the 1990s.

Bush to Clinton

For months after the Persian Gulf War in 1991, George H. W. Bush seemed unbeatable. But the aftermath of Desert Storm was mixed, with Saddam Hussein's grip on Iraq still intact. Despite his image of strength abroad, Bush began to look weak even on foreign policy. The Soviet Union, meanwhile, stumbled on to its surprising end. On December 25, 1991, the Soviet flag over the Kremlin was replaced by the flag of the Russian Federation.

The Persian Gulf War

Iraqi soldiers surrender to the Allied forces in Kuwait.

The cold war had ended not just with the collapse of the Soviet Union but with the dismemberment of its fifteen constituent republics. As a result, the United States had become the world's only superpower.

"Containment" of the Soviet Union, the bedrock of American foreign policy for more than four decades, had lost its reason for being. Bush struggled to interpret the fluid new international scene. He spoke of a "new world order" but never defined it. By his own admission he had trouble with "the vision thing." By the end of 1991, a listless Bush faced a challenge in the Republican primary from the feisty television commentator and former White House aide Patrick Buchanan.

RECESSION AND DOWNSIZING   For the Bush administration and for the nation, the most devastating development in the early 1990s was a prolonged economic recession. The first major economic setback in more than eight years, it grew into the longest, if not the deepest, since the Great Depression. During 1991, 25 million workers—about 20 percent of the labor force—were unemployed at some point. The euphoria over the allied victory in the Gulf War quickly gave way to anxiety and to resentment generated by the depressed economy. At the end of 1991, *Time* magazine declared that "no one, not even George Bush" could deny "that the economy was sputtering." With his domestic policies in disarray and his foreign policy abandoned, George Bush tried a clumsy balancing act in addressing the recession, on the one hand acknowledging that "people are hurting" while on the other telling Americans that "this is a good time to buy a car."

TAX TURMOIL   President Bush had already set a political trap for himself when he declared at the 1988 Republican Convention: "Read my lips. No new taxes." Fourteen months into his presidency, he decided that the growing federal budget deficit was a greater risk than violation of his no-new-taxes pledge. After intense negotiations with congressional Democrats, Bush announced that reducing the federal deficit required "tax revenue increases." His backsliding set off a revolt among House Republicans, but a bipartisan majority (with most Republicans still opposed) finally approved a tax increase, raising the top personal rate from 28 to 31 percent, disallowing certain deductions in the upper brackets, and raising various excise taxes. Conservative Republicans would not let George Bush forget his abandoned pledge.

DEMOCRATIC RESURGENCE   As the Republicans divided over tax policy and social issues, the Democrats sought to present an image of centrist forces in control. For several years the Democratic Leadership Council, in which Arkansas governor William Jefferson Clinton figured prominently, had been pushing the party from the liberal left to the center of the political spectrum. Clinton strove to move the Democrats closer to the mainstream of political opinion. A graduate of Georgetown University, he had won a Rhodes scholarship to Oxford University and then earned a law degree from Yale, where he met his future wife, Hillary Rodham. By 1979, at age thirty-two, Bill Clinton was back in his native Arkansas, having been elected the youngest governor in the country. He served three more terms as governor and in the process emerged as a dynamic young leader committed to winning back the middle-class whites who had voted Republican during the 1980s. Democrats had grown so liberal, he argued, that they had alienated their key constituency, the "vital center."

A self-described moderate seeking the Democratic presidential nomination in 1992, Clinton promised to cut the defense budget, provide tax relief for the middle class, and create a massive economic-aid package for the former republics of the Soviet Union seeking to embrace democratic capitalism. Handsome, witty, intelligent, and a compelling speaker, Clinton projected an

The 1992 presidential campaign
Presidential candidate Bill Clinton and his running mate, Al Gore, brought youthful enthusiasm to the campaign trail.

image of youthful energy and optimism, reminding many political observers of John F. Kennedy. But underneath the veneer of Clinton's charisma were several flaws. He often seemed so determined to become president that he was willing to sacrifice consistency and principle. He made extensive use of polls to shape his stance on issues, pandered to special-interest groups, and flip-flopped on controversial subjects, leading critics to label him Slick Willie. Said one former opponent in Arkansas: "He'll be what people want him to be. He'll do or say what it will take to get elected." Even more enticing to the media and more embarrassing to Clinton were charges that he was a chronic adulterer and that he had manipulated the ROTC program during the Vietnam War to avoid the draft. Clinton's evasive denials of both allegations could not dispel a lingering distrust of his character.

Yet after a series of bruising party primaries, Clinton emerged as the front-runner at the Democratic nominating convention in the summer of 1992. Once nominated, Clinton chose Senator Albert Gore Jr. of Tennessee as his running mate. So the candidates were two southern Baptists from adjoining states.

Flushed with their convention victory and sporting a ten-point lead in the polls, the Clinton-Gore team stressed economic issues to win over working-class white and African American voters. Clinton won the election with

370 electoral votes and about 43 percent of the vote; Bush received 168 electoral votes and 39 percent of the vote; and off-and-on independent candidate H. Ross Perot of Texas garnered 18 percent of the popular vote but no electoral votes. A puckish billionaire, Perot found a large audience for his simplified explanations of public problems and his offers to just "get under the hood and fix them."

DOMESTIC POLICY IN CLINTON'S FIRST TERM

Clinton's inexperience in international affairs and congressional maneuvering led to several missteps in his first year as president. Like George Bush before him, he reneged on several campaign promises. He abandoned his proposed middle-class tax cut in order to keep down the federal deficit. Nine days into office he backed down when the Pentagon and Congress opposed his attempt to allow professed homosexuals to serve in the military; subsequently he announced an ambiguous policy concerning gays in the military that came to be known as "don't ask, don't tell." In Clinton's first two weeks in office, his approval rating dropped 20 percent.

THE ECONOMY   Clinton entered office determined to reduce the federal deficit without damaging the economy. To this end, on February 17, 1993, he proposed higher taxes for corporations and for individuals in higher tax brackets and called for an economic stimulus package for "investment" in public works (transportation, utilities, and the like) and "human capital" (education, skills, health, and welfare). Clinton's hotly contested deficit-reduction package passed by 218 to 216 in the House and 51 to 50 in the Senate, with Vice President Gore breaking the tie.

Equally contested was the North American Free Trade Agreement (NAFTA), which the Bush administration had negotiated with Canada and Mexico. The debate over its congressional approval revived old arguments on the tariff. Clinton stuck with his party's tradition of low tariffs and urged approval of NAFTA, which would make North America the largest free-trade area in the world. He and his supporters argued that tariff reductions would open up foreign markets to American industries. Opponents of the bill, including gadfly Ross Perot and organized labor, favored barriers that would discourage cheaper foreign products and believed that with NAFTA the country would hear the "giant sucking sound" of American jobs being drawn to Mexico. Yet Clinton prevailed, winning solid Republican support while losing a sizable minority of Democrats, mostly from the South, where executives predicted that textile mills would lose business to "cheap-labor" countries.

NAFTA protesters

Protesters going to a rally where House Majority Leader Richard Gephardt spoke to hundreds of opponents.

HEALTH-CARE REFORM

Clinton's major public-policy initiative was a federal health-care plan. Sentiment for health-care reform spread as annual medical costs skyrocketed and some 39 million Americans went without insurance either by choice or out of necessity. Universal medical coverage as proposed by Clinton would entitle every citizen and documented immigrant to health insurance. First Lady Hillary Clinton chaired the plan's task force and became the administration's lead witness on the plan before congressional committees. The bill aroused intense opposition from the pharmaceutical and insurance industries, and by the summer of 1994 Clinton's health-insurance plan was doomed. Lacking the votes to stop a filibuster by Senate Republicans, the Democrats acknowledged defeat and gave up the fight for universal medical coverage.

REPUBLICAN INSURGENCY

During 1994, Bill Clinton began to see his presidency unravel. Unable to get either health-care reform or welfare-reform bills through the Democratic Congress and having failed to carry out his campaign pledge for middle-class tax relief, he and his party found themselves on the defensive. In the midterm elections of 1994, the Democrats suffered a humbling defeat. It was the first election since 1952 in which Republicans captured both houses of Congress. Not a single Republican incumbent was defeated. Republicans also won a net gain of eleven governorships and fifteen state legislatures.

THE CONTRACT WITH AMERICA A Georgian named Newton Leroy Gingrich led the Republican insurgency in Congress. Gingrich, a brilliant former history professor with an oversize ego, had helped mobilize religious and social conservatives associated with the Christian Coalition. In early 1995 he became the first Republican Speaker of the House in forty-two years. Gingrich announced that "we are at the end of an era." Liberalism, he claimed, was dead, and the Democratic party was dying. Gingrich pledged to start a new reign of congressional Republican dominance that would dismantle the "corrupt liberal welfare state." He was aided by freshman Republicans promoting what he called the Contract with America. The ten-point contract outlined an anti-big-government program with less regulation, less environmental conservation, term limits for members of Congress, a line-item veto for the president, welfare reform, and a balanced-budget amendment.

Yet the much-ballyhooed GOP revolution and the Contract with America fizzled out. The revolution that the imperious Gingrich touted was far too ambitious to be carried out in so limited a time with so slim a majority and so little sense of crisis. What is more, many of the Republican freshman representatives were scornful of compromise and were amateurs at legislative procedure; they limited Gingrich's ability to maneuver. The Senate, whose members were less spellbound by Gingrich and not party to the Contract with America anyway, rejected many of the bills that had been passed in the House. The "Republican revolution" of 1994 fizzled out, too, because Newt Gingrich became such an unpopular figure, both in Congress and among the electorate. He was too ambitious, too slick, too aggressive, too rambunctious. Clinton's lieutenants effectively portrayed him as an extremist.

LEGISLATIVE BREAKTHROUGH In the late summer of 1996, as lawmakers were preparing to adjourn and participate in the presidential nominating conventions, the 104th Congress broke through its partisan gridlock and passed a flurry of important legislation that President Clinton quickly signed, including bills increasing the minimum wage and broadening access to health insurance.

Even more significant was a comprehensive welfare-reform measure that ended the federal government's open-ended guarantee of aid to the poor, a guarantee that had been in place since 1935. The Personal Responsibility and Work Opportunity Act of 1996 turned over the major federal welfare programs to the states, which would receive federal grants to fund them. The bill also limited the amount of time during which a person could receive welfare benefits funded by federal money and required that at least half of a state's welfare recipients have jobs or be enrolled in job-training programs by 2002. States failing to meet the deadline would have their federal funds cut.

The Republican-sponsored welfare-reform legislation passed the Senate by a vote of 74 to 24. When Clinton signed the bill, liberals charged that he was abdicating Democratic social principles in order to gain reelection amid the conservative climate of the times. Clinton and his centrist advisers dismissed the criticism, however. With his reelection bid at stake, the president was determined to live up to his 1992 campaign pledge to "end welfare as we know it." Clinton also knew that most voters in both parties were eager to see major cuts in federal entitlement programs.

THE 1996 CAMPAIGN   After clinching the Republican presidential nomination in 1996, Senate majority leader Bob Dole resigned his seat in order to devote himself to defeating Bill Clinton. As the 1996 presidential campaign unfolded, however, Clinton maintained a large lead in the polls. With an improving economy and no major foreign-policy crises to confront, personal and partisan issues surged into prominence. Concern about Dole's age (seventy-three) and his acerbic personality, as well as rifts in the Republican party between economic and social conservatives over issues such as abortion and gun control, hampered Dole's efforts to generate widespread support.

On November 5, 1996, Clinton won again, with an electoral vote of 379 to 159 and 49 percent of the popular vote. Dole received 41 percent of the popular vote, and independent candidate Ross Perot got 8 percent. The Republicans lost eight seats in the House but retained a 227 to 207 advantage over the Democrats in the House; in the Senate, Republicans gained two seats for a 55–45 majority.

The Clinton Years at Home

As the twentieth century came to a close, the United States benefited from a prolonged period of unprecedented prosperity. Buoyed by low inflation, high employment, declining federal budget deficits, dramatic improvements in productivity, the rapid globalization of economic life, and the leadership of Federal Reserve Board chairman Alan Greenspan, business and industry witnessed record profits.

THE "NEW ECONOMY"   During the late 1990s the stock market soared. In 1993 the Dow Jones Industrial Average hit 3,500. By 1996 it had topped 6,000. During 1998 it reached 9,000, defying the predictions of experts that the economy could not sustain such performance. In 1998, unemployment was only 4.3 percent, the lowest since 1970. Inflation was a measly 1.7 percent. People talked of the onset of a new economy, one that was centered on high-tech companies and would defy the boom-and-bust cycles of the previous hundred years. "It is possible," Greenspan suggested, "that we have moved 'beyond history.'"

In the 1990s much of the growth in the economy resulted from efforts to promote favored free markets on a world scale: global markets without tariffs and other barriers to free trade. More and more gigantic corporations such as IBM and General Electric had become international in scope. This phenomenon encouraged free-trade agreements such as NAFTA as well as most-favored-nation treatment for Communist China and other countries. With such agreements in place, American companies could easily "outsource" much of their production to plants in countries with lower labor costs. Increasingly, therefore, blue-collar labor lost ground to cheap foreign labor in assembly plants or "sweatshops" elsewhere in the world.

RACE INITIATIVES   After the triumphs of the civil rights movement in the 1960s, the momentum for minority advancement had run out—except for gains in college admissions and employment under the rubric of affirmative action. The conservative mood during the mid-1990s manifested itself in the Supreme Court. In 1995 the Court ruled against election districts redrawn to create African American or Hispanic majorities and narrowed federal affirmative-action programs.

In 1996 two major steps were taken against affirmative action in college admissions. In *Hopwood v. Texas*, a federal court ruled that considering race to achieve a diverse student body at the University of Texas was "not a compelling interest under the Fourteenth Amendment." Later that year the state of California passed Proposition 209, an initiative that ruled out race, sex, ethnicity, and national origin as criteria for preferring any group. These rulings eviscerated affirmative-action programs and drastically reduced African American enrollments, thereby prompting second thoughts. In addition, the nation still had not addressed intractable problems that lay beyond civil rights—that is, problems of dependency: illiteracy, poverty, unemployment, urban decay, and slums.

THE SCANDAL MACHINE   During his first term, President Clinton was dogged by allegations of improper involvement in the Whitewater Development Corporation. In 1978, as governor of Arkansas, he had invested in a resort to be built in northern Arkansas. The project turned out to be a fraud and a failure, and the Clintons took a loss on their investment. In 1994, Kenneth Starr, a Republican, was appointed to serve as independent counsel in an investigation of the Whitewater case. Starr's exhaustive investigation did not uncover evidence that the Clintons were directly involved in the fraud, although several of their close associates had been caught in the web and convicted of various charges, some related to Whitewater and some not.

Besides Whitewater, Starr's team of investigators looked into the allegations of Paula Jones that Clinton had sexually harassed her while he was governor of Arkansas and she was a state employee. In the course of the investigation, it surfaced that the president may have had a sexual affair with a former White House intern, Monica Lewinsky, and may have pressed her to lie about it under oath. Clinton publicly denied the affair, but the tawdry scandal would not disappear. In August 1998, President Clinton agreed to appear before a grand jury convened to investigate the sexual allegations. He was the first president in history to testify before a grand jury. On August 17, with the nation anxiously awaiting the results, Clinton recanted his earlier denials and acknowledged having had "inappropriate intimate physical contact" with Monica Lewinsky. Public reaction to Clinton's stunning about-face was mixed. A majority of Americans expressed sympathy for the president because of his public humiliation and wanted the matter dropped. Clinton's credibility had suffered a serious blow on account of his reckless lack of self-discipline and his efforts to deny and then cover up the sordid scandal.

Meanwhile, on September 9, 1998, Kenneth Starr submitted to Congress a 445-page report and eighteen boxes of supporting material. The Starr Report found "substantial and creditable" evidence of presidential wrongdoing. Drawing upon the evidence, the Republican-controlled House Judiciary Committee voted 21 to 16 to recommend a full impeachment inquiry into the allegations of perjury and obstruction of justice by the president. On October 8 the House of Representatives voted 258 to 176 to begin a wide-ranging impeachment inquiry of the president. Thirty-one Democrats joined the Republicans in supporting the investigation. On December 19, 1998, William Jefferson Clinton became the second president to be impeached by the House of Representatives. The House officially approved two articles of impeachment, charging Clinton with lying under oath to a federal grand jury and obstructing justice.

The Senate trial of President Clinton began on January 7, 1999. Five weeks later, on February 12, the Senate acquitted the president. Rejecting the first charge of perjury, 10 Republicans and all 45 Democrats voted "not guilty." On the charge of obstruction of justice, the Senate split 50–50 (which meant

Impeachment

Representative Edward Pease, a member of the House Judiciary Committee, covers his face during the vote on the third of four articles of impeachment charging President Clinton with "high crimes and misdemeanors," December 1998.

acquittal, since 67 votes were needed for conviction). In both instances, senators had a hard time interpreting Clinton's philandering as constituting "high crimes and misdemeanors," the constitutional requirement for removal of a president from office. Clinton's supporters portrayed him as the victim of a puritanical special prosecutor and a partisan conspiracy run amok. His critics lambasted him as a lecherous man without honor or integrity. Both characterizations were incomplete. Politically astute, charismatic, and well-informed, Clinton had as much ability and potential as any president. Yet he was also shamelessly self-indulgent. The result was a scandalous presidency punctuated by dramatic achievements in welfare reform, economic growth, and foreign policy.

FOREIGN-POLICY CHALLENGES

Like Woodrow Wilson, Lyndon Johnson, and Jimmy Carter before him, Bill Clinton was a Democratic president who came into office determined to focus on the nation's domestic problems only to find himself mired in foreign

Clinton and the Middle East

President Clinton presides as Israeli prime minister Yitzhak Rabin (left) and PLO leader Yasir Arafat (right) agree to a peace accord between Israel and the Palestinians, September 1993.

entanglements. Clinton continued the Bush administration's intervention in Somalia, on the northeastern horn of Africa, where collapse of the government early in 1991 had left the country in anarchy, prey to tribal marauders. President Bush in 1992 had gained UN sanction for a military force led by American troops to relieve hunger and restore peace. In early 1993, U.S. troop levels peaked and began to shrink with the arrival of international forces. The Somalian operation proved successful at its primary mission, but it never solved the political problems that lay at the root of the population's starvation and civil strife.

THE MIDDLE EAST   Clinton also continued George Bush's policy of sponsoring patient negotiations between the Arabs and the Israelis. A new development was the inclusion of the PLO in the negotiations. In 1993 a draft agreement between Israel and the PLO provided for the restoration of Palestinian self-rule in the occupied Gaza Strip and in Jericho, on the West Bank of the Jordan River, in an exchange of land for peace as provided in UN Security Council resolutions. A formal signing occurred at the White House on September 13, 1993. With President Clinton presiding, Israeli prime minister Yitzhak Rabin and PLO leader Yasir Arafat exchanged handshakes, and their foreign ministers signed the agreement.

The Middle East peace process suffered a terrible blow in early November 1995, however, when Yitzhak Rabin was assassinated at a peace rally in Tel Aviv by an Israeli Jewish zealot who resented Rabin's efforts to negotiate with the Palestinians. Some observers feared that the assassin had killed the peace process as well when seven months later conservative hard-liner Benjamin Netanyahu narrowly defeated the U.S.-backed Shimon Peres in the Israeli elections. Yet in October 1998, Clinton brought Arafat, King Hussein of Jordan, and Netanyahu together at a conference center in Wye Mills, Maryland, where they reached an agreement. Under the Wye River Memorandum, Israel surrendered land in return for security guarantees by the Palestinians. As hard-liners attempted to derail the tenuous peace process, Netanyahu called elections early, and the Israeli public swept into power former general Ehud Barak, who promised to jump-start the peace process.

THE BALKANS Clinton's foreign policy also addressed the chaotic transition in eastern Europe from Soviet domination to independence. When Yugoslavia imploded in 1991, fanatics and tyrants incited ethnic conflict as four of its six republics seceded. Serb minorities, backed by Serbia itself, stirred up civil wars in Croatia and Bosnia. In Bosnia especially, the war involved "ethnic cleansing"—driving Muslims from their homes and towns. In 1995, American negotiators finally persuaded the foreign ministers of Croatia, Bosnia, and the new Federal Republic of Yugoslavia to agree to a comprehensive peace plan. To enforce the agreement, 60,000 NATO troops would be dispatched to Bosnia as part of a peacekeeping operation. A cease-fire went into effect in October 1995.

In 1998 the Balkan tinderbox flared up again, this time in the Yugoslav province of Kosovo, a region long considered sacred by Christian Serbs. By 1989, however, over 90 percent of the 2 million Kosovars were ethnic Albanian Muslims. In that year, Yugoslav president Slobodan Milošević decided to reassert Serbian control over the province. He stripped Kosovo of its autonomy and established de facto martial law. When the Albanian Kosovars resisted and large numbers of Muslim men began to join the Kosovo Liberation Army, Serbian soldiers and state police ruthlessly suppressed them and launched another program of "ethnic cleansing," burning Albanian villages, murdering men, raping women, and displacing hundreds of thousands of Muslim Albanian Kosovars.

On March 24, 1999, NATO, relying heavily upon American military resources and leadership, launched air strikes against Yugoslavia. After seventy-two days of unrelenting bombardment, Milošević sued for peace on NATO's terms. An agreement was reached on June 3, 1999. As the Albanian Kosovars began to return to Kosovo, however, large numbers of Serbs, fearful of Muslim retribution, began to leave, and some of them were killed. Members of the Kosovo Liberation Army stepped into the vacuum left by the departing Serbs and began to take control of the province.

GLOBALIZATION   The deepening involvement of the United States in the complex affairs of eastern Europe symbolized the broadening scope of globalization. As the proliferation of globe-spanning information and communications technologies shrank time and distance, a cornucopia of consumer goods was produced, distributed, marketed, and sold by multinational companies all over the world, not just in the United States. As more nations entered the world economy and experienced prosperity, they benefited corporations in the United States by buying more American products and sending more and better goods to the United States. U.S. exports rose dramatically in the last twenty years of the twentieth century. By the end of the twentieth century, the American economy had become dependent on the global economy; foreign trade had become central to American prosperity—and to American politics. By 2000 over a third of the production of American multinational companies was occurring abroad, compared with only 9 percent in 1980. By the end of the twentieth century, the American economy had become internationalized to such a profound extent that global concerns exercised an overwhelming influence on American domestic and foreign policies.

THE ELECTION OF 2000

The election of 2000 revealed that American voters were split evenly along partisan lines. The two major-party candidates for president, Vice President Al Gore, the Democrat, and Texas governor George W. Bush, the Republican and son of the former president, presented sharply contrasting views on the role of the federal government, tax cuts, environmental policies, and the best way to preserve Social Security and Medicare. Gore, a Tennessee native and Harvard graduate whose father had been a senator, favored an active federal government that would preserve Social Security and subsidize prescription-medicine expenses for the elderly. He criticized proposed Republican tax cuts for catering to the wealthy. An environmental activist, Gore reaffirmed his support for the Environmental Protection Agency and the Interior Department.

Bush, on the other hand, proposed to transfer power from the federal government to the states, particularly in regard to the environment and education. He promoted more drilling for oil on federal land, and he endorsed the use of vouchers (cash grants) to enable parents to send their children to private schools. In international affairs, Bush questioned the need to maintain U.S. peacekeeping forces in Bosnia and the continuing expense of other global military commitments.

In the end the election was the one of the closest—and most controversial—in history. The television networks initially reported that Gore had narrowly won the state of Florida and its decisive twenty-five electoral votes. Later in the evening, however, the networks reversed themselves, saying that

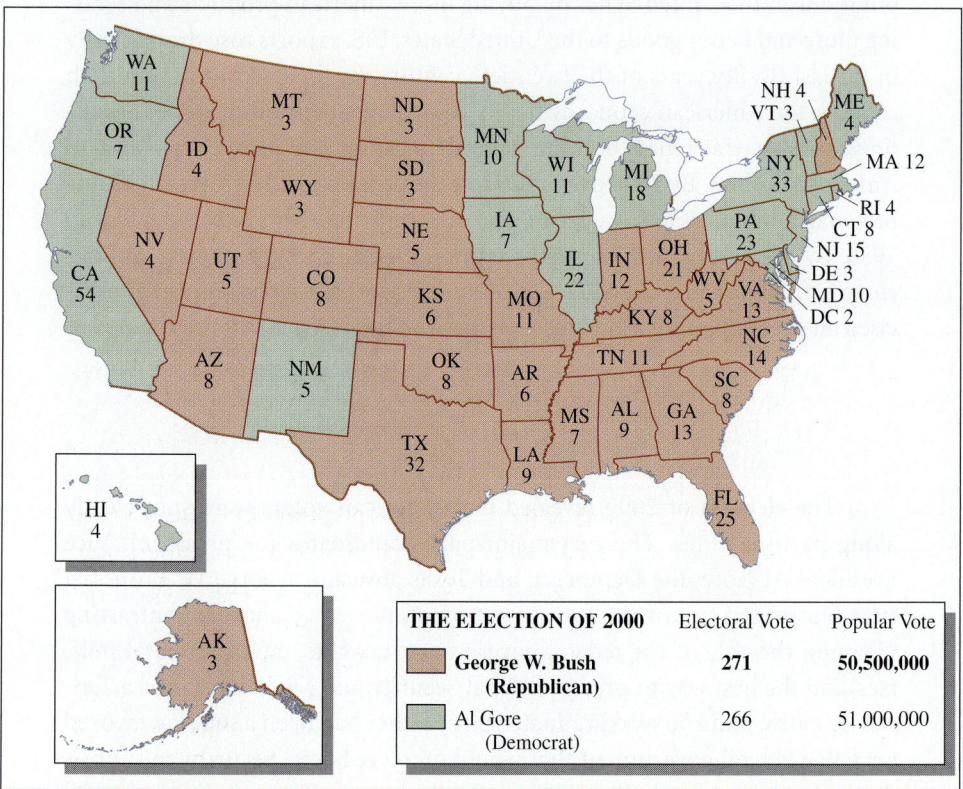

THE ELECTION OF 2000	Electoral Vote	Popular Vote
George W. Bush (Republican)	271	50,500,000
Al Gore (Democrat)	266	51,000,000

Why was the 2000 presidential election so close? How was the conflict over the election results resolved? How were differences between urban and rural voters key to the outcome of the election?

Florida was too close to call. The final tally in Florida showed Bush with a razor-thin lead, and state law required a recount. For the first time in 125 years, the results of a presidential election remained in doubt for weeks after the voting.

As a painstaking hand count of presidential ballots proceeded in Florida, supporters of Bush and Gore pursued victory through legal maneuvers in the Florida courts and the U.S. Supreme Court; each side accused the other of trying to steal the election. The political drama remained stalemated for five weeks. At last, on December 12, 2000, the Supreme Court halted the statewide manual recounts in Florida. In the case known as *Bush v. Gore,* a bare 5–4 majority ruled that any new recount would clash with existing Florida law. Bush was deemed the winner in Florida by the slimmest of margins: 537 votes. Although Gore amassed a 540,000-vote lead nationwide, he lost in the Electoral College by two votes when he lost Florida.

COMPASSIONATE CONSERVATISM

THE SECOND BUSH PRESIDENCY George W. Bush arrived in the White House amid the controversy of a disputed election to confront a sputtering economy and a falling stock market. By the spring of 2000, the high-tech companies that had led the soaring stock market during the 1990s had begun to stall. Many of the dazzling new dot-com businesses declared bankruptcy. Greed fed by record profits and speculative excesses had led businesses, investors, and consumers to take dangerous risks; many leading corporate executives, it turned out, had engaged in unethical practices that undermined the economy. The Internet bubble burst in 2001. Stock values collapsed, stealing over $2 trillion from household wealth. Consumer confidence and capital investment plummeted with the stock market. By March 2001 the economy was in recession for the first time in over a decade.

Yet Bush's disputed election and the political balance in Congress did not prevent the new president from launching an ambitious legislative agenda. Confident that he could win over Democrats, he promised within months of his inauguration to provide "an explosion of legislation" promoting his goal of "compassionate conservatism." The top item on Bush's wish list was a $1.6-trillion tax cut intended to stimulate the sagging economy. The Senate eventually trimmed the cut to $1.35 trillion over eleven years, and Bush signed it into law on June 7, 2001.

NO CHILD LEFT BEHIND   In addition to tax reduction, one of President Bush's top priorities was education reform. In late 2001, Congress passed a comprehensive education-improvement plan called No Child Left Behind, and the president signed the bill in early 2002. It required states to set new learning standards and ensure that all students were "proficient" at reading and math by 2014. It also mandated that all teachers be "highly qualified" in their subject area by 2005, allowed children in low-performing schools to transfer to other schools, and required states to submit annual reports of students' scores on standardized tests. Schools and school districts that fell short of the new standards were eligible for financial and technical assistance, but if progress did not occur, the federal government would issue a series of sanctions; ultimately a chronically failing school district would be taken over by the state. States soon criticized the program, noting that it provided insufficient funds for remedial programs and that poor school districts, many of them in blighted inner cities or rural areas, would be especially hard-pressed to meet the guidelines.

EXPLOITING THE ENVIRONMENT   The Bush administration's environmental policies ignited a firestorm of controversy. The president sought to roll back restrictions on economic development posed by long-standing environmental regulations. In addition, he allowed more logging in national forests and opened up more federal land, including wildlife sanctuaries, to exploration for energy sources in the face of dramatic increases in oil and gasoline prices. Like Ronald Reagan before him, Bush appointed former industry executives to federal agencies responsible for enforcing environmental regulations, and he exempted the Defense Department from many environmental restrictions. James Jeffords, a Republican turned independent and the ranking minority member of the Senate Environment and Public Works Committee, predicted that the Bush administration would "go down in history as the greatest disaster for public health and the environment in the history of the United States."

GLOBAL TERRORISM

With the collapse of the Soviet Union and the end of the cold war, world politics had grown more unstable during the 1990s. Where ideologies such as capitalism and communism had earlier been the cause of conflict and tension in foreign relations, issues of religion, ethnicity, and clashing cultural values now divided peoples. Nations were no longer the sole actors on the stage of world politics. Instead, nebulous multinational groups inspired by religious fanaticism and anti-American rage were using high-tech terrorism to gain notoriety and exact vengeance. Well-financed and well-armed terrorists flourished in the cracks of foundering nations such as Sudan, Somalia, Pakistan, Yemen, and Afghanistan. Throughout the 1990s the United States fought a losing secret war against global terrorism. The ineffectiveness of Western intelligence agencies in tracking the movements and intentions of militant extremists became tragically evident in the late summer of 2001.

SEPTEMBER 11, 2001: A DAY OF INFAMY At 8:45 A.M. on September 11, 2001, the world watched in horror as a commercial airliner hijacked by Islamic terrorists slammed into the north tower of the World Trade Center in New York City. A second hijacked jumbo jet, traveling at 500 miles per hour, hit the south tower eighteen minutes later. The fuel-laden planes turned the majestic buildings into infernos. The iconic twin towers, both 110 stories tall and occupied by thousands of people, collapsed from the intense heat. Surrounding buildings also crumpled. The entire southern end of Manhattan—ground zero—became a hellish scene of twisted steel, suffocating smoke, and wailing sirens.

While the catastrophic drama in New York was unfolding, a third hijacked plane crashed into the Pentagon in Washington, D.C. A fourth commandeered airliner, thought to be headed for the White House, missed its mark when passengers, who had heard reports of the earlier incidents via cell phones, assaulted the hijackers to prevent the plane from being used as a weapon. During the struggle in the cockpit, the plane went out of control and plummeted into the Pennsylvania countryside, killing all on board.

The hijackings represented the costliest terrorist assault on the United States in the nation's history. There were 266 passengers and crew members aboard the crashed jets. More than 100 civilians and military personnel were killed at the Pentagon. The death toll at the World Trade Center was over 2,600, with many firefighters, police officers, and rescue workers among the dead. Hundreds of those killed were foreign nationals working in the financial district; some eighty nations lost citizens in the attacks. The terrorists also destroyed a powerful symbol of America: the World Trade Center towers were the central offices of global capitalism.

The terrorist attacks of September 11 created shock and chaos, grief and anger. They also prompted an unprecedented display of national unity and patriotism. People rushed to donate blood, food, and money. Volunteers clogged military-recruiting centers. American flags were in evidence everywhere. Citizens around the world held vigils at U.S. embassies. World leaders offered condolences and support. For the first time in its history, NATO invoked Article 5 of its charter, which states that an attack on any member will be considered an attack on all.

Within hours of the hijackings, officials had identified the nineteen terrorists as members of al Qaeda (the Base), a well-financed worldwide network of Islamic extremists led by a wealthy Saudi renegade, Osama bin Laden. Years before, bin Laden had declared holy war on the United States, Israel, and the Saudi monarchy. For several years he had been using remote bases in war-torn Afghanistan as terrorist training centers. Collaboring with bin Laden's terrorist network was Afghanistan's ruling Taliban, a coalition of radical Islamists that had emerged in the mid-1990s following the forced withdrawal of Soviet troops from Afghanistan. Taliban leaders provided bin Laden with a safe haven in exchange for his financial and military support

September 11, 2001

Smoke pours out of the north tower of the World Trade Center as the south tower bursts into flames after being struck by a second hijacked airplane. Both towers collapsed about an hour later.

against the Northern Alliance, a cluster of rebel groups opposed to Taliban rule. Bin Laden sought to mobilize into a global army Muslim militants energized by local causes. As many as 20,000 recruits from twenty countries circulated through his Afghan training camps. Most of the terrorists received religious indoctrination and basic infantry training to prepare them to fight for the Taliban. A smaller group was selected by al Qaeda for elite training to organize secret cells around the world and engage in urban warfare, assassination, demolition, and sabotage, with Western Europe and the United States as the primary target.

WAR ON TERRORISM   The September 11 assault on the United States changed the course of the new presidency, the nation, and the world. The economy, already in decline, went into a free fall. President Bush, who had never professed to know much about international relations or world affairs and had shown only disdain for Bill Clinton's "multilateralism," was thrust onto center stage as commander in chief of a wounded nation eager for vengeance. The Bush administration immediately forged an international

Operation Enduring Freedom

Smoke rises from the Taliban village of Khanaqa, fifty-five miles from the Afghan capital Kabul, after a U.S. aircraft released bombs.

coalition to strike at terrorism worldwide. The coalition demanded that Afghanistan's Taliban government surrender the terrorists or risk military attack. In a televised address on September 20, Bush warned Americans that the war against terrorism would be a lengthy campaign involving covert action as well as conventional military forces, which would target not only terrorists but also the groups and governments that abet them. "Every nation in every region," he said, "now has a decision to make: either you are with us or you are with the terrorists."

On October 7, after the Taliban defiantly refused to turn over bin Laden, the United States and its allies launched a ferocious military campaign— Operation Enduring Freedom—to locate and punish terrorists or "those harboring terrorists." U.S. and British cruise missiles and bombers destroyed Afghan military installations and al Qaeda training camps. The coalition found key allies in neighboring Pakistan and in Afghanistan's Northern Alliance. On December 9, only two months after the American-led military campaign in Afghanistan had begun, the Taliban regime collapsed. With its collapse, the war in Afghanistan devolved into a high-stakes manhunt for the elusive Osama bin Laden and an international network of terrorists operating in sixty countries.

TERRORISM AT HOME   While the military campaign continued in Afghanistan, officials in Washington worried that terrorists might launch additional attacks in the United States with biological, chemical, or even nuclear weapons. To address the threat and to help restore public confidence, President Bush created a new federal agency, the Office of Homeland Security. Another new federal agency, the Transportation Security Administration, assumed responsibility for screening airline passengers. At the same time, President Bush and a supportive Congress created new legislation, known as the USA Patriot Act, which gave government agencies the right to eavesdrop on confidential conversations between prison inmates and their lawyers and permitted suspected terrorists to be tried in secret military courts. Civil liberties groups voiced grave concerns that the measures jeopardized constitutional rights and protections. But the crisis atmosphere after September 11 caused most people to support these extraordinary steps.

THE BUSH DOCTRINE   In the fall of 2002, President Bush unveiled a new national security doctrine that marked a distinct shift from that of previous administrations. Containment and deterrence had been the guiding strategic concepts of the cold war. Now, President Bush declared, the growing menace posed by "shadowy networks" of terrorist groups and unstable

Bush's defense policy

President George W. Bush addresses soldiers in July 2002 as part of an appeal to Congress to speed approval of increased defense spending after the September 11 terrorist attacks.

rogue nations with "weapons of mass destruction" required a new doctrine of preemptive military action. "If we wait for threats to fully materialize," he explained, "we will have waited too long. In the world we have entered, the only path to safety is the path of action. And this nation will act."

A SECOND PERSIAN GULF WAR During 2002 and 2003, Iraq emerged as the focus of the Bush administration's new policy of "preemptive" military action to prevent terrorism and destroy presumed weapons of mass destruction. In September 2002, President Bush urged the United Nations to confront the "grave and gathering danger" posed by Saddam Hussein's dictatorial regime in Iraq. He warned that the United States would act alone if the UN did not respond. In October, Congress approved a resolution proposed by Bush authorizing him to use "all means that he determines to be appropriate, including force," to defend the United States against the threat posed by Iraq's supposed possession of biological and chemical weapons. On November 8 the UN Security Council passed Resolution 1441 ordering Iraq to disarm immediately or face "serious consequences." Faced with growing international pressure, Hussein grudgingly allowed UN weapons inspectors to return to Iraq "without conditions."

On March 17, 2003, President Bush issued an ultimatum to Saddam Hussein: he and his sons must leave Iraq within forty-eight hours or face a U.S.-led invasion. Hussein refused. Two days later, on March 19, American and British forces, supported by what George Bush called the "coalition of the willing," attacked Iraq. Operation Iraqi Freedom involved a massive bombing campaign followed closely by a fast-moving invasion across the Iraqi desert from bases in Kuwait. Some 250,000 American soldiers, sailors, and marines were joined by 50,000 British troops as well as small contingents from other countries, including Australia and Poland. On April 9, after three weeks of intense fighting amid sweltering heat and blinding sandstorms, allied forces occupied Baghdad, the capital of Iraq. Saddam's Baathist regime and his inept army collapsed and fled a week later. On May 1, 2003, an exuberant President Bush declared that the war was essentially over. "The battle of Iraq," he said, "is one victory in a war on terror that began on September 11, 2001, and still goes on."

A continued presence in Iraq

U.S. military police patrol the market in Abu Ghraib, on the outskirts of Baghdad.

The complicated Iraqi military campaign was a brilliantly orchestrated demonstration of intense firepower, daring maneuver, and complex logistical support. No one had predicted such a quick and decisive victory—or so few casualties among the allied forces. The six-week war came at a cost of fewer than 200 combat deaths among the 300,000 coalition troops. Over 2,000 Iraqi soldiers were killed; civilian casualties numbered in the tens of thousands.

REBUILDING IRAQ   It proved easier to win the war than to rebuild Iraq, however. Secretary of Defense Donald Rumsfeld saw the Iraq War as an opportunity to showcase America's new military strategy, with its focus on airpower, precision weaponry, sophisticated communications, and mobile ground forces adept at stealth and speed. Yet winning the peace proved far more difficult than winning the war. No sooner had Saddam Hussein's tyranny been destroyed than the allies faced the daunting task of restoring order and installing a democratic government in a chaotic Iraq torn by age-old religious feuds and ethnic tensions. Looting was rampant and basic services nonexistent. Saddam Hussein and many of his lieutenants evaded capture and organized insurgent attacks against the allied forces and the interim Iraqi government. Violence engulfed the war-torn country. Vengeful Islamic jihadists (holy warriors) from around the world streamed into Iraq to wage a merciless campaign of terror and sabotage against the coalition forces and their Iraqi allies.

Defense Department analysts had greatly underestimated the difficulty of pacifying and reconstructing postwar Iraq. As Secretary Rumsfeld told his staff in October 2003, the invasion of Iraq was the easy part. The allies now faced "a long, hard slog" in their effort to install a new Iraqi government and restore basic services in the midst of a growing guerrilla insurgency. By the fall of 2003, President Bush was forced to admit that substantial numbers of American troops (around 150,000) would remain in Iraq much longer than originally anticipated and that rebuilding the fractured nation would take much longer than expected. Victory on the battlefields of Iraq did not bring peace to the Middle East. Militant Islamic groups seething with hatred for the United States remained a constant global threat. In addition, the dispute over the Iraq War strained relations between the Anglo-American alliance and France, Germany, and Russia, all of which opposed the war.

Throughout 2003 and 2004 the Iraqi insurgency and its campaign of terror grew in scope and savagery. Near-daily suicide car bombings and roadside ambushes of U.S. military convoys wreaked havoc among Iraqi civilians and allied troops. Terrorists kidnapped foreign civilians and beheaded several of them in grisly rituals videotaped for the world to see. In the United States the euphoria of battlefield victory turned to dismay as the number of casualties and the expense of the occupation soared. In the face of mounting criticism, President Bush urged Americans to "stay the course," insisting that a democratic Iraq would bring stability to the volatile Middle East and thereby blunt the momentum of Islamic terrorism.

But the president's credibility suffered a sharp blow in January 2004 when administration officials admitted that no weapons of mass destruction—the primary reason for launching the invasion—had been found in Iraq. The chief weapons inspector told Congress that the intelligence reports about Hussein's supposed secret weapons were "almost all wrong." Furthermore, shocking revelations in April 2004 of American soldiers torturing Iraqi prisoners further eroded public confidence in Bush's handling of the war and its aftermath.

By September 2004, U.S. military deaths in Iraq had reached 1,000, and during 2006 the number was well over 2,500. Although Saddam Hussein had been captured in December 2003 and Iraqi citizens elected their first democratic government in January 2005 and approved a new constitution nine months later, Iraq seemed less secure than ever. The continuing guerrilla war in Afghanistan and the new one in Iraq strained American military resources and the federal budget.

THE ELECTION OF 2004   Growing public concern about the mayhem in Iraq complicated George Bush's campaign for a second presidential term. Throughout 2004 his approval rating plummeted. And in the new century the electorate had become deeply polarized. A ferocious partisanship dominated civic commentary in the early years of the century. Democrats still fumed over the contested election results of 2000. When asked about the intensity of his critics, a combative George Bush declared the furor "a compliment. It means I'm willing to take a stand." One of his advisers explained it more bluntly: "He likes being hated. It lets him know he's doing the right thing."

The 2004 presidential campaign was punctuated by negative attacks on each candidate as the two parties sought to galvanize their loyalists. The Democratic nominee, Senator John Kerry of Massachusetts, lambasted the Bush administration for misleading the nation on the issue of weapons of mass destruction in Iraq and for its inept handling of the Iraq occupation. Kerry also highlighted the record budget deficits occurring under the Republican leadership. Bush countered that the tortuous efforts to create a democratic government in Iraq would enhance America's long-term security.

The 2004 election

President George W. Bush (center) and Democratic candidate Senator John Kerry (left) participate in the second presidential debate, a town-hall-style exchange held at Washington University in St. Louis, Missouri.

On election day the exit polls suggested a Kerry victory, but in the end the election hinged on the crucial swing state of Ohio. No Republican had ever lost Ohio and still won the presidency. After an anxious night viewing returns from Ohio and even considering the contested ballots, Kerry conceded the election. "The outcome," he stressed, "should be decided by voters, not a protracted legal battle." By narrowly winning Ohio, Bush garnered 286 electoral votes to Kerry's 251. The 2004 election was remarkable for its high voter turnout. Almost 120 million people voted, some 15 million more than in the disputed 2000 election.

Bush won the popular vote by 50.73 to 48.27 percent, the narrowest margin won by any incumbent president. Yet in some respects the close election was not so close. Bush received 3.5 million more votes nationwide than Kerry, and Republicans increased their control of both the House and the Senate. Trumpeting "the will of the people at my back," Bush pledged to bring democracy to Iraq, overhaul the tax code and eliminate the estate tax, revamp Social Security, trim the federal deficit, limit financial awards for medical malpractice lawsuits, pass an energy bill, and create more jobs. "I earned capital in the campaign, political capital, and now I intend to spend it," he told reporters.

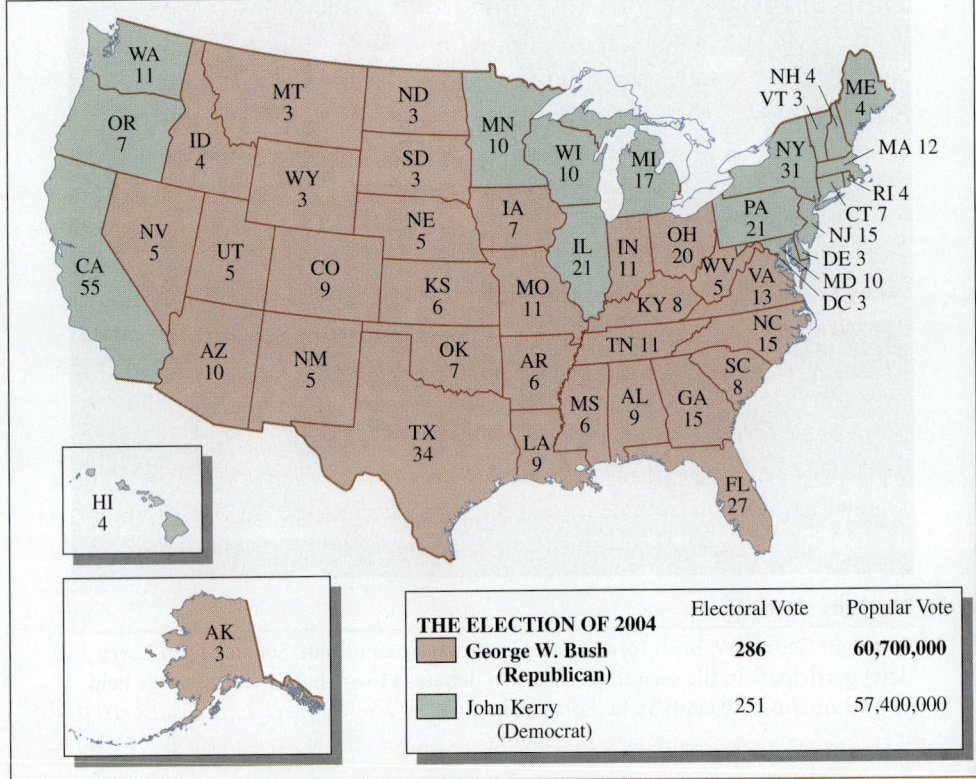

THE ELECTION OF 2004	Electoral Vote	Popular Vote
George W. Bush (Republican)	286	60,700,000
John Kerry (Democrat)	251	57,400,000

How did the war in Iraq polarize the electorate? In what ways did the election of 2004 give Republicans a mandate?

SECOND-TERM BLUES

Yet like many modern presidents, George Bush sputtered in his second term. In 2005 he pushed through Congress an energy bill and a Central American Free Trade Act. But his effort to privatize Social Security retirement accounts went nowhere, and soaring budget deficits made repeal of the estate tax politically impossible.

The retirement of Sandra Day O'Connor from the Supreme Court in July 2005 ignited a fierce political debate over combustible issues such as abortion, gay marriage, and affirmative action. Militants on the left and on the right exerted unrelenting pressure on the White House, but Bush's shrewd decision to nominate John G. Roberts Jr., a socially conservative circuit court judge, stalemated critics because Roberts's legal credentials were impeccable. Yet the fractious cultural debates did not subside. No sooner had the Senate overwhelmingly confirmed Roberts (78 to 22) than Chief Justice William Rehnquist died. Bush then named Roberts the new chief justice and nominated Harriet E. Miers, a longtime friend and former personal lawyer turned White House legal counsel, to replace O'Connor. Critics, many of them Republican conservatives, denounced Miers as a legal mediocrity and a presidential crony. The furor led Miers to withdraw her nomination in late October 2005, a humiliating development for President Bush that further hobbled his stalled legislative efforts. Her withdrawal coincided with the indictment of Vice President Richard Cheney's chief of staff, Lewis Libby, for perjury and obstruction of justice relating to an investigation of administration officials who purportedly revealed the identity of a covert CIA agent in a supposed act of political revenge. To address concerns that the Bush administration was sputtering in its second term and to heal the ruptures within the Republican coalition, Bush nominated to the Supreme Court Samuel Alito Jr., a federal judge and a favorite of conservatives.

HURRICANE KATRINA   In the summer of 2005, President Bush's eroding public support suffered another blow, this time when a natural disaster turned into a political crisis. In late August a killer hurricane named Katrina slammed into the Gulf coast, devastating large areas of Alabama, Mississippi, and Louisiana. The sultry metropolis of New Orleans was virtually destroyed as levees and flood walls holding back the Mississippi River and Lake Pontchartrain burst, inundating three quarters of the city. Katrina's awful wake left over 1,000 people dead in three states and millions homeless and hopeless.

Local political officials and the Federal Emergency Management Agency (FEMA) were caught unprepared as the catastrophe unfolded. Disaster plans were incomplete; confusion and incompetence abounded. A wave of public outrage crashed against the Bush administration. In the face of blistering criticism, President Bush accepted responsibility for the balky federal response to the disaster and accepted the resignation of the FEMA director. Rebuilding the Gulf coast would take a long time and a lot of money.

A STALLED PRESIDENCY   George Bush bore the brunt of public indignation over the federal response to the Katrina disaster. Thereafter,

Hurricane Katrina
Cars and buildings are partially submerged on Canal Street, a central thoroughfare in New Orleans, September 3, 2005.

his second presidential term was beset by political problems, a sputtering economy, and growing public dissatisfaction with performance and the continuing war in Iraq. Even his support among Republicans crumbled, and many social conservatives felt betrayed by his sporadic attention to their concerns. The editors of the *Economist*, an influential conservative newsmagazine, declared that Bush had become "the least popular re-elected president since Richard Nixon became embroiled in the Watergate fiasco." The skyrocketing gasoline prices and the federal budget deficit fueled public frustration. President Bush and Congress had overseen the largest increase in federal spending since Franklin Roosevelt. The president's efforts to reform the tax code, Social Security, and immigration laws languished during his second term, and the turmoil and violence in Iraq showed no signs of abating. Senator Chuck Hagel, a Nebraska Republican, declared in 2005 that "we're losing in Iraq." The drumbeat of disillusionment prompted President

Bush to acknowledge "setbacks" in Iraq and flaws in the intelligence reports that provided the rationale for going to war.

VOTER REBELLION In the November 2006 congressional elections the Democrats capitalized on the public disapproval of the Bush administration to win control of the House of Representatives, the Senate, and a majority of governorships and state legislatures. The election results were so lopsided that for the first time in history the vic-

House Speaker Nancy Pelosi

At a news conference on Capitol Hill.

torious party (the Democrats) did not lose a single incumbent or open congressional seat or governorship. Former Republican congressman Dick Armey said that "the Republican Revolution of 1994 officially ended" with the 2006 election. "It was a rout." George Bush admitted that the voters had given him and his party a "thumpin'" that would require a "new era of cooperation" with the victorious Democrats. As it turned out, however, the Bush White House and the Democratic Congress became mired in partisan gridlock. Stalemate trumped bipartisanship.

The transformational election also included a significant milestone: Californian Nancy Pelosi, the leader of the Democrats in the House of Representatives, became the highest-ranking woman in the history of the U.S. Congress upon her election as House Speaker in January 2007.

THE "SURGE" IN IRAQ The 2006 election was largely a referendum on the lack of progress in the Iraq War. Throughout the fall the violence and casualties in Iraq had spiked. The newly elected Iraqi government remained unstable, and fighting among the various religious and ethnic factions grew more chaotic. Bush remained stubbornly "committed to victory" in Iraq. But he responded to declining public and political support by replacing Donald Rumsfeld, the combative secretary of defense, with Robert Gates, a former head of the CIA. The president also created the Iraq Study Group, a nonpartisan task force co-chaired by Lee H. Hamilton, a former Democratic congressman, and James A. Baker III, secretary of state under the first President Bush. The group's report recommended that the United States step up the training of Iraqi troops and withdraw virtually all U.S. combat forces from a "grave and deteriorating Iraq" by the spring of 2008.

President Bush disagreed with the findings of the Iraq Study Group and others, including key military leaders, who urged a phased withdrawal. On January 10, 2007, he announced that he was sending a "surge" of 20,000 (eventually 30,000) additional American troops to Iraq, bringing the ultimate total to almost 170,000. Most Democrats opposed the escalation and instead called for an exit strategy. Senate majority leader Harry Reid, a Nevada Democrat, proclaimed in April 2007 that the United States had "lost" the war in Iraq and should beat a hasty retreat. During the summer of 2007, congressional Democrats tried to force the withdrawal of U.S. forces from Iraq, but Bush held firm. The "surge" of additional soldiers, he explained,

General David Petraeus

General Petraeus salutes U.S. soldiers during his visit at the village of Jadihah northeast of Baghdad, Iraq.

would involve a change in strategy as well as additional soldiers. The U.S. troops would shift their focus from offensive operations to the protection of Iraqi civilians from attacks by terrorist insurgents and sectarian militias. Bush hoped that the additional security would enable Iraqi leaders to promote political reconciliation among the war-torn country's major factions, the Shiites, Sunnis, and Kurds.

From a military perspective, the "surge" strategy succeeded. By the fall of 2008, the convulsive violence in Iraq had declined dramatically, and the U.S.-supported Iraqi government had grown in stature and confidence. But the financial expenses and human casualties of American involvement in Iraq continued to generate widespread criticism, and the "surge" failed to attain its political objectives. Iraqi leaders had yet to build a stable, self-sustaining democracy. The U.S. general who masterminded the "surge" strategy admitted that the gains remained "fragile and reversible." In 2008, as the number of U.S. combat deaths in Iraq passed 4,000, President Bush acknowledged that the conflict was "longer and harder and more costly than we anticipated." During 2008 over 60 percent of Americans said that going to war in Iraq had been a mistake.

The "surge"

An Iraqi reads a pamphlet asking for information on insurgents, handed to him by U.S. troops brought to Baghdad in an attempt to bring security to the city.

ECONOMIC WOES   After the intense but brief 2001 recession, the American economy had begun a period of prolonged expansion. Prosperity was fueled primarily by a prolonged housing boom, ultra-low interest and mortgage rates, easy credit, and reckless consumer spending. Home values across the nation had risen at rates that were unprecedented—and, as it turned out, unsustainable. Between 1997 and 2006, home prices in the United States, especially in the Sunbelt states, rose 85 percent, leading to a frenzy of irresponsible lending and building—and a debt-fueled consumer spending spree. Tens of millions of people bought houses that were more expensive than they could afford, refinanced their mortgages, or tapped home-equity loans to make discretionary purchases. The irrational confidence in soaring housing prices also led government regulatory agencies and mortgage lenders to ease credit restrictions so that more people could buy homes. Predatory lenders offered an array of so-called subprime loans with low initial "teaser" rates to home buyers with weak credit ratings and a low annual income. Investment banks and brokerage firms exacerbated the housing bubble by buying and selling bundles of home mortgages and other complex financial instruments, which they marketed as safe forms of "securitized" investments.

Such mortgage-backed securities were viable assets as long as home prices kept rising faster than personal income. In 2007, however, home values and housing sales began a precipitous decline. By the fall of 2007, the housing bubble had burst. Sales of new homes plummeted—as did asking prices. During 2008 the loss of trillions of dollars in home-equity value set off a seismic shock across the economy. Record numbers of mortgage borrowers defaulted on their payments. Foreclosures soared, adding to the glut of homes for sale and further reducing home prices. Banks lost billions, first on shaky subprime mortgages, then on most other categories of debt: credit cards, car loans, student loans, and an array of commercial mortgage-backed securities.

Capitalism depends on access to capital; short-term credit is the lifeblood of the economy. In 2008, however, the nation's credit supply froze up. Concerned about their own insolvency as well as their ability to gauge credit risks, banks essentially stopped lending—to the public and to each other. So people stopped buying; businesses stopped selling; industries slashed production and postponed investment. The sudden contraction of consumer credit, corporate spending, and consumer purchases triggered by the financial crisis pushed the economy into a deepening recession in 2008. The scale and suddenness of the slump caught economic experts and business leaders by surprise. Some of the nation's most prestigious banks, investment firms, and insurance companies went belly-up. The price of food and gasoline spiked. Unemployment soared. "Almost all businesses are in a survival mode," said one economist, "and they're slashing payrolls and investments. We're in store for some big job losses." Indeed, some two million jobs disappeared in 2008.

The high-flying stock market, itself fed by artificially low interest rates, began to tremble in September 2008; during October the bottom fell out. The Dow Jones Industrial Average lost a third of its value. Panic set in amid the turmoil. By late fall 2008 the United States was facing its greatest financial crisis since the Great Depression of the 1930s. What had begun as a decline in home prices had become a global economic meltdown—fed by the paralyzing fright of insecurity. No investment seemed safe. As people saw their retirement savings accounts gutted, they were left confused, anxious, and angry. A Missouri couple expressed a common concern: "We were always optimistic when we were young. We thought that every year, things would get better." Now the bubble had burst. Even Alan Greenspan, the former chairman of the Federal Reserve Board, found himself in a state of "shocked disbelief."

Amid what quickly became a global financial crisis, policy makers faced the challenge of shoring up the financial system and dealing with the social effects (panic) of a deepening recession. The crisis demanded decisive action.

The financial bailout

President Bush (left) and Treasury Secretary Henry Paulson speak to reporters from the steps of the Treasury Department after the House passed the $700 billion financial bailout bill (TARP).

On October 3, 2008, after two weeks of contentious and often emotional congressional debate, President Bush signed into law a far-reaching historic bank bailout fund called the Troubled Asset Relief Program (TARP). The TARP called for the Treasury Department to spend $700 billion to keep banks and other financial institutions from collapsing. "By coming together on this legislation, we have acted boldly to prevent the crisis on Wall Street from becoming a crisis in communities across our country," Bush said after the House voted 263 to 171 to pass the TARP bill. Despite such unprecedented government investment in the private financial sector, the economy still sputtered. In early October, stock markets around the world began to crash. Economists warned that the world was at risk of careening into a depression.

A HISTORIC ELECTION

The economic crisis had potent political effects. As two preeminent economists noted, "In the eight years since George W. Bush took office, nearly every component of the U.S. economy has deteriorated." Budget

The Clinton campaign

Democratic presidential hopeful Senator Hillary Clinton speaks at the Fort Worth Stockyards.

deficits, trade deficits, and consumer debt had reached record levels, and the total expense of the American war in Iraq was projected to top $3 trillion. During the president's last year in office, just 29 percent of the voters "approved" of his leadership. And more than 80 percent said that the nation was headed in the "wrong direction." Even a prominent Republican strategist, Kevin Phillips, deemed Bush "perhaps the least competent president in modern history."

Bush's vulnerability excited Democrats about the possibility of regaining the White House in the 2008 election. As a journalist predicted in November 2007, "It looks highly likely that this will be the Democrats' year." Not only was the Bush presidency floundering, but the once-indomitable Republican party was in disarray, plagued by scandals, riven by factions, and lacking effective leadership. In 2004 the American electorate had been evenly divided by party identification: 43 percent for both the Democratic and the Republican parties. By 2008 the Democrats were leading the Republicans 50 percent to 35 percent.

The early front-runner for the Democratic nomination was New York senator Hillary Clinton, the highly visible spouse of ex-president Bill Clinton. Like her husband, she displayed an impressive command of policy issues and mobilized a well-funded campaign team. And as the first woman with a serious chance of gaining the presidency, she garnered widespread support among voters eager for female leadership. But in the end an overconfident Clinton was upset in the Democratic primaries and caucuses by little-known first-term senator Barack Obama of Illinois, an inspiring speaker who attracted huge crowds by promising a "politics of hope" and bolstering their

The Obama campaign

Democratic presidential hopeful, Senator Barack Obama waves to supporters at Waterfront Park in Portland, Oregon.

desire for "change." While the Clinton campaign courted the powerful members of the party establishment, Obama mounted an innovative Internet-based campaign directed at grassroots voters, donors, and volunteers. Obama was especially popular among young people. In early June, 2008, Obama gained enough delegates to secure the Democratic nomination.

Obama was the first African American presidential nominee of either party, the gifted biracial son of a white mother from Kansas and a black Kenyan father who left the household and returned to Africa when Barack was a toddler. The forty-seven-year-old Harvard Law School graduate and former professor, community organizer, and state legislator presented himself as a conciliator who could inspire and unite a diverse people and forge bipartisan collaborations.

Obama exuded poise, confidence, and energy. By contrast, his Republican opponent, seventy-two-year-old Arizona senator John McCain, was the oldest presidential candidate in history. The son and grandson of distinguished Navy admirals, McCain had graduated from the U.S. Naval Academy

The 2008 presidential debates

Republican presidential candidate John McCain (left) and Democratic presidential candidate Barack Obama (right) focused on foreign policy, national security, and the financial crisis at the first of three presidential debates.

before serving as a pilot in the Vietnam War. Captured after his plane was shot down, he spent over five years as a prisoner of war in Hanoi, suffering frequent torture. As a twenty-five-year veteran of Congress, a leading Republican senator, and a 2004 candidate for the Republican presidential nomination, he had developed a reputation as a bipartisan maverick willing to work with Democrats to achieve key legislative goals. McCain had voted against President Bush's tax cuts for the wealthy in 2001 and 2003, and he criticized the religious right for being "agents of intolerance."

Concerns about McCain's support among Republican conservatives led him to select Alaska governor Sarah Palin as his running mate, the first woman on a Republican ticket. Although hardly known outside party circles, Palin held the promise of winning over religious conservatives nervous about McCain's ideological purity. She opposed abortion, gay marriage (Obama opposed it too), and stem-cell research, and she endorsed the teaching of creationism in public schools. For his part, Barack Obama rejected calls to choose Hillary Clinton as his running mate. Instead, he selected veteran Delaware senator Joseph Biden.

THE 2008 ELECTION   The presidential campaign started in August 2008 with polls suggesting a very tight race. But the dramatic economic downturn in September and October gave Obama and the Democrats a powerful partisan weapon. Obama shrewdly capitalized on widespread dissatisfaction with the Republicans and centered his campaign on the echoing promise of "change." He repeatedly linked McCain with the unpopular George W. Bush. His pledge to avoid politics as usual and adopt a "post-partisan" approach resonated with voters tired of attack politics. Obama denounced the prevailing Republican "economic philosophy that says we should give more and more to those with the most and hope that prosperity trickles down to everyone else." He described the 2008 financial meltdown as the "final verdict on this failed philosophy."

While Obama's campaign projected a youthful, vibrant, energetic, disciplined, and consistent tone, John McCain struggled to define himself and his message. With each successive televised debate, the calm and confident Obama widened his lead. Meanwhile, as the editors of *Newsweek* magazine noted, the "U.S. economy went from being *an* issue in the presidential election to the *only* issue." With the country's finances in a tailspin, McCain made a clumsy statement in September—"the fundamentals of our economy are strong"—that would come back to haunt him. Within ten days, McCain reversed himself, announcing that the economic crisis was so serious that he needed to suspend his campaign in order to return to the Senate.

Election night rally

President-elect Barack Obama, his wife Michelle, and two daughters, Sasha and Malia wave to the crowd of supporters in Chicago's Grant Park.

Still floundering, he tried to refocus the campaign debate on his support for the Iraq War and the success of the "surge" strategy. Obama parried by promising a phased withdrawal of American forces. The Obama campaign also pledged to broaden health-insurance coverage, promote renewable energy, raise taxes on the wealthy, and get the economy growing again.

On November 4, 2008, Barack Obama made history by becoming the nation's first person of color elected president. "Change has come to America," he announced in his victory speech. His triumph was decisive and sweeping. The inspirational Obama won the popular vote by seven points: 53 percent to 46 percent. His margin in the electoral vote was even more impressive: 365 to 173. The president-elect won big among his core supporters—voters under age thirty, women, minorities, the very poor, and first-time voters. He collected 95 percent of the African American vote and 66 percent of voters aged eighteen to twenty-nine, and he won the Hispanic vote. Obama also helped the Democrats win solid majorities in the House and Senate races.

Within days of his electoral victory, Barack Obama had adopted a bipartisan approach in selecting his new cabinet members. He appointed Hillary

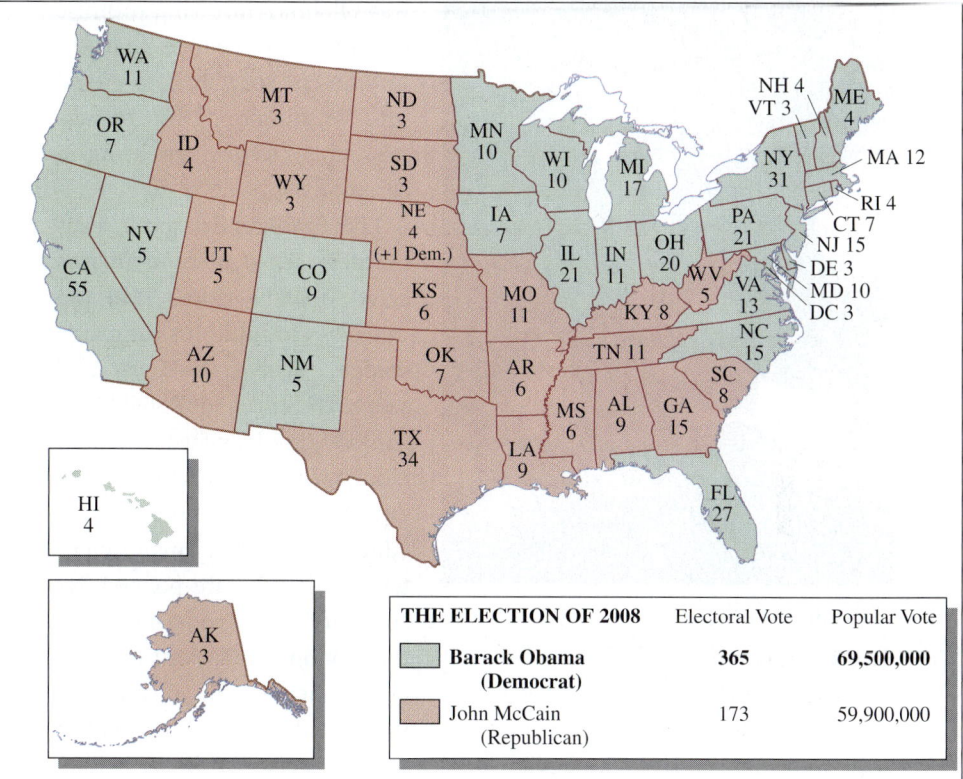

THE ELECTION OF 2008

	Electoral Vote	Popular Vote
Barack Obama (Democrat)	365	69,500,000
John McCain (Republican)	173	59,900,000

How did the economic crisis affect the outcome of the election? What are the similarities and differences between the map of the 2004 election and the map of the 2008 election?

Clinton secretary of state, renewed Republican Robert Gates as secretary of defense, selected retired general James Jones, who had campaigned for McCain, as his national security adviser, and appointed Eric Holder as the nation's first African American attorney general.

THE FIRST ONE HUNDRED DAYS

On January 20, 2009, President Obama delivered a sobering inaugural address in frigid weather amid daunting challenges. The United States was embroiled in two wars, in Iraq and Afghanistan. The economy was in shambles, unemployment was soaring, and the national debt was hemorrhaging. Yet it

The Oath of Office

Barack Obama takes the oath as the forty-fourth President of the United States.

was Obama's inspiring promise of hope and change that led millions of spectators to crowd into Washington, D.C., to witness the historic swearing-in ceremony.

Like Franklin Roosevelt, a supremely self-confident Obama acted quickly—some said too quickly—to fulfill his campaign pledges. With a boldness and scope reminiscent of Ronald Reagan, Obama launched an audacious agenda. He would overhaul government regulations, reform education, energy, environmental, and health-care policies, restructure the tax code, invigorate the economy, and recast U.S. foreign policy. On his second day in office, he issued an executive order to begin a case-by-case review of all suspected terrorists being held at the U.S. detention center at the Guantánamo Bay Naval Base in Cuba. The prisoners were to be released or transferred to other prisons, and the detention center would be closed within a year. In March, Obama eased restrictions on the federal funding of human embryonic stem-cell research. His doing so outraged abortion opponents but pleased those who believe that stem-cell research can lead to medical cures for many diseases. Obama also lifted restrictions on American travel to Cuba that had been in place for nearly fifty years. And he offered to talk with the totalitarian leaders of Iran and North Korea, something his predecessors had refused to do.

REVIVING THE ECONOMY The new Obama administration's main challenge was to keep the deepening recession from becoming a prolonged depression. Unemployment in early 2009 had passed 8 percent and was still rising. More than 5 million people had lost their jobs since 2007. The financial sector remained paralyzed. At the same time, U.S. military forces remained embroiled in the conflicts in Iraq and Afghanistan. Like Franklin Roosevelt, Obama wanted to be a "transformative" president. To do so, he needed to move swiftly to enact his ambitious agenda while still enjoying widespread public support. Like Roosevelt in 1933, the new president sought to restore public confidence during these "difficult and uncertain times" by acting "boldly and wisely" to fulfill his campaign pledges and stimulate the stagnant economy. He assured the nation that "we will rebuild, we will recover."

In mid-February, after a prolonged and often strident debate, Congress passed, and Obama signed, a $787-billion economic stimulus bill—the largest in history—called the American Recovery and Reinvestment Act. The gargantuan bill (over 1,000 pages long) included cash distributions to the states, funds for food stamps, unemployment benefits, construction projects to renew the nation's infrastructure (roads, bridges, levees, government buildings, and the electricity grid), funds for renewable-energy systems, and tax reductions. But the passage of the stimulus bill showed no evidence that Obama was successful in implementing a "bipartisan" presidency. Only three Senate Republicans voted for the bill. Not a single House Republican voted for it, and eleven House Democrats opposed it as well. In February, Obama continued his calibrated boldness by ordering the Treasury Department to implement tax cuts for 95 percent of Americans (all but the most wealthy), and he announced plans to let the tax cuts for the rich implemented by George W. Bush expire in 2010. During the summer of 2009, Congressional Democrats began working with the White House to develop the two largest and most controversial of Obama's proposals: health-care reform and climate-change legislation.

LEAVING IRAQ? President Obama announced on February 27, 2009, that all U.S. combat troops would be withdrawn from Iraq by the end of 2011. A "transitional force" of 35,000 to 50,000 troops would assist Iraqi security forces, protect Americans and fight terrorism, Obama said. "The drawdown of our military should send a clear signal that Iraq's future is now its own responsibility. The long-term success of the Iraqi nation will depend on decisions made by Iraq's leaders and the fortitude of the Iraqi people," Obama said. At the same time that he was reducing U.S. military involvement in Iraq, Obama dispatched 21,000 additional troops to Afghanistan, which he called "ground zero" in the battle against terrorism. Obama's Iraqi withdrawal plan prompted many hard questions: Did his timetable provide enough time for Iraqis to forge a self-reliant government and economy? Could the U.S. withdrawal trigger a civil war between Sunnis and Shiites? Only time would tell.

End of Chapter Review

- **Changing Demographics**   From 1980 to 2009 the population of the United States grew by 20 percent to 290 million. The South and the West lured residents from the Midwest and the Northeast. The number of traditional family units continued to decline; the poverty rate was especially high among African Americans. A wave of immigrants caused Latinos to surpass African Americans as the nation's largest minority.

- **Divided Government**   The popularity of President George H. W. Bush waned after the Gulf War an economic recession, and his decision to raise taxes. The election of William Jefferson Clinton and the Democratic victory was short-lived, however. Speaker Newt Gingrich mobilized the Christian Coalition against "liberalism" with his Contract with America to achieve the Republican landslide of 1994.

- **Economic Prosperity and Crises**   The United States benefited from a period of unprecedented prosperity during the 1990s, fueled by the dramatic effect of the new computer-based industries on the economy. The collapse of high-tech companies in 2000 betrayed the underlying insecurity of the market. Economic growth soon surged again primarily because of consumers' ability to borrow against the skyrocketing value of their home mortgages. In 2007 the country experienced an unparalleled crisis when the global financial markets collapsed under the weight of "toxic" financial securities.

- **Global Terrorism**   The September 11 attacks led President George W. Bush to declare a war on terrorism and enunciate the Bush Doctrine. In 2002 the Bush administration shifted its focus to Saddam Hussein. The American-led Operation Iraqi Freedom succeeded in removing Hussein from power but was fully unprepared to establish order in a country that was soon riven by sectarian violence. The American public became bitterly divided over the Iraq War.

- **2008 Presidential Election**   The 2008 presidential campaigns included the first major female candidate, Senator Hillary Clinton; an African American, Senator Barack Obama; and Senator John McCain, the oldest candidate in history. Obama won the popular vote and a landslide victory in the Electoral College, becoming the nation's first African American president. His victory was fueled by the collapse of the economy, an unprecedented Internet- and grassroots-based campaign, and voters' weariness with President Bush and the Republican policies of the preceding eight years.

CHRONOLOGY

1971	Microprocessor (computer chip) is invented
1989	Pat Robertson forms the Christian Coalition
1991	Ethnic conflict explodes in Yugoslavia
1995	Republicans promote the Contract with America
1996	Congress passes the Personal Responsibility and Work Opportunity Act
1998	Kenneth Starr issues his report on the Whitewater investigation
1998	Bill Clinton brokers the Wye Mills Accord with Israel, the Palestine Liberation Organization, and Jordan
1999	Bill Clinton is impeached and acquitted
2000	Supreme Court issues *Bush v. Gore* decision
September 11, 2001	Terrorists hijack four commercial jets to carry out the deadliest terrorist attacks in the nation's history
March 2003	Iraq War begins with the staging of Operation Iraqi Freedom
August 2005	Hurricane Katrina
January 2007	Nancy Pelosi becomes the first female Speaker of the House of Representatives
2007	President Bush calls for a surge in Iraq, in an attempt to quell sectarian violence
2008	Global financial markets collapse
January 2009	Barack Obama becomes the forty-fourth president of the United States and the nation's first African American president

KEY TERMS & NAMES

GLOSSARY

36°30′ According to the Missouri Compromise, any part of the Louisiana Purchase north of this line (Missouri's southern border) was to be excluded from slavery.

54th Massachusetts Regiment After President Abraham Lincoln's Emancipation Proclamation, the Union army organized all black military units, which white officers led. The 54th Massachusetts Regiment was one of the first of such units to be organized.

Abigail Adams (1744–1818) As the wife of John Adams, she endured long periods of separation from him while he served in many political roles. During these times apart, she wrote often to her husband; and their correspondence has provided a detailed portrait of life during the Revolutionary War.

abolition In the early 1830s, the anti-slavery movement shifted its goal from the gradual end of slavery to the immediate end or abolition of slavery.

John Adams (1735–1826) He was a signer of the Declaration of Independence and a delegate to the First and Second Continental Congress. During the Revolutionary War, he worked as a diplomat in France and Holland and negotiated the peace treaty with Britain. After the Revolutionary War, he served as the minister to Britain as well as the vice president and the second president of the United States. As president, he passed the Alien and Sedition Acts and endured a stormy relationship with France, which included the XYZ affair.

John Quincy Adams (1767–1848) As secretary of state under President Monroe, he negotiated agreements to define the boundaries of the Oregon country and the Transcontinental Treaty. He urged President Monroe to issue the Monroe Doctrine, which incorporated Adams's views. As president, Adams envisioned an expanded federal government and a broader use of federal powers. Adams's nationalism and praise of European leaders caused a split in his party. Some Republicans suspected him of being a closet monarchist and left to form the Democrat party. In the presidential election 1828, Andrew Jackson claimed that Adams had gained the presidency through a "corrupt bargain" with Henry Clay, which helped Jackson win the election.

Samuel Adams (1722–1803) A genius of revolutionary agitation, he believed that English Parliament had no right to legislate for the colonies. He organized the Sons of Liberty as well as protests in Boston against the British.

Jane Addams (1860–1935) As the leader of one of the best known settlement houses, she rejected the "do-goodism" spirit of religious reformers. Instead, she focused on solving the practical problems of the poor and tried to avoid the assumption that she and other social workers knew what was best for poor immigrants. She established child care for working mothers, health clinics, job training, and other social programs. She was also active in the peace movement and was awarded the Noble Peace Prize in 1931 for her work on its behalf.

Agricultural Adjustment Act (1933) New Deal legislation that established the Agricultural Adjustment Administration (AAA) to improve agricultural prices by limiting market supplies; declared unconstitutional in *United States v. Butler* (1936).

Emilio Aguinaldo (1869?–1964) He was a leader in Filipino struggle for independence. During the war of 1898, Commodore George Dewey brought Aguinaldo back to the Philippines from exile to help fight the Spanish. However, after the Spanish surrendered to Americans, America annexed the Philippines and Aguinaldo fought against the American military until he was captured in 1901.

Alamo, Battle of the Siege in the Texas War for Independence of 1836, in which the San Antonio mission fell to the Mexicans. Davy Crockett and Jim Bowie were among the courageous defenders.

Alien and Sedition Acts (1798) Four measures passed during the undeclared war with France that limited the freedoms of speech and press and restricted the liberty of noncitizens.

American Federation of Labor Founded in 1881 as a federation of trade unions made up of skilled workers, the AFL under president Samuel Gompers successfully pushed for the eight-hour workday.

American Indian Movement Fed up with the poor conditions on Indian reservations and the federal government's unwillingness to help, Native Americans founded the American Indian Movement (AIM) in 1963. In 1973, AIM led 200 Sioux in the occupation of Wounded Knee. After a ten-week standoff with the federal authorities, the government agreed to reexamine Indian treaty rights and the occupation ended.

American Protective Association Nativist, anti-Catholic secret society founded in Iowa in 1887 and active until the end of the century.

American Recovery and Reinvestment Act Hoping to restart the weak economy, President Obama signed this $787-billion economic stimulus bill in February of 2009. The bill included cash distributions to states, funds for food stamps, unemployment benefits, construction projects to renew the nation's infrastructure, funds for renewable-energy systems, and tax reductions.

American System Program of internal improvements and protective tariffs promoted by Speaker of the House Henry Clay in his presidential campaign of 1824; his proposals formed the core of Whig ideology in the 1830s and 1840s.

anaconda strategy Union General Winfield Scott developed this three-pronged strategy to defeat the Confederacy. Like a snake strangling its prey, the Union army would crush its enemy through exerting pressure on Richmond, blockading Confederate ports, and dividing the South by invading its major waterways.

Annapolis Convention In 1786, all thirteen colonies were invited to a convention in Annapolis to discuss commercial problems, but only representatives from five states attended. However, the convention was not a complete failure because the delegates decided to have another convention in order to write the constitution.

anti-Federalists Forerunners of Thomas Jefferson's Democratic-Republican party; opposed the Constitution as a limitation on individual and states' rights, which led to the addition of a Bill of Rights to the document.

Anti-Masonic party This party grew out of popular hostility toward the Masonic fraternal order and entered the presidential election of 1832 as a third party. It was the first party to run as a third party in a presidential election as well as the first to hold a nomination convention and announce a party platform.

Benedict Arnold (1741–1801) A traitorous American commander who planned to sell out the American garrison at West Point to the British, but his plot was discovered before it could be executed and he joined the British army.

Atlanta Compromise Speech to the Cotton States and International Exposition in 1895 by educator Booker T. Washington, the leading black spokesman of the day; black scholar W. E. B. Du Bois gave the speech its derisive name and criticized Washington for encouraging blacks to accommodate segregation and disenfranchisement.

Atlantic Charter Issued August 12, 1941, following meetings in Newfoundland between President Franklin D. Roosevelt and British Prime Minister Winston Churchill, the charter signaled the allies' cooperation and stated their war aims.

Crispus Attucks (1723–1770) During the Boston Massacre, he was supposedly at the head of the crowd of hecklers who baited the British troops. He was killed when the British troops fired on the crowd.

Stephen F. Austin (1793–1836) He established the first colony of Americans in Texas, which eventually attracted 2,000 people.

Axis powers In World War II, the nations of Germany, Italy, and Japan.

Aztec Empire Mesoamerican people who were conquered by the Spanish under Hernando Cortés, 1519–1528.

baby boom Markedly higher birth rate in the years following World War II; led to the biggest demographic "bubble" in American history.

Bacon's Rebellion Unsuccessful 1676 revolt led by planter Nathaniel Bacon against Virginia governor William Berkeley's administration, because it had failed to protect settlers from Indian raids.

Bank of the United States Proposed by the first Secretary of the Treasury Alexander Hamilton, the bank opened in 1791 and operated until 1811 to issue a uniform currency, make business loans, and collect tax monies. The second Bank of the United States was chartered in 1816 but was not renewed by President Andrew Jackson twenty years later.

barbary pirates Plundering pirates off the Mediterranean coast of Africa; President Thomas Jefferson's refusal to pay them tribute to protect

American ships sparked an undeclared naval war with North African nations, 1801–1805.

Battle of the Bulge On December 16, 1944, the German army launched a counter attack against the Allied forces, which pushed them back. However, the Allies were eventually able to recover and breakthrough the German lines. This defeat was a great blow to the Nazi's morale and their army's strength. The battle used up the last of Hitler's reserve units and opened a route into Germany's heartland.

Bear Flag Republic On June 14, 1846, a group of Americans in California captured Sonoma from the Mexican army and declared it the Republic of California whose flag featured a grizzly bear. In July, the commodore of the U.S. Pacific Fleet landed troops on California's shores and declared it part of the United States.

Beats A group of writers, artists, and musicians whose central concern was the discarding of organizational constraints and traditional conventions in favor of liberated forms of self expression. They came out of the bohemian underground in New York's Greenwich Village in the 1950s and included the writers Jack Kerouac, Allen Ginsberg, and William Burroughs. Their attitudes and lifestyles had a major influence on the youth of the 1960s.

beatnik A name referring to almost any young rebel who openly dissented from the middle-class life. The name itself stems from the Beats.

Nicholas Biddle (1786–1844) He was the president of the second Bank of the United States. In response to President Andrew Jackson's attacks on the bank, Biddle curtailed the bank's loans and exchanged its paper currency for gold and silver. He was hoping to provoke an economic crisis to prove the bank's importance. In response, state banks began printing paper without restraint and lent it to speculators, causing a binge in speculating and an enormous increase in debt.

Bill of Rights First ten amendments to the U.S. Constitution, adopted in 1791 to guarantee individual rights and to help secure ratification of the Constitution by the states.

Osama bin Laden (1957–) He is the leader of al Qaeda whose members attacked America on September 11, 2001. Years before the attack, he had declared *jihad* (holy war) on the United States, Israel, and the Saudi monarchy. In Afghanistan, the Taliban leaders gave Osama bin Laden a safe haven in exchange for aid in fighting the Northern Alliance, who were rebels opposed to the Taliban. After the 9/11 terrorist attacks, the United States asked the Taliban to turn over bin Laden. Following their refusal, America and multinational coalition invaded Afghanistan and overthrew the Taliban, but they did not capture bin Laden.

black codes Laws passed in southern states to restrict the rights of former slaves; to combat the codes, Congress passed the Civil Rights Act of 1866 and the Fourteenth Amendment and set up military governments in southern states that refused to ratify the amendment.

black power A more militant form of protest for civil rights that originated in urban communities, where nonviolent tactics were less effective than in the South. Black power encouraged African Americans to take pride in their racial heritage and forced black leaders and organizations to focus attention on the plight of poor inner-city blacks.

James Gillepsie Blaine (1830–1893) As a Republican congressman from Maine, he developed close ties with business leaders, which contributed to him losing the presidential election of 1884. He later opposed President Cleveland's efforts to reduce tariffs, which became a significant issue in the 1888 presidential election. Blaine served as secretary of state under President Benjamin Harrison and his flamboyant style often overshadowed the president.

"bleeding" Kansas Violence between pro- and antislavery settlers in the Kansas Territory, 1856.

blitzkrieg The German "lightening war" strategy used during World War II; the Germans invaded Poland, France, Russia, and other countries with fast-moving, well-coordinated attacks using aircraft, tanks, and other armored vehicles, followed by infantry.

Bolsheviks Under the leadership of Vladimir Lenin, this Marxist party led the November 1917 revolution against the newly formed provisional government in Russia. After seizing control, the Bolsheviks negotiated a peace treaty with Germany, the Treaty of Brest-Litovsk, and ended their participation in World War I.

Bonus Expeditionary Force Thousands of World War I veterans, who insisted on immediate payment of their bonus certificates, marched on Washington in 1932; violence ensued when President Herbert Hoover ordered their tent villages cleared.

Daniel Boone (1734–1820) He found and expanded a trail into Kentucky, which pioneers used to reach and settle the area.

John Wilkes Booth (1838?–1865) He assassinated President Abraham Lincoln at the Ford's Theater on April 14, 1865. He was pursued to Virginia and killed.

Bourbons In post–Civil War southern politics, the opponents of the Redeemers were called Bourbons. They were known for having forgotten nothing and learned nothing from the ordeal of the Civil War.

Joseph Brant (1742?–1807) He was the Mohawk leader who led the Iroquois against the Americans in the Revolutionary War.

brinkmanship Secretary of State John Foster Dulles believed that communism could be contained by bringing America to the brink of war with an aggressive communist nation. He believed that the aggressor would back down when confronted with the prospect of receiving a mass retaliation from a country with nuclear weapons.

John Brown (1800–1859) He was willing to use violence to further his antislavery beliefs. In 1856, a pro-slavery mob sacked the free-state town of Lawrence, Kansas. In response, John Brown went to the pro-slavery settlement of Pottawatomie, Kansas and hacked to death several people, which led to a guerrilla war in the Kansas territory. In 1859, he attempted to raid the federal arsenal at Harpers Ferry. He had hoped to use the stolen weapons to arm slaves, but he was captured and executed. His failed raid instilled panic throughout the South, and his execution turned him into a martyr for his cause.

***Brown v. Board of Education of Topeka* (1954)** U.S. Supreme Court decision that struck down racial segregation in public education and declared "separate but equal" unconstitutional.

William Jennings Bryan (1860–1925) He delivered the pro-silver "cross of gold" speech at the 1896 Democratic Convention and won his party's nomination for president. Disappointed pro-gold Democrats chose to walk out of the convention and nominate their own candidate, which split the Democratic party and cost them the White House. Bryan's loss also crippled the Populist movement that had endorsed him.

"Bull Moose" Progressive party In the 1912 election, Theodore Roosevelt was unable to secure the Republican nomination for president. He left the Republican party and formed his own party of progressive Republicans, called the "Bull Moose" party. Roosevelt and Taft split the Republican vote, which allowed Democrat Woodrow Wilson to win.

Bull Run, Battles of (First and Second Manassas) First land engagement of the Civil War took place on July 21, 1861, at Manassas Junction, Virginia, at which surprised Union troops quickly retreated; one year later, on August 29–30, Confederates captured the federal supply depot and forced Union troops back to Washington.

Martin Van Buren (1782–1862) During President Jackson's first term, he served as secretary of state and minister to London. He often politically fought Vice President John C. Calhoun for the position of Jackson's successor. A rift between Jackson and Calhoun led to Van Buren becoming vice president during Jackson's second term. In 1836, Van Buren was elected president, and he inherited a financial crisis. He believed that the government should not continue to keep its deposits in state banks and set up an independent Treasury, which was approved by Congress after several years of political maneuvering.

General John Burgoyne (1722–1792) He was the commander of Britain's northern forces during the Revolutionary War. He and most of his troops surrendered to the Americans at the Battle of Saratoga.

burned-over district Area of western New York strongly influenced by the revivalist fervor of the Second Great Awakening; Disciples of Christ and Mormons are among the many sects that trace their roots to the phenomenon.

Aaron Burr (1756–1836) Even though he was Thomas Jefferson's vice president, he lost favor with Jefferson's supporters who were Republicans. He sought to work with the Federalists and run as their candidate for the governor of New York. Alexander Hamilton opposed Burr's candidacy and his stinging remarks on the subject led to Burr challenging him to duel in which Hamilton was killed.

George H. W. Bush (1924–) He had served as vice president during the Reagan administration and then won the presidential election of 1988. During his presidential campaign, Bush promised not to raise taxes. However, the federal deficit had become so big that he had to raise taxes. Bush chose to make fighting illegal drugs a priority. He created the Office of National Drug Control Policy, but it was only moderately successful in stopping drug use. In 1989, Bush ordered the invasion of Panama and the capture of Panamanian leader Manuel Noriega, who was wanted in America on drug charges. He was captured, tried, and convicted. In 1990, Saddam Hussein invaded Kuwait; and Bush sent the American military to Saudi Arabia on a defensive mission. He assembled a multinational force and launched Operation Desert Storm, which took Kuwait back from Saddam in 1991. The euphoria over the victory in Kuwait was short lived as the country slid into a recession. He lost the 1992 presidential election to Bill Clinton.

George W. Bush (1946-) In the 2000 presidential election, Texas governor George W. Bush ran as the Republican nominee against Democratic nominee Vice President Al Gore. The election ended in controversy over the final vote tally in Florida. Bush had slightly more votes, but a recount was required by state law. However, it was stopped by Supreme Court and Bush was declared president. After the September 11 terrorist attacks, he launched his "war on terrorism." President George W. Bush adapted the Bush Doctrine, which claimed the right to launch preemptive military attacks against enemies. The United States invaded Afghanistan and Iraq with unclear outcomes leaving the countries divided. In the summer of 2006, Hurricane Katrina struck the Gulf Coast and left destruction across several states and three-quarters of New Orleans flooded. Bush was attacked for the unpreparedness of the federal government to handle the disaster as well as his own slowness to react. In September 2008, the nation's economy nosedived as a credit crunch spiraled into a global economic meltdown. Bush signed into law the bank bailout fund called Troubled Asset Relief Program (TARP), but the economy did not improve.

Bush Doctrine Believing that America's enemies were now terrorist groups and unstable rogue nations, President George W. Bush adapted a foreign policy that claimed the right to launch preemptive military attacks against enemies.

***Bush v. Gore* (2000)** The close 2000 presidential election came down to Florida's decisive twenty-five electoral votes. The final tally in Florida gave Bush a slight lead, but it was so small that a recount was required by state law. While the votes were being recounted, a legal battle was being waged to stop the recount. Finally, the case, *Bush v. Gore*, was present to the Supreme Court who ruled 5–4 to stop the recount and Bush was declared the winner.

buying (stock) on margin The investment practice of making a small down payment (the "margin") on a stock and borrowing the rest of money need for the purchase from a broker who held the stock as security against a down market. If the stock's value declined and the buyer failed to meet a margin call for more funds, the broker could sell the stock to cover his loan.

John C. Calhoun (1782–1850) He served in both the House of Representatives and the Senate for South Carolina before becoming secretary of war under President Monroe and then John Quincy Adams's vice president. He introduced the bill for the second national bank to Congress and led the minority of southerners who voted for the Tariff of 1816. However, he later chose to oppose tariffs. During his time as secretary of war under President Monroe, he authorized the use of federal troops against the Seminoles who were attacking settlers. As John Quincy Adams's vice president, he supported a new tariffs bill to win presidential candidate Andrew Jackson additional support. Jackson won the election, but the new tariffs bill passed and Calhoun had to explain why he had changed his opinion on tariffs.

Camp David Accords Peace agreement between Israeli Prime Minister Menachem Begin and Egyptian President Anwar Sadat, brokered by President Jimmy Carter in 1978.

"Scarface" Al Capone (1899–1947) He was the most successful gangster of the Prohibition era whose Chicago-based criminal empire included bootlegging, prostitution, and gambling.

Andrew Carnegie (1835–1919) He was a steel magnate who believed that the general public benefited from big business even if these companies employed harsh business practices. This philosophy became deeply ingrained in the conventional wisdom of some Americans. After retiring, he devoted himself to philanthropy in hopes of promoting social welfare and world peace.

carpetbaggers Northern emigrants who participated in the Republican governments of the reconstructed South.

Jimmy Carter (1924–) Jimmy Carter, an outsider to Washington, capitalized on the post-Watergate cynicism and won the 1976 presidential election. He created departments of Energy and Education and signed into law several environmental initiatives. However, his efforts to support the Panama Canal Treaties and his unwillingness to make deals with legislators caused other bills to be either gutted or stalled in Congress. Despite his efforts to improve the economy, the recession continued and inflation increased. In 1978, he successfully brokered a peace agreement between Israel and Egypt called the Camp David Accords. Then his administration was plagued with a series of crises. Fighting in the Middle East produced a fuel shortage in the United States. The Soviets invaded Afghanistan and Carter responded with the suspension of an arms-control treaty with the Soviets, the halting of grain shipments to the Soviet Union, and a call for a boycott of the Olympic Games in Moscow. In Iran, revolutionaries toppled the shah's government and seized the American embassy, taking hostage those inside. Carter struggled to get the hostages released and was unable to do so until after he lost the 1980 election to Ronald Reagan. He was awarded the Nobel Peace Prize in 2002 for his efforts to further peace and democratic elections around the world.

Jacques Cartier (1491–1557) He led the first French effort to colonize North America and explored the Gulf of St. Lawrence and reached as far as present day Montreal on the St. Lawrence River.

Bartolomé de Las Casas (1484–1566) A Catholic missionary who renounced the Spanish practice of coercively converting Indians and advocated the better treatment for them. In 1552, he wrote *A Brief Relation of the Destruction of the Indies*, which described the Spanish's cruel treatment of the Indians.

Fidel Castro (1926–) In 1959, his Communist regime came to power in Cuba after two years of guerrilla warfare against the dictator Fulgenico Batista. He enacted land redistribution programs and nationalized all foreign-owned property. The latter action as well as his political trials and summary executions damaged relations between Cuba and America. Castro was turned down when he asked for loans from the United States. However, he did receive aid from the Soviet Union.

Carrie Chapman Catt (1859–1947) She was a leader of a new generation of activists in the women's suffrage movement who carried on the work started by Elizabeth Cady Stanton and Susan B. Anthony.

Cesar Chavez (1927–1993) He founded the United Farm Workers (UFW) in 1962 and worked to organize migrant farm workers. In 1965, the UFW joined Filipino farm workers striking against corporate grape farmers in California's San Joaquin Valley. In 1970, the strike and a consumer boycott on grapes compelled the farmers to formally recognize the UFW. As the result of Chavez's efforts, wages and working conditions improved for migrant workers. In 1975, the California state legislature passed a bill that required growers to bargain collectively with representatives of the farm workers.

Chinese Exclusion Act (1882) The first federal law to restrict immigration on the basis of race and class. Passed in 1882, the act halted Chinese immigration for ten years, but it was periodically renewed and then indefinitely extended in 1902. Not until 1943 were the barriers to Chinese immigration finally removed.

Church of Jesus Christ of Latter-day Saints / Mormons Founded in 1830 by Joseph Smith, the sect was a product of the intense revivalism of the burned-over district of New York; Smith's successor Brigham Young led 15,000 followers to Utah in 1847 to escape persecution.

Winston Churchill (1874–1965) The British prime minister who led the country during World War II. Along with Roosevelt and Stalin, he helped shape the post-war world at the Yalta Conference. He also coined the term "iron curtain," which he used in his famous "The Sinews of Peace" speech.

"city machines" Local political party officials used these organizations to dispense patronage and favoritism amongst voters and businesses to ensure their loyal support to the political party.

Civil Rights Act of 1957 First federal civil rights law since Reconstruction; established the Civil Rights Commission and the Civil Rights Division of the Department of Justice.

Civil Rights Act of 1964 Outlawed discrimination in public accommodations and employment.

Henry Clay (1777–1852) In the first half of the nineteenth century, he was the foremost spokesman for the American system. As speaker of the House in the 1820s, he promoted economic nationalism, "market revolution," and the rapid development of western states and territories. He formulated the "second" Missouri Compromise, which denied the Missouri state legislature the power to exclude the rights of free blacks and mulattos. In the deadlocked presidential election of 1824, the House of Representatives decided the election. Clay supported John Quincy Adams, who won the presidency and appointed Clay to secretary of state. Andrew Jackson claimed that Clay had entered into a "corrupt bargain" with Adams for his own selfish gains.

Hillary Rodham Clinton (1947–) In the 2008 presidential election, Senator Hillary Clinton, the spouse of former President Bill Clinton, initially was the front-runner for the Democratic nomination, which made her the first woman with a serious chance to win the presidency. However,

Senator Barack Obama's Internet based and grassroots-orientated campaign garnered him enough delegates to win the nomination. After Obama became president, she was appointed secretary of state.

William Jefferson Clinton (1946–) The governor of Arkansas won the 1992 presidential election against President George H. W. Bush. In his first term, he pushed through Congress a tax increase, an economic stimulus package, the adoption of the North America Free Trade Agreement, welfare reform, a raise in the minimum wage, and improved public access to health insurance. However, he failed to institute major health-care reform, which had been one of his major goals. In 1996, Clinton defeated Republican presidential candidate Bob Dole. Clinton was scrutinized for his investment in the fraudulent Whitewater Development Corporation, but no evidence was found of him being involved in any wrongdoing. In 1998, he was revealed to have had a sexual affair with a White House intern. Clinton had initially lied about the affair and tried to cover up it, which led to a vote in Congress on whether or not to begin an impeachment inquiry. The House of Representatives voted to impeach Clinton, but the Senate found him not guilty. Clinton's presidency faced several foreign policy challenges. In 1994, he used U.S. forces to restore Haiti's democratically elected president to power after he had been ousted during a coup. In 1995, the Clinton Administration negotiated the Dayton Accords, which stopped the ethnic strife in the former Yugoslavia and the Balkan region. Clinton sponsored peace talks between Arabs and Israelis, which culminated in Israeli Prime Minister Yitzhak Rabin and the Palestine Liberation Organization leader Yasir Arafat signing the Oslo Accords in 1993. This agreement provided for the restoration of Palestinian self-rule in specific areas in exchange for peace as provided in UN Security Council resolutions.

Coercive Acts / Intolerable Acts (1774) Four parliamentary measures in reaction to the Boston Tea Party that forced payment for the tea, disallowed colonial trials of British soldiers, forced their quartering in private homes, and set up a military government.

coffin ships Irish immigrants fleeing the potato famine had to endure a six-week journey across the Atlantic to reach America. During these voyages, thousands of passengers died of disease and starvation, which led to the ships being called "coffin ships."

Christopher Columbus (1451–1506) The Italian sailor who persuaded King Ferdinand and Queen Isabella of Spain to fund his expedition across the Atlantic to discover a new trade route to Asia. Instead of arriving at China or Japan, he reached the Bahamas in 1492.

Committee on Public Information During World War I, this committee produced war propaganda that conveyed the Allies' war aims to Americans as well as attempted to weaken the enemy's morale.

Committee to Re-elect the President (CREEP) During Nixon's presidency, his administration engaged in a number of immoral acts, such as attempting to steal information and falsely accusing political appointments of sexual improprieties. These acts were funded by money illegally collected through CREEP.

Thomas Paine's *Common Sense* This pamphlet refocused the blame for the colonies' problems on King George III rather than on Parliament and advocated a declaration of independence, which few colonialists had considered prior to its appearance.

Compromise of 1850 Complex compromise mediated by Senator Henry Clay that headed off southern secession over California statehood; to appease the South it included a stronger fugitive slave law and delayed determination of the slave status of the New Mexico and Utah territories.

Compromise of 1877 Deal made by a special congressional commission on March 2, 1877, to resolve the disputed presidential election of 1876; Republican Rutherford B. Hayes, who had lost the popular vote, was declared the winner in exchange for the withdrawal of federal troops from the South, marking the end of Reconstruction.

Conestoga wagons These large horse-drawn wagons were used to carry people or heavy freight long distances, including from the East to the western frontier settlements.

conquistadores Spanish term for "conqueror," applied to European leaders of campaigns against indigenous peoples in central and southern America.

consumer culture In the post–World War II era, affluence seemed to be forever increasing in America. At the same time, there was a boom in construction as well as products and appliances for Americans to buy. As a result, shopping became a major recreational activity. Americans started spending more, saving less, and building more shopping centers.

containment U.S. strategy in the cold war that called for containing Soviet expansion; originally devised in 1947 by U.S. diplomat George F. Kennan.

Continental army Army authorized by the Continental Congress, 1775–1784, to fight the British; commanded by General George Washington.

Contras The Reagan administration ordered the CIA to train and supply guerrilla bands of anti-Communist Nicaraguans called Contras. They were fighting the Sandinista government that had recently come to power in Nicaragua. The State Department believed that the Sandinista government was supplying the leftist Salvadoran rebels with Soviet and Cuban arms. A cease-fire agreement between the Contras and Sandinistas was signed in 1988.

Calvin Coolidge "Silent Cal" (1872–1933) After President Harding's death, his vice president, Calvin Coolidge, assumed the presidency. Coolidge believed that the nation's welfare was tied to the success of big business, and he worked to end government regulation of business and industry as well as reduce taxes. In particular, he focused on the nation's industrial development.

Hernán Cortés (1485–1547) The Spanish conquistador who conquered the Aztec Empire and set the precedent for other plundering conquistadores.

General Charles Cornwallis (1738–1805) He was in charge of British troops in the South during the Revolutionary War. His surrendering to George Washington at the Battle of Yorktown ended the Revolutionary War.

Corps of Discovery Meriwether Lewis and William Clark led this group of men on an expedition of the newly purchased Louisiana territory, which took them from Missouri to Oregon. As they traveled, they kept detailed journals and drew maps of the previously unexplored territory. Their reports attracted traders and trappers to the region and gave the United States a claim to the Oregon country by right of discovery and exploration.

"corrupt bargain" A vote in the House of Representatives decided the deadlocked presidential election of 1824 in favor of John Quincy Adams, who Speaker of the House Henry Clay had supported. Afterward, Adams appointed Clay secretary of state. Andrew Jackson charged Clay with having made a "corrupt bargain" with Adams that gave Adams the presidency and Clay a place in his administration. There was no evidence of such a deal, but it was widely believed.

the counterculture "Hippie" youth culture of the 1960s, which rejected the values of the dominant culture in favor of illicit drugs, communes, free sex, and rock music.

court-packing plan President Franklin D. Roosevelt's failed 1937 attempt to increase the number of U.S. Supreme Court justices from nine to fifteen in order to save his Second New Deal programs from constitutional challenges.

covenant theory A Puritan concept that believed true Christians could enter a voluntary union for the common worship of God. Taking the idea one step further, the union could also be used for the purposes of establishing governments.

Coxey's Army Jacob S. Coxey, a Populist, led this protest group that demanded the federal government provide the unemployed with meaningful employment. In 1894, Coxey's Army joined other protests groups in a march on Washington D.C. The combination of the march and the growing support of Populism scared many Americans.

Credit Mobilier scandal Construction company guilt of massive overcharges for building the Union Pacific Railroad were exposed; high officials of the Ulysses S. Grant administration were implicated but never charged.

George Creel (1876–1953) He convinced President Woodrow Wilson that the best approach to influencing public opinion was through propaganda rather than censorship. As the executive head of the Committee on Public Information, he produced propaganda that conveyed the Allies' war aims.

"Cross of Gold" Speech In the 1896 election, the Democratic party split over the issue of whether to use gold or silver to back American currency. Significant to this division was the "Cross of Gold" speech that William Jennings Bryan delivered at the Democratic convention. This pro-silver speech was so well received that Bryan won the nomination to be their presidential candidate. Disappointed pro-gold Democrats chose to walk out of the convention and nominate their own candidate.

Cuban missile crisis Caused when the United States discovered Soviet offensive missile sites in Cuba in October 1962; the U.S.–Soviet confrontation was the cold war's closest brush with nuclear war.

cult of domesticity The belief that women should stay at home to manage the household, educate their children with strong moral values, and please their husbands.

George A. Custer (1839–1876) He was a reckless and glory-seeking Lieutenant Colonel of the U.S. Army who fought the Sioux Indians in the Great Sioux War. In 1876, he and his detachment of soldiers were entirely wiped out in the Battle of Little Bighorn.

D-day June 6, 1944, when an Allied amphibious assault landed on the Normandy coast and established a foothold in Europe from which Hitler's defenses could not recover.

Jefferson Davis (1808–1889) He was the president of the Confederacy during the Civil War. When the Confederacy's defeat seemed invitable in early 1865, he refused to surrender. Union forces captured him in May of that year.

Eugene V. Debs (1855–1926) He founded the American Railway Union, which he organized against the Pullman Palace Car Company during the Pullman strike. Later he organized the Social Democratic party, which eventually became the Socialist Party of America. In the 1912 presidential election, he ran as the Socialist party's candidate and received more than 900,000 votes.

Declaratory Act Following the repeal of the Stamp Act in 1766, Parliament passed this act which asserted Parliament's full power to make laws binding the colonies "in all cases whatsoever."

deism Enlightenment thought applied to religion; emphasized reason, morality, and natural law.

détente In the 1970s, the United States and Soviet Union began working together to achieve a more orderly and restrained competition between each other. Both countries signed an agreement to limit the number of Intercontinental Long Range Ballistic Missiles (ICBMs) that each country could possess and to not construct antiballistic missiles systems. They also signed new trade agreements.

George Dewey (1837–1917) On April 30, 1898, Commodore George Dewey's small U.S. naval squadron defeated the Spanish warships in Manila Bay in the Philippines. This quick victory aroused expansionist fever in the United States.

John Dewey (1859–1952) He is an important philosopher of pragmatism. However, he preferred to use the term *instrumentalism*, because he saw ideas as instruments of action.

Ngo Dinh Diem (1901–1963) Following the Geneva Accords, the French, with the support of America, forced the Vietnamese emperor to accept Dinh Diem as the new premier of South Vietnam. President Eisenhower sent advisors to train Diem's police and army. In return, the United States expected Diem to enact democratic reforms and distribute land to the peasants. Instead, he suppressed his political opponents, did little or no land distribution, and let corruption grow. In 1956, he refused to participate in elections to reunify Vietnam. Eventually, he ousted the emperor and declared himself president.

Dorothea Dix (1802–1887) She was an important figure in increasing the public's awareness of the plight of the mentally ill. After a two-year investigation of the treatment of the mentally ill in Massachusetts, she presented her findings and won the support of leading reformers. She eventually convinced twenty states to reform their treatment of the mentally ill.

Dixiecrats Deep South delegates who walked out of the 1948 Democratic National Convention in protest of the party's support for civil rights legislation and later formed the States' Rights (Dixiecrat) party, which nominated Strom Thurmond of South Carolina for president.

dollar diplomacy The Taft administration's policy of encouraging American bankers to aid debt-plagued governments in Haiti, Guatemala, Honduras, and Nicaragua.

Donner party Forty-seven surviving members of a group of migrants to California were forced to resort to cannibalism to survive a brutal winter trapped in the Sierra Nevadas, 1846–1847; highest death toll of any group traveling the Overland Trail.

Stephen A. Douglas (1812–1861) As a senator from Illinois, he authored the Kansas-Nebraska Act. Once passed, the act led to violence in Kansas between pro- and antislavery factions and damaged the Whig party. These damages prevented Senator Douglas from being chosen as the presidential candidate of his party. Running for senatorial reelection in 1858, he engaged Abraham Lincoln in a series of public debates about slavery in the territories. Even though Douglas won the election, the debates gave Lincoln a national reputation.

Frederick Douglass (1818–1895) He escaped from slavery and become an eloquent speaker and writer against slavery. In 1845, he published his autobiography entitled *Narrative of the Life of Frederick Douglass* and two years later he founded an abolitionist newspaper for blacks called the *North Star*.

dot-coms In the late 1990s, the stock market soared to new heights and defied the predictions of experts that the economy could not sustain such a performance. Much of the economic success was based on dot-com enterprises, which were firms specializing in computers, software, telecommunications, and the internet. However, many of the companies' stock market values were driven higher and higher by speculation instead of financial success. Eventually the stock market bubble burst.

Dred Scott v. Sandford (1857) U.S. Supreme Court decision in which Chief Justice Roger B. Taney ruled that slaves could not sue for freedom and that Congress could not prohibit slavery in the territories, on the grounds that such a prohibition would violate the Fifth Amendment rights of slaveholders.

W. E. B. Du Bois (1868–1963) He criticized Booker T. Washington's views on civil rights as being accommodationist. He advocated "ceaseless agitation" for civil rights and the immediate end to segregation and an enforcement of laws to protect civil rights and equality. He promoted an education for African Americans that would nurture bold leaders who were willing to challenge discrimination in politics.

John Foster Dulles (1888–1959) As President Eisenhower's secretary of state, he institutionalized the policy of containment and introduced the strategy of deterrence. He believed in using brinkmanship to halt the spread of communism. He attempted to employ it in Indochina, which led to the United States' involvement in Vietnam.

dust bowl Great Plains counties where millions of tons of topsoil were blown away from parched farmland in the 1930s; massive migration of farm families followed.

Peggy Eaton (1796–1879) The wife of John Eaton, President Jackson's secretary of war, was the daughter of a tavern owner with an unsavory past. Supposedly her first husband had committed suicide after learning that she was having an affair with John Eaton. The wives of members of Jackson's cabinet snubbed her because of her lowly origins and past. The scandal that resulted was called the Eaton Affair.

Jonathan Edwards (1703–1758) New England Congregationalist minister, who began a religious revival in his Northampton church and was an important figure in the Great Awakening.

Election of 1912 The presidential election of 1912 featured four candidates: Wilson, Taft, Roosevelt, and Debs. Each candidate believed in the basic assumptions of progressive politics, but each had a different view on how progressive ideals should be implemented through policy. In the end, Taft and Roosevelt split the Republican party votes and Wilson emerged as the winner.

Queen Elizabeth I of England (1533–1603) The protestant daughter of Henry VIII, she was Queen of England from 1558-1603 and played a major role in the Protestant Reformation. During her long reign, the doctrines and services of the Church of England were defined and the Spanish Armada was defeated.

General Dwight D. Eisenhower (1890–1969) During World War II, he commanded the Allied Forces landing in Africa and was the supreme Allied commander as well as planner for Operation Overlord. In 1952, he was elected president on his popularity as a war hero and his promises to clean up Washington and find an honorable peace in the Korean War. His administration sought to cut the nation's domestic programs and budget, but he left the basic structure of the New Deal intact. In July of 1953, he announced the end of fighting in Korea. He appointed Earl Warren to the Supreme Court whose influence helped the court become an important force for social and political change. His secretary of state, John Foster Dulles, institutionalized the policies of containment and deterrence. Eisenhower supported the withdrawal of British forces from the Suez Canal and established the Eisenhower doctrine, which promised to aid any nation against aggression by a communist nation. Eisenhower preferred that state and local institutions to handle civil rights issues, and he refused to force states to comply with the Supreme Court's civil rights decisions. However, he did propose the legislation that became the Civil Rights Act of 1957.

Ellis Island Reception center in New York Harbor through which most European immigrants to America were processed from 1892 to 1954.

Emancipation Proclamation (1863) President Abraham Lincoln issued a preliminary proclamation on September 22, 1862, freeing the slaves in the Confederate states as of January 1, 1863, the date of the final proclamation.

Ralph Waldo Emerson (1803–1882) As a leader of the transcendentalist movement, he wrote poems, essays, and speeches that discussed the sacredness of nature, optimism, self-reliance, and the unlimited potential of the individual. He wanted to transcend the limitations of inherited conventions and rationalism to reach the inner recesses of the self.

encomienda System under which officers of the Spanish conquistadores gained ownership of Indian land.

Enlightenment Revolution in thought begun in the seventeenth century that emphasized reason and science over the authority of traditional religion.

enumerated goods According to the Navigation Act, these particular goods, like tobacco or cotton, could only be shipped to England or other English colonies.

Erie Canal Most important and profitable of the barge canals of the 1820s and 1830s; stretched from Buffalo to Albany, New York, connecting the Great Lakes to the East Coast and making New York City the nation's largest port.

ethnic cleansing The act of killing an entire group of people in a region or country because of its ethnic background. After the collapse of the former Yugoslavia in 1991, Serbs in Bosnia attacked communities of Muslims, which led to intervention by the United Nations. In 1998, fighting broke out again in the Balkans between Serbia and Kosovo. Serbian police and military attacked, killed, raped, or forced Muslim Albanian Kosovars to leave their homes.

Fair Employment Practices Commission Created in 1941 by executive order, the FEPC sought to eliminate racial discrimination in jobs; it possessed little power but represented a step toward civil rights for African Americans.

Farmers' Alliance Two separate organizations (Northwestern and Southern) of the 1880s and 1890s that took the place of the Grange, worked for similar causes, and attracted landless, as well as landed, farmers to their membership.

Federal Writers' Project During the Great Depression, this project provided writers, such as Ralph Ellison, Richard Wright, and Saul Bellow, with work, which gave them a chance to develop as artists and be employed.

The Federalist Collection of eighty-five essays that appeared in the New York press in 1787–1788 in support of the Constitution; written by Alexander Hamilton, James Madison, and John Jay but published under the pseudonym "Publius."

Geraldine Ferraro (1935–) In the 1984 presidential election, Democratic nominee, Walter Mondale, chose her as his running mate. As a member of the U.S. House of Representatives from New York, she was the first woman to be a vice-presidential nominee for a major political party. However, she was placed on the defensive because of her husband's complicated business dealings.

Fifteenth Amendment This amendment forbids states to deny any person the right to vote on grounds of "race, color or pervious condition of servitude." Former Confederate states were required to ratify this amendment before they could be readmitted to the Union.

the "final solution" The Nazi party's systematic murder of some 6 million Jews along with more than a million other people including, but not limited to, gypsies, homosexuals, and handicap individuals.

Food Administration After America's entry into World War I, the economy of the home front needed to be reorganized to provide the most efficient means of conducting the war. The Food Administration was a part of this effort. Under the leadership of Herbert Hoover, the organization sought to increase agricultural production while reducing civilian consumption of foodstuffs.

force bill During the nullification crisis between President Andrew Jackson and South Carolina, Jackson asked Congress to pass this bill, which authorized him to use the army to force South Carolina to comply with federal law.

Gerald Ford (1913–2006) He was President Nixon's vice president and assumed the presidency after Nixon resigned. President Ford issued Nixon a pardon for any crimes related to the Watergate scandal. The American public's reaction was largely negative; and Ford never regained the public's confidence. He resisted congressional pressure to both reduce taxes and increase federal spending, which sent the American economy into the deepest recession since the Great Depression. Ford retained Kissinger as his secretary of state and continued Nixon's foreign policy goals, which included the signing of another arms-control agreement with the Soviet Union. He was heavily criticized following the collapse of South Vietnam.

Fort Laramie Treaty (1851) Restricted the Plains Indians from using the Overland Trail and permitted the building of government forts.

Fort Necessity After attacking a group of French soldiers, George Washington constructed and took shelter in this fort from vengeful French troops. Washington eventually surrendered to them after a day-long battle. This conflict was a significant event in igniting the French and Indian War.

Fort Sumter First battle of the Civil War, in which the federal fort in Charleston (South Carolina) Harbor was captured by the Confederates on April 14, 1861, after two days of shelling.

"forty-niners" Speculators who went to northern California following the discovery of gold in 1848; the first of several years of large-scale migration was 1849.

Fourteen Points President Woodrow Wilson's 1918 plan for peace after World War I; at the Versailles peace conference, however, he failed to incorporate all of the points into the treaty.

Fourteenth Amendment (1868) Guaranteed rights of citizenship to former slaves, in words similar to those of the Civil Rights Act of 1866.

Franciscan Missions In 1769, Franciscan missioners accompanied Spanish soldiers to California and over the next fifty years established a chain of missions from San Diego to San Francisco. At these missions, friars sought to convert Indians to Catholicism and make them members of the Spanish empire. The friars stripped the Indians of their native heritage and used soldiers to enforce their will.

Benjamin Franklin (1706–1790) A Boston-born American, who epitomized the Enlightenment for many Americans and Europeans, Franklin's wide range of interests led him to become a publisher, inventor, and statesman. As the latter, he contributed to the writing of the Declaration of Independence, served as the minister to France during the Revolutionary War, and was a delegate to the Constitutional Convention.

Free-Soil party Formed in 1848 to oppose slavery in the territory acquired in the Mexican War; nominated Martin Van Buren for president in 1848, but by 1854, most of the party's members had joined the Republican party.

Freedmen's Bureau Reconstruction agency established in 1865 to protect the legal rights of former slaves and to assist with their education, jobs, health care, and landowning.

freedom riders In 1961, the Congress of Racial Equality had this group of black and white demonstrators ride buses to test the federal court ruling that had banned segregation on buses and trains and in terminals. Despite being attacked, they never gave up. Their actions drew national attention and generated respect and support for their cause.

John C. Frémont "the Pathfinder" (1813–1890) He was an explorer and surveyor who helped inspire Americans living in California to rebel against the Mexican government and declare independence.

French and Indian War Known in Europe as the Seven Years' War, the last (1755–1763) of four colonial wars fought between England and France for control of North America east of the Mississippi River.

Sigmund Freud (1865–1939) He was the founder of psychoanalysis, which suggested that human behavior was motivated by unconscious and irrational forces. By the 1920s, his ideas were being discussed more openly in America.

Fugitive Slave Act of 1850 Gave federal government authority in cases involving runaway slaves; so much more punitive and prejudiced in favor of slaveholders than the 1793 Fugitive Slave Act had been that Harriet Beecher Stowe was inspired to write *Uncle Tom's Cabin* in protest; the new law was part of the Compromise of 1850, included to appease the South over the admission of California as a free state.

fundamentalism Anti-modernist Protestant movement started in the early twentieth century that proclaimed the literal truth of the Bible; the name came from *The Fundamentals*, published by conservative leaders.

"gag rule" In 1831, the House of Representatives adopted this rule, which prevented the discussion and presentation of any petitions for the abolition of slavery to the House. John Quincy Adams, who was elected to the House after his presidency ended, fought the rule on the grounds that it violated the First Amendment. In 1844, he succeeded in having it repealed.

William Lloyd Garrison (1805–1879) In 1831, he started the anti-slavery newspaper *Liberator* and helped start the New England Anti-Slavery Society. Two years later, he assisted Arthur and Lewis Tappan in the founding of the American Anti-Slavery Society. He and his followers believed that America had been thoroughly corrupted and needed a wide range of reforms. He embraced every major reform movement of the day: abolition, temperance, pacifism, and women's rights. He wanted to go beyond just freeing slaves and grant them equal social and legal rights.

Marcus Garvey (1887–1940) He was the leading spokesman for Negro Nationalism, which exalted blackness, black cultural expression, and black exclusiveness. He called upon African Americans to liberate themselves from the surrounding white culture and create their own businesses, cultural centers, and newspapers. He was also the founder of the Universal Negro Improvement Association.

Citizen Genêt (1763–1834) As the ambassador to the United States from the new French Republic, he engaged American privateers to attack British ships and conspired with frontiersmen and land speculators to organize an attack on Spanish Florida and Louisiana. His actions and the French radicals excessive actions against their enemies in the new French Republic caused the French Revolution to lose support among Americans.

Geneva Accords In 1954, the Geneva Accords were signed, which ended French colonial rule in Indochina. The agreement created the independent nations of Laos and Cambodia and divided Vietnam along the 17th parallel until an election in 1956 would reunify the country.

German U-boat German submarines, or U-boats, were used to attack enemy merchant ships in the waters around the British Isles during World War I. The sinking of the ocean liner *Lusitania* by a German submarine caused a public outcry in America, which contributed to the demands to expand the United States' military.

Gettysburg, Battle of Fought in southern Pennsylvania, July 1–3, 1863; the Confederate defeat and the simultaneous loss at Vicksburg spelled the end of the South's chances in the Civil War.

Ghost Dance movement This spiritual and political movement came from a Paiute Indian named Wovoka (or Jack Wilson). He believed that a messiah would come and rescue the Indians and restore their lands. To hasten the arrival of the messiah, the Indians needed to take up a ceremonial dance at each new moon.

Newt Gingrich (1943–) He led the Republican insurgency in Congress in the mid 1990s through mobilizing religious and social conservatives. Along with other Republican congressmen, he created the Contract with America, which was a ten-point anti-big government program. However, the program fizzled out after many of its bills were not passed by Congress.

The Gilded Age Mark Twain and Charles Dudley Warner's 1873 novel, the title of which became the popular name for the period from the end of the Civil War to the turn of the century.

glasnost Soviet leader Mikhail Gorbachev instituted this reform, which brought about a loosening of censorship.

Glorious Revolution In 1688, the Protestant Queen Mary and her husband, William of Orange, took the British throne from King James II in a bloodless coup. Afterward, Parliament greatly expanded its power and passed the Bill of Rights and the Act of Toleration, both of which would influence attitudes and events in the colonies.

Barry Goldwater (1909–1998) He was a leader of the Republican right whose book, *The Conscience of a Conservative*, was highly influential to that segment of the party. He proposed eliminating the income tax and overhauling Social Security. In 1964, he ran as the Republican presidential candidate and lost to President Johnson. He campaigned against Johnson's war on poverty, the tradition of New Deal, the nuclear test ban and the Civil Rights Act of 1964. He advocated the wholesale bombing of North Vietnam.

Samuel Gompers (1850–1924) He served as the president of the American Federation of Labor from its inception until his death. He focused on achieving concrete economic gains such as higher wages, shorter hours, and better working conditions.

"good neighbor" policy Proclaimed by President Franklin D. Roosevelt in his first inaugural address in 1933, it sought improved diplomatic relations between the United States and its Latin American neighbors.

Mikhail Gorbachev (1931–) In the late 1980s, Soviet leader Mikhail Gorbachev attempted to reform the Soviet Union through his programs of *perestroika* and *glasnost*. He pursued a renewal of détente with America and signed new arms-control agreements with President Reagan. Gorbachev chose not to involve the Soviet Union in the internal affairs of other Communist countries, which removed the threat of armed Soviet crackdowns on reformers and protesters in Eastern Europe. Gorbachev's decision allowed the velvet revolutions of Eastern Europe to occur without outside interference. Eventually the political, social, and economic upheaval he had unleashed would lead to the break-up of the Soviet Union.

Al Gore (1948–) He served as a senator of Tennessee and then as President Clinton's vice president. In the 2000 presidential election, he was the Democratic candidate and campaigned on preserving Social Security, subsidizing prescription-medicine expenses for the elderly, and protecting the environment. His opponent was Governor George W. Bush, who promoted compassionate conservatism and the transferring of power from the federal government to the states. The election ended in controversy. The close election came down to Florida's electoral votes. The final tally in Florida gave Bush a slight lead, but it was so small that a recount was required by state law. While the votes were being recounted, a legal battle was being waged to stop the recount. Finally, the case, *Bush v. Gore*, was presented to the Supreme Court who ruled 5–4 to stop the recount and Bush was declared the winner.

Jay Gould (1836–1892) As one of the biggest railroad robber barons, he was infamous for buying rundown railroads, making cosmetic improvements and then reselling them for a profit. He used corporate funds for personal investments and to bribe politicians and judges.

gradualism This strategy for ending slavery involved promoting the banning of slavery in the new western territories and encouraging the release of slaves from slavery. Supporters of this method believed that it would bring about the gradual end of slavery.

Granger movement Political movement that grew out of the Patrons of Husbandry, an educational and social organization for farmers founded in 1867; the Grange had its greatest success in the Midwest of the 1870s, lobbying for government control of railroad and grain elevator rates and establishing farmers' cooperatives.

Ulysses S. Grant (1822–1885) After distinguishing himself in the western theater of the Civil War, he was appointed general in chief of the Union army in 1864. Afterward, he defeated General Robert E. Lee through a policy of aggressive attrition. He constantly attacked Lee's army until it was grind down. Lee surrendered to Grant on April 9th, 1865 at the Appomattox Court House. In 1868, he was elected President and his tenure suffered from scandals and fiscal problems including the debate on whether or not greenbacks, paper money, should be removed from circulation.

Great Awakening Fervent religious revival movement in the 1720s through the 1740s that was spread throughout the colonies by ministers like

New England Congregationalist Jonathan Edwards and English revivalist George Whitefield.

great black migration After World War II, rural southern blacks began moving to the urban North and Midwest in large numbers in search of better jobs, housing, and greater social equality. The massive influx of African American migrants overwhelmed the resources of urban governments and sparked racial conflicts. In order to cope with the new migrants and alleviate racial tension, cities constructed massive public-housing projects that segregated African Americans into overcrowded and poor neighborhoods.

Great Compromise (Connecticut Compromise) Mediated the differences between the New Jersey and Virginia delegations to the Constitutional Convention by providing for a bicameral legislature, the upper house of which would have equal representation and the lower house of which would be apportioned by population.

Great Depression Worst economic depression in American history; it was spurred by the stock market crash of 1929 and lasted until World War II.

Great Sioux War In 1874, Lieutenant Colonel Custard led an exploratory expedition into the Black Hills, which the United States government had promised to the Sioux Indians. Miners soon followed and the army did nothing to keep them out. Eventually, the army attacked the Sioux Indians and the fight against them lasted for fifteen months before the Sioux Indians were forced to give up their land and move onto a reservation.

Great Society Term coined by President Lyndon B. Johnson in his 1965 State of the Union address, in which he proposed legislation to address problems of voting rights, poverty, diseases, education, immigration, and the environment.

Horace Greeley (1811–1872) In reaction to Radical Reconstruction and corruption in President Ulysses S. Grant's administration, a group of Republicans broke from the party to form the Liberal Republicans. In 1872, the Liberal Republicans chose Horace Greeley as their presidential candidate who ran on a platform of favoring civil service reform and condemning the Republican's Reconstruction policy.

greenbacks Paper money issued during the Civil War. After the war ended, a debate emerged on whether or not to remove the paper currency from circulation and revert back to hard-money currency (gold coins).

Opponents of hard-money feared that eliminating the greenbacks would shrink the money supply, which would lower crop prices and make it more difficult to repay long-term debts. President Ulysses S. Grant, as well as hard-currency advocates, believed that gold coins were morally preferable to paper currency.

Greenback party Formed in 1876 in reaction to economic depression, the party favored issuance of unsecured paper money to help farmers repay debts; the movement for free coinage of silver took the place of the greenback movement by the 1880s.

Nathanael Greene (1742–1786) He was appointed by Congress to command the American army fighting in the South during the Revolutionary War. Using his patience and his skills of managing men, saving supplies, and avoiding needless risks, he waged a successful war of attrition against the British.

Sarah Grimké (1792–1873) and **Angelina Grimké (1805–1879)** These two sisters gave anti-slavery speeches to crowds of mixed gender that caused some people to condemn them for engaging in unfeminine activities. The sisters rejected this opinion and made the role of women in the anti-slavery movement a prominent issue. In 1840, William Lloyd Garrison convinced the Anti-Slavery Society to allow women equal participation in the organization. A group of members that did not agree with this decision left the Anti-Slavery Society to form the American and Foreign Anti-Slavery Society.

Half-Way Covenant Allowed baptized children of church members to be admitted to a "halfway" membership in the church and secure baptism for their own children in turn, but allowed them neither a vote in the church, nor communion.

Alexander Hamilton (1755–1804) His belief in a strong federal government led him to become a contributor to *The Federalist* and leader of the Federalists. As the first secretary of the Treasury, he laid the foundation for American capitalism through his creation of a federal budget, funded debt, a federal tax system, a national bank, a customs service, and a coast guard. His "Reports on Public Credit" and "Reports on Manufactures" outlined his vision for economic development and government finances in America. He died in a duel against Aaron Burr.

Warren Harding (1865–1923) In the 1920 presidential election, he was the Republican nominee who promised Americans a "return to normalcy," which would mean a return to conservative values and a turning away from President Wilson's internationalism. His message resonated with voters' conservative postwar mood; and he won the election. Once in office, Harding's administration dismantled many of the social and economic components of progressivism and pursued a pro-business agenda. Harding appointed four pro-business Supreme Court Justices and his administration cut taxes, increased tariffs and promoted a lenient attitude towards government regulation of corporations. However, he did speak out against racism and ended the exclusion of African Americans from federal positions. His administration did suffer from a series of scandals as the result of him appointing members of the Ohio gang to government positions.

Harlem Renaissance African American literary and artistic movement of the 1920s and 1930s centered in New York City's Harlem district; writers Langston Hughes, Jean Toomer, Zora Neale Hurston, and Countee Cullen were among those active in the movement.

Hartford Convention Meeting of New England Federalists on December 15, 1814, to protest the War of 1812; proposed seven constitutional amendments (limiting embargoes and changing requirements for officeholding, declaration of war, and admission of new states), but the war ended before Congress could respond.

Patrick Henry (1736–1799) He inspired the Virginia Resolves, which declared that Englishmen could only be taxed by their elected representatives. In March of 1775, he met with other colonial leaders to discuss the goals of the upcoming Continental Congress and famously declared "Give me liberty or give me death." During the ratification process of the U.S. Constitution, he became one of the leaders of the anti-federalists.

Hideki Tōjō (1884–1948) He was Japan's war minister and later prime minister during World War II.

Alger Hiss (1904–1996) During the second Red Scare, Alger Hiss, who had served in several government departments, was accused of being a spy for the Soviet Union and was convicted of lying about espionage. The case was politically damaging to the Truman administration because the president called the charges against Hiss a "red herring." Richard

Nixon, then a California congressman, used his persistent pursuit of the case and his anti-Communist rhetoric to raise his national profile and to win election to the Senate.

Adolph Hitler "Führer" (1889–1945) The leader of the Nazis who advocated a violent anti-Semitic, anti-Marxist, pan-German ideology. He started World War II in Europe and orchestrated the systematic murder of some 6 million Jews along with more than a million others.

HIV/AIDS Human Immunodeficiency Virus (HIV) is a virus that attacks the body's T-cells, which are necessary to help the immune system fight off infection and disease. Acquired Immunodeficiency Syndrome (AIDS) occurs after the HIV virus has destroyed the body's immune system. HIV is transferred when body fluids, such as blood or semen, which carry the virus, enter the body of an uninfected person. The virus appeared in America in the early 1980s. The Reagan administration was slow to respond to the "AIDS Epidemic," because effects of the virus were not fully understood and they deemed the spread of the disease as the result of immoral behavior.

Homestead Act (1862) Authorized Congress to grant 160 acres of public land to a western settler, who had only to live on the land for five years to establish title.

Herbert Hoover (1874–1964) Prior to becoming president, Hoover served as the secretary of commerce in both the Harding and Coolidge administrations. During his tenure at the Commerce Department, he pursued new markets for business and encouraged business leaders to share information as part of the trade-association movement. The Great Depression hit while he was president. Hoover believed that the nation's business structure was sound and sought to revive the economy through boosting the nation's confidence. He also tried to restart the economy with government constructions projects, lower taxes and new federal loan programs, but nothing worked.

House Un-American Activities Committee (HUAC) Formed in 1938 to investigate subversives in the government; best-known investigations were of Hollywood notables and of former State Department official Alger Hiss, who was accused in 1948 of espionage and Communist party membership.

Sam Houston (1793–1863) During Texas's fight for independence from Mexico, Sam Houston was the commander in chief of the Texas forces, and he led the attack that captured General Antonio López de Santa Anna. After Texas gained its independence, he was name its first president.

Jacob Riis' *How the Other Half Lives* Jacob Riis was an early muckraking journalist who exposed the slum conditions in New York City in his book *How the Other Half Lives*.

General William Howe (1729–1814) As the commander of the British army in the Revolutionary War, he seized New York City from Washington's army, but failed to capture it. He missed several more opportunities to quickly end the rebellion, and he resigned his command after the British defeat at Saratoga.

Saddam Hussein (1937–2006) The former dictator of Iraq who became the head of state in 1979. In 1980, he invaded Iran and started the eight-year-long Iran-Iraq War. In 1990, he invaded Kuwait, which caused the Gulf War of 1991. In 2003, he was overthrown and captured when the United States invaded. He was sentenced to death by hanging in 2006.

Anne Hutchinson (1591–1643) The articulate, strong-willed, and intelligent wife of a prominent Boston merchant, who espoused her belief in direct divine revelation. She quarreled with Puritan leaders over her beliefs; and they banished her from the colony.

impressment The British navy used press-gangs to kidnap men in British and colonial ports who were then forced to serve in the British navy.

indentured servant Settler who signed on for a temporary period of servitude to a master in exchange for passage to the New World; Virginia and Pennsylvania were largely peopled in the seventeenth and eighteenth centuries by English indentured servants.

"Indian New Deal" This phrase refers to the reforms implemented for Native Americans during the New Deal era. John Collier, the commissioner of the Bureau of Indian Affairs (BIA), increased the access Native Americans had to relief programs and employed more Native Americans at the BIA. He worked to pass the Indian Reorganization Act. However, the version of the act passed by Congress was a much-diluted version of

Collier's original proposal and did not greatly improve the lives of Native Americans.

Indian Removal Act (1830) Signed by President Andrew Jackson, the law permitted the negotiation of treaties to obtain the Indians' lands in exchange for their relocation to what became Oklahoma.

Indochina This area of Southeast Asian consists of Laos, Cambodia, became and Vietnam and was once controlled by France as a colony. After the Viet Minh defeated the French, the Geneva Accords were signed, which ended French colonial rule. The agreement created the independent nations of Laos and Cambodia and divided Vietnam along the 17th parallel until an election would reunify the country. Fearing a communist take over, the United States government began intervening in the region during the Truman administration, which led to President Johnson's full-scale military involvement in Vietnam.

Industrial Workers of the World A radical union organized in Chicago in 1905, nicknamed the Wobblies; its opposition to World War I led to its destruction by the federal government under the Espionage Act.

internationalists Prior to the United States' entry in World War II, internationalists believed that America's national security depended on aiding Britain in its struggle against Germany.

internment of Japanese Americans In 1942, President Roosevelt issued an executive order to have all Japanese Americans forcibly relocated to relocation camps. More than 60 percent of the more than 100,000 internees were American citizens.

interstate highway system In the late 1950s, construction began on a national network of interstate superhighways for the purpose of commerce and defense. The interstate highways would enable the rapid movement of military convoys and the evacuation of cities after a nuclear attack.

Iranian Hostage Crisis In 1979, a revolution in Iran placed the Ayatollah Ruhollah Khomeini, a fundamental religious leader, in power. In November 1979, revolutionaries seized the American embassy in Tehran and held those inside hostage. President Carter struggled to get the hostages. He tried pressuring Iran through appeals to the United Nations, freezing Iranian assets in the United States and imposing a trade embargo. During an aborted rescue operation, a helicopter collided with a transport plane and killed eight U.S. soldiers. Finally, Carter unfroze several billion dollars in Iranian assets, and the hostages were released after being held for 444 days; but not until Ronald Reagan had become president of the United States.

Iran-Contra affair Scandal of the second Reagan administration involving sale of arms to Iran in partial exchange for release of hostages in Lebanon and use of the arms money to aid the Contras in Nicaragua, which had been expressly forbidden by Congress.

Irish Potato Famine In 1845, an epidemic of potato rot brought a famine to rural Ireland that killed over 1 million peasants and instigated a huge increase in the number or Irish immigrating to America. By 1850, the Irish made up 43 percent of the foreign-born population in the United States; and in the 1850s, they made up over half the population of New York City and Boston.

iron curtain Term coined by Winston Churchill to describe the cold war divide between western Europe and the Soviet Union's Eastern European satellites.

Iroquois League An alliance of the Iroquois tribes that used their strength to force Europeans to work with them in the fur trade and to wage war across what is today eastern North America.

Andrew Jackson (1767–1837) As a major general in the Tennessee militia, he defeated the Creek Indians, invaded the panhandle of Spanish Florida and won the Battle of New Orleans. In 1818, his successful campaign against Spanish forces in Florida gave the United States the upper hand in negotiating for Florida with Spain. As president, he vetoed bills for the federal funding of internal improvements and the re-chartering of the Second National Bank. When South Carolina nullified the Tariffs of 1828 and 1832, Jackson requested that Congress pass a "force bill" that would authorize him to use the army to compel the state to comply with the tariffs. He forced eastern Indians to move west of the Mississippi River so their lands could be used by white settlers. Groups of those who opposed Jackson come together to form a new political part called the Whigs.

Jesse Jackson (1941–) An African American civil rights activist who had been one of Martin Luther King Jr.'s chief lieutenants. He is most famous for founding the social justice organization the Rainbow

Coalition. In 1988, he ran for the Democratic presidential nomination, which became a race primarily between him and Michael Dukakis. Dukakis won the nomination, but lost the election to Republican nominee Vice President George H. W. Bush.

Thomas "Stonewall" Jackson (1824–1863) He was a Confederate general who was known for his fearlessness in leading rapid marches, bold flanking movements, and furious assaults. He earned his nickname at the Battle of the First Bull Run for standing courageously against Union fire. During the battle of Chancellorsville, his own men accidently mortally wounded him.

William James (1842–1910) He was the founder of Pragmatism and one of the fathers of modern psychology. He believed that ideas gained their validity not from their inherent truth, but from their social consequences and practical application.

Jay's Treaty Treaty with Britain negotiated in 1794 by Chief Justice John Jay; Britain agreed to vacate forts in the Northwest Territories, and festering disagreements (border with Canada, prewar debts, shipping claims) would be settled by commission.

Thomas Jefferson (1743–1826) He was a plantation owner, author, the drafter of the Declaration Independence, ambassador to France, leader of the Republican party, secretary of state, and the third president of the United States. As president, he purchased the Louisiana territory from France, withheld appointments made by President Adams leading to *Marybury v. Madison*, outlawed foreign slave trade, and was committed to a "wise and frugal" government.

Jesuits A religious order founded in 1540 by Ignatius Loyola. They sought to counter the spread of Protestantism during the Protestant Reformation and spread the Catholic faith through work as missionaries. Roughly 3,500 served in New Spain and New France.

"Jim Crow" laws In the New South, these laws mandated the separation of races in various public places that served as a way for the ruling whites to impose their will on all areas of black life.

Andrew Johnson (1808–1875) As President Abraham Lincoln's vice president, he was elevated to the presidency after Lincoln's assassination. In order to restore the Union after the Civil War, he issued an amnesty proclamation and required former Confederate states to ratify the Thirteenth Amendment. He fought Radical Republicans in Congress over whether he or Congress had the authority to restore states rights to the former Confederate states. This fight weakened both his political and public support. In 1868, the Radical Republicans attempted to impeach Johnson but fell short on the required number of votes needed to remove him from office.

Lyndon B. Johnson (1908–1973) Former member of the United States House of Representatives and the former Majority Leader of the United States Senate, Vice President Lyndon Johnson, assumed the presidency after President Kennedy's assassination. He was able to push through Congress several pieces of Kennedy's legislation that had been stalled including the Civil Rights Act of 1964. He declared "war on poverty" and promoted his own social program called the Great Society, which sought to end poverty and racial injustice. In 1965, he signed the Immigration and Nationality Service Act, which abolished the discriminatory quotas system that had been the immigration policy since the 1920s. Johnson greatly increased America's role in Vietnam. By 1969, there were 542,000 U.S. troops fighting in Vietnam and a massive anti-war movement had developed in America. In 1968, Johnson announced that he would not run for re-election.

Kansas-Nebraska Act (1854) Law sponsored by Illinois senator Stephen A. Douglas to allow settlers in newly organized territories north of the Missouri border to decide the slavery issue for themselves; fury over the resulting nullification of the Missouri Compromise of 1820 led to violence in Kansas and to the formation of the Republican party.

Florence Kelley (1859–1932) As the head of the National Consumer's League, she led the crusade to promote state laws to regulate the number of working hours imposed on women who were wives and mothers.

George F. Kennan (1904–2005) While working as an American diplomat, he devised the strategy of containment, which called for the halting of Soviet expansion. It became America's choice strategy throughout the cold war.

John F. Kennedy (1917–1963) Elected president in 1960, he was interested in bringing new ideas to the White House. Despite the difficulties he had in getting his legislation through Congress, he did establish the Alliance for Progress programs to help Latin America, the Peace Corps, the Trade

Expansion Act of 1962, and funding for urban renewal projects and the space program. He mistakenly proceeded with the Bay of Pigs invasion, but he successfully handled the Cuban missile crisis. In Indochina, his administration became increasingly involved in supporting local governments through aid, advisors, and covert operations. In 1963, he was assassinated by Lee Harvey Oswald in Dallas, Texas.

Kent State During the spring of 1970, students on college campuses across the country protested the expansion of the Vietnam War into Cambodia. At Kent State University, the National Guard attempted to quell the rioting students. The guardsmen panicked and shot at rock-throwing demonstrators. Four student bystanders were killed.

Kentucky and Virginia Resolutions (1798–1799) Passed in response to the Alien and Sedition Acts, the resolutions advanced the state-compact theory that held states could nullify an act of Congress if they deemed it unconstitutional.

Francis Scott Key (1779–1843) During the War of 1812, he watched British forces bombard Fort McHenry, but fail to take it. Seeing the American flag still flying over the fort at dawn inspired him to write "The Star-Spangled Banner," which became the American national anthem.

Keynesian economics A theory of economics developed by John Maynard Keynes. He argued that increased government spending, even if it increased the nation's deficit, during an economic downturn was necessary to reinvigorate a nation's economy. This view was held by Harry Hopkins and Harold Ickes who advised President Franklin Roosevelt during the Great Depression.

Martin Luther King Jr. (1929–1968) As an important leader of the civil rights movement, he urged people to use nonviolent civil disobedience to demand their rights and bring about change. He successfully led the Montgomery bus boycott. While in jail for his role in demonstrations, he wrote his famous "Letter from Birmingham City Jail," in which he defended his strategy of nonviolent protest. In 1963, he delivered his famous "I Have a Dream Speech" from the steps of the Lincoln Memorial as a part of the March on Washington. A year later, he was awarded the Nobel Peace Prize. In 1968, he was assassinated.

King William's War (War of the League of Augsburg) First (1689–1697) of four colonial wars between England and France.

King Philip (?–1676) or Metacomet The chief of the Wampanoages, who the colonists called King Philip. He resented English efforts to convert Indians to Christianity and waged a war against the English colonists in which he was killed.

Henry Kissinger (1923–) He served as the secretary of state and national security advisor in the Nixon administration. He negotiated with North Vietnam for an end to the Vietnam War. In 1973, an agreement was signed between America, North and South Vietnam, and the Viet Cong to end the war. The cease-fire did not last; and South Vietnam fell to North Vietnam. He helped organize Nixon's historic trips to China and the Soviet Union. In the Middle East, he negotiated a cease-fire between Israel and its neighbors following the Yom Kippur War and solidified Israel's promise to return to Egypt most of the land it had taken during the 1967 war.

Knights of Labor Founded in 1869, the first national union picked up many members after the disastrous 1877 railroad strike, but lasted under the leadership of Terence V. Powderly, only into the 1890s; supplanted by the American Federation of Labor.

Know-Nothing party Nativist, anti-Catholic third party organized in 1854 in reaction to large-scale German and Irish immigration; the party's only presidential candidate was Millard Fillmore in 1856.

Ku Klux Klan Organized in Pulaski, Tennessee, in 1866 to terrorize former slaves who voted and held political offices during Reconstruction; a revived organization in the 1910s and 1920s stressed white, Anglo-Saxon, fundamentalist Protestant supremacy; the Klan revived a third time to fight the civil rights movement of the 1950s and 1960s in the South.

Marquis de Lafayette (1757–1834) A wealthy French idealist excited by the American cause, he offered to serve in Washington's army for free in exchange for being named a major general. He overcame Washington's initial skepticism to become one of his most trusted aides.

Land Ordinance of 1785 Directed surveying of the Northwest Territory into townships of thirty-six sections (square miles) each, the sale of the sixteenth section of which was to be used to finance public education.

Bartolomé de Las Casas (1484–1566) A Catholic missionary who renounced the Spanish practice of coercively converting Indians and advocated the better treatment for them. In 1552, he wrote *A Brief Relation of the Destruction of the Indies*, which described the Spanish's cruel treatment of the Indians.

League of Nations Organization of nations to mediate disputes and avoid war established after World War I as part of the Treaty of Versailles; President Woodrow Wilson's "Fourteen Points" speech to Congress in 1918 proposed the formation of the league.

Mary Elizabeth Lease (1850–1933) She was a leader of the farm protest movement who advocated violence if change could not be obtained at the ballot box. She believed that the urban-industrial East was the enemy of the working class.

Robert E. Lee (1807–1870) Even though he had served in the United States Army for thirty years, he chose to fight on the side of the Confederacy and took command of the Army of North Virginia. Lee was excellent at using his field commanders; and his soldiers respected him. However, General Ulysses S. Grant eventually wore down his army, and Lee surrendered to Grant at the Appomattox Court House on April 9, 1865.

Lend-Lease Act (1941) Permitted the United States to lend or lease arms and other supplies to the Allies, signifying increasing likelihood of American involvement in World War II.

John Dickinson's "Letters from a Farmer in Pennsylvania" These twelve letters appeared in the *Pennsylvania Chronicle* and argued that Parliament could regulate colonial commerce and collect duties that related to that purpose, but it did not have the right to levy taxes for revenue.

Levittown First low-cost, mass-produced development of suburban tract housing built by William Levitt on Long Island, New York, in 1947.

Lexington and Concord, Battle of The first shots fired in the Revolutionary War, on April 19, 1775, near Boston; approximately 100 Minutemen and 250 British soldiers were killed.

Liberator William Lloyd Garrison started this anti-slavery newspaper in 1831 in which he renounced gradualism and called for abolition.

Queen Liliuokalani (1838–1917) In 1891, she ascended to the throne of the Hawaiian royal family and tried to eliminate white control of the Hawaiian government. Two years later, Hawaii's white population revolted and seized power with the support of American marines.

Abraham Lincoln (1809–1865) His participation in the Lincoln-Douglas debates gave him a national reputation and he was nominated as the Republican party candidate for president in 1860. Shortly after he was elected president, southern states began succeeding from the Union and in April of 1861 he declared war on the succeeding states. On January 1, 1863, Lincoln signed the Emancipation Proclamation, which freed all slaves. At the end of the war, he favored a reconstruction strategy for the former Confederate states that did not radically alter southern social and economic life. However, before his plans could be finalized, John Wilkes Booth assassinated Lincoln at Ford's Theater on April 14, 1865.

Lincoln-Douglas debates Series of senatorial campaign debates in 1858 focusing on the issue of slavery in the territories; held in Illinois between Republican Abraham Lincoln, who made a national reputation for himself, and incumbent Democratic senator Stephen A. Douglas, who managed to hold onto his seat.

John Locke (1632–1704) An English philosopher whose ideas were influential during the Enlightenment. He argued in his *Essay on Human Understanding* (1690) that humanity is largely the product of the environment, the mind being a blank tablet, *tabula rasa*, on which experience is written.

Henry Cabot Lodge (1850–1924) He was the chairman of the Senate Foreign Relations Committee who favored limiting America's involvement in the League of Nations' covenant and sought to amend the Treaty of Versailles.

de Lôme letter Spanish ambassador Depuy de Lôme wrote a letter to a friend in Havana in which he described President McKinley as "weak" and a seeker of public admiration. This letter was stolen and published in the *New York Journal*, which increased the American public's dislike of Spain and moved the two countries closer to war.

Lone Star Republic After winning independence from Mexico, Texas became its own nation that was called the Lone Star Republic. In 1836, Texans drafted themselves a constitution, legalized slavery, banned free blacks, named Sam Houston president, and voted for the annexation to the United States. However, quarrels over adding a slave state and fears of instigating a war with Mexico delayed Texas's entrance into the Union until December 29, 1845.

March on Washington Civil rights demonstration on August 28, 1963, where the Reverend Martin Luther King Jr. gave his "I Have a Dream" speech on the steps of the Lincoln Memorial.

George C. Marshall (1880–1959) As the chairman of the Joint Chiefs of Staff, he orchestrated the Allied victories over Germany and Japan in World War II. In 1947, he became President Truman's secretary of state and proposed the massive reconstruction program for western Europe called the Marshall Plan.

Chief Justice John Marshall (1755–1835) During his long tenure as chief justice of the supreme court (1801–1835), he established the foundations for American jurisprudence, the authority of the Supreme Court, and the constitutional supremacy of the national government over states.

Marshall Plan U.S. program for the reconstruction of post–World War II Europe through massive aid to former enemy nations as well as allies; proposed by General George C. Marshall in 1947.

massive resistance In reaction to the *Brown v. Board of Education* decision of 1954, U.S. Senator Harry Byrd encouraged southern states to defy federally mandated school integration.

Senator Joseph R. McCarthy (1908–1957) In 1950, this senator became the shrewdest and most ruthless exploiter of America's anxiety of communism. He claimed that the United States government was full of Communists and led a witch hunt to find them, but he was never able to uncover a single communist agent.

George B. McClellan (1826–1885) In 1861, President Abraham Lincoln appointed him head of the Army of the Potomac and, later, general in chief of the U.S. Army. He built his army into well trained and powerful force. However, he often delayed taking action against the enemy even though Lincoln wanted him to attack. After failing to achieve a decisive victory against the Confederacy, Lincoln removed McClellan from command in 1862.

Cyrus Hall McCormick (1809–1884) In 1831, he invented a mechanical reaper to harvest wheat, which transformed the scale of agriculture. By hand a farmer could only harvest a half an acre a day, while the McCormick reaper allowed two people to harvest twelve acres of wheat a day.

William McKinley (1843–1901) As a congressman, he was responsible for the McKinley Tariff of 1890, which raised the duties on manufactured products to their highest level ever. Voters disliked the tariff and McKinley, as well as other Republicans, lost their seats in Congress the next election. However, he won the presidential election of 1896 and raised the tariffs again. In 1898, he annexed Hawaii and declared war on Spain. The war concluded with the Treaty of Paris, which gave America control over Puerto Rico, Guam, and the Philippines. Soon America was fighting Filipinos, who were seeking independence for their country. In 1901, McKinley was assassinated.

Robert McNamara (1916–) He was the secretary of defense for both President Kennedy and President Johnson and a supporter of America's involvement in Vietnam.

McNary-Haugen Bill Vetoed by President Calvin Coolidge in 1927 and 1928, the bill to aid farmers would have artificially raised agricultural prices by selling surpluses overseas for low prices and selling the reduced supply in the United States for higher prices.

Andrew Mellon (1855–1937) As President Harding's secretary of the Treasury, he sought to generate economic growth through reducing government spending and lowering taxes. However, he insisted that the tax reductions mainly go to the rich because he believed the wealthy would reinvest their money and spur economic growth. In order to bring greater efficiency and nonpartisanship to the government's budget process, he persuaded Congress to pass the Budget and Accounting Act of 1921, which created a new Bureau of the Budget and a General Accounting Office.

mercantile system A nationalistic program that assumed that the total amount of the world's gold and silver remained essentially fixed with only a nation's share of that wealth subject to change.

James Meredith (1933–) In 1962, the governor of Mississippi defied a Supreme Court ruling and refused to allow James Meredith, an African American, to enroll at the University of Mississippi. Federal marshals were sent to enforce the law which led to clashes between a white mob and the marshals. Federal troops intervened and two people were killed and many others were injured. A few days later, Meredith was able to register at the university.

Merrimack* (ship renamed the *Virginia*) and the *Monitor First engagement between ironclad ships; fought at Hampton Roads, Virginia, on March 9, 1862.

Metacomet (?–1676) or King Philip The chief of the Wampanoages, who the colonists called King Philip. He resented English efforts to convert Indians to Christianity and waged a war against the English colonists in which he was killed.

militant nonviolence After the success of the Montgomery bus boycott, people were inspired by Martin Luther King Jr.'s use of this nonviolent form of protest. Throughout the civil rights movement, demonstrators used this method of protest to challenge racial segregation in the South.

Ho Chi Minh (1890–1969) He was the Vietnamese communist resistance leader who drove the French and the United States out of Vietnam. After the Geneva Accords divided the region into four countries, he controlled North Vietnam, and ultimately became the leader of all of Vietnam at the conclusion of the Vietnam War.

minstrelsy A form of entertainment that was popular from the 1830s to the 1870s. The performances featured white performers who were made up as African Americans or blackface. They performed banjo and fiddle music, "shuffle" dances and lowbrow humor that reinforced racial stereotypes.

Minutemen Special units organized by the militia to be ready for quick mobilization.

***Miranda v. Arizona* (1966)** U.S. Supreme Court decision required police to advise persons in custody of their rights to legal counsel and against self-incrimination.

Mississippi Plan In 1890, Mississippi instituted policies that led to a near-total loss of voting rights for blacks and many poor whites. In order to vote, the state required that citizens pay all their taxes first, be literate, and have been residents of the state for two years and one year in an electoral district. Convicts were banned from voting. Seven other states followed this strategy of disenfranchisement.

Missouri Compromise Deal proposed by Kentucky senator Henry Clay to resolve the slave/free imbalance in Congress that would result from Missouri's admission as a slave state; in the compromise of March 20, 1820, Maine's admission as a free state offset Missouri, and slavery was prohibited in the remainder of the Louisiana Territory north of the southern border of Missouri.

Model T Ford Henry Ford developed this model of car so that it was affordable for everyone. Its success led to an increase in the production of automobiles which stimulated other related industries such steel, oil, and rubber. The mass use of automobiles increased the speed goods could be transported, encouraged urban sprawl, and sparked real estate booms in California and Florida.

modernism As both a mood and movement, modernism recognized that Western civilization had entered an era of change. Traditional ways of thinking and creating art were being rejected and replaced with new understandings and forms of expression.

Molly Maguires Secret organization of Irish coal miners that used violence to intimidate mine officials in the 1870s.

Monroe Doctrine President James Monroe's declaration to Congress on December 2, 1823, that the American continents would be thenceforth closed to colonization but that the United States would honor existing colonies of European nations.

Montgomery bus boycott Sparked by Rosa Parks's arrest on December 1, 1955, a successful year-long boycott protesting segregation on city buses; led by the Reverend Martin Luther King Jr.

Moral Majority Televangelist Jerry Falwell's political lobbying organization, the name of which became synonymous with the religious right—conservative evangelical Protestants who helped ensure President Ronald Reagan's 1980 victory.

J. Pierpont Morgan (1837–1913) As a powerful investment banker, he would acquire, reorganize, and consolidate companies into giant trusts. His biggest achievement was the consolidation of the steel industry into the United States Steel Corporation, which was the first billion-dollar corporation.

James Monroe (1758–1831) He served as secretary of state and war under President Madison and was elected president. As the latter, he signed the Transcontinental Treaty with Spain which gave the United States Florida and expanded the Louisiana territory's western border to the Pacific coast. In 1823, he established the Monroe Doctrine. This foreign policy proclaimed the American continents were no longer open to colonization and America would be neutral in European affairs.

Robert Morris (1734–1806) He was the superintendent of finance for the Congress of the Confederation during the final years of the Revolutionary War. He envisioned a national finance plan of taxation and debt management, but the states did not approve the necessary amendments to the Articles of Confederation need to implement the plan.

Samuel B. Morse (1791–1872) In 1832, he invented the telegraph and revolutionized the speed of communication.

mountain men Inspired by the fur trade, these men left civilization to work as trappers and reverted to a primitive existence in the wilderness. They were the first whites to find routes through the Rocky Mountains, and they pioneered trails that settlers later used to reach the Oregon country and California in the 1840s.

muckrakers Writers who exposed corruption and abuses in politics, business, meat-packing, child labor, and more, primarily in the first decade of the twentieth century; their popular books and magazine articles spurred public interest in progressive reform.

Mugwumps Reform wing of the Republican party that supported Democrat Grover Cleveland for president in 1884 over Republican James G. Blaine, whose influence peddling had been revealed in the Mulligan letters of 1876.

Benito Mussolini "Il Duce" (1883–1945) The Italian founder of the Fascist party who came to power in Italy in 1922 and allied himself with Adolf Hitler and the Axis powers during World War II.

My Lai Massacre In 1968, Lieutenant William Calley and his soldiers massacred 347 Vietnamese civilians in the village of My Lai. Twenty-five army officers were charged with complicity in the massacre and its cover-up but only Calley was convicted. Later, President Nixon granted him parole.

NAFTA Approved in 1993, the North American Free Trade Agreement with Canada and Mexico allowed goods to travel across their borders free of tariffs; critics argued that American workers would lose their jobs to cheaper Mexican labor.

National Industrial Recovery Act (1933) Passed on the last of the Hundred Days; it created public-works jobs through the Federal Emergency Relief Administration and established a system of self-regulation for industry through the National Recovery Administration, which was ruled unconstitutional in 1935.

National Recovery Administration This organization's two goals were to stabilize business and generate purchasing power for consumers. The first goal was to be achieved through the implementation industry-wide codes that set wages and prices, which would reduce the chaotic competition. To provide consumers with purchasing power, the administration would provide jobs, define workplace standards, and raise wages.

National Socialist German Workers' (Nazi) party Founded in the 1920s, this party gained control over Germany under the leadership of Adolf Hitler in 1933 and continued in power until Germany's defeat at the end of World War II. It advocated a violent anti-Semitic, anti-Marxist, pan-German ideology. The Nazi party systematically murdered some 6 million Jews along with more than a million others.

nativism Anti-immigrant and anti-Catholic feeling in the 1830s through the 1850s; the largest group was New York's Order of the Star-Spangled Banner, which expanded into the American, or Know-Nothing party in 1854. In the 1920, there was a surge in nativism as Americans grew to fear immigrants who might be political radicals. In response, new strict immigration regulations were established.

nativist A native-born American who saw immigrants as a threat to his way of life and employment. During the 1880s, nativist groups worked to stop the flow of immigrates into the United States. Of these groups, the most successful was the American Protective Association who promoted government restrictions on immigration, tougher naturalization requirements, the teaching of English in schools and workplaces that refused to employ foreigners or Catholics.

Navigation Acts Passed by the English Parliament to control colonial trade and bolster the mercantile system, 1650–1775; enforcement of the acts led to growing resentment by colonists.

new conservatism The political philosophy of those who led the conservative insurgency of the early 1980s. This brand of conservatism was personified in Ronald Reagan who believed in less government, supply-side economics, and "family values."

New Deal Franklin D. Roosevelt's campaign promise, in his speech to the Democratic National Convention of 1932, to combat the Great Depression with a "new deal for the American people;" the phrase became a catchword for his ambitious plan of economic programs.

New France The name used for the area of North America that was colonized by the French. Unlike Spanish or English colonies, New France had a small number of colonists, which forced them to initially seek good relations with the indigenous people they encountered.

New Freedom Democrat Woodrow Wilson's political slogan in the presidential campaign of 1912; Wilson wanted to improve the banking system, lower tariffs, and, by breaking up monopolies, give small businesses freedom to compete.

New Frontier John F. Kennedy's program, stymied by a Republican Congress and his abbreviated term; his successor Lyndon B. Johnson had greater success with many of the same concepts.

New Jersey Plan The delegations to the Constitutional Convention were divided between two plans on how to structure the government: New Jersey wanted one legislative body with equal representation for each state.

New Nationalism Platform of the Progressive party and slogan of former President Theodore Roosevelt in the presidential campaign of 1912; stressed government activism, including regulation of trusts, conservation, and recall of state court decisions that had nullified progressive programs.

"new Negro" In the 1920s, a slow and steady growth of black political influence occurred in northern cities where African Americans were freer to speak and act. This political activity created a spirit of protest that expressed itself culturally in the Harlem Renaissance and politically in "new Negro" nationalism.

New Netherlands Dutch colony conquered by the English to become four new colonies New York, New Jersey, Pennsylvania, and Delaware.

New South *Atlanta Constitution* editor Henry W. Grady's 1886 term for the prosperous post–Civil War South: democratic, industrial, urban, and free of nostalgia for the defeated plantation South.

William Randolph Hearst's *New York Journal* In the late 1890s, the *New York Journal* and its rival, the *New York World*, printed sensationalism on the Cuban revolution as part of their heated competition for readership. The *New York Journal* printed a negative letter from the Spanish ambassador about President McKinley and inflammatory coverage of the sinking of the *Maine* in Havana Harbor. These two events roused the American public's outcry against Spain.

Joseph Pulitzer's *New York World* In the late 1890s, the *New York World* and its rival, *New York Journal*, printed sensationalism on the Cuban revolution as part of their heated competition for readership.

Admiral Chester Nimitz (1885–1966) During World War II, he was the commander of central Pacific. Along with General Douglas MacArthur, he dislodged the Japanese military from the Pacific Islands they had occupied.

Nineteenth Amendment (1920) Granted women the right to vote.

Richard Nixon (1913–1994) He first came to national prominence as a congressman involved in the investigation of Alger Hiss. Later he served as vice president during the Eisenhower administration. In 1960, he ran as the Republican nominee for president and lost to John Kennedy. In 1968, he ran and won the presidency against Democratic nominee Hubert Humphrey. During his campaign, he promised to bring about "peace with honor" in Vietnam. He told southern conservatives that he would slow the federal enforcement of civil rights laws and appoint pro-southern justices to the Supreme Court. After being elected, he fulfilled the latter promise attempted to keep the former. He opened talks with the North Vietnamese and began a program of Vietnamization of the war. He also bombed Cambodia. In 1973, America, North and South Vietnam, and the Viet Cong agreed to end the war and the United States withdrew. However, the cease-fire was broken, and the South Vietnam fell to North Vietnam. In 1970, Nixon changed U.S. foreign policy. He declared that the America was no longer the world's policemen and he would seek some partnerships with Communist countries. With his historic visit to China, he ended twenty years of diplomatically isolating China and he began taking steps towards cultural exchanges and trade. In 1972, Nixon travelled to Moscow and signed agreements with the Soviet Union on arms control and trade. That same year, Nixon was reelected, but the Watergate scandal erupted shortly after his victory. When his knowledge of the break-in and subsequent cover-up was revealed, Nixon resigned the presidency under threat of impeachment.

No Child Left Behind President George W. Bush's education reform plan that required states to set and meet learning standards for students and make sure that all students were "proficient" in reading and writing by 2014. States had to submit annual reports of students' standardized test scores. Teachers were required to be "proficient" in their subject area.

Schools who failed to show progress would face sanctions. States criticized the lack of funding for remedial programs and noted that poor school districts would find it very difficult to meet the new guidelines.

Lord North (1732–1792) The first minister of King George III's cabinet whose efforts to subdue the colonies only brought them closer to revolution. He helped bring about the Tea Act of 1773, which led to the Boston Tea Party. In an effort to discipline Boston, he wrote, and Parliament passed, four acts that galvanized colonial resistance.

North Atlantic Treaty Organization (NATO) Defensive alliance founded in 1949 by ten western European nations, the United States, and Canada to deter Soviet expansion in Europe.

Northwest Ordinance Created the Northwest Territory (area north of the Ohio River and west of Pennsylvania), established conditions for self-government and statehood, included a Bill of Rights, and permanently prohibited slavery.

nullification Concept of invalidation of a federal law within the borders of a state; first expounded in the Kentucky and Virginia Resolutions (1798), cited by South Carolina in its Ordinance of Nullification (1832) of the Tariff of Abominations, used by southern states to explain their secession from the Union (1861), and cited again by southern states to oppose the *Brown v. Board of Education* decision (1954).

Nuremberg trials At the site of the annual Nazi party rallies, twenty-one major German offenders faced an international military tribunal for Nazi atrocities. After a ten-month trial, the court acquitted three and sentenced eleven to death, three to life imprisonment, and four to shorter terms.

Barack Obama (1961–) In the 2008 presidential election, Senator Barack Obama mounted an innovative Internet based and grassroots orientated campaign that garnered him enough delegates to win the Democratic nomination. As the nation's economy nosedived in the fall of 2008, Obama linked the Republican economic philosophy with the country's dismal financial state and promoted a message of "change" and "politics of hope," which resonated with voters. He decisively won the presidency and became America's first person of colored to be elected president.

Sandra Day O'Connor (1930–) She was the first woman to serve on the Supreme Court of the United States and was appointed by President Reagan. Reagan's critics charged that her appointment was a token gesture and not a sign of any real commitment to gender equality.

Ohio gang In order to escape the pressures of the White House, President Harding met with a group of people, called the "Ohio gang," in a house on K Street in Washington D.C. Members of this gang were given low-level positions in the American government and they used their White House connection to "line their pockets" by granting government contracts without bidding, which led to a series of scandals, most notably the Teapot Dome Scandal.

Frederick Law Olmsted (1822–1903) In 1858, he constructed New York's Central Park, which led to a growth in the movement to create urban parks. He went on to design parks for Boston, Brooklyn, Chicago, Philadelphia, San Francisco, and many other cities.

Opechancanough (?–1644) The brother and successor of Powhatan who led his tribe in an attempt to repel the English settlers in Virginia in 1622.

Open Door Policy In hopes of protecting the Chinese market for U.S. exports, Secretary of State John Hay unilaterally announced in 1899 that Chinese trade would be open to all nations.

Operation Desert Shield After Saddam Hussein invaded Kuwait in 1990, President George H. W. Bush sent American military forces to Saudi Arabia on a strictly defensive mission. They were soon joined by a multinational coalition. When the coalition's mission changed to the retaking of Kuwait, the operation was renamed Desert Storm.

Operation Desert Storm Multinational allied force that defeated Iraq in the Gulf War of January 1991.

Operation Overlord The Allies' assault on Hitler's "Atlantic Wall," a seemingly impregnable series of fortifications and minefields along the French coastline that German forces had created using captive Europeans for laborers.

J. Robert Oppenheimer (1904–1967) He led the group of physicists at the laboratory in Los Alamos, New Mexico, who constructed the first atomic bomb.

Oregon Country The Convention of 1818 between Britain and the United States established the Oregon Country as being west of the crest of the

Rocky Mountains and the two countries were to jointly occupy it. In 1824, the United States and Russia signed a treaty that established the line of 54°40′ as the southern boundary of Russia's territorial claim in North America. A similar agreement between Britain and Russia finally gave the Oregon Country clearly defined boarders, but it remained under joint British and American control.

Oregon fever Enthusiasm for emigration to the Oregon Country in the late 1830s and early 1840s.

Osceola (1804?–1838) He was the leader of the Seminole nation who resisted the federal Indian removal policy through a protracted guerilla war. In 1837, he was treacherously seized under a flag of truce and imprisoned at Fort Moultrie, where he was left to die.

Overland (Oregon) Trail Route of wagon trains bearing settlers from Independence, Missouri, to the Oregon Country in the 1840s to 1860s.

A. Mitchell Palmer (1872–1936) As the attorney general, he played an active role in government's response to the Red Scare. After several bombings across America, including one at Palmer's home, he and other Americans became convinced that there was a well-organized Communist terror campaign at work. The federal government launched a campaign of raids, deportations, and collecting files on radical individuals.

Panic of 1819 Financial collapse brought on by sharply falling cotton prices, declining demand for American exports, and reckless western land speculation.

panning A method of mining that used a large metal pan to sift gold dust and nuggets from riverbeds during the California gold rush of 1849.

Rosa Parks (1913–2005) In 1955, she refused to give up her seat to a white man on a city bus in Montgomery, Alabama, which a local ordinance required of blacks. She was arrested for disobeying the ordinance. In response, black community leaders organized the Montgomery bus boycott.

Alice Paul (1885–1977) She was a leader of the women's suffrage movement and head of the Congressional Committee of National Women Suffrage Association. She instructed female suffrage activists to use more militant tactics, such as picketing state legislatures, chaining themselves to public buildings, inciting police to arrest them, and undertaking hunger strikes.

Norman Vincent Peale (1898–1993) He was a champion of the upbeat and feel-good theology that was popular in the 1950s religious revival. He advocated getting rid of any depressing or negative thoughts and replacing them with "faith, enthusiasm and joy," which would make an individual popular and well liked.

"peculiar institution" This term was used to describe slavery in America because slavery so fragrantly violated the principle of individual freedom that served as the basis for the Declaration of Independence.

Pentagon papers Informal name for the Defense Department's secret history of the Vietnam conflict; leaked to the press by former official Daniel Ellsberg and published in the *New York Times* in 1971.

Pequot War Massacre in 1637 and subsequent dissolution of the Pequot Nation by Puritan settlers, who seized the Indians' lands.

perestroika Soviet leader Mikhail Gorbachev introduced these political and economic reforms, which included reconstructing the state bureaucracy, reducing the privileges of the political elite, and shifting from a centrally planned economy to a mixed economy.

Commodore Matthew Perry (1794–1858) In 1854, he negotiated the Treaty of Kanagawa, which was the first step in starting a political and commercial relationship between the United States and Japan.

John J. Pershing (1860–1948) After Pancho Villa had conducted several raids into Texas and New Mexico, President Woodrow Wilson sent troops under the command of General John J. Pershing into Mexico to stop Villa. However, after a year of chasing Villa and not being able to catch him, they returned to the United States. During World War I, Pershing commanded the first contingent of U.S. soldiers sent to Europe and advised the War Department to send additional American forces.

"pet banks" During President Andrew Jackson's fight with the national bank, Jackson resolved to remove all federal deposits from it. To comply with Jackson's demands, Secretary of Treasury Taney continued to draw on government's accounts in the national bank, but deposit all new federal receipts in state banks. The state banks that received these deposits were called "pet banks."

Dien Bien Phu The defining battle in the war between French colonialists and the Viet Minh. The Viet Minh's victory secured North Vietnam for

Ho Chi Minh and was crucial in compelling the French to give up Indochina as a colony.

Pilgrims Puritan Separatists who broke completely with the Church of England and sailed to the New World aboard the *Mayflower*, founding Plymouth Colony on Cape Cod in 1620.

Gifford Pinchot (1865–1946) As the head of the Division of Forestry, he implemented a conservation policy that entailed the scientific management of natural resources to serve the public interest. His work helped start the conservation movement. In 1910, he exposed to the public the decision of Richard A. Ballinger's, President Taft's secretary of the interior, to open up previously protected land for commercial use. Pinchot was fired, but the damage to Taft's public image resulted in the loss of many pro-Taft candidates in 1910 congressional election.

Elizabeth Lucas Pinckney (1722? –1793) One of the most enterprising horticulturists in colonial America, she began managing her family's three plantations in South Carolina at the age of sixteen. She had tremendous success growing indigo, which led to many other plantations growing the crop as well.

Pinckney's Treaty Treaty with Spain negotiated by Thomas Pinckney in 1795; established United States boundaries at the Mississippi River and the 31st parallel and allowed open transportation on the Mississippi.

Francisco Pizarro (1478?–1541) In 1531, he lead his Spanish soldiers to Peru and conquered the Inca Empire.

planters In the antebellum South, the owner of a large farm worked by twenty or more slaves.

James Knox Polk "Young Hickory" (1795–1849) As President, his chief concern was the expansion of the United States. In 1846, his administration resolved the dispute with Britain over the Oregon Country border. Shortly, after taking office, Mexico broke off relations with the United States over the annexation of Texas. Polk declared war on Mexico and sought to subvert Mexican authority in California. The United States defeated Mexico; and the two nations signed the Treaty of Guadalupe Hidalgo in which Mexico gave up any claims on Texas north of the Rio Grande River and ceded New Mexico and California to the United States.

Pontiac's Rebellion The Peace Treaty of 1763 gave the British all French land east of the Mississippi River. This area included the territory of

France's Indian allies who were not consulted about the transfer of their lands to British control. In an effort to recover their autonomy, Indians captured British forts around the Great Lakes and in the Ohio Valley as well as attacked settlements in Pennsylvania, Maryland, and Virginia.

popular sovereignty Allowed settlers in a disputed territory to decide the slavery issue for themselves.

Populist / the People's party Political success of Farmers' Alliance candidates encouraged the formation in 1892 of the People's party (later renamed the Populist party); active until 1912, it advocated a variety of reform issues, including free coinage of silver, income tax, postal savings, regulation of railroads, and direct election of U.S. senators.

Chief Powhatan Wahunsonacock He was called Powhatan by the English after the name of his tribe, and was the powerful, charismatic chief of numerous Algonquian-speaking towns in eastern Virginia representing over 10,000 Indians.

pragmatism William James founded this philosophy in the early 1900s. Pragmatists believed that ideas gained their validity not from their inherent truth, but from their social consequences and practical application.

Proclamation of 1763 Royal directive issued after the French and Indian War prohibiting settlement, surveys, and land grants west of the Appalachian Mountains; although it was soon over-ridden by treaties, colonists continued to harbor resentment.

proprietary colonies A colony owned by an individual, rather than a joint-stock company.

pueblos The Spanish term for the adobe cliff dwellings of the indigenous people of the southwestern United States.

Pullman Strike Strike against the Pullman Palace Car Company in the company town of Pullman, Illinois, on May 11, 1894, by the American Railway Union under Eugene V. Debs; the strike was crushed by court injunctions and federal troops two months later.

Puritans English religious group that sought to purify the Church of England; founded the Massachusetts Bay Colony under John Winthrop in 1630.

Quakers George Fox founded the Quaker religion in 1647. They rejected the use of formal sacraments and ministry, refused to take oaths and embraced pacifism. Fleeing persecution, they settled and established the colony of Pennsylvania.

Radical Republicans Senators and congressmen who, strictly identifying the Civil War with the abolitionist cause, sought swift emancipation of the slaves, punishment of the rebels, and tight controls over the former Confederate states after the war.

Raleigh's Roanoke Island Colony English expedition of 117 settlers, including Virginia Dare, the first English child born in the New World; colony disappeared from Roanoke Island in the Outer Banks sometime between 1587 and 1590.

A. Philip Randolph (1889–1979) He was the head of the Brotherhood of Sleeping Car Porters who planned a march on Washington D.C. to demand an end to racial discrimination in the defense industries. To stop the march, Roosevelt administration negotiated an agreement with the Randolph group. The demonstration would be called off and an executive order would be issued that forbid discrimination in defense work and training programs and set up the Fair Employment Practices Committee.

range wars In the late 1800s, conflicting claims over land and water rights triggered violent disputes between farmers and ranchers in parts of the western United States.

Ronald Reagan (1911–2004) In 1980, the former actor and governor of California was elected president. In office, he reduced social spending, cut taxes, and increased defense spending. He was criticized for cutting important programs, such as housing and school lunches and increasing the federal deficit. By 1983, prosperity had returned to America and Reagan's economic reforms appeared to be working, but in October of 1987 the stock market crashed. Some blamed the federal debt, which had tripled in size since Reagan had taken office. In the early 1980s, HIV/AIDS cases were beginning to be reported in America, but the Reagan administration chose to do little about the growing epidemic. Reagan believed that most of the world's problems came from the Soviet Union, which he called the "evil empire." In response, he conducted a major arms build up. Then in 1987, he signed an arms-control treaty with the Soviet Union. He authorized covert CIA operations in Central America. In 1986, the Iran-Contra scandal came to light which revealed arms sales were being conducted with Iran in a partial exchange for the release of hostages in Lebanon. The arms money was being used to aid the Contras.

Reaganomics Popular name for President Ronald Reagan's philosophy of "supply side" economics, which combined tax cuts, less government spending, and a balanced budget with an unregulated marketplace.

Reconstruction Finance Corporation Federal program established in 1932 under President Herbert Hoover to loan money to banks and other institutions to help them avert bankruptcy.

Red Scare Fear among many Americans after World War I of Communists in particular and noncitizens in general, a reaction to the Russian Revolution, mail bombs, strikes, and riots.

Redeemers In post–Civil War southern politics, redeemers were supporters of postwar Democratic leaders who supposedly saved the South from Yankee domination and the constraints of a purely rural economy.

Dr. Walter Reed (1851–1902) His work on yellow fever in Cuba led to the discovery that the fever was carried by mosquitoes. This understanding helped develop more effective controls of the worldwide disease.

Reformation European religious movement that challenged the Catholic Church and resulted in the beginnings of Protestant Christianity. During this period, Catholics and Protestants persecuted, imprisoned, tortured, and killed each other in large numbers.

reparations As a part of the Treaty of Versailles, Germany was required to confess its responsibility for World War I and make payments to the victors for the entire expense of the war. These two requirements created a deep bitterness among Germans.

Alexander Hamilton's Report on Manufactures First Secretary of the Treasury Alexander Hamilton's 1791 analysis that accurately foretold the future of American industry and proposed tariffs and subsidies to promote it.

"return to normalcy" In the 1920 presidential election, Republican nominee Warren G. Harding campaigned on the promise of a "return to normalcy," which would mean a return to conservative values and a turning away from President Wilson's internationalism.

Paul Revere (1735–1818) On the night of April 18, 1775, British soldiers marched towards Concord to arrest American Revolutionary leaders and seize their depot of supplies. Paul Revere famously rode through the night and raised the alarm about the approaching British troops.

Roaring Twenties In 1920s, urban America experienced an era of social and intellectual revolution. Young people experimented with new forms of recreation and sexuality as well as embraced jazz music. Leading young urban intellectuals expressed a disdain for old-fashioned rural and small-town values. The Eastern, urban cultural shift clashed with conservative and insular midwestern America, which increased the tensions between the two regions.

Jackie Robinson (1919–1972) In 1947, he became the first African American to play major league baseball. He won over fans and players and stimulated the integration of other professional sports.

rock-and-roll music Alan Freed, a disc jockey, noticed white teenagers were buying rhythm and blues records that had been only purchased by African Americans and Hispanic Americans. Freed began playing these records, but called them rock-and-roll records as a way to overcome the racial barrier. As the popularity of the music genre increased, it helped bridge the gap between "white" and "black" music.

John D. Rockefeller (1839–1937) In 1870, he founded the Standard Oil Company of Ohio, which was his first step in creating his vast oil empire. Eventually, he perfected the idea of a holding company: a company that controlled other companies by holding all or at least a majority of their stock. During his lifetime, he donated over $500 million in charitable contributions.

Romanticism Philosophical, literary, and artistic movement of the nineteenth century that was largely a reaction to the rationalism of the previous century; Romantics valued emotion, mysticism, and individualism.

Eleanor Roosevelt (1884–1962) She redefined the role of the presidential spouse and was the first woman to address a national political convention, write a nationally syndicated column and hold regular press conferences. She travelled throughout the nation to promote the New Deal, women's causes, organized labor, and meet with African American leaders. She was her husband's liaison to liberal groups and brought women activists and African American and labor leaders to the White House.

Franklin D. Roosevelt (1882–1945) Elected during the Great Depression, Roosevelt sought to help struggling Americans through his New Deal programs that created employment and social programs, such as Social Security. Prior to American's entry into World War II, he supported Britain's fight against Germany through the lend-lease program. After the bombing of Pearl Harbor, he declared war on Japan and Germany and led the country through most of World War II before dying of cerebral hemorrhage. In 1945, he met with Winston Churchill and Joseph Stalin at the Yalta Conference to determine the shape of the post-War world.

Theodore Roosevelt (1858–1919) As the assistant secretary of the navy, he supported expansionism, American imperialism and war with Spain. He led the First Volunteer Cavalry, or Rough Riders, in Cuba during the war of 1898 and used the notoriety of this military campaign for political gain. As President McKinley's vice president, he succeeded McKinley after his assassination. His forceful foreign policy became known as "big stick diplomacy." Domestically, his policies on natural resources helped start the conversation movement. Unable to win the Republican nomination for president in 1912, he formed his own party of progressive Republicans called the "Bull Moose" party.

Roosevelt Corollary to the Monroe Doctrine (1904) President Theodore Roosevelt announced in what was essentially a corollary to the Monroe Doctrine that the United States could intervene militarily to prevent interference from European powers in the Western Hemisphere.

Rough Riders The First U.S. Volunteer Cavalry, led in battle in the Spanish-American War by Theodore Roosevelt; they were victorious in their only battle near Santiago, Cuba; and Roosevelt used the notoriety to aid his political career.

Nicola Sacco (1891–1927) In 1920, he and Bartolomeo Vanzetti were Italian immigrants who were arrested for stealing $16,000 and killing a paymaster and his guard. Their trial took place during a time of numerous bombings by anarchists and their judge was openly prejudicial. Many liberals and radicals believe that the conviction of Sacco and Vanzetti was based on their political ideas and ethnic origin rather than the evidence against them.

"salutary neglect" Edward Burke's description of Robert Walpole's relaxed policy towards the American colonies, which gave them greater independence in pursuing both their economic and political interests.

Sandinista Cuban-sponsored government that came to power in Nicaragua after toppling a corrupt dictator. The State Department believed that the Sandinistas were supplying the leftist Salvadoran rebels with Cuban and Soviet arms. In response, the Reagan administration ordered the CIA to train and supply guerrilla bands of anti-Communist Nicaraguans called Contras. A cease-fire agreement between the Contras and Sandinistas was signed in 1988.

Margaret Sanger (1883–1966) As a birth-control activist, she worked to distribute birth control information to working-class women and opened the nation's first family-planning clinic in 1916. She organized the American Birth Control League, which eventually changed its name to Planned Parenthood.

General Antonio López de Santa Anna (1794–1876) In 1834, he seized political power in Mexico and became a dictator. In 1835, Texans rebelled against him and he led his army to Texas to crush their rebellion. He captured the missionary called the Alamo and killed all of its defenders, which inspired Texans to continue to resistance and Americans to volunteer to fight for Texas. The Texans captured Santa Anna during a surprise attack and he bought his freedom by signing a treaty recognizing Texas's independence.

Saratoga, Battle of Major defeat of British general John Burgoyne and more than 5,000 British troops at Saratoga, New York, on October 17, 1777.

scalawags White southern Republicans—some former Unionists—who served in Reconstruction governments.

Phyllis Schlafly (1924–) She was a right-wing Republican activist who spearheaded the anti-feminism movement. She believed feminist were "anti-family, anti-children, and pro-abortion." She worked against the equal-rights amendment for women and civil rights protection for gays.

Winfield Scott (1786–1866) During the Mexican War, he was the American general who captured Mexico City, which ended the war. Using his popularity from his military success, he ran as a Whig party candidate for President.

Sears Roebuck and Company By the end of the nineteenth century, this company dominated the mail-order industry and helped create a truly national market. Its mail-order catalog and low prices allowed people living in rural areas and small towns to buy products that were previously too expensive or available only to city dwellers.

secession Shortly after President Abraham Lincoln was elected, southern states began dissolving their ties with the United States because they believed Lincoln and the Republican party were a threat to slavery.

second Bank of the United States In 1816, the second Bank of the United States was established in order to bring stability to the national economy, serve as the depository for national funds, and provide the government with the means of floating loans and transferring money across the country.

Second Great Awakening Religious revival movement of the early decades of the nineteenth century, in reaction to the growth of secularism and rationalist religion; began the predominance of the Baptist and Methodist churches.

Second New Deal To rescue his New Deal program form judicial and political challenges, President Roosevelt launched a second phase of the New Deal in 1935. He was able to convince Congress to pass key pieces of legislation including the National Labor Relations act and Social Security Act. Roosevelt called the latter the New Deal's "supreme achievement" and pensioners started receiving monthly checks in 1940.

Seneca Falls Convention First women's rights meeting and the genesis of the women's suffrage movement; held in July 1848 in a church in Seneca Falls, New York, by Elizabeth Cady Stanton and Lucretia Coffin Mott.

"separate but equal" Principle underlying legal racial segregation, which was upheld in *Plessy v. Ferguson* (1896) and struck down in *Brown v. Board of Education* (1954).

separation of powers The powers of government are split between three separate branches (executive, legislative, and judicial) who check and balance each other.

September 11 On September 11, 2001, Islamic terrorists, who were members of al Qaeda terrorist organization, hijacked four commercial airliners. Two were flown into the World Trade Center and a third into the Pentagon. A fourth plane was brought down in Shanksville, Pennsylvania, when its passengers attacked the cockpit. In response, President George W. Bush launched his "war on terrorism." His administration assembled an international coalition to fight terrorism, and they invaded Afghanistan after the country's government would not turn over al Qaeda's leader, Osama bin Laden. However, bin Laden evaded capture. Fearful of new attacks, Bush created the Office of Homeland Security and the Transportation Security Administration.

Bush and Congress passed the U.S.A. Patriot Act, which allowed government agencies to try suspected terrorists in secret military courts and eavesdrop on confidential conversations.

settlement houses Product of the late nineteenth-century movement to offer a broad array of social services in urban immigrant neighborhoods; Chicago's Hull House was one of hundreds of settlement houses that operated by the early twentieth century.

Shakers Founded by Mother Ann Lee Stanley in England, the United Society of Believers in Christ's Second Appearing settled in Watervliet, New York, in 1774 and subsequently established eighteen additional communes in the Northeast, Indiana, and Kentucky.

sharecropping Type of farm tenancy that developed after the Civil War in which landless workers—often former slaves—farmed land in exchange for farm supplies and a share of the crop; differed from tenancy in that the terms were generally less favorable.

Share-the-Wealth program Huey Long, a critic of President Roosevelt, offered this program as an alternative to the New Deal. The program proposed to confiscate large personal fortunes, which would be used to guarantee every poor family a cash grant of $5,000 and every worker an annual income of $2,500. Under this program, Long promised to provide pensions, reduce working hours, pay veterans' bonuses, and ensures a college education to every qualified student.

Shays's Rebellion Massachusetts farmer Daniel Shays and 1,200 compatriots, seeking debt relief through issuance of paper currency and lower taxes, stormed the federal arsenal at Springfield in the winter of 1787 but were quickly repulsed.

William T. Sherman's March through Georgia Union General William T. Sherman believed that there was a connection between the South's economy, morale, and ability to wage war. During his March through Georgia, he wanted to demoralize the civilian populace and destroy the resources they needed to fight. His army seized food and livestock that the Confederate Army might have used as well as wrecked railroads and mills and burned plantations.

Sixteenth Amendment (1913) Legalized the federal income tax.

Alfred E. Smith (1873–1944) In the 1928 presidential election, he won the Democratic nomination, but failed to win the presidency. Rural voters distrusted him for being Catholic and the son of Irish immigrants as well as his anti-Prohibition stance.

Captain John Smith (1580–1631) A swashbuckling soldier of fortune with rare powers of leadership and self-promotion, he was appointed to the resident council to manage Jamestown.

Joseph Smith (1805–1844) In 1823, he claimed that the Angel Moroni showed him the location of several gold tablets on which the Book of Mormon was written. Using the Book of Mormon as his gospel, he founded the Church of Jesus Christ of Latter-day Saints, or Mormons. Joseph and his followers upset non-Mormons living near them so they began looking for a refuge from persecution. In 1839, they settled in Commerce, Illinois, which they renamed Nauvoo. In 1844, Joseph and his brother were arrested and jailed for ordering the destruction of a newspaper that opposed them. While in jail, an anti-Mormon mob stormed the jail and killed both of them.

social Darwinism Application of Charles Darwin's theory of natural selection to society; used the concept of the "survival of the fittest" to justify class distinctions and to explain poverty.

social gospel Preached by liberal Protestant clergymen in the late nineteenth and early twentieth centuries; advocated the application of Christian principles to social problems generated by industrialization.

social justice An important part of the Progressive's agenda, social justice sought to solve social problems through reform and regulation. Methods used to bring about social justice ranged from the founding of charities to the legislation of a ban on child labor.

Sons of Liberty Organized by Samuel Adams, they were colonialists with a militant view against the British government's control of the colonies.

Hernando de Soto (1500?–1542) A conquistador who explored the west coast of Florida, western North Carolina and along the Arkansas river from 1539 till his death in 1542.

Southern Christian Leadership Conference (SCLC) Civil rights organization founded in 1957 by the Reverend Martin Luther King Jr., and other civil rights leaders.

"southern strategy" This strategy was a major reason for Richard Nixon's victory in the 1968 presidential election. To gain support in the South, Nixon assured southern conservatives that he would slow the federal enforcement of civil rights laws and appoint pro-southern justices to the Supreme Court. As president, Nixon fulfilled these promises.

Spanish flu Unprecedentedly lethal influenza epidemic of 1918 that killed more than 22 million people worldwide.

Herbert Spencer (1820–1903) As the first major proponent of social Darwinism, he argued that human society and institutions are subject to the process of natural selection and that society naturally evolves for the better. Therefore, he was against any form of government interference with the evolution of society, like business regulations, because it would help the "unfit" to survive.

spoils system The term—meaning the filling of federal government jobs with persons loyal to the party of the president—originated in Andrew Jackson's first term; the system was replaced in the Progressive Era by civil service.

stagflation During the Nixon administration, the economy experienced inflation and a recession at the same time, which is syndrome that defies the orthodox laws of economics. Economists named this phenomenon "stagflation."

Joseph Stalin (1879–1953) The Bolshevik leader who succeeded Lenin as the leader of the Soviet Union in 1924 and ruled the country until his death. During his totalitarian rule of the Soviet Union, he used purges and a system of forced labor camps to maintain control over the country. During the Yalta Conference, he claimed vast areas of Eastern Europe for Soviet domination. After the end of World War II, the alliance between the Soviet Union and the Western powers altered into the tension of the cold war and Stalin erected the "iron curtain" between Eastern and Western Europe.

Stalwarts Conservative Republican party faction during the presidency of Rutherford B. Hayes, 1877–1881; led by Senator Roscoe B. Conkling of New York, Stalwarts opposed civil service reform and favored a third term for President Ulysses S. Grant.

Stamp Act Congress Twenty-seven delegates from nine of the colonies met from October 7 to 25, 1765 and wrote a Declaration of the Rights and Grievances of the Colonies, a petition to the King and a petition to Parliament for the repeal of the Stamp Act.

Standard Oil Company of Ohio John D. Rockefeller found this company in 1870, which grew to monopolize 90 to 95 percent of all the oil refineries in the country. It was also a "vertical monopoly" in that the company controlled all aspects of production and the services it needed to conduct business. For example, Standard Oil produced their own oil barrels and cans as well as owned their own pipelines, railroad tank cars, and oil-storage facilities.

Elizabeth Cady Stanton (1815–1902) She was a prominent reformer and advocate for the rights of women, and she helped organize the Seneca Falls Convention to discuss women's rights. The convention was the first of its kind and produced the Declaration of Sentiments, which proclaimed the equality of men and women.

staple crop, or cash crop A profitable market crop, such as cotton or tobacco.

Thaddeus Stevens (1792–1868) As one of the leaders of the Radical Republicans, he argued that the former Confederate states should be viewed as conquered provinces, which were subject to the demands of the conquerors. He believed that all of southern society needed to be changed, and he supported the abolition of slavery and racial equality.

Adlai E. Stevenson (1900–1965) In the 1952 and 1956 presidential elections, he was the Democratic nominee who lost to Dwight Eisenhower. He was also the U.S. Ambassador to the United Nations and is remembered for his famous speech in 1962 before the UN Security Council that unequivocally demonstrated that the Soviet Union had built nuclear missile bases in Cuba.

Strategic Defense Initiative ("Star Wars") Defense Department's plan during the Reagan administration to build a system to destroy incoming missiles in space.

Levi Strauss (1829–1902) A Jewish tailor who followed miners to California during the gold rush and began making durable work pants that were later dubbed blue jeans or Levi's.

Students for a Democratic Society (SDS) Major organization of the New Left, founded at the University of Michigan in 1960 by Tom Hayden and Al Haber.

suburbia The postwar era witnessed a mass migration to the suburbs. As the population in cities areas grew, people began to spread further out within the urban areas, which created new suburban communities. By 1970 more people lived in the suburbs (76 million) than in central cities (64 million).

sunbelt The label for an arc that stretched from the Carolinas to California. During the postwar era, much of the urban population growth occurred in this area.

the "surge" In early 2007, President Bush decided he would send a "surge" of new troops to Iraq and implement a new strategy. U.S. forces would shift their focus from offensive operations to the protection of Iraqi civilians from attacks by terrorist insurgents and sectarian militias. While the "surge" reduced the violence in Iraq, Iraqi leaders were still unable to develop a self-sustaining democracy.

Taliban A coalition of ultraconservative Islamists who rose to power in Afghanistan after the Soviets withdrew. The Taliban leaders gave Osama bin Laden a safe haven in their country in exchange for aid in fighting the Northern Alliance, who were rebels opposed to the Taliban. After September 11 terrorist attacks, the United States asked the Taliban to turn over bin Laden. After they refused, America invaded Afghanistan, but bin Laden evaded capture.

Tammany Hall The "city machine" used by "Boss" Tweed to dominate politics in New York City until his arrest in 1871.

Tariff of 1816 First true protective tariff, intended strictly to protect American goods against foreign competition.

Tariff of 1832 This tariff act reduced the duties on many items, but the tariffs on cloth and iron remained high. South Carolina nullified it along with the tariff of 1828. President Andrew Jackson sent federal troops to the state and asked Congress to grant him the authority to enforce the tariffs. Henry Clay presented a plan of gradually reducing the tariffs until 1842, which Congress passed and ended the crisis.

TARP In 2008 President George W. Bush signed into law the bank bailout fund called Troubled Asset Relief Program (TARP), which required the Treasury Department to spend $700 billion to keep banks and other financial institutions from collapsing.

Zachary Taylor (1784–1850) During the Mexican War, he scored two quick victories against Mexico, which made him very popular in America. President Polk chose him as the commander in charge of the war. However, after he was not put in charge of the campaign to capture Mexico City, he chose to return home. Later he used his popularity from his military victories to be elected the president as a member of the Whig party.

Taylorism In his book *The Principles of Scientific Management*, Frederick W. Taylor explained a management system that claimed to be able to reduce waste through the scientific analysis of the labor process. This system called Taylorism, promised to find the optimum technique for the average worker and establish detailed performance standards for each job classification.

Teapot Dome Harding administration scandal in which Secretary of the Interior Albert B. Fall profited from secret leasing to private oil companies of government oil reserves at Teapot Dome, Wyoming, and Elk Hills, California.

Tecumseh (1768–1813) He was a leader of the Shawnee tribe who tried to unite all Indians into a confederation that could defend their hunting grounds. He believed that no land cessions could be made without the consent of all the tribes since they held the land in common. His beliefs and leadership made him seem dangerous to the American government and they waged war on him and his tribe. He was killed at the Battle of the Thames.

Tejanos Texas settlers of Spanish or Mexican descent.

Teller Amendment On April 20, 1898, a joint resolution of Congress declared Cuba independent and demanded the withdrawal of Spanish forces. The Teller amendment was added to this resolution, and it declaimed any designs the United States had on Cuban territory.

Tenochtitlán The capital city of the Aztec Empire. The city was built on marshy islands on the western side of Lake Tetzcoco, which is the site of present-day Mexico City.

Tet offensive Surprise attack by the Viet Cong and North Vietnamese during the Vietnamese New Year of 1968; turned American public opinion strongly against the war in Vietnam.

Thirteenth Amendment This amendment to the U.S. Constitution freed all slaves in the United States. After the Civil War ended, the former confederate states were required to ratify this amendment before they could be readmitted to the Union.

Gulf of Tonkin incident On August 2 and 4 of 1964, North Vietnamese vessels attacked two American destroyers in Gulf of Tonkin off the coast of North Vietnam. President Johnson described the attacks as unprovoked. In reality, the U.S. ships were monitoring South Vietnamese attacks on North Vietnamese islands that America advisors had planned. The incident spurred the Tonkin Gulf resolution.

Tonkin Gulf resolution (1964) Passed by Congress in reaction to supposedly unprovoked attacks on American warships off the coast of North Vietnam; it gave the president unlimited authority to defend U.S. forces and members of SEATO.

Tories Term used by Patriots to refer to Loyalists, or colonists who supported the Crown after the Declaration of Independence.

Trail of Tears Cherokees' own term for their forced march, 1838–1839, from the southern Appalachians to Indian lands (later Oklahoma); of 15,000 forced to march, 4,000 died on the way.

Transcendentalism Philosophy of a small group of mid-nineteenth-century New England writers and thinkers, including Ralph Waldo Emerson, Henry David Thoreau, and Margaret Fuller; they stressed "plain living and high thinking."

Transcontinental railroad First line across the continent from Omaha, Nebraska, to Sacramento, California, established in 1869 with the linkage of the Union Pacific and Central Pacific railroads at Promontory, Utah.

triangular trade Means by which exports to one country or colony provided the means for imports from another country or colony. For example, merchants from colonial New England shipped rum to West Africa and used it to barter for slaves who were then taken to the West Indies. The slaves were sold or traded for materials that the ships brought back to New England including molasses which is need to make rum.

Treaty of Ghent The signing of this treaty in 1814 ended the War of 1812 without solving any of the disputes between Britain and the United States.

Harry S. Truman (1884–1972) As President Roosevelt's vice president, he succeeded him after his death near the end of World War II. After the war, Truman wrestled with the inflation of both prices and wages, and his attempts to bring them both under control led to clashes with organized labor and Republicans. He did work with Congress to pass the National Security Act, which made the Joint Chiefs of Staff a permanent position and created the National Military Establishment and the Central Intelligence Agency. He banned racial discrimination in the hiring of federal employees and ended racial segregation in the armed forces. In foreign affairs, he established the Truman Doctrine to contain communism and the Marshall Plan to rebuild Europe. After North Korea invaded South Korea, Truman sent the U.S. military to defend

South Korea under the command of General Douglas MacArthur. Later in the war, Truman expressed his willingness to negotiate the restoration of prewar boundaries which MacArthur attempted to undermine. Truman fired MacArthur for his open insubordination.

Truman Doctrine President Harry S. Truman's program of post–World War II aid to European countries—particularly Greece and Turkey—in danger of being undermined by communism.

Sojourner Truth (1797? –1883) She was born into slavery, but New York State freed her in 1827. She spent the 1840s and 1850s travelling across the country and speaking to audiences about her experiences as slave and asking them to support abolition and women's rights.

Harriet Tubman (1820–1913) She was born a slave, but escaped to the North. Then she returned to the South nineteen times and guided 300 slaves to freedom.

Nat Turner (1800–1831) He was the leader of the only slave revolt to get past the planning stages. In August of 1831, the revolt began with the slaves killing the members of Turner's master's household. Then they attacked other neighboring farmhouses and recruited more slaves until the militia crushed the revolt. At least fifty-five whites were killed during the uprising and seventeen slaves were hanged afterwards.

Tuskegee Airmen During World War II, African Americans in the armed forces usually served in segregated units. African American pilots were trained at a separate flight school in Tuskegee, Alabama, and were known as Tuskegee Airmen.

Mark Twain (1835–1910) Born Samuel Langhorne Clemens in Missouri, he became a popular humorous writer and lecturer and established himself as one of the great American authors. Like other authors of the local-color movement, his stories expressed the nostalgia people had for rural culture and old folkways as America became increasingly urban. His two greatest books, *The Adventures of Tom Sawyer* and *The Adventures of Huckleberry Finn*, drew heavily on his childhood in Missouri.

"Boss" Tweed (1823–1878) An infamous political boss in New York City, Tweed used his "city machine," the Tammany Hall ring, to rule, plunder and sometimes improve the city's government. His political domination of New York City ended with his arrest in 1871 and conviction in 1873.

Twenty-first Amendment (1933) Repealed prohibition on the manufacture, sale, and transportation of alcoholic beverages, effectively nullifying the Eighteenth Amendment.

Underground Railroad Operating in the decades before the Civil War, the "railroad" was a clandestine system of routes and safehouses through which slaves were led to freedom in the North.

Unitarianism Late eighteenth-century liberal offshoot of the New England Congregationalist church; Unitarianism professed the oneness of God and the goodness of rational man.

United Nations Security Council A major agency within the United Nations which remains in permanent session and has the responsibility of maintaining international peace and security. Originally, it consisted of five permanent members, (United States, Soviet Union, Britain, France, and the Republic of China), and six members elected to two-year terms. After 1965, the number of rotating members was increased to ten. In 1971, the Republic of China was replaced with the People's Republic of China and the Soviet Union was replaced by the Russian Federation in 1991.

Utopian communities These communities flourished during the Jacksonian era and were attempts to create the ideal community. They were social experiments conducted in relative isolation, so they had little impact on the world outside of their communities. In most cases, the communities quickly ran out of steam and ended.

Cornelius Vanderbilt (1794–1877) In the 1860s, he consolidated several separate railroad companies into one vast entity, New York Central Railroad.

Bartolomeo Vanzetti (1888–1927) In 1920, he and Nicola Sacco were Italian immigrants who were arrested for stealing $16,000 and killing a paymaster and his guard. Their trial took place during a time of numerous bombings by anarchists and their judge was openly prejudicial. Many liberals and radicals believe that the conviction of Sacco and Vanzetti was based on their political ideas and ethnic origin rather than the evidence against them.

Amerigo Vespucci (1455–1512) Italian explorer who reached the New World in 1499 and was the first to suggest that South America was a new continent. Afterward, European mapmakers used a variant of his first name, America, to label the New World.

Viet Cong In 1956, these guerrilla forces began attacking South Vietnam's government and in 1960 the resistance groups coalesced as the National Liberation Front.

Vietnamization President Nixon's policy of equipping and training the South Vietnamese so that they could assume ground combat operations in the place of American soldiers. Nixon hoped that a reduction in U.S. forces in Vietnam would defuse the anti-war movement.

Vikings Norse people from Scandinavia who sailed to Newfoundland about A.D. 1001.

Pancho Villa (1877–1923) While the leader of one of the competing factions in the Mexican civil war, he provoked the United States into intervening. He hoped attacking the United States would help him build a reputation as an opponent of the United States, which would increase his popularity and discredit Mexican President Carranza.

Virginia Company A joint stock enterprise that King James I chartered in 1606. The company was to spread Christianity in the New World as well as find ways to make a profit in it.

Virginia Plan The delegations to the Constitutional Convention were divided between two plans on how to structure the government: Virginia called for a strong central government and a two-house legislature apportioned by population.

George Wallace (1919–1998) An outspoken defender of segregation. As the governor of Alabama, he once attempted to block African American students from enrolling at the University of Alabama. He ran as the presidential candidate for the American Independent party in 1968. He appealed to voters who were concerned about rioting anti-war protestors, the welfare system, and the growth of the federal government.

War Hawks In 1811, congressional members from the southern and western districts who clamored for a war to seize Canada and Florida were dubbed "war hawks."

Warren Court The U.S. Supreme Court under Chief Justice Earl Warren, 1953–1969, decided such landmark cases as *Brown v. Board of Education* (school desegregation), *Baker v. Carr* (legislative redistricting), and *Gideon v. Wainwright* and *Miranda v. Arizona* (rights of criminal defendants).

Booker T. Washington (1856–1915) He founded a leading college for African Americans in Tuskegee, Alabama, and become the foremost black educator in America by the 1890s. He believed that the African American community should establish an economic base for its advancement before striving for social equality. His critics charged that his philosophy sacrificed educational and civil rights for dubious social acceptance and economic opportunities.

George Washington (1732–1799) In 1775, the Continental Congress named him the commander in chief of the Continental Army. He had previously served as an officer in the French and Indian War, but had never commanded a large unit. Initially, his army was poorly supplied and inexperienced, which led to repeated defeats. Washington realized that he could only defeat the British through wearing them down, and he implemented a strategy of evasion and selective confrontations. Gradually, the army developed into an effective force and, with the aid of the French, defeated the British. In 1787, he was the presiding officer over the Constitutional Convention, but participated little in the debates. In 1789, the Electoral College chose Washington to be the nation's first president. He assembled a cabinet of brilliant minds, which included Thomas Jefferson, James Madison, and Alexander Hamilton. Together, they would lay the foundations of American government and capitalism. Washington faced the nation's first foreign and domestic crises. In 1793, the British and French were at war. Washington chose to keep America neutral in the conflict even though France and the United States had signed a treaty of alliance. A year later, the Whiskey Rebellion erupted in Pennsylvania, and Washington sent militiamen to suppress the rebels. After two terms in office, Washington chose to step down; and the power of the presidency was peacefully passed to John Adams.

Watergate Washington office and apartment complex that lent its name to the 1972–1974 scandal of the Nixon administration; when his knowledge of the break-in at the Watergate and subsequent cover-up was revealed, Nixon resigned the presidency under threat of impeachment.

Daniel Webster (1782–1852) As a representative from New Hampshire, he led the New Federalists in opposition to the moving of the second national bank from Boston to Philadelphia. Later, he served as representative and a senator for Massachusetts and emerged as a champion of a stronger national government. He also switched from opposing to supporting tariffs because New England had built up its manufactures with the understanding tariffs would protect them from foreign competitors.

Webster-Ashburton Treaty Settlement in 1842 of U.S.–Canadian border disputes in Maine, New York, Vermont, and in the Wisconsin Territory (now northern Minnesota).

Webster-Hayne debate U.S. Senate debate of January 1830 between Daniel Webster of Massachusetts and Robert Hayne of South Carolina over nullification and states' rights.

Ida B. Wells (1862–1931) After being denied a seat on a railroad car because she was black, she became the first African American to file a suit against such discrimination. As a journalist, she criticized Jim Crow laws, demanded that blacks have their voting rights restored and crusaded against lynching. In 1909, she helped found the National Association for the Advancement of Colored People (NAACP).

western front The military front that stretched from the English Channel through Belgium and France to the Alps during World War I.

Whig party Founded in 1834 to unite factions opposed to President Andrew Jackson, the party favored federal responsibility for internal improvements; the party ceased to exist by the late 1850s, when party members divided over the slavery issue.

Whigs Another name for revolutionary Patriots.

Whiskey Rebellion Violent protest by western Pennsylvania farmers against the federal excise tax on corn whiskey, 1794.

George Whitefield (1714–1770) A true catalyst of the Great Awakening, he sought to reignite religious fervor in the American congregations. During his tour of the American Colonies in 1739, he gave spellbinding sermons and preached the notion of "new birth"—a sudden, emotional moment of conversion and salvation.

Eli Whitney (1765–1825) He invented the cotton gin which could separate cotton from its seeds. One machine operator could separate fifty times more cotton than worker could by hand, which led to an increase in cotton production and prices. These increases gave planters a new profitable use for slavery and a lucrative slave trade emerged from the coastal South to the Southwest.

Wilderness Road Originally an Indian path through the Cumberland Gap, it was used by over 300,000 settlers who migrated westward to Kentucky in the last quarter of the eighteenth century.

Roger Williams (1603–1683) Puritan who believed that the purity of the church required a complete separation between church and state and freedom from coercion in matters of faith. In 1636, he established the town of Providence, the first permanent settlement in Rhode Island and the first to allow religious freedom in America.

Wendell L. Willkie (1892–1944) In the 1940 presidential election, he was the Republican nominee who ran against President Roosevelt. He supported aid to the Allies and criticized the New Deal programs. Voters looked at the increasingly dangerous world situation and chose to keep President Roosevelt in office for a third term.

Wilmot Proviso Proposal to prohibit slavery in any land acquired in the Mexican War, but southern senators, led by John C. Calhoun of South Carolina, defeated the measure in 1846 and 1847.

Woodrow Wilson (1856–1924) In the 1912 presidential election, Woodrow Wilson ran under the slogan of New Freedom, which promised to improve of the banking system, lower tariffs, and break up monopolies. He sought to deliver on these promises through passage of the Underwood-Simmons Tariff, the Federal Reserve Act of 1913, and new antitrust laws. Though he was weak on implementing social change and showed a little interest in the plight of African Americans, he did eventually support some labor reform. At the beginning of World War I, Wilson kept America neutral, but provided the Allies with credit for purchases of supplies. However, the sinking of U.S. merchant ships and the news of Germany encouraging Mexico to attack America caused Wilson to ask Congress to declare war on Germany. Following the war, Wilson supported the entry of America into the League of Nations and the ratification of the Treaty of Versailles; but Congress would not approve the entry or ratification.

John Winthrop Puritan leader and Governor of the Massachusetts Bay Colony who resolved to use the colony as a refuge for persecuted Puritans and as an instrument of building a "wilderness Zion" in America.

Women Accepted for Voluntary Emergency Services (WAVES) During World War II, the increased demand for labor shook up old prejudices about gender roles in workplace and in the military. Nearly 200,000 women served in the Women's Army Corps or its naval equivalent, Women Accepted for Volunteer Emergency Service (WAVES).

Women's Army Corps (WAC) During World War II, the increased demand for labor shook up old prejudices about gender roles in workplace and in the military. Nearly 200,000 women served in the Women's Army

Corps or its naval equivalent, Women Accepted for Volunteer Emergency Service (WAVES).

Woodstock In 1969, roughly a half a million young people converged on a farm near Bethel, New York, for a three-day music festival that was an expression of the flower children's free spirit.

Wounded Knee, Battle of Last incident of the Indians Wars took place in 1890 in the Dakota Territory, where the U.S. Cavalry killed over 200 Sioux men, women, and children who were in the process of surrender.

XYZ affair French foreign minister Tallyrand's three anonymous agents demanded payments to stop French plundering of American ships in 1797; refusal to pay the bribe led to two years of sea war with France (1798–1800).

Yalta Conference Meeting of Franklin D. Roosevelt, Winston Churchill, and Joseph Stalin at a Crimean resort to discuss the postwar world on February 4–11, 1945; Soviet leader Joseph Stalin claimed large areas in eastern Europe for Soviet domination.

yeomen Small landowners (the majority of white families in the South) who farmed their own land and usually did not own slaves.

surrender at Yorktown Last battle of the Revolutionary War; General Lord Charles Cornwallis along with over 7,000 British troops surrendered at Yorktown, Virginia, on October 17, 1781.

Brigham Young (1801–1877) Following Joseph Smith's death, he became the leader of the Mormons and promised Illinois officials that the Mormons would leave the state. In 1846, he led the Mormons to Utah and settled near the Salt Lake. After the United States gained Utah as part of the Treaty of Guadalupe Hidalgo, he became the governor of the territory and kept the Mormons virtually independent of federal authority.

youth culture The youth of the 1950s had more money and free time than any previous generation which allowed a distinct youth culture to emerge. A market emerged for products and activities that were specifically for young people such as transistor radios, rock records, *Seventeen* magazine, and Pat Boone movies.

APPENDIX

THE DECLARATION OF INDEPENDENCE (1776)

WHEN IN THE COURSE OF HUMAN EVENTS, it becomes necessary for one people to dissolve the political bands which have connected them with another, and to assume the Powers of the earth, the separate and equal station to which the Laws of Nature and of Nature's God entitle them, a decent respect to the opinions of mankind requires that they should declare the causes which impel them to the separation.

We hold these truths to be self-evident, that all men are created equal, that they are endowed by their Creator with certain unalienable rights, that among these are Life, Liberty, and the pursuit of Happiness. That to secure these rights, Governments are instituted among Men, deriving their just powers from the consent of the governed. That whenever any Form of Government becomes destructive of these ends, it is the Right of the People to alter or to abolish it, and to institute new Government, laying its foundation on such principles and organizing its powers in such form, as to them shall seem most likely to effect their Safety and Happiness. Prudence, indeed, will dictate that Governments long established should not be changed for light and transient causes; and accordingly all experience hath shown, that mankind are more disposed to suffer, while evils are sufferable, than to right themselves by abolishing the forms to which they are accustomed. But when a long train of abuses and usurpations, pursuing invariably the same Object evinces a design to reduce them under absolute Despotism, it is their right, it is their duty, to throw off such Government, and to provide new Guards for their future security.—Such has been the patient sufferance of these Colonies; and such is now the necessity which constrains them to alter their former Systems of Government. The history of the present King of Great Britain is a history of repeated injuries and usurpations, all having in direct object the establishment of an absolute Tyranny over these States. To prove this, let Facts be submitted to a candid world.

He has refused his Assent to Laws, the most wholesome and necessary for the public good.

He has forbidden his Governors to pass Laws of immediate and pressing importance, unless suspended in their operation till his Assent should be obtained; and when so suspended, he has utterly neglected to attend to them.

He has refused to pass other Laws for the accommodation of large districts of people, unless those people would relinquish the right of Representation in the Legislature, a right inestimable to them and formidable to tyrants only.

He has called together legislative bodies at places unusual, uncomfortable, and distant from the depository of their public Records, for the sole purpose of fatiguing them into compliance with his measures.

He has dissolved Representative Houses repeatedly, for opposing with manly firmness his invasions on the rights of the people.

He has refused for a long time, after such dissolutions, to cause others to be elected; whereby the Legislative powers, incapable of Annihilation, have returned to the People at large for their exercise; the State remaining in the mean time exposed to all dangers of invasion from without, and convulsions within.

He has endeavoured to prevent the population of these States; for that purpose obstructing the Laws of Naturalization of Foreigners; refusing to pass others to encourage their migrations hither, and raising the conditions of new Appropriations of Lands.

He has obstructed the Administration of Justice, by refusing his Assent to Laws for establishing Judiciary powers.

He has made Judges dependent on his Will alone, for the tenure of their offices, and the amount and payment of their salaries.

He has erected a multitude of New Offices, and sent hither swarms of Officers to harass our People, and eat out their substance.

He has kept among us, in times of peace, Standing Armies without the Consent of our legislatures.

He has affected to render the Military independent of and superior to the Civil Power.

He has combined with others to subject us to a jurisdiction foreign to our constitution, and unacknowledged by our laws; giving his Assent to their Acts of pretended Legislation:

For quartering large bodies of armed troops among us:

For protecting them, by a mock Trial, from Punishment for any Murders which they should commit on the Inhabitants of these States:

For cutting off our Trade with all parts of the world:

For imposing taxes on us without our Consent:

For depriving us of many cases, of the benefits of Trial by jury:

For transporting us beyond Seas to be tried for pretended offences:

For abolishing the free System of English Laws in a neighbouring Province, establishing therein an Arbitrary government, and enlarging its

Boundaries so as to render it at once an example and fit instrument for introducing the same absolute rule into these Colonies:

For taking away our Charters, abolishing our most valuable Laws, and altering fundamentally the Forms of our Governments:

For suspending our own Legislatures, and declaring themselves in vested with Power to legislate for us in all cases whatsoever.

He has abdicated Government here, by declaring us out of his Protection and waging War against us.

He has plundered our seas, ravaged our Coasts, burnt our towns, and destroyed the lives of our people.

He is at this time transporting large armies of foreign mercenaries to compleat the works of death, desolation, and tyranny, already begun with circumstances of Cruelty & perfidy scarcely paralleled in the most barbarous ages, and totally unworthy the Head of a civilized nation.

He has constrained our fellow Citizens taken Captive on the high Seas to bear Arms against their Country, to become the executioners of their friends and Brethren, or to fall themselves by their Hands.

He has excited domestic insurrections amongst us, and has endeavoured to bring on the inhabitants of our frontiers, the merciless Indian Savages, whose known rule of warfare, is an undistinguished destruction of all ages, sexes, and conditions.

In every stage of these Oppressions We have Petitioned for Redress in the most humble terms: Our repeated Petitions have been answered only by repeated injury. A Prince, whose character is thus marked by every act which may define a Tyrant, is unfit to be the ruler of a free people.

Nor have We been wanting in attention to our British brethren. We have warned them from time to time of attempts by their legislature to extend an unwarrantable jurisdiction over us. We have reminded them of the circumstances of our emigration and settlement here. We have appealed to their native justice and magnanimity, and we have conjured them by the ties of our common kindred to disavow these usurpations, which, would inevitably interrupt our connections and correspondence. They too must have been deaf to the voice of justice and of consanguinity. We must, therefore, acquiesce in the necessity, which denounces our Separation, and hold them, as we hold the rest of mankind, Enemies in War, in Peace Friends.

WE, THEREFORE, the Representatives of the UNITED STATES OF AMERICA, in General Congress, Assembled, appealing to the Supreme Judge of the world for the rectitude of our intentions, do, in the Name, and by Authority of the good People of these Colonies, solemnly publish and declare, That these United Colonies are, and of Right ought to be FREE AND INDEPENDENT STATES; that they are Absolved from all Allegiance to the

British Crown, and that all political connection between them and the State of Great Britain, is and ought to be totally dissolved; and that as Free and Independent States, they have full Power to levy War, conclude Peace, contract Alliances, establish Commerce, and to do all other Acts and Things which Independent States may of right do. And for the support of this Declaration, with a firm reliance on the Protection of Divine Providence, we mutually pledge to each other our Lives, our Fortunes, and our sacred Honor.

The foregoing Declaration was, by order of Congress, engrossed, and signed by the following members:

John Hancock

NEW HAMPSHIRE
Josiah Bartlett
William Whipple
Matthew Thornton

MASSACHUSETTS BAY
Samuel Adams
John Adams
Robert Treat Paine
Elbridge Gerry

RHODE ISLAND
Stephen Hopkins
William Ellery

CONNECTICUT
Roger Sherman
Samuel Huntington
William Williams
Oliver Wolcott

NEW YORK
William Floyd
Philip Livingston
Francis Lewis
Lewis Morris

NEW JERSEY
Richard Stockton
John Witherspoon
Francis Hopkinson
John Hart
Abraham Clark

PENNSYLVANIA
Robert Morris
Benjamin Rush
Benjamin Franklin
John Morton
George Clymer
James Smith
George Taylor
James Wilson
George Ross

DELAWARE
Caesar Rodney
George Read
Thomas M'Kean

MARYLAND
Samuel Chase
William Paca
Thomas Stone
Charles Carroll, of Carrollton

VIRGINIA
George Wythe
Richard Henry Lee
Thomas Jefferson
Benjamin Harrison
Thomas Nelson, Jr.
Francis Lightfoot Lee
Carter Braxton

NORTH CAROLINA
William Hooper
Joseph Hewes
John Penn

SOUTH CAROLINA
Edward Rutledge
Thomas Heyward, Jr.
Thomas Lynch, Jr.
Arthur Middleton

GEORGIA
Button Gwinnett
Lyman Hall
George Walton

Resolved, that copies of the declaration be sent to the several assemblies, conventions, and committees, or councils of safety, and to the several commanding officers of the continental troops; that it be proclaimed in each of the united states, at the head of the army.

ARTICLES OF CONFEDERATION (1778)

To all to whom these Presents shall come, we the undersigned Delegates of the States affixed to our Names send greeting.

Whereas the Delegates of the United States of America in Congress assembled did on the fifteenth day of November in the Year of our Lord One Thousand Seven Hundred and Seventy-seven, and in the Second Year of the Independence of America agree to certain articles of Confederation and perpetual Union between the States of Newhampshire, Massachusetts-bay, Rhodeisland and Providence Plantations, Connecticut, New York, New Jersey, Pennsylvania, Delaware, Maryland, Virginia, North-Carolina, South-Carolina and Georgia in the Words following, viz.

Articles of Confederation and perpetual Union between the States of Newhampshire, Massachusetts-bay, Rhodeisland and Providence Plantations, Connecticut, New-York, New-Jersey, Pennsylvania, Delaware, Maryland, Virginia, North-Carolina, South-Carolina and Georgia.

Article I. The stile of this confederacy shall be "The United States of America."

Article II. Each State retains its sovereignty, freedom and independence, and every power, jurisdiction and right, which is not by this confederation expressly delegated to the United States, in Congress assembled.

Article III. The said States hereby severally enter into a firm league of friendship with each other, for their common defence, the security of their liberties, and their mutual and general welfare, binding themselves to assist each other, against all force offered to, or attacks made upon them, or any of them, on account of religion, sovereignty, trade or any other pretence whatever.

ARTICLE IV. The better to secure and perpetuate mutual friendship and inter-course among the people of the different States in this Union, the free inhab-itants of each of these States, paupers, vagabonds and fugitives from justice excepted, shall be entitled to all privileges and immunities of free citizens in the several States; and the people of each State shall have free ingress and regress to and from any other State, and shall enjoy therein all the privileges of trade and commerce, subject to the same duties, impositions and restric-tions as the inhabitants thereof respectively, provided that such restrictions shall not extend so far as to prevent the removal of property imported into any State, to any other State of which the owner is an inhabitant; provided also that no imposition, duties or restriction shall be laid by any State, on the property of the United States, or either of them.

If any person guilty of, or charged with treason, felony, or other high mis-demeanor in any State, shall flee from justice, and be found in any of the United States, he shall upon demand of the Governor or Executive power, of the State from which he fled, be delivered up and removed to the State having jurisdiction of his offence.

Full faith and credit shall be given in each of these States to the records, acts and judicial proceedings of the courts and magistrates of every other State.

ARTICLE V. For the more convenient management of the general interests of the United States, delegates shall be annually appointed in such manner as the legislature of each State shall direct, to meet in Congress on the first Monday in November, in every year, with a power reserved to each State, to recall its delegates, or any of them, at any time within the year, and to send others in their stead, for the remainder of the year.

No State shall be represented in Congress by less than two, nor by more than seven members; and no person shall be capable of being a delegate for more than three years in any term of six years; nor shall any person, being a delegate, be capable of holding any office under the United States, for which he, or another for his benefit receives any salary, fees or emolument of any kind.

Each State shall maintain its own delegates in a meeting of the States, and while they act as members of the committee of the States.

In determining questions in the United States, in Congress assembled, each State shall have one vote.

Freedom of speech and debate in Congress shall not be impeached or questioned in any court, or place out of Congress, and the members of Con-gress shall be protected in their persons from arrests and imprisonments, during the time of their going to and from, and attendance on Congress, except for treason, felony, or breach of the peace.

ARTICLE VI. No State without the consent of the United States in Congress assembled, shall send any embassy to, or receive any embassy from, or enter into any conference, agreement, alliance or treaty with any king, prince or state; nor shall any person holding any office of profit or trust under the United States, or any of them, accept of any present, emolument, office or title of any kind whatever from any king, prince or foreign state; nor shall the United States in Congress assembled, or any of them, grant any title of nobility.

No two or more States shall enter into any treaty, confederation or alliance whatever between them, without the consent of the United States in Congress assembled, specifying accurately the purposes for which the same is to be entered into, and how long it shall continue.

No State shall lay any imposts or duties, which may interfere with any stipulations in treaties, entered into by the United States in Congress assembled, with any king, prince or state, in pursuance of any treaties already proposed by Congress, to the courts of France and Spain.

No vessels of war shall be kept up in time of peace by any State, except such number only, as shall be deemed necessary by the United States in Congress assembled, for the defence of such State, or its trade; nor shall any body of forces be kept up by any State, in time of peace, except such number only, as in the judgment of the United States, in Congress assembled, shall be deemed requisite to garrison the forts necessary for the defence of such State; but every State shall always keep up a well regulated and disciplined militia, sufficiently armed and accoutred, and shall provide and constantly have ready for use, in public stores, a due number of field pieces and tents, and a proper quantity of arms, ammunition and camp equipage.

No State shall engage in any war without the consent of the United States in Congress assembled, unless such State be actually invaded by enemies, or shall have received certain advice of a resolution being formed by some nation of Indians to invade such State, and the danger is so imminent as not to admit of a delay, till the United States in Congress assembled can be consulted: nor shall any State grant commissions to any ships or vessels of war, nor letters of marque or reprisal, except it be after a declaration of war by the United States in Congress assembled, and then only against the kingdom or state and the subjects thereof, against which war has been so declared, and under such regulations as shall be established by the United States in Congress assembled, unless such State be infested by pirates, in which case vessels of war may be fitted out for that occasion, and kept so long as the danger shall continue, or until the United States in Congress assembled shall determine otherwise.

ARTICLE VII. When land-forces are raised by any State of the common defence, all officers of or under the rank of colonel, shall be appointed by the Legislature of each State respectively by whom such forces shall be raised, or in such manner as such State shall direct, and all vacancies shall be filled up by the State which first made the appointment.

ARTICLE VIII. All charges of war, and all other expenses that shall be incurred for the common defence or general welfare, and allowed by the United States in Congress assembled, shall be defrayed out of a common treasury, which shall be supplied by the several States, in proportion to the value of all land within each State, granted to or surveyed for any person, as such land and the buildings and improvements thereon shall be estimated according to such mode as the United States in Congress assembled, shall from time to time direct and appoint.

The taxes for paying that proportion shall be laid and levied by the authority and direction of the Legislatures of the several States within the time agreed upon by the United States in Congress assembled.

ARTICLE IX. The United States in Congress assembled, shall have the sole and exclusive right and power of determining on peace and war, except in the cases mentioned in the sixth article—of sending and receiving ambassadors—entering into treaties and alliances, provided that no treaty of commerce shall be made whereby the legislative power of the respective States shall be restrained from imposing such imposts and duties on foreigners, as their own people are subjected to, or from prohibiting the exportation or importation of and species of goods or commodities whatsoever—of establishing rules for deciding in all cases, what captures on land or water shall be legal, and in what manner prizes taken by land or naval forces in the service of the United States shall be divided or appropriated—of granting letters of marque and reprisal in times of peace—appointing courts for the trial of piracies and felonies committed on the high seas and establishing courts for receiving and determining finally appeals in all cases of captures, provided that no member of Congress shall be appointed a judge of any of the said courts.

The United States in Congress assembled shall also be the last resort on appeal in all disputes and differences now subsisting or that hereafter may arise between two or more States concerning boundary, jurisdiction or any other cause whatever; which authority shall always be exercised in the manner following. Whenever the legislative or executive authority or lawful agent of any State in controversy with another shall present a petition to Congress, stating the matter in question and praying for a hearing, notice thereof shall be given by order of Congress to the legislative or executive authority of the other State in controversy, and a day assigned for the appearance of the parties by their lawful agents, who shall then be directed to appoint by joint consent, commissioners or judges to constitute a court for hearing and determining the matter in question: but if they cannot agree, Congress shall name three persons out of each of the United States, and from the list of such persons each party shall alternately strike out one, the petitioners beginning, until the number shall be reduced to thirteen; and from that number not less than seven, nor more than nine names as Congress shall direct, shall in the presence of Congress be drawn out by lot, and the persons whose names shall be so drawn or any five of them, shall be commissioners or judges, to hear and finally determine the controversy, so always as a major part of the judges who shall hear the cause shall agree in the determination: and if either party shall neglect to attend at the day appointed, without reasons, which Congress shall judge sufficient, or being present shall refuse to strike, the Congress shall proceed to nominate three persons out of each State, and the Secretary of Congress shall strike in behalf of such party absent or refusing; and the judgment and sentence of the court to be appointed, in the manner before prescribed, shall be final and conclusive; and if any of the parties shall refuse to submit to the authority of such court, or to appear or defend their claim or cause, the court shall nevertheless proceed to pronounce sentence, or judgment, which shall in like manner be final and decisive, the judgment or sentence and other proceedings being in either case transmitted to Congress, and lodged among the acts of Congress for the security of the parties concerned: provided that every commissioner, before he sits in judgment, shall take an oath to be administered by one of the judges of the supreme or superior court of the State where the case shall be tried, "well and truly to hear and determine the matter in question, according to the best of his judgment, without favour, affection or hope of reward:" provided also that no State shall be deprived of territory for the benefit of the United States.

All controversies concerning the private right of soil claimed under different grants of two or more States, whose jurisdiction as they may respect such lands, and the states which passed such grants are adjusted, the said grants or either of them being at the same time claimed to have originated antecedent to such settlement of jurisdiction, shall on the petition of either party to the Congress of the United States, be finally determined as near as may be in the same manner as is before prescribed for deciding disputes respecting territorial jurisdiction between different States.

The United States in Congress assembled shall also have the sole and ex-clusive right and power of regulating the alloy and value of coin struck by their own authority, or by that of the respective States—fixing the standard of weights and measures throughout the United States—regulating the trade and managing all affairs with the Indians, not members of any of the States, provided that the legislative right of any State within its own limits be not in-fringed or violated—establishing and regulating post-offices from one State to another, throughout all of the United States, and exacting such postage on the papers passing thro' the same as may be requisite to defray the expenses of the said office—appointing all officers of the land forces, in the service of the United States, excepting regimental officers—appointing all the officers of the naval forces, and commissioning all officers whatever in the service of the United States—making rules for the government and regulation of the said land and naval forces, and directing their operations.

The United States in Congress assembled shall have authority to appoint a committee, to sit in the recess of Congress, to be denominated "a Committee of the States," and to consist of one delegate from each State; and to appoint such other committees and civil officers as may be necessary for managing the general affairs of the United States under their direction—to appoint one of their number to preside, provided that no person be allowed to serve in the office of president more than one year in any term of three years; to ascertain the necessary sums of money to be raised for the service of the United States, and to appropriate and apply the same for defraying the public expenses—to borrow money, or emit bills on the credit of the United States, transmitting every half year to the respective States an account of the sums of money so borrowed or emitted,—to build and equip a navy—to agree upon the num-ber of land forces, and to make requisitions from each State for its quota, in proportion to the number of white inhabitants in such State; which requisi-tion shall be binding, and thereupon the Legislature of each State shall appoint the regimental officers, raise the men and cloath, arm and equip them in a sol-dier like manner, at the expense of the United States; and the officers and men so cloathed, armed and equipped shall march to the place appointed, and within the time agreed on by the United States in Congress assembled: but if the United States in Congress assembled shall, on consideration of circum-stances judge proper that any State should not raise men, or should raise a smaller number of men than the quota thereof, such extra number shall be raised, officered, cloathed, armed and equipped in the same manner as the quota of such State, unless the legislature of such State shall judge that such extra number cannot be safely spared out of the same, in which case they shall raise officer, cloath, arm and equip as many of such extra number as they judge can be safely spared. And the officers and men so cloathed, armed and equipped, shall march to the place appointed, and within the time agreed on by the United States in Congress assembled.

The United States in Congress assembled shall never engage in a war, nor grant letters of marque and reprisal in time of peace, nor enter into any treaties or alliances, nor coin money, nor regulate the value thereof, nor ascertain the sums and expenses necessary for the defence and welfare of the United States, or any of them, nor emit bills, nor borrow money on the credit of the United States, nor appropriate money, nor agree upon the number of vessels to be built or purchased, or the number of land or sea forces to be raised, nor appoint a commander in chief of the army or navy, unless nine States assent to the same: nor shall a question on any other point, except for adjourning from day to day be determined, unless by the votes of a majority of the United States in Congress assembled.

The Congress of the United States shall have power to adjourn to any time within the year, and to any place within the United States, so that no period of adjournment be for a longer duration than the space of six months, and shall publish the journal of their proceedings monthly, except such parts thereof relating to treaties, alliances or military operations, as in their judgment require secresy; and the yeas and nays of the delegates of each State on any question shall be entered on the Journal, when it is desired by any delegate; and the delegates of a State, or any of them, at his or their request shall be furnished with a transcript of the said journal, except such parts as are above excepted, to lay before the Legislatures of the several States.

ARTICLE X. The committee of the States, or any nine of them, shall be authorized to execute, in the recess of Congress, such of the powers of Congress as the United States in Congress assembled, by the consent of nine States, shall from time to time think expedient to vest them with; provided that no power be delegated to the said committee, for the exercise of which, by the articles of confederation, the voice of nine States in the Congress of the United States assembled is requisite.

ARTICLE XI. Canada acceding to this confederation, and joining in the measures of the United States, shall be admitted into, and entitled to all the advantages of this Union: but no other colony shall be admitted into the same, unless such admission be agreed to by nine States.

ARTICLE XII. All bills of credit emitted, monies borrowed and debts contracted by, or under the authority of Congress, before the assembling of the United States, in pursuance of the present confederation, shall be deemed and considered as a charge against the United States, for payment and satisfaction whereof the said United States, and the public faith are hereby solemnly pledged.

ARTICLE XIII. Every State shall abide by the determinations of the United States in Congress assembled, on all questions which by this confederation are submitted to them. And the articles of this confederation shall be inviolably observed by every State, and the Union shall be perpetual; nor shall any alteration at any time hereafter be made in any of them; unless such alteration be agreed to in a Congress of the United States, and be afterwards confirmed by the Legislatures of every State.

And whereas it has pleased the Great Governor of the world to incline the hearts of the Legislatures we respectively represent in Congress, to approve of, and to authorize us to ratify the said articles of confederation and perpetual union. Know ye that we the undersigned delegates, by virtue of the power and authority to us given for that purpose, do by these presents, in the name and in behalf of our respective constituents, fully and entirely ratify and confirm each and every of the said articles of confederation and perpetual union, and all and singular the matters and things therein contained: and we do further solemnly plight and engage the faith of our respective constituents, that they shall abide by the determinations of the United States in Congress assembled, on all questions, which by the said confederation are submitted to them. And that the articles thereof shall be inviolably observed by the States we respectively represent, and that the Union shall be perpetual.

In witness thereof we have hereunto set our hands in Congress. Done at Philadelphia in the State of Pennsylvania the ninth day of July in the year of our Lord one thousand seven hundred and seventy-eight, and in the third year of the independence of America.

THE CONSTITUTION OF THE UNITED STATES (1787)

WE THE PEOPLE OF THE UNITED STATES, in order to form a more perfect Union, establish Justice, insure domestic Tranquility, provide for the common defence, promote the general Welfare, and secure the Blessings of Liberty to ourselves and our Posterity, do ordain and establish this Constitution for the United States of America.

ARTICLE. I.

Section. 1. All legislative Powers herein granted shall be vested in a Congress of the United States, which shall consist of a Senate and House of Representatives.

Section. 2. The House of Representatives shall be composed of Members chosen every second Year by the People of the several States, and the Electors in each State shall have the Qualifications requisite for Electors of the most numerous Branch of the State Legislature.

No Person shall be a Representative who shall not have attained to the Age of twenty five Years, and been seven Years a Citizen of the United States, and who shall not, when elected, be an Inhabitant of that State in which he shall be chosen.

Representatives and direct Taxes shall be apportioned among the several States which may be included within this Union, according to their respective Numbers, which shall be determined by adding to the whole Number of free Persons, including those bound to Service for a Term of Years, and excluding Indians not taxed, three fifths of all other Persons. The actual Enumeration shall be made within three Years after the first Meeting of the Congress of the United States, and within every subsequent Term of ten Years, in such

Manner as they shall by Law direct. The Number of Representatives shall not exceed one for every thirty Thousand, but each State shall have at Least one Representative; and until such enumeration shall be made, the State of New Hampshire shall be entitled to chuse three, Massachusetts eight, Rhode-Island and Providence Plantations one, Connecticut five, New-York six, New Jersey four, Pennsylvania eight, Delaware one, Maryland six, Virginia ten, North Carolina five, South Carolina five, and Georgia three.

When vacancies happen in the Representation from any state, the Executive Authority thereof shall issue Writs of Election to fill such Vacancies.

The House of Representatives shall chuse their Speaker and other Officers; and shall have the sole Power of Impeachment.

Section. 3. The Senate of the United States shall be composed of two Senators from each State, chosen by the legislature thereof, for six Years; and each Senator shall have one Vote.

Immediately after they shall be assembled in Consequence of the first Election, they shall be divided as equally as may be into three Classes. The Seats of the Senators of the first Class shall be vacated at the Expiration of the second Year, of the second Class at the Expiration of the fourth Year, and of the third Class at the Expiration of the sixth Year, so that one third maybe chosen every second Year; and if Vacancies happen by Resignation, or otherwise, during the Recess of the Legislature of any State, the Executive thereof may make temporary Appointments until the next Meeting of the Legislature, which shall then fill such Vacancies.

No Person shall be a Senator who shall not have attained to the Age of thirty Years, and been nine Years a Citizen of the United States, and who shall not, when elected, be an Inhabitant of that State for which he shall be chosen.

The Vice President of the United States shall be President of the Senate, but shall have no Vote, unless they be equally divided.

The Senate shall chuse their other Officers, and also a President pro tempore, in the Absence of the Vice President, or when he shall exercise the Office of President of the United States.

The Senate shall have the sole Power to try all Impeachments. When sitting for that Purpose, they shall be on Oath or Affirmation. When the President of the United States is tried, the Chief Justice shall preside: And no Person shall be convicted without the Concurrence of two thirds of the Members present.

Judgment in Cases of Impeachment shall not extend further than to removal from Office, and disqualification to hold and enjoy any Office of honor, Trust or Profit under the United States: but the Party convicted shall nevertheless be liable and subject to Indictment, Trial, Judgment and Punishment, according to Law.

Section. 4. The Times, Places and Manner of holding Elections for Senators and Representatives, shall be prescribed in each State by the Legislature thereof; but the Congress may at any time by Law make or alter such Regulations, except as to the Places of chusing Senators.

The Congress shall assemble at least once in every Year, and such Meeting shall be on the first Monday in December, unless they shall by Law appoint a different Day.

Section. 5. Each House shall be the Judge of the Elections, Returns and Qualifications of its own Members, and a Majority of each shall constitute a Quorum to do Business; but a smaller Number may adjourn from day to day, and may be authorized to compel the Attendance of absent Members, in such Manner, and under such Penalties as each House may provide.

Each House may determine the Rules of its Proceedings, punish its Members for disorderly Behaviour, and, with the Concurrence of two thirds, expel a Member.

Each House shall keep a Journal of its Proceedings, and from time to time publish the same, excepting such Parts as may in their Judgment require Secrecy; and the Yeas and Nays of the Members of either House on any question shall, at the Desire of one fifth of those Present, be entered on the Journal.

Neither House, during the Session of Congress, shall, without the Consent of the other, adjourn for more than three days, not to any other Place than that in which the two Houses shall be sitting.

Section. 6. The Senators and Representatives shall receive a Compensation for their Services, to be ascertained by Law, and paid out of the Treasury of the United States. They shall in all Cases, except Treason, Felony and Breach of the Peace, be privileged from Arrest during their Attendance at the Session of their respective Houses, and in going to and returning from the same; and for any Speech or Debate in either House, they shall not be questioned in any other Place.

No Senator or Representative shall, during the Time for which he was elected, be appointed to any civil Office under the Authority of the United States, which shall have been created, or the Emoluments whereof shall have been encreased during such time; and no Person holding any Office under the United States, shall be a Member of either House during his Continuance in Office.

Section. 7. All Bills for raising Revenue shall originate in the House of Representatives; but the Senate may propose or concur with Amendments as on other Bills.

Every Bill which shall have passed the House of Representatives and the Senate shall, before it become a Law, be presented to the President of the United States; If he approve he shall sign it, but if not he shall return it, with his Objections to that House in which it shall have originated, who shall enter the Objections at large on their Journal, and proceed to reconsider it. If after such Reconsideration two thirds of that House shall agree to pass the Bill, it shall be sent, together with the Objections, to the other House, by which it shall likewise be reconsidered, and if approved by two thirds of that House, it shall become a Law. But in all such Cases the Votes of both Houses shall be determined by yeas and Nays, and the Names of the Persons voting for and against the Bill shall be entered on the Journal of each House respectively. If any Bill shall not be returned by the President within ten Days (Sundays excepted) after it shall have been presented to him, the Same shall be a Law, in like Manner as if he had signed it, unless the Congress by their Adjournment prevent its Return, in which Case it shall not be a Law.

Every Order, Resolution, or Vote to which the Concurrence of the Senate and House of Representatives may be necessary (except on a question of Adjournment) shall be presented to the President of the United States; and before the Same shall take Effect, shall be approved by him, or being disapproved by him, shall be repassed by two thirds of the Senate and House of Representatives, according to the Rules and Limitations prescribed in the Case of a Bill.

Section. 8. The Congress shall have Power To lay and collect Taxes, Duties, Imposts and Excises, to pay the Debts and provide for the common Defence and general Welfare of the United States; but all Duties, Imposts and Excises shall be uniform throughout the United States;

To borrow Money on the credit of the United States;

To regulate Commerce with foreign Nations, and among the several States, and with the Indian Tribes;

To establish an uniform Rule of Naturalization, and uniform Laws on the subject of Bankruptcies throughout the United States;

To coin Money, regulate the Value thereof, and of foreign Coin, and fix the Standard of Weights and Measures;

To provide for the Punishment of counterfeiting the Securities and current Coin of the United States;

To establish Post Offices and Post Roads;

To promote the Progress of Science and useful Arts, by securing for limited Times to Authors and Inventors the exclusive Right to their respective Writings and Discoveries;

To constitute Tribunals inferior to the supreme Court;

To define and punish Piracies and Felonies committed on the high Seas, and Offences against the Law of Nations;

To declare War, grant Letters of Marque and Reprisal, and make Rules concerning Captures on land and Water;

To raise and support Armies, but no Appropriation of Money to that Use shall be for a longer Term than two Years;

To provide and maintain a Navy;

To make Rules for the Government and Regulation of the land and naval Forces;

To provide for calling forth the Militia to execute the Laws of the Union, suppress Insurrections and repel Invasions;

To provide for organizing, arming, and disciplining, the Militia, and for governing such Part of them as may be employed in the Service of the United States, reserving to the States respectively, the Appointment of the Officers, and the Authority of training the Militia according to the discipline prescribed by Congress.

To exercise exclusive Legislation in all Cases whatsoever, over such District (not exceeding ten Miles square) as may, by Cession of Particular States, and the Acceptance of Congress, become the Seat of the Government of the United States, and to exercise like Authority over all Places purchased by the Consent of the Legislature of the State in which the Same shall be, for the Erection of Forts, Magazines, Arsenals, dock-Yards, and other needful Buildings;—And

To make all Laws which shall be necessary and proper for carrying into Execution the foregoing Powers, and all other Powers vested by this Constitution in the Government of the United States, or in any Department or Officer thereof.

Section. 9. The Migration or Importation of such Persons as any of the States now existing shall think proper to admit, shall not be prohibited by the Congress prior to the Year one thousand eight hundred and eight, but a Tax or duty may be imposed on such Importation, not exceeding ten dollars for each Person.

The Privilege of the Writ of Habeas Corpus shall not be suspended, unless when in Cases of Rebellion or Invasion the public Safety may require it.

No Bill of Attainder or ex post facto Law shall be passed.

No Capitation, or other direct, Tax shall be laid, unless in Proportion to the Census or Enumeration herein before directed to be taken.

No Tax or Duty shall be laid on Articles exported from any State.

No Preference shall be given by any Regulation of Commerce or Revenue to the Ports of one State over those of another: nor shall Vessels bound to, or from, one State, be obliged to enter, clear, or pay Duties in another.

No Money shall be drawn from the Treasury, but in Consequence of Appropriations made by Law; and a regular Statement and Account of the Receipts and Expenditures of all public Money shall be published from time to time.

No Title of Nobility shall be granted by the United States: And no Person holding any Office of Profit or trust under them, shall, without the Consent of the Congress, accept of any present, Emolument, Office, or Title, of any kind whatever, from any King, Prince, or foreign State.

Section 10. No State shall enter into any Treaty, Alliance, or Confederation; grant Letters of Marque and Reprisal; coin Money; emit Bills of Credit; make any Thing but gold and silver Coin a Tender in Payment of Debts; pass any Bill of Attainder, ex post facto Law, or Law impairing the Obligation of Contracts, or grant any Title of Nobility.

No State shall, without the Consent of the Congress, lay any Imposts or Duties on Imports or Exports, except what may be absolutely necessary for executing its inspection Laws: and the net Produce of all Duties and Imposts, laid by any State on Imports or Exports, shall be for the Use of the Treasury of the United States; and all such Laws shall be subject to the Revision and Controul of the Congress.

No State shall, without the Consent of Congress, lay any Duty of Tonnage, keep Troops, or Ships of War in time of Peace, enter into any Agreement or Compact with another State, or with a foreign Power, or engage in War, unless actually invaded, or in such imminent Danger as will not admit of delay.

ARTICLE. II.

Section. 1. The executive Power shall be vested in a President of the United States of America. He shall hold his Office during the term of four Years, and, together with the Vice President, chosen for the same Term, be elected, as follows:

Each State shall appoint, in such Manner as the Legislature thereof may direct, a Number of Electors, equal to the whole Number of Senators and Representatives to which the State may be entitled in the Congress: but no Senator or Representative, or Person holding an Office of Trust or Profit under the United States, shall be appointed an Elector.

The Electors shall meet in their respective States, and vote by Ballot for two Persons, of whom one at least shall not be an Inhabitant of the same State with themselves. And they shall make a List of all the Persons voted for, and of the Number of Votes for each; which List they shall sign and certify, and transmit sealed to the Seat of the Government of the United States, directed to the President of the Senate. The President of the Senate shall, in the Presence of the Senate and House of Representatives, open all the Certificates, and the Votes shall then be counted. The Person having the greatest Number of Votes shall be the President, if such Number be a Majority of the whole Number of Electors appointed; and if there be more than one who have such Majority, and have an equal Number of Votes, then the House of Representatives shall immediately chuse by Ballot one of them for President; and if no Person have a Majority, then from the five highest on the List the said House shall in like Manner chuse the President. But in chusing the President, the Votes shall be taken by States, the Representation from each State having one Vote; A quorum for this Purpose shall consist of a Member or Members from two thirds of the States, and a Majority of all the States shall be necessary to a Choice. In every Case, after the Choice of the President, the Person having the greatest Number of Votes of the Electors shall be the Vice President. But if there should remain two or more who have equal Votes, the Senate shall chuse from them by Ballot the Vice President.

The Congress may determine the Time of chusing the Electors, and the Day on which they shall give their Votes; which Day shall be the same throughout the United States.

No Person except a natural born Citizen, or a Citizen of the United States, at the time of the Adoption of this Constitution, shall be eligible to the Office of President; neither shall any Person be eligible to that Office who shall not have attained to the Age of thirty five Years, and been fourteen Years a Resident within the United States.

In Case of the Removal of the President from Office, or of his Death, Resignation, or Inability to discharge the Powers and Duties of the said Office, the Same shall devolve on the Vice President, and the Congress may by Law provide for the Case of Removal, Death, Resignation or Inability, both of the President and Vice President, declaring what Officer shall then act as President, and such Officer shall act accordingly, until the Disability be removed, or a President shall be elected.

The President shall, at stated Times, receive for his Services, a Compensation, which shall neither be encreased or diminished during the Period for which he shall have been elected, and he shall not receive within that Period any other Emolument from the United States, or any of them.

Before he enters on the Execution of his Office, he shall take the following Oath or Affirmation:—"I do solemnly swear (or affirm) that I will faithfully execute the Office of President of the United States, and will to the best of my Ability, preserve, protect and defend the Constitution of the United States."

Section. 2. The President shall be Commander in Chief of the Army and Navy of the United States, and of the Militia of the several States, when called into the actual Service of the United States; he may require the Opinion, in writing, of the principal Officer in each of the executive Departments, upon any Subject relating to the Duties of their respective Offices, and he shall have Power to grant Reprieves and Pardons for Offences against the United States, except in Cases of Impeachment.

He shall have Power, by and with the Advice and Consent of the Senate, to make Treaties, provided two thirds of the Senators present concur; and he shall nominate, and by and with the Advice and Consent of the Senate, shall appoint Ambassadors, other public Ministers and Consuls, Judges of the supreme Court, and all other Officers of the United States, whose Appointments are not herein otherwise provided for, and which shall be established by Law; but the Congress may by Law vest the Appointment of such inferior Officers, as they think proper, in the President alone, in the Courts of Law, or in the Heads of Departments.

The President shall have Power to fill up all Vacancies that may happen during the Recess of the Senate, by granting Commissions which shall expire at the End of their next Session.

Section. 3. He shall from time to time give to the Congress Information of the State of the Union, and recommend to their Consideration such Measures as he shall judge necessary and expedient; he may, on extraordinary Occasions, convene both Houses, or either of them, and in Case of Disagreement between them, with Respect to the Time of Adjournment, he may adjourn them to such Time as he shall think proper; he shall receive Ambassadors and other public Ministers; he shall take Care that the Laws be faithfully executed, and shall Commission all the Officers of the United States.

Section. 4. The President, Vice President and all civil Officers of the United States, shall be removed from Office on Impeachment for, and Conviction of, Treason, Bribery, or other high Crimes and Misdemeanors.

Article. III.

Section. 1. The judicial Power of the United States, shall be vested in one supreme Court, and in such inferior Courts as the Congress may from time to time ordain and establish. The Judges, both of the supreme and inferior Courts, shall hold their Offices during good Behavior, and shall, at stated Times, receive for their Services, a Compensation, which shall not be diminished during their Continuance in Office.

Section. 2. The judicial Power shall extend to all Cases, in Law and Equity, arising under this Constitution, the Laws of the United States, and Treaties made, or which shall be made, under their Authority;—to all Cases affecting Ambassadors, other public Ministers and Consuls;—to all Cases of admiralty and maritime Jurisdiction;—the Controversies to which the United States shall be a Party;—to Controversies between two or more States;—between a State and Citizens of another State;—between Citizens of different States;—between Citizens of the same State claiming Lands under Grants of different States, and between a State, or the Citizens thereof, and foreign States, Citizens or Subjects.

In all cases affecting Ambassadors, other public Ministers and Consuls, and those in which a State shall be Party, the supreme Court shall have original Jurisdiction. In all the other Cases before mentioned, the supreme Court shall have appellate Jurisdiction, both as to Law and Fact, with such Exceptions, and under such Regulations as the Congress shall make.

The Trial of all Crimes, except in Cases of Impeachment, shall be by Jury; and such Trial shall be held in the State where the said Crimes shall have been committed; but when not committed within any State, the Trial shall be at such Place or Places as the Congress may by Law have directed.

Section. 3. Treason against the United States, shall consist only in levying War against them, or in adhering to their Enemies, giving them Aid and Comfort. No Person shall be convicted of Treason unless on the Testimony of two Witnesses to the same overt Act, or on Confession in open Court.

The Congress shall have Power to declare the Punishment of Treason, but no Attainder of Treason shall work Corruption of Blood, or Forfeiture except during the Life of the Person attainted.

ARTICLE. IV.

Section. 1. Full Faith and Credit shall be given in each State to the public Acts, Records, and judicial Proceedings of every other State. And the Congress may by general Laws prescribe the Manner in which such Acts, Records and Proceedings shall be proved, and the Effect thereof.

Section. 2. The Citizens of each State shall be entitled to all Privileges and Immunities of Citizens in the several States.

A Person charged in any State with Treason, Felony, or other Crime, who shall flee from Justice, and be found in another State, shall on Demand of the executive Authority of the State from which he fled, be delivered up, to be removed to the State having Jurisdiction of the Crime.

No Person held to Service or Labour in one State, under the Laws thereof, escaping into another, shall, in Consequence of any Law or Regulation therein, be discharged from such Service or Labour, but shall be delivered up on Claim of the Party to whom such Service or Labour may be due.

Section. 3. New States may be admitted by the Congress into this Union; but no new State shall be formed or erected within the Jurisdiction of any other State; nor any State be formed by the Junction of two or more States, or Parts of States, without the consent of the Legislatures of the States concerned as well as of the Congress.

The Congress shall have Power to dispose of and make all needful Rules and Regulations respecting the Territory or other Property belonging to the United States; and nothing in this Constitution shall be so construed as to Prejudice any Claims of the United States, or of any particular States.

Section. 4. The United States shall guarantee to every State in this Union a Republican Form of Government, and shall protect each of them against Invasion; and on Application of the Legislature, or of the Executive (when the Legislature cannot be convened) against domestic Violence.

ARTICLE. V.

The Congress, whenever two thirds of both Houses shall deem it necessary, shall propose Amendments to this Constitution, or, on the Application of the

Legislatures of two thirds of the several States, shall call a Convention for proposing Amendments, which, in either Case, shall be valid to all Intents and Purposes, as Part of this Constitution, when ratified by the Legislatures of three fourths of the several States, or by Conventions in three fourths thereof, as the one or the other Mode of Ratification may be proposed by the Congress; Provided that no Amendment which may be made prior to the Year One thousand eight hundred and eight shall in any Manner affect the first and fourth Clauses in the Ninth Section of the first Article; and that no State, without its Consent, shall be deprived of its equal Suffrage in the Senate.

Article. VI.

All Debts contracted and Engagements entered into, before the Adoption of this Constitution, shall be as valid against the United States under this Constitution, as under the Confederation.

This Constitution, and the Laws of the United States which shall be made in Pursuance thereof; and all Treaties made, or which shall be made, under the Authority of the United States, shall be the supreme Law of the Land; and the Judges in every State shall be bound thereby, any Thing in the Constitution or Laws of any State to the Contrary notwithstanding.

The Senators and Representatives before mentioned, and the Members of the several State Legislatures, and all executive and judicial Officers, both of the United States and of the several States, shall be bound by Oath or Affirmation, to support this Constitution; but no religious Test shall ever be required as a Qualification to any Office or public Trust under the United States.

Article. VII.

The Ratification of the Conventions of nine States, shall be sufficient for the Establishment of this Constitution between the States so ratifying the Same.

Done in Convention by the Unanimous Consent of the States present the Seventeenth Day of September in the Year of our Lord one thousand seven hundred and Eighty seven and of the Independence of the United States of America the Twelfth. In witness thereof We have hereunto subscribed our Names,

Go. WASHINGTON—Presdt.
and deputy from Virginia.

New Hampshire	{ John Langdon Nicholas Gilman
Massachusetts	{ Nathaniel Gorham Rufus King
Connecticut	{ Wm Saml Johnson Roger Sherman
New York: . . .	Alexander Hamilton
New Jersey	{ Wil: Livingston David A. Brearley. Wm Paterson. Jona: Dayton
Pennsylvania	{ B Franklin Thomas Mifflin Robt Morris Geo. Clymer Thos FitzSimons Jared Ingersoll James Wilson Gouv Morris

Delaware	{ Geo: Read Gunning Bedford jun John Dickinson Richard Bassett Jaco: Broom
Maryland	{ James McHenry Dan of St Thos Jenifer Danl Carroll
Virginia	{ John Blair— James Madison Jr.
North Carolina	{ Wm Blount Richd Dobbs Spaight. Hu Williamson
South Carolina	{ J. Rutledge Charles Cotesworth Pinckney Charles Pinckney Pierce Butler.
Georgia	{ William Few Abr Baldwin

AMENDMENTS TO THE CONSTITUTION

ARTICLES IN ADDITION TO, and Amendment of the Constitution of the United States of America, proposed by Congress, and ratified by the Legislatures of the several States, pursuant to the fifth Article of the original Constitution.

AMENDMENT I.

Congress shall make no law respecting an establishment of religion, or prohibiting the free exercise thereof; or abridging the freedom of speech, or of the press; or the right of the people peaceably to assemble, and to petition the Government for a redress of grievances.

AMENDMENT II.

A well regulated Militia, being necessary to the security of a free State, the right of the people to keep and bear Arms, shall not be infringed.

AMENDMENT III.

No Soldier shall, in time of peace be quartered in any house, without the consent of the Owner, nor in time of war, but in a manner to be prescribed by law.

AMENDMENT IV.

The right of the people to be secure in their persons, houses, papers, and effects, against unreasonable searches and seizures, shall not be violated, and no Warrants shall issue, but upon probable cause, supported by Oath or affirmation, and particularly describing the place to be searched, and the persons or things to be seized.

Amendment V.

No person shall be held to answer for a capital, or otherwise infamous crime, unless on a presentment or indictment of a Grand Jury, except in cases arising in the land or naval forces, or in the Militia, when in actual service in time of War or public danger; nor shall any person be subject for the same offence to be twice put in jeopardy of life or limb; nor shall be compelled in any criminal case to be a witness against himself, nor be deprived of life, liberty, or property, without due process of law; nor shall private property be taken for public use, without just compensation.

Amendment VI.

In all criminal prosecutions, the accused shall enjoy the right to a speedy and public trial, by an impartial jury of the State and district wherein the crime shall have been committed, which district shall have been previously ascertained by law, and to be informed of the nature and cause of the accusation; to be confronted with the witnesses against him; to have compulsory process for obtaining witnesses in his favor, and to have the Assistance of Counsel for his defence.

Amendment VII.

In Suits at common law, where the value in controversy shall exceed twenty dollars, the right of trial by jury shall be preserved, and no fact tried by a jury, shall be otherwise re-examined in any Court of the United States, than according to the rules of the common law.

Amendment VIII.

Excessive bail shall not be required, nor excessive fines imposed, nor cruel and unusual punishments inflicted.

AMENDMENT IX.

The enumeration in the Constitution, of certain rights, shall not be construed to deny or disparage others retained by the people.

AMENDMENT X.

The powers not delegated to the United States by the Constitution, nor prohibited by it to the States, are reserved to the States respectively, or to the people. [The first ten amendments went into effect December 15, 1791.]

AMENDMENT XI.

The Judicial power of the United States shall not be construed to extend to any suit in law or equity, commenced or prosecuted against one of the United States by Citizens of another State, or by Citizens or Subjects of any Foreign State. [January 8, 1798.]

AMENDMENT XII.

The Electors shall meet in their respective states, and vote by ballot for President and Vice-President, one of whom, at least, shall not be an inhabitant of the same state with themselves; they shall name in their ballots the person voted for as President, and in distinct ballots the person voted for as Vice-President, and they shall make distinct lists of all persons voted for as President, and of all persons voted for as Vice President, and of the number of votes for each, which lists they shall sign and certify, and transmit sealed to the seat of the government of the United States, directed to the President of the Senate;—The President of the Senate shall, in the presence of the Senate and House of Representatives, open all the certificates and the votes shall then be counted;—The person having the greatest number of votes for President, shall be the President, if such number be a majority of the whole number of Electors appointed; and if no person have such majority, then from the persons having the highest numbers not exceeding three on the list of those voted for as President, the House of Representatives shall choose immediately, by ballot, the President. But in choosing the President, the votes shall be taken by states, the representation from each state having one vote; a quorum for this purpose shall consist of a member or members from two-thirds of the states, and a majority of all the states shall be necessary to a choice. And if the House of Representatives shall not choose a President whenever the right of choice shall devolve upon them, before the fourth day of March next following, then the Vice-President shall act as President, as in the case of the death or other constitutional disability of the President.— The person having the greatest number of votes as Vice-President, shall be the Vice-President, if such number be a majority of the whole number of Electors appointed, and if no person have a majority, then from the two highest numbers on the list, the Senate shall choose the Vice-President; a quorum for the purpose shall consist of two-thirds of the whole number of Senators, and a majority of the whole number shall be necessary to a choice. But no person constitutionally ineligible to the office of President shall be eligible to that of Vice-President of the United States. [September 25, 1804.]

AMENDMENT XIII.

Section 1. Neither slavery nor involuntary servitude, except as a punishment for crime whereof the party shall have been duly convicted, shall exist within the United States, or any place subject to their jurisdiction.

    Section 2. Congress shall have power to enforce this article by appropriate legislation. [December 18, 1865.]

AMENDMENT XIV.

Section 1. All persons born or naturalized in the United States, and subject to the jurisdiction thereof, are citizens of the United States and of the State wherein they reside. No State shall make or enforce any law which shall abridge the privileges or immunities of citizens of the United States; nor shall any State deprive any person of life, liberty, or property, without due process of law; nor deny to any person within its jurisdiction the equal protection of the laws.

Section 2. Representatives shall be apportioned among the several States according to their respective numbers, counting the whole number of persons in each State, excluding Indians not taxed. But when the right to vote at any election for the choice of electors for President and Vice President of the United States, Representatives in Congress, the Executive and Judicial officers of a State, or the members of the Legislature thereof, is denied to any of the male inhabitants of such State, being twenty-one years of age, and citizens of the United States, or in any way abridged, except for participation in rebellion, or other crime, the basis of representation therein shall be reduced in the proportion which the number of such male citizens shall bear to the whole number of male citizens twenty-one years of age in such State.

Section 3. No person shall be a Senator or Representative in Congress, or elector of President and Vice President, or hold any office, civil or military, under the United States, or under any State, who, having previously taken an oath, as a member of Congress, or as an officer of the United States, or as a member of any State legislature, or as an executive or judicial officer of any State, to support the Constitution of the United States, shall have engaged in insurrection or rebellion against the same, or given aid or comfort to the enemies thereof. But Congress may by a vote of two-thirds of each House, remove such disability.

Section 4. The validity of the public debt of the United States, authorized by law, including debts incurred for payment of pensions and bounties for services in suppressing insurrection or rebellion, shall not be questioned. But neither the United States nor any State shall assume or pay any debt or obligation incurred in aid of insurrection or rebellion against the United States, or any claim for the loss or emancipation of any slave; but all such debts, obligations and claims shall be held illegal and void.

Section 5. The Congress shall have power to enforce, by appropriate legislation, the provisions of this article. [July 28, 1868.]

Amendment XV.

Section 1. The right of citizens of the United States to vote shall not be denied or abridged by the United States or by any State on account of race, color, or previous condition of servitude—

Section 2. The Congress shall have power to enforce this article by appropriate legislation.—[March 30, 1870.]

Amendment XVI.

The Congress shall have power to lay and collect taxes on incomes, from whatever source derived, without apportionment among the several

States, and without regard to any census or enumeration. [February 25, 1913.]

AMENDMENT XVII.

The Senate of the United States shall be composed of two senators from each State, elected by the people thereof, for six years; and each Senator shall have one vote. The electors in each State shall have the qualifications requisite for electors of the most numerous branch of the State legislature.

When vacancies happen in the representation of any State in the Senate, the executive authority of such State shall issue writs of election to fill such vacancies: *Provided,* That the legislature of any State may empower the executive thereof to make temporary appointments until the people fill the vacancies by election as the legislature may direct.

This amendment shall not be so construed as to affect the election or term of any senator chosen before it becomes valid as part of the Constitution. [May 31, 1913.]

AMENDMENT XVIII.

After one year from the ratification of this article, the manufacture, sale, or transportation of intoxicating liquors within, the importation thereof into, or the exportation thereof from the United States and all territory subject to the jurisdiction thereof for beverage purposes is hereby prohibited.

The Congress and the several States shall have concurrent power to enforce this article by appropriate legislation.

This article shall be inoperative unless it shall have been ratified as an amendment to the Constitution by the legislatures of the several States, as provided in the Constitution, within seven years from the date of the submission thereof to the States by Congress. [January 29, 1919.]

AMENDMENT XIX.

The right of citizens of the United States to vote shall not be denied or abridged by the United States or by any State on account of sex.

The Congress shall have power by appropriate legislation to enforce the provisions of this article. [August 26, 1920.]

AMENDMENT XX.

Section 1. The terms of the President and Vice-President shall end at noon on the twentieth day of January, and the terms of Senators and Representatives at noon on the third day of January, of the years in which such terms would have ended if this article had not been ratified; and the terms of their successors shall then begin.

Section 2. The Congress shall assemble at least once in every year, and such meeting shall begin at noon on the third day of January, unless they shall by law appoint a different day.

Section 3. If, at the time fixed for the beginning of the term of the President, the President-elect shall have died, the Vice-President-elect shall become President. If a President shall not have been chosen before the time fixed for the beginning of his term, or if the President-elect shall have failed to qualify, then the Vice-President-elect shall act as President until a President shall have qualified; and the Congress may by law provide for the case wherein neither a President-elect nor a Vice-President-elect shall have qualified, declaring who shall then act as President, or the manner in which one who is to act shall be selected, and such person shall act accordingly until a President or Vice-President shall have qualified.

Section 4. The Congress may by law provide for the case of the death of any of the persons from whom the House of Representatives may choose a President whenever the right of choice shall have devolved upon them, and for the case of the death of any of the persons from whom the Senate may choose a Vice-President whenever the right of choice shall have devolved upon them.

Section 5. Sections 1 and 2 shall take effect on the 15th day of October following the ratification of this article.

Section 6. This article shall be inoperative unless it shall have been ratified as an amendment to the Constitution by the legislatures of three-fourths of the several States within seven years from the date of its submission. [February 6, 1933.]

AMENDMENT XXI.

Section 1. The eighteenth article of amendment to the Constitution of the United States is hereby repealed.

Section 2. The transportation or importation into any State, Territory or possession of the United States for delivery or use therein of intoxicating liquors, in violation of the laws thereof, is hereby prohibited.

Section 3. This article shall be inoperative unless it shall have been ratified as an amendment to the Constitution by convention in the several States, as provided in the Constitution, within seven years from the date of the submission thereof to the States by the Congress. [December 5, 1933.]

AMENDMENT XXII.

Section 1. No person shall be elected to the office of the President more than twice, and no person who has held the office of President, or acted as President, for more than two years of a term to which some other person was elected President shall be elected to the office of the President more than once. But this Article shall not apply to any person holding the office of President when this Article was proposed by the Congress, and shall not prevent any person who may be holding the office of President, or acting as President, during the term within which this Article becomes operative from holding the office of President or acting as President during the remainder of such term.

Section 2. This article shall be inoperative unless it shall have been ratified as an amendment to the Constitution by the legislatures of three-fourths of the several states within seven years from the date of its submission to the States by the Congress. [February 27, 1951.]

AMENDMENT XXIII.

Section 1. The District constituting the seat of government of the United States shall appoint in such manner as the Congress may direct:

A number of electors of President and Vice-President equal to the whole number of Senators and Representatives in Congress to which the District would be entitled if it were a State, but in no event more than the least populous State; they shall be in addition to those appointed by the States, but they shall be considered, for the purposes of the election of President and Vice-President, to be electors appointed by a State; and they shall meet in the District and perform such duties as provided by the twelfth article of amendment.

Section 2. The Congress shall have the power to enforce this article by appropriate legislation. [March 29, 1961.]

AMENDMENT XXIV.

Section 1. The right of citizens of the United States to vote in any primary or other election for President or Vice President, for electors for President or Vice President, or for Senator or Representative in Congress, shall not be denied or abridged by the United States or any State by reason of failure to pay any poll tax or other tax.

Section 2. The Congress shall have power to enforce this article by appropriate legislation. [January 23, 1964.]

AMENDMENT XXV.

Section 1. In case of the removal of the President from office or of his death or resignation, the Vice President shall become President.

Section 2. Whenever there is a vacancy in the office of Vice President, the President shall nominate a Vice President who shall take office upon confirmation by a majority vote of both Houses of Congress.

Section 3. Whenever the President transmits to the President pro tempore of the Senate and the Speaker of the House of Representatives his written declaration that he is unable to discharge the powers and duties of his office, and until he transmits to them a written declaration to the contrary, such powers and duties shall be discharged by the Vice President as Acting President.

Section 4. Whenever the Vice President and a majority of either the principal officers of the executive departments or of such other body as Congress may by law provide, transmit to the President pro tempore of the Senate and the Speaker of the House of Representatives their written declaration that the President is unable to discharge the powers and duties of his office, the Vice President shall immediately assume the powers and duties of the office as Acting President.

Thereafter, when the President transmits to the President pro tempore of the Senate and the Speaker of the House of Representatives his written declaration that no inability exists, he shall resume the powers and duties of his office unless the Vice President and a majority of either the principal officers of the executive departments or of such other body as Congress may by law provide, transmit within four days to the President pro tempore of the Senate and the Speaker of the House of Representatives their written declaration that the President is unable to discharge the powers and duties of his office. Thereupon Congress shall decide the issue, assembling within forty-eight hours for that purpose if not in session. If the Congress, within twenty-one days after receipt of the latter written declaration, or, if Congress is not in session, within twenty-one days after Congress is required to assemble, determines by two-thirds vote of both Houses that the President is unable to discharge the powers and duties of his office, the Vice President shall continue to discharge the same as Acting President; otherwise, the President shall resume the powers and duties of his office. [February 10, 1967.]

AMENDMENT XXVI.

Section 1. The right of citizens of the United States, who are eighteen years of age or older, to vote shall not be denied or abridged by the United States or by any State on account of age.

Section 2. The Congress shall have power to enforce this article by appropriate legislation [June 30, 1971.]

AMENDMENT XXVII.

No law, varying the compensation for the services of the Senators and Representatives shall take effect, until an election of Representatives shall have intervened. [May 8, 1992.]

PRESIDENTIAL ELECTIONS

Year	Number of States	Candidates	Parties	Popular Vote	% of Popular Vote	Electoral Vote	% Voter Participation
1789	11	**GEORGE WASHINGTON**	No party designations			69	
		John Adams				34	
		Other candidates				35	
1792	15	**GEORGE WASHINGTON**	No party designations			132	
		John Adams				77	
		George Clinton				50	
		Other candidates				5	
1796	16	**JOHN ADAMS**	Federalist			71	
		Thomas Jefferson	Democratic-Republican			68	
		Thomas Pinckney	Federalist			59	
		Aaron Burr	Democratic-Republican			30	
		Other candidates				48	
1800	16	**THOMAS JEFFERSON**	Democratic-Republican			73	
		Aaron Burr	Democratic-Republican			73	
		John Adams	Federalist			65	
		Charles C. Pinckney	Federalist			64	
		John Jay	Federalist			1	
1804	17	**THOMAS JEFFERSON**	Democratic-Republican			162	
		Charles C. Pinckney	Federalist			14	

Year	Number of States	Candidates	Parties	Popular Vote	% of Popular Vote	Electoral Vote	% Voter Participation
1808	17	**JAMES MADISON**	Democratic-Republican			122	
		Charles C. Pinckney	Federalist			47	
		George Clinton	Democratic-Republican			6	
1812	18	**JAMES MADISON**	Democratic-Republican			128	
		DeWitt Clinton	Federalist			89	
1816	19	**JAMES MONROE**	Democratic-Republican			183	
		Rufus King	Federalist			34	
1820	24	**JAMES MONROE**	Democratic-Republican			231	
		John Quincy Adams	Independent			1	
1824	24	**JOHN QUINCY ADAMS**	Democratic-Republican	108,740	30.5	84	26.9
		Andrew Jackson	Democratic-Republican	153,544	43.1	99	
		Henry Clay	Democratic-Republican	47,136	13.2	37	
		William H. Crawford	Democratic-Republican	46,618	13.1	41	
1828	24	**ANDREW JACKSON**	Democratic	647,286	56.0	178	57.6
		John Quincy Adams	National-Republican	508,064	44.0	83	

Year	Number of States	Candidates	Parties	Popular Vote	% of Popular Vote	Electoral Vote	% Voter Participation
1832	24	**ANDREW JACKSON**	Democratic	688,242	54.5	219	55.4
		Henry Clay	National-Republican	473,462	37.5	49	
		William Wirt	Anti-Masonic	101,051	8.0	7	
		John Floyd	Democratic			11	
1836	26	**MARTIN VAN BUREN**	Democratic	765,483	50.9	170	57.8
		William H. Harrison	Whig			73	
		Hugh L. White	Whig	739,795	49.1	26	
		Daniel Webster	Whig			14	
		W. P. Mangum	Whig			11	
1840	26	**WILLIAM H. HARRISON**	Whig	1,274,624	53.1	234	80.2
		Martin Van Buren	Democratic	1,127,781	46.9	60	
1844	26	**JAMES K. POLK**	Democratic	1,338,464	49.6	170	78.9
		Henry Clay	Whig	1,300,097	48.1	105	
		James G. Birney	Liberty	62,300	2.3		
1848	30	**ZACHARY TAYLOR**	Whig	1,360,967	47.4	163	72.7
		Lewis Cass	Democratic	1,222,342	42.5	127	
		Martin Van Buren	Free Soil	291,263	10.1		
1852	31	**FRANKLIN PIERCE**	Democratic	1,601,117	50.9	254	69.6
		Winfield Scott	Whig	1,385,453	44.1	42	
		John P. Hale	Free Soil	155,825	5.0		
1856	31	**JAMES BUCHANAN**	Democratic	1,832,955	45.3	174	78.9
		John C. Frémont	Republican	1,339,932	33.1	114	
		Millard Fillmore	American	871,731	21.6	8	

Year	Number of States	Candidates	Parties	Popular Vote	% of Popular Vote	Electoral Vote	% Voter Participation
1860	33	**ABRAHAM LINCOLN**	Republican	1,865,593	39.8	180	81.2
		Stephen A. Douglas	Democratic	1,382,713	29.5	12	
		John C. Breckinridge	Democratic	848,356	18.1	72	
		John Bell	Constitutional Union	592,906	12.6	39	
1864	36	**ABRAHAM LINCOLN**	Republican	2,206,938	55.0	212	73.8
		George B. McClellan	Democratic	1,803,787	45.0	21	
1868	37	**ULYSSES S. GRANT**	Republican	3,013,421	52.7	214	78.1
		Horatio Seymour	Democratic	2,706,829	47.3	80	
1872	37	**ULYSSES S. GRANT**	Republican	3,596,745	55.6	286	71.3
		Horace Greeley	Democratic	2,843,446	43.9	66	
1876	38	Rutherford B. Hayes	Republican	4,036,572	48.0	185	81.8
		Samuel J. Tilden	Democratic	4,284,020	51.0	184	
1880	38	**JAMES A. GARFIELD**	Republican	4,453,295	48.5	214	79.4
		Winfield S. Hancock	Democratic	4,414,082	48.1	155	
		James B. Weaver	Greenback-Labor	308,578	3.4		
1884	38	**GROVER CLEVELAND**	Democratic	4,879,507	48.5	219	77.5
		James G. Blaine	Republican	4,850,293	48.2	182	
		Benjamin F. Butler	Greenback-Labor	175,370	1.8		
		John P. St. John	Prohibition	150,369	1.5		
1888	38	**BENJAMIN HARRISON**	Republican	5,477,129	47.9	233	79.3
		Grover Cleveland	Democratic	5,537,857	48.6	168	
		Clinton B. Fisk	Prohibition	249,506	2.2		
		Anson J. Streeter	Union Labor	146,935	1.3		

Year	Number of States	Candidates	Parties	Popular Vote	% of Popular Vote	Electoral Vote	% Voter Participation
1892	44	**GROVER CLEVELAND**	Democratic	5,555,426	46.1	277	74.7
		Benjamin Harrison	Republican	5,182,690	43.0	145	
		James B. Weaver	People's	1,029,846	8.5	22	
		John Bidwell	Prohibition	264,133	2.2		
1896	45	**WILLIAM MCKINLEY**	Republican	7,102,246	51.1	271	79.3
		William J. Bryan	Democratic	6,492,559	47.7	176	
1900	45	**WILLIAM MCKINLEY**	Republican	7,218,491	51.7	292	73.2
		William J. Bryan	Democratic; Populist	6,356,734	45.5	155	
		John C. Wooley	Prohibition	208,914	1.5		
1904	45	**THEODORE ROOSEVELT**	Republican	7,628,461	57.4	336	65.2
		Alton B. Parker	Democratic	5,084,223	37.6	140	
		Eugene V. Debs	Socialist	402,283	3.0		
		Silas C. Swallow	Prohibition	258,536	1.9		
1908	46	**WILLIAM H. TAFT**	Republican	7,675,320	51.6	321	65.4
		William J. Bryan	Democratic	6,412,294	43.1	162	
		Eugene V. Debs	Socialist	420,793	2.8		
		Eugene W. Chafin	Prohibition	253,840	1.7		
1912	48	**WOODROW WILSON**	Democratic	6,296,547	41.9	435	58.8
		Theodore Roosevelt	Progressive	4,118,571	27.4	88	
		William H. Taft	Republican	3,486,720	23.2	8	
		Eugene V. Debs	Socialist	900,672	6.0		
		Eugene W. Chafin	Prohibition	206,275	1.4		

Year	Number of States	Candidates	Parties	Popular Vote	% of Popular Vote	Electoral Vote	% Voter Participation
1916	48	**WOODROW WILSON**	Democratic	9,127,695	49.4	277	61.6
		Charles E. Hughes	Republican	8,533,507	46.2	254	
		A. L. Benson	Socialist	585,113	3.2		
		J. Frank Hanly	Prohibition	220,506	1.2		
1920	48	**WARREN G. HARDING**	Republican	16,143,407	60.4	404	49.2
		James M. Cox	Democratic	9,130,328	34.2	127	
		Eugene V. Debs	Socialist	919,799	3.4		
		P. P. Christensen	Farmer–Labor	265,411	1.0		
1924	48	**CALVIN COOLIDGE**	Republican	15,718,211	54.0	382	48.9
		John W. Davis	Democratic	8,385,283	28.8	136	
		Robert M. La Follette	Progressive	4,831,289	16.6	13	
1928	48	**HERBERT C. HOOVER**	Republican	21,391,993	58.2	444	56.9
		Alfred E. Smith	Democratic	15,016,169	40.9	87	
1932	48	**FRANKLIN D. ROOSEVELT**	Democratic	22,809,638	57.4	472	56.9
		Herbert C. Hoover	Republican	15,758,901	39.7	59	
		Norman Thomas	Socialist	881,951	2.2		
1936	48	**FRANKLIN D. ROOSEVELT**	Democratic	27,752,869	60.8	523	61.0
		Alfred M. Landon	Republican	16,674,665	36.5	8	
		William Lemke	Union	882,479	1.9		
1940	48	**FRANKLIN D. ROOSEVELT**	Democratic	27,307,819	54.8	449	62.5
		Wendell L. Willkie	Republican	22,321,018	44.8	82	
1944	48	**FRANKLIN D. ROOSEVELT**	Democratic	25,606,585	53.5	432	55.9
		Thomas E. Dewey	Republican	22,014,745	46.0	99	

Year	Number of States	Candidates	Parties	Popular Vote	% of Popular Vote	Electoral Vote	% Voter Participation
1948	48	**HARRY S. TRUMAN**	Democratic	24,179,345	49.6	303	53.0
		Thomas E. Dewey	Republican	21,991,291	45.1	189	
		J. Strom Thurmond	States' Rights	1,176,125	2.4	39	
		Henry A. Wallace	Progressive	1,157,326	2.4		
1952	48	**DWIGHT D. EISENHOWER**	Republican	33,936,234	55.1	442	63.3
		Adlai E. Stevenson	Democratic	27,314,992	44.4	89	
1956	48	**DWIGHT D. EISENHOWER**	Republican	35,590,472	57.6	457	60.6
		Adlai E. Stevenson	Democratic	26,022,752	42.1	73	
1960	50	**JOHN F. KENNEDY**	Democratic	34,226,731	49.7	303	62.8
		Richard M. Nixon	Republican	34,108,157	49.5	219	
1964	50	**LYNDON B. JOHNSON**	Democratic	43,129,566	61.1	486	61.9
		Barry M. Goldwater	Republican	27,178,188	38.5	52	
1968	50	**RICHARD M. NIXON**	Republican	31,785,480	43.4	301	60.9
		Hubert H. Humphrey	Democratic	31,275,166	42.7	191	
		George C. Wallace	American Independent	9,906,473	13.5	46	
1972	50	**RICHARD M. NIXON**	Republican	47,169,911	60.7	520	55.2
		George S. McGovern	Democratic	29,170,383	37.5	17	
		John G. Schmitz	American	1,099,482	1.4		

Year	Number of States	Candidates	Party	Popular Vote	% Popular Vote	Electoral Vote	% Voter Participation
1976	50	**JIMMY CARTER**	Democratic	40,830,763	50.1	297	53.5
		Gerald R. Ford	Republican	39,147,793	48.0	240	
1980	50	**RONALD REAGAN**	Republican	43,901,812	50.7	489	52.6
		Jimmy Carter	Democratic	35,483,820	41.0	49	
		John B. Anderson	Independent	5,719,437	6.6		
		Ed Clark	Libertarian	921,188	1.1		
1984	50	**RONALD REAGAN**	Republican	54,451,521	58.8	525	53.1
		Walter F. Mondale	Democratic	37,565,334	40.6	13	
1988	50	**GEORGE H. W. BUSH**	Republican	47,917,341	53.4	426	50.1
		Michael Dukakis	Democratic	41,013,030	45.6	111	
1992	50	**BILL CLINTON**	Democratic	44,908,254	43.0	370	55.0
		George H. W. Bush	Republican	39,102,343	37.4	168	
		H. Ross Perot	Independent	19,741,065	18.9		
1996	50	**BILL CLINTON**	Democratic	47,401,185	49.0	379	49.0
		Bob Dole	Republican	39,197,469	41.0	159	
		H. Ross Perot	Independent	8,085,295	8.0		
2000	50	**GEORGE W. BUSH**	Republican	50,455,156	47.9	271	50.4
		Al Gore	Democrat	50,997,335	48.4	266	
		Ralph Nader	Green	2,882,897	2.7		
2004	50	**GEORGE W. BUSH**	Republican	62,040,610	50.7	286	60.7
		John F. Kerry	Democrat	59,028,444	48.3	251	
2008	50	**BARACK OBAMA**	Democrat	69,456,897	52.92%	365	63.0
		John McCain	Republican	59,934,814	45.66%	173	

Candidates receiving less than 1 percent of the popular vote have been omitted. Thus the percentage of popular vote given for any election year may not total 100 percent.

Before the passage of the Twelfth Amendment in 1804, the electoral college voted for two presidential candidates; the runner-up became vice president.

ADMISSION OF STATES

Order of Admission	State	Date of Admission	Order of Admission	State	Date of Admission
1	Delaware	December 7, 1787	26	Michigan	January 26, 1837
2	Pennsylvania	December 12, 1787	27	Florida	March 3, 1845
3	New Jersey	December 18, 1787	28	Texas	December 29, 1845
4	Georgia	January 2, 1788	29	Iowa	December 28, 1846
5	Connecticut	January 9, 1788	30	Wisconsin	May 29, 1848
6	Massachusetts	February 7, 1788	31	California	September 9, 1850
7	Maryland	April 28, 1788	32	Minnesota	May 11, 1858
8	South Carolina	May 23, 1788	33	Oregon	February 14, 1859
9	New Hampshire	June 21, 1788	34	Kansas	January 29, 1861
10	Virginia	June 25, 1788	35	West Virginia	June 30, 1863
11	New York	July 26, 1788	36	Nevada	October 31, 1864
12	North Carolina	November 21, 1789	37	Nebraska	March 1, 1867
13	Rhode Island	May 29, 1790	38	Colorado	August 1, 1876
14	Vermont	March 4, 1791	39	North Dakota	November 2, 1889
15	Kentucky	June 1, 1792	40	South Dakota	November 2, 1889
16	Tennessee	June 1, 1796	41	Montana	November 8, 1889
17	Ohio	March 1, 1803	42	Washington	November 11, 1889
18	Louisiana	April 30, 1812	43	Idaho	July 3, 1890
19	Indiana	December 10, 1816	44	Wyoming	July 10, 1890
20	Mississippi	December 10, 1817	45	Utah	January 4, 1896
21	Illinois	December 3, 1818	46	Oklahoma	November 16, 1907
22	Alabama	December 14, 1819	47	New Mexico	January 6, 1912
23	Maine	March 15, 1820	48	Arizona	February 14, 1912
24	Missouri	August 10, 1821	49	Alaska	January 3, 1959
25	Arkansas	June 15, 1836	50	Hawaii	August 21, 1959

POPULATION OF THE UNITED STATES

Year	Number of States	Population	% Increase	Population per Square Mile
1790	13	3,929,214		4.5
1800	16	5,308,483	35.1	6.1
1810	17	7,239,881	36.4	4.3
1820	23	9,638,453	33.1	5.5
1830	24	12,866,020	33.5	7.4
1840	26	17,069,453	32.7	9.8
1850	31	23,191,876	35.9	7.9
1860	33	31,443,321	35.6	10.6
1870	37	39,818,449	26.6	13.4
1880	38	50,155,783	26.0	16.9
1890	44	62,947,714	25.5	21.1
1900	45	75,994,575	20.7	25.6
1910	46	91,972,266	21.0	31.0
1920	48	105,710,620	14.9	35.6
1930	48	122,775,046	16.1	41.2
1940	48	131,669,275	7.2	44.2
1950	48	150,697,361	14.5	50.7
1960	50	179,323,175	19.0	50.6
1970	50	203,235,298	13.3	57.5
1980	50	226,504,825	11.4	64.0
1985	50	237,839,000	5.0	67.2
1990	50	250,122,000	5.2	70.6
1995	50	263,411,707	5.3	74.4
2000	50	281,421,906	6.8	77.0
2008	50	304,059,724	8.0	79.6

IMMIGRATION TO THE UNITED STATES, FISCAL YEARS 1820–2008

Year	Number	Year	Number	Year	Number	Year	Number
1820–1989	**55,457,531**	**1871–80**	**2,812,191**	**1921–30**	**4,107,209**	**1971–80**	**4,493,314**
1820	8,385	1871	321,350	1921	805,228	1971	370,478
1821–30	**143,439**	1872	404,806	1922	309,556	1972	384,685
1821	9,127	1873	459,803	1923	522,919	1973	400,063
1822	6,911	1874	313,339	1924	706,896	1974	394,861
1823	6,354	1875	227,498	1925	294,314	1975	386,914
1824	7,912	1876	169,986	1926	304,488	1976	398,613
1825	10,199	1877	141,857	1927	335,175		103,676
1826	10,837	1878	138,469	1928	307,255	1977	462,315
1827	18,875	1879	177,826	1929	279,678	1978	601,442
1828	27,382	1880	457,257	1930	241,700	1979	460,348
1829	22,520	**1881–90**	**5,246,613**	**1931–40**	**528,431**	1980	530,639
1830	23,322	1881	669,431	1931	97,139	**1981–90**	**7,338,062**
1831–40	**599,125**	1882	788,992	1932	35,576	1981	596,600
1831	22,633	1883	603,322	1933	23,068	1982	594,131
1832	60,482	1884	518,592	1934	29,470	1983	559,763
1833	58,640	1885	395,346	1935	34,956	1984	543,903
1834	65,365	1886	334,203	1936	36,329	1985	570,009
1835	45,374	1887	490,109	1937	50,244	1986	601,708
1836	76,242	1888	546,889	1938	67,895	1987	601,516
1837	79,340	1889	444,427	1939	82,998	1988	643,025
1838	38,914	1890	455,302	1940	70,756	1989	1,090,924
1839	68,069	**1891–1900**	**3,687,564**	**1941–50**	**1,035,039**	1990	1,536,483
1840	84,066	1891	560,319	1941	51,776	**1991–2000**	**9,090,857**
1841–50	**1,713,251**	1892	579,663	1942	28,781	1991	1,827,167
1841	80,289	1893	439,730	1943	23,725	1992	973,977
1842	104,565	1894	285,631	1944	28,551	1993	904,292
		1895	258,536	1945	38,119	1994	804,416
		1896	343,267	1946	108,721		

Year	Number	Year	Number	Year	Number	Year	Number
1843	52,496	1897	230,832	1947	147,292	1995	720,461
1844	78,615	1898	229,299	1948	170,570	1996	915,900
1845	114,371	1899	311,715	1949	188,317	1997	798,378
1846	154,416	1900	448,572	1950	249,187	1998	660,477
1847	234,968					1999	644,787
1848	226,527	**1901–10**	**8,795,386**	**1951–60**	**2,515,479**	2000	841,002
1849	297,024	1901	487,918	1951	205,717	**2001–8**	**8,330,011**
1850	369,980	1902	648,743	1952	265,520	2001	1,058,902
		1903	857,046	1953	170,434	2002	1,059,356
1851–60	**2,598,214**	1904	812,870	1954	208,177	2003	705,827
1851	379,466	1905	1,026,499	1955	237,790	2004	957,883
1852	371,603	1906	1,100,735	1956	321,625	2005	1,122,373
1853	368,645	1907	1,285,349	1957	326,867	2006	1,266,129
1854	427,833	1908	782,870	1958	253,265	2007	1,052,415
1855	200,877	1909	751,786	1959	260,686	2008	1,107,126
1856	200,436	1910	1,041,570	1960	265,398		
1857	251,306						
1858	123,126	**1911–20**	**5,735,811**	**1961–70**	**3,321,677**		
1859	121,282	1911	878,587	1961	271,344		
1860	153,640	1912	838,172	1962	283,763		
		1913	1,197,892	1963	306,260		
1861–70	**2,314,824**	1914	1,218,480	1964	292,248		
1861	91,918	1915	326,700	1965	296,697		
1862	91,985	1916	298,826	1966	323,040		
1863	176,282	1917	295,403	1967	361,972		
1864	193,418	1918	110,618	1968	454,448		
1865	248,120	1919	141,132	1969	358,579		
1866	318,568	1920	430,001	1970	373,326		
1867	315,722						
1868	138,840						
1869	352,768						
1870	387,203						

Source: U.S. Department of Homeland Security.

IMMIGRATION BY REGION AND SELECTED COUNTRY OF LAST RESIDENCE, FISCAL YEARS 1820–2008

Region and country of last residence	1820 to 1829	1830 to 1839	1840 to 1849	1850 to 1859	1860 to 1869	1870 to 1879	1880 to 1889	1890 to 1899
Total	128,502	538,381	1,427,337	2,814,554	2,081,261	2,742,137	5,248,568	3,694,294
Europe	99,272	422,771	1,369,259	2,619,680	1,877,726	2,251,878	4,638,677	3,576,411
Austria-Hungary	—	—	—	—	3,375	60,127	314,787	534,059
Austria	—	—	—	—	2,700	54,529	204,805	268,218
Hungary	—	—	—	—	483	5,598	109,982	203,350
Belgium	28	20	3,996	5,765	5,785	6,991	18,738	19,642
Bulgaria	—	—	—	—	—	—	—	52
Czechoslovakia	—	—	—	—	—	—	—	—
Denmark	173	927	671	3,227	13,553	29,278	85,342	56,671
Finland	—	—	—	—	—	—	—	—
France	7,694	39,330	75,300	81,778	35,938	71,901	48,193	35,616
Germany	5,753	124,726	385,434	976,072	723,734	751,769	1,445,181	579,072
Greece	17	49	17	32	51	209	1,807	12,732
Ireland	51,617	170,672	656,145	1,029,486	427,419	422,264	674,061	405,710
Italy	430	2,225	1,476	8,643	9,853	46,296	267,660	603,761
Netherlands	1,105	1,377	7,624	11,122	8,387	14,267	52,715	29,349
Norway-Sweden	91	1,149	12,389	22,202	82,937	178,823	586,441	334,058
Norway	—	—	—	—	16,068	88,644	185,111	96,810
Sweden	—	—	—	—	24,224	90,179	401,330	237,248
Poland	19	366	105	1,087	1,886	11,016	42,910	107,793
Portugal	177	820	196	1,299	2,083	13,971	15,186	25,874
Romania	—	—	—	—	—	—	5,842	6,808
Russia	86	280	520	423	1,670	35,177	182,698	450,101
Spain	2,595	2,010	1,916	8,795	6,966	5,540	3,995	9,189
Switzerland	3,148	4,430	4,819	24,423	21,124	25,212	81,151	37,020
United Kingdom	26,336	74,350	218,572	445,322	532,956	578,447	810,900	328,759
Yugoslavia	—	—	—	—	—	—	—	—
Other Europe	3	40	79	4	9	590	1,070	145

Asia	34	55	121	36,080	54,408	134,128	71,151	61,285
China	3	8	32	35,933	54,028	133,139	65,797	15,268
Hong Kong	—	—	—	—	—	166	247	102
India	9	38	33	42	50	—	—	102
Iran	—	—	—	—	—	—	—	—
Israel	—	—	—	—	138	193	1,583	13,998
Japan	—	—	—	—	—	—	—	—
Jordan	—	—	—	—	—	—	—	—
Korea	—	—	—	—	—	—	—	—
Philippines	—	—	—	—	—	—	—	—
Syria	—	—	—	—	—	—	—	—
Taiwan	19	8	45	94	129	382	2,478	27,510
Turkey	—	—	—	—	—	—	—	—
Vietnam	3	1	11	11	63	248	1,046	4,407
Other Asia	—	—	—	—	—	—	—	—
America	9,655	31,905	50,516	84,145	130,292	345,010	524,826	37,350
Canada and Newfoundland	2,297	11,875	34,285	64,171	117,978	324,310	492,865	3,098
Mexico	3,835	7,187	3,069	3,446	1,957	5,133	2,405	734
Caribbean	3,061	11,792	11,803	12,447	8,751	14,285	27,323	31,480
Cuba	—	—	—	—	—	—	—	—
Dominican Republic	—	—	—	—	—	—	—	—
Haiti	—	—	—	—	—	—	—	—
Jamaica	—	—	—	—	—	—	—	—
Other Caribbean	3,061	11,792	11,803	12,447	8,751	14,285	27,323	31,480
Central America	57	94	297	512	70	173	279	649
Belize	—	—	—	—	—	—	—	—
Costa Rica	—	—	—	—	—	—	—	—
El Salvador	—	—	—	—	—	—	—	—
Guatemala	—	—	—	—	—	—	—	—
Honduras	—	—	—	—	—	—	—	—
Nicaragua	—	—	—	—	—	—	—	—
Panama	—	—	—	—	—	—	—	—
Other Central America	57	94	297	512	70	173	279	649
South America	405	957	1,062	3,569	1,536	1,109	1,954	1,389
Argentina	—	—	—	—	—	—	—	—
Bolivia	—	—	—	—	—	—	—	—

Region and country of last residence	1820 to 1829	1830 to 1839	1840 to 1849	1850 to 1859	1860 to 1869	1870 to 1879	1880 to 1889	1890 to 1899
Brazil	—	—	—	—	—	—	—	—
Chile	—	—	—	—	—	—	—	—
Colombia	—	—	—	—	—	—	—	—
Ecuador	—	—	—	—	—	—	—	—
Guyana	—	—	—	—	—	—	—	—
Paraguay	—	—	—	—	—	—	—	—
Peru	—	—	—	—	—	—	—	—
Suriname	—	—	—	—	—	—	—	—
Uruguay	—	—	—	—	—	—	—	—
Venezuela	—	—	—	—	—	—	—	—
Other South America	405	957	1,062	3,569	1,536	1,109	1,954	1,389
Other America	—	—	—	—	—	—	—	—
Africa	15	50	61	84	407	371	763	432
Egypt	—	—	—	—	4	29	145	51
Ethiopia	—	—	—	—	—	—	—	—
Liberia	1	8	5	7	43	52	21	9
Morocco	—	—	—	—	—	—	—	—
South Africa	—	—	—	—	35	48	23	9
Other Africa	14	42	56	77	325	242	574	363
Oceania	3	7	14	166	187	9,996	12,361	4,704
Australia	2	1	2	15	—	8,930	7,250	3,098
New Zealand	—	—	—	—	—	39	21	12
Other Oceania	1	6	12	151	187	1,027	5,090	1,594
Not Specified	19,523	83,593	7,366	74,399	18,241	754	790	14,112

Total	8,202,388	4,295,510	699,375	856,608	2,499,268	3,213,749	6,244,379
Europe	7,572,569	2,560,340	444,399	472,524	1,404,973	1,133,443	668,866
Austria-Hungary	2,001,376	60,891	12,531	13,574	113,015	27,590	20,437
Austria	532,416	31,392	5,307	8,393	81,354	17,571	15,374
Hungary	685,567	29,499	7,224	5,181	31,661	10,019	5,063
Belgium	37,429	21,511	4,013	12,473	18,885	9,647	7,028
Bulgaria	34,651	2,824	1,062	449	97	598	1,124
Czechoslovakia	—	101,182	17,757	8,475	1,624	2,758	5,678
Denmark	61,227	34,406	3,470	4,549	10,918	9,797	4,847
Finland	—	16,922	2,438	2,230	4,923	4,310	2,569
France	67,735	54,842	13,761	36,954	50,113	46,975	32,066
Germany	328,722	386,634	119,107	119,506	576,905	209,616	85,752
Greece	145,402	60,774	10,599	8,605	45,153	74,173	37,729
Ireland	344,940	202,854	28,195	15,701	47,189	37,788	22,210
Italy	1,930,475	528,133	85,053	50,509	184,576	200,111	55,562
Netherlands	42,463	29,397	7,791	13,877	46,703	37,918	11,234
Norway-Sweden	426,981	170,329	13,452	17,326	44,224	36,150	13,941
Norway	182,542	70,327	6,901	8,326	22,806	17,371	3,835
Sweden	244,439	100,002	6,551	9,000	21,418	18,779	10,106
Poland	—	223,316	25,555	7,577	6,465	55,742	63,483
Portugal	65,154	44,829	3,518	6,765	13,928	70,568	42,685
Romania	57,322	67,810	5,264	1,254	914	2,339	24,753
Russia	1,501,301	61,604	2,463	605	453	2,329	33,311
Spain	24,818	47,109	3,669	2,774	6,880	40,793	22,783
Switzerland	32,541	31,772	5,990	9,904	17,577	19,193	8,316
United Kingdom	469,518	341,552	61,813	131,794	195,709	220,213	153,644
Yugoslavia	514	49,215	6,920	2,039	6,966	17,990	16,267
Other Europe	299,836	22,434	9,978	5,584	11,756	6,845	3,447
Asia	19,884	126,740	19,231	34,532	135,844	358,605	2,391,356
China	—	30,648	5,874	16,072	8,836	14,060	170,897
Hong Kong	3,026	—	—	—	13,781	67,047	112,132
India	—	2,076	554	1,692	1,850	18,638	231,649
Iran	—	208	198	1,144	3,195	9,059	98,141
Israel	—	—	—	98	21,376	30,911	43,569

Region and country of last residence	1900 to 1909	1910 to 1919	1920 to 1929	1930 to 1939	1940 to 1949	1950 to 1959	1960 to 1969	1980 to 1989
Japan	139,712	77,125	42,057	2,683	1,557	40,651	40,956	44,150
Jordan	—	—	—	—		4,899	9,230	28,928
Korea	—	—	—	—	83	4,845	27,048	322,708
Philippines	—	—	5,307	391	4,099	17,245	70,660	502,056
Syria	—	—		2,188	1,179	1,091	2,432	14,534
Taiwan	—	—				721	15,657	119,051
Turkey	127,999	160,717	40,450	1,327	754	2,980	9,464	19,208
Vietnam	—	—				290	2,949	200,632
Other Asia	9,215	7,500	5,994	6,016	7,854	14,084	40,494	483,601
America	277,809	1,070,539	1,591,278	230,319	328,435	921,610	1,674,172	2,695,329
Canada and Newfoundland	123,067	708,715	949,286	162,703	160,911	353,169	433,128	156,313
Mexico	31,188	185,334	498,945	32,709	56,158	273,847	441,824	1,009,586
Caribbean	100,960	120,860	83,482	18,052	46,194	115,661	427,235	790,109
Cuba	—	—	12,769	10,641	25,976	73,221	202,030	132,552
Dominican Republic	—	—		1,026	4,802	10,219	83,552	221,552
Haiti	—	—		156	823	3,787	28,992	121,406
Jamaica	—	—				7,397	62,218	193,874
Other Caribbean	100,960	120,860	70,713	6,229	14,593	21,037	50,443	120,725
Central America	7,341	15,692	16,511	6,840	20,135	40,201	98,560	339,376
Belize	77	40	285	193	433	1,133	4,185	14,964
Costa Rica	—	—		431	1,965	4,044	17,975	25,017
El Salvador	—	—		597	4,885	5,094	14,405	137,418
Guatemala	—	—		423	1,303	4,197	14,357	58,847
Honduras	—	—		679	1,874	5,320	15,078	39,071
Nicaragua	—	—		405	4,393	7,812	10,383	31,102
Panama	—	—		1,452	5,282	12,601	22,177	32,957
Other Central America	7,264	15,652	16,226	2,660	—	—	—	—

South America	15,253	39,938	43,025	9,990	19,662	78,418	250,754	399,862
Argentina	—	—	—	1,067	3,108	16,346	49,384	23,442
Bolivia	—	—	—	50	893	2,759	6,205	9,798
Brazil	—	—	4,627	1,468	3,653	11,547	29,238	22,944
Chile	—	—	—	347	1,320	4,669	12,384	19,749
Colombia	—	—	—	1,027	3,454	15,567	68,371	105,494
Ecuador	—	—	—	244	2,207	8,574	34,107	48,015
Guyana	—	—	—	131	596	1,131	4,546	85,886
Paraguay	—	—	—	33	85	576	1,249	3,518
Peru	—	—	—	321	1,273	5,980	19,783	49,958
Suriname	—	—	—	25	130	299	612	1,357
Uruguay	—	—	—	112	754	1,026	4,089	7,235
Venezuela	—	—	—	1,155	2,182	9,927	20,758	22,405
Other South America	15,253	39,938	38,398	4,010	7	17	28	61
Other America	—	—	29	25	25,375	60,314	22,671	83
Africa	6,326	8,867	6,362	2,120	6,720	13,016	23,780	141,990
Egypt	—	8,867	1,063	781	1,613	1,996	5,581	26,744
Ethiopia	—	—	—	10	28	302	804	12,927
Liberia	—	—	—	35	37	289	841	6,420
Morocco	—	—	—	73	879	2,703	2,880	3,471
South Africa	6,326	—	5,299	312	1,022	2,278	4,360	15,505
Other Africa	—	—	—	909	3,141	5,448	9,314	76,923
Oceania	12,355	12,339	9,860	3,306	14,262	11,353	23,630	41,432
Australia	11,191	11,280	8,404	2,260	11,201	8,275	14,986	16,901
New Zealand	—	1,059	935	790	2,351	1,799	3,775	6,129
Other Oceania	1,164	—	521	256	710	1,279	4,869	18,402
Not Specified	33,493	488	930	—	135	12,472	119	305,406

Region and country of last residence	1990 to 1999	2000	2001	2002	2003	2004	2005	2006	2007	2008
Total	9,775,398	841,002	1,058,902	1,059,356	703,542	957,883	1,122,257	1,266,129	1,052,415	1,107,126
Europe	1,348,612	131,920	176,892	177,059	102,546	135,663	180,396	169,156	120,759	121,146
Austria-Hungary	27,529	2,009	2,303	4,004	2,176	3,689	4,569	2,991	2,057	2,576
Austria	18,234	986	996	2,650	1,160	2,442	3,002	1,301	849	1,505
Hungary	9,295	1,023	1,307	1,354	1,016	1,247	1,567	1,690	1,208	1,071
Belgium	7,077	817	997	834	515	746	1,031	891	733	829
Bulgaria	16,948	4,779	4,273	3,476	3,706	4,042	5,451	4,690	3,766	2,805
Czechoslovakia	8,970	1,407	1,911	1,854	1,472	1,871	2,182	2,844	1,851	1,650
Denmark	6,189	549	732	651	435	568	714	738	505	551
Finland	3,970	377	497	365	230	346	549	513	385	287
France	35,945	4,063	5,379	4,567	2,926	4,209	5,035	4,945	3,680	5,246
Germany	92,207	12,230	21,992	20,977	8,061	10,270	12,864	10,271	8,640	8,456
Greece	25,403	5,113	1,941	1,486	900	1,213	1,473	1,544	1,152	943
Ireland	65,384	1,264	1,531	1,400	1,002	1,518	2,083	2,038	1,599	1,499
Italy	75,992	2,652	3,332	2,812	1,890	2,495	3,179	3,406	2,682	2,738
Netherlands	13,345	1,455	1,888	2,296	1,321	1,713	2,150	1,928	1,482	1,423
Norway-Sweden	17,825	1,967	2,544	2,082	1,516	2,011	2,264	2,111	1,604	1,557
Norway	5,211	508	582	460	385	457	472	532	388	386
Sweden	12,614	1,459	1,962	1,622	1,131	1,554	1,792	1,579	1,216	1,171
Poland	172,249	9,750	12,308	13,274	11,004	14,048	14,836	16,704	9,717	7,896
Portugal	25,497	1,373	1,611	1,301	808	1,062	1,084	1,439	1,054	781
Romania	48,136	6,506	6,206	4,515	3,305	4,078	6,431	6,753	5,240	4,563
Russia	433,427	43,156	54,838	55,370	33,513	41,959	60,344	59,720	41,593	45,092
Spain	18,443	1,390	1,875	1,588	1,102	1,453	2,002	2,387	1,810	1,970
Switzerland	11,768	1,339	1,786	1,493	862	1,193	1,465	1,199	885	936
United Kingdom	156,182	14,427	20,118	17,940	11,155	16,680	21,956	19,984	16,113	16,189
Yugoslavia	57,039	11,960	21,854	28,051	8,270	13,213	19,249	11,066	6,364	5,812
Other Europe	29,087	3,337	6,976	6,723	6,377	7,286	9,485	10,994	7,847	7,347

Asia	2,859,899	254,932	336,112	325,749	235,339	319,025	382,707	411,746	359,387	369,339
China	342,058	41,804	50,677	55,901	37,342	50,280	64,887	83,590	70,924	75,410
Hong Kong	116,894	7,181	10,282	7,938	5,015	5,421	5,004	4,514	4,450	4,389
India	352,528	38,938	65,673	66,644	47,032	65,507	79,139	58,072	55,371	59,728
Iran	76,899	6,481	8,003	7,684	4,696	5,898	7,306	9,829	8,098	9,920
Israel	41,340	3,871	4,892	4,907	3,686	5,206	6,963	6,667	4,999	6,682
Japan	66,582	7,688	10,424	9,106	6,702	8,655	9,929	9,107	7,213	7,510
Jordan	42,755	4,476	5,106	4,774	4,008	5,186	5,430	5,512	5,516	5,692
Korea	179,770	15,107	19,728	19,917	12,076	19,441	26,002	24,472	21,278	26,155
Philippines	534,338	40,465	50,644	48,493	43,133	54,651	57,654	71,133	68,792	52,391
Syria	22,906	2,255	3,542	3,350	2,046	2,549	3,350	3,080	2,550	3,310
Taiwan	132,647	9,457	12,457	9,932	7,168	9,314	9,389	8,545	9,053	9,237
Turkey	38,687	2,702	3,463	3,914	3,318	4,491	6,449	6,433	4,728	4,953
Vietnam	275,379	25,159	34,537	32,372	21,227	30,074	30,832	29,701	27,510	29,807
Other Asia	637,116	49,348	56,684	50,817	37,890	52,352	70,373	91,091	68,905	74,155
America	5,137,743	392,461	470,794	477,363	305,996	408,972	432,726	548,812	434,272	491,045
Canada and Newfoundland	194,788	21,289	29,991	27,142	16,447	22,439	29,930	23,913	20,324	22,366
Mexico	2,757,418	171,445	204,032	216,924	114,758	173,711	157,992	170,042	143,180	188,015
Caribbean	1,004,687	84,250	96,384	93,914	67,498	82,116	91,371	144,477	114,318	134,744
Cuba	159,037	17,897	25,832	27,435	8,685	15,385	20,651	44,248	25,441	48,057
Dominican Republic	359,818	17,373	21,139	22,386	26,112	30,063	27,365	37,997	27,875	31,801
Haiti	177,446	21,977	22,470	19,151	11,924	13,695	13,491	21,625	29,978	25,522
Jamaica	177,143	15,603	15,031	14,507	13,045	13,581	17,774	24,538	18,873	18,077
Other Caribbean	181,243	11,400	11,912	10,435	7,732	9,392	12,090	16,069	12,151	11,287
Central America	610,189	60,331	72,504	66,298	53,283	61,253	52,629	74,244	53,834	49,741
Belize	12,600	774	982	983	616	888	901	1,263	1,089	1,113
Costa Rica	17,054	1,390	1,863	1,686	1,322	1,811	2,479	3,459	2,722	2,287
El Salvador	273,017	22,301	30,876	30,472	27,854	29,297	20,891	31,258	20,009	18,937
Guatemala	126,043	9,861	13,399	15,870	14,195	18,655	16,466	23,674	17,198	15,791
Honduras	72,880	5,851	6,546	6,355	4,582	5,339	6,825	8,036	7,300	6,389

Region and country of last residence	1990 to 1999	2000	2001	2002	2003	2004	2005	2006	2007	2008
Nicaragua	80,446	18,258	16,908	9,171	3,503	3,842	3,196	4,035	3,587	3,486
Panama	28,149	1,896	1,930	1,761	1,211	1,421	1,869	2,519	1,929	1,738
Other Central America	—	—	—	—	—	—	—	—	—	—
South America	570,624	55,143	67,880	73,082	53,946	69,452	100,803	136,134	102,616	96,178
Argentina	30,065	2,472	3,426	3,791	3,193	4,672	6,945	7,239	5,375	5,170
Bolivia	18,111	1,744	1,804	1,660	1,365	1,719	2,164	4,000	2,326	2,350
Brazil	50,744	6,767	9,391	9,034	6,108	10,247	16,329	17,741	13,546	11,813
Chile	18,200	1,660	1,881	1,766	1,255	1,719	2,354	2,727	2,202	1,988
Colombia	137,985	14,125	16,234	18,409	14,400	18,055	24,705	42,017	32,055	29,349
Ecuador	81,358	7,624	9,654	10,524	7,022	8,366	11,528	17,624	12,011	11,541
Guyana	74,407	5,255	7,835	9,492	6,373	5,721	8,771	9,010	5,288	6,302
Paraguay	6,082	394	464	413	222	324	523	725	518	489
Peru	110,117	9,361	10,838	11,737	9,169	11,369	15,205	21,300	17,056	14,873
Suriname	2,285	281	254	223	175	170	287	341	193	225
Uruguay	6,062	396	516	499	470	750	1,110	1,639	1,340	1,380
Venezuela	35,180	5,052	5,576	5,529	4,190	6,335	10,870	11,758	10,696	10,689
Other South America	28	12	7	5	4	5	12	13	10	9
Other America	37	3	3	3	4	1	2	—	—	1
Africa	346,416	40,790	50,009	56,002	45,559	62,623	79,697	112,100	89,277	100,881
Egypt	44,604	4,323	5,333	6,215	3,928	6,590	10,296	13,163	10,178	10,728
Ethiopia	40,097	3,645	4,620	6,308	5,969	7,180	8,378	13,390	11,340	11,703
Liberia	13,587	1,225	1,477	1,467	1,081	1,540	1,846	3,736	3,771	3,478
Morocco	15,768	3,423	4,752	3,188	2,969	3,910	4,165	4,704	4,311	4,187
South Africa	21,964	2,814	4,046	3,685	2,088	3,335	4,425	3,173	2,842	2,638
Other Africa	210,396	25,360	29,781	35,139	29,524	40,068	50,587	73,934	56,835	68,147
Oceania	56,800	5,928	7,201	6,495	5,076	6,954	7,432	8,000	6,639	5,926
Australia	24,288	2,694	3,714	3,420	2,488	3,397	4,090	3,770	3,026	3,031
New Zealand	8,600	1,080	1,347	1,364	1,030	1,420	1,457	1,344	1,234	1,092
Other Oceania	23,912	2,154	2,140	1,711	1,558	2,137	1,885	2,886	2,379	1,803
Not Specified	25,928	14,971	17,894	16,688	9,086	24,646	39,299	16,315	42,081	18,789

— Represents zero or not available.

PRESIDENTS, VICE PRESIDENTS, AND SECRETARIES OF STATE

	President	Vice President	Secretary of State
1.	George Washington, Federalist 1789	John Adams, Federalist 1789	Thomas Jefferson 1789 Edmund Randolph 1794 Timothy Pickering 1795
2.	John Adams, Federalist 1797	Thomas Jefferson, Dem.-Rep. 1797	Timothy Pickering 1797 John Marshall 1800
3.	Thomas Jefferson, Dem.-Rep. 1801	Aaron Burr, Dem.-Rep. 1801 George Clinton, Dem.-Rep. 1805	James Madison 1801
4.	James Madison, Dem.-Rep. 1809	George Clinton, Dem.-Rep. 1809 Elbridge Gerry, Dem.-Rep. 1813	Robert Smith 1809 James Monroe 1811
5.	James Monroe, Dem.-Rep. 1817	Daniel D. Tompkins, Dem.-Rep. 1817	John Q. Adams 1817
6.	John Quincy Adams, Dem.-Rep. 1825	John C. Calhoun, Dem.-Rep. 1825	Henry Clay 1825
7.	Andrew Jackson, Democratic 1829	John C. Calhoun, Democratic 1829 Martin Van Buren, Democratic 1833	Martin Van Buren 1829 Edward Livingston 1831 Louis McLane 1833 John Forsyth 1834
8.	Martin Van Buren, Democratic 1837	Richard M. Johnson, Democratic 1837	John Forsyth 1837
9.	William H. Harrison, Whig 1841	John Tyler, Whig 1841	Daniel Webster 1841

	President	Vice President	Secretary of State
10.	John Tyler, Whig and Democratic 1841	None	Daniel Webster 1841 Hugh S. Legaré 1843 Abel P. Upshur 1843 John C. Calhoun 1844
11.	James K. Polk, Democratic 1845	George M. Dallas, Democratic 1845	James Buchanan 1845
12.	Zachary Taylor, Whig 1849	Millard Fillmore, Whig 1848	John M. Clayton 1849
13.	Millard Fillmore, Whig 1850	None	Daniel Webster 1850 Edward Everett 1852
14.	Franklin Pierce, Democratic 1853	William R. King, Democratic 1853	William L. Marcy 1853
15.	James Buchanan, Democratic 1857	John C. Breckinridge, Democratic 1857	Lewis Cass 1857 Jeremiah S. Black 1860
16.	Abraham Lincoln, Republican 1861	Hannibal Hamlin, Republican 1861 Andrew Johnson, Unionist 1865	William H. Seward 1861
17.	Andrew Johnson, Unionist 1865	None	William H. Seward 1865
18.	Ulysses S. Grant, Republican 1869	Schuyler Colfax, Republican 1869 Henry Wilson, Republican 1873	Elihu B. Washburne 1869 Hamilton Fish 1869
19.	Rutherford B. Hayes, Republican 1877	William A. Wheeler, Republican 1877	William M. Evarts 1877

	President	*Vice President*	*Secretary of State*
20.	James A. Garfield, Republican 1881	Chester A. Arthur, Republican 1881	James G. Blaine 1881
21.	Chester A. Arthur, Republican 1881	None	Frederick T. Frelinghuysen 1881
22.	Grover Cleveland, Democratic 1885	Thomas A. Hendricks, Democratic 1885	Thomas F. Bayard 1885
23.	Benjamin Harrison, Republican 1889	Levi P. Morton, Republican 1889	James G. Blaine 1889 John W. Foster 1892
24.	Grover Cleveland, Democratic 1893	Adlai E. Stevenson, Democratic 1893	Walter Q. Gresham 1893 Richard Olney 1895
25.	William McKinley, Republican 1897	Garret A. Hobart, Republican 1897 Theodore Roosevelt, Republican 1901	John Sherman 1897 William R. Day 1898 John Hay 1898
26.	Theodore Roosevelt, Republican 1901	Charles Fairbanks, Republican 1905	John Hay 1901 Elihu Root 1905 Robert Bacon 1909
27.	William H. Taft, Republican 1909	James S. Sherman, Republican 1909	Philander C. Knox 1909
28.	Woodrow Wilson, Democratic 1913	Thomas R. Marshall, Democratic 1913	William J. Bryan 1913 Robert Lansing 1915 Bainbridge Colby 1920
29.	Warren G. Harding, Republican 1921	Calvin Coolidge, Republican 1921	Charles E. Hughes 1921
30.	Calvin Coolidge, Republican 1923	Charles G. Dawes, Republican 1925	Charles E. Hughes 1923 Frank B. Kellogg 1925

	President	Vice President	Secretary of State
31.	Herbert Hoover, Republican 1929	Charles Curtis, Republican 1929	Henry L. Stimson 1929
32.	Franklin D. Roosevelt, Democratic 1933	John Nance Garner, Democratic 1933 Henry A. Wallace, Democratic 1941 Harry S. Truman, Democratic 1945	Cordell Hull 1933 Edward R. Stettinius, Jr. 1944
33.	Harry S. Truman, Democratic 1945	Alben W. Barkley, Democratic 1949	Edward R. Stettinius, Jr. 1945 James F. Byrnes 1945 George C. Marshall 1947 Dean G. Acheson 1949
34.	Dwight D. Eisenhower, Republican 1953	Richard M. Nixon, Republican 1953	John F. Dulles 1953 Christian A. Herter 1959
35.	John F. Kennedy, Democratic 1961	Lyndon B. Johnson, Democratic 1961	Dean Rusk 1961
36.	Lyndon B. Johnson, Democratic 1963	Hubert H. Humphrey, Democratic 1965	Dean Rusk 1963
37.	Richard M. Nixon, Republican 1969	Spiro T. Agnew, Republican 1969 Gerald R. Ford, Republican 1973	William P. Rogers 1969 Henry Kissinger 1973
38.	Gerald R. Ford, Republican 1974	Nelson Rockefeller, Republican 1974	Henry Kissinger 1974
39.	Jimmy Carter, Democratic 1977	Walter Mondale, Democratic 1977	Cyrus Vance 1977 Edmund Muskie 1980

	President	Vice President	Secretary of State
40.	Ronald Reagan, Republican 1981	George H. W. Bush, Republican 1981	Alexander Haig 1981 George Schultz 1982
41.	George H. W. Bush, Republican 1989	J. Danforth Quayle, Republican 1989	James A. Baker 1989 Lawrence Eagleburger 1992
42.	William J. Clinton, Democratic 1993	Albert Gore, Jr., Democratic 1993	Warren Christopher 1993 Madeleine Albright 1997
43.	George W. Bush, Republican 2001	Richard B. Cheney, Republican 2001	Colin L. Powell 2001 Condoleezza Rice 2005
44.	Barack Obama, Democratic 2009	Joseph R. Biden, Democratic 2009	Hillary Rodham Clinton 2009

FURTHER READINGS

CHAPTER 1

A fascinating study of pre-Columbian migration is Brian M. Fagan's *The Great Journey: The Peopling of Ancient America*, rev. ed. (2004). Alice B. Kehoe's *North American Indians: A Comprehensive Account*, 2nd ed. (1992), provides an encyclopedic treatment of Native Americans. See also Alvin M. Josephy, Jr., ed., *America in 1492: The World of the Indian Peoples before the Arrival of Columbus* (1992), and Daniel K. Richter, *Facing East from Indian Country: A Native History of Early America* (2001).

The conflict between Native Americans and Europeans is treated well in James Axtell's *The Invasion Within: The Contest of Cultures in Colonial North America* (1986) and *Beyond 1492: Encounters in Colonial North America* (1992). Colin G. Calloway's *New Worlds for All: Indians, Europeans, and the Remaking of Early America* (1997) explores the ecological effects of European settlement.

The most comprehensive overviews of European exploration are two volumes by Samuel Eliot Morison: *The European Discovery of America: The Northern Voyages, A.D. 500–1600* (1971) and *The Southern Voyages, A.D. 1492–1616* (1974).

The voyages of Columbus are surveyed in William D. Phillips Jr. and Carla Rahn Phillips's *The Worlds of Christopher Columbus* (1992). For sweeping overviews of Spain's creation of a global empire, see Henry Kamen's *Empire: How Spain Became a World Power, 1492–1763* (2003) and Hugh Thomas's *Rivers of Gold: The Rise of the Spanish Empire, from Columbus to Magellan* (2004). David J. Weber examines Spanish colonization in *The Spanish Frontier in North America* (1992). For the French experience, see William J. Eccles's *France in America*, rev. ed. (1990). For an insightful comparison of Spanish and English modes of settlement, see J. H. Elliott, *Empires of the Atlantic World: Britain and Spain in America, 1492–1830* (2006).

CHAPTER 2

Two excellent surveys of early American history are Peter C. Hoffer's *The Brave New World: A History of Early America,* 2nd ed. (2006), and William R. Polk's *The Birth of America: From before Columbus to the Revolution* (2006).

Bernard Bailyn's *Voyagers to the West: A Passage in the Peopling of America on the Eve of the Revolution* (1986) provides a comprehensive view of migration to the New World. Jack P. Greene offers a brilliant synthesis of British colonization in *Pursuits of Happiness: The Social Development of Early Modern British Colonies and the Formation of American Culture* (1988). The best overview of the colonization of North America is Alan Taylor's *American Colonies: The Settling of North America* (2001). On the interactions among Indian, European, and African cultures, see Gary B. Nash's *Red, White, and Black: The Peoples of Early North America,* 5th ed. (2005). See Daniel K. Richter's *The Ordeal of the Longhouse: The Peoples of the Iroquois League in the Era of European Colonization* (1992) and Daniel P. Barr's *Unconquered: The Iroquois League at War in Colonial America* (2006) for a history of the Iroquois Confederacy.

Andrew Delbanco's *The Puritan Ordeal* (1989) is a powerful study of the tensions inherent in the Puritan outlook. For information regarding the Puritan settlement of New England, see Virginia DeJohn Anderson's *New England's Generation: The Great Migration and the Formation of Society and Culture in the Seventeenth Century* (1991). The best biography of John Winthrop is Francis J. Bremer's *John Winthrop: America's Forgotten Founding Father* (2003).

The pattern of settlement in the middle colonies is illuminated in Barry Levy's *Quakers and the American Family: British Settlement in the Delaware Valley* (1988). On the early history of New York, see Russell Shorto's *The Island at the Center of the World: The Epic Story of Dutch Manhattan and the Forgotten Colony That Shaped America* (2004). Settlement of the areas along the Atlantic in the South is traced in James Horn's *Adapting to a New World: English Society in the Seventeenth-Century Chesapeake* (1994). For a study of race and the settlement of South Carolina, see Peter H. Wood's *Black Majority: Negroes in Colonial South Carolina from 1670 through the Stono Rebellion* (1974). A brilliant book on relations between the Catawba Indians and their black and white neighbors is James H. Merrell's *The Indians' New World: Catawbas and Their Neighbors from European Contact through the Era of Removal* (1989). On the flourishing trade in captive Indians, see Alan Gallay's *The Indian Slave Trade: The Rise of the English Empire in the American South,*

1670–1717 (2002). On the Yamasee War, see Steven J. Oatis's *A Colonial Complex: South Carolina's Frontiers in the Era of the Yamasee War, 1680–1730* (2004).

CHAPTER 3

The diversity of colonial societies may be seen in David Hackett Fischer's *Albion's Seed: Four British Folkways in America* (1989). On the economic development of New England, see Christine Leigh Heyrman's *Commerce and Culture: The Maritime Communities of Colonial Massachusetts, 1690–1750* (1984) and Stephen Innes's *Creating the Commonwealth: The Economic Culture of Puritan New England* (1995). John Frederick Martin's *Profits in the Wilderness: Entrepreneurship and the Founding of New England Towns in the Seventeenth Century* (1991) indicates that economic concerns rather than spiritual motives were driving forces in many New England towns. For a fascinating account of the impact of livestock on colonial history, see Virginia DeJohn Anderson's *Creatures of Empire: How Domestic Animals Transformed Early America* (2004).

Paul Boyer and Stephen Nissenbaum's *Salem Possessed: The Social Origins of Witchcraft* (1974) connects the notorious witch trials to changes in community structure. Bernard Rosenthal challenges many myths concerning the Salem witch trials in *Salem Story: Reading the Witch Trials of 1692* (1993). Mary Beth Norton's *In the Devil's Snare: The Salem Witchcraft Crisis of 1692* (2002) emphasizes the role of Indian violence.

Discussions of women in the New England colonies can be found in Laurel Thatcher Ulrich's *Good Wives: Image and Reality in the Lives of Women in Northern New England, 1650–1750* (1980), Joy Day Buel and Richard Buel, Jr.'s *The Way of Duty: A Woman and Her Family in Revolutionary America* (1984), and Carol F. Karlsen's *The Devil in the Shape of a Woman: Witchcraft in Colonial New England* (1987). On women and religion, see Susan Juster's *Disorderly Women: Sexual Politics and Evangelicalism in Revolutionary New England* (1994). John Demos describes family life in *A Little Commonwealth: Family Life in Plymouth Colony*, new ed. (2000).

For an excellent overview of Indian relations with Europeans, see Colin G. Calloway's *New Worlds for All: Indians, Europeans, and the Remaking of Early America* (1997). On New England Indians, see Kathleen J. Bragdon's *Native People of Southern New England, 1500–1650* (1996). For analyses of Indian wars, see Alfred A. Cave's *The Pequot War* (1996) and Jill Lepore's *The Name of War: King Philip's War and the Origins of American Identity* (1998). The story of the Iroquois is told well in Daniel K. Richter's *The Ordeal of the Longhouse: The Peoples of the Iroquois League in the Era of European Colonization* (1992). Indians in the southern colonies are the focus of James Axtell's *The Indians' New South: Cultural Change in the Colonial Southeast* (1997).

For the social history of the southern colonies, see Allan Kulikoff's *Tobacco and Slaves: The Development of Southern Cultures in the Chesapeake, 1680–1800* (1986) and Kathleen M. Brown's *Good Wives, Nasty Wenches, and Anxious Patriarchs: Gender, Race, and Power in Colonial Virginia* (1996). Family life along the Chesapeake Bay is described in Gloria L. Main's *Tobacco Colony: Life in Early Maryland, 1650–1720* (1982) and Daniel Blake Smith's *Inside the Great House: Planter Family Life in Eighteenth-Century Chesapeake Society* (1980).

Edmund S. Morgan's *American Slavery, American Freedom: The Ordeal of Colonial Virginia* (1975) examines Virginia's social structure, environment, and labor patterns in a biracial context. On the interaction of the cultures of blacks and whites, see Mechal Sobel's *The World They Made Together: Black and White Values in Eighteenth-Century Virginia* (1987). African American viewpoints are presented in Timothy H. Breen and Stephen Innes's *"Myne Owne Ground": Race and Freedom on Virginia's Eastern Shore, 1640–1676*, new ed. (2004). David W. Galenson's *White Servitude in Colonial America: An Economic Analysis* (1981) looks at the indentured labor force.

Henry F. May's *The Enlightenment in America* (1976) and Donald H. Meyer's *The Democratic Enlightenment* (1976) examine intellectual trends in eighteenth-century America. Lawrence A. Cremin's *American Education: The Colonial Experience, 1607–1783* (1970) surveys educational developments.

On the Great Awakening, see Patricia U. Bonomi's *Under the Cope of Heaven: Religion, Society, and Politics in Colonial America*, updated ed. (2003), Timothy D. Hall's *Contested Boundaries: Itinerancy and the Reshaping of the Colonial American Religious World* (1994), and Frank Lambert's *Inventing the "Great Awakening"* (1999). For evangelism in the South, see Christine Leigh Heyrman's *Southern Cross: The Beginnings of the Bible Belt* (1997).

CHAPTER 4

The economics motivating colonial policies is covered in John J. McCusker and Russell R. Menard's *The Economy of British America, 1607–1789*, rev. ed. (1991). The problems of colonial customs administration are explored in Michael Kammen's *Empire and Interest: The American Colonies and the Politics of Mercantilism* (1970).

The Andros crisis and related topics are treated in Jack M. Sosin's *English America and the Revolution of 1688: Royal Administration and the Structure of Provincial Government* (1982). Stephen Saunders Webb's *The Governors-General: The English Army and the Definition of the Empire, 1569–1681* (1979) argues that the Crown was more concerned with military administration than with commercial regulation, and Webb's *1676: The End of American Independence* (1984) shows how the Indian wars undermined the autonomy of the colonial governments.

On the Jesuits, see Nicholas P. Cushner's *Why Have You Come Here? The Jesuits and the First Evangelization of Native America* (2006). The early Indian wars are treated in Jill Lepore's *The Name of War: King Philip's War and the Origins of American Identity* (1998) and in Francis Jennings's *The Invasion of America: Indians, Colonialism, and the Cant of Conquest* (1975). See also Richard Aquila's *The Iroquois Restoration: Iroquois Diplomacy on the Colonial Frontier, 1701–1754* (1983). Gregory Evans Dowd describes the unification efforts of Indians east of the Mississippi in *A Spirited Resistance: The North American Indian Struggle for Unity, 1745–1815* (1992). See also James H. Merrell's *Into the American Woods: Negotiators on the Pennsylvania Frontier* (1999).

A good introduction to the imperial phase of the colonial conflicts is Howard H. Peckham's *The Colonial Wars, 1689–1762* (1964). More analytical is Douglas Edward Leach's *Arms for Empire: A Military History of the British Colonies in North America, 1607–1763* (1973). Fred Anderson's *Crucible of War: The Seven Years' War and the Fate of Empire in British North America, 1754–1766* (2000) is the best history of the Seven Years' War. On the French colonies in North America, see Allan Greer's *The People of New France* (1997).

CHAPTER 5

For a narrative survey of the events leading to the Revolution, see Edward Countryman's *The American Revolution,* rev. ed. (2003). For Great Britain's perspective on the imperial conflict, see Ian R. Christie's *Crisis of Empire: Great Britain and the American Colonies, 1754–1783* (1966).

The intellectual foundations of revolt are traced in Bernard Bailyn's *The Ideological Origins of the American Revolution,* enlarged ed. (1992). To understand how these views were connected to organized protest, see Pauline Maier's *From Resistance to Revolution: Colonial Radicals and the Development of American Opposition to Britain, 1765–1776* (1972) and Jon Butler's *Becoming America: The Revolution before 1776* (2000).

Several books deal with specific events in the crisis. Oliver M. Dickerson's *The Navigation Acts and the American Revolution* (1951) stresses the change from trade regulation to taxation in 1764. Edmund S. Morgan and Helen M. Morgan's *The Stamp Act Crisis: Prologue to Revolution*, rev. ed. (1962), gives the colonial perspective on that crucial event. Also valuable are Hiller B. Zobel's *The Boston Massacre* (1970), Benjamin Woods Labaree's *The Boston Tea Party, 1773; Catalyst for Revolution* (1964), and David Ammerman's *In the Common Cause: American Response to the Coercive Acts of 1774* (1974). On the efforts of colonists to boycott the purchase of British goods, see T. H. Breen's *The Marketplace of Revolution: How Consumer Politics Shaped American Independence* (2004). An excellent overview of the political turmoil leading to war is John Ferling's *A Leap in the Dark: The Struggle to Create the American Republic* (2003). A fascinating account of the smallpox epidemic during the Revolutionary War is Elizabeth A. Fenn's *Pox Americana: The Great Smallpox Epidemic of 1775–1782* (2001).

Pauline Maier's *American Scripture: Making the Declaration of Independence* (1997) is the best analysis of the framing of that document. For accounts of how the imperial controversy affected individual colonies, see Edward Countryman's *A People in Revolution: The American Revolution and Political Society in New York, 1760–1790* (1981), Richard L. Bushman's *King and People in Provincial Massachusetts* (1985), James H. Hutson's *Pennsylvania Politics, 1746–1770: The Movement for Royal Government and Its Consequences* (1972), Rhys Isaac's *The Transformation of Virginia, 1740–1790* (1982), and A. Roger Ekirch's *"Poor Carolina": Politics and Society in Colonial North Carolina, 1729–1776* (1981).

Events west of the Appalachians are chronicled concisely by Jack M. Sosin in *The Revolutionary Frontier, 1763–1783* (1967). Military affairs in the early phases of the war are handled in John W. Shy's *Toward Lexington: The Role of the British Army in the Coming of the American Revolution* (1965) and in works described in Chapter 6.

CHAPTER 6

The Revolutionary War is the subject of Colin Bonwick's *The American Revolution*, 2nd ed. (2005), Gordon S. Wood's *The Radicalism of the American Revolution* (1991), and Jeremy Black's *War for America: The Fight for Independence, 1775–1783* (1991). John Ferling's *Setting the World Ablaze Washington, Adams, Jefferson, and the American Revolution* (2000) highlights the roles played by key leaders.

On the social history of the Revolutionary War, see John W. Shy's *A People Numerous and Armed: Reflections on the Military Struggle for American Independence*, rev. ed. (1990), Charles Royster's *A Revolutionary People at War: The Continental Army and American Character, 1775–1783* (1979), and E. Wayne Carp's *To Starve the Army at Pleasure: Continental Army Administration and American Political Culture, 1775–1783* (1984). Colin G. Calloway tells the neglected story of the Indian experiences in the Revolution in *The American Revolution in Indian Country: Crisis and Diversity in Native American Communities* (1995). The imperial, aristocratic, and racist aspects of the Revolution are detailed in Francis Jennings's *The Creation of America: Through Revolution to Empire* (2000).

Why some Americans remained loyal to the Crown is the subject of Robert M. Calhoon's *The Loyalists in Revolutionary America, 1760–1781* (1973) and Mary Beth Norton's *The British-Americans: The Loyalist Exiles in England, 1774–1789* (1972).

The definitive study of African Americans during the Revolutionary era remains Benjamin Quarles's *The Negro in the American Revolution* (1961). Mary Beth Norton's *Liberty's Daughters: The Revolutionary Experience of American Women, 1750–1800*, new ed. (1996), Linda K. Kerber's *Women of the Republic: Intellect and Ideology in Revolutionary America* (1980), and Carol Berkin's *Revolutionary Mothers: Women in the Struggle for America's Independence* (2005) document the role that women played in securing independence. Joy Day Buel and Richard Buel Jr.'s *The Way of Duty: A Woman and Her Family in Revolutionary America* (1984) shows the impact of the Revolution on one New England family.

The Standard introduction to the diplomacy of the Revolutionary era is Jonathan R. Dull's *A Diplomatic History of the American Revolution* (1985).

CHAPTER 7

A good overview of the Confederation period is Richard B. Morris's *The Forging of the Union, 1781–1789* (1987). Another useful analysis of this period is Richard Buel Jr.'s *Securing the Revolution: Ideology in American Politics, 1789–1815* (1972).

David P. Szatmary's *Shays's Rebellion: The Making of an Agrarian Insurrection* (1980) covers that fateful incident. For a fine account of cultural change during the period, see Joseph J. Ellis's *After the Revolution: Profiles of Early American Culture* (1979).

Excellent treatments of the post-Revolutionary era include Edmund S. Morgan's *Inventing the People: The Rise of Popular Sovereignty in England and America* (1988), Michael Kammen's *Sovereignty and Liberty: Constitutional Discourse in American Culture* (1988), and Joyce Appleby's *Inheriting the Revolution: The First Generation of Americans* (2000). On the political philosophies contributing to the drafting of the Constitution, see Ralph Lerner's *The Thinking Revolutionary: Principle and Practice in the New Republic* (1987). Woody Holton's *Unruly Americans and the Origins of the Constitution* (2007) emphasizes the role of taxes and monetary policies in the crafting of the Constitution. Among the better collections of essays on the Constitution are *Toward a More Perfect Union: Six Essays on the Constitution* (1988), edited by Neil L. York, and *The Framing and Ratification of the Constitution* (1987), edited by Leonard W. Levy and Dennis J. Mahoney.

Bruce Ackerman's *We the People,* vol. 1, *Foundations* (1991) examines Federalist political principles. For the Bill of Rights that emerged from the ratification struggles, see Robert A. Rutland's *The Birth of the Bill of Rights, 1776–1791* (1955).

CHAPTER 8

The best introduction to the early Federalists remains John C. Miller's *The Federalist Era, 1789–1801* (1960). Other works analyze the ideological debates among the nation's first leaders. Richard Buel Jr.'s *Securing the Revolution: Ideology in American Politics, 1789–1815* (1972), Joyce Appleby's *Capitalism and a New Social Order: The Republican Vision of the 1790s* (1984), Drew R. McCoy's *The Last of the Fathers: James Madison and the Republican Legacy* (1989), and Stanley Elkins and Eric McKitrick's *The Age of Federalism: The Early American Republic, 1788–1800* (1993) trace the persistence and transformation of ideas first fostered during the Revolutionary crisis. On the first ten constitutional amendments, see Leonard W. Levy's *Origins of the Bill of Rights* (1999).

The 1790s may also be understood through the views and behavior of national leaders. Joseph J. Ellis's *Founding Brothers: The Revolutionary Generation* (2000) is a superb group study. See also the following biographies: Richard Brookhiser's *Founding Father: Rediscovering George Washington* (1996) and *Alexander Hamilton, American* (1999) and Joseph J. Ellis's *Passionate Sage: The Character and Legacy of John Adams* (1993). For a female perspective, see Phyllis Lee Levin's *Abigail Adams: A Biography* (1987). The Republican viewpoint is the subject of Lance Banning's *The Jeffersonian Persuasion: Evolution of a Party Ideology* (1978).

Federalist foreign policy is explored in Jerald A. Comb's *The Jay Treaty: Political Battleground of the Founding Fathers* (1970) and William Stinchcombe's *The XYZ Affair* (1980). For specific domestic issues, see Thomas P. Slaughter's *The Whiskey Rebellion: Frontier Epilogue to the American Revolution* (1986) and Harry Ammon's *The Genet Mission* (1973). The treatment of Indians in the Old Northwest is explored in Richard H. Kohn's *Eagle and Sword: The Federalists and the Creation of the Military Establishment in America, 1783–1802* (1975). For the Alien and Sedition Acts, consult James Morton Smith's *Freedom's Fetters: The Alien and Sedition Laws and American Civil Liberties* (1956).

Several books focus on social issues of the post-Revolutionary period, including *Keepers of the Revolution: New Yorkers at Work in the Early Republic* (1992), edited by Paul A. Gilje and Howard B. Rock; Ronald Schultz's *The Republic of Labor: Philadelphia Artisans and the Politics of Class, 1720–1830* (1993); and Peter Way's *Common Labour: Workers and the Digging of North American Canals, 1780–1860* (1993).

The African American experience in the Revolutionary era is detailed in Mechal Sobel's *The World They Made Together: Black and White Values in Eighteenth-Century Virginia* (1987) and Gary B. Nash's *Forging Freedom: The Formation of Philadelphia's Black Community, 1720–1840* (1988).

CHAPTER 9

Marshall Smelser's *The Democratic Republic, 1801–1815* (1968) presents an overview of the Republican administrations. The standard biography of Jefferson is Joseph J. Ellis's *American Sphinx: The Character of Thomas Jefferson* (1996). On the life of Jefferson's friend and successor, see Drew R. McCoy's. *The Last of the Fathers: James Madison and the Republican Legacy* (1989). Joyce Appleby's *Capitalism and a New Social Order: The Republican Vision of the 1790s* (1984) minimizes the impact of Republican ideology.

Linda K. Kerber's *Federalists in Dissent: Imagery and Ideology in Jeffersonian American* (1970) explores the Federalists while out of power. The concept of judicial review and the courts can be studied in Richard E. Ellis's *The Jeffersonian Crisis: Courts and Politics in the Young Republic* (1971). On John Marshall, see G. Edward White's *The Marshall Court and Cultural Change, 1815–1835* (1988) and James F. Simon's *What Kind of Nation: Thomas Jefferson, John Marshall, and the Epic Struggle to Create a United States* (2002). Milton Lomask's two volumes, *Aaron Burr: The Years from Princeton to Vice President, 1756–1805* (1979) and *The Conspiracy and the Years of Exile, 1805–1836* (1982) trace the career of that remarkable American.

For the Louisiana Purchase, consult Jon Kukla's *A Wilderness So Immense: The Louisiana Purchase and the Destiny of America* (2003). For a captivating account of the Lewis and Clark expedition, see Stephen Ambrose's *Undaunted Courage: Meriwether Lewis, Thomas Jefferson, and the Opening of the American West* (1996). Bernard W. Sheehan's *Seeds of Extinction: Jeffersonian Philanthropy and the American Indian* (1973) is more analytical in its treatment of the Jeffersonians' Indian policy and the opening of the West.

Burton Spivak's *Jefferson's English Crisis: Commerce, Embargo, and the Republican Revolution* (1979) discusses Anglo-American relations during Jefferson's administration; Clifford L. Egan's *Neither Peace Nor War: Franco-American Relations, 1803–1812* (1983) covers America's relations with France. An excellent revisionist treatment of the events that brought on war in 1812 is J. C. A. Stagg's *Mr. Madison's War: Politics, Diplomacy, and Warfare in the Early American Republic, 1783–1830* (1983). The war itself is the focus of Donald R. Hickey's *The War of 1812: A Forgotten Conflict* (1989). See also David Curtis Skaggs and Gerard T. Altoff's *A Signal Victory: The Lake Erie Campaign, 1812–1813* (1997).

CHAPTER 10

The standard overview of the Era of Good Feelings remains George Dangerfield's *The Awakening of American Nationalism, 1815–1828* (1965). A classic summary of the economic trends of the period is Douglass C. North's *The Economic Growth of the United States, 1790–1860* (1961). An excellent synthesis of the era is Charles Sellers's *The Market Revolution: Jacksonian America, 1815–1846* (1991).

On diplomatic relations during James Monroe's presidency, see William Earl Weeks's *John Quincy Adams and American Global Empire* (1992). For relations after 1812, see Ernest R. May's *The Making of the Monroe Doctrine* (1975).

Background on Andrew Jackson can be obtained from works cited in Chapter 11. The campaign that brought Jackson to the White House is analyzed in Robert Vincent Remini's *The Election of Andrew Jackson* (1963).

CHAPTER 11

An excellent survey of events covered in this chapter is Daniel Feller's *The Jacksonian Promise: America, 1815–1840* (1995). Even more comprehensive surveys of politics and culture during the Jacksonian era are Daniel Walker Howe's *What Hath God Wrought: The Transformation of America,*

1815–1848 (2007) and David S. Reynolds's *Waking Giant: America in the Age of Jackson* (2008). A more political focus can be found in Harry L. Watson's *Liberty and Power: The Politics of Jacksonian America* (1990).

A still-valuable standard introduction to the development of the political parties of the 1830s is Richard Patrick McCormick's *The Second American Party System: Party Formation in the Jacksonian Era* (1966). For an outstanding analysis of women in New York City during the Jacksonian period, see Christine Stansell's *City of Women: Sex and Class in New York, 1789–1860* (1986). In *Chants Democratic: New York City and the Rise of the American Working-Class, 1788–1850* (1984), Sean Wilentz analyzes the social basis of working-class politics. More recently, Wilentz has traced the democratization of politics in *The Rise of American Democracy: Jefferson to Lincoln*, abridged college ed. (2009).

The best biography of Jackson remains Robert Vincent Remini's three-volume work: *Andrew Jackson: The Course of American Empire, 1767–1821* (1977), *Andrew Jackson: The Course of American Freedom, 1822–1832* (1981), and *Andrew Jackson: The Course of American Democracy, 1833–1845* (1984). A more critical study of the seventh president is Andrew Burstein's *The Passions of Andrew Jackson* (2003). On Jackson's successor, consult John Niven's *Martin Van Buren: The Romantic Age of American Politics* (1983) and Ted Widmer's *Martin Van Buren* (2005). Studies of other major figures of the period include John Niven's *John C. Calhoun and the Price of Union: A Biography* (1988), Merrill D. Peterson's *The Great Triumvirate: Webster, Clay, and Calhoun* (1987), and Robert Vincent Remini's *Henry Clay: Statesman for the Union* (1991) and *Daniel Webster: The Man and His Time* (1997).

The political philosophies of Jackson's opponents are treated in Michael F. Holt's *The Rise and Fall of the American Whig Party: Jacksonian Politics and the Onset of the Civil War* (1999) and Harry L. Watson's *Andrew Jackson vs. Henry Clay: Democracy and Development in Antebellum America* (1998).

On the Eaton affair, see John F. Marszalek's *The Petticoat Affair: Manners, Mutiny, and Sex in Andrew Jackson's White House* (1998). Two studies of the impact of the bank controversy are William G. Shade's *Banks or No Banks: The Money Issue in Western Politics, 1832–1865* (1972) and James Roger Sharp's *The Jacksonians versus the Banks: Politics in the States after the Panic of 1837* (1970).

The outstanding book on the nullification issue remains William W. Freehling's *Prelude to Civil War: The Nullification Controversy in South Carolina, 1816–1836* (1965). John M. Belohlavek's *"Let the Eagle Soar!": The Foreign Policy of Andrew Jackson* (1985) is a thorough study of Jacksonian diplomacy. Ronald N. Satz's *American Indian Policy in the Jacksonian Era* (1974) surveys the controversial relocation policy.

CHAPTER 12

On economic development in the nation's early decades, see Stuart Bruchey's *Enterprise: The Dynamic Economy of a Free People* (1990). The classic study of transportation and economic growth is George Rogers Taylor's *The Transportation Revolution, 1815–1860* (1951). A fresh view is provided in Sarah H. Gordon's *Passage to Union: How the Railroads Transformed American Life, 1829–1929* (1996). On the Erie Canal, see Carol Sheriff's *The Artificial River: The Erie Canal and the Paradox of Progress, 1817–1862* (1996).

The impact of technology is traced in David J. Jeremy's *Transatlantic Industrial Revolution: The Diffusion of Textile Technologies between Britain and America, 1790–1830s* (1981). On the invention of the telegraph, see Kenneth Silverman's *Lightning Man: The Accursed Life of Samuel F. B. Morse* (2003). For the story of steamboats, see Andrea Sutcliffe's *Steam: The Untold Story of America's First Great Invention* (2004). The best treatment of public works, such as the Erie Canal in the development of nineteenth-century America, is John Lauritz Larson's *Internal Improvement: National Public Works and the Promise of Popular Government in the Early United States* (2001).

Paul E. Johnson's *A Shopkeeper's Millenium: Society and Revivals in Rochester, New York, 1815–1837* (1978) studies the role religion played in the emerging industrial order. The attitude of the worker during this time of transition is surveyed in Edward E. Pessen's *Most Uncommon Jacksonians: The Radical Leaders of the Early Labor Movement* (1967). Detailed case studies of working communities include Anthony F. C. Wallace's *Rockdale: The Growth of an American Village in the Early Industrial Revolution* (1978), Thomas Dublin's *Women at Work: The Transformation of Work and Community in Lowell, Massachusetts, 1826–1860* (1979), and Sean Wilentz's *Chants Democratic: New York and the Rise of the American Working Class, 1788–1850* (1984). Walter Licht's *Working for the Railroad: The Organization of Work in the Nineteenth Century* (1983) is rich in detail.

For a fine treatment of urbanization, see Charles N. Glaab and A. Theodore Brown's *A History of Urban America* (1967). On immigration, see *The Irish in America,* edited by Michael Coffey with text by Terry Golway (1997).

CHAPTER 13

Russel Blaine Nye's *Society and Culture in America, 1830–1860* (1974) provides a wide-ranging survey of the Romantic movement. On the reform impulse, consult Ronald G. Walter's *American Reformers, 1815–1860,* rev. ed.

(1997). Revivalist religion is treated in Nathan O. Hatch's *The Democratization of American Christianity* (1989), Christine Leigh Heyrman's *Southern Cross: The Beginnings of the Bible Belt* (1997), and Ellen Eslinger's *Citizens of Zion: The Social Origins of Camp Meeting Revivalism* (1999). On the Mormons, see Leonard Arrington's *Brigham Young: American Moses* (1985).

The best treatments of transcendentalist thought are Paul F. Boller's *American Transcendentalism, 1830–1860: An Intellectual Inquiry* (1974) and Philip F. Gura's *American Transcendentalism: A History* (2007). Several good works describe various aspects of the antebellum reform movement. For temperance, see W. J. Rorabaugh's *The Alcoholic Republic: An American Tradition* (1979) and Barbara Leslie Epstein's *The Politics of Domesticity: Women, Evangelism, and Temperance in Nineteenth-Century America* (1981). Stephen Nissenbaum's *Sex, Diet, and Debility in Jacksonian America: Sylvester Graham and Health Reform* (1980) looks at a pioneering reformer concerned with diet and lifestyle. On prison reform and other humanitarian projects, see David J. Rothman's *The Discovery of the Asylum: Social Order and Disorder in the New Republic*, rev. ed. (2002), and Thomas J. Brown's biography *Dorothea Dix: New England Reformer* (1998). Lawrence A. Cremin's *American Education: The National Experience, 1783–1876* (1980) traces early school reform.

On women during the antebellum period, see Nancy F. Cott's *The Bonds of Womanhood: "Woman's Sphere" in New England, 1780–1835*, rev. ed. (1997), and Ellen C. DuBois's *Feminism and Suffrage: The Emergence of an Independent Women's Movement in America, 1848–1869* (1978). Michael Fellman's *The Unbounded Frame: Freedom and Community in Nineteenth-Century American Utopianism* (1973) surveys the utopian movements.

CHAPTER 14

For background on Whig programs and ideas, see Michael F. Holt's *The Rise and Fall of the American Whig Party: Jacksonian Politics and the Onset of the Civil War* (1999). On John Tyler, see Edward P. Crapol's *John Tyler: The Accidental President* (2006). Several works help interpret the expansionist impulse. Frederick Merk's *Manifest Destiny and Mission in American History: A Reinterpretation* (1963) remains a classic. A more recent treatment of expansionist ideology is Thomas R. Hietala's *Manifest Design: Anxious Aggrandizement in Late Jacksonian America* (1985).

The best survey of western expansion is Richard White's *"It's Your Misfortune and None of My Own": A New History of the American West* (1991). Robert M. Utley's *A Life Wild and Perilous: Mountain Men and the Paths to the Pacific* (1997) tells the dramatic story of the rugged pathfinders who discovered corridors over the Rocky Mountains. The movement of settlers to the West is ably documented in John Mack Faragher's *Women and Men on the Overland Trail,* 2nd ed. (2001), and David Dary's *The Santa Fe Trail: Its History, Legends, and Lore* (2000). On the tragic Donner party, see Ethan Rarick's *Desperate Passage: The Donner Party's Perilous Journey West* (2008).

Gene M. Brack's *Mexico Views Manifest Destiny, 1821–1846: An Essay on the Origins of the Mexican War* (1975) takes Mexico's viewpoint on U.S. designs on the West. For the American perspective on Texas, see Joel H. Silbey's *Storm over Texas: The Annexation Controversy and the Road to Civil War* (2005). On the siege of the Alamo, see William C. Davis's *Three Roads to the Alamo: The Lives and Fortunes of David Crockett, James Bowie, and William Barret Travis* (1998). An excellent biography related to the emergence of Texas is Gregg Cantrell's *Stephen F. Austin: Empresario of Texas* (1999). On James K. Polk, see John H. Schroeder's *Mr. Polk's War: American Opposition and Dissent, 1846–1848* (1973). The best survey of the military conflict is John S. D. Eisenhower's *So Far from God: The U.S. War with Mexico, 1846–1848* (1989). The Mexican War as viewed from the perspective of the soldiers is ably described in Richard Bruce Winders's *Mr. Polk's Army: American Military Experience in the Mexican War* (1997). On the diplomatic aspects of Mexican-American relations, see David M. Pletcher's *The Diplomacy of Annexation: Texas, Oregon, and the Mexican War* (1973).

CHAPTER 15

Those interested in the problem of discerning myth and reality in the southern experience should consult William R. Taylor's *Cavalier and Yankee: The Old South and American National Character* (1961). Three recent efforts to understand the mind of the Old South and its defense of slavery are Eugene D. Genovese's *The Slaveholders' Dilemma: Freedom and Progress in Southern Conservative Thought, 1820–1860* (1992), Eric H. Walther's *The Fire-Eaters* (1992), and William W. Freehling's *The Road to Disunion: Secessionists Triumphant, 1854–1861* (2007).

Contrasting analyses of the plantation system are Eugene D. Genovese's *The World the Slaveholders Made: Two Essays in Interpretation,* with a new introduction (1988), and Gavin Wright's *The Political Economy of the Cotton South: Households, Markets, and Wealth in the Nineteenth Century* (1978). Stephanie McCurry's *Masters of Small Worlds: Yeoman Households, Gender Relations, and the Political Culture of the Antebellum South Carolina Low Country* (1995) greatly enriches our understanding of southern households, religion, and political culture.

Other essential works on southern culture and society include Bertram Wyatt-Brown's *Honor and Violence in the Old South* (1986), Elizabeth Fox-Genovese's *Within the Plantation Household: Black and White Women of the Old South* (1988), Catherine Clinton's *The Plantation Mistress: Woman's World in the Old South* (1982), Joan E. Cashin's *A Family Venture: Men and Women on the Southern Frontier* (1991), and Theodore Rosengarten's *Tombee: Portrait of a Cotton Planter* (1986).

A provocative discussion of the psychology of African American slavery can be found in Stanley M. Elkins's *Slavery: A Problem in American Institutional and Intellectual Life,* 3rd ed. (1976). John W. Blassingame's *The Slave Community: Plantation Life in the Antebellum South,* rev. and enlarged ed. (1979), Eugene D. Genovese's *Roll, Jordan, Roll: The World the Slaves Made* (1974), and Herbert G. Gutman's *The Black Family in Slavery and Freedom, 1750–1925* (1976) all stress the theme of a persisting and identifiable slave culture. On the question of slavery's profitability, see Robert William Fogel and Stanley L. Engerman's *Time on the Cross: The Economics of American Negro Slavery* (1974).

Other works on slavery include Lawrence W. Levine's *Black Culture and Black Consciousness: Afro-American Folk Thought from Slavery to Freedom* (1977); Albert J. Raboteau's *Slave Religion: The "Invisible Institution" in the Antebellum South* (1978); *We Are Your Sisters: Black Women in the Nineteenth Century,* edited by Dorothy Sterling (1984); Deborah Gray White's *Ar'n't I a Woman? Female Slaves in the Plantation South,* rev. ed. (1999); and Joel Williamson's *The Crucible of Race: Black-White Relations in the American South since Emancipation* (1984). Charles Joyner's *Down by the Riverside: A South Carolina Slave Community* (1984) offers a vivid reconstruction of one community.

Useful surveys of abolitionism include James Brewer Stewart's *Holy Warriors: The Abolitionists and American Slavery,* rev. ed. (1997), and Julie Roy Jeffrey's *The Great Silent Army of Abolitionism: Ordinary Women in the Antislavery Movement* (1998). On William Lloyd Garrison, see Henry Mayer's *All on Fire: William Lloyd Garrison and the Abolition of Slavery* (1998). For the pro-slavery argument as it developed in the South, see Larry E. Tise's *Proslavery: A History of the Defense of Slavery in America, 1701–1840* (1987) and James Oakes's *The Ruling Race: A History of American Slaveholders* (1982). The problems southerners had in justifying slavery are explored in Kenneth S. Greenberg's *Masters and Statesmen: The Political Culture of American Slavery* (1985).

CHAPTER 16

The best surveys of the forces and events leading to the Civil War include James M. McPherson's *Battle Cry of Freedom: The Civil War Era* (1988), Stephen B. Oates's *The Approaching Fury: Voices of the Storm, 1820–1861* (1997), Bruce Levine's *Half Slave and Half Free: The Roots of Civil War* (1992), and David M. Potter's *The Impending Crisis, 1848–1861* (1976). The most recent narrative of the political debate leading to secession is Michael A. Morrison's *Slavery and the American West: The Eclipse of Manifest Destiny and the Coming of the Civil War* (1997).

Mark J. Stegmaier's *Texas, New Mexico, and the Compromise of 1850: Boundary Dispute and Sectional Crisis* (1996) probes that crucial dispute, while Michael F. Holt's *The Political Crisis of the 1850s* (1978) traces the demise of the Whigs. Eric Foner, in *Free Soil, Free Labor, Free Men: The Ideology of the Republican Party before the Civil War* (1970), shows how events and ideas combined in the formation of a new political party. A more straightforward study of the rise of the Republicans is William E. Gienapp's *The Origins of the Republican Party, 1852–1856* (1987). The economic, social, and political crises of 1857 are examined in Kenneth M. Stampp's *America in 1857: A Nation on the Brink* (1990). On the Anthony Burns case, see Albert J. von Frank's *The Trials of Anthony Burns: Freedom and Slavery in Emerson's Boston* (1998). The *Dred Scott* case is ably assessed in Earl M. Maltz's *Dred Scott and the Politics of Slavery* (2007). For an assessment of the Revival of 1857–1858, see Kathryn Teresa Long, *The Revival of 1857–1858: Interpreting an American Religious Awakening* (1998).

Robert W. Johannsen's *Stephen A. Douglas* (1973) analyzes the issue of popular sovereignty. A more national perspective is provided in James A. Rawley's *Race and Politics: "Bleeding Kansas" and the Coming of the Civil War* (1969). On the role of John Brown in the sectional crisis, see Stephen B. Oates's *To Purge This Land with Blood: A Biography of John Brown* (1970) and David S. Reynolds's *John Brown, Abolitionist: The Man Who Killed Slavery, Sparked the Civil War, and Seeded Civil Rights* (2005). An excellent study of the South's journey to secession is William W. Freehling's *The Road to Disunion*, vol. 1, *Secessionists at Bay, 1776–1854* (1990), and *The Road to Disunion*, vol. 2, *Secessionists Triumphant, 1854–1861* (2007).

On the Buchanan presidency, see Jean H. Baker's *James Buchanan* (2004). On Lincoln's role in the coming crisis of war, see Don E. Fehrenbacher's *Prelude to Greatness: Lincoln in the 1850s* (1962). Harry V. Jaffa's *Crisis of the House Divided: An Interpretation of the Issues in the Lincoln-Douglas Debate*, 50th anniversary ed. (2009), details the debates, and Maury Klein's *Days of Defiance: Sumter, Secession, and the Coming of the Civil War* (1997) treats the

Fort Sumter controversy. An excellent collection of interpretive essays is *Why the Civil War Came* (1996), edited by Gabor S. Boritt.

CHAPTER 17

The best one-volume overview of the Civil War period is James M. McPherson's *Battle Cry of Freedom: The Civil War Era* (1988). A good introduction to the military events is Herman Hattaway's *Shades of Blue and Gray: An Introductory Military History of the Civil War* (1997). The outlook and experiences of the common soldier are explored in James M. McPherson's *For Cause and Comrades: Why Men Fought in the Civil War* (1997) and Earl J. Hess's *The Union Soldier in Battle: Enduring the Ordeal of Combat* (1997).

For emphasis on the South, turn first to Gary W. Gallagher's *The Confederate War* (1997). For a sparkling account of the birth of the Rebel nation, see William C. Davis's *"A Government of Our Own": The Making of the Confederacy* (1994). The same author provides a fine biography of the Confederate president in *Jefferson Davis: The Man and His Hour* (1991). On the best Confederate commander, see John M. Taylor's *Duty Faithfully Performed: Robert E. Lee and His Critics* (1999). On the key Union generals, see Lee Kennett's *Sherman: A Soldier's Life* (2001) and Josiah Bunting III's *Ulysses S. Grant* (2004).

Analytical scholarship on the military conflict includes Joseph L. Harsh's *Confederate Tide Rising: Robert E. Lee and the Making of Southern Strategy, 1861–1862* (1998), Steven E. Woodworth's *Jefferson Davis and His Generals: The Failure of Confederate Command in the West* (1990), and Paul D. Casdorph's *Lee and Jackson: Confederate Chieftains* (1992). Lonnie R. Speer's *Portals to Hell: Military Prisons of the Civil War* (1997) details the ghastly experience of prisoners of war.

The history of the North during the war is surveyed in Philip Shaw Paludan's *A People's Contest: The Union and Civil War, 1861–1865,* 2nd ed. (1996), and J. Matthew Gallman's *The North Fights the Civil War: The Home Front* (1994).

The central northern political figure, Abraham Lincoln, is the subject of many books. See Harry V. Jaffa's *A New Birth of Freedom: Abraham Lincoln and the Coming of the Civil War* (2000). On Lincoln's great speeches, see Ronald C. White Jr.'s *The Eloquent President: A Portrait of Lincoln through His Words* (2005). The election of 1864 is treated in John C. Waugh's *Reelecting Lincoln: The Battle for the 1864 Presidency* (1997). On Lincoln's assassination, see William Hanchett's *The Lincoln Murder Conspiracies* (1983).

Concerning specific military campaigns, see Larry J. Daniel's *Shiloh: The Battle That Changed the Civil War* (1997), Thomas Goodrich's *Black*

Flag: Guerrilla Warfare on the Western Border, 1861–1865 (1995), Stephen W. Sears's *To the Gates of Richmond: The Peninsula Campaign* (1992), James M. McPherson's *Crossroads of Freedom: Antietam* (2002), James Lee McDonough and James Pickett Jones's *"War So Terrible": Sherman and Atlanta* (1987), Robert Garth Scott's *Into the Wilderness with the Army of the Potomac*, rev. and enl. ed. (1992), Albert Castel's *Decision in the West: The Atlanta Campaign of 1864* (1992), and Ernest B. Furgurson's *Not War but Murder: Cold Harbor, 1864* (2000). On the final weeks of the war, see William C. Davis's *An Honorable Defeat: The Last Days of the Confederate Government* (2001).

The experience of the African American soldier is surveyed in Joseph T. Glatthaar's *Forged in Battle: The Civil War Alliance of Black Soldiers and White Officers* (1990) and Ira Berlin, Joseph P. Reidy, and Leslie S. Rowland's *Freedom's Soldiers: The Black Military Experience in the Civil War* (1998). For the African American woman's experience, see Jacqueline Jones's *Labor of Love, Labor of Sorrow: Black Women, Work and the Family, from Slavery to the Present* (1985).

Recent gender and ethnic studies include *Divided Houses: Gender and the Civil War*, edited by Catherine Clinton and Nina Silber (1992), Drew Gilpin Faust's *Mothers of Invention: Women of the Slaveholding South in the American Civil War* (1996), George C. Rable's *Civil Wars: Women and the Crisis of Southern Nationalism* (1989), and William L. Burton's *Melting Pot Soldiers: The Union's Ethnic Regiments*, 2nd ed. (1998).

CHAPTER 18

The most comprehensive treatment of Reconstruction is Eric Foner's *Reconstruction: America's Unfinished Revolution, 1863–1877* (1988). On Andrew Johnson, see Hans L. Trefousse's *Andrew Johnson: A Biography* (1989). An excellent brief biography of Grant is Josiah Bunting III's *Ulysses S. Grant* (2004).

Scholars have been sympathetic to the aims and motives of the Radical Republicans. See, for instance, Herman Belz's *Reconstructing the Union: Theory and Policy during the Civil War* (1969) and Richard Nelson Current's *Those Terrible Carpetbaggers: A Reinterpretation* (1988). The ideology of the Radicals is explored in Michael Les Benedict's *A Compromise of Principle: Congressional Republicans and Reconstruction, 1863–1869* (1974). On the black political leaders, see Phillip Dray's *Capitol Men: The Epic Story of Reconstruction through the Lives of the First Black Congressmen* (2008).

The intransigence of southern white attitudes is examined in Michael Perman's *Reunion without Compromise: The South and Reconstruction, 1865–1868* (1973) and Dan T. Carter's *When the War Was Over: The Failure of*

Self-Reconstruction in the South, 1865–1867 (1985). Allen W. Trelease's *White Terror: The Ku Klux Klan Conspiracy and Southern Reconstruction* (1971) covers the various organizations that practiced vigilante tactics. On the massacre of African Americans, see Charles Lane's *The Day Freedom Died: The Colfax Massacre, the Supreme Court, and the Betrayal of Reconstruction* (2008). The difficulties former slaves had in adjusting to the new labor system are documented in James L. Roark's *Masters without Slaves: Southern Planters in the Civil War and Reconstruction* (1977). Books on southern politics during Reconstruction include Michael Perman's *The Road to Redemption: Southern Politics, 1869–1879* (1984), Terry L. Seip's *The South Returns to Congress: Men, Economic Measures, and Intersectional Relationships, 1868–1879* (1983), and Mark W. Summers's *Railroads, Reconstruction, and the Gospel of Prosperity: Aid under the Radical Republicans, 1865–1877* (1984).

Numerous works study the freed blacks' experience in the South. Start with Leon F. Litwack's *Been in the Storm So Long: The Aftermath of Slavery* (1979). Joel Williamson's *After Slavery: The Negro in South Carolina during Reconstruction, 1861–1877* (1965) argues that South Carolina blacks took an active role in pursuing their political and economic rights. The Freedmen's Bureau is explored in William S. McFeely's *Yankee Stepfather: General O. O. Howard and the Freedmen* (1968). The situation of freed slave women is discussed in Jacqueline Jones's *Labor of Love, Labor of Sorrow: Black Women, Work and the Family, from Slavery to the Present* (1985).

The politics of corruption outside the South is depicted in William S. McFeely's *Grant: A Biography* (1981). The political maneuvers of the election of 1876 and the resultant crisis and compromise are explained in C. Vann Woodward's *Reunion and Reaction: The Compromise of 1877 and the End of Reconstruction* (1951) and in William Gillette's *Retreat from Reconstruction, 1869–1879* (1979). The role of religion in determining the fate of Reconstruction is the focus of Edward J. Blum's *Reforging the White Republic: Race, Religion, and American Nationalism, 1865–1898* (2005).

CHAPTER 19

The classic study of the emergence of the New South remains C. Vann Woodward's *Origins of the New South, 1877–1913* (1951). A more recent treatment of southern society after the end of Reconstruction is Edward L. Ayers's *Southern Crossing: A History of the American South, 1877–1906* (1995). A good survey of industrialization in the South is James C. Cobb's *Industrialization and Southern Society, 1877–1984* (1984).

C. Vann Woodward's *The Strange Career of Jim Crow,* commemorative ed. (2002), remains the standard on southern race relations. Some of Woodward's points are challenged in Howard N. Rabinowitz's *Race Relations in the Urban South, 1865–1890* (1978). Leon F. Litwack's *Trouble in Mind: Black Southerners in the Age of Jim Crow* (1998) treats the rise of legal segregation, while Michael Perman's *Struggle for Mastery: Disfranchisement in the South, 1888–1908* (2001) surveys efforts to keep African Americans from voting. An award-winning study of white women and the race issue is Glenda Elizabeth Gilmore's *Gender and Jim Crow: Women and the Politics of White Supremacy in North Carolina, 1896–1920* (1996). On W. E. B. Du Bois, see David Levering Lewis's *W. E. B. Du Bois: Biography of a Race, 1868–1919* (1993).

For stimulating reinterpretations of the frontier and the development of the West, see William Cronon's *Nature's Metropolis: Chicago and the Great West* (1991), Patricia Nelson Limerick's *The Legacy of Conquest: The Unbroken Past of the American West* (1987), Richard White's *"It's Your Misfortune and None of My Own": A New History of the American West* (1991), and Walter Nugent's *Into the West: The Story of Its People* (1999). An excellent overview is James M. McPherson's *Into the West: From Reconstruction to the Final Days of the American Frontier* (2006).

The role of African Americans in western settlement is the focus of William Loren Katz's *The Black West: A Documentary and Pictorial History of the African American Role in the Westward Expansion of the United States,* rev. ed. (2005), and Nell Irvin Painter's *Exodusters: Black Migration to Kansas after Reconstruction* (1977). The best account of the conflicts between Indians and whites is Robert M. Utley's *The Indian Frontier of the American West, 1846–1890* (1984). On Sitting Bull, see Utley's *The Lance and the Shield: The Life and Times of Sitting Bull* (1993). For a presentation of the Native American side of the story, see Peter Nabokov's *Native American Testimony: A Chronicle of Indian-White Relations from Prophecy to the Present, 1492–2000,* rev. ed. (1999). On the demise of the buffalo herds, see Andrew C. Isenberg's *The Destruction of the Bison: An Environmental History, 1750–1920* (2000).

CHAPTER 20

For masterly syntheses of post–Civil War industrial development, see Walter Licht's *Industrializing America: The Nineteenth Century* (1995) and Maury Klein's *The Genesis of Industrial America, 1870–1920* (2007). On the growth of railroads, see Albro Martin's *Railroad Triumphant: The Growth, Rejection, and Rebirth of a Vital American Force* (1992). A monumental study of the transcontinental railroad is David Haward Bain's *Empire Express: Building the First Transcontinental Railroad* (1999). On the 1877 railroad strike, see David O. Stowell's *Streets, Railroad, and the Great Strike of 1877* (1999).

On entrepreneurship in the iron and steel sector, and Thomas J. Misa's *A Nation of Steel: The Making of Modern America, 1865–1925* (1995). The best biographies of the leading business tycoons are Ron Chernow's *Titan: The Life of John D. Rockefeller, Sr.* (1998), David Nasaw's *Andrew Carnegie* (2006), and Jean Strouse's *Morgan: American Financier* (1999). Nathan Rosenberg's *Technology and American Economic Growth* (1972) documents the growth of invention during the period.

Much of the scholarship on labor stresses the traditional values and the culture of work that people brought to the factory, Hebert G. Gutman's *Work, Culture, and Society in Industrializing America: Essays in American Working-Class and Social History* (1975) best introduces these themes. The leading survey remains David Montgomery's *The Fall of the House of Labor: The Workplace, the State, and American Labor Activism, 1865–1925* (1987).

For the role of women in the changing workplace, see Alice Kessler-Harris's *Out to Work: A History of Wage-Earning Women in the United States* (1982) and Susan E. Kennedy's *If All We Did Was to Weep at Home: A History of White Working-Class Women in American* (1979).

As for the labor unions, Gerald N. Grob's *Workers and Utopia: A Study of Ideological Conflict in the American Labor Movement, 1865–1900* (1961) examines the difference in outlook between the Knights of Labor and the American Federation of Labor. For the Knights, see Leon Fink's *Workingmen's Democracy: The Knights of Labor and American Politics* (1983). Also useful is Susan Levine's *Labor's True Woman: Carpet Weavers, Industrialization, and Labor Reform in the Gilded Age* (1984), on the role of women in the Knights. On Mother Jones, see Elliott J. Gorn's *Mother Jones: The Most Dangerous Woman in America* (2001). To trace the rise of socialism among organized workers, see Nick Salvatore's *Eugene V. Debs: Citizen and Socialist* (1982). The key strikes are discussed in Paul Arvich's *The Haymarket Tragedy* (1984) and Paul Krause's *The Battle for Homestead, 1880–1892: Politics, Culture, and Steel* (1992).

CHAPTER 21

For a survey of urbanization, see David R. Goldfield's *Urban America: A History*, 2nd ed. (1989). Gunther Barth discusses the emergence of a new urban culture in *City People: The Rise of Modern City Culture in Nineteenth-Century America* (1980). John Bodnar offers a synthesis of the urban immigrant experience in *The Transplanted: A History of Immigrants in Urban America* (1985). See also Roger Daniels's *Guarding the Golden Door: American Immigration Policy and Immigrants since 1882* (2004). Walter Nugent's *Crossings: The Great Transatlantic Migrations, 1870–1914* (1992) provides a wealth of demographic information and insight. Efforts to stop Chinese immigration are described in Erika Lee's *At America's Gates: Chinese Immigration during the Exclusion Era* (2003).

On urban environments and sanitary reforms, see Martin V. Melosi's *The Sanitary City: Urban Infrastructure in America from Colonial Times to the Present* (2000), Joel A. Tarr's *The Search for the Ultimate Sink: Urban Pollution in Historical Perspective* (1996), and Suellen Hoy's *Chasing Dirt: The American Pursuit of Cleanliness* (1995).

For the growth of urban leisure and sports, see Roy Rosenzweig's *Eight Hours for What We Will: Workers and Leisure in an Industrial City, 1870–1920* (1983) and Steven A. Riess's *City Games: The Evolution of American Urban Society and the Rise of Sports* (1989). Saloon culture is examined in Madelon Powers's *Faces along the Bar: Lore and Order in the Workingman's Saloon, 1870–1920* (1998).

Richard Hofstadter's *Social Darwinism in American Thought,* rev. ed. (1969), and Cynthia Eagle Russett's *Darwin in America: The Intellectual Response, 1865–1912* (1976) examine the impact of the theory of evolution. On the rise of realism in thought and the arts during the second half of the nineteenth century, see David E. Shi's *Facing Facts: Realism in American Thought and Culture, 1850–1920* (1995). Pragmatism is the focus of Louis Menand's *The Metaphysical Club: A Story of Ideas in America* (2001).

Eleanor Flexner and Ellen Fitzpatrick's *Century of Struggle: The Woman's Rights Movement in the United States,* enl. ed. (1996), surveys the condition of women in the late nineteenth century. The best study of the settlement house movement is Jean Bethke Elshtain's *Jane Addams and the Dream of American Democracy: A Life* (2002).

CHAPTER 22

A good overview of the Gilded Age is Vincent P. De Santis's *The Shaping of Modern America, 1877–1916* (1973). Nell Irvin Painter's *Standing at Armageddon: The United States, 1877–1919* (1987) focuses on the experience of the working class. For a stimulating overview of the political, social, and economic trends during the Gilded Age, see Jack Beatty's *Age of Betrayal: The*

Triumph of Money in America, 1865–1900 (2007). On the development of city rings and bosses, see Kenneth D. Ackerman's *Boss Tweed: The Rise and Fall of the Corrupt Pol Who Conceived the Soul of Modern New York* (2005). Excellent presidential biographies include Hans L. Trefousse's *Rutherford B. Hayes* (2002), Zachary Karabell's *Chester Alan Arthur* (2004), Henry F. Graff's *Grover Cleveland* (2002), and Kevin Phillips's *William McKinley* (2003).

Scholars have also examined various Gilded Age issues and interest groups. Gerald W. McFarland's *Mugwumps, Morals, and Politics, 1884–1920* (1975) examines the issue of reforming government service. Tom E. Terrill's *The Tariff, Politics, and American Foreign Policy, 1874–1901* (1973) lends clarity to that complex issue. The finances of the Gilded Age are covered in Walter T. K. Nugent's *Money and American Society, 1865–1880* (1968).

One of the most controversial works on populism is Lawrence Goodwyn's *The Populist Movement: A Short History of the Agrarian Revolt in America* (1978). A more balanced account is Robert C. McMath Jr.'s *American Populism: A Social History, 1877–1898* (1992). On the role of religion in the agrarian protest movements, see Joe Creech's *Righteous Indignation: Religion and the Populist Revolution* (2006). The best biography of Bryan is Michael Kazin's *A Godly Hero: The Life of William Jennings Bryan* (2006).

CHAPTER 23

An excellent survey of the diplomacy of the era is Charles S. Campbell's *The Transformation of American Foreign Relations, 1865–1900* (1976). For background on the events of the 1890s, see Walter LaFeber's *The American Search for Opportunity, 1865–1913* (1993) and David Healy's *U.S. Expansionism: The Imperialist Urge in the 1890s* (1970). The dispute over American policy in Hawaii is covered in Thomas J. Osborne's *"Empire Can Wait": American Opposition to Hawaiian Annexation, 1893–1898* (1981).

Ivan Musicant's *Empire by Default: The Spanish-American War and the Dawn of the American Century* (1998) is the most comprehensive volume on the conflict. For the war's aftermath in the Philippines, see Stuart Creighton Miller's *"Benevolent Assimilation": The American Conquest of the Philippines, 1899–1903* (1982). Robert L. Beisner's *Twelve against Empire: The Anti-Imperialists, 1898–1900* (1968) handles the debate over annexation. On the Philippine-American War, see David J. Silbey's *A War of Frontier and Empire: The Philippine-American War, 1899–1902* (2007).

A good introduction to American interest in China is Michael H. Hunt's *The Making of a Special Relationship: The United States and China to 1914* (1983). Kenton J. Clymer's *John Hay: The Gentleman as Diplomat* (1975) examines the role of this key secretary of state in forming policy.

For U.S. policy in the Caribbean and Central America, see Walter LaFeber's *Inevitable Revolutions: The United States in Central America*, 2nd ed. (1993). David McCullough's *The Path between the Seas: The Creation of the Panama Canal, 1870–1914* (1977) presents the fullest account of how the United States secured the Panama Canal.

CHAPTER 24

A splendid analysis of progressivism is John Whiteclay Chambers II's *The Tyranny of Change: America in the Progressive Era, 1890–1920*, rev. ed. (2000). On Ida Tarbell and the muckrakers, see Steve Weinberg's *Taking on the Trust: The Epic Battle of Ida Tarbell and John D. Rockefeller* (2008). The evolution of government policy toward business is examined in Martin J. Sklar's *The Corporate Reconstruction of American Capitalism, 1890–1916: The Market, the Law, and Politics* (1988). Mina Carson's *Settlement Folk: Social Thought and the American Settlement Movement, 1885–1930* (1990) and Jack M. Holl's *Juvenile Reform in the Progressive Era: William R. George and the Junior Republic Movement* (1971) examine the social problems in the cities. An excellent study of the role of women in progressivism's emphasis on social justice is Kathryn Kish Sklar's *Florence Kelley and the Nation's Work: The Rise of Women's Political Culture, 1830–1900* (1995). On the tragic fire at the Triangle Shirtwaist Company, see David Von Drehle's *Triangle: The Fire That Changed America* (2003).

There is a rich body of scholarship focused on the conservation movement. See especially Rebecca Conard's *Places of Quiet Beauty: Parks, Preserves, and Environmentalism* (1997), Samuel P. Hays's *Conservation and the Gospel of Efficiency: The Progressive Conservation Movement, 1890–1920* (1959), Karl Jacoby's *Crimes against Nature: Squatters, Poachers, Thieves, and the Hidden History of American Conservation* (2001), John F. Reiger's *American Sportsmen and the Origins of Conservation* (1975), and Ted Steinberg's *Down to Earth: Nature's Role in American History* (2002). Robert Kanigel's *The One Best Way: Frederick Winslow Taylor and the Enigma of Efficiency* (1997) highlights the role of efficiency in the Progressive Era.

On the pivotal election of 1912, see James Chace's *1912: Wilson, Roosevelt, Taft, and Debs—The Election That Changed the Country* (2004). Excellent biographies include Kathleen Dalton's *Theodore Roosevelt: A Strenuous Life* (2002) and H. W. Brands's *Woodrow Wilson* (2003). For banking developments, see Allan H. Meltzer's *A History of the Federal Reserve*, vol. 1, *1913–1951* (2003).

CHAPTER 25

A lucid overview of international events covered in this chapter is Robert H. Ferrell's *Woodrow Wilson and World War I, 1917–1921* (1985). On Wilson's stance toward war, see Ross Gregory's *The Origins of American Intervention in the First World War* (1971). An excellent brief biography is H. W. Brands's *Woodrow Wilson* (2003).

Edward M. Coffman's *The War to End All Wars: The American Military Experience in World War I* (1968) is a detailed presentation of America's military involvement. See also Gary Mead's *The Doughboys: America and the First World War* (2000). David M. Kennedy's *Over Here: The First World War and American Society* (1980) surveys the impact of the war on the home front, as does Meirion Harries and Susie Harries's *The Last Days of Innocence: America at War, 1917–1918* (1997). One of the best overviews of the European context of the war is John Keegan, *The First World War* (1998). Maurine Weiner Greenwald's *Women, War, and Work: The Impact of World War I on Women Workers in the United States* (1980) discusses the role of women. Ronald Schaffer's *America in the Great War: The Rise of the War Welfare State* (1991) shows the effect of war mobilization on business organization. Richard Polenberg's *Fighting Faiths: The Abrams Case, the Supreme Court, and Free Speech* (1987) examines the prosecution of a case under the 1918 Sedition Act.

How American diplomacy fared in the making of peace has received considerable attention. Thomas J. Knock interrelates domestic affairs and foreign relations in his explanation of Wilson's peacemaking in *To End All Wars: Woodrow Wilson and the Quest for a New World Order* (1992).

The problems of the immediate postwar years are chronicled by a number of historians. The best overview is Ann Hagedorn's *Savage Peace: Hope and Fear in America, 1919* (2007). On the Spanish flu, see John M. Barry's *The Great Influenza: The Epic Story of the Deadliest Plague in History* (2004). Labor tensions are examined in David E. Brody's *Labor in Crisis: The Steel Strike of 1919* (1965) and Francis Russell's *A City in Terror: Calvin Coolidge and the 1919 Boston Police Strike* (1975). On racial strife, see William M. Tuttle Jr.'s *Race Riot: Chicago in the Red Summer of 1919* (1970). The fear of

Communists is analyzed in Robert K. Murray's *Red Scare: A Study in National Hysteria, 1919–1920* (1955).

CHAPTER 26

For a lively survey of the social and cultural changes during the interwar period, start with William E. Leuchtenburg's *The Perils of Prosperity, 1914–32*, 2nd ed. (1993). The best introduction to the culture of the 1920s remains Loren Baritz's *The Culture of the Twenties* (1970). See also Lynn Dumenil's *The Modern Temper: American Culture and Society in the 1920s* (1995).

John Higham's *Strangers in the Land: Patterns of American Nativism, 1860–1925*, 2nd ed. (2002) details the story of immigration restriction. The controversial Sacco and Vanzetti case is thoroughly explored in *Kill Now, Talk Forever: Debating Sacco and Vanzetti*, edited by Richard Newby (2001). For analysis of the revival of Klan activity, see Nancy MacLean's *Behind the Mask of Chivalry: The Making of the Second Ku Klux Klan* (1994). The best analysis of the Scopes trial is Edward J. Larson's *Summer for the Gods: The Scopes Trial and America's Continuing Debate over Science and Religion* (1997). On Prohibition, see Michael A. Lerner's *Dry Manhattan: Prohibition in New York City* (2007).

Women's suffrage is treated extensively in Eleanor Flexner and Ellen Fitzpatrick's *Century of Struggle: The Woman's Rights Movement in the United States*, enlarged ed. (1996). The best study of the birth-control movement is Ellen Chesler's *Woman of Valor: Margaret Sanger and the Birth Control Movement in America* (1992). See Charles Flint Kellogg's *NAACP: A History of the National Association for the Advancement of Colored People* (1967) for his analysis of the pioneering court cases against racial discrimination. Nathan Irvin Huggins's *Harlem Renaissance* (1971) assesses the cultural impact of the Great Migration on New York City. The emergence of jazz is ably documented in Burton W. Peretti's *The Creation of Jazz: Music, Race, and Culture in Urban America* (1992). On the African American migration to Chicago, see James R. Grossman's *Land of Hope: Chicago, Black Southerners, and the Great Migration* (1989). Nicholas Lemann's *The Promised Land: The Great Black Migration and How It Changed America* (1991) is a fine exposition of the changes brought about by the migration in both the South and the North.

On southern modernism, see Daniel Joseph Singal's *The War Within: From Victorian to Modernist Thought in the South, 1919–1945* (1982). Stanley Coben's *Rebellion against Victorianism: The Impetus for Cultural Change in*

1920s America (1991) surveys the appeal of modernism among writers, artists, and intellectuals.

CHAPTER 27

A fine synthesis of events immediately following the First World War is Ellis W. Hawley's *The Great War and the Search for a Modern Order: A History of the American People and Their Institutions, 1917–1933*, 2nd ed. (1992). On the election of 1920, see David Pietrusza, *1920: The Year of the Six Presidents* (2006).

On Harding, see Robert K. Murray's *The Harding Era: Warren G. Harding and His Administration* (1969). On Coolidge, see Robert H. Ferrell's *The Presidency of Calvin Coolidge* (1998). On Hoover, see Martin L. Fausold's *The Presidency of Herbert C. Hoover* (1985). The Democratic candidate for president in 1928 is explored in Robert A. Slayton's *Empire Statesman: The Rise and Redemption of Al Smith* (2001). The influential secretary of the Treasury during the 1920s is ably analyzed in David Cannadine's *Mellon: An American Life* (2006).

Overviews of the depressed economy are found in Charles P. Kindleberger's *The World in Depression, 1929–1939*, rev. and enlarged ed. (1986) and Peter Fearon's *War, Prosperity, and Depression: The U.S. Economy, 1917–1945* (1987). John A. Garraty's *The Great Depression: An Inquiry into the Causes, Course, and Consequences of the Worldwide Depression of the Nineteen-Thirties* (1986) describes how people survived the Depression. On the removal of the Bonus Army, see Paul Dickson and Thomas B. Allen's *The Bonus Army: An American Epic* (2004).

CHAPTER 28

A comprehensive overview of the New Deal is David M. Kennedy's *Freedom from Fear: The American People in Depression and War, 1929–1945* (1999). On the critics of the New Deal, see Alan Brinkley's *Voices of Protest: Huey Long, Father Coughlin, and the Great Depression* (1982).

James N. Gregory's *American Exodus: The Dust Bowl Migration and Okie Culture in California* (1989) describes the migratory movement's effect on American culture. On the environmental and human causes of the dust bowl, see Donald Worster, *Dust Bowl: The Southern Plains in the 1930s* (1979).

Chapter 29

The best overview of interwar diplomacy remains Selig Adler's *The Uncertain Giant, 1921–1941: American Foreign Policy between the Wars* (1965). Joan Hoff's *American Business and Foreign Policy, 1920–1933* (1971) highlights the efforts of Republican administrations during the 1920s to promote international commerce. Robert Dallek's *Franklin D. Roosevelt and American Foreign Policy, 1932–1945* (1979) provides a judicious assessment of Roosevelt's foreign policy during the 1930s.

A noteworthy study is Waldo Heinrichs's *Threshold of War: Franklin D. Roosevelt and American Entry into World War II* (1988). See also David Reynolds's *From Munich to Pearl Harbor: Roosevelt's America and the Origins of the Second World War* (2001). Bruce M. Russett's *No Clear and Present Danger: A Skeptical View of the United States Entry into World War II*, 25th anniversary ed. (1997), provides a critical account of American actions.

On Pearl Harbor, see Gordon W. Prange's *Pearl Harbor: The Verdict of History* (1986). Japan's perspective is described in Akira Iriye's *The Origins of the Second World War in Asia and the Pacific* (1987).

Chapter 30

John Keegan's *The Second World War* (1989) surveys the European conflict, while Charles B. MacDonald's *The Mighty Endeavor: The American War in Europe* (1986) concentrates on U.S. involvement. Roosevelt's wartime leadership is analyzed in Eric Larrabee's *Commander in Chief: Franklin Delano Roosevelt, His Lieutenants, and Their War* (1987).

Books on specific European campaigns include Stephen E. Ambrose's *D-Day, June 6, 1944: The Climactic Battle of World War II* (1994) and Charles B. MacDonald's *A Time for Trumpets: The Untold Story of the Battle of the Bulge* (1985). On the Allied commander, see Carlo D'Este's *Eisenhower: A Soldier's Life* (2002).

For the war in the Far East, see John Costello's *The Pacific War, 1941–1945* (1981), Ronald H. Spector's *Eagle against the Sun: The American War with Japan* (1985), John W. Dower's award-winning *War without Mercy: Race and Power in the Pacific War* (1986), and Dan van der Vat's *The Pacific Campaign: The U.S.-Japanese Naval War, 1941–1945* (1991).

An excellent overview of the war's effects on the home front is Michael C. C. Adams's *The Best War Ever: America and World War II* (1994). On economic effects, see Harold G. Vatter's *The U.S. Economy in World War II* (1985).

Susan M. Hartmann's *The Home Front and Beyond: American Women in the 1940s* (1982) treats the new working environment for women. Neil A. Wynn looks at the participation of blacks in *The Afro-American and the Second World War* (1976). The story of the oppression of Japanese Americans is told in Peter Irons's *Justice at War: The Story of the Japanese American Internment Cases* (1983).

A sound introduction to U.S. diplomacy during the conflict can be found in Gaddis Smith's *American Diplomacy during the Second World War, 1941–1945* (1965). To understand the role that Roosevelt played in policy making, consult Warren F. Kimball's *The Juggler: Franklin Roosevelt as Wartime Statesman* (1991).

The issues and events that led to the deployment of atomic weapons are addressed in Martin J. Sherwin's *A World Destroyed: The Atomic Bomb and the Grand Alliance* (1975).

CHAPTER 31

The cold war remains a hotly debated topic. The traditional interpretation is best reflected in John Lewis Gaddis's *The United States and the Origins of the Cold War, 1941–1947* (1972) and *We Now Know: Rethinking Cold War History* (1997). Both superpowers, Gaddis argues, were responsible for causing the cold war, but the Soviet Union was more culpable. The revisionist perspective is represented by Gar Alperovitz's *Atomic Diplomacy: Hiroshima and Potsdam: The Use of the Atomic Bomb and the American Confrontation with Soviet Power*, 2nd ed. (1994). Alperovitz places primary responsibility for the conflict on the United States. Also see H. W. Brands's *The Devil We Knew: Americans and the Cold War* (1993) and Melvyn P. Leffler's *A Preponderance of Power: National Security, the Truman Administration, and the Cold War* (1992). On the architect of containment, see David Mayers's *George Kennan and the Dilemmas of U.S. Foreign Policy* (1988).

Arnold A. Offner indicts Truman for clumsy statesmanship in *Another Such Victory: President Truman and the Cold War, 1945–1953* (2002). For a positive assessment of Truman's leadership, see Alonzo L. Hamby's *Beyond the New Deal: Harry S. Truman and American Liberalism* (1973). The domestic policies of the Fair Deal are treated in William C. Berman's *The Politics of Civil Rights in the Truman Administration* (1970), Richard M. Dalfiume's *Desegregation of the U.S. Armed Forces: Fighting on Two Fronts, 1939–1953* (1969), and Maeva Marcus's *Truman and the Steel Seizure Case: The Limits of*

Presidential Power (1977). The most comprehensive biography of Truman is David McCullough's *Truman* (1992).

For an introduction to the tensions in Asia, see Akira Iriye's *The Cold War in Asia: A Historical Introduction* (1974). For the Korean conflict, see Callum A. MacDonald's *Korea: The War before Vietnam* (1986) and Max Hasting's *The Korean War* (1987).

The anti-Communist syndrome is surveyed in David Caute's *The Great Fear: The Anti-Communist Purge under Truman and Eisenhower* (1978). Arthur Herman's *Joseph McCarthy: Reexamining the Life and Legacy of America's Most Hated Senator* (2000) covers McCarthy himself. For a well-documented account of how the cold war was sustained by superpatriotism, intolerance, and suspicion, see Stephen J. Whitfield's *The Culture of the Cold War*, 2nd ed. (1996).

CHAPTER 32

Two excellent overviews of social and cultural trends in the postwar era are William H. Chafe's *The Unfinished Journey: America since World War II*, 6th ed. (2006), and William E. Leuchtenburg's *A Troubled Feast: America since 1945*, rev. ed. (1979). For insights into the cultural life of the 1950s, see Jeffrey Hart's *When the Going Was Good! American Life in the Fifties* (1982) and David Halberstam's *The Fifties* (1993).

The baby boom generation and its impact are vividly described in Paul C. Light's *Baby Boomers* (1988). The emergence of the television industry is discussed in Erik Barnouw's *Tube of Plenty: The Evolution of American Television*, 2nd rev. ed. (1990), and Ella Taylor's *Prime-Time Families: Television Culture in Postwar America* (1989).

A comprehensive account of the process of suburban development is Kenneth T. Jackson's *Crabgrass Frontier: The Suburbanization of the United States* (1985). Equally good is Tom Martinson's *American Dreamscape: The Pursuit of Happiness in Postwar Suburbia* (2000).

The middle-class ideal of family life in the 1950s is examined in Elaine Tyler May's *Homeward Bound: American Families in the Cold War Era*, rev. ed. (2008). Thorough accounts of women's issues are found in Wini Breines's *Young, White, and Miserable: Growing Up Female in the Fifties* (1992). For an overview of the resurgence of religion in the 1950s, see George M. Marsden's *Religion and American Culture*, 2nd ed. (2000).

A lively discussion of movies of the 1950s can be found in Peter Biskind's *Seeing Is Believing: How Hollywood Taught Us to Stop Worrying and Love the*

Fifties (1983). The origins and growth of rock and roll are surveyed in Carl Belz's *The Story of Rock,* 2nd ed. (1972). Thoughtful interpretive surveys of postwar literature include Josephine Hendin's *Vulnerable People: A View of American Fiction since 1945* (1978) and Malcolm Bradbury's *The Modern American Novel* (1983). The colorful Beats are brought to life in Steven Watson's *The Birth of the Beat Generation: Visionaries, Rebels, and Hipsters, 1944–1960* (1995).

CHAPTER 33

Scholarship on the Eisenhower years is extensive. A carefully balanced overview of the period is Chester J. Pach, Jr. and Elmo Richardson's *The Presidency of Dwight D. Eisenhower,* rev. ed. (1991). For the manner in which Eisenhower conducted foreign policy, see Robert A. Divine's *Eisenhower and the Cold War* (1981). Tom Wicker deems Eisenhower a better person than a president in *Dwight D. Eisenhower* (2002).

For the buildup of U.S. involvement in Indochina, consult Lloyd C. Gardner's *Approaching Vietnam: From World War II through Dienbienphu, 1941–1954* (1988) and David L. Anderson's *Trapped by Success: The Eisenhower Administration and Vietnam, 1953–61* (1991). How the Eisenhower Doctrine came to be implemented is traced in Stephen E. Ambrose and Douglas G. Brinkley's *Rise to Globalism: American Foreign Policy since 1938,* 8th ed. (1997).

The impact of the Supreme Court during the 1950s is the focus of Archibald Cox's *The Warren Court: Constitutional Decision as an Instrument of Reform* (1968). A masterly study of the important Warren Court decision on school desegregation is James T. Patterson's *Brown v. Board of Education: A Civil Rights Milestone and Its Troubled Legacy* (2001).

For the story of the early years of the civil rights movement, see Taylor Branch's *Parting the Waters: America in the King Years, 1954–1963* (1988) and Robert Weisbrot's *Freedom Bound: A History of America's Civil Rights Movement* (1990).

CHAPTER 34

A dispassionate analysis of John Kennedy's life is Thomas C. Reeves's *A Question of Character: A Life of John F. Kennedy* (1991). The best study of the Kennedy administration's domestic policies is Irving Bernstein's *Promises Kept: John F. Kennedy's New Frontier* (1991). For details on the still swirling conspiracy theories about the assassination, see David W. Belin's *Final Disclosure: The Full Truth about the Assassination of President Kennedy* (1988).

The most comprehensive biography of Johnson is Robert Dallek's two-volume work, *Lone Star Rising: Lyndon Johnson and His Times, 1908–1960* (1991) and *Flawed Giant: Lyndon Johnson and His Times, 1961–1973* (1998). On the Johnson administration, see Vaughn Davis Bornet's *The Presidency of Lyndon B. Johnson* (1984).

Among the works that interpret liberal social policy during the 1960s, John E. Schwarz's *America's Hidden Success: A Reassessment of Twenty Years of Public Policy* (1983) offers a glowing endorsement of Democratic programs. For a contrasting perspective, see Charles Murray's *Losing Ground: American Social Policy, 1950–1980,* rev. ed. (1994).

On foreign policy, see *Kennedy's Quest for Victory: American Foreign Policy, 1961–1963* (1989), edited by Thomas G. Paterson. To learn more about Kennedy's problems in Cuba, see Mark J. White's *Missiles in Cuba: Kennedy, Khrushchev, Castro and the 1962 Crisis* (1997). See also Aleksandr Fursenko and Timothy Naftali's *"One Hell of a Gamble": Khrushchev, Castro and Kennedy, 1958–1964* (1997).

American involvement in Vietnam has received voluminous treatment from all political perspectives. For an excellent overview, see Larry Berman's *Planning a Tragedy: The Americanization of the War in Vietnam* (1983) and *Lyndon Johnson's War: The Road to Stalemate in Vietnam* (1989), as well as Stanley Karnow's *Vietnam: A History,* 2nd rev. ed. (1997). An analysis of policy making concerning the Vietnam War is David M. Barrett's *Uncertain Warriors: Lyndon Johnson and His Vietnam Advisors* (1993). A fine account of the military involvement is Robert D. Schulzinger's *A Time for War: The United States and Vietnam, 1941–1975* (1997). On the legacy of the Vietnam War, see Arnold R. Isaacs's *Vietnam Shadows: The War, Its Ghosts, and Its Legacy* (1997).

Many scholars have dealt with various aspects of the civil rights movement and race relations in the 1960s. See especially Carl M. Brauer's *John F. Kennedy and the Second Reconstruction* (1977), David J. Garrow's *Bearing the Cross: Martin Luther King, Jr., and the Southern Christian Leadership Conference* (1986), and Adam Fairclough's *To Redeem the Soul of America: The Southern Christian Leadership Conference and Martin Luther King, Jr.* (1987). William H. Chafe's *Civilities and Civil Rights: Greensboro, North Carolina, and the Black Struggle for Freedom* (1980) details the original sit-ins. An award-winning study of racial and economic inequality in a representative American city is Thomas J. Sugrue's *The Origins of the Urban Crisis: Race and Inequality in Postwar Detroit* (1996).

CHAPTER 35

An engaging overview of the cultural trends of the 1960s is Maurice Isserman and Michael Kazin's *America Divided: The Civil War of the 1960s,* 3rd ed. (2007). The New Left is assessed in Irwin Unger's *The Movement: A History of the American New Left, 1959–1972* (1974). On the Students for a Democratic Society, see Kirkpatrick Sale's *SDS* (1973) and Allen J. Matusow's *The Unraveling of America: A History of Liberalism in the 1960s* (1984). Also useful is Todd Gitlin's *The Sixties: Years of Hope, Days of Rage,* rev. ed. (1993).

Two influential assessments of the counterculture by sympathetic commentators are Theodore Roszak's *The Making of a Counter-culture: Reflections on the Technocratic Society and Its Youthful Opposition* (1969) and Charles A. Reich's *The Greening of America: How the Youth Revolution Is Trying to Make America Livable* (1970). A good scholarly analysis that takes the hippies seriously is Timothy Miller's *The Hippies and American Values* (1991).

The best study of the women's liberation movement is Ruth Rosen's *The World Split Open: How the Modern Women's Movement Changed America,* rev. ed. (2006). The organizing efforts of Cesar Chavez are detailed in Ronald B. Taylor's *Chavez and the Farm Workers* (1975). The struggles of Native Americans for recognition and power are sympathetically described in Stan Steiner's *The New Indians* (1968).

On Nixon, see Melvin Small's *The Presidency of Richard Nixon* (1999). For a solid overview of the Watergate scandal, see Stanley I. Kutler's *The Wars of Watergate: The Last Crisis of Richard Nixon* (1990). For the way the Republicans handled foreign affairs, consult Tad Szulc's *The Illusion of Peace: Foreign Policy in the Nixon Years* (1978).

The loss of Vietnam and the end of American involvement there are traced in Larry Berman's *No Peace, No Honor: Nixon, Kissinger, and Betrayal in Vietnam* (2001). William Shawcross's *Sideshow: Kissinger, Nixon and the Destruction of Cambodia,* rev. ed. (2002), deals with the broadening of the war, while Larry Berman's *Planning a Tragedy: The Americanization of the War in Vietnam* (1982) assesses the final impact of U.S. involvement. The most comprehensive treatment of the anti-war movement is Tom Wells's *The War Within: America's Battle over Vietnam* (1994).

A comprehensive treatment of the Ford administration is contained in John Robert Greene's *The Presidency of Gerald R. Ford* (1995). The best overview of the Carter administration is Burton I. Kaufman's *The Presidency of James Earl Carter, Jr.,* 2nd rev. ed. (2006). A work more sympathetic to the Carter administration is John Dumbrell's *The Carter Presidency: A*

Re-evaluation, 2nd ed. (1995). Gaddis Smith's *Morality, Reason, and Power: American Diplomacy in the Carter Years* (1986) provides an overview. Background on how the Middle East came to dominate much of American policy is found in William B. Quandt's *Decade of Decisions: American Policy toward the Arab-Israeli Conflict, 1967–1976* (1977).

CHAPTER 36

Two brief accounts of Reagan's presidency are David Mervin's *Ronald Reagan and the American Presidency* (1990) and Michael Schaller's *Reckoning with Reagan: America and Its President in the 1980s* (1992). A more substantial biography is John Patrick Diggins's *Ronald Reagan: Fate, Freedom, and the Making of History* (2007). An excellent analysis of the 1980 election is Andrew E. Busch's *Reagan's Victory: The Presidential Election of 1980 and the Rise of the Right* (2005). A more comprehensive summary of the Reagan years is Sean Wilentz's *The Age of Reagan: A History, 1974–2008* (2008).

On Reaganomics, see David A. Stockman's *The Triumph of Politics: Why the Reagan Revolution Failed* (1986) and Robert Lekachman's *Greed Is Not Enough: Reaganomics* (1982). On the issue of arms control, see Strobe Talbott's *Deadly Gambits: The Reagan Administration and the Stalemate in Nuclear Arms Control* (1984).

For Reagan's foreign policy in Central America, see James Chace's *Endless War: How We Got Involved in Central America—and What Can Be Done* (1984) and Walter LaFeber's *Inevitable Revolutions: The United States in Central America*, 2nd ed. (1993). Insider views of Reagan's foreign policy are offered in Alexander M. Haig Jr.'s *Caveat: Realism, Reagan, and Foreign Policy* (1984) and Caspar W. Weinberger's *Fighting for Peace: Seven Critical Years in the Pentagon* (1990).

On Reagan's second term, see Jane Mayer and Doyle McManus's *Landslide: The Unmaking of the President, 1984–1988* (1988). For a masterly work on the Iran-Contra affair, see Theodore Draper's *A Very Thin Line: The Iran Contra Affairs* (1991). Several collections of essays include varying assessments of the Reagan years. Among these are *The Reagan Revolution?* (1988), edited by B. B. Kymlicka and Jean V. Matthews; *The Reagan Presidency: An Incomplete Revolution?* (1990), edited by Dilys M. Hill, Raymond A. Moore, and Phil Williams, and *Looking Back on the Reagan Presidency* (1990), edited by Larry Berman.

On the 1988 campaign, see Jack W. Germond and Jules Witcover's *Whose Broad Stripes and Bright Stars? The Trivial Pursuit of the Presidency, 1988*

(1989) and Sidney Blumenthal's *Pledging Allegiance: The Last Campaign of the Cold War* (1990). For a social history of the decade, see John Ehrman's *The Eighties: America in the Age of Reagan* (2005).

CHAPTER 37

On George H. W. Bush's presidency, see *Leadership and the Bush Presidency: Prudence or Drift in an Era of Change?*, edited by Ryan J. Barilleaux and Mary E. Stuckey (1992), and Charles Tiefer's *The Semi-Sovereign Presidency: The Bush Administration's Strategy for Governing without Congress* (1994). Among the journalistic accounts of the presidential election of 1992, the best narrative is Jack W. Germond and Jules Witcover's *Mad as Hell: Revolt at the Ballot Box, 1992* (1993). The best scholarly study is Theodore J. Lowi and Benjamin Ginsberg's *Democrats Return to Power: Politics and Policy in the Clinton Era* (1994).

Analysis of the Clinton years can be found in Joe Klein's *The Natural: The Misunderstood Presidency of Bill Clinton* (2002). Clinton's impeachment is assessed in Richard A. Posner's *An Affair of State: The Investigation, Impeachment, and Trial of President Clinton* (1999).

On changing demographic trends, see Sam Roberts's *Who We Are Now: The Changing Face of America in the Twenty-First Century* (2004). On social and cultural life in the 1990s, see Haynes Johnson's *The Best of Times: America in the Clinton Years* (2001). The onset and growth of the AIDS epidemic are traced in *And the Band Played On: Politics, People, and the AIDS Epidemic*, 20th anniversary ed. (2007), by Randy Shilts.

Aspects of fundamentalist and apocalyptic movements are the subject of Paul Boyer's *When Time Shall Be No More: Prophecy Belief in Modern American Culture* (1992), George M. Marsden's *Understanding Fundamentalism and Evangelicalism*, new ed. (2006), and Ralph E. Reed's *Politically Incorrect: The Emerging Faith Factor in American Politics* (1994).

On the invention of the computer and the Internet, see Paul E. Ceruzzi's *A History of Modern Computing*, 2nd ed. (2003), and Janet Abbate's *Inventing the Internet* (1999). The booming economy of the 1990s is well analyzed in Joseph E. Stiglitz's *The Roaring Nineties: A New History of the World's Most Prosperous Decade* (2003). On the rising stress within the workplace, see Jill Andresky Fraser's *White-Collar Sweatshop: The Deterioration of Work and Its Rewards in Corporate America* (2001). Aspects of corporate restructuring and downsizing are the subject of Bennett Harrison's *Lean and Mean: The Changing Landscape of Corporate Power in the Age of Flexibility* (1994).

For further treatment of the end of the cold war, see Michael R. Beschloss and Strobe Talbott's *At the Highest Levels: The Inside Story of the End of the Cold War* (1993) and Richard Crockatt's *The Fifty Years War: The United States and the Soviet Union in World Politics, 1941–1991* (1995). On the Persian Gulf conflict, see Lester H. Brune's *America and the Iraqi Crisis, 1990–1992: Origins and Aftermath* (1993). On the transformation of American foreign policy, see James Mann's *Rise of the Vulcans: The History of Bush's War Cabinet* (2004), Claes G. Ryn's *America the Virtuous: The Crisis of Democracy and the Quest for Empire* (2003), and Stephen M. Walt's *Taming American Power: The Global Response to U.S. Primacy* (2005).

The disputed 2000 presidential election is the focus of Jeffrey Toobin's *Too Close to Call: The Thirty-Six-Day Battle to Decide the 2000 Election* (2001). On the attacks of September 11, 2001, and their aftermath, see *The Age of Terror: America and the World after September 11*, edited by Strobe Talbott and Nayan Chanda (2001).

On the environmental history of New Orleans, see Craig E. Colten's *An Unnatural Metropolis: Wresting New Orleans from Nature* (2004). For a devastating account of the Bush administration by a White House insider, see Scott McClellan's *What Happened: Inside the Bush White House and Washington's Culture of Deception* (2008). On the historic 2008 election, see Michael Nelson's *The Elections of 2008* (2009).

CREDITS

PART 1: p. 1, The New York Public Library/Art Resource, NY; **p. 3,** Granger Collection;

CHAPTER 1: p. 5, Bettmann/Corbis; **p. 12,** Bridgeman Art Library; **p. 14,** The Benson Latin American Collection, University of Texas; **p. 15,** Atlantide Phototravel/Corbis; **p. 19,** Werner Forman/Art Resource, NY.

CHAPTER 2: p. 26, The Granger Collection; **p. 28,** Bridgeman Art Library; **p. 102,** The Granger Collection; **p. 35,** The Granger Collection; **p. 39,** Library of Congress; **p. 40,** The Mariners' Museum/Corbis; **p. 44,** The Royal Library of Copenhagen; **p. 47,** Bettmann/Corbis; **p. 49,** Stapleton Collection/Corbis.

CHAPTER 3: p. 58, The Granger Collection; **p. 60,** The Granger Collection; **p. 63,** Connecticut Historical Society Museum; **p. 65,** Granger Collection; **p. 68,** Abby Aldrich Rockefeller Folk Art Center Colonial Williamsburg; **p. 71,** Granger Collection; **p. 72,** The Granger Collection; **p. 81,** Library Company of Philadelphia; **p. 84,** Granger Collection; **p. 87,** National Portrait Gallery, London; **p. 89,** Bettmann/Corbis.

CHAPTER 4: p. 94, Granger Collection; **p. 96,** I. N. Phelps Stokes Collection Miriam and Ira D. Wallach Division of Art, Prints and Photographs, The New York Public Library Astor, Lenox and Tilden Foundations; **p. 100,** Granger Collection; **p. 104,** Snark/Art Resource, NY; **p. 108,** Library of Congress.

CHAPTER 5: p. 116, Library of Congress; **p. 117,** Granger Collection; **p. 119,** Library of Congress; **p. 123,** Library of Congress; **p. 126,** Library of Congress; **p. 127,** I. N. Phelps Stokes Collection, Miriam and Ira D. Wallach Division of Art, Prints and Photographs, The New York Public Library, Astor, Lenox and Tilden Foundations; **p. 130,** Library of Congress; **p. 133,** Granger Collection; **p. 135,** Library of Congress; **p. 138,** American Antiquarian Society; **p. 139,** Library of Congress.

PART 2: p. 145, Giraudon/Art Resource; **p. 146,** Library of Congress.

CHAPTER 6: p. 149, Giraudon/Art Resource NY; **p. 150,** Library of Congress; **p. 152,** U.S. Senate Collection; **p. 154,** Anne S. K. Brown Military Collection, Brown University Library; **p. 157,** Granger Collection; **p. 159,** Granger Collection; **p. 165,** Library of

Congress; **p. 171,** Courtesy of the Maryland Historical Society 1960.108.3.11; **p. 172,** Granger Collection; **p. 174,** Granger Collection.

CHAPTER 7: **p. 178,** Bettmann/Corbis; **p. 183,** Library Company of Philadelphia; **p. 185,** Historical Society of Pennsylvania; **p. 186,** Granger Collection; **p. 187,** Library of Congress; **p. 189,** Library of Congress; **p. 193,** Independence National Historical Park.

CHAPTER 8: **p. 200,** Art Resource, NY; **p. 201,** Library of Congress; **p. 203,** Library of Congress; **p. 206,** Independence National Historical Park; **p. 210,** Historical Society of Pennsylvania; **p. 212,** Granger Collection; **p. 216,** Granger Collection; **p. 220,** Granger Collection; **p. 223,** National Portrait Gallery NPG.71.4; **p. 224,** The Granger Collection; **p. 225,** The Granger Collection.

CHAPTER 9: **p. 232,** Giraudon/Art Resource NY; **p. 235,** Miriam and Ira D. Wallach Division of Art, Prints and Photographs. NYPL; **p. 240,** Copyright American Philosophical Society; **p. 241,** Copyright American Philosophical Society; **p. 242,** Library of Congress; **p. 245,** Library of Congress; **p. 249,** Library of Congress; **p. 254,** Library of Congress; **p. 256,** Collection of Davenport West, Jr.

PART 3: **p. 261,** Library of Congress; **p. 263,** Library of Congress.

CHAPTER 10: **p. 265,** Library of Congress; **p. 268,** Maryland Historical Society 1934.2.1; **p. 281,** Henry Clay Memorial Foundation; **p. 277,** Bettmann/Corbis; **p. 280,** Gerard W. Gawalt and Janice E. Ruth, Manuscript Division, Library of Congress; **p. 283,** Corbis.

CHAPTER 11: **p. 290,** Library of Congress; **p. 292,** Saint Louis Art Museum, Gift of Bank of America; **p. 295,** Library of Congress; **p. 297,** Granger Collection; **p. 299,** National Portrait Gallery; **p. 301,** Library of Congress; **p. 306,** Alamy; **p. 309,** Collection of the New York Historical Society; **p. 313,** Library of Congress.

CHAPTER 12: **p. 320,** Granger Collection; **p. 327,** Granger Collection; **p. 333,** American Textile History Museum, Lowell, MA; **p. 334,** Granger Collection; **p. 335,** Library of Congress; **p. 338,** Board of Trustees, National Gallery of Art, Washington 1980.62.9.(2794)/PA; **p. 339,** Library of Congress; **p. 340,** National Park Service, Ellis Island Collection; **p. 344,** Library of Congress; **p. 346,** Library of Congress; **p. 348,** John W. Bennett Labor Collection, Special Collections and University Archives, W. E. B. Du Bois Library, University of Massachusetts, Amherst; **p. 349,** Courtesy Pennsylvania Hospital Historic Collections, Philadelphia.

CHAPTER 13: **p. 354,** Bettmann/Corbis; **p. 357,** Alamy; **p. 360,** Library of Congress; **p. 362,** Alamy; **p. 365,** Bettmann/Corbis; **p. 366,** Bettmann/Corbis; **p. 367,** American Antiquarian Society; **p. 368,** The Walters Art Museum, Baltimore; **p. 370,** Granger Collection; **p. 374,** Warder Collection.

CHAPTER 14: **p. 380,** Granger Collection; **p. 381,** Granger Collection; **p. 385,** Library of Congress; **p. 386,** Library of Congress; **p. 390,** Richard Collier, Wyoming

Department of State Parks and Cultural Resources; **p. 393,** Macduff Everton/Corbis; **p. 396,** National Archives; **p. 399,** Library of Congress.

PART 4: **p. 411,** Granger Collection; **p. 412,** Library of Congress.

CHAPTER 15: **p. 415,** Bettmann/Corbis; **p. 418,** Prints and Photographs Division, Schomburg Center for Research, The New York Public Library; **p. 420,** Bettmann/Corbis; **p. 423,** The Charleston Museum; **p. 424,** Library of Congress; **p. 428,** Library of Congress; **p. 431,** Granger Collection; **p. 432,** Library of Congress; **p. 432,** Library of Congress; **p. 434,** Granger Collection; **p. 434,** Library of Congress; **p. 435,** Granger Collection.

CHAPTER 16: **p. 440,** Granger Collection; **p. 443,** Library of Congress; **p. 445,** Granger Collection; **p. 447,** Library of Congress; **p. 449,** Granger Collection; **p. 451,** Granger Collection; **p. 453,** Granger Collection; **p. 458,** Library of Congress; **p. 465,** Granger Collection; **p. 467,** Library of Congress; **p. 469,** Library of Congress; **p. 464,** Granger Collection; **p. 476,** Library of Congress.

CHAPTER 17: **p. 477,** Library of Congress; **p. 481,** Medford Historical Society Collection/Corbis; **p. 483,** Bettmann/Corbis; **p. 484,** Granger Collection; **p. 494 (both),** Library of Congress; **p. 495,** Bettmann/Corbis; **p. 497,** Library of Congress; **p. 498,** Library of Congress; **p. 501,** Granger Collection; **p. 503,** Library of Congress; **p. 504,** National Archives; **p. 505,** Library of Congress; **p. 508,** Library of Congress; **p. 510,** Bettmann/Corbis; **p. 512,** Bettmann/Corbis; **p. 516,** Library of Congress.

CHAPTER 18: **p. 520,** Library of Congress; **p. 522,** Library of Congress; **p. 523,** Library of Congress; **p. 527,** Library of Congress; **p. 530,** Library of Congress; **p. 537,** Bettmann/Corbis; **p. 540,** Library of Congress; **p. 544,** Library of Congress; **p. 545,** Library of Congress; **p. 549,** Library of Congress.

PART 5: **p. 555,** Granger Collection; **p. 556,** Granger Collection.

CHAPTER 19: **p. 559,** Library of Congress; **p. 565,** Granger Collection; **p. 567,** Library of Congress; **p. 570,** Special Collections, University of Chicago Library; **p. 571,** Library of Congress; **p. 572,** Warder Collection; **p. 574,** Kansas State Historical Society; **p. 579,** Warder Collection; **p. 582,** Bettmann/Corbis; **p. 585,** Corbis; **p. 587,** Western Historical Collections University of Oklahoma Library.

CHAPTER 20: **p. 590,** Library of Congress; **p. 592,** Alfred Stieglitz, The Hand of Man 1902, hotogravure, P.1978.112, Amon Carter Museum; **p. 593,** Bettmann/Corbis; **p. 595** Union Pacific Museum; **p. 599,** Warder Collection; **p. 607,** American Petroleum Institute Historical Photo Collection; **p. 601,** Carnegie Library of Pittsburgh; **p. 602,** Pierpont Morgan Library; **p. 603,** Granger Collection; **p. 609,** T. V. Powderly Photographic Collection, The American Catholic History Research Center University Archives, The Catholic University of America, Washington, D.C.; **p. 613,** Walter P. Reuther Library, Wayne State University.

CHAPTER 21: **p. 618,** Library of Congress; **p. 622,** The Art Archive/Culver Pictures; **p. 623,** Bettmann/Corbis; **p. 626,** The Bryon Collection, Museum of the City of New York;

p. 627, William Williams Papers, Manuscripts and Archives Division, The New York Public Library, Astor, Lenox and Tilden Foundations; **p. 630,** Bettmann/Corbis; **p. 632,** Brown Brothers; **p. 633,** Old York Library; **p. 634,** Library of Congress; **p. 636,** Special Collections, Vassar College Libraries; **p. 638,** American Museum of Natural History; **p. 640,** Time Life Pictures/Getty Images; **p. 643,** The Salvation Army National Archives; **p. 644,** University of Illinois at Chicago.

CHAPTER 22: **p. 650,** Library of Congress; **p. 651,** Library of Congress; **p. 655,** Library of Congress; **p. 658,** Warder Collection; **p. 660,** Bettmann/Corbis; **p. 662,** Bettmann/Corbis; **p. 665,** Library of Congress; **p. 666,** Library of Congress; **p. 669,** Kansas State Historical Society; **p. 672,** Library of Congress; **p. 674,** Library of Congress.

PART 6: **p. 681,** Library of Congress; **p. 683,** Library of Congress.

CHAPTER 23: **p. 685,** Bettmann/Corbis; **p. 689,** Hawaii State Archives; **p. 692,** Library of Congress; **p. 693,** Bettmann/Corbis; **p. 699,** National Archives; **p. 698,** Photo: Corporal George J. Vennage; Courtesy of OSU Rare Books & Manuscripts Library; **p. 696,** Library of Congress; **p. 702,** Granger Collection; **p. 706,** Bettmann/Corbis; **p. 707,** Bettmann/Corbis.

CHAPTER 24: **p. 712,** Library of Congress; **p. 715,** Granger Collection; **p. 717,** Library of Congress; **p. 718,** Bettmann/Corbis; **p. 719,** Corbis; **p. 722 (top),** Collection of The New York Historical Society; **p. 722 (bottom),** Library of Congress; **p. 725,** Library of Congress; **p. 728,** Library of Congress; **p. 729,** Library of Congress; **p. 730,** Granger Collection; **p. 731,** Library of Congress; **p. 734,** Warder Collection; **p. 737,** Warder Collection; **p. 739,** Corbis.

CHAPTER 25: **p. 744,** Library of Congress; **p. 746,** Bettmann/Corbis; **p. 749,** Alamy; **p. 753,** The New York Times; **p. 755,** Bettmann/Corbis; **p. 757,** Swim Ink 2, LLC/Corbis; **p. 760,** Everett Collection; **p. 750,** National Archives; **p. 762,** Bettmann/Corbis; **p. 766,** Mary Evans Picture Library; **p. 769,** Courtesy of the Ding Darling Wildlife Society.

CHAPTER 26: **p. 776,** Bettmann/Corbis; **p. 778,** Bettmann/Corbis; **p. 780,** Bettmann/Corbis; **p. 782,** Bettmann/Corbis; **p. 784,** Ramsey Archive; **p. 785,** Bettmann/Corbis; **p. 786,** Bettmann/Corbis; **p. 789,** AP Photos.

CHAPTER 27: **p. 798,** Bettmann/Corbis; **p. 800,** Hulton Archive/Getty Images; **p. 803,** The Washington Post. Reprinted with permission; **p. 805,** Hulton Archive/Getty Images; **p. 807,** Bettmann/Corbis; **p. 809,** From the Collections of The Henry Ford Museum; **p. 812,** Bettmann/Corbis; **p. 813,** David J. & Janice L. Frent Collection/Corbis; **p. 814,** Herbert Hoover Presidential Library; **p. 819,** Bettmann/Corbis; **p. 821,** New York Daily News.

CHAPTER 28: **p. 824,** Bettmann/Corbis; **p. 827,** AP Photos; **p. 830,** National Archives; **p. 835,** Library of Congress; **p. 838,** National Archives; **p. 840,** Library of Congress; **p. 843,** Bettmann/Corbis; **p. 844,** Hulton Archives/Getty Images; **p. 845,**

Bettmann/Corbis; **p. 846,** Bettmann/Corbis; **p. 848,** Library of Congress; **p. 851,** Corbis; **p. 856,** Granger Collection; **p. 857,** Bettmann/Corbis.

CHAPTER 29: **p. 862,** Bettmann/Corbis; **p. 864,** AP Photo; **p. 868,** National Archives; **p. 872,** 1938, The Washington Post; **p. 874,** British Information Services; **p. 875,** Granger Collection; **p. 878,** Bettmann/Corbis, **p. 882,** Library of Congress.

CHAPTER 30: **p. 886,** Bettmann/Corbis; **p. 888,** Warder Collection; **p. 890,** Swim Ink 2, LLC/Corbis; **p. 892,** Library of Congress; **p. 893,** AP Photo; **p. 895,** Bettmann/Corbis; **p. 903,** Eisenhower Presidential Library; **p. 904,** National Archives; **p. 910,** National Archives; **p. 913,** National Archives; **p. 915,** Bettmann/Corbis; **p. 917,** Hulton Archives/ Getty Images.

PART 7: **p. 923,** Bill Eppridge/Getty Images; **p. 925,** Peter Turnley/Corbis.

CHAPTER 31: **p. 927,** Bettmann/Corbis; **p. 929,** University of Louisville; **p. 931,** Granger Collection; **p. 935,** Library of Congress; **p. 937,** Hartford Courant; **p. 939,** Hy Peskin/Getty Images; **p. 940,** 1948, Washington Post; **p. 941,** Bettmann/Corbis; **p. 948,** Bettmann/Corbis; **p. 950,** Yale Joel/Getty Images.

CHAPTER 32: **p. 954,** Hulton Archives/Getty Images; **p. 956,** William Joseph O'Keefe Collection, Veterans History Project, Library of Congress; **p. 958,** AP Photo; **p. 959,** AP Photo; **p. 961,** Library of Congress; **p. 963,** Fogg Art Museum, Harvard University; **p. 964,** PNI/Archive Museum of Art; **p. 960,** William Gottlieb/Corbis; **p. 971,** AP Photos; **p. 966,** Art Shay/Time Life Pictures/Getty Images; **p. 968,** Hulton/Getty Images; **p. 969,** AP Photos.

CHAPTER 33: **p. 976,** Bettmann/Corbis; **p. 981,** Bettmann/Corbis; **p. 982,** AP Photo; **p. 983,** "Don't Be Afraid—I Can Always Pull You Back" from Herblock's *Special for Today* (Simon & Schuster 1958); **p. 984,** Photoworld; **p. 985,** AP Photo; **p. 993,** AP Photo; **p. 995,** University of Louisville; **p. 997,** Black Star/Stock Photo; **p. 998,** Joseph Scherschel/Time Life Pictures/Getty Images.

CHAPTER 34: **p. 1004,** Bettmann/Corbis; **p. 1008,** National Archives; **p. 1010,** National Archives; **p. 1012,** Hulton Archives/Getty Images; **p. 1016,** Time Life Pictures/Getty Images; **p. 1017,** AP Photo; **p. 1021,** Bettmann/Corbis; **p. 1024,** National Archives; **p. 1028,** Newark Star-Ledger; **p. 1027,** Bettmann/Corbis.

CHAPTER 35: **p. 1036,** Bettmann/Corbis; **p. 1037,** Ted Streshinsky/Corbis; **p. 1039,** Magnum Photos; **p. 1041,** John Dominis/Getty Images; **p. 1042,** Bettmann/Corbis; **p. 1045,** AP Photos; **p. 1050,** Howard Ruffner/Time Life Pictures/Getty Images; **p. 1055,** Bettmann/Corbis; **p. 1056,** NASA Kennedy Space Center; **p. 1057,** John Dominis/Getty Images; **p. 1058,** AP Photo; **p. 1061,** AP Photo; **p. 1063,** Wally McNamee/Corbis; **p. 1066,** AP Photo.

CHAPTER 36: **p. 1070,** Bettmann/Corbis; **p. 1071,** Bettmann/Corbis; **p. 1072,** Bettmann/Corbis; **p. 1077,** Bettmann/Corbis; **p. 1078,** Los Angeles Times Syndicate;

p. 1082, Bettmann/Corbis; **p. 1080,** AP Photo; **p. 1087,** Woodfin Camp; **p. 1088,** AP Photo; **p. 1091,** Bettmann/Corbis.

CHAPTER 37: **p. 1094,** Smiley N. Pool/Dallas Morning News/Corbis; **p. 1096,** AP Photo; **p. 1097,** Library of Congress; **p. 1099,** Durand-Hudson-Langevin-Orban/Sygma/Corbis; **p. 1101,** Chris Wilkins/Getty Images; **p. 1103,** AP Photo; **p. 1108,** AP Photo; **p. 1109,** AP Photo; **p. 1116,** Sean Adair/Reuters/Corbis; **p. 1117,** AP Photo; **p. 1119,** Reuters/Corbis; **p. 1120,** Bettmann/Corbis, **p. 1123,** Brooks Kraft/Corbis; **p. 1126,** Reuters/Corbis; **p. 1127,** AP Photo; **p. 1128,** AP Photo; **p. 1129,** AP Photo; **p. 1131,** AP Photo; **p. 1132,** Michael Ainsworth/Dallas Morning News/Corbis; **p. 1133,** AP Photo; **p. 1134,** Shawn Thew/epa/Corbis; **p.1136,** AP Photo; **p. 1138,** Jim Young/Reuters/Corbis.

INDEX

Page numbers in *italics* refer to illustrations.

ARCTIC OCEAN

160° 140° 120° 100° 80° 60° 40° 20°

80°

GREENLAND
(DENMARK)

Arctic Ci
ICEL

ALASKA
(U.S.)

60°

NORTH
AMERICA
CANADA

DENMAR
UNITED KINGD
IRELAND

FRANC

Vancouver

40°

Ottawa
Toronto

Chicago
New York
Washington, D.C.

NORTH
ATLANTIC
OCEAN

PORTUGAL

S

NORTH
PACIFIC
OCEAN

UNITED STATES

Los Angeles

MOROCCO

MIDWAY
ISLAND
(U.S.)

Tropic of Cancer

Gulf of Mexico

BAHAMAS
HAITI
DOMINICAN REPUBLIC
Puerto Rico (U.S.)
VIRGIN ISL. (US & UK)
ST. KITTS & NEVIS
ANTIGUA & BARBUDA
DOMINICA
ST. LUCIA
ST. VINCENT & THE GRENADINES
BARBADOS

MAURITANIA
BURKINA FASO
CAPE VERDE   SENEGAL
GAMBIA
GUINEA-BISSAU
GUINEA
SIERRA LEONE
LIBERIA
CÔTE D'IVOIRE
GHANA

20°

HAWAII
(U.S.)

MEXICO

Mexico
City

BELIZE

GUATEMALA
EL SALVADOR
HONDURAS
NICARAGUA
COSTA RICA
PANAMA

CUBA
JAMAICA

CARIBBEAN
SEA

COLOMBIA

VENEZUELA   GUYANA
SURINAME
FRENCH GUIANA
(FR)

TRINIDAD & TOBAGO

0° Equator

ECUADOR

WESTERN
SAMOA
AMERICAN
SAMOA
TONGA (U.S.)

20°

PERU

SOUTH
AMERICA

BOLIVIA

PARAGUAY

BRAZIL

Rio de Janeiro
São Paulo

CAMER
SÃO TOMÉ AND PRÍN
EQUATORIAL GU
CENTRAL AFRICAN REPU
GA
CONGO REPU

Tropic of Capricorn

SOUTH
PACIFIC
OCEAN

CHILE

A
R
G
E
N
T
I
N
A

URUGUAY

Buenos Aires

SOUTH
ATLANTIC
OCEAN

40°

60°

FAULKLAND
ISLANDS (U.K.)

0   250   500 Miles
0   250   500 Kilometers

NORWAY
Bergen

FINLAND

Oslo

SWEDEN

Helsinki

St. Petersburg

RUSSIA

Stockholm

Tallinn

ESTONIA

Nizhniy
Novgorod

NORTH
SEA

Göteborg

Riga

LATVIA

Moscow

Belfast

GREAT
BRITAIN

DENMARK

Copenhagen

LITHUANIA

IRELAND
Dublin

NETHERLANDS

Hamburg

Gdansk

RUSSIA   Vilnius

Minsk

BELARUS

ATLANTIC

OCEAN

London Amsterdam

Brussels

BELGIUM

Berlin

GERMANY

POLAND
Warsaw

Baltic Sea

Kiev

Kharkov

Paris

LUXEMBOURG

CZECH
REPUBLIC

Prague

UKRAINE

FRANCE

Munich

Bern

SWITZ.

AUSTRIA

Vienna
Ljubljana

SLOVENIA

Milan

Venice

SLOVAKIA
Bratislava
Budapest

HUNGARY

Zagreb

CROATIA

MOLDOVA

Chisinau   Odessa

ROMANIA

Belgrade

Bucharest

BLACK SEA

PORTUGAL

Lisbon

SPAIN

Madrid

BALEARIC
ISLANDS

CORSICA

ITALY

Sarajevo

SERBIA

Rome

BOSNIA &
HERZEGOVINA

MONTENEGRO

SARDINIA

Naples

Podgorica

ALBANIA

BULGARIA

Sofia

Skopje

MACEDONIA

Tiranë

Istanbul

Ankara

TURKEY

MEDITERRANEAN

GREECE

SEA

SICILY

Athens

MOROCCO

ALGERIA

TUNISIA

CRETE

RHODES

CYPRUS

LEBANON

Short Loan Collection

WITHDRAWN

UNIVERSITY OF GLASGOW LIBRARY